To Carol, Madison, and Daniel

Constitutional Law, Administrative Law, and Human Rights

A Critical Introduction

Eighth edition

IAN LOVELAND

Professor of Public Law, City, University of London

OXFORD
UNIVERSITY PRESS

OXFORD
UNIVERSITY PRESS

Great Clarendon Street, Oxford, OX2 6DP,
United Kingdom

Oxford University Press is a department of the University of Oxford.
It furthers the University's objective of excellence in research, scholarship,
and education by publishing worldwide. Oxford is a registered trade mark of
Oxford University Press in the UK and in certain other countries

Fifth edition 2009
Sixth edition 2012
Seventh edition 2015

Impression: 1

Published in the United States of America by Oxford University Press
198 Madison Avenue, New York, NY 10016, United States of America

British Library Cataloguing in Publication Data
Data available

Library of Congress Control Number: 2017959721

ISBN 978-0-19-880468-0

Printed in Great Britain by
Bell & Bain Ltd., Glasgow

Preface

Early in 2017, I concluded a review of the collection of essays on *Entick v Carrington* edited by Adam Tomkins and Paul Scott with the comment: 'The primary achievement of the book . . . is surely to stand as a welcome corrective to the temptation to conclude that the primary responsibility of public law scholarship—and especially its teaching element—is to provide students with evermore condensed introductions to evermore extensive bodies of substantive material'.[1] The eighth edition to this book has made some significant changes to its seventh version, but I hope in ways that have resisted that undesirable temptation. The alterations are in part a response to reviews of and comments on the seventh edition from teachers at other English law schools, and are designed to enhance the effectiveness of the book as a primary text both to students on GDL or graduate LLB programmes and to LLB students whose law degree is their first exposure to university level education.

In this edition, the need to deal in some detail with the UK's (proposed as of autumn 2017) departure from the European Union has led to a substantial culling of the historical material about the EU's development in what were chapters eleven and twelve, which are replaced with a single chapter. That chapter also omits much of the previous discussion of the ECJ's effet utile jurisprudence, which is a topic perhaps now rarely taught in a constitutional law module. The previous chapters are available on the Online Resource Centre attached to the book, and readers will also find all of the material that was in chapters eleven and twelve of the ORC casebook in the new chapter eleven of the online casebook. In this edition, the brexit issue is considered in a new final chapter, and is dealt with in a fashion which draws together many of the themes explored in earlier parts of the book. This edition also condenses the coverage of human rights protection prior to the enactment of the Human Rights Act 1998 to allow for more extensive discussion of recent issues.

Keeping the book to a manageable length necessarily means that much detailed material which many observers would regard as important is omitted. Those of us who teach public law must now perhaps be reconciled to the reality that there are now far too many issues to be fitted within a year-long class on the subject.

That said, I continue to hold the view that public law is a challenging, multi-disciplinary topic, and that attempts to simplify it in analytical terms do a disservice both to the subject and to the reader. This edition therefore retains the first edition's initial concern to provide a cross-disciplinary introduction to the subject of public law, with a continuing emphasis placed on material drawn from political theory, political science, and legal and social history. Insofar as the book has a particular target audience, that audience would be able and industrious undergraduate and graduate students who have an innate enthusiasm for thinking about the moral and political underpinnings of our constitutional system, a willingness to read widely and critically around the core of their subject, and also a readiness to accept that much of what they learn about that subject will seem to be (at least initially) confusing and contradictory. That is perhaps what makes the subject so interesting.

Ian Loveland
London, Autumn 2017

---

[1] Loveland I (2017) 'Review of *Entick v Carrington: 250 years of the Rule of Law*', Adam Tomkins and Paul Scott (eds), *Public Law* 528.

Guide to the online resources

The online resources that accompany this book provide students and lecturers with ready-to-use teaching and learning resources. They are free of charge, and are designed to complement the book and maximize the teaching and learning experience.

www.oup.com/uk/loveland8e/

Outline Contents

Part Six Conclusions

Detailed Contents

Part Two The Institutions and Operation of National Government

Part Four Administrative Law

Part Five Human Rights

Table of Legislation

Table of Treaties and Conventions

Table of Cases

Decisions of the European Court of Justice are listed below numerically. These decisions are also included in the preceding alphabetical list.

Part One

Theoretical Principles

Chapter 1

Defining the Constitution?

We hold these truths to be self-evident. That all men are created equal. That they are endowed by their creator with certain inalienable rights. That among these are life, liberty and the pursuit of happiness. That to secure these rights, governments are instituted among men, deriving their just powers from the consent of the governed. That whenever any form of government becomes destructive of those ends, it shall be the right of the people to alter or abolish it, and to institute new government, laying its foundations upon such principles, and organising its powers in such form, as shall seem to them most likely to effect their safety and happiness.

Thomas Jefferson, Philadelphia, 4 July 1776.

It may seem odd to begin a textbook analysing the British constitution by quoting from the United States' Declaration of Independence, a document drafted by Thomas Jefferson in 1776. The Declaration was written because the American colonists rejected the British constitutional system under which they had previously been governed. Jefferson's words were intended firstly to justify the American colonists' decision to rebel against British rule, and secondly to outline the broad moral principles that the revolutionaries would try to preserve in their new country.

This book begins with Jefferson's words partly because there is much common ground between American and British perceptions as to the moral principles which should underpin a country's constitutional arrangements.[1] However, they have been chosen primarily because they continue to provide a succinct, eloquent statement of the issues with which constitutional lawyers in any modern democratic country should be concerned.

We might contrast the sentiments of the Declaration with definitions of the British constitution offered by authors of several textbooks. Colin Turpin suggests that the constitution is: 'a body of rules, conventions and practices which regulate or qualify the organisation and operation of government in the United Kingdom'; de Smith's classic introductory text regards the constitution as 'a central, but not the sole feature, of the rules regulating the system of

---

[1] See Harlow C (1995) 'A special relationship? American influences on judicial review in England'; and Allan T (1995) 'Equality and moral independence: public law and private morality', both in Loveland I (ed) *A special relationship?*

government'.[2] A longer version is offered by Vernon Bogdanor, for whom the constitution is: 'a code of rules which aspire to regulate the allocation of functions, powers and duties among the various agencies and officers of government, and defines the relationship between these and the public'.[3]

These authors are trying to tell us what the constitution *is*—to *describe* the *form* that it takes. The Declaration, in contrast, is telling us what a constitution *is for*—to *analyse* the *functions* it performs. This book presents a functionalist view of the British constitution, concerned more with the 'Why?' than with the 'What?' of contemporary arrangements. It assumes that the purpose of a constitution is to articulate and preserve a society's fundamental moral principles. This is not to suggest that knowledge of the form that the constitution takes is unimportant, nor that issues of form and function are unrelated; it is simply to stress that one cannot understand the law of the constitution without looking beyond its surface image.

The book does not offer a one sentence 'definition' of the constitution. Rather, the entire book may be seen as a 'definition'. But this book amounts to only one definition, no more conclusive than any other formula that a student may encounter. British constitutional law is a subject as much concerned with history and politics as with legal rules. Definitive answers to particular problems are often elusive, and it is almost always possible to advance plausible alternatives to the solutions that have apparently been adopted.

This introductory chapter identifies certain evaluative criteria which readers might keep in mind when considering the description and analysis of Britain's current constitutional arrangements. The following pages explore several abstract questions concerning the functions that a constitution might perform to illustrate the complex nature of the subject. We also devote some attention to the solutions which the American revolutionaries adopted to resolve the constitutional difficulties which they faced when the United States became an independent country. This is not a comparative book, nor is it suggested that the American solution is necessarily 'better' than the British model. The British and American systems are however very different in the form that they take. This is highly significant for our purposes, because the Americans claimed that their revolution was fought not against the moral principles of the British constitution, but against the corruption of those principles by the British Parliament, the British government, the British judiciary, and the British people.[4]

We return to these historical matters shortly. Before doing so however, we may usefully spend some time considering the meaning of what we might (from an early-twenty-first century vantage point) intuitively regard as the most important function a constitution should perform—to ensure that a country is governed according to 'democratic principles'.

I. The meaning(s) of 'democracy'?

That modern Britain is a democratic country is perhaps a contemporary 'self-evident truth': the point is so obvious that few observers would ever question it. But if we dig beneath the surface of that assumption, we may find that we hold different views about the essential features of a democratic state,[5] and would reach different conclusions about how democratic a country Britain actually is. That, however, is a judgement best reserved to later chapters. At this point, we might more sensibly ask what yardsticks we might use in answering these questions.

---

[2] Respectively in (2nd edn, 1990) *British government and the constitution* p 3; Street H and Brazier R (5th edn, 1985) *de Smith's Constitutional and administrative law* p 15.

[3] Bogdanor V (1988) 'Introduction' p 4 in Bogdanor V (ed) *Constitutions in democratic politics*.

[4] See generally the marvelous study by Bernard Bailyn (1967) *The ideological origins of the American revolution*.

[5] Cf Bealey F (1988) *Democracy in the contemporary state* esp chs 1 and 2; Holden B (1988) *Understanding liberal democracy* esp ch 1.

What is democratic governance? Some hypothetical examples

The following hypothetical example assumes that the constitution of the countries concerned (countries A and B) provide that laws be made by referendums, in which all adult citizens are granted one vote. A law is passed if 50%+1 of those citizens who vote support the proposal. Assume that a majority of citizens in both countries A and B decide that they are not prepared to tolerate the poverty caused by an economic depression which has left many people unemployed.

Economic policy as a constitutional issue?

In country A, a new law provides a generous scheme of unemployment benefits, financed by imposing heavy income taxes on the wealthiest 30% of the population. In doing this, the law frees the poorest members of society from the threat of starvation and homelessness. But it deprives the richest citizens of a substantial slice of their income, which they had planned to spend pursuing their own favoured forms of happiness.

In country B, the law requires that men and women aged over 60 retire from work. A small retirement pension will be paid to retired people. The law thus reduces the problem of unemployment at a modest financial cost to the majority of the population, but imposes substantial hardship on people over 60 years old who do not want to retire.

How would we decide if these laws were 'democratic'? Should we ask only if the law has majority support, and if the answer is yes, go no further? If so, both laws (and presumably the constitutional arrangements under which they were passed) would be democratic. Or should we demand that there be an inter-relationship between the level of support a law attracts and the severity of its consequences for particular minorities—the more severe the law, the greater the degree of support it must attract to be democratic? If we accepted that principle, could we then agree that forcing people to retire from work is more 'severe' than imposing heavy taxes on the rich? If so, could we further agree that forced retirement would be 'democratic' if it enjoyed 55% (or 66% or 75% or 100%) support, while 50%+1 would be sufficient to 'democratise' large tax increases? Or thirdly, should we conclude that there are some laws whose consequences are so severe that they may never be enacted by a democratic society, even if supported by 100% of the population? If so, would either forcing people to retire from work at 60 or imposing large tax increases on the wealthiest sections of the population fall into that category?

Waging war as a constitutional issue?

Alternatively, let us suppose that country C declares war on countries E and F. The majority of voters in country E decide that they attach more importance to winning the war than to safeguarding personal liberty, and so enact a law (we might call it the War Emergency Powers Detention Law) which allows the government to imprison (without trial, and for an indefinite period, but in humane conditions) anybody suspected by specified government employees of having connections with the enemy country, for fear that such people might be spies or saboteurs. Country C's attacks are eventually repelled. Several thousand people are imprisoned under the law for the three years that the war lasts. No investigation is ever carried out to establish if the government's suspicions about those people detained are well-founded.

In country F, the majority of the population decides that it must accord moral priority to liberty of the person over winning the war, and rejects the proposed War Emergency Powers Detention Law. Subsequently, enemy agents succeed in sabotaging military facilities and undermining the citizenry's morale to such an extent that country F is defeated, and subjugated by country C.

Which country has acted in a democratic fashion here? Does a desire to preserve the country's independence justify interference with people's physical liberty? Does the answer to this question depend on the severity of the interference—or on the severity of the threat from the aggressor? Or on the outcome of the war? Would we need to know the size of the majority supporting each measure before deciding if it was democratic?

Combating terrorism as a constitutional issue?

Let us suppose, as a third example, that country X has recently been subjected to several terrorist attacks by an extremist political group. The attacks involved the planting of bombs in crowded shopping areas, and have killed and injured many people. The following Prevention of Terrorism Law is proposed. It has five sections. The proposed law is approved by 51% of voters on a 90% turnout. The sections provide that:

1. Any police officer may arrest and question any person she/he suspects of being a terrorist or of being a supporter of terrorist activity. The person may be detained for up to seventy-two hours without being charged with a crime.

2. Any police officer of the rank of Inspector or above may authorize the continued detention for a period of up to twenty-eight days of any person detained under section 1.

3. Any police officer may inflict mild beatings on any person detained under section 1 or section 2 if any police officer believes this would uncover information which would prevent a future terrorist attack.

4. Any police officer police may torture and/or severely beat any person detained under section 1 or section 2 if any police officer believes this would uncover information which would prevent an imminent terrorist attack.

5. No action claimed by any police officer to be taken under any section of this law may be the subject of any legal proceedings in any court.

We might accept that the people who voted for the law are motivated by a sincerely held belief that its enactment will save many people from being killed or injured by terrorist attacks. Many of the law's supporters also believe that the police would never actually detain anyone not involved in some way with a terrorist group. Other supporters take the view that the law is bound to be applied to wholly innocent people, some of whom will be severely injured by torture; but that is a price worth paying to reduce the number of terrorist attacks. Should we pay any attention in evaluating the law to the motivations of the voters who support it? And if so, is the first or second group acting in the more 'democratic' fashion?

The various sections of the law clearly interfere to different degrees with the physical liberty and well-being of individuals detained under it. Should our evaluation of the 'democratic' nature of each provision turn on the level of support each received? If so could we accept, if only in the context of country X being subject to terrorist attack, that a three day detention is such a trivial matter that the barest of majorities would lend section 1 a democratic character? And if we accept the principle that more severe interferences demand higher levels of support, what criteria should we use to assess severity? Is a twenty-eight day detention in humane conditions more 'severe', for example, than a mild beating and release after three days? Would our views on the acceptability of the law change significantly if section 5 were removed?

Complicating the question

Such questions—and such laws—can provoke endless argument as to the proper meaning of 'democratic' governance. It might be suggested that the central function performed by a society's constitutional law is how it reconciles its people's divergent beliefs about issues of great moral significance.

Moreover, we can rapidly make the questions raised by such 'laws' and the constitutional orders in which they are made more elaborate by bringing the hypothetical law-making process under closer scrutiny. Would our conclusions about 'democracy' alter if it transpired that the law enacted in country A was supported by the 70% of the population who would not have to pay extra taxes to finance it, but opposed by the 30% who would suffer reduced income if the new system was introduced? Or alternatively, that it was supported by all of the richest 30% but opposed by many of the unemployed, who regarded it as a patronising erosion of their dignity? Similarly, would our views as to the democratic nature of the new law made in country B change if we learned that it was enthusiastically supported by almost all people over the age of sixty? Would either law become more or less democratic in our eyes if we discover that neither country permits unemployed people to vote in the law-making process?

How relevant to our evaluation of the democratic credentials of country X's Prevention of Terrorism Law would it be to know that many of the people who supported the law had no clear understanding of what was meant by the term 'torture' used in section 3; or had not appreciated that a person who was released after having been detained for the maximum twenty-eight days permitted by section 2 could be detained again the day after being released?

A constitution as a social and political contract?

We might readily agree that the issue of 'consent' permeates the many plausible answers that could be offered to those hypothetical questions. As a statement of general principle, it is difficult to find fault with Jefferson's suggestion that 'government derives its just powers from the consent of the governed'. Problems arise when we go further and ask what exactly the concept of 'consent' actually means.

The notion of a constitution as some form of 'contract', negotiated either among the citizenry themselves, or between the citizenry and its rulers, was not a novel idea, if only in philosophical terms, in 1776. The French philosopher Jean-Jacques Rousseau had explored the concept of 'direct democracy' through an idealised small city state, in which all citizens participated personally in fashioning the laws under which they lived.[6] In such a society, the legitimacy of all laws would rest on the citizenry's constant, express consent to the process of government. Rousseau rejected the idea of a divine, or natural, or God-given system of government; his men and women were not sculpted by their creator and endowed with those 'inalienable rights' that the American revolutionaries were so keen to defend. Rousseau's social order resulted from agreements between every individual citizen and the citizenry as a whole, from which government was formed. All government action therefore had a 'contractual' base; the citizens' rights and obligations under their constitution derived from covenants that they willingly made.

John Locke's celebrated *Second Treatise on Government*, first published in 1690, pursued the concept of constitutions as contracts in a slightly different form. Unlike Rousseau, Locke maintained that society was subject to a form of natural or divine law which imposed limits on individual behaviour. Government existed to provide mechanisms for enforcing the substance of such natural laws, the terms of which would serve as the constitution within which the government operated:

> it is unreasonable for Men to be Judges in their own Cases . . . Self-love will make Men partial to themselves and their friends . . . Ill Nature, Passion and Revenge will carry them too far in punishing others. And hence nothing but Confusion or Disorder will follow, and therefore God hath certainly appointed government to restrain the partiality and violence of Men.[7]

Locke and Rousseau were engaging in an exercise in abstract, academic philosophising: they were sketching ideal solutions to hypothetical problems, rather than offering a detailed programme capable of immediate implementation in their respective countries.[8] Indeed, in

---

[6] Rousseau J (1987) *The social contract* (edited and translated by Betts C).

[7] Laslett P (ed) Locke—*Two treatises of government*, II para 13.

[8] There is debate among Lockean scholars as to whether the *Second treatise* was written as an ex post facto justification for the 1688 English revolution, of which more will be said in ch 2; see Laslett P (1988) 'Two Treatises of Government and the revolution of 1688', in Laslett (ed) op cit.

the early 1700s it was difficult to identify any historical examples of such idealised sentiments being put into practice. David Hume's famous 1748 essay on the formation of constitutions and governments, 'Of the Original Contract', recorded that:

> Almost all governments which exist at present, or of which there remains any record in story, have been founded originally either on usurpation or conquest, or both, without any pretence of a fair consent or voluntary subjection of the people.[9]

Nonetheless, Locke's and Rousseau's writings provided an important reference for the American and French revolutionaries whose armed struggles were waged so that their countries might try to construct a new, 'ideal' form of constitutional order. But even at a hypothetical, abstract level, the idea of constitutions as political contracts or covenants raises major difficulties. The foremost among these is, as Rousseau recognised, 'to determine what those covenants are'.

Locke presented the emergence of government as a prerequisite for protecting individual citizens' 'property', a concept construed broadly as encompassing their lives, their physical and spiritual liberty, and their land and possessions.[10] These matters could thus be construed as entitlements which citizens derived from 'natural law', and are an obvious source of inspiration for Jefferson's notion of 'inalienable rights'. The terms are too vague to permit any exhaustive definition. Yet by focusing on the specific objectives of the American revolutionaries we can gain some indication of the issues they might encompass.

The Declaration's complaints against the British government concerned both the way that laws were made and their content. The overall thrust of the argument was that Britain was seeking to establish 'an absolute Tyranny over these States', but the general accusation comprised many specific complaints. Jefferson accused the British of, for example, 'imposing taxes on us without our consent' and '[keeping] among us, in times of peace, standing armies without the consent of our legislatures'. Jefferson is not arguing here that the levying of taxation or the maintenance of an army in peace-time are per se unacceptable features of government power, but that they are acceptable only if 'the people' affected by the measures have agreed to them.

Jefferson also identified British actions which apparently were unacceptable per se. The British had, for instance:

> dissolved Representative Houses repeatedly. . . . [and] refused for a long time, after dissolutions, to cause others to be elected. . . . [and] refused to pass laws for the accommodation of large districts of people, unless those people would relinquish the right of Representation in the Legislature, a right inestimable in them and formidable to tyrants only.[11]

This grievance, so keenly felt, suggests that Jefferson considered that no part of the government process can be acceptable if 'the people' cannot choose their preferred law-makers at regular intervals. Without this power of choice, the people could not 'consent' to the laws, and therefore those laws could not be 'just'.

A third category of complaints suggests that there were some laws to which 'the people' could not consent even if they wished to. The Americans were outraged, for example, that Britain subjected them to laws which 'depriv[ed] us in many cases of the benefits of Trial by Jury' and 'transport[ed] us beyond seas to be tried for pretended offences'. The presumption that one's guilt in criminal matters be established by a jury of one's peers, and that the scope of the criminal law be clear and stable, were seemingly regarded as fundamental principles of

---

[9] Reproduced in Hume D (1994) *Political writings* p 168 (edited by Warner D and Livingston D).

[10] See Laslett P (1988) 'The social and political theory of *Two Treatises of Government*', in Laslett (ed) op cit.

[11] For the Lockean roots of this complaint see the *Second treatise on government* paras 215–216.

social organisation by the colonists. One might attach similar importance to Jefferson's claim that the British King had:

> obstructed the Administration of Justice, by refusing his Assent to Laws for establishing Judiciary powers. He has made Judges dependent on his Will alone, for the tenure of their offices, and the amount and payment of their salaries.

But it is perhaps easier to identify precisely those aspects of government behaviour which the revolution was fought against, than those it was fought for. The rhetoric of 'All men being created equal' and sharing 'inalienable rights to life, liberty and the pursuit of happiness' is beguiling, almost perhaps bewitching. We might (again intuitively) regard such sentiments as integral ingredients of a democratic constitutional order. But what do they mean? Their concern, broadly stated, appears to be with the nature both of the legal powers that a government possesses and of the processes through which that power is exercised. The bulk of this book explores those concerns in the British context, but we might first consider the answers which Jefferson and his contemporaries offered to these questions.

II. The first 'modern' constitution?

The following pages offer a simplistically drawn picture of the constitutional settlement at which the American revolutionaries finally arrived in 1791.[12] It is intended to operate not as a yardstick against which to measure the adequacy of the details of the British constitution, but as a comparator which indicates alternative ways in which modern societies might organise their constitutional structures.

The problem—majoritarianism

A central principle informing the deliberations of the framers of the American constitution was a pervasive distrust of human nature. This sentiment was best expressed by one of Jefferson's contemporaries, James Madison, in *The Federalist Papers No 10*:

> As long as the reason of man continues fallible, and he is at liberty to exercise it, different opinions will be formed. . . . A zeal for different opinions concerning religion, concerning government and [above all] the unequal distribution of property . . . have, in turn, divided mankind into parties, inflamed them with mutual animosity, and rendered them much more disposed to vex and oppress each other than to co-operate for their common good.[13]

Madison saw no merit in trying to suppress diversity of opinion per se. That men would take different views on all manner of questions was an inevitable component of both individual and collective liberty. He was however greatly concerned to draw lessons from history concerning the dangers that a country faced from within its own borders by the combination of citizens sharing the same 'vexatious' or 'oppressive' sentiments into distinct political 'factions', a faction being:

> a number of citizens, whether amounting to a majority or minority of the whole, who are united and actuated by some common impulse of passion, or of interest, adverse to the rights of other citizens, or to the permanent and aggregate interests of the community.[14]

---

[12] For a more detailed introduction see McKay D (1989) *American politics and society* chs 3 and 4.

[13] *The Federalist Papers* were essays written by James Madison, Alexander Hamilton, and John Jay in the mid-1780s. The US Constitution which exists today was the second Constitution which the revolutionaries adopted after the War of Independence. *The Federalist Papers* were part of an intense argument between advocates of the new Constitution and defenders of the first Constitution, the so-called Articles of Confederation. The papers can be accessed at <http://www.foundingfathers.info/federalistpapers/>.   [14] *The Federalist Papers No 10.*

A form of government in which laws expressed the wishes of the electoral majority would ensure that irrational or oppressive schemes favoured by minority factions would not be given legal effect. But, Madison suggested, this 'majoritarian' system of law-making offered no protection to society when oppressive or irrational ideas were favoured by a majority. That an idea enjoyed majority support did not necessarily make it conducive to the 'public good': majorities might be misinformed about important issues, or be temporarily persuaded to abandon their better judgement by the seductive rhetoric of charismatic leaders, or simply be prepared to sacrifice their country's long-term welfare to gain a short-term, sectional advantage. Consequently, Madison argued that the most important characteristic of the Constitution he was urging his fellow Americans to adopt was its attempt to ensure that 'the majority . . . be rendered unable to concert and carry into effect schemes of oppression'.

The solutions—representative government, federalism, a separation of powers, and supra-legislative 'fundamental' rights

Madison suggested that the dangers of faction could be reduced by adopting a form of 'representative government', in which laws would be made not directly by the people themselves, but by representatives who the people chose to exercise law-making power on their behalf in a legislative assembly. Madison hoped:

> to refine and enlarge the public views by passing them through the medium of a chosen body of citizens, whose wisdom may best discern the true interest of their country and whose patriotism and love of justice will be least likely to sacrifice it to temporary or partial considerations.[15]

We might take something of a diversion at this point, and wonder how Madison's notions of 'wise' legislators fits with contemporary understandings of 'democratic' government. Let us return to countries A and B, and assume that laws are made not by the people directly, but by 100 legislators who are selected by the people to act on their behalf; a law is enacted if a simple majority of legislators support it. We may further assume that for the purposes of selecting its legislators, both countries are divided into electoral districts with equal populations, each of which returns one member to the legislature; all adult citizens have one vote in choosing their representatives, and the legislative seat is won by whichever candidate receives the most votes.

Would we consider the law enacted in country A as democratic if we learned that ten of the fifty-five legislators who voted for it represented areas where the majority of electors opposed any tax increase, and that the ten legislators concerned had promised their electors they would vote against any such measure? Would it make any difference to our answer if the reason for the ten legislators' change of heart was the force of arguments presented in favour of the law during a debate in the legislature? The answer to this question presumably depends on how we answer the logically precedent question of whether the role of a legislator is simply to transmit the wishes of her electors into law, or is rather to exercise her judgement as to the 'best' response to particular issues, even if her electors would wish her to reach a different conclusion?

A constitution in which law-making power is delegated or entrusted to a small number of citizens makes the task of judging the democratic nature of laws more complex, for we immediately become concerned not just with the merits of the particular law per se, but also with the merits of those laws which determine the way that legislators are selected and the ways that they behave during the law-making process. Might we question the 'democratic' basis of every law country A enacted, for example, if some electoral districts contained twice as many electors as others, but still returned only one member? Or, to revisit a familiar question, if unemployed people were not permitted to vote? Might we also feel uneasy about the

---

[15] Ibid.

law-making process if we learned that many seats in the legislature had been contested by four or five candidates, all of whom attracted approximately equal electoral support, so that the winner was voted for by barely 30% of the people qualified to vote?

A less contentious matter, at least from the American revolutionaries' perspective, was the presumption that the people's representatives, once elected, should enjoy unimpeded freedom to discuss any subject they chose, and to cast their law-making votes in any manner they wished. The colonists' aforementioned complaints over British interference with the operation of their colonial legislatures have clear philosophical roots in Locke's suggestion that 'consent' to government demanded that the people's legislature should not be hindered by any legal rules:

> from assembling in its due time, or from acting freely, pursuant to those ends for which it was constituted, the Legislative is altered. For tis not a certain number of men, no nor their meeting, unless they have also Freedom of Debating, and Leisure of perfecting, what is for the good of the Society wherein the Legislature exists. . . . For it is not Names that Constitute governments, but the use and exercise of those powers that were intended to accompany them.[16]

The issue of representative government invites us to consider further dimensions of the concept of liberty adverted to in the Declaration. Jefferson's condemnation of imprisonment for 'pretended offences' addresses liberty in a physical and individual sense. Yet the Declaration also suggests that liberty bears more abstract and collective meanings, particularly in respect of matters concerning freedom of speech and conscience.

This leads us once again to consider the notion of 'consent' to government. Jefferson and his contemporaries assumed that 'man' was a rational, autonomous being; the preservation of his liberty demanded that 'he' make decisions on the basis of full and accurate knowledge. Consent had to be *informed consent*. The American revolutionaries thus placed a considerable premium on safeguarding individual citizens' freedom of conscience and expression in relation to political matters. Consequently, the restrictions which Britain had placed on the activities of representative colonial legislatures were perceived by the colonists as an intolerable infringement of their collective liberty.

This particular strand of 'liberty' can be compromised in many ways, and it is intimately tied to our contemporary understandings of 'democratic government'. Would we conclude, for example, that no law made by the legislative assembly of our hypothetical country A could be democratic if it was a criminal offence for any person to reveal details of legislators' speeches or votes on the proposals before them? In such circumstances, electors would not know which legislators had supported or opposed tax increases, and so could not make informed choices as to their preferred candidate at the next election? Would we draw the same conclusion about country B if we learned it was a crime in that society for anyone to voice criticisms of the laws enacted by the legislature, with a view to convincing electors to choose different representatives at the next election? These issues are obviously of major significance to any attempt to gauge the adequacy of the mechanism through which legislatures are elected.

Madison's particular vision of 'representative government' clearly demands that one accept the desirability of fostering a certain degree of elitism in one's governors, and as such demands that law-makers ignore the irrational or oppressive sentiments of the citizens they represent. But this elitism may substantially dilute the 'representativeness' of the laws enacted. The preamble to the US Constitution begins with the words: 'We the people of the United States, in order to form a more perfect union . . . '. Yet 'the people' who chose the legislators who framed the Constitution comprised barely 10% of the populace of the colonies.[17] Voters were

---

[16] Locke J (1690) *Second treatise on government* para 215 (reproduced in Laslett op cit).

[17] See, for contrasting views, Beard C (1990) 'An economic interpretation of the Constitution', in Ollman B and Birmbaum J (eds) *The United States Constitution* and Brown R (1987) 'The Beard thesis attacked: a political approach', in Levy L (ed) *The making of the Constitution*.

all male, almost all were white, and the great majority were atypically well educated and afflu-ent. The consent of the poor, the uneducated, and women was not presumed necessary to the establishment of the United States' newly created form of government, seemingly because the framers of the Constitution doubted that such groups, which comprised the mass of the populace, could be relied upon to support 'rational' (from the framers' perspectives) con-stitutional provisions.

Such discriminatory principles might lead us to conclude that the 'consent' which the revo-lutionaries sought was somewhat illusory. This question is one to which we will frequently return in the context of British constitutional history and practice. Yet we may also consider it prudent to be concerned with the powers that legislators might wield once they have assumed (in accordance with whatever notion of popular consent determines their selection) their law-making powers. Madison recognised that it was by no means a complete answer to the spectre of tyranny simply to hope that a system of representative government, in which legis-lators were selected by an elitist electorate, would invariably produce rulers who would have the wisdom and capacity always to forswear sectional objectives favoured by factions of the population. One could not always rely on 'patriotism and love of justice' rather than 'tem-porary and partial considerations' being the dominant forces in the minds of one's chosen law-making representatives, no matter how carefully they were selected. Madison considered that it was: 'In vain to say that enlightened statesmen will be able to adjust . . . clashing interests and render them all subservient to the public good. Enlightened statesmen will not always be at the helm'.[18]

In those circumstances, the problem of majoritarianism was simply displaced from the arena of 'the people' themselves to the much smaller number of citizens who served as legisla-tors. For the designers of the US Constitution, this indicated that preserving 'the public good' might demand that the helmsmen steering the ship of state either be precluded from embark-ing on voyages to undesirable destinations, or at the very least, be subject to constraints that made such journeys very difficult.

Federalism and the separation of powers

The American colonists' sense of themselves as citizens of a single nation was not well devel-oped. Each colony had been created, in the legal sense, by 'Charters' granted by the British monarchy.[19] These had been granted at different times, and on rather different terms. By 1776, the (then) thirteen colonies (from a British perspective) or States (in the revolutionaries' eyes) had developed distinctive political and social cultures, which were expressed in their respec-tive laws.[20] Yet the colonists also shared many common practical and philosophical concerns. The most pressing was obviously justifying and then succeeding in their revolutionary war: a task that could be achieved only if the colonies acted in a co-ordinated manner; aspects of their individual identities would have to be surrendered to a 'national' military and political project. But having won their independence through such unified action, the revolutionaries then faced the dilemma of how best to structure the inter-relationships between the nation, the States, and the people. Their eventual solution was to fashion a 'federal' constitution.

In the modern era, 'federalism' is a concept bearing many meanings. As perceived by the American revolutionaries, their federal constitution would have the positive virtue of creating a multiplicity of powerful political societies within a single nation State, each wielding significant political powers within precisely defined geographical boundaries. However, the Constitution placed limits on the political autonomy of each State by granting sole responsibility for certain

---

[18] *Federalist Papers No 10.*

[19] The grant of Charters was a part of what were known as the Monarch's 'prerogative' powers. We examine these powers more closely in ch 4.

[20] See Bailyn op cit. pp 191–193. A contemporaneous perspective is offered by Madison in *The Federalist Papers No 39.*

types of governmental power to the newly created national government. Those matters left within the sole competence of the States, while important in themselves, were not regarded as crucial to the well-being of the entire nation. It would not therefore be dangerous to allow the people of each State to devise their own 'internal' constitutional arrangements to determine their respective preferences on these issues: if they chose to indulge factional sentiment within their own borders, so be it; but their choices would have no legal force in the other States. Each State could quite lawfully enact different laws to deal with matters within their geographical and functional jurisdiction.

The principle underlying the creation of a federal nation again derives from a particular view of the meaning of 'consent'. It assumes that a 'people' within which divergent factions held differing views on major (if not fundamental) political matters would be more likely to agree to live under a constitutional order which offered many opportunities for those views to be given legal effect at the same time, albeit within limited geographical areas, than under a system which allowed a majority of the entire population, acting through a national legislature, to impose its preferences on all issues on the entire country.

Even if one accepts this principle as desirable, however, there remains the problem of deciding which powers should be allocated to which sphere of government. The American revolutionaries initially adopted a constitution known as the Articles of Confederation, which gave virtually no powers to the national government. The Articles were rejected within ten years, in favour of a new constitutional settlement which granted the national government considerably more authority.[21] The national government would be empowered to conduct foreign policy, to grant national citizenship, to maintain military forces and wage war, to issue the national currency, to impose customs duties on imported and exported goods, to levy sales taxes (but not income taxes) on a uniform basis throughout the country, to run the nation's postal service, and to regulate commerce among the States and with foreign nations. The States were not permitted to enact laws concerning these matters.

Thus, if our hypothetical countries A and E were organised on the same federal lines as the US Constitution, country A's central legislature would apparently have been unable to introduce its proposed anti-unemployment law, irrespective of how many legislators supported it, since the constitution seemingly did not give it the power to levy income taxes. Alternatively, if we accepted that the law introduced by country E was an element of the central legislature's war powers, it could be enacted even if the majority of people in several States heartily disapproved of it.

Madison's concern with the dangers of faction and majoritarianism was initially directed at placing limits on the power of national government, acting at the behest of either a majority of the people or a majority of the States,[22] to produce irrational or oppressive laws. This safeguard was to be achieved in part by a further development on the theme of representative government. The Constitution eventually devised a representative form of national government which produced a balance between the people as a whole and the people as citizens of their respective States. The framers of the Constitution created an elaborate separation (or fragmentation) of powers within the institutions of the national government. The national legislature, the Congress, would have two component parts. Seats in the House of Representatives were to be apportioned among the States in proportion to their respective populations. In contrast, each State, irrespective of its population size, would have two members in the Senate. The approval of a majority in both chambers would be required to enact laws.[23] Thus, in simple

---

[21] See Jensen M (1990) 'The Articles of Confederation', in Birmbaum and Ollman op cit; Levy L (1987) 'Introduction—the making of the Constitution 1776–1789', in Levy op cit.

[22] Since the States were not of equal (population) size, the two concepts are not coterminous.

[23] Jefferson's aforementioned reiteration of Locke's analysis of the prerequisites of effective legislatures was met by the Constitution's requirements that Congress meet at least once every year, and that its proceedings, including the voting behaviour of its members, be published.

terms, neither a majority of the legislative representatives of the States nor a majority of the population could impose its wishes on the other. The dual nature of the national legislature did not however exhaust the fragmentation of power to which the Constitution subjected the national government.

The task of implementing Congressional legislation was granted not to the Congress itself, but to a separate, 'executive' branch of government headed by an elected President. In addition to possessing a limited array of personal powers, the President was also afforded a significant role in the legislative process. Measures attracting majority support in both chambers of Congress would become laws only when signed by the President. Should he refuse his assent, a measure would be enacted only if then approved by a two-thirds majority in the Senate and the House. The President was thus empowered to block the law-making preferences of a small Congressional majority, but not the wishes of an overwhelming majority in both houses.

The framers' initial distrust of populist sentiment was further emphasised by the electoral arrangements made for choosing the President and the legislators who staffed the two chambers of Congress. While members of the House were to be elected directly by electors in each State, Senators would be selected by each State's own legislative assembly, and the President would be chosen by an 'electoral college' of representatives from each State.

Thus two branches of the national government were chosen by what was in effect an 'electorate within an electorate', whose members might be thought likely to (in Madison's words) 'refine and enlarge the public views'. Madison assumed that this elitist process would much reduce the possibility that the occupants of the most important national government offices would be motivated by 'temporary or partial considerations' when they performed the task of enacting and implementing laws made within the boundaries of their respective constitutional competence. But the Constitution took one further step in its efforts to guarantee that the federal and institutional separation of powers which the revolutionaries considered fundamental to the nation's long-term security and prosperity would be preserved against the threat of internal factions, even if that faction should be large enough to control the national law-making process.

Fundamental rights and a supra-legislative constitution

It perhaps sounds fatuous to record that the Americans assumed that their Constitution would function as a 'constituent' document, but the point is of considerable significance. The framers regarded the rules they had created as 'the highest form of law' within American society. The Constitution was the source of all governmental powers; its terms identified the fundamental moral and political principles according to which society should be managed.

Federalism was clearly a fundamental political value to the framers of the Constitution. This was evident not only in the proposed allocation of powers between the national and State governments, but also in the procedures through which the Constitution itself was to gain legal force. As Madison explained in *The Federalist Papers No 39*:

> assent and ratification is to be given by the people, not as individuals composing one entire nation, but as composing the distinct and independent States to which they respectively belong. . . . The act, therefore, establishing the Constitution will not be a *national* but a *federal* act.[24]

Constitutional values as fundamental law

Madison and the other architects of the Constitution rejected the Lockean notion of 'divine' law in the sense of considering human beings subservient to a rigid set of rules emanating from a deity. Similarly, they were not persuaded that the moral values which they wished to control the government of their new nation should be subject to an eternally fixed code of 'natural'

---

[24] Original emphasis.

law, which could never be altered. They nevertheless concluded that once they had succeeded in identifying the mutually acceptable principles according to which the foundations of government should be laid, those 'fundamental laws' should enjoy considerable fixity. The moral principles expressed in the Constitution had not lightly been arrived at: they were not lightly to be discarded; they were not to be left at the mercy of the ordinary institutions of government.

But the framers were not so arrogant as to assume that the views they held in 1789–1791 amounted to eternal truths, which would control the government of American society forever. The federal Congress, the federal President, and the various State governments would all be bodies of limited legal competence: they possessed only those powers which 'the people' had granted to them in the Constitution, and had no capacity to create new powers for themselves. The ultimate, or sovereign legal authority, was 'the people'. If the Congress, or the President, or the States wished to acquire new powers, they would have to persuade 'the people' to amend the Constitution. The framers of the Constitution decided that 'the people' would express themselves for this purpose through a special law-making process, involving both the Congress and the States, which demanded extremely large majorities. Article 5 of the Constitution permits amendments only if proposed changes attract the support of a two-thirds majority of both houses of Congress and three quarters of the States.[25] Madison and his colleagues had concluded that the fundamental moral values identified in the Constitution had to be deeply *entrenched* within society's governmental structure.

'The people' was therefore not a law-making body that would be in constant, or even regular session. It would act only on those rare occasions when the overwhelming majority of members of Congress, and an even larger majority of the States, considered that the time had come for aspects of the country's fundamental laws to be altered. 'The people' was not an ordinary, but a quite *extraordinary* law-making body.

The Bill of Rights

The Constitution was in fact substantially altered almost as soon as it was introduced. The Constitution was adopted on the assumption that Congress' first task would be to formulate amendment proposals to send to the States for their approval.

Ten amendments, colloquially referred to as the 'Bill of Rights', were introduced in 1791. The first eight amendments listed various individual liberties (much influenced by the litany of complaints in the Declaration) with which the institutions of national government could not interfere. These need not be listed in their entirety here, but we might note some of their most important provisions. The First Amendment precluded Congress from enacting laws which abridged freedom of speech, the freedom of the press, and freedom of religious belief. The Fourth Amendment forbade national government officials from conducting arbitrary searches of citizens' houses and seizing of their possessions. The Fifth Amendment prevented the national government from appropriating citizens' property, or interfering with their lives or liberty, without 'due process of law'. The Sixth Amendment guaranteed the right to trial by jury in criminal cases while the Eighth Amendment prohibited the infliction of 'cruel and unusual punishments'.

Madison and his supporters had initially argued that the 'Bill of Rights' was superfluous. Congress and the Presidency possessed only those powers which the Constitution had granted them. Since no powers had been given to infringe the 'liberties' listed in the Bill of Rights, the Constitution implicitly forbade the national government acting in such a manner. The Madisonian 'faction' was later convinced that giving such liberties explicit protection was a beneficial course to follow. In part this shift of position was for the tactical reason of assuaging opposition to the new Constitution and thereby facilitating its adoption. However Madison also accepted that the Bill of Rights would have an intrinsic, declaratory value, further

---

[25] This somewhat oversimplifies the position, but the description is adequate for our limited purposes.

emphasising the basic moral principles the revolution had been fought to defend. These provisions themselves could only be altered through the Article 5 amendment process.

The importance which the framers accorded to maximising the political autonomy of the States within the Constitution's federal structure is illustrated by their decision to apply the provisions of the Bill of Rights only against the national government, not against the States. If the people of the States wished to impose similar restraints on their respective State governments, they were free to do so. Madison himself, once he accepted the desirability in principle of the Bill of Rights, had favoured its extension to State as well as Federal governments. He found little support for this argument either in Congress or among the States; nothing in the text of the first eight amendments indicated that they were to control the States as well as Congress and the Presidency.

The constitutional role of the Supreme Court

The Constitution could be no more than a framework document. It outlined the broad principles within which the government process should be conducted. It did not promulgate detailed rules which would provide answers to every foreseeable (or unforeseeable) problem that might arise. The framers anticipated that there would frequently be ambiguity concerning the national/State separation of powers. Alternatively, within the context of the Bill of Rights, doubt might arise as to whether a Congressional law or Presidential action 'abridged the freedom of the press', or imposed a 'cruel and unusual punishment'. The framers entrusted the task of answering such questions to the US Supreme Court.

The intended role of the Supreme Court was outlined by Alexander Hamilton in *The Federalist Papers No 78*. Hamilton envisaged that the Court would serve as the ultimate arbiter of the meaning of the Constitution. 'The people' had intended that the Constitution would impose agreed limitations on the powers of government bodies, and in Hamilton's view:

> Limitations of this kind can be preserved in practice no other way than through the medium of courts of justice, whose duty it must be to declare all acts contrary to the manifest tenor of the Constitution void.

The Court would therefore stand:

> between the people and the legislature, to keep the latter within the limits assigned to their authority . . . A constitution is, in fact, and must be regarded by the judges as fundamental law. . . . the Constitution ought to be preferred to the [legislature's] statute, the intention of the people to the intention of their agents.

This did not mean that the Supreme Court was to be in any sense 'superior' to the Congress:

> It only supposes that the power of the people is superior to both, and that where the will of the legislature [or the Presidency] . . . stands in opposition to that of the people, the judges ought to be governed by the latter and not the former.

Unlike the Presidency, the legislature, or the States, the Court had 'neither sword nor purse'; the effectiveness of its judgments would depend not on any coercive power, but on their legitimacy, which we may construe as their capacity to convince the citizenry that they were in conformity with the meaning of the Constitution.

Great care would thus have to be exercised in selecting the judges who sat on the Supreme Court, for they bore a heavy constitutional burden. Hamilton suggested that:

> there can be but few men in the society who will have sufficient skill in the laws to qualify them for the stations of judges. And making the proper deductions for the ordinary depravity of human nature, the number must be still smaller of those who unite the requisite integrity with the requisite knowledge.

The Constitution did not specify either the intellectual or moral qualifications that Supreme Court nominees should possess, but involved both the President and the Senate in their selection. The President would nominate candidates for judicial office, but his nominees could assume their seats only after receiving the approval of the Senate. The President could thus not 'pack' the Court with appointees who did not enjoy the confidence of the legislature, although a President and Senate majority who adhered to the same faction could do so. Hamilton had placed much emphasis on a pre-revolutionary custom or tradition, developed (as discussed in chapter three) within the British constitution, but corrupted in the colonies, that both politicians and the judiciary themselves should regard the courts' 'interpretation' of the law as a matter above factional politics. Politicians should thus forswear considerations of personal or party advantage in selecting members of the judiciary, while the judges themselves should exclude such considerations from their judgments.

But the framers did not rely solely on Presidential and Congressional self-restraint to safeguard the independence of the Supreme Court. Once the Judges were in office, neither the President nor the Congress would be able to remove them simply because they disapproved of the decisions the Court subsequently reached. Unless convicted of criminal offences, or guilty of grossly immoral behaviour, Supreme Court Justices were to enjoy lifetime tenure, with payment of their salaries expressly guaranteed in the Constitution itself.

The significance of judicial power

The enormous power and responsibility entrusted to the Supreme Court under the American Constitution can be illustrated by returning to our hypothetical nations. If countries A and E had federal constitutions modelled on the initial American settlement, country A's tax-raising law if enacted by the country's Congress would seem to have been illegal as the Congress had no power to levy income tax. In contrast, the detention measures enacted by the Congress of nation E would seem a constitutional exercise of its war powers.

Suppose, however, that the Supreme Court of country A concluded that the law in question was in reality a measure to regulate commerce among the nation's various States (a matter clearly within the national legislature's competence) by stimulating economic growth, and the tax thereby raised was merely an incidental side effect. As such, the measure would be constitutional. Similarly let us suppose that the Supreme Court of country E held that the law introducing indefinite imprisonment without trial was cruel and unusual punishment and thereby breached the Eighth Amendment. Would we conclude that such judgments represented a judicial attempt to subvert the fundamental principles of the Constitution, or that they were a surprising but nevertheless defensible interpretation of an ambiguous constitutional text?

It would be misleading to suggest that Supreme Court decisions which frustrated the wishes of the elected Congress or President were necessarily 'undemocratic' simply because the Judges themselves were not elected officials. Such accusations would have conclusive force only if one equates 'democracy' with a constitutional order which gives unfettered supremacy to a bare legislative majority. They would be less convincing if one took a view of 'democracy' which entailed the protection of 'higher laws' against the possibly transient and ill-informed views of the greater number of one's legislators. Within that constitutional context, accusations of 'anti-democratic' conduct might as readily be levelled at the elected politicians apparently seeking to subvert the wishes of 'the people' from whom their powers derived.

Conclusion

Over 200 years ago, it took a revolutionary war for the American colonists to rid themselves of what they considered an unacceptable constitutional order. The new constitution which the United States subsequently fashioned marked a radical departure from traditional British understandings of the appropriate way for a country to regulate the relationship between its people and its government. The principles adopted in the US Constitution have been widely copied by many nations which have created or redesigned their own constitutional arrangements in the modern era. Lest it be assumed that the Americans created an 'ideal' constitutional order, we might note that the framers preserved the institution of negro slavery by leaving its abolition to the individual States. Thus while slave-owners had 'property' (guaranteed by the Fifth Amendment) in their slaves, slaves themselves enjoyed no inalienable rights, either of a physical or spiritual nature. Jefferson, for whom all men were supposedly created equal, was himself a slave-owner. And those framers who found slavery morally abhorrent were prepared to tolerate its continued existence in the southern States rather than take the risk that some States would reject the new constitutional settlement.[26]

But, as we shall begin to see in chapter two, the contemporary British constitution retains many important elements of the system which the Americans rejected as tyrannical and oppressive in 1776. In modern Britain, there is no likelihood of a violent revolution to overhaul our constitutional arrangements. The country has largely[27] avoided the difficulties posed by armed conflict between factions of its population for over 300 years. For some observers, that basic political reality might be sufficient grounds for concluding that there is no need even to question the adequacy of the constitution, still less to expend energy on proposals advocating fundamental reforms to its substance. Yet as we enter the twenty-first century, the workings of the constitution are the subject of wide-ranging and critical debate. We examine the sources and nature of that debate throughout the remainder of this book. The modest objective of this opening chapter has been to identify some of the general ideas we might use to evaluate Britain's existing constitutional arrangements. Chapter two turns to what many commentators regard as perhaps the most important part of Britain's constitutional heritage—the doctrine of parliamentary sovereignty.

Suggested further reading

Academic and political commentary

BAILYN B (1967) *The ideological origins of the American revolution* ch 2; pp 198–229

MADISON J (1787) *The federalist papers No. 10* (<http://www.foundingfathers.info/federalistpapers/>)

HAMILTON A (1787) *The federalist papers no. 78* (<http://www.foundingfathers.info/federalistpapers/>)

CORWIN E (1928) 'The higher law background of American constitutional law (part I)' *Harvard LR* 149

HOLDEN B (1988) *Understanding liberal democracy* ch 1

MAIER P (1963) 'John Wilkes and American disillusionment with Britain' *William and Mary Quarterly* 373

Case law and legislation

Marbury v Madison (1803) 1 Cranch 137

---

[26] See particularly Madison's *Federalist Papers No 54*; Du Bois W (1990) 'Slavery and the Founding Fathers', in Ollman and Birmbaum op cit; Kelly A, Harbison W and Belz H (1983) *The American Constitution* ch 14.

[27] The history of Britain's relationship with Ireland demands that we qualify the notion of internal peace to an appreciable extent.

Chapter 2

Parliamentary Sovereignty

In analysing how constitutions work, it is helpful to think of 'laws' as a formal way in which 'democratic' societies express consent to the way they are governed. The US Constitution is a clear example of a society making fundamental changes to its legal structures because its people no longer consented to their existing form of government. The US Constitution reflects its architects' commitment to what many modern western societies regard as a basic, if contentious, point of democratic theory; namely that the more important that a particular law is to the way society is governed, the more difficult it should be for that law to be changed. One might suggest the reason for this is that it would be undesirable for fundamental laws to be vulnerable to reform which does not attract the 'consent' of the governed. The difficult questions facing designers of modern constitutions are: firstly, how much importance should one ascribe to particular values; secondly, how much consent should one need to change those values; and thirdly, how should that consent be expressed?

The US Constitution can only be amended with the consent of two-thirds of the members of the federal Congress and the legislatures of three quarters of the fifty states. Because this level of consent is difficult to obtain, the Constitution has been amended fewer than thirty times. This degree of permanence might justifiably lead us to say that the Constitution marks out stable legal boundaries which define the nature of the American people's consent to the powers of their government. This does not mean that the US Constitution invariably prevents a tyranny of the majority—but it precludes a tyranny of minorities and of *small* majorities.

Most law-making in the United States takes place *within* the boundaries of consent outlined by the Constitution. These laws affect issues not fundamental to society's basic values, and so can be changed in less difficult ways. Some can be altered by the Congress, some by individual States. A straightforward majority vote in the particular legislature is often enough to change those laws not regarded as essential to society's continued welfare.

Pre-1688—natural or divine law

The American system protects fundamental values by making their reform subject to a cumbersome, super-majoritarian law-making process. An analysis of early-seventeenth-century English case law reveals several judgments in which courts suggested that there were certain values that were *so fundamental* to the English constitution that they could not be changed at all. These principles are perhaps analogous to the 'inalienable rights' Thomas Jefferson identified in the US *Declaration of Independence*. Some judges seemed ready to suggest that there was a system of 'natural law' or 'divine law' which limited what the various branches of government might do.

For example in *Dr Bonham's Case*[1] in 1610, Coke CJ had said:

> And it appears in our books, that in many cases, the common law will control Acts of Parliament, and sometime adjudge them to be utterly void: for when an Act of Parliament is against common right or reason, or repugnant, or impossible to be performed, the common law will control it, and adjudge such Act to be void.

Five years later, in *Day v Savadge*, Hobart CJ concluded that; 'even an Act of Parliament, made against natural equity, as to make a man judge in his own case, is void in itself, for jura naturae sunt immutabilia, and they are leges legum'.[2] Similarly in 1653 in *R v Love*, Keble J had pronounced that; 'Whatsoever is not consonant to the law of God, or to right reason which is maintained by scripture, . . . be it Acts of Parliament, customs, or any judicial acts of the Court, it is not the law of England'.[3]

The intricacies of the legal arguments expounded in these cases need not detain us here. The point to stress is that there have been periods in English constitutional history when it seems that it was widely believed that there were basic moral or political principles that it was not within the power of any number of the people, through any type of law-making process, to change in any way at all; and that the substance of those principles would be protected by the courts.[4]

The Diceyan (or orthodox) theory

Modern Britain does not have such a complex constitutional structure. We no longer recognise natural law doctrines. And unlike the Americans, we have not accepted that fundamental constitutional values should be safeguarded by a complex amendment process. The 'basic principle' of the British constitution can be summed up fairly bluntly. A statute, that is a piece of legislation produced by Parliament, is the highest form of law within the British constitutional structure. The British Parliament, it is said, is a *sovereign* law-maker.

In describing this concept of parliamentary sovereignty, we draw mainly on two sources. The first is the political events of the late-seventeenth century, when England experienced its last civil war.[5] The second is a legal theory articulated in the 1880s by an Oxford law professor, A V Dicey, in a celebrated textbook, *An introduction to the study of the law of the constitution*.

---

[1] (1610) 8 Co Rep 114a at 118a. The case concerned legislation passed in 1561, which gave the College of Physicians control over the practice of medicine in London.

[2] (1614) Hob 85; 80 ER 235 at 237. Loosely translated: 'natural law is immutable and the highest form of law'. The case concerned, prosaically, trespass to a bag of nutmegs. The legal point in issue was whether a governmental body could act as a judge in a cause to which it was also a party even if given that competence by statute.

[3] (1653) 5 State Tr 825 at 828.

[4] The cautious language indicates that commentators hold divergent views as to the principles the judges were espousing. Several analysts suggest that *Bonham* is merely advancing an unusual rule of statutory interpretation; see Thorne S (1938) 'Dr Bonham's case' *LQR* 543; Plucknett T (1928) 'Doctor Bonham's Case and judicial review' *Harvard LR* 30. In contrast see Dike C (1976) 'The case against parliamentary sovereignty' *Public Law* 283; Maitland F (1908) *The constitutional history of England* at p 300; 'It is always difficult to pin Coke to a theory, but he does seem to claim distinctly that the common law is above the statute'.

Goldsworthy's study—(1999) *The sovereignty of Parliament*—should now perhaps be the primary point of reference on seventeenth-century understandings and practice. Goldsworthy's critique also subscribes to the view that Coke was asserting a power of interpretation rather than invalidation of statutory provisions; see especially Goldsworthy op cit ch 5.

[5] For a helpful introduction to the period see Wicks E (2006) *The evolution of a constitution* ch 1.

Dicey wields an enormous influence on British constitutional law. This is in many senses unfortunate. Some of the political views which Dicey held when *The law of the constitution* was first published would be considered entirely unacceptable from a contemporary moral standpoint. Dicey certainly did not approve of democracy as that concept is now understood. For example, he opposed allowing women or the working class to vote in parliamentary elections.[6] Nevertheless, it is important to understand the basic features of his theory. Dicey suggested that the concept of parliamentary sovereignty has two parts—a positive limb and a negative limb.

The positive and negative limbs of Dicey's theory

The principle articulated in the *positive limb* is that Parliament can make or unmake any law whatsoever. If a majority of members of the House of Commons approve a particular Bill, and this is then approved by both a majority in the House of Lords and by the Monarch, that Bill becomes an Act,[7] irrespective of its contents. In legal terms there are no limits to the substance of statute law; Parliament can make any law that it wishes. Nor does it matter how big the majority is in support of a particular measure; an Act passed by a majority of one in both the Commons and Lords is as authoritative as legislation which receives unanimous support. Relatedly, no distinction is drawn between 'ordinary' and 'constitutional' (or 'fundamental') law. Parliament legislates in the same way for trivial matters as for vitally important issues.

The proposition advanced in the *negative limb* is that the legality of an Act of Parliament cannot be challenged in a court. There is no mechanism within the British constitution for declaring an Act of Parliament legally invalid. Dicey's theory rejects the idea that the courts could invoke natural law or divine law to conclude that a statute was 'unconstitutional': the substantive moral content of legislation is in legal terms irrelevant.[8]

The negative and positive limbs of Dicey's theory offer us a simple principle upon which to base analysis of the constitution. As we examine the subject further, it will become evident that the picture is not quite as clear as Diceyan theory would suggest. But before examining criticisms of this orthodox theory, it is useful to consider the sources invoked by contemporary adherents to Dicey's thesis. Why have we accepted that statute is the highest form of law?

The political source of parliamentary sovereignty—the 'glorious revolution'

The central theme of seventeenth-century English political history is a struggle for power between the House of Commons and House of Lords and the Monarchy. In its most acute form, the conflict produced the civil war, the execution of Charles I, the brief rule of Oliver Cromwell, the restoration of Charles II to the throne, the subsequent overthrow of his brother, James II, in 1688, and the installation of William of Orange and his wife Mary as joint Monarchs.[9] But less dramatically, seventeenth-century England was continually beset by squabbles between the King, Commons, and Lords over the extent of their respective powers. This argument was waged as frequently in the courts as on the battlefield: both the King and the respective houses of Parliament hoped that the courts would supply rulings which favoured their own

---

[6] See McEldowney J (1985) 'Dicey in historical perspective', in McAuslan P and McEldowney J (eds) *Law, legitimacy and the constitution*; Loughlin M (1992) *Public law and political theory* ch 7.

[7] The terms 'Act', 'statute', and 'legislation' are used interchangeably.

[8] Cf Dicey op cit at p 39: 'These then are the three traits of Parliamentary sovereignty as it exists in England: first, the power of the legislature to alter any law, fundamental or otherwise, as freely and in the same manner as other laws; secondly, the absence of any legal distinction between constitutional and other laws; thirdly, the non-existence of any judicial or other authority having the right to nullify an Act of Parliament, or to treat it as void or unconstitutional'.

[9] See further Wicks (2006) op cit ch 1; Russell C (1971) *The crisis of Parliaments*; Miller J (1983) *The glorious revolution*.

preferences. As chapter four suggests, the courts switched their allegiance in these disputes as expediency and principle demanded. But on some occasions they struck an independent line; in the natural or divine law cases mentioned earlier, the judges were effectively saying that neither Acts of Parliament nor the actions of the Monarch were supreme. Both were subject to the laws of God and nature, and of course only the judges could identify the content of these immutable principles. In functionalist terms, this principle would have made the judiciary the 'highest source of law' within the English constitution.

Such reasoning did not commend itself to the Stuart Monarchs, who believed in the doctrine of the divine right of kings,[10] which placed complete legal authority in the King himself. James I explained the rationale behind this theory in 1610:

> Kings are not only God's lieutenants on earth . . . but even by God himself they are called Gods. . . . [They] exercise a manner or resemblance of divine power on earth. . . . they make and unmake their subjects; they have power of raising and casting down; of life and of death; judges over all their subjects, and in all causes, and yet accountable to none but God only.

James I would have rejected any assertion that this claimed power amounted to tyranny; he considered himself bound by an oath he took to exercise his powers in accordance with the law. Yet since he also claimed the power to alter such laws at will, the substantive value of the oath was limited. The previous Tudor dynasty, in which the foundations of a recognisably modern government structure were laid,[11] made no such sweeping claims. Nor was James' doctrine uncontested by the Commons and the Lords. Both bodies invoked constitutional principles of considerable antiquity to limit the Stuart Kings' effective legal powers.

Since the signing of the Magna Carta in the thirteenth century it had been accepted that the King could not levy taxation without 'Parliament's' approval.[12] The production of the Magna Carta could be compared to the American revolution in some respects. Both events represented a severe rupture in the fabric of society's previously dominant political values. They signalled that the present government no longer commanded the consent of 'the people', and they led to the digging of new political foundations upon which the constitution's legal structure was based. Magna Carta was not a democratic constitutional settlement as we now understand the term.[13] It simply transferred some powers from one person, the King, to the few aristocrats who effectively controlled 'Parliament'.[14] Nevertheless, Magna Carta broadened, slightly, the basis of consent required to make law in English society. The Monarch's grip on the reins of constitutional power remained particularly firm because she retained the personal legal power (or 'prerogative') to summon and dissolve Parliament when she thought fit.

By 1600, the Commons and Lords had become increasingly reluctant to approve taxes without a guarantee that Monarchs accepted limits on their personal powers. Although (as chapter four notes) the Stuart Monarchs found ways to subvert this principle, Charles II and James II generally sought to govern the country by proclamation or prerogative powers, bypassing Parliament and entrusting the administration of government to their own appointees.

---

[10] See Plucknett T (11th edn, 1960) Taswell-Langmead's *English constitutional history* pp 329–333.

[11] See Elton G (1953) *The Tudor revolution in government*; Loach J (1990) *Parliament under the Tudors*.

[12] Article 14 of Magna Carta. 'Parliament' did not then exist in a recognisably modern form; Article 14 refers to 'the archbishops, bishops, abbots, earls, and greater barons, by writ addressed to each severally, and all other tenants *in capite* by a general writ addressed to the sheriff of each shire'. One can discern here the outline of the subsequent distinction between the Lords and the Commons.

[13] Professor John Millar argued for example that Magna Carta was intended 'to establish the privileges of a few individuals. A great tyrant on one side [King John], and a set of petty tyrants on the other, seem to have divided the kingdom, and the great body of people, disregarded and oppressed on all hands, were beholden for any privileges bestowed on them, to the jealousy of their masters' (1803) *Historical view* vol II pp 80–81, quoted in Loughlin (1992) op cit p 7.

[14] On the events leading to the signing of Magna Carta, and the terms of the document see Plucknett (1960) op cit ch 4.

This became very difficult whenever the Crown needed money above and beyond its own resources—whenever it wanted to go to war for example.

The Triennial Act of 1641 was a measure passed by Parliament which purportedly required the Monarch to summon Parliament at least once every three years. Yet, following the restoration of the Stuart Monarchy in 1660, Charles II did not regard himself as obliged to obey its terms. The many causes of the 1688 revolution cannot sensibly be addressed in detail here. It is nevertheless clear that James II's evident contempt for the (admittedly limited) notion of citizen 'consent' to the government process, made apparent by his disinclination to allow Parliament to sit on a regular basis,[15] was a major contributor to his eventual downfall.

The complaints of the English revolutionaries were outlined in the 1688 '*Declaration of Right*', the broad thrust of which was that: 'the late King James, by the assistance of diverse evill councellors, judges, and ministers imployed by him, did endeavour to subvert and extirpate the Protestant religion, and the laws and liberties of this kingdom'.

Like the American revolutionaries' *Declaration of Independence*, the English revolutionaries' *Declaration of Right* supported its general accusation with numerous specific charges, and the similarities between the two documents extended to matters of substance as well as methodology. James II had allegedly infringed upon the 'liberties' of the English people in, inter alia, the following ways:[16]

> By levying money for and to the use of the Crown by pretence of prerogative for other time and in other manner than . . . granted by Parliament;
>
> By assuming and exercising a power of dispensing with and suspending of lawes and the execution of laws without consent of Parliament;
>
> By violating the freedom of elections of members to serve in Parliament;
>
> By raising and keeping a standing army within this kingdom in time of peace without consent of Parliament and quartering soldiers contrary to law;
>
> Corrupt and unqualified persons have been returned and served on juries in trials;
>
> And excessive fines have been imposed and illegal and cruell punishments inflicted.

The 1688 revolution, like Magna Carta and the Civil War before it, marked the crossing of a political watershed. A new political 'contract'[17] was struck between Parliament and the Monarchy, and consequently a new constitutional foundation was laid. Having deposed James II, the victorious revolutionaries offered the throne to James II's (protestant) daughter Mary and her (protestant) husband, William Prince of Orange. In return, William and Mary accepted that the Crown's ability to govern the English nation through its prerogative powers would be severely limited. The Monarch might still be responsible for governing the country, and she/he could appoint the Ministers who would assist her in carrying out that task, but the Monarch and her Ministers would govern the country according to laws defined by Parliament. And if Parliament changed the law, the Monarch's government would have to respond accordingly.

The initial 'terms' of the contract were specified in the text of the Bill of Rights produced by the Parliament of 1689. Those terms address directly the complaints made in the *Declaration of Right*:[18]

> 1. That the pretended power of suspending of laws or the execution of laws by regall authority without consent of Parliament is illegal;

---

[15] See Pluckett (1960) op cit pp 524–526.

[16] The following quotations are drawn from the Bill of Rights 1688, a statute passed by the post-revolutionary Parliament. The phraseology of the *Declaration* and the Bill of Rights is virtually identical; Pluckett (1960) op cit pp 447–450.

[17] See Slaughter T (1981) 'Abdicate' and 'contract' in the Glorious Revolution' 24 *The Historical Journal* 323; Miller J (1982) 'The Glorious Revolution: 'contract' and 'abdication' reconsidered' 25 *The Historical Journal* 541.

[18] The numbers are those used in the Bill; they have been re-ordered thematically here.

13. And that for redresse of all grievances and for the amending, strengthening and preserving of the laws Parliaments ought to be held frequently;

8. That elections of members of Parliament ought to be free;

9. That the freedome of speech, and debates or proceedings in Parliament ought not to be impeached or questioned in any court or place out of Parliament;

4. That levying of money for or to the use of the Crown by pretence of prerogative without grant of Parliament . . . is illegal;

6. That the raising or keeping of a standing army within the kingdom in time of peace unlesse it be with consent of Parliament is against law;

11. That jurors ought to be duly impannelled and returned . . .

10. That excessive bail ought not to be required nor excessive fines imposed nor cruel and unusual punishment inflicted.

Once enacted in the Bill of Rights, these moral principles would possess a superior legal status to any personal legal powers retained by the Monarchy. Furthermore, in addition to placing the Monarch's prerogative powers beneath statute in the hierarchy of constitutional importance, the 1688 revolution is generally regarded as having settled the question of the relationship between Parliament and the courts.[19] The notion aired in *Dr Bonham's Case* and *R v Love* that 'natural' or 'divine' law provided the courts with a constitutional authority superior to statute was disregarded. And it was also assumed that the common law was subordinate in terms of its legal authority to legislation. We examine the constitutional importance of the royal prerogative and the common law further in chapter four; the basic principle to remember at this point is that both are assumed to be less important than statute.

Despite the evident similarities between the functional underpinnings of the *Declaration of Independence* and the *Declaration of Right*, the English revolutionary settlement expressed in the 1688 Bill of Rights is substantially different from the American settlement articulated in the 1789–1791 Constitution. While the American revolutionaries presumed that sovereignty should lie with the American 'people', their English predecessors assumed that sovereignty would rest with 'Parliament'. The Bill of Rights could not be regarded as a constituent framework for the country's subsequent governance in the legal sense provided for by the US Constitution.

This is not to say that the English revolutionaries were less sincere in the moral principles they expressed than the Americans were. Rather it means that there was nothing 'special' in the legal sense about the terms of the English settlement. Parliament, as the country's sovereign law-making power, could alter, repeal, or add to the supposedly 'fundamental' provisions of the Bill of Rights whenever it chose, through exactly the same process as it might enact laws on the most trivial subject. The English Bill of Rights was not secured against attack by the national legislature in the same way as its American namesake was protected against infringement by Congress. Parliament was England's ordinary as well as extraordinary legislature. It would sit in regular, perhaps almost constant session. And it alone would wield all the law-making powers subsequently so carefully and elaborately divided by Madison and his colleagues among the Presidency, the Congress, the States, and the people of the United States.

Moreover, England was a unitary rather than federal state. If people in geographically discrete parts of the country wished to be governed in different ways, in order to reflect local traditions or political sentiments, they could be so only with Parliament's permission. Parliament could pass legislation designating the boundaries of any sub-central units of government in England, determining the powers such bodies might possess, and specifying the manner in which the officials running them were to be chosen. And Parliament might whenever it chose enact a new statute containing different provisions. There were no constitutional rights which a citizen or group of citizens could expect the English courts to enforce

---

[19] See Goldsworthy (1999) op cit pp 159–166.

against Parliament, for the wishes of Parliament were 'the highest form of law' known to the English constitution.

That the American revolutionaries framed their rebellion against Britain's post-revolutionary constitution in much the same terms as the architects of that constitution framed their own complaints against the Stuart Kings ninety years earlier might suggest that the 1688 settlement had not provided effective protection for 'the liberties of the people'. We might therefore wonder if the sovereignty of Parliament, a constitutional device created to safeguard the nation and its empire against the tyranny of its King, had succeeded merely in transferring tyrannical authority into different hands. In what sense, if any, did the English revolution ensure that the laws of England enjoyed the consent of the governed?

What is (was) 'Parliament'?

The 1688 Parliament was not 'representative' of the English population as we would now understand that term. But it would be rash to dismiss the principles underlying the 1688 settlement too quickly. In some ways it was based on ideas that we might consider valid today. It is important to clarify what the revolutionaries of 1688 meant by the institution of 'Parliament' for instance. Parliament was not a single body, but had three parts: the House of Commons, the House of Lords, and the Monarch. At that time, all three parts of Parliament had equal powers within the law-making process. If one part refused to approve a Bill, that Bill could not become law.

From a modern day perspective, we might think that the 1688 Parliament simply represented the views of elite groups and effectively excluded the mass of the population from any means of consenting to the law-making process. However some late-seventeenth-century political theorists sincerely believed that a Parliament composed of these three bodies was the most effective way to secure that laws accurately expressed the national interest.[20] We should recall that Jefferson used a very selective definition of 'the people' in the *Declaration of Independence*; for law-making purposes, many poor men, all women and all slaves were not 'people' in late-eighteenth-century America. Similarly, in seventeenth-century England, it was assumed that only the King, the aristocracy, the Church, and the affluent merchant and landowning class which elected members of the Commons, had any legitimate role to play in fashioning the laws. Orthodox political theory argued that the Commons, the Lords, and the Monarch formed the three 'Estates of the Realm'. These estates, acting in concert, were presumed to be the only legitimate arbiters of the national interest.

So the 1688 settlement could be perceived as democratic in a primitive sense; not because it gave all citizens a role in the law-making process, but because it gave such a role to everyone who was presumed entitled to participate. This might be seen as a more extreme version of Madison's subsequent advocacy of elitist representative assemblies, staffed only by legislators trusted to act in the national interest. But the 1688 settlement had a further purpose. The objective of the 1688 revolution was to create a 'balanced' law-making process within a 'balanced' constitution.[21] Because Acts of Parliament could only be made if the Commons, Lords, and King agreed, the legislature could not produce statutes which represented the interests of only one or two of the three Estates of the Realm.[22] This supposed solution to the problem

[20] See particularly Judson M (1936) 'Henry Parker and the theory of parliamentary sovereignty', in Wittke C (ed) *Essays in history and political theory in honour of Charles Howard McIlwain*; Bailyn op cit pp 198–229; Goldsworthy op cit pp 109–124.

[21] See Vile M (1967) *Constitutionalism and the separation of powers* ch 3.

[22] Contemporary commentators expressed the principle in more hyperbolic language; 'Lest . . . the Crown should lead towards arbitrary government, or the tumultuary licentiousness of the people should incline towards a democracy, the wisdom of our ancestors hath instituted a middle state of nobility . . . The excellence of this government consists in the due balance of the several constituent parts of it, for if either one of them should be too hard for the other two, there is an actual dissolution of the constitution'; Trenchard J and Moyle W (1697) *An argument showing that a standing army is inconsistent with a free government*, quoted in Miller (1983) op cit p 114.

of potentially tyrannical law-makers did not spring, Athena like, from the heads of the 1688 revolutionaries. Rather it represented the culmination of a long process of theorisation and practice which had exercised the minds of philosophers and politicians throughout the seventeenth century.[23]

We should also remember that the Parliament of 1688 was not organised along party political lines. There were some fairly firm party based alliances among groups of members;[24] but the seventeenth-century Parliament was intended to function as an arena both for local interests to be aired and for discussion of national priorities—the House of Commons was initially conceived as the *House of Communities*. Many individual members came to the Commons as representatives not of a political party, but of their town or county.

From a contemporary perspective, one might readily ask how the formal structure of our constitution has responded to changing definitions of 'the people', and to what we might call the growing 'nationalisation' of politics? As chapter seven will explain, it is now a fundamental tenet of modern British society that virtually every adult can vote in parliamentary elections. It is also clear that parliamentary elections are contested by nationally organised political parties, and are won and lost primarily on national rather than local issues. It might seem obvious that a constitutional structure designed to adduce the consent of a tiny minority of the small population of an agrarian country would be ill-suited to securing the consent of some forty million people in a modern industrialised society. It is perhaps instructive to observe for instance that no other modern democracy has fully copied the British constitutional model: the American system has proved much the more influential blueprint. But in many respects, the formal constitutional principles which emerged as a result of political revolution in England in 1688 remain largely unchanged today. And it is probably accurate to say that parliamentary sovereignty is the most significant of those unchanged principles. It is therefore important that we consider how the doctrine has been both criticised and vindicated in recent times.

I. Legal authority for the principle of parliamentary sovereignty

Our constitution no longer offers any role for the courts to invoke natural law or common law as a source of legal authority having a higher constitutional status than Acts of Parliament. One must look very hard to find any suggestion that after 1688 the courts entertained the idea that statutes might be invalidated if they conflicted with natural law. The 1701 case *City of London v Wood*[25] offers some, albeit confused, support for the *Bonham* principle. At one point, Holt CJ argued that:

> What my Lord Coke says in *Dr Bonham's Case* is far from any extravagancy, for it is a very reasonable and true saying, that if an Act of Parliament should ordain the same person should be party and judge, it would be a void Act of Parliament.[26]

But Holt CJ then concluded that; 'an Act of Parliament can do no wrong, though it may do several things that look pretty odd'.[27] So contradictory a judgment cannot be considered a powerful authority for natural law ideas. Nor can one find more helpful precedents in the post-revolutionary case law. The principle was last seen in *Forbes v Cochrane* in 1824, when the Court suggested it would not enforce a law permitting slavery, as this would be 'against the law of nature and God'.[28]

---

[23] See Sharp A (1983) *Political ideas of the English civil war.*

[24] Plucknett (1960) op cit pp 436–438. On the strength of party loyalties in the revolution Parliament see Horwitz H (1974) 'Parliament and the glorious revolution' *Bulletin of the Institute of Historical Research* 36–52; Plumb J (1937) 'Elections to the Convention Parliament of 1689' *Cambridge Historical Journal* 235.

[25] (1701) 12 Mod Rep 669. See Plucknett (1928) op cit.   [26] (1701) 12 Mod Rep 669 at 687.

[27] Ibid, at 688.   [28] (1824) 2 B & C 448 at 470, 107 ER 450.

Yet nor will one find much case law prior to 1800 which lends explicit support to the idea of parliamentary sovereignty. In his celebrated *Commentaries*, first published in 1765, Blackstone drew the following conclusion about the constitutional status of legislation:

> I know it is generally laid down . . . that acts of parliament contrary to reason are void. But if the parliament will positively enact a thing to be done which is unreasonable, I know of no power that can control it . . . for that were to set the judicial power above that of the legislature, which would be subversive of all government.[29]

As noted in chapter one, the American colonists were contemporaneously trying to fashion a constitutional order which avoided the problem of subversion by setting the power of the people above both legislature and judiciary. Blackstone was manifestly unimpressed by such theorisation, but one might also note that he could find little direct judicial authority for his proposition as to Parliament's supremacy. The dearth of authority may be because everybody took it for granted that this was the way things were; sometimes the most important values are those which go unspoken and unexamined. However, several strands of case law supporting the orthodox understanding of parliamentary sovereignty appear in the nineteenth century. The first deals with 'the enrolled bill rule'.

Substance or procedure? The enrolled Bill rule

The plaintiff in *Edinburgh and Dalkeith Rly Co v Wauchope*[30] was a landowner affected by a private Act of Parliament[31] authorising construction of a railway. He claimed that the Court should invalidate the legislation because its promoters had not given notice to affected parties in accordance with the House of Commons' standing orders which regulated its internal procedures in respect of such measures. Lord Campbell thought that judging the constitutional adequacy of proceedings in either the Commons or the Lords was entirely beyond the court's powers:

> All that a court . . . can do is to look to the Parliamentary Roll: if from that it should appear that a Bill has passed both Houses and received the Royal Assent, no court . . .can inquire into the mode in which it was introduced . . . or what passed . . . during its progress in its various stages through Parliament.[32]

A similar conclusion was reached in *Lee v Bude and Torrington Junction Rly Co* where Wile J commented that; 'if an Act of Parliament has been obtained improperly it is for the legislature to correct it by repealing it; but so long as it exists as law, the Courts are bound to obey it'.[33]

This principle was also forcefully restated by the House of Lords in 1974 in *British Railways Board v Pickin*.[34] Mr Pickin alleged that British Rail had steered a private Bill through Parliament without giving the necessary notices to affected landowners. Somewhat surprisingly, the Court of Appeal thought this raised a triable issue: Lord Denning indicated that one could draw a valid distinction between public Bills and private Bills. That view was rapidly overruled by the House of Lords. Lord Reid explicitly denied that the courts had any power to question the legality of a Bill's passage through Parliament: 'the whole trend of authority for over a century is clearly against permitting such an investigation'.[35] In Lord Simon's opinion:

> a concomitant of the sovereignty of Parliament is that the houses of Parliament enjoy certain privileges . . . Among the privileges of the Houses of Parliament is the exclusive right to determine their own proceedings.[36]

The enrolled Bill rule has been widely construed as unambiguously affirming the principle of parliamentary sovereignty. Whether this view is analytically defensible (in either formal

---

[29] Ibid, at 62.   [30] (1842) 8 Cl & Fin 710, 8 ER 279, HL.
[31] On the distinction between private and public Acts see 'Private Bills', ch 5, p 120.
[32] (1842) 8 ER 279 at 285.   [33] (1871) LR 6 CP 576 at 582.   [34] [1974] AC 765.   [35] Ibid, at 788.
[36] Ibid, at 788–789. We address the 'privileges of Parliament' in ch 8.

or functionalist terms) is a question to which we shall return. For the moment, we consider a second series of cases, setting out what is known as the 'doctrine of implied repeal'.

The doctrine of implied repeal

Vauxhall Estates Ltd v Liverpool Corpn[37] and *Ellen Street Estates Ltd v Minister of Health*[38] both focused on the Acquisition of Land Act 1919, a slum clearance measure which laid down levels of compensation for property owners. The Housing Acts of 1925 and 1930 made these provisions less generous. The landowners affected sought to have compensation assessed on the basis used in the 1919 Act.

The landowners seized on s 7 of the 1919 Act. This said that any Act affecting compensation provisions would 'cease to have or *shall not have effect*' (emphasis added) if inconsistent with the 1919 legislation. That phraseology arguably looks towards future Acts as well as those already existing. But the plaintiffs did not argue that the 1919 Act was completely protected from amendment by a subsequent Parliament. Instead they drew a *distinction between express and implied repeal*.

The landowners conceded that if a subsequent Act said expressly that the 1919 Act was overturned, the courts could not challenge the new Act's effect. However, they argued that the courts could safeguard the 1919 Act against *accidental or implied repeal*; if Parliament did not expressly say it was changing a statute that seemed to have been intended to prevent future amendment, the court should assume that the original Act should be upheld.

This argument reaches out towards constitutional principles founded on consent theory. It suggests that it would be unconstitutional to allow legislation to have unintended effects because 'the people' could not have knowingly consented to the law that had been passed. This seems to offer a variation on the theme of 'functionalist' approaches to parliamentary sovereignty; if that function is to ensure that laws enjoy the consent of the governed, it would be logical to assume that the courts should not permit Parliament to enact legislation premised on false information.

The argument reached the Court of Appeal in *Ellen Street*—where it was uncategorically dismissed. The courts rejected any notion of a functionalist interpretation of the parliamentary sovereignty doctrine. The judges adopted instead a formalist approach. That formal rule simply demanded that the courts unquestioningly obey the most recent Act of Parliament. And if that Act appeared inconsistent with previous legislation, the previous legislation must give way.[39] Questions about the existence of the people's consent, or Parliament's unspoken intentions, were not something the courts would entertain.

Scrutton LJ dismissed the landowners' argument as:

> [A]bsolutely contrary to the constitutional position that Parliament can alter an Act previously passed, and it can do so by repealing in terms the previous Act—[the plaintiff] agrees that it can do so—and it can do it also in another way—namely, by enacting a provision which is clearly inconsistent with the previous Act.[40]

Maugham LJ was similarly unreceptive:

> The Legislature cannot, according to our constitution, bind itself as to the form of subsequent legislation, and it is impossible for Parliament to enact that in a subsequent statute dealing with the same subject matter there can be no implied repeal. If in a subsequent statute Parliament makes it plain that the earlier statute is being to some extent repealed, effect must be given to that intention just because it is the will of the Legislature.[41]

Despite the vigour with which the Court of Appeal delivered its opinion, it could not draw on much past case law to support its proposition. The main precedent it relied on was the

---

[37] [1932] 1 KB 733.   [38] [1934] 1 KB 590, CA.
[39] The rule is sometimes expressed in the Latin maxim 'lex posterior derogat priori' (a later law overrules an earlier one).   [40] [1934] 1 KB 590 at 595–596.

decision in *Vauxhall Estates* two years earlier. That seems a flimsy legal base on which to build so important a constitutional principle.[42] We can however find a further line of supportive decisions in cases dealing with the relationship between British statutes and international law.

Inconsistency with international law

The first case we might consider is *Mortensen v Peters*.[43] One of the most important areas of international law relates to defining the extent of a country's jurisdiction over the oceans which surround it. By 1906, most nations accepted that their respective jurisdictions should extend for three miles from their coastline and had signed treaties with each other to that effect. In 1889, the British Parliament passed the Herring Fishery (Scotland) Act. This Act gave Scotland's Fishery Board the power to make bye-laws to control fishing in the Moray Firth. Much of the Moray Firth is more than three miles from land, so the 1889 Act would seem inconsistent with international law obligations to which Britain was party.

Mortensen was the captain of a Norwegian trawler. He was arrested for breaching the bye-laws that the Fishery Board had made. His defence was that the Act was 'unconstitutional' because it breached accepted international law standards, and therefore had no legal effect. The House of Lords peremptorily dismissed this argument:

> In this Court we have nothing to do with . . . whether an act of the legislature is *ultra vires* as in contravention of generally acknowledged principles of international law. For us, an Act of Parliament duly passed by Lords and Commons and assented to by the King, is supreme, and we are bound to give effect to its terms.[44]

This conclusion is entirely consistent with both traditional Diceyan theory and the political outcome of the 1688 revolution. Under Britain's constitutional arrangements, treaties are negotiated and formally entered into by the Crown (or 'the government') through its prerogative powers, not by Parliament. Orthodox constitutional theory maintains that a treaty signed by the British government can only have legal effect in Britain if it is *incorporated* into British law by an Act of Parliament. This is a logical consequence of the parliamentary sovereignty doctrine. The 1688 revolution produced an agreement between William of Orange and Parliament which provided that the constitutional role of the King's government was to govern within the laws made by Parliament. The government itself could not create new laws simply by coming to an agreement with foreign countries. If one allowed that to happen, one would essentially be saying that it is the government rather than Parliament that is the sovereign law-maker, as the government could bypass the refusal of the Commons and/or the Lords to consent to its proposed laws.

Quite how much effect a particular Treaty might have within domestic law would be a matter for Parliament to determine. The notion of 'incorporation' is a broad one, and really means no more than that Parliament has chosen to enact a statute which provides some indigenous legal force for some or all of the political principles agreed by the countries which signed the Treaty. In 'incorporating' international law into the domestic legal system, Parliament could make whatever choice it wished on such matters as which parts of the Treaty should be given a statutory base, which courts could apply those provisions, which claimants could invoke them and against whom or what they could be invoked, and, perhaps most importantly, how a competent court should resolve any litigation in which it found that the Treaty terms incorporated in the relevant Act conflicted with other rules of domestic law. Strictly speaking, however,

---

[41] Ibid, at 597.

[42] See Marshall G (1954) 'What is Parliament? The changing concept of Parliamentary Sovereignty' *Political Studies* 193.   [43] (1906) 14 SLT 227.

[44] Ibid, at 230. The term ultra vires literally means 'beyond the legal powers'. If a body is legally sovereign, nothing can be beyond its powers. The ultra vires doctrine thus could not be applied to Parliament.

whatever effect the Treaty has in domestic law arises simply because a domestic court is applying the terms of the relevant incorporating statute, not of the Treaty itself.[45]

The principle is further illustrated by *Cheney v Conn*.[46] Mr Cheney was a taxpayer who appealed against the Inland Revenue's assessment of his income tax liability. The Inland Revenue made its assessment in accordance with the Finance Act 1964. Mr Cheney claimed that some of his tax money was being used to build nuclear weapons, contrary to the principles of the Geneva Convention, a treaty the British government had signed. Parts of the Treaty were incorporated into British law, but these were not helpful to Mr Cheney's argument. His case rested on sections of the Treaty that remained unincorporated. Mr Cheney argued that since these parts of the Treaty forbade the use of nuclear weapons, it must be illegal for Parliament to enact a statute that raised money so that such weapons could be built. The judge, Ungoed-Thomas J, had no doubt that this was a pointless argument:

> [W]hat the statute itself enacts cannot be unlawful, because what the statute says is itself the law, and the highest form of law that is known to this country. It is the law which prevails over every other form of law, and it is not for the court to say that a parliamentary enactment, the highest law in this country, is illegal.[47]

Having addressed the basic political and legal foundations of the parliamentary sovereignty doctrine, we now turn to the various challenges to the Diceyan theory that have been aired before the courts and in academic fora. None of these challenges has thus far proved effective—but that does not mean that one will not become so in the future. We consider three arguments. Firstly, we look at the 'manner and form' technique of safeguarding certain basic constitutional values against reform by a simple majority vote in Parliament. Secondly, we assess the status of the Treaty of Union of 1707 between England and Scotland. And thirdly, we explore the notion that there might be some moral values which Parliament can only change through *express* legislative statements.

II. Entrenching legislation—challenges to the orthodox position

The positive limb of Dicey's theory suggests that Parliament can enact any moral values it considers desirable. But there appears to be a basic flaw in this formulation of the parliamentary sovereignty doctrine. Simply put, how can Parliament have supreme legislative power if there is one thing it cannot do, namely pass an Act which binds successor Parliaments. If Parliament is

---

[45] We can illustrate the point by varying the facts of *Mortensen*. If Parliament had enacted 'The Law of the Sea Act 1902', which simply provided that all Treaties relating to the law of the sea to which the United Kingdom is a party are from January 1 1903 to be applied by domestic courts, then Captain Mortensen would have had an effective defence. The Law of the Sea Act 1902, being a statute enacted after the Herring Fishery (Scotland) Act 1899, would impliedly repeal the 1899 Act to the extent of any inconsistency between them. But Mr Mortensen would be relying for his defence on the 1902 Act, not on the Treaty. (Had the Law of the Sea Act been passed in 1897, it would not have provided a defence, since its terms would have been impliedly repealed by the 1899 Act.)

[46] [1968] 1 WLR 242.   [47] Ibid, at 782.

[48] This does not mean the same thing however, as asserting that a sovereign Parliament must be an ever-present feature of Britain's constitutional landscape; cf Dicey op cit p 24:

> A sovereign power can divest itself of authority in two ways ... It may simply put an end to its own existence. Parliament could extinguish itself by legally dissolving itself and leaving no means whereby a subsequent Parliament could be legally summoned ... A sovereign body may again transfer sovereign authority to another person or body of persons ... A sovereign power can divest itself of authority in two ways ... It may simply put an end to its own existence. Parliament could extinguish itself by legally dissolving itself and leaving no means whereby a subsequent Parliament could be legally summoned ... A sovereign body may again transfer sovereign authority to another person or body of persons ...
>
> Whether the previously sovereign Parliament could then in some fashion be 'resurrected' at a future date is a nice question.

truly a sovereign law-maker, then one would have assumed that it must have the power to limit its own law-making capacity?[48] This conundrum presents us with the distinction between the *continuing* and *self-embracing* theories of parliamentary sovereignty.[49]

The *continuing* theory maintains that the sovereign Parliament is a *perpetual institution*. Its unconfined legislative power is created anew every time it meets, irrespective of previous enactments. This is the Diceyan position. Parliament need pay no heed at all to what its predecessors have done.

The *self-embracing* theory advocates a radical position. It has aroused much academic interest. With one important exception,[50] it has not had any practical political effect in this country, but it has had considerable influence in former British colonies. The self-embracing theory holds that Parliament's sovereignty includes the power to bind itself and its successors. Supporters of the self-embracing theory argue that Parliament can enact legislation safe from subsequent amendment—that certain measures can be legally *entrenched* and rendered immune from repeal by a future Parliament.

Entrenchment simply means any constitutional mechanism which makes some laws immune to repeal by the usual legislative formula of a simple majority in the Commons and the Lords plus the Royal Assent. In principle, a particular political value might be entrenched in either a *substantive* or *procedural* sense.

Substantive entrenchment entails acceptance of the principle that *Parliament cannot legislate at all* about specific subjects. It implies that there are basic human values which can never be changed. This argument has not been vigorously pursued in recent times. The obvious drawback to substantive entrenchment would be that a society would be stuck with particular values forever; it is a completely rigid form of safeguard.

Modern commentators who oppose Dicey's theory have sought to limit Parliament's power through *procedural entrenchment*. Procedural entrenchment would not necessarily produce a rigid constitution—it lends a relative rather than absolute degree of permanence to certain laws. In theory, one would entrench a particular piece of legislation if a Commons majority of two rather than one was needed to change it. That legislation would not be entrenched very firmly; but as one makes reform procedures more rigorous, so legislation becomes more securely entrenched. Constitutional values only changeable with the support of, for example 70% of MPs, would be deeply entrenched; if amendment required near unanimous support within each house, then change might be virtually impossible.[51]

Jennings' critique and the 'rule of recognition'

The starting point for analysis of this theory is to ask ourselves why courts recognise statutes as the highest form of law. There is no supra-legislative constitution which articulates this rule. Similarly, we cannot find the doctrine of parliamentary sovereignty laid down in a statute. But the haziness surrounding the legal status of this so-called '*rule of recognition*' has assisted constitutional lawyers opposed to the Diceyan view.[52]

The most forceful exponent of the so-called '*manner and form*' strategy of procedural entrenchment was Sir Ivor Jennings.[53] Jennings based his critique of the orthodox theory on a version of the self-embracing understanding of sovereignty. His argument takes three apparently logical steps. Firstly, the rule of recognition is a common law concept. Secondly, statute is legally superior to the common law. Thirdly, Parliament can therefore enact legislation

---

[49] Winterton G (1976) 'The British grundnorm: parliamentary sovereignty re-examined' 92 *LQR* 591.

[50] This relates to the UK's membership of the European Community. The development is of recent origin, and is discussed in ch. 11.

[51] Thus the terms of the United States' Constitution are deeply, but not permanently entrenched.

[52] The term is Professor H Hart's; see (1961) *The concept of law* p 161. For an overview of related theories see Winterton (1976) op cit.   [53] See especially (5th edn, 1958) *The law and the constitution* pp 140–145.

changing the rule of recognition and requiring the courts to accept that some Acts are protected from repeal by a simple majority vote. Jennings formulated the argument in the following terms:

> Legal sovereignty is merely a name indicating that the legislature has for the time being power
> to make laws of any kind in the manner required by law. That is, a rule expressed to be made by
> the Queen, [the House of Commons and the House of Lords] will be recognised by the courts,
> *including a rule which alters this law itself* . . . The power of a legislature derives from the law by
> which it is established . . . In the United Kingdom . . . it derives from the accepted law, which is the
> common law.[54]

There seems an obvious logic to this argument. Jennings' analysis also appears to make sound
political sense. If the judges are subordinate to Parliament, then surely Parliament can tell
them what rules they should follow when assessing if a statute is constitutional.

The manner and form argument draws its theoretical basis largely from Jennings' work. His
ideas rely heavily on three cases,[55] all rooted in the process of former British colonies gaining independence. The first, *A-G for New South Wales v Trethowan*,[56] was an Australian case
decided by the Australian High Court and Privy Council in 1932.

A-G for New South Wales v Trethowan (1931)

The New South Wales Parliament was created by a British statute; 'The Constitution Statute
1855'. In many respects, the New South Wales constitution followed the British model.
Legislation required the support of a simple majority in an upper house (the Legislative
Council) and lower house (the Legislative Assembly), and the Royal Assent was provided by
the Governor-General qua the Monarch's representative. However, s 5 of a subsequent British
statute, the Colonial Laws Validity Act 1865, provided that statutes enacted by certain colonial legislatures (including the New South Wales Parliament) which sought to alter their own
'constitution, powers or procedures' would have legal effect only if passed 'in such manner or
form' as the law then in force in the colony demanded. The terms of s 5 were left unchanged
when the New South Wales' Constitution Act was passed by the New South Wales Legislature
in 1902. The 1902 Act, inter alia, made provisions concerning the composition and respective
powers of the two houses.

In 1929, the Liberal Party government, which had majorities in both houses of the NSW
Parliament, promoted the Constitution (Legislative Council Amendment) Bill 1929. The Bill
was passed by both houses, received the Royal Assent, and thus became an Act. The Act introduced a new s 7A into the Constitution Act 1902, to the effect that a Bill seeking to abolish
the Legislative Council could not be sent for Royal Assent unless it had been approved by a
majority of both houses and by a majority of the electorate in a referendum. Section 7A therefore seemed to change the 'manner and form' of the legislation needed to abolish the upper
chamber, by adding an additional step to the usual legislative process. Furthermore, s 7A(6)
provided that s 7A itself could not be repealed unless the repealing legislation had also been
approved by a majority of electors in a special referendum. It appeared that the government
expected to lose the imminent general election, and wished to ensure that the opposition
Labour Party could not carry out its stated intention to abolish the upper house without first
putting that specific question to the electorate.

At the 1930s elections, the Labour Party secured a majority in both houses. Both houses
thereafter approved Bills respectively repealing s 7A and abolishing the Legislative Council.
Neither measure was subjected to a referendum before it was submitted for the Royal Assent.

---

[54] Op cit pp 152–153 and 156; original emphasis.
[55] Jennings relied on the first two cases discussed here. The third was decided after the 1958 edition of Jennings'
book *The law and the constitution* was written.   [56] (1931) 44 CLR 394; affd [1932] AC 526, PC.

Several members of the Legislative Council immediately began an action before the New South Wales courts requesting an injunction to prevent the Bills being sent for the Royal Assent; if granted, the injunction would therefore prevent the Bills becoming legislation. Their argument was that s 7A could be repealed only in the 'manner and form' which it had itself specified.

The new government argued that successive New South Wales Parliaments, just like the British Parliament, were not bound by any legislation passed by their predecessors. A Parliament might pass any 'manner and form' provisions it thought fit, but those provisions would have no effect when a future Parliament, acting by the 'simple majority plus Royal Assent formula', passed legislation to repeal them. That had happened here, and thus s 7A had been lawfully repealed.

In the High Court of Australia,[57] two of the five judges accepted that argument. However the majority held that the Court was bound to prevent any Bill dealing with the subject matter of s 7A being sent for the Royal Assent unless approved in a referendum. The special 'manner and form' of s 7A provided an effective form of procedural entrenchment, safeguarding the existence of the Legislative Council. The majority reasoned that, unlike the British Parliament, the New South Wales legislature owed its existence and powers to two British statutes, the Constitution Statute 1855 and the Colonial Laws Validity Act 1865. Those Acts provided the basis of the New South Wales Constitution, and until s 5 of the 1865 Act was itself repealed, the New South Wales legislature was subject to its terms. The majority saw this as a straight-forward *legal rule*, which, Rich J explained (in terms very reminiscent of Madison's warnings about factionalism) served an obvious *political purpose*:

> There is no reason why a Parliament representing the people should be powerless to determine whether the constitutional salvation of the State is to be reached by cautious and well considered steps rather than by rash and ill considered measures.[58]

On further appeal to the Privy Council, the majority opinion, and the reasoning underlying it, was upheld.[59]

Harris v Dönges (Minister of the Interior) (1952)

The second case, *Harris v Dönges (Minister of the Interior)*,[60] was decided by the Appellate Division of South Africa's Supreme Court in 1952. Once again, the story begins with the slow process of Britain disengaging itself from its former Empire. In 1909 the British Parliament passed the South Africa Act, which united the four South African colonies under a single legislature. The South African Parliament mirrored that of Britain in most respects. It had a lower house (the house of assembly) and an upper house (the senate) and retained the King's power of Royal Assent (given on the King's behalf by an appointed Governor-General). In respect of almost all laws, South Africa's legislature had the same legal competence as the British Parliament—a Bill receiving a simple majority in both the house and the senate and receiving the Royal Assent was generally the 'highest form of law' within South Africa's constitution. However the 1909 Act contained some exceptions to the 'simple majority in both houses plus Royal Assent' formula.

Firstly, the South African Parliament could not, under any circumstances, pass laws 'repugnant' to British statutes intended to have effect within South Africa. The supremacy of British law vis-à-vis South African law was a substantively entrenched feature of South Africa's 1909 constitutional settlement. Secondly, ss 33–34 of the 1909 Act prevented the South African

---

[57] (1931) 44 CLR 394.   [58] Ibid, at 420.   [59] [1932] AC 526, PC.
[60] (1952) 1 TLR 1245. See Griswold E (1952) 'The "coloured vote case" in South Africa' 65 *Harvard LR* 1361; Note (1952) 68 *LQR* 285; Cowen D (1952) and (1953) 'Legislature and judiciary: parts I and II' *MLR* 282 and 273; Loveland I (1999) *By due process of law? Racial discrimination and the right to vote in South Africa 1850–1960*.

Parliament altering the composition of the house or the senate for ten years. Those provisions were thus substantively, but temporarily, entrenched. Thirdly, s 35 provided that a person could not be deprived of his right to vote on the basis solely of his race unless that legislation had been supported by a two-thirds majority of the house and senate sitting in joint session. Fourthly, s 137 provided that the status of both Afrikaans and English as the country's official languages could only be changed by the two-thirds majority procedure. Section 152 thereafter provided that s 35 and s 137 themselves could be amended only by a South African statute also attracting a two-thirds majority in a joint session. Section 35 and s 152 imply that the British Parliament in 1909 considered that non-white citizens' 'right' to vote on the same basis as whites was too important a political value to be left at the mercy of a bare legislative majority. It was not an 'inalienable right', but would be more difficult to change than most other aspects of the South African constitution.[61]

In 1931, the British Parliament passed the Statute of Westminster which recognised South Africa (and several other former colonies) as independent sovereign states, possessing what was termed 'Dominion' status within the British Empire. The Statute of Westminster made, inter alia, the following provisions. Section 2 released the newly created Dominions from the controls imposed by the Colonial Laws Validity Act 1865. Section 4 then provided that:

> No Act of Parliament of the United Kingdom passed after the commencement of this Act shall extend, or be deemed to extend, to a Dominion as part of the law of that Dominion unless it is expressly declared in that Act that that Dominion has requested and consented to the enactment thereof.

As a matter of British constitutional law, s 4 might be thought to have little significance. Although on its face s 4 offers a form of 'linguistic entrenchment' (ie the Act must state there has been Dominion consent), if Parliament passed legislation contravening s 4, the statute concerned would presumably have been applied in the orthodox fashion by domestic courts. The point is perhaps best conveyed by the comment of Lord Sankey in *British Coal Corpn v R*:

> It is doubtless true that the power of the Imperial Parliament to pass on its own initiative any legislation that it thought fit extending to [a Dominion] remains in theory unimpaired: indeed, the Imperial Parliament could as a matter of abstract law, repeal or disregard s 4 of the Statute. But that is [legal] theory and has no relation to [political] realities.[62]

As Lord Sankey suggested, the Statute of Westminster may more sensibly be seen as an exercise in *constitutional politics rather than constitutional law*. It affirmed an existing practical reality—namely that the Dominions could now act as independent States in respect both of their internal affairs and their international relations. Some Dominions modified their constitutions at the time that they gained independence. However, no changes were made to the South Africa Act 1909 at this time. Indeed, both houses of the South African legislature had resolved that the terms of the 1931 Act should 'in no way derogate from the entrenched provisions of the South Africa Act'.[63]

From the late 1940s onwards, the white Afrikaaner National Party possessed a majority in both houses. The National Party had committed itself to introducing apartheid, a policy demanding rigid and (to non-whites) oppressive separation of different racial groups.[64] One element of this policy was to create separate electoral registers and voting systems for white and Cape coloured citizens. The Separate Representation of Voters Act was passed in 1951 by a simple majority, with both houses sitting separately. The Act's 'constitutionality' was then challenged by several coloured voters, on the basis that the procedures used to enact it did not comply with the 'manner and form' specified in s 35.

[61] For insight into why see Loveland (1999) op cit ch 4; Lewin J (1956) 'The struggle for law in South Africa' 27 *Political Quarterly* 176.   [62] [1935] AC 500 at 520, PC.

[63] See Loveland (1999) op cit pp 179–187.   [64] Ibid, at 231–247.

Before the Appellate Division of South Africa's Supreme Court, the South African government argued that this special procedure was no longer necessary. The government maintained that after the Statute of Westminster was passed in 1931 South Africa had become a sovereign state, and therefore its Parliament was not bound by the country's initial constitution, which was enacted while South Africa was still a colony. As a matter of South African constitutional law, the government argued, the South African legislature had acquired all the legal attributes of Britain's Parliament: it could enact any law whatsoever by a simple majority; and no domestic court could question the legality of any such Act.

All five judges then sitting in the Appellate Division rejected this argument, and concluded that the Act was invalid. The Court did accept that South Africa was a sovereign country, and also held that the South African courts would no longer consider British legislation superior to South African statutes. The Court also accepted that South Africa had a sovereign Parliament. The Appellate Division nevertheless held that the Separate Representation of Voters Act was an illegal measure.

The judgment hinges on two presumptions. The first is that a sovereign country need not have a sovereign legislature. Pointing to the United States, Centlivres CJ observed it was entirely feasible for a country's constitutional arrangements to withhold some legal powers from its central legislature. The second presumption, in respect of which the US model is not a helpful analogy, is that a country can have a sovereign Parliament without according sovereignty to a simple majority procedure. The Court held that South Africa had adopted ss 35 and 152 of the 1909 Act as part of its constitutional settlement when it gained independence in 1931. Its Parliament therefore existed in two forms. For every purpose but three, Parliament could pass an Act by a simple majority with the houses sitting separately. But for those three purposes of repealing s 35, or s 137, or s 152, Parliament had to act by a two-thirds majority in joint session. Until that high percentage of the legislature's members wished to repeal those provisions, they remained entrenched within South Africa's constitution.

Bribery Commissioner v Ranasinghe (1965)

Ceylon, yet another former British colony, became an independent country in 1947. The terms of its Constitution were initially set by British law. On many issues, Ceylon's Parliament (comprised of the House of Representatives and Senate plus the Royal Assent given by the Governor-General) could legislate by simple majority.[65] However the Constitution also contained several principles (dealing primarily with religious discrimination) which were permanently and substantively entrenched. In addition, the Constitution contained various procedurally entrenched provisions. Section 29 of the Constitution provided that the procedurally entrenched provisions could be altered by legislation passed by at least two-thirds of the members of the house. Among the entrenched provisions was s 55, which provided that junior members of the judiciary could be appointed only by a body called the Judicial Services Commission, comprised entirely of senior judges.

In 1958, Ceylon's Parliament passed the Bribery Amendment Act. The Act was not passed in accordance with s 29. The Act established a body known as the Bribery Tribunal, which was in effect a court exercising jurisdiction over alleged bribery offences. Its members were appointed by the Ceylonese government, not by the Judicial Services Commission. Ranasinghe had been convicted by the Bribery Tribunal. He then appealed against his conviction on the basis that the Bribery Amendment Act—since it was not passed in the manner and form specified by s 29—was inconsistent with s 55 of the Constitution and therefore void.

---

[65] See Jennings I and Tambiah H (1952) *The dominion of Ceylon* pp 73–75.

At that time, Ceylon's Constitution retained the House of Lords (sitting in its capacity as the Privy Council) as the country's highest court of appeal. Lord Pearce, delivering the Privy Council's sole judgment, concluded that Mr Ranasinghe's argument was well-founded:

> [A] legislature has no power to ignore the conditions of law-making that are imposed by the instrument which itself regulates its [ie the legislature's] power to make law . . . [T]he proposition which is not acceptable is that a legislature, once established, has some inherent power derived from the mere fact of its establishment to make a valid law by the resolution of a bare majority which its own constituent instrument has said shall not be a valid law unless made by a different type of majority . . . [66]

Lord Pearce echoed the point made by Centlivres CJ in *Harris* that this conclusion did not mean that Ceylon lacked a sovereign Parliament, or that it was not a sovereign state:

> No question of sovereignty arises. A Parliament does not cease to be sovereign whenever its component members fail to produce among themselves a requisite majority. . . . The minority are entitled under the constitution of Ceylon to have no amendment of it which is not imposed by a two-thirds majority. The limitation thus imposed on some lesser majority does not limit the sovereign powers of Parliament itself which can always, whenever it chooses, pass the amendment with the requisite majority.[67]

Are *Trethowan*, *Harris*, and *Ranasinghe* relevant to the British situation?

Initially it might seem that *Ranasinghe*, *Harris*, and *Trethowan* provide a model to bind Parliament in Britain. Suppose Parliament enacts a statute—the Bill of Rights Act 2020— which replicates the terms of the United States' Bill of Rights, for example, and includes within the statute a section which specifies that Parliament may legislate in a way inconsistent with the Bill of Rights only if at least two-thirds of the members of the House of Commons and House of Lords vote in favour of the Act concerned.[68] If a subsequent Parliament wished to enact a statute which contravened the terms of the new Bill of Rights Act, surely *Harris*, *Ranasinghe*, and *Trethowan* are precedents for saying that it could not do so by a simple majority: the 'manner and form' of two-thirds support would be required before a British court would enforce any subsequently enacted statute breaching the provisions of the Bill of Rights. This proposition has attracted the support of several eminent commentators, in addition to Jennings himself.[69]

However there would seem little force to such arguments. The more persuasive analysis is that these cases are irrelevant to questions concerning the sovereignty of the British Parliament. This position, forcefully argued by Wade in 1955,[70] contends that if one transposes these cases to the British context, they are revealed simply as instances of statutory bodies created by Parliament acting beyond the confines of the authority Parliament has bestowed upon them. In both cases there was a 'higher law' to which the Acts in question were subordinate, namely an Act of the British Parliament: the New South Wales' and South African legislatures were acting 'ultra vires' (beyond their legal powers). If these two *subordinate legislatures* had acted beyond the legal limits of the powers granted by the legislature which created them, it was quite consistent with the theory of parliamentary sovereignty for the courts

---

[66] *Bribery Comr v Ranasinghe* [1965] AC 172 at 198, PC.

[67] Ibid, at 200.

[68] We might also assume that the two-thirds majority provision is also protected by another two-thirds majority clause.

[69] See Friedmann W (1950) 'Trethowan's case, parliamentary sovereignty and the limits of legal change' 24 *Australian Law Journal* 103; Keir D (6th edn, 1978) *Cases in constitutional law* p 7; Griswold op cit. Heuston R (1964) *Essays in constitutional law* ch 1; Barendt E (1998) *An introduction to constitutional law* pp 86–93.

[70] Wade HRW (1955) 'The basis of legal sovereignty' *Cambridge LJ* 172.

to intervene. Indeed, the courts in those countries would as a matter of law be obliged to intervene—even if the countries had by then become independent states—for so long as the sovereign law-making power within each jurisdiction had not removed or amended the terms of the initial British statutes.[71]

Britain, in contrast, has no higher source of law than Parliament. Nor is there any obvious colonial master to which the British Parliament owes its existence. Per *Ranasinghe*, there is no 'constituent instrument' specifying the way in which Parliament should make laws on particular subjects. Consequently it would not seem possible for Parliament ever to exceed its legal authority. Indeed, it is puzzling that *Trethowan* was invoked to suggest that the British Parliament could enact manner and form limitations on its own sovereignty, given the comments of the Australian judges. Rich J stated clearly that: 'The Legislature of New South Wales is not sovereign, and no analogy can be drawn from the position of the British Parliament'.[72] Similarly, in Starke J's opinion: 'the Parliaments of the Dominions or Colonies are not sovereign and omnipotent bodies. They are subordinate bodies; their powers are limited by the Imperial [British] or other Acts which created them'.[73] In the same vein, Dixon J observed that:

> The incapacity of the British legislature to limit its own power . . . has been explained as a necessary consequence of a true conception of sovereignty. But in any case it depends on considerations which have no application to the legislature of New South Wales, which is not a sovereign body and has a purely statutory origin.[74]

Advocates of the Jennings thesis might however draw on the following passage from Dixon J's judgment:

> It must not be supposed, however, that all difficulties would vanish if the full doctrine of parliamentary supremacy could be invoked. [If] an Act of the British Parliament . . . contained a provision that no Bill repealing any part of the Act . . . should be presented for the Royal Assent unless the Bill were first approved by the electors. . . . [i]n strictness it would be an unlawful proceeding to present such a Bill before it had been approved by the electors. . . . [T]he Courts would be bound to pronounce it unlawful to do so.[75]

Dixon J's statement was merely obiter, and while one should acknowledge his subsequent reputation as one of the foremost of constitutional scholars, his opinion has yet to be embraced in the English courts.

The logic of the manner and form argument rests on the assumption made by Professor Jennings that the 'rule of recognition' is a common law principle. But as Professor Wade suggests, that logic disintegrates if one regards the *rule of recognition as a political fact rather than a legal principle*. In Wade's view, the rule of recognition is not part of the common law, but something prior to and superior to the common law. It is in essence a basic political reality, not a technical legal rule. It represents the courts' acceptance of the new political consensus brought about by the 1688 revolution. Following that revolution, the political underpinnings of British society were radically changed. Parliament was in a position to establish its superiority over both the King and the courts—and both the King and the courts had no choice but to acquiesce to these new circumstances.

Thus from Wade's 1955 perspective, the theory and practice of parliamentary sovereignty could not be altered by 'legal' means at all. The only thing that could have removed the legislative sovereignty of Parliament was another revolution. This need not be a war or a violent

---

[71] Jennings acknowledged that neither *Trethowan* nor *Harris* were determinative authorities in the British context, but did maintain that they illustrated the principle that; 'the power of a legislature derives from the law by which it was established'; op cit p 156. And, as noted earlier, Jennings asserted that 'the law' in issue in relation to the UK's Parliament was the common law.   [72] (1931) 44 CLR 394 at 418.

[73] Ibid, at 422.   [74] Ibid, at 425–426.   [75] Ibid, at 426.

insurrection, but it would have to be some momentous break in legal and political continuity, some fundamental redefinition of the way that the country's citizens bestow law-making power on their legislature.[76]

Subsequently,[77] Wade adopted a rather different position. He suggested that the only feasible way forward was the very simple device of Parliament introducing legislation to change the judiciary's oath of loyalty. The new oath would require the judges to swear eternal obedience to a statute entrenching certain fundamental rights or liberties that we would never want to have removed, or which could only be removed by a special form of parliamentary procedure above and beyond the bare majority plus Royal Assent formula. If the courts subsequently found themselves presented with a situation analogous to the one the South African Supreme Court faced in *Harris*, their loyalty to the new oath would require them to declare the so-called legislation unconstitutional. The obvious drawback of that proposal is that one could envisage a future Parliament introducing legislation to change the oath back again. The idea does indeed look very simple—but perhaps that is because it seems most unlikely that it would work unless part of a more wide-ranging revolutionary overhaul of the constitution that Wade talked of in 1955.

Is parliamentary sovereignty a British or English concept?

The mid-1950s also lent new impetus to a Scots challenge to the legal supremacy of the British Parliament. This chapter has stressed that parliamentary sovereignty initially emerged in *England, not in Britain*. The Glorious Revolution happened in 1688. England and Scotland then shared a King, and had done so since 1603. But each country had its own Parliament. Scotland and England were at that time both sovereign states, each with its own particular constitutional structure. *Britain* was not created until 1707, when the Scots and English Parliaments each passed an Act of Union approving the terms of a Treaty of Union negotiated between the governments of each country. Between 1688 and 1707, parliamentary sovereignty may have been accepted as the foundation of the constitution in England, but it is far from certain that the idea enjoyed that status in Scotland.[78] Quite what happened in legal and political (and hence constitutional) terms when Britain was created as a country is open to several interpretations.[79]

Orthodox British theory suggests that what happened in 1707 was essentially a *takeover* or absorption of the Scots Parliament by the English Parliament; that is, the constitution of the newly created country of Britain was based on the same principles that underpinned the English constitution between 1688 and 1707. This analysis presumably rests at least in part on the brute fact that the British Parliament sat in the same place as the English Parliament, and while Scots MPs were admitted to both the Commons and the Lords, no English seats in either house were removed.[80]

An alternative perspective would be that what happened in 1707 was *not a takeover, but a merger*.[81] This argument would further maintain that the merger terms were set out in the Treaty of Union itself, and that the Treaty does provide a form of higher law which limits the legal powers of the British Parliament.

---

[76] For an insightful analysis of the Wade/Jennings debate see Gordon M (2009) 'The conceptual foundations of parliamentary sovereignty . . .' *Public Law* 519.

[77] (1980) *Constitutional fundamentals*.

[78] Smith T (1957) 'The Union of 1707 as fundamental law' *Public Law* 99; Munro C (1987) *Studies in constitutional law* ch 4; MacCormick N (1978) 'Does the United Kingdom have a constitution?' 29 *Northern Ireland Law Quarterly* 1; Goldsworthy op cit pp 165–173.

[79] For a fascinating analysis see Upton M (1989) 'Marriage vows of the elephant: the constitution of 1707' *LQR* 79.

[80] The Treaty of Union Art XXII made provision for forty-five Scots MPs to sit in the Commons, and sixteen in the Lords.   [81] See especially MacCormick, op cit.

A third, and perhaps more appropriate characterisation of the events of 1707 is that; 'The union . . . cannot be described as the merging of two states. It was more accurately two renunciations of title and a new state acquiring title over the same territory immediately thereafter'.[82] As with the second perspective, this view of the union maintains that the Treaty should be seen as a 'constituent instrument', restricting the legislative powers of the British Parliament.

'Entrenched' provisions within the Treaty of Union?

The Treaty does not specify how Parliament should make laws: that is, there are no enhanced majority or manner and form provisions to suggest that certain political values were to be entrenched in *procedural* terms. However, if interpreted literally, parts of the Treaty of Union create the impression that various types of *substantive* entrenchment were intended by the framers of the Treaty.

Art XXV certainly confirms that the Treaty should supersede all existing laws incompatible with its terms—be they statutory or common law in origin—in both England and Scotland:

> Article XXV. That all Laws and Statutes in either Kingdom so far as they are contrary to or inconsistent with the Terms of these Articles . . . shall from and after the Union cease and become void . . .

This is of course a repealing rather than entrenching provision, but nonetheless a term that speaks to the supremacy of future legislation over existing law.

Various substantive entrenchment provisions are however easily identifiable. Article I provided that:

> That the Two Kingdoms of England and Scotland shall upon the First Day of May which shall be in the Year One thousand seven hundred and seven and for ever after be united into One Kingdom by the name of Great Britain.

Article II contained the following rule: ' . . . [A]ll Papists and Persons marrying Papists shall be excluded from and forever incapable to inherit possess or enjoy the Imperial Crown of Great Britain . . . .'.

The permanent entrenchment of assorted religious principles was continued in an annex to the Treaty, which reproduced the text of an Act passed by the Scots Parliament in 1706. This included, inter alia, terms to the effect that the form of Protestantism then used in the Church of Scotland; 'shall remain and continue unalterable'. Relatedly, the Act provided that only adherents to this particular faith could hold positions in the then existing Scots universities.

Article VI was concerned with matters of fiscal rather than religious policy:

> That all Parts of the United Kingdom for ever from and after the Union shall . . . be under the same Prohibitions Restrictions and Regulations of Trade and liable to the Same Customs and Duties on Import and Export . . .

The Treaty also contained what might best be termed 'substantively but contingently' entrenched provisions. For example, Article XVIII indicated that the British Parliament could alter all laws concerning matters of public law and private law in Scotland. But this provision was limited in two ways. Firstly, alterations to matters of private law were permissible only if they were for the 'evident Utility of the Subjects within Scotland'.[83] Relatedly, Article XIX stated that Scotland's Court of Session should; 'remain in all time coming within Scotland as it is now constituted by the Laws of that Kingdom'. However, this unequivocal pronouncement was then qualified by the proviso that the British Parliament could modify the Court of Session in any fashion for; 'the better Administration of Justice'.[84]

---

[82] Wicks E (2001) 'A new constitution for a new state? The 1707 union of England and Scotland' *LQR* 109.

[83] The Treaty did not explain what was meant by 'evident utility' or who would decide if a new law satisfied that test.

[84] Nor did the Treaty explain by who or against what criteria the notion of 'better administration of justice' would be gauged.

Notwithstanding these provisions, obvious criticisms can be levelled against both the second and third perspectives on the legal consequences of the Anglo-Scots union. Two such criticisms are schematic in nature. Firstly, the Treaty does not contain any suggestion as to how the entrenched provisions might be safeguarded against subsequent statutory infringement. Certainly no jurisdiction is expressly given to any Court to invalidate any such legislation. Secondly, if the higher law perspective is correct, Britain was created without the benefit of a sovereign law-maker. Article III of the Treaty expressly abolishes the Scots and English Parliaments in creating the British Parliament. But the Treaty contains no mechanism for resummoning those Parliaments, nor for amending or removing the entrenched provisions. A third criticism is rooted in practical historical fact. Most of the supposedly entrenched provisions of the Treaty of Union are apparently no longer in force.[85] Successive generations of parliamentarians and of judges seem to have accepted unquestioningly until the 1950s that the legal status of the Treaty of Union was the same as any other statute—its provisions were open to amendment by either express or implied repeal by subsequent legislation.[86]

McCormick v Lord Advocate (1953)

However, the constituent instrument understanding of the Treaty has been tested several times in the Scots courts, and Scots judges have not dismissed it entirely. *McCormick v Lord Advocate*[87] concerned a challenge to the constitutionality of the Royal Titles Act 1953. Under this Act, the former Princess Elizabeth succeeded to the British throne with the title of Elizabeth II. McCormick argued that Britain had never had a Queen Elizabeth I—the woman who stepped on Walter Raleigh's cloak in the sixteenth century was Elizabeth I of England— and so could not have an Elizabeth II.

The Scots Court of Session rejected McCormick's claim, but offered some unexpected opinions on the wider issue of the constitutional status of the Act of Union. The leading judgment was delivered by Lord Cooper, who observed that:

> The principle of the unlimited sovereignty of Parliament is a distinctively English principle which has no counterpart in Scottish constitutional law . . . Considering that the Union legislation extinguished the Parliaments of Scotland and England and replaced them by a new Parliament, I have difficulty in seeing why it should have been supposed that the new Parliament of Great Britain must inherit all the peculiar characteristics of the English Parliament but none of the Scottish Parliament, as if all that happened in 1707 was that Scottish representatives were admitted to the Parliament of England. That is not what was done.[88]

Lord Cooper then alluded to the various 'entrenched' provisions of the Treaty:

> I have never been able to understand how it is possible to reconcile with elementary canons of construction[89] the adoption by the English constitutional theorists of the same attitude towards those markedly different types of provisions.

While many of the terms of the Act of Union have been repealed, some of its most important provisions remain in place. Scotland retains its own legal system for example, and its own established Church. It is interesting to speculate how the courts in England and Scotland would

---

[85] Wicks notes some disagreement between Scots constitutional scholars on the extent of the repeal; (2001) op cit p 18.

[86] Cf Dicey's comment in *The Law of the Constitution* concerning the 'entrenched' provisions of the Treaty; 'The history of legislation in respect of these very Acts affords the strongest proof of the futility inherent in every attempt of one sovereign body to restrain the action of another equally sovereign body'. One need not be a rigorous critic of Dicey's position to see that in this passage he assumes rather than proves that the British Parliament possesses sovereign powers.

[87] 1953 SC 396.   [88] Ibid, at 411.

[89] By which is meant the principles that 'British' courts have traditionally invoked to ascertain the meaning of statutory provisions. This point is addressed in ch 3.

respond if Parliament passed legislation changing either of these two features of Scottish soci-ety.[90] It would seem unlikely that Parliament would ever enact legislation with that intended effect. But *McCormick* offers at least the theoretical possibility that an argument before a court questioning the validity of a statute might succeed.

Women's enfranchisement

The common law also provides one often overlooked example of the courts disapplying ortho-dox notions of parliamentary sovereignty in defence of the traditional moral values. As we shall see in chapter seven, the 1832 Great Reform Act extended the parliamentary franchise to affluent middle class men. Further nineteenth-century reforms gave the right to vote to an increasing percentage of the male population. Parliament declined explicitly to enfran-chise women: but in the 1860s, women's suffrage campaigners formulated an argument that Parliament had done so impliedly.

Section 4 of Lord Brougham's Act of 1850, provided that 'in all Acts words importing the masculine gender shall be deemed and taken to include females . . . unless the contrary as to gender is expressly provided'. The 1867 Reform Act did not expressly exclude women. John Stuart Mill, then an MP and supporter of women's suffrage, suggested during the Bill's passage that such phraseology impliedly extended the vote to women. The government did not intro-duce a clause expressly disapplying Lord Brougham's Act to the franchise issue, suggesting that establishing the effect of the statute on this point was to be left to the courts.[91]

Chorlton v Lings (1868)

In *Chorlton v Lings*,[92] a woman who satisfied all the criteria entitling a man to vote argued that women had been impliedly enfranchised by the 1867 Act. However, the Court of Common Pleas held that Parliament could not possibly have intended to enfranchise women. To do so would overturn centuries of constitutional tradition and practice. Willes J explained the essentially moral reasoning behind this practice, in language no doubt considered diplomatic at the time:

> [T]he absence of such a right is referable to the fact that . . . chiefly out of respect to women, and a sense of decorum, and not from their want of intellect, or their being for any other reason unfit to take part in the government of the country, they have been excused from taking any share in this department of public affairs.[93]

The Court's unanimous rejection of the argument that Parliament could impliedly amend basic constitutional values was most clearly expressed by Keating J; the legislature, 'if desirous of making an alteration so important and extensive, would have said so plainly and distinctly'.[94]

Nairn v University of St Andrews (1909)

The *Chorlton v Lings* scenario was replayed forty years later in *Nairn v University of St Andrews*.[95] The Representation of the People (Scotland) Act 1868 extended the franchise in university constituencies to all of the university's graduates. The Universities (Scotland) Act 1889 empowered Scots universities to award degrees to women. Nairn was a woman graduate who contended that the 1889 legislation necessarily implied that she was now entitled to vote. The House of Lords saw little merit in such an argument. Lord Loreburn LC was adamant that female suffrage could be introduced only by the *most explicit* of statutory provisions: 'It would

---

[90] Cf the comment by Lord Cooper in *McCormick*; 'it is of little avail to ask whether the Parliament of Great Britain "can" do this or that, without going on to inquire who can stop them if they do'; 1953 SC 396 at 412.

[91] Kent S (1989) *Sex and suffrage in Britain 1860–1914* ch 8.   [92] (1868) LR 4 CP 374.

[93] Ibid, at 392.   [94] Ibid, at 395.

[95] [1909] AC 147. See Leneman L (1991) 'When women were not "persons": the Scottish women graduates case 1906–1908' *Juridical Review* 109.

require a convincing demonstration to satisfy me that Parliament intended to effect a constitutional change so momentous and far-reaching by so furtive a process.'[96]

Keating J's holding in *Chorlton* that Parliament may introduce 'important and extensive' changes to the nature of a citizen's relationship to the state only through 'plain and distinct' statutory language is a principle of potentially wide application. One could draw the same conclusion about Lord Loreburn's observation that the common law does not permit Parliament to achieve policy objectives relating to matters of fundamental political and/or moral significance through 'furtive' legislative devices.

What the courts seem to be saying in these two cases does not seem easy to reconcile with the legal principles advanced in orthodox interpretations of the decisions in *Vauxhall Estates* and *Ellen Street Estates*, which are assumed to have established the doctrine of implied repeal. However, one can see convincing 'democratic' reasons for preferring the *Chorlton/Nairn* rationale. If we assume that Parliament derives its political authority from the consent of the people, it would seem sensible that Parliament is candid about the objectives it is seeking. Without such honesty in the legislative process, it would not be possible for citizens to decide whether or not they wished to continue to consent to what Parliament was doing. That is however essentially a political argument rather than a legal one, and as yet it is one that the British courts have not been prepared to accept.

Conclusion

We might draw some initial conclusions about the status of parliamentary sovereignty within our constitution. Perhaps the most important point to remember is that the principle was not designed for a modern, democratic society which has large political parties which contest general elections on a nationwide basis. It is a 300-year-old idea.

To do justice to Dicey's theorisation of the principle in the 1880s, we ought to note that his concern was to illustrate the relationship between Acts of Parliament and the courts—to stress that as *a matter of legal principle* the courts were invariably subordinate to the will of Parliament. Dicey accepted that political sovereignty was a very different thing. When it came to the practicalities of government, it was nonsense to say that Parliament could enact legislation on any subject it chose. Because one part of Parliament, the House of Commons, was an elected body, and its members could periodically be changed by its citizens, MPs would always have to be conscious of what measures the electorate would accept, and temper legislation accordingly. Thus, to evaluate the *political acceptability* of Dicey's legal doctrine we must examine long-term changes in other areas of Britain's law-making and government processes. In particular, we must assess the *voting system* through which members of the Commons are elected, the *relationship between the House of Commons and the government*, and the *changing balance of power within Parliament* between the Commons, Lords, and Monarch.

These inquiries will repeatedly lead us to a point of considerable importance which frequently resurfaces in any study of the British constitution; namely a *distinction between legal formality and political reality*. These two concepts do not always coincide, and one of the great difficulties facing constitutional lawyers is deciding in what circumstances law gives way to politics, and vice-versa.

But for the present, we might leave our discussion of parliamentary sovereignty with a quotation from the 1969 case of *Madzimbamuto v Lardner-Burke*.[97] Lord Reid observed that:

> it is often said that it would be unconstitutional for . . . Parliament to do certain things, meaning that
> the moral, political and other reasons against doing them are so strong that most people would

---

[96] [1909] AC 147 at 161.   [97] [1969] 1 AC 645, PC.

regard it as highly improper if Parliament did these things. But that does not mean it is beyond the power of Parliament to do such things. If Parliament chose to do any of them, the courts could not hold the Act of Parliament invalid.[98]

As later chapters suggest, the UK's accession to the European Economic Community in 1973 cast considerable doubt on the orthodox theory of parliamentary sovereignty. But it would be an adventurous lawyer who suggested that we can currently find purely *domestic* limitations to the principle that Parliament's legal powers are unconfined. Yet as we shall begin to see in the following chapter, it would be rash to assume that the continued dominance of the orthodox theory of parliamentary sovereignty invariably places obvious limits on the constitutional authority of the courts.

Suggested further reading

Academic and political commentary

WADE HRW (1955) 'The basis of legal sovereignty' *Cambridge LJ* 172

GORDON M (2009) 'The conceptual foundations of parliamentary sovereignty: reconsidering Jennings and Wade' *Public Law* 519

GOLDSWORTHY J (1999) *The sovereignty of Parliament* chs 5 and 8

WICKS E (2006) *The evolution of a constitution* ch 1

WINTERTON G (1976) 'The British grundnorm; parliamentary sovereignty re-examined' *LQR* 591

WICKS E (2001) 'A new constitution for a new state? The 1707 union of England and Scotland' *LQR* 109

SLAUGHTER T (1981) 'Abdicate and contract in the Glorious Revolution' 24 *Historical Journal* 323

Case law and legislation

Harris v (Dönges) Minister of the Interior (1952) 1 TLR 1245

Trethowan v Attorney-General for New South Wales (1931) 44 CLR 394

Mortensen v Peters (1906) 14 SLT 227

McCormick v Lord Advocate (1953) SC 396

British Railways Board v Pickin [1974] AC 765

---

[98] [1969] 1 AC 645 at 723, PC.

Chapter 3

The Rule of Law and the Separation of Powers

The 'rule of law' is another taken-for-granted element of the British constitution, invoked—like 'democracy'—to convey the essential adequacy of Britain's constitutional arrangements. But 'the rule of law', like 'democracy', has no single meaning: it is not a legal rule, but a moral principle, meaning different things to different people according to their particular moral positions. We might view the rule of law as a vehicle for expressing 'the people's' preferences about two essentially political issues. Firstly, it relates to the *substance* of the relationship between citizens and government. Secondly, it deals with the *processes* through which that relationship is conducted. More simply, the rule of law is concerned with what government can do—and how government can do it.

Many theorists have presented variations on these two themes.[1] In addition to analysing several seminal cases, in which one can discern the varying ways in which principles are put into practice, this chapter addresses three theoretical analyses, those of A V Dicey, Friedrich Hayek, and Harry Jones, which span the spectrum of mainstream debate about the nature of the rule of law in Britain's modern constitution.

I. The Diceyan perspective: the rule of law in the pre-welfare state

Dicey's account of the rule of law might be viewed guardedly. Dicey was the product of an undemocratic society in the modern sense: as noted in chapter seven, few adults were entitled to vote in parliamentary elections when Dicey completed his famous *Study of the law of*

---

[1] Cf Harlow C and Rawlings R (1984) *Law and administration* chs 1–2; Munro op cit ch 9; Thompson E (1975) *Whigs and hunters* pp 258–266; Raz J (1977) 'The rule of law and its virtue' *LQR* 191.

the constitution in the 1880s. Dicey opposed the nineteenth-century trend towards increased government intervention in social and economic affairs.[2] Nevertheless, in respect of parliamentary sovereignty, the British constitution rests on foundations which pre-dated modern concepts of democracy. Consequently, Dicey's theories provide a good starting point to examine the meaning of the rule of law.

The essence of Dicey's approach appears in several short passages in the *Law of the constitution*:

> We mean, in the first place, that no man is punishable or can be lawfully made to suffer in body or goods except for a distinct breach of the law established in the ordinary legal manner before the ordinary courts of the land.... [And] we mean in the second place ... that every official, from the Prime Minister down to a constable or collector of taxes, is under the same responsibility for every act done without legal justification as any other citizen.[3]

This definition has three parts. Firstly, 'no man can lawfully be made to suffer in body or goods'. That indicates that Dicey's primary concern is with protecting individual rights and liberties (ie a more modern restatement of Lockean principles). Dicey stressed that this protection had to be effective against both other citizens and against the government. A government official, like every other citizen, had to find some legal justification for behaving in an apparently unlawful way. Secondly, 'except for a distinct breach of the law'. This reinforces the conclusion that government has to operate within a framework of laws superior to the mere actions of government officials: behaviour does not become lawful simply because a government official claims so. The third factor is that any breach of the law 'must be established in the ordinary legal manner before the ordinary courts of the land'. The courts, rather than the government, must determine whether or not the law has been broken. These three elements of Dicey's rule of law lead towards another taken-for-granted constitutional principle: the separation of powers.

Philosophical works such as Locke's *Second Treatise of Civil Government* (1690) and Montesquieu's *Spirit of the Laws* (1748) had a profound influence on theoretical analyses of the British constitution, and, in a different way, on the constitutional principles adopted by the American revolutionaries.[4] For introductory purposes, the basic point to distill from the separation of powers doctrine in the British context is that the government function has three discrete elements.

The first is legislation. One part of government makes the laws under which people live. Returning to the idea of the British constitution as a social contract, the legislative function is to produce the terms of the contract under which government is conducted. In Britain, the legislative function rests with Parliament. But if a society drafts a contract, the people must also design some way of carrying that contract out.

This second element, carrying out or 'executing' of the laws, is undertaken by the executive branch of government. Diceyans regards the second function of government with suspicion. Their assumption is that the executive will always try to do things that the legislature has not authorised. According to orthodox British understandings of the rule of law, the executive branch of government has no autonomous power to make law through legislation.[5] That power rests exclusively with Parliament. Consequently, a third element of government must offer citizens a remedy if the executive acts incompatibly with the laws the legislature has enacted.

---

[2] McEldowney (1985) op cit.

[3] Dicey A (1915, 8th edn) *Introduction to the study of the law of the constitution* pp 110 and 114.

[4] On the differential impact of these theories on Britain, France, and the United States see Vile op cit. See also Goldsworthy op cit pp 151–153.

[5] As noted in ch 2, the Monarch (whom for present purposes we may treat as the head of the executive branch of government) has the power to make international law through signing of Treaties. But international law has no direct force in domestic law until the relevant Treaty has been 'incorporated' by an Act of Parliament; see 'Inconsistency with International law', ch 2, pp 29–30.

This third element is the courts. The citizen can seek a remedy 'in the ordinary courts of the land' if she believes herself the victim of unlawful government action. In addition to determining if executive action falls within the limits approved by parliament, courts possess a limited law-making power through developing the common law. Executive action with no legislative foundation may be lawful if rooted in common law.

This threefold division within Dicey's version of the rule of law is helpfully illustrated by a celebrated eighteenth-century case—*Entick v Carrington*.[6]

Entick v Carrington (1765)

The mid-eighteenth century was a turbulent time in British constitutional history. In addition to facing rebellion in America, the government was under continuous pressure from an indigenous radical movement which accused it of corruption and incompetence. Technological advances in the printing industry enabled radicals to spread their ideas far and wide. London in the 1760s was awash with numerous pamphlets criticising the government.

The focus of much opposition was John Wilkes, a radical politician elected to the House of Commons several times. On each occasion the Commons had refused to permit him to take his seat.[7] This made him a hero to many American colonists, who felt he shared their struggle against an increasingly tyrannical government and Parliament.[8] The British government adopted various draconian tactics to stem the flow of Wilkes' critical literatures. One technique that the Home Secretary deployed was to issue a 'general warrant' empowering his civil servants to raid the premises of radicals suspected of producing seditious material. The warrant purportedly authorised government officials to enter private premises without the owner's permission and to seize everything they found there. In 1764, the Home Secretary authorised such a raid by government officials on Mr Entick, a Wilkes sympathiser.

The government's action ostensibly contravened some basic principles of consensual constitutional government discussed in chapters one and two. There was little point in electors choosing Wilkes as their MP if the 'government'[9] prevented him from taking his seat. And it would be difficult for electors to make an informed choice about their law-makers if the government suppressed radical publications. Eighteenth-century Britain was not a democratic country in the modern sense. But was it a society subject to the rule of law as Dicey later defined it?

Entick had obviously 'suffered in goods'—his property had been broken into and taken away. But had he committed 'a distinct breach of the law established in the ordinary manner before the ordinary courts of the land'? Evidently not. He had not been accused nor convicted of a crime, nor brought before any court. In contrast, the government's officials appeared to have contravened the common law by trespassing on Mr Entick's land and seizing his property.

Consequently, Mr Entick sued the officials for trespass to his land and goods. Their defence was that the Home Secretary's warrant provided a lawful excuse for their actions. However, the defence proved difficult to sustain. There was no legislation in force which authorised the Home Secretary to grant such a warrant. Nor was there any common law precedent making this government activity lawful.

Lacking clear statutory or common law authority to justify their actions, the government officials invoked two further defences. The first was an argument of 'state necessity'. The Home Secretary essentially claimed that he thought Entick's papers presented a serious threat to public order; it was necessary to seize the papers to prevent political unrest. The second argument might be described as one of 'custom and tradition'. The power had been used many

---

[6] (1765) 19 State Tr 1029.   [7] This is explored further in ch 8.

[8] See Maier P (1963) 'John Wilkes and American disillusionment with Britain' *William and Mary Quarterly* 373.

[9] The word is used guardedly; see 'John Wilkes', ch 8, pp 203–204.

times, and had never been challenged by anyone. So, surely the practice could not be unlawful? Camden CJ was not interested in what the government thought was necessary, or in what it had done before, but in finding the law. One element of 'the law' was entirely clear:

> By the laws of England, every invasion of private property, be it ever so minute is a trespass. No man can set his foot upon my ground without my licence. . . . If he admits the fact, he is bound to show by way of justification, that some positive law has empowered or excused him. . . .[10]

Furthermore, so 'exorbitant' a power as that deployed against Mr Entick could be justified only by clear statutory or common law authority. Camden CJ put the point simply: 'If it is law, it will be found in our books. If it is not to be found there, it is not law'.[11] The lawyers arguing the Mr Carrington's case[12] could not find any such authority. In consequence, the entry to Mr Entick's property and seizure of his papers were a trespass. Mr Entick was entitled to recover damages for his loss. The jury awarded the then substantial sum of £300.

Decisions such as *Entick v Carrington* led one legal philosopher to characterise the courts as the 'lions under the throne' of the British constitution.[13] The aphorism lends itself to several interpretations, but for our purposes might be seen as suggesting that the judges would spring out and fiercely defend the rights and liberties of individual citizens from unlawful government interference. *Entick* provides a classic example of the courts upholding the Diceyan version of the rule of law. The theory does not entail that government always acts lawfully, but that citizens have a legal remedy when the government acts unlawfully.

Lord Camden's reasoning reveals the depths to which Lockean notions of 'property' and 'liberty' were embedded within the eighteenth-century common law tradition: 'The great end, for which men entered into society, was to secure their property. That right is preserved sacred and incommunicable in all instances, where it has not been taken away or abridged by some public law for the good of the whole'.[14] But even if we accept that defence of 'property' and 'liberty' against arbitrary government is the courts' primary constitutional responsibility—and that is itself a controversial moral proposition—we again encounter the problem of just what 'liberty' and 'property' might mean?

Dicey's rule of law–process or substance?

The concept of the separation of powers, as applied in *Entick*, might suggest that Diceyan theories of the rule of law concern only the processes through which laws are administered, and not their substance.[15] However Dicey's overt focus on process co-existed with a political view about the 'correct' substance of the laws which Parliament makes. Dicey was much concerned that laws had a high degree of *predictability or forseeability*. People needed to know where they stood if they were to run a business, get involved in politics, or start certain types of social relationships. Dicey thought the rule of law demanded that Parliament did not give government any arbitrary or wide discretionary powers. A statute which said, for instance, that the Home Secretary can imprison anyone she likes, whenever she likes, for as long as she likes, would not meet the tests of predictability and forseeability, and would seemingly contradict Dicey's version of rule of law.

But we automatically encounter a major problem here. Dicey seems to be saying that there are limits to the type of governmental powers which Parliament can create if society is to remain subject to the rule of law. Yet the theory of parliamentary sovereignty tells us that there are no legal limitations on the statutes Parliament can enact. One cannot go to court and

---

[10] (1765) 19 State Tr 1029 at 1066.   [11] (1765) 19 State Tr 1029.
[12] Although Mr Carrington was formally the defendant, since he actually committed the trespass, in the broader constitutional sense the Minister's action was in issue.
[13] Heuston R (1970) '*Liversidge v Anderson* in retrospect' *LQR* 33–68.   [14] (1765) 19 State Tr 1029 at 1066.
[15] See generally Craig P (1997) 'Formal and substantive conceptions of the rule of law' *Public Law* 467.

ask for a statute which (for example) bestows very wide discretionary powers on the Home Secretary to search people's homes and seize their papers to be declared unconstitutional in a legal sense because it contravenes the Diceyan rule of law. Had Parliament in 1760 passed a statute authorising the Home Secretary to issue warrants allowing civil servants to enter people's premises and to seize people's papers whenever he thought such action desirable, Carrington's 'trespass' would have been lawful, and Entick's suit would have failed. While notions of the inviolability of 'property' and 'liberty' were by then 'embedded' in the common law, they were not 'entrenched' in the constitution, since Parliament might impinge upon property rights and personal liberties whenever and however it thought fit. After *Entick*, Parliament could if it had wished have passed legislation affording 'general warrants' an entirely lawful status.

The logical conclusion might therefore be that the rule of law is a less important constitutional principle than the sovereignty of Parliament. But both the Diceyan rule of law and Dicey's theory of parliamentary sovereignty are at root moral concepts. Perhaps they are both, per Professor Wade, 'ultimate political facts'. The difficult question which then arises is how can one have two 'ultimate' facts?[16] Later in this chapter, and in subsequent chapters, we consider the ways in which this apparent tension has been addressed.

The 'independence of the judiciary'

A second tension between the rule of law and parliamentary sovereignty appears when we consider the 'independence of the judiciary'. Before 1688, and in the years immediately thereafter, English judges held office 'at the King's pleasure'. This meant simply that not only did the King appoint the judges, but also that judges who subsequently displeased the King or his government could be dismissed. This fate befell Coke in the early-seventeenth century when his judgments led him into great disfavour with the Crown.[17]

The continuance of this situation after the 1688 revolution would have undermined parliamentary sovereignty, since the King could have used his dismissal powers to 'persuade' judges to interpret laws in a manner inconsistent with Parliament's intentions. The solution to this problem, the Act of Settlement 1700, provided that while the Crown had the power to appoint judges,[18] judges would hold office 'during good behaviour'. This means a judge could only be removed by a joint address of the House of Lords and House of Commons, after the judge has committed a crime or engaged in some gross form of moral misbehaviour. She cannot simply be sacked by the Crown for producing judgments that the government does not like.

A chief complaint of the American revolutionaries was that the Act of Settlement did not extend to the colonies. Their judges were appointed for limited terms by colonial Governors, acting on behalf of the Crown, and could be dismissed if they made decisions the Governor disliked. In contrast, Lord Camden could produce a judgment of which the government disapproved in *Entick v Carrington* because, unlike colonial judges, he was not dismissible at the government's whim.

However the Act of Settlement only secured the independence of the judiciary against the Crown, not against Parliament. Parliamentary sovereignty meant both that an individual judge could be dismissed by a majority in the Commons and Lords, and that the rules in the Act of Settlement could be changed by new legislation. This theoretical possibility has yet to emerge in reality: only one High Court judge has ever been dismissed (in 1830); and while the Act of Settlement has been subjected to minor modifications, its basic provisions remain

---

[16] See Allan T (1985) 'Legislative supremacy and the rule of law: democracy and constitutionalism' *Cambridge LJ* 111.

[17] See Plucknett (1928) op cit; Corwin E (1928) 'The higher law background of American constitutional law (parts I and II)' *Harvard LR* 149–182 and 365–409.

[18] This appointment method survived until the early twenty-first century; see 'Conclusion', ch 6, pp 168–169.

intact. We might therefore plausibly conclude that in practice the British constitution affords the judiciary independence (from both government and Parliament) in the tenure of their office. The force of this tradition in the 'British' context is perhaps best illustrated by returning to the *Harris* controversy in South Africa.

Harris v Minister of the Interior—the aftermath

The only entrenched clauses in South Africa's constitution in 1952 were s 35, s 137, and s 152. Everything else could seemingly be changed by a simple majority house plus senate vote (and the Royal Assent). The government decided to use its parliamentary majorities to bypass the Supreme Court's defence of the constitution. Its first initiative was to promote the High Court of Parliament Act 1952, which purported to turn Parliament itself into a new Court, empowered to hear appeals from the Appellate Division. The 'Act' was passed by simple majority. The plaintiffs in *Harris* immediately challenged this legislation, arguing that any such measure could only be enacted through the s 152 procedures. In *Harris (No 2)*,[19] the Appellate Division Court invalidated the 1952 Act, using a more inventive strategy than in *Harris (No 1)*.

The Court found that s 152 impliedly required that any legislation dealing with matters protected by s 35 or s 137 be subject to scrutiny by a 'court'. This implied term was a necessary inheritance of the British constitutional tradition on which South Africa's own constitution was based. Furthermore, a 'court' in this sense had to be institutionally independent from the legislature and the government, and had to be staffed by legally qualified 'judges'. The supposed 'High Court of Parliament' met neither criteria. To entrust such a body with the legal protection of s 35 and s 137 would render that protection illusory. A 'High Court of Parliament' with jurisdiction to hear cases involving the entrenched clauses could only be created via the s 152 procedures.[20]

The government's second strategy was more straightforward. The Constitution did not prevent the legislature increasing the size of the Appellate Division. Consequently, the government invited the legislature to enact the Appellate Division Quorum Act 1955. This legislation—passed by simple majority—added six further judges, appointed by the government, to the existing five. All six ostensibly met the requirement identified in *Harris (No 2)* that they be legally qualified: they were all either judges in lower courts or law professors. All six were also, however, known supporters of government policy. Parliament then enacted, again by simple majority, the Senate Act 1955. This enlarged the senate from forty-eight to eighty-nine members, chosen by a method which ensured that they were almost all government supporters. The government thereby gained a two-thirds parliamentary majority. Then, in 1956, Parliament re-enacted the Separate Representation of Voters Act in the manner and form required by s 35. The new eleven judge Supreme Court promptly held that the new Act was constitutional in *Collins v Minister of the Interior*.[21]

All these steps were 'legal' in the formal sense, although we would from a contemporary British perspective question their moral acceptability.[22] The message conveyed by the Appellate Division Quorum Act 1955 and the judgment in *Collins* is that there is more to the concept of an 'independent' judiciary than job security. Legislatures may create compliant courts by packing them with new judges. 'Independence' may be as much a question of a judge's state of mind as of the fixity of her legal hold on office.[23]

---

[19] 1952 (4) SA 769 (A).   [20] See Loveland (1999) op cit ch 9.   [21] 1957 (1) SA 552 (A).

[22] See Lewin op cit; Le May G (1957) 'Parliament, the Constitution and the doctrine of the mandate' 74 *South African Law Journal* 33; Loveland (1999) op cit ch 10.

[23] This episode suggests there are no simple solutions to the entrenchment conundrum in the British context. A legal device which safeguarded basic moral values by demanding that they could be infringed only by super-majorities within Parliament, would be worthless if the power to appoint judges and select members of Parliament was not regulated in a similar way.

II. The rule of law in the welfare state

Dicey's constitutional theories were shaped by the experience of living in a society which permitted few citizens to vote in parliamentary elections, and in which government performed few functions. By the 1950s, virtually all adults were enfranchised,[24] and government had assumed a significant role in managing economic and social affairs. At virtually the same time that Dicey was writing his *Law of the constitution*, Parliament began to enact legislation which gave government bodies loosely defined discretionary powers and duties. This trend accelerated markedly after 1900. It is beyond this book's scope to consider questions of political theory and history in depth, but it is important that we grasp the rudiments of the two dominant theories which have informed modern British political history.[25]

The first theory, representing right wing political views, we might call 'market liberalism', to which Dicey was an early adherent. Its most celebrated modern defence was authored by Friedrich Hayek in a 1944 book, *The Road to Serfdom*. The second theory, social democracy, emerged from the centre-left of the political spectrum, and from a lawyer's viewpoint, is best explained by the American jurist Harry Jones in a 1958 article in the *Columbia Law Review*.[26]

Hayek—the road to serfdom

Hayek is a latter day exponent of the orthodox Diceyan viewpoint. For Hayek, the function of the rule of law is to ensure that: 'government in all its actions is bound by rules fixed and announced beforehand'.[27] This concern encompasses both process and substance.

In respect of process, Hayek follows Dicey in demanding that all citizens must have access to an independent judiciary before which they can challenge the legality of government action to establish if what government has done accords with a pre-existing common law or statutory rule? The courts' only duty when deciding a case of this sort is to protect the citizen against the government; judges must not ignore or bend legal rules in order to facilitate the government process. Hayek's reference to 'rules' is fundamental to his analysis. He sees minimal scope for laws which give government discretionary powers, as such powers make it impossible for citizens to predict the exact extent of government authority. This preference for a rule-bound government process co-exists with a desire for a government minimalist in substance. Hayekians believe that society's interests are best served by reducing the power and size of government to a minimum, thereby giving individual citizens as much freedom as possible to organise their social and economic affairs. Government must provide an army to defend the country; a police force to uphold the criminal law; and a court system to settle disputes over crimes, contracts, and property. But it should have no role at all in the provision of health services, education, housing, or social security. If such things were beneficial to society, they would be provided by private entrepreneurs.

Hayekian theorists accept that there will be great inequalities of wealth in such a society. This is regarded as a natural consequence of people's varying attitudes and abilities. Such inequality is a lesser evil than the intrusion upon individual freedom which would result if the government took positive steps to address this 'natural' state of affairs. The bottom line of the Hayekian analysis is that society cannot have both the rule of law and a welfare state. Since Parliament is sovereign, it may choose one value or the other, but legislators cannot

---

[24] The historical development of this element of the constitution is traced in ch 7.
[25] See George V and Wilding P (1976) *Ideology and state welfare*.
[26] Jones H (1958) 'The rule of law and the welfare state' 58 *Columbia LR* 143. For a contextualised explanation see Crosland C (1952) 'The transition from capitalism'; and Jenkins R (1952) 'Equality', both in Crossman R (ed) *New Fabian Essays*.   [27] (1944) op cit p 54.

simultaneously pursue both ideals. The *rule of law is an absolute value*, which can exist only in constitutions which prevent legislators intervening in social and economic affairs. From this viewpoint, the rule of law: 'has little to do with the question whether all actions of government are legal in the juridical sense'; rather 'it implies limits to the scope of legislation'.[28] In Hayek's view: 'any policy aiming directly at a substantive ideal of redistributive justice must lead to the destruction of the rule of law'.[29]

Jones—the rule of law in the welfare state

While Hayek's theory was influential in Britain in the 1980s, it enjoyed little support among either the Conservative or Labour Parties between 1945 and 1975. The political consensus in that era fell within the broad confines of a *social democratic* approach to government. The period is often referred to as 'Butskellism'. This is a combination of the names of R A Butler and Hugh Gaitskell, leading figures in the Conservative and Labour Parties respectively, and stresses the similarity of the political objectives which the two parties pursued.[30] This perspective assumes firstly that government should play an extensive role in economic affairs, and secondly that individuals must accept significant limits on their autonomy if the legislature deems such restraints in the public interest.

Early examples of this theory of government were introduced by the Gladstone and Disraeli administrations in the late-nineteenth century, in legislation which limited the use of child labour for example, or which prevented factories from emptying their effluent into rivers. The justification for such government intervention comes from two sources. Firstly, it is considered 'just' and 'fair' in so far as it protects individuals from exploitation. Secondly, it is thought to be rational for society as a whole; for example the cost of ill health resulting from not having controls on pollution outweighs the expense involved in regulating waste disposal.

By the 1950s, this twin rationale underpinned an immense network of government activities; a national health service, millions of publicly owned houses; government control of the coal, steel, water, gas, and electricity industries; old age pensions; unemployment benefits; and free schooling for all children. This clearly represented, in Hayek's words, a 'substantive ideal of redistributive justice'. The welfare state also required Parliament to give government officials many discretionary powers; it was not feasible to run a complex welfare state in accordance with legislative 'rules'. Government was now doing so much, and dealing with so many different issues, that it would be impossible for legislators to produce a rule for every foreseeable situation. This meant that there was some reduction in the precision with which citizens could predict the limits of government's powers. However, some constitutional lawyers denied that this meant that society could not be governed in accordance with the rule of law.

Unlike Hayek, Jones suggests that the *rule of law is a relative rather than absolute political value*; that one can dilute Dicey's model without removing its basic features. Like Hayek, Jones accepts that 'the rule of law's great purpose is protection of the individual against state power holders'.[31] But he also suggested that the rule of law would continue to exist as long as legislators, government officials, and the judiciary accepted an 'adjudicative ideal'.

While legislation in Hayekian society would take the form of rigid rules, the statutory basis of a welfare state would also contain flexible standards, permitting government to make various responses to given situations. However the adjudicative ideal demands that although the legislature bestows wide discretion on government bodies, it may not grant them arbitrary powers. Jones' version of the rule of law does not dismiss the importance of

[28] (1944) op cit at pp 61–62. [29] Ibid, at 59. [30] See George and Wilding op cit chs 2–4.
[31] Op cit at p 145.

predictability; rather it accepts that in some areas of government activity it is only necessary that citizens can foresee the general boundaries rather than the precise location of government authority.

Nor does Jones' theory reject the need for a separation of powers. Citizens must be able to challenge the legality of government action through a 'meaningful day in court'. Jones differs from Hayek in assuming that this need not entail resort to the 'ordinary courts'; specialist tribunals could serve this purpose in respect of some government functions, since they might be more informal, more expert, and less expensive than the normal judicial process.

The task which faces the courts and tribunals in social democratic society is not to protect the individual at all costs. Since Parliament has given the government discretionary powers, the courts must accept that the legislature intends that individuals might suffer some restraint on their autonomy in order to further the public interest. This may present courts with a difficult problem—how much discretion did Parliament intend the government to have? Jones recognised that this set 'a harder and wider task for the rule of law', but he suggested that Hayek was being unduly pessimistic in suggesting that the concept had to be abandoned altogether.

Although a welfare state may be difficult to reconcile with a Diceyan or Hayekian view of the rule of law, it is consistent with some of the notions of democracy in the sense of government by consent discussed in chapter one. If 'the people' have decided that they are willing to dilute the Diceyan ideal to achieve certain social objectives, there would seem to be no obvious barrier to them doing so. Whether that conclusion is sound from a political perspective is a question to which we shall return. It would be quite possible for a society to adhere to Hayek/Dicey's version of the rule of law without being a democracy. A dictator who preserved market autonomy and stuck rigidly to pre-announced limits on his powers would pass Hayek's test. Whether one can have a democratic constitution without respect for at least a diluted version of the rule of law is a more difficult question, which we shall pursue at a later stage.

'Red light' and 'green light' theories

Jones' and Hayek/Dicey's competing viewpoints about the 'what and the how' of modern government are neatly encapsulated in what Harlow and Rawlings term the 'red light' and 'green light' theories of legal control of executive behaviour.[32] Red light theorists such as Hayek, echoing Dicey's suspicion of the executive, maintain that the rule of law's primary concern should be to stop government interfering with individual autonomy. Green light theorists such as Jones, in contrast, believe that the Diceyan preoccupation with individual rights is misplaced. They assume that Parliament and the courts should loosen the legal constraints on government discretion, enabling government to curb individual autonomy in order to promote society's collective well-being.

The reality of court regulation of government action in the modern British constitutional context does not fit neatly into one or other of these theoretical perspectives. Harlow and Rawlings suggest that we can identify a third theoretical position—'amber light' theory—lying between the two extremes. This does not mean that, in practice, legal controls lie at the precise mid-point of the theoretical continuum, but that individual cases are located at various positions on the spectrum.

Within this theoretical framework, legal controls provide government with some flexibility, but not too much flexibility. That naturally raises the question of 'How much is too much?'. The issue is perhaps best explored by gradual accumulation of many examples; a task to which, after a brief diversion, we shall return.

---

[32] Op cit chs 1 and 2.

III. Judicial regulation of government behaviour: the constitutional rationale

The origins, structure, and powers of the present judicial system is a subject best explored in detail in textbooks dealing with the English legal system. However some broad points must be made here about the nature of both the court system and the 'judicial law-making process'. All courts in Britain are now in technical terms statutory creations. Prior to the revolution, the legal landscape was littered with many different courts, each exercising nominally independent but frequently overlapping jurisdictions. Numerous piecemeal reforms affecting the court system (such as the Act of Settlement 1700) were introduced during the next 200 years, but for our purposes the most significant legislative initiative was the passage of the Judicature Acts of 1873 and 1875. These Acts merged the many so-called 'superior' courts into the newly created High Court and Court of Appeal, and defined both the new courts' respective jurisdictions and the qualifications required of the judges who would sit in them. Subsequent statutes confirmed the House of Lords' position (in its judicial capacity) at the apex of the British judicial system, where it functioned as the final court of appeal until superseded by the Supreme Court in 2010.[33]

However, while Parliament has periodically altered the structure and jurisdiction of the courts, and while the 'common law'[34] is undoubtedly inferior to statute in circumstances where a statutory and common law rule seemingly demand different solutions to particular problems, Parliament has never enacted legislation which has sought systematically to control the method or outcome of the judiciary's law-making process. The 1688 revolution established that statute could alter or abolish any common law principles whenever Parliament wished, but virtually all of those principles initially remained in place. The content of the common law remains a matter for the courts to control. And within the modern court system, it has been the House of Lords (and now the Supreme Court) which has determined the substance of common law principles.

Such judicial power is not inconsistent with the notion of parliamentary sovereignty, because it is assumed that Parliament always intends that government will exercise its statutory powers in accordance with common law requirements. One might say that common law principles are the implied terms of the government process, and that Parliament is considered to 'contract in' to these limits on executive autonomy. If Parliament does not want a particular government action to be subject to judicial control, it must say so in the statute which grants the power. Because Parliament is sovereign, it would seem that in theory Parliament can 'contract out' of the common law principles which allow the court to regulate government activities. Such legislation might seem (to adapt Lord Reid's terminology in *Madzimbamuto v Lardner-Burke*) 'politically or morally improper', in that it derogates from orthodox understandings of the rule of law, but there is no *legal* impediment to Parliament enacting it.

This book uses the term 'administrative law' to encompass the various common law controls that the courts place on the government process. The concept of *judicial review* is the main component of administrative law. We explore that concept in detail in later chapters; but, it is necessary at this point to consider the fundamental ingredients of, and justification for the doctrine.

Broadly stated, the modern form of judicial review is designed to uphold a certain interpretation of the rule of law—its function is to ensure that executive bodies remain within the limits of the powers that the legislature has granted, or which are recognised by the courts as existing at common law.

---

[33] The reform is discussed further in 'Conclusion', ch 6, pp 168–169.

[34] The term is used here loosely, to denote laws made by courts rather than by Parliament.

An early judicial statement of the principle is provided by Coke CJ in *Baggs Case*,[35] which concerned the attempts of the Mayor and Burgesses of Plymouth to expel one of their number from the city's council. In holding that the expulsion was unlawful, Coke CJ made a more general statement of the scope of the court's powers:

> [T]his court hath not only jurisdiction to correct errors in judicial proceedings, but other misde-meanours extrajudicial tending to the breach of the peace or the oppression of the subject . . . or any other manner of misgovernment; so that no wrong or injury, either publick or private, can be done but this shall be reformed or punished.[36]

The intricacies and complexities of the emergence and consolidation of the judicial review jurisdiction merit closer examination than they can be given here.[37] For our limited pur-poses, a preliminary understanding is perhaps best gleaned from the 1948 Court of Appeal decision in *Associated Provincial Picture Houses Ltd v Wednesbury Corporation*[38] which is often invoked as the clearest restatement both of the constitutional basis for judicial review of government action and of the principles courts deploy to establish if a government body's action is lawful.

The case itself concerned a substantive issue of minor importance. Local councils in England and Wales were empowered by s 1 of the Sunday Entertainments Act 1932 to place 'such con-ditions as the authority think fit to impose' on cinemas in the council's area which wished to open on Sundays. The Wednesbury Corporation imposed a condition which forbade children under the age of 15 from attending cinemas on Sundays. The cinema company, facing an obvi-ous threat to its profits, argued that the condition was unlawful.

The judgment in *Wednesbury* identifies three grounds on which a court may find that exec-utive action is 'ultra vires', that is to say 'beyond the limits' of parliamentary (or sometimes common law) authority.

The first ground could be described as 'illegality'. If Parliament passes a statute for instance which allows the government to provide schools, the government could not invoke that stat-ute as a justification to build houses. Similarly, a government body empowered by a statute to employ teachers could not invoke the legislation to justify employing nurses or train drivers. Clearly, the Corporation's condition in the *Wednesbury* case did not fall into this category.

A government body also exceeds its statutory powers if it uses them to produce 'unreasonable' or 'irrational' results. This ground of review is particularly important in respect of discretionary powers. The concept of 'unreasonableness' or 'irrationality' bears a special meaning in adminis-trative law.[39] A government decision is only unreasonable/irrational if its content is so bizarre that no reasonable person could have assumed Parliament would have intended it to happen. As an example, assume that a statute empowers government to employ teachers in primary schools 'on such terms as it thinks fit'. The exercise of that power would only be unreasonable if it produced an outcome that bore no relation at all to rational objectives; if the government body decided not to employ anyone with red hair for instance. In contrast, reasonable people might reach different conclusions about precisely how much teachers should be paid, or what level of qualifications teachers should have. Such diversity is perfectly lawful: administrative law accepts that when a statute uses a discretionary term, Parliament assumes there will be variation in the substance of decisions reached. The notion of irrationality functions to ensure that those variations remain within the boundaries of political consensus that Parliament envisaged. The condition attached by the council in the *Wednesbury* case could not plausibly be classified as 'irrational' in this sense, even if it was more restrictive than conditions imposed by other nearby local authorities.

---

[35] (1615) 11 Co Rep 93b.   [36] Ibid, at 98a.
[37] See de Smith S (1951) 'The prerogative writs' *Cambridge LJ* 40; Jaffe L and Henderson G (1956) 'Judicial review and the rule of law: historical origins' *LQR* 345.   [38] [1948] 1 KB 223, CA.
[39] 'Irrationality' is the more modern term. See further 'Irrationality', ch 13, pp 370–375.

The third ground of review is sometimes referred to as 'natural justice'. This ground of review is not concerned with the substance of a given decision, but rather with the way in which the decision has been reached. Administrative law requires that government bodies exercise their statutory or common law powers through fair procedures. Broadly stated, this means firstly that decision-makers should not have a personal interest in the decision being made; and secondly that people affected by the decision should have an opportunity to state their case before a conclusion is reached.

Judicial review is a *supervisory* rather than *appellate* jurisdiction. A court which holds a government action unlawful will not substitute its own decision for the one made by the government body concerned, but will return the question to the original decision-maker so that the decision can be made again, this time in accordance with legal requirements. In contrast, in an action for (for example) trespass or breach of contract, the court will impose its solution on the dispute before it.

The theoretical rationale for judicial control of government behaviour derives from the constitution's 'ultimate political fact' of parliamentary sovereignty. This requires that the government may only perform those tasks that Parliament (or the common law) permits. The courts' constitutional role is therefore to police the boundaries of legislative intent,[40] and ensure that government cannot overstep those boundaries without incurring legal liability.

Yet one should beware of concluding from this that the courts' role is one of mere mechanical obeisance to legislative texts. We return to this point in more detail later. But here we might note that since the *Wednesbury* grounds of review are common law concepts, the courts may amend, abolish, or add to those grounds. We will shortly, when examining the concept of *stare decisis*, encounter the moral principles which have led the courts to be cautious in developing new grounds of review or redefining existing ones. But until Parliament enacts legislation on the issue, there is no legal barrier to radical judicial reform of any existing common law principle.

This necessarily leads us to ask to whom, or to what, does a judge's constitutional loyalty ultimately lie? This is less a question of a judge's personal predisposition than of the principles which judges deploy when interpreting the meaning of statutes and deciding the content of the common law. Both issues are more appropriately discussed in detail in textbooks on jurisprudence or the English legal system, but they are integral elements of the contemporary constitutional order, and merit at least brief consideration.[41]

IV. Principles of statutory interpretation

While the words of a statute have traditionally been regarded as the 'highest form of law' known to the British constitution, the task of attaching a specific legal meaning to those words has generally fallen to the courts. The inherent imprecision of language necessarily entails that even legislation expressed as rigid rules may sometimes raise questions concerning its applicability to particular situations. Such uncertainty increases when Parliament employs statutory formulae bestowing discretionary powers on government bodies. Since resolving such uncertainty is a judicial function, the process of statutory interpretation is a crucial element both of the rule of law and the sovereignty of Parliament.

Parliament has on occasion enacted legislation instructing the courts as to the meaning to be accorded to particular words or phrases which constantly reappear in various statutes. We saw one example of a so-called 'interpretation act' in chapter two when we looked at the role played by Lord Brougham's Act of 1850 in *Chorlton v Lings*. However, such legislation pertains

---

[40] This point applies also to legal justifications for government behaviour rooted in common law, for one assumes that particular common law rules exist only because Parliament has not abolished or amended them.
[41] See Michael Zander's (4th edn, 1994) *The law-making process* chs 3–4.

to technicalities rather than to sweeping instructions as to broad interpretative techniques. That latter component of the constitution is one historically left by Parliament to be controlled by the courts as an element of the common law. Three techniques of interpretation, respectively referred to as the 'literal rule', the 'golden rule', and the 'mischief rule' have traditionally been recognised as legitimate.

The literal rule

While judges often suggest that in interpreting statutes they are seeking to find Parliament's 'intentions', the reference to intentions is generally taken to mean not that a court is considering what was in the minds of the legislators who voted for a particular measure, but what is the ordinary meaning of the words used in the text of the Act. What has been termed the 'literal rule' of statutory interpretation has been by far the dominant approach taken by the courts. The literal rule suggests that the court's duty is to attach the orthodox, grammatical meaning to the statute's phraseology, even if that leads to ostensibly bizarre results.

The literal rule was most clearly expressed by Lord Esher in 1892 in *R v Judge of the City of London Court*: 'If the words of the Act are clear, you must follow them, even though they lead to a manifest absurdity. The court has nothing to do with the question of whether the legislature has committed an absurdity'.[42]

The literal rule betokens a dogmatic judicial acceptance of the common law's constitutional inferiority to statute. Since Parliament may if it wishes enact 'absurdities', the court would be questioning Parliament's sovereignty if it tried to attach a 'sensible' interpretation to statutory formulae whose literal meaning pointed in a different direction. If the 'absurdity' is a mistake rather than an intended consequence, the solution is for Parliament to enact a new statute amending the former Act. The point was made in grand theoretical terms by Lord Diplock in *Duport Steel v Sirs*:

> [I]t cannot be too strongly emphasised that the British constitution, though largely unwritten, is firmly based upon the separation of powers; Parliament makes the laws, the judiciary interpret them. When Parliament legislates to remedy what the majority of its members at the time perceive to be a defect or a lacuna in the existing law (whether it be the written law enacted by existing statutes or the unwritten common law as it has been expounded by the judges in decided cases), the role of the judiciary is confined to ascertaining from the words that Parliament has approved as expressing its intention what that intention was, and to giving effect to it. Where the meaning of the statutory words is plain and unambiguous it is not for the judges to invent fancied ambiguities as an excuse for failing to give effect to its plain meaning because they themselves consider that the consequences of doing so would be inexpedient, or even unjust or immoral. . . . Under our constitution it is Parliament's opinion on these matters that is paramount.
>
> A statute passed to remedy what is perceived by Parliament to be a defect in the existing law may in actual operation turn out to have injurious consequences that Parliament did not anticipate at the time the statute was passed. . . . But if this be the case it is for Parliament, not for the judiciary, to decide whether any changes should be made to the law as stated in the Acts.[43]

---

[42] [1892] 1 QB 273 at 290, CA. See also Lord Reid in *Inland Revenue Commissioners v Hinchy* [1960] AC 748 at 767:
What we must look for is the intention of Parliament, and I also find it difficult to believe that Parliament ever really intended the consequences which flow from the [commissioners'] contention. But we can only take the intention of Parliament from the words which they have used in the Act, and therefore the question is whether these words are capable of a more limited construction.
If not, then we must apply them as they stand, however unreasonable or unjust the consequences, and however strongly we may suspect that this was not the real intention of Parliament . . .

[43] [1982] 1 WLR 142 at 157. The case involved statutory protection given to trade unions and their members against actions in tort for losses caused by the unions' actions in furtherance of trade disputes. Lord Diplock's judgment made it clear that he disapproved of the Act, which literally construed, afforded trade unions very extensive protection. Such disapproval was however irrelevant to the question of the Act's meaning.

We should not however assume that such a clear statement of principle will necessarily produce similar clarity in practice. Judges may take different views of the 'literal' meaning of particular words or phrases and thence as to the legal effect of particular statutory provisions.[44]

Complicating the literal rule: (most) statutory provisions are 'always speaking'

The scope for uncertainty as to the 'literal' meaning of words or phrases in Acts increases when we ask if the literal meaning the court is seeking is the one which would have prevailed when the provision was enacted or when the provision is being construed by the court. It is possible that the ordinary or natural meaning of words will alter over long—or even short—periods of time. Parliament might, in recognition of the dynamic nature of language, alter legislation accordingly. If it has not done so, the question which arises is whether it is appropriate for the courts to 'update' the provision by giving its words their 'new' rather than 'original' meaning.

One might readily think that Diceyan notions of the sovereignty of Parliament and the separation of powers—particularly when restated in the forceful fashion deployed by Lord Diplock in *Duport Steel*—would lead the courts to accept that the common law would require that when interpreting a statutory term the judge should lend that term the meaning it bore when enacted. However, the constitutional orthodoxy which has developed is that statutes should (generally) be presumed to be 'always speaking'.[45] The position is put in this way in Bennion's influential text, *Statutory interpretation*:

> [T]he interpreter is to presume that Parliament intended the original Act to be applied at any future time in such a way as to give effect to the original intention. Accordingly the interpreter is to make allowances for any relevant changes that have occurred, since the Act's passing, in law, social conditions, technology, the meaning of words and other matters.[46]

The application of the 'always speaking' doctrine is helpfully illustrated in *R v Ireland; R v Burstow*.[47] The principal issue before the court in *Burstow* was the meaning of the Offences Against the Person Act 1861 s 20 and s 47, which provide:

> 20. Whosoever shall unlawfully and maliciously . . . inflict any grievous bodily harm upon any other person, either with or without any weapon or instrument, shall be guilty of a misdemeanour, and being convicted therefore shall be liable to imprisonment . . . for not more than five years.
> 47. Whosoever shall be convicted upon an indictment of any assault occasioning actual bodily harm shall be liable . . . to imprisonment for not more than five years.

Both defendants had engaged in conduct, primarily by making silent and/or threatening telephone calls, which had caused their respective victims serious psychiatric harm. The point of interpretation which arose was whether 'bodily harm' included psychiatric injury, or was limited to non-psychiatric bodily injury. If the latter view was correct, neither defendant would have committed an offence.

The defendants' primary argument was that the phrase 'bodily harm' should be construed as it would have been understood in 1861 when the statute was enacted. At that time, it was contended, the state of medical knowledge and opinion would not have recognised psychiatric injury as bodily harm.

The House of Lords rejected that argument in principle. Lord Steyn's leading judgment suggested that the method underling the defendant's case would in most cases be misconceived, since: 'statues will generally be found to be of the 'always speaking' variety'.[48] It was thus to the medical understandings of 1980, not of 1861, that the Court would look to ascertain the meaning of 'bodily harm'. In the Court's view, the then prevalent opinion was that severe psychiatric distress could amount to bodily harm, and so the defendants' convictions were upheld.

---

[44] See Ingman T (2011) *The English legal process* pp 140–143.
[45] Bennion F (1997) *Statutory interpretation* p 686.   [46] Ibid, at 687.   [47] [1998] AC 147.
[48] Ibid, at 158.

The 'always speaking' technique was deployed in *Burstow* to answer a newly emergent question. However the approach can also be used to alter previously authoritative rulings as to what particular statutory provisions mean. In 2010, in *Yemshaw v Hounslow LBC*,[49] the Supreme Court considered the meaning of the term 'violence' in the Housing Act 1996. Five years earlier, in *Danesh v Kensington and Chelsea Royal London Borough Council*,[50] the Court of Appeal had rejected submissions that 'violence', literally construed, could include actions which did not involve physical contact between the perpetrator and the victim. Actions which caused the victim severe fear or distress, or even (psychiatric) bodily harm in the *Burstow, Ireland* sense, would not be violent in the absence of physical contact. That conclusion was reversed in *Yemshaw*. The Supreme Court suggested that *Danesh* was wrongly decided at the time, but even if it was correct in 2006, it could not be so regarded in 2011. The Court referred to a substantial range of sources (including government policy statements, Law Commission reports, and United Nations resolutions) to justify lending the notion of 'violence' a much broader meaning which could include psychological and emotional abuse.

Neither Lord Steyn's opinion in *Burstow* nor Baroness Hale's judgment in *Yemshaw* indicated how we know if a statute is of the 'always speaking variety'.[51] That is an unfortunate omission. But the more significant point is that if we accept most statutes to be 'always speaking', then as a statute ages, and as the social, cultural, and economic contexts in which its terms are applied change, so we might defensibly suggest that in a practical sense the moral beliefs to which 'the law' gives effect are those of the courts rather than the legislature.

This proposition might be reconciled with orthodox notions of parliamentary sovereignty if we assume an initial (and continuing) tacit acceptance by legislators that the statutes they enact (and leave formally unamended) are indeed 'always speaking'. It is less easy to reconcile the proposition as a principle, and its practical effect in *Burstow*, with Diceyan notions of the rule of law which demand a high degree of predictability in the content of the law.

The golden rule

The so-called 'golden rule' credits the legislature with a greater degree of rationality than does the literal rule. It suggests that when a literal reading of a particular statutory provision would lead to an absurdity, the court should examine the statute in its entirety to see if another, more sensible meaning might be attached to the relevant words in the light of the legislative context in which they appear.

An interesting modern example of the application of the golden rule is provided by *Royal College of Nursing of the United Kingdom v DHSS*.[52] The Offences Against the Person Act 1861 s 58 criminalised the practice of abortion.[53] The statute did not contain any explicit defence on the basis that an abortion might be necessary to safeguard the life or health of the pregnant woman. However in *R v Bourne*,[54] the High Court concluded that the word 'unlawfully' in s 58 embraced a defence; a qualified medical practitioner who performed an abortion to preserve the life or health of the pregnant woman was not acting unlawfully.[55]

Parliament did not alter the law on abortion until 1967. The Abortion Act of that year significantly relaxed the previous law, providing in effect that abortion would be available whenever

---

[49] [2011] UKSC 3, [2011] 1 WLR 433.   [50] [2006] EWCA Civ 1404, [2007] 1 WLR 69.

[51] Like Lord Steyn in *Burstow/Ireland*, Baroness Hale in *Yemshaw* indicated that most statutes were of the 'always speaking' kind.   [52] [1981] AC 800.

[53] 'Whosoever, with intent to procure the miscarriage of any woman, whether she be or be not with child, shall unlawfully administer to her or cause to be taken by her any poison or other noxious thing, or shall unlawfully use any instrument or other means whatsoever with the like intent, shall be guilty of felony.'

[54] [1939] 1 KB 687.

[55] *Bourne* was in effect a test case, brought at the initiative of a consultant obstetrician, Aleck Bourne, who performed an abortion on a 15-year-old girl pregnant because of rape and invited the police to prosecute him. See de Costa C (2009) 'The King versus Aleck Bourne' *Medical Journal of Australia* 230.

two doctors confirmed that continuing the pregnancy would adversely affect the health of the woman. The Act also imposed controls on where and by whom abortions could be carried out. Section 1(1) provided that a criminal offence would be committed if the pregnancy was 'terminated by' a person other than a doctor.

In 1967, abortion was exclusively a surgical procedure. However by the late 1970s a new technique had developed which induced abortion by the use of intravenously administered drugs. The new procedure had many discrete stages, and could last for as long as thirty hours. The then prevailing medical opinion was that the new procedure could be conducted safely by nurses as long as a doctor oversaw the process and could attend the patient in the event of complications. The Department of Health favoured the new procedure as it made fewer demands on doctors' time (and thence on the National Health Service's budget). Several thousand such procedures were being conducted each year. Many nurses were however concerned that since they were not doctors, they would be committing a criminal offence under s 1(1) if they actually administered the drugs.

The narrow question before the House of Lords in the *Royal College of Nursing* case was the meaning of the phrase 'when a pregnancy is terminated by a registered medical practitioner' in s 1(1).[56] The construction contended for by the government was apparently two steps removed from a narrowly literalist reading of the text. The first step was to argue that the word 'terminated' actually meant: 'course of treatment resulting in termination'. The second was that 'by a registered medical practitioner' meant: 'overseen by a registered medical practitioner in accordance with accepted standards of good medical practice'.

Neither Lord Wilberforce nor Lord Edmund-Davies accepted this line of argument. As Lord Wilberforce put it: 'But with all respect, this is not construction, it is rewriting'.[57] Lord Edmund-Davies took a similar view: 'My Lords, this is redrafting with a vengeance'.[58]

The dissenting judges considered that the government was seeking to extend the law, and that such a result could only properly be achieved by new legislation.[59] Given the morally controversial nature of any such 'relaxation' of the abortion laws, it is likely that the government (then the first Thatcher administration) had no wish to follow this course even if it were confident that a parliamentary majority would support a change.

The government was however spared that political difficulty by the majority decision. Lord Diplock identified an absurdity (although he did not use that term expressly) which would flow from a literal construction of s 1(1); namely that a doctor would commit an offence in any case where the procedure did not result in an abortion.[60] Lords Keith and Roskill were more concerned by the fact that a literal reading would mean that thousands of nurses who had carried out the procedure already had committed a criminal offence. These consequences were apparently sufficiently undesirable to justify a more extensive search for the meaning of s 1(1) than merely looking at its words.

The majority opinions focused on the fact that various other provisions in the statute use the term 'treatment' rather than 'termination'. There was no obvious rationale for the different terminology, and so it was proper to assume that the terms were interchangeable.[61] The majority then reasoned that 'treatment' could be conducted as a 'team effort' involving many different types of hospital staff each performing roles consistent with her qualifications and experience. Such treatment would be undertaken 'by' a doctor for the purposes of s 1(1) as long as it was: 'prescribed by [her] and carried out in accordance with his directions'.[62]

That the House of Lords was divided 3/2 not just on the outcome of the litigation but also on the appropriate interpretive technique forcefully illustrates the simplistic nature of the

---

[56] It was accepted by all parties that 'registered medical practitioner' meant a doctor licensed to practise in the United Kingdom.   [57] [1981] AC 800, at 823.

[58] Ibid, at 831.   [59] See especially Lord Wilberforce at 822.

[60] This was dismissed as 'fanciful' by Lord Wilberforce and 'in reality non-existent' by Lord Edmund-Davies: Ibid, at 823 and 833.   [61] See Lord Diplock at 827–828; Lord Roskill at 837–838.

[62] See Lord Diplock at 828; Lord Keith at 835; Lord Roskill at 838.

constitutional homily that Parliament legislates and the courts interpret. The reality—if by reality we mean which constitutional actors effectively determine the moral content of the law—is much more complicated than that.

The mischief rule

The third strategy, the 'mischief rule' requires that the court ask itself which 'mischief' or defect in the common law or a previous statute the statutory provision in issue was intended to remove, and thereafter to construe the Act in a manner that minimises the possibility of the mischief recurring.

The mischief rule has pre-revolutionary roots. Its origin is frequently identified as the 1584 judgment in *Heydon's Case*,[63] which concerned the construction of legislation passed by Parliament to assist Henry VIII's ambitions to gain control of lands owned by monasteries. The rule formulated in *Heydon's Case* required a court to conduct a four stage inquiry:

> 1st. What was the common law before the making of the Act.
> 2nd. What was the mischief and defect for which the common law did not provide.
> 3rd. What remedy the Parliament hath resolved and appointed to cure the disease of the commonwealth; and.
> 4th. The true reason of the remedy; and then the office of all the Judges is always to make such construction as shall suppress the mischief, and advance the remedy, and to suppress subtle inventions and evasions for continuance of the mischief . . .

In its initial form, the judges' interpretation of the mischief rule did not empower them to look beyond the statute and the relevant common law rules to ascertain the 'mischief' Parliament was supposedly trying to remove. Thus, if a logical parliamentary intent could not be deduced from the words of the Act itself, the rule could not be applied.[64] By the mid-1970s, the courts had begun to refer to government policy documents explaining the policies underlying particular legislative reforms as an aid to interpretation.[65] That initiative certainly enhanced the potency of the mischief rule. But its utility continued to be greatly limited by the courts' presumption that their search for Parliament's intentions did not permit them to clarify the meaning of statutory texts by referring to speeches made about the legislation during its passage through the Commons and the Lords. We consider that principle, and the House of Lords' more recent departure from it, at a later stage, for neither can be fully understood until we have examined the nature of the legislative process in rather greater detail.[66]

Purposive (or 'teleological') interpretation

All three traditional strategies draw a clear distinction between the legislative and judicial role, and emphasise the subordinancy of the latter to the former. They did not, however, find favour with all members of the judiciary, some of whom thought a more radical approach was sometimes desirable. Lord Denning, in the 1950 case of *Magor and St Mellons RDC v Newport Corpn*, advanced (in a dissenting judgment) a rather different understanding of the court's 'interpretative' duty:

> We do not sit here to pull the language of Parliament and of Ministers to pieces and make nonsense of it. . . . We sit here to find out the intention of Parliament and of Ministers and carry it out, and we do this better by filling in the gaps and making sense of the enactment than by opening it up to destructive analysis.[67]

---

[63] [1584] EWHC Exch J36, 76 ER 637.
[64] For a forceful criticism see Smith H (1926) 'The residue of power in Canada' *Canadian Bar Review* 432.
[65] *Black-Clawson International Ltd v Papierwerke Waldhof-Aschaffenburg AG* [1975] AC 591, HL.
[66] In ch 8.   [67] [1949] 2 KB 481 at 498–499, CA.

Lord Denning's initiative may be seen as an example of a fourth interpretative technique, now known as the 'purposive' or 'teleological' approach. This strategy rejects the presumption that a judge should restrict her search for the meaning of law to the statute itself, but rather tries to imagine what the framers of the legislation would have done if facing the problem before the court. The teleological strategy was by then already a common feature of many continental European legal systems, and was widely used in the United States. But Lord Denning's efforts to 'import' it so transparently into the English constitutional tradition found little favour with the House of Lords, which rebutted Lord Denning's presumptions as to the judiciary's appropriate constitutional role. According to Lord Simonds:

> [T]he general proposition that it is the duty of the court to find out the intention of Parliament—and not only of Parliament but of Ministers also—cannot by any means be supported. The duty of the court is to interpret the words that the legislature has used.[68]

As to Lord Denning's suggestion that the court might 'fill in the gaps' left by the statute's text, Lord Simonds identified fundamental constitutional objections. Such action would be: 'a naked usurpation of the legislative function under the thin guise of interpretation . . . If a gap is disclosed, the remedy lies in an amending Act'.[69]

Lord Simonds somewhat overstated the 'naked usurpation' criticism. In the absence of legislation specifically forbidding 'purposive' interpretative techniques, the House of Lords (as the ultimate arbiter of common law principles) was in theory quite competent to jettison the three traditional rules and adopt Lord Denning's preferred option. That the majority in *Magor* chose not to was an indication that they considered such an innovation 'unconstitutional' in the sense of its political illegitimacy, not of its legal impossibility.

The case does however emphasise the point that the dividing line between 'interpretation' and 'legislation' may be difficult to draw. We can confidently state that, as a matter of constitutional theory, Parliament legislates and the courts interpret. It is more difficult to ascertain whether, as a matter of constitutional practice, that theory is always respected. That difficulty is compounded by the fact that the common law recognizes a range of different interpretive techniques as being acceptable. This problem is perhaps best illustrated by examining the judgments delivered in two leading cases: *Liversidge v Anderson* from 1942 and *R v IRC, ex p Rossminster* from 1980.

Liversidge v Anderson (1942)

Liversidge v Anderson[70] arose out of the Defence Regulations 1939, a measure enacted during World War II to strengthen the government's powers to protect the country from sabotage or treason by enemy agents. Regulation 18b provided that:

> If the Home Secretary has reasonable cause to believe any person to be of hostile origins or association . . ., he may make an order against that person directing that he be detained.

Between May and August 1940, the Home Secretary, Sir John Anderson, used reg 18b to detain 1,500 people.[71] One person detained was Robert Liversidge. Liversidge sued Anderson for false imprisonment. Liversidge had obviously been made (to borrow from Dicey's formulation of the rule of law) to 'suffer in body'—he had been confined in prison. The question before the Court was whether the executive action which led to Liversidge's detention was lawful. Was there a statutory or common law power which entitled the government to lock Mr Liversidge up? Liversidge's contention was that although the Defence Regulations empowered the Home

---

[68] [1952] AC 189 at 191.   [69] Ibid.   [70] [1942] AC 206, HL.
[71] See the fascinating study by Simpson A (1991) *In the highest degree odious*.

Secretary to detain people in some circumstances, those circumstances did not exist in this particular case. The detention was therefore 'illegal' in the *Wednesbury* sense.

To understand the basis of Mr Liversidge's argument, we must examine the precise wording of reg 18b. It says that the Home Secretary can detain an individual if: 'he has reasonable cause to believe' that person is of hostile origin or association. The insertion of the 'reasonable cause to believe' clause seems to fit with the Diceyan idea of the rule of law which disapproves of any statute in which Parliament grants the government wide discretionary powers. The clause seems to limit the possibility of the Home Secretary using the power arbitrarily. Detention would not be lawful unless a court was satisfied that the Home Secretary's beliefs were under-pinned by 'reasonable cause'. Regulation 18b would therefore implicitly seem to require the Home Secretary to show the court the evidence on which his suspicions were based, and to convince the judges that the evidence did indeed amount to a 'reasonable cause'. The obvious meaning of reg 18b would seem to be that if there was insufficient evidence to support the conclusion that a detainee had hostile origins or associations, the power could not lawfully be used.

The government itself had acknowledged that this was the correct interpretation of the regulations in the first case challenging their use, *Lees v Anderson*.[72] Subsequently, in, *R v Home Secretary, ex p Budd*,[73] the government changed its argument, and contended that no such evidence need be presented. In short, the government's contention was that as long as the Home Secretary believed that a person was of 'hostile origins or association', that belief was necessarily 'reasonable'. That argument did not initially succeed; the Court had ordered Mr Budd to be released because the Home Secretary produced no evidence of his 'hostility'. Mr Budd then suffered the misfortune of being detained again. On this occasion, the Court accepted the government's arguments as to the effect of reg 18b and saw no need to examine the sufficiency of the evidence which led the Home Secretary to exercise his powers.

When *Liversidge v Anderson* reached the House of Lords, the meaning of reg 18b was therefore uncertain. Four[74] of the five members of the House of Lords accepted the govern-ment's interpretation of reg 18b. They concluded that the Home Secretary could use reg 18b to imprison anyone he thought was of hostile origins. He did not need to offer the Court any evidence to show that his belief was reasonable. He could imprison anyone at all. He did not have to say why. And anyone who was detained was wasting her time coming to the courts to challenge the adequacy of the Home Secretary's belief. Lord Wright encapsulated the majority sentiment by concluding that:

> All the word 'reasonable', then, means is that the minister must not lightly or arbitrarily invade the liberty of the subject, He must be reasonably satisfied before he acts, but it is still his decision, and not the decision of anyone else. . . . No outsider's decision is invoked, nor is the issue within the competence of any court.[75]

One law lord took a different view. Lord Atkin thought that reg 18b could bear only one possible meaning. If Parliament said 'reasonable cause to believe', it must have intended that there be *some* plausible evidence on which that view was based. If legislators had intended to give the Home Secretary an arbitrary power, they would simply have said 'if the Home Secretary believes'. Regulation 18(b)'s parliamentary history seems to support Lord Atkin's view. The original version of the regulation had not included the 'reason-able cause' requirement. The requirement had been inserted as an amendment because MPs had feared that leaving it out would give the Home Secretary too arbitrary a power.

---

[72] (1940) *The Times*, 13 and 21 August; discussed in Simpson op cit pp 62–63 and ch 14.
[73] [1942] 1 All ER 373. See Simpson op cit pp 318–321.
[74] Viscount Maugham, Lord Macmillan, Lord Wright, and Lord Romer.   [75] [1942] AC 206 at 268–270.

This suggests that the majority judgment effectively permitted the government both to disregard the principle of parliamentary sovereignty and to contravene Dicey's version of the rule of law. It seems that only Lord Atkin had upheld the orthodox tradition that the courts should interpret the words used in legislation in accordance with their literal meaning.[76]

But despite the apparently 'unconstitutional' nature of the majority judgment, it was Lord Atkin who received considerable criticism from the government, from fellow judges, and from the public. In part, this criticism was directed at the substance of his opinion. The country was after all at war. People were greatly concerned about saboteurs, traitors, and spies. Lord Atkin was accused of wanting to tie the government's hands in its efforts to root out these potential enemies. Hayekian theory, for example, would accept that the rule of law could legitimately be 'suspended' during war, on the grounds that the most important political value (another 'ultimate political fact'?) was the preservation of the country's very existence as an independent state.[77]

However, Lord Atkin also antagonised many people (including fellow judges) by the language that he used.[78] He accused his four colleagues in the Lords of being 'more executive minded than the executive'.[79] Lord Atkin had found only one possible 'authority' to justify the majority's interpretation of reg 18b. There is a scene in *Alice through the looking glass* where Alice and Humpty Dumpty discuss the use of language:

> When I use a word,' Humpty Dumpty said in rather a scornful tone, 'it means just what I choose it to mean, neither more nor less.' 'The question is,' said Alice, 'whether you can make words mean different things.' 'The question is,' said Humpty Dumpty, 'which is to be master—that's all.[80]

The important inference to draw from Lord Atkin's dissent is that there is little point in regarding the relationship between citizens and the government as a 'political contract' in which Parliament creates a legal framework to which the people consent, nor to assume that the constitution rests on the twin bedrocks of parliamentary sovereignty and the Diceyan rule of law, if the words that the legislature uses in statutes to express its wishes can be interpreted by the courts to mean things that legislators did not 'intend'. Such an outcome might be seen as a judicial subversion of the power of Parliament.

One might meet this point by suggesting that the majority decision in *Liversidge* must have been 'correct', because Parliament did not reverse it. As we shall later see, that argument rather oversimplifies the nature of the relationship between Parliament and the courts. It also fails to meet the objection that the House of Commons, the House of Lords, or the Monarch might seek to mislead each other (or combine to mislead the people) by deliberately passing Bills in the expectation that the courts will lend the resultant statute an interpretation that defies accepted understandings as to the meaning of language.

Following *Liversidge*, one of Lord Atkin's fellow judges (Stable J) wrote to him to say the majority decision brought the judiciary into disrepute. The judges were no longer 'lions under the throne, but mice squeaking under a chair in the Home Office'.[81] The case once again suggests that effective functioning of the rule of law, at least as Dicey understood it, requires judges who possess an independence of mind, as well as an independence of office.[82]

[76] The division of opinion on the Court was reflected in contemporaneous academic critique. In support of the majority see Holdsworth W (1942) 'Note' *LQR* 1 and Goodhart A (1942) 'Note' *LQR* 3. For an analysis supportive of Lord Atkin see Allen C. (1942) 'Regulation 18B and reasonable cause . . .' *LQR* 232.

[77] The principle is sometimes expressed in the latin maxim *salus populi est suprema lex*.

[78] See Heuston op cit.   [79] [1942] AC 206 at 244.   [80] Ibid, at 245, HL.

[81] Quoted in Heuston op cit at p 51.

[82] For a fascinating account of the WWI equivalent of reg 18b see Foxton D (2003) '*R v Halliday ex parte Zadig* in retrospect' *LQR* 455.

R v IRC, ex p Rossminster Ltd (1980)

The Taxes Management Act 1970 s 20C seemed to bestow sweeping search and seizure powers on Inland Revenue employees. Section 20C—added to the original Act in
1976—empowered the Inland Revenue to seek a search warrant from a circuit judge. If
the judge was satisfied that there were reasonable grounds to assume that evidence of a
tax fraud might be found on particular premises, she could issue a warrant authorising
a named officer to: 'Seize and remove any things whatsoever found there which he has
reasonable cause to believe may be required as evidence . . .'. The Act did not explicitly
require that the warrant specify the precise offence being investigated, nor identify the
suspected perpetrator(s).

Acting under such a warrant, Inland Revenue officials raided Rossminster's premises and,
without offering details of the matter under investigation, seized many documents. The legal
background to the *Rossminster* seizure is distinguishable from the background to the *Entick*
case, since the seizure was purportedly rooted in a statutory power. Rossminster nevertheless
claimed that Lord Camden's reasoning was relevant to interpretation of s 20C. Rossminster
argued that the court should presume that Parliament intended s 20C to be construed consistently with the common law principles informing *Entick*—namely that the power would
only be used in a precisely targeted way, and would not be invoked by Revenue officials to
enable them to embark upon a speculative trawl through all of a company's or an individual's
private papers.

The Court of Appeal accepted this argument.[83] Lord Denning's leading judgment was particularly forceful, portraying the Inland Revenue's behaviour as incompatible both with contemporary moral standards and long established legal principle:

> [T]here has been no search like it—and no seizure like it—in England, since that Saturday, April 30
> 1763, when the Secretary of State issued a general warrant by which he authorised the King's mes-
> sengers to arrest John Wilkes and seize all his books and papers. . . .[84]

Denning's judgment rested on the presumption that the bare words of the Act had to be read
against a background (or contextual) legal principle; namely that Parliament would always be
sensitive to the need to protect individual liberty when enacting legislation. As Lord Denning
put it: 'it is, as I see it, the duty of the courts so to construe the statute as to see that it encroaches
as little as possible upon the liberties of the people of England'.[85]

This was in effect a teleological or purposive approach to the interpretation of s 20C. The
'purpose' being served was ensuring that government behaviour did not interfere unduly with
citizens' common law entitlements. This interpretative strategy then led Lord Denning to the
following conclusion:

> . . . as a matter of construction of the statute and therefore of the warrant—in pursuance of our
> traditional role to protect the liberty of the individual—it is our duty to say that the warrant must
> particularise the specific offence which is charged as being fraud on the revenue.[86]

Since the warrant did not do so, it was invalid.

The Court of Appeal's judgment was subsequently reversed in the House of Lords, which
adopted a straightforwardly literalist approach to s 20C. Lord Wilberforce, delivering the leading opinion, saw no point in referring to old cases such as *Entick* to support Rossminster's
contention. He concluded that the 'plain words' of s 20C authorised the Inland Revenue to
engage in behaviour which could not be justified at common law. Nor could he see any basis
for finding an implied term in the statute which required much greater specificity in the terms
of the warrant: Parliament's intention had been to override common law principles. Lord

---

[83] [1980] AC 952.   [84] Ibid, at 970.   [85] Ibid, at 972.   [86] Ibid, at 974.

Wilberforce's invocation of the literal rule was entirely orthodox, and quite consistent with traditional understandings of the separation of powers:

> while the courts may look critically at legislation which impairs the rights of citizens and should resolve any doubt of interpretation in their favour, it is no part of their duty, or power, to restrict or impede the working of legislation, even of unpopular legislation; to do so would be to weaken rather than advance the democratic process.[87]

Lord Wilberforce nevertheless cast some doubt on the political acceptability of the legal rule which the statute had enacted, by observing that: 'I cannot believe that this does not call for a fresh look by Parliament'.[88] Lord Dilhorne expressed similar sentiments: 'It may be that there are many persons who think that in 1976 too wide a power was given to the revenue. If it was, and I express no opinion on that, it must be left to Parliament to narrow the power it gave'.[89]

The House of Lords evidently considered that the judges in the Court of Appeal had allowed their moral distaste for s 20C to push them into adopting illegitimate interpretative strategies, and thus to overstep the boundaries of their proper constitutional role. This is most clearly illustrated by Lord Wilberforce's comment that courts should not 'restrict or impede the working of legislation'. That is however a simplistic view. Lord Denning would no doubt have agreed with the sentiment that courts should not impede the working of legislation. Where he differed from Lord Wilberforce was in his understanding of how the legislation was supposed to work. In Denning's opinion it would work as Parliament intended if it did not trample over established common law principles. In Wilberforce's view it was designed to have just that intensely intrusive effect. Neither perspective can be regarded as legally 'correct' in any definitive sense. Rather the case further underlines the point that there is much unpredictability in the way that courts may approach their constitutional responsibility of giving meaning to the provisions of statutes.

Conclusion

It is also helpful to compare *Liversidge* and *Rossminster* to illustrate the point that a court's adoption of a particular interpretative strategy does not determine the substantive character of the result that the court produces in a given case. If one looked solely at *Rossminster*, one might be tempted to assume that teleological interpretation would restrain governmental power to a greater degree than literal interpretation. Yet in *Liversidge*, Lord Atkin's robust defence of individual liberty against government interference is founded on a literalist interpretative technique. In that case, it was the majority who engaged in teleological strategies. The 'purpose' the majority sought to promote was the successful prosecution of the war, which led them to construe the literal words of reg 18b against a background or context which demanded that government powers be very generously interpreted. In Lord Macmillan's view: 'The purpose of the regulation is to ensure public safety, and it is right so to interpret emergency legislation as to promote, rather than to defeat, its efficacy for the defence of the realm'.[90]

Lord Atkin—in contrast—(and much like Lord Wilberforce in *Rossminster*) seemed to consider resort to those background principles illegitimate, and invoked an alternative context against which to construe reg 18b:

> In this country, amid the clash of arms, the laws are not silent. They may be changed, but they speak the same language in war as in peace. It has always been one of the pillars of freedom, one of the principles of liberty for which on recent authority we are now fighting, that the judges are no respecters of persons and stand between the subject and any attempted encroachment on his liberty by the executive.[91]

---

[87] Ibid, at 988.   [88] Ibid, at 999.   [89] Ibid, at 1006.   [90] Ibid, at 251.
[91] [1980] AC 952 at 244.

To put the matter in rather more abstract terms, cases such as *Burstow*, *Royal College of Nursing*, *Rossminster*, and *Liversidge* tell us that while *Parliament may do anything* it wishes, the constitutional responsibility to tell us *what Parliament actually has done* rests with the courts. If one bears that point in mind, it might be at best simplistic and at worst entirely misleading to characterise the normative relationship between Parliament and the courts as a simple hierarchy in which the judiciary occupies the inferior position.

V. *Stare decisis*

The principle of legal certainty—that citizens be able to predict the limits the law places on individual and governmental behaviour—is an essential ingredient (albeit respected with varying stringency) in all theoretical analyses of the rule of law. The principle has only a precarious legal basis in the British constitution, since Parliament may at any time change any law in any way whatsoever. For much of the modern era, the common law has, in contrast, possessed—at least in formal terms—an almost absolute degree of legal certainty.

The *London Tramways* judgment (1898)

The common law's attachment to an inflexible doctrine of *stare decisis* ('let the previous decision stand') was confirmed in the 1898 case of *London Tramway Co v LCC*.[92] For a unanimous House of Lords, Lord Halsbury claimed that the judgments of that court bound not only all inferior courts, but also the House of Lords itself. He acknowledged that such rigidity might on occasion produce substantively unjust solutions to given problems because the common law could not be adapted to meet changing social conditions:

> but what is that . . . as compared with the inconvenience—the disastrous inconvenience—of having each question subject to being reargued and the dealings of mankind rendered doubtful by reason of different decisions, so that in truth and in fact there would be no final court of appeal.[93]

Lord Halsbury's reasoning obviously has strong roots in Diceyan perceptions of the need to avoid unpredictability and arbitrariness in the content of the legal framework within which citizens live. It may thus be seen as a legal expression of the political principles underpinning red light variants of the rule of law. It should however be emphasised that the courts' adherence to a rigid *stare decisis* principle (like its preference for a literal rule of statutory interpretation) was a common law rule, fashioned by the House of Lords itself, not a requirement imposed by Parliament. Clearly, in cases involving intolerable injustice in which the House of Lords felt itself bound by a previous decision, Parliament could pass legislation altering the substantive law. Similarly, Parliament could at any time enact a statute ordering the courts to depart from the *London Tramways* rule on any occasions they thought fit, or to abandon the principle altogether. But furthermore, in the absence of any legislation on the point, the House of Lords itself retained the power to amend or reject the rule: common law rules are as much at the mercy of the final court of appeal as of the legislature.

Lord Halsbury's suggestion that the House of Lords could bind itself is therefore a nonsense, as a matter both of abstract logic and constitutional principle. Binding legal rules depend for their force on the existence of a higher source of law than the rules themselves. The members of the House of Lords qua final court of appeal in 1898 could no more 'bind' their successors than the Parliament of that year could 'bind' future Parliaments. Lord Halsbury might expect his successors to respect his rule because of its intrinsic merits; he could in no legal sense compel them to do so.[94]

---

[92] [1898] AC 375.   [93] Ibid, at 380.

[94] Of course, Parliament might enact legislation which gives the Supreme Court such a power.

The 1966 Practice Statement

The House of Lords did not use its undoubted constitutional power to overrule *London Tramways* until 1966. In a Practice Statement issued on 26 July,[95] the Lord Chancellor announced that the House of Lords would modify its approach to *stare decisis*, and depart from its previous decisions to avoid injustice and to facilitate the development of common law principles in a way that reflected changing social and economic conditions:

> Their Lordships regard the use of precedent as an indispensable foundation upon which to decide what is the law and its application to individual cases. It provides at least some degree of certainty upon which individuals can rely in the conduct of their affairs, as well as a basis for orderly development of legal rules.
>
> Their Lordships nevertheless recognise that too rigid adherence to precedent may lead to injustice in a particular case and also unduly restrict the proper development of the law. They propose, therefore, to modify their present practice and, while treating former decisions of this House as normally binding, to depart from a previous decision when it appears right to do so.
>
> In this connection they will bear in mind the danger of disturbing retrospectively the basis on which contracts, settlements of property and fiscal arrangements have been entered into and also the especial need for certainty as to the criminal law.

The House of Lords has however rarely deployed this power, and has developed rigorous criteria which must be met before a previous decision is overruled.[96] The initiative may thus be seen as a classic example of the green light approach to the rule of law, in which red light principles are not abandoned entirely, but are nevertheless appreciably diluted. While important in itself, the significance of the 1966 Practice Statement should not be exaggerated. The House of Lords/Supreme Court will only infrequently find itself faced by legal problems which cannot in some way be distinguished from previous decisions on similar points. And for constitutional lawyers, the more pressing question is not what the House of Lords/Supreme Court does when faced with a common law rule it considers unpalatable,[97] but what it does when its distaste is triggered by a statutory provision.

VI. Parliamentary sovereignty v the rule of law

Dicey's notions of parliamentary sovereignty and the rule of law only function in the sense that he intended if the courts accept that their allegiance lies not to the people, nor to a supra-legislative constitution, but simply to the will of Parliament as expressed in a statutory text. But as our knowledge of the law of the constitution increases, so we come to see that orthodox theory may present a misleading picture. *Liversidge* seemingly provides an example of the courts in effect giving allegiance to the executive rather than to Parliament. Insofar as the constitution places the task of interpreting legislation in the hands of the courts, *Liversidge* respects parliamentary sovereignty because it is only the court which can tell us what Parliament intended. But that is a very formalistic view of 'law'; if we look behind this legal facade to the political principles underpinning traditional views of the rule of law and the separation of powers, *Liversidge* can plausibly be portrayed as a manifestly 'unconstitutional' decision.

But one can also find episodes in constitutional history when the judiciary apparently considered that its ultimate allegiance lay not to the executive, nor even to Parliament, but rather to a version of the rule of law which possessed a higher constitutional status than

---

[95] *Practice Statement (Judicial Precedent)* [1966] 1 WLR 1234.   [96] See Zander (1994) op cit pp 190–199.
[97] An issue we consider in 'Rape within marriage: *R v R (rape: marital exemption)* (1991)', pp 72–74.

the clear words of legislation. Such appears to be the lesson offered by the judgment of the House of Lords in the 1969 case of *Anisminic Ltd v Foreign Compensation Commission*[98] and the Court of Appeal's decision a decade earlier in *R v Medical Appeal Tribunal, ex p Gilmore*.[99]

Ouster clauses—*Gilmore* (1957) and *Anisminic* (1969)

In the 1950s and 1960s, Parliament made increasing use of statutes seeming to oust the courts' common law power of review. These so-called 'ouster clauses' were a logical ingredient of the drift towards 'green light' theories of administrative law. Often Parliament sought to exclude the courts because the legislation concerned established alternative fora for review, appeal, or inquiry. Relatedly, it was widely felt that much government activity did not lend itself to resolution by judicial methods.[100] Such statutes would contradict the Diceyan version of the rule of law, but since Parliament can make any law whatsoever, there is theoretically no impediment to it passing legislation which excludes the common law power of review.

R v Medical Appeal Tribunal, ex p Gilmore (1957)

Under the National Insurance (Industrial Injuries) Act 1948 decisions as to a claimant's entitlement were initially made by a government employee. The Act allowed applicants dissatisfied with the original decisions to appeal to a specialised medical tribunal. Section 36(3) provided that the tribunal's decision 'shall be final', a formula which seemed to remove the individual's right to seek review of the tribunal's decision in the courts. However in *R v Medical Appeal Tribunal, ex p Gilmore* Lord Denning, faced with an apparent error of law on the tribunal's part, concluded that, notwithstanding s 36(3)'s apparently unambiguous instruction, judicial review: 'is never to be taken away by any statute except by the most clear and explicit words. The word 'final' is not enough. That only means 'without appeal'. It does not mean without recourse to [review]'.[101]

This apparently presents us with a modification to the doctrine of implied repeal, which we discussed in chapter two. Section 36(3) implies that Parliament had decided to 'contract out' of judicial review with respect to industrial injury compensation. Lord Denning's judgment appears to echo the decisions in *Chorlton v Lings* and *Nairn v University of St Andrews*, where the courts held that the enfranchisement of women would represent such a fundamental reform to society's political order that Parliament could not effect it through implied or 'furtive' legislative terms. In *Gilmore*, Denning seems to attribute the same high political status to a Diceyan principle of the rule of law—namely that individual citizens should always be able to challenge the decisions of government bodies before 'the ordinary courts'. Denning suggests that Parliament may 'suspend' this principle if it wishes, but only by adopting absolutely unambiguous statutory formulae.

Anisminic Ltd v Foreign Compensation Commission (1969)

One might have assumed that Parliament had adopted 'the most clear and explicit words' in the ouster clause in s 4(4) of the Foreign Compensation Act 1950. The Act established a Commission to distribute limited funds among British nationals whose overseas property had been seized by foreign governments. Section 4(4) stated that the Commission's 'determinations . . . shall not be called in question in any court of law'. 'Calling into question' would appear to reach both appeal and review. Nevertheless, in *Anisminic Ltd v Foreign Compensation Commission*,[102] the House of Lords assumed jurisdiction to review the Commission's activities.

---

[98] [1969] 2 AC 147.   [99] [1957] 1 QB 574.
[100] See particularly Titmuss R (1971) 'Welfare rights, law and discretion' *Political Quarterly* 113.
[101] [1957] 1 QB 574.   [102] [1969] 2 AC 147.

It did so on the grounds that the Commission had made an error of law in its decision-making process. Consequently, the decision that the Commission had produced was not a determination, but 'a purported determination'. Since the ouster clause made no reference to 'purported determinations', the Court was not challenging parliamentary sovereignty by declaring the Commission's action unlawful.

Like the majority judgment in *Liversidge*, such reasoning commends itself only to the most formalistic of constitutional analyses. *Gilmore* and *Anisminic* can more plausibly be presented as examples of the judges steeling themselves to resist orthodox understandings of the hierarchy of legal authority in order to safeguard a political principle—that government action always be subject to judicial review, irrespective of Parliament's intentions. In each case, the judges adopted a narrow view of legislative sovereignty. Parliament could indeed exclude judicial review; but only by initiating the protracted and highly visible process of passing legislation explicitly overturning the courts' decisions. One might say that the House of Lords was rejecting a formal, legalistic interpretation of parliamentary sovereignty in favour of a functionalist, political interpretation—namely to ensure that the exclusion of judicial review really did attract the consent of the people.

The House of Lords' judgment might lead us to note the oft-quoted words of Bishop Hoadly, delivered in a sermon to the King in 1717:

> Whoever hath an absolute authority to interpret any written or spoken laws, it is he who is truly the lawgiver, to all intents and purposes, and not the person who first spoke or wrote them.

Anisminic clearly presented a judicial challenge to Parliament's sovereignty, but that challenge lay in the sphere of the legitimacy rather than legality of parliamentary intentions. Parliament could reverse *Anisminic*, but only at the risk of being seen to abrogate orthodox understandings of the rule of law. The government initially seemed prepared to take that risk, and prepared a Bill containing a more extensive ouster clause applying not only to the 'determinations' of the Commission, but also to any 'purported determinations'. Whether the courts would have been prepared to 'defy' that legislation by a further exercise in creative statutory 'interpretation' is a matter for speculation. Lord Reid might, for example, have concluded that what was before the court was not a 'determination', nor even a 'purported determination', but only 'purportedly a purported determination', which on a literal reading of the amended statute would not be protected from judicial review. The proposal was abandoned in the face of opposition within Parliament, and replaced by a measure granting the Court of Appeal appellate jurisdiction over the Commission's determinations.[103]

Leading constitutional theorists took different views of *Anisminic's* implications. Professor John Griffiths felt that the courts were intruding 'unconstitutionally' on the sovereignty of Parliament.[104] In contrast, Professor Wade suggested that the threat to the constitution came not from the judges' apparent challenge to parliamentary sovereignty, but from Parliament's increasing predisposition to deploy ouster clauses to limit or remove the courts' powers of judicial review. In Wade's view, such legislation showed an unhealthy disrespect for orthodox principles of the rule of law.[105] Both viewpoints are obviously defensible, a fact which further strengthens the presumption that constitutional analysis must operate as much in the realm of practical politics as of legal theory. That suggestion gains further force when we consider the contentious issue of 'retrospective law-making'.

---

[103] Foreign Compensation Act 1969 s 3. See Wade HRW and Forsyth C (1994) *Administrative law* pp 734–739.

[104] (1977) *The politics of the judiciary* pp 123–124.

[105] (1969) 'Constitutional and administrative aspects of the *Anisminic* case' LQR 198; (1980) *Constitutional fundamentals* pp 65–66.

VII. 'Retrospective' law-making

The objection that Diceyans would make to Parliament's growing preference for granting the executive discretionary powers in statutes is that citizens may find it difficult to predict what government bodies are legally entitled to do. That objection is met only in part by the *Wednesbury* principles of administrative law; those principles enable the citizen to predict the outer limits of lawful government action, but not the precise point where a given decision may be located. But unpredictability would be taken to an extreme degree if Parliament enacted legislation which had retrospective effect; for example by enacting a statute in 2020 which provided that everybody who had bought a foreign car since 2012 had to pay a 'patriotism levy' of £50; or by introducing legislation in 2018 which made it a criminal offence to have written anything critical of government policy at any time in the past. Since Parliament is sovereign, there is no legal impediment to it introducing such legislation. In doing so however, Parliament would surely be undermining all versions of the rule of law discussed in this chapter. For students who might suppose Parliament could never do such a thing, the events which followed the 1964 case of *Burmah Oil Co (Burmah Trading) v Lord Advocate*[106] may come as a surprise.

Retrospectivity in legislation—the War Damage Act 1965

In 1942, the British government, acting under what it presumed to be a common law power,[107] ordered its army in Burma to destroy one of Burmah Oil's refineries to prevent it falling into the hands of the advancing Japanese forces. After the war, the government offered Burmah Oil *ex gratia* compensation of £4.6m. The oil company began legal proceedings, claiming some £31m compensation, and arguing that the common law power used required that owners be fully reimbursed by the government for any loss suffered. There was no clear authority for the House of Lords to follow. The judges thus faced the task of deciding the extent of the government's common law power to destroy property in war-time. The details of the judgment need not concern us;[108] suffice to say that the majority upheld Burmah Oil's claim.

The government (a Labour administration headed by Harold Wilson) was alarmed by this decision, since it might mean that not only Burmah Oil, but also many other individuals or companies whose property had been destroyed in similar circumstances, would be entitled to large sums of compensation. Such claims could have major implications for public expenditure. The government therefore introduced the War Damage Bill into Parliament to reverse the judgment. There could be no objection in terms of constitutional principle, whether from a parliamentary sovereignty or rule of law perspective, to Parliament changing the common law by statute in the sense of providing that *in future* the payment of compensation in such circumstances will be determined by statutory rule *x* rather than common law rule *y*. However, the War Damage Bill was intended to overrule the common law not just for future instances of property loss, but also for those that had already happened—the statute was to have retrospective as well as prospective effect.

Diceyan theory tells us that such legislation is entirely consistent with the legal doctrine of parliamentary sovereignty, but utterly inconsistent with the political principle of the rule of law. The Bill generated appreciable controversy as it progressed through Parliament.[109] That it emerged as the War Damage Act 1965 provides further compelling evidence that the rule of law, in so far as it can be construed as a moral code embedding certain political values in

---

[106] [1965] AC 75.   [107] These 'royal prerogative powers' are considered in ch 4.

[108] A useful summary is provided by Jackson P (1964) 'The royal prerogative' *MLR* 709.

[109] See Jackson P (1965) 'War Damage Act 1965' *MLR* 574.

Britain's democratic structure, may on occasions be regarded by our sovereign legislature as an expendable rather than indispensable ingredient of Britain's constitutional recipe. But one might also identify controversies of relatively recent origin where the same accusation might plausibly be levelled at the courts.

'Retrospectivity at common law'? Rape within marriage and conspiracy to corrupt public morals

The House of Lords 1966 practice direction on precedent attached particular importance to the need for certainty in the criminal law. This was not a new concern, but one we might credibly assert to have long been axiomatic to British understandings of the rule of law. But it is not difficult to identify common law principles which are hard to reconcile in both an abstract and practical sense with a strong respect for legal certainty. The majority and dissenting opinions in the House of Lords in the 1962 judgment in *DPP v Shaw*[110] and the court's unanimous decision in *R v R (rape-marital exemption)*[111] in 1991 provide powerful illustrations of this point.

A new or old offence at common law? Conspiracy to corrupt public morals

Mr Shaw displayed some entrepreneurial spirit in the early 1960s by publishing what he called a 'Ladies' Directory'. This was a magazine detailing the names, photos, addresses, and practices of prostitutes in particular neighbourhoods. He was subsequently charged with and convicted of various statutory offences but he was also charged with the supposed common law offence of 'conspiracy to corrupt public morals'. Mr Shaw's defence to this charge was the blunt claim that the alleged crime simply did not exist as there was no previous authority upholding it. Alternatively he argued that even if such a crime had once been recognised, it should no longer be applied as it was an umbrella concept of such width that it would be impossible to predict what kind of behaviour might fall within it. In abstract terms, these are very much substantive rule of law/legal certainty arguments. Mr Shaw was convicted at trial. On appeal, the majority in the House of Lords did not find either argument an impediment to upholding the conviction.

Viscount Simonds—so alert to the dangers of the judiciary usurping the legislative function in *Magor*—concluded that it was entirely proper for the courts to fashion new offences at common law to deal with what the judges regarded as newly emergent social problems:

> I entertain no doubt that there remains in the courts of law a residual power to enforce the supreme and fundamental purpose of the law, to conserve not only the safety and order but also the moral welfare of the State, and that it is their duty to guard it against attacks which may be the more insidious because they are novel and unprepared for.[112]

The suggestion that the offence was objectionable because of its potential width and thence uncertainty was firmly dispatched by Lord Morris:

> It is said that there is a measure of vagueness in a charge of conspiracy to corrupt public morals, and also that there might be peril of the launching of prosecutions in order to suppress unpopular or unorthodox views. My Lords, I entertain no anxiety on these lines. Even if accepted public standards may to some extent vary from generation to generation, current standards are in the keeping of juries, who can be trusted to maintain the corporate good sense of the community and to discern attacks upon values that must be preserved.[113]

Lord Reid issued a powerful dissent premised on an evident attachment to orthodox understandings of the rule of law and the separation of powers. In respect of the separation of powers

---

[110] [1962] AC 220.   [111] [1992] 1 AC 599.   [112] [1962] AC 220 at 267–268.   [113] Ibid, at 292.

issue, Lord Reid concluded that the nature of the supposed offence was one which was better suited to criminalisation by Parliament than by the courts:

> Even if there is still a vestigial power of this kind it ought not, in my view, to be used unless there appears to be general agreement that the offence to which it is applied ought to be criminal if committed by an individual. Notoriously, there are wide differences of opinion today as to how far the law ought to punish immoral acts which are not done in the face of the public. Some think that the law already goes too far, some that it does not go far enough. Parliament is the proper place, and I am firmly of opinion the only proper place, to settle that. When there is sufficient support from public opinion, Parliament does not hesitate to intervene. Where Parliament fears to tread it is not for the courts to rush in. . . .[114]

He was equally concerned that the majority's conclusion was offensive to a proper understanding of legal certainty and thus of the rule of law:

> Finally I must advert to the consequences of holding that this very general offence exists. It has always been thought to be of primary importance that our law, and particularly our criminal law, should be certain: that a man should be able to know what conduct is and what is not criminal, particularly when heavy penalties are involved.[115]

One might criticise the majority judgment in *Shaw* for resolving an uncertainty in the content of the common law in a fashion which imposed a criminal penalty on an individual. This criticism in terms of constitutional principle is perhaps easy to make because on the particular facts of the case we could readily assume that many people (even in 1960) would not have regarded Mr Shaw's action as morally reprehensible. The debate over the legitimacy of common law innovation becomes more complicated however if the behaviour in question would be almost universally regarded as unacceptable and/or if the innovation concerned does not resolve an uncertainty but rather reverses a long established rule.

Rape within marriage: *R v R (rape: marital exemption)* (1991)

To modern day observers, an obviously objectionable moral principle informing social and legal affairs in the mid-eighteenth century was the proposition advanced by Sir Matthew Hale in his *History of the Pleas of the Crown*:

> [a] husband cannot be guilty of a rape committed by himself upon his lawful wife, for by their mutual matrimonial consent and contract the wife hath given herself up in this kind unto her husband which she cannot retract.[116]

The notion that a woman was legally obliged to accommodate her husband's desire to have sex with her whenever he wished rested on the moral assumption that a wife was the 'subservient chattel'[117] of her husband. The questions before the House of Lords in *R v R (rape: marital exemption)*[118] in 1991 were whether that assumption remained valid, and—if it was not—whether the common law should alter to reflect new cultural or moral assumptions.[119]

In *R v R*, the House of Lords accepted the view that the common law could legitimately be regarded as a dynamic and flexible source of legal rules. As Lord Keith put it:

> The common law is, however, capable of evolving in the light of changing, social, economic and cultural developments. Hale's proposition reflected the state of affairs in these respects at the time

---

[114] Ibid, at 287.   [115] Ibid, at 291.

[116] Quoted in *R v R (rape: marital exemption)* [1992] 1 AC 599 at 615 per Lord Keith.

[117] [1992] 1 AC 599 at 616.   [118] [1992] 1 AC 599.

[119] The rule had been narrowed somewhat by subsequent case law of fairly modern vintage. A husband could be convicted of raping his wife if they were legally separated prior to the finalisation of divorce proceedings; see *R v R*, ibid, at 616–619.

it was enunciated. . . . Since then, the status of women, and particularly of married women, has changed out of all recognition. . . . In modern times any reasonable person must regard [Hale's proposition] as quite unacceptable.[120]

The Court then concluded that the overturning of the previous common law rule was a task that could appropriately be undertaken by the courts. There was no need to wait for Parliament to enact legislation changing the law.

R v R is a significant judgment in many respects.[121] For present purposes, the key question arising is *when* it became a crime for a husband to rape his wife. The House of Lords settled the legal question in October 1991. The (attempted) 'rape' in issue was committed some two years earlier. The change in the law could thus be seen as retrospective, in the sense that any person who consulted law reports or legal textbooks in 1989 would understandably have concluded that—notwithstanding the morally abhorrent nature of such an action—a husband could not, save in very limited circumstances, be convicted of raping his wife. To put it in Diceyan terms, such an action would seemingly not have involved any breach—and certainly not a distinct one—of the law.

We would presumably have expected—if the House of Lords had felt it appropriate for the law to be changed by Parliament rather than the courts—that any legislation attaching criminal liability to a husband's rape of his wife would have only prospective effect. Had such a statute been given retrospective effect, sufficient to bring R (and presumably any other husband who had raped his wife since October 1989) within its terms, it would no doubt have attracted criticism on the grounds that it infringed the rule of law.

But innovative judicial law-making—which either alters rules of common law or attaches new meanings to existing statutory provisions—is generally retrospective in nature. One might in formalistic terms rebut that contention by pointing out that when R attempted to rape his wife the law had already changed. We (and he) just did not find out about that change until two years later when the House of Lords finally delivered judgment on the issue. And quite when the law changed is a mystery.[122]

It is perhaps curious that the British constitutional tradition has so normalised the retrospective impact of common law innovation that it is evidently not seen as 'really' retrospective at all. It might be suggested that most sensible observers in the 1980s would have anticipated that the marital rape exemption would soon be substantially amended or even abolished by the courts, given that the rule rested on such obsolete and objectionable moral foundations and had already been narrowed by modern judicial decisions. But if one's understanding of the rule of law incorporates a concern with establishing with certainty the substantive content of laws—or at least those laws whose breach imposes heavy costs on a defendant—*R v R* can readily be regarded as a problematic decision in both specific and general terms.

R v C (2004)

That difficulty becomes more pronounced when one considers the Court of Appeal's subsequent judgment in *R v C*.[123] The defendant in *C* had been convicted in 2002 of—inter alia—raping his wife. The rape in issue had occurred in 1970; over twenty years prior to the House of Lords' decision in *R v R*. On appeal, C's counsel argued that the prosecution of the offence of rape should be regarded as an abuse of process and therefore be quashed by the Court of Appeal. C's argument conceded the propriety of the House of Lords' conclusion in *R v R* that by *1989* it was entirely foreseeable that courts would be prepared to reject Hale's

---

[120] Ibid, at 616.   [121] For further analysis see Laird V (1992) 'Reflections on R. v R' *MLR* 386.
[122] Cf the comment in the *Practice Statement (Judicial Precedent)* 1966 that the House of Lords would bear in mind; 'the especial need for certainty in the criminal law'; [1966] 1 WLR 1234.
[123] [2004] 1 WLR 2098.

assumption as to the legal impossibility of a man raping his wife. The argument asserted however that no such conclusion could sensibly have been drawn in *1970*. This contention might be thought to be reinforced by the observation that three significant judgments which weakened the general applicability of Hale's doctrine by disavowing its relevance in respect of spouses who were undergoing divorce or separation proceedings had been issued in 1974, 1976, and 1986 respectively.[124] In more prosaic terms, C's submission was that while the law had indeed changed prior to *R v R*, it had not changed by the time he 'raped' his wife in 1970.

The Court of Appeal saw no need to engage with the question left open by the House of Lords in *R v R*; namely when precisely did it become a crime for a man to rape his wife. The Court nonetheless had little difficulty concluding that the law had certainly changed by 1970. The judgment posed the question of what a solicitor might then have been expected to say to a client who inquired if he might be guilty of rape if he forced his wife to have non-consensual sexual intercourse. In the Court's view:

> The solicitor would have started by pointing out to his client that to rape his wife would be barbaric, and that he would not condone it. He would then have told his client that the courts had developed and could be expected to continue to develop exceptions to the supposed rule of irrevocable consent, and that if ever the issue were considered in this court, the supposed immunity of a husband from a successful prosecution for rape of his wife might be recognised for what it was, a legal fiction.[125]

The judgment did not offer any evidence to support this perhaps rather extravagant conclusion. It is certainly difficult to reconcile it with the observation of the Court of Appeal in 1986 in *R v Roberts* to the effect that the general presumption that a husband could not rape his wife remained valid, albeit subject to a growing number of exceptions:

> In our judgment the law is now quite plain on this topic. The status of marriage involves that the woman has given her consent to her husband having intercourse with her during the subsistence of the marriage. She cannot unilaterally withdraw it. The cases show that in a number of circumstances that consent can be terminated. If it has been terminated and the husband has intercourse with his wife without her consent he is guilty of rape.[126]

The Court of Appeal did not invoke any other authority supporting its assertion as to common understandings of the law on this point in 1970, an omission which rather undermines the persuasiveness of its conclusion. We still do not know of course when the law on this point changed. We know simply that it had changed by 1970. Perhaps it had changed by 1960? Or 1950? This presumably means that there are many men now in principle liable to prosecution and conviction for having committed an act which was not identified as a crime by either statute or common law at the relevant time, but which carries a sentence of life imprisonment.

It may readily be conceded that C's behaviour was utterly barbaric. But that point should not be allowed to obscure the broader question of constitutional principle which the case raises; namely the aforementioned 'retrospective' impact of change in the substantive content of the common law.[127] The principle might be thought difficult to reconcile with Diceyan notions of the rule of law, which demand inter alia that governmental interferences with the 'body or goods' of citizens are justifiable only if authorised by 'distinct' laws.[128]

---

[124] *R v O'Brien* [1974] 3 All ER 663; *R v Steele* (1976) 65 Cr App R 22; *R v Roberts* [1985] Crim LR 188.
[125] [2004] 1 WLR 2098 at 2013.   [126] [1985] Crim LR 188.
[127] See Lawrence I (2006) 'Punishment without law: how ends justify the means in marital rape' Denning LJ 37.
[128] See 'Dicey's rule of law—process or substance?', ch 3, pp 47–48.

'Retrospective' or 'prospective' overruling?

The common law's attachment to what is often termed 'retrospective overruling' was prem-ised largely on the theoretical proposition that the courts simply 'declare' what the law is. According to this declaratory theory of the common law, courts never actually make law when promulgating new rules or principles; rather they draw our attention to a state of legal affairs which has existed unnoticed for some (perhaps considerable) time. The modern status of this declaratory theory may be best illustrated by Lord Browne-Wilkinson's judgment in *Kleinwort Benson Ltd v Lincoln City Council*:

> According to this theory, when an earlier decision is overruled the law is not changed; its true nature is disclosed, having existed in that form all along. This theoretical position is, as Lord Reid said, a fairy tale in which no-one any longer believes. In truth, judges make and change the law.[129]

The 'fairy tale' reference relates to Lord Reid's comments in a lecture delivered in 1972, in which he observed:

> There was a time when it was thought almost indecent to suggest that judges make law –they only declare it. Those with a taste for fairy tales seem to have thought that in some Aladdin's cave there is hidden the common law in all its splendour and that on a judge's appointment there descends on him knowledge of the magic words Open Sesame. Bad decisions are given when the judge has muddled the password and the wrong door opens. But we do not believe in fairy tales any more. So we must accept the fact that for better or worse judges do make law, and tackle the question how do they approach their task. . . .[130]

Lord Reid's comments are obviously wholly consistent with the views he expressed in *Shaw*. But even if we have left the era of fairy tales behind us, the constitutional presump-tion that it is legitimate for innovation at common law to make new law which has in practical terms a retrospective effect remains problematic from a rule of law perspective. The difficulties which attend the practice of retrospective overruling in cases such as *R v R* or *R v C* might be avoided if the House of Lords/Supreme Court were to accept (or Parliament were to require through statute) that overruling of previous decisions or the fashioning of entirely new common law principles would have only 'prospective effect'. That is to say that the law would become effective only in respect of factual situations which occurred after the judgment was issued. This approach to the temporal effect of judicially created change to the law is by no means uncommon in modern western legal systems.[131] Given its sovereign law-making power, Parliament could at any time impose such a requirement on the courts, either in general or selective terms. Similarly, since our constitution's attachment to retrospective judicial innovation is a common law phenom-enon, the House of Lords/Supreme Court qua final court of appeal could alter the rule. From the late 1990s onwards, the question received continued judicial scrutiny. In *Re Spectrum Plus Ltd*[132] the House of Lords acknowledged that there was no insurmountable obstacle preventing a change of traditional practice. Giving only prospective effect to a change in the previously accepted meaning of the law could be appropriate in 'exceptional' or 'extreme' circumstances. But neither the courts nor Parliament have as yet shown any obvious enthusiasm for making prospective overruling a principle of even extensive let alone general application.

---

[129] [1992] AC 349 at 358.

[130] 'The judge as lawmaker' (1972–1973) *Journal of the Society of Public Teachers of Law* 22 at 22.

[131] See the discussion in Ingman (2002) op cit pp 387–388; Rodger A (2005) 'A time for everything under the law: some reflections on retrospectivity' *LQR* 57; and Atrill S (2005) 'Nulla poena sine lege in comparative per-spective . . .' *Public Law* 107.   [132] [2005] UKHL 41, [2005] 2 AC 680

Conclusion

We will revisit the legitimacy of the *R v R* judgment in chapter eighteen. At this stage, our conclusions might sensibly be limited to observing that we should exercise caution when presented with the general proposition that Britain's constitutional tradition rests securely on the three supporting pillars of parliamentary sovereignty, the rule of law, and the separation of powers, which are themselves securely rooted in the foundation stone of democracy. Chapters one and two indicated that our constitution's foundation is itself shifting and unstable; in addition, the theoretical analyses and historical events discussed in this chapter have suggested that those pillars may at times lean in contradictory rather than complementary directions. Whether this is a desirable situation is a question to which we shall return; it may be that one can argue it is preferable for a constitution to bend to the wind of changing times, rather than to stand rigid and so risk destruction in the face of a political or social hurricane. To sustain or refute that argument however, we need to gather more knowledge of the constitution's historical and contemporary make-up. In chapter four, we begin that task by examining the royal prerogative.

Suggested further reading

Academic and political commentary

HARLOW C and RAWLINGS R (1984) *Law and administration* chs 1 and 2

JONES H (1958) 'The rule of law and the welfare state' 58 *Columbia LR* 143

HOLDSWORTH W (1942) 'Note' [on *Liversidge*] *LQR* 1

GOODHART A (1942) 'Note' [on *Liversidge*] *LQR* 3

ALLEN C (1942) 'Regulation 18B and reasonable cause . . .' *LQR* 232

HEUSTON R (1974) '*Liversidge v Anderson* in retrospect' *LQR* 33

HAYEK F (1944) *The road to serfdom* ch 6

JAFFE L and HENDERSON G (1956) 'Judicial review and the rule of law: historical origins' *LQR* 345

Case law and legislation

Liversidge v Anderson [1942] AC 206

Entick v Carrington (1765) 19 St Tr 1029

R v R (marital rape exemption) [1992] 1 AC 599

DPP v Shaw [1962] AC 220

Harris v Dönges (Minister of the Interior No. 2) (1952) (4) SA 769 (A)

Chapter 4

The Royal Prerogative

The courts' acceptance of Diceyan notions of parliamentary sovereignty leaves no scope for judges overtly to challenge the substance of legislation. Decisions such as *Anisminic* suggest there are instances in our constitutional history when judges *in effect* dispute Parliament's supremacy. But, the Court took care in *Anisminic* to root its arguments in a theoretically legitimate constitutional framework.

The gap between theoretical and practical legitimacy in judicial behaviour is less evident in respect of review of government action taken under statute. That government bodies be subject to judicial review is clearly necessary to maintain Parliament's sovereignty. If the courts permitted government to cross the legal boundaries which Parliament has enacted, they would be recognising government action, not legislation, as the constitutional hierarchy's most important value.

As *Anisminic* and *Liversidge* suggest, one sometimes finds cases where, in practice, the court's interpretation of a statute seems impossible to reconcile with the Act's text. In such circumstances, we might plausibly argue that the theory of parliamentary sovereignty—in so far as it rests upon judicial obeisance to the literal wording of an Act—is being subverted. A more subtle, but more prevalent analytical complication arises when we note the variety of interpretive techniques courts might deploy to determine the meaning of statutory provisions. It is a trite point, but one of immense significance, that we cannot conclude that an executive body has overstepped the limits of its statutory powers until the courts qua interpreters of statutes tell us what those limits are. However, statute is not the only source of the British government's legal authority. The government also possesses various common law powers. Constitutional lawyers gather these powers together under the label of the royal prerogative.

The source of prerogative powers

In its, pre-1688 form, the 'royal prerogative' comprised the Monarch's personal powers. Despite the apparent wishes of some[1] Stuart Kings, the English Monarchy was never absolutist—medieval kings had neither the financial nor the military resources to rule without the active support of the nobility. That support depended upon the Monarch accepting some constraints on her/his power to govern. Those constraints were articulated in both statute and the common law—neither of which the Monarch could change without the support of Parliament or the courts.

Seventeenth-century political history was marked by recurrent disputes between the King and Parliament over the distribution of governmental power. There was an ongoing struggle between the King's effort to rule by prerogative powers or 'proclamations', and Parliament's power to restrain the King's autonomy through statute. And until that struggle degenerated into civil war, the courts were usually the site of the battle.

Prerogative cases before the 1688 revolution

Seventeenth-century, pre-revolutionary case law on how and for what purpose prerogative powers could be used was riven with ambiguity. The fundamental legal issue was whether, in principle and in practice, the Monarch's prerogative powers had a superior constitutional status to legislation. Judges tended to produce opinions which adopted inconsistent positions, which, given the era's political instability, is readily understandable.

The Case of Prohibitions (1607); the Case of Impositions (1610); and the Case of Proclamations (1611)

Before 1688, the courts had sometimes robustly resisted the King's preferences. In the 1607 *Case of Prohibitions*,[2] James I had claimed a right to sit as a judge; 'The King said that he thought the law was founded upon reason, and that he and others had reason, as well as the judges'. The judges, led by Coke, rejected this claim. While the judges confirmed that the King was not subject to any man, he was subject to the law, and until he had gained sufficient expertise in the law's many rules he had no entitlement to sit as a judge. This expertise was not a matter of 'natural reason' or 'common sense', but demanded mastery of 'an artificial reason . . . which requires long study and experience, before that a man can attain to the cognizance of it'.[3]

As well as placing restraints on the Monarch, this ruling enhanced the powers of the courts. 'Common reason' was the formula invoked in *Dr Bonham's Case* to overrule statute; if 'common reason' was something that only judges could discern, one would be saying in effect that the courts were the ultimate source of law in the pre-revolutionary constitution.

Similarly, in the 1611 *Case of Proclamations*,[4] Coke seemingly placed stringent limits on the King's ability to rule by prerogative powers. He held that the King only had those prerogative powers which the common law *already recognised*; he could not grant himself new ones. The issue before the Court was whether the King could use his prerogative powers to impose controls on the building of new houses in London and on the use of wheat, and to attach criminal penalties to any breach of those controls. Despite the antiquity of Coke's language, the constitutional principles underlying the judgment are clear:

---

[1] Tomkins A (2005) *Our republican constitution* pp 91–93 suggests that Charles I favoured a more broadly based consensual approach to governance.

[2] (1607) 12 Co Rep 63.

[3] One sees here an early statement of a trend in constitutional theory which ties the 'independence' of the judiciary to its competence; cf Alexander Hamilton in *The Federalist Papers No 78* ('The constitutional role of the Supreme Court', ch 1, pp 16–17) and Centlivres CJ in *Harris (No 2)* ('*Harris v Minister of the Interior*—the aftermath', ch 3, p 49).   [4] (1611) 12 Co Rep 74.

[T]he King by his proclamation or other ways cannot change any part of the common law, or statute law, or the customs of the realm, . . . : also the King cannot create any offence by his prohibition or proclamation, which was not an offence before, for that was to change the law, and to make an offence which was not . . . [T]he King hath no prerogative, but that which the law of the land allows him.

Not all judges were as committed to keeping the King's personal powers within legal boundaries. There are several seventeenth-century examples of judges interpreting prerogative powers in a way that completely undermined the principles laid down in the *Case of Proclamations*.

The *Case of Impositions*,[5] or *Bate's Case*, in 1606, centred on the King's prerogative power to regulate foreign trade, and Parliament's statutory power to levy taxation. Bate had refused to pay an import duty that the King had placed on currants, his argument being that the tax was illegal. The King's response was that this was not a tax, but a measure to regulate trade, the money raised was just an incidental side effect of the regulatory power. The integrity of that argument is obviously questionable. However, the Court accepted it, and so provided a back door route for prerogative powers to override statutory provisions. That was not necessarily unconstitutional at the time; the supremacy of statute had not been established by then. Condemnation of this type of monarchical behaviour was a major component of the 1688 *Declaration of Right*; and it was expressly prohibited by Art 4 of the Bill of Rights.[6]

Ship Money (1637)

A similar scenario arose in *Ship Money (R v Hampden)*[7] in 1637. It was then generally accepted that the Monarch possessed a power to compel coastal areas of the country to furnish him with ships in times of military emergency so that he could better defend his realm. In the 1630s, Charles I sought to establish that this power extended to all parts of the country and permitted him to charge money (in effect a tax) rather than simply insist on provision of a ship. When Charles I levied such a charge in 1637, John Hampden—a member of the Commons and an opponent of much of the King's policy—refused to pay. Hampden accepted that the prerogative power existed, and accepted that it could be levied throughout the country in the form of a tax. However he argued that it could only be invoked when a military emergency was imminent.

The case was heard by a court of twelve judges.[8] Ten found in the King's favour. The majority opinion rested essentially on the presumption that only the King could assess if an imminent emergency existed. The Court would not address concerns relating either to the good faith or the accuracy of the King's conclusion. In effect, the judgment provided the King with a legal mechanism to bypass the generally accepted principle that levying taxation required statutory authorisation.

That narrow conclusion was unacceptable to many members of Parliament. But *Ship Money* raised broader concerns. Several judges made very sweeping statements as to the locus of sovereign legal power. Judge Vernon went so far as to say: '[T]he king may charge pro bono publico notwithstanding any Act of Parliament . . . [A] statute derogating from the prerogative doth not bind the King, and the King may dispense with any laws in the case of necessity'.[9] Finch CJ put the point in this way: 'They are void Acts of Parliament [which seek] to bind the King not to command the subjects, their persons and goods, and I say their money too; for no Acts of Parliament make any difference'.[10]

---

[5] (1610) 2 State Tr 371.
[6] See 'The political source of parliamentary sovereignty—the "glorious revolution"', ch 2, pp 21–25.
[7] (1637) 3 State Tr 826.　　[8] See Keir D (1936) 'The case of shipmoney' *LQR* 546.
[9] (1637) St Tr iii 1125; cited in Keir op cit pp 568–569.　　[10] Ibid, at 569.

The *Ship Money* saga is a graphic example of the ongoing struggle in seventeenth-century English history to establish where sovereign power lay. Within a few years of the judgment, Charles I responded to parliamentary discontent on the narrow implication of the judgment by assenting to a Bill which not only purported to abolish the ship money power, but also asserted that no such power had ever existed. Several judges who found in his favour in the case were removed from office and imprisoned. If, however, the King did indeed possess a power to dispense with Acts of Parliament whenever he thought it necessary—and if necessity was a matter only the King could assess—the efficacy of any such statute might prove rather limited.

Habeas corpus, the *Resolutions in Anderson* (1592) and *Darnel's Case* (1627)

Protection against unlawful taxation was an important element of the citizens' property rights in pre-revolutionary England. It was however perhaps less important than 'property' in one's physical liberty, in the sense of being able to call upon the courts for protection against unlawful imprisonment. The writ of *habeas corpus* has common law origins which predate even Magna Carta. Its purpose, crudely put, was to empower the common law courts to order any person detaining a citizen to bring that person before the court and show lawful authority for the detention. If no such authority could be shown in the gaoler's 'return', the prisoner would be released.

Habeas corpus was, in practice, hedged about with limitations. Its utility was particularly compromised during Elizabeth I's reign. Elizabeth and her Privy Councillors[11] claimed an arbitrary power to imprison anyone who displeased them, without charge or trial, for as long as they wished. The constitutionality of such commitment was widely questioned, and caused sufficient disquiet for the judges to deliver an opinion to the Crown assessing its legality. The so-called *Resolutions in Anderson*[12] began with what seems a spirited defence of individual liberty: 'her highnesses subjects may not be detained in prison, by commandment of any nobleman or councillor, against the laws of the realm'. This suggests that the judges were claiming authority to examine the justification for any such detention and pronounce upon its legality. However, the *Resolutions* concluded by accepting that the courts could not question the factual basis of the Crown's claim that the person detained had committed treason.[13] Thus, as long as Privy Councillors complied with this formality, their actions would be within 'the laws of the realm'.[14]

Anderson offers an obvious precedent for the *Bate's Case* and *Ship Money* principle that only the Monarch could judge if the factual prerequisites of a prerogative power existed. Unsurprisingly, Charles I invoked the opinion to justify imprisoning his subjects who declined to pay the 'unlawful' taxes levied. Sir Thomas Darnel was one of five knights who refused to pay a compulsory loan to the King. Charles I immediately ordered their arrest and imprisonment. In *Darnel's Case*,[15] the knights' application for writs of *habeas corpus* were met by a return stating simply that they were held 'by special command of the King'. Darnel's counsel argued that this was insufficient justification for committal, since it disclosed no breach of any known law. The Court however concluded that the King's power fell within that considered acceptable in the *Resolutions in Anderson*: the judges would not investigate either the factual or legal basis of the King's opinion. In effect, the King retained an arbitrary power.

---

[11] On the status of the Privy Council see 'The fusion of powers, the rise of the party system and cabinet dominance of the Commons', ch 5, pp 108–109.

[12] See Crawford C (1915) 'The suspension of the Habeas Corpus Act and the Revolution of 1689' *The English Historical Review* 613.

[13] Plucknett (1960) op cit pp 308–311.

[14] Precisely perhaps the conclusion reached by the House of Lords in *Liversidge* as to the Home Secretary's powers under reg 18b.　　　　　　　　　　　　　　　　　　　[15] (1627) 3 State Tr 1.

Godden v Hales (1686)

Following the Civil War, the Commons and Lords persuaded Charles II and James II to assent to several *Habeas Corpus* Acts which appeared to extend the remedy and curb the Crown's capacity to evade it. But the then uncertain status of statute vis-à-vis the prerogative cast considerable doubt on the efficacy of any such legislation.

James II was eager to take advantage of the courts' flexibility to rule by prerogative powers rather than with parliamentary consent in the 1680s. *Godden v Hales*[16] in 1686 is the most obvious example of this trend. James was a King with strong Catholic sympathies in a country whose houses of Parliament were dominated by Protestants. Parliament had passed several Acts disqualifying Catholics from government office. James attempted to override these acts on behalf of a Catholic, Sir Edward Hales, by announcing that Hales need not swear loyalty to Protestantism before assuming office. Although this obviously breached an Act of Parliament, the Court (by a majority of eleven to one) held that it was part of the Monarch's prerogative to dispense with laws if it was necessary to do so. And as in *Ship Money*, the King was the sole judge of necessity. The Court concluded its judgment with a succinct summary of the constitutional position:

> [T]he judges go upon these grounds:
>
> 1   that the kings of England are sovereign princes;
> 2   that the laws of England are the king's laws;
> 3   that therefore it is an inseparable prerogative in the kings of England to dispense with penal laws in particular cases and upon particular necessary reasons;
> 4   that of those reasons and those necessities, the king himself is sole judge; and then, which is consequent upon all;
> 5   that this is not a trust invested in, or granted to, the king by the people, but the ancient remains of the sovereign power and prerogative of the kings of England; which never yet was taken from them, nor can be.

The obvious implication of *Godden v Hales*—an implication intolerable to many members of the Commons and Lords—was that sovereign legal power rested with the King. Under this analysis, the enactment of legislation in which the Commons, Lords, and Monarch had reached and expressed a consensual position on particular political issues would be a legally futile endeavour, since the King could at any point 'dispense' with the measure that Parliament had produced.

Post 1688—the revolutionary settlement

It was arguably James II's persistent disregard of parliamentary authority that triggered the 1688 revolution. The Bill of Rights 1689, which we could plausibly regard as the 'contract of government' between William and Mary and the revolutionary Commons and Lords, placed clear statutory limits on the extent of prerogative powers.

Reversing *Godden v Hales*—and denying the correctness of the judgment when it was made—were important elements of the revolutionary settlement. *Godden v Hales* is clearly the target of Art 1 of the Bill of Rights of 1689: 'That the pretended power of suspending the laws or the execution of laws by regal authority without consent of Parliament is illegal.' The correctness of the judgments in cases such as *Ship Money* and the *Case of Impositions* was also forcefully repudiated by the Bill of Rights; Art 4 provided that: 'levying money for or to the use of the Crown by pretence of prerogative, without grant of Parliament, for longer time, or

---

[16] (1686) 11 State Tr 1166.

in other manner than the same is or shall be granted, is illegal.' Two further points of great significance emerged from the political deal that was struck.

Firstly, the *scope of prerogative powers was fixed*—it was not open to the King to claim new ones. What William and Mary received in 1688 was the *residue* of the previous King's powers. That residue has been shrinking ever since. As Diplock LJ observed in the 1965 case of *BBC v Johns*:

> [it was] 350 years and a civil war too late for the Queen's courts to broaden the prerogative. The limits within which the executive government may impose obligations or restraints on citizens of the UK without any statutory authority are now well settled and incapable of extension.[17]

One must however note that while it is generally accepted that the 1688 settlement had imbued the prerogative with a residual character, the exact extent of that residue was unclear. As we saw in *Burmah Oil*,[18] the courts have on occasion been called upon to decide the precise limits of prerogative powers, which, even 330 years after the revolution, remain poorly defined. *Burmah Oil* provides another example of the loose fit between the form and the reality of constitutional principles; while the Crown cannot de jure[19] create new prerogative powers or duties, the courts could achieve that result by holding that the Crown had rediscovered a 'forgotten' part of the 1688 residue.

The second point, and the reason why the residue has been getting smaller, is that the 1688 settlement acknowledged that Parliament can amend or abolish prerogative powers through legislation. The prerogative was recognised as being a common law power, subordinate to statute. Thus, as in the *Burmah Oil* saga, Parliament may always respond to inconvenient judicial decisions concerning the scope of an existing prerogative power by introducing legislation to alter or reverse the courts' decisions.

Similarly, Parliament may create statutory frameworks which limit how prerogative powers may be used. This principle is perhaps best illustrated in the immediate post-revolutionary era by legislative regulation of the Monarch's power to summon and dissolve Parliament. We may recall that Art 13 of the Bill of Rights had provided that 'Parlyaments ought to be held frequently'. Parliament defined that timescale more precisely in the Triennal Act 1694. This statute required the King to summon a new Parliament within three years of the dissolution of the previous Parliament, and also obliged him not to permit Parliament to sit for more than three years before the next dissolution. Within these statutory time limits, the Monarch enjoyed unfettered legal power to summon or dismiss the Commons and the Lords; but he/she had no legal power to exceed those periods. Parliament could alter the time scale if it wished, and in the Septennial Act of 1715 it chose to increase its maximum duration to seven years.

While the Bill of Rights clearly addressed the issue of the prerogative's status vis-à-vis Acts of Parliament, it was less explicit about the question of how the Monarch's common law powers should be approached by the courts. Both *Bate's Case*, and *Darnel's Case* can be read as judgments in which the courts held that the judiciary could not question the way a power that the King was accepted to possess was used. A common law principle which effectively excused some of the Monarch's personal powers from judicial regulation presented an obvious threat to the sovereignty of Parliament. Moreover, the principle would not seem compatible with the various theories of the rule of law which subsequently emerged within the British constitutional tradition.

Since 1688, the Monarch's personal political powers have declined significantly in practical terms. The Queen is now largely just a figurehead, performing ceremonial and symbolic functions within the contemporary constitution. But this does not mean that the prerogative powers have disappeared. For most practical purposes, prerogative powers are exercised on

---

[17] [1965] Ch 32 at 79.   [18] See 'Retrospectivity in legislation—the War Damage Act 1965', ch 3, pp 70–71.
[19] 'De jure' meaning 'as a matter of law', in contrast to 'de facto' meaning as a matter of practicality.

the Monarch's behalf by the government. But before considering a brief list of the residue of prerogative powers which the government retains, we ought to make some reference to a *definitional problem*. What was originally meant by the notion of the *personal powers* of the sovereign?

What is the prerogative? A definitional controversy

There are two schools of thought on this point.[20] The first, 'narrow' interpretation was advanced by Blackstone. For Blackstone, prerogative powers were only those 'singular and eccentrical' to the King himself—things which only the King could do. So for example the power to enter into contracts, to lend money, to employ people, should not be considered as part of the prerogative because any other citizen could do those things. Only powers such as declaring war, or granting peerages were exclusive to the King, and so correctly labelled as prerogative powers.

In Dicey's wider view everything that government can lawfully do that does not have its roots in a statute, but which could be enforced in the courts was a prerogative power. Dicey's usage is generally accepted today—although there are still some influential commentators who favour the Blackstone version.[21] But assuming we take the wider view as the more authoritative version, which prerogative powers does the government still possess?

The most important one is probably the conduct of foreign affairs and the signing of treaties. In the domestic sphere such actions as the summoning and dissolution of Parliament, the appointment of Ministers, the granting of peerages, appointing judges, giving pardons to convicted criminals or stopping criminal proceedings, and the terms and conditions of civil servants' employment were all components of this residual source of legal authority. This is not an exhaustive list, but it is sufficient to convey the point that the prerogative remains a substantively important source of governmental authority.

Most of these powers can be exercised in two ways, either directly or indirectly. Direct exercise of the prerogative need not take any documentary form. Foreign policy for example is usually carried on in this way. The prerogative is exercised indirectly through a device known as the Order in Council, which is in some respects analogous to a statute, in that it often grants Ministers the legal authority to exercise a range of discretionary powers.

Irrespective of the way they are used, the continued existence of prerogative powers raises two substantial constitutional issues—one legal, the other political. The legal issue is essentially the question of the relationship between the government and the judiciary; which prerogative powers will the courts subject to judicial review, and in what circumstances and according to which criteria will the courts intervene to regulate government activity? The political issue centres on the relationship between the government and the houses of Parliament. Is it desirable that important political decisions such as going to war, signing treaties, or granting pardons be taken without the explicit prior approval of a majority of MPs? We will return to the political issue in later chapters. This chapter considers the fate of the prerogative in the courts during the twentieth century.

I. The relationship between statute, the prerogative, and the rule of law

In the early-twentieth century, the House of Lords produced two forceful opinions curbing the way that prerogative powers could be exercised. One of the most sweeping prerogative powers exercised by Monarchs was to seize property for military reasons in times of war, if

---

[20] See generally Markesenis B (1973) 'The royal prerogative revisited' *Cambridge LJ* 287.
[21] See particularly Wade HRW (1985) 'The civil service and the prerogative' *LQR* 190.

the seizure was necessary to safeguard national security.[22] The power was invoked frequently during World War I. The government evidently believed its actions to be legal, but the lawfulness of seizures was challenged in the courts. The most controversial point was whether such requisition of private property obliged the government to compensate the owners.[23]

Re Petition of Right (1915)

Re Petition of Right[24] concerned the army's seizure of a commercial airfield for military purposes. The owners contended that the prerogative power to requisition the property without compensation arose only in emergency situations such as an actual invasion, and not for the long-term purpose of establishing an airbase. The High Court and Court of Appeal accepted that the power existed only in 'invasion' situations. The owners' claim nonetheless failed, as the judges considered that the notion of 'invasion' was to be interpreted in the light of modern military technology. A German plane or airship flying into British airspace was as much an invasion in 1915 as the disembarkation of belligerent troops at Dover would have been in 1637. This interpretive principle is important, for it means that the practical reach of the supposedly residual prerogative could legitimately be extended as a result of changing social, political, or technological development. In essence, the judgment tells us that prerogative powers are 'always speaking' in the same way as statutory provisions.

The *Petition of Right* judgment was also significant in another respect. In *Ship Money*, the question of deciding what was 'necessary' to protect national security was held to be the sole preserve of the Monarch. In *Petition of Right*, the courts seemed to require that the government demonstrate that an 'invasion' situation actually existed and that the requisition of the property concerned was necessary to counter the threat. However this was not a taxing obligation; the judges expressed no willingness to allow any challenge to a senior military officer's assertion that the seizure of the airport was necessary.

The Zamora (1916)

This approach was modified in *The Zamora*.[25] *The Zamora* was a ship from a neutral country carrying a cargo of copper. The government seized the ship and its cargo when it docked at a British port. The Court accepted that judges were neither sufficiently expert, nor constitutionally entitled to argue the case with the government as to the adequacy of the national security justification for using this prerogative power. National security was still regarded as a matter in respect of which the court could not evaluate the legal adequacy of the government's decision. However, in this case the government had not produced any evidence that the copper was needed for national security reasons. The Court therefore held that the government had not shown that the factual prerequisite for using the power had arisen, and so the power could not be invoked.[26]

The Zamora displays a shift from the position which the courts adopted in *Ship Money*. The decision seems to make essentially the same point as Lord Atkin's subsequent dissent in *Liversidge*; namely in the absence of a clear legislative provision to the contrary, the executive must convince the court that the facts which trigger the use of a legal power do indeed exist. What is less clear is how much evidence would be required to confirm that national security issues were involved, a point to which we devote further attention later in the chapter.

[22] *R v Hampden* (1637) 3 State Tr 826. This was the power at issue in *Burmah Oil*; see '"Retrospective" law making', ch 3, pp 70–71.

[23] The government's practice was to offer compensation *ex gratia*, ie not as a matter of right.

[24] [1915] 3 KB 649, CA.   [25] [1916] 2 AC 77, PC.

[26] See Holdsworth W (1919) 'The power of the Crown to requisition British ships in a national emergency' *LQR* 12–42.

The superiority of statute over prerogative:
A-G v De Keyser's Royal Hotel Ltd (1920)

The judgment in *A-G v De Keyser's Royal Hotel Ltd*[27] makes this among the most instructive of all constitutional law cases. In addition to dealing authoritatively with the nature of the relationship between statute and prerogative powers, the Court's use of principles of statutory interpretation tells us much about the interaction between the doctrines of parliamentary sovereignty and the rule of law.

The 'property' at stake in *De Keyser* was a hotel, which the government wished to use to accommodate the administrative headquarters of the Royal Flying Corps. The owners did not dispute that the government had the legal power to requisition it. Two questions were however in issue. Firstly, did that power derive from statute or the prerogative? And secondly—whatever its source—was the power one which required the government to pay compensation to the owners? The House of Lords dealt with these questions in an holistic way, but for our purposes the decision may be divided into three parts; dealing respectively with the existence (or non-existence) of specific prerogative powers, the precise meaning of relevant statutory provisions, and the general issue of the relationship between statute and the prerogative.

On the first issue, two subsidiary questions arose: did the prerogative power identified in *Re Petition of Right* extend to these particular circumstances; and if it did not, did the Crown possess an alternative prerogative power to take property without compensation in war-time which did arise on these facts?

The Court did not accept that this case fell within the *Re Petition of Right* principle. The property was not being commandeered to form an immediate defence against invasion (even in the modern sense). Lord Sumner also made it quite clear—in an obvious departure from the *Ship Money* principle—that the court would inquire if the factual circumstances amounting to an emergency actually existed; it would not simply defer to the government's view on that question.[28]

Nor was any member of the Court convinced that the Crown ever possessed a prerogative power to take property without paying compensation in non-emergency war-time situations. The power to take property in such circumstances was undoubtedly part of the residue of prerogative powers left to the Crown after the revolution; what was not so readily evident was whether the power could be exercised without granting compensation. The Court explored this issue through historical rather than legal analysis, as it could find no case law which offered clear guidance. The Court's inquiries into the practical conduct of such requisitions indicated that they had all been accompanied by the payment of compensation. As Lord Atkinson put it:

> The conclusion, as I understand it, is that it does not appear that the Crown has ever taken for these purposes the land of the subject, without paying for it, and that there is no trace of the Crown having, even in the time of the Stuarts, exercised or asserted the power or right to do so.[29]

In effect, the Attorney-General was arguing that the Court should grant the government a new prerogative power. This was a request to which the Court was not constitutionally competent to accede. This conclusion necessarily meant that if the government was empowered to requisition the hotel without paying compensation, that power had to derive from statute.

---

[27] [1920] AC 508. The Attorney-General is the senior of the government's two 'law officers'; (the Solicitor-General is the junior officer). He/she is generally an MP sitting in the Commons, and will on occasion argue for the government in the courts. He/she is not usually a member of the Cabinet.

[28] '[This] seems to me to be an ... obvious proposition—namely that when the court can see from the character and circumstances of the requisition itself that the case cannot be one of imminent danger, it is free to inquire whether the conditions, resting on necessity, which were held to exist in [*Re Petition of Right*] are applicable to the case in hand' [1920] AC 508 at 565. The principle would be of no practical significance if the inquiry was satisfied by the mere statement of a government official that 'imminent danger' existed.   [29] [1920] AC 508 at 539.

The Court also engaged in a history lesson in deciding just what statutory powers the government possessed. Its conclusion on this point is not directly pertinent to the question of prerogative powers. Nonetheless, it merits attention here because it enables us to embellish our understanding of the way in which the courts' use of techniques of statutory interpretation can reconcile ostensible tensions between the principles of parliamentary sovereignty and the rule of law.

Their Lordships' judgments suggested that Parliament began to legislate on this matter in the eighteenth century primarily because the limited prerogative powers of emergency requisition were inadequate to deal with the growing complexities of modern warfare. At the outbreak of World War I, the main legislation in this field had been the Defence Act 1842. The Act gave the government very substantial powers of requisition. It also attached quite rigorous procedural conditions to the exercise of those powers, and also provided that the owners of requisitioned property should be compensated, the amount to be decided by a jury.

The Court's presumption was that the legislation was enacted to achieve three objectives which—to borrow Harlow and Rawlings' terminology—mixed green and red light concerns. The extended powers of requisition were intended to enhance the country's capacity to conduct war successfully; the procedural conditions to reduce the likelihood that the power could be used arbitrarily; and the compensation provisions to place the cost of conducting a war on the whole population rather than on the few people whose property was taken.

The 1842 Act was not repealed in 1914. Its effect was however extended by the powers contained in the Defence of the Realm (Consolidation) Act 1914. Section 1 of that Act provided that: 'His Majesty in Council has power to issue regulations for securing the public safety and the defence of the realm . . .'. Section 1(2) detailed a more specific example of that general power: 'Any such regulations may provide for the suspension of any restrictions on the acquisition or user of land . . . or any other power under the Defence Acts 1842–1875 . . .'. A regulation was subsequently passed in November 1914 which empowered an authorised military officer to take possession of any land or building when it was necessary to do so 'for the purpose of securing the public safety or the defence of the realm'.

The government's contention in *De Keyser* was that the duty to pay compensation laid down in the 1842 Act was a 'restriction' on the government's ability to acquire land for defence purposes, and as such could be suspended by regulation. The regulation passed in November was claimed to have this effect. De Keyser's response to this argument was that the notion of 'restrictions' reached only to the procedural conditions contained in the 1842 Act, and not to the separate issue of compensation.

The way in which the judges addressed this issue illustrates forcefully how blurred the edges might be between the literal and teleological approaches to statutory interpretation. It is not fanciful to argue that having to pay for something is likely to operate as a 'restriction' on one's readiness to take it; the cost may act as a disincentive to acquisition. However the House of Lords rejected that interpretation. Lord Moulton's reasoning on the point was cursory, implying that the literal meaning of 'restriction' simply could not bear that construction:

> The duty of paying compensation cannot be regarded as a restriction. It is a consequence of the taking, but in no way restricts it, and therefore . . . [De Keyser] are entitled to the compensation provided by that [1842] Act.[30]

This is assertion rather than explanation. The explanation for the conclusion is best provided in Lord Atkinson's judgment. One way of characterising his reasoning would be that the literal meaning of 'restriction' was conditioned by a contextual (or background) principle

---

[30] Ibid, at 551.

derived from a rigorous understanding of the rule of law intended to protect the property of private citizens:

> The recognised rule for the construction of statute is that, unless the words of the statute clearly so demand, the statute is not to be construed so as to take away the property of a subject without compensation.[31]

One might alternatively characterise his reasoning (and here one slips into the then heresy of teleological interpretation) as 'making sense'[32] of the 1914 Act and subsequent regulation by regarding them as devices to sweep away procedural impediments to the effective conduct of the war without compromising the substantive principle that its cost should be borne by the entire country.

The judgment also addressed several issues of broader significance. Lord Atkinson firmly rejected the Attorney-General's contention that a prerogative power and a statutory power dealing with the same issue could co-exist—that they were as the Attorney-General put it 'merged'—and that the government could choose to deploy whichever power best suited its purpose. Lord Atkinson considered the notion of 'merger' inapposite. Rather a statute:

> abridges the royal prerogative while it is in force to this extent—that the Crown can only do the particular thing under and in accordance with the statutory provisions, and that its prerogative power to do that thing is in abeyance.[33]

The notion that the passage of a statute sends the affected prerogative power into some form of constitutional suspended animation was not shared by all members of the court. Lord Dunedin implied that he thought the prerogative power remained in place, but the place it now occupied was distinctly inferior to that inhabited by the new statutory provisions. This distinction is of little functional significance. The essential point common to both views concerns the hierarchical relationship between statute and the prerogative. On this question, Lord Dunedin and Lord Atkinson agreed. While Lord Dunedin indicated that the prerogative retained some degree of constitutional sentience: 'it is equally certain that if the whole ground of something which could be done by the prerogative is covered by the statute, it is the statute that rules'.[34]

Both standpoints accept that Parliament can expressly provide that prerogative powers covering a matter now affected by statutory rules continue to exist side-by-side with the Act concerned. There is nothing in the judgments to suggest that Parliament can only override the prerogative by express suspension of the relevant prerogative powers. Any such rule would contradict the implied repeal facet of the parliamentary sovereignty doctrine. If statute is a superior form of law to the prerogative, and if existing statutes must give way if inconsistent with later legislation, it would be a nonsense if an existing prerogative power was considered more authoritative than an inconsistent statute. Yet there is some illogicality about the 'abeyance' argument. It would not be maintained that a 1920 Act which amended a statute passed in 1910 'suspended' the earlier legislation, in the sense that the 1910 provisions would regain their legal effect if the 1920 Act were itself repealed. Nor would it be argued that the 1910 Act retained a legal status, albeit one inferior to the 1920 Act. Rather, the presumption would be that the 1910 Act no longer existed at all. It would seem peculiar that the prerogative, a common law power, should enjoy greater legal longevity than a statutory provision covering the same point. The illogicality can perhaps be reasoned away by suggesting that the courts could legitimately conclude that it would always be Parliament's

---

[31] Ibid, at 542. The court's methodology resembles that subsequently deployed in *Gilmore* and *Anisminic* (see 'Ouster clauses—*Gilmore* (1957) and *Anisminic* (1969)', ch 3, pp 68–69), where the contextual principle concerned the jurisdictional question of access to the courts rather than the substantive issue of receiving compensation for property.   [32] Cf. Denning LJ's opinion in *Magor*; 'Purposive (or "teleological") interpretation', ch 3, pp 60–61.   [33] [1920] AC 508 at 540, per Lord Atkinson.   [34] Ibid, at 526.

(unspoken) intention that a 'suspended' prerogative power would be reactivated whenever an Act repealed an earlier Act which had itself put a prerogative power into abeyance. Such reasoning is however difficult to reconcile with orthodox understandings of the courts' interpretive role.

Extending *De Keyser*: *Laker Airways Ltd v Department of Trade* (1977)

The Court of Appeal's judgment in *Laker Airways*[35] further emphasised the prerogative's inferior constitutional status relative to statutes by extending the *De Keyser* principle. Following the passage of the Civil Aviation Act 1971, airlines which wished to operate a service between Britain and the United States required two forms of authorisation. Firstly, the airline needed a licence from the Civil Aviation Authority (CAA). The CAA exercised powers under the 1971 Act, and awarded licences according to criteria laid down in s 3(1), which required the CAA to promote low fares, high safety standards, and competition on major routes. Under s 3(2) the Department of Trade (DoT) could give the CAA 'guidance' concerning the way it exercised its licensing function. Under s 4(3), the DoT could give the CAA 'directions' concerning matters which affected national security or diplomatic relations. Secondly, the airline had to be granted landing rights in the United States. These derived from a Treaty called the Bermuda Agreement which the government, using its prerogative powers, had negotiated with the United States.

In 1972 Laker Airways applied for a licence to operate a cheap London-to-New York service. The only British companies then flying these routes were British Airways and British Caledonian. The CAA granted Laker a licence under s 3(1), and the DoT used its prerogative power to arrange for Laker to be given landing rights in New York. After the 1974 general election, the new Labour government decided that it wanted to protect British Airways and British Caledonian from Laker's competition, and sought to withdraw Laker's permission to fly. The government could not use s 4(3) to give 'directions' to the CAA to revoke Laker's licence, since no questions of national security or diplomatic relations arose. Consequently, the DoT attempted to use its prerogative powers to cancel Laker's landing rights under the Bermuda Agreement, and issued the CAA with 'guidance' under s 3(2) instructing it to withdraw Laker's licence. Laker claimed both actions were ultra vires.

The Court of Appeal supported Laker's contention; neither statute nor prerogative provided a lawful basis for the government's action. Lord Denning first considered the meaning of 'guidance' in s 3(2). He felt that Parliament's intention in using this term had been to empower the government to 'explain', 'amplify' or 'supplement' the policy of the Act, not to 'reverse' or 'contradict' it. However, Denning concluded that the government's new policy would reduce competition and so raise prices on the London–New York route. This was entirely inconsistent with the s 3(1) objectives, namely to encourage competition and reduce prices. The policy could not therefore be 'guidance', and so lacked a statutory foundation.

Lord Denning also rejected the argument that the government's prerogative power provided a lawful justification for withdrawing Laker's landing rights. He reasoned that the government was trying to use its prerogative powers to contradict a statutory objective. Unlike *De Keyser*, *Laker* presented a situation in which statutory and prerogative powers were not overlapping, but interlocking. The statute was not intended to replace the prerogative, but to be used in conjunction with it. Nevertheless, in such circumstances, statute's superior constitutional status demanded that the prerogative be exercised only in ways that furthered, rather than obstructed Parliament's intentions. If the government wished to pursue a policy contradicting the objectives of the 1971 Act, it would have to persuade Parliament to enact new legislation which amended the DoT's powers.[36]

---

[35] [1977] QB 643   [36] See Wade HRW (1977) 'Judicial control of the prerogative' *LQR* 325.

The judgment protected the 'sovereignty' of Parliament in a political as well as legal sense. The government then had only a tiny majority in the Commons and was in a minority in the Lords. It was clear that some Labour Party MPs would not support any Bill designed to stop Laker Airways flying, and that any such Bill would attract little public support. Unsurprisingly, no such measure was introduced.

Extending *Laker: R v Secretary of State for the Home Department, ex p Fire Brigades Union* (1995)

This principle was further extended in 1995, in a judgment concerning the administration of the Criminal Injuries Compensation scheme. The Criminal Injuries Compensation Board (CICB) was established in 1964 to provide compensation to the victims of violent crime or to their dependents. It was not set up under statute, but under the prerogative. The then Labour government also publicised criteria which the Board would use to assess compensation; criteria broadly based on the compensation that a person would receive if she had suffered a similar injury as a result of tortious action. Some twenty years later, Parliament enacted the Criminal Justice Act 1988. Sections 108–117 gave a statutory basis to the existing common law scheme. However, the sections were not brought into force immediately. Rather, under s 171(1) of the Act, the Home Secretary was empowered to place the original entitlement criteria on a statutory basis 'on such day as he may appoint'. The government chose not to exercise this power immediately. In 1993, the government concluded that the existing scheme was proving too expensive. Consequently, rather than exercise his s 171 power, the then (Conservative) Home Secretary Michael Howard concluded that he would use his prerogative powers to amend the original scheme and introduce a cheaper system. The government felt that it could amend the existing scheme without infringing the 1988 Act, as ss 108–117 had no legal force until the Home Secretary exercised his s 171 power to implement them.

The Fire Brigades Union challenged the decision on various grounds, one being that the Home Secretary was attempting to disregard a statutory limit on his prerogative powers. The argument was rejected in the High Court,[37] but accepted in the Court of Appeal,[38] which reasoned that while s 171 did not require the Home Secretary to place the scheme on a statutory basis by any particular date, it did restrict the Home Secretary's prerogative powers in respect of the scheme, so that they could no longer be used in a way that contradicted Parliament's intentions. By enacting s 171, Parliament had given a statutory seal of approval to the prerogative scheme introduced in 1964. For the Home Secretary to alter the scheme would therefore conflict with Parliament's wishes. If the government wished to introduce different entitlement criteria, it would have to ask Parliament to repeal ss 108–117.

The Court of Appeal's decision was subsequently upheld in the House of Lords, albeit only by a three to two majority.[39] Lords Mustill and Keith suggested that ss 108–117 had as yet no legal force, and thus could not curb the Home Secretary's prerogative powers. The majority (Lords Browne-Wilkinson, Lloyd, and Nicholls) disagreed. The rationale underpinning the majority's conclusion is best put by Lord Lloyd, who considered it mistaken to assume that ss 108–117 had no legal existence at all until the s 171 power was deployed:

> True, they do not have statutory force. But that does not mean that they are writ in water. They contain a statement of Parliamentary intention, even though they create no enforceable rights . . . The Home Secretary has power to delay the coming into force of the statutory provisions, but he has no power to reject them or set them aside, as if they had never been passed.[40]

---

[37] [1994] PIQR P320.   [38] [1995] 2 AC 513.   [39] Ibid, at 544.
[40] Ibid, at 570–571. See Barendt E (1995) 'Constitutional law and the criminal injuries compensation scheme' *Public Law* 357.

Shortly thereafter, the government announced that it would introduce a Bill to modify the existing scheme. The Bill was promptly enacted. The episode thus provides us with an example of the practical operation of the constitution coinciding perfectly with its theoretical base.

II. The traditional perspective on judicial review of prerogative powers: and its erosion

Orthodox constitutional theory assumes that Parliament 'contracts in' to administrative law when creating government powers through statute. If Parliament does not wish the implied terms of administrative law to apply to particular statutory activities, it must make that intention clear in the legislation. Absent such express 'contracting out', a government body's exercise of statutory power will (according to the *Wednesbury* principles) be ultra vires if no such power has been granted, if the power has been exercised 'unreasonably', or if decisions have been made through 'unfair procedures'. Such government decisions attract what we might term 'full review' by the courts.

'Limited' rather than 'full' review of prerogative powers

However, in relation to judicial review of government action taken under the prerogative, the courts traditionally applied only the first of the *Wednesbury* principles. The judges would say, as in *De Keyser* or *BBC v John*, whether a claimed prerogative power actually existed. This is clearly consistent with the notion that the prerogative was a collection of residual powers—the courts would not permit the government to claim new ones. Relatedly, as Lord Atkinson stressed in *De Keyser*, a court would examine if the requisite factual triggers for an exercise of the power were present.

But prior to the 1980s, the concepts of 'unreasonableness' or 'procedural fairness' to which the use of statutory powers was subjected were seemingly not applied to the prerogative. Thus while the courts were concerned with the *existence and extent* of a claimed prerogative power, they were not concerned with the way that power was *exercised*.

This differential treatment of prerogative and statutory powers would seem difficult to reconcile with orthodox understandings of the function performed by the principle of the rule of law within democratic constitutions—namely to minimise the possibility of government being able lawfully to exercise power in arbitrary or procedurally unfair ways. From a functionalist perspective, such a dichotomy would be defensible only if prerogative powers were qualitatively distinct from powers exercised under statute. Absent such a distinction, the common law's varying treatment of these two types of government powers could be justified only on purely formalist grounds—that prerogative powers were not fully reviewable simply because they were prerogative powers. (See Table 4.1.)

One can thus discern a 'rule of law' as well as a 'parliamentary sovereignty' basis for the *De Keyser* principle which forbade the co-existence of prerogative and statutory powers. To permit co-existence would allow the government to evade the judicial review principles to which it was assumed Parliament had subjected it by passing legislation in an area where executive powers previously derived solely from the prerogative.

The principle that prerogative powers be subject to only limited review is given ringing endorsement in Blackstone's *Commentaries*:

> In the exertion therefore of those prerogatives, which the law has given him, the King is irresistible and absolute, according to the forms of the constitution. And yet if the consequence of that exertion be manifestly to the grievance or dishonour of the kingdom, the Parliament will call his advisers to a just and severe account.[41]

[41] Volume 1 p 251. See also Chitty's 1820 *Prerogatives of the Crown* p 6: 'in the exercise of his lawful prerogatives, an unbounded discretion is, generally speaking, left to the King'.

Table 4.1 The differential scope of judicial review of prerogative and statutory powers

Ground of review	Statutory power	Prerogative power
Illegality	Yes	Yes
Irrationality	Yes	No
Procedural unfairness	Yes	No

Blackstone's observation indicated that he regarded the imposition of accountability on Ministers for the way in which prerogative powers were exercised as a matter for political pressure in the Commons or Lords rather than legal argument before the courts. This would however seem to have been an orthodoxy which rested on somewhat shaky foundations: judicial authority for the rule is rather less forthright. This is perhaps unsurprising, given that the rule seems to provide the government with a sweeping exemption from having to comply with an expansive understanding of the rule of law. In an influential article,[42] Markesenis pointed to two oft-cited authorities for the proposition: *R v Allen*[43] and *China Navigation Co Ltd v A-G*.[44] Both cases sustain the conclusion that the particular prerogative powers in issue should receive only limited review. Yet neither supports the rule that all prerogative powers should be subjected to this diluted conception of the rule of law.

R v Allen (1862)

R v Allen concerned the *nolle prosequi* power retained by the Attorney-General, a device which enables her to end any ongoing criminal trial. Allen had been charged with perjury. His trial was however halted when the Attorney-General issued a *nolle prosequi*. This intervention was challenged by the prosecuting authorities, on the ground that the *nolle prosequi* had been issued in a procedurally incorrect way, in so far as the Attorney-General had breached his usual practice of allowing the prosecution to give its views on the desirability of continuing the case before reaching his decision. The prosecuting authorities thus contended that the *nolle prosequi* should be quashed. The Court clearly viewed the Attorney-General's failure to consult the prosecution lawyers with disfavour,[45] but nonetheless saw no grounds for reviewing his decision:

> Suppose it is possible that there could be an abuse of his power by the Attorney-General or injustice in the exercise of it, the remedy is by holding him responsible for his acts before the great tribunal of this country, the High Court of Parliament.[46]

Echoing Blackstone, Cockburn CJ suggested that control over the exercise of this prerogative powers was a matter for the political rather than legal process. But it is not possible to extract from the (extremely short) judgments any clear reason as to why the *nolle prosequi* should be treated in this way. Cockburn CJ alluded to the 'great inconvenience' that would result if the power were to be subject to full review, but did not explain how this 'inconvenience' would arise. It is however clear that the various opinions in the case were all limited to the specific power of *nolle prosequi*: none of the judges made any reference to the prerogative in general.

China Navigation (1932)

The Court of Appeal's 1932 judgment in *China Navigation* was similarly specific. The prerogative power in issue was the government's control of the armed forces. The Court of Appeal noted that in some specific respects, this prerogative power had been restricted by statute. Those powers that remained, however, were: 'left to the uncontrolled discretion which [the

---

[42] (1973) op cit.   [43] (1862) 12 ER 929.   [44] [1932] 2 KB 197, CA.
[45] '[The Attorney-General] would act wisely in calling the prosecutor before him . . . I think that is a wholesome practice' (1862) 12 ER 929 at 931; per Cockburn CJ.   [46] Ibid.

King] exercises through his Ministers. The Courts cannot question it . . . '.[47] As in *R v Allen*, there is no indication that the Court regarded this conclusion as applicable to all prerogative powers.

Developments in the 1960s and 1970s

From the late 1960s, the courts' attachment to the orthodox proposition that prerogative powers were subjected only to limited review began to change. Several cases merit close attention. The first is the 1967 decision in *R v Criminal Injuries Compensation Board, ex p Lain*.[48]

Lain (1967)—a break with orthodoxy?

Mrs Lain was the widow of a policeman. She claimed that the amount of compensation she had been offered in respect of her husband's injuries and subsequent death had not been properly assessed in accordance with the published criteria. In other words, she was questioning the way in which the Board had exercised its powers. The Board contended that the court had no power to review the exercise of the prerogative.

However, the Court held that this particular prerogative power should be reviewed as if derived from a statute. The main reason for this was that the Board was performing an essentially 'judicial' task. It had the straightforward duty of awarding compensation on the basis of the published rules. Unlike the complex national security question raised in cases like *Ship Money*, this was an issue which the courts were well equipped to decide.

Lain apparently made a distinct break with traditional theory, although it received little attention in the academic press. The judgment lent itself to one of three interpretations. Firstly, that it was an aberrant decision, which if not overruled would be confined solely to the CICB and not extended to other prerogative actions. Secondly, that it laid the ground for future judgments to conclude that all prerogative powers should be fully reviewable. Or thirdly, that it intimated that full review should apply only to prerogative powers raising issues that the court regarded as intrinsically well-suited to be subject to judicial scrutiny.

Laker Airways (1977)—a rejection of orthodoxy?

Several years later, in *Laker Airways*, Denning lent further weight to the argument that prerogative powers per se should not be subject only to limited review. In that case, Denning again restricted his judgment to a particular prerogative power—designation of an airline under the Bermuda Agreement—but this time concluded that the power should be subject to full review:

> Seeing that the prerogative is a discretionary power to be exercised for the public good, it follows that its exercise can be examined by the courts just as any other discretionary power which is vested in the executive [ie by statute].[49]

Gouriet (1978)—a division of judicial opinion

Gouriet v Union of Post Office Workers[50] suggests that the higher courts had adopted different interpretations of the *Lain* decision. One prerogative power exercised on behalf of the government by the Attorney-General is the *relator* proceeding. This enables the Attorney-General to initiate civil proceedings in defence of the public interest in situations where an individual is either unable or unwilling to take action.

---

[47] [1932] 2 KB 197 at 217, CA, per Scrutton LJ. See also Lawrence LJ at 229: 'The manner in which the Crown exercises its powers is not a matter which can be inquired into by a Court of law'.   [48] [1967] 2 QB 864.
[49] [1977] QB 643 at 705.   [50] [1978] AC 435, HL.

The Post Office Union had decided to boycott mail to and from South Africa for twenty-four hours, as a gesture of disapproval of the South African government's apartheid regime. This constituted a criminal offence under the Post Office Acts. However, for political reasons, the government decided that the union would not be prosecuted. Mr Gouriet was a member of a group called the Freedom Association, which disapproved of the union's activities and of the government's failure to prosecute. Consequently, Mr Gouriet approached the Attorney-General, asking him to initiate a *relator* action for an injunction to stop the mail embargo going ahead. When the Attorney-General refused, Mr Gouriet asked the courts to review his decision.

Before *Gouriet* there was no case law supporting the argument that the *relator* power could be reviewed. There was however precedent for the converse proposition; namely whether or not to launch *relator* proceedings was a prerogative power solely within the control of the Attorney-General. *Gouriet* produced a divergence of opinion between Lord Denning in the Court of Appeal and the House of Lords. Denning thought that the time had come to question traditional perceptions of the *relator* action as being completely beyond judicial supervision. Denning drew a distinction between a situation where the Attorney-General launched *relator* proceedings, and circumstances where he refused to do so. In the former case, use of the prerogative power was not open to question in the courts. However a refusal to begin proceedings could be challenged; Denning suggested that if the courts did not intervene in situations like this it would allow the criminal law to be infringed with impunity. In such circumstances, Denning asked himself; 'Are the courts to stand idly by?'. In his opinion, the answer was: 'No'.

There was nothing unconstitutional, in the legal sense, about Denning's analysis. Since the prerogative is a common law concept, and since the common law is dynamic and open to constant amendment by the courts, Denning's innovative judgment could be thought legally defensible. He was not overriding a statute—but simply saying that an old common law rule should be replaced by a new one.

However, as far as the House of Lords was concerned, the courts should indeed stand idly by when this particular prerogative power was being employed—and when it was not being employed. In the House of Lords' opinion, whether or not to launch a *relator* action was a public interest question which only the government was competent to decide. It was another example (like the test of 'necessity' in *Ship Money* perhaps) of a legal power which could not be subjected to review on the basis of either irrationality or procedural unfairness. The judgment suggested that it would be unconstitutional, in the political if not legal sense, to overturn government policy over this issue.[51]

Denning's perception of constitutionality accorded the highest priority to seeing that the criminal law was not ignored. In contrast, the House of Lords' version was most concerned with not overruling the policy preferences of an elected government. Despite the House of Lords' strong stance, there was a suggestion that the judges' reluctance to intervene owed more to the highly contentious nature of the power concerned rather than simply its source in the prerogative. Unlike *Lain*, *Gouriet* raised an issue which had immense party political implications. For the court to have told the government that it could not act in the way it wished would have exposed the judges to accusations of subverting the democratic process.

Conclusion—the 'constitutionality' of reform

But would the courts infringe parliamentary sovereignty by changing the common law in order to place review of the prerogative on the same basis as review of action taken under statute? Clearly, any such alteration in the common law would be unconstitutional if it contradicted the clear terms of a statute. But even in the absence of an expressly contradictory

---

[51] This was perhaps the 'great inconvenience' to which Cockburn CJ alluded in *Allen*.

statute, the constitutionality of such a reform to the law could perhaps be questioned. One might argue that if Parliament was dissatisfied with the courts' traditional reluctance to subject prerogative powers to full review, it could do one of two things. Either it could pass a statute saying that all prerogative powers would henceforth be reviewable in the same way as statutory powers. Or, less radically, it could place specific prerogative powers on a statutory basis, and so make them amenable to full *Wednesbury* review. If the legislature took neither of these steps, it would seem plausible to assume that Parliament approved of the present situation of limited review. Consequently, if the courts changed the common law, they might in effect, if not in theory, be 'usurping the legislative function'.

Nevertheless, the suggestion was being floated in the early 1980s that the time was ripe for the courts to reject the traditional idea that all exercises of the prerogative were beyond judicial supervision. If the courts could say that executive action taken under statute was unlawful in some circumstances, surely the same argument could be applied to the less party-politicised aspects of prerogative power. This is another illustration of a constitutional argument rooted in a functionalist rather than formalist conceptual framework. If the function of the rule of law is to protect citizens from arbitrary or unpredictable government activity, why should the source of that government power be of any relevance? Use of the prerogative could impact just as seriously on individuals as action taken under statute. There was no logical, functional reason why the two sources of governmental authority should be distinguished. The scene was set therefore for the courts to question the orthodox constitutional theory. The opportunity to do so was provided by *Council of Civil Service Unions v Minister for the Civil Service*.

III. Full reviewability—the *GCHQ* case (1983)

Council of Civil Service Unions v Minister for the Civil Service,[52] generally known as the *GCHQ* case, concerned employees at the Government Communication Headquarters in Cheltenham. GCHQ monitored radio and satellite transmissions in overseas countries; it was linked in some ill-defined way with the security services. Many of its employees belonged to a civil service trade union. At that time, civil servants did not have contracts of employment. Their terms and conditions of work were generally regulated by Orders in Council, the indirect exercise of the prerogative.[53] One term under which civil servants at GCHQ worked was that their conditions of service should not be altered until the Minister for the Civil Service had consulted with the trade unions about the proposed change.

In the early 1980s, the trade unions engaged in industrial action which disrupted GCHQ's intelligence gathering activities. The then Prime Minister, Margaret Thatcher, was also Minister for the Civil Service. She responded to the disruption by forbidding GCHQ employees from belonging to a trade union. Employees who refused to resign from their union would be redeployed to less sensitive posts. The Prime Minister did not consult the trade unions before introducing this change.

The trade unions challenged the action on the grounds that the Prime Minister had acted in a procedurally unfair way by failing to consult them (their argument was essentially that employed by the prosecuting authorities in *Allen*). In effect, the unions were asking the courts to apply standards of statutory review to prerogative powers. The government advanced two defences. The first was simply that this was a prerogative power, not subject to review on grounds of procedural unfairness. The second defence was that even if principles of procedural

---

[52] [1985] AC 374. See Lee S (1985) 'Prerogative and public law principles' *Public Law* 186.
[53] For subsequent developments see Morris G and Fredman S (1991) 'Judicial review and civil servants: contracts of employment declared to exist' *Public Law* 485.

fairness did apply to this prerogative power, the court should not intervene because the issue concerned 'national security'.

The 'nature' not the 'source' of power as the determinant of reviewability

Overturning traditional doctrine, the House of Lords rejected the government's first defence. Lord Fraser perhaps put the point most clearly:

> There is no doubt that if the Order in Council of 1982 had been made under the authority of a statute, the power delegated to the Minister would have been . . . subject to a duty to act fairly. I am unable to see why the words conferring the same powers should be construed differently merely because their source was an Order in Council made under the prerogative.[54]

This point was made with similar force by Lord Roskill, who could not see:

> any logical reason why the fact that the source of the power is the prerogative and not statute should today deprive the citizen of that right of challenge to the manner of its exercise which he would possess were the source of power statutory. In either case the act in question is the act of the executive. To talk of that act as the act of the sovereign savours of the archaism of past centuries.[55]

Such comments confirmed that the availability of judicial review would depend upon *the nature of government powers, not their source*. But victory on this point of general constitutional principle did not mean that the trade unions were ultimately successful. The House of Lords' concern with the nature of government powers takes us to the second important part of the *GCHQ* decision. Lord Diplock suggested that government powers would not be what he termed 'justiciable', and so would not be subject to review on the basis of irrationality or of procedural impropriety, if the dispute was of a sort which does not lend itself to resolution by judicial type methods. The non-justiciable issue is not simply a case of A versus B. Rather it presents a great many competing points of view, all of which have to be weighed and balanced in the search for an overall political solution. Elected politicians, rather than non-elected judges, are the appropriate people to make these kinds of decisions. Lord Diplock described this type of decision as 'a balancing exercise which judges by their upbringing and experience are ill-qualified to perform'.[56] He considered that national security was 'par excellence a non-justiciable question. The judicial process is totally inept to deal with the sort of problems which it involves'.[57] (See Table 4.2.)

In effect, the House of Lords refused to investigate either the honesty or the reasonableness of the Prime Minister's claim that she had revoked trade union membership without consultation because of national security reasons. If we are looking for old parallels to elements of the *GCHQ* decision, it might be more appropriate to focus on the court's approach to this question of national security. In the pre-revolutionary *Ship Money* case, the Court held that the King need not offer any evidence to support his assertion that the security of the realm was in jeopardy. In the 1916 *Zamora* case, in contrast, the Court had required at least some evidence that the government had bona fide grounds for believing national security to be threatened.

Table 4.2 The differential scope of judicial review of justiciable and non-justiciable powers

Ground of review	Justiciable	Non-justiciable
Illegality	Yes	Yes
Irrationality	Yes	No
Procedural unfairness	Yes	No

[54] [1985] AC 374 at 399.   [55] Ibid, at 417.   [56] Ibid, at 411.   [57] Ibid, at 412.

The *GCHQ* decision seems to follow the *Zamora* principle. The Court required the government to produce an affidavit confirming that the Minister had genuinely considered the issue. But this does not seem to be a very difficult hurdle for the government to clear, and it implies that we have to trust the government never to invoke national security reasons for dishonest or bizarre reasons.

The final important point advanced in *GCHQ* was the court's conclusion that it was not just national security issues which were non-justiciable. Lord Roskill produced a list of what we might call 'excluded' categories—aspects of the prerogative where review would relate only to the existence of the claimed power, not to its exercise. The powers that Lord Roskill had in mind were: 'the making of treaties, the defence of the realm, the prerogative of mercy, the grant of honours, the dissolution of Parliament and the appointment of Ministers'.[58]

This list perhaps suggests that the court's definition of non-reviewable prerogative powers closely resembles Blackstone's old notion of the prerogative as consisting solely of those powers 'singular and eccentrical to the Crown', which indicates that one may always find a historical precedent for supposedly radical developments in constitutional law.

IV. Post-*GCHQ* developments

Cases decided since 1985 seem to build on rather than contradict the more functionalist analysis the House of Lords adopted in *GCHQ*. The central question the case raised was whether 'justiciability' was a concept with a fixed meaning, or whether if, like other common law principles, it would be an unstable concept, prone to sudden and substantial change. Before the courts offered answers to that question however, the Court of Appeal took an unexpected approach to the issues both of the existence of claimed prerogative powers and the capacity of such powers to co-exist with statutory provisions.

R v Secretary of State for the Home Department, ex p Northumbria Police Authority (1988)

The legal structure of the police forces in this country has traditionally been complex; but to put the matter simply, before 2011 some powers rested with central government, some with local police authorities, and some with the Chief Constable of each force.[59] The *Northumbria* case[60] arose when the central government decided to set up a central supply store for plastic bullets and CS gas, on which Chief Constables could draw when they thought it necessary. Northumbria Police Authority did not want its Chief Constable to use these weapons without its approval, and so it initiated judicial review proceedings in an effort to establish that central government had no legal power to pursue this policy. The government claimed such power emanated from the Police Act 1964 and/or the old prerogative power 'to keep the peace'.

The Court of Appeal eventually decided that the 1964 Act included the power to set up a central weapons depot. That was a controversial conclusion, but we need not dwell on it here. What we consider is the court's answer to the questions of whether there was a prerogative power to keep the peace, and if so, what types of action it embraced in the mid-1980s.

The Police Authority's case rested on two main contentions. The first argument was that there was no mention in nineteenth-century textbooks or case law of a prerogative power

---

[58] Ibid, at 418.

[59] See Lustgarten L (1989) *The governance of police*. See also Marshall G and Loveday B (1994) 'The police: independence and accountability', in Jowell and Oliver op cit. Under the terms of the Police and Social Responsibility Act 2011 police authorities were replaced by directly elected 'Police and Crime Commissioners'.

[60] [1988] 1 All ER 556, CA. See also Bradley A (1988) 'Police powers and the prerogative' *Public Law* 298.

to keep the peace. This would seem a strong argument in the Police Authority's favour. If we recall Lord Camden's judgment in *Entick v Carrington*, we will remember that he was quite clear about how to determine if the Crown had a legal power to seize Mr Entick's papers; 'If it is law, it will be found in our books. If it is not to be found there, it is not law'. In effect, the Police Authority was contending that the residue of prerogative powers left to the Crown after 1688 never extended to equipping a police force.

The Court of Appeal dismissed this contention. Its innovative attitude is perhaps best expressed by Nourse LJ:

> [The] scarcity of reference in the books to the prerogative of keeping the peace within the realm does not disprove that it exists. Rather it may point to an unspoken assumption that it does.[61]

It is not difficult to agree with the first of those sentences; we should be cautious about assuming that eighteenth-century textbooks and law reports offered a comprehensive map of that era's legal landscape. But the meaning of the second sentence seems odd. Nourse LJ appears to argue that we should assume a legal power exists because no judge or textbook writer has ever recognised it. It seems hard to reconcile that reasoning with definitions of the rule of law which demand predictability and certainty in the scope of government's legal powers. Nevertheless, as we have already stressed, the *Burmah Oil* case serves as a salutary reminder that while there is no doubt that the prerogative is residual, there yet remains considerable uncertainty that all parts of that residue have thus far been identified. Nourse LJ's analysis in *Northumbria* might therefore be defended (unconvincingly) on the basis that he was perspicacious enough to find a 'lost' power which no other judge had previously managed to spot.

The Police Authority's second argument drew on *De Keyser* and *Laker*. The first police force was created by statute in the early-nineteenth century. So Northumbria contended that whatever prerogative powers to keep the peace may have existed between 1688 and 1800 would have been superseded by any overlapping statutory provisions. Section 4 of the Police Act 1964 granted the power to provide clothing and equipment to the police to police authorities. *Northumbria* argued that if one applied the *De Keyser* principle to s 4, one could only conclude that whatever prerogative power to supply equipment the Home Secretary might have had before 1964 had now been removed.

But the Court of Appeal also rejected this argument. It held that s 4 did not 'expressly grant a monopoly' in respect of equipment provision to the Police Authority, but rather created a situation in which the Police Authority's statutory power co-existed with the Home Secretary's prerogative power. But unlike the situation in *Laker*, the co-existence appeared to be contradictory rather than interlocking. This is a rather surprising argument, for it seems to be saying that the doctrine of implied repeal does not apply to prerogative powers. The Court is apparently suggesting that Parliament can only abolish or curtail the prerogative through express statutory provisions.[62]

This initially appears to take us into a seemingly illogical train of thought. Firstly, we accept that statute has a superior legal status to the prerogative. Secondly, we accept that statutes can be impliedly repealed by subsequent, impliedly inconsistent legislation. Thirdly, we accept that prerogative powers cannot be impliedly repealed by subsequent, impliedly inconsistent legislation. The third contention obviously contradicts points one and two. It is difficult to reconcile the Court of Appeal's decision about the status of the prerogative with orthodox constitutional theory, which might perhaps lead us to conclude that if we look hard enough we will usually find that our constitution harbours exceptions to even the most evidently straightforward of rules.

---

[61] [1988] 1 All ER 556 at 575, CA.

[62] It is unlikely that the 1964 Parliament would have expressly abolished a prerogative power not then known to exist.

On further reflection however, *Northumbria's* acceptance of the co-existence of statutory and prerogative powers is, post-*GCHQ*, arguably unproblematic. Since the nature of the Crown's prerogative power to keep the peace and the powers afforded to the Home Secretary by the Police Act 1964 is the same, whichever method the government chose to apply its preferred policies would receive the same degree of judicial scrutiny. There is thus no longer any functionalist justification, from a rule of law perspective, for assuming the grant of statutory powers impliedly suspends analogous prerogative authority.

Foreign affairs?

The courts have also given further guidance as to the reach of the justiciability principle. Three cases merit attention; the first two nominally fall under the excluded category of 'foreign policy' to which Lord Roskill referred in *GCHQ*; the third concerns the grant of pardons for the commissions of crimes which—per *GCHQ*—would also seem to be a non-justiciable power.

Ex p Molyneaux[63] arose from the Anglo-Irish Agreement signed by the British and Irish governments in 1985. The Agreement established an Inter-Governmental Conference which would meet to try to develop initiatives to resolve the problems afflicting Northern Ireland. Molyneaux was one of several Protestant Northern Irish politicians who opposed the Agreement. He sought judicial review of the Agreement on the grounds that it implemented policies which could only be achieved through legislation. This was a speculative argument, and the Court readily dismissed it. The Agreement was a treaty with a foreign state; it was quite clear that the government had a prerogative power to negotiate treaties; and it was equally clear that the exercise of that power was not justiciable.

The Court of Appeal reached a different conclusion in *R v Secretary of State for Foreign and Commonwealth Affairs, ex p Everett*.[64] Mr Everett was an alleged criminal who had taken up residence in Spain, a country with which Britain did not then have an extradition agreement. When Mr Everett's passport expired, the Foreign Office declined to renew it. The government maintained a policy of not renewing passports when the applicant was the subject of an arrest warrant. The issuance of passports has not been put on a statutory basis, and so was clearly a prerogative power. The Foreign Office's refusal meant that Mr Everett could not leave Spain. The Foreign Office did offer him a one-way trip back to Britain, but since he would have been arrested on his return, this was an offer which Mr Everett decided to refuse.

Mr Everett subsequently sought a review of the Foreign Office's decision. The government's primary defence was that the issue of passports was a question of foreign policy, and so within Lord Roskill's 'excluded categories'. The Court of Appeal rejected this argument. O'Connor LJ held that:

> the issue of a passport fell into an entirely different category. [I]t would seem obvious to me that the exercise of the prerogative . . . is an area where common sense tells one that, if for some reason a passport is wrongly refused for a bad reason, the court should be able to inquire into it.[65]

'Common sense' is not a precise legal tool. Taylor LJ's reasoning is more helpful. He suggested that non-justiciability in foreign relations issues only extended to questions of 'high policy'. He did not define this precisely, but he seems to mean matters which had national security implications or which directly affected Britain's relationship with a foreign state. Issuing a passport was not a matter of high policy, but merely an administrative decision. As such, it should be subject to full review.

---

[63] [1986] 1 WLR 331.   [64] [1989] QB 811.   [65] [1989] 2 WLR 224 at 228.

Excluded categories: a shrinking list?

The prerogative of mercy figured prominently in Lord Roskill's list of non-justiciable prerogative powers in *GCHQ*. But barely ten years later, in *R v Secretary of State for the Home Department, ex p Bentley*,[66] the Court extended its power of review to this aspect of the prerogative. Derek Bentley, a 19-year-old youth of very limited intellectual capacity, had been convicted of murder in 1952 and hanged in 1953. Bentley had been an accomplice to the actual murderer, a 16 year old, who was too young to be executed. Despite a recommendation from the jury that Bentley not be executed, the trial judge imposed the death sentence. The then Home Secretary declined to grant mercy.

The *Bentley* case was a final step in a forty-year campaign fought by Iris Bentley, the accused's sister, to establish either that her brother was innocent, or, at the very least, that he should not have received a capital sentence. By the early 1990s, Iris Bentley had convinced many people that her brother had been unjustly treated, and in 1992 she asked the Home Secretary to grant her brother a posthumous pardon. The Home Secretary (then Kenneth Clarke) refused to do so. Mr Clarke suggested that he personally believed that Bentley should not have been hanged, but that he could not grant a pardon because he had not been presented with any evidence indicating that Bentley was innocent of the murder.

Before the High Court, Iris Bentley argued that the Home Secretary had misdirected himself in law, by failing to appreciate that 'a pardon' could take several forms, not all of which required a presumption of innocence. The Court rejected the Home Secretary's assertion that this particular prerogative power was per se unreviewable, concluding that Lord Roskill's apparent assertion to that effect in *GCHQ* was simply obiter. The Court based its analysis on a seemingly logical extension of the *GCHQ* principle that: 'the powers of the court cannot be ousted merely by invoking the word 'prerogative'.[67] The issue before the Court in *Bentley* was not the essentially non-justiciable question of how the Home Secretary should have balanced the various moral and political factors involved in determining whether a pardon should be granted in this case, but the eminently 'legal' question of whether the Home Secretary should be required to re-make his decision when his original response was based on a fundamental misunderstanding of the scope of his power. In such circumstances, the Court saw no constitutional barrier to full review.

But having assumed the power to declare that Mr Clarke's decision was unlawful, the Court then declined to use it. Rather, Watkins LJ 'invited' the Home Secretary to look at the question again and 'devise some formula which would amount to a clear acknowledgment that an injustice was done'.[68] In such circumstances, the distinction between an 'invitation' and an 'order' is perhaps merely semantic: the practical effect of the Court's decision was to pull a hitherto legally unregulated aspect of the government process within a recognisably Diceyan notion of the rule of law.

V. 'Justiciability' revisited—are all statutory powers subject to full review?

The notion of justiciability is a two-edged sword. If, post-*GCHQ*, the courts' concern is now with the nature of a government power rather than its source, it would seem plausible to assume that there are (and always have been) some statutory powers whose nature makes them unsuitable for review. Once more therefore, we are drawn towards a functionalist rather than formalist interpretation of constitutional principle. *Chandler v DPP*[69] offers an example of this principle being put into practice.

---

[66] [1994] QB 349.   [67] Ibid, at 452.   [68] [1994] QB 349 at 366.   [69] [1964] AC 763, HL.

Section 1 of the Official Secrets Act 1911 made it an offence for anybody to enter any prohibited place 'for any purpose prejudicial to the safety . . . of the state'. This is obviously a national security issue, but one dealt with by statute rather than the prerogative. As part of a political campaign against nuclear weapons, Chandler entered such a prohibited place, a military airfield, and tried to immobilise planes by sitting on the runway. He was subsequently prosecuted under s 1.

His defence was that his efforts to publicise the cause of disarmament were beneficial to the safety of the state. However the House of Lords declined to be drawn into this argument. The Court held that the question of evaluating threats to national security was not justiciable. The gravity of any claimed threat to national security was an issue that could only be evaluated by the government.

This was not quite a judicial retreat back to the *Ship Money* situation. At least technically, the Court seemed to follow the precedent set in the *Zamora* case by requiring some evidence that the protestors' activities had jeopardised national security. That requirement did not seem to be very demanding however—the Court was satisfied by an affidavit from an Air Commodore simply saying that the air strip was an important defence installation, and that any intrusion into it was 'prejudicial to the safety of the state'.

This result is obviously similar to that reached twenty years later in *GCHQ*. In theory, the government is subjected to a burden of proof to demonstrate that it was indeed motivated by national security considerations. But in practice, that requirement is a formality, discharged by the most flimsy evidence. So one must beware of falling into the trap of assuming that simply putting prerogative powers on a statutory basis will make them subject to full review. National security, whether invoked under a statute or under the prerogative, seems likely always to be a non-justiciable issue.

There may perhaps come a point where there seems to be no justification for claiming that national security issues arise. One might speculate for example how the Court of Appeal would have responded in *Laker Airways* to a DoT claim that it was indeed entitled to issue 'directions' under s 4(3)—a power which arose only in respect of national security or diplomatic concerns—because in the Minister's considered opinion Laker's service did have adverse national security implications. However this theory has not yet been tested.

The post-*GCHQ* focus on the nature rather than source of governmental power also means that one should not attach great significance to the suggestions made by the (Gordon Brown led) Labour government in 2007 that some prerogative powers, notably to sign treaties and to deploy military forces might be placed on a statutory basis or subjected to statutory restrictions which would require the government to gain the express approval of the House of Commons before such powers could be used.[70] A draft 'Constitutional Renewal' document which included those proposals was published early in 2008.[71]

Conclusion

The courts supervise the government's use of prerogative powers more closely now than in the pre-revolutionary era. It is also quite clear that there has been some increase in the *theoretical* reach of the courts' power of review since the 1967 decision in *Lain*. We can also conclude that administrative law now seems to treat prerogative and statutory powers in the same way.

[70] Ministry of Justice (2007) *The governance of Britain*. For an overview of the proposals see Le Sueur A (2008) 'Gordon Brown's new constitutional settlement' *Public Law* 21.

[71] Some were enacted in the Constitutional Reform and Governance Act 2010. See further 'VII. Turning convention into law; the Ponsonby rule and the Constitutional Reform and Governance Act 2010', ch 9, pp 246–247.

The more difficult issue is to decide if the concept of non-justiciability is too widely defined. Are the courts allowing too much government action to take place free from the control of judicial review? The courts' control of the common law concept of judicial review gives the judges considerable power. By extending the scope of justiciability, the courts can place tighter controls on government's ability to behave in ways that seem inconsistent with traditional understandings of the rule of law. That looks very much like a 'red light' interpretation of the judicial function, and is a desirable result if one is suspicious of government, and fears that government powers might be used for unmeritorious ends. Alternatively, if one favours a 'green light' judicial role, believing that it is important for government to have great freedom to pursue policies which it thinks advance the national interest, one might prefer that the courts decide that more types of government action are non-justiciable. At present, the common law's power to extend review to currently non-justiciable issues obviously exists, but it is not clear under what circumstances, if any, it will be used.

The limits of the courts' willingness to expand the notion of justiciability were indicated by the Court of Appeal's 2002 judgment in *R (Abbasi) v Secretary of State for Foreign and Commonwealth Affairs.*[72] Abbasi was a British national, alleged by the US government to be a Taliban fighter, and imprisoned without trial in the Guantanamo Bay prison camp. His mother began judicial review proceedings on his behalf, seeking to establish that the Foreign Secretary was obliged to use his foreign policy prerogative to urge the US government to treat Mr Abbasi more favourably. The Court of Appeal saw little scope for intervention:

> Whether to make any representations in a particular case and if so, in what form, was left entirely to the Secretary of State's discretion. The Secretary of State had to be free to give full weight to foreign policy considerations, which were not justiciable.[73]

The scope both of judicial power to control the prerogative and of judicial unwillingness to use that power were graphically revealed by the litigation involving the Chagos Islands between 2000 and 2009. The Chagos Islands are a small archipelago in the Indian Ocean, which until the mid-1960s were formally part of the then British colony of Mauritius. The islands had some 1500 inhabitants, many of whose families had lived there for several generations, who made a very modest living in agricultural activities. In the mid-1960s, the American government decided it would like a military base on Diego Garcia, the largest of the islands. To accommodate this, the British government issued an Order in Council[74] which established the islands as a separate colony, the British Indian Ocean Territory. The Order created a 'Commissioner' to govern the islands, and granted her powers (in s 1) to make laws for the 'peace order and good government' of the islands. The Commissioner—in effect the Foreign Secretary—then issued an immigration order purportedly under the s 11 power which provided for the forcible deportation of the inhabitants and their relocation in Mauritius. The Americans were subsequently granted a lease to build their base on Diego Garcia.

After years of effort, the displaced islanders succeeded in extracting a modest amount of compensation for their removal. Some however wished to establish a right to return. The claimant in *R (Bancoult) v Secretary of State for Foreign and Commonwealth Affairs*[75] advanced several challenges to the lawfulness of the government's actions.[76] The High Court's judgment revealed a history of duplicity and casual racism in the government's[77] treatment of the

---

[72] [2002] EWCA Civ 1598, [2002] 47 LS Gaz R 29, (2002) *The Times* 8 November.

[73] Ibid, per Lord Phillips MR.   [74] The British Indian Ocean Territory Order 1965.

[75] [2001] QB 1067.

[76] It will often be the case in litigation heard many years after the actions complained of, that the 'government' which is the formal defendant in legal proceedings may have little in common (ideologically or in terms of personnel) with the 'government' which actually took the decisions in issue.

[77] The government at the relevant time was a Labour administration headed by Harold Wilson. Para 13 of the judgment of Laws LJ is the most revealing.

islanders in the 1960s. More significantly, the Court held that the immigration order was per se unlawful, on the simple basis that it could not be within the power to make law for the 'peace order and good government' of a territory to produce a law which emptied the land concerned of people who might be governed.[78]

The government in 2000 (the first Blair Labour government) responded to the judgment by accepting that its predecessors had behaved unconscionably towards the islanders and by (apparently) committing itself to allow the islanders to return. The commitment was not how-ever honoured. The ostensible basis for this was that it would not be economically feasible for the population to return, although the relatively clear reason for the government's evident change of heart was political pressure from the American government which did not wish there to be any indigenous population near its military base.

The government sought to give effect to this policy by issuing an Order in Council in 2004 which purported to create a new 'constitution' for the islands. Section 9 of the Order provided that no-one would have the right of abode in the colony other than in accordance with rules prescribed by the government. A subsequently promulgated Immigration Ordinance made it evident that the islanders themselves would not be permitted to return.

Mr Bancoult's subsequent efforts to establish that s 9 of the Order in Council was unlawful succeeded in both the High Court and the Court of Appeal,[79] essentially on the basis that the Crown did not possess a common law power wholly to depopulate a particular colony. Such a drastic political objective could only be achieved by Parliament qua sovereign law-maker.

That rationale was also supported by Lord Bingham[80] and Lord Mance[81] in the House of Lords. Unhappily for Mr Bancoult however, the majority took a different view. Lord Rodger expressed the point most clearly:

> 109 Assuming, then, that Her Majesty's constituent power can properly be described as a power to make 'laws for the peace, order and good government of the territory', such a power is equal in scope to the legislative power of Parliament . . . [I] it is not open to the courts to hold that legislation enacted under a power described in those terms does not, in fact, conduce to the peace, order and good government of the territory. Equally, it cannot be open to the courts to substitute their judgment for that of the Secretary of State advising Her Majesty as to what can properly be said to conduce to the peace, order and good government of BIOT. This is simply because such questions are not justiciable. The law cannot resolve them: they are for the determination of the responsible ministers rather than judges. In this respect, the legislation made for the colonies is in the same position as legislation made by Parliament for this country . . . In both cases, the sanction for inap-propriate use of the legislative power is political, not judicial. . . .

---

[78] See paras 53–60.

[79] *R (Bancoult) v Secretary of State for Foreign Affairs (No 2)*; [2006] EWHC 1038 in the High Court; in the Court of Appeal [2007] EWCA Civ 498, [2008] QB 365; and in the House of Lords [2008] UKHL 61, [2009] 1 AC 453. For an insightful analysis see Cohn M (2009) 'Judicial review of non-statutory executive powers after Bancoult: a unified anxious model' *Public Law* 260.

[80] [2009] 1 AC 453 at para 70: 'This is not a surprising conclusion, since the relationship between the citizen and the Crown is based on reciprocal duties of allegiance and protection and the duty of protection cannot ordi-narily be discharged by removing and excluding the citizen from his homeland. It is not, I think, suggested that those whose homes are in former colonial territories may be treated in a way which would not be permissible in the case of citizens in this country . . . . Nor is it to the point that the Queen in Parliament could have legislated to the effect of section 9: it could, but not without public debate in Parliament and democratic decision.'

[81] Ibid, at para 157: 'A colony . . . [c]onsists, first and foremost, of people living in a territory, with links to a parent state. The Crown's 'constituent' power to introduce a constitution for a ceded territory is a power intended to enable the proper governance of the territory, at least among other things for the benefit of the people inhabit-ing it. A constitution which exiles a territory's inhabitants is a contradiction in terms. The absence of any prec-edent for the exercise of the royal prerogative to exclude the inhabitants of a colony from the colony is significant, although to my mind entirely unsurprising. Until the present case, no-one can have conceived of its exercise for such a purpose'.

This might be thought a very problematic conclusion. In jurisprudential terms, its effect is essentially to place the government on an equal footing with Parliament; to suggest, in effect, that there are two sovereign law-makers. More prosaically, the majority's reasoning means that it is for the citizen to persuade Parliament to prevent the government from depriving her of even so basic an entitlement as the right to live in her homeland, rather than for the government to persuade Parliament to allow it to do so. It is, we might suggest, an example of the courts subjecting the government to the rule of politics rather than the rule of law.[82]

Lord Rodger's position does however alert us to the fact that resort to the courts is not the only means to regulate the government's use of prerogative or statutory powers. In addition to having analysed the legal mechanism of judicial review, we must also assess political methods of control; methods alluded to in Blackstone's *Commentaries* and Cockburn CJ's judgment in *Allen*. As subsequent chapters suggest, political controls of governmental behaviour can take various forms, both in shaping the way that such power is used and in providing mechanisms of accountability in respect of powers that have been 'improperly' (if not unlawfully) exercised. In chapters five and six, we consider two of those forms—the House of Commons and the House of Lords.

Suggested further reading

Academic and political commentary

TOMKINS A (2005) *Our republican constitution* ch 3

ELLIOT M and PERREAU-SAUSSINE A (2009) 'Pyrrhic public law: Bancoult and the sources, status and content of common law limitations on prerogative power' *Public Law* 697

MARKESENIS B (1973) 'The royal prerogative re-visited' *Cambridge LJ* 287

KEIR D (1936) 'The case of Shipmoney' *LQR* 546

WADE HRW (1985) 'The civil service and the prerogative' *LQR* 190

WADE HRW (1977) 'Judicial control of the prerogative' *LQR* 325

Case law and legislation

Attorney-General v De Keyser Royal Hotel [1920] AC 508

Bancoult v Secretary of State for Foreign Affairs (No.2) [2008] UKHL 61, [2009] 1 AC 453

R v Criminal Injuries Compensation Board, ex parte Lain [1967] 2 QB 864

Laker Airways v Dept of Trade [1977] 2 All ER 182

Council for Civil Service Unions v Minister for the Civil Service (GCHQ) [1985] AC 374

R v Secretary of State for Home Affairs, ex parte the Fire Brigades Union [1995] 2 AC 513

---

[82] Cf the comment that: 'the majority in *Bancoult* interprets English public law as offering a dismally modest check on the Executive's extra-territorial exercise of prerogative power'; Elliot M and Perreau-Saussine A (2009) 'Pyrrhic public law: Bancoult and the sources, status and content of common law limitations on prerogative power' *Public Law* 697 at 722.

Part Two

The Institutions and Operation of National Government

Chapter 5

The House of Commons

This chapter does not offer a comprehensive picture of the historical development and modern role of the House of Commons.[1] Rather, it sketches aspects of the relationship between the government and the legislature to develop arguments concerning the doctrines of parliamentary sovereignty and the separation of powers within the contemporary constitution.

Crown and commons—the original intent and the subsequent rise of 'party' politics

The fragmentary historical records of medieval England make it impossible to state with certainty when a body which might be regarded as the predecessor of the Commons first emerged.[2] By 1270, several national assemblies, whose members included 'commoners' and aristocrats had met under the King's authority to assist in devising solutions to political difficulties.[3] The consolidation of the Commons, Lords, and Monarch as the three 'Estates of the Realm' occurred by 1300. Members of the Lords were individually summoned by the Monarch; the members of the Commons comprised representatives of each county and borough.[4] If we accept 1688 as the birth date of the modern constitution, it is helpful to focus briefly on then prevailing perceptions of the Commons' correct constitutional functions, and, relatedly, the moral source of its governmental authority.

The Commons initially performed two distinct legislative roles. The first, inherent in its status as one Estate of the Realm, safeguarded the interests of non-aristocratic elite groups in society against the possible incursions of the Lords and/or the Crown.[5] As such, it provided

---

[1] See Silk P (1992) *How Parliament works*; Rogers R and Walters R (eds) *How Parliament works* (6th edn, 2006), esp. chs 2 and 3; Adonis A (1991) *Parliament today*; Walkland S and Ryle M (eds) (1977) *The Commons in the seventies*; Ryle M and Richards P (1988) *The Commons under scrutiny*; Norton P (2005) *Parliament in British politics* chs 2 and 5.

[2] For a brief overview see Norton (2005) op cit ch 2.   [3] Plucknett (1960) op cit pp 130–140.

[4] The electoral system through which members of the Commons are chosen is discussed in ch 7. The Commons is often referred to as the 'lower house' or 'lower chamber' of Parliament; the Lords as the 'upper house' or 'upper chamber'. The book uses these labels inter-changeably.

[5] As ch 7 suggests, this rather oversimplifies the reality.

a weak representative base to the governmental process. As explained in chapter seven, 'the people' from which the Commons was drawn prior to 1832 was a narrowly defined concept. But the notion that legitimate government demanded the consent of 'the people' rather than merely their submission was then an accepted (if flexible) principle of constitutional morality. The Commons' second legislative role was to represent local interests within the national legislature. Members were 'elected' on a geographical basis, as representatives of particular areas known as 'constituencies' and were expected to act as advocates for those areas: the Commons was as much an aggregation of localities as a 'national' forum.

The MP—representative or delegate?

By 1688, the 'national' dimension of the Commons' role was becoming dominant.[6] This is illustrated by subsequently accepted perceptions of the nature of the relationship between an MP and his electors, a perception famously articulated by Edmund Burke in his 1774 *Address to the electors of Bristol*:

> it ought to be the happiness and glory of a representative to live in the strictest union, the closest correspondence, and the most unreserved communication with his constituents. It is his duty to sacrifice his repose, his pleasures, his satisfaction to theirs; . . . and in all cases to prefer their interest to his own. But his unbiased opinion, his mature judgement, his enlightened conscience, he ought not to sacrifice . . . to any set of men living. . . . Your representative owes you, not his industry only, but his judgement: and he betrays, instead of serving you, if he sacrifices it to your opinion.

Burke's thesis is echoed in Madison's notion of representative government.[7] Legislators were not the mere delegates of their electors. Madison's words would fit unproblematically into Burke's rationale; as representatives, MPs' legislative task would be to 'refine and enlarge the public view', to 'discern the true interest of their country' and to resist pressure from their electors to sacrifice that interest to 'temporary or partial considerations'. Electors who concluded that their MP had succumbed to such pressures, or, alternatively, who favoured 'temporary and partial considerations' which their representative did not support, might subsequently choose a different MP. But what Parliament had thus far never done was pass legislation which empowered disgruntled electors to dismiss an MP who failed to follow their instructions.

Burke offers an idealised picture of the Commons; a legislative chamber in which independently minded MPs address every question in an enlightened, impartial manner, free from the fetters both of parochialism and factional allegiances. In such circumstances, one might plausibly assume that the decisions the house reached would indeed represent the 'national interest'. Whether such a governmental idyll ever did (or could) exist within the British constitution (or any other) is a moot point; more certain is that the practicalities of political life in the Parliaments which sat from 1750 onwards contained the seeds of a countervailing trend, which by 1900 had hardened into a rigid orthodoxy. In formal, legal terms the Burkean position still exists today. MPs are not legally obliged to structure their voting behaviour or work in the Commons in accordance with anybody else's wishes. Yet, in practice, the contemporary MP can defensibly be portrayed as a delegate; not of her constituents, but of her party.

The fusion of powers, the rise of the party system, and cabinet dominance of the Commons

The concept of the 'independent' MP fits comfortably with idealised versions of the separation of powers, in which the legislature and the executive were entirely discrete bodies. Yet a pure

---

[6] Plucknett (1960) op cit pp 618–619.

[7] See 'The solutions—representative government, federalism, a separation of powers, and supra-legislative "fundamental" rights', ch 1, pp 10–11.

separation of powers has always been a myth within the English (and later British) constitution. The 1688 settlement did not effect an extreme separation of powers. The Monarch, then
the formal and functional core of the executive branch of government, was also part of the
legislature. Similarly, many of his/her advisers and Ministers were members of the Lords or
Commons. The Monarch's advisers were collectively known as the Privy Council,[8] a body with
as many as fifty members. Two of the three branches of government were from the outset of
the post-revolutionary era 'fused' rather than separated.

Yet it would be simplistic to assume that an overlap of personnel necessarily precluded
an effective divergence, if not quite separation, of powers between the Commons and the
executive in the immediate post-revolutionary period. Given the turbulence of seventeenth-
century political history, it is apparent that many members of the Commons would regard
the Monarch with suspicion, even though his/her legal powers were now inferior to those
of Parliament.

The emergence of the parliamentary sovereignty doctrine produced a substantial redefinition of contemporary constitutional understandings. Yet as noted in discussing the royal
prerogative, certain pre-revolutionary principles continued to structure judicial perceptions
of the relationships between the other two branches of government. Such continuities had
political and legal dimensions.[9]

Charles II introduced the first recognisably modern 'Cabinet' when, in 1671, he effectively marginalised the Privy Council and chose to formulate government policy with a
'Cabal' of just five Ministers. Charles' initiative attracted considerable criticism; the Cabal
was seen as a factional vehicle, rather than, like the larger Privy Council, a source of diverse
and disinterested counsel. Yet despite the revolution's apparent distrust of factional government, the more centralised 'Cabinet' rather than the Privy Council formed the core of the
executive in the immediate post-revolutionary era. Furthermore, the nature of the relationship between the Monarch and his/her Ministers within the core also began to shift. Neither
George I nor George II took much interest in government affairs. By 1740, practical control
of the Cabinet rested with the occupant of the newly emergent office of 'Prime Minister'.
Sir Robert Walpole is generally regarded as the first holder of the post, but his position had
no legal basis, and it was not until 1800 that the label came into common usage.[10] George
III took close control of the government process, but since he suffered periodic bouts of
insanity, his ability to reverse the drift towards Prime Ministerial pre-eminence within the
government was limited.

The eighteenth-century Monarchs' disinclination and/or inability to lead 'their' Cabinets
coincided with the emergence of a sophisticated system of party political organisation. Outside
the Commons, the rise of the national political party was facilitated by advances in technology.
Improved transport facilities and cheaper printing meant that, for the first time, like-minded
citizens throughout the country could constantly act in concert on political issues.

The perception of the two houses containing 'a government' and 'an opposition' is again
associated with Walpole, who from 1717 led a group of MPs which for the first time saw its
raison d'etre as being to 'oppose' the government, although it is not until the 1820s that the label
'The Opposition' (meaning the second largest grouping of MPs in the house) became commonplace.[11] By then, the Cabinet, comprised almost exclusively of members of the Commons
and/or Lords, was generally formed from the leading members of the party commanding
majority support in the lower house.

---

[8] The term was in common usage by 1540; Plucknett (1960) op cit p 255. The Privy Council still exists, but
has little practical relevance except when (staffed by law lords) it sits as a final Court of Appeal for some
Commonwealth countries.

[9] See Plucknett (1960) op cit pp 610–647.   [10] See Wicks (2006) op cit ch 3.

[11] Norton P (1988) 'Opposition to government' p 100, in Ryle and Richards op cit.

As chapters six and seven suggest, the Commons had in practice become the dominant chamber within Parliament by the 1830s. By then, the Commons was beginning to be controlled by a majority party pursuing a coherent set of policy objectives, over which the Cabinet and the Prime Minister exercised substantial control. For modern observers, the perception that the Commons is little more than an arena within which the Labour and Conservative Parties alternately form the government and the opposition is a strong one. It is given considerable force simply by the physical layout of the Commons' main chamber. The 'floor of the house' places government and opposition members directly opposite each other on several rows of benches. Government Ministers and their opposition 'shadows' occupy the front benches on each side, with the rest of their party members sitting behind them.[12] That the lower house is now a body in which party factions are clearly demarcated and constantly jostle for advantage cannot seriously be disputed. Equally clearly, that contemporary reality bears little relation to the Commons' initial role in the post-revolutionary constitution.

Party discipline in the Commons: the whips and the appointment of Ministers

MPs have never been legally obliged to support their party within the house. Parties are in effect voluntary organisations, within which maintaining co-operation between members is an entirely internal matter. Within the Commons, the larger parties have developed a relatively sophisticated control mechanism known as the 'whipping system'.[13] Several MPs in each party serve as whips. They function as the party's personnel managers, ensuring that their party's MPs are deployed to maximise achievement of party objectives.

'The whip' is also used to refer to the weekly timetable of Commons business produced by each party. This alerts MPs to the significance which their party's leadership attaches to particular issues. Specific items of business will be marked with 'one line', 'two line', and 'three line' whips; the higher the number, the more important it is presumed to be that MPs participate and vote. Not all house business is whipped. For issues on which a party's leadership has no particular view, it may permit a 'free vote' in which MPs follow whichever course they consider appropriate.

Party whips are often portrayed as a purely coercive force, whose role is to persuade or threaten MPs to support party policy. That is a role they frequently perform; but they also serve as a channel for exchanging information between the front and backbenches, and will sometimes be concerned more with convincing the Cabinet that its plans will not attract sufficient backbench support than with compelling backbenchers to support party preferences. Party whips also oversee their MPs' 'pairing' arrangements, whereby two MPs of opposing parties who expect to vote in different ways agree with each other not to vote on particular occasions, thereby freeing themselves to undertake activities elsewhere. Like most aspects of Commons procedures, 'pairing' is not a legally enforceable concept, and pairs have on occasion been broken in close votes.

MPs who consistently flout party policy may have the whip withdrawn.[14] This can have severe long-term consequences. Since an MP is legally the representative of her constituency not her party, losing the party whip has no impact on her presence in the Commons. However, as chapter eight suggests, election to the Commons is now determined primarily by a candidate's party allegiance. A member not adopted as her party's candidate at the next general election is unlikely to retain her seat.

---

[12] Hence ministers and shadow ministers are often referred to as 'frontbenchers'. Members not holding such positions are 'backbenchers'.

[13] See generally Rogers and Walters op cit ch.5; Norton P (1979) 'The organisation of parliamentary parties', in Walkland S (ed) *The House of Commons in the twentieth century*.

[14] See Cross J (1967) 'Withdrawal of the Conservative Party whip' *Parliamentary Affairs* 169.

If the whipping system is in some senses the stick with which parties discipline their MPs, granting governmental or shadow office may be seen as the carrot. The power to appoint people to ministerial office nominally rests with the Monarch through her prerogative powers. The government is technically 'Her Majesty's Government'. In effect, the appointment, promotion, transfer, demotion, and dismissal of Ministers are matters for the Prime Minister. An MP's progress up (or down) what is disparagingly referred to as 'the greasy pole' is contingent on many factors, relating both to the qualities of the individual concerned and the wider political situation. But MPs who regularly diverge from party policies are unlikely to enter ministerial ranks, or to rise within them. Not all MPs seek to hold ministerial office; some will have returned to the backbenches after having previously served in government. For such members, the influence of the lure of office on their loyalty to their party is limited. For the careerist MP, however, the prospect of promotion is a powerful incentive for tailoring her own political cloth to the pattern drawn up by the party leadership.

There are no formal degrees of seniority within the Cabinet, but there is an informal hierarchy. Cabinet members are generally 'Secretaries of State' of particular government departments. The three most important (often referred to as the 'great offices of state') are Home Secretary, Foreign Secretary, and the Chancellor of the Exchequer. There is no fixed limit to the number of Ministers who may serve in the Cabinet (although at present no more than twenty-one Cabinet members may hold paid posts as Secretaries of State).[15] The number has risen over the past 150 years, from barely a dozen in the 1870s to as many as two dozen now. Nor is there any legal requirement that Cabinet Ministers be members of either house, although it is now unheard of for a Minister not to be a Member of Parliament.

'Ministers of State', several of whom are appointed for each department, occupy a lower rung of the ministerial ladder, and are rarely Cabinet members. They may nevertheless wield very substantial executive responsibilities, and if their particular Secretary of State is a member of the Lords, they will bear primary responsibility for representing their department in the Commons. At a lower level, are junior ministers known as 'Parliamentary Under Secretaries'. At the bottom of the ministerial hierarchy are 'Parliamentary Private Secretaries' (PPSs), often pejoratively referred to as ministerial 'bag carriers'.

The House of Commons Disqualification Act 1975 currently precludes the government from having more than ninety-five Ministers drawn from the Commons. The number was periodically increased throughout the twentieth century. This may be attributed in part to the post-war era's growing acceptance of green light theories of the state; since twentieth-century governments have assumed greater responsibilities than their predecessors, it is unsurprising that they need more Ministers. However, the increase may also be explained by successive governments' wishes to exercise more control over party members.[16] This argument has the force of numbers behind it; since a party needs only 340 MPs to enjoy a comfortable Commons majority, the presence of nearly 100 members in the government points to a significant merging of the executive and legislative branches. Sections II and III below consider whether this merging might defensibly be presented as an executive takeover of the lower house by assessing the Commons' roles as a contributor to the legislative process, and as a mechanism to scrutinise government behaviour.

I. Setting the context

This section focuses on three elements of the Commons' constitutional identity. The first concerns the roots of its procedural rules; the second addresses the role of 'the Speaker'; while the third considers the resources MPs have to carry out their duties.

---

[15] Ministerial and other Salaries Act 1975 s 1.   [16] de Smith op cit pp 264–265.

The sources of the Commons' procedural rules

Parliament has passed little legislation controlling the Commons' proceedings. Nor has there been any significant judicial intervention through the common law in this area.[17] Such questions have been left primarily to the house itself. Its rules currently derive from three main sources: traditional customs or 'ancient usage'; various 'standing orders' passed by the house; and Speakers' rulings.

In the absence of legislation controlling the matter in issue, the house may amend any of its procedures by a simple majority vote. Significant changes are rarely introduced so peremptorily. The notion that the house's procedures should rest on the basis of consensual reciprocity has generally been a strongly held moral principle among MPs. Major reforms are generally instigated at the recommendation of the Commons Procedure Committee.[18]

The leading source of guidance on Commons' procedure is *Erskine May's Treatise on the Law, Privileges, Proceedings and Usage of Parliament*.[19] But it would be misleading to consider such guidance, or indeed the procedures themselves, as 'laws'. The most important element of the house's working practices is the phenomenon known as 'the usual channels'—the various informal agreements made between the government and opposition parties as to how the Commons' time should be allocated. Managing the usual channels is a task allocated primarily to the Leader of the House (a senior member of the Cabinet) and the government chief whip, together with their opposition counterparts.

The house's procedural rules can be regarded as presumptions to which members voluntarily acquiesce: in part because they consider the rules intrinsically correct; in part because they feel the wishes of a majority of members should be respected; and in part because they would hope that should they form part of the Commons majority in future, the then minority would be similarly co-operative. The presumptions are not, however, irrebuttable.

The dominant presumption is that government business takes priority in each parliamentary session. This presumption is currently given force in a standing order—but that merely reflects rather than creates the government's ability to control the house's proceedings. The crucial informants of the way the Commons conducts its business are the willingness of its members to respect traditional practices, and, should that respect break down, the government's capacity to marshal majority support for its preferences.

The Commons generally sits for between 150 and 200 days per session; sessions usually begin in the autumn and run for eleven months. Each begins with 'The Queen's Speech', in which the Monarch outlines the government's planned legislative programme. There is no rigid rule as to how precisely time will be divided between the Commons' various functions. In recent years, 30%–35% of time spent on the floor of the house has been devoted to government Bills; 15%–17% has been used for motions (general debates) and ministerial statements on subjects of the government's choosing; 7%–8% has been granted to Opposition motions; 8%–10% has been for backbenchers' Bills and motions, and similar amounts have been devoted to questions to Ministers, and passing delegated legislation.

There is great scope for inter-party disagreement as to the propriety of government efforts to manage the house's workflow. Since the Commons' procedural rules are not legal phenomena, and so not subject to judicial oversight, some other arbiter is required to resolve disputes. That function is one of several performed by the Speaker.

The Speaker

The Speaker's office dates from 1376. It is her task to interpret and apply the various customs and standing orders structuring the house's proceedings. To some extent, her role is that of

---

[17] See 'Substance or procedure? the enrolled Bill rule', ch 2, pp 27–28.　　[18] Griffith and Ryle op cit pp 174–175.
[19] References here to *Erskine May* are to the 21st edition, edited by Boulton C (1989).

judge whenever disputes arise as to how parliamentary business should be managed; when, for example, the usual channels cannot produce agreement, or backbenchers feel that the government and opposition front benches are paying insufficient attention to backbench concerns. Her jurisdiction is both extensive and multi-faceted. It embraces such diverse issues as deciding which amendments are to be debated (and for how long) at the report and third reading stages of a Bill's passage; choosing which members may speak; and disciplining members whose behaviour breaches accepted standards.[20]

Before 1688, the Speaker often functioned largely as an emissary of the Crown. It was not until 1750 (when the fusion rather than separation of the executive and legislature was becoming apparent), that the Speaker had clearly become a defender of the Commons' interests against the wishes of the government.[21]

The Speaker is elected by members of the house. It is now accepted that the office is a non-party political post. The Speaker resigns from her political party on election. She nevertheless remains an MP, and acts on behalf of her constituents. She must also seek re-election to the Commons at subsequent elections, in which she stands as 'the Speaker'. She does not vote except when there is a tie; in such circumstances, tradition requires her to vote for the status quo. In the modern era, Speakers have generally been members of the majority party. However, one recent incumbent, Betty Boothroyd, was a Labour MP prior to assuming office in 1992, even though the Commons then contained a Conservative majority. Ms Boothroyd could not have won the election without significant cross-party support, a forceful indicator of the extent to which the Speaker is now perceived, in functional as well as formal terms, to be above party politics.[22] Similarly in June 2009 the Conservative MP John Bercow was elected Speaker by a house which had a substantial Labour majority.[23]

It would be inaccurate to characterise the Speaker as exercising coercive powers. Insofar as a Speaker effectively controls the house, she does so because members voluntarily submit to her authority, even when it might appear that their immediate party political interests would be better served by defiance. As such, the Speaker performs the important (if largely symbolic) task of stressing that the Commons should function as more than a vehicle for dogmatic pursuit of short-term factional advantage.

Resources

MPs are poorly resourced in comparison to their legislative contemporaries in other modern democracies.[24] In the USA, members of Congress enjoy substantial research and administrative staffs. The rationale underpinning such expansive provision is rooted in the notion of informed consent to government. Legislators are unlikely effectively to contribute to the legislative process, nor searchingly evaluate the merits of government behaviour, if they lack access to expert analysis of relevant information.[25]

Yet in the mid-1980s, the Commons offered only 350 offices to its 650 members. Many MPs were consequently forced to share office space. Many offices were extremely small—few could accommodate secretarial and research staff. MPs are not richly endowed with supporting

---

[20] See Borthwick R (1988) 'The floor of the house', in Ryle and Richards op cit; Adonis (1990) op cit ch 4; Silk op cit pp 71–76; Laundy P (1979) 'The Speaker and his office in the twentieth century', in Walkland op cit.

[21] We examine this issue further in ch. 8.

[22] The Speaker is not always in the chair when the Commons is in session. Her presence is generally reserved only for the most important parts of the Commons' timetable. Often, her role is taken by one of three deputy speakers, first among whom is the 'Chairman of Ways and Means'.

[23] <http://www.timesonline.co.uk/tol/news/politics/article6556617.ece>

[24] See generally Bennet P and Pullinger S (1991) *Making the Commons work*; Rogers and Walters op cit ch 3.

[25] For a more expansive account see Lock G (1988) 'Information for Parliament' in Ryle and Richards op cit; Griffith J (1974) *Parliamentary scrutiny of government bills* ch 8.

staff. Members presently receive an allowance of some £190,000 per year for office and staff expenses,[26] a sum insufficient to employ an extensive administrative and research staff.

The Commons has what might initially seem a substantial library. The library employs some 150 staff, many of whom devote all their time to researching MPs' queries. The Commons library is however a modest affair compared to the US Library of Congress. In the 1990s, the Commons employed fewer than 700 staff to service its 650 MPs; the slightly smaller number of legislators in the US Congress had some 20,000 employees.[27]

It is difficult to accept that successive governments' unwillingness to afford MPs more substantial logistical support is motivated by financial considerations: facilities comparable to those in the USA would add only a tiny amount to public expenditure. Adequate resourcing would impose a 'cost' upon a government, but the cost would be political rather than financial. A comment from *The Economist* offers a cynical explanation of the current situation:

> the government of the day has little to gain by giving Parliaments their own source of knowledge and advice. Why spend money providing information for backbenchers, when ignorance keeps them so much more malleable?[28]

Any substantial increase in expenditure would require the support of a majority of MPs, which is unlikely to be forthcoming without government approval. By the mid-1990s, repeated expressions of backbench dissatisfaction with Commons' working conditions had apparently borne some fruit; the government accepted that sufficient resources should be provided to ensure that every MP at least had her own office within or adjacent to the Palace of Westminster.

Nor are MPs' salaries particularly high. They are currently about £75,000 per year, which obviously would not permit the member to finance the research and secretarial assistance she might consider appropriate.[29] MPs have traditionally also been entitled to claim various expenses, relating to travel and, for those representing constituencies outside London, up to £22,000 towards the cost of maintaining a second home in the London area. Notwithstanding this supplement to the basic salary, an MP's remuneration may compare poorly with that paid to senior members of the professions. MPs were not paid at all until the early-twentieth century. The present rather low level of salaries perhaps provides members with a financial incentive for seeking ministerial office, for which a substantial additional salary is payable. However, being a backbench MP need not be a 'full-time job': many backbench MPs derive income from other forms of employment, such as journalism, legal practice, directorships of companies, or 'consultancies' for commercial organisations.

The case for more expansive (and expensive) provision of financial support for MPs was substantially undermined by a minor scandal in 2008. The house's rules for the payment of administrative and personal expenses had always been remarkably lax, and a succession of press stories emerged suggesting that some MPs had been taking improper advantage of the system.[30] The episode led to a thorough overhaul of the expenses system, involving both a restriction of the items and amounts for which claims could be made and greatly increased transparency in respect of claims submitted. The Brown government promoted a Bill enacted as the Parliamentary Standards Act 2009. The Act created an Independent Parliamentary Standards Authority (IPSA) with responsibility for monitoring expenses claims, and—in the longer term—making recommendations about MPs' salaries and other payments.[31]

---

[26] See generally Rogers and Walters op cit pp 64–67. For a detailed breakdown of the current figures see <http://www.theipsa.org.uk/media/1617/9-mps-scheme-of-business-costs-and-expenses-2017-18-updated.pdf>.

[27] Adonis (1990) op cit p 62.   [28] Cited in Lock op cit at p 52.

[29] MPs with substantial personal wealth who spend some of it on assistance in carrying out their political duties, have a distinct advantage over their less affluent counterparts.

[30] For details see the seventh edition of this book at pp 129–130.

[31] See the IPSA website at: <http://www.parliamentarystandards.org.uk/about%20us/Pages/default.aspx>; both for an explanation of IPSA's role and regular publication of MPs' expenses claims.

The involvement of many MPs in paid extra-parliamentary activities also has some bearing on the Commons' traditionally bizarre working hours. Until recently, activity on the floor of the house generally did not begin until 2.30pm and frequently did not end until the early hours of the morning. Mornings would thus be free for other activities. This was very convenient if an MP was in legal practice or serving as a director or consultant for commercial interests. Modest timetable reforms were introduced in 1994. The reforms introduced a limited number of morning sittings in the chamber, abolished some Friday sittings, and proposed an earlier end to business on Thursdays. The change marked at least a modest first step towards a more far-reaching normalisation of MPs' working hours. Further steps in this direction were taken in 2002.

Some MPs do regard membership of the Commons as a full-time occupation. When not in the chamber, they will be attending to matters arising in their respective constituencies, or participating in the work of the Commons' various committees. Such backbenchers appear to be a minority however. This may be because some members now see election to the Commons as a means to other professional or financial ends, rather than as an end in itself. But it may also be, as is suggested in section III of this chapter, because realistic backbench MPs doubt that their individual and collective presence in the house will often have a significant impact, either on the content of legislation or the behaviour of the government.[32] What has been said so far might suggest that the balance of power between the government and the Commons is weighted heavily in the government's favour. This is unsurprising given the fused nature of the government/Commons relationship: in that context, the notion of a meaningful separation between the house and the executive is a misleading dichotomy. The following sections consider whether the dichotomy currently has any merit at all.

II. The passage of legislation

Commentators now seem to agree that the modern House of Commons is rarely a law-*making* body in any meaningful sense. Norton suggests, for example:

> Although some writers continue to list 'legislation' as one of the functions of the House of Commons, it is a function which for all intents and purposes has not been exercised by the house in the twentieth century.[33]

Gavin Drewry expresses a similar scepticism:

> [S]ome would question whether in reality the Westminster Parliament, dominated as it is by a powerful executive, able in most circumstances to mobilise majority support in the division lobbies, can properly be called a 'legislature' at all.[34]

John Griffith's comprehensive study of the Commons in the 1967–1971 sessions, concluded that:

> [T]he direct impact of the House on Government proposals for legislation was unimpressive. . . . On no occasion was the government either defeated or forced to make a tactical retreat . . . [T]he visible result of a great deal of Opposition and Government backbench activity was very small indeed.[35]

Such critiques contend that the content of legislation is effectively determined in Cabinet. Governments formulate policies which they expect to command the support of their party's members in the Commons, and it is rare that their preferences will be significantly amended

---

[32] (1976) *Report of the Committee on financial aid to political parties* (Cmnd 6601).
[33] Norton (1985) op cit p 81.   [34] Drewry (1988) op cit p 122.   [35] (1974) op cit p 206.

during a Bill's passage. Thus one might suggest that in examining the significance of the Commons' legislative role, one should direct attention to considering its efficacy in influencing or pressurising the government to modify or withdraw its proposals.

The various stages a Bill undergoes in its Commons passage now possess a sacrosanct constitutional status.[36] The process begins with the 'first reading'; a purely formal step, in which the measure is introduced to the house. Consideration of the Bill's main principles occurs during 'second reading', a major set piece debate on the floor of the house. If the Bill is approved,[37] its details are addressed in a 'standing committee', which is empowered to amend the original text. On leaving the standing committee, the Bill returns to the floor for its 'report stage', when any committee amendments (or new ones proposed by the government) are considered. On completing its report stage, the Bill (as amended) enters its 'third reading'. If approved by the house, it is then sent to the Lords.[38] This process has no legal basis. It is a matter purely of custom and tradition.

There are no rigid rules concerning the time taken for a Bill to pass through the legislative process, although until 2003 a government or private member's Bill had to complete all its stages in a single parliamentary session. In emergency situations, a Bill may be passed in days or even hours. Such measures are unlikely to have received mature consideration. Conversely, controversial Bills on major issues may spend six months or more in the Commons.[39]

A government with majority support may at any stage of a Bill's passage subject it to an 'allocation of time order', colloquially called the 'guillotine'.[40] The guillotine specifies in advance precisely how long shall be allocated to discussion of a Bill's provisions. Once that time expires, debate ends, irrespective of how much of a Bill remains undiscussed.

Allocation of time orders raises sensitive issues. They may from one perspective be viewed as elevating governmental expediency above the principle that proposed legislation should receive rigorous Commons discussion. Alternatively, they can be seen as a legitimate means for the government to overcome bloody-minded obstructionism by minority parties. Before 1980, governments were most reluctant to deploy the guillotine, evidently for fear of the adverse publicity such a move might generate.[41] However, recent Conservative governments had fewer qualms about the constitutional propriety of doing so.[42] Feelings in the house over this issue were sufficiently inflamed in 1994 for the Labour Party to withdraw from the usual channels and commit itself to being as obstructive as possible to the conduct of government business.

Second reading

Second reading debates on government Bills are opened and closed by speeches from the Bill's sponsoring Ministers, each of whom is followed by her opposition counterpart. During the central period of the debate, the Speaker controls the order in which MPs are called to speak, although tradition demands that she alternately chooses members of the government and opposition parties. In major debates, demand to speak is intense. This demand has been met to some extent since 1988, when a standing order was introduced which permitted the Speaker to limit individual speeches to a maximum of ten minutes.[43] This helps to ensure that the house is exposed to a wide range of views on the merits of the government's proposed policy.

---

[36] A helpful introduction is provided by Norton (2005) op cit ch 5 and by Rogers and Walters op cit ch 7.

[37] At all stages, a bare majority of members voting in favour amounts to approval.

[38] A Bill may originate in the Lords, in which case it would be sent for the Royal Assent after the Commons' third reading. For an informative study of the passage of a controversial measure see Rose H (1973) 'The Immigration Act 1971: a case study in the work of Parliament' *Parliamentary Affairs* 69.

[39] See Adonis (1990) op cit ch 5; Silk op cit pp 138–139.

[40] See Erskine May op cit pp 409–416; Griffith and Ryle op cit pp 225–228.

[41] For the 1974–1988 period see the helpful table in Griffith and Ryle op cit p 303.

[42] Adonis op cit p 70.   [43] Silk op cit p 92.

It is unlikely that a contribution by an individual MP, or even a series of like-minded speeches, will persuade members to vote other than on party lines. To some degree, labelling the second reading stage as a 'debate' is misleading. Proceedings are rarely characterised by the cut and thrust of attack and immediate defence. Many members merely recite prepared speeches which outline a particular element of party policy. This is not to say second reading debates are worthless—but that they have little immediate impact on the content of a Bill.

Second readings are also valuable simply because of their visibility to the wider public. Debates on major Bills are widely reported in the press and on radio and television. Such coverage does not alert voters to the details of government and opposition arguments, but the glare of publicity may prompt both government and opposition to ensure that their policies do not markedly diverge from the wishes of the general public.[44]

Standing committees

The Commons' capacity to pass Bills would be much reduced if their details, as well as their principles, had to be debated on the floor of the house. Thus, while measures of major constitutional significance may undergo their committee stage on the floor, most Bills are sent 'upstairs' to be examined by a standing committee of between sixteen and fifty MPs.

Membership of standing committees reflects the party balance in the whole house. Thus a government with a comfortable majority is assured of a proportionate advantage at the committee stage. Standing committees on government Bills always include the sponsoring Minister and her shadow. Other members are formally chosen by the house's own Committee of Selection, which takes into account a member's fields of expertise when making its choices. But selection is in practice controlled by the party whips, and it is unlikely that the whips would support inclusion of an MP whose expertise might lead her to reject party policy.

That said, Ministers face more rigorous questioning in committee than on the floor. This is due in part to the nature of the committee's task: effective scrutiny of detail demands expertise and intellectual precision, rather than the rhetorical skills that may suffice on the floor. In addition, committee proceedings generally attract less media attention than second reading debates. Insofar as MPs are playing to an audience when in committee, it is to an audience of colleagues, most likely to be impressed by an incisive and knowledgeable dissection of the Bill's provisions.[45]

At the committee stage (unless a guillotine has been imposed), the allocation of time to particular clauses is determined by the Chairman. The Chairman also decides which amendments may be moved. Amendments may not contradict the Bill's main principles as approved at second reading, but should be directed at questions of detail.[46] In practice, it appears that most committee amendments are introduced by the government itself, either to correct previously unnoticed errors, or to respond to what the government regards as acceptable concerns expressed by MPs or other interest groups.[47]

There must however be doubt as to the efficacy even of the standing committee's more searching and informed deliberations when dealing with a government dogmatically attached to the details as well as principles of its legislative programme. This point is forcefully made by Adonis' discussion of the passage of the Thatcher government's Bills to privatise the water and electricity services.[48] The electricity Bill consumed over 100 hours of committee time. It was amended 114 times. 113 amendments were moved by the government. The other was one (of twenty-two) moved by a Conservative backbencher. None of the 227 opposition amendments were carried.

---

[44] Cf Lord Bingham's dissenting judgment in *Bancoult (No 2)*; see 'Conclusion', ch 4, pp 100–103.

[45] See eg the account of the impression made in 1992 by the then junior backbench Labour MPs Gordon Brown and Tony Blair on the Conservative Minister Alan Clark; Clark A (1993) *Diaries* pp 53–54.

[46] Although so-called 'wrecking amendments' are occasionally introduced at other stages of the legislative process.

[47] See especially Griffith (1974) op cit ch 3; Norton (1985) op cit ch 5.   [48] (1990) op cit pp 103–104.

Report and third reading

Since the mid-1960s, the report stage of government Bills has consumed some 10% of time spent on the floor of the house.[49] This gives some indication of its potential importance within the legislative process. The report stage enables the house to consider a Bill in its entirety as amended in committee. It also offers the opportunity for further amendments to be moved. Controversial Bills may require several days of the house's time.

For most Bills which complete the report stage, the third reading is a mere formality. A debate may be held if six members request one. It is possible for a government Bill to be rejected at the third reading debate, but it is difficult to conceive of circumstances (other than those where a government has only a minority of MPs in the house) when this might occur.

Conclusion

It has become a cliché to suggest that the Common's role in respect of government Bills is now 'legitimation rather than legislation'. The inference seems to be that because the Commons is an elected body, the wishes of the majority of its members necessarily ensure that its decisions have a 'democratic' basis. As chapter seven will suggest, that assumption is itself problematic: as was noted in chapter one, legitimacy and democracy may demand rather more than simple majoritarianism.

Yet, seemingly paradoxically, there now also appears to be an academic consensus that backbench MPs have become more assertive since 1970 in resisting government policies of which they disapprove.[50] An MP's capacity to do this effectively depends in part on the size of the government's majority, and in part on the number of like-minded colleagues who support her cause. The first Wilson government (1964–1966), which had a majority of only four, found its plans to bring the steel industry into public ownership were blocked by the refusal of two Labour MPs to vote with the government.[51] One may also identify several instances in the mid-1980s when the Thatcher government, with substantial Commons majorities, misread the mood of its backbenchers and found itself obliged to abandon Bills. The most spectacular example was provided by the Shops Bill 1986, a measure designed to liberalise Sunday trading laws. The government had correctly anticipated that Labour MPs would oppose the measure because of its impact on shopworkers. The government had not expected that many backbench Conservatives would support a campaign orchestrated by religious groups to 'Keep Sunday Special'. Squeezed by this unlikely alliance, the Bill was defeated on second reading.[52]

We will examine several more examples of such behaviour over significant policy issues (by Labour, Liberal, and Conservative MPs) in subsequent chapters. Such episodes may defensibly be regarded as exceptions to a more general rule; namely that the passage of government Bills through the Commons is dependent not so much on the intrinsic merit of their contents, nor on the skill which Ministers display in defending them on the floor or in committee, but on the size and cohesiveness of the governing party's majority. An intriguing study of standing committee activity since 2000 suggests that committees are devoting more time to their task and generating rather more media attention, yet are having no discernibly more significant effect on the content of government Bills.[53] But government measures are not the only Bills which the Commons considers. In respect of 'private members' Bills, different considerations may apply.

---

[49] Griffith and Ryle op cit p 237; Silk op cit p 135.

[50] For statistical information see Griffith and Ryle op cit pp 118–130. More generally see Johnson N (1988) 'Departmental select committees', in Ryle and Richards op cit; Norton P (1980) *Dissension in the House of Commons* 1974–1979.   [51] See Pimlott B (1992) *Harold Wilson* pp 357–359.

[52] Three other Bills were withdrawn during that Parliament. None could be regarded as of great importance. See Drewry (1988) op cit pp 134–136.

[53] See Thompson L (2013) 'More of the same or a period of change? The impact of Bill Committees in the twenty first century House of Commons' *Parliamentary Affairs* 459.

Private members' Bills

A few Bills are introduced every session by backbench members. Twelve Friday sittings per session are currently allocated for dealing with such measures. There is in theory no limit to the number of Bills that an MP can introduce. Many Bills are presented to the house simply because the sponsoring MP may wish to draw attention to herself or to a particular issue. But if the Bill is to have any realistic prospect of being enacted, it must be initiated through one of two mechanisms.

The most significant is the annual ballot under SO 13. Any backbencher may enter the ballot. Twenty 'winners' are drawn. The first six are allocated top place in the order of business on a given Friday for a second reading. These six then assume priority on subsequent Fridays for their report and third reading over the second readings of the other fourteen Bills. The popularity of the procedure is due in part to the high profile that a full second reading debate can give to its sponsor. But the attractiveness is not solely a matter of publicity. Almost 200 Bills introduced through this method were enacted between 1974 and 1989.[54] It thus offers some MPs a good opportunity to make a legislative mark.

Such Bills have sometimes introduced important legislative reforms in areas which generate considerable moral controversy, but in respect of which opinion does not divide along traditional party lines. The most obvious (and oft-quoted) example of such legislation is the Abortion Act 1967 (sponsored by David Steel MP).[55] The process is also frequently deployed to rationalise archaic legislation, or to introduce a regulatory framework around newly emergent social or legal problems.[56]

There is little immediate point in backbenchers launching initiatives to which the government is opposed. The carrot and stick modes of intra-party discipline wielded by the Prime Minister and the whips do not suddenly disappear just because a Bill emanates from a backbencher. The government has no obligation to allow free votes on such Bills, although there is perhaps some moral pressure to do so. However, allowing a free vote may sometimes suit a government's purposes very well. An obvious benefit of so doing is to foster the impression that the government respects the independence of MPs as individuals, and of the Commons as a collectivity. On issues about which the government has no strong policy preferences, such action is a substantively painless way of rebutting suggestions that the executive wields an unhealthy degree of control over the legislative process. Equally, a government may conclude that facilitating the passage of a private member's Bill in respect of a policy which it supports, but which might be unpopular among its MPs or the electorate, is a useful way of achieving preferred outcomes without having to take responsibility for having done so.

The backbencher's need for government support also has a more mundane dimension. Pressures on the Commons' legislative timetable make it unlikely that Bills other than the first three or four in the ballot could be passed if the government does not allocate some of its own time for their passage. For a government with time to spare, making a little available to backbench initiatives is a painless way to curry favour with the house. The Labour governments of 1964–1970 offered time to over twenty backbench Bills.[57] In contrast, during the 1980s, successive Conservative governments did not appear concerned to facilitate such expression of backbench opinion: the Thatcher administrations were notably reluctant to devote government time to private members' Bills.[58]

---

[54] Silk op cit p 117.

[55] For an illuminating discussion see Richards P (1970) *Parliament and conscience* ch 5. The effect of the Act was discussed at 'The golden rule', ch 3, p 56.

[56] See Silk op cit pp 117–118; Griffith and Ryle op cit pp 386–390.

[57] Norton (1985) op cit p 102.   [58] Griffith and Ryle op cit p 398.

Conversely, the private member's Bill can also offer governments with over-full legislative programmes a means to grab an even greater share of the Commons' time. A backbencher promoting a Bill with which the government sympathises may find herself invited to modify her measure in accordance with ministerial preferences in return for assistance in finding the necessary Commons time to push it through.[59]

Backbenchers may also try to initiate legislation though the 'ten-minute rule Bill' process provided by SO 19. One such Bill may be introduced each Tuesday and Wednesday. Its sponsoring member makes a brief (hence 'ten minute' rule) statement to the house outlining its objectives; an equal time is given to a member wishing to oppose the measure.

The procedure offers MPs a public platform when the house is often packed. But ten minute rule Bills are not a serious component of the legislative process. While most are formally allowed to proceed by the house, there is minimal chance that they will be enacted as there is so little time available for them. It is not unusual for periods of several years to pass without a single ten minute rule reaching the statute book. Their function might more sensibly be seen as affording an MP a high profile public forum from which to raise an issue of current concern, in the hope that either a government department or another MP who tops the private member's ballot will introduce a like measure. There are, as always, exceptions to the general rule. The Sexual Offences Act 1967, which repealed legislation criminalising homosexual acts between consenting adults, emerged from the ten minute rule. It is however clear that its passage was largely dependent on the government's willingness to find time for it to be enacted.[60]

Private members' Bills are quantitatively insignificant compared to government Bills. Equally, many of them address minor issues. Nevertheless they do occasionally effect major changes on matters of considerable substance. What they do not do is provide a vehicle through which the 'independence' of the Commons is promoted over and above party loyalties on a substantial and systematic scale.

Private Bills

'Private' Bills are a different form of legislative creature than private members' Bills, which are technically, like government Bills, 'public' measures. Private Bills confer certain benefits or obligations on a narrowly defined class of persons or companies, or authorise specific works or activities in a particular area.[61]

Bills are introduced to the Commons not by a government department or an MP, but by the interested parties themselves. The parties are represented in the house by lawyers styled as 'parliamentary agents'. As chapter two suggested when discussing the *Wauchope* litigation, the house's standing orders require the promoters to notify any affected third parties of the Bill's intentions. After second reading, a private Bill is sent to a special committee of four members which examines it in detail. It is at this stage that the significance of the need to notify affected parties becomes apparent. Clearly, if affected persons have not been notified of the Bill's passage, they cannot present their point of view to the Committee, which will thus proceed on the basis of incomplete information.

The very different process used to enact private statutes, and the generally sectional interests which they serve, perhaps lend force to Lord Denning's suggestion in *Pickin* that the courts should reconsider their traditional refusal to assess the procedural propriety of the legislative process. The mechanism was subject to an intensive investigation by a joint Lords/Commons select committee in the late-1980s, but as yet no significant reforms have been introduced.

[59] eg the Chronically Sick and Disabled Persons Act 1970 and Sexual Offences Act 1967; see Griffith and Ryle op cit pp 392–393 and Silk op cit pp 116–117.   [60] Richards (1970) op cit ch 4.
[61] As noted in ch 2, the device was often used in respect of the construction of railways.

Delegated legislation

It would be inaccurate to suggest that most laws under which the British people now live have received searching Commons scrutiny. This is due only in part to the logistical and party political constraints operating on the house's analysis of Bills. Its major cause is the government's increasing tendency to promote Bills which delegate secondary law-making power to Ministers through the mechanism of 'regulations' or 'statutory instruments' (SIs).[62] Under this form of law-making, the 'parent' Act sketches the broad confines of the power conferred upon the government, leaving the Minister to fill in the details in SIs. The mechanism represents something of a half-way house in procedural terms between purely legislative and purely executive law-making.

SIs spare Ministers the time-consuming and potentially problematic task of putting their policy preferences into a Bill and trying to pilot it through the Commons. SIs have been favoured by governments of both parties in the modern era, largely because the growing scope of government intervention in social and economic life means that the house would not have time to deal with all matters through primary legislation. Since 1980, the government's resort to SIs has continued apace: over 1,000 per year have been passed on average. Some are exceedingly trivial—a favourite example being the Baking and Sausage Making (Christmas and New Year) Regulations 1985.[63] Others have profound constitutional implications; the law under which Mr Liversidge was imprisoned was an SI. Delegated legislation can afford Ministers sweeping powers in important areas of governmental activity.

A political party's protests (when in opposition) against SIs should consequently be regarded sceptically—it seems likely that any 'principles' which underlie them would be quietly forgotten when that party next formed a government. For constitutional lawyers, however, the issues of principle have more force, since they bear directly on the questions of the sovereignty of 'Parliament' and the separation of powers, and indirectly on the question of what type of 'democracy' the constitution currently upholds. Are statutory instruments a substratum of the legislative process, or would it be more realistic to regard them as 'law-making by the executive'?

Contemporary principles and practice

Use of delegated legislation assumed considerable prominence in the late 1920s, following publication of a book called *The new despotism* by Lord Chief Justice Hewart.[64] Hewart, in a Diceyan vein, deplored Parliament's practice of affording Ministers what he regarded as arbitrary bureaucratic powers. The critique was hyperbolic, but focused attention on the distinction between substantive and procedural conceptions of the rule of law. In theoretical terms, a parent Act does not (and indeed cannot) bestow an unfettered power upon a Minister: she does not thereby become in any sense a 'sovereign legislature'; her powers are confined by the terms of the 'parent' legislation. Consequently, the terms of statutory instruments are subject to judicial review to ensure that they do not exceed the competence Parliament has granted.[65] But neither does the process require that the Commons consider every detail of each SI 'enacted'.

Hewart might be seen as concerned entirely with matters of process; it is not what government does that is the problem, but how government does it. Its intervention would be acceptable if only it had exposed its plans to the rigorous scrutiny attaching to the passage of primary legislation. An obvious response to such an argument would be to highlight the Commons' limited role even in respect of most statutes.

---

[62] This somewhat oversimplifies the terminology; see Griffith and Ryle op cit p 245; *Erskine May* pp 539–541.
[63] See Silk op cit pp 148–149.
[64] See Harlow and Rawlings (1984) op cit pp 119–130.   [65] See *Chester v Bateson* [1920] 1 KB 829.

That dichotomy is somewhat misleading. Issues of process and substance are necessarily linked. It is not possible to govern a highly interventionist unitary state solely through primary legislation.[66] To reject altogether the process of delegated legislation therefore is to reject the substance of social democratic government. Hewart's attack led the government to establish the Donoughmore Committee,[67] which responded to Hewart much as Harry Jones later critiqued Hayek's minimalist notion of the rule of law.[68] Delegated legislation was a necessity in modern society. The issue therefore becomes how best to ensure that this unavoidable fact of political life departed as little as possible from orthodox constitutional understandings of the legislative/executive relationship.

Donoughmore recommended that Standing Committees on delegated legislation be created in both the Lords and Commons to examine the technicalities and vires of proposed SIs. Their purpose would not be to question the merits of government policy per se, but to 'supply the private member with knowledge which he lacks at present and thus enable him to exercise an informed discretion whether to object or criticise himself'.[69]

The Statutory Instruments Act 1946

Neither Parliament as a whole, nor the Commons itself made an immediate, far-reaching response to the Donoughmore report. A Commons Committee on Statutory Instruments was established in 1944, and the procedures through which SIs were to pass were rationalised by the Statutory Instruments Act 1946. The Act sketches out principles as to the processes to be followed; subsequent parent Acts may opt out of the 1946 Act if the enacting Parliament so wishes, and (ironically) ss 8–9 allow the legislation's scope to be altered by subsequent delegated legislation. A further step supposedly intended to enhance MPs' awareness of and control over the contents of SIs was made in 1972, when a Joint Commons/Lords Committee on Statutory Instruments (the 'scrutiny committee') was established.

Some SIs receive no consideration in the house at all. Most are however dealt with by either the 'affirmative' or 'negative' resolution procedure specified in the 1946 Act. The affirmative procedure prevents the passage of an SI into law unless it is approved by majority vote in the house. The initiative thus rests with the government (within forty days) both to defend the measure in debate, and to ensure it is voted through. Debates on affirmative resolutions on the floor are infrequent and short in duration. Most examination is undertaken 'upstairs' in the Standing Committee on Statutory Instruments, although the support of twenty members is sufficient to compel the Minister to schedule debate for the floor of the house. Committee debates rarely exceed ninety minutes per SI. The Committee's role is merely that of consideration. It cannot amend the SI: nor does it exercise delegated power to pass the measure; the subsequent vote is still taken by the whole house.

It is accepted that the more important SIs should be subject to the affirmative procedure, although this is not a legally enforceable provision, and there is obvious scope for disagreement between government and opposition on how to gauge an SI's importance. During the 1980s, some 20% of SIs were subject to affirmative resolutions.[70]

The 'negative resolution' procedure passes the initiative to the opposition parties, who may invite the house to vote against the instrument's passage into law, again within a forty-day period. Debate may be taken either on the floor of the house (generally late at night) or in standing committee. Once again, access to both fora is controlled by the government. Little time is allocated for debate before the whole house: Silk notes for example that the 9,500 SIs

---

[66] The problem of 'legislative overload' is less acute in a federal state; its scale varying in inverse proportion to the scope of the powers afforded to the central legislature.

[67] Donoughmore, Lord (1932) *Report of the Committee on Ministers' Powers* (Cmnd 4060).

[68] See 'II. The rule of law in the welfare state, ch 3', pp 51–52.

[69] Donoughmore op cit at pp 63–64; quoted in Himsworth C (1995) 'The delegated powers scrutiny committee' *Public Law* 34 at p 37.   [70] Silk op cit p 151.

subject to the negative resolution procedure between 1974 and 1985 attracted barely 200 hours of debate.[71] One might therefore be forgiven for thinking that the process serves little useful purpose beyond enabling a determined opposition to inconvenience a government with a small majority by disrupting its parliamentary timetable.[72]

The Joint Committee on Statutory Instruments plays, in quantitative terms, a more significant role. It is generally chaired by an opposition MP, which lends it an aura of independence. Its members are supposed to eschew party political issues, and to refrain from questioning the merits of a given SI's policy, and to focus instead on the narrower, legal question of the SI's compatibility with its parent Act. In the event of apparent inconsistency, the Committee will draw the SI to the house's attention, which may then proceed as it wishes. Neither the government nor the house is obliged to accept the Committee's opinions. Nor would a court be precluded from holding an SI ultra vires because the Committee had concluded its contents lay within the Minister's powers.

The vast quantity of SIs approved by the house each year, and the obvious limitations which attach to MPs' scrutiny of such measures, forcefully illustrate the extent to which the government effectively controls the legislative process. They are not however the most draconian example of the constitution's seeming capacity to reconcile the de jure sovereignty of 'Parliament' with the de facto supremacy of the executive.

'Henry VIII clauses'

The Donoughmore Committee expressed grave reservations about the growing (but still quantitatively insignificant) parliamentary practice of enacting 'Henry VIII' clauses in primary legislation. Such provisions empower a government Minister to use SIs to amend or even repeal existing Acts of Parliament. The label stems from the Statute of Proclamations 1539. Henry VIII, presumably having doubts about the constitutional status of his prerogative powers vis-à-vis legislation and other common law rules, prevailed upon an unwilling Commons and Lords to pass a Bill confirming that the Monarch's proclamations were equal in force to Acts. Once enacted, this legislation would, by virtue of the *lex posterior* rule, enable the King to repeal or alter existing statutes without further recourse to Parliament; to—as Plucknett put it—'play the despot by the co-operation of Parliament'.[73] The language of the Act is obviously archaic, but its meaning is nonetheless clear:

> Be it therefore enacted . . . that always the king for the time being, with the advice of his honourable council, . . . may set forth at all times by authority of this act his proclamations, under such penalties and pains and of such sort as to his highness and his said honourable council or the more part of them shall see[m] necessary and requisite; and that those same shall be obeyed, observed, and kept as though they were made by act of parliament.

Applying the Henry VIII nomenclature to contemporary manifestations of this practice has the unfortunate tendency of belittling their constitutional significance. The relative superiority of statute to the prerogative was not established in the sixteenth century; the King might plausibly have achieved the same result through direct exercise of his proclamatory power. Furthermore, the Statute of Proclamations itself was hedged about with restrictions which substantially compromised its utility.[74] And, most importantly, neither Henry VIII, nor Tudor Parliaments, had any need to justify their behaviour in terms of 'democratic' principle.

---

[71] Op cit p 152. See also Griffith and Ryle op cit pp 345–350.

[72] See Punnet R (1968) *British government and politics* p 333. See also Drewry (1988) op cit.

[73] Plucknett (1960) op cit p 233.

[74] Plucknett (1960) op cit pp 233–234; Elton G (1960) 'Henry VIII's Act of Proclamations' *English Historical Review* 208; Bush M (1983) 'The Act of Proclamations: a reinterpretation' *American Journal of Legal History* 33.

There is no legal impediment to Parliament granting what is formally a 'circumscribed portion of legislative competence to a subordinate Minister'.[75] The power may at any time be withdrawn, and subsequent Parliaments may undo whatever 'legislative' work the designated Minister has done. Different issues arise if one asks if the practice is politically legitimate in modern society.

Until recently, the dubious moral basis of Henry VIII clauses seems to have led Parliament to enact them sparingly. The authors of the 1985 edition of de Smith's *Constitutional and Administrative Law* concluded that:

> this formulation is not widely used, and it is normally innocuous if the grant of power is confined to a limited period for the purpose of enabling draftsmen to make consequential adaptations to miscellaneous enactments that may have been overlooked when the principal Act was passed.[76]

This view of Henry VIII clauses sees them essentially as time-saving devices for remedying unintended errors in primary legislation. As such they would be only mildly objectionable, as they spare the government the consequences of its own incompetence. More recently however, governments have seemingly regarded Henry VIII clauses as an acceptable means to implement sweeping policy programmes. This trend scaled new heights of executive law-making in the Deregulation and Contracting Out Act 1994 introduced by the Major government.[77] The Act empowered the Secretary of State for Trade and Industry to make regulations to suspend any existing legislation which he/she considered imposes a burden on any economic activity, and to transfer many government functions allocated by statute to a Minister to any private sector organisation.

The Act suggested that the Major government regarded the legislative process as an unwelcome obstacle which it was entitled to circumvent whenever convenient. Whether that is construed as a welcome development depends presumably on the observer's party affiliation; and that is in itself perhaps a telling indictment of the extent to which the Commons is prone, even on significant issues, to operate simply as a vehicle for promoting the wishes of whichever faction currently forms a majority of its members.

Conclusion

From a legislative perspective, therefore, a Commons 'independent' of the executive is likely to occur only when the government cannot command a reliable majority. Yet it would seem likely that such circumstances will promote paralysis rather than consensus in the house. The implications that the Commons' essentially factional, antagonistic approach to the legislative process has for the democratic basis of the constitution cannot fully be appreciated until we explore in later chapters the relationship between the Commons and the Lords, and between the Commons and the people. In the remainder of this chapter, we address another dimension of the relationship between the Commons and the government.

III. Controlling the executive

Although a government's legislative programme is often viewed as its *raison d'être*, much government activity does not require legislative initiative. Ministers retain substantial legal powers under the prerogative, through which important policy decisions may be taken. Similarly, Ministers may also deploy existing statutory powers, which, if cast in sufficiently

---

[75] Turpin C (2nd edn, 1990) *British government and the constitution* p 369.   [76] Op cit p 352.
[77] See Freedland M (1995) 'Privatising *Carltona*: Part II of the Deregulation and Contracting Out Act 1994' *Public Law* 21.

loose terms, may permit the government lawfully to pursue quite different objectives from those favoured by its predecessors. In neither case is the government legally dependent on maintaining majority Commons support to exercise its authority. Nevertheless, the house may play an important constitutional role by monitoring the government's implementation of its preferred policies.[78]

Motions on the floor of the house

Approximately twenty days per session are devoted to general debates on topics chosen by the opposition parties.[79] These occasions are directed towards a critical attack on particular aspects of government policy. Governments with a reliable majority have no difficulty in defeating such motions, but the outcome of the vote is insignificant. The main purpose of 'Opposition days' is to provide a visible forum in which to display the adversarial character of the British political system. Leading speeches are made by Ministers and by senior opposition frontbenchers. Backbenchers depend on 'catching the Speaker's eye' if they wish to contribute.

One might doubt if 'debate' is the correct label to apply to such proceedings. Observers are more frequently presented with the recitation of a collection of opposing views rather than an intimately interactive argument. Nevertheless, the process serves certain tangential purposes. Impressive (or poor) speeches can further (or undermine) an MP's prospects of government or shadow frontbench office. Additionally, the high profile such debates attract offers the wider public some opportunity to form opinions about the merits of government and opposition policies.

Questions to Ministers

The adversarial character of party politics in modern Britain is well illustrated by oral questions to Ministers put by backbenchers and shadow ministers. The procedure was an established feature of the Commons' working practices by the mid-nineteenth century, and by 1900 the government fielded some 5,000 questions each year on the floor of the house.[80] Questions were taken as the first item of business, and 'question time' continued until all had been answered. This meant that other business was frequently not reached until the early evening. While this practice emphasised (literally as well as metaphorically) the principle that the government should be answerable to the Commons, it offered great opportunities for opposition MPs to upset the government's timetable.

Proposals for reform were introduced by Arthur Balfour, Leader of the House in the 1901 Conservative government.[81] Balfour's plans generated considerable controversy in the house, which eventually accepted that question time would in future be held before the commencement of public business, but for a limited time of between forty-five and fifty-five minutes. Questions not reached on the floor would receive a prompt written answer. Individual MPs were limited to a maximum of eight questions per day.[82]

Questions are now taken at the beginning of business on Mondays to Thursdays, for around forty-five minutes. Ministers answer in rotation, so that the conduct of each government department is examined at three to four-week intervals. At present, up to 150 questions may be tabled for answer every day. It is unlikely that many more than two dozen will be dealt with in the short time available. Those questions not reached on the floor are answered in writing.

---

[78] See Norton (2005) op cit ch 6.

[79] See generally Norton (1985) op cit ch 6; Irwin H (1988) 'Opportunities for backbenchers', in Richards and Ryle op cit. [80] Chester N (1977) 'Questions in the house', in Walkland and Ryle op cit.

[81] See Chester N and Bowring M (1962) *Questions in parliament* p 58.

[82] The daily maximum is now two per member per day, and no more than eight may be tabled in any ten sitting days.

Oral proceedings attract considerable attention, both from MPs and the media. Members are thus extremely keen to ensure that their particular question is delivered and answered on the floor. To have any chance of securing this objective, members must submit questions ten days in advance to the 'Table Office', which numbers them at random. Ministers thus have the opportunity to arrange for their officials to provide them with detailed answers to the specific questions raised, and to anticipate follow-up questions ('supplementaries') which might be put immediately after the Minister gives her reply.

Both the content and the style of questions to Ministers are subject to convoluted rules, overseen by the Speaker.[83] The Speaker exercises virtually unconfined discretion over the number of supplementary questions which may be put, both by the mover of the question and other MPs. The Speaker also chooses which members will speak. Successive Speakers have adhered to rather different policies on this issue, with some favouring more expansive exploration of a small number of questions, and others preferring to maximise the number of members called upon to speak.[84]

Erskine May tells us that: 'the purpose of a question is to obtain information or press for action'.[85] However one might doubt whether such sentiments underlie many of the questions currently tabled. Griffith and Ryle suggest that in the past fifty years questions have become considerably less specific. Rather than request that a Minister comment upon a particular detailed issue, often affecting the member's constituency, contemporary questions and the associated supplementaries are increasingly likely to be couched at a general level.[86] One might now be forgiven for thinking that the primary purpose of questions moved by opposition MPs is to use a supplementary to expose a Minister's inability to think on her feet, while government backbenchers offer Ministers the opportunity to engage in self-congratulation.

Despite the evidently increasing frequency of sycophantic questions from government backbenchers,[87] it would be an oversimplification to suggest that party loyalties create an absolute rule, rather than merely a strong presumption, of deference between a government's backbench MPs and its Ministers during questions. Small handfuls of MPs, generally acting in collective defence of their individual constituency interests can deploy the high public profile that question time provides to severely undermine a Minister's standing in the house and in Cabinet. A forceful modern example is provided by the furore which met the announcement in April 1995 by the then Health Secretary (Virginia Bottomley) that several London hospitals were to be closed to curb rising public expenditure. The policy was substantively unpalatable to Conservative MPs whose constituencies contained such hospitals. MPs were however further aggrieved by the procedures used for the announcement—a written answer in Hansard rather than orally in the house. Peter Brooke MP (a former Cabinet colleague of Bottomley) accused her in the house of 'lacking moral courage' by not making a personal statement. The insult ensured that the episode gained considerable publicity, to the extent that rumours circulated suggesting Bottomley would be sacked by the Prime Minister. No such consequences immediately ensued, but it was widely assumed that Bottomley's chances of assuming higher office had been fundamentally damaged by her humiliation in the house.

Vigorous defence of isolated constituency interests has always been a hallmark of backbench behaviour, and serves as a constant reminder that the localist origins of the Commons' representative system has not been entirely subsumed beneath the demands of party politics. Government whips may take a benevolent view of individual members who defy party policy in order to be seen to support their constituents' concerns, especially when such a 'rebellion' raises no prospect of defeat for the government. It would take an unusual combination of

---

[83] Griffith and Ryle op cit pp 254–258. The most important rule is that the question's subject matter must fall within the particular Minister's sphere of departmental responsibility.

[84] Griffith and Ryle op cit pp 369–70; Laundy op cit.   [85] Op cit at p 337.   [86] Op cit pp 254–258.

[87] See eg Hattersley R (1992) 'The beggaring of PM's question time' *The Guardian* 28 January.

circumstances for this aspect of the MP's role to present a serious threat even to an individual Minister, still less to the government as a whole. The Bottomley incident was noteworthy because the government then had a Commons majority of barely a dozen, and had announced hospital closures in the constituencies of several of its backbench MPs.

Prime Ministerial accountability on the floor of the house

Between 1960 and 1997, the Prime Minister took questions on the floor for fifteen minute periods on Tuesday and Thursday afternoons. This practice began following a recommendation of the Select Committee on Procedure. Prior to that date, questions to the Prime Minister enjoyed no special priority over and above questions to other Ministers, which meant that on many days the Prime Minister was never called upon to give oral answers.[88]

Proceedings are now generally dominated by a ritualised clash between the Prime Minister and the Leader of the Opposition. The Leader of the Opposition is generally permitted to put as many as six questions consecutively to the Prime Minister. The opportunity this offers for immediate argument is perhaps as close as the house ever gets to witnessing a debate in the cut-and-thrust sense of the word. The exchanges are perhaps most significant for the impact they have on MPs' perceptions of their respective leader's abilities. In the factionalised arena the house offers, a Prime Minister who continually bests the Leader of the Opposition is unlikely to find her ascendancy in her party under threat, while opposition MPs may be tempted to conclude that their prospects of future electoral success are much hampered by their Leader's evident inadequacies on the floor. All recent Prime Ministers have devoted much time and effort to preparing themselves for this brief exposure to the house.

For opposition MPs, the opportunity to speak is little more than a chance to attract a good deal of publicity by indulging in splenetic rhetoric designed to demonstrate their ideological purity either to their party leaders or their local constituency activists. Government backbenchers, in contrast, are likely to produce questions which enable the Prime Minister to lavish praise on particular aspects of government policy.

Immediately after the 1997 general election, Prime Minister Blair appeared to favour a more thoughtful approach to Prime Minister's question time by proposing that the previous two fifteen-minute slots be replaced with a single half-hour session, evidently to enable issues to be examined in more depth. In practice, that worthy ambition seems to have been disregarded. The first years of the Blair government saw question time used increasingly by Labour MPs to indulge the government's apparent fondness for being showered with meaningless compliments couched in inane language, many of which were evidently extracted by the backbenchers concerned from lists of prepared questions produced by the government.[89]

The copious media attention which Prime Minister's Question Time attracts both in the house and in the media may create a rather misleading impression. A revealing study published in 1990 noted that since 1945 Prime Ministers have contributed far less frequently to life on the floor of the house than their predecessors.[90] James Callaghan, Labour Prime Minister from 1976 to 1979, and Margaret Thatcher were particularly reluctant to participate in general debates. The study suggests that both Prime Ministers (but especially Thatcher) saw their role predominantly as that of running the executive rather than making themselves answerable to the Commons. Tony Blair's premiership seemingly continued this trend. If this view is correct, it identifies a thus far overlooked but nevertheless highly significant aspect of the executive's contemporary dominance of the Commons.

---

[88] See Jones G (1973) 'The Prime Minister and parliamentary questions' *Parliamentary Affairs* 260.

[89] For examples see the seventh edition of this book at p 147.

[90] Dunleavy P, Jones G, and O'Leary B (1990) 'Prime Ministers and the Commons: patterns of behaviour 1868–1987' *Public Administration* 123.

Questions for written answer

For MPs whose main concern is with eliciting information from the government rather than simply confronting a Minister, the 'question for written answer' may prove a more effective tool than seeking an oral answer.[91] There is no limit on the number of such questions that MPs may table. As many as 40,000 have been raised in a single session. Questions for written answer are often less partisan than proceedings on the floor. They are often more precisely targeted and more fully answered than their oral counterparts. As such, they represent a valuable resource for backbenchers, since in effect they force the government to undertake research which neither the member herself nor the Commons' library may have the capacity to carry out.[92]

Informal processes

It may be that the most important vehicle for backbench influence on government behaviour is one that defies any straightforward calibration—namely the informal (and often invisible) processes of consultation and lobbying of Ministers by individual members on matters of constituency or general concern. Quite often, such influence will be pre-emptive—potential conflicts between frontbench policy and backbench opinion are filtered out by modification to government policies before they make even an initial appearance. Party whips play an important part in this process, by acting as a conduit of backbench sentiment to the Cabinet and individual Ministers.

One can only speculate on the extent to which such pressure is effectively applied through channels hidden from public view.[93] Equally, there is no reliable way of knowing whether governments engage in self-censorship of some of their preferred policy objectives simply because they doubt their proposals would find favour in the house.

Thus far, this section has been concerned with the role MPs play in an individual capacity, or as members of ad hoc alliances over specific policy issues. But the Commons' efforts to oversee and influence executive behaviour are also expressed in a more formal, collective manner through the mechanisms of 'select committees'.

The departmental select committee system

'Select committees' have a potted parliamentary history. Their modern origins derive from an *ad hoc* Committee established in 1855 to examine the government's conduct of the Crimean War, when the Army frequently found itself lacking basic supplies. The initiative came from John Roebuck, a radical MP, and was staunchly resisted by the government which considered it incompatible with orthodox understandings of the separation of powers. Gladstone, in seeking to persuade the house not to establish the Committee, condemned it as an unprecedented and unconstitutional intrusion into the sphere of executive responsibility. On being overwhelmingly defeated in the subsequent vote, the government resigned, expecting that the Committee's inquiry would reveal grave errors in its policies.[94]

The Crimea Committee was a single issue body of limited duration. The Public Accounts Committee (PAC), created in 1861, has in contrast been a permanent feature of the Commons' organisational landscape. The PAC scrutinises the implementation of the government's expenditure plans. It is chaired by an opposition MP, frequently one who was formerly a

---

[91] For a useful guide see Borthwick R (1979) 'Questions and debates', in Walkland op cit.

[92] Although the government does sometimes decline to answer questions on the grounds that the cost of doing so would be prohibitive; see Griffith and Ryle op cit pp 373–374.

[93] See Norton P (1982) '"Dear Minister" . . . The importance of MP to minister correspondence' *Parliamentary Affairs* 59.   [94] See Magnus P (1963) *Gladstone* pp 118–119.

Treasury Minister. It has extensive investigatory powers and substantial resources to carry out its tasks. Its reports invariably attract a prompt and considered Treasury reply, and many of its recommendations have influenced subsequent government practice. In consequence, the PAC has gradually acquired a formidable reputation, and is widely regarded as an effective tool for the Commons to raise concerns about government expenditure.[95] But as we shall see later in the chapter, it might justly be regarded as something of an exception to the general trend.

The Crossman reforms

It would be inaccurate to suggest that there was a select committee *system* until the 1960s. Before then, most such committees were established for short periods to deal with specific problems. In 1965, the Labour Prime Minister Harold Wilson supported proposals formulated by one of his Ministers, Richard Crossman, that the house should create two permanent select committees, which would scrutinise government policy in the areas of Science and Agriculture. Crossman presented his initiative as in part a means of enhancing government performance. He envisaged committees of a dozen or so backbench members, who would gain some expertise in a particular policy field. The committees would have a functional rather than departmental remit, and could conceivably find themselves examining the behaviour of several Ministries. Their membership would reflect party balance in the house, but it was intended that their members would put aside party loyalties and advance the collective interest of the Commons overall. Thus constituted, the Committees 'could provide an astringent stimulus to . . . our Departments by ventilating issues and exploring corners which had been covered up in the past'.[96]

Crossman was concerned to redress what he saw as an undesirable imbalance of power between the Commons and the Cabinet:

> Ministers aren't bothered by Parliament, indeed they're hardly ever there . . . The amount of time a Minister spends on the front bench is very small. The Executive reigns supreme in Britain and has minimum trouble from the legislature.[97]

The policy had been strongly opposed by some Ministers. The Treasury feared that Committees would act as lobbyists for additional departmental expenditure, while others resented in principle the notion that their Departments' workings should be exposed to constant Commons scrutiny. Crossman records the First Secretary to the Treasury, Michael Stewart, as arguing in Cabinet that:

> [A] backbench MP has a perfectly satisfactory job to do and there is no reason to create work for him to keep him happy. Indeed, our backbenchers should be thankful that . . . we want to keep the Executive strong, not to strengthen Parliamentary control. Michael's remarks had been applauded by many people around the table.[98]

It is not clear if Crossman and Wilson were sincere about enhancing the Commons' role vis-à-vis the Cabinet. Wilson's biographer records that they saw the Committees as: 'a means for keeping bored backbenchers out of mischief, rather than as a rod for their own backs'.[99] Four further Committees were established.[100] But the government quickly displayed little

---

[95] See Bates St J (1988) 'Scrutiny of administration'; and Robinson R (1988) 'The House of Commons and public money', both in Ryle and Richards op cit; McEldowney J (1988) 'The contingencies fund and the Parliamentary scrutiny of public finance' *Public Law* 232.

[96] Crossman R (1979) *Diaries* pp 200–201.   [97] Ibid, at 275.   [98] Crossman R (1979) *Diaries* p 275.

[99] Pimlott op cit p 518. Note also the extract from Crossman's *Diaries* with which Griffith and Ryle preface their book on Parliament: 'The government has had its summer recess—a delicious time for any government. Now we have got to settle down to the dreary nagging strain of Parliament'.

[100] Dealing respectively with Education and Science, Race Relations and Immigration, Scottish Affairs, and Overseas Aid.

tolerance for Committee activities which effectively questioned government policy. The chief casualty of Wilson's disenchantment was the Agriculture Committee, which was disbanded after displaying considerable investigative independence on the issue of the impact that British accession to the EEC would have on the domestic farming industry.

This episode also demonstrates how our constitutional culture has normalised the presumption that the government should control the Commons. Technically, of course, the government could neither create nor disband a Commons committee. That is a matter for the house itself. It seems however quite clear that when the house did indeed vote to abolish the Agriculture Committee, the Labour majority in favour of doing so was responding more to pressure from government whips rather than to a considered review of the merits of the case.

The 1979 reforms

It is perhaps no coincidence that the Crossman reforms were promoted by a government with (initially) a very small Commons majority. The 1974–1979 Labour government which accepted far more systematic proposals from the Commons' Procedure Committee had similarly precarious support. This might suggest that governments are more likely to accommodate the supposed independence of the Commons when they cannot invariably rely on a working majority.[101] However, the proposals were adopted by the subsequent Conservative government (which did enjoy a sizeable majority),[102] and were implemented (in part) under the tutelage of the then Leader of the House, Norman St John Stevas.

The reform's supposed objective (according to both St John Stevas and his Labour predecessor Michael Foot) was to reverse a perception that the Commons was becoming increasingly impotent in the face of government majorities in the house: the Procedure Committee had argued in 1978 that: 'the day-to-day working of the Constitution is now weighted in favour of the government to a degree which arouses widespread anxiety'.[103]

The method adopted to address this supposed problem was to create a dozen select committees, each having eleven to thirteen members, which would closely scrutinise the work of particular departments.[104] Membership was to be fixed for the life of a Parliament, so that MPs could develop specialised knowledge of particular issues. Members were to be chosen by a special Committee of Selection rather than by party whips. A principle nevertheless emerged to the effect that a government with a majority in the house would retain a majority on each committee. It also appears that both government and opposition whips have in practice succeeded in gaining de facto control of the appointment process.[105] Ministers could not serve on committees, and there was a hope, if not an expectation, that members would approach their task in an independent and fair-minded spirit. Their activities were to be overseen and coordinated by a Liaison Committee comprising the chairpersons of the individual committees.

The new select committees have been in operation long enough for us to form an impression about their impact on the government/Commons relationship by noting several issues of general applicability and by focusing on some of the more significant episodes in their thus far brief history.[106]

---

[101] Although the then Labour chief whip, Michael Cocks, had little empathy with the proposals: 'I didn't want any bloody select committee examining what we were up to!' quoted by White M and Norton-Taylor R (1995) 'Commons watchdogs lack full set of teeth' *The Guardian* 22 March.   [102] For the figures see Table 7.5.

[103] Quoted in Drewry (1985a) op cit p 136. See Baines P (1985) 'The history and rationale of the 1979 reforms', in Drewry G (ed) *The new select committees*; Johnson op cit.

[104] The Committees being Agriculture, Defence, Education, Employment, Energy, Environment, Foreign Affairs, Home Affairs, Scottish Affairs, Social Services, Trade and Industry, Transport, Treasury and Civil Service, and Welsh Affairs.   [105] See Griffith and Ryle op cit pp 417–420.

[106] For examples see Nixon J and Nixon N (1983) 'The social services committee' *Journal of Social Policy* 331; Hawes D (1992) 'Parliamentary select committees: some case studies in contingent influence' Policy and Politics 227. More generally see Drewry (1985) (ed) op cit.

The committees have been prolific in terms of the number and diversity of reports which they have produced. On a few occasions, these reports seem to have led directly to shifts in government policy. Others are intended either to filter in the longer term into the general process of governmental policy-making, or merely to draw attention to issues whose complexities have thus far remained unappreciated.[107] This gradual accumulation of expert knowledge on a wide variety of issues is perhaps the most successful area of committee activity thus far. In other respects, their impact has been far more limited.

Unlike the PAC, the departmental select committees are not well-resourced. The committees do not control any resources of their own; their expenditure is determined by the House of Commons Commission. In this respect, they fare very poorly in comparison with the legislative committee system of the US Congress, which enjoys considerable power and prestige within the US government process. The two systems are not of course directly comparable, since the US constitution adheres to a more rigid separation of powers than Britain's, and often finds itself accommodating a national executive and legislature controlled by different political parties. Nevertheless, the select committees' paucity of resources undermines their capacity to be fully informed on relevant aspects of government policy.

A further significant constraint on the committees' efficacy derives from their (practically) limited powers to extract information from unwilling government departments. St John Stevas announced to the house in 1979 that:

> I give the House the pledge on the part of the government that every Minister from the most senior Cabinet Minister to the most junior Under-Secretary will do all in his or her power to co-operate with the new system of Committees and make it a success.[108]

One cannot know if such a promise was made in good faith. Nor can one know if committee members exercise their power 'to send for persons, papers and records' in fearless disregard of Ministerial sensibilities. But it is evident that a Minister may simply refuse to attend a committee inquiry. Or she may decline to answer questions on particular subjects. It may be politically embarrassing for a Minister to behave in this way, and may expose her to both parliamentary and public criticism. But one must surely assume that she is unco-operative because a candid discussion would reveal information of an even more embarrassing or damaging nature.

Ministers are frequently reluctant to permit senior civil servants to contribute to committee inquiries. The Employment Committee's inquiry into the GCHQ affair was severely hindered by the government's refusal to allow the Director of GCHQ to give evidence. Similarly, the controversy engendered by the so-called Westland Affair,[109] prompted inquiries by both the Defence Committee and the Treasury and Civil Service Committee; both were hampered by the government's decision not to allow particular civil servants to appear.[110]

A further indication of the government's somewhat restrictive interpretation of 'full co-operation' was provided by a 1980 *Memorandum of Guidance* which indicated that certain types of documentary evidence would not be available. The text of the Memorandum lent itself to extremely broad interpretation. The forbidden territory included, for example: 'Questions in the field of political controversy'; 'advice given to Ministers by their departments'; the discussions of Cabinet committees; and 'inter-departmental exchanges on policy issues'.

The list suggests that the Thatcher government was no more willing than previous administrations to open its activities up to searching Commons' scrutiny. It is technically within the power of the house to insist that persons attend committee hearings, or that documents be

---

[107] See generally Griffith and Ryle op cit pp 423–428.

[108] *HCD* 25 June 1979 c 45; quoted in Turpin op cit p 384.   [109] We revisit Westland in ch 9.

[110] Hennessy P (1986) 'Helicopter crashes into Cabinet: Prime Minister and constitution hurt' *Journal of Law and Society* 423.

produced. It is however difficult to envisage circumstances in which a government could not persuade its MPs to vote against any such action. Thus while the power may be significant in respect of private individuals, it is largely illusory in the context of government/Commons relations.

Most commentators seem to suggest that while the committees have become accepted as a legitimate part of the parliamentary landscape, it is only the PAC which exercises a continuously significant influence over government behaviour: the reform clearly does not merit the label of a 'revolution' in the workings of government with which St John Stevas initially cloaked it.[111] The suggestion that governments would tolerate select committees only for so long as they did not prove a constant thorn in the executive's side was reinforced after the 1992 general election. Prior to the election, the Health Committee was chaired by Nicholas Winterton MP, an independently minded Conservative who frequently criticised government health policy. The government seemingly wished to remove him from this post, but did not want to do so candidly. Conservative whips thus formulated a rule that Conservative MPs could not serve for more than twelve years on the same Committee. Not, one assumes, by coincidence, it transpired that Winterton fell into this category. His initial reaction was one of blustering indignation, couched in the rhetoric of constitutional impropriety:

> What we have now is government by whips' dictat. They are now saying free speech and an independent mind can have no role in Parliament. . . . They [the Cabinet] are being seen as dictators who will not brook any dissent.[112]

Yet Mr Winterton did not feel compelled to demonstrate his commitment to 'free speech and independence' by resigning from the Conservative Party. Nor was his outrage shared by a sufficient number of his colleagues for the Conservative whips to doubt that a Commons majority would support their new policy. The episode may indeed have been, as one anonymous Conservative MP complained, 'a gross interference with the work of Parliament'.[113] Yet in formal terms, the government has no power to determine the rules controlling Committee membership; that is a matter for the house itself. That the whips' gambit was successful reveals the true significance of the Winterton 'sacking'—namely that so very few Conservative members regarded maintaining the independence of their house as a higher loyalty than pandering to the convenience of their party.

Perhaps curiously, given the size of the New Labour government's Commons majority, the significance of select committees within the house seemed to grow after the 1997 election. This resulted in part from a decision to experiment with the idea of using select committees to explore the merits of proposed legislation prior to its introduction to the house: an experiment which, in respect of the government's proposed freedom of information legislation, proved something of an embarrassment to Ministers. But some committees also seemed to pursue their traditional role with increased vigour. The Treasury Committee became notably more assertive in its attempts to monitor the mechanics of the government's economic policy. More significantly, the Foreign Affairs Committee subjected the Foreign Secretary and his officials to aggressive questioning over the government's involvement in the supply of arms—in breach of a United Nations embargo—to the government of Sierra Leone. The next year, the Deputy Prime Minister, John Prescott, was sufficiently rattled by the Transport Select Committee's strong criticism of government transport policy to launch an intemperate attack on the Committee's members. Simultaneously, the Trade and Industry Committee accused the government of a systematic failure to respect human rights concerns by promoting the sale of arms to repressive foreign regimes.

---

[111] See Johnson op cit; Drewry (1985a) op cit; Griffith and Ryle op cit pp 430–434.
[112] *The Guardian* 14 July 1992.   [113] Ibid.

Conclusion

The Labour Party's sweeping victory at the 1997 general election (producing a Commons majority of some 180 seats) did not herald any radical changes in the Commons' de facto subordination to the government. The Blair government did establish a cross party committee to investigate ways in which the Commons might modernise its internal procedures. Its proposals were mild. Foremost among them were the scheduling of more Commons business for the mornings and—in a nod to MPs' family commitments—short closures of the Commons during school half term holidays. MPs whose constituencies were far from London would be assisted by a decision to make minimal use of Friday sittings, thereby offering MPs the chance to depart for their constituencies on Thursday evenings. The committee also suggested that more MPs should be enabled to speak in debates by empowering the Speaker to place stricter time limits on the duration of each speech. Whether that proposal would actually enhance the quality of debate, rather than just permit a greater number of anodyne contributions by inexpert speakers, remains to be seen. Some indication of how absurdly archaic the Commons' procedures are is given by press coverage of the cross-party committee's recommendations; the proposal that attracted most attention was the abolition of the requirement that an MP could only make a point of order during a division if she was wearing a top hat.

A government with a Commons majority of 180 is unlikely to find its legislative timetable substantially inconvenienced by the lower house. The first Blair government suffered few episodes of major backbench rebellion. All came from the left of the party, in response to what rebels regarded as unacceptably harsh social policy initiatives. The most serious arose late in 1997, in respect of a Bill designed to cut welfare payments to single parent families. Some 120 Labour MPs publicly opposed the changes. Only forty-seven eventually voted against the second reading, another fourteen abstained. One junior Minister, Malcolm Chisholm, preferred to resign his office rather than support the government. The government did not make any significant concession to the rebels; but the episode was sufficiently embarrassing for the Prime Minister to feel obliged to sack the then Secretary of State for Social Security, Harriet Harman, shortly afterwards.

No such draconian consequences ensued in June 1998, when forty Labour MPs voted against the government's plans to abolish student grants. Once again, backbench pressure was insufficient to persuade the government to alter its policy. In contrast, the Home Secretary was persuaded by the prospect of fifty or so Labour MPs voting against the government to modify the contents of his decidedly illiberal Bill to discourage refugees from seeking asylum in Britain. Planned cuts in welfare benefits—this time to the disabled—caused further difficulties to the Blair administration late in 1999. The government offered minor concessions to the rebels, but refused to countenance major modifications. Fifty-four Labour MPs eventually opposed the Bill at third reading, reducing the government's majority to sixty. A further substantial revolt was triggered in May 2000 by the government's plan to privatise the air traffic control system, a policy which it had condemned as wholly undesirable when in opposition.

Notwithstanding such episodes, which attracted much press coverage, the first Blair government ended its term without having been defeated even once on a whipped vote. No other post-war government had achieved such a feat.[114]

The first Blair government also appeared unwilling to enhance the power of Commons' select committees. In 2000, the Liaison Committee (comprised of the chairs of other select committees) produced a report which urged, inter alia, that party whips should no longer play

---

[114] Cowley and Stuart (2001) op cit.

any part in choosing committee members and that committee membership should be structured in a fashion that offered an alternative career structure to the ministerial greasy pole. The government dismissed the proposals. Labour backbenchers were sufficiently quiescent to allow the government to resist demands that the report should be subject to a vote in the house.

The Commons appeared to have become more assertive in defence of its committees in the immediate aftermath of the 2001 general election. In a manner reminiscent of the Major government's treatment of Nicholas Winterton, the government attempted to remove two of its most effective backbench critics, Donald Anderson and Gwyneth Dunwoody, from their respective Chairs of the Foreign Affairs and Transport Select Committees. The risible justification for the proposal was that Anderson and Dunwoody had sat on the committees for too long. Ms Dunwoody had recently expressed the view that the government was so irritated by her Committee's behaviour that Ministers were co-ordinating a smear campaign among MPs and in the press to undermine her credibility. The government then suffered the ignominy of a substantial defeat on the floor of the house when both MPs were voted back into their chairs. It should perhaps be stressed however that the election of committee chairs is, at least in principle, a matter for a free vote. Whether Labour MPs would have proved such staunch proponents of the Commons' autonomy in the face of a whip is a matter for speculation.[115]

Hopes were raised that more extensive reforms might attract government support when the former Foreign Secretary, Robin Cook, was appointed as Leader of the House in the second Blair government. In an interview given shortly after his appointment, Cook professed himself much concerned to increase the authority and effectiveness of the house vis-à-vis the government. Shortly thereafter, he announced that the government favoured change along the lines proposed by the Liaison Committee two years earlier. The plans were enthusiastically received in the press. Mr Cook had evidently failed however to convince his Cabinet colleagues and the Prime Minister of the benefits of his ideas. In May 2002, government whips succeeded in persuading Labour backbenchers to vote against the reforms.[116] The only change of any note introduced in the first year of the second Blair government's term was that the Prime Minister agreed to undertake a regular, televised question-and-answer session on all facets of government policy with the Liaison Committee.

A more assertive and independent house?

A forceful argument has however been made by Philip Cowley that backbench Labour MPs demonstrated considerable independence from (or opposition to) the Blair government since 2001.[117] The point is overtly evidenced by the decision of 139 Labour MPs in March 2003 to vote against the government's motion in the House of Commons seeking approval of its planned invasion of Iraq. The motion was ultimately carried only because the government was supported by the Conservative opposition. A perhaps more graphic illustration is provided by the government's first defeat on a whipped vote in the Commons in November 2005, over its wish to have legislation enacted which would authorise the detention of terrorists suspects for up to ninety days without charge or trial. Forty-nine Labour backbenchers joined the opposition parties in voting against the government's proposal.[118]

---

[115] See Cowley P and Stuart M (2002) 'Parliament: mostly continuity, but more change than you'd think' *Parliamentary Affairs* 270.

[116] One Labour MP who favoured change, Gordon Prentice, subsequently asked on the floor of the house; 'Is it in order for government whips to be standing outside the voting lobbies on a free vote and pointing to the No lobby and saying "parliamentary Labour Party this way"?'; *The Guardian* 15 May 2002.

[117] Cowley P (2005) *The rebels*. The book offers a very detailed and engaging portrait of the realities of the law-making process within our modern Parliament.   [118] Ibid, ch 5.

Cowley's study suggests that backbench Labour MPs exerted influence over government policy in more subtle ways. He identifies several major bills promoted by the government during the 2001–2005 Parliament which were substantially amended during their passage as a result of government concerns that backbench Labour support might not be forthcoming. After the 2005 general election, the government's majority in the Commons fell to sixty-one; a scenario which suggested that Prime Minister Blair's third administration (and subsequently Gordon Brown's first government from 2007) might have to be more accommodating to the wishes of its backbenchers than its predecessors had been. A strong illustration of this supposition was provided in the spring of 2008, when a substantial number of Labour backbenchers indicated that they would oppose a budget proposal removing the lowest rate of income tax. The proposal would have significantly raised the tax liability of a substantial number of people on low incomes. The government took the threat of rebellion sufficiently seriously to pre-empt the possibility of defeat in the Commons by putting forward a package of measures to compensate the people affected.

The 2010 general election produced a house in which no party had a single majority, and led to the formation of Conservative/Liberal coalition government. Although the parties produced a 'Coalition Agreement' outlining their intended legislative programme,[119] by mid-2011 that there was significant disagreement between both Minister and backbenchers of both parties on the merits of various legislative proposals. These tensions were particularly acute over proposed reforms to the National Health Service, with the result that the government announced there would be a 'pause' in the passage of a Bill which had already completed most of its Commons stages so that further consultation could take place on its contents. The episode certainly raised the possibility that the Commons might play a more significant role both as legislator and scrutinser of the government than it had for much of the modern era.

Notwithstanding this recent trend, it is clear that for most of the modern era the Commons has been a body in which party politics is the dominant determinant both in the legislative process and in respect of executive accountability.[120] The house is manifestly now a factional rather than national assembly for most purposes. But it would as yet be premature to conclude that the constitution therefore permits factional concerns to determine both the content of legislation and the parliamentary accountability of government behaviour. To answer that question, our analysis must consider several further issues. Firstly, the constitutional role played by the House of Lords—the second limb of our tripartite Parliament. Secondly, the nature of the relationship between factional Commons majorities and 'the people'. And thirdly, the uses to which factional governments put whatever power is at their disposal. This last question is perhaps the most important of all. For even if one accepts that a factional constitution is undesirable in a modern democracy, it does not necessarily follow that such a constitution will lead to the production of factional laws, nor, in the event that it does, that the laws concerned do not attract the consent of the governed.

Suggested further reading

Academic and political commentary

Cowley P (2005) *The rebels*

Norton P (2005) *Parliament in British politics* ch 5

---

[119] <http://www.cabinetoffice.gov.uk/news/coalition-documents>. The election result is considered at 'Counting the Vote', ch 7, pp 190–193.

[120] A recent critique to this effect is offered by the Hansard Society (2000) *The challenge for Parliament: making government accountable.*

Rogers R and Walters R (eds) (2006) *How Parliament works* chs 2 and 3

Kenny M (2009) 'Taking the temperature of the British political elite 3: when grubby is the order of the day' *Parliamentary Affairs* 503

Norton P (1979) 'The organisation of parliamentary parties', in Walkland S (ed) *The House of Commons in the twentieth century*

Borthwick R (1988) 'The floor of the house', in Ryle M and Richards P (eds) *The Commons under scrutiny*

Bates S et al (2012) 'Questions to the Prime Minister: a comparative study of PMQs from Thatcher to Cameron' *Parliamentary Affairs* 1.

Laundy P (1979) 'The Speaker and his office in the twentieth century', in Walkland S (ed) *The House of Commons in the twentieth century*

Chapter 6

The House of Lords

Chapter five began to explore how accurately Parliament's current role reflects the intentions of the 1688 settlement; those being to secure that elite groups monopolised law-making power, and to ensure that no faction(s) within that elite could seize legislative power to pursue majoritarian or minoritarian ends. It was suggested there has been a significant change in the Commons' role since 1688, from a body providing the voice of one distinct segment of society, counterposed to the Lords and Monarch, to a forum which expressed the divergent political philosophies of the entire population. The rise of nationwide party politics, and the fusion rather than separation of powers between the legislature and the government, create the danger of a majoritarian lower chamber, in which pursuing factional party advantage rather than safeguarding national interests could be legislators' main occupation. Chapter seven considers how development of the parliamentary electoral system has affected this trend. This chapter asks whether the upper chamber plays an effective anti-majoritarian legislative role.

Bicameral legislatures: a functionalist justification

Most modern democracies have two houses in their central legislature. They are referred to as having a bicameral Parliament: countries with only one legislative assembly have unicameral Parliaments.[1] The Americans' division of their central legislature into the House and the Senate was a continuation of the theme of the separation of powers. By requiring that federal legislation attracted the consent of more than one body, Madison and Jefferson hoped to reduce still further the likelihood that Congress could enact tyrannical laws. The two houses of Congress fulfil different representative functions. The Senate has two Senators from each State, irrespective of the size of the State's population. Senators represent State interests within the national legislature, thereby stressing the Constitution's federal nature. In contrast, members of the House are chosen on a population basis; the number from each State reflects that State's share

---

[1] On the reasoning behind other countries' choice of this framework see Shell D (1992) *The House of Lords* ch 1.

of the national population. This emphasises that the US' Federal legislature was responsible to individual citizens as well as to the States. Bicameralism is intended to maximise the chances that Congress, acting within its constitutional powers, produces laws that acceptably balance the interests of the States and of individual citizens.

For practical purposes, the two parts of the UK's legislature are the Commons and the House of Lords. In theory, Parliament has a third part—the Monarch. As a matter of legal theory, the Monarch retains the power to veto proposed legislation by withholding the Royal Assent. However, as a matter of practical politics, this power is no longer used.[2]

Appreciating the distinction between *theory and practice*, or between what is sometimes referred to as *law and convention*, is essential to understanding the constitutional status and function of the House of Lords. By pursuing this 'gap' between theory and practice here, we raise ideas which later chapters suggest are central to understanding how and why the constitution functions as it does. For present purposes, we might distinguish law and convention in the following simple way. Both are vehicles through which political power is exercised in an effective and legitimate manner. However, while laws may be enforced by an action before the courts, conventions have no actionable legal basis. Rather, they control the exercise of political power because the wielders of that power either believe that conventional restraints are morally correct, or fear the political consequences of breaching them.

I. The historical background

The House of Lords' origins may be traced to the 'Great Council', a body which assumed a recognisably modern shape in the fifteenth century.[3] In the pre-revolutionary era, the Lords was regarded as a 'fundamental' element of the English constitution.[4] In 1688, the Lords and Commons were, in terms of their legal powers, co-equal partners in the legislative process. The 1688 revolution established the legal supremacy of Parliament, not of the Commons. If the House of Lords disapproved a Commons Bill, that Bill could not go any further.

Co-equality extended to the formation of governments as well as enacting legislation. Until the late-nineteenth century, the Cabinet was as likely to contain a majority of members from the Lords as from the Commons: only one member of Lord Grey's 1830 Cabinet was not either a peer or the son of a peer: Gladstone assembled a Cabinet of twelve members in 1880; one was a duke, one a marquess, and five were earls.[5] Not until 1900 had the conventional practice arisen that the Prime Minister should be a member of the Commons.

In 1688, the peers in the Lords were either hereditary peers or bishops. The Lords was a combination of the church and the land-owning aristocracy: it was not a democratic chamber in the modern sense. But neither was the Commons, whose members were then 'elected' (the word is used guardedly) by a tiny minority of the (male) population.[6] Co-equality was a co-equality of elites, not of the mass of the population. Such elitism was readily understandable from a functionalist perspective. The constitutional morality of that era discerned a vital purpose for an aristocratic veto within the legislative process: to preserve existing patterns of political and economic power.

---

[2] We assess the nature of the Monarch's power in ch 9.

[3] See Adonis (1993) op cit p 193; Weston C (1965) *English constitutional theory and the House of Lords* ch 1.

[4] England had a unicameral legislature between 1649 and 1657, when Cromwell's revolutionary House of Commons purported to abolish the Lords. Charles II, when restored to his throne in 1660, recalled the Lords, accepting that the upper house should again enjoy 'that authority and jurisdiction which hath always belonged to you by your birth, and the fundamental law of the land': see Smith E (1992) *The House of Lords in British Politics and Society 1815–1911* p 1.

[5] Turbeville A (1958) *The House of Lords in the Age of Reform* p 256; Jenkins R (1968) *Mr Balfour's Poodle* p 27; Smith op cit p 64.   [6] The electoral process is examined in detail in ch 7.

As discussed in chapter seven, the impact of the industrial revolution on the nature and distribution of wealth was immense, and led to equally significant realignments in the basis of political influence. However even as late as 1800, land ownership was the predominant form of economic power: and members of the House of Lords were the predominant class of landowners. In 1876, almost half of the country's thirty million acres was owned by barely 500 peers,[7] many of whom also derived substantial incomes from industrial, commercial, and residential development and agriculture.

Co-equality to complementarity: a conventional change

The situation of equal status between the two houses within both the legislative process and the formation of the government continued in legal terms until the twentieth century. But it very quickly began to undergo a political change. From the outset of the post-revolutionary period, both houses appeared to accept that the Lords should not veto legislation dealing with the raising of government revenue. The original sources of this conventional understanding are obscure,[8] but its scope was clearly delineated in a 1678 Commons resolution:

> [A]ll Bills for granting such Aids and Supplies ought to begin with the Commons: And that it is the undoubted and sole right of the Commons to direct limit and appoint in such Bills the Ends, Purposes, Considerations, Conditions, Limitations, and Qualifications of such Grants: which ought not to be changed or altered by the House of Lords.

Quite how effective this principle, or indeed any other conventional understandings, have proven in regulating the legislative process is a question perhaps best answered by example.

The Treaty of Utrecht

A major conflict between the post-revolution Lords and Commons arose in the early-eighteenth century. The immediate cause was a disagreement between the government, which commanded a majority in the Commons, and the majority of peers in the Lords over the terms of the Treaty of Utrecht. The stalemate was resolved when the government asked Queen Anne to use her prerogative powers to create enough new peers who supported the government to ensure that it had a reliable Lords majority. The Queen accepted that she should follow her Ministers' advice, and created twelve new peers.[9]

The Utrecht episode demonstrated that the Lords' theoretical co-equality could be undermined if the Monarch supported a government which enjoyed majority Commons support. The affair is constitutionally significant, for it reveals a pro-majoritarian legal loophole sewn into the fabric of the 1688 settlement. For a government and Monarch to collude in this way would undermine the anti-majoritarian sentiment informing the original understanding of parliamentary sovereignty, but it would not be illegal.

A more important focus for constitutional change was provided by the Great Reform Act 1832. This legislation is examined closely in chapter seven. Here we might simply note that the Act was vigorously opposed by many Tory peers, who feared it undermined the traditional 'balance' of the constitution and thereby threatened the distribution of economic power on which they assumed the security of the nation to rest. The reasons behind the Lords' eventual acquiescence to the Bill are also discussed in chapter eight. That acquiescence meant however that from 1832 onwards one can begin to see a democratic justification for regarding the Lords as constitutionally subordinate to the Commons. The Commons was increasingly a body which could plausibly claim to derive its authority from the consent of the governed.

---

[7] Turbeville (1958) op cit p 408.   [8] Smith op cit p 34.

[9] Plucknett (1960) op cit pp 540–542; Turbeville A (1927) *The House of Lords in the eighteenth century* pp 111–118.

It would be misleading to suggest that the Commons in 1833 was a truly representative body. But after 1832, the legislative trend headed steadily in that direction.

The doctrine of the mandate

The more 'democratic' basis of the post-Reform Act Commons had significant implications for the power that a non-elected Lords could expect to wield. By the 1880s the two houses were in legal theory still equal partners, but in practice their relationship had changed profoundly. By 1900 a convention had emerged that the Lords would not block Bills passed by the Commons unless it seemed that the Commons was promoting measures that could not command popular support. The legitimate limits to the Lords' intransigence were described by Lord Lyndhurst in 1858:

> I never understood, nor could such a principle be acted upon, that we were to make a firm, determined and persevering stand against the opinion of the other House of Parliament when that opinion is backed by the opinion of the people.[10]

Lord Lyndhurst viewed the Lords' capacity to block legislation as a power, which it might deploy when it thought the Commons was pursuing policies which lacked electoral support.

In contrast, Lord Salisbury, then leader of the Tory peers, suggested in 1872 that the veto was a constitutional duty. The upper house was obliged to defy the Commons on major issues unless 'the judgement of the nation has been challenged at the polls and decidedly expressed'.[11] This so-called 'doctrine of the mandate' or 'referendal theory' emerged in the late 1860s, when the Lords vetoed a government Bill to reform the Irish Church. Lord Salisbury justified the Lords' position on the grounds that the policy was not part of the proposed legislative programme on which the Liberal government had fought the last general election, and that another general election was shortly to be held.[12]

The defensibility of this position rested largely on the hardening of party allegiances in both the Commons and the country which had occurred by then. Party membership was all-pervasive in the Lords in 1880: E A Smith notes that 280 peers described themselves as 'Conservative and 203 as Liberal, against only thirteen of no party'.[13]

Party discipline was less rigidly enforced in the Lords than in the Commons, but was nevertheless sufficiently effective to assure the Conservatives of a majority whenever required.[14] Unsurprisingly, Tory governments experienced fewer problems in piloting Bills through the Lords than their Liberal counterparts. The administrations led by Sir Robert Peel in the 1840s and Lord Derby and Disraeli in the 1860s and 1870s generally secured Lords majorities for modest programmes of social, economic, and political reform.[15]

The doctrine of the mandate presents a paradox—a body composed primarily of the landed gentry[16] saw one of its crucial constitutional roles as upholding 'democratic' principles against the elected chamber. The Lords portrayed itself as the 'watchdog of the constitution', able to 'overreach' the House of Commons and seek the views of the people by insisting that a government with radical proposals test its popularity in a general election. Cynical observers might wonder if the upper house's defence of public opinion would be staunch only when public sentiment coincided with that of the majority of Tory peers. Salisbury was certainly prepared to amend his formula when the original version did not meet his needs. The Lords rejected

---

[10] Cited in Jenkins (1968) op cit p 28.   [11] Jenkins (1968) op cit p 31.

[12] Smith op cit pp 166–168; Jenkins (1968) op cit pp 28–31.   [13] Smith op cit p 157.

[14] Smith op cit ch 5; Large D (1963) 'The decline of the "Party of the Crown" and the rise of parties in the House of Lords, 1783–1837' *English Historical Review* 669; Brock M (1973) *The Great Reform Act* pp 216–217.

[15] See Turbeville op cit pp 347–351, 397–399, 411–416.

[16] From the mid-nineteenth century onwards newly created peers had a slightly more meritocratic profile—outstanding service in the law, armed forces or government service were seen as legitimate ladders up which commoners could climb to the lower ranks of the aristocracy: Turbeville (1958) op cit pp 369–370.

the Liberal government's Irish Home Rule Bill on the basis that it had been approved by the Commons only with the support of Irish MPs. Most MPs from England, which was the 'predominant partner' in Parliament, opposed the measure, which Salisbury considered sufficient justification to force the Liberals to put the issue to the electorate again.[17] This 'predominant partner' principle emphasises the general point that the substance of a convention may be unilaterally altered by the individuals or groups who have considered themselves bound to it.

The Lords and Commons clashed on several issues during the late-Victorian era—especially policy towards Ireland[18]—but disputes were always defused before reaching a constitutional crisis. But the Lords' deference was a matter of political self-regulation. The Lords chose not to frustrate the Commons. This choice may have been influenced by the fear that the government might ask the Monarch to swamp the upper chamber with new peers if the Lords rejected a Commons Bill. But there was no legal impediment to the Lords simply blocking government policy.

There was perhaps an inverse correlation between the Lords' conventional power and the breadth of the parliamentary franchise; as more people obtained the right to vote for members of the Commons, it became more difficult for the Lords to find a 'democratic' justification for obstructing the lower house. By 1900 almost all adult men were entitled to vote in parliamentary elections and, simultaneously, the Lords' political role was shifting from *co-equality* to *complementarity*.

The Lords complemented the Commons by acting as a scrutiniser of Bills, a forum for debate on issues of general significance, and a vehicle to bring important questions to the nation's attention. As *The Times* had predicted in 1831, the Lords' political role was drifting towards one in which it might persuade, but not compel the Commons to forgo factional legislative programmes; to act in effect as a 'watchdog of the constitution':

> among the uses of an Upper Chamber ought to be accounted that of . . . subjecting that which may be but a light or transient caprice, to the test of calm, laborious, and reiterated deliberation.[19]

Between 1909 and 1911 however, the Lords appeared to reject its new conventional role of complementarity in favour of its traditional legal status of co-equality.

Lloyd George and the 'people's budget'

A convention cannot be legally enforced. It is effective only while the people supposedly bound by it agree to be bound. By 1909, the Lords no longer accepted conventional constraints on its formal legal power to veto Bills passed in the Commons. The long-term cause of this problem was the consolidation of the party system within national politics, in which substantial blocs of opinion had developed irreconcilable views around several major issues. An acute political fault line appeared over matters of social and economic policy, which, put simplistically, offers an early empirical example of the dichotomy between social democratic and liberal market theories of the state.

In 1906, the House of Commons had 671 members. In the 1906 general election, the Liberals and the smaller parties supporting them won 514 seats. The opposition Conservative and Unionist parties had 157 seats. This gave the government an effective majority of 357. The party balance in the Lords was very different however: the Conservatives had a majority of 391.[20] (See Table 6.1.)

[17] Smith op cit pp 168–169.   [18] See Smith op cit ch 9.

[19] 3 October 1831; quoted in Smith op cit p 118. One could find few better British examples of a recipe to counter Madisonian fear of faction.

[20] Wicks (2006) op cit p 83. The substantial increase in the number of Conservative peers between 1880 and 1906—and the corresponding decline in Liberal representation—was the result of many former Liberal peers switching allegiance to the Conservatives because they opposed Liberal Party policy to grant Home Rule to Ireland.

Table 6.1 House of Lords: historical shifts in party allegiance

	1880	1906	1930	1955	1975	1992	2001
Conservative	280	354	489	507	507	475	222
Labour	–	–	17	55	149	119	197
Liberal	203	98	79	42	30	58	62
Cross-bench	13	43	140	251	281	263	216

Sources: Compiled from information in Shell (1992) op cit p 67; Adonis (1993) op cit p 205; Butler D and Sloman A (1975) op cit p 175; *The Guardian*, 8 November 2001.

Between 1906 and 1909 the Liberal government promoted various radical social policy programmes.[21] Although the Conservative majority was in a clear minority in the Commons, the party leader Arthur Balfour was able effectively either to block or substantially amend government Bills by mobilising the Lords' Conservative majority.[22]

Matters came to a head over the Finance Bill of 1909, popularly known as Lloyd George's 'People's Budget'. The Bill would raise taxes substantially to pay for an expanded welfare state. From a modern viewpoint, Lloyd George's tax plans seem very modest; income tax would be levied at only nine pence in the pound. Nevertheless, as Roy Jenkins records, the plans provoked furious Tory opposition:

> It 'means the beginning of the end of all rights of property' said Sir Edward Carson. 'It is a monument of reckless and improvident finance,' said Lord Lansdowne [leader of the Conservative peers]. 'It is inquisitorial, tyrannical and socialistic,' said Lord Roseberry.[23]

The opposing views of the 1906 budget neatly encapsulate one difficulty inherent in applying Jeffersonian constitutional principles to modern government. Carson might be seen as espousing the wealthy's 'inalienable right' not to have their property taken away by taxation. Lloyd George, in contrast, might plausibly have argued that the Liberals' substantial Commons majority made it clear that 'the people' had now consented to a more egalitarian route in their 'pursuit of happiness'.

Given the size of the Liberal majority, one might have thought that convention demanded that the Lords should not obstruct the Finance Bill. However, the Lords' Conservative majority persistently refused to pass it, claiming that since its provisions had not been clearly put to the electorate the doctrine of the mandate required the government to call a general election to decide if the citizenry supported the policy.

The Liberal government requested the King to create enough Liberal peers for the government to push the Bill through the Lords. Edward VII would not do this, and he was supported by Balfour. Balfour had urged the Lords' Conservative majority to block the government's Bill. This led Lloyd George to suggest that the Lords was not the 'watchdog of the constitution', but 'Mr Balfour's poodle. It fetches and carries for him. It barks for him. It bites anybody that he sets it on to'.[24] The Conservative's upper house majority was almost as substantial as that of the Liberals in the Commons. 354 peers took the Conservative whip, fewer than 100 were Liberals, and only 43 claimed no party allegiance (the so-called 'cross-benchers').[25]

One might here pause to consider which party was acting 'unconstitutionally'. From a contemporary perspective, we might readily accuse the Conservatives, since the Liberals had won the 1906 general election. But to suggest that the Liberal government and its small party allies represented the mass of the people is misleading. We have already referred to the limited

---

[21] See Hay J (1975) *The origins of the Liberal welfare reforms 1906–1914.*   [22] Wicks (2006) op cit pp 84–85.
[23] (1968) op cit p 76.   [24] Quoted in Butler D and Sloman A (1975) *British political facts* p 223.
[25] Smith op cit p 157; Jenkins (1968) op cit pp 24–25.

Table 6.2 The 1906 and 1910 general elections

	1906		1910 (1)		1910(2)	
	Seats	(% vote)	Seats	(% vote)	Seats	(% vote)
Liberal	400	(49.0%)	275	(43.2%)	272	(43.9%)
Labour*	30	(5.9%)	78	(7.6%)	56	(7.1%)
Irish Nat*	83	(0.6%)	82	(1.9%)	84	(2.5%)
Conservative	157	(43.6%)	273	(46.9%)	272	(46.3%)
Turnout		82.6%		86.6%		81.1%
Electorate		7,264,608		7,694,741		7,709,981

* Aligned with the Liberals
Source: Compiled from information in Butler D and Sloman A (1975) op cit pp 182–183.

franchise which then existed; over half of the adult population were not entitled to vote in 1906. Moreover, as noted in Table 6.2, only 55% of voters supported the Liberal bloc; 45% of voters preferred an opposition party. The Liberal position was therefore democratic only in the narrow sense of commanding majority support among a 'people' which was in itself only a minority of the population.

One might argue, (as did Professor Dicey)[26] that it was the Conservative peers who remained true to the traditional constitution. The tripartite, sovereign Parliament was created to preclude enactment of factional legislation. The factionalist label could clearly be attached to the People's Budget. In vetoing a Bill of which a substantial minority of 'the people' apparently disapproved, the Lords was presumably upholding the spirit of the 1688 settlement. The Liberal government assumed that majoritarianism in the Commons was the constitution's 'ultimate political fact'. Accusing the Lords of 'a breach of the Constitution' in blocking the Finance Bill, Prime Minister Asquith requested a dissolution of Parliament in December 1909.

The general election of January 1910 was fought primarily on the issue of the People's Budget. The Liberals achieved a substantial (albeit reduced) effective majority, and proposed a Parliament Bill greatly reducing the Lords' veto powers. While the Lords subsequently accepted the Finance Bill, it refused to approve a Bill reducing its own legal powers. King Edward VII also appeared hostile to the latter Bill, and equivocated about whether to create the hundreds of new peers needed to outvote the Conservative majority. His successor (as of 6 May 1910) George V seemed equally reluctant to follow the Utrecht precedent.

Asquith called another general election for December 1910, squarely on the issue of constitutional reform to curb the Lords' power. The Liberals 'won' this election as well. In the aftermath of this the King had agreed to create enough new peers to force the Bill through both houses.

A moderate grouping of Tory peers had proposed reform of the composition rather than the powers of the upper house.[27] Lord Lansdowne, Tory leader in the Lords, introduced a Bill in May 1911. The Bill proposed an upper house of some 350 members; one third elected by MPs, one third appointed by the government in proportion to parties' strength in the Commons, and one third comprised of so-called 'Lords of Parliament'—hereditary peers who had previously held important public office. The Bill did not envisage reduction in the Lords' powers. Lansdowne's initiative was designed to reinforce the Lords' legitimacy as a chamber co-equal to the Commons by reducing the obviously unrepresentative character of its members, and simultaneously increasing their expertise and political impartiality. The Lords would become a meritocratic rather than an aristocratic assembly, designed to restrain the potentially

[26] Jenkins (1968) op cit p 96.   [27] Jenkins (1968) op cit pp 139–144, 200–205.

impetuous wishes of a factional Commons majority by embodying a national interest owing more to sagacity and public service than wealth and genealogy.

The reform proposal was rebuffed by the government, which maintained that its plans to reduce the Lords' power would remain unchanged irrespective of the upper house's composition. Asquith recognised that Lansdowne's new house would still contain an in-built Conservative majority. Had the Cabinet supported the Bill, it would have created a chamber no less powerful and potentially obstructive to Liberal policy than the existing house, but better positioned to defend any such obstruction by pointing to its reformed composition. At this point, a substantial number of moderate peers decided that further resistance to government policy was futile, and the Parliament Bill 1911 was passed in the upper house, albeit by only seventeen votes.[28]

The Parliament Act 1911

The Act's preamble announced that the Act was an interim measure, pending more thoroughgoing reform of the Lords on 'a popular instead of hereditary basis'. The World War I coalition government established the Bryce Commission to explore the question of reform. The Commission's recommendations were not acted upon, but its analysis of the functions a second chamber should perform has attracted widespread support.[29] Bryce identified four main tasks for the Lords: examining and revising Commons Bills; initiating Bills on non-party political subjects; offering a forum for debate on major issues; and, perhaps most importantly, delaying Bills for sufficient time to allow public sentiment to be made clear.[30] We will shortly assess the success with which the Lords has performed these functions. Before doing so we consider an argument thrown up by the 1911 Act concerning the nature of 'Parliament' and its supposedly 'sovereign' law-making powers.

One 'Parliament'? Or three?

The Act introduced several innovations in the way laws might be made. The most significant provision was the grant of law-making powers to the Commons and King in circumstances where the Lords refused to pass a Bill approved in the lower house. Two distinct scenarios were identified in which the Commons and King would acquire this new authority.

Section 1 dealt with 'Money Bills':

> If a Money Bill, having been passed by the House of Commons, and sent up to the House of Lords at least one month before the end of the session, is not passed by the House of Lords without amendment within one month after it is so sent up to that House, the Bill shall, unless the House of Commons direct to the contrary, be presented to His Majesty and become an Act of Parliament on the Royal Assent being signified, notwithstanding that the House of Lords have not consented to the Bill.

Section 1(2) contained examples of the type of Bill that would be regarded as a 'Money Bill'. However s 1(3) further provided that the Speaker would certify whether a Bill did indeed fall within the 'Money Bill' definition.

Section 2 then addressed certain measures other than 'Money Bills':

> (1) If any Public Bill (other than a Money Bill or a Bill containing any provision to extend the maximum duration of Parliament beyond five years) is passed by the House of Commons in three successive sessions (whether of the same Parliament or not), and, having been sent up to the House of Lords at least one month before the end of the session, is rejected by the House of Lords in each of those sessions, that Bill shall, on its rejection for the third time by the House of Lords,

---

[28] The most informative guide is Jenkins (1968) op cit.

[29] (1918) (Cd 9038); see Shell op cit pp 11–13.   [30] Jenkins (1968) op cit pp 280–282.

unless the House of Commons direct to the contrary, be presented to His Majesty and become an Act of Parliament on the Royal Assent being signified thereto, notwithstanding that the House of Lords have not consented to the Bill: Provided that this provision shall not take effect unless two years have elapsed between the date of the second reading in the first of those sessions of the Bill in the House of Commons and the date on which it passes the House of Commons in the third of those sessions.[31]

Section 2(2) required that the Speaker attach a certificate to any Bill sent to the King under this provision, confirming that the necessary events had occurred.

Section 3 further provided that the Speaker's certificate on this matter (as in respect of a s 1(3) certificate) 'shall be conclusive for all purposes, and shall not be questioned in any court of law'. Section 4 then added the requirement that any law produced under the s 1 or s 2 procedures should contain the following statement:

Be it enacted by the King's most Excellent Majesty, by and with the advice and consent of the Commons in this present Parliament assembled, in accordance with the provisions of the Parliament Act 1911, and by authority of the same, as follows . . .

Section 7 of the Act reduced the maximum period between general elections to five years from the previous maximum of seven years.

If interpreted in accordance with either the literal or golden rule, the 1911 Act produces quite peculiar results. Perhaps the Act's most notable textual provision was the characterisation in both s 1 and s 2 of the laws produced by the Commons and King as 'Acts of Parliament'. Read in conjunction with the statement in the preamble to the Act that the Act's objective was, inter alia, 'to restrict the powers of the House of Lords', the 'Act of Parliament' label in ss 1–2 indicates that legislators may have presumed that the 1911 Act created two 'new' or 'alternative' 'Parliaments'; these being the 'Money Bill Parliament' per s 1 (ie Commons and King after a one-month delay) and the 'other public Bill Parliament' per s 2 (ie Commons and King after a three-session/two-year delay). This is, for three reasons, a difficult presumption to accept.

Firstly, the presumption is irreconcilable with the orthodox notion that Parliament qua enacter of statutes is a tripartite institution, and that the assent of each of its three parts is required for a measure to be recognisable as an Act of Parliament. We might readily concede that there can be no objection in legal terms to the proposition that Parliament can create law-making bodies which exercise almost unlimited law-making powers; nor to the suggestion that the laws produced by such a body may be equivalent in terms of hierarchical legal status to Acts of Parliament. Such laws might also be called 'Acts of Parliament'; albeit that so styling them would be confusing, misleading, and constitutionally ill-informed. But whatever form that body might take, and whatever its powers might be, that body would be the creation of Parliament and its laws would be the progeny of the 1911 Act. The body would be a subordinate 'legislature' and the laws it produced would be delegated legislation. From this perspective, a 'better' way for Parliament to have expressed its wishes would have been for the 1911 Act to have characterised the laws made by the Commons and King as measures 'equivalent in effect to Acts of Parliament' and to have styled them not as 'Acts of Parliament' but as 'Parliament Act legislation'.

The second reason relates to the intrinsic illogicality of s 1 and s 2. The 'Money Bill Parliament' is manifestly stated—in unambiguously literal terms—to be a law-making body of very limited competence: its powers are restricted to measures dealing with the subject matter identified in s 1 itself. Similarly, s 2(1) places express limitations on the results that can be

---

[31] The original version of the Bill had not included the 'duration of Parliament' provision. During the Bill's passage, Conservative peers in the Lords proposed many additional restrictions on the powers of the Commons and King qua law-maker. None save the duration of Parliament clause were accepted by the Commons.

produced by the 'other public Bill Parliament'; namely that it cannot 'enact' a Money Bill or a Bill which would extend the duration of a Parliament (ie the period between general elections) beyond five years. The notion expressed in both s 1 and s 2 that a law-maker can be both sovereign and subject to clear restraints on the scope of its powers is inherently oxymoronic.

The third reason—again stemming from the text of the Act itself—is the presence of the s 3 ouster clause. The purpose of an ouster clause is to protect governmental bodies from judicial review.[32] And the purpose of judicial review is to provide a mechanism for establishing that governmental bodies are acting within the limits of their powers. But there is no need to protect 'Parliament' from judicial review, since Parliament's powers are unlimited. In seeking to protect the 'Money Bill Parliament' and the 'other public Act Parliament' from judicial review, the 1911 Act necessarily acknowledges that it was creating law-makers of limited competence.

These difficulties might indicate that any attempt to discern the meaning of the Act would have to attempt to reconcile its text with the purpose that it was intended to serve; or to frame the issue in another way, to identify the 'mischief' the Act was intended to cure. Perhaps the clearest indication of the way in which Asquith's government saw the issue is found in Asquith's addresses to his constituency voters in the January and December 1910 general elections.

In January, Asquith identified the problem in the following terms:

> The claim of the House of Lords to control finance is novel, and a mere usurpation. But the experience of the Parliament which has today been dissolved shows that the possession of an unlimited veto by a partisan people, however clearly expressed, is always liable to be rendered inoperative . . . [A] Liberal majority in the House of Commons, as has been demonstrated during the last four years, is, under existing conditions, impotent to place on the Statute-book the very measures which it was sent to Westminster to carry in to law.
>
> It is absurd to speak of this system as though it secured to us any of the advantages of a Second Chamber, in the sense in which that term is understood and practically interpreted in every other democratic country.
>
> The limitation of the veto is the first and most urgent step to be taken; for it is the condition precedent to the attainment of the great legislative reforms which our party has at heart . . .

In December, he argued:

> The appeal which is now being made to you and to the country at large may almost be said to be narrowed to a single issue. But upon its determination, in one sense or the other, hangs the whole future of Democratic government.
>
> Are the people, through their freely chosen representatives, to have control, not only over finance and administrative Policy, but over the making of their law? Or are we do continue in the one-sided system under which a Tory majority, however small in size and casual in creation, has a free run of the Statute Book, while from Liberal legislation, however clear may be the message of the polls, the forms of the Constitution persistently withhold a fair and even chance?

The 'mischief' which Asquith identifies here is a narrow one; namely that the House of Lords has the capacity to prevent legal effect being given to government-promoted Bills ('Liberal legislation') addressing policy matters attracting discernible popular approval ('the message of the polls').

The legal question raised by the 1911 Act is essentially this: would the courts accept that the Commons and Monarch (using either the s 1 or s 2 procedure) were in legal terms a 'subordinate legislature', and thus entertain the possibility that a measure produced by the Commons and Monarch could be ultra vires their law-making power? The consequential question arising if the first proposition was accepted would be: 'Just what was the extent of the vires granted to the Commons and King by the 1911 Act?'

---

[32] See 'Ouster clauses—*Gilmore* (1957) and *Anisminic* (1969)', ch 3, pp 68–69.

The s 2 procedure was used twice shortly after the 1911 Act came into force. The Government of Ireland Act 1914, which provided for the creation of an Irish Parliament with substantial law-making powers was 'enacted' in 1914 under s 2. The same procedure was used for the Welsh Church Disestablishment Act 1915. Neither measure was subjected to any legal challenge as being used to achieve an objective beyond the powers of the King and Commons.

The Salisbury Doctrine and the Parliament Act 1949

The scope for conflict between the Commons and Lords was reduced virtually to vanishing point for much of the period between 1916 and 1945. For many of these years, the government was a multi-party coalition involving the Conservative, Liberal, and Labour parties. In that political context, the government had no need to resort to law-making powers granted to the Commons and King by the 1911 Act. The evident convergence of policy objectives for Conservative, Liberal, and (most) Labour MPs necessarily meant that there was no obvious opposition faction for Conservative peers to represent, and little scope for the Lords to claim it represented the national interest against a partisan Commons. In one commentator's view, the Lords in 1945 was 'a wasted and powerless assembly. It had long ceased to play any remotely significant role in government.'[33] The failure of successive governments since 1911 to promote legislation to give effect to the declaration in the 1911 Act's preamble that the composition of the Lords would be given a representative basis also lent the upper house an increasingly anachronistic character. From 1930 onwards, the electorate had embraced virtually all adult men and women; the Commons could plausibly be portrayed as the representative of 'the people' in a comprehensive sense. The upper house, in contrast remained an almost entirely hereditary body.

The Salisbury doctrine

The 1945 general election produced a large Commons majority for the Labour Party. The Labour Party had fought that election on the basis of a radical policy programme which included commitments to introduce a comprehensive welfare state and to nationalise many private sector industries. It was not however clear that the Lords, whose members remained overwhelmingly Conservative,[34] would pass the necessary Bills. The prospect arose that the Lords would exercise its powers under the 1911 Act to delay such Bills for two parliamentary sessions.

This stance would have been quite legal. Moreover, the Labour Party's massive Commons majority had been achieved with only 48% of the popular vote. One could see, as in 1906, some basis for arguing that the Labour government's radical plans did not enjoy universal support. Nonetheless, in recognition of these changed political circumstances, Conservative peers adopted a new convention concerning their powers under the 1911 Act. The convention, known as the Salisbury doctrine (after the fifth Marquess of Salisbury, then leader of the Conservative peers and a descendant of the Lord Salisbury mentioned earlier), was that the Lords would not even delay any Bill canvassed in the government's 1945 election manifesto.

The inverse correlation between the degree of 'democracy' shaping the composition of the Commons and the conventional extent of the Lords' powers again seems to explain this change. But the Salisbury doctrine structured the Lords' legislative role only while the majority of peers accepted its principles. For the 1945–1950 Labour government, the doctrine had two flaws. The first was that a Lords' majority for self-restraint could not always be relied upon. The second was a question of time. Because the Lords retained a three-session/two-year suspensory power in respect of public Bills other than Money Bills, the government could only be sure of getting its proposed legislation through both houses if it began more than two sessions before the end of Parliament's five-year term.

[33] Adonis (1993) op cit p 230.   [34] See Table 6.1.

The Parliament Act 1949

The Labour government found this possible obstacle to 'enactment' of its planned legislative programme unacceptably restrictive, so used the 1911 Act procedure to introduce the Parliament Act 1949. This second Parliament Act reduced the Lords' delaying power to two sessions/one year. The Bill was introduced in 1947, and was rejected three times in the House of Lords. The Lords' refusal to pass the Bill was arguably quite consistent with the new Salisbury doctrine convention, as the Labour Party had not expressly intimated prior to the 1945 election that it wished to see the 1911 Act amended in this way. The Labour Party's 1945 election manifesto had included the statement that: '[W]e give clear notice that we will not tolerate obstruction of the people's will by the House of Lords.' This might readily be thought to fall some way short of being 'clear notice' that the electorate was being asked to approve a governmental programme which might involve further curtailment of the upper house's powers by use of the 1911 Act. Some suggestions were made during the Bill's passage that use of the 1911 Act procedure would be 'unconstitutional', in that the 1911 Act had not been intended to be used to curb the Lords' powers any further. As in 1914 and 1915, however, that assertion was not put to a legal test.

The 1949 Act coincided with a cross-party initiative to produce agreement on reforms to the Lords' composition and powers. The Bryce recommendations as to functions of a second chamber were broadly approved; agreement was reached on the principles that this body should be a reformed House of Lords rather than a new institution, and that its composition 'should be such as to secure as far as practicable that a permanent majority is not secured for any one political party'.[35]

No significant changes were made, and it appeared that the Lords might simply fade into obsolescence. In the mid-1950s, attendance averaged sixty members. It seemed the upper house would become a quaint historical relic. However things did not turn out like that.

II. The House of Lords in the modern era

This section examines four episodes in the Lords' recent history: the introduction of life peerages; the proposed 1968 reforms; the Lords' role in the 1974–1979 Parliament; and some aspects of the relationship between the upper house and the Thatcher governments.

Life peerages

In the late 1800s, the constitutional theorist Walter Bagehot had observed that:

> with a perfect Lower House it is certain that an Upper House would scarcely be of any value. But . . . beside the actual House [of Commons] a revising and leisured legislature is extremely useful.[36]

By the mid-1950s, the House of Commons was getting evermore overloaded, both as a legislator and as a scrutiniser of the executive. We saw in chapter five that successive governments have promoted various changes to the Commons' internal workings to try to address this problem; a task which, we might defensibly conclude, was undertaken with varying degrees of sincerity. In the 1950s, rather than radically reform the lower house, the Conservative government looked to the Lords to lighten the Commons' burden.

The 1958 Life Peerages Act introduced a new category of member to the Lords. 'Life peers' were appointed by the Monarch on the advice of the Prime Minister. They were entitled to sit, speak, and vote in the upper house, but could not pass on their titles when they died. Life Peers

---

[35] Jenkins op cit pp 281–282.   [36] Quoted in Griffith and Ryle op cit p 455.

have generally been people who made distinguished contributions to public life, such as MPs, trade unionists, military personnel, businessmen and women, and a smaller number from the arts or universities.[37] The new class of peer meant that the upper chamber was better equipped to perform its complementary function. The infusion of life peers with broad expertise and experience enabled the Lords to counter criticism that it was just peopled by elderly landowners. The characteristics of life peers do not mirror those of the general population—but neither of course do those of MPs.[38]

The shift by 1911 in the Lords' role from co-equality with the Commons to complementarity lent impetus to arguments in favour of diluting the hereditary element in the upper house. As expertise and ability became increasingly important requirements for the second chamber, so the intellectual shortcomings of hereditary peers caused greater dissatisfaction, and the pressure for adding appointed members intensified. The 1958 Act enjoyed some cross-party support, and was designed to strengthen the Lords' complementary relationship to the Commons. Complementarity was not viewed solely as a matter of doing some of the Commons' work. Viscount Samuel, 87 years old and a Minister in Asquith's 1911 government, attributed the need for reform to the entrenchment of party politics in the Commons. While regarding parties as a necessity, he feared that the rigidity of party discipline had produced: 'a considerable crushing of the independent mind' thereby excluding 'men and women who might be of the greatest value to the community, but who have not the time or the temperament . . . to face the turmoil and the preoccupations of strenuous Parliamentary life'.[39]

How effective life peers have been in equipping the Lords to perform its complementary functions is considered later. We might conclude this section by making a simple party political point. Even by 1990 life peers remained very much a minority within the Lords,[40] and so made little impact on the Conservative majority, given the Conservative predispositions of most hereditary members.

Labour Prime Ministers made substantial efforts to increase non-Conservative representation (see Table 6.3), but among Conservative governments, only the Macmillan and Home administrations followed suit. Barely a quarter of the peers created by the Thatcher governments took the Labour or Liberal whip,[41] and since cross-benchers voted predominantly for Conservative policies,[42] it is difficult to avoid the conclusion that the introduction of life peers led the Lords some way towards the situation advocated by Lord Lansdowne, and feared by Asquith, in 1911—namely a Conservative house which could invoke its more expert members as a partial justification for obstructing Labour government policy. Appointing peers remained a non-justiciable issue, although a 'political honours committee', comprising three privy councillors, played a limited role in ensuring that the Prime Minister's nominees were not entirely unsuitable.

The 1968 reforms

In 1964, Labour Prime Minister Harold Wilson warned the upper house that if it delayed government Bills: 'we shall seek a mandate to amend the Parliament Act so as to end the Lords' power to block Commons legislation'.[43] The Salisbury convention made such

---

[37] Shell notes that of 601 life peers created between 1958 and 1991 204 were formerly MPs, 86 businessmen/women, 26 trade unionists, 65 academics, 35 local councillors, 19 civil servants, 9 military personnel, 30 lawyers, 11 doctors, 15 journalists, and 50 other types of public servant: (1992) op cit p 40.

[38] See Adonis (1993) op cit ch 3; Silk op cit ch 2.

[39] Quoted in Weare V (1964) 'The House of Lords—prophecy and fulfilment' *Parliamentary Affairs* 422.

[40] In July 1992, the house had 1,205 members. 26 were clerics, 20 were law lords, 382 were life peers. 777 were hereditary peers; Adonis (1993) op cit p 194.

[41] Adonis op cit pp 232–233.   [42] Shell op cit pp 91–92.   [43] Quoted in Weare op cit p 432.

Table 6.3 Party allegiance of life peers created between 1958 and 1991

Prime Minister	Period	C	L	Lib	CB	Total	Hereditary Peers
Macmillan/Home	1958–64	17	29	1	18	65	870
Wilson	1964–70	11	78	6	46	141	850
Heath	1970–74	23	5	3	15	46	820
Wilson/Callaghan	1974–79	17	82	6	34	139	805
Thatcher	1979–90	99	45	10	45	199	780
Major	1990	6	5	1	1	13	777

Key: C = Conservative: L = Labour: Lib = Liberal/SDP: CB = Cross-bench. Figures for hereditary peers are approximate only.
Source: Compiled from information in Shell D (1992) op cit, Table 2.2; Griffiths and Ryle op cit p 457; Adonis (1993) op cit p 194.

obstruction unlikely. However the Lords initially rejected the War Damage Bill 1965, which, as noted in chapter four, retrospectively reversed *Burmah Oil*. A Lords amendment removed the Bill's retrospective element, but this was promptly reversed by the Commons, whereupon the Marquess of Salisbury, defending the convention bearing his name, persuaded peers to allow the Bill to proceed. The Act provides an interesting example of a dispute between the Lords and Commons which did not have a simple party political basis, since the Bill enjoyed cross-party Commons support. Given the Act's incompatibility with most perceptions of the rule of law, the Lords' stance might be thought consistent with the role of 'watchdog of the constitution'. Equally important however, is the indication the controversy gives of the Lords' impotence when opposing policies supported by Conservatives in the Commons.

The episode may have strengthened the government's resolve to maintain a bipartisan approach to reform, for it established an All Party Committee to consider the future of the upper house. The Committee's main innovation was to recommend dividing the Lords into two categories—voting and non-voting peers. Only life peers would be entitled to vote. The Monarch could bestow life peerages on hereditary Lords, but they would have to give up their titles to vote in the new house.

The bipartisan approach collapsed in June 1967 when the Lords used, for the first time, the power left to them by the 1949 Parliament Act to veto delegated legislation. In November 1968 the Labour government produced a White Paper, *House of Lords Reform*.[44] The continuity in this area of constitutional development is well illustrated by the close correspondence between the White Paper's view of the Lords' appropriate legislative role, and that of the Bryce Commission. The second chamber should serve as a forum for public debate; as a reviser of Bills introduced in the Commons; as an initiator of Bills on less party politicised issues; and as a scrutiniser of the executive and of delegated legislation.

The White Paper's proposals closely resembled the ideas of the All Party Committee, and was enthusiastically endorsed by the Lords. However the Bill introducing the proposals encountered substantial Commons opposition. Right-wing Conservatives attacked it for going too far, while Labour's left wing thought that it did not go far enough.[45] The government subsequently withdrew the Bill in 1969. Between 1969 and 1999 there were no governmental attempts to promote legislation to alter the upper house's powers or composition. This does not mean, however, that the Lords did not generate appreciable constitutional controversy in that period.

[44] Cmnd 3799.   [45] Shell op cit pp 21–23.

The 1974–1979 parliament

Between 1974 and 1979, Britain had a Labour government which never had a Commons majority of more than four. Consequently, the government found it very difficult even to get Bills through the lower house. It faced even more difficulties in the Lords. As Table 6.4 shows, these Labour governments enjoyed only minoritarian support in terms of the share of the vote they won at the two general elections of that year. Furthermore, the government suffered several by-election defeats and defections in the course of the Parliament, which temporarily left it in a Commons minority.

For a brief period after 1977, the Labour and Liberal parties formed a 'pact', in which the Liberals guaranteed their support in return for some policy concessions. This might be argued to have enhanced the government's legitimacy (in a crude majoritarian sense), as the parties combined share of the vote at the last general election exceeded 50%. Despite its weak Parliamentary and electoral position, the 1974–1979 government pursued radical economic policies. This combination of a clearly factional legislative programme by a government with a precarious Commons majority and limited popular support presented the upper house with several difficult questions as to its 'correct' constitutional role.

During the 1959–1964 Parliament, when the Conservatives were in government, there were 299 votes in the Lords. The government was defeated on eleven occasions—3.7% of the time. Between 1974 and 1979, the Lords had 445 divisions. The Labour government was defeated on some 355 occasions—80% of the time. See Table 6.5.

Such bald statistics obviously support arguments that the Lords continued to be a Conservative chamber. However we ought to qualify those figures a little. In almost all cases between 1974 and 1979 the Lords gave way if the Commons sent the Bill back. The government's policies were not being vetoed (a power which the Lords no longer possessed), nor even being delayed for the full period permitted by the 1949 Act. Nevertheless, they were being obstructed. Passing a Bill can be a protracted process, and the Commons only has limited time for this task. By constantly refusing to approve government measures, and requiring the Commons to consider issues again, the Lords significantly impeded government policy. Whether it was constitutionally acceptable for the Lords to do so raises a difficult

Table 6.4 The 1974 general elections—seats won and share of vote

	February	October
Labour	301 (37.1%)	319 (39.2%)
Liberal	14 (19.3%)	13 (18.3%)
Conservative	297 (37.9%)	277 (35.8%)
Others	23 (5.7%)	26 (6.7%)

Source: Butler and Sloman op cit p 186.

Table 6.5 Government defeats in the Lords 1964–1986

Period	Governing Party	Number of defeats
1964–70	Labour	116
1970–74	Conservative	26
1974–79	Labour	355
1979–86	Conservative	100

Source: Brazier R (1990) *Constitutional texts* p 527.

question, which we might try to answer by briefly considering two of the measures on which the houses disagreed.

The Trade Union and Labour Relations (Amendment) Bill and the Aircraft and Shipbuilding Industries Bill

The first Bill was intended to amend the 1974 Trade Union and Labour Relations Act. The Act was concerned with regulating compulsory trade union membership (the 'closed shop') in the workplace; the amending Bill was intended to restrict the circumstances in which employees could refuse to join a union without risking dismissal from their jobs.

The substantive issue seized upon by Conservative and cross-bench peers was their wish to provide additional safeguards for newspaper editors whose freedom of expression was thought to be jeopardised if they had to join a trade union. The government proposed a 'Charter' safeguarding editorial independence, but declined to give it legal force. A Lords amendment to make the Charter enforceable in the courts was passed, reversed in the Commons, but then insisted upon by the Lords. Amid government threats both of a mass creation of peers and of resort to the Parliament Acts, the government's position was eventually accepted by a Lords majority of thirty-seven.

The controversy over the Aircraft and Shipbuilding Industries Bill, intended to bring these industries into public ownership, was equally intense. This policy was an acute source of disagreement between the Conservative and Labour Parties. The Bill's Commons passage, during which the government's proposals were substantially amended, provoked furious controversy. The government frequently guillotined debate, and on one occasion a government whip was accused of deliberately breaking a pairing agreement in a division which the government won on the Speaker's casting vote. Conservative peers, joined by cross-benchers and some Labour members, insisted upon several wrecking amendments. The government then initiated the Parliament Act procedures, but following consultation with the opposition, a much amended Bill was passed some months later.

The constitutionality of the Lords' behaviour on these occasions is debatable.[46] Both measures were included in the Labour Party's 1974 election manifesto, and so were nominally within the Salisbury convention. Yet both were highly contentious Bills, for which there were only the barest Commons majorities. Lord Carrington, then leader of the Conservative peers, saw no shortcomings in the Lords' position. The Lords was invoking its powers: 'for the purpose for which they were given to us—that is as an opportunity for further consultation, for second thoughts.'[47]

Again, however, we are drawn to the impact of convention in undermining the legitimacy of undoubtedly legal behaviour. Shell has suggested that the Lords committed a tactical blunder in the years following World War II by adopting the conventional practice of appearing unwilling to use its delaying powers. Shell argues that this lent an unwarranted degree of constitutional significance to a power envisaged by the framers of the 1911 and 1949 Parliaments as a routine part of the legislative process. It was precisely because this power had become delegitimised through disuse that the events of 1976 and 1977 provoked such a constitutional furore.[48]

The experience of the 1974–1979 Parliament led the Labour Party to pledge to abolish the House of Lords altogether if it won the next general election. It did not succeed at the polls however, and subsequent Conservative governments displayed no inclination formally to amend the status quo. Yet one would be mistaken in assuming that the relationship between the upper house and the Thatcher governments was unproblematic.

---

[46] See Burton I and Drewry G (1978) 'Public legislation: a survey of the sessions of 1975/76 and 1976/77' *Parliamentary Affairs* 140.

[47] Quoted in Adonis (1993) op cit p 227.   [48] Shell (1992) op cit pp 246–253.

The House of Lords and the Thatcher governments

The Thatcher governments of 1979–1990 assumed office, as did Asquith's Liberals in 1906, and Attlee's Labour Party in 1945, committed to implementing a radical policy agenda. Furthermore, just like Asquith's and Atlee's administrations, the Thatcher governments enjoyed substantial Commons majorities gained with less than 50% electoral support. See Table 6.6.

Shell records that the Thatcher administrations were defeated 155 times in the Lords between 1979 and 1990. Sixty-three defeats were accepted by the government, and on thirty occasions a compromise was reached; the remainder were rejected.[49] As the decade progressed, the government became increasingly unwilling to accommodate their Lordships' opinions, with the result that Conservative MPs experienced the inconveniences engendered by the need to be present in the Commons to vote to reverse Lords' amendments.[50]

The reasons for the frequency of conflict between the Lords and Commons in this era are difficult to quantify precisely. One contributory explanation may be that Conservatives in the Commons had become significantly more right wing in their political beliefs than the Conservative peers; such differences of opinion were clearly evident in respect of criminal justice legislation in the early 1980s. Another factor may have been the profound disarray among the Labour, Liberal, and Social Democrat parties in the Commons, which perhaps convinced some peers that they were the only people capable of providing effective parliamentary opposition to Thatcherite policies.

The most acute cause of tension between the Thatcher government and the Lords arose over differences in opinion as to the appropriate constitutional role of local government (an issue considered in detail in chapter ten). The government suffered temporary defeats on several minor issues, such as an attempt to abolish free bus passes for schoolchildren in rural areas, and a clause in the 1985 Housing Bill which sought to force local authorities and housing associations to sell special sheltered accommodation for the elderly. The Lords inflicted more significant reversals on government plans to reform the structure of local government in 1985, and the system of local taxation in 1987 and 1988.[51]

Backwoodsmen—the voting house and the working house

The government's eventual success on the latter issues required it to draw on the so-called 'backwoodsmen'—hereditary Tory peers who took no real part in the life of the house. They rarely attended or contributed to debates but were occasionally prepared to vote when a Conservative government faced defeat on a major issue. No such resource was ever available to a Labour government, but backwoodsmen were a weapon of last resort even for a

Table 6.6 The 1979, 1983, and 1987 elections—seats won and share of vote

	1979	1983	1987
Conservative	339 (43.1)	397 (42.4)	376 (42.3)
Labour	269 (36.9)	209 (27.6)	292 (30.8)
Liberal*	11 (13.8)	23 (25.4)	22 (22.6)

* 1983 and 1987 includes the SDP.
Source: Compiled from information in Norton P (1991) *The British Polity* pp 97–99.

[49] Shell (1992) op cit ch 7.
[50] See particularly Shell D (1985) 'The House of Lords and the Thatcher government' *Parliamentary Affairs* 16; Adonis A (1988) 'The House of Lords in the 1980s' *Parliamentary Affairs* 380.
[51] See Welfare D (1992) 'The Lords in defence of local government' *Parliamentary Affairs* 205; and ch 10.

Conservative government in serious parliamentary difficulties. Because these peers were so disinterested in the day-to-day responsibilities of legislative activity, they were not very responsive to the government whip. Two or three calls in any parliamentary session was the most that a Conservative government could rely on.

For many observers, even one call was one too many. Since the Lords' continued legitimacy depended upon its members gaining a reputation for independent thought and expert abilities, the rapid influx of peers who never demonstrated any legislative skills, and who were clearly acting under party orders, enhanced neither the dignity nor the authority of the house.

The problem of backwoodsmen led to the suggestion that one could draw a distinction between the 'working house' and the 'voting house'.[52] In the 1980s, the working house—those peers who attended regularly and contributed to debate—was fairly evenly divided between government and the opposition. This can create the impression that the Lords could be as powerful an obstacle to a Conservative government as to a Labour administration. However the voting house, which included the backwoodsmen, was so heavily Conservative that government policies were not seriously threatened.[53] This led to the apparently unsatisfactory circumstance in which Lords debates suggested that majority sentiment opposed the government, only for the non-working Lords to appear and safeguard government policy when the vote was held.

The backwoodsmen problem would have disappeared had the 1968 reforms been enacted. It would no doubt have been a simple matter for a determined government with a reliable Commons majority to enact a third Parliament Act to achieve that objective. A more difficult question is how effectively the 'working house' performed its role.

III. The work of the House of Lords today

The Lords became a more important element of the government process from 1960 onwards. Adonis speaks of a 'remarkable revival'; Shell of a 'much better attended and a partly professional House'.[54] As Table 6.7 indicates, the time the Lords devotes to its tasks has increased markedly since 1950. This section centres on four areas in which the Lords might have played an obviously complementary role to the Commons, areas canvassed in the Bryce Report and/or the 1967 White Paper; deliberation on matters of public concern; revision and initiation of legislation; consideration of delegated legislation; and scrutiny of the executive.

Table 6.7   House of Lords: sitting hours and attendance 1950–2006

Session	Sitting Days	Sitting Hours	Attendance
1950–1951	96	292	86
1960–1961	125	599	142
1970–1971	153	966	265
1980–1981	143	920	296
1985–1986	165	1213	317
1995–1996	136	885	372
2005–2006	206	1370	403

Source: Griffith and Ryle op cit p 472; Baldwin N (1999) 'The membership and work of the House of Lords', p 47, in Dickson and Carmichael (eds) *The House of Lords: its parliamentary and judicial roles.*

[52] Adonis (1993) op cit pp 198–199; Griffith and Ryle op cit pp 465–466.

[53] See particularly Adonis' demolition of the claim made by Lord Denham, government chief whip, that: 'However you calculate it, the Conservative Party has no overall majority in your Lordship's House' (1988) op cit pp 381–382.

[54] (1993) op cit p 226; (1992) op cit p 28.

Several characteristics of the Lords distinguish it from the Commons. Perhaps most significant was its less structured party discipline. In part this resulted from peers' non-elected status, which freed them from any need to cater to the prejudices of their local constituency associations. The weaker grip exercised by party loyalties over peers' behaviour also accrued from their age and backgrounds; for peers at the end of their careers or with substantial extra-parliamentary interests 'the bait of Ministerial office dangled so effectively in the Commons is missing'.[55] The major parties maintain formal organisations within the house, for which they receive limited public funds, and also have a whipping system, albeit of an exhortatory rather than directory nature. A peer's behaviour must be egregious before he/she suffers withdrawal of the whip.[56]

The Lords preserved a more negotiatory approach to timetabling its business than the Commons. Government business has no formal priority; that it enjoys that status de facto is the result of the maintenance of conciliatory relations between the parties and cross-benchers through the upper house's variant of the 'usual channels'.

The more loosely disciplined nature of the Lords was further evidenced by the absence of a Speaker with coercive powers over procedure. The Lord Chancellor presided over the House in a formal sense, but regulation of peers' behaviour was a matter for the peers themselves. The chamber was 'guided' on such matters by the Leader of the House. The Lords sporadically considered the desirability of creating an office similar to that of the Speaker of the Commons, but until 2006 preferred to rely on members' good manners to maintain decorous standards. The Lords did establish the post of 'Lord Speaker' in 2006. The Lord Speaker now has responsibility for presiding over debates in the house, although she lacks the disciplinary powers wielded by the Speaker in the Commons. She also plays a prominent ambassadorial role, representing the house to the outside world and receiving visitors on the house's behalf. The rules relating to the post provide for the Lord Speaker to be elected by the members of the house, to serve for up to two five-year terms. The Lord Speaker must foreswear any party political allegiance while she occupies the post, and may not vote on any matters.

Deliberation

It is often said that debates on matters of general public concern in the Lords are of a higher quality than in the Commons. This is partly because many members have considerable expertise in particular areas, and partly because party loyalty is not as unswerving as in the Commons. As Griffith and Ryle suggest: 'such subjective judgements are impossible either to prove or to refute'.[57] One can undoubtedly point to debates on major issues where speakers have brought a formidable body of knowledge and experience to bear on the issue concerned; reform of the legal profession, the administration of justice, and foreign and commonwealth relations are areas where the upper house possesses considerable expertise.[58] The quality of debate, in the sense of its capacity fully to explore the substance of the issue in question, rather than simply advance a partisan response, is aided by the more muted nature of party politics and the more relaxed procedural regime. However, if one construes the 'quality' of debate in terms of its influence on subsequent policy, the Lords' success is far more difficult to quantify. Adonis concludes that Lords' debates 'rarely have an impact on policy which is more than minor and indirect'; while Shell maintains that: 'Almost everyone involved with the House acknowledges that a great deal of what is said there is worthless'.[59]

Less cynically, one might suggest that as a deliberative chamber the Lords functions more as a sounding board than as crucial contributor to policy formation over the full range of

[55] Griffith and Ryle op cit p 510.   [56] For examples see Shell (1992) op cit pp 93–94.
[57] Op cit p 497.   [58] Shell (1992) op cit pp 188–194; Adonis (1993) op cit p 194.
[59] Adonis (1993) op cit p 216; Shell (1992) op cit p 198.

government activities. Debate in the upper house seems to have significant influence only in areas where the Lords combines expertise with personal interests in matters which are fairly non-contentious in the party political sense, such as legal reform, issues concerning the elderly, and policies affecting agriculture and the countryside. The percentage of the Lords' workload devoted to deliberative activities has declined since 1980; from over 25% in 1979 to barely 14% in 1988.[60] This could be construed as an indication that the upper house has become less enamoured with its reflective role in recent years, but it may also be due to rather more practical pressures.

Revision of legislation

The reduction in the percentage of Lords' time spent on general debate has been more than matched by an increase in attention devoted to its purely legislative role. By 1989, 60% of the house's sitting hours were consumed by the revision of legislation, the overwhelming majority of which originated in the Commons.[61] We have already considered the (now limited) circumstances in which the Lords might reject a Bill. In quantitative terms, the Lords' revisionary role is primarily concerned with constructive rather than destructive amendment.

The lower profile of party loyalty and greater procedural flexibility in the Lords supposedly enables the upper house to do a better job of revising proposed legislation than the Commons. Peers are assumed to be less firmly wedded to party ideology, and so more willing to accept that Bills may contain technical flaws. The presence of a substantial number of cross-bench peers reinforces this assumption. Relatedly, the growing breadth of experience and expertise among life peers make it likely that the upper house can muster an informed audience for even the most esoteric of government legislative proposals.

Superficially, a Bill's passage through the Lords mirrors that in the Commons. There are however certain important differences. The house does not have a guillotine procedure: rather it relies on peers themselves to ensure that their spoken contributions are pertinent and concise. Perhaps more importantly, the Lords traditionally did not have a standing committee structure: the committee stage is generally taken on the floor of the house. The committee stage is presided over by the Chairman of Committees, a salaried post, to which a peer is appointed by the house each parliamentary session. During this period, the Chairman must detach her/himself from any party political activities.

The committee stage has latterly accounted for almost half of the time the upper chamber has given to its legislative functions.[62] The Lords has conducted sporadic experiments with standing committees in the past forty years, but none were regarded as a success.[63] In 1993–1994, the Lords made a further effort in this regard, by considering five relatively uncontroversial Bills under the so-called 'Jellicoe procedure'. Pressure on time is further increased, almost comically, by the physical process of walking through division lobbies whenever a vote on an amendment is taken: forty hours were spent simply on voting in the 1985–1986 session.[64]

Table 6.7 charts the apparently substantial growth in the Lords' activities. One should not read too much into workload statistics, for crude figures often conceal vast variations in the complexity or importance of nominally equivalent subject matter. Many amendments may be introduced at the government's request, to remedy defects which escaped the Commons' attention. While this may be a valuable function for the upper house to fulfill, it raises the danger of the Lords becoming a convenient dumping ground for dealing with legislative minutiae which the Commons is unwilling to address. A related problem is the government's recurring failure to spread the Lords legislative load evenly through the parliamentary session, with the

---

[60] Griffith and Ryle op cit p 473. [61] Ibid. [62] Griffith and Ryle op cit p 483.
[63] Shell (1992) op cit pp 140–142; Borthwick R (1973) 'Public Bill Committees in the House of Lords' *Parliamentary Affairs* 440.   [64] Adonis (1993) op cit p 241.

result that the upper house faces impossibly onerous tasks which cannot be discharged in any meaningful way.[65]

Given the then Conservative majority in the Lords, it is safe to conclude that many of the amendments carried against government wishes during the 1980s were not motivated by simple party political bias. Yet as Adonis observed in 1993: 'On not a single occasion since 1979 has the Lords insisted on one of its amendments once overturned by the Commons'.[66] A Lords amendment against the government may be significant when the government has only a small Commons majority, for the reasoning behind the Lords' decision might persuade wavering backbench MPs not to follow the party line. But when faced with a cohesive Conservative majority in the lower house, the Lords latterly resembled a constitutional watchdog long deprived of any significant bite, and rarely willing to bark.

One notable recent exception was the Lords' refusal to pass the War Crimes Bill. This Bill was intended to impose retrospective criminal liability for war crimes committed in World War II by foreign nationals who had subsequently become British citizens. The Bill received clear cross-party support in the Commons. However a similar cross-party consensus in the Lords rejected it for what would appear to be, *pace* the War Damage Act, 'rule of law' type reasons—namely opposition in principle to retrospective legislation.[67] The Lords' behaviour prompted even some Conservative MPs to question the constitutional defensibility of a non-elected chamber frustrating the elected house, but predictions of a constitutional crisis when the government used the Parliament Acts procedure proved unfounded.

The upper house also inflicted several defeats on the Major government's Criminal Justice Bill in 1994, relating to matters of sentencing policy and the conduct of criminal trials. Most defeats were reversed in the Commons, but the government made several concessions to the upper house. The Bill had been announced as a major plank of government policy by Home Secretary Michael Howard at the 1993 Conservative Party Conference. The Lords' intransigence might be seen either as an unacceptable barrier to the wishes of an elected government, or as a prudent means to ensure that important legislation was not unduly influenced by improperly partisan objectives. (See Table 6.8.)

Control of delegated legislation

The Lords retains co-equal status with the Commons over private Bills, although this is perhaps insufficiently important a topic to merit attention here. A more significant issue is the Lords' continued co-equality in respect of statutory instruments. Given the much greater resort made to such measures by modern governments, and the Commons' obvious shortcomings

Table 6.8 Lords amendments to government Bills 1970–1990

Period	Bills	Bills amended	Total amendments
1970–1973	79	31	2366
1974–1977	68	49	1859
1979–1982	82	39	2231
1983–1986	69	43	4137
1987–1990	61	38	5181

Source: Shell (1992) op cit, p 144.

---

[65] The problem has been posed by governments of both parties; see Shell (1992) op cit pp 139–141; Drewry and Burton op cit.

[66] (1993) op cit p 237.   [67] See Richardson (1995) op cit.

in monitoring their use, one might have expected this to be an area in which the upper house might function as a meaningful curb on government excesses. The formal parity between the two houses is emphasised by their equality of representation on the joint select committee which examines the technical propriety of such measures.

In respect of the substantive policy merits of delegated legislation, however, we can once again discern a large gap between the Lords' legal and conventional authority. Between 1949 and 1999 the Lords only once (in 1967) vetoed an order. By the mid-1980s, it appeared widely accepted that a repeat of such behaviour would breach convention.[68] The Lords' reticence may spring from a fear that exercising its veto would simply lead to a third Parliament Act removing their legal co-equality, but quite what purpose is served by possessing a legal power one will never use is unclear. This is perhaps another situation in which the Lords' legal powers have been delegitimised through disuse.

The house has fashioned several devices for expressing disapproval of government proposals without rejecting them. Motions signalling disagreement with or regret at an instrument may be moved and voted upon. Such devices may prove an embarrassment to the government, especially if they attract press publicity, but their value would appear to be more a symbolic affirmation of the Lords' independence than a practical constraint on executive action.

Scrutiny of the executive

There would be little need for upper house scrutiny of executive behaviour if the Commons adequately performed that task. But the intensity of party discipline and paucity of investigatory resources in the lower house places stringent restrictions on the effectiveness of MPs' supervisory capacities. Consequently, there is appreciable scope for the Lords to complement the Commons in this respect.

Like the Commons, however, the Lords' scrutinising role is subject to resource constraints. These arise not simply, as in the Commons, from the limited office space and research assistance financed by the government, but also from more structural institutional sources. While it was commonplace for as many Ministers to sit in the Lords as in the Commons in the nineteenth century, almost all Ministers are now members of the lower house. Although modern Conservative governments have included several senior Ministers from the Lords, it is likely for a Labour government that the Lord Chancellor and Leader of the House will be the Lords' only two Cabinet Ministers. This poses obvious problems of accountability, simply because the politician responsible for the activities of most government departments is never present in the chamber. Occasional suggestions have been floated that all senior Ministers should be entitled to speak in either house, but none has been adopted.

The government's limited representation in the house also poses problems of competence. The practice which has consequently evolved is for politicians of sometimes limited experience to assume substantial departmental responsibilities at an early stage of their careers. The Labour Party suffered particular problems in finding sufficient frontbench spokespersons, particularly in opposition. Almost all Labour members were life peers, and as well as being older than many of their hereditary Conservative counterparts, they were ending their political careers—a junior ministerial or shadow post was therefore not an attractive proposition.

With the exception of a limited number of Ministerial posts, Leader of the Opposition, and Opposition Chief Whip, and the non-party political offices of Chairman and Principal Deputy Chairman of Committees, membership of the Lords is not salaried. While peers may claim reasonably generous expense allowances (£300 per day) for days on which they attend the house, those lacking independent means cannot afford to be full-time politicians, a factor which necessarily reduces the time peers can devote to examining government activities.

[68] Shell (1992) op cit p 219.

IV. The 1999 reforms

Both the Labour and Liberal parties fought the 1992 general election on manifestos which included proposals to replace the Lords with some form of elected assembly. The Conservatives' victory at that election forestalled any possibility of reform, but did nothing to reduce the Lords' obvious weaknesses. The most evident of these derived from the house's composition. The Labour and Liberal parties saw no defensible basis for an hereditary form of membership in our modern society—expert and independent judgement is not a genetically transmitted trait.

The Labour Party's 1997 election manifesto included a pledge that a Labour government would introduce a Bill that would remove hereditary peers from the Lords, although the manifesto did not make it clear if the party's preference was to simply retain the Lords on a life peer only basis, or to transform the Lords into an elected chamber. The Bill's prominent place in the manifesto should, in principle, have ensured that its passage was not blocked in the upper house. For peers to have rejected the Bill would have been a clear breach of the Salisbury convention. If the convention were to be respected, there would be no need for the government to invoke the Parliament Acts to bypass the Lords' refusal to approve the Bill.

The Lords' Conservative majority did not however defer to the government's overwhelming Commons' majority. In 1998, the government introduced its sweeping Crime and Disorder Bill in the House of Lords. The Bill's initial passage through the upper house was uncontroversial. However, when the Bill came to the Commons, a Labour MP moved an amendment intended to equalise the age of consent to sexual relations for people of both heterosexual and homosexual orientation. The amendment received a majority of over 200 in the Commons in July 1998. On 23 July, the Bill was rejected by 290 votes to 122 in the Lords. Rather than risk losing the entire Bill, the government withdrew the amendment. The amendment had not been part of Labour's election manifesto, so its rejection by the Lords could not be regarded as a breach of the Salisbury convention. However the sentiments expressed by many peers who had opposed equalising the age of consent were distinctly bigoted and intolerant, which rather undermined the suggestion that the Lords served as a moderating force against a narrowly partisan Commons.

The Blair government subsequently affirmed its support for the equal age amendment by including an identical provision in its Sexual Offences (Amendment) Bill in 1998. This measure was supported by all three major parties in the Commons, but was rejected by the Lords. And once again, the rejection was cast in such intolerant and antediluvian terms that one might wonder if the government had deliberately offered the upper house the opportunity to discredit itself in public opinion; an opportunity which—if taken—would reduce any public disquiet about subsequent Lords reform.

By late 1998 the Conservative majority in the Lords had angered the government substantially by failing to respect the terms of the Salisbury convention. The Labour Party's 1997 election manifesto had promised that a Bill to reform the electoral system used to select British members of the European Parliament would be introduced for elections scheduled in May 1999. In autumn 1998, the Lords consistently refused to pass the Bill, on the disingenuous grounds that since the Labour manifesto had not specified precisely the new system that would be introduced, rejecting the measure did not breach the Salisbury convention. As in 1910 and 1911, the Conservative majority in the Lords was fully supported by the Conservative opposition in the Commons—characterising the Lords' majority as 'Mr Hague's poodle'[69] would seem entirely apposite.

---

[69] William Hague replaced John Major as leader of the Conservative Party in 1997.

Had the Blair government harboured any doubts about proceeding with reform of the Lords, the European elections controversy would have dispelled it. The details of the reform emerged late in 1998, amid an extraordinary breakdown of discipline within the Conservative shadow Cabinet. In an attempt to forestall opposition to reform in the upper house, the Blair government had negotiated an agreement with the leader of the Conservative peers, Lord Cranborne, that ninety-two hereditary peers could continue to sit in the house. Cranborne had not informed his shadow Cabinet colleagues of these negotiations, and was promptly dismissed from the shadow Cabinet when they were revealed. Bizarrely, the Conservative Party then decided to support the arrangement.

The last weeks of the unreformed Lords' life were a farrago of pantomime and farce. The government had decided that the ninety-two hereditary members who would sit in the new house should be 'elected' by the hereditary peers.[70] Candidates were permitted to issue a seventy-five word 'manifesto' supporting their cause. The documents which emerged prompted the thought that the Blair government had again taken the chance to allow the hereditary peers to make themselves appear ridiculous. Viscount Monckton's manifesto announced:

> I support the Queen and all the royal family . . . All cats to be muzzled outside to stop the agonising torture of small birds. . . . LEVEL UP, not level down. God willing.

Earl Alexander of Tunis invoked more nationalistic sentiments:

> By the living God who made me, but I love this country. . . . I will struggle with all I have to offer: For her democracy, her integrity, her sovereignty, her independence, her self-government, her crown and the rights and ancient freedoms of her people.

Having entered the realms of the absurd in the run-up to the hereditaries' 'election', the house then moved to the surreal on 27 October 1999 at the Bill's third reading. As the debate began, the Earl of Burford leapt onto the Lord Chancellor's seat to shout out a tirade of hysterical nonsense. As peers from all sides of the house watched in stunned silence, soon followed by mutters of disapproval, Burford informed his audience the Bill was 'Treason', promoted by Prime Minister Blair as a first step in the abolition of Britain: 'Before us lies the wasteland. No Queen, no culture, no sovereignty, no freedom. Stand up for your Queen and country and vote this down'. Had supporters of the reform of the Lords been invited to conjure a scenario in which the upper house's anachronisms were revealed most starkly to the public, they could hardly have imagined anything quite so effective as Burford's intervention. His pleas fell—unsurprisingly—on deaf ears. The Cranborne deal was respected by most peers, and the Bill passed its third reading by a majority of 140.

The house saved a final irritation to the government for the next day, when peers voted again against some provisions of the government's contentious welfare reform Bill—a measure already promoting rebellion among Labour MPs in the Commons. Perhaps ironically, the house's behaviour on this matter offered a perfect example of the role a subordinate second chamber might legitimately play. The arguments against the Bill were calm and measured, the votes against it drawn from all sides of the house.

The 'reformed' House of Lords

Given the significance of its impact on the composition of Parliament, the House of Lords Act 1999 is a remarkably slender document. Section 1 provides simply that: 'No-one shall be a member of the House of Lords by virtue of a hereditary peerage'. Section 2 permits up to ninety-two persons to be exempted from s 1. Hereditary peers not exempted under s 2 may stand for election to the Commons and vote in Commons elections.

---

[70] The government had indicated that the reform legislation would contain retrospective authorisation for this 'election'.

The Act creates a second chamber with obvious similarities to the 1911 Landsdowne proposals, which Asquith rejected for fear that a more legitimately composed house would be more obstructive to the Commons than an hereditary chamber. The Blair government had evidently overlooked this possibility, as it appeared wholly surprised in January 2000 when a multi-party grouping (including prominent Labour peers) in the Lords blocked by a majority of 100 the government's proposals to restrict the right to trial by jury. The legislation seemed an ideal candidate to be legitimately delayed in the new upper house. It was controversial in substance, impacted heavily on civil liberties, and raised the type of question which many life peers—by virtue of their legal experience—were well-equipped to evaluate. The government did not accept this proposition however. Home Secretary Jack Straw complained that the Lords' threat was 'undemocratic'. This comment was rather ill-conceived. Since the Blair government had presumably promoted the Lords reform Bill in the belief that the house's new composition was (if only temporarily) the most appropriate for a body possessing delaying and scrutinising powers, it could hardly be 'undemocratic' for those powers to be used; unless, of course, the government accepted that the reformed house was per se an 'undemocratic' institution. The episode rather indicated that the Blair government's view of the Lords' democratic credentials rested primarily on a majority in the upper house agreeing with the majority in the Commons; a perspective which suggests there is little point in having a second chamber at all.

The 1999 Act did however immediately much reduce the Conservative Party's strength in the upper chamber. As of November 2001, the Conservatives held 222 Lords seats, the Labour Party 197, the Liberals 62, and the cross-benchers (including bishops and law lords) 216. Given the (C)conservative predispositions of many cross-benchers,[71] the government could certainly not expect to command reliable majority support in the upper house. Frequently aired objections that the Blair government had 'packed' the Lords with its own supporters therefore had little basis in fact; rather the Prime Minister had used 'his' powers of appointment to begin to redress the huge historical imbalance within the house in favour of the Conservative Party.

The recommendations of the Wakeham Commission

The Royal Commission established in 1999 to make recommendations for long-term reform to the House of Lords published its report, *A house for the future*, in January 2000. The Wakeham Commission had proceeded on the assumption that the powers of the upper chamber would remain largely unchanged. Its task was therefore to consider how to reform the composition of the Lords in ways which would enhance its existing complementary role to the Commons.

Effective complementarity would require independence and expertise within the upper house. If we accept that the Lords should be both subordinate to the Commons and independent of the prevailing patterns of party affiliation in the lower house, there is no need for its members to be elected. Indeed, for those purposes an elected second chamber could be quite dysfunctional. If elected on the same basis as the Commons, the Lords might simply reproduce its party alignment, and so lose any plausible claim to independence. If chosen through a different electoral system, the Lords might be construed as a more legitimate expression of the people's wishes, and so pose a threat to the lower house's 'democratically' justified superiority. And whatever form of election was used, there remains the risk that members would be elected because of their appeal to transient popular prejudice, and so produce a chamber intellectually unsuited for its role of exerting a supra-party political influence on legislative and governmental processes.

---

[71] The point should not be overstated; see Russell M and Sciara M (2009) 'Independent parliamentarians en masse: the changing nature and role of the 'crossbenchers' in the House of Lords' *Parliamentary Affairs* 32.

The life peerage system therefore appears well suited as a selection process for a complementary house. Reform to the Life Peerage Act to place some justiciable limits on the Prime Minister's powers to nominate peers might seem desirable, but the greatest weakness in the membership of the Lords that selection through life peerages would produce would seem to be not one of political bias or limited ability, but of age: a more vigorous house may demand that we have a younger house.

Given the predominance of the party in modern political life, it would be facile to think one could remove party politics from the Lords. Even if one abolished formal party organisation, it is certain that members' behaviour would continue to be structured by their party loyalties. And, indeed, since one of the functions we wish the Lords to perform is scrutiny of the executive, there must be a sufficient number of competent Ministers in the house for other peers to question. Consequently, rather than wondering how to abolish party influence, a more pertinent inquiry would be to ask how much influence should be accorded to party discipline in respect of each of the house's various functions.

Objections to the Lords' powers to delay or amend government Bills derive not so much from the delay per se, as from its differential party impact. That the Lords indulged in such behaviour prior to 2000 far more frequently when a Labour government controlled the Commons suggests that their Lordship's stance owed less to a principled belief in the integrity of their position than to a knee-jerk mobilisation of their Conservative majority. There is no justification for according party ideology such scope in a complementary chamber. This suggests the Lords' composition as a corporate entity would have to be based on a quota system which ensured that a government Bill could be delayed or amended only if opposition peers won over a substantial body of cross-bench opinion, and perhaps some governing party peers as well. One would thereby increase the likelihood that any legislative difficulties the government encountered derived from flaws in its policies, rather than the simple factional opposition intransigence. Nor should a house of life peers experience any conventional reluctance to use such legal powers—their very purpose would be to cause the government difficulties if it appeared that legislative policy ignored public sentiment. In this context, as with its scrutinising functions, the Lords' role is to expose government policy to the oxygen of publicity by alerting the electorate to criticism of the government's position.

The Wakeham Commission did not propose any increase in the upper chamber's legislative powers. Indeed, to the contrary, the Commission recommended that the Lords' veto power over delegated legislation be replaced with a much lesser power to delay such measures for up to three months. It did recommend a modest extension of the Lords' role in scrutinising executive behaviour, primarily through an expansion of the house's select committee system. The Commission also suggested that—while members should not be salaried—they should receive enhanced attendance allowances, which raised the possibility that some members would be able to sit in the chamber on much more than an occasional basis.

The modesty of these proposals was matched by the Commission's recommendations for altering the house's composition. Wakeham saw no place for the remaining ninety-two 'hereditary' peers in a reformed house. The Commission suggested that the great majority of members of the new house, of whom there would be some 550, should be appointed to office. The Commission saw no valid role for the Prime Minister in the appointment process. Rather appointments should be made by an independent 'Appointments Commission', with ten members selected on a non-partisan basis. Appointees would serve for a fifteen-year fixed term. The Appointments Commission would ensure that the party balance among appointed members bore a close resemblance to each party's share of the vote at the most recent general election. In a further break with tradition, the Commission proposed that the overall composition of the house should better represent women and ethnic minorities than had been the case in the previous house and in the Commons. The Commission also recommended that a small proportion of the new house's members should be elected. The various commissioners could not agree on how many members should be chosen in this way. Three options were suggested, ranging from barely 10% of the house to a maximum of around 35%. These modest figures led Shell to observe; 'One senses throughout the report a fundamental antipathy towards including elected members'.[72] The proposals attracted little enthusiasm from the opposition parties or constitutional reform pressure groups, most of whom favoured the creation of a wholly elected second house. That perspective has little to commend it. That it was appointed peers who rejected the government's jury trial proposals so decisively (coincidentally on the same day that the Wakeham report was published) provides compelling evidence that an elected house is not necessary to ensure that the second chamber makes an effective contribution to the legislative process. The Commission was perhaps ill-advised in suggesting that any members be elected. In so doing, it implicitly acknowledged that it saw force in this argument yet, by recommending that so few members be chosen in this way, it opened itself to the criticism of being hypocritical or fainthearted. That view was strengthened by repeated rumours that the Cabinet had made it known to Lord Wakeham that a wholly or predominantly appointed house would be its preferred option. Despite its preferences being granted, the government made no immediate attempt to promote legislation further reforming the upper house. It seemed likely that any such proposal would be delayed until after the next general election.[73]

The 2001 White Paper

That the second Blair government harboured no great enthusiasm for radical Lords reform was clearly evident from the contents of the white paper published in 2001, *Completing the reform*.[74] The government had formed the view that creating an entirely or substantially elected upper house was not a viable option, as this might lead to a situation of legislative 'gridlock' between the houses.[75] While there is undoubtedly some force in this position, the government rather undermined the potency of its own favoured reform by proposing a house whose members would be selected in an incoherent mish-mash of ways.

The white paper accepted that hereditary peers should be removed from the house. It then recommended a chamber composed of some 600 peers: 120 would be elected on a regional basis; 120 would be appointed by a statutory, non-partisan Appointments Commission; and 360 would be selected by party leaders in shares approximately equal to the parties' popularity at the previous general election. This represented a significant dilution of the Wakeham proposals, which had envisaged that all non-elected peers be selected by the Appointments Commission.[76]

The white paper attracted little positive comment in the press or within Parliament. More radical proposals were advanced, including—with breathtaking hypocrisy—a suggestion from the Conservative Party that a reformed house be entirely elected. More significantly, in a rare display of independence, substantial numbers of backbench Labour MPs voiced strong opposition to the white paper, with many seemingly favouring a largely or wholly elected upper house.

---

[72] Shell D (2000) 'Reforming the House of Lords' *Public Law* 193.

[73] See especially Bogdanor V (1999) 'Reform of the House of Lords: a sceptical view' *Political Quarterly* 375.

[74] Lord Chancellor's Department (2001) *Completing the reform*.

[75] Whether such 'gridlock' would be of a symbolic or practical kind would of course depend on the powers that the reformed Lords would exercise. The government did embrace Wakeham's proposals that the Lords' powers over delegated legislation be reduced. No enhancement of powers in respect of primary legislation was proposed. Any gridlock that might ensue if this weakened house were to be composed of elected members would be of a sort that would embarrass a government with a Commons majority rather than block its legislative programme.

[76] Prompting the unflattering comment that the white paper would; 'allow the party leaders to use the Lords as a patronage bin'; Constitution Unit (2001—December) *Monitor* p 2.

The Blair government apparently did not see the question of further reform to the House of Lords as a matter of sufficient importance to warrant an open fight with its backbenchers, and in May 2002 the government announced that more far-reaching proposals for reform would be considered by a joint Commons and Lords Committee. Quite how receptive the Blair government would be to the Committee's plans remained to be seen. The Leader of the House, Robin Cook, announced in May 2002 that; 'The matter is now in the hands of parliament and the speed and the radicalism with which we can now move is very much down to how MPs proceed in this matter and how they subsequently vote'.[77] Notwithstanding this statement of intent, press stories in June 2002 suggested that the government had been at some pains to place its own supporters on the joint committee, to be chaired by Jack Cunningham, a Cabinet Minister in the first Blair government.

The Joint Committee's report, published in the autumn of 2002,[78] concluded that there was little point in addressing the issue of whether any changes should be made to the powers of the Lords until the matter of its composition was settled. The Joint Committee also identified various criteria which the reformed house should meet; 'legitimacy'; 'representativeness'; 'no domination by any one party'; 'independence'; and 'expertise'.[79] Those criteria, while undeniably vague, would seem wholly unobjectionable. On the question of altering the composition of the house, however, the Joint Committee was rather more opaque. Its core recommendation was that MPs should be given a free vote on various reform options, ranging from creating a fully elected chamber to retaining a fully appointed body through a number of hybrid elected/appointed options.

The government nominally accepted that the matter should be left to a free vote. However, shortly before the Commons addressed the issue, the Prime Minister made it clear that he was firmly supportive of a fully appointed second chamber. Mr Blair appeared concerned that a fully or partly elected upper house would act in effect as a rival rather than revising chamber to the Commons. His intervention was criticised both in the media and within Parliament, on the grounds that some of the more quiescent Labour MPs would not visibly vote against his wishes irrespective of their own views on the merits.

The Commons' subsequent vote on reform descended into farce. MPs were eventually presented with seven proposals for reform. Amid allegations that Labour whips were exerting pressure on Labour MPs to follow the Prime Minister's line, none of the proposals mustered majority support.[80] It was expected that the Joint Committee would make further attempts to fashion a proposal that would carry a majority in the Commons, but no successful reform emerged.

Notwithstanding the press criticism levied at the Blair government for its failure to take a radical lead on this issue, the status quo might be thought to have certain benefits. The partially reformed house has continued to prove a more potent obstacle to government policy than the Commons. As the reform debate raged at the end of 2002, the Lords succeeded in persuading the government to make several important changes to Bills dealing with asylum and animal health issues. In 2003, the upper house proved similarly obstructive towards the government's flagship Bill to reform the National Health Service[81]; and in both 2004 and 2005 the Lords inflicted defeats on the government in respect of proposed anti-terrorism legislation. It might also be suggested that the current house had by then become reasonably representative of the public at large, at least in respect of the issue of party political affiliation. In the 2001 general election, the proportion of eligible voters who supported the Labour, Conservative, and Liberal parties were 24%, 19%, and 11% respectively. At that time, Labour peers held 28%

---

[77] *The Guardian* 14 May 2002.   [78] Joint Committee on House of Lords Reform (2002) *First report*.

[79] On the notions of 'democratic', 'representative', and 'legitimate' in this context see Kelso A (2006) 'Reforming the House of Lords: navigating representation, democracy and legitimacy at Westminster' *Parliamentary Affairs* 563.

[80] See Cowley (2005) op cit pp 34–36; 97–100.   [81] Cowley op cit pp 152–154.

of seats in the Lords; the Conservatives 32%; and the Liberals 9%; with the balance held by cross-benchers. As we shall see in chapter seven, the Lords might plausibly claim to be better representative of contemporary voting patterns than is the Commons.

One parliament or three? *Jackson v Attorney-General*

While neither Parliament nor the Blair government displayed enthusiasm for further Lords reform, the courts offered, in 2004 and 2005, answers to the legal questions raised by the Parliament Act 1911; namely were the Commons and King a 'subordinate legislature'; and, if so, what were the limits on their legislative power?

In the postwar era, two distinct views had emerged among academic commentators. The first, championed by Professor de Smith was that the Parliament Act had 'redefined Parliament' in a way which; 'provided a simpler, optional procedure for legislation on most topics'.[82] Any measure produced by the Commons and King was indeed therefore as much an 'Act of Parliament' as a statute enacted in the orthodox manner. de Smith's view on this point appeared to be much influenced by the Commonwealth legislature cases discussed in chapter two.[83] Quite why these cases should be regarded as relevant to the nature of the British Parliament is, for reasons outlined in chapter two,[84] something of a mystery.

The second view, proposed by William Wade, seems more persuasive. That view, initially advanced in 1955 and reiterated in 1980[85] was that measures passed by the Commons and King under the Parliament Act procedures were delegated legislation. While the Commons and Monarch might indeed be a 'legislature', they could only be a subordinate legislature; their subordinacy being to the Parliament that created their law-making power:

> The acid test of primary legislation, surely, is that it is accepted by the courts at its own face value, without needing support from any superior authority. But an Act passed by Queen and Commons only has no face value of its own. As Coke put it in The Prince's Case, 'If an Act be penned, that the King with the assent of the Lords, or with the assent of the Commons, it is no Act of Parliament for three ought to assent to it *scil*. The King, the Lords and the Commons.' An Act of Queen and Commons alone is accepted by the courts only because it is authorised by the Parliament Act—and indeed it is required to recite that it is passed 'in accordance with the Parliament Acts 1911 and 1949 and by authority of the same'. This is the hall-mark of subordinate legislation.[86]

The matter was eventually subjected to judicial analysis in 2004 and 2005. The episode was triggered by the passage of a measure styled as the Hunting Act 2004. The law stemmed from an attempt by the Blair government to persuade Parliament in 2002 to regulate the hunting of wild animals by groups of people who chased their prey on horseback accompanied by packs of dogs which tracked and killed the pursued animals. The proposal attracted considerable controversy in both Houses of Parliament and in the press. An amendment moved by a backbench Labour MP to ban such hunting entirely was approved in the Commons but then rejected in the Lords. The government was unenthusiastic about pursuing the issue at all. There was nonetheless substantial support for the hunting ban among many Labour, and opposition, party MPs in the Commons, and the Bill was re-introduced into the Commons in September 2004. Majority opinion in the Lords opposed the measure however and, when efforts to find a broadly acceptable compromise measure failed, the Lords again refused to pass

---

[82] de Smith S (5th edn, 1985) *Constitutional and administrative law* p 100.

[83] See 'Jennings' critique and the 'rule of recognition' ff, ch 2, pp 31–36.

[84] 'Are *Trethowan*, *Harris* and *Ranasinghe* relevant to the British situation?', ch 2, pp 36–38.

[85] (1955) op cit; (1980) *Constitutional fundamentals*.

[86] (1995) op cit pp 27–28. See Mirfield P (1979) 'Can the House of Lords be lawfully abolished' *LQR* 36; Winterton G (1979) 'Is the House of Lords immortal?' *LQR* 386.

the Bill even though the proposal had attracted a very large Commons majority. The measure was therefore sent to the Queen for her approval under the Parliament Act 1949.

Having lost the political argument in the Commons, opponents of the Hunting Act 2004 then made a legal argument before the courts. The core of their case was that the Parliament Act 1949 was a legally invalid measure. If this contention was correct, then any subsequent measure purportedly enacted under the Parliament Act 1949 procedure—including the Hunting Act 2004—would also be invalid. The argument endorsed Wade's analysis, to the effect that the law-making body—the Commons by simple majority plus the Royal Assent—created by the 1911 Act was a 'subordinate' not 'sovereign' legislature. As such, there were limits on its powers. One such limit was laid out expressly in the text of the 1911 Act; namely that the Commons and Queen could not extend the period between general elections beyond five years. It was further contended that the powers of the Monarch and Commons were also subject to implied limits, in particular the limit that they could not increase the scope of their own law-making authority. It was then suggested that because the Parliament Act 1949 sought to increase the powers of the Commons and Monarch by further reducing the Lords' power of delay, it was a measure beyond the powers of the Monarch and Commons to produce.

The judgment of the House of Lords

The House of Lords regarded the issue raised in *Jackson* as of sufficient importance to merit consideration by nine judges rather than the usual five.[87] The Court unanimously held that the 1949 Act was not invalid, but did so on the basis of different—and rather unsatisfactory—reasoning.[88]

Lord Bingham delivered the longest judgment, which began with a careful study of the historical context within which the 1911 Act was produced. In Lord Bingham's view:

> [24] . . . The 1911 Act did, of course, effect an important constitutional change, the change lay not in authorising a new form of sub-primary parliamentary legislation, but in creating a new way of enacting primary legislation. . . .
>
> [25] [T]he overall object of the Act was not to enlarge the powers of the Commons but to restrict those of the Lords.

Lord Bingham was apparently led to this conclusion in part by his reading of the historical background to the Act. But his reasoning seemed to rest primarily on a literal construction of the text of the 1911 Act—and especially of ss 1(1) and 2(1) which provide that any measure passed by the Commons and Monarch would be an 'Act of Parliament'. In Lord Bingham's opinion, there are thus no substantive limits on the legislative competence of the Commons and Monarch. Acting in concert, they could enact a statute on any subject matter whatsoever. This would include a measure which overrode the express provision in s 2(1) of the 1911 Act that the new procedure did not apply to Bills which extended the duration of a parliament beyond five years. There are substantial deficiencies in this analysis.

The first difficulty is that Lord Bingham's reasoning necessarily accepts the presumption that the United Kingdom now has two sovereign law-makers. This is a logical absurdity. Lord Bingham is evidently not offering a scenario in which sovereignty is divided between differently identified Parliaments, as was the case in South Africa in the 1950s.[89] Each of Lord Bingham's Parliaments is evidently legally omnipotent.

---

[87] [2005] UKHL 56[[2006] 1 AC 262. Unsurprisingly, the judgment prompted a voluminous body of academic literature. See especially Jowell J (2006) 'Parliamentary sovereignty under the new constitutional hypothesis' *Public Law* 562; McHarg A (2006) 'What is delegated legislation?' *Public Law* 539; Ekins R (2007) 'Acts of Parliament and the Parliament Acts' *LQR* 91.   [88] [2005] UKHL 56, [2006] 1 AC 262.

[89] See '*Harris v Dönges (Minister of the Interior)* (1952)', ch 2, pp 33–34.

The second flaw is evident when one considers the practical consequences of Lord Bingham's unquestioning reliance on the literal wording of s 1(1) and s 2(1). On this reasoning, had the 1911 Act dispensed altogether with any need for the Lords or Monarch to assent to legislation, and had provided simply that any measure approved by a bare majority in the Commons at third reading was 'an Act of Parliament', then the Commons alone would have become a(nother) sovereign legislature. And had the 1911 Act attributed 'Act of Parliament' status to a written government policy proposal supported by a majority of the Cabinet and certified as such by the Prime Minister, then it seems a Cabinet majority would also be 'Parliament' and thus a sovereign law-maker. Moreover, according to Lord Bingham's analysis, either of those additional 'sovereigns' could now be brought into being by the Commons and Queen acting under the 1911 or 1949 Act procedures; and the additional sovereigns would then, since their wishes would be 'Acts of Parliament', have the legal capacity to create yet more sovereign law-makers.

The judgment offered by Lord Nicholls is even more problematic. Like Lord Bingham, Lord Nicholls relies on the use of the 'Act of Parliament' label in s 1(1) and s 2(1) to support his assertion that the Commons and Monarch are not a subordinate legislature: 'To describe an Act of Parliament made by this procedure as 'delegated' or 'subordinate' legislation, with all the connotations attendant on those expressions, would be an absurd and confusing mis-characterisation.'[90] Rather the 1911 Act created 'a parallel route' for the creation of legislation. However, Lord Nicholls—unlike Lord Bingham—also held that his 'parallel route' could not be used by the Commons and Lords to repeal the substantive restrictions on its use laid out in s 2(1).[91] This must mean that the Commons and Monarch are a law-maker of limited competence. Yet they are also apparently not 'subordinate' to the Parliament composed of the Commons, Monarch, and Lords. This is an intrinsically incoherent position to adopt. Lord Nicholls then offers as; 'the second source of confirmation'[92] of his conclusion the peculiar suggestion that any measures produced by the Parliament Act 1911 or 1949 procedures must be 'Acts of Parliament' because laws produced in such fashion have been recognised as such or amended by subsequent statutes enacted by (the three-part) Parliament.

Lord Steyn's judgment began in terms which seemed rather more sophisticated than those deployed by his colleagues. He appeared to take some care to avoid characterising the legal measures produced by the Commons and Queen as 'Acts' which were 'enacted' by Parliament. Instead he referred to: 'the manner and form in which laws may be made . . . [T]he new method of making law . . . [T]his new method of expressing the will of Parliament'.[93] However, he eventually adopted the view that the 1911 Act had 'redefined Parliament', and rejected the suggestion that the Commons and Queen were a subordinate legislature: 'in manner and form the 1911 Act simply provides for an alternative mode by which Parliament, as reconstituted for specific purposes, may make laws'.[94]

An unsatisfactory judgment?

The reasoning—and thence the conclusions—of the members of the House of Lords are problematic. At root, the problem lies in the Court's evident unwillingness to accept the point so clearly made by William Wade that the sovereignty of Parliament is *not a phenomenon that derives from a legal source*, and as such *neither is it a phenomenon that can be altered by a legal source*. The 'ultimate political fact' of the constitution is that Parliament's sovereign power cannot by non-revolutionary means be restricted nor given away. However powerful qua law-maker the Commons and Monarch might be, they are not and cannot be Parliament and so cannot possess sovereign power.

---

[90] [2005] UKHL 56, [2006] 1 AC 262 at para 64.

[91] ie that it did not apply to money Bills or Bills seeking to extend the duration of Parliaments beyond five years.

[92] [2006] 1 AC 262 at para 67.   [93] Ibid, at para 75.

[94] Ibid, at para 94. He also held however that the lifetime of a parliament could not be extended either directly or indirectly by the Commons and Queen.

Conclusion

We return to the implications of *Jackson* for the continuing force of orthodox theories of Parliamentary sovereignty in the final chapter. At this juncture we might simply conclude that the number of variations on the theme of reforming the powers and composition of the House of Lords qua legislative body are legion.[95] But most reform plans present a paradox. The more we ask a second chamber to perform functions complementary to those of the Commons, the more we demand of its members that they be (as individuals and as a body) 'expert', 'experienced', and 'non-partisan', and so the more we reveal the crushing dominance of party politics in the lower house, and the incapacity and/or unwillingness of backbench MPs to exert a restraining influence on government activities. Thus it is difficult to identify effective reforming strategies for the Lords without simultaneously considering the merits and draw-backs of 'Parliament' more broadly, in terms both of its legislative powers and its relationship with the 'people'. Discussion of Lords reform frequently proceeds on the assumption that the upper house's legal and conventional subordination to the Commons is desirable because of what one might intuitively regard as 'democratic' reasons. The Lords may be portrayed as an elitist, unelected body, which has no legitimate power to obstruct the wishes of 'the people', such wishes invariably being accurately expressed by the elected representatives in the lower house. The Wakeham Commission recommendations, and the proposals outlined in the 2001 White Paper, do not go very far towards meeting that criticism.

Further reform was identified as an element of the Conservative/Liberal coalition govern-ment's reform agenda in 2010: 'We will establish a committee to bring forward proposals for a wholly or mainly elected upper chamber on the basis of proportional representation'.[96] A draft Bill proposing an 80% elected chamber was published in May 2011. The Bill proposed a much smaller house, comprising only 300 members. Elected members would serve fifteen-year terms, with a third of the seats to be contested every five years. The Bill appeared initially to receive a hostile reception from backbench MPs of all parties. The Bill passed its second reading in July 2012. However a substantial number of Conservative MPs voted against the measure and the Labour Party indicated it wished to see the Bill significantly amended. Faced with these difficulties, the government decided not to press the matter.[97]

The most notable feature of the Cameron government's treatment of the Lords is perhaps the huge number of people appointed to sit in it. Prime Minister Cameron appointed 117 peers in his first year in office, prompting suggestions that the house now had too many mem-bers to function effectively.[98] Although the pace of appointments slowed in subsequent years, the house was a larger chamber in 2014 than in 1999. The Lords had 805 members in early 2017: 254 were Conservatives, 202 Labour, 178 cross-bench, and 102 Liberal.[99]

Alterations to the judicial role of the House of Lords were however completed in 2010. Part 3 of The Constitutional Reform Act 2005 made provision for the creation of a new 'Supreme Court' which would exercise the jurisdiction of the appellate committee of the House of Lords. The Supreme Court has twelve members; the initial members being those law lords then holding office. The Act creates an elaborate selection process for subsequent members of the Supreme Court. The initial power of recommendation lies with a non-partisan 'selection

---

[95] See for example Oliver D (1990) *United Kingdom government and constitution* ch 3; Brazier R (1992) *Constitutional reform* ch 4; Bogdanor (1999) op cit; Shell D (1999) 'The future of the second chamber' *Political Quarterly* 390; Dickson B and Carmichael P (eds) *The House of Lords: its parliamentary and judicial roles*; Russell M (2000) *Reforming the House of Lords. Lessons from overseas.*

[96] <http://www.cabinetoffice.gov.uk/sites/default/files/resources/coalition_programme_for_government.pdf> at p 27.

[97] <http://www.parliament.uk/business/publications/research/briefing-papers/SN06405/house-of-lords-reform-bill-201213-decision-not-to-proceed>.   [98] See the discussion in Russell M (2011) *House full.*

[99] <http://www.parliament.uk/mps-lords-and-offices/lords/composition-of-the-lords/>.

commission'. Although the Commission's proposals may be rejected by the Lord Chancellor and Prime Minister, the power of initiative has been removed from the government, which in an institutional sense reinforces the independence of the judiciary. That institutional independence is also underlined—in a symbolic sense—by the provision of a new building outside the Houses of Parliament in which the Supreme Court sits.

Of more significance perhaps were the provisions in Part 4 of the Act creating a new Judicial Appointments Commission (JAC). The JAC was to be a non-partisan body which would assume substantial responsibility for selecting judges at all levels of the judicial hierarchy. Although there has been no serious suggestion in recent years that Prime Ministers have appointed judges for biased party political reasons, the 2005 reforms effectively remove any scope for the appointment power to be abused in that way.

Reform of the Lords in its legislative capacity evidently presents a considerably more intractable problem. But before we conclude that it is only the House of Lords (in both its unreformed and reformed states) that lacks a 'democratic' underpinning within Parliament, we ought to revisit the House of Commons, and consider not its powers, but the methods through which its members are chosen. The question raised in chapter seven is a stark one: to what extent can we credibly assert that the composition of the Commons accurately represents the wishes of 'the people'?

Suggested further reading

Academic and political commentary

MIRFIELD P (1979) 'Can the House of Lords be lawfully abolished' *LQR* 36

SHELL D (1992) *The House of Lords*

JENKINS R (1968) *Mr Balfour's Poodle*

KELSO A (2006) 'Reforming the House of Lords: navigating representation, democracy and legitimacy at Westminster' *Parliamentary Affairs* 563

SHELL D (1985) 'The House of Lords and the Thatcher government' *Parliamentary Affairs* 16

JOWELL J (2006) 'Parliamentary sovereignty under the new constitutional hypothesis' *Public Law* 562

SHELL D (2000) 'Reforming the House of Lords' *Public Law* 193

BOGDANOR V (1999) 'Reform of the House of Lords: a sceptical view' *Political Quarterly* 375

EKINS R (2007) 'Acts of Parliament and the Parliament Acts' *LQR* 91

Case law and legislation

Parliament Act 1911

Jackson v Attorney General [2005] UKHL 56; [2006] 1 AC 262

Chapter 7

The Electoral System

This book began by suggesting various ways to assess if a society's constitution was 'democratic', in the substantive sense of the content of its laws, and the procedural sense of the way laws are made. The first six chapters sketched some characteristics of the British version of democracy. Parliament has traditionally been regarded as sovereign, capable of amending all laws by the simple majority in both houses plus royal assent formula. The Life Peerages Act 1958 and the House of Lords Act 1999 show that Parliament can alter the membership of its component parts. There is no obvious reason why the parliamentary sovereignty doctrine should not also apply to the Commons' electoral system. The questions we might therefore ask are why Parliament has exercised its powers in this area in the way that it has; and how far this choice satisfies democratic requirements.

To begin, we might return to Jefferson's claim that governments 'derive their just powers from the consent of the governed'. The claim is one most people would consider fundamental to any democratic society. But how do citizens choose their law-makers? How effective is that choice in controlling the legislature's composition? And how do we decide if our choice ensures that the law's substance attracts our consent?

A recent survey of electoral laws in modern societies identified six fundamental characteristics of democratic systems.[1] Firstly, that virtually all adults may vote; secondly, that elections are held regularly; thirdly, that no large group of citizens is prohibited from fielding candidates; fourthly, that all legislative seats are contested; fifthly, that election campaigns are conducted fairly; and sixthly, that votes are secretly cast and accurately counted.

This chapter asks how well Britain's electoral system satisfies these tests. Section two reviews the contemporary picture. Section one traces the route Britain has followed in reaching its present position, picking up the threads of issues previously encountered but left untied, and weaving a more tightly knit picture of the constitution.

I. The evolution of a 'democratic' electoral system?

This section focuses on two issues: the Great Reform Act 1832 and the reforms of 1867–1884.

---

[1] Butler D, Penniman H, and Ranney A (1981) *Democracy at the polls* ch 1.

The Great Reform Act 1832

The Commons' progress towards becoming a fully representative institution dates from the 1832 Great Reform Act. The Act retained many features of earlier electoral law.[2] Nevertheless, its passage provoked a constitutional crisis. This arose in part from the House of Lords' decision to wreck a Bill that had majority Commons support, from the Monarch's (William IV) unwillingness to exercise his prerogative powers to create new pro-government peers, and in the apparent readiness of middle and working class communities to use violence to secure the Bill's enactment. This complex web of forces makes the Act a useful vehicle for exploring the meaning of 'democracy' in British constitutional history.

By 1830, the nature of elite groups in British society was undergoing rapid change. Wealth had moved away from the landed and merchant classes towards manufacturing industry.[3] The technological advance which triggered this trend also facilitated the 'nationalisation of politics'; improved communications and transport systems permitted people in different regions to identify common interests transcending 'local concerns'. One can identify 'public opinion' as a distinct political force from 1800.[4] The Commons may still have been a 'House of Communities'; but the nation's political demography was one in which the division of the population by economic class into several large segments, rather than division by physical geography into the inhabitants of innumerable cities, towns, and villages, was becoming evermore important.

Dissatisfaction with the electoral system had four principal foci. The first related to the geographical distribution of seats; the second concerned the qualifications needed to vote; the third centred on candidate selection; the fourth on the conduct of election campaigns.

The constituency system

The Commons now has around 650 members, each representing a given geographical area, or 'constituency'. This geographical division was a firmly embedded principle by 1688. Constitutional theory then accepted that the Commons existed as much to protect local interests as to define national issues. In 1830, 658 MPs sat in the Commons. The country's population was approximately sixteen million. Representation was divided between counties and boroughs, with most English counties (39) and boroughs (around 200) each returning two members, and each Scots and Welsh county and borough returning one member. Ireland had two-member counties (32) and (mostly) one-member boroughs (31). This framework was established in 1675, and had remained broadly unchanged ever since.[5]

Seat allocation bore no relation to population patterns; Parliament had not established any mechanism for altering representation to reflect demographic trends. In 1830, large industrial towns such as Birmingham and Manchester had no representatives at all (see Tables 7.1 and 7.2). In contrast, over 100 so-called 'rotten boroughs' had fewer than 100 voters. Boroughs were created by the Monarch's exercise of prerogative powers; the way in which the Monarch exercised the power was not subject to judicial control.

Qualification for the franchise

Entitlement to vote arose in many ways, most deriving from land ownership. The value of land required was set high enough to exclude most local residents. Residence was generally not required, which meant that many so-called 'out-voters' possessed votes in several places. The English county qualification was more straightforward—freehold ownership of land worth £2 per year; (the sum was fixed in 1430). Residence was not needed.[6]

---

[2] Gash N (1953) *Politics in the age of Peel* p x; Mandler P (1990) *Aristocratic government in the age of reform* ch 4.
[3] Hobsbawm op cit chs 2–3.   [4] Brock op cit p 17.
[5] Cannon J (1973) *Parliamentary reform 1640–1832* p 29.   [6] See Brock op cit ch 1.

Table 7.1 The size of the electorate

	Adult Population	Electorate	% Enfranchised
1830	13,900,000	435,000	3.2%
1840	15,900,000	700,000	4.4%
1870	22,700,000	1,900,000	8.7%
1900	24,930,000	6,730,935	27.0%
1919	27,900,000	21,755,583	78.0%
1949	34,970,000	34,269,770	98.2%

Source: Compiled from data in Seymour C (1970) *Electoral reform in England and Wales* Appendix 1: Coleman D and Salt J (1992) *The British population* p 41; Butler and Sloman op cit p 200. Figures prior to 1900 are approximate only and are for England and Wales only. Later dates are for the United Kingdom.

Table 7.2 Voting population of two member English boroughs 1830

Number of electors	Number of boroughs
0–50	56
51–100	21
101–300	36
301–600	24
601–1000	22
1001–5000	36
5000 +	7

Source: adapted from Brock op cit p 20.

Defenders of the status quo invoked the theory of 'virtual representation' to justify the non-enfranchisement of most citizens. This saw no need for most citizens to have a vote, since there would be some MPs whose dominant constituency interest would coincide with those of the disfranchised group (generally defined in occupational terms), thus ensuring that representations would be made on that group's behalf within the Commons.[7] The British government had made this argument to the American colonists in the 1770s when dismissing their demand for seats in Parliament; the colonists considered the theory specious.[8] By 1830, its efficacy in countering domestic discontent had also substantially weakened.

The conduct of election campaigns

Three 'traditional' activities attracted considerable criticism by 1830: bribery, 'treating', and intimidation.[9] Bribery is a self-explanatory term. The explicit purchase of votes for cash had technically been illegal since 1696, but the law was so rarely enforced that the practice had almost acquired conventional status. Offers of employment, public office, or advantageous transfers of land in return for votes were also widespread.

'Treating' was indirect bribery, in which voters were 'persuaded' to support a candidate by lavish provision of food, drink, and entertainments. Although treating had technically been a crime since 1696, it was so routine a part of elections that candidates who could not afford to 'entertain' voters were effectively debarred from entering contested elections. Treating was

---

[7] See Rawlings H (1988) *Law and the electoral process* ch 1.   [8] Bailyn op cit pp 161–170.
[9] O'Leary C (1962) *The elimination of corrupt practices in British general elections 1868–1911* ch 1.

further encouraged by the fact that many constituencies had only one polling booth. However, voters had many days to register their choice. This was a necessity for out-voters, who needed time to journey to their various electoral homes. Out-voters could also expect to have their travel, accommodation, and refreshment bills met by their preferred candidate.[10]

The cost of candidacy was further increased by the rule that candidates themselves paid all the administrative costs of the election, such as hiring the polling station. This particular provision survived until well into the twentieth century.

Intimidation took various forms. Mob violence was common, as was assault of voters by supporters of particular candidates. Somewhat more subtle was economic intimidation, entailing dismissal from employment or eviction from property if the employer/landlord's voting instructions were not followed.

The impact of these practices was exacerbated by the lack of a secret ballot. Public voting was justified on the basis that the right to vote was akin to a trust, and so necessarily open to scrutiny.[11] Reformers regarded this as a guarantor of corruption and intimidation: candidates who bought votes could check they gained value for money and penalise voters of independent inclinations.

The incentive for candidates to engage in corruption was magnified by the political, rather than legal, nature of the way corruption was policed. Until 1604, defeated candidates alleging malpractice pursued their case before the courts. From 1604 to 1770, disputed election petitions were heard by the Commons sitting as a whole house. Since so many MPs owed their seats to corrupt practices, only the most egregious misbehaviour led to disqualification. In 1770, a private members' Bill was enacted which granted jurisdiction to a thirteen-member Commons committee, in the hope that the task could be approached in a less partisan manner.[12]

A corrupt contest was a lesser ground for concern than having no contest at all. Elections with just one candidate per seat were the norm rather than the exception of pre-1832 practice, and frequently resulted from an agreement by groups of candidates of opposing parties to allow each other a clear run in neighbouring constituencies.

Selecting candidates

Since 1710, MPs representing county constituencies had to own landed property worth at least £600; for borough members the sum was £300. These criteria clearly excluded most of the population, including many of the emergent middle classes, from the electoral contest, and indicates the formal influence of landed wealth on the Commons' composition. More noteworthy was the informal influence exercised by members of the Lords. The lack of contestation in many seats, the exorbitant cost of contested campaigns, the small size of many electorates and the open voting process, combined to enhance local aristocrats' control of voters' behaviour.

There would have been little point in peers controlling voter behaviour if they could not subsequently control the MP's behaviour. For many local magnates, 'their' MP was as much a part of their property as their land or their livestock. In 'nomination' or 'pocket' boroughs, voters were economically dependent on the local aristocrat, and the candidates were often his sons. Such familial feeling frequently ensured a coincidence of political opinion between the members of the lower and upper house. Similarly, candidates were frequently proteges of peers. In 1830, 270 MPs represented such constituencies. Some senior peers reputedly controlled as many as twelve MPs.[13] And for patrons whose interest in politics might wane, a pocket borough was a saleable commodity, fetching as much as £180,000 (at 1830 prices).[14] One would err in assuming that nomination boroughs ensured that the Commons automatically followed the Lords' wishes. But their existence on such a scale undermined the Commons' supposed role as a balancing force arraigned against the aristocracy and the Monarch.

---

[10] Cannon op cit p 209.　　[11] O'Leary op cit p 26.　　[12] Ibid, at 9–12.
[13] Turbeville (1958) op cit pp 244–247.　　[14] Brock op cit ch 1.

The original Bill

The Bill presented by Lord Grey's Whig (Liberal) government[15] sought to shift the formal balance of power in the Commons away from the landowning aristocracy towards the newly emergent manufacturing and professional classes. Grey was not, however, advocating a 'democratic' society. As Brock suggests, the government wished 'to make aristocratic government acceptable by purging away its most corrupt and expensive features'.[16] Grey himself was candid as to his intentions:

> A great change has taken place . . . in the distribution of property, and unless a corresponding change can be made in the legal mode by which that property can act upon government, revolutions must necessarily follow. This change requires a greater influence to be yielded to the middle classes, who have made wonderful advances both in property and intelligence.[17]

Grey established a four-member Committee to produce a reform plan sufficiently radical to defuse popular discontent, yet sufficiently conservative to ensure the continued dominance of aristocratic ideas within the lower house. The Committee recommended that large counties should gain two extra MPs; boroughs with fewer than 2,000 inhabitants would lose both members; boroughs with fewer than 4,000 would lose one; unrepresented towns with over 10,000 residents would gain one MP. The Committee retained the property qualification, but recommended a uniform £10 freehold threshold. Out-voting was to be abolished by introducing a residence requirement, and voting would be by secret ballot. These plans would produce a substantially increased electorate, voting in constituencies which acknowledged contemporary population patterns, under conditions encouraging independent voting behaviour.

While agreeing to most of these proposals, the Cabinet rejected the secret ballot. Grey personally opposed secrecy, as did William IV, considering it: 'inconsistent with the manly spirit and free avowal of opinion which distinguish the people of England'.[18]

The Bill's parliamentary passage

In the Commons, the Bill passed second reading by 302 votes to 301. In Committee, however, the Tories carried a wrecking amendment. Grey subsequently resigned, and was granted a dissolution by William IV. At the ensuing election, fought entirely on the basis of reform, the government gained a majority of 130 seats. The legislative battleground subsequently shifted to the Lords.

As chapter six suggested, Conservative peers who regarded Liberal policies as revolutionary were not persuaded even in 1911 to defer to a newly elected Commons majority. In 1831, the convention that the Lords should do so had yet to be established. The Commons was asking the Lords to approve a measure which would have greatly reduced the aristocracy's direct control over the lower house's composition. Tory peers lacked Grey's faith that a middle class electorate would vote for aristocratic principles of government, and remained intransigent.

One way to view the constitutional function of the Lords' (then) legislative co-equality was as a guarantor of traditional distributions of 'property'. The common law had accepted that an entitled voter could maintain a tortious action against a government official who unlawfully prevented him from exercising the right.[19] Casting one's vote could therefore be seen as 'property' in the same sense as security in one's home (*Entick*) or one's physical liberty (*Liversidge*).

But for many Tories, the vote was regarded as 'property' in a rather different sense, belonging not to the individual voter, but to the aristocrat on whom the voter was economically dependent, as tenant or employee. In 1829, the Duke of Newcastle responded to criticism of his decision to evict tenants who voted against his preferred candidate by saying: 'Is it presumed

[15] See Cannon op cit pp 206–210.   [16] Brock op cit p 44.   [17] Ibid, at 152.
[18] Quoted in Cannon op cit p 211.   [19] *Ashby v White* (1703) 2 Ld Raym 938.

then that I am not to do what I will with my own'.[20] The point was clearly put by Lord Eldon when criticising the Bill's plan to abolish pocket boroughs: 'Parliament had no more right, Eldon told the Lords in 1832, "to take away the elective franchise from the present holders of it, than . . . to take away from them the property in houses or land which conferred it"'.[21] The idea that voting for one's legislators was a 'right' that all citizens possessed was accepted only by the radical fringes of early-nineteenth-century society.

The first weeks after the election were taken up with negotiations between Grey and William IV concerning a mass creation of peers to ensure the Bill would be passed. William was unwilling to create the fifty peers needed to ensure a government majority, and the Lords rejected the Bill by forty-one votes at second reading. The veto triggered widespread public protest. Riots in Bristol led to over 400 deaths, and several Tory peers found themselves and their property under attack.[22] Many observers feared violent revolution was at hand.

Rather than resign again, the government produced a modified Bill, designed to mollify its Tory opponents. As in 1909 and 1911, the Tory Party split into two factions—the 'waverers' and the 'die-hards'. The former, fearing either that a further government defeat would lead either to its resignation and possibly civil war, or to a mass creation of peers, advocated amendment rather than veto. The latter favoured resistance, irrespective of the consequences. Initially, the die-hards kept the upper hand.

The amended Bill received a Commons majority of 162, but was subject to a wrecking amendment in the Lords. William continued to refuse a mass creation, whereupon Grey once more resigned. Given the party balance in the Commons, there was no prospect of a Tory government being formed, although this was William's preferred solution. The King asked the Tory leader, the Duke of Wellington, to form a government, but he could not muster sufficient Commons support. 'Public opinion' voiced many protests against a possible Wellington administration. Grey subsequently agreed to continue in office if the King agreed to create as many peers as necessary to push the Bill through. Eventually, sufficient Tory peers capitulated for the Bill to pass.

For Wellington, the Act was 'a revolution by due process of law'.[23] What Professor Wade later termed the 'ultimate political fact' of parliamentary sovereignty remained unchanged—but Parliament now reflected a changed concept of 'the people' upon whose consent the stability of constitutional government would depend.[24]

The 1867–1884 reforms: towards a universal 'right' to vote and a 'fair' electoral contest

Minor reforms were enacted in the thirty-five years following 1832. The requirement that MPs be substantial landowners was abolished altogether, without opposition from the Lords, in 1858. More systematic revision occurred in 1867.

Disraeli's 1867 Reform Bill attracted no substantial opposition in the Lords.[25] Its Commons passage, in contrast, was extraordinarily tortuous. Disraeli led a minority Tory Party in the Commons in an administration headed by Lord Derby. It assumed office following the resignation of Lord John Russell's Liberal government when a backbench Liberal rebellion defeated Russell's own reform plans; the rebels (known as 'the Cave') thought Russell's proposals too extensive. The 1867 Act introduced a modest redistribution to reflect demographic trends. Its main focus, however, was on qualification for the franchise. Over a million voters joined the electoral roll, doubling its size. This was more than twice as many as envisaged by Russell's

[20] Brock op cit p 63.   [21] Ibid, at 36.
[22] Cannon op cit pp 226–228; Brock op cit pp 247–259.   [23] Brock op cit p 204.
[24] Previous editions of this book addressed the nineteenth-century Chartist movement for electoral reform. Readers interested in that issue should refer to the 5th edition, ch 7, p 207 at www.oxfordtextbooks.co.uk/orc/loveland7e.   [25] Turbeville (1958) op cit pp 422–425.

measure. Yet those very MPs who had voted against Russell subsequently supported Disraeli. Perhaps the most striking feature of the 1867 controversy is that a matter of such great constitutional significance was resolved not according to its substantive merits per se, but according to what Disraeli calculated would best serve his party's short term survival in government.[26]

Disraeli's great achievement was to produce a Bill supported not only by moderate Conservatives, but also by radical Liberals and reactionary Tories. The centre ranks of the Tories and Liberals (the Liberals led in effect by Gladstone) had become so mutually antagonistic that it was inconceivable either would support the other on any reform measure. It was also generally believed (as a legacy of 1832) that the Liberals favoured more far-reaching reform than the Tories.

The Bill detached the radicals from the Liberal Party by proposing to reduce the county franchise qualification from £50 to £15, and to extend the borough franchise to any adult male paying poor rates. However it simultaneously placated reactionary Tories by creating 'fancy franchises' to give additional votes to individuals with certain property or educational qualifications. Furthermore, borough ratepayers could vote only if they paid their rates personally: those who paid their rates to their landlord within their rent (predominantly poorer tenants) would not be enfranchised. Initially one might think Disraeli's concessions would have alienated radical support. But Disraeli had tacitly agreed with radical MPs to acquiesce if they removed those restrictions in Committee, where the government was in a minority. The Committee stage modified the Bill in both progressive and reactionary directions. The personal payment and fancy franchise provisions were removed, and the county franchise reduced to £12, but the radicals could not muster majority support for the secret ballot, for government subsidy of election expenses, and for the explicit enfranchisement of women.[27]

Neither Disraeli nor Gladstone were then 'democrats'. Gladstone's Liberalism did not then extend to enfranchising 'the poorest, the least instructed and the most dependent members of the community'.[28] Nevertheless, barely twenty years later, Gladstone led Parliament a considerable way along such a path.

The dawning of the democratic age?

Shortly after the passage of the 1867 Act, Disraeli steered the Election Petitions and Corrupt Practices at Elections Act through Parliament. The Act returned jurisdiction over disputed elections to the courts. The measure had both practical and symbolic effects; the former in ensuring that a coherent body of precedent defining unacceptable behaviour would emerge; the latter in suggesting that the electoral process was henceforth subject to orthodox rule of law principles.

The secret ballot was introduced in 1872. The 1868 general election had been attended by substantial corruption and intimidation.[29] A Select Committee established in 1869 identified the secret ballot as the most effective anti-corruption device. Gladstone's Liberal administration introduced a Bill in 1871, opposed by the Tories in the Commons, and vetoed by the Lords. Gladstone submitted a similar Bill in 1872, and threatened a dissolution if it was rejected. The Bill was grudgingly approved. Equally significant was the Corrupt and Illegal Practices Prevention Act 1883. This limited the amount of money that individual candidates could spend on their local campaign, the amount based on a (small) *per capita* sum for each voter.

Both measures indicated a further cultural shift towards a meritocratic rather than aristocratic constitutional morality. The political process itself was increasingly structured by middle class values of fair competition, in which political power was won on the basis of rational

---

[26] Fascinating studies are provided by Cowling M (1967) *1867: Disraeli, Gladstone, and revolution* and Turbeville (1958) op cit pp 396–428.   [27] Cowling op cit pp 223–226.

[28] Ibid, at 40.   [29] See Rover C (1967) *Women's suffrage and party politics in Britain 1866–1914* pp 40–41.

Table 7.3 Uncontested seats in general elections

1906	1910*	1918	1924	1929	1931	1935	1945	1951
114	163	107	32	7	67	40	3	4

*Second election.
Source: Adapted from Butler and Sloman op cit pp 180–182.

argument, rather than the unthinking deference previously accorded to landowning interests. By the mid-1880s, that rationality had led Parliament to include a substantial proportion of working class men within the electorate.

The key element of Gladstone's 1884 reform was a uniform borough/county voting qualification, set at the lower borough level, which would enfranchise two million additional voters.[30] The Tories initially opposed the Bill. Although the Liberals had a reliable Commons majority, they were a minority in the Lords. Lord Salisbury, leader of the Tory peers, was ready to apply his 'referendal theory' of the veto power,[31] and force a dissolution. Many Liberal MPs relished the prospect of a veto, seeing an opportunity to curb the upper chamber's powers. Gladstone himself described any such veto as 'A precedent against Liberty'.[32] As in 1832, the Lords' intransigence provoked widespread public agitation in support of reform. In the Commons Tory MPs failed to follow Salisbury's advice to give the Bill 'a good parting kick at third reading'.[33] The Lords was thus unable to point to a clear split in electoral opinion on the issue. Crisis was avoided by negotiation between a handful of each party's leaders, with little debate in either house, which prompted the leading Liberal newspaper (*The Manchester Guardian*) to describe the outcome as 'a usurpation of the office and powers of Parliament'.[34] This contrasted markedly with the passage of the 1867 Bill, where the Commons committee stage was of paramount importance to the Act's final shape.

The reforms introduced in the RPA 1918 had a more bipartisan air. For the first time, women were granted the right to vote. In the same year, Parliament also accepted that women could sit as members of the Commons.[35] Adult male suffrage was granted solely on the basis of six months' residence in a constituency (women under thirty had to wait until further reform was enacted in 1928). The Act also acknowledged the desirability of maintaining constituencies with electorates of equal size, although it did not demand exact mathematical equality. Additionally, the RPA 1918 made several significant financial innovations. Parliament finally accepted that the government, not the candidates, should bear the administrative costs of the election. To discourage frivolous candidates, a deposit of £150 (then a substantial sum) was required. This was returned if a candidate attracted more than 12.5% of the vote. To impose further economic equality on candidates, the spending limits introduced by the 1883 Act were almost halved in real terms. It was nevertheless not until 1955 that all seats were contested (see Table 7.3).

II. The contemporary electoral process

Despite the evidently 'democratic' credentials of Britain's electoral system, the contemporary political environment has contained many voices in recent years advocating electoral reform. Critics have three foci of discontent. The first relates to constituency apportionment. The second concerns the conduct of election campaigns, especially the cost and content of party political advertising. The third, and most significant, is the counting system through which citizens' choices are transmitted.

---

[30] See generally Jones A (1972) *The Politics of reform 1884*.
[31] See 'The doctrine of the mandate', ch 6, pp 140–141.   [32] Jones op cit p 149.
[33] Ibid, at 148.   [34] Ibid, at 221.   [35] Parliament (Qualification of Women Act) 1918.

Apportionment—drawing constituency boundaries

The Parliamentary Constituencies Act 1986 is a consolidating statute which defines the powers and responsibilities of a body called the Boundary Commission. The Commission determines the size and shape of constituencies in Scotland, Northern Ireland, Wales, and England. This is obviously a task which must be sensitive to accusations of political bias. Boundaries could intentionally be drawn in ways that bestow a political advantage on one party. To minimise this problem, each country's Commission (nominally chaired by the Speaker) is headed by a high court judge. She is assisted by two other members. Members are appointed by the government, but, as a matter of convention, are also approved by the opposition parties. A Commission taking this form was first established in 1944. Earlier legislation had created bodies with less clearly structured apportionment responsibilities, staffed by party politicians, which consequently had great difficulty rebutting accusations that they could not be objective.[36] At eight to twelve year intervals, the Commission holds local inquiries concerning reapportionment proposals. The Commission then presents a report to the Home Secretary making recommendations. The Home Secretary must then lay the report, with an implementing Order In Council (which may amend the proposals), before the Commons and Lords for approval.

Apportionment criteria—a non-justiciable issue?

The Commission's discretion is structured by 'rules' contained in the Parliamentary Constituencies Act 1986 Sch 2. The 'rule' label is a misnomer, since the legal status of Sch 2 provisions is frequently merely guidance to which the Commission must have regard. Rule 1 specifies (with some precision) the total number of constituencies. Rule 7 requires the Commission to calculate an electoral quota—a figure arrived at by dividing the total number of registered voters by the number of constituencies. At present, the quota is approximately 66,000.

Thereafter, the Commission must apply rather more discretionary criteria, seemingly ranked in the following order of importance. Rule 4 provides that, 'as far as practicable', constituencies should not cross county or London borough boundaries. Rule 5 then directs the Commission, subject to rule 4, to make all constituencies as near to the electoral quota as possible: it may only depart from rule 4 if respecting county or London borough boundaries would produce 'excessive disparity' between a constituency's size and the electoral quota. Rule 6 then permits the Commission to override rules 4 and 5 if 'special considerations, including in particular the size, shape and accessibility of a constituency, appear to render a departure desirable'.

The legislation therefore does not require mathematical equivalence in constituency sizes.[37] In practice, the Act produces substantial discrepancies. Prior to the 1983 reapportionment, Buckingham constituency had 116,000 voters, while Newcastle Central had only 24,000.[38] In 1987 over 100 seats deviated from the quota by more than 20%. At the various extremes were the Orkney and Shetland constituency with 31,000 voters, and the Isle of Wight with over 98,000.[39]

Such variations provoke criticisms of anti-democratic practice, on the grounds that the system ignores the principle of 'one vote one value'.[40] This complaint has a collective and individuated dimension. Collectively, the votes of Orkney residents were 'worth' more than three times as much as those of Isle of Wight residents, since both constituencies returned only one MP. More generally, the 'value' of a given constituency's voting power increases/decreases according to the extent by which its electorate is smaller/larger than the electoral quota. All communities are not created equal for electoral purposes.

---

[36] See eg Cowling op cit pp 231–232.

[37] See Craig J (1959) 'Parliament and Boundary Commissions' *Public Law* 23.

[38] Alder J (1994) *Constitutional and administrative law* p 161.

[39] Norton (1991) op cit p 94.   [40] See especially Wade (1980) op cit ch 2.

The effective 'value' of an individual vote is more difficult to gauge. If, for example, residents in Newcastle Central and Buckingham voted in 1983 in identical proportions for the Conservative, Labour, and Liberal Parties, the relative sizes of the constituencies would not affect the parties' overall performance. However, if a party had only 12,001 supporters in the two areas combined (ie 9% of the total electorate), it could nonetheless win one (50%) of the two seats if they all lived and voted in Newcastle Central. This is an extreme illustration of the more general point that a party benefits greatly if its supporters are disproportionately concentrated in small constituencies.

The apportionment criteria undoubtedly contain appreciable scope for unintended political bias, and, thus, one might have thought, wide scope for legal challenges to the Commission's recommendations. However Parliament sought to curtail litigation by providing in s 4(7) that any Order in Council *purportedly* made under the Act 'shall not be questioned in any legal proceedings'. The use of 'purports' presumably safeguards the Act against the judicial 'threat' posed by *Anisminic*. This suggests that legislators see apportionment as a non-justiciable issue, to which Diceyan notions of the rule of law cannot apply. Thus far the courts appear to agree with that analysis.[41]

The 1969 controversy

The courts' limited supervisory role has contributed to an explicitly partisan mode of dispute settlement within Parliament, as evidenced by events in 1969. The Commission's 1969 recommendations, reflecting population movement away from the cities, seemed likely to cost the Labour Party a dozen seats in the next election. James Callaghan, the Home Secretary, decided not to introduce an implementing Order. Instead, the government introduced a Bill effecting only some of the Commission's proposals, and also removing the Home Secretary's statutory obligation to lay the Order. The government (feebly) defended its strategy on the basis that constituency reapportionment should be carried out alongside the redrawing of local government boundaries expected within the next few years.

The Conservative opposition considered the government was acting for partisan purposes. Consequently, the Lords' Conservative majority passed several wrecking amendments to the Bill, which was then withdrawn. Rather than reintroduce the Bill and invoke the Parliament Act procedures, the government instructed Labour MPs to vote against the Orders when Callaghan laid them before the Commons. The boundary changes could therefore not be introduced before the next election. This was perfectly legal; the Act did not require either House to approve the Orders, it merely commanded the Home Secretary to present them. The cynicism underlying the Cabinet's strategy is neatly revealed in Crossman's Diaries:

> We agreed to have all the Orders put to the Commons and the trick would be to put them but not approve them, so that . . . we would negate the lot. Wilson has won. We have not been discredited because the ordinary public are convinced that both the Government and the Tories are concerned for our own self-interest . . . .[42]

The 1983 controversy

While Orders cannot be challenged in court, there is no ouster clause preventing litigation trying to stop the Commission presenting its report to the Home Secretary. Whether such litigation enjoyed any prospects of success was, until 1983, an open question—to which the courts then offered a curt answer.

The Labour Party feared that the Commission's recommendations for the 1983 election would significantly benefit the Conservative Party. In *R v Boundary Commission for England,*

---

[41] See *Harper v Home Secretary* [1955] Ch 238, CA. See Craig J op cit; de Smith S (1955) 'Boundaries between Parliament and the courts' *MLR* 281.   [42] Op cit p 660.

ex p Foot,[43] the party's leader, Michael Foot, sought a judicial review of the Commission's findings. Mr Foot contended that the Commission had misconstrued its responsibilities by regarding the statutory 'rule' requiring approximate parity in constituency sizes as subordinate to the 'rule' that constituencies should not straddle county or London borough boundaries. Mr Foot argued that the substantial divergences in constituency size envisaged by the proposals: 'offend[ed] against the principle of equal representation for all electors which is required by our modern system of Parliamentary representation'.[44] The applicants sought a court order to prevent the Commission from submitting its recommendations to the Home Secretary.

Given the wording of the 1949 Act, the applicants were advancing an optimistic argument. Whether the constitution recognises a principle of 'equal representation' in electoral districting which demands mathematical equality is a moot (and political) point, but not one expressed unambiguously in the Act. In effect, Mr Foot was asking the Court to attach the same constitutional significance to the moral principle of 'one vote one value' as it had attached to the moral principle of the 'rule of law' in *Anisminic*. The Court declined to do so. Sir John Donaldson MR categorised the Commission's task as presumptively non-justiciable in the absence of all but the most egregious malfeasance.

The Political Parties, Elections and Referendums Act 2000

In 1999, the Labour government introduced the Political Parties, Elections and Referendums Bill which would transfer the Boundary Commissions' function to a new statutory body, the Electoral Commission.[45] The Commission would consist of between five and nine members, nominally appointed by the Queen (in effect by the Prime Minister) following approval by the Commons. The Bill also proposed creation of a body called the Speaker's Committee to oversee the activities of the Commission. Rather bizarrely, the Speaker would not sit on the Committee, which would comprise the Home Secretary, the Minister responsible for local government, the Chair of the Home Affairs Select Committee, and six backbench MPs. The Bill requires the Committee to approve candidates selected to sit on the Commission. The proposal seems to be an attempt not so much to depoliticise the apportionment question as to ensure that it functions on the basis of multi-party agreement. The Bill was enacted in 2000 as the Political Parties, Elections and Referendums Act (hereafter the PPERA 2000). The timetable for the Electoral Commission to take on the functions of the Boundary Commission was relaxed. The Commission took over responsibility for delineating local government boundaries in April 2002; its powers in respect of parliamentary constituencies have yet to be assumed.

To that point, the notion of 'one vote one value' was an idea whose time had not yet come within the British constitution. We consider a more recent initiative to address this issue at the end of this chapter. However, the potential shortcomings of the apportionment process should not be seen in isolation from other aspects of electoral law, especially the vote-counting method discussed later. But before broaching that question, we briefly explore the conduct of election campaigns.

The contents and conduct of election campaigns

This section discusses four subjects: the voters, the candidates, and the financing and content of electoral advertising. Jurisdiction over disputed elections is still vested in the High Court, which is empowered to invalidate results and disqualify malfeasors from subsequent elections. Few petitions are now presented, a state of affairs primarily attributable to an apparently pervasive acceptance of the moral propriety of electoral law.

---

[43] [1983] QB 600, CA.   [44] Ibid, at 617.

[45] See Oliver D (1999) 'An Electoral Commission: an ingenious idea' *Public Law* 585.

The voters

Voter registration was introduced in 1832 to minimise fraudulent voting. The RPA 1918 introduced a more rigorous process, giving local authorities responsibility for ensuring the register's accuracy. In the modern era, there have been few suggestions that the registration process is significantly abused.

Constitutional morality now accepts that voting is not a privilege earned through property or educational qualifications, but a right extending to virtually all adult citizens, forfeited only in very limited circumstances. The principle now underlying the grant of the franchise is that of residence. Since the passage of the RPA 1948, all citizens over 21 years old (reduced to 18 in 1969) may vote if their names are entered on the electoral register of the constituency(ies) where they have a place of residence.[46] Until 2000, the register was compiled annually in October by local government officials. This had the unfortunate consequence that prospective voters who just missed the October deadline could not register in their new constituencies until the next October, and so would be unable to vote there if an election was held in the interim. The RPA 2000 removed this difficulty by permitting the register to be updated on a continual basis. While there is no legal obligation compelling registered citizens to vote, failure to respond to registration forms is an offence.

In recent years, several minor initiatives have been undertaken to increase the size of the electorate still further. The RPA 1985 enabled previously registered voters living overseas to maintain a vote in their old constituencies. The RPA 2000 promoted by the first Blair government made it possible for homeless people to register a notional residence for electoral purposes. A homeless person may give as his/her address; 'a place in the UK where he commonly spends a substantial part of his time . . . '.[47] The 2000 Act also entitles prisoners held in gaol on remand to use the prison as their residential address.

The only citizens presumptively excluded from the franchise because of their status are the Monarch, life peers, and the remaining hereditary members of the Lords. Other disqualifications are premised on failings of behaviour or competence. Individuals may not vote if they are serving prison sentences, or have recently been convicted of electoral malpractice. Some parliamentary consideration was given during the passage of the RPA 2000 to enfranchising convicted prisoners, but the Blair government held the view that disenfranchisement was a logical additional penalty to be suffered by persons gaoled for having committed crimes.[48] The issue was again under consideration, this time by the Conservative/Liberal coalition government, in 2010 and 2011. The RPA 2000 also removed the previous disqualification of people detained in hospital under the Mental Health Act 1983.

The candidates

There are few collective prohibitions on candidacy.[49] Parties advocating extremist political philosophies such as the British National Party and Socialist Workers Party regularly field candidates, albeit never victorious ones. Nor is there any prohibition on parties such as Plaid Cymru, the Scottish Nationalists, or Sinn Fein, whose primary policy objective has often been to secure their respective country's independence. The entitlement to contest elections does not however extend to certain 'proscribed organisations', designated under the Prevention of Terrorism Acts. The justification for this is presumably that the groups concerned have chosen to pursue their political objectives outside the democratic process.

---

[46] 'Residence' is a justiciable concept. See *Ferris v Wallace* 1936 SC 561; *Fox v Stirk* [1970] 2 QB 463, CA; *Hipperson v Newbury District Electoral Registration Officer* [1985] QB 1060, CA.

[47] RPA 2000 s 6, amending RPA 1983 s 7.

[48] See Lardy H (2001) 'Representation of the People Act 2000' *MLR* 63.

[49] See the helpful guidance published by the Electoral Commission at: <http://www.electoralcommission.org.uk/__data/assets/pdf_file/0019/173017/UKPGE-Part-1-Can-you-stand-for-election.pdf>.

The requirement that MPs be wealthy was abolished in 1872. Current electoral law retains a modest financial barrier to candidacy itself. All candidates must produce a deposit of £500, which is forfeit if they fail to gain 5% of the vote. The rationale for the election deposit is not that impecunious candidates are per se unsuitable legislators, but that it prevents frivolous candidates from belittling the election process and/or making it harder to administer.

Candidates need not reside in their chosen constituency, but must be nominated by ten registered voters. Various statutes[50] also disqualify a miscellaneous collection of citizens from candidacy, including those under 18 years old, holders of judicial office, and members of various government bodies. Church of England and Roman Catholic clergymen were banned from candidacy until 2001.[51] Prohibitions are also placed on bankrupt debtors, and some categories of criminals and the mentally ill. These are overall residual and quantitatively insignificant restrictions.

The legal framework regulating candidacy is directed towards the candidate as an individual. Unlike most other 'democratic countries', Britain has no legislation dealing explicitly with such issues as the selection of parliamentary candidates, the formation of party policy, and the election of party leaders. Nor is there as yet anything to indicate that the courts consider such matters justiciable. An opportunity to test that assumption arose in 1990, when the Conservative Party ignored its rules for electing its leader when John Major succeeded Margaret Thatcher.[52] No challenge was issued however. Nor do constitutional lawyers appear to consider the question important: intra-party democracy is an issue few legal commentators have examined.[53]

In 1994 it was suggested that legislation prohibiting gender and race discrimination might apply to political parties' internal membership and candidate selection practices, but this has yet to be confirmed by the courts. This raises a further dimension of the 'electoral equality' principle: women and citizens of minority ethnicity are severely under-represented both as MPs and candidates, and, as candidates, are disproportionately concentrated in unwinnable seats.[54]

Sanders v Chichester

A further lacuna in electoral law was revealed by a curious episode in 1994. The plaintiff in *Sanders v Chichester*[55] was a Liberal Democrat candidate in the 1994 election for members of the European Parliament, although the issue the case raised was of equal relevance in elections to the Commons. Mr Sanders was seeking to have the result of his constituency's election set aside.

The defendant was the successful candidate for the seat, although his behaviour was not in question. A Mr Huggett had stood in the election as a 'Literal Democrat'. In Mr Sanders' view, Mr Hugget was seeking to mislead careless Liberal Democrat supporters into voting for him rather than Mr Sanders to enhance the Conservative candidate's chances of winning. If that was Huggett's intention, he succeeded admirably. He attracted some 10,000 votes. The seat was won by Mr Chichester, the Conservative candidate, by fewer than 800 votes.[56]

The judgment turned on the meaning of rule 6(2) and (3) of Sch 1 of the RPA 1983. These rules required candidates to list their full name and address on the ballot paper. Candidates

---

[50] Primarily the House of Commons Disqualification Act 1975 and Electoral Administration Act 2005.

[51] House of Commons (Removal of Clergy Disqualification) Act 2001.

[52] See Alderman R and Smith M (1990) 'Can British Prime Ministers be given the push by their parties?' *Parliamentary Affairs* 260; Alderman R and Carter N (1991) 'A very Tory coup: the ousting of Mrs Thatcher' *Parliamentary Affairs* 125.

[53] The notable exception being Dawn Oliver; see her chapter in successive editions of Jowell and Oliver op cit.

[54] Norton op cit pp 101–103.   [55] [1995] 03 LS Gaz R 37.

[56] Mr Huggett denied this was his intention. There was no suggestion that he was encouraged to stand by the Conservative Party.

did not need to list any further information, but could if they wished add a description of up to six words. The description was generally used to confirm a candidate's party political affiliation.[57]

The Court concluded that it could invalidate an election result only if a candidate mis-stated her full name and address, since Parliament had made this aspect of candidate identification mandatory. However, the Court held that Parliament had not intended that the permissive, description element of the information that candidates might enter on the ballot form could provide grounds for overturning an election result. The Act did not provide a legal mechanism to protect voters and candidates against potentially misleading entries on the ballot form: 'the rules did not prohibit candidates, whether out of spite or a wicked sense of fun, from describing themselves in a confusing way or indulging in spoiling tactics'.[58]

This was an unfortunately sterile interpretation of the statute. Parliament's failure to grant explicit protection against spoiling candidates to parties (and, more importantly, their supporters) was reprehensible in the context of a modern party-based electoral contest, but this was not necessarily a barrier to the court producing that result. Teleologically construed, the candidate's power to add a description to his/her name and address could readily be seen as a device intended to aid electors to make an informed decision when casting their votes. Descriptions which manifestly hampered that outcome would thus be unlawful.

The scope for abuse left open by *Sanders* was reduced by the Registration of Political Parties Act 1998. The Act permitted parties to register particular emblems with the Registrar of Companies, and empowered them to prevent other parties using the emblem. More importantly, the Act prohibited candidates from describing themselves on the ballot paper in terms likely to mislead voters into assuming the candidate represents a registered party. The PPERA 2000 introduced a more extensive system of party registration, overseen by the Electoral Commission, which effectively precludes candidates standing for non-existent or 'spoiling' parties. This would seem a welcome—if belated—reform to electoral law, which clearly recognises the primacy of party affiliation in guiding voter behaviour.

Financing elections

A similar conclusion might now be drawn in respect of laws regulating electoral finance.[59] British campaigns are no longer marked by the violence and intimidation which so concerned the 1832 reformers. Nor do bribery or treating affect the contemporary process.[60] Such threats would technically be caught by the crime of 'undue influence' (now RPA 1983 s 115), but s 115 prosecutions are more likely in respect of activities such as defacing a candidate's posters or pulling leaflets from voters' letterboxes.[61]

But there is more to fairness than an absence of physical force and financial corruption. This becomes apparent when one observes that until enactment of the PPERA 2000 the discrepancy between the historically local form of the electoral system and the nationalisation of political choice evident in the apportionment process was also apparent in the laws governing the amounts of money that parties and candidates can spend on election campaigns.

The reasoning behind the limits on expenditure first introduced by the Corrupt and Illegal Practices Prevention Act 1883 makes obvious democratic sense. The restrictions ensure that the merits of a candidate's arguments, rather than the size of her advertising budget, determine her electoral popularity. The letter of the 1883 law has been retained,

[57] Permission to add the description was only introduced in 1968. Until then, candidates had not been allowed to identify their party on the ballot paper.   [58] [1995] 03 LS Gaz R 37 at 39.

[59] On the pre-2000 position see particularly Rawlings op cit ch 5; Ewing K (1987) *The funding of political parties in Britain*.

[60] See Rawlings op cit pp 146–149.   [61] *Roberts v Hogg* [1971] SLT 78.

with regularly updated financial thresholds. In the early 2000s, each candidate was allowed by RPA 1983 s 76 to spend around £9,000, plus a few pence for every registered voter in the constituency. Rich candidates thus could not derive an advantage from their wealth by, for example, employing dozens of full time helpers, or sending out glossy leaflets for weeks on end. Doubts existed as to when the expenditure clock started ticking. The announcement of the dissolution of Parliament would appear the most likely point. This means of course that a wealthy candidate could have spent unlimited amounts of money on publicity prior to the dissolution.

The rules on this issue were altered with effect from 2010. Provision is now made for candidates' spending to be split between what are termed 'the long campaign' and the 'short campaign'. The 'long campaign' runs for some three months prior to the dissolution of Parliament. During this period, candidates could spend (in 2015) £30,000 plus 5p/7p per registered voter in urban/rural constituencies. The short campaign runs for some three weeks immediately prior to the election. Candidates (in 2015) were permitted to spend some £8,700 plus 6p/9p per registered voter in urban/rural constituencies in this period.[62]

Early efforts to enforce expenditure limits were handicapped by the law's limited focus. Only the candidate himself or his agent were covered by the rule: expenditure by 'independent' individuals or companies was not subject to any ceiling. This provoked ingenious efforts by candidates and their supporters to establish 'independent' financial relationships, and much litigation ensued as defeated opponents sought to disprove the supporter's allegedly autonomous status.[63] This loophole was plugged by RPA 1918 s 34(1) (now RPA 1983 s 75), which prohibited any expenditure intended to promote a candidate unless written authorisation was received from the candidate's agent. Any such expenditure counts towards the candidate's overall limit.[64] The candidate's agent must compile an election return detailing all expenses. This is a public document, open to inspection by other candidates. Failure to produce the return is also an offence. However there is no mechanism for independent official scrutiny of returns. Any challenge to the legality of a candidate's expenditure is dependent upon the initiative of other candidates or voters.

The *Fiona Jones* case

Before 2000, the law on this question was markedly ambiguous. This was illustrated by an episode involving Fiona Jones, the successful Labour candidate for Newark in 1997. The defeated Liberal candidate accused Ms Jones of falsifying her expenses. Jones was convicted under s 82 of the RPA 1983 for dishonestly making a false declaration of her election expense. Jones protested her innocence, and announced she would appeal. The Act seemed to require that any person convicted of such a crime vacate her Commons seat. The Speaker subsequently declared the seat vacant. Shortly thereafter, before any by-election was held, the Court of Appeal quashed the conviction.[65]

The Court's judgment dwelt primarily on the law's extraordinarily imprecise nature. Section 76(1) of the 1983 Act provides that:

(1) No sum shall be paid and no expense shall be incurred by a candidate at an election or his election agent, whether before, during or after an election, on account of or in respect of the conduct or management of the election, in excess of the maximum amount specified in this section.

Section 118 then defined 'election expenses' as: 'expenses incurred, whether before, during or after the election, on account of or in respect of the conduct or management of the election'.

---

[62] Electoral Commission (2011) *UK general election 2010 campaign spending report* p 3.

[63] O'Leary op cit pp 54–55.

[64] For the background to the 1918 reform see *R v Hailwood and Ackroyd Ltd* [1928] 2 KB 277, CCA.

[65] [1999] 2 Cr App Rep 253, CA.

Lord Bingham CJ suggested that the meaning of ss 76 and 118 was obscure:

There is no simple and decisive test to determine whether an expense is or is not an election expense. . . . Some expenses obviously are, some obviously not. But there may be some expenses about which reasonable people, applying themselves to the question in all good faith, could reach different conclusions. . . . In this intermediate area, questions of judgment may arise.[66]

The Court accepted that it was possible that certain expenditures that Ms Jones had incurred were indeed 'election expenses' such as the cost of renting an office, shared with candidates in local elections, prior to the general election being called, and the use on polling day of a pre-existing database recording names and addresses of likely Labour voters. But there was room for doubt on that point. And given that doubt, there was no evidence to suggest that Jones had acted *dishonestly* by *knowingly* making a false declaration.[67]

The issue then before the High Court in *A–G v Jones*[68] was whether Ms Jones' vacation of the seat should be regarded as invalidating the Newark election or whether it was merely a temporary incapacity, which if removed by a successful appeal against conviction under s 82, did not prevent Ms Jones resuming her seat.

It seems unfortunate, on a matter so significant to the MP concerned, her opponents, and their electors, that the RPA 1983 did not offer a clear answer to this question. In a short, very technical judgment, the Court held that the Act imposed different consequences on candidates who filed false returns dependent on the forum before which the impugned behaviour was challenged. The Court held that the RPA provided for invalidation of the election only if proceedings were undertaken before an election court. A criminal conviction did not invalidate the election result, and an MP in Ms Jones' position could resume her seat as long as a by-election had not been held in the interim. The result makes obvious sense, but required some ingenuity on the Court's part, which suggested that a more streamlined statutory scheme might be desirable.

The PPERA 2000 proposed some amendments to this area of the law. But these did not obviously cure the uncertainties highlighted by the *Jones* case, particularly in the way that account is taken of what might be termed 'spending in kind'; that is to say a candidate's use of office space or campaign personnel donated by supporters.[69]

A local not national limit on party spending

Until 2000, spending limits only applied to local campaigns. As Alder observes: 'The kind of campaign envisaged by the law is centred upon knocking on doors and holding meetings in public halls'.[70] As with apportionment, the law did not recognise the concept of a 'general election' for financial purposes; rather it saw 650 individual elections.

This is illustrated by the *Tronoh Mines* case.[71] Shortly before the 1951 General Election, the Tronoh Mines company placed an advertisement in *The Times*, part of which read:

The coming general election will give us all the opportunity of saving the country from being reduced, through the policies of the Socialist government, to a bankrupt 'Welfare State'. . .

The advert clearly disparaged the Labour Party, and thus indirectly boosted the Conservatives' prospects. The company and *The Times* were prosecuted (under what is now RPA 1983 s 75)

---

[66] Ibid, at 260, CA.

[67] 'It is not a crime to declare an honest belief in a declaration of election expenses in which some expenses which should have been included have been omitted . . . unless the person making the declaration knows that it is false in one or other respect or both. Honest belief in the truth of the declaration, and thus in the completeness and accuracy of the figures disclosed, is a complete defence': [1999] 2 Cr App Rep 253, CA, per Lord Bingham CJ.

[68] [2000] QB 66.

[69] See Ewing K (2000) 'Transparency, accountability and equality: the Political Parties, Elections and Referendums Act 2000' *Public Law* 542.

[70] Alder op cit p 163.   [71] *R v Tronoh Mines Ltd* [1952] 1 All ER 697, CA.

for making unauthorised expenditure designed to promote the candidacy of the Conservative in the constituency where the paper was printed. McNair J held that there was no case to answer. He considered that the advert's purpose was 'to advance the prospects of the anti-Socialist cause generally' by influencing public opinion as a whole.[72] The Act however, addressed only efforts to promote 'a candidate at a particular election, and not candidates at elections generally'.[73] Since the advert played to a national, not constituency audience, it was not prohibited.

The inference of the judgment was that there was no legal limit to the funds a party could spend on its national campaigns. Parties could put as many adverts as they could afford in national newspapers; or buy as many poster sites they as could afford all over the country. Rawlings observed that *Tronoh Mines* 'is an excellent illustration of the blindness of our electoral law to the realities of national election campaigning'.[74] That is an unduly harsh criticism of McNair J, whose interpretation of the Act was entirely logical. If the law was unsatisfactory, blame was more appropriately laid at Parliament's feet.[75]

In the Britain of 1883, a concept of financial equality limited to local campaigns was perhaps defensible. The party system was clearly well-established by then, but one still had 'independent' candidates, and the relative technological backwardness of the news media and transport infrastructure made local campaigns an important contributor to voter choice. Party loyalties influenced voter behaviour, but they were not obviously the dominant factor.

In modern Britain, political realities are very different. General elections are fought and won and lost in the national arena. Voter choice is motivated primarily by party affiliation. Similarly, the information on which that choice is based is more likely to have been gleaned from the national news media than from localised techniques such as listening to a candidate's local speeches or reading her election literature. One might plausibly conclude therefore that the more money a party spends on its national campaign, the more likely it is to persuade people all over the country that they should vote for that party's local candidate. There is no guarantee that spending lots of money will win a party lots more support. But as Table 7.4 indicates, campaign expenditure has been rising in recent years.

Whether one can establish a correlation between the Conservative Party's higher spending and its electoral success in the 1983, 1987, and 1992 elections is a question offering no easy answer. Deciding whether the constitution should tolerate the possibility of electoral choice being swayed by party wealth would seem more straightforward. The spirit of the 1883 Act was to sever the direct link between financial and political power; the retention merely of its letter in a quite different political context ensured that that objective was no longer being effectively achieved.

Table 7.4 Party campaign spending in recent general elections

	1987	1992	1997	2001	2005	2010	2015
Conservative	£9.0m	£11.2m	£20.0m	£12.8m	£17.85m	£16.6m	£15.6m
Labour	£4.2m	£10.2m	£13.0m	£11.1m	£17.93m	£8.0m	£12.1m
Liberal/SDP	£2.0m	£1.8m	£0.7m	£1.4m	£4.3m	£4.7m	£3.5m

Source: Compiled from data in Butler D and Kavanagh D (1988) *The British general election of 1987* pp 235–236; (1993) *The British general election of 1992* p 260; (1998) *The British general election of 1997* p 242: *The Guardian* 17 December 2001; Electoral Commission (2005) 'Spending by political parties and campaign groups at the 5 May UK parliamentary election'; (2011) *UK general election 2010 campaign spending report* p 11; (2016) *UK general election 2015 campaign spending report* p 20.

[72] [1952] 1 All ER 697 at 698.   [73] Ibid, at 699.   [74] Op cit p 135.
[75] See also See Munro C (1976) 'Elections and expenditure' *Public Law* 300.

An equally significant omission was the absence of any legal requirement that parties reveal the sources of their income. This raised the possibility that powerful economic interests could 'buy' legislative influence. Neither were there any limits on the size of contributions that individuals or corporations might make to a political party. In the 1980s and 1990s, stories occasionally appeared in the national press alleging that life peerages have in effect been 'bought' by leading industrialists whose companies have made large donations to Conservative Party funds. Such allegations were unproven, but if substantiated would clearly further undermine the Lords' legitimacy. A greater concern was that substantial numbers of MPs might favour policies benefiting a substantial donor, irrespective of the policies' intrinsic merits. In the mid-1990s, particular concern was engendered by reports that the Conservative Party consistently accepted huge sums of money from overseas business interests, which created the suspicion that the donors were attempting to buy legislative influence. Such suspicions were intensified during the first term of the Blair government. Particular controversy arose over the gift of £1m given to the Labour Party by Bernie Ecclestone, the motor racing tycoon. The gift 'coincided' with an apparent abandonment by the government of a plan to ban tobacco advertising. Since Ecclestone derived vast amounts of his fortune from tobacco advertising, the inference arose that he had bought the change in government policy. That the Labour Party subsequently returned the donation did little to allay suspicion that its financial integrity was compromised.

The Political Parties, Elections and Referendums Act 2000

Such gaps in the law emphasised that the formal structure of this part of the constitution had not kept pace with changing political circumstances. The PPERA made a wide-ranging attempt to bring the rules of electoral finance law into line with contemporary political realities. Several important initiatives were introduced. Most significantly, Part V and Sch 8 of the Act place limits on a party's national campaign expenditure.[76] The sum was fixed at £30,000 per constituency contested. Parties contesting only a few seats may spend a maximum of £810,000 in England, £120,000 in Scotland, and £60,000 in Wales. The Act requires that each party would have to appoint a Treasurer and Deputy Treasurers who are the only persons permitted to authorise campaign expenditure. Following the campaign, the party Treasurer must submit detailed accounts to the Electoral Commission which are available for public inspection. Exceeding the limits is now a criminal offence.

The Act also provides that only individuals registered to vote in the United Kingdom and corporate bodies established in the United Kingdom can make donations to political parties. Any donations from non-permitted donors must be returned, and a knowing breach of the rules by a party Treasurer or a donor would be a criminal offence. All donations of over £200 must be recorded in the party's accounts, which must be submitted to the Electoral Commission and made available for public inspection at the end of each financial year.

These are valuable initiatives.[77] The rationale underlying the Bill was that political parties should be entirely candid about the sources of their income, thereby enabling voters to make a more informed choice about who to support. Importantly, the Bill enjoyed multi-party support in the Commons and the Lords and was enacted in largely unchanged form. In so far as the original Bill had an obvious weakness, it was in limiting penalties for breach of its provisions to individuals (in particular the party Treasurer). A penalty which involved invalidation of general election results in their entirety would not be practical. But the deterrent effect of the provisions might have been enhanced if their breach led to large fines being imposed on a party.

Both the Labour and Conservative Parties fell short of spending the maximum permissible amount in the 2005 and 2010 general elections.[78] This rather suggests that the concern evinced by the Act that the larger parties might augment their vote through unrestrained spending on

---

[76] These sums would be additional to sums spent by individual candidates in constituency campaigns.
[77] For a helpful analysis see Ewing (2001) op cit.   [78] See Table 7.4.

campaigning was exaggerated. However the Act has brought more intense public and press focus to bear on the ways political parties raise their money. The Electoral Commission maintains an online database which contains detailed listings of all registrable donations to the political parties. This innovation substantially enhances the transparency of party funding by making the relevant information widely available and thereby enabling other political parties, the press, or interested individuals to raise questions about the legality of donations made.

In 2002, continuing scandals over the main parties' (but especially the Labour Party's) evident predilections to take large sums of money in dubious circumstances from commercial sources led to renewed calls in the press, and within Parliament, for state financing of political parties, accompanied by calls for low limits on the amounts that individuals or companies could donate. The suggestion is a sound one. On the surface it appears profligate to allocate several million pounds of public money each year to political parties. But such expenditure would be substantially less damaging to the public purse than the status quo, in which it seems that parties in government are willing to channel large amounts of public expenditure in the form of subsidies, or sell-offs of public property, or contracts for services which represent poor value for money but whose beneficiaries made a proportionately miniscule donation to party funds.

The Electoral Commission reviewed the matter in 2002. Its subsequent report[79] did not advocate any radical changes to the existing system, offering instead the modest suggestion that individuals should be encouraged to make small donations to political parties either by the provision of matching public funds to supplement such gifts or by making donations eligible for tax relief.

However, pressure for further legislative reform arose early in 2006. A series of stories ran in the press claiming that Prime Minister Blair had either solicited or accepted on the Labour Party's behalf very substantial loans from wealthy businessmen. These loans were not declared to the public, nor even it seems to the Labour Party's Treasurer and some senior members of the Cabinet. Strictly speaking, there was no legal requirement that the loans be declared, as the PPERA is concerned only with donations. It is of course conceivable that the terms of the 'loans' were so beneficial to the Labour Party that they might credibly be regarded as being at least partial donations. But the main criticism levelled at the Prime Minister was that it appeared that the makers of some of the loans were subsequently nominated by the Prime Minister for life peerages. The obvious—and to many observers essentially corrupt—inference to be drawn from this was that Prime Minister Blair was selling seats in Parliament to wealthy Labour Party supporters. Accusations were also raised that the other main political parties had engaged in a similarly distasteful attempt to evade the spirit of the PPERA regime. To contain the criticism made of the Prime Minister, the government announced in March 2006 that it would promote an amendment to the PPERA rules that would make loans declarable in future.

Television and radio broadcasting

The British approach to the regulation of television and radio broadcasting by political parties has been a markedly non-legal affair. There has long been widespread acceptance that candidates' and parties' wealth should have no bearing on their access to the public. Broadcasting time is not for sale to politicians. Parliament has consistently legislated to this effect in the modern era.[80] Air time was initially allocated by a body called the Committee on Party

---

[79] The Electoral Commission (2004) *The funding of political parties*. For comment see Rowbottom J (2005) 'The electoral Commission's proposals on the funding of political parties' *Public Law* 468. For a sophisticated analysis of the issue see Marriot J (2005) 'Alarmist or relaxed? Election expenditure limits and free speech' *Public Law* 764.

[80] The Communications Act 2003 s 319 is the current version. See especially Lewis T and Cumper P (2009) 'Balancing freedom of political expression against equality of opportunity: the courts and the UK broadcasting ban on political advertising' *Public Law* 89.

Political Broadcasting, composed of representatives from television and radio organisations, and members of the main political parties. The Committee allocated small amounts of air time to each party, the share being roughly in accordance with the party's portion of the vote at the last general election.

While both the BBC and the IBA are legally obliged to maintain political impartiality in their programming decisions, the Committee itself has no explicit legal basis. Nor could the Committee be described as a 'conventional' institution in the formal sense. The process in fact broke down in 1987, when decisions were made solely by the broadcasting organisations themselves. In the run up to the 1987 general election, the three main parties had five television broadcasts and the Greens one. It may seem anomalous that so important a part of the electoral process is not regulated by statute. Yet paradoxically this is one of the few aspects of the system attuned to the realities of contemporary campaigns. There are no technical obstacles preventing Parliament intervening in this area; as yet no government has invited it to do so.[81] It may be there is little practical need for such regulation, as the broadcasts themselves seem to have little (and declining) influence on voter behaviour: those in the 2005 election were described by one commentator as: '[A] shrunken shadow of their former selves.'[82]

There is no indication that the broadcasts made in the 2010 election period reversed this trend.[83] The potentially significant innovation in that campaign was that the leaders of the main parties held a televised debate along the lines of the presidential debates long held in the USA. The initiative attracted much press interest, and an impressive performance by the Liberal Democrat leader Nick Clegg appeared to boost his party's standing in the opinion polls. That boost did not however translate into a commensurate increase in seats won at the ensuing vote.[84]

'Decent, honest and truthful'? The content of political advertising

Parliament has yet to try to regulate the content of party advertising. Hyperbolic claims and vitriolic abuse now seem a staple ingredient of election campaigns, as are lurid tales of opposing parties' hidden political agendas. Clearly one would not wish voters' choices to be influenced by lies. But 'truth' is an elusive concept, and has little bearing on matters of political opinion such as 'A Labour government would ruin the economy' or 'A Conservative government will produce increased unemployment'.

In 1895, a private member's Bill was enacted which forbade the making of a 'false statement of fact' intended to hamper a candidate's prospects of success. Matters such as a circular letter falsely announcing a candidate's withdrawal from the contest, and press accusations of salmon poaching, were offered by MPs as evidence of such unworthy practices. The courts subsequently held that the Act extended only to statements concerning a candidate's personal characteristics, not his political views. A private members' Bill to reverse this decision failed through lack of government support in 1911.[85] The present law, RPA 1983 s 106, maintains the personal/political distinction: falsely calling a candidate a 'communist' or 'fascist' does not contravene the Act.

The provision has rarely been invoked. This may be due less to the intrinsic integrity of candidates' campaign literature and speeches than to a rather fatalistic acceptance by both politicians and the public that honesty and accuracy are invariably qualities that are in short supply in elections. However, s 106 came to prominence following the 2010 election. A former Labour Minister, Phil Woolas, won the marginal seat of Oldham East by 103 votes from his

---

[81] See generally Boyle A (1986) 'Political broadcasting, fairness and administrative law' *Public Law* 562.

[82] Butler and Kavanagh (2005) op cit p 111.

[83] See Kavanagh D and Cowley P (2010) *The British general election of 2010* ch 13.

[84] Ibid. See also Chadwick A (2001) 'Britain's first live televised leaders' debate: from the news cycle to the political information cycle' *Parliamentary Affairs* 24.   [85] O'Leary op cit pp 179–181, 216–226.

Liberal Democrat opponent Robert Watkins. Watkins claimed that Woolas had knowingly made untrue claims about him, including assertions that he was seeking support from violent Muslim extremists, and that he had accepted unlawful donations from a Saudi Arabian sheikh. The litigation[86] turned essentially on whether such comments should be regarded as referring to Mr Watkins' 'personal character' or be viewed instead as relating to his political beliefs or conduct. The conclusion reached by the Court was while the assertions concerned political issues, they did so in a way which called Mr Watkins' personal honour into question and so fell within s 106.

The penalty for breaching s 106 is that the election concerned is held to be void and the defendant is barred from election to the Commons for three years.[87] Mr Woolas' political career has likely been ended by the episode. But perhaps ironically, the new Labour candidate won the subsequent by-election with a much increased majority. The episode may however encourage candidates to be more careful about how they attack their opponents in future elections.

Counting the vote

There is no evidence to suggest that the integrity of modern elections is significantly compromised by irregularities in the physical process of adding up individual votes. Ballot slips are not altered after the voter fills them in; forged papers are not added to the ballot box; and ballot boxes do not go astray. The count is an open process, which all candidates may scrutinise. But the concept of 'counting' votes can also bear a rather wider meaning. The most frequently voiced complaint concerning the present system is the limited correlation between the votes that a party receives and the number of seats it wins. Chapter one adverted to the problems posed in a democratic state by the tyranny of the majority. Table 7.5 reveals that modern Britain did not suffer from the problem of majoritarian government between 1945 and 2009, since (except for the dubious exception of the 1977 Lib/Lab pact) it did not have a government enjoying majority electoral support. No single party government elected since 1945 has secured over 50% of the vote. The best Conservative performance was 49.7% in 1955. Labour's highest ever share was 48.8% in 1951. However, Labour lost the 1951 election. The Conservatives, with fewer votes, gained seven more Commons seats. Moreover, by no means does everybody choose to vote. While over 80% of eligible voters took part in the 1950 and 1951 elections, that percentage has declined dramatically in recent elections. The Thatcher governments elected in 1979, 1983, and 1987 had the positive support of one third of the population. The Blair governments elected in 1997 and 2001 enjoyed even lower levels of active support. In 2001, the Labour Party won a Commons majority of over 160 on just 40% of the vote. Since turnout slumped to less than 60%, the Labour Party was actually voted for by less than 25% of the registered electorate.

The figures for the 2005 general election appear similarly startling. Turnout was again very low. Only 61.2% of eligible electors voted. The Labour Party won 356 seats—and a majority in the Commons of over 60 seats—with a 35.2% share of the votes cast. The Conservatives' 32.4% share yielded 198 seats. The Liberal Democrats attracted 22% of the popular vote, yet secured only 62 seats. The third Blair administration thus enjoyed the dubious distinction of having won the lowest share of the eligible vote of any twentieth-century government.[88]

In the 2010 election, in which some 65% of eligible voters participated, the Conservative Party's 32% share of the vote yielded 307 (47%) of the seats in the Commons. The Liberal Democrats once again fared poorly on the vote cast/seats won index. Despite winning 23% of

---

[86] *Watkins v Woolas* [2010] EWHC 2702 (QB). See the discussion in Hoar F (2011) 'Public or personal character in election campaigns: a review of the implications of the judgment in Watkins v Woolas' *MLR* 607.

[87] RPA 1983 ss 159–160.   [88] Butler D and Kavanagh D (2005) *The British general election of 2005*, App 1.

Table 7.5 Votes gained and seats won at general elections since 1945

Year	Conservative		Labour		Liberal *		Turnout
	Vote %	Seats	Vote %	Seats	Vote %	Seats	
1945	39.8	213	47.8	393	9.0	12	72.7%
1950	43.5	298	46.1	315	9.1	9	84.0%
1951	48.0	321	48.8	295	2.5	6	82.5%
1955	49.7	344	46.4	277	2.7	6	76.7%
1959	49.4	365	43.8	258	5.9	6	78.8%
1964	43.4	304	44.1	317	11.2	9	77.1%
1966	41.9	253	47.9	363	8.5	12	75.8%
1970	46.4	330	43.0	287	7.5	6	72.0%
1974 [1]	37.9	297	37.1	301	19.3	14	78.7%
1974 [2]	35.8	277	39.2	319	18.3	13	72.8%
1979	43.9	339	36.9	269	13.8	11	76.0%
1983	42.4	397	27.6	209	25.4	23	72.7%
1987	42.3	376	30.8	292	22.6	22	75.3%
1992	41.9	336	34.4	271	17.8	20	77.7%
1997	30.7	165	43.2	418	16.8	46	71.2%
2001	31.7	166	40.7	412	18.3	52	59.8%
2005	32.4	198	35.2	356	22.0	62	61.2%
2010	36.1	307	29.0	258	23.0	57	65.1%
2015	36.9	331	30.4	232	7.9	8	66.1%

*1983 and 1987 votes include the Social Democratic Party (SDP).
Source: Compiled from data in Norton (1991) op cit pp 97–99; Butler and Kavanagh (1993) op cit p 246; (1998) op cit p 255; (2002) op cit p 261; 2006 op cit; Kavanagh and Cowley (2010) op cit pp 350–351.

votes cast, the party ended up with only 53 (8%) of the seats. David Cameron's Conservative Party secured a small (twelve-seat) majority at the 2015 election, having won 36.9% of a 66% turnout. Once again, therefore, a government was formed on the basis of the active support of barely 25% of eligible voters.

These ostensibly extraordinary results arise because the British electoral system permits minority rule, not simply majoritarianism. If one's concern as a constitutional lawyer is to ensure that government derives its powers from the consent of the governed, this may seem unsatisfactory, especially since that government frequently has de facto control of Parliament's supposedly unlimited legal competence.

The vote/seat discrepancy situation is an almost inevitable consequence of a country where most electoral support is closely divided between two political parties choosing the 'plurality' counting system in single-member constituencies. The 'plurality' or 'first past the post' rule means that one wins a constituency simply by polling more votes than any other candidate. In a two-party contest, the winner must gain 50%+1 of the votes cast, an outcome which raises the prospect of barely majoritarian government. However, should four candidates compete, the seat could be won with as few as 25%+1 votes. The more candidates, and the more evenly balanced their support, the fewer votes needed to win.

Supporters of defeated parties in our hypothetical four-candidate constituency have exercised only indirect, negative power over the selection of their MP, in so far as if they

Table 7.6 Minoritarianism in parliamentary constituency elections

Constituency	Year	Con	Lab	Lib*	Nat
Carlisle	1983	37.3%	37.5%	25.1%	–
Stockton North	1983	33.3%	37.1%	29.6%	–
Brecon and Radnor	1987	34.7%	29.2%	34.8%	1.3%
South Stockton	1987	35.0%	31.3%	33.7%	–
Nairn and Lochaber	1992	22.6%	25.1%	26.0%	24.7%
Renfrew West	1992	32.9%	36.6%	10.0%	20.2%
Falmouth and Cambourne	1997	28.8%	33.8%	25.2%	–
Colchester	1997	31.4%	30.6%	34.4%	–
Hastings and Rye	1997	29.2%	34.4%	28.0%	–
Ochil and South Perthshire	2005	21.5%	31.4%	13.3%	29.9%
Perthshire North	2005	30.4%	18.7%	16.1%	33.7%
Camden, Hampstead, and Kilburn	2010	32.7%	32.8%	31.2%	–
Sutton and Devonport	2010	34.3%	31.7%	24.7%	–
Argyll and Bute	2010	24.0%	22.7%	31.6%	18.9%

*Includes the SDP.
Source: Com.piled from data in Butler and Kavanagh (1984); (1988); (1993); (1998); (2005) op cit.

did not vote for losing candidates A, B, or C, winning candidate D would need fewer votes to succeed. But these 75%–1 voters have not exercised any direct, positive control over the choice of their legislative representative. This is often referred to as the 'wasted vote' problem. In legal terms, one votes not for a party on a national basis, but for an individual representative of a party in an individual constituency. The 'general election' label is a misnomer; rather one has 650 simultaneous local elections. Supporters of defeated parties cannot pick up their wasted votes and use them to support another of their party's candidates somewhere else.

Within an individual constituency, there will always be a mismatch between votes cast and seats won in contested elections unless every voter supports one candidate, since there is only one seat to win. But the potential shortcomings of the single member plurality system are magnified when one aggregates the results of all constituencies to determine whose representatives gain de facto control of Parliament's unlimited legal sovereignty. If modern Britain had only two political parties, enjoying approximately equal popular support, a party could theoretically take every seat by winning each constituency with 50%+1 votes: the party which won 50%–1 votes in every constituency would have no MPs at all.

Such theoretical extremes do not occur in practice. But candidates regularly win constituencies with only 40% of the votes, because the majority of electors have split their vote among several other parties: (see Table 7.6). A constituency is rarely won by a candidate who gains more than 65% support. Consequently at least a substantial minority of votes are always 'wasted'. In the 2005 general election, 419 of the 646 constituencies were won by candidates who attracted fewer than 50% of the votes cast. The problem was particularly acute in Scottish constituencies in the 2005 general election. Of the fifty-nine seats contested in Scotland, forty-two were won by candidates (twenty-six of whom were Labour candidates) with under 50% of the vote. And of those forty-two newly returned MPs, thirteen (eight of them Labour candidates) failed to reach the 40% level.[89]

In a two-party system, where each party enjoys approximately equal support, the parties' wasted votes may cancel each other out. If one examines just the Conservative and Labour performances in Table 7.5, one sees that the party with more votes generally (but not always) wins more seats, and that the Commons majority increases as the voting share expands. But Table 7.5 also shows that the percentage of the total vote shared between the Labour and Conservative Parties has declined since 1945.[90] Other parties have attracted growing electoral support. They have not as a consequence gained growing parliamentary representation. The Liberal Party has suffered acutely from the vote/seat discrepancy. In 1983 the SDP/Liberal Alliance won 25.4% of the vote but only twenty-three seats. In 1987, their 22.6% of the vote produced only twenty-two MPs. Liberal support is spread relatively evenly throughout Britain. Consequently, Liberals often come second in both Labour and Conservative constituencies. But in a single MP constituency system, there are no direct rewards for coming second. Unusually in 2010 however, there were some indirect ones.

The 2010 election: a hung Parliament and a coalition government

The opinion polls in the run-up to the 2010 election had consistently predicted that no party would manage to win an overall Commons majority.[91] The predictions proved well-founded. Of the 650 seats, 307 were won by the Conservatives, 258 by Labour, 57 by the Liberals, 27 by Scots/Welsh/Northern Irish parties and 1 by the Greens.

This result threw up several possibilities for the formation of the next government. One outcome might be a minority Conservative government. A second alternative would be a formal or informal (majority) coalition government between the Conservatives and the Liberals. A third outcome could be a minority Conservative-led coalition with the Democratic Unionist Party from Northern Ireland. A fourth option might be a Labour/Liberal minority coalition, perhaps bolstered by the support of some of the smaller parties.

None of the parties had campaigned on the basis of with which other parties and on what terms they might enter a coalition agreement. It might therefore be suggested that any outcome other than the first one would produce a government for which indeed no-one had actually voted. Immediately after the results were finalised, the Liberal Democrats indicated that they would explore the possibility of coalition with either the Conservative or Labour Parties. Negotiations continued for five days between the parties, during which time the Brown government remained in office. The negotiations eventually led to the creation of a formal coalition between the Conservative and Liberal parties, which at least in simple arithmetical terms commanded a clear majority in the Commons.[92]

Alternative voting systems

The plurality model is generally contrasted with a voting mechanism described as 'proportional representation' (PR). PR is an umbrella term, embracing many electoral systems. In so far as these systems share a common theme, it is to produce a closer relationship between the votes cast for and seats won by parties attracting substantial national or regional voter support.

---

[89] Butler and Kavanagh (2005) op cit App 1.

[90] On the reasons for this decline, which appear broadly to reflect a breakdown of traditional working class/middle class divisions, see Norton op cit pp 105–115.

[91] Kavanagh and Cowley op cit ch 12.   [92] See Kavanagh and Cowley op cit ch 10.

PR is not a novel idea in British constitutional theory.[93] John Stuart Mill coupled his advocacy of women's enfranchisement with support for the 'Hare' scheme of PR (named after its inventor).[94] This system was adopted in Tasmania shortly thereafter,[95] and a variant of it is described below.

PR generated a particular flurry of parliamentary and extra-parliamentary activity during the passage of the 1884 Reform Act. Many proponents were motivated by a purely sectarian desire to safeguard the representation of the minority protestant community in Ireland. Others, including E C Clark, then Regius Professor of Civil Law at Cambridge, saw PR as a Madisonian guard against factional legislation, which would remove any incentive for parties to offer sensationalist policies appealing to the bigotry or ignorance of an 'impulsive' electorate.[96] The Speaker's Conference established during World War I had indeed recommended that the plurality method be replaced by a PR scheme. This was put to a free vote in both houses, where it attracted substantial, if not sufficient support.[97]

It is not entirely sensible to consider electoral reform in isolation from other constitutional issues; the method one adopts to choose one's legislature may well be affected by one's choice as to its powers. It is nonetheless helpful to outline the basic features of alternatives to the plurality/single member model.

The party list system

A national list system maximises the correlation between seats cast and votes won; a party gaining x% of the votes wins x% of the seats. There is in effect only one constituency—namely the entire country—under a national list system. Voters choose a party, not an individual candidate. The parties themselves draw up lists of candidates. Parties which gained sufficient votes for ten, twenty, or fifty seats respectively would send the first ten, twenty, and fifty members on their list to the legislature. Israel operates the purest list system. In its 120-member Knesset, a party will gain a legislative seat with only 1% of the popular vote.

A national list system eliminates both the wasted vote problem and the difficulties of apportionment. Whether it is however more 'democratic' is a complex question. The Israeli system affords legislative representation to extremist political parties, thereby lending an unwarranted legitimacy to their policies. In the British system, in contrast, given the existence of three mainstream parties, an extremist candidate will need at least 25%+1 support in a given constituency to win its seat. This danger may be countered by having a representation threshold: a party would not receive any seats at all unless it passes 5% or 10% or 15% of the vote barrier. The higher the threshold, the more difficult it becomes for extremist parties to gain representation.

The list method also offers opportunities for small parties to enter government by forming coalitions with larger parties. If such coalitions result from post-election negotiation, one may end up with a government for which no-one has actually voted. That objection could be overcome if parties were to announce their prospective coalition partners prior to the poll.

Critics also point out that the list places complete control of candidate selection in the hands of party officials, although this criticism may be met by a legal framework which opens up parties' selection processes to all of their members. Similarly, accusations that the list precludes any identification between a given legislator and particular parts of the country can be reduced (if not eliminated) by compiling lists on a regional rather than national basis.

---

[93] See Hart J (1992) *Proportional representation: critics of the British electoral system 1820–1945*.
[94] Hart (1992) op cit ch 2.   [95] Brown W (1899) 'The Hare system in Tasmania' *LQR* 51.
[96] Jones op cit pp 99–100.   [97] See Butler (1953) op cit ch 1.

The single transferable vote

The single transferable vote (STV) method, (a development of the Hare system), offers the advantage of being tried, tested, and evidently approved in Ireland, Malta, and Australia. STV employs multi-member constituencies. Parties field as many candidates as they wish, while voters mark candidates in order of preference. A candidate is successful if she attains first preference votes equivalent to one more than the number of electors divided by the number of candidates +1. In a four member constituency this figure would be 20%+1; in a three member constituency 25%+1, and so on. That candidate's second preference votes are then allocated as new first preference votes to the remaining candidates. Any candidates thereby reaching the quota are also elected, and their second preferences are in turn divided among remaining candidates until all seats are filled.

STV is time-consuming and complex, and also requires large and potentially unwieldy constituencies. Nevertheless, particularly in constituencies returning four or more members, it minimises the wasted vote problem. It also enables voters not wishing to support a straight party line to express a preference between individual candidates as well as between parties.

Absolute majority systems

Absolute majority systems are not strictly concerned with proportionality, but with ensuring that the winning candidate in a single-member constituency attracts majority electoral support, thereby reducing but not eliminating the wasted vote problem. This may be achieved through the 'alternative vote' method. Voters list candidates in order of preference. If a candidate secures 50%+1 first preference votes she is elected. If no candidate does so, the least popular is eliminated and her second preference votes are re-allocated to the remaining candidates. This process is repeated until one candidate passes the 50% barrier.

Another route to a similar end is offered by the 'second ballot' method. Should more than two candidates run, the first ballot operates solely to eliminate all but the two most popular. These two candidates then contest a run-off election shortly after the initial contest. This both ensures majority support, and also offers voters the chance to reflect on their final choice.

The German system

Elections to Germany's *Bundestag* employ a mixed method of plurality voting in one member constituencies coupled with a regional list.[98] Half of the *Bundestag* seats are allocated to candidates gaining a plurality in their constituencies, half to candidates on the lists. However, voters also have a second vote in which they express a party preference. After the constituency candidates take their seats, each party's representation in the *Bundestag* is increased to that number which equates in percentage terms to its share of the party votes.

The process can usefully be illustrated by returning to the absurd example canvassed earlier in which Party A gains 50%+1 votes in every constituency, while Party B gains 50%–1. In Britain, Party A wins every seat. In Germany, (assuming voters follow a straight party line), Party A wins every constituency seat, but only one party seat, the rest of which go to Party B. Party A thus gains the slimmest of *Bundestag* majorities to reflect its tiny lead in the popular vote.

The German method offers the benefits of almost perfect proportionality along with constituency representation. It also addresses the criticisms made of national list systems that MP selection is utterly dominated by parties, and that legislators have no ties to particular areas.

---

[98] See Bogdanor V (1983) *What is proportional representation?* ch 4; Pulzer P (1983) 'Germany' in Butler D and Bogdanor V (eds) *Democracy and elections.*

The prospects of reform

One can identify shortcomings as well as benefits in all voting systems. This section has thus far dwelt solely on the drawbacks of our single-member plurality system; one ought also to focus on its claimed merits. One would assume these are considerable, given that since 1945 both Labour and Conservative controlled Houses of Commons have chosen to retain an electoral system in which unlimited legal power is bestowed upon the representatives of a minority of the citizenry.[99]

The first is the so-called 'strong government' thesis. This stresses the importance of ensuring that the country always has a stable government, able to implement a clearly defined set of legislative priorities, unencumbered by the need to compromise its beliefs to maintain the support of minority parties. Relatedly, the electorate knows where to attribute responsibility for failure or success, and can react accordingly at the next election. A second argument points to the simplicity and transparency of the present system. It is easy both for voters to understand and for government to administer. A third dwells on the importance of small constituency representation, which ensures both that MPs are not too distanced from the concerns of ordinary voters, and that all candidates are directly exposed to popular, rather than simply party scrutiny.

Those points may be promptly rebutted. The strong government thesis is unconvincing if one views the project of government as a long- rather than short-term process. Firstly, it may not be beneficial for a country to march strongly in one direction during the lifetime of one or two Parliaments, and then equally strongly in an altogether different direction for the next five or ten years. Secondly, if alternative systems are deemed too complex for the electorate to understand, the appropriate solution may be more extensive voter education. Thirdly, the necessity or desirability of having members of the national legislature play a substantial role as constituency representatives is contingent on the powers and structure of sub-central elected government, an issue addressed in chapter ten.

Voting reform has long been a central element of the Liberal Democrat's political ideology, the party having traditionally favoured a form of STV. The Party's entry into the coalition government offered some opportunity to put the issue to the electorate. The Conservative Party was willing however only to countenance the holding of a referendum on the question of whether the 'first past the post' system should be replaced with the 'alternative vote'. A commitment to this effect was made in the coalition agreement, and subsequently enacted as the Parliamentary Voting Systems and Constituencies Act 2010. A referendum was held in the spring of 2011. To the chagrin of the Liberal Party, the proposal was defeated by some 68%–32%, albeit on a very low turnout of just 42%.[100] In the medium term at least, it appears that the 'first past the post' constituency system will continue in robust political health.[101]

The coalition government also proposed that legislation be enacted to place the electoral cycle on a five-year fixed term basis, subject to an override by a two-thirds majority vote in the Commons or the passing (presumably by simple majority) of a vote of no confidence in the government. The Bill was enacted in September 2011 as the Fixed Term Parliaments Act 2011. Section 1 of the Act identified the presumptive date for the next general election as 7 May 2015.

---

[99] For the defence see Maude A and Szemerey J (1981) *Why electoral reform? The case for electoral reform examined)*. For a demolition of the defence see Oliver D (1982) 'Why electoral reform? The case for electoral reform examined' *Public Law* 236.

[100] <http://www.electoralcommission.org.uk/elections/referendums/referendum>.

[101] As noted in ch 12, rather different systems have latterly been introduced for elections to the newly created Scots Parliament and Welsh Assembly.

In legal terms, the Act replaces the Monarch's (de facto the Prime Minister's) non-justiciable prerogative power to dissolve parliament whenever she thinks fit with a strictly defined statutory rule. The Act's political effect is to preclude a government from manipulating the electoral cycle in whatever way it thinks best serves its party political interests. As such, it amounts to a welcome—albeit modest—enhancement to the representative basis of the electoral system.

Perhaps rather more significant however was the coalition government's proposal, enacted as the Parliamentary Voting Systems and Constituencies Act 2010 ss 10–14, that the size of the House of Commons be reduced for the 2015 election from 650 seats to 600. The government's rationale was evidently that the general public might become more favourably disposed towards the Commons if the house had fewer members and was therefore (slightly) less expensive to run. A more principled objective was that the previously tolerated wide disparities in voter numbers between constituencies should be removed.[102] Save for a handful of geographically atypical constituencies, the Act provided that the size of each constituency's electorate should not be more than 5% above or below the electoral quota;[103] an acceptance at last of the 'one vote, one value' principle.[104]

The Boundary Commission for England published its initial plans in September 2011. The intended charges were unsurprisingly not well received by many MPs, especially those whose seats were being substantially withdrawn or abolished altogether. The Commission's consultation process continued until late 2011 and culminated (unsurprisingly) in a decision to leave constituency boundaries unchanged for the 2015 election.

Conclusion

It would be facile to assume that there is an 'ideal' electoral system waiting to be discovered. In leaving this topic, we might again try to assess the extent to which electoral law ensures that the political party controlling the legislature enjoys the consent of the governed. In chapters five to seven, it has been suggested that the sovereignty of Parliament is in effect the sovereignty of the Commons, which is in turn the sovereignty of the majority party in the lower house, which is in turn the sovereignty of the minority of voters supporting that party. The constitution is, in legal terms, a vehicle facilitating factional government on all issues.

Yet factionalism in the law-making process need not lead to factionalism in the law's content. We must also consider what objectives factional parties pursue when they control Parliament's sovereign legal authority. If major parties share similar views on those elements of the constitution regarded as 'higher law' in other democracies, majoritarian or minoritarian control of the Commons is less problematic—factional differences will only be given legal expression in respect of non-fundamental issues. Supporters of the losing party may find such policies unpalatable, but not intolerable, and accept defeat because they anticipate that their opponents would do likewise if they lost the next election. The thorny question of how one identifies a 'fundamental' law is returned to repeatedly in subsequent chapters. Before doing so however, we return in chapter eight to the topic of parliamentary privilege.

---

[102] Cf the point made earlier ('Apportionment criteria—a non-justiciable issue?', p 178) that: 'a party benefits greatly if its supporters are disproportionately concentrated in small constituencies'. In the previous two elections it appeared that the Labour party had benefited from that rather anti-egalitarian reality.

[103] Which would be some 76,000 electors.

[104] For a helpful review of the proposal see White I and Gay O (2010) *Reducing the size of the House of Commons.*

Suggested further reading

Academic and political commentary

BOGDANOR V (1983) *What is proportional representation?* ch 4

EWING K (2000) 'Transparency, accountability and equality: the Political Parties, Elections and Referendums Act 2000' *Public Law* 542

THE ELECTORAL COMMISSION (2004) *The funding of political parties*

OLIVER D (1999) 'An Electoral Commission: an ingenious idea' *Public Law* 585

WADE HRW (1980) *Constitutional fundamentals* ch 2

LARDY H (2001) 'Representation of the People Act 2000' *MLR* 63

Case law and legislation

Watkins v Woolas [2010] EWHC 2702 (QB)

R v Boundary Commission for England, ex p Foot [1983] QB 600

R v Tronoh Mines Ltd [1952] 1 All ER 697

R v Jones [1999] 2 Cr App Rep 253

Chapter 8

Parliamentary Privilege

'Parliamentary privilege' began to assume a coherent form on the constitutional landscape by 1450, from when the Speaker of Commons began each session of Parliament with an address to the Monarch claiming 'the ancient rights and privileges of the Commons'. Early analysis of privilege assumed the Commons and Lords were superior 'courts', possessing exclusive, inherent power over matters within their claimed jurisdiction. As Coke CJ put it:

> Every court of justice hath rules and customs for its directions . . . It is lex et consuetudo parliamenti that all weighty matters in any Parliament moved concerning the peers of the realm, or commons in parliament assembled, ought to be determined, adjudged, and discussed by the course of the parliament, not by the civil law nor yet by the common laws of this realm used in more inferior courts.[1]

Coke's treatise was written in the pre-revolutionary era, and offers no clear guidance on the legal status of the *lex et consuetudo parliamenti* (law and custom of Parliament) vis-à-vis statute and the common law. This is partly the consequence of a misleading use of terminology. Coke's attention focused not on 'Parliament', but on two of its component parts—the Commons and Lords—qua independent constitutional actors.

The revolutionary settlement left unanswered several theoretical questions (with significant practical consequences) in relation to parliamentary privilege. How far did the privileges of each house extend? Were they residual powers, or could each house create new ones? Were such powers constitutionally superior to Acts of Parliament and/or the common law whenever a clash occurred? And would responsibility for answering the third question rest with the courts or with the house?[2]

There is no scope here to analyse in detail the pre-revolutionary history of the houses' respective privileges. However, one significant episode merits discussion, with a view to identifying issues which assumed considerable importance after 1688.[3]

---

[1] 1 Inst 15; cited in Keir and Lawson op cit p 251.

[2] The Commons generally assigns questions concerning its privileges to its Committee of Privileges (recently renamed as the Committee on Standards and Privileges). The report of the Committee is then considered by the whole house. See Griffith and Ryle op cit ch 3; Marshall G (1979) 'The House of Commons and its privileges', in Walkland op cit.

[3] Further episodes are discussed in the seventh edition at pp 234–235.

The Case of the Five Members (1641)

Notwithstanding Elizabeth's evident enthusiasm for invoking the *Resolutions in Anderson*, and her similarly pronounced distaste for liberty of discussion in the Commons, neither she nor her Tudor predecessors sought to rule as entirely absolutist Monarchs. Under that form of constitutional arrangement, there would be no legal protection for legislation, for the common law, or for the privileges of each house against the prerogative.

Charles I had ruled between 1629 and 1640 without summoning Parliament. By 1640, his political weakness made that course unsustainable. The newly summoned houses rapidly addressed what they perceived as the worst abuses wrought by the King. MPs agreed to levy taxation only after securing (reluctant) royal support for the Triennial Act, an act abolishing ship money (which also gaoled the judges who had found for the King), and legislation subjecting the Monarch's detention power under *Anderson* to (limited) judicial scrutiny.

For many MPs however, such measures inadequately expressed what they perceived as the growing significance of Parliament within the constitution (and of the Commons within Parliament). A motion was subsequently moved in the house to present to the King (and for publication) the 'Grand Remonstrance' of 1641 which detailed many political and religious grievances. The motion offers the first recorded instance of the house 'dividing' on a vote, rather than presenting a united front behind which its internal divisions were hidden. A narrow majority of members voted in favour of publishing the Remonstrance. An enraged Charles I demanded of the Commons that the five leaders of this 'opposition' be tried for treason. The Commons did not comply with this request, regarding it as a gross interference with its deliberative autonomy.

The house prepared to equip itself with an armed guard, fearing that the King would abduct the five members by force. Charles subsequently entered the house, backed by 400 armed men, and commanded that the MPs identify the impugned members. No MP would do so. In an act of some personal courage, the Speaker William Lenthell (in words frequently invoked to demonstrate the Speaker's role as the Commons' defender against executive interference) defied the King's direct command to reveal the five members' whereabouts: 'May it please your majesty, I have neither eyes to see, nor tongue to speak in this place but as this House is pleased to direct, whose servant I am here.'

Charles' 'invasion' of the Commons was perhaps the precipitate cause of the civil war. His Stuart successors nevertheless remained reluctant to accept that the constitution forbade such direct Monarchical interference with the house's internal proceedings. The *Declaration of Right* stressed the constitutional importance of the Commons' 'independence' from interference either from the Crown directly or (since judges were then appointed by the King and dismissable at his pleasure) indirectly via the courts. The crucial provision was subsequently expressed in Art 9 of the Bill of Rights.

Article 9 of the Bill of Rights 1689

> That the freedom of speech, and debates or proceedings in Parliament ought not to be impeached or questioned in any court or place out of Parliament.

Quite what status Art 9 possessed in England's revised constitutional order was uncertain. One interpretation would suggest that, by enacting Art 9, Parliament abolished all pre-existing privileges and replaced them with a new statutory formula. The meaning to be attached to 'freedom of speech', 'debates', 'proceedings', 'Parliament', 'impeached' and 'questioned' would then become a question of statutory interpretation for the courts, in respect of which the previous *lex et consuetudo parliamenti* might serve as a persuasive authority.

Much academic, judicial, and political opinion has until very recently rejected such an interpretation. The preferred view appears to have been that Art 9 was merely 'declaratory' of the legitimacy of the pre-revolutionary situation.[4] That opinion is conceptually very problematic. The Bill of Rights, like any other post-revolutionary legislation, enjoys a different constitutional status to any pre-revolutionary statute. In respect of Acts passed before 1688 'declaring' the extent of privilege, there is no difficulty in assuming that Parliament was merely bestowing added legitimacy on a political concept which arguably enjoyed equal but separate status to legislation. But one might readily assume that legislation passed by the newly sovereign Parliament could no longer be merely declaratory, but necessarily transformed the constitutional status of the issues it addressed.

Any claim by the Commons or Lords that the interpretation of Art 9 was a matter for them alone has no textual basis in the Bill of Rights. Such a claim would also contradict orthodox understandings of parliamentary sovereignty and the rule of law, which entrust the task of interpreting statutes to the ordinary courts. But one can discern a contextual basis for the Commons' wish to exclude judicial interpretation of Art 9. This would derive in part from a suspicion that the Crown could interfere indirectly with the Commons' operations through its power to appoint and dismiss the judges. However, that contextual justification would largely have disappeared following the Act of Settlement 1700, which empowered the Commons to veto the dismissal of members of the judiciary.

The Act of Settlement displaced rather than extinguished the Commons' understandable fears about losing control of its claimed interpretive power. Despite the then eclectic structure of the English court system, the House of Lords unarguably enjoyed a dual 'judicial' status, exercising jurisdiction over its own *lex parliamenti* but also over interpretation of statutes and most facets of the common law. For the scope of the Commons' privileges to be determinable by the common law would mean that they were controlled by the Lords. It was not until the passage of the Judicature Acts of 1873 and 1875 that one could plausibly argue that the House of Lords qua 'ordinary court' was both formally and functionally independent of the Lords qua legislative assembly; although as suggested later in the chapter, this initiative was not sufficient to induce the Commons to disclaim its purported interpretive authority.

We revisit the conceptual problems flowing from the uncertain status and meaning of Art 9 later. But other issues also merit attention. The following pages sweep broadly over 300 years of the history of parliamentary privilege in three general areas. Firstly, the houses' power to regulate their own composition through the admission, retention, and expulsion of their members; secondly, the admissibility before the courts of parliamentary material; and thirdly the regulation of MPs' ethical standards.

I. The admission, retention, and expulsion of members

The tortuous development of the Commons' electoral system was traced in chapter seven. However the Acts which gradually extended the franchise do not fully identify the constitutional principles which have determined the lower house's composition. The relationship between the 'people' and the Commons has also been affected by questions of privilege.

---

[4] Thus in *Pickin v British Railways Board* (see 'Substance or procedure? the enrolled Bill rule', ch 2, pp 27–28) Lord Simon denied that Art 9 'created' the enrolled Bill rule. Rather, Art 9 'reflected' an existing functional imperative—namely preserving uninhibited discussion in a democratic Parliament. This analysis is inept. The 1688 revolutionaries had no inclination to produce a 'democratic' legislature as we now understand that term; (and see 'What is (was) Parliament?', ch 2, p 25). Article 9 could not 'reflect' democratic sentiment, because no such sentiment existed. The judgment does however raise important methodological issues, in that it suggests the scope of privilege falls to be determined by judicial (rather than house) perceptions of what is 'necessary' for the conduct of parliamentary business.

Ashby v White

The courts accepted shortly after the revolution that enfranchised citizens enjoyed common law 'rights of property' in their entitlement to vote. Thus the plaintiff in *Ashby v White* could maintain an action in tort against the returning officer in Aylesbury who had prevented him from voting.[5] The judges hearing the litigation had however held sharply divergent views. As noted in chapter seven, the Commons enjoyed statutory authority to determine the outcome of disputed elections between 1604 and 1868.[6] The result in the Aylesbury election was not in doubt, and thus the Commons had no statutory jurisdiction over Ashby's suit. The point of contention raised was whether a freeholder's right to vote derived from common law, or from the Commons' power to control its own composition. The question had profound consequences; if the latter claim were accepted, it would effectively empower the Commons alone to determine the allocation of the franchise.

The majority of the judges hearing Ashby's case at first instance accepted that latter viewpoint. His claim bore directly on an established Commons privilege, with which the court could not interfere. For White and Gould JJ, the matter was a question of hierarchy—in these matters, the *lex parliamenti* overrode common law. Holt CJ dissented. Ashby's claimed right to vote was firmly based in common law. The judges' duty was to uphold that law. The court should thus hear his claim, and if the case was well-founded, decide in his favour. For Holt, the extent of privilege was for the courts, not the house to decide.

Paty's case

The House of Lords (qua final court of appeal) supported Holt's dissent, and reversed the judgment. It is tempting to see this as a victory for the 'rule of law' over the arbitrary inclinations of the Commons. For the lower house, it perhaps appeared as an illegitimate intrusion by the upper house (qua judicial body) into its sphere of responsibility. The Commons immediately passed a resolution rejecting the Lords' decision in *Ashby*:

> [N]either the qualifications of any elector, or the right of any person elected, is cognisable or determinable elsewhere, than before the commons of England. . . . whoever shall presume to commence any action [before] any other jurisdiction . . . except in cases especially provided for by act of parliament . . . are guilty of a high breach of privilege of this house.[7]

Five other Aylesbury voters then initiated legal actions. The Commons immediately held them to have breached its privileges and gaoled them. The courts' equivocal role was illustrated by a majority judgment which declined jurisdiction over writs of *habeas corpus*.[8] Holt again dissented, stressing the subordinacy of privilege to both common law and statute:

> bringing such actions was declared by the house of Commons to be a breach of their privilege; but that declaration will not make that a privilege that was not so before. . . . The privileges of the house of Commons . . . are nothing but the law. . . . This privilege of theirs concerns the liberty of the people in a high degree, by subjecting them to imprisonment, which is what the people cannot be subjected to without an act of Parliament.[9]

Substantively, *Ashby* and *Paty's Case* have little contemporary relevance. Conceptually, however, they retain significance because of Holt's assertion of parliamentary sovereignty and the rule of law as constitutional principles superior to privilege. As the following

---

[5] (1703) 1 Bro Parl Cas 62.   [6] See 'The contents and conduct of election campaigns', ch 7, p 180.
[7] Quoted in Plucknett (1960) op cit pp 582–583.   [8] *R v Paty* (1705) 91 ER 431.
[9] Ibid at 433. Holt's method provides an obvious precedent for Lord Camden's reasoning in *Entick*; see '*Entick v Carrington*', ch 3, pp 46–47.

pages suggest, Holt's analysis has gradually gained greater conceptual legitimacy and practical endorsement.

John Wilkes

The grievances of the American colonists were not all engendered by British action undertaken in the colonies. The Americans' disenchantment was added to by the treatment meted out by the Commons and successive British governments to British politicians sympathetic to the Americans' cause. John Wilkes' role as a critic of government policy has already been alluded to;[10] his career now merits further consideration.

Wilkes' early attachment to 'democratic' principles seemed tenuous; in 1757 he bought his way into the Commons by bribing and treating the electors of (ironically) Aylesbury. Wilkes nevertheless moved in radical political circles, and in the 1760s edited a journal, *The North Briton*, which disseminated vehement criticism of the government. Issue No 45 castigated the measures contained in the King's Speech opening the 1763 parliamentary session:

> Every friend of this country must lament that a prince of so many great and admirable qualities . . . can be brought to give the sanction of his sacred name to the most odious measures and the most unjustifiable public declarations . . .

Wilkes then published a potentially blasphemous and seditious tract called *An Essay on Women*. The combined effect of the two publications provoked the government to prosecute him for libel and the Commons to expel him. Wilkes meanwhile fled the country. On returning to England in June 1768, he was sentenced to two years' imprisonment.

To modern eyes, subsequent events have a farcical hue, but they were of considerable significance to shaping emergent understandings of the relationship between the Commons, statute, and the electorate. If a member is expelled, the seat becomes vacant and a by-election is held. Wilkes did not contest his Aylesbury seat after his first expulsion. But Wilkes' status as a convicted prisoner was not then a legal impediment to standing for election or taking a seat.[11] Thus in 1769, Wilkes stood as a candidate for Middlesex, where many electors endorsed his views. Wilkes was elected to the house on 16 February—and expelled by the Commons on 17 February. Wilkes was returned again on 16 March—and was expelled the next day. In April, he was again elected. This time, rather than expel Wilkes and trigger another election, the Commons declared Wilkes' defeated opponent the 'winner', and admitted him to the house. One of Wilkes' supporters tabled a motion inviting the Commons to resolve that; 'no person eligible by law can be incapacitated from election by a vote of the House, but by Act of Parliament alone'. The motion was defeated by 226 to 186. The house carried a government motion that Wilkes' expulsion was 'agreeable to the law of the land'.[12] That conclusion was not put to a legal test. Wilkes did not challenge his exclusion in the courts, and thereby missed the opportunity to set up a potentially momentous dispute between the 'rights' of the electorate and the 'privileges' of the Commons.

One might initially attribute the house's conduct towards Wilkes to the era's political context. The Commons then made no claim to be 'democratic'; sixty years had still to pass before the Great Reform Act would set Britain on the long, slow path towards a universal franchise. In formal terms, Wilkes' repeated expulsion was a defensible expression of the Commons' traditional autonomy. From a functional perspective, the house's action could be construed as

---

[10] See '*Entick v Carrington*', ch 3, pp 46–47. See generally Rude G (1962) *Wilkes and Liberty*; Maier op cit.

[11] See the discussion of *Goodwin and Fortescue's Case* (1604) in Plucknett op cit pp 372–374; Keir D (8th ed 1966) *The constitutional history of modern Britain* pp 175–177.

[12] Rude op cit pp 119, 133. See also Wittke op cit pp 115–123. This was perhaps an early example of effective government control of the lower house.

a collective expression of Burke's portrayal of the MP as representative rather than delegate: MPs were sparing an ill-advised, intemperate electorate from the consequences of its folly. If so, one might then assume that as the franchise became more extensive and the electorate more 'mature', and the legitimacy of the Commons' legislative role rested increasingly on the assumption that it represented 'the people', the house could no longer defensibly invoke its privileges to exclude an elected member. But as the experience of Charles Bradlaugh suggests, any such assumption would be ill-founded.

Charles Bradlaugh

Bradlaugh, a radical political campaigner, achieved notoriety by 1870 both for founding the atheistic National Secular Society, and for being prosecuted for publishing a book on birth control.[13] Such notoriety apparently appealed to the voters of Northampton; in 1880 they returned Bradlaugh as their MP.

Bradlaugh's difficulties began when he tried to take his seat. MPs had been placed under a statutory obligation during Elizabeth I's reign to take an oath of allegiance to the Monarch and the Protestant faith before assuming their seats.[14] The oath (administered by the Speaker on the floor of the house) was intended to exclude Roman Catholics from the Commons, but also caught Protestant non-conformists and Jews. The oath was modified to admit Catholics in 1829; legislation in 1866 introduced an oath acceptable to members of the Jewish faith, and the Promissory Oaths Act 1868 permitted members of dissentient religious sects to 'affirm' their loyalty rather than swear it. The legislation did not actually exclude members from the house if they had not taken the oath or affirmed, but fined them £500 (in 1880 an enormous sum) for each occasion when they sat and voted without having done so.

On entering the house, Bradlaugh (having previously announced himself an atheist) wished to affirm rather than swear his loyalty. The house, however, resolved that he could not do so. Bradlaugh's subsequent attempt to take the oath instead was also blocked by a resolution. On declining to leave the house, Bradlaugh was forcibly ejected. The majority in the Commons then expelled him in April 1881. He was returned at a by-election a week later, when the Speaker had evidently concluded that: 'the house would do well and wisely, according to the constitution, to admit him without question'.[15] The majority nevertheless expelled him again. Bradlaugh was subsequently physically ejected by Commons' officials. Undeterred, he re-entered the house and adopted the extraordinary course of administering the oath to himself and then assuming his place on the backbenches. He was again expelled; and again returned at the ensuing by-election.

The Commons' continued refusal to admit Bradlaugh seemingly negated the impact of the Great Reform Act and Disraeli's 1867 franchise legislation in respect of the electors of Northampton. For those voters, the extended franchise was worthless, since their chosen candidate was unable to represent them. For Bradlaugh the legal and moral position was clear. He and his electors were the victims of:

> the arbitrary and illegal action of the House of Commons. It is a melancholy exhibition of the tyranny of orthodoxy when we see one branch of the legislature taking upon itself to nullify laws which the whole legislature itself has sanctioned.[16]

He then challenged this 'arbitrary and illegal action' before the courts. The suit in *Bradlaugh v Gossett*[17] was directed against the Commons' Serjeant-at-Arms, who, obeying a Commons resolution, had intimated that he would use physical violence to prevent Bradlaugh entering

---

[13] Arnstein W (1983) *The Bradlaugh Case* ch 1. See also Wittke op cit pp 160–169; Anson W (5th edn 1922) *The law and custom of the constitution* pp 93–98, 195–196.　　　　　　[14] See Anson op cit pp 93–95.

[15] Arnstein op cit p 104.　　　[16] Ibid, at 147.　　　[17] (1884) 12 QBD 271.

in future. Bradlaugh's suit asked the Court to issue an injunction preventing the Serjeant-at-Arms from so doing. As Stephen J indicated, the case raised a straightforward clash between the authority of statute and of privilege:

> Suppose that the House of Commons forbids one of its members to do that which an Act of Parliament requires him to do . . . is such an order one which we can declare to be void and restrain the executive officer of the House from carrying out.[18]

The judgment held that no statute could impliedly alter the Commons' power to control its internal proceedings. Neither was the house's jurisdiction in such matters overridden by common law. In reaching this conclusion, Stephen J was influenced by a sense of judicial deference to the Commons:

> The House of Commons is not a Court of Justice, but the effect of its privilege to regulate its own internal concerns practically invests it with a judicial character when it has to apply to particular cases the provisions of Acts of Parliament. . . . If its determination is not in accordance with the law, this resembles the case of an error by a judge whose decision is not subject to appeal . . . [I]f we were to attempt to erect ourselves into a Court of Appeal from the House of Commons, we should consult neither the public interest, nor the interests of Parliament and the constitution, nor our own dignity.[19]

Since swearing or affirming were procedures conducted entirely within the house, their regulation was a matter solely for the house. In contrast, the house would have no authority to interfere with processes affecting its composition which occurred outside its boundaries; for example, a citizen's common law or statutory entitlement to vote in a parliamentary election. This would be consistent with Holt's opinions in *Ashby* and *Paty's Case*, and reiterates the point that the courts claimed the power to identify the extent of privilege, but not to interfere with its exercise within those identified boundaries. But Stephen J seemed uncertain as to the courts' response if the house chose to exceed its jurisdiction in this way:

> I should in any case feel a reluctance almost invincible to declaring a resolution of the House of Commons to be beyond the powers of the house . . . Such a declaration would in every case be unnecessary and disrespectful.[20]

In effect, the Court was abdicating its role as the guardian of the rule of law and allowing the Commons to determine the meaning of legislation. Given the vituperative clashes between the Commons, Lords, and Monarch over the terms of nineteenth-century enfranchisement legislation, which had led to considerable modification of the initial Bills,[21] it is implausible to assume that Parliament impliedly granted such jurisdiction to the Commons. The judgment thus entirely subverts orthodox understandings of parliamentary sovereignty.

The Bradlaugh saga was eventually ended after the 1885 general election, when Bradlaugh was for the seventh time returned as Northampton's MP. The solution was, from a legal perspective, unsatisfactory. After the election, the house had chosen a new Speaker, the former Liberal MP Sir Arthur Peel. When the house assembled, Peel maintained that the house's previous resolutions preventing Bradlaugh from taking the oath had lapsed. The Speaker also refused to accept any new motion on the same issue:

> I have no right, original or delegated to interfere between an honourable member and his taking of the oath. . . . It is not for me, I respectfully say, it is not for the House, to enter into any inquisition as to what may be the opinions of a Member when he comes to the table to take the oath.[22]

---

[18] Ibid, at 278.   [19] Ibid, at 286.   [20] Ibid, at 282.   [21] See 'The original Bill' ff, ch 7, pp 174–175.
[22] Quoted in Arnstein op cit p 310.

That Peel ended the controversy so simply forcefully illustrates the disciplinary authority a determined Speaker may exercise over the house, even when his/her views are not supported by most members. Yet the solution, as much as the controversy itself, also indicates the extent to which both the Commons and the courts considered themselves competent to deny the electors of Northampton the services of their chosen representative.

The Bradlaugh episode neatly illustrates the so-called 'dualism' which attaches to the constitutional status of the houses' privileges:

> Thus there may be at any given moment two doctrines of privilege, the one held by the courts, the other by either House, the one to be found in the law reports, the other in Hansard, and no way of resolving the real point at issue should conflict arise.[23]

The practical problems raised by dualism are not limited solely to the question of the admission of members to their respective house.

Freedom from imprisonment, arrest, and molestation

The first recorded instance of the Commons asserting its privilege to force the release of an imprisoned member seems to be *Ferrer's Case* in 1543.[24] The privilege has an obvious functional basis in the pre-revolutionary era, namely to ensure that the members summoned by the King were not impeded from travelling to London and thereafter going about their parliamentary business, whether by unlawful interference or by legal proceedings initiated in a court. A 1604 statute 'recognised' the privilege as encompassing both a power to set free a member duly imprisoned by a court, and the power to punish any person arresting a member.[25] Neither house was obliged to protect its members from detention: the privilege was a power the house might waive.

The privilege was not invoked in respect of criminal charges, even if the impugned conduct occurred within the Commons or Lords itself. Until the recent expenses scandal,[26] there had been relatively few occasions in the modern era on which MPs have faced criminal charges. Several Irish MPs were imprisoned during the 1880s and again in 1918 for criminal activities arising from the Irish struggle for independence. On none of these occasions did the house make any suggestion that it would interfere with the court proceedings.

The Parliamentary Privilege Act 1770

The arrest privilege nevertheless had considerable practical significance for civil suits, especially while it remained possible to be imprisoned for debt. Immediately after the revolution, the houses' growing sense of self-importance led them to claim a greater scope for the arrest privilege, encompassing not just the persons of members, but also their land, their moveable property, and their servants. The extended privilege was frequently invoked as an expedient way for MPs and their retinues to evade numerous legal obligations—a practice which provoked considerable public criticism.[27]

Public pressure eventually led Parliament to reduce the privilege's scope. In 1700, legislation was enacted entitled 'An Act for preventing any inconveniences that may happen by privilege of Parliament'. Its main provision, as restated in the Parliamentary Privilege Act 1770 s 1, was that:

> Any person may at any time commence and prosecute any action or suit against any Lord of Parliament or any . . . [member] of the House of Commons . . . or any other person intitled to the privilege of Parliament . . . and no such action shall at any time be impeached, stayed or delayed by or under colour or pretence of any privilege of Parliament.

---

[23] Keir and Lawson op cit p 255.   [24] Plucknett op cit pp 249–250. See also Wittke op cit pp 33–35.

[25] Plucknett (1960) op cit pp 333–334.

[26] This episode is considered at 'Parliamentary privilege and the expenses scandal', pp 219–220.

[27] See Wittke op cit pp 39–43.

If interpreted literally (ie *any* privilege), s 1 seems to abolish all aspects of privilege which restricted access to the courts, including Art 9. The Commons and the judiciary appeared to have reached a shared (and less expansive) understanding of the Act's impact in 1958, when the Commons (without surrendering its claimed jurisdiction to judge the extent of privilege) invited the Privy Council (in its judicial capacity) to interpret the 1770 Act.[28]

The Court applied the mischief rule rather than the literal rule to s 1. It considered that the 'mischief' in issue was solely MPs' increasing predilection to invoke privilege as a blanket immunity against all civil actions, and not MPs' entitlement to freedom of speech in the house. The Privy Council considered this freedom to have been so central a value in the 1688 settlement that it was inconceivable that Parliament would have curtailed its scope just twelve years later. The Court thus concluded that the Act reached only those legal actions whose origins did not lie in a 'proceeding in Parliament'.

But this opinion left a crucial question unanswered: namely who decided if the action concerned had been precipitated by a 'proceeding in Parliament'—the Commons or the courts? It is generally assumed that the constitution confers the responsibility of statutory interpretation on the courts. Determining the meaning of 'proceedings' would thus be a judicial function. This presumption could however be rebutted in two ways. Firstly, one might argue that this privilege (or indeed privilege in general) enjoyed a special constitutional status, which (unlike the prerogative or other common law rules) rendered it immune to implied repeal. The Court seemed to accept this viewpoint, by observing that the free speech privilege was 'solemnly *reasserted* in the Bill of Rights'.[29] The notion of 'reassertion' suggests that the legal status of privilege was such that it co-existed with Art 9—that the statutory provision was declaratory and not transformative of the substantive entitlements the house had hitherto enjoyed. A second argument, which the Court did not entertain, was that the Bill of Rights itself (or indeed any other statute touching upon privilege) impliedly ousted the courts' jurisdiction and bestowed it on the house.

Lord Denning dissented from the Court's opinion.[30] He concluded that the clear meaning of the 1770 Act was that the Commons would be acting illegally if it made any attempt to interfere with a legal action initiated against one of its members. The Act was a command from Parliament to one of its component parts not to undertake such action. But this did not mean such a suit could be argued, still less succeed. For Lord Denning also held that the courts remained obliged by Art 9 to refuse to entertain action which 'questioned' a 'proceeding in Parliament'.

Denning nonetheless made the important point that whatever jurisdiction the Commons might have possessed to determine the extent and meaning of its free speech privilege before 1689 had been overridden by Parliament when Art 9 was enacted. Art 9 therefore did not 'reassert' the house's privilege. Rather it extinguished the privilege and created a new statutory protection. Nor did Art 9 contain any implied grant of interpretive authority to the Commons. Privilege thus enjoyed no higher status vis-à-vis statute than did the common law:

> This means of course that it is for the courts to say what is a 'proceeding in Parliament' within the Bill of Rights—which is just what the House of Commons do not wish to concede.[31]

Support for Denning's analysis was offered by Scarman J in *Stourton v Stourton*, a 1963 case concerning the applicability of the freedom of arrest privilege to peers:

> I do not think however, that I, sitting in the High Court . . . must necessarily take the law that I have to apply from what would be the practice of the House. I think I have to look to the common law as deduced in judicial decisions in order to determine in the particular case whether the privilege arises, and if so its scope and effect.[32]

---

[28] *Re Parliamentary Privilege Act 1770* [1958] AC 331. [29] Ibid at 350 (emphasis added).
[30] The Privy Council did not then permit dissents. Denning's opinion was neither recorded nor published in the report itself. See Lord Denning 'Re Parliamentary Privilege Act 1770' (1985) *Public Law* 80. [31] Ibid, at 85.
[32] [1963] 1 All ER 606 at 608. See also Leopold P (1989) 'The freedom of peers from arrest' *Public Law* 398.

We revisit this issue later in the chapter. Before doing so however, we might usefully turn to a second facet of the role played by the Commons' privileges in regulating the relationship between the house and the courts.

II. The justiciability of 'proceedings in Parliament'

Speeches made by MPs in either house which defame other citizens clearly raise a potential conflict with the courts. The fear of losing a defamation action could act as a considerable impediment to MPs' freedom of speech, yet the common law has always provided extensive remedies enabling people to protect their 'right' to a good reputation.[33] In such circumstances, the conceptual problem of 'dualism' is particularly acute. In practice however, the courts and the houses appeared to have reached a shared understanding of the scope of law and privilege on this question.

The plaintiff in *Dillon v Balfour*[34] was a midwife in Ireland. Balfour[35] was then a Minister in Ireland. During the passage of the Criminal Procedure (Ireland) Bill in 1887, Balfour made remarks about Dillon which she felt undermined her professional reputation, in respect of which she sought substantial damages. Balfour applied for the action to be struck out, contending that speeches made in the house could not be the subject of a defamation suit.

The judgment offers a paradigmatic example of the conceptual obfuscation which attends many analyses of the legal status of such speeches. Palles CB began his judgment by turning to Art 9. However he construed Art 9 not as creating a statutory protection, but as declaratory of pre-revolutionary privilege. To complicate matters further, he then observed that the privilege was an 'ancient right and liberty of the realm',[36] suggesting it had a common law source.

The basis of his judgment, which struck out the plaintiff's action, was equally unclear. Palles CB held that the courts had jurisdiction in a defamation action only to ask if the words in issue were spoken/written as a 'proceeding in Parliament'. Whatever its source, the court's jurisdiction was 'ousted' (though by what he did not explain) if it determined that the words were a 'proceeding in Parliament'. Any such statement enjoyed complete immunity from actions in defamation.[37]

What are 'proceedings in parliament'?

The Privy Council had stressed in *Re the Parliamentary Privilege Act 1770* that it offered no view on the meaning of 'proceedings in Parliament'. Nor did it address the more contentious question of whether the power to determine that meaning lay within the jurisdiction of the courts or the respective houses. The Commons' reference to the Privy Council had been triggered by an episode involving Labour MP George Strauss. Strauss had sent a letter to a Minister criticising the London Electricity Board (LEB). The Minister forwarded the letter to the Chairman of the LEB. The Chairman considered Strauss' comments defamatory, and threatened a libel action. Strauss thereupon referred the matter to the house, claiming the threat was a breach of privilege.

---

[33] See Brazier M (9th edn, 1993) *Street on Torts* ch 23.   [34] (1887) 20 LR Ir 600.

[35] See 'Lloyd George and the "people's budget"', ch 6, pp 141–144.   [36] (1887) 20 LR Ir 600 at 612.

[37] In 1868, the courts concluded that similar protection extended to newspapers which produced accurate reports of such 'defamatory' proceedings, if the report was circulated to inform the citizenry of what was happening in Parliament rather than as a malicious attempt to discredit the person criticised: see *Wason v Walter* (1868) LR 4 QB 73.

The issue turned on whether the letter was a 'proceeding in Parliament'. There are strong arguments for assuming that it was. Such communications about matters within a Minister's competence would be a frequently occurring and important part of the MP's role, both as a party politician and as a constituency representative. The Committee of Privileges concluded that the letter was a 'proceeding', and that a breach had occurred. However the house rejected the Committee's conclusion. In contrast, the house had accepted in 1938–1939 that communications between members and Ministers initiated with a view to placing a question would be 'proceedings'. A fortiori, oral or written questions themselves would also be privileged. Even if we accept that the houses are constitutionally competent to give an authoritative definition of the concept, they clearly have not done so. Griffith and Ryle's suggestion that there are many 'grey areas' is a polite understatement.[38]

The Commons Committee of Privileges recommended in 1977 that the concept be given a clearer, legislative meaning. However the house chose not to act upon the proposal, presumably because the passage of such legislation would imply that Parliament had removed the houses' claimed competence to interpret the term. 'Proceedings in parliament' thus remains a legally obscure area of the constitution. That obscurity has in the past triggered acute controversy.

Stockdale v Hansard (1839)

The constitutional clash between the courts and the Commons that was avoided over Wilkes' admission in the 1760s eventually occurred in the late 1830s. The trigger for the dispute was mundane. A report by the Inspector of Prisons, published on the house's instructions, had made libellous comments about a medical textbook circulating in a gaol. Stockdale, the book's author, commenced defamation proceedings against Mr Hansard, the Commons' printer.[39]

The house instructed Mr Hansard not to contest the case on its merits, but to inform the court that the house had resolved that the report was a proceeding in Parliament, and as such not subject to judicial jurisdiction.[40] The Court, for which Lord Denman CJ gave the leading judgment, rejected the Commons' assertion of privilege, categorising it as:

> a claim for an arbitrary power to authorise the commission of any act whatever, on behalf of a body which in the same argument is admitted not to be the supreme power in the state.[41]

Lord Denman concluded that the claim was irreconcilable with orthodox understandings of parliamentary sovereignty and the rule of law. The Commons' (or Lords') constitutional competence in matters of privilege stretched only to the application of existing privilege. With that jurisdiction, the courts would not interfere. But neither house could grant itself new privileges. Furthermore, the power to determine the boundaries of existing privileges lay not with either house through resolutions, but with the courts through the common law. Parliament might grant either house a jurisdiction which exceeded the existing boundaries, and give the house the power that it claimed in this case, but the Commons could not achieve that result itself:

> The House of Commons is not Parliament, but only a co-ordinate and component part of the Parliament. That sovereign power can make and unmake the laws; but the concurrence of the three legislative estates is necessary; the resolution of any one of them cannot alter the law . . .[42]

Lord Denman's reasoning follows that of Holt CJ in *Ashby v White* and *Paty's Case*. Just as Holt saw the right to vote as a common law entitlement that could only be overridden by Parliament, so Lord Denman viewed the common law right to protect one's reputation against libellous criticism as immune to anything other than statutory regulation. Lord Denman considered

---

[38] Op cit p 88.   [39] *Stockdale v Hansard* (1839) 9 Ad & El 1.
[40] The house was evidently not offering an interpretation of Art 9 qua statute, but construing it as declaratory of a continuing privilege with pre-revolutionary origins.   [41] (1839) 9 Ad & El 1 at 107–108.
[42] Ibid, at 108.

that 'proceedings in Parliament' could not form the subject of a defamation action. However he would not accept that reports subsequently circulated outside the house enjoyed such protection. Lord Denman adopted what to modern eyes would be a teleological interpretive strategy by suggesting that the protections the houses possessed under Art 9 extended only to matters 'necessary' for them to perform their duties. He also held, crucially, that assessing the issue of necessity was a matter for the courts, not for the Commons. Since Lord Denman saw no 'necessity' for the publishers of this particular report to be immune from a libel action, Stockdale could proceed with his action.

The *Case of the Sheriff of Middlesex* (1840)

Stockdale won his action. However, the Commons did not accept the Court's conclusion. Acting on the house's instructions, Mr Hansard refused to comply with the judgment. The Sheriff of Middlesex, an officer of the court, then sought to enforce the judgment. The Commons ordered that the Sheriff be committed to the Tower for having breached the house's privileges. The Commons' stance on this question is obviously hypocritical, given its long history of opposition in the pre-revolutionary era to the Crown's repeated efforts to invoke a similarly arbitrary power to detain anyone who displeased it. The Sheriff had been detained because he was complying with the Court's instructions. In crude terms, he had been punished by the Commons for upholding the rule of law. One might therefore have expected that his subsequent *habeas corpus* action would lead the courts to order his immediate release.[43]

The Serjeant at Arms' return to the writ stated simply that the Sheriff had been committed for 'a breach of privilege and contempt'. The Court, Lord Denman giving the leading judgment, declined to question the return. Lord Denman held that so long as the Commons complied with the mere formality of stating that the committal was for 'contempt', no court was competent to order the prisoner's release. It would be, he suggested, 'unseemly' for a court to doubt the Commons' bona fides in such circumstances.

The decision is closely comparable to the opinion in the *Resolutions in Anderson* 300 years earlier; the only difference being that the court was now permitting the Commons rather than the Crown to make a mockery of *habeas corpus*. The decision also completely undermined *Stockdale*. Lord Denman began his opinion in *Middlesex* by observing that *Stockdale* was 'in all respects correct'. Yet there is little point in a judgment being 'correct' if the same court subsequently permits it to be evaded.

Neither the Commons nor the judiciary emerge with credit from the *Stockdale* controversy. The specific legal problem that the case raised was subsequently resolved by Parliament in the Parliamentary Papers Act 1840. The Act empowered the Speaker to issue a certificate staying any legal proceedings in respect of documents published by order of either house.

'Redefining parliament'—*Pepper v Hart* (1993)

One rule to which students of British law were traditionally exposed was that judges would not refer to the records of debates in *Hansard* to clarify the meaning of legislative terminology.[44] The legal roots of the 'exclusionary rule' are obscure.[45] It might be simply a common law rule concerning the admissibility of evidence. An alternative perspective

---

[43] (1840) 11 Ad & El 273. For a fuller discussion see Wittke op cit pp 152–156; Stockdale E (1989) 'The unnecessary crisis: the background to the Parliamentary Papers Act 1840' *Public Law* 30.

[44] See 'The mischief rule', ch 3, p 60.

[45] The exclusionary rule was of late Victorian rather than venerable vintage. One can find both pre- and post-revolutionary cases in which the courts made explicit reference to parliamentary debate as an aid to statutory interpretation; see *Ash v Abdy* (1678) 3 Swan 664; *Millar v Taylor* (1769) 4 Burr 2303; *Re Mew and Thorne* (1862) 31 LJ Bcy 87.

is that the courts were deferring to a statutory command in Art 9 of the Bill of Rights, wherein the notion of 'questioned' extended to considering the content of debate to aid statutory interpretation. A third argument contends that the courts' refusal to consult *Hansard* was an element of privilege, existing alongside the common law but immune to judicial jurisdiction.

The rule's source is significant when considering whether and how it might be revised. If it was a common law concept, there would be no constitutional barrier to prevent the House of Lords changing it. In contrast, if the rule derived from Art 9, the courts could not simply overrule it. That would be inconsistent with parliamentary sovereignty. However, as a law-maker in the interpretative sense, the House of Lords could alter its previous definition of Art 9. The concept of 'questioned' could, for example, be narrowed, perhaps so that it embraced only a defence to defamation proceedings.[46] If the rule was part of privilege, judicial amendment would be constitutionally problematic rather than impossible. If we accept (per *Stockdale*, Denning's dissent in *Re the Parliamentary Privilege Act 1770*, and *Stourton*) that the common law sets the boundaries to privilege, the courts might legitimately conclude that they had previously misinterpreted those boundaries and that the correct scope of privilege did not preclude reference to *Hansard*. This could however provoke a conflict between the houses and the courts, since it is unlikely that either house would wish to cede its claimed jurisdiction over such questions.

The rule's purposes are more readily discernible. Four reasons have been advanced. Lord Wilberforce in *Beswick v Beswick*[47] fastened on a question of 'constitutional principle'. The task of interpreting legislation rested solely on the courts; for the judiciary to allow their view of the meaning of a statute to be determined by the speech of a Minister would in effect delegate their interpretative role to that Minister. This would turn parliamentary sovereignty into government sovereignty. This reason is perhaps overstated, and loses force if one suggests that *Hansard* should merely be of persuasive not determinative authority.

In the same case, Lord Reid identified 'purely practical reasons' for the rule. Access to *Hansard* would increase the time and expense of litigation, since lawyers would read debates in their entirety in pursuit of statements supporting their clients' cases. This, too, seems a weak justification. The same reasoning might plausibly be applied to law reports; counsel might avidly scrutinise every judgment ever delivered on the point in issue, hoping to uncover some helpful forgotten judicial subtlety. Moreover, it seems unlikely that lawyers would not prioritise their use of information cost-effectively.

Lord Scarman offered a third justification in *Davis v Johnson*.[48] He suggested that *Hansard* was an unreliable guide to a statute's meaning. The content of debate, suffused with the need to score party political points, would be unlikely to convey governmental intent precisely. This objection ostensibly seems convincing, but on reflection is overly simplistic. While many Commons or Lords exchanges may lack the rationality with which one might hope to find laws expressed, *Hansard* also contains calm, deliberate speeches in which ministers precisely describe the objectives they expect a bill to achieve. Lord Scarman's point might be met by selective resort to debate; total abstinence seems unnecessary.

A fourth reason, noted by Lord Diplock in *Fothergill v Monarch Airlines Ltd*,[49] was that 'elementary justice' demanded that all the materials on which the citizen might depend in litigation should be readily accessible. Lord Diplock felt *Hansard* did not meet this criterion. This is also a weak argument. One would doubt that citizens would find *Hansard* any more esoteric or inaccessible than the *All England Law Reports*. In so far as Lord Diplock's point raised a

---

[46] This interpretation appealed to Popplewell J in *Rost v Edwards* [1990] 2 QB 460. However, he considered himself bound to accept the broad meaning. Re-interpretation would have to await a decision by the House of Lords.   [47] [1968] AC 58.

[48] [1979] AC 264.   [49] [1981] AC 251.

valid informed consent issue, it amounted to an argument not for excluding *Hansard* from the courts but for ensuring that its contents were more widely known and more easily available.

Sporadic challenges to the traditional position were made in the 1960s and 1970s. Dissenting in *Warner v Metropolitan Police Comr*, Lord Reid reaffirmed the rule but added: 'there is room for an exception where examining the proceedings in Parliament would almost certainly settle the matter immediately one way or the other'.[50] Lord Denning also appeared reluctant to accept the rule, sometimes disregarding it or circumventing it by referring not to *Hansard* itself, but to extracts from debates reproduced in legal textbooks or periodicals, or by taking illicit peeks at *Hansard* when not in court.[51]

Perhaps more significantly (from a practical if not 'legal' perspective), the Commons resolved in 1980 that the courts need no longer petition the house for permission to make 'reference' to *Hansard*. The Commons appeared to root the rule solely in Art 9 of the Bill of Rights, though it was not clear if the house was waiving what it perceived to be a statutory protection or an aspect of its privilege.[52] It subsequently became clear that the Commons' interpretation of 'reference' was restricted: the house would regard use of *Hansard* to clarify the meaning of an ambiguous statute as exceeding the concept of 'reference'. The stage nevertheless seemed set for revision of the rule.

Opening Pandora's box?

Pepper v Hart[53] was triggered by a textual ambiguity in legislation concerning the taxation of a particular benefit. The taxpayers maintained that a Minister had made a clear statement during debate which favoured their interpretation. This argument could not be sustained without recourse to *Hansard*. The taxpayers were therefore asking the Court to overturn the exclusionary rule.

Lord Browne-Wilkinson's leading judgment departed substantially if cautiously, from previous orthodoxy. His central conclusion was that:

> reference to parliamentary material should be permitted as an aid to the construction of legislation which is ambiguous or obscure or the literal meaning of which leads to an absurdity . . . where such material clearly discloses . . . the legislative intention lying behind the ambiguous or obscure words.[54]

The rationale underpinning Lord Browne-Wilkinson's judgment lay in what he referred to as an issue of constitutional principle. His principle, however, appeared at odds with the principle advanced by Lord Wilberforce in *Beswick*. He observed that legislators might sometimes be genuinely mistaken as to the legal meaning of the statutory formula they enacted. In such circumstances, the courts would frustrate rather than fulfill their constitutional subordination to 'Parliament' by not referring to *Hansard*. This analysis requires one to define parliamentary sovereignty not in the formalistic, Diceyan sense of blind obedience to statutory words, but in a more functionalist vein of giving effect to legislative intent, in which the courts assume responsibility for protecting citizens from legislators' readily ascertainable mistakes.

Lord Browne-Wilkinson attempted to meet Lord Scarman's aforementioned concerns by limiting the type of speech to which judges may refer to statements by the Minister or member promoting the Bill. He was, however, less accommodating to other previous judicial justifications for the rule. He observed that New Zealand and Canada had both recently allowed

---

[50] [1969] 2 AC 256 at 279.

[51] See *Davis v Johnson* [1979] AC 264 at 276–277. Such peeking perhaps explains his observation in *Magor* some twenty years earlier that the judicial function was to make sense of Ministers' words as well as Parliament's.

[52] This again returns us to the question of whether Art 9 is declaratory or transformative of pre-revolutionary privilege. See Leopold P (1981) 'References in court to Hansard' *Public Law* 316; Miers D (1983) 'Citing Hansard as an aid to interpretation' *Statute LR* 98.   [53] [1993] AC 593.

[54] Ibid, at 634.

their courts to refer to legislative proceedings; neither jurisdiction had found that the cost or duration of litigation had increased unacceptably as a result. Nor did Lord Browne-Wilkinson attach any weight to the argument that *Hansard* was insufficiently accessible to litigants, for such a weakness was equally attributable to legislation.

His Lordship was uncertain about the rule's source, suggesting it could derive from all three sources previously outlined. He consequently dealt with each in turn. If the rule was judge-made self-regulation, the House of Lords could remake it in a more contemporarily relevant form. Should the rule have a statutory base, Lord Browne-Wilkinson concluded that Art 9 should be reinterpreted in the narrow sense canvassed in *Rost v Edwards*:

> In my judgment, the plain meaning of art 9, viewed against the historical background in which it was enacted, was to ensure that members of Parliament were not subjected to any penalty, civil or criminal for what they said [in either House].[55]

Finally his Lordship addressed the question of parliamentary privilege. Referring to the 1980 Commons' resolution, he suggested that the house viewed its privileges as co-extensive with the scope of Art 9. Consequently, given his redefinition of Art 9, recourse to *Hansard* could not impinge upon privilege. One might doubt that the house would accept this reasoning, for it 'confirms' the subordinacy of privilege to the common law. Whether this last point has now joined the constitution's array of 'ultimate political facts' is at present an unanswerable question, determinable only when the Commons and the courts again adopt contradictory positions over a question of the magnitude of those posed by Wilkes, Stockdale, and Bradlaugh.

Lord Browne-Wilkinson framed his judgment in cautious terms.[56] However the tests that he laid out were quite rapidly relaxed both by the House of Lords itself and by lower courts.[57] Lord Browne-Wilkinson seemed to take the view that this relaxation had gone too far. In *Melluish (Inspector of Taxes) v BMI (No 3) Ltd*,[58] he confirmed that *Pepper v Hart* should not be read as a justification for making reference to *Hansard* a routine element of the process of statutory interpretation.

This evident unease with the way in which the case was being used was forcefully reiterated by the House of Lords in *R v Secretary of State for the Environment, Transport and the Regions ex p Spath Holme Ltd*[59] The Court was unanimous in stressing that the principle in *Pepper v Hart* should be used sparingly and cautiously. The point was perhaps put most clearly by Lord Bingham:

> I think it important that the conditions laid down by the House in *Pepper v Hart* should be strictly insisted upon. Otherwise, the cost and inconvenience feared by Lord Mackay, whose objections to relaxation of the exclusionary rule were based on considerations of practice not principle, will be realised. The worst of all worlds would be achieved if parties routinely combed through Hansard, and the courts dredged through conflicting statements of parliamentary intention, only to conclude that the statutory provision called for no further elucidation or that no clear and unequivocal statement by a responsible minister could be derived from Hansard.

The Court's circumspection in *Spath Holme* about using *Hansard* was enthusiastically endorsed in a forceful analysis of the *Pepper v Hart* principle by Aileen Kavanagh.[60] Kavanagh suggests that the case may be read as elevating ministerial statements to the status of a source of law. This is seen to be problematic in two respects. Firstly, it undermines the role of Parliament as a collective assembly in which MPs engage in a careful and informed process of debate

---

[55] Ibid, at 638.   [56] Zander op cit pp 153–157.

[57] See generally Marshall G (1998) 'Hansard and the interpretation of statutes', in Oliver and Drewry op cit; Mullan K (1999) 'The impact of *Pepper v Hart*', in Carmichael and Dickson op cit.   [58] [1996] AC 454.

[59] [2001] 2 AC 349.

[60] Kavanagh A (2005) '*Pepper v Hart* and matters of constitutional principle' 121 *LQR* 98.

and evaluation which eventually leads to the production of a legislative text which accurately expresses the wishes of members who voted for it. Secondly, it undermines the role of the courts as the body with responsibility for determining the meaning of the laws that Parliament has enacted.

This argument has much to commend it in terms of abstract constitutional theory. In a more practical sense, it ought perhaps to be qualified somewhat. Two points might be made.

Firstly, the notion that MPs uniformly and consistently make informed choices as to the measures for which they vote is poorly based empirically. Cowley's previously discussed study of the voting behaviour of backbench Labour MPs since 1997 casts an illuminating and rather unsettling light on the realities of this part of the law-making process.[61] Some of Cowley's findings are almost comic. He cites for example occasions when MPs mistakenly walk through the wrong door when casting their votes. A more frequently occurring scenario is illustrated by a discussion of the extraordinarily esoteric contents of an obscure provision in the Finance Bill 2005. The provision was so complicated, and an understanding of its impact so thoroughly contingent on an understanding of the existing complicated law, that it is simply absurd to assume that many MPs appreciated the effect the measure would have when enacted. The matter is put in rather more prosaic and systemic terms by one of Cowley's MP respondents: 'I go through the lobby a great number of times not knowing a fuck about what I am voting for'.[62] The reality in such cases is that MPs simply do whatever party whips ask them to do.[63]

The second point is that one might as readily argue that *Pepper v Hart* enhances rather than reduces the power of the courts vis-à-vis the 'executive'. If one means by 'the executive' the government currently in power, invocation of *Hansard* as an interpretive aid may well *reduce* executive power. It is entirely possible that the legislative text in issue was promoted by a previous government with different political views from the present administration, and with different understanding from the present government as to the meaning of the relevant 'ambiguous or obscure' statutory provision. A judgment which attached determinative significance to a ministerial statement in such circumstances would also enhance the role of the Commons and Lords qua legislative assemblies, since in order to change the law in issue the present government would have to promote new legislation.

More broadly, the conditions which *Pepper v Hart* attaches to use of *Hansard* are all discretion-laden and thus open to judicial manipulation. Is a statutory term ambiguous if literally construed? Would such construction led to an absurd result? Did a Minister make a clear statement as to the government's intended meaning of the provision? Such questions will often be answerable quite defensibly as either 'yes' or 'no'. This means that the courts have a choice as to whether *Hansard* is to be used, and if so, as to what significance is attached to the information it contains.

Pepper v Hart has significant constitutional implications. This relates in part to its recognition of the political reality of government dominance of the legislative process and thus of shifts in the nature of the separation of powers within the contemporary constitution. But in respect of the rather narrower issue of parliamentary privilege, the judgment's greater importance lies in the court's implicit claim that it, rather than the two houses, is the only body possessing the constitutional competence to determine the meaning of privilege. This means that the courts are in effect denying that the Commons has any authority to claim immunity from orthodox understandings of parliamentary sovereignty and the rule of law. There may well be many aspects of privilege with which the courts feel unable to interfere. But that decision would be based on the functionalist criterion of the non-justiciable nature of the privilege in question, not formalist consideration of its source.

---

[61] (2005) op cit.   [62] Ibid, at 34.   [63] Ibid, at 28–34.

However Lord Browne-Wilkinson's judgment has deeper implications. Paradoxically, by asserting the supremacy of Parliament over its component parts, *Pepper v Hart* bolsters arguments which attack the doctrine of parliamentary sovereignty itself. We return to this argument in the final chapter. But as the following section suggests, it might readily be assumed that many MPs would be reluctant to tolerate further judicial intrusion into the houses' regulation of privilege.

III. The regulation of MPs' ethical standards

The summer of 1995 presented the British public with the extraordinary spectacle of a backbench Conservative MP, Sir Jerry Wiggin, tabling amendments during the committee stage of a Bill's passage in the name of another Conservative, Sebastian Coe, without Coe's permission. Wiggin had a financial interest in the issue; he was a consultant for an organisation which would benefit from the amendment. He had used Coe's name for fear that the amendment's prospects of success would be compromised if the house knew its mover had been paid by a commercial organisation to promote it. Press coverage of the episode was hugely critical of Wiggin, and he found few supporters even on the Conservative benches. However the Speaker declined to refer the matter to the Committee of Privileges; in her opinion Wiggin's misbehaviour merited no greater punishment than that he apologise to the house.

Until 1975, MPs were under no obligation to declare either the sources or amounts of any income they received over and above their MP's salary. Parliament had not enacted legislation on the subject. Nor had the house concluded that it should itself require such disclosure. This lacuna had significant implications for the concepts of informed consent, both within the Commons itself and in terms of the relationship between an MP and her electors. One could not be sure, for example, that individual MPs were not supporting particular pieces of legislation, making speeches, or putting questions to Ministers because they had been paid to do so by commercial interests rather than because they honestly believed in the intrinsic rectitude of the course they were following. It is quite plausible to conclude that many electors might decline to support a particular candidate if they knew that she was receiving financial benefits from sources of which they disapproved.

The register of members' interests

A considerable scandal broke in the early 1970s, when a prominent Labour politician, T Dan Smith,[64] was convicted of various offences of corruption. The scandal was exacerbated by the revelation that Edward Short, then Labour Leader of the House, had accepted a 'gift' of £250 from Mr Smith in 1963 'provided it can be kept a confidential matter between the two of us'.[65]

The episode generated extensive press coverage dwelling on the many opportunities for corrupt practice which became available to MPs as a result of their membership of the house. There was never any suggestion that such behaviour was endemic or even widespread within the Commons. However given the effective dominance of the legislative process which the Commons by then possessed, even one MP who was prepared to engage in improper financial relationships would be one too many. Without an effective mechanism to regulate such matters, the house could not realistically claim to be above suspicion.

Among the more far-reaching proposals aired in the aftermath of the Smith affair was the suggestion that legislation should be introduced requiring MPs to make their income tax returns available for public inspection. The house apparently regarded this as an intolerable

---

[64] Smith was not an MP, but the leader of Newcastle city council.   [65] See *The Economist* 4 May 1974.

intrusion into MPs' private affairs, and opted for a far more modest system of self-regulation. In May 1974 the Commons resolved that:

> in any debate or proceeding of the house ... or communications which a Member may have with other Members or Ministers or servants of the Crown, he shall disclose any relevant pecuniary interest or benefit of whatever nature, whether direct or indirect, that he may have or may be expecting to have.[66]

The house also resolved to create a Register of Members' Interest, on which MPs would record certain sources of income. An ad hoc select committee was established to produce detailed proposals. It is perhaps worth recalling that the Labour government then had only a bare Commons majority; there was thus no prospect of the government simply pushing through its own preferences. That the house endorsed such anodyne reforms is perhaps a powerful indication of its members' (irrespective of party) arrogance and self-righteousness.

The house adopted the select committee's recommendations in 1975. The Register would serve:

> to provide information of any pecuniary interest or other material benefit which a Member of Parliament may receive which might be thought to affect his [sic] conduct as a member of Parliament or influence his [sic] actions, speeches or votes in Parliament.[67]

The Register covers a wide range of financial interests, including such matters as directorships of companies, income from practice in the professions, paid employment (which includes 'public relations' and 'consultancy' activities), and overseas visits not financed from public funds.[68] The names of any employers or clients should also be disclosed whenever the income the member derives from the relationship pertains 'in any manner' to her/his membership of the house. However, there was no requirement that members disclose how much income they received from each source. The information that the Register disclosed was thus of limited value. The house also created a 'Select Committee on Members' Interests' to consider amendments to the Register and hear complaints about alleged breaches of its terms. But it was not clear what sanctions, if any, would be imposed on MPs whose entries in the Register were found to be inaccurate. Nevertheless, the measures still proved too much for some MPs. Thus the Conservative MP John Stokes, seemingly oblivious to press coverage and public opinion, argued that: 'there is no demand for all this cumbersome machinery to register Members' interests'.[69]

Quite how effective the Register proved is an open question. One MP, Enoch Powell, simply refused to disclose any interests. No action was taken against him. Nor does it appear that the Register became more effective with age. Appreciable controversy arose in 1994, when press stories suggested that Conservative MP Neil Hamilton had failed to disclose that he had enjoyed an expensive six-day stay at the Ritz hotel in Paris paid for by a foreign businessman, Mohammed Al-Fayed, who was then under investigation by the Department of Trade and Industry. The Privilege Committee's 'investigation' of the Hamilton episode thoroughly undermined any contention that the house eschewed party political considerations in such matters. Conservative MPs acquiesced in the government's wish to have a whip on the committee. His presence could serve no purpose but to ensure that other Conservative members did nothing to jeopardise party interests. Opposition MPs eventually walked out of the Committee, which then reached the extraordinary conclusion that while Hamilton had failed to make a relevant disclosure, this amounted to no more than 'imprudence' and did not merit any punishment. This particular case was however merely symptomatic of an apparently wider malaise.

---

[66] *Erskine May* p 384.   [67] Ibid, at 386.   [68] For a full list see *Erskine May* pp 386–387.
[69] 12 June 1975 c 737 at c 749.

'Cash for questions' and the report of the Nolan Commission

In the early 1990s, acting on rumours about some MPs' rather lax ethical standards, two *Sunday Times* journalists posed as representatives of a foreign company wishing to raise a question in the house and willing to pay £1,000 to the MP who placed it. The journalists approached ten Labour MPs and ten Conservative MPs. The Labour members refused to take money for such purposes, as did seven Conservatives. The eighth Conservative, Bill Walker, agreed to table a question for a fee given to charity. Two Conservatives, Graham Riddick and David Tredinnick (both parliamentary private secretaries), agreed to table a question and accept the fee. In the ensuing furore, the Speaker granted an emergency debate to discuss the issue, and referred the case to the Privileges Committee. After a lengthy investigation, the Privileges Committee, dominated by a Conservative majority, imposed a rather lenient punishment of ten and twenty days' suspension on the offending MPs.

However, the 'cash for questions' scandal generated such hostile press coverage that the government established a committee of inquiry, chaired by Nolan LJ, with a wide-ranging remit to inquire into 'Standards in Public Life'.[70] Rumours rapidly began to circulate that the Committee would recommend extensive reforms, whereupon Conservative MPs equally rapidly began to cast aspersions on its impartiality and competence. Yet the recommendations contained in the Committee's first report were feeble. Its most significant proposal was that MPs should in future disclose not just the source but also the amount of income they received for the performance of services arising from their membership of the house. Nolan also urged the creation of a body 'independent' of the Commons to investigate MPs' behaviour. The model he favoured was that of a 'Parliamentary Commissioner for Standards', who would report to the Privileges Committee. The obvious weakness of the recommendation was that the Nolan Committee had apparently accepted that MPs' ethical standards should remain a matter for the house. Neither proposal was to have a statutory basis; rather they were to be matters for the Commons itself to introduce.

Although the Conservative government initially welcomed the report, many of its back-benchers (those, one assumes, who received substantial 'consultancy' payments) signalled that they would not support its implementation. Rather than carry the proposals into force by relying on opposition votes, the government decided to refer the Nolan Report to a special select committee for further consideration.

The Committee had a Conservative majority. It divided on party lines on the main question before it. The Conservative members rejected—while all the Opposition members accepted—the Nolan proposal that the house's rules should require MPs to divulge the amount as well as the source of their 'consultancy' payments. The Committee's recommendation was subsequently endorsed by the Cabinet. However, when the Committee's report was put before the house, some twenty-three Conservative MPs voted with the Opposition in support of requiring disclosure of the amount of income MPs received for these activities. The Commons did accept that the post of Parliamentary Commissioner for Standards (PCS) should be created. It also subsumed the former role of the Privileges Committee and the Committee on Members Interests into a new Committee on Standards and Privileges (CSP).

Whether this new regime would prove more effective than its predecessor was open to question. The disclosure requirement was not a 'law' enforceable in the independent arena of the courts; it was merely an internal rule of the house. Its adequacy would be entirely dependent on MPs attaching greater importance to financial candour than to party loyalties. The new rule would presumably be most effective if the house were to expel or suspend those members who fail to make accurate disclosures. But one might doubt that MPs in a governing party with a small Commons majority would take such drastic steps should some of their number be found

---

[70] See Rush M (1998) 'The law relating to members' conduct', in Oliver and Drewry op cit.

wanting on a question of financial integrity. The outcome of the 'cash for questions' scandal was thus something of a damp squib.

The Blair government took no steps to place the Nolan Commission's recommendations on a statutory basis, nor to strengthen the controls on MPs' disclosure of financial rewards. The Nolan Committee has however metamorphosised into a long-term feature on the political landscape, subsequently chaired by Lord Neill and charged with a general remit to investigate ethical standards in a wide range of governmental bodies. But the need for financial candour had evidently yet to impress itself fully on MPs; the press continued to field a steady stream of stories reporting members' failures to declare relevant sources of income.[71]

Many of these stories related to extremely trivial issues, and indicated that the rather serious questions of MPs' financial ethics had been subsumed beneath the cloak of party political bickering. But in a more serious vein, some Labour Ministers proved little less susceptible to the temptation to engage in financial practices of dubious ethicality than their Conservative predecessors. Elizabeth Filkin succeeded the first PCS, Sir Gordon Downey. She rapidly made it clear that she would take a vigorous and rigorous approach to her duties. This included conducting investigations into the affairs of Keith Vaz, a Minister of State at the Foreign Office, and John Reid, then Secretary of State for Northern Ireland. Ms Filkin considered that both men had deliberately obstructed her inquiries. In her view, Reid had gone so far as to threaten a witness whom Ms Filkin wished to interview. She received little support from the Commons however, or from the government. The CSP rejected her highly critical report on John Reid, and she left her post in 2002 amid press stories of a concerted effort by the government and many backbenchers to sabotage her work.[72]

In 1975, Enoch Powell MP had opposed the creation of the Register of Interests on the grounds that: 'we degrade ourselves by implying that our honour and traditions are not adequate to maintain proper standards in this house'.[73] Similar sentiments were voiced in 1995 by Conservative MPs who opposed the Nolan recommendations. Yet MPs' 'honour and tradition' are clearly entirely inadequate guarantors of 'proper standards'. The circumstances surrounding Ms Filkin's departure from her post would suggest that—most unfortunately—the majority of MPs continued to refuse to accept this.

It should nonetheless be noted that in 2009 Parliament did enact the Parliamentary Standards Act.[74] Section 3 of the Act created a body (presumptively) independent of the House of Commons called the Independent Parliamentary Standards Authority ('IPSA'), which would be responsible for revising the content of the expenses system and thereafter administering it. Section 3 also established a 'Commissioner for Parliamentary Investigations' who would police the administration of the scheme to ensure that inappropriate or fraudulent claims were not made. A new criminal offence was introduced by s 10 of the Act, dealing with MPs making claims on the basis of what they know to be false or misleading information. Rather surprisingly, the new offence would carry a maximum sentence of only one year, rather than the seven years available under s 17 of the Theft Act.

The new system, introduced in 2010, was notably more restrictive than its predecessor,[75] especially in relation to the payment of allowances for second homes. The new scheme prompted howls of outrage from many MPs, and was criticised as 'anti-family' by the Prime Minister (David Cameron) in December 2010. The notion that IPSA was an independent body was rather undermined by the Prime Minister's blunt assertion that if IPSA did not

[71] See Rush (1998) op cit pp 115–116.

[72] See generally Doig A (2002) 'Sleaze fatigue in "The House of ill-repute"' *Parliamentary Affairs* 389.

[73] *HCD* 12 June 1975 c 743.

[74] For an overview of the Act see Parpworth N (2010) 'The Parliamentary Standards Act 2009: a constitutional dangerous dogs measure' *MLR* 262.

[75] Details of the scheme, and of the claims made under it, are available on the IPSA website at: <http://www. parliamentary-standards.org.uk/>.

change the rules then IPSA itself would be changed. That impression was reinforced when modifications were subsequently made in 2011, particularly in respect of the number of MPs who would be entitled to claim expenses for running a second home.

The 2009 Act certainly marks an advance in the transparency of the expenses scheme and its administrations. The Act nonetheless has obvious weaknesses. It does not apply at all to the House of Lords, and leaves the Commons' Privileges and Standards Committee with a significant role to play in overseeing the Commissioner's investigatory processes. More importantly, as Mr Cameron's 2010 intervention made clear, IPSA operates under the cloud of a government threat of reform if it pursues its task too rigorously.

The report of the Nicholls Committee

Shortly after the 1997 general election, the two houses established a Joint Committee, chaired by a law lord, Lord Nicholls, to review the whole area of privilege. The Committee produced an extensive report, which contained significant proposals for change.[76] Most importantly, the Committee advocated that many issues relating to privilege—and in particular the various elements of Art 9 (ie 'proceedings in Parliament'; 'questioned'; 'place out of Parliament')—now be given a much more tightly defined statutory base. Responsibility for interpreting those provisions would presumably therefore rest with the courts, not with either house. In an attempt to allay public concern about corruption, the Committee also proposed a new statutory offence of bribery of MPs be created. This would, again, be a matter for the courts to control. The Report also addressed some of the evident weaknesses in the houses' internal disciplinary procedures by proposing that the CSP's hearings should in future adopt a more 'judicial' approach in its investigations. These were all worthy recommendations. But they would be of little value if they were not put on a statutory basis. There was little indication that Parliament would take any such steps quickly. That any significant reform was enacted appears to be attributable to the substantial press and public criticism of MPs' ethical standards in the expenses scandal in 2007–2010.

Parliamentary privilege and the expenses scandal

The Parliamentary Standards Act 2009 expressly states in s 1 that; 'Nothing in this Act shall be construed by any court in the United Kingdom as affecting Article IX of the Bill of Rights 1689'. Section 1 was inserted during the Bill's passage following concern being expressed (primarily by Commons officials) over the original version of the Bill which expressly disapplied Art 9 to IPSA's activities and those of the Commissioner. The concern was evidently that this would deter MPs from co-operating with IPSA and the Commissioner for fear that any information provided might subsequently be used against them in criminal proceedings.[77] What was perhaps not appreciated at the time was that several of the MPs accused of false accounting in respect of their expenses under the pre-IPSA scheme would argue that their prosecution was prohibited by Art 9 on the basis that the administration of the expenses scheme and their claims under it were proceedings in Parliament. In *R v Chaytor* that contention was rejected by the Supreme Court.[78]

The litigation is of limited value as a guide to the nature and extent of privilege in circumstances where privilege is being invoked by the House of Commons collectively to resist what would appear prima facie to be clear statutory or common law rules. The Commons offered

---

[76] See generally Leopold P (1999) 'Report of the Joint Committee on parliamentary privilege' *Public Law* 604; Lock G (1999) 'Report of the Joint Committee on parliamentary privilege' *Study of Parliament Group Newsletter*, Summer, 13.

[77] See Parpworth op cit at pp 974–976.   [78] [2010] UKSC 52; [2010] 3 WLR 1707.

no support to any of the defendants, being content to assume that the Theft Act charges were properly brought. This stance perhaps made the courts' task rather easier.

The leading judgment in the Supreme Court was given by Lord Phillips. His opinion is interesting in a jurisdictional sense, insofar as he held that Art 9 co-existed with, rather than replaced, privilege as a concept having neither a statutory or common law basis. In respect of Art 9, Lord Phillips had no doubt that the definition of 'proceedings in parliament' was a matter for the courts as part of its general constitutional duty to interpret statutes. Echoing the judgment of Lord Denman in *Stockdale*, Lords Phillips took a relatively narrow approach to the issue:

> 61 There are good reasons of policy for giving article 9 a narrow ambit that restricts it to the important purpose for which it was enacted—freedom for Parliament to conduct its legislative and deliberative business without interference from the Crown or the Crown's judges . . .
> 62 . . . Submitting claims for allowances and expenses does not form part of, nor is it incidental to, the core or essential business of Parliament, which consists of collective deliberation and decision making. The submission of claims is an activity which is an incident of the administration of Parliament; it is not part of the proceedings in Parliament.

Lord Phillips' conclusion in respect of what he termed the 'exclusive cognisance' of each house to regulate its internal proceedings was similarly unhelpful to the defendants. His reasoning however seemed to be driven largely by the fact that the Commons itself did not seem to consider that its privileges extended to a matter of this sort. Such a deferential approach may be unproblematic where the view of the courts as to 'exclusive cognisance' coincides with that of the majority of the Commons. It may however prove much less palatable in circumstances where the view of the Commons is ostensibly inconsistent with statutory or common law requirements.

Lord Rodger's opinion, while concurring in the result, was more blunt in its reasoning. He seemed doubtful that Art 9 and 'exclusive cognisance' were separate phenomena. But even if they were, neither could provide immunity from prosecution in respect of 'an ordinary crime'. And while making a seditious speech in the house would not be an 'ordinary crime', fiddling one's expenses was, just as an MP would commit an 'ordinary crime' by assaulting a fellow MP in the chamber or stealing money from the till in one of the house's dining rooms.

The Bribery Act 2010

The enactment of the Parliamentary Standards Act 2009 was followed by Parliament's evident, albeit not explicit, acceptance that it should be a criminal offence for an MP to accept a bribe in relation to the performance of her/his parliamentary activities. This had been proposed by the Joint Committee on Parliamentary Privilege in 1999, but the measure was not enacted until 2010. The offences created under the Act—essentially both of giving and accepting a bribe—are however crimes of general application, and do not identify MPs as a specific category.[79]

The original version of the Bill (in cl 15) provided in explicit terms that the new offence would apply to MPs, and that Art 9 would not provide an MP with any protection against prosecution:

> 15. Proceedings in Parliament
>
> (1) No enactment or rule of law preventing proceedings in Parliament being impeached or questioned in any court or any place out of Parliament is to prevent any evidence of
>   (a) words spoken by a member of either house of Parliament in proceedings in Parliament, or
>   (b) any other conduct of such a member in such proceedings
>
> from being admissible in proceedings against the member for a bribery offence or in related proceedings.

[79] See the discussion in Munro C (2011) 'Parliamentarians, privilege and prosecutions' *Scots Law Times* 1.

The draft Bill was however subject to pre-legislative scrutiny by a joint Lords and Commons committee, which promptly recommended that cl 15 be deleted. The rather feeble basis for this was that the privilege issue should not be dealt with in a 'piecemeal' way, but should instead be the subject of more comprehensive consideration and reform. Given that ten years had by then passed since the Nicholls Committee had made such a recommendation, one might credibly think that successive majorities of members in the Commons were in no hurry for comprehensive reform to be broached.

Although this recommendation to remove cl 15 was accepted when the Bill began its passage, the (Labour) Minister promoting the Bill gave a clear indication at second reading that MPs' parliamentary activities fell within its scope:

> There is one point that is not in the Bill but which the House would expect me to mention. The general offences in the Bill apply to all those performing functions of a public nature. As such, we intend that the Bill would apply to Members of this House and of the other place. The Joint Committee did not demur from this. It is, I believe, axiomatic that no Peer or Member of Parliament should be above the law.

Should any MP prosecuted under the Act seek to shelter behind Art 9—or indeed the 'exclusive cognisance' of the house—reference will presumably be made to this passage under the *Pepper v Hart* principle. However, the removal of cl 15 has unfortunate implications, and one need not be overly cynical to wonder if these were both understood and seen as desirable by the then government and many MPs.

The main difficulty is that to make out an offence under the 2010 Act, the prosecution will often need to prove not just that an MP received an improper payment or benefit, but that she did so in return for a parliamentary activity, be it the casting of a vote for or against a particular legislative proposal, the moving of an amendment to a Bill, the content of a speech, or the asking of a spoken or written question to a Minister. The trial court would therefore have to form a view on the content of, and motives underlying, the MP's speech and conduct. Unlike the submission of an expenses claim, such activities might be thought to fall within the narrow (per *Chaytor*) construction of Art 9.[80] We might wonder if bribery will be considered by a court to be an 'ordinary crime' (to borrow Lord Rodger's terminology) if it can only be made out after careful judicial examination of what an MP said and why she/he said it during the legislative process or in her/his dealings with Ministers. More importantly perhaps, we might wonder if a majority of members in the Commons would regard it in such a fashion. Given the track record of MPs in recent years, it may not be too long before the question arises.

Conclusion

Media coverage of the cash for questions scandal and the Nolan Report was perhaps most notable for revealing the casual equation frequently made, both by seasoned media commentators and by MPs themselves of the House of Commons with Parliament, and relatedly of the privileges of the house with legislation. This may perhaps be seen as a realistic interpretation of the contemporary balance of power between Parliament's three constituent parts. As noted in chapter six, the Commons is now much the more powerful of the two houses, and we shall see in chapter nine that the Monarch no longer plays a meaningful role in the legislative process.

---

[80] Presumably most attempts to bribe an MP would be prompted by the briber's hope to secure political advantage, and so necessarily relate to the MP's political activities. One could envisage 'non-political' bribes in this sense, a company seeking to 'persuade' MPs to choose a particular supplier of catering facilities to the Commons for example, which would fall outside the sphere of what Lord Phillips in *Chaytor* termed 'core' or 'essential' parliamentary activities.

The equation is, however, theoretically inept, and in practical terms both dangerous and underdeveloped, because it fails to take the further realistic step of observing that the Commons is generally just a vehicle for the promotion of factional, party interest. The Commons alone (except on those very rare occasions when no single party commands a reliable majority) does not in any sense perform the role that the revolution bestowed upon Parliament. The notion that the Commons plays a significantly independent role either as an actor within the legislative process or as a monitor of executive behaviour is generally quite fallacious in the contemporary political context.

It is perhaps an exaggeration to suggest that our examination of the Commons' legislative and supervisory roles, of the electoral system through which its members are chosen, and of the privileges within which MPs wrap themselves, leads to the conclusion that the lower house as presently constituted and regulated can defensibly be described as unrepresentative, incompetent, and corrupt. Such hyperbole perhaps contains more than a grain of truth, but it would as yet be premature to form firm conclusions as to the adequacy of our present parliamentary institutions. The next two chapters take us further towards the position from which a firm conclusion might more plausibly be drawn. Chapter nine addresses a further set of non-legal principles of the constitution which regulate governmental and parliamentary behaviour, while chapter ten assesses the uses to which the executive's dominance of the legislature has been put in respect of perhaps the most important of constitutional values in a nominally democratic society—namely the extent to which 'the people' can effectively express the divergent political and moral beliefs which they hold.

Suggested further reading

Academic and political commentary

LEOPOLD P (1998) 'The application of the civil and criminal law to members of Parliament and parliamentary proceedings', in DREWRY G and OLIVER D (eds) *The law and Parliament*

ARNSTEIN W (1983) *The Bradlaugh case* ch 1

LOCK G (1989) 'The 1689 Bill of Rights' *Political Studies* 541

MARSHALL G (1998) 'Hansard and the interpretation of statutes', in DREWRY G and OLIVER D (eds) *The law and Parliament*

DOIG A (2002) 'Sleaze fatigue in "The House of ill-repute"' *Parliamentary Affairs* 389

LEOPOLD P (1999) 'Report of the Joint Committee on parliamentary privilege' *Public Law* 604

STOCKDALE E (1989) 'The unnecessary crisis: the background to the Parliamentary Papers Act 1840' *Public Law* 30

Case law and legislation

Bradlaugh v Gossett (1884) 12 QBD 271

Stockdale v Hansard (1839) 9 Ad & El 1

Pepper v Hart [1993] AC 593

R v Chaytor [2010] UKSC 52, [2010] 3 WLR 1707

Chapter 9

Constitutional Conventions

Thus far we have focused primarily on legal regulation of constitutional behaviour. Such controls may be construed as performing a political or moral function—to ensure that the constitution respects the demands of democracy and the rule of law. Chapter six addressed more clearly the constitutional inter-relationship between legal principle and political practice by discussing the changing functions of the House of Lords, especially instances of tension between the Lords' *legal* powers and shifting *conventional* understandings of its legitimate legislative role. This chapter assesses the nature and purpose of constitutional conventions more systematically.

We might begin by considering several hypothetical situations. Assume, for example, that the Queen opposes a government's policy to cut old age pensions. She decides that when the Bill promoting the policy is sent for the Royal Assent she will not sign it. She justifies her action on the grounds that 'the people' dislike the policy (observing that the government did not win a majority of votes at the last election) and claims her first loyalty is to her people, not to the Houses of Parliament or the government. Alternatively, assume that the Queen no longer wants Theresa May as Prime Minister, and concludes that if the Conservative Party (alone or in coalition) has a majority of Commons seats after the next election she will invite Boris Johnson to be Prime Minister, even though May remains Conservative Party leader.

Giving the Royal Assent and appointing a Prime Minister are prerogative powers still exercised by the Monarch personally. The courts have never indicated that such prerogatives are justiciable. Thus, if the Queen adopted either course, there is no apparent legal obstacle in her way. Nor does it answer this problem to suggest that Parliament could pass legislation preventing such behaviour—for such legislation could only emerge if the Queen assented to the relevant Bill. But it is not just the Queen who wields potentially important yet clearly non-justiciable constitutional powers.

Suppose, as a third hypothetical scenario, that at the next general election Labour wins a two-seat Commons majority, but has a smaller share of the vote than the Conservatives. Theresa May claims that the Conservative Party has 'won' the election, refuses to resign as Prime Minister, and she and her party colleagues resolve (with the Queen's support) to stay in office as a minority government.

We will find neither an Act nor a common law rule indicating that the law of the constitution has been breached in those situations. But it seems most unlikely such events could ever occur. Could the Queen override the wishes of the Commons and Lords? Or impose an unwanted Prime Minister on the Commons' majority party? Would a Prime Minister really have to be dragged out of Downing Street after a general election defeat? That such hypotheses belong in the realm of fantasy is a result of their political impracticality—or, in other words, of their 'unconstitutionality'. They indicate that vital pillars of our constitutional structure rest upon foundations with no obvious legal basis—foundations which we might call constitutional conventions.

The Diceyan perspective—laws and conventions distinguished

Dicey's *Law of the Constitution* identified two distinct types of constitutional rule:

> The one set of rules are in the strictest sense 'laws', since they are rules (whether derived from statute or . . . the common law) enforced by the courts; . . . The other set of rules consists of conventions, understandings, habits or practices which, though they may regulate the conduct of . . . officials, are not in reality laws at all since they are not enforced by the courts.[1]

Dicey does not distinguish laws from conventions because of their importance, or their role, but in terms of whether they are enforceable by the courts. The utility of that proposition is discussed later. But first, it may be useful to approach constitutional conventions from another angle. In Jennings' view, a convention was characterised not just by its legal non-enforceability, but also because there was a reason for the rule.[2] We might therefore ask what constitutional role conventions supposedly play.

The functions and sources of conventions

A simple, if incomplete, way to characterise conventions' constitutional function is that they fill in the gaps within the legal structure of the governmental system. This notion operates at different levels of generality. Very narrowly, conventions provide a moral framework within which government Ministers or the Monarch should exercise non-justiciable legal powers. Slightly more broadly, they function as one means of regulating the relationship between Ministers within central government. More widely, conventions also regulate the relationship between the different branches of government—especially between the Monarch and the Cabinet, between central government and the Commons and Lords, and between central government and local government. We analyse that final relationship in chapter ten. This chapter explores the first three. Before turning to conventions' function and substance however, we should give some thought to their source.

The sources of constitutional conventions

As noted in chapter six, George V refused Asquith's requests for a mass creation of Liberal peers to overcome the Lords' Conservative majority during the 1909–1911 controversies. The King had sought advice from senior Conservative politicians. Asquith had described the Lords' intransigence as 'a breach of the constitution'. That breach was of a conventional, not

---

[1] (1915) op cit pp 23–24.   [2] (1959) op cit p 136.

legal nature. Asquith took a similar view of George V's recourse to opposition party politicians for advice. In a minute to the King, Asquith explained why:

> The part to be played by the Crown, in such a situation as now exists, has happily been settled by the accumulated traditions and unbroken practice of more than 70 years. It is to act upon the advice of the Ministers who for the time being possess the confidence of the House of Commons. . . . It follows that it is not the function of a Constitutional Sovereign to act as arbiter or mediator between rival parties and policies, still less to take advice from the leaders on both sides, with the view to forming a conclusion of his own.

Asquith assumed that the reason for the convention that the Monarch 'act upon the advice of the Ministers who possess the confidence of the Commons' was to ensure that the preferences of the party with majority Commons support were always given legal effect whenever personal prerogatives were deployed. We can see an obvious 'democratic' (albeit majoritarian) justification for the convention, since the party with a Commons majority usually represents the largest section (if not a majority) of the electorate.

Asquith also suggests three possible sources of conventions: 'tradition', 'unbroken practice', and a lengthy time span, here seventy years.[3] We might reasonably assume that if a particular (non-legal) aspect of the government process possesses all three characteristics it can be regarded as a convention.

The idea that there are minimum requirements for practice to become a convention is reinforced by the argument that there are also a set of non-legal constitutional rules inferior to conventions. Dicey used such phrases as customs, practices, and usages to describe these lesser rules of behaviour. Jennings agreed with Dicey on this point. He suggested that these informal practices could be divided into those that eventually became conventions and those that did not. As already noted, Jennings additionally insisted that a convention only arose if there was an important 'reason' for its existence, that is, that its provisions had substantial political significance.

Determining when a practice matures sufficiently to be a convention is a question defying authoritative answer. Chapter six suggested the Salisbury doctrine was a convention. Griffith and Ryle's *Parliament* approves that classification. But another eminent commentator, Colin Turpin, concludes: 'It may be doubted whether these principles have sufficient clarity, or are supported by a sufficient agreement to give them the status of conventions'.[4]

Such disagreement over so important an element of constitutional history implies we may never find analytical tools which tell us when a custom assumes conventional status. We might nonetheless proceed by assuming that a crucial test of whether a custom is a convention is whether the rule is respected by the people it supposedly controls. This suggests that convention spotting is more an empirical than a theoretical task. Consequently, the only way to decide how to classify rules of political behaviour is to examine situations where a supposed convention has either been respected or ignored. The rules on which we initially focus are the concepts of collective and individual ministerial responsibility.[5]

I. Collective ministerial responsibility

The Cabinet, like the office of Prime Minister, has no identifiable legal source. It assumed a recognisably modern form after about 1720, when we can also see the Prime Minister emerging as the 'first among equals' within it. Both the office of Prime Minister and the institution of the Cabinet are therefore creatures of convention. Except in periods when a ruling party has a small Commons majority, and must be acutely sensitive to its MPs' wishes, the Cabinet is the hub of the

---

[3] A period which (from 1909) takes us back to the enactment of the Great Reform Act.
[4] (1990) op cit p 491.   [5] See generally Diana Woodhouse (1994) *Ministers and Parliament*.

legislative and executive arms of government: it is there that government policies are formulated and refined. Consequently, for a government with a reliable Commons majority, parliamentary sovereignty is in effect Cabinet sovereignty. Given the Cabinet's obvious importance, it may seem odd that it operates without any appreciable legal structure. But the absence of legal controls on Cabinet behaviour does not mean that there are no principles regulating its activities.

The convention of ministerial responsibility is perhaps the most important non-legal rule within our constitution. It regulates the conduct of government (and especially Cabinet) activities, both in respect of Ministers' relations with each other, and with the two Houses of Parliament. The convention is divided into collective and individual branches. We consider individual responsibility in section IV. Firstly, however, we address collective responsibility. This convention has three sub-divisions: the confidence rule; the unanimity rule; and the confidentiality rule.

Confidence

The confidence rule originally required a government to resign if it could not command majority Commons support—if the house had 'lost confidence' in the government. Initially the rule applied if a government was defeated on a major policy issue.[6] During the mid-nineteenth century such resignations were commonplace: Jennings records five between 1852 and 1859.[7]

It is difficult to define 'major' issues. Presumably the Shops Bill on which the Thatcher government was defeated in 1986 did not meet that criterion. But this does no more than tell us that an issue is not sufficiently important to require a government's resignation if the government does not resign when it is defeated. That test would be entirely circular. Furthermore, there have been several instances of modern governments enduring Commons defeats on important issues, but continuing in office regardless. The 1974–1979 Labour administrations suffered frequent defeats. Its expenditure plans were rejected by the Commons in March 1976. It is difficult to disagree with the then Leader of the Opposition, Margaret Thatcher, that this policy was so fundamental a part of the government's *raison d'être* that defeat demanded resignation. The Cabinet declined to do so however. The government also refused to resign when defeated in an attempt to raise income tax levels in 1977, clearly a matter of major importance.

The experiences of the mid-1970s suggest that the convention's initial form no longer binds Cabinet behaviour. If a necessary feature of conventional status is that politicians consider themselves obliged to follow a given course of action, the confidence rule of the 1850s is clearly not a conventional feature of the contemporary constitution. But it would be inaccurate to claim the convention has disappeared entirely; rather, it has evolved into a different form.

The rule's modern version seems to require the government to resign only if defeated on an explicit no-confidence motion. The function of this shift in conventional understandings is readily discernible. Governments are rarely elected because of their policy on a single issue, but because of the overall package of policies and personalities they offer. A government's failure to command a Commons majority on one issue need not mean it cannot do so in other policy areas. Defeat in an explicit no-confidence motion, in contrast, implies the Commons considers the government wholly incompetent.

The reason behind the new convention is clear. In one, somewhat abstract sense, it stresses that the executive is accountable to the Commons, and so provides a different illustration of the principle of legislative supremacy. More prosaically, in the age of nationalised party politics, it provides an indirect means for the people, via their MPs, to signify withdrawal of their consent to a particular government.[8] However we have only rather barren historical soil

---

[6] Norton P (1978) 'Government defeats in the House of Commons: myth and reality' *Public Law* 360.

[7] (1959) op cit pp 512–519.

[8] Although, a successful no-confidence motion might lead not to a dissolution, but to formation of a new administration from within the existing Parliament.

in which to root the new convention. There has been just one occasion since 1945 when the convention has been tested. James Callaghan's minority Labour government resigned in 1979 when defeated by one vote on an explicit no-confidence motion. One might doubt that this amounts to a tradition or long-term unbroken practice.

Only one other Prime Minister has resigned in comparable circumstances in the twentieth century, that one being Stanley Baldwin in 1924. Baldwin led a minority Conservative administration, which failed to gain Commons approval for the legislative programme outlined in the King's speech. (At the 1923 election the Conservatives won 258 seats, Labour 191, and the Liberals 159). Ramsay MacDonald subsequently formed a minority Labour administration from within the same Parliament, which survived for barely eleven months. That administration was also defeated on a confidence vote, although that vote led to a dissolution rather than simply a change of government.[9] It thus seems that the contemporary confidence rule, if rarely invoked in practice, is straightforward in principle. The second limb of collective responsibility, the unanimity rule, seems quite the opposite.

Unanimity

The unanimity rule requires all Cabinet Ministers to offer public support for all Cabinet decisions, even if a Minister opposed the policy concerned in Cabinet. Ministers who find a particular policy unacceptable should resign from office. As Lord Salisbury explained in 1878:

> For all that passes in Cabinet every member of it who does not resign is absolutely and irretrievably responsible and has no right afterwards to say that he agreed in one case to a compromise, while in another he was persuaded by his colleagues.[10]

The rule also supposes that ministerial differences of opinion have been aired in Cabinet. The convention demands collective loyalty to collective decisions. It could therefore be undermined either by Ministers who openly signalled their disagreement with government policy, or by Cabinet decision-making procedures which prevent Ministers having any say in policy formation.

The rule originally arose in the seventeenth century to protect Ministers from the King's attempts to undermine their power by exposing or encouraging public arguments. Since the Cabinet is no longer in conflict with the Monarch, the rationale for the rule has changed. The contemporary argument suggests the rule is needed to maintain public and business confidence in the unity and purpose of government. It is alleged that public Cabinet divisions would trigger such dire consequences as reduced investment from overseas, a run on the pound, or various other forms of economic or political instability.

There seem to be three ways to test whether the rule has conventional status. The first, and most elusive, would be to identify occasions when a Minister strongly opposed a particular policy, made and lost her argument in Cabinet, and then resolutely kept her dissent a secret from outside observers. Unfortunately, it is in the nature of a secret event that we do not know that it happened. We may, in retrospect, gain some insight by the eventual release of Cabinet papers (currently embargoed for at least thirty years), or (more promptly) by the memoirs of former Ministers, although the latter may present a skewed interpretation of events. The second test would seek instances when irreconcilable disagreement between Cabinet members led to resignations or dismissals of Ministers. Such episodes would reinforce the claim that the convention effectively determined government behaviour. The third test, which would seem to disprove the rule's conventional status, would search political history for public intra-Cabinet

---

[9] Norton (1978) op cit; Jennings (1959) op cit pp 28–30.
[10] Quoted in Ellis D (1980) 'Collective ministerial responsibility and collective solidarity' *Public Law* 367.

disputes in which all protagonists stayed in office. It is an indicator of the unfortunate indeterminacy of conventional rules that one readily finds examples to satisfy all three tests.

Michael Heseltine's resignation from Thatcher's second administration in 1985 over the Westland affair offers a powerful illustration of the convention taking effect. Heseltine, then Defence Secretary, was embroiled within Cabinet in an argument as to whether the financially troubled Westland helicopter company should be rescued by American or European firms. Heseltine favoured the European option, but the Cabinet majority preferred the American bid. It is not clear if Heseltine would have resigned solely because of his disagreement with the substance of Cabinet policy. His own account stresses that he left office because the Cabinet did not accept the second limb of the unanimity convention—namely that a Minister may argue her case fully before her colleagues. Heseltine alleged that a Cabinet meeting scheduled for him to make his argument had been cancelled by the Prime Minister in order to force through the American takeover, a strategy which he interpreted as confirming that the Cabinet no longer operated in a collective manner.[11]

A similar accusation that Margaret Thatcher rejected collective forms of decision-making was made by Nigel Lawson. Lawson resigned as Chancellor of the Exchequer in 1989, claiming his position had been undermined by the Prime Minister's preference for taking advice on economic policy from her personal adviser, Professor Alan Walters, rather than from her Chancellor. Lawson's decision to leave office has several obvious Conservative predecessors. In 1886, Lord Randolph Churchill, Chancellor in Lord Salisbury's administration, was isolated in Cabinet over his plans to cut military spending. Rather than defer to majority sentiment, Churchill quit the government altogether.[12] A similarly principled stand was taken by Chancellor Peter Thorneycroft and two junior Ministers in 1958, who felt the Cabinet was not committed to sufficiently rigorous anti-inflation policies. Neither the Churchill nor Thorneycroft departures dealt a fatal blow to their respective government's stability. Prime Minister Harold Macmillan famously minimised the impact of the 1958 events by referring to them as 'a little local difficulty'. The impact of Lawson's resignation is considered further later in the chapter.

Illustrations supportive of the rule are not limited solely to the Conservative Party. In 1951, two members of the Labour Cabinet (Nye Bevan and Harold Wilson) resigned from Attlee's government in protest at plans to introduce prescription charges into the newly founded National Health Service. The action was widely construed as revealing a deep ideological split within the party.[13] More recently, the resignation of both Robin Cooke and Clare Short from Tony Blair's Cabinet in 2003 in protest at the government's decision to join a military invasion of Iraq exemplified deep division within the governing party.

These episodes pale in comparison, however, to the events of 1931. The 1929–1931 Labour government was a minority administration. Its tenure coincided with the Great Depression, which wrought severe distress on most western economies. A Cabinet committee proposed large cuts in public expenditure to address the crisis. These were opposed by eight Cabinet members. Faced with so profound a split in his government, the then Labour Prime Minister, Ramsay MacDonald, tendered his administration's resignation to the King.

At the Prime Minister's invitation, George V played a pivotal role in brokering a solution to the crisis. The suggestion for a coalition government headed by MacDonald was made by Sir Herbert Samuel, the leader of the Liberal Party, and enthusiastically pressed on Stanley Baldwin, the Conservative leader, by the King. The Liberals and Conservatives agreed to join a coalition administration, on the understanding that Parliament would be dissolved as soon as emergency legislation enacting the Cabinet committee's recommendation was passed. Only three of the Labour Cabinet's eighteen Ministers agreed to serve in a 'National' coalition

---

[11] The episode merits close attention; see especially Hennessy (1986) op cit.
[12] For further details see Madgwick P (1966) 'Resignations' *Parliamentary Affairs* 59.
[13] Pilot op cit pp 160–165; Hennessy P (1992) *Never again* pp 415–417.

government, in which MacDonald led what he described as 'a Cabinet of Individuals'—most of whom were Conservatives. At the subsequent general election, the 'National Government', led by MacDonald, was returned with a substantial Commons majority.

Reactions to Disraeli's proposals for the 1867 Reform Act also illustrate the operation of the unanimity rule. Three members of Lord Derby's Cabinet, all opposing further democratisation, resigned rather than support the Bill.[14] Similarly, Richard Crossman's *Diaries* reveal that the 1966–1970 Labour Cabinet was deeply divided over lowering the voting age to 18.[15] Such disagreement was not made public (at least not until the *Diaries* were published some years later!). Ministers opposed to the reform stifled their dissent; the government could thus present the Bill as a measure enjoying unanimous Cabinet support.

But electoral reform also provides quite contradictory examples, seemingly disproving the convention's existence. In 1883, for example, Joseph Chamberlain campaigned vigorously for continued extension of the franchise, to which the rest of Gladstone's Cabinet was clearly opposed.[16]

In recent years, several examples have arisen of collective solidarity being 'suspended' in respect of particular issues. This 'suspension' principle has latterly been deployed by both Labour and Conservative Cabinets over government policies towards the European Community.[17] In 1975, the Labour Prime Minister Harold Wilson allowed Cabinet members to campaign on both sides in the referendum on whether Britain should remain in the EEC. Wilson explained his decision by saying that the split reflected a similar rift within public opinion.[18] James Callaghan, Labour Prime Minister between 1976 and 1979, supported the idea of selectively applied conventions. Callaghan permitted his Cabinet openly to hold differing views in 1979 about the type of electoral system to be used for elections to the EEC Parliament. When accused of acting unconstitutionally, he replied that collective responsibility would always apply 'except in cases where I announce that it does not'.[19] More informally, the second Major government was noticeably divided between 'Euro-sceptics' and 'Euro-enthusiasts', a point explored more fully in chapter eleven. Members of the Conservative/Liberal coalition government saw no difficulty in campaigning in favour of opposing views during the 2011 referendum on electoral reform,[20] although since this had been foreshadowed in the coalition negotiations it is perhaps not apposite to see it as a further erosion of the unanimity convention.

As an organising principle, 'suspension' has little merit—a practice cannot be a binding rule if it can be disregarded at the whim of those it purportedly controls. Moreover, such arguments do not explain the 1883 Cabinet's tolerance of Chamberlain's independent line. The Cabinet portrayed Chamberlain's dissent as an example of a principle of 'Ministerial freedom of speech', but such a concept is manifestly incompatible with a unanimity convention. Chamberlain's behaviour was accepted because his dismissal or resignation was impractical from a party political perspective; it would have alienated many Liberal voters, with dire electoral results. He could thus defy the supposed convention and advance both his own prospects within the party and the prospects of more radical electoral reform being enacted.

A similar combination of personal ambition and policy preference seems to underlie James Callaghan's very evident dissent, when Home Secretary, from the industrial relations policies of the second (1966–1970) Wilson administration. The government wished to impose legal sanctions on workers who took industrial action without trade union approval. Callaghan clearly aligned himself with trade union opposition to this proposal. Subsequently, he announced, without having sought Cabinet approval, that the government would take no new measures to regulate wage and price inflation. Many Cabinet members apparently considered that Callaghan was seeking to establish himself as the trade unions' preferred successor to

---

[14] Cowling op cit pp 163–165.   [15] Op cit pp 493–494, 500–501.   [16] Jones op cit p 106.
[17] See ch 11.   [18] This episode is discussed more fully in ch 11.   [19] *HCD* 16 June 1977 c 552.
[20] See 'Prospects of reform', ch 7, pp 196–197.

Harold Wilson, and demanded he be disciplined for disregarding the unanimity rule.[21] No action was taken however, since the government, facing an imminent general election, could not risk losing the political and financial support the unions provided.

The inference we might draw from these examples is that whatever 'reason' one might adduce for the rule of Cabinet unanimity, it is ignored for reasons of party political expediency too frequently for us to conclude that Asquith's threefold test for conventional status is met. One might refine the convention by suggesting it operates differently for Conservative and Labour governments. Writing in 1980, Ellis argued Labour governments contained a wider range of opinion than Conservative administrations, and their members were less inclined than Conservatives to compromise ideological preferences to preserve party unity.[22] So fractious an atmosphere was inimical to effective functioning of the unanimity rule, especially since, as noted in chapter seven, until the Blair/Brown era from 1997 to 2010 most Labour governments had precarious Commons majorities. Ministers representing distinct party factions may see no need to respect the unanimity rule if their faction's continued support is a prerequisite of the government's survival.

Confidentiality

Lawson and Heseltine withheld their explanation of their departures from Cabinet until after they had resigned. In so doing, they respected the unwritten letter of the unanimity rule. It is also however a convention of the constitution that Ministers who resign are afforded the opportunity to offer reasons for their action to the Commons (or, if peers, to the Lords). This is another manifestation of the confidence rule, since it enables MPs to evaluate the government's performance after having heard both sides of the argument.

Once out of Cabinet, Lawson and Heseltine explained their actions in detail, both in the Commons and in the media. In so doing, they drew attention to another facet of collective responsibility, namely that all Ministers owe their Cabinet colleagues a duty of confidentiality. Ministers should not reveal how colleagues argued or voted in particular disputes: to do so would seriously undermine the unanimity rule and also inhibit Ministers from speaking their minds.

To date this rule seems to have been respected, at least formally. However, reports of Cabinet discussions are leaked to the press with sufficient regularity to suggest that in practice some Ministers ignore it. A more contentious issue is whether confidentiality should continue after a Minister leaves the Cabinet. And if so for how long, and how stringently? The rule's status, and the political and legal consequences which flowed from ignoring it, arose in *A-G v Jonathan Cape Ltd*—the *Crossman Diaries* case.[23]

Can conventions become laws? 1: The *Crossman Diaries* case

Crossman, a member of Wilson's Cabinet between 1964 and 1970, wanted to provide a detailed account of Cabinet government in operation. Consequently, he kept a comprehensive diary of Cabinet decisions, intending to publish it following his retirement. Unfortunately for Crossman, he died prematurely; but his widow decided to publish the *Diaries*.

After extracts appeared in *The Sunday Times*, the government sought an injunction preventing further publication. It argued that the courts should preserve the confidentiality of three types of ministerial information: firstly, the views of individual Ministers; secondly, confidential advice to Ministers from civil servants; and thirdly, discussions about the appointment or transfer of senior officials. Crossman's publishers argued that the duty of Cabinet

---

[21] According to Crossman's *Diaries*; op cit at pp 497–500. Crossman notes that Callaghan protested that there was nothing unconventional about his behaviour.   [22] Op cit.

[23] [1976] QB 752.

confidentiality had no legal basis; it was merely a moral obligation, respected or ignored according to the Minister's conscience.

Lord Widgery did not find history a helpful guide: 'I find overwhelming evidence that the doctrine of joint responsibility is generally understood and practiced, and equally strong evidence that it is on occasion ignored'.[24] Widgery eventually delivered a puzzling judgment. Firstly, he accepted that Ministers owed each other a legally enforceable duty of confidentiality. However, this duty did not derive from the convention turning into a law. It was created by 'stretching' existing common law principles about confidentiality in respect of other types of relationship, particularly marriage and commercial undertakings.[25] But secondly, Widgery held that unless the disclosures threatened national security, the duty would disappear ten years after the relevant events occurred.

The government subsequently established a committee of inquiry, headed by Lord Radcliffe, to make recommendations concerning the publication of Ministers' diaries or autobiographies.[26] The committee proposed a fifteen-year delay on publication of sensitive material. The proposal has not been given statutory force: given the rapidity with which retired Ministers have subsequently marketed their memoirs,[27] it seems safe to assume that it should not be regarded as a convention.

If analysed formalistically, the judgment does not sweep away Dicey's claim that conventions are not enforceable by the courts. Technically, the case is not an example of a court enforcing a convention, but accepting that a convention was coincidentally underpinned by existing common law rules. That may seem a semantic distinction. In functionalist terms, we might argue that the court enforced a convention by cloaking it with a common law label. There is no legal impediment to the courts doing so. The common law is recognised to be dynamic. In cases such as *Burmah Oil*, *Lain*, and *GCHQ*, 'new' common law principles emerged when judges considered that applying traditional ideas would have produced unsatisfactory results. Parliament may restore the former law by legislation reversing a court decision, but (short of passing legislation forbidding the courts from altering common law principles) it has no power to pre-empt judicial innovation. This inter-relationship between convention and common law within the courts is something to which we shall return. For the present, before concluding our discussion of collective responsibility, we divert our attention to an ostensibly non-justiciable issue—the relationship between the Monarch and her Ministers.

II. The Monarch

In formal terms, the Monarch retains substantial legal powers. Unlike the House of Lords, she has the legal capacity to veto any Bill passed by the Commons. The Monarch also seems to have the legal authority to appoint whomsoever she wishes to be Prime Minister, and to appoint and dismiss other Ministers at will; she may dismiss an entire government if she wishes. And she may at any time, without fear of legal reversal, dissolve Parliament and so force a general election to be held. All such actions are elements of the royal prerogative 'peculiar and eccentrical' to the Monarch herself, and which, per *GCHQ*, appear non-justiciable. Nor could such prerogatives be altered or abolished by statute without the Monarch's consent. As a legal creature, the Monarchy possesses (at least) co-equal status with the Commons.

---

[24] Ibid, at 770.

[25] *Argyll v Argyll* [1967] Ch 302; *Saltman Engineering Co Ltd v Campbell Engineering Co Ltd* (1948), but not reported until [1963] 3 All ER 413, CA, respectively.

[26] Radcliffe (1976) *Report on Ministerial Memoirs*, (Cmnd 6386).

[27] eg Clark A (1993) *Diaries*—the most revealing of the genre; Baker K (1993) *The turbulent years*; Lawson N (1992) *The view from No 11*.

Yet there is no part of the contemporary constitution in which the mismatch between legal principle and political fact is more pronounced than in respect of the personal prerogatives. The notion that a single individual should wield substantial legal powers bestowed solely by accident of birth is entirely antithetic to the particular form of parliamentary democracy on which the legitimacy of the constitution rests. This is not to say that one could not invoke alternative conceptions of 'democracy' to justify such powers in some circumstances. But as a matter of political instinct, one might readily infer that there would be very convincing reasons for the presence of constitutional conventions which subjected the exercise of the personal prerogatives to the wishes of the government which enjoyed the confidence of the Commons. A brief survey of the past 150 years suggests that such a convention has indeed emerged.

'On the advice of her Ministers'? The conventional 'democratisation' of the personal prerogatives

As noted in chapter seven, William IV did not acknowledge that the Great Reform Act's tentative push towards constitutional democratisation affected his power to remove a government which displeased him. In 1834, he dismissed Lord Melbourne's Whig administration, which he regarded as unacceptably radical.[28] William invited Sir Robert Peel to lead a minority Conservative administration. Peel was more sensitive to the Act's implications, and requested an immediate dissolution, hoping to legitimise both his own position and the King's by winning the subsequent general election. The electorate, however, returned the Whigs and their allies with a workable Commons majority. William subsequently deferred to the Commons majority, and did not obstruct the formation of a new Whig administration.

There have been no subsequent examples of such blatant interference by the Monarch. However, Queen Victoria engaged in secretive manoeuvrings to keep Gladstone out of power in 1886. Victoria, like many Liberal MPs, opposed Gladstone's policy of granting home rule to Ireland. She subsequently approached several prominent anti-Gladstonian Liberals to try and ensure that a Gladstone administration could not enact that policy. Her tone was explicitly partisan:

> I appeal to you and to all moderate loyal and patriotic men, who have the safety and well-being of the Empire and the Throne at heart, and who wish to save them from destruction, with which, if the government again fell into the reckless hands of Mr Gladstone, they would be threatened, to rise above party and to be true patriots.[29]

One might defend the Queen's action by characterising her appeal that politicians should forswear party allegiances in pursuit of greater national interests as echoing a Madisonian fear of faction. As an abstract exercise in democratic theorisation, that viewpoint has some substantive attractions, although one might doubt that the process through which such a national interest was defined, namely the Monarch's individual preferences, would satisfy even the most dilute notions of democratic process. But in the context of historical trends in the late-nineteenth century, Victoria's initiative was undoubtedly 'unconstitutional'.

By 1886, the Monarch's conventional capacity to engage in independent exercise of her legal powers had been substantially undermined by both the gradual extension of the Commons' electoral franchise to ever greater numbers of 'the people'—and relatedly—by the increasing ascendancy of the Commons vis-à-vis the Lords within Parliament. Neither trend formally affected the Monarch's legal powers, but both emphasised that electoral accountability rather than accident of birth should regulate access to governmental power. In so far as the legitimacy of her constitutional role depended on her maintaining a studied neutrality between those

---

[28] Brock op cit pp 315–317; Jennings (1959) op cit pp 403–405.

[29] Cited in Jennings (1959) op cit p 34. Gladstone suggested of Victoria that there was 'no greater Tory in the land'; quoted in Arnstein op cit p 151.

political parties which each enjoyed substantial electoral support, Victoria's machinations in 1886 revealed a distinct failure to accept (or understand) the constitutional implications of the social changes the country was undergoing.

This gradual process of subordinating legal power to political practice is demonstrated by subsequent Monarchs' increasingly tentative interventions in situations of political instability. As noted in chapter seven, the behaviour of Edward VII and George V in 1909–1911 was less than fully supportive of Asquith's wishes. At that point, the legal context in which the personal prerogatives were to be exercised was virtually the same as in 1886—the House of Lords remained a co-equal partner to the Commons, and the franchise had not been substantially extended since 1884. Twenty years later, that context had altered significantly. The passive role played by George V in forming the 1931 National government can be explained largely by the virtual completion of the democratisation process; since 1928, Britain had had a universal franchise for elections to the Commons, and since 1911 the Lords' inferior status within Parliament was a matter of law, not merely convention. Elizabeth II was admittedly intimately involved in the choice of a Conservative Prime Minister in the mid-1950s, but that was because the Conservative Party had no formal arrangements to choose its leader; the leader traditionally 'emerged' in some mysterious fashion after consultation among the party's senior figures. In the mid-1960s, the Conservative Party established a system in which its leader was chosen through a ballot of its MPs. The Labour Party already had such a process, and it seems inconceivable that it would now be legitimate for a Monarch to appoint as Prime Minister someone who was not the leader of her party. The principle powerfully illustrates not just the primacy of party interests over national interests within Parliament, but also of the ascendancy of convention over law at the heart of Britain's constitutional identity.

Refusing the Royal Assent

If we borrow Jennings' 'reason' test for conventional status, and (mis)apply it to the 1688 settlement, we might assume that the Monarch's formal co-equality with the Commons and the Lords served to protect both the Queen herself from an alliance of the two houses, and 'the people' from a lower and upper house temporarily seized by a desire to enact oppressive legislation. To suggest that the Queen might ever invoke her veto power would, however, seem utterly to contradict the trend towards democratisation which we employed to explain why the Monarch generally cannot use her personal prerogatives in an independent manner. This leads us yet again to examine the meaning of democracy in the contemporary constitution. If the concept means simply that a political party commanding a reliable Commons majority can pass any law whatsoever, a refusal of the Royal Assent to any Bill would be 'undemocratic'. Yet it is not difficult to imagine scenarios in which we might intuitively regard such action as essential to defend democratic ideals.

Assume, for example, that a government, fearing it will lose the next general election, promotes a Bill to extend the lifetime of a Parliament without opposition party agreement. At present the Lords may veto such a Bill, and so, in its anachronistic way, can operate as a 'democratic' safeguard against a dictatorial Commons majority. But the Lords does not (apparently) possess a veto over a third Parliament Act removing that veto power. What conventional understandings should guide the Queen's decision about granting the Royal Assent in the following situations?

Firstly if the Lords also approved the Bill extending the lifetime of the Parliament? Secondly to a new Parliament Bill, introduced against the Lords' wishes under the 1949 procedures, which removed the Lords' veto power on all legislation? And thirdly, if she assented to the second Bill, to a subsequent Bill extending the lifetime of the present Parliament? Alternatively, what course should the Queen follow in respect of a Bill which requires that the next general election be fought on constituency boundaries designed to secure a vast majority for the governing party?

We might suggest all such Bills would be 'unconstitutional', and so the Queen could legitimately withhold her assent. But the argument is a difficult one to sustain. One could contend, for instance, that refusing the Royal Assent would be legitimate because any such Bill would be seeking to change the basis of consent to government within the constitution—to effect, as the Duke of Wellington put it, 'a revolution by due process of law'. The flaw in this argument is that it entrenches contemporary understandings of 'consent', and suggests that we have now arrived at the ultimate form of democratic government. Yet these allegedly 'unconstitutional' Bills may be no more radical from our perspective than were Grey's Reform Bill or Asquith's Parliament Bill in the eyes of contemporaneous conservative opinion. In the absence of a supra-parliamentary constitution, we simply lack an authoritative yardstick against which to measure the substantive legitimacy of radical constitutional reform.

It is some answer to these questions to observe that no such Bills are ever likely to appear. In all reasonably foreseeable circumstances, there appears to be no difficulty in concluding that the Monarch's personal prerogatives are exercised according to the wishes of a Prime Minister whose government enjoys the confidence of the Commons. The reason for that convention is to subject the Queen's legal powers to democratic control—insofar as we consider Prime Ministerial control democratic. But that reason disappears when a Prime Minister's government does not possess the lower house's confidence. In such situations, the conventional constraints on the Monarch's legal powers are decidedly ambiguous. One such scenario relates to the appointment of the Prime Minister following a general election in which no party has won a majority of Commons seats.

Choosing a Prime Minister in a hung Parliament

In the February 1974 general election, Edward Heath's outgoing Conservative government failed to win an overall majority. But although Harold Wilson's Labour Party had the largest number of Commons' seats, it too had no majority. The balance of power was held by small parties, which had only thirty-seven seats.

There is no legal requirement that a government resign after a general election defeat. It does so, as a matter of convention, in deference to an electoral sentiment which indicates that another party is the people's preferred choice. That choice was however far from clear in 1974. While the electorate may have signalled displeasure with the Conservatives, it had not shown obvious enthusiasm for Labour. In these circumstances, Heath decided not to resign, but to negotiate with the smaller parties to see if they would offer him support in a coalition government. None did so. Heath then concluded that the correct course was for him to resign, and advise the Queen to invite Wilson to form a minority administration.

It is possible to argue that Heath should have automatically resigned, on the grounds firstly that Labour had won more seats than the Conservatives and, secondly, that the prospect of a Conservative/Liberal coalition had not been put to the electorate. However, there is neither a legal nor a conventional basis for the claim, in circumstances where no single party has a Commons majority, that the leader of the party with the most seats has any immediate entitlement to a favourable exercise of the personal prerogatives. Heath, and the Queen, faced a somewhat unusual situation; it would be difficult to describe their behaviour as constitutionally indefensible.[30]

That the Monarch has in effect been wholly removed from this aspect of the operation of the constitution seems to be underlined by events following the 2010 general election.[31] The process of negotiation and consultation between the Conservative, Labour, and Liberal Democrat Parties was played out without any involvement from the Queen or her personal advisers.[32]

[30] See generally Brazier R (1982) 'Choosing a Prime Minister' *Public Law* 395.
[31] See 'The 2010 election: a hung Parliament and a coalition government', ch 7, p 193.
[32] See the discussion in Kavanagh and Cowley (2010) op cit ch 10.

III. Collective ministerial responsibility revisited: from Cabinet to Prime Ministerial government . . .?

It is perhaps an apocryphal tale that when the Duke of Wellington became Prime Minister, after a career spent in the army rather than the Commons, he remarked on his first Cabinet meeting: 'An extraordinary affair. I gave them their orders and they wanted to stay and discuss them'.[33] We might doubt if there ever was a 'golden age' of Cabinet government in which all Ministers participated fully in decision-making. But in the modern era, James Callaghan's aforementioned belief that he could suspend constitutional conventions whenever he saw fit provides lucid support for the argument that Britain's government is controlled by the Prime Minister rather than the Cabinet.

That argument was first aired in the nineteenth century in Walter Bagehot's leading work on the constitution.[34] Bagehot suggested that the Cabinet was becoming a 'dignified' rather than 'efficient' part of the constitution. Its role was increasingly ceremonial or symbolic, while real power was shifting to the Prime Minister and a few of his colleagues.

Bagehot's ideas were forcefully restated in a new edition of his book by Richard Crossman in the 1960s. Crossman's introduction, written before he became a Cabinet Minister, argued that the Prime Minister effectively dominated the Cabinet rather than being just 'first among equals'. Prime Ministers achieved this through three main powers: firstly, by being able to appoint and dismiss Ministers; secondly, by setting the agenda for Cabinet discussions, which permitted the Prime Minister to avoid challenges over particular issues by leaving them off the agenda altogether; and thirdly, by controlling the remit and membership of Cabinet committees.

Crossman argued that collective responsibility had assumed a new meaning by 1960. It no longer meant that all Cabinet Ministers were involved in making the decisions which they were obliged to support, but rather that all Ministers were expected to lend unquestioning support to decisions reached by Cabinet Committees, or a so-called inner Cabinet of senior Ministers, or the Prime Minister. The unanimity rule would thus have undergone a marked shift. If a Minister disagreed with Cabinet policy she would still be expected to either stifle her dissent or resign; she should not however expect to be a full participant in a collective decision-making process.

As we saw earlier, Michael Heseltine felt this trend had become an established, and (to him) unacceptable feature of the Thatcher Cabinets. His resignation was premised, we might say, on his refusal to accept the legitimacy of a Cabinet in which collective decision-making had become entirely a 'dignified' rather than 'efficient' part of the constitution.

Harold Wilson did not invent the committee-based form of Cabinet decision-making, but did use it more systematically than his predecessors. Nevertheless, Wilson himself disputed the Prime Ministerial government thesis. Writing in 1972, while in opposition, he suggested that 'The Prime Minister's task is to get a consensus of Cabinet or he cannot reasonably ask for loyalty and collective responsibility'.[35]

There are undoubtedly sound justifications for a drift away from a fully collegiate model of Cabinet decision-making. As the government's workload has grown, it has become increasingly implausible to expect all Cabinet members to have the time or expertise to comment usefully on all fields of government activity. One is nevertheless left with the problem of deciding how best to enhance governmental efficiency without concentrating power in too few ministerial hands. The only satisfactory way to gauge the accuracy of Crossman's thesis would be to study the intimacies of Cabinet decision-making over a protracted period. Such a task is beyond the

---

[33] Quoted in Hennessy P (1986a) *Cabinet* p 121.
[34] (1867) *The English constitution* (1963 edn by Crossman R).   [35] Quoted in Ellis op cit at p 372.

scope of this work;[36] we can however advert briefly to certain important episodes which indicate one can readily find examples which both underpin and undermine Crossman's argument.

There have been perhaps few more important policy decisions made in the post-war era than the 1945–1951 Attlee governments' conclusion that Britain should develop its own atomic weapons capacity. But to talk of this as a decision of the government, or even of the Cabinet, would be quite misleading. Attlee had permitted only a handful of his Cabinet to know about this policy. He recalled some years later that: 'I thought some of them [the Cabinet] were not fit to be trusted with secrets of this kind'.[37] Similarly, James Callaghan preferred to formulate the major strands of economic policy not in Cabinet, but in a small 'Economic Seminar', containing just a handful of Ministers. The role of Cabinet was merely to agree to whatever conclusions the 'Seminar' had reached.

Such dismissive Prime Ministerial treatment of Cabinet colleagues has not been a trait solely of Labour Prime Ministers. A graphic example of the apparently paradoxical way in which the Prime Minister's use of his great power within Cabinet can actually much weaken his position is provided by the notorious 'night of the long knives' in July 1962. As Prime Minister, the Conservative leader Harold Macmillan had cultivated an air of 'unflappability'. The party's electoral appeal was felt to depend largely on public perception that Macmillan would always act in a calm, rational fashion. That perception was shattered in just one day when Macmillan dismissed one third of his Cabinet. Macmillan's initial concern had simply been to replace his Chancellor of the Exchequer, Selwyn Lloyd, who he considered insufficiently interventionist on economic policy issues. However several Conservative defeats in by-elections, coupled with the government's poor standing in public opinion polls, and press rumours of an impending Cabinet reshuffle, led Macmillan to panic rather, and end up sacking seven Ministers, hoping that a new look government would be more electorally appealing.

That a Prime Minister can dismiss so many Ministers in so cursory a fashion cogently illustrates her short-term dominance of the Cabinet. Yet, since that Prime Minister may have appointed those Ministers in the first place, their removal casts doubt on the Prime Minister's own competence, for one of her most important tasks is surely to select able colleagues. Macmillan subsequently described the sacked Ministers as 'worn out', and replaced them with much younger colleagues, but his strategy did not attract substantial backbench support. Whether Macmillan could have survived as party leader in the long term after antagonising so large a section of his party, and whether he could have led the Conservatives to victory in another general election, remained unanswered questions; he resigned as a result of ill health the following year.[38]

There are no legal rules controlling the identity of individuals appointed to ministerial office. Nor does it seem likely that there could be. It seems clear that the Prime Minister's choices are motivated by two factors: maximising her own standing within her party, while simultaneously maximising her party's standing with the electorate. Neither criterion seems justiciable. We might wonder if the constitution should require a Prime Minister to appoint the most able of her party's members to ministerial office, but 'ability' is a concept which cannot be objectively defined. There would seem little alternative but to leave evaluation of the Prime Minister's selection and management of her Cabinet to her parliamentary party, and ultimately to the electorate. Both MPs and voters might plausibly be thought to place pre-emptive limits on the extent to which Prime Ministers can amend conventional understandings of collective responsibility. The difficulty, as Margaret Thatcher's tenure of 10 Downing Street eventually revealed, is predicting where those boundaries lie.

Thatcher was often portrayed as placing little faith in the idea of full Cabinet participation in policy-making. Shortly before the 1979 election, she had announced that her government would 'not waste time having any internal arguments'. Her first Cabinet contained many

---

[36] The most accessible and informative guide is perhaps Hennessy (1986a) op cit.
[37] Quoted in Hennessy (1986a) op cit p 123.   [38] See generally Horne A (1987) *Macmillan 1957–1986*.

so-called 'wet' Ministers, who were not entirely supportive of her preferred economic policies. To some extent, these Ministers were simply bypassed. Peter Hennessy observes that the Thatcher Cabinet met far less frequently than its post-war predecessors, and also considered far fewer policy documents.[39] A further tactic which the new Prime Minister deployed to control policy-making more tightly was to have Ministers present their initial ideas to her and her personal advisers, rather than to the Cabinet or even to a Cabinet Committee. This occasionally proved problematic. The decision to withdraw union recognition from GCHQ workers was made by only five Ministers.[40] Wider consultation may have identified the constitutional implications that the decision subsequently proved to have.

After the 1983 election, when the Conservative majority increased to over 140 seats, Thatcher 'purged' her Cabinet in a manner almost as draconian as the 'night of the long knives', secure in the knowledge that she would be antagonising only a limited section of the parliamentary party. By the late 1980s some commentators were suggesting that she had effectively instituted a form of Presidential government.[41] This substantial shift in constitutional arrangements was achieved without any formal legal changes whatsoever. Peter Hennessy concluded his discussion of Thatcher's style of Cabinet government more cautiously:

> At worst she has put Cabinet government temporarily on ice. . . . the old model could, and probably will, be restored in the few minutes it takes a new Prime Minister to travel from Buckingham Palace to Downing Street.[42]

Events were subsequently to prove that the 'old model' had merely been chilled, rather than deep frozen, in the Thatcher years.

. . . And back again?

At the 1987 general election, the Conservative Party retained a Commons majority of over 100 seats. In such circumstances, one might have expected Thatcher's control of her third government to have become even more personalised in both style and substance. However, while that may indeed have been the Prime Minister's intention, her belief that she could amend still further the conventional notion of collective Cabinet government proved misplaced.

Nigel Lawson's resignation as Chancellor, on the grounds that the Prime Minister was simply ignoring his advice, can be bracketed with Heseltine's earlier suggestion that the Prime Minister was crossing conventional constitutional boundaries. Both resignations threatened the Prime Minister's authority within the Conservative Party, in that they offered figureheads around which dissident backbench opinion might coalesce. However their true significance was subsequently seen to lie in the individual contribution they made to a growing sense of collective unease within the parliamentary party. That unease was given an acute focus by the resignation of Sir Geoffrey Howe as Deputy Prime Minister in 1990, an event which had serious and immediate implications, both for Thatcher herself and the Prime Ministerial government thesis.

Howe resigned because he could no longer accept the Prime Minister's avowedly hostile attitude towards the EC (a matter explored in chapter eleven). In his resignation speech to the Commons,[43] Howe maintained that the Prime Minister had consistently and deliberately undermined the collective decisions which the Cabinet assumed it had reached on EC matters. Howe's account reinforced Michael Heseltine's earlier claims that Thatcher held conventional understandings as to the conduct of Cabinet business in some contempt, and the speech precipitated

---

[39] Hennessy (1986a) op cit ch 3.   [40] See 'III. Full reviewability—the *GCHQ* case (1983)', ch 4, pp 94–96.
[41] Doherty M (1988) 'Prime Ministerial power and ministerial responsibility in the Thatcher era' *Parliamentary Affairs* 49.   [42] (1986a) op cit p 122.
[43] *HCD* 13 November 1990 c 461; <http://www.publications.parliament.uk/pa/cm199091/cmhansrd/1990-11-13/Debate-1.html>.

Heseltine's challenge to Thatcher for leadership of the Conservative Party. That challenge led rapidly to Thatcher's resignation as party leader (and thence as Prime Minister) and her eventual replacement by John Major. Her fate would suggest that her preference for an increasingly Presidential style of government amounted (eventually) to a serious error of political judgement: even the most powerful of Prime Ministers, it seems, must retain the support of senior Ministers.

In reviewing Thatcher's resignation, it is difficult to be sure where the effective political power that removed her actually lay.[44] Was it in the combined resignations of Heseltine, Lawson, and Howe? Or with those remaining Cabinet Ministers who intimated to Thatcher that they would resign if she did not? If it was the latter, we might plausibly conclude that the convention of collective Cabinet government had merely been dormant during the 1980s, and simply required a sudden jolt to reawaken it. Or did that power lie with the many Conservative MPs who did not vote for Thatcher in the first round of the leadership election? If so, we see a further manifestation of the pre-eminence of party politics within the constitution. Or did the power lie (indirectly) in the electorate, who had indicated in many opinion polls that a Thatcher government could not hope to win another general election, and thereby frightened Conservative MPs in marginal seats into withdrawing support from their Prime Minister?

What is clear, however, is that Thatcher's successor, John Major, did adopt a more collective style of Cabinet government.[45] Michael Heseltine's return to Cabinet was one manifestation of this trend, as was Major's apparent concern to ensure that his ministerial team reflected the various factional groupings within his parliamentary party.

Recent history would suggest that Prime Ministerial styles—and the capacity of other Cabinet ministers to influence those styles—are not determined by party political allegiance. Tony Blair's premiership was characterised by one leading commentator as a 'command and control' approach to governance.[46] Hennessy cites as a particularly cogent illustration of this style the decision taken by Blair, and his Chancellor of the Exchequer, Gordon Brown, to relinquish governmental control of interest rate policy to the Bank of England. This extremely important economic policy decision was taken without any Cabinet discussion at all. Indeed, Hennessy notes, the decision was taken before the first Blair Cabinet had even met.[47] Cabinet meetings in the Blair government were of far shorter duration that under previous administrations, and were frequently conducted without the benefit (or perhaps, in the Prime Minister's view, the constraint) of a formal agenda.

IV. Individual ministerial responsibility

The second strand of the ministerial responsibility convention is individual ministerial responsibility, which supposedly identifies the situations in which Ministers should resign from government office. Its modern form has two parts. The first addresses the Minister's political or administrative competence; the second her personal morality.

Issues of competence

The competence rule originally held Ministers answerable to the Commons for every action undertaken by their departments' civil servants. Ministers took the credit when their officials got things right. Relatedly they took the blame when their staff got things wrong; if the error was sufficiently grave, a Minister would be expected to resign. A corollary of this proposition was that individual civil servants would not face parliamentary scrutiny or public criticism for

---

[44] For various perspectives see Brazier R (1991) 'The downfall of Margaret Thatcher' 54 *MLR* 471; Alderman and Carter op cit.   [45] Marshall G (1991) 'The end of Prime Ministerial government?' *Public Law* 1.
[46] Henessy P (2001) *The Prime Minister* ch 18.   [47] Ibid, at 480–481.

their own failures. This is not to say that incompetent civil servants would find their careers unaffected, but that sanctions attached to failure were a managerial matter resolved within the executive, not, as for a Minister, a political matter resolved within Parliament.

Even by the early 1800s, the idea that a Minister should be personally responsible for everything done in his department was barely credible. But the scale of government has grown so much since 1850 that it has become completely impracticable for a Minister to know everything that is being done by her department's civil servants. So the initial form of this supposed convention has altered. It now seems necessary that a Minister has been personally involved in a particular decision before she must resign.

This redefinition of conventional boundaries began in a series of late-nineteenth-century episodes,[48] and had hardened sufficiently to merit being described as a rule by the mid-1950s. The resignation of Sir Thomas Dugdale as Minister of Agriculture in 1954 following the Crichel Down controversy is a good illustration. Crichel Down involved a government department's failure to resell land to the family from whom it had been compulsorily purchased for military use just before World War II, in breach of assurances to that effect. Dugdale resigned when it became clear he had specific knowledge of his civil servants' activities, but had failed to appreciate the problematic nature of the action being undertaken.

Crichel Down's ramifications went beyond the issue of a Minister's personal culpability.[49] The episode triggered a crisis of confidence in the 'green light' variant of the rule of law which had increasingly structured the government process in the immediate post-war era. The response of the then Conservative government was to promote a wide-ranging 'judicialisation' of many aspects of the administrative process, entailing more tightly defined legislative rules for executive bodies to follow, the creation of quasi-judicial appeal tribunals for citizens dissatisfied with certain types of government decision, and somewhat easier access to judicial review. The change in emphasis was encapsulated in the Tribunals and Inquiries Act 1958, whose provisions corresponded closely to the theoretical perceptions of the rule of law advanced by analysts such as Harry Jones.[50]

For present purposes, Crichel Down's significance lies in the clear indication that a Minister need not resign in response to the failings of civil servants of which he was not, and could not reasonably be expected to have been aware, irrespective of the gravity of the consequences. This suggests resignation is more likely to be triggered by a failure of policy, rather than implementation, since the former remains more obviously the province of Ministers themselves.

James Callaghan's 1967 resignation as Chancellor from Harold Wilson's second Labour government was clearly precipitated by policy failure, even though the failure was determined largely by matters beyond his control. The government had struggled for some years to maintain sterling's dollar exchange rate at $2.80. After repeated rumours of devaluation, followed by repeated government denials of any such intention, sterling was devalued. As Chancellor, Callaghan was the chief architect of a manifestly unsuccessful economic strategy. Nevertheless the devaluation arguably owed far more to previous governments' refusal to acknowledge Britain's declining economic status than to Callaghan's errors per se.

A more pertinent, more recent, example is offered by Lord Carrington's resignation as Foreign Secretary following the Argentinean invasion of the Falkland Islands in 1982. Carrington considered he had underestimated the severity of the Argentinean threat, and thought it necessary that somebody accept responsibility for the governmental failure that the invasion betokened.

This redefinition of the convention to require personal knowledge is strengthened by instances when Ministers have not resigned following gross errors by their civil servants. In 1982, for example, a man named Michael Fagan breached security at Buckingham Palace

---

[48] See Finer S (1956) 'The individual responsibility of Ministers' *Public Administration* 377.

[49] Hamson C (1954) 'The real lesson of Crichel Down' *Public Administration* 383.

[50] See '*Jones*—the rule of law in the welfare state', ch 3, pp 51–52.

and wandered around unchallenged for hours before having a conversation with the Queen in her bedroom. William Whitelaw, the Home Secretary, was formally 'responsible' for the Metropolitan Police, who provided security at the Palace. Fagan's escapade revealed that security precautions were quite inadequate. Whitelaw's initial instinct was to go, but he was talked out of this by the Prime Minister. Her argument was firstly that no harm had befallen the Queen and, secondly, the Home Secretary could not be expected personally to supervise the minutiae of the Metropolitan Police's activities.

James Prior, Secretary of State for Northern Ireland, invoked a similar argument when thirty-eight IRA prisoners broke out of the Maze prison in 1983. Prior felt that convention would require his resignation only if the escape had resulted from a policy initiative he had taken—for example if he had given instructions to relax prison security measures. When an inquiry concluded that the escape resulted from management errors made by the prison governor, Prior decided not to resign. He sacked the prison governor instead.

The experience of one of Whitelaw's successors as Home Secretary, Kenneth Baker, suggests a Minister need not resign over such errors even when they happen with disquieting frequency. The most serious incident occurred in 1991, when several IRA prisoners escaped from Brixton prison, using a gun which had been smuggled into the gaol. The Chief Inspector of Prisons had reported some months earlier that security at Brixton was inadequate for high-risk prisoners. However the Home Office had neither stopped using Brixton for such detainees, nor improved its security facilities. One might have assumed this was a high level policy matter within the Home Secretary's personal sphere of responsibility. However, Mr Baker contended that responsibility lay with the prison governor.

Baker subsequently resigned from the government when offered the less important post of Welsh Secretary in 1992. But his failings in office continued to haunt him. In 1993, he achieved the unenviable distinction of being held by the House of Lords in *M v Home Office*[51] to have committed contempt of court by authorising the expulsion of a political refugee in defiance of a court order. We can only speculate as to whether Baker would have seen this as a resigning matter.[52] It seems possible that he would have argued that he was just following the advice of his departmental lawyers. If so, it becomes difficult to conceive of any decision-making error which would require a Minister's resignation.

The competence limb of the convention now seems to be in a fluid, or perhaps fragile, state of health. It may however be rash to conclude that it has now evolved to the point where only the most calamitous incompetence will necessitate resignation. We should perhaps focus our attention not simply on the scale of the mistake, but also on the strength or weakness of the Minister's position within the governing party.

Errors of judgement

The sanction of resignation seems to attach more firmly to Ministers making severe errors of judgement rather than policy or administrative mistakes. In recent times, the Westland Affair provides a graphic example of this convention. The then Trade Secretary, Leon Brittan, had authorised the leaking of a letter from the Solicitor-General criticising the constitutional propriety of Michael Heseltine's behaviour. This leak breached another convention—that Law Officers' advice to Ministers should remain confidential within the government. Although the Cabinet initially disclaimed knowledge of the leak's source, the Solicitor-General's threat to resign if a leak inquiry was not conducted led to the revelation that Brittan had condoned a decision by his Press Officer to release the letter. Facing such evidence, Brittan had no option

---

[51] [1994] 1 AC 377.

[52] He had declined to do so when held in contempt by the Court of Appeal; see Marshall G (1992) 'Ministerial responsibility, the Home Office, and Mr Baker' *Public Law* 7.

but to resign, albeit amid suspicions that his departure was intended to conceal the Prime Minister's reputed approval of the leak.[53]

Westland provided yet another illustration of ministerial responsibility when the Prime Minister, Margaret Thatcher, was subsequently compelled to defend her own role before the Commons in an emergency debate. The potential importance of debate in the house as a mechanism to control executive behaviour is revealed by Thatcher's own belief that a poor performance might result in her own resignation that evening. But an inept speech by Neil Kinnock, then Leader of the Opposition, enabled the Prime Minister successfully both to distance herself from the Westland intrigues and to downplay their constitutional importance.[54]

Westland is an unusually important episode in modern constitutional history. Other recent resignations over errors of judgement have been more mundane. Nicholas Ridley, for example, resigned as Secretary of State for Trade and Industry in 1990 after expressing hostile attitudes towards Germany in a press interview. Such sentiments were considered quite inappropriate for a Minister, given the closeness of Anglo-German relations within both the EEC and NATO. Similarly, in 1988, Edwina Currie, a junior Minister, left the government after alleging that almost all UK egg production was infected by salmonella. The statement's accuracy was questionable. Its devastating effect on British egg producers was not. Protracted vilification from the farming industry, and repeated media questioning of her abilities, persuaded Mrs Currie to resign. The episode need not have ended her ministerial career. She was invited to join the second Major administration, but declined to do so.

The Blair government did not escape such difficulties. Peter Mandelson, the Secretary of State for Trade and Industry, and Geoffrey Robinson, the Paymaster-General, both resigned from the government in 1999 when it transpired that Robinson had lent Mandelson some £370,000 to buy a house. Concealing the loan was manifestly an error of judgement on both men's part, given that the Department of Trade was conducting investigations into the running of companies with which Robinson was closely involved. Mandelson's 'punishment' was however a light one. He returned to the Cabinet less than a year later. Somewhat bizarrely, Mandelson was subsequently compelled by prime ministerial and backbench pressure to resign from the Cabinet a second time, following accusations that he had sought to assist the Indian billionaire Hinduja brothers to gain British citizenship in return for them making a substantial contribution to the government's ill-fated Millennium Dome project.[55]

It is difficult to extract a 'rule' (qua a predictable, binding behavioural code) from these or any other examples of resignation. Finer's celebrated study of the issue suggested party political expediency rather than moral principle was the critical factor in determining both whether a Minister should resign and her eventual fate.[56] It certainly appears that subsequent resignations have been intended to have symbolic rather than practical effects. Callaghan's aforementioned resignation as Chancellor in 1967 was essentially a sideways transfer, for he simply swapped offices with the Home Secretary, Roy Jenkins. One thus gains the impression that the reason for the resignation was an attempt to wipe the government's economic slate clean before the next general election. Such an interpretation reinforces Finer's earlier (1956) suggestion that a Minister's errors will not invariably precipitate resignation unless her conduct has alienated a substantial body of opinion within her own party.

That even a high level of support from one's party colleagues will not necessarily suffice to save a ministerial career is however shown by the resignation of the Liberal Democrat

---

[53] Brittan's case illustrates that resignation even on the grounds of gross personal culpability need not end a Minister's political career. Shortly after resigning, Brittan was appointed as an EEC Commissioner, a post of considerable political importance.　　[54] See Young H (1991) *One of us* pp 454–457; Clark op cit pp 132–135.

[55] Resignation led not to the end of Mandelson's political career, but to his appointment by Prime Minster Blair as an EC Commissioner. Indeed, Mandelson was once again reappointed to the Cabinet, by Blair's successor as Prime Minister, Gordon Brown.　　[56] (1956) op cit.

MP David Laws from the coalition government in 2010. Laws was an evidently very popular figure with both Liberal Democrat and Conservative MPs when it became known that he was embroiled in the expenses scandal. Laws had claimed some £40,000 in rent payments to which he was not entitled, given that his 'landlord' was his (male) partner. Laws had apparently decided not to reveal that fact to the Commons' authorities to conceal his sexual orientation from public view.[57] As well as feeling compelled to resign from the government, Laws was subsequently suspended from the Commons for seven days.

But it is not just professional or political misjudgement that can bring the convention of individual ministerial responsibility into play. Questions as to moral or personal conduct have also been a regular recent source of ministerial resignations. In these circumstances, questions of party solidarity seem less important.

Issues of morality

Few resignations have generated as much public curiosity as John Profumo's in 1963. Profumo, Minister of War in Macmillan's government, had an affair with a call girl, Christine Keeler. The liaison had obvious security implications, since Ms Keeler was simultaneously sleeping with a Russian Naval Attaché. The affair itself may have been enough to have forced Profumo from office. To choose a mistress who was also a lover of an enemy agent would presumably also have amounted to a gross error of judgement. But Profumo's greatest sin was to lie to the Commons when Richard Crossman raised the matter in the house. When the truth was subsequently revealed, Profumo had no choice but to resign.

The resignations of Lord Lambton and Earl Jellicoe in 1973 from Edward Heath's government also had salacious and security-related overtones. Both peers had been conducting relationships with prostitutes, and Lambton was also reputed to have been using illegal drugs. Neither Minister returned to the government. But sexual indiscretion need not always end a ministerial career. Cecil Parkinson resigned from the Cabinet in 1983 when it was disclosed that he had an affair with Sara Keays, who eventually bore his child. Parkinson's behaviour was considered the more reprehensible as he had allegedly promised Keays he would leave his wife, a promise on which he reneged. However after some years on the backbenches, Parkinson re-entered the Cabinet in 1987.

It is too soon to conclude that the morality rule now demands only that Ministers interrupt rather than abandon their career, although the Mellor and Yeo resignations suggest immediacy in resigning is a fast disappearing element of the convention. Mellor, then a married man with several young children, served in John Major's Cabinet. He attracted voluminous media publicity in 1992 following his affair with a young actress. There was no suggestion of any threat to national security. The episode did however cast doubt on his fitness for office, in the sense both of his personal integrity (or lack thereof) and allegations that he felt too 'knackered' to devote as much energy as previously to government responsibilities. Tim Yeo, a junior environment Minister, suffered similarly extensive and critical publicity over an affair with a young Conservative Party worker, by whom he fathered a child.[58] Both Ministers, evidently with Prime Ministerial support, clung to office for several months hoping to ride out the media storm. Mellor decided to resign only when his adultery and apparent exhaustion were coupled with the revelation that he had accepted gifts from a prominent associate of the Palestine Liberation Organization. Yeo did not resign until his local party members made it clear that they wished him to do so.

Most 'moral' resignations are triggered by the sexual 'misbehaviour' of male Ministers. The weight of evidence suggests there is a respected convention that such activities should lead to

---

[57] *Daily Telegraph* 29 May 2010.
[58] See Brazier R (1994) 'It is a constitutional issue: fitness for Ministerial office in the 1990s' *Public Law* 431.

resignation, albeit only temporarily. The reason behind the rule is less clear, given that Britain's contemporary social mores indicate that adultery is an activity in which many citizens engage. One suggestion would be that Ministers should set a shining moral example, and are unfit for office if they cannot meet such exacting standards. Another argument would be that resignation is a 'punishment' not for sexual immorality per se, but for the hypocrisy of participating in activities of which the government supposedly disapproves. This contention is especially persuasive in respect of Parkinson, Mellor, and Yeo; all broke their marriage vows while members of Conservative administrations which laid great stress on 'traditional' family values. That Prime Minister John Major was revealed after leaving office to have been conducting an adulterous affair while Prime Minister with one of his junior Ministers, Edwina Currie, lends further force to that contention.

Whether a Minister's personal life compromises his discharge of public duties is a large question. An answer is more easily found when one asks if individual ministerial responsibility could assume a legal basis. Designating behaviour as grossly immoral, or quite immoral, or not really immoral at all, is a highly value laden decision. One might assume that when opposition MPs express outrage at a Minister's misbehaviour they are more concerned with embarrassing the government than protecting the nation's moral fibre. The obvious political delicacy of these questions of ministerial morality provides a strong argument against having this aspect of the government process overseen by legal rules. It would be extremely contentious for a judge to say that a Minister was unfit for office because of the way he conducts his personal life.

That point seems equally applicable to questions of ministerial competence or misjudgement. There are no obvious criteria against which a court could measure a Minister's incompetence to decide if it was sufficiently grave to merit dismissal. Nor could a judge reach that conclusion without being accused of taking sides in what will invariably be a party political dispute.

This might indicate we could begin to construct some definition of conventions in terms of those parts of the constitution with which the courts could not interfere without jeopardising their supposedly impartial political status. This pushes us towards a suggestion that 'non-justiciability' may be an essential ingredient of conventional status. If a rule is important to the operation of the government process, and can be framed in a justiciable manner, the diluted Diceyan version of the rule of law to which the constitution adheres would suggest it should be given legal form. In the following sections we pursue this argument in greater depth.

To conclude our analysis of conventions, we return to the question of the relationship between convention, statute, and the common law—and find that it may be less straightforward than we might have thought.

V. Can conventions become laws? 2: Patriating the Canadian constitution

As chapter seven suggested in discussing the Lords' disinclination to invoke its delaying powers under the Parliament Act 1949, there may be areas of constitutional practice in which conventional reluctance to deploy legal authority eventually leads to the law shedding its political legitimacy. This chapter indicates that conventions might plausibly be seen as a melting pot in which differing concentrations of legal and political ingredients are constantly mixed. If so, we might ask if a diametrically opposite process to delegitimisation could occur? Might it ever be possible for conventions to have been respected for so long, become so precisely defined, and be so important, that they could 'crystallise' into laws?

One obvious way to give conventions legal effect is to enact them as statutes. The Parliament Acts are themselves an illustration of that process. A more radical proposition is that the courts can achieve that effect through the common law. *Crossman Diaries* suggests the courts can de facto do so by finding that the common law 'coincidentally' mirrors conventional understandings. This is not the same however, either in symbolic or practical terms, as de jure acknowledgement of crystallisation. Events in the early 1980s offered an opportunity for that constitutional development to occur.

Patriating the Canadian constitution

The country of Canada, as a legal entity, was created by the UK Parliament's British North America Act 1867. The Act gave Canada a federal structure, which, reflecting the USA's system, granted some powers to the national Parliament and government, and others to the (now) ten provincial governments and legislatures. However, while the USA's Constitution could be amended by its 'people', the British North America Act required 'Canada' to ask Westminster to enact amending legislation. In the 1931 Statute of Westminster, the UK Parliament recognised that several of its former colonies had de facto achieved the status of independent nations. Section 4 provided:

> No Act of Parliament of the United Kingdom passed after the commencement of this Act shall extend . . . to a Dominion as part of the law of that Dominion unless it is expressly declared in that Act that that Dominion has requested, and consented, to the enactment thereof.

Section 4's political consequence seemed to be that Parliament had sought to bind its successors never to legislate on Canadian issues unless requested to do so by 'Canada'. That consequence would of course be a legal impossibility if one adhered to orthodox notions of parliamentary sovereignty.[59] The 1931 Act also permitted the Canadian national Parliament to amend some parts of the Canadian constitution through domestic procedures. But 'Canada' was still obliged to place a Bill before the UK Parliament to amend the balance of power between the national and provincial spheres of government.

However, the Act did not specify what was meant by 'Canada'. Was this just the national Parliament, or the national government; or some or all of the Provinces as well; and/or the country's various racial and ethnic sub-groups? Nor did the Act say if there were circumstances in which the British Parliament might refuse to enact a measure passed from 'Canada'.

During the next fifty years, two conventions filled these legal gaps in the Canadian and UK constitutions. The first was that the Canadian national government would not send a Bill to Britain which altered the national/provincial division of power unless it enjoyed the support of all Provinces. The second was that the British Parliament would always enact Bills sent by the Canadian national government. The conventions arose (to adopt Asquith's typology) through 'tradition', 'unbroken practice' (several amendments had been effected in this way), and a lengthy passage of time (some fifty years). Their force was further strengthened by codification in a national government white paper published in the 1960s.

The reasons for the conventions are readily apparent. The first ensures that the federal nature of Canada's governmental system was safeguarded against unilateral amendment by the central legislature, or factional alteration by a majority or even minority of provincial governments. The particular form of federalism provided for by the allocation of powers between the national government and the provinces, in other words, sat atop Canada's hierarchy of constitutional principles. The second acknowledges that 'Canada' had achieved sufficient economic and political maturity to wield de facto, if not de jure control of its own constitutional destiny.

---

[59] As a matter of Canadian constitutional law however, one may safely assume that Canadian courts would not obey a subsequent British statute purporting to restore Parliament's previous authority. Nor, one assumes, would Parliament ever legislate in such a way. This 'transfer of sovereignty' to Canada was the source of Lord Sankey's oft-quoted dictum in *British Coal Corpn v R* [1935] AC 500 at 520, PC: 'It is doubtless true that the power of the [UK] Parliament to pass on its own initiative any legislation that it thought fit extending to Canada remains in theory unimpaired . . . But that is theory and bears no relation to realities'.

In the late 1970s, Pierre Trudeau's national government wished to 'patriate' the Canadian constitution—to make all amendments a matter solely of domestic law. The patriation Bill also contained proposals significantly to amend federal/provincial relations. The Bill provoked considerable controversy in Canada; its contents had been supported by only two provincial governments.[60] The Bill's opponents pursued two strategies to prevent its passage. The first attempted to convince the British Houses of Parliament that the Bill had not been sent by 'Canada', and should therefore not be enacted. The second involved litigation before the Canadian Supreme Court to establish firstly that the Canadian constitution recognised a convention that demanded unanimous provincial consent before the Bill could be sent to Westminster; and secondly that the Canadian courts could give that convention legal effect.

The opinion of the British House of Commons

The Canadian crisis presented Mr St John Stevas' newly invigorated Commons Select Committee system[61] with an opportunity to engage in a non-partisan investigation of constitutional principle and practice. The first Thatcher government had indicated that it had no power to look behind a Bill sent from the Canadian national government to examine the basis of consent which the measure had attracted. Any such Bill, would, per the second aforementioned convention, be introduced into Parliament. But as we have already established, there is no legal mechanism through which the three constituent parts of Parliament can be compelled to approve a Bill.[62] The question the Select Committee addressed was whether the Commons was morally or politically obliged simply to approve any Canadian Bill, or whether it should satisfy itself that the first of the aforementioned conventions (that the Bill enjoyed unanimous provincial support) had been satisfied. After taking evidence from many expert academic and political sources, the Committee produced a report rejecting the Trudeau government's presumption that Parliament should unquestioningly enact any Canadian Bill.[63] The Committee suggested that the Commons was under no conventional obligation to approve a Bill enjoying so little provincial support. But nor need it withhold approval until unanimous support was obtained. Rather, it concluded:

> All Canadians (and thus the governments of the provinces too) have, and always have had, a right to expect the UK Parliament to exercise its amending powers in a manner consistent with the federal nature of the Canadian constitutional system...[64]

This expectation could be met if Parliament required Canadian Bills to enjoy a 'substantial' degree of provincial consent. The Committee proposed a complex formula, relating to geographical location and population patterns to determine if substantial consent had been achieved. Without such consent, Parliament could properly refuse to enact a Canadian Bill.

The Select Committee report nevertheless left several important questions unanswered. For example, if the two houses approved the Bill, would British courts override traditional understandings as to parliamentary privilege and Art 9 of the Bill of Rights and prevent the Bill being sent for the Royal Assent in a manner reminiscent of the *Trethowan* scenario?[65] Equally fascinating was the question of whether, if the British courts refused to intervene, the Queen would breach the convention of acting on her Ministers' advice and withhold her assent. Or, assuming assent was given, would a British court disregard the enrolled Bill rule and refuse to apply the statute? No doubt to the regret of constitutional lawyers, most of these questions never required a concrete answer. The eventual solution to Canada's difficulties was provided by its own Supreme Court.

---

[60] For a detailed examination of the background see Romanov R, Whyte J, and Leeson H (1984) *Canada notwithstanding*, esp chs 3–4.

[61] For a detailed account of this stage of the episode see Romanov et al op cit ch 5.

[62] Although the Lords' objections could be by-passed by use of the Parliament Act 1949.

[63] House of Commons Foreign Affairs Committee (1981) *British North America Acts: the role of Parliament*.

[64] House of Commons Foreign Affairs Committee (1981) op cit at para 103.

[65] See '*A-G for New South Wales v Trethowan* (1931)', ch 2, pp 32–33.

The judgment of the Canadian Supreme Court

In *A-G of Manitoba v A-G of Canada*[66] the Canadian Supreme Court confirmed that there was a convention, established by years of practice and acknowledged by former federal governments, that the British Parliament should only be sent Bills supported by a substantial number of provinces. Two out of ten was not substantial. Consequently the federal government was breaching this constitutional convention. The reason for the convention was to ensure that 'Canada' retained its distinctively federal system of government.

Having recognised a convention of substantial provincial consent, the Court concluded that while a convention could be admissible as evidence in helping judges decide the correct legal response to a particular problem, it could not become a law, no matter how long it had been respected and no matter how important a principle it embodied. Conventions were not justiciable, and could not become so. 'Crystallisation' was a figment of overactive legal imaginations. The Supreme Court could not stop the Trudeau government sending the Bill to Britain.

But by laying such stress on the importance of the convention of substantial provincial consent, the Supreme Court completely undermined the legitimacy of the federal government's efforts to ignore the Provinces. It was not possible as a matter of morality or political practicality for the government to go ahead.[67] The initial Bill was therefore withdrawn, and the Trudeau government re-opened negotiations with the Provinces in order to produce a conventionally legitimate patriation proposal. A Bill was eventually produced which attracted the support of nine Provinces. This Bill was subsequently sent to the Westminster Parliament, where it was enacted as the Canada Act 1982.

We can only speculate as to how a British court would have viewed an 'Act' which seemed to alter Canadian law but did not contain any reference to Canadian consent to its terms. The Diceyan view would be that any such reference is unnecessary—for the courts to demand it would amount to recognition of 'manner and form' entrenchment as a valid principle of British constitutional law, and thereby create a new 'ultimate political fact'. The whole basis of the constitution would then be undermined; for if we accept one statute is 'special' because of the political substance of its subject matter, there is no logical barrier to prevent other 'special' statutes emerging, and indeed for different statutes to enjoy different degrees of 'specialness' according to the enacting Parliaments' and interpreting courts' perceptions of their political importance. As a political or moral principle, such a 'revolution' may be no bad thing: yet as a matter of orthodox legal theory, it would seem unachievable. But the question of whether constitutional lawyers should regard legal theory as more important than political practice is one which we might consider once more in the final section of this chapter.

VI. Turning convention into law: the 'Ponsonby rule' and the Constitutional Reform and Governance Act 2010

The suggestion made earlier that the primary function of conventions is to lend a 'democratic' character to the government's exercise of non-justiciable powers is well-illustrated by the emergence and consolidation of the so-called 'Ponsonby rule' in the early-twentieth century. As noted in chapter four, the government's power to make the United Kingdom a party to international law agreements derives from the personal prerogative powers of the Monarch. Thus far, even in the post-*GCHQ* era, the courts have not indicated that this power is one that might be subject to judicial review.[68] As a matter of legal theory therefore, it would have been entirely possible for a

---

[66] [1981] 1 SCR 753, sub nom *Reference re Amendment of Constitution of Canada (Nos 1, 2, 3)* 125 DLR (3d) 1. For other critiques from a British perspective see Turpin (1990) op cit pp 102–115; Allan T (1986) 'Law, convention, prerogative: reflections prompted by the Canadian constitutional case' *Cambridge LJ* 305.

[67] See Romanov et al op cit pp 183–190.   [68] 'Foreign Affairs?', ch 4, pp 98–99.

government to conclude treaties which are opposed by a majority of members of the Commons or Lords. Such action might lead to the government facing and losing a confidence vote, but there has traditionally been no legal barrier to the government acting in this way.

The 'Ponsonby rule' was introduced in the 1920s at the initiative of the then Foreign Office Minister in the first Labour government, Arthur Ponsonby. The purpose of the rule was to enable both houses to consider and form a view on the merits of any proposed treaty before it was ratified by the government.[69] A draft treaty would be formally laid before each house, with the government undertaking not to proceed to ratification for at least twenty-one days and to allow debate on the terms of the treaty if there was any significant demand to do so from members in either house. The rule appears to have been adhered to with sufficient consistency by governments of all parties to merit the description of being an established constitutional convention.[70]

In response at least in part to backbench pressure for the Commons to subject government behaviour to closer scrutiny which emerged during the latter parts of the Blair/Brown government era,[71] the Brown government invited Parliament to give the convention a statutory basis. The subsequently enacted Constitutional Reform and Governance Act 2010 made various provisions in this regard. At first glance, s 20 seems to place the government's treaty-making power under the control of each house:

20 Treaties to be laid before Parliament before ratification

(1) Subject to what follows, a treaty is not to be ratified unless—
   (a) a Minister of the Crown has laid before Parliament a copy of the treaty,
   (b) the treaty has been published in a way that a Minister of the Crown thinks appropriate, and
   (c) period A has expired without either House having resolved, within period A, that the treaty should not be ratified.
(2) Period A is the period of 21 sitting days beginning with the first sitting day after the date on which the requirement in subsection (1)(a) is met.

However s 20(4) allows the government to override a resolution of the House of Lords. More significantly, s 22 permits a Minister if she considers that 'exceptional circumstances' apply to a particular treaty, to by-pass the s 20 procedure altogether.

It is very difficult to envisage a situation in which a court would accept jurisdiction to assess if 'exceptional circumstances' did indeed exist. In contrast, a justiciable issue would presumably arise if a government which triggers the s 20 process then sought to ignore a Commons' resolution, since that issue is quite distinct from the substance of the treaty and/or whether it is desirable for the country to become a signatory to the treaty concerned. The resolution acquires statutory force by virtue of s 20(1)(c), and the first clause of s 20(1) is quite unambiguous (a treaty is not to be ratified) as to the consequences of such a resolution. As a matter of legal theory, one would expect the courts to resolve any such dispute in accordance with the *DeKayser/Laker/Fire Brigades Union* rationale.[72] Whether a court would be willing to do in the context of what would undoubtedly be an extremely volatile political situation is open to doubt. Section 20 is perhaps best seen as a statutory initiative operating in the realm of legitimacy rather than legality. In giving the Ponsonby rule a statutory base, Parliament has made it politically much more difficult for a government to depart from the moral purpose which the convention was intended to serve.

---

[69] <http://www.publications.parliament.uk/pa/ld200506/ldselect/ldconst/236/23612.htm>.

[70] See Barret J (2011) 'The United Kingdom and Parliamentary scrutiny of treaties: recent reforms' *International and Comparative Law Quarterly* 225, and the sources cited at fn 5 therein.

[71] 'Conclusion', ch 5, pp 133–135.

[72] See 'Extending *Laker: R v Secretary of State for the Home Department, ex p Fire Brigades Union*' (1995), ch 4, pp 89–90.

Conclusion—the conventional basis of parliamentary sovereignty?

It was suggested in chapters five to eight that the sovereignty of Parliament was de facto the sovereignty of whichever political faction controlled majority support in the Commons. Much of the argument advanced in this chapter has indicated that the concentration of effective political power is often very intense even within a political party; small groups of senior Ministers or even the Prime Minister alone may occasionally be, to all intents and purposes, 'elected dictators'.[73]

One might think that this type of institutional structure would be a recipe for oppressive, if not tyrannical law-making. But while we may question complacent claims that Britain's form of democracy is incapable of improvement, it is absurd to claim that our constitution has proven profoundly insensitive to its citizens' wishes. Yet this result has seemingly been achieved in spite of, rather than because of, the constitution's legal structure. This might prompt us to adopt the argument made by Geoffrey Marshall that:

> the most obvious and undisputed convention of the British constitutional system is that Parliament does not use its unlimited sovereign power of legislation in an oppressive or tyrannical way. That is a vague but clearly accepted conventional rule resting on the principle of constitutionalism and the rule of law.[74]

In the light of the analysis presented thus far in this book, we might qualify that assertion somewhat. Firstly we might wonder whether avoiding tyranny and oppression is a sufficiently ambitious target for a modern constitution to set itself? That a democratic constitution may avoid such gross evils does not mean that there is no scope for further improvement in the structure and powers of its governing process.

The second qualification relates to the nature of 'Parliament'. We have now established that legislative sovereignty is frequently de facto wielded by a small faction within a single political party that enjoys only minoritarian electoral support. In that context, we might plausibly conclude that the most important of all constitutional principles are that governing parties (and within them, Cabinets and Prime Ministers) resist the temptation to use Parliament's unfettered legal powers to enact policies intolerable to the majority of the electorate and, moreover, that the electoral majority is not predisposed to consent to laws which impinge substantially on the liberty of minority factions.

The American revolutionaries, and the constitutional architects of most other western democracies, did not have so optimistic a view of their legislators' or their citizenries' political culture. Indeed, Madison and Jefferson saw sound reasons for taking a particularly pessimistic view of the political morality of Britain's ruling elites. It was precisely because they considered that conventional constraints on governmental power could not be relied upon that the American framers erected so elaborate a system of procedural entrenchment of basic values to safeguard them against majoritarian intolerance or irrationality. The great paradox of British constitutional development is that its basic principle, the sovereignty of Parliament, was initially premised on a perceived need to protect fundamental values through an even more rigorous form of procedural entrenchment. In 1688, each faction of 'the people' (as then very narrowly defined) could veto legislation of which it disapproved. Yet now 'the people' comprise virtually the entire adult population and, in so far as the people are ridden by factions, their alliances derive from loyalties to a political party. If we transposed the 1688 revolutionaries' 'Three Estates of the Realm' methodology to contemporary British society, the tripartite

---

[73] The phrase is Lord Hailsham's, being the title of a lecture he delivered in 1976; Hailsham, Lord (1976) 'Elective dictatorship' *The Listener* (21 October) 496. The speech can be listened to at <http://www.bbc.co.uk/programmes/p00fr9gh/broadcasts>.   [74] Marshall G (1984) *Constitutional conventions* p 9.

Parliament in which each limb exercised veto powers would not be the Commons, Monarch, and Lords, but the Conservative, Labour, and Liberal Democrat Parties. Yet the constitution currently empowers a government to ignore rather than accommodate the wishes of those among the people who support opposition parties.

It would thus seem that the long-term legitimacy of our modern constitutional arrangements rests on the assumption that we have no need for a system of 'higher' or entrenched laws, protecting fundamental constitutional values against the whims of electoral majorities, because government and opposition parties are in broad agreement as to the basic political and moral principles which the constitution should express. In such circumstances, it would not greatly matter if one's preferred party lost a general election, for one could be sure that while the new government would pursue policies with which one disagreed, that disagreement would be of degree rather than kind. A political party might readily be expected to consent to laws that its supporters found unpalatable, but not intolerable. This may be because it accepts the intrinsic legitimacy of majoritarian law-making in respect of non-fundamental issues, and/or (more cynically) because it hopes to win the next general election and expects that its own consent to defeat would be reciprocated in respect of its own unpalatable laws by supporters of the previous government.

It is not possible in this book to delve in great detail into Britain's post-war political history. But at the risk of oversimplification, most commentators accept that the 1945–1975 period was marked by appreciable agreement between Labour and Conservative administrations about both the substance and the style of government.[75] The era is often referred as one of 'Butskellite' consensus. 'Butskell' is an amalgam of the surnames of R A Butler and Hugh Gaitskell, respectively leading figures in the Conservative and Labour Parties. Both men adhered to the Keynesian school of economic policy, which advocated extensive government interference in the economy to smooth out the peaks and troughs of the economic cycle. Butskellism embraced a commitment to maintaining full employment; to government ownership of public utilities such as rail, telecommunications, gas, water, electricity and coal; to an extensive network of social security benefits for the elderly and unemployed; and to a comprehensive, government controlled national health service.

The first Thatcher administration embraced quite different political values, and subscribed enthusiastically to the model of government advocated by Hayek's *Road to Serfdom*, and just as previous Labour governments had used their de facto control of Parliament's sovereignty to 'nationalise' private industries, so the first Thatcher government used its Commons majority to return them to the private sector. The Thatcher administrations regarded activities such as shipbuilding, and car and aerospace manufacturing as purely economic in nature, and thus no legitimate part of the government's responsibilities. Similarly, it was thought that services such as the telephone system, the railways, gas, electricity, and water provision were better run as profit-making private businesses rather than some form of public sector social service.

In addition, the Thatcher, Major, and Blair governments also believed that more overtly 'governmental' services should also be managed by private sector companies. Privatisation does not dilute the House of Commons' control over service management, but rather removes it altogether. In persuading Parliament to privatise formerly public services, the government effectively abolishes ministerial responsibility for matters which may have a significant impact on citizens' lives and welfare. If we regard the constitution as being concerned essentially with structuring both the substance and the processes of the relationship between a country's government and its citizens, it seems that a major part of the constitution has undergone substantial reform in the past thirty years. Chapter six used the changing historical role of the House of Lords as a vehicle to explore the notion of democracy as a matter of procedural politics—the co-equal legislative status of the upper house had become politically

[75] See George and Wilding op cit chs 3–4; Gamble (1981) op cit chs 3–4.

unacceptable because of the consolidation of a conventional principle that 'consent' to government demanded legislators be electorally accountable. But we should be wary, especially given the characteristics of our electoral system, of assuming that periodic voting for members of the Commons is a sufficient guarantor of a democratic constitution. Chapter ten returns to the idea that democracy may also be a matter of substantive politics, by focusing not on the House of Lords, but on the institution of local government, in exploring the importance of inter-party consensus to the legitimacy of our constitutional arrangements.

Suggested further reading

Academic and political commentary

BRAZIER R (1991) 'The downfall of Margaret Thatcher' 54 *MLR* 471

HENNESY P (1986) 'Helicopter crashes into cabinet: Prime Minister and constitution hurt' *Journal of Law and Society* 423

BRAZIER R (1994) 'It is a constitutional issue: fitness for Ministerial office in the 1990s' *Public Law* 431

NORTON P (1978) 'Government defeats in the House of Commons: myth and reality' *Public Law* 360

FINER S (1956) 'The individual responsibility of Ministers' *Public Administration* 377

ALLAN T (1986) 'Law, convention, prerogative: reflections prompted by the Canadian constitutional case' *Cambridge LJ* 305

BRAZIER R (1982) 'Choosing a Prime Minister' *Public Law* 395

Case law and legislation

Attorney-General v Jonathan Cape [1976] QB 752

A-G of Manitoba v A-G of Canada [1981] 1 SCR 753

Part Three
The Geographical Separation of Powers

Chapter 10

Local Government

We have thus far encountered federalism in several different forms. Chapter one noted the inter-relationship in the United States between the people, the national government, and the State governments. The geographical separation of powers between national and State government and the subordination of both spheres of governance to the sovereign power of 'the people'[1] were fundamental political principles underpinning the constitutional settlement, afforded explicit legal protection in the Constitution's text. Chapter nine discussed how the Canadian constitution developed a similarly profound attachment to a national/provincial division of powers as a matter of constitutional convention.

Both Canadian and American federalism rest on the moral premise that the constitutions of large, democratic nations should permit 'the people's' inevitably varying political sentiments to be given constant expression on matters of substantial political significance. Within the United States, the individual States may have quite different laws in place in respect of important as well as trivial political or moral issues.

---

[1] In the sense of the amendment process in Art 5.

A unitary state where legislators face periodic re-election may provide its people with the opportunity to consent in a *sequential* sense, at a national level, to different governmental philosophies. It may have supra-legislative constitutional provisions which ensure that opposition parties have realistic prospects of winning future general elections if they formulate attractive policies. But such societies cannot provide their people, as does the United States, with any legally constituent basis for the *simultaneous* co-existence of alternative governmental programmes.

It is also possible, in theory, for a unitary state with a legislature exercising sovereign powers on a bare majority basis to offer its people substantial sequential and simultaneous pluralism within the government process. This would require that whichever political faction controlled a central legislative majority regarded allowing legal effect to be given to differing political preferences in different parts of the country as a fundamental principle of constitutional morality. Such legislators would maintain a governmental system facilitating effective expression of divergent political opinion. The fewer the powers that the national legislature gave to the national government, and the more it allocated to locally elected bodies, the less unitary and thence more 'federal' or 'pluralist' the constitution's moral, functional basis would be. A country could be very federalist in functional terms, while formally being entirely unitary.

Post-revolutionary England adopted a constitutional structure recognising a unitary state, within which Parliament possessed total legislative competence. Presumptively therefore, any geographical division of governmental power within English (and later British) society could not have a constituent legal status; it could have only a moral (or, to use familiar terminology, conventional) basis.

That the American and English revolutionaries adopted (and that their successors subsequently maintained) such divergent approaches to the geographical separation of powers might suggest either or both of two things. Firstly, that British society did not then (and has not since) contained geographically based divisions of political sentiment among its people; and/or, secondly, that it has such divisions, and they have been respected by successive parliamentary majorities. The rest of this chapter explores those issues.

I. Localism, tradition, and the 'modernisation' of local government

'Localism' was an important element of seventeenth-century English political culture. By then, some areas could already claim several hundred years of self-government. Kingston-upon-Hull was recognised as a unit of local government by 1299, while the town of Beverley traces its local government history back to 1129.[2] Much local government activity was based on a fusion rather than separation of powers. Its origins frequently lay in the need to enforce and maintain law and order, so government officials frequently occupied posts which now appear as much judicial as executive in nature.[3] Indeed, the English '*common law*' emerged from efforts by successive monarchs to impose uniform legal principles on the many divergent inferior jurisdictions which flourished in England since the Middle Ages.[4]

The twin socio-economic forces of urbanisation and industrialisation[5] placed increasing demands on government from 1750 onwards, particularly regarding maintaining public health and law and order, and providing transport infrastructure. Initially however, Parliament did

---

[2] Elcock H (2nd edn, 1986) *Local government* ch 1.
[3] See Jennings I (4th edn, 1960) *Principles of local government law* ch 2.   [4] Plucknett (1960) op cit ch 3.
[5] See Loughlin M (1985) 'Municipal socialism in a unitary state', in McAuslan and McEldowney op cit; (1986) *Local government in the modern state* ch 1.

not address these pressures systematically. Rather, it created ad hoc units of local government in response to perceived social needs in particular areas. Often these government bodies had only one responsibility: for poor relief, or sewerage works, for example. Some, but not all of these office holders were elected (and electorates were then extremely small and unrepresentative of local populations). Most were appointed by central government, which had often delegated that responsibility to powerful locally based politicians. In terms both of the type of powers that its office holders exercised, and the way that they were chosen, local government at this time might more appropriately be described as a form of 'magistracy' rather than of representative democracy.

The preponderance of single function authorities produced a very complex governmental structure. As well as presenting difficulties in co-ordinating service provision, the profusion of small single issue bodies prevented local government deriving the advantages of economies of scale, and offered many opportunities for corruption and patronage in allocating offices and the performance of public duties. It was not a system well-suited to the social, economic, and political demands of a country in the throes of the world's first industrial revolution.

The Municipal Corporations Act 1835

Following the passage of the 1832 Great Reform Act, the Whigs (Liberals), then led by Lord Melbourne, promised further reform of the country's governmental structures, this time at the local level. Such radicalism triggered one of the last exercises of explicitly partisan monarchical intervention in the political process. William IV dismissed Melbourne's government and dissolved Parliament in the hope that an election would produce a Tory majority. However the January 1835 election returned the Whigs (with Melbourne as Prime Minister with an adequate Commons majority). Melbourne resumed office only after having extracted a pledge of support from the King,[6] and immediately promoted a Bill to reform the country's system of sub-central government.

While the Bill's Commons passage was uneventful, it met determined opposition in the Lords. This is perhaps surprising, given the obvious 'defeat' that the Lords had suffered over the 1832 Great Reform Act. It seems more readily understandable, however, when one considers the Act's impact on aristocratic control over the country's governance. To some contemporary observers, it amounted to revolution:

> There never was such a coup as this Bill. . . . It marshalls all the middle classes in all the towns . . . in the ranks of reform: aye, and gives them monstrous power too. I consider it a much greater blow to Toryism than the Reform Bill itself.[7]

While the 1832 Act had cut a swathe through the foliage of the landed classes' political influence, the 1835 Bill promised to attack that influence at its roots: it signified that the twin economic forces of urbanisation and industrialisation had been joined by the political catalyst of increased pressure for the democratisation of the country's constitutional arrangements. The functionally haphazard, aristocratically dominated structure of sub-central government which then existed offended the emergent middle classes' attachment to the principles of both efficiency and representativeness in public affairs.

The Tories in the Lords campaigned vigorously against the Bill,[8] passing numerous wrecking amendments. The government offered no resistance, seemingly believing that if given enough legislative rope the Tory peers would hang themselves from the scaffold of reformist, middle class public opinion. One contemporary commentator suggested that the government was:

---

[6] Brock op cit p 317.   [7] See Turbeville (1958) op cit p 351; Brock op cit p 317.
[8] See generally Turbeville (1958) op cit pp 351–358.

content to exhibit its paltry numbers in the House of Lords in order that the world may see how essentially it is a Tory body, that it hardly fulfils the conditions of a great independent legislative assembly, but presents the appearance of a dominant party faction.[9]

As in 1832, the intransigence of reactionary Tory peers finally foundered on Peel's refusal to condone their obstruction of an elected government's policy. Shorn of lower house support, Tory peers subsequently contented themselves with fashioning amendments which the Whig government would accept. This was not however the end of the legal battle over the Act.

The courts as defenders of local democracy—the emergence of the 'fiduciary duty doctrine'

Prior to enactment of the legislation, the officials of several boroughs attempted to prevent corporation assets falling into the hands of the newly enfranchised middle classes by disposing of corporation property to themselves or their nominees. Once the Act came into force, the newly elected authorities (acting through the Attorney-General) sought recovery of the assets.

A-G v Aspinall[10] was the first of these cases. The application succeeded, the nub of the judgment being that the controllers of the corporation, whoever they might be, held its property on trust for their successors and that dispositions of such property; 'made collusively for less than full value' were unlawful.[11] Lord Cottenham CJ analysed the case by drawing an analogy from the law of trusts, in which a trustee holding financial resources on trust for a beneficiary is placed under an implied 'fiduciary duty' to exercise her management powers over the resources to the best advantage of the beneficiary:

> I cannot doubt that a clear trust was created by this Act for public, and therefore in the legal sense of the term, charitable purposes of all the property belonging to the corporation at the time of the passing of this Act; and that the corporation in its former state . . . were in the situation of trustees for these purposes . . . and subject to the general obligations and duties of persons in whom such property is vested.[12]

A clearer indication of what Lord Cottenham CJ had meant by 'collusive' in *Aspinall* was provided in *A-G v Wilson*.[13] The Mayor and Aldermen of the borough of Leeds had greeted the 1835 Bill with a resolution to the effect that:

> [T]his Court views with alarm the sweeping measure of corporation reform introduced into the House of Commons by Lord John Russell, as calculated to throw municipal government into the hands of political parties and religious sectaries, opposed to the best and most sacred institutions of the country.

The Mayor and Aldermen then transferred a substantial portion of the borough's assets to three of their number. On the basis of the evidence before the Court, Lord Cottenham CJ concluded that:

> The deed of the 30th May 1835 was avowedly made for the purpose of stripping the corporation of all its property before the bill then in Parliament could pass . . . These five defendants, being agents and trustees of the corporation funds, though the legal title was not vested in them, by an illegal exercise of the authority of the corporation, procured the funds to be diverted from their legal custody and purpose, and to be placed in other hands . . .[14]

These cases indicate that the fiduciary duty doctrine in relation to local authorities emerged within English law to deal with an extreme political problem; namely an attempt by appointed

---

[9] Quoted in Ibid, at 354.   [10] (1837) 40 ER 773, 2 My & Cr 613.   [11] (1837) 40 ER 773 at 777.
[12] Ibid.   [13] (1840) 41 ER 389.   [14] Ibid, at 398.

holders of public office to sabotage an Act of Parliament and to undermine the significance of the newly created local electoral process.

An incremental approach to reform

The 1835 legislation reformed only urban areas—the system of rural local government remained intact. Nor did the Act effect a significant transfer of powers to the new borough councils from existing single function bodies. Its importance lay rather in its recognition that councillors should hold office on the basis of periodic elections, and that their continued occupancy of that office should depend on their winning the consent of a local electorate whose right to vote was defined by a uniform, national franchise based on low levels of property ownership.[15]

Parliament nevertheless continued to create single issue bodies to address new social and economic problems at a local level. The Poor Law Amendment Act 1834 had vested responsibility for the administration of poor relief in local 'Boards of Guardians', rather than granting it to the soon to be reformed boroughs. Similarly, following acute public anxiety in the 1850s over the spread of cholera, Parliament created local 'Boards of Health', rather than bestow such powers on the boroughs. It was not until the 1870s that the legislature was ultimately convinced of the desirability of allocating this task to the boroughs.

By the 1880s, the boroughs' 'multi-functional'[16] nature was firmly established. In addition to their public health powers, they gained extensive responsibilities in the areas of housing provision and town planning. Relatedly, Parliament had in 1871 created a central government department, originally titled the Local Government Board, to co-ordinate and oversee local authority activities.[17]

The system of rural local government was not rationalised in the sense of becoming multi-functional and elected according to a uniform franchise until the enactment of the Local Government Act 1888. A county council for London was created in 1899. The 1902 Education Act further reinforced councils' multi-functional importance by transferring responsibility for state elementary schooling from the specialist school boards established in 1870 to the county councils and the larger boroughs.

During the next two decades, Parliament made further significant extensions to local government's responsibilities for administering the newly emergent welfare state. There were then some 1,500 units of elected, multi-functional local government. They were divided on the basis of powers as well as geography. Many authorities existed within a two-tier structure, in which different types of authority had different responsibilities.[18] Thus a county council, which provided education and social services throughout its area, might contain within its boundaries several borough councils, each controlling such issues as housing and town planning. The picture was further complicated by some areas which had only a single-tier structure; larger boroughs might be granted 'county borough status', and thereby take over the county's responsibilities within the borough's boundaries.

Given their profusion, there was no scope for local councils to exercise powers on a scale comparable to those possessed by the State governments of the United States, or the Canadian provinces. But this does not mean that their powers were politically insignificant. In a welfare

[15] The local electoral franchise was more expansive than its parliamentary counterpart. The property qualification was lower and women were enfranchised some years before being permitted to vote for members of the Commons.

[16] See Loughlin M (1994) 'The restructuring of central–local government relations', in Jowell and Oliver op cit.

[17] This role successively passed to the Ministry of Health, the Ministry of Housing and Local Government, and, from the 1970s onwards, the Department of the Environment (DoE). The relevant department is now the Department of Communities and Local Government.

[18] For more detail see Hampson W (2nd edn, 1991) *Local government and urban politics* pp 17–20.

state, citizens will be intimately and acutely affected by governmental decisions in such fields as education, housing, social services, and town planning. Moreover, the combined impact of these services would be sufficient to enable electors to express appreciably divergent opinions as to the precise content and conduct of citizen-government relations in their respective areas.

By 1920, the democratisation of British society was firmly established. Parliament had introduced a near universal franchise, and the legal reduction in the Lords' powers under the Parliament Act 1911 stressed the elected chamber's dominance in the legislative process. It was also the case that the 'people's' political allegiance was almost equally divided between the Conservative and Liberal/Labour parties. A powerful local government sector, enjoying appreciable independence from central control, would thus offer defeated voters the opportunity to see their preferred policies given some effect. If our concept of democracy rests on reasonably sophisticated notions of popular consent to government, it is of crucial importance to consider, as a matter both of law and of convention, the principles which structured the relationship between central government, local authorities, and the national and local electorates from the 1920s onwards.

II. Local government's constitutional status in the early-twentieth-century—law and convention

The sophisticated understanding of consent might provide us with (per Jennings) a 'reason' for parliamentary self-restraint in respect of local political pluralism. From this perspective, it makes little sense to search for conventional understandings of central/local relations prior to 1918. That date does offer, from a contemporary vantage point, the advantage of giving us (to borrow from Asquith) a sufficiently lengthy time span to scrutinise to see if any clear 'traditions and settled practices' have emerged.

Several strong presumptions as to the 'correct' allocation of power between central and local government were consolidated among politicians of all parties during World War II, when Britain was governed by a Conservative-Labour-Liberal coalition. The parliamentary roots of the Butskellite consensus are highly significant for consent-based theories of constitutional law, since Churchill's war-time administration is the only modern government which can plausibly be portrayed as commanding the level of popular support which, in democracies such as the United States, would be sufficient to redefine 'fundamental' constitutional values. The depth of the consensus between mainstream Conservative and Labour policies is well illustrated by Churchill's first Commons speech following his return as Prime Minister in 1951: 'What the nation needs is several years of quiet, steady administration, if only to allow the socialist [ie Labour government's] legislation to reach its full fruition'.[19]

The 'socialist legislation' to which Churchill referred had entailed significant transfers of formerly local responsibilities to newly created national bodies, especially in the fields of health care and the management of gas, water, and electricity supplies. In terms of the multiplicity of its functions, local government in the Butskellite era was thus less important than it had been immediately before the war. It was also subject to more central oversight, in so far as legislation increasingly contained explicit powers which would enable Ministers to interfere with or override council decisions in certain circumstances.[20] However in terms of the scale of its activities, local government had become more important than ever. Local responsibilities lay primarily in the fields of housing, education, land-use planning, and social work services.

---

[19] *HCD* 4 November 1951; quoted in Jenkins R (1994) 'Churchill: the government of 1951–1955' at p 497, in Blake R and Louis W (eds) *Churchill*.

[20] Hampson op cit ch 10; Buxton R (1971) *Local government* ch 5.

Given the substantive importance of such functions in a modern welfare state, their reservation to elected local government could be seen as a guarantor of political pluralism within the government process. Should the Labour, Liberal, or Conservative parties win control of councils endowed by Parliament with such significant responsibilities, they might reasonably assume that their respective political preferences would be implemented in some areas, irrespective of the outcome of general elections. This is not to suggest that local councils would enjoy complete independence in these spheres of activity, but rather that they would possess sufficient autonomy to exceed or modify centrally determined standards.[21]

There was a readily discernible party split along regional lines in general elections during the post-war era. Crudely stated, more electors in London, Wales, Scotland, and northern England consistently voted Labour rather than Conservative, and that tendency was reversed in the rest of southern England. Powerful, autonomous local councils would ensure that this geographically based divergence of opinion was constantly accommodated within the country's overall government structure. It is plausible to conclude that 'the people' in these regions would more readily consent to defeat at the national level if their respective political preferences influenced the government process on a significant, if limited scale in their particular areas.

The Butskellite view of government also acknowledged reasons of a less profoundly 'constitutional' nature for preserving a powerful and vibrant local government sector.[22] The first might be called the 'local knowledge' factor. This argument assumes that one will improve the efficiency of service provision if it is entrusted to an organisation with intimate knowledge of local social and economic conditions, especially if one is dealing with a package of services where trade-offs need to be made between the resources each is allocated.

A second justification falls under the heading of political education. Councils can serve as training grounds for politicians before they move on to central government. In another sense, local government's role as a political educator draws more people into the government process, thereby making them aware of their rights and responsibilities as citizens. This can be achieved by becoming a councillor, getting involved with local pressure groups, or even individual lobbying over such issues as school closures or housing repairs.

A third justification sees local government as a vehicle for experimental social policies. The sheer diversity of political opinion to which local councils offer expression makes it likely that some authorities will formulate innovative policies. Relatedly, the small geographical scope of any such authority's jurisdiction offers a guarantee of damage limitation if experimental policies prove unsuccessful.

Broadly stated, this Butskellite perception of local government suggests that there is more to the concept of 'democracy' in a modern multi-party state than a five-yearly stroll to the ballot box to express a preference concerning the party composition of national government. Rather, it indicates that democracy in post-war Britain was widely perceived as a perpetual and multi-faceted process, within which various sub-groups of 'the people' would push and pull 'government' at all levels in contradictory directions, and to which a geographical separation of powers could make a vital contribution.

The physical boundaries of local authorities

In terms of their physical boundaries, no less than in respect of their powers, local authorities have not enjoyed a sacrosanct, conventional status in the modern era. The Macmillan government had persuaded Parliament to create a Local Government Boundary Commission in

---

[21] See especially Griffith J (1966) *Central departments and local authorities* ch 1.
[22] See Sharpe J (1970) 'Theories and value of local government' *Political Studies* 153.

1958, which exercised powers analogous to those of its parliamentary namesake.[23] Boundary redrawing had previously been undertaken on an ad hoc basis, a process clearly vulnerable to accusations of political bias. Macmillan's initiative lent the issue a consensual rather than factional character.

However, the Commission was abolished during Harold Wilson's first administration. Wilson established a Royal Commission (the Redcliffe-Maud Commission) to review the structure of local government in England. Richard Crossman, then Minister of Local Government, was largely responsible for determining the Commission's personnel and terms of reference.[24]

Redcliffe-Maud recommended radical reforms. It proposed as a first principle that England should contain just fifty-eight local councils, each exercising all the powers formerly divided between counties, county boroughs, and boroughs. A two-tier system would be retained only in London and several other large conurbations. The Commission also advocated the creation of eight 'provinces', whose governments (indirectly elected from the other local authorities) would exercise broad, strategic economic planning powers.

Redcliffe-Maud suggested that these reforms would eliminate conflict and confusion between different types of authorities with geographically overlapping responsibilities, heighten people's awareness of which government body was responsible for local service provision, and by enhancing both the geographical size and range of powers each council wielded significantly increase the political importance of local government. Had they been implemented, the proposals would have lent the overall structure of English government a distinctly more 'federal' character.

The Labour and Conservative parties were divided on the merits of the Redcliffe-Maud proposals, although both rejected the proposal for provincial government. Labour's initial Bill watered down the proposals significantly, although it did not reject in principle the extension of single-tier local government. However the Wilson government lost office in the 1970 general election before its measures could be enacted. The Heath government, in contrast, while accepting that England contained too many small authorities, remained attached to the multi-tier principle. The Local Government Act 1972 (which came into force in 1974) abolished many of the 1,500 or so small councils which then existed, and merged them into larger units. The 'larger units' were still however numerous and therefore often quite small. In 1974 there were forty-seven county councils in England and Wales, thirty-six metropolitan district councils, and 333 district councils.[25] Only the metropolitan districts were single-tier authorities in the sense envisaged by Redcliffe-Maud and apparently preferred by the Labour Party. The Bill had been appreciably amended, at least in matters of detail, during its passage, when the government accepted that its original proposals should be adjusted to accommodate local sensitivities.[26] The Bill was nevertheless opposed at second reading by both the Labour and Liberal parties.

The size and range of powers exercised by local councils has obvious implications for the sector's efficacy as a representative of divergent political opinion. The larger a council, and the more extensive its powers, the greater scope it possesses to act as a meaningful 'alternative' to central government for a local electorate which opposes the party commanding a Commons majority. Neither the Conservative nor Labour parties during the Butskellite era saw any merit in creating a conventionally federal model (in the US or Canadian sense) of central/local

---

[23] Local Government Act 1958. See Jennings (1960) op cit pp 88–94.

[24] Crossman's *Diaries* suggest that his zeal for 'modernisation' in this process did not always override his concern with party political electoral advantage: op cit p 201.

[25] For a helpful explanation (and even more helpful maps) of the eventual structure see Hampson op cit ch 2.

[26] See Burton I and Drewry G (1972) 'Public legislation a survey of the session 1971–1972' *Parliamentary Affairs* 145.

relations; councils remained too small, too numerous and too functionally heterogeneous for that argument to have any force. But this is not to say either that local authorities therefore lacked a significant degree of political autonomy, or that the British constitution was insensitive to the pluralist nature of its people's political beliefs. Before introducing its Bill, the Heath government had stated that:

> A vigorous local democracy means that authorities must be given real functions—with powers of decision and the ability to take action without being subjected to excessive regulation by central government through financial or other controls . . . [A]bove all else, a genuine local democracy implies that decisions should be taken—and should be seen to be taken—as locally as possible.[27]

The following pages address the extent to which such rhetoric reflected the realities of central/local relations.

III. Taxation and representation: the fiscal autonomy of local government

There is a close connection between fiscal and political autonomy within the 'government' process. The notion of 'government' carries within it the idea that elected representatives have the power to raise sufficient revenue to put the policies preferred by their electorate into practice: such limits as were imposed on this power would be a purely political matter regulated by the electoral process. An elected body whose revenue and expenditure was determined entirely by another government organisation would not in any meaningful sense be a 'government' at all, but would be merely an administering agency doing the bidding of its fiscal master. This point illustrates a proposition of general applicability to the British constitution in the modern era; that the more fiscal autonomy the council sector possessed, the greater its capacity to express pluralist political sentiment, and hence the more 'governmental' and less 'administrative' its constitutional role.

The multi-functional, elected local authorities with which Britain entered the modern era derived their funding from three sources. The first was grants from central government. The second was income from trading operations, especially rents from council houses. The third was a locally levied property tax, colloquially known as 'the rates', paid by local businesses and householders.

As Table 10.1 suggests, the trend during the twentieth century until 1980 was for an increasingly larger part of local government's income to be central government grant. By the mid-1970s over 40% of a council's income came from grants; barely 25% derived from the rates.

One reason for this heavy financial input from central government lay in the need to avoid massive inequality in service provision between various councils. Local authorities obviously cover very different areas. There can be significant discrepancies both in their wealth and their needs for welfare services. In general, poorer areas will need more services but have less capacity to pay for them than more affluent regions. Central grants were allocated according to various complex formulae which tried to take these factors into account—in effect the process involved a transfer of wealth from richer to poorer areas to enable all councils to meet minimum standards of service provision.

But while greater central funding may enhance equality, it threatens local authorities' political independence from central government. If a council could levy and spend only the funds which central government provided, the local electoral process would be a mere charade; the constitution might just as well provide for a local office of a central government department to

---

[27] DoE (1971) *Local government in England* p 6.

Table 10.1 Sources of local authority income 1945–1970

Year	Income (£m)	Rates %	Grants %	Trading operations %
1950	966	34	34	32
1955	1415	33	36	31
1960	2182	33	37	30
1966	3767	33	38	29
1970	5511	31	40	29

Source: Extracted from data in Layfield/DoE (1976) *Local government finance.*

administer whatever services central government wished to offer, and abolish local elections altogether.

Several steps were taken to reduce this risk. From the 1950s onwards,[28] central grants were paid in a 'block', rather than being earmarked for specific services. This permitted councils to prioritise expenditure on different activities according to their particular political preferences. More significant was the apparent existence of a conventional rule that central government would not use statute to limit the revenue that local authorities raised through the rates. The question of local taxation levels was presumed to be a matter for a council and its electors. If rates were too high, the appropriate means to reduce them was for local electors to vote the party controlling the council out of office, and replace it with a party committed to lower levels of expenditure on local services. Central government might request an authority to keep its rates within certain limits; it might negotiate about total spending plans and the amounts allocated to particular services; it might even threaten to reduce the grants it provided; but it did not ask Parliament to place legal limits on councils' tax levying 'independence'.

The significance of Parliament's conventional self-restraint on the question of local taxation was forcefully stressed by Jennings in 1960:

> Local authorities are elected by the people of the area not to carry out as agents of the central government the policy of that government, but to carry out the policy of the electors of the area. The furtherance of that policy needs expenditure, and for the expenditure and the means of meeting it the local authority is again responsible, not to the central government . . . but to the electors. . . . The importance of this principle cannot be overestimated. . . . so long as the rating power is independent of [central government] control, local government as a whole must be, to a large extent, independent.[29]

One must beware of exaggerating this degree of 'independence'. Indeed, independence is perhaps an inappropriate word to use here. 'Autonomy' may be a better term to describe local government's constitutional relationship vis-à-vis central government, given that so substantial a proportion of its financial resources derived from central grants. But 'autonomy' is a complicated concept. Its extent may depend as much on precisely how a council is permitted to spend its resources as on the amount of revenue itself. To explore this issue, we must examine the legal framework regulating council behaviour in rather more detail.

IV. The role of the judiciary

Councils are statutory creations, susceptible to judicial review to ensure that the powers that Parliament has granted them are not exceeded. However the absence of explicit legal limits on

---

[28] Loughlin (1994) op cit.   [29] (1960) op cit pp 184–186.

a council's rate levying power typified a general trend in legislation defining local government powers before 1980. Many local government statutes were drafted in very loose language, reflecting the fact that Parliament accepted both the need for local variation in service provision, and the competence of elected councillors to reach those exact decisions.

Consequently, we can find several important cases which suggest that the courts might be reluctant to apply the ultra vires doctrine to councils acting under loosely drafted statutes. In *Kruse v Johnson*,[30] the local authority had passed a bye-law[31] making it an offence to play an instrument on the highway within fifty yards of a dwelling house if asked to stop by an occupant or constable. The bye-law apparently expressed the wish of local electors to maintain peace and quiet in their neighbourhoods. Kruse was charged with the offence, but raised in his defence the assertion that the bye-law was invalid because it was 'unreasonable'. In addressing this question, the Court held that because councils were elected bodies accountable to their voters, bye-laws should be 'benevolently' interpreted. While a bye-law would be ultra vires if unreasonable, unreasonable bore a special meaning in this context. The substance of a decision would only be ultra vires if it was 'manifestly unjust; or contained elements of bad faith or fraud; or involved gratuitous and oppressive interference with citizens' rights'.[32]

This expansive concept of substantive reasonableness in relation to local authority discretion was reiterated in 1948 in *Associated Provincial Picture Houses Ltd v Wednesbury Corpn*, a case briefly noted in chapter three.[33] In *Wednesbury*, the Court of Appeal refused to interfere with a council decision to use its statutory power to license cinemas to prohibit children from attending shows on Sundays. The Court considered the policy was well within the range of opinions that reasonable people might hold. The courts should only invalidate the substance of such a decision if it was so grossly unreasonable that no reasonable person could have thought it within the powers conferred by the Act.

These two cases both seemed to accept that the courts should be slow to question the merits of council policy decisions. Their rationale appears to be that Parliament has entrusted these democratically elected bodies to govern their particular areas in certain fields. This process necessarily involves the making of value judgements about political issues, a task which, in accordance with traditional notions of the separation of powers, one might reasonably assume that politicians are better equipped to make than judges. But *Kruse* and *Wednesbury* co-existed with another line of cases in which judges placed more restrictive limits on a council's power to pursue its preferred policies. The best known is *Roberts v Hopwood*, which reached the House of Lords in 1925.

The 'fiduciary duty' doctrine revisited (and subverted?)

Poplar Council, a small inner-London authority, was controlled by a radical faction of the Labour Party in the 1920s. The councillors had an uneasy relationship with central government over their social policies. This conflict came to a head when the council decided to pay all its employees a flat rate wage much higher than that offered for similar private sector jobs or by many other local authorities.[34]

Section 62 of the Metropolis Management Act 1855 empowered the council to pay its employees 'such wages as it thinks fit'. The council assumed this meant either that there were no limits on its discretion, or at most, that its policy should be 'benevolently' interpreted per *Kruse*. This was the view taken by the Court of Appeal in *Roberts*.

---

[30] [1898] 2 QB 91.

[31] In effect a piece of delegated legislation whose geographical reach was confined within the council's boundaries.

[32] [1898] 2 QB 91 at 99.   [33] [1948] 1 KB 223.

[34] [1925] AC 578, HL. For background to the case see Keith-Lucas B (1962) 'Poplarism' *Public Law* 52; Jones G (1973) 'Herbert Morrison and Poplarism' *Public Law* 11.

However the House of Lords decided that the council's apparently unfettered statutory power to pay 'such wages as it thinks fit' was subject to a common law 'fiduciary duty' to local ratepayers, analogous to the duty a limited company owes to its shareholders, or trustees owe to the trust's beneficiaries. As noted earlier, this principle emerged within British constitutional law in order to protect the interests of the local population against the behaviour of electorally unaccountable municipal office holders. The origins of the principle seem to have been either overlooked or disregarded in the House of Lords. Neither *Aspinall* nor *Wilson* was cited in any of the opinions delivered by the Court. As construed by the House of Lords in *Roberts*, the fiduciary duty doctrine apparently required that local authorities be construed as businesses, operating on a profit and loss basis, rather than as governments which can redistribute wealth in whatever way attracts electoral support. The House of Lords characterised Poplar's policy as the pursuit of 'eccentric principles of socialist philanthropy'. Councillors should not allow their personal political or philosophical preferences to influence their policy choices.

This reasoning entirely ignores the argument that giving effect to local partisan political preferences is one of the main justifications for having elected sub-central government in a democratic unitary state. The decision attracted a stinging rebuke from Harold Laski, then a professor at the LSE:

> the council's theory of what is 'reasonable' in the exercise of discretion is, even though affirmed by its constituents, seemingly inadmissible if it does not square with the economic preconceptions of the House of Lords; it is, it appears, a function of the courts to protect the electorate from the consequences of its own ideas.[35]

Several Poplar councillors were gaoled for contempt of court after refusing to amend their policies.[36] However, central government (then Conservative-controlled) considered this an extreme sanction, and introduced legislation enabling councillors who approved unlawful expenditure to be personally surcharged and disqualified from office for five years.[37]

Conclusion

One might safely suggest that judicial supervision of council policy-making in the first half of the twentieth century displayed both very expansive and extraordinarily stunted[38] perceptions of local government's role in a modern, 'democratic' state. The next section adds more historical flesh to this analytical skeleton by examining how central government and judicial control of local authorities was exercised in the Butskellite era in respect of one of the most important areas of council activity: the provision of housing.

V. Council housing

By 1974, the council sector contained over six million properties and housed seventeen million people.[39] Council housing performed several governmental functions in the Butskellite era in addition to the obvious concern of providing reasonable quality, low-cost accommodation for individual families. The 1945 Labour government regarded an expanding council sector

---

[35] Laski H (1926) 'Judicial review of social policy in England' *Harvard LR* 832 at p 844. See Fennel P (1986) '*Roberts v Hopwood*: the rule against socialism' *JLS* 401.   [36] See Branson N (1979) *Poplarism*.

[37] Board of Guardians (Default) Act 1926; Audit (Local Authorities) Act 1927. For comment see Keith-Lucas op cit.

[38] This is perhaps best illustrated by Lord Sumner's comment in *Roberts* that the limits of a council's discretion was reached in such matters as deciding 'the necessity for a urinal, and the choice of its position'; [1925] AC 578 at 605, HL.

[39] See Bowley M (1985) *Housing and the state 1919–1945* ch 1; Merret S (1979) *State housing in Britain*; Malpass P and Murie A (1987) *Housing policy and practice* (1987) ch 2; Forrest R and Murie A (1988) *Selling the welfare state* ch 2.

as a useful tool for wealth redistribution. Conservative administrations were less attached to this principle, but shared enthusiasm for public housing's role in shaping the environment. And both parties found the labour intensive nature of house building a useful tool to regulate overall demand in the economy.

The public sector's style and scope varied considerably across the country. Local discretion over such macro-issues as stock size and design was not formally structured by tightly defined legislative rules;[40] decisions on such matters were largely determined by local election results. The absence of a precise legal framework might appear peculiar given council housing's important role in central government economic and land development policy. Legal compulsion was however largely unnecessary; councils formulated policies in close consultation with Ministers and civil servants at the Ministry of Housing and Local Government (MHLG) and (subsequently) the Department of the Environment (DoE), in a process which typified the consensual, negotiatory ethos informing central–local government relations between 1945–1970.

However, the 'national–local government system'[41] which dominated housing policy did not offer tenants any significant legal or political control over the management of their homes. Parliament's allocation of power to local authorities in this area was a paradigmatic example of 'green light theory', which afforded individual citizens few legal 'rights'. The Housing Act 1936 had simply placed the 'general management, regulation and control' of public housing within the discretion of the local authority with no discernible substantive or procedural constraints. With respect both to macro-issues such as the number and types of dwellings built, and to such micro-questions as allocation mechanisms, rent levels, maintenance standards, tenancy conditions, and management styles, council discretion was not closely regulated by statute.

Nor were the courts eager to subject local authorities' housing powers to the *Wednesbury* principles of substantive and procedural ultra vires. In *Shelley v LCC*,[42] the plaintiff was a tenant summarily served with an eviction notice. Shelley had no opportunity to argue against eviction, nor was evidence offered of any breach of the tenancy agreement. The council's decision would thus seem both procedurally and substantively ultra vires. The House of Lords however declined to intervene, asserting that housing authorities could 'pick and choose their tenants at will',[43] and evict them in similar fashion.

Both Parliament and the courts adopted a similarly non-directive role over the issue of the rents that councils charged. Section 83 of the Housing Act 1936 required that rents be 'reasonable'. This did not make it clear to what extent councils might 'subsidise' rents from local taxation. In *Belcher v Reading Corpn*,[44] the Court held that 'reasonableness' required councils to balance tenants' interests, (the presumed beneficiaries of public subsidy), with those of ratepayers (the supposed financiers of the subsidy). Romer J held that rent levels would be unreasonably high only if significantly more costly than similar private sector dwellings.[45] Tenants thus had no legal right to subsidised rents. *Belcher* nevertheless upheld local authorities' politically accepted role to use rent policies to *ameliorate* market forces—council house rents would be unreasonably low, and thus breach the council's fiduciary duty, only if *significantly* less expensive than comparable private dwellings. The decision thus took a more 'benevolent' view of local fiscal autonomy than *Roberts v Hopwood*.

---

[40] Although in the 1960s central government 'encouraged' councils to build particular types of dwelling by variations in the financial support offered; see Cullingworth J (1979) *Essays on housing policy* ch 1; Malpass and Murie op cit pp 78–81.

[41] See Loughlin (1985a) 'The restructuring of central–local government legal relations' *Local Government Studies* 59; Hampson op cit ch 9; and Rhodes R (1986) *The national world of local government*.

[42] [1949] AC 56.   [43] Ibid, at 66.

[44] [1950] Ch 380. See also *Summerfield v Hampstead Borough Council* [1957] 1 WLR 167; *Luby v Newcastle-under-Lyme Corpn* [1965] 1 QB 214, CA.   [45] [1950] Ch 380 at 392.

Litigation over council tenancies presented the courts both with a question of administrative law between an authority and its tenants, and a question of constitutional convention concerning local autonomy from central control. The 'hands-off' approach adopted by both Parliament and the courts towards public housing administration reflected the wider norms regulating central–local government relations between 1945 and 1975. Tightly drafted statutes or interventionist case law would have overridden the traditional expectation that councils should *govern* their local areas, rather than simply *administer* centrally defined services on an agency basis. The inference one might draw from this is that legalisation of council/tenant relations might have to await a redefinition of the constitutional relationship between central and local government. Such a redefinition appeared to occur in 1972.

The Housing Finance Act 1972

Notwithstanding its evident commitment to principles of local fiscal autonomy prior to introducing the Local Government Bill 1972 to the Commons, the Heath government adopted a more directive policy towards rental levels in the Housing Finance Act 1972. This legislation sought to raise council house rents to levels analogous to those in the private rented sector, while providing rent rebates to poorer tenants. For many councils, this required a substantial rent increase. The government had anticipated that many councils might not wish to implement this legislation; consequently, the Act also gave the DoE stringent enforcement powers against obstructive authorities.[46]

Several Labour-controlled councils threatened not to apply the Act. Only one authority eventually refused to do so. Clay Cross council in Derbyshire, whose eleven councillors were all Labour Party members, resolutely refused to raise rents.[47] DoE attempts to persuade the councillors to implement the Act failed, and they were subsequently surcharged and disqualified. At the subsequent election, local voters returned eleven new Labour councillors, all committed to maintaining the unlawful policy. The conflict was eventually resolved indirectly, in that Clay Cross was one of the many authorities merged into larger councils when the Local Government Act 1972 came into force in 1974.

The Clay Cross episode raises interesting questions both about the relationship between law and convention, and about the nature of the central–local government partnership convention itself. Clay Cross councillors clearly broke the law. In that legalistic sense, the council's behaviour was obviously unconstitutional. In terms of convention, the picture is less clear. The traditional approach to housing policy had been that local authorities should have considerable freedom to set rent levels. Thus the Clay Cross councillors considered the Housing Finance Act conventionally 'unconstitutional'. Relatedly, they regarded their own illegal refusal to implement the Act as entirely legitimate. The practical difficulty which this stance presented for them was of course that they could not draw on the Heath government's alleged breach of convention as a defence in legal actions arising from their own breach of the law.

Nor was it clear that convention was on the council's side. There is no great weight of historical practice supporting the notion that councils might legitimately defy the law so flagrantly. From the perspective of conventional practice, the 'constitutional' course of action for the council to follow would have been (reluctantly) to have enforced the Act and hope that the Heath government's breach of convention would lead voters to turn it out of office at the next general election.

---

[46] Which the courts proved reluctant to question; see *Asher v Secretary of State for the Environment* [1974] Ch 208, CA.

[47] Mitchell A (1974) 'Clay Cross' 45 *Political Quarterly* 165–175; Sklair L (1975) 'The struggle against the Housing Finance Act', in Miliband R and Smith J (eds) *Socialist Register*.

The objection to such a strategy is that it suggests the disputed policy is tolerable to the factions which oppose it, and thereby dilutes or diffuses popular antagonism to central government's preferences. One then faces the argument that had the American revolutionaries, or the 1832 electoral reformers, in this country adopted similarly quiescent tactics, they might not have achieved the results we would now regard as entirely justified. It may of course be argued that the issue of local electoral control of council house rents in 1972 is qualitatively distinct from the enfranchisement struggles of the 1830s: we might assume that 'democracy' within the British constitution is a concept that reached its fullest expression in 1930, when all adults became entitled to vote in parliamentary elections. From that perspective, there would be no justification for any defiance of any statute, for one would remain at liberty to argue and campaign for its repeal. This is a question to which we will return.

VI. From 'ambivalence' to 'authoritarianism'

It is difficult to draw firm conclusions about the constitutional position of local government in the period up to 1980. It is tempting simply to categorise central–local relations in the post-war era as a 'partnership' model,[48] in which governments of both parties adhered to a principle of constitutional morality which accepted that elected local authorities should enjoy appreciable political freedom, and should be persuaded rather than legally compelled to follow central government preferences on those occasions when central government regarded uniformity as desirable. From this viewpoint, we might plausibly conclude that the constitution did indeed by 1975 contain a convention that legislative majorities should generally tolerate a significant, geographically defined separation of powers—that parliamentary self-restraint in deference to the preservation of political pluralism had, as a matter of 'tradition and settled practice', become a matter of fundamental moral significance.

We should however recall that there was considerable consensus between the main political parties on major issues in this period. It is not politically intolerable from central government's perspective for Parliament to maintain a legal structure which allows local councils to pursue their own preferred policies over such important issues as housing if those policies diverge only mildly from central preferences. But in situations where that divergence was significant it is clear that central government would try to invoke formal legal powers in an attempt to force councils to comply with its wishes. Anthony Crosland, a member of Harold Wilson's Cabinets, offered a more cynical explanation of Ministers' attitudes towards local autonomy:

> On the one hand, they genuinely believe the ringing phrases they use about how local government should have more power and freedom. . . . On the other hand a Labour government hates it when Tory councils pursue education or housing policies of which it disapproves, and exactly the same is true of a Tory government with a Labour council. This ambivalence exists in everybody I know who is concerned with relations between central and local government.[49]

The 'ambivalence' adverted to by Crosland swung markedly in favour of greater central control by 1975. Both the Heath (Conservative) government in 1970 to 1974, and the Wilson and Callaghan's Labour administrations between 1974 and 1979 had been much concerned to control public expenditure in response to an economic crisis. Many areas of government activity, including local authority service provisions, were cut back. The Labour governments sought to control council expenditure through the negotiatory model of central–local relations.

---

[48] See Loughlin (1985a) op cit.
[49] Quoted in Bogdanor V (1976) 'Freedom in education' *Political Quarterly* 149, 156.

Authorities were requested or cajoled to reduce spending, but were not legally obliged to do so. Relatedly, the amount of tax revenue that a council raised was left to be determined at local elections.

Wilson's government had established a Committee of Inquiry (the Layfield Committee) to investigate local government finance. Layfield suggested that the issue raised profound questions about the nature of British democracy. Close central control over finance and meaningful political diversity could not co-exist. A choice as to which was the more important moral value was required. Layfield's preference was clear: '[T]he only way to sustain a vital local democracy is to enlarge the share of local taxation in total local revenue'.[50]

The Labour government appeared unwilling to accept the pluralist argument. The 1977 DoE policy paper, *Local government finance*, analysed local government's role in a way which relegated localised forms of democracy almost to an afterthought.[51] The 1979–1983 Conservative government also wished to reduce local authority spending, but for the Thatcher government tight control of local government expenditure was one part of a systematic attempt to restructure the constitution's conventional basis.

The first Thatcher administration rejected the Keynesian orthodoxies favoured by previous Labour and Conservative administrations. It adhered instead to a Hayekian philosophy stressing a much reduced social and economic role for state institutions.[52] This philosophy entailed substantial reductions in public expenditure on welfare services, areas where local authorities traditionally exercised significant responsibilities and enjoyed appreciable discretion. The Thatcher administration was also determined to impose its preferred moral principles on all levels of government.

This authoritarian outlook did not fit easily with the pluralist model of central–local relations. Nor did it reflect the wishes of even a small majority of the electorate. In the United Kingdom as a whole, the Thatcher government had the support of barely 33% of eligible voters. In Scotland, Wales, and northern England its levels of support were under 25%. The geographical fragmentation of support for Thatcherism was reinforced by the fact that many local authorities were controlled by opposition parties: the Conservatives suffered further considerable losses in the local government elections of 1980 and 1981.[53] But the limited nature of the 'consent' which 'Thatcherism' enjoyed did not persuade the government that it should moderate its wishes to impose its policies on the entire country. For local authorities, this absence of governmental self-restraint had profound consequences.

The legitimacy of the Thatcher government's plans lay partly in the argument that local authorities were not really 'democratic' institutions. Turnout for local elections since 1945 was low: it rarely exceeded 50%, and in 1975 fell below 33% in England. This compares unfavourably with turnout in general elections, which averaged 70%–80% since 1945.[54] The Thatcher administrations suggested these figures revealed a 'silent majority' of local electors who needed to be 'saved' by national government from the unrepresentative, extremist views of the small minority of political activists controlling local councils.[55] Given that the Thatcher governments had themselves attracted the support of barely one third of the national electorate, such arguments might not appear to withstand close scrutiny. The government nonetheless chose to 'protect' local people from elected councils by substantially reducing the powers that authorities could wield.

---

[50] Layfield/DoE (1976) *Report of the Committee of Enquiry into local government finance*, p 300 (Cmnd 6453).
[51] See para 2.3.   [52] See particularly Hall S (1983) 'The great moving right show', in Hall and Jacques op cit.
[53] See Butler D, Adonis A, and Travers T (1994) *Failure in British government: the politics of the poll tax*, p 29.
[54] For detailed figures see the first edition of this book at pp 428–429.
[55] See Jenkins J (1987) 'The green sheep in Colonel Gadaffi Drive' *New Society*, 9 January 1987.

VII. Financial 'reform' 1: grant penalties and ratecapping

The Local Government, Planning and Land Act 1980 introduced 'grant penalties'. The DoE calculated a total spending plan for each authority. Councils were not legally obliged to respect the spending target, but if expenditure exceeded the DoE's expenditure target, the DoE withdrew a specified amount of grant. This meant that ratepayers had to finance both 100% of extra expenditure and the resultant loss of grant.

Many councils nevertheless continued to spend at higher levels than the DoE wished. Consequently, the Local Government Finance Act 1982 increased the rate of grant withdrawal. From the government's perspective, this measure was little more successful than its predecessor. Some councils simply imposed ever-higher rates on local voters, and so received ever-lower central government grants, yet still attracted electoral approval.

Some penalised authorities also initiated judicial review proceedings to challenge expenditure targets. This strategy met with mixed results. In *R v Secretary of State for the Environment, ex p Hackney London Borough Council*,[56] the council argued that expenditure targets should be attainable; if the reductions could not be achieved without large cuts in services, surely the target must be substantively ultra vires? The Court refused to enter what it saw as essentially a political dispute between central and local government; this was evidently another non-justiciable issue. Subsequently, in *Nottinghamshire County Council v Secretary of State for the Environment*,[57] the House of Lords indicated that it had no wish to enter this political controversy. Lord Templeman observed that judicial review was not 'just a move in an interminable game of chess'; rather than commence litigation, councils should 'bite on the bullet' and govern their areas within whatever financial constraints the DoE thought appropriate. Notwithstanding the courts' reluctance to participate in this dispute, the DoE rapidly concluded that the grant penalties system was not very effective either in curbing council expenditure or in 'persuading' local electorates not to vote for high spending parties. Some councils overcame the threat of penalties by raising rates to such high levels that they no longer received any grant at all. That situation presumably enhances a council's accountability to its local electorate, given that voters would pay almost the entire cost of locally provided services. It would also seem to insulate a council from central government control; threats to withdraw grant will not work if councils receive no grant anyway. Thus the government introduced more direct methods to curb council expenditure.

Ratecapping

The post-revolutionary constitution seemed always to have harboured a conventional rule that Parliament would not impose direct legal limits on a council's power to raise revenue through the rates. The grant penalties legislation undermined that convention. In the Rates Act 1984, the Thatcher government cast it aside. The 1984 Act introduced the practice of 'ratecapping'. This simply permitted the DoE to impose a ceiling on the amount of rates revenue a council could raise. The new control was placed on income rather than expenditure. Twenty authorities were originally targeted for capping; eighteen were Labour controlled.

The 'democratic' implications of ratecapping were profound; local voters wishing to choose a council providing extensive services simply could not do so, even if they were prepared to finance such services through increased local taxation. They might vote for any party they

---

[56] (1985) *The Times*, 11 May, CA.   [57] [1986] AC 240, CA.

chose, but their chosen councillors could raise only that amount of revenue which central government deemed appropriate.[58]

The government had some difficulty in pushing the 1984 Act through Parliament. A few Conservative MPs, and rather more Conservative peers, felt the Act would take too much power away from local authorities and their voters. They shared the sentiments of opposition parties that local government's conventional status as an independent political organ was being too severely undermined. But with a Commons majority of 140, the government's problems in the lower house were only minor, particularly as ready resort was made to the guillotine to stifle debate.[59] In the Lords, opposition, cross-bench and some Conservative peers were sufficiently alarmed by the 1984 Bill's anti-pluralist implications to mount a determined amendment campaign, which on occasion reduced the government's majority to single figures.[60] The Bill nevertheless emerged virtually unscathed. The focus of political opposition then shifted to its implementation.

Some Labour councils attacked the Rates Act as constitutionally illegitimate, and resolved to refuse to apply it. They hoped that widespread defiance would trigger a constitutional crisis which would force the government to return to the conventional, fiscally pluralist model of central–local relations. As the deadline for compliance approached, however, support for illegal defiance melted away. Only two councils eventually refused to abide by the Act's provisions—the London borough of Lambeth and Liverpool city council.[61] Many Lambeth and Liverpool councillors were eventually surcharged and disqualified from office as a result of their non-compliance.

Given the utter inconsistency of the ratecapping principle with conventional understandings of local government's constitutional role, it is understandable that several authorities declined to take Lord Templeman's earlier advice to 'bite the bullet' of government decisions which denied their electorates the power to vote for local services to be administered as they preferred. Both Birmingham and Greenwich councils initiated successful judicial review proceedings against ratecapping in 1986.[62] But these proved short-lived successes. The government had by now tired of defending its policies in the courts; judicial review was a time-consuming process, in which favourable outcomes could apparently not be guaranteed. Consequently, the government began to respond to defeats in the courts by promoting retrospective legislation.

The highly unconventional constitutional character of retrospective legislation has already been adverted to.[63] The Thatcher government saw no impediment to using retrospective legislation to curb local government's financial independence; what had previously been regarded as a presumptively 'unconstitutional' exercise of Parliament's sovereign power, invoked on a cross-party basis in response to extraordinary situations, had become a routinised, partisan feature of government policy.

Grant penalties and ratecapping comprised the first two phases of the Thatcher governments' efforts to redefine conventional constitutional understandings about central–local financial relations. We address the third phase later in the chapter. Before doing so however, we devote some further attention to the courts' role in determining the limits of local authorities' political and economic autonomy.

---

[58] On the background to the Bill, and for a detailed description of its mechanics, see Jackman R (1984) 'The Rates Bill: a measure of desperation' *Political Quarterly* 161.   [59] See Loughlin (1994) op cit at n 49.

[60] See Welfare op cit.   [61] Butler, Adonis, and Travers op cit p 65.

[62] *R v Secretary of State for the Environment, ex p Birmingham City Council* (15 April 1986, unreported); *R v Secretary of State for the Environment, ex p Greenwich London Borough Council* (17 December 1986, unreported). Neither case is reported, but both are noted in Loughlin (1994) op cit.

[63] See 'VII. Retrospective law-making.' ch 3, pp 70–75.

VIII. Collective politics and individual rights: the judicial role

A notable consequence of the grant penalty and ratecapping policies was that it became a normal aspect of central–local relations for councils to challenge the legality of government action. Between 1945 and 1980 it was rare for disagreements between central and local government to be resolved in this way.[64] Disputes were generally settled through negotiations which eventually produced acceptable compromise. After 1980, such compromises proved less readily attainable. But the so-called 'juridification'[65] of the financial relationship between central and local government was not the only issue relating to local democracy in which the courts were embroiled.

'Fares fair': *Bromley London Borough Council v Greater London Council*

While most of the country had waited until the Local Government Act 1972 for its Victorian local government structures to be modernised, local government in London was overhauled in the mid-1960s. Many small councils were abolished, and new larger authorities created. The London county council was also replaced by a strategic council with limited functions for the entire capital. The 'Greater London Council' (GLC) assumed responsibility for, among other things, public transport systems, waste collection, major planning proposals, and housing provision. An elected 'Inner London Education Authority' (ILEA) was also created, with wide-ranging education functions. The GLC's creation was the result of a prolonged process of negotiation, initiated by a Royal Commission investigation. The Commission's proposals were subsequently introduced as a Bill and, following substantial amendment in response to the wishes of the opposition and various local authorities, enacted in 1965.[66]

The GLC's most noteworthy policy in the 1980s attempted to shift the burden of transport provision in London away from cars towards greater use of buses, tubes, and trains. The GLC's transport role was set out in the London (Transport) Act 1969, a statute introduced by Wilson's second Labour government. Section 1 required the GLC to provide an 'economic, efficient and integrated' transport system for Greater London. The Act did not give the GLC direct control of London's bus and underground networks; rather it created a body called the London Transport Executive (LTE) to co-ordinate and manage services. Following the 'green light' philosophy then prevailing in parliamentary circles, the 1969 Act did not specify precisely how the LTE should operate; but s 7 indicated that the LTE should as far as practicable avoid making a financial loss in successive years. The Act envisaged that the LTE and the GLC would work closely together, and in particular s 3 empowered the GLC to make grants to the LTE for 'any purpose'.

At this point we might ask what 'purposes' the 1969 Parliament intended London Transport to serve. From a social democratic perspective, the system might be seen as a social service, with operating losses subsidised by ratepayers. By encouraging people to use trains and buses rather than cars one presumably reduces traffic congestion and air pollution, speeds up journey times, reduces overcrowding on trains, and makes public transport a more pleasant and reliable way to travel to work and to leisure activities. An alternative, Hayekian view would see London Transport as a business like any other, providing a system that made an overall profit. If the LTE or GLC wanted to run loss-making routes, they would have to subsidise them through profits on other routes, not by taking subsidies from ratepayers.

---

[64] Loughlin (1985) op cit; (1994) op cit.   [65] The term is Martin Loughlin's; see (1985) op cit.
[66] See Hampson op cit, pp 23–26.

Scrutiny of the Act, and of *Hansard*, indicates that Wilson's government was unclear about its preferences. When introducing the Bill, the sponsoring Minister had said that:

> . . . the GLC might wish . . . the LTE to run services at a loss for social or planning reasons. It might wish to keep fares down at a time when costs are rising and there is no scope for economies. It is free to do so. But it has to bear the costs.[67]

But the Minister also stressed that the LTE should attempt to break even. Consequently, one could find neither a legislative nor governmental answer to the crucial question of whether the GLC could use s 3 to cancel out successive deficits the LTE might incur if it ran London Transport as a 'social service' rather than a 'business'.

In its manifesto for the 1981 GLC elections, Labour put forward a programme (called 'Fares Fair') to increase bus and tube services, and simultaneously cut fares by 25%. 'Fares Fair' would cost £120m per year; a sum comprising a £69m operating deficit, and a £50m loss in central government grant because the programme took the GLC over its expenditure target. The Labour group planned to raise this money by levying a special rate on all the London boroughs.

Labour won a majority in the GLC elections. A legal challenge to Fares Fair was immediately launched by the Conservative controlled Bromley council, a suburban London borough liable to pay the supplementary rate. The issue before the Court was straightforward: what had Parliament meant when it ordered the GLC to maintain 'economic, efficient and integrated' transport services? Was London Transport a social service, heavily subsidised by London ratepayers? Or a business, whose primary concern should be to avoid operating losses? Or was that choice a matter for the GLC's elected representatives to make?

The House of Lords decided unanimously against the GLC.[68] The majority held that s 1's reference to an 'economic' service required the GLC to ensure that the LTE ran on a 'break even' basis. The GLC could use s 3 to provide a subsidy to make up for unforeseen losses, or to compensate for exceptional circumstances, but it was not 'economic' deliberately to adopt a s 3 subsidy policy which underwrote a long-term operating deficit. Lord Diplock adopted a slightly different argument. He considered that the argument over the first component of the policy's cost, the £69m rating loss, was finely balanced. However he did not feel obliged to resolve this question, for the second element of the cost, the loss of £50m of government grant, clearly breached the council's fiduciary duty to its ratepayers.

The judgments obviously owe much to the *Roberts v Hopwood* misapplication of the fiduciary duty doctrine. As in *Roberts*, the House of Lords did not consider that electoral approval had any bearing on the policy's legality. There is a temptation to explain the outcome of *Bromley* simply in terms of judicial bias; the GLC lost because a conservative House of Lords did not approve of cheap bus fares. This rather simplistic political reductionism (which in effect alleges that the courts are constantly engaged in an anti-Labour conspiracy which subverts the sovereignty of Parliament, the separation of powers, and conventional models of central–local relations) has attracted some support from authoritative commentators.[69] The argument is difficult to sustain. In respect of *Bromley*, one cannot avoid the conclusion that Wilson's government presented Parliament with an ambiguous Bill, which neither house clarified. The Act's text lent itself to two irreconcilable interpretations; it is unsurprising that the judiciary favoured the more fiscally conservative meaning.

---

[67] *HCD* 17 December 1968 cc 1247–1248.   [68] [1983] 1 AC 768.

[69] See Griffith J (1985) 'Judicial decision-making in public law' *Public Law* 564; Pannick D (1984) 'The Law Lords and the needs of contemporary society' *Political Quarterly* 318; McAuslan P (1983) 'Administrative law, collective consumption and judicial policy' *MLR* 1.

Nevertheless, the re-emergence of the warped version of the fiduciary duty doctrine intensified the juridification process. Its high profile in *Bromley* led many councils routinely to seek counsel's opinions on the legality of their expenditure plans.[70] Yet it was not simply questions of fiscal autonomy that made local government such a significant area of constitutional controversy in the1980s.

IX. Institutional 'reform'; the abolition of the GLC and metropolitan counties

The Local Government Act 1985 was a straightforward measure to abolish the GLC. The commitment to do this was belatedly slipped into the Conservative Party's 1983 election manifesto by the Prime Minister.[71] The governmental investigations preceding the creation of the GLC had lasted several years and comprised several thousand pages of investigation and proposals. The DoE report recommending abolition, *Streamlining the cities*,[72] took two months to produce, spanned thirty-one pages, and involved no significant consultation with opposition parties, local authorities, or the people of London. Its recommendation was that the council should be abolished and its functions given to the London boroughs or boards appointed by central government. The GLC was simply presumed to be an unnecessary tier of government, which added to bureaucracy without producing any worthwhile benefits.[73]

The GLC campaigned skilfully against abolition. The campaign questioned the constitutional legitimacy of simply doing away with an elected local authority which represented over five million people, and on the technical efficiency of scrapping an authority which provided co-ordinated strategic services for one of the world's most important cities. The GLC attracted considerable public support. It also seemed that some Conservative MPs and many Conservative peers would vote against the government on this issue, as they had over ratecapping. The government's abolition timetable had two parts. The Local Government (Interim Provisions) Bill 1984 proposed that the GLC elections scheduled for May 1985 would be scrapped. Arrangements for transferring the GLC's powers to new bodies would not be effective until April 1986, and would be introduced in a subsequent Bill early in 1985. Parliament was thus being asked to approve the details of abolition before debating the merits of the central question. This procedural objection was compounded by the Bill's substantive effect. During the eleven-month gap between May 1985 and April 1986, the GLC's powers would be wielded by 'interim councils' based on the various London boroughs, which in effect would give the Conservative Party majority control of powers which the GLC's electorate had bestowed on the Labour Party.

The Lords inflicted a substantial defeat (191 votes to 143) on the government in Committee. The government then conceded that the existing GLC councillors could remain in office until the abolition in 1986.[74] The government did not however concede on the cancellation of the 1985 elections, presumably because it feared that London's voters might use it to signify massive popular disapproval of the abolition proposal. The Lords' stance did much to enhance its resurgent reputation; *The Times* hailed the government's defeat as 'a triumph for the principles of constitutionalism and specifically for the principle of a bicameral Parliament'.[75] Upper house opposition continued when the abolition Bill itself was debated. An amendment creating an

---

[70] Bridges L et al (1987) *Legality and local politics.*   [71] Butler, Adonis, and Travers op cit pp 37–39.

[72] (1983) (Cmnd 9063).

[73] For an analysis of the motives behind abolition see O'Leary B (1987) 'Why was the GLC abolished?' *International Journal of Urban and Regional Research* 192; (1987) 'British farce, French drama and tales of two cities' *Public Administration* 369.   [74] See Welfare op cit; Shell (1992) op cit pp 168–173.

[75] 30 June 1984; quoted in Shell (1992) op cit p 69.

elected 'co-ordinating authority' to supervise all of the GLC's former powers was lost by only seventeen votes.

That the Bill was ultimately enacted virtually unscathed illustrates the fragility of conventional constitutional principles when they are opposed by a determined central government with a large Commons majority. The geographical boundaries of local government have been restructured many times before. But in the modern era, the process has not been conducted in so pre-emptory a way, nor on the basis of substantive terms prompting so much party political dispute and public opposition, and not without the creation of a new elected body to assume the powers of the abolished authorities.

X. Privatising local government

The abolition of the capital city's elected council is perhaps the most graphic example of local government's declining constitutional significance since 1980. But it is merely one part of a more complex tapestry. The GLC abolition Bill, seen in conjunction with the previous reforms to local government finance, was described in 1984 as the 'most determined assault on local government autonomy in recent history'.[76] It is overly simplistic to suggest that this assault was 'anti-democratic' in nature. Rather it represented the triumph of a highly centralised, authoritarian perception of minoritarian democracy over a decentralised, consensual perception of pluralist democracy. This trend raises large questions as to the adequacy of Britain's contemporary constitutional arrangements; but before turning to that issue it is appropriate to examine several other legislative innovations enacted from the mid-1980s onwards.

The Widdicombe Report

The Widdicombe Committee of Inquiry into the Conduct of Local Authority Business,[77] was established by the DoE in 1985 following the GLC abolition imbroglio. The Committee's title perhaps hints at the kind of recommendations the government was hoping the report would produce—the concern apparently being more with 'business' than with 'government'. If so, the government was disappointed both by the Committee's investigations and its conclusions. Widdicombe identified an important role for party politics in the local government sector, and produced a package of recommendations which would seemingly have strengthened councils' capacities to pursue distinctive political agendas.[78]

The resultant legislation, the Local Government and Housing Act 1989,[79] was highly selective in the principles it accepted from the Widdicombe report. The DoE policy statement which preceded the Act announced that the reforms were intended 'to ensure that local democracy and local accountability are substantially strengthened'.[80] However, the government defined 'democracy' in terms which increased the likelihood that the outcome of locally based decision-making procedures would accord with central government preferences.

Thus the Act responded to the fact that many Labour councillors were the employees of other councils by prohibiting such 'twin-tracking', but refusing to accept that councillors should be paid for the tasks they performed. Relatedly, the Act created so-called 'politically

[76] Jackman op cit p 61.

[77] (1986) (Cmnd 9797). For comment see McAuslan P (1987) 'The Widdicombe Report: local government business or politics' *Public Law* 154.

[78] See Leach S (1989) 'Strengthening local democracy? the government's response to Widdicombe', in Stewart J and Stoker G (eds) *The future of local government.*

[79] See Ganz G (1990) 'The depoliticisation of local authorities: the Local Government and Housing Act 1989, Part I' *Public Law* 224.   [80] DoE (1988) *The conduct of local authority business* p v.

restricted' posts in local authorities. Citizens employed in such jobs were not permitted to engage in such political activities as holding office in a political party, canvassing at elections, or speaking or writing in public in a way that might affect support for a political party. The Act made several other significant intrusions into local authorities' internal management processes, often by simply making provision for the DoE to issue regulations to control particular aspects of council behaviour. The Act exemplifies, as McAuslan suggests, a perception of democracy in a unitary state in which 'in so far as local government has a role in the governance of the United Kingdom . . . it is to carry out and obey central government policies in the manner required by central government'.[81]

Forcing local government to conduct its activities along business lines is one method by which a government with a legislative majority can ensure that local electorates which prefer social democratic forms of government cannot vote for councils which can implement those principles. It is not however the only method. Rather than force elected councils to act like businesses, central government might simply decide to remove certain powers from the council sector altogether, and give them to individuals or bodies more likely to share central government's political predispositions. This following section examines how the Thatcher and Major governments applied this ideology to the management of council housing.

Housing—individuated and collective privatisation

A corollary of councils' traditional autonomy in housing management was that neither Parliament nor the courts granted tenants legally enforceable rights against their landlords over the way that their homes were managed. Many councils evidently thought that tenants' 'rights' were unnecessary, considering councils' 'democratic accountability . . . a sufficient safeguard against any abuses'.[82] But by 1975, it was widely accepted that council house management could often justifiably be accused of inefficiency and insensitivity to tenants' wishes.[83]

The Callaghan government's 1979 Housing Bill included a 'Tenant's Charter'. The Charter limited councils' eviction powers, forbade certain restrictive tenancy conditions, and would have required authorities to establish a Tenants' Committee which was to be consulted on all aspects of housing management, including allocation policies and rent levels. The Bill fell with the Labour government in 1979.

The Tenants' Charter subsequently promoted by the first Thatcher government, enacted in the Housing Act 1980, superficially resembled Labour's Bill. The new legislation added a 'right to buy' for existing tenants, and dropped the Tenants' Committees proposal. The 1980 Act fundamentally recast the legal basis of a council's relationship with its tenants. In granting tenants legally enforceable rights and significant security of tenure, the Act necessarily curtailed local authority autonomy in respect of its remaining tenants. But equally significantly the 'right to buy' provided a mechanism for tenants to become owners of their homes. The 'right to buy' entitled council tenants of three years standing to buy their home at a discount of 33% on its market value, with an extra 1% for each year of additional occupancy, to a 70% maximum. Over a million units were sold during the 1980s.

The right to buy was a controversial policy in 1980. Some Labour councils decided they did not want to apply it: several decided to make it difficult for tenants to become owner-occupiers.[84] The 1980 Act had given the DoE sweeping interventionist powers against authorities suspected of obstructing sales. Section 23 provided that where it appears, to the Minister,

---

[81] (1988) op cit pp 157–158.   [82] Cited in Laffin op cit, n 6, p 194.
[83] See eg Cullingworth op cit pp 38–47; Merret op cit, ch 8.
[84] Ascher K (1983) 'The politics of administrative opposition—council house sales and the right to buy' *Local Government Studies* 12.

that the tenants are experiencing difficulty in buying their houses, the Minister may send in centrally appointed Housing Commissioners to take over the sales process.

Following complaints from tenants in Norwich, the Minister invoked s 23. The council challenged the use of this power, arguing it had deployed staff on other responsibilities which it was obliged to undertake and so there was nothing 'unreasonable' about the delays that tenants experienced. In *Norwich City Council v Secretary of State for the Environment*, the Court of Appeal characterised s 23 as: 'draconian . . . without precedent in legislation of this nature'.[85] But whether the council's action was reasonable was irrelevant. The person whose conduct was in question was the Minister—was his intervention *Wednesbury* unreasonable? As no sales at all had been completed in Norwich in the first seven months of the Act being in force it would seem difficult to categorise his action in that way. His intervention was clearly a 'legal' exercise of executive power. Whether s 23 was itself a 'legitimate' exercise of legislative power is a different and more difficult question.

The right to buy enabled many less wealthy householders to become owners, and therefore to benefit from long-term increases in property values and to escape from a restrictive landlord–tenant relationship. The policy's full impact on local government's role as a housing provider is, however, only evident when one also considers central government policies towards the building of new council housing. The Thatcher administrations placed significant restrictions on new construction. Proceeds from the right to buy exceeded £9b by 1986. But councils were permitted to spend only a fraction of those receipts on new housing. Fewer council houses were built in the 1980s than in any decade since 1920. While over one million units were sold, only 330,000 were built.[86]

'Opting out' and Housing Action Trusts

Nevertheless, over 20% of the population still lived in council houses in 1988. Few of these tenants could afford to buy their homes. Consequently the DoE sought other methods further to reduce the local authority's landlord role. The Housing Act 1988 empowered tenants to 'opt out' of local authority control and 'vote' for a new, government approved landlord. Early votes indicated little tenant support for wholesale privatisation. This perhaps suggests that tenants, if not central government, continued to see councils as legitimate and desirable providers of subsidised housing.

Part III of the 1988 Act also introduced the 'Housing Action Trust' (HAT). HATs were government appointed boards which assumed control of public housing and land use planning in government designated inner-city areas. HATs were to act as temporary landlords, responsible for upgrading the housing and thereafter selling it, either to current occupants or new private sector landlords. HATs attracted little support from council tenants initially. Seven estates were originally targeted for HAT schemes. By late 1990, none had voted to leave council control. Several estates subsequently chose HAT status in 1991. This was perhaps not an entirely 'free' choice, in so far as prospective HATs were offered funds for refurbishment and redevelopment not available to local authorities.[87]

'Ring-fencing' housing revenue accounts

Legislative initiatives also reduced local authorities' traditionally loosely confined discretion to set rent levels. Significant reductions in DoE rent subsidies since 1980[88] compelled many councils to raise rents well above prevailing inflation rates. Councils' scope to subsidise rents

    [85] [1982] 1 All ER 737 at 748, per Kerr LJ. For an analysis of events see Murie and Maplass op cit pp 233–240.

    [86] See Loveland I (1992) 'Square pegs, round holes: the "right" to council housing in the post-war era' *Journal of Law and Society* 339.

    [87] Woodward R (1991) 'Mobilising opposition: the campaign against housing action trusts in Tower Hamlets' *Housing Studies* 44.   [88] Loughlin (1985) op cit p 104; Malpass and Murie op cit pp 110–113.

from their general revenue was obviously curbed by general DoE expenditure constraints during the 1980s. The Local Government and Housing Act 1989 reinforced this indirect pressure by 'ring fencing' councils' housing budgets. Local authorities could no longer use their general revenue for housing purposes; council stock would have to run on a 'break even' basis. Ring fencing provoked vigorous criticism from Labour and Conservative authorities. Many considered it an unwarranted, further limitation on council autonomy. Twenty authorities increased rents by over 30% in 1990, with Conservative controlled Canterbury DC and South Buckinghamshire DC levying 54% and 53% rises respectively.

Conclusion

The Thatcher and Major reforms to local authority housing provision system were concerned with curtailing ideological as well as fiscal pluralism, but it is frequently difficult to disentangle the two issues. The penultimate section of this chapter consequently returns to questions of local government finance, in discussing the rise and fall of the 'poll tax'.

XI. Financial 'reform' 2: the community charge

By 1980, the rates were seen by all political parties as having several defects. Since rates were levied on householders, many citizens were not legally obliged to pay them. Consequently many people were presumed to be immune from the financial consequences of voting for increased local authority spending. And since business ratepayers had no vote at all, their only way to register disapproval of council policies was to relocate—an often impractical option. A second flaw was that there was no direct link between the size of a rates bill and the services provided. Since rates were based primarily on property values, the amount a householder or business paid could depend more on the value of her house or shop than her council's spending plans. Thirdly, rates were not sensitively related to ability to pay. People could live in an expensive house but have only a limited income: the apocryphal little old lady living in her family home on a widow's pension is the obvious example. On the positive side, rates were easy to administer, and, since they were levied on properties not people, were difficult to evade. Rates reform was thus a popular but impractical political slogan. When Leader of the Opposition, Thatcher had promised her first administration would abolish the rates; that pledge was quietly forgotten.[89] Indeed, the Thatcher government concluded in 1983 that: 'rates should remain for the foreseeable future the main source of local revenue for local government'.[90]

Reform reappeared on the political agenda in 1986, when a DoE report, *Paying for Local Government*, recommended replacing the rates with a 'community charge' or 'poll tax'. The government's volte-face seems to have been triggered by the evident failure of grant penalties and ratecapping to curb the spending of Labour controlled local authorities. The poll tax would be levied on a flat rate basis on everyone resident in a local authority area, and would thus require councils to compile a residence register. Some groups would be exempt, and there would be a limited rebate scheme for people on low incomes. Local councils would set the community charge for their respective voters; central government would set a uniform rate for businesses. Under the rates, councils had set both figures.

The government assumed that a flat rate, universal tax would convey to voters the true cost of electing a council providing expansive (and expensive) services. What is less clear is whether the government intended that such transparency would ensure that local electoral choices would be made on the basis of fully informed consent (in which case they would

---

[89] Butler, Adonis, and Travers op cit, p 22.   [90] DoE (1983) *Rates*, p 14 (Cmnd 9008).

presumably have to be respected as meaningful exercises in democratic practice), or whether it hoped that opposition parties would be 'priced out' of office.

As originally conceived, the community charge would not be subject to capping. This suggests that the government was willing to give local electorates unimpeded freedom to determine their council's expenditure. However when it became apparent that many councils still proposed to finance high spending through very high community charge levels, the government introduced capping powers into the Bill.[91] Charge capping seems completely inconsistent with the principle of increased political accountability between a council and its electorate. If a council is capped, voters who want lots of services and are prepared to pay for them cannot do so.

Furthermore, the poll tax's very nature suggests the latter objective was predominant. A flat rate tax is necessarily highly regressive—it falls with disproportionate severity on taxpayers with low incomes. This evidently led some Cabinet Ministers, foremost among them Nigel Lawson, to regard it as an ill-advised venture. Leon Brittan (then Home Secretary) also voiced doubts, on the basis that compulsory registration for the tax might lead some people to 'disappear' from the electoral register to evade payment: the charge might thus be portrayed as a tax on voting. But in accordance with the unanimity limb of the convention of collective ministerial responsibility, neither Lawson nor Brittan resigned over the issue; their dissent was kept secret until they published their memoirs.

The Bill which eventually became the Local Government Finance Act 1988 met sustained opposition in the Commons and the Lords. In the Commons, the government's greatest difficulties were caused by one of its own backbenchers, Michael Mates, who moved an amendment relating the amount of poll tax levied to the individual's ability to pay. Government whips exerted considerable pressure on Mates to withdraw. When he declined to do so, they turned their attention (with more success) to Conservative MPs expressing support for the amendment. Notwithstanding such efforts at 'persuasion', thirty-eight Conservative MPs voted with Mates, while thirteen abstained.[92] In the Lords, a similar amendment was defeated by mobilising the backwoodsmen. Local authorities' legal efforts to challenge the Act's implementation were unsuccessful.[93] However a more broadly based political campaign against the poll tax proved considerably more effective.

A step too far? The demise of the poll tax

Many local authorities had opposed the poll tax because of its regressive nature and the threat that it posed to their political autonomy. This disquiet straddled party boundaries; Conservative councillors were among the fiercest of critics, some resigning the party whip in protest. Concern among councils increased markedly when they faced the prospect of collecting the tax.

The legislation subjected householders to fines, initially of £50, and thereafter £10 per day, for not providing details of people living in their properties. If registered individuals refused to pay the tax, a local authority could seek a 'liability order' from the magistrates' court. This allowed councils to use various enforcement measures, including attachment of earnings, deductions from welfare benefits, and distress—an archaic remedy which enables private bailiffs to seize and sell a debtor's property. Refusal to pay the poll tax could (and did) ultimately lead to imprisonment. Moreover, since the legislation made a designated individual liable for his/her spouse/cohabitee's payment, it was also possible to be jailed for someone else's non-payment.

---

[91] See Himsworth (1991) op cit.   [92] Butler, Adonis, and Travers op cit pp 118–121.

[93] See *R v Secretary of State for the Environment, ex p Hammersmith and Fulham London Borough Council* [1991] 1 AC 521, sub nom *Hammersmith and Fulham London Borough Council v Secretary of State for the Environment* [1990] 3 All ER 589; and more generally Himsworth op cit.

The Labour Party had pledged to repeal the legislation if it won the next general election, but did not advocate non-payment. This reflected a legalistic interpretation of appropriate constitutional behaviour; how could the party present itself as an alternative government if it set a precedent for ignoring legislation, a precedent which might be used against future Labour administrations? Unofficially, however, many Labour Party members (including several MPs and many councillors) supported non-payment.

Opposition to the tax was magnified by a loose-knit group called the 'All-Britain Anti-Poll Tax Federation'.[94] Its leaders had links to far-left parties, but the membership appeared to cross party lines and included people who had not previously been politically active. The Federation's techniques included encouragement of non-payment, marches and demonstrations, offering legal assistance to individuals facing court action, and a practice called 'scum-busting', in which members formed a human barrier around the houses of people issued with liability orders, thereby preventing bailiffs from seizing goods.

Due in part to the success of the Federation's activities, non-payment rates reached 50% in some areas.[95] There was initially appreciable variation in the enthusiasm with which local authorities approached the collection process. However, when faced with the income shortfall caused by mass non-payment, even some of the more radical Labour councils began to make full resort to all collection processes. The Audit Commission, a central government watchdog of local authority finance, predicted that as many as four million people might have to be prosecuted in 1991 and 1992 to collect poll tax arrears.[96]

Conclusion

If the story ended here, it would be difficult not to regard the poll tax policy as revealing major deficiencies in Britain's constitutional structure. One might point to minority electoral approval for the principle; to rebellions within the parliamentary Conservative Party when the tax was enacted; to clear public opposition to the policy in opinion polls; to the display of more overt dissatisfaction through widespread non-payment; and to very limited enthusiasm on the part of the local politicians and professional officers responsible for the tax's collection. Despite all this, the poll tax's legality remained beyond challenge. As previous chapters have already suggested however, the operation of the British constitution is shaped as much, if not more, by issues concerning the legitimacy of government behaviour than questions over its legality. And from the perspective of legitimacy, the poll tax proved to have significant defects.

As chapter eleven reveals, Thatcher's fall from power in 1990 was caused in part by her attitude towards the European Community. But her association with the poll tax also made her an electoral liability for many Conservative MPs, who feared that they would lose their seats at the next general election if the tax was not removed. Unsurprisingly, therefore, Michael Heseltine's challenge to Thatcher for the party leadership in 1990 was coupled with an announcement that he would, if elected, institute a thorough review of the community charge. John Major made a similar commitment when announcing his candidacy for the leadership. His government subsequently introduced a Bill replacing the poll tax with a so-called 'council tax', based primarily on property values. While less regressive and easier to collect than its predecessor, the council tax did not indicate any resurgence of pre-Thatcherite conventions concerning local authority fiscal autonomy: the DoE retained the power to 'cap' council tax levels. Nor did the Major government make any attempt to restore local autonomy in such as areas as housing

---

[94] See Nally S and Dear J (1990) 'No surrender' *Municipal Journal*, 12–18 October.
[95] Institute of Fiscal Studies (1990) *Local government finance: the 1990 reforms*.
[96] Audit Commission (1990) *The administration of the community charge*.

and education policy. Notwithstanding the demise of the community charge, the 'partnership', pluralist model of central–local relations was by 1997 becoming evermore clearly a feature of past constitutional history rather than current constitutional practice.

XII. The Blair government's reforms

The Blair governments did not promote any substantial reversal of this general trend. Labour's 1997 election manifesto offered several abstract statements which might be thought to herald the restoration of much of local government's former autonomy, for example that: 'Local decision-making should be less constrained by central government, and also more accountable to local people'.[97] But on the crucial issue of councils' fiscal powers, the manifesto promised only minor tinkering with, rather than reversal of, the existing legal position: 'Although crude and universal council tax capping should go, we will retain reserve powers to control excessive council tax rises'.[98] Nor did the manifesto envisage any substantial restoration of local authorities' influence over education policy, housing provision, or transport services.[99] The suggestion that the Labour Party had accepted the Thatcherite position that councils' freedom of political judgement extended only to doing things of which central government approved was powerfully conveyed by the following passage:

> Every council will be required to publish a local performance plan with targets for service improvement, and be expected to achieve them. The Audit Commission will be given additional powers to monitor performance and promote efficiency. On its advice, [central] government will where necessary send in a management team with full powers to remedy failure.[100]

In a major policy statement, published in 1998 as a pamphlet entitled *Leading the Way*,[101] Prime Minister Blair suggested that local authorities' proper constitutional role is to serve as the agents of central government:

> However much government does at the centre it will often be dependent on others to make things happen on the ground where it matters. And that is where local government comes in. The delivery of the government's key pledges and policies also requires modern local government helping to make change happen.[102]

The Prime Minister's message was blunt. If councils did just what the government wants them to do:

> You can look forward to an enhanced role and new powers. Your contribution will be recognised. Your status enhanced. If you are unwilling or unable to work to the modern agenda then the government will have to look to other partners to take on your role.[103]

The notion that local government has a legitimate constitutional role to play in enabling voters to express opposition or antagonism to central government policy did not enter the Prime Minister's argument. In that very important respect, Prime Minister Blair seemed to share common constitutional ground with his two immediate predecessors. The policy objectives underlying the Local Government Acts 1999 and 2000 went some way, albeit only a short way, towards refuting that assumption.

---

[97] At 34.   [98] Ibid.
[99] For a suggestion that there has been a shift in degree, if not quality, see Vincent-Jones P (2000) 'Central-local relations under the Local Government Act 1999' *MLR* 84.
[100] Ibid.   [101] The pamphlet was published by the Institute for Public Policy Research (IPPR).
[102] *Leading the Way* op cit p 6.   [103] Ibid, at 22.

The Local Government Acts 1999 and 2000

The central policy objective contained in the 1999 Act was to subject all local authority deci-sion-making to a 'Best Value' regime. The 'Best Value' principle was rather more expansive than a crude statutory reassertion of the *Roberts/Bromley* notion of the fiduciary duty, but was essen-tially a notion of 'efficiency' in which central government had the sole responsibility to deter-mine what 'efficient' actually means. Councils were subject to rigorous inspection by central government bodies—primarily the bizarrely named Best Value Inspectorate—to establish that these efficiency targets were being met. Those councils which were successful when measured against this yardstick would be rewarded with extra responsibilities and resources. Those which failed might find that their powers removed and transferred to government-appointed boards.

The Blair governments' understanding of 'efficiency' in the local government context did not encompass the principle that local electorates should be able to instruct their authorities to pursue policies with which central government disagrees. The Best Value regime indicated that the Blair administration were as contemptuous as their immediate Conservative prede-cessors of the principle that local councils should govern rather than simply administer their areas.[104]

A second innovation provided for by the 2000 Act pointed however in a potentially more pluralist direction. The Act permits local authorities to hold a referendum in which voters may decide if they wish their council to be headed by a directly elected Mayor, who would wield a substantial portion of the authority's (admittedly very limited powers). A directly elected Mayor of cities such as Manchester, Birmingham, or Leeds would exercise significant political authority, even though she would actually wield few governmental powers. The new policy did not however seem to attract much enthusiasm from local voters. By February 2002, refer-enda had been held in only twenty-two areas. In fifteen of those areas, voters had rejected the directly elected Mayor option.[105]

The governance of London

In this general context, the Blair government's plans to introduce a new tier of elected local administration in London seem oddly out of place; for they raised the very real possibility that the Blair government would create a new locus of political power which might afford it substantial discomfort in both the short and longer term.

A Mayor and Assembly for London

A government white paper published in 1998, began by suggesting that:

> Since the abolition of the GLC in 1986, London has lacked strategic direction and leadership. Lon-doners and London organisations have complained about confused responsibilities, duplication of effort, conflicting policies and programmes and a general sense of drift. No one was in charge or able to speak up for London.[106]

Rather than recreate the GLC, the government proposed to establish a 'Greater London Authority' (GLA), composed of a directly elected Mayor and an elected Assembly of twenty-five members. The proposals were subsequently enacted virtually unamended in the Greater London Authority Act 1999. The Assembly would be the junior partner in the enterprise; it seemed likely to be a body possessing little political influence and even less political power.[107]

---

[104] See Wilson D (2001) 'Local government: balancing diversity and uniformity' *Parliamentary Affairs* 289.
[105] *The Times*, 18 February 2002.
[106] Department of the Environment, Transport and the Regions (1998) *A Mayor and Assembly for London*, para 1.6.
[107] Greater London Authority Act 1999 ss 59–60.

The proposals for the Mayor, in contrast, presented a considerable constitutional curiosity, for the government's plans envisaged an office which exercises little practical political authority but which could prove important in terms of political influence.

The GLA has been given some practical responsibility for several areas of governmental activity—including transport, land planning, economic development, environmental protection, and policing.[108] The Mayor is empowered to act both as the formulator and executor of most policy decisions, advised by a 'Cabinet' of her own choosing. The Assembly has a potentially significant checking and amendment role in respect of the GLA's budget, and some entitlement to be consulted by the Mayor over the formulation of policy. The Assembly may also initiate reports and investigations on matters of concern to the administration of the city, and is empowered to require the Mayor to explain and defend her activities in an annual report to its members.

Financial autonomy

The government's explanation of the motives behind the financial system it intended to impose on the GLA sounded distinctly Thatcherite in tone:

> The new finance system will. . . . meet the government's objectives of efficiency and value for money in public spending, while keeping the overall tax burden as low as possible. The finance system will incorporate incentives to be efficient, be durable and robust, and seek to minimise the scope for conflict with central government.[109]

The GLA has not been granted any powers to levy income tax, or a property tax, or a sales tax directly on local residents and businesses. It can raise income through the council tax, but it will do this indirectly by charging a precept to local authorities within the GLA area which will be quantified on each borough's own council tax forms.[110] The GLA's precepting power is subject to capping under the same rules as currently apply to other local authorities' council tax levies. The GLA will also derive income from government grants, charges for services, and the sale of capital assets. The white paper made no attempt to quantify the relative importance of these various sources of finance within the GLA's overall budget, which it suggested would initially be some £3.3b.

The GLA's fiscal power is limited to decisions about viring sums of money within its overall budget from one function to another. Even here, however, the GLA's discretion is tightly restrained. A substantial proportion of the GLA's grant revenue—particularly in respect of transport and economic development matters—is earmarked by central government for specific capital or recurrent expenditure. The GLA has no viring power at all over such monies. Bluntly put, the GLA has no significant degree of budgetary autonomy.

This lacuna strikes a powerful blow at the heart of the Blair government's claim that the GLA would substantially enhance the democratic basis of London governance. A meaningful notion of 'government' surely demands that multi-function government institutions enjoy appreciable autonomy to raise and spend tax revenues, while a meaningful notion of democratic accountability surely demands that voters have some appreciable say in how much tax revenue their elected representatives raise and spend on their behalves. The GLA demonstrably fails both tests.

The electoral process

The Mayor is chosen by the supplementary vote (SV) system.[111] Electors may select a first and second choice candidate. Should any candidate not receive 50%+1 of the first preference

---

[108] Policing powers are among the more important of the GLA's functions, if only because the Police Authority for London was previously the Home Secretary: see Part VI of the Act.

[109] Department of the Environment, Transport and the Regions op cit para 6.7 (hereafter cited as DETR op cit).

[110] Greater London Authority Act 1999 ss 82–84.

[111] Greater London Authority Act 1999 ss 3–4, 17, and Sch 2.

votes, all but the two candidates attracting the most first preference votes are eliminated. Any second preference votes of defeated candidates which were given to the top two candidates will then be reallocated, leaving the person with the greater number of first and second preference votes as the winner. To discourage frivolous or crank candidates, a 'significant deposit' would be required, which would be returned only if the candidate gains 5% or more of the vote. Candidates also have to be nominated by a 'significant number' of registered voters from each borough. These proposals will presumably restrict the field to the representatives of established political parties.

Assembly candidates must pay a 5% threshold deposit and be nominated by a set number of voters in their chosen constituency. The Assembly is elected by the additional member system (AMS). Fourteen seats are allocated to constituencies, which will return members on a first past the post basis. The remaining eleven members are drawn from party lists, in numbers which ensure that party representation closely reflects the overall distribution of the vote. The use of AMS means it is improbable that the Assembly will contain a single party majority, a fact which may have some significant impact in the way in which the Assembly goes about discharging its (limited) governmental duties.

Conclusion

In an interesting break with tradition, the government had promoted legislation allowing a referendum to be staged in London on the desirability of proceeding with the GLA proposals. The vote was held on 7 May 1998. Some 70%+ of those voting supported the government's plans. Turnout however was barely 35%, so the government could hardly claim a ringing democratic mandate for its plans.

The low turnout is not inconsistent with the participation levels recorded in local authority elections in general in recent years. Nor indeed was the Blair government's response to that low turnout significantly out of line with that of previous Conservative governments. It appeared unimpressed by the argument that voters may not turn out for local elections because they believe (quite justifiably) that local authorities no longer have any substantial political role. A substantial expansion of local power as a cure for low turnout was not on the government's agenda.

Conclusion

The Liberal Democrat Party had consistently championed a more expansive role for local authorities during the last third of the twentieth century, and that sentiment appeared to be endorsed in the Conservative/Liberal coalition's 2010 *Programme for government*:

> We will promote the radical devolution of power and greater financial autonomy to local government and community groups. This will include a review of local government finance.[112]

However, the Localism Act which was enacted in 2011 seemed designed to reduce local authorities' powers still further by devolving some of their existing powers to sub-local bodies. While there is certainly eminent support for the notion that this initiative may be an effective way of encouraging more citizens to engage with political questions,[113] it is difficult to see that enactment of the Bill will better equip local authorities to function as a meaningful counterweight to central government on important political issues.[114] Section 1 of the Act granted

---

[112] <http://www.cabinetoffice.gov.uk/sites/default/files/resources/coalition_programme_for_government.pdf> at p 11.

[113] See Bogdanor's analysis in (2009) *The new British constitution* ch 10.

[114] See generally on this point Loveland I (1999) 'Local authorities' in Blackburn R and Plant R (eds) *Constitutional reform*.

local authorities a 'general power of competence', which would enable them to do 'anything that individuals generally may do'. This might be thought to enhance council's political powers, insofar as they would no longer have to find an explicit grant of statutory authority to pursue innovative policies. Section 2 however provides that s 1 may not be used to bypass existing restrictions on local authority powers, and—more importantly—the Act has not loosened central government controls over local council's financial autonomy. Section 1 cannot credibly be seen as reversing the post-1980 legislative trend towards reducing the political significance of the local government sector.

It was suggested in chapter nine that legislative self-restraint in deference to 'traditionally fundamental' political and moral principles might be the most important of Britain's constitutional conventions. There is room to dispute the precise conventional understanding of central–local relations in the modern era, but the preponderance of evidence suggests that prior to 1980 governments of both parties considered that maintaining some significant simultaneous political pluralism within the overall structure of government was an important constitutional principle.

We might argue whether that principle should be regarded as a 'convention' in the orthodox sense, but there is little scope for disagreement as to its importance in the context of modern British society. The recent history of local government suggests that the pluralist principle was ignored by the Conservative administrations which enjoyed a Commons majority from 1979 onwards and by the Blair and Brown Labour governments which succeeded them.

Yet it is a profound paradox of constitutional history that just as the Thatcher and Major governments so successfully deployed their Commons' and Lords' majorities to dismantle the country's internal structures of post-war pluralism and eradicate the influence of Butskellite philosophy on the government process, so they faced increasingly formidable opposition to their ideological agenda from a hitherto unexpected quarter. Chapter eleven addresses the impact on traditional constitutional understandings of governmental power of Britain's membership of the European Community.

Suggested further reading

Academic and political commentary

SHARPE J (1970) 'Theories and value of local government' *Political Studies* 153

BOGDANOR V (2009) *The new British constitution* ch 10

LOVELAND I (1999) 'Local authorities' in BLACKBURN R and PLANT R (eds) *Constitutional reform*

LOUGHLIN M (1986) *Local government in the modern state* ch 1

LASKI H (1926) 'Judicial review of social policy in England' *Harvard LR* 832 p 844

KEITH-LUCAS B (1962) 'Poplarism' *Public Law* 52

MITCHELL A (1974) 'Clay Cross' *Political Quarterly* 165

BUTLER D, ADONIS A, and TRAVERS T (1994) *Failure in British government: the politics of the poll tax*

WILSON D (2001) 'Local government: balancing diversity and uniformity' *Parliamentary Affairs* 289

Case law and legislation

Bromley LBC v GLC [1983] 1 AC 768

Roberts v Hopwood [1925] AC 578

Associated Provincial Picture Houses Ltd v Wednesbury Corpn [1948] 1 KB 223

A-G v Aspinall (1837) 40 ER 773

Chapter 11

Parliamentary Sovereignty within the European Union

As chapter two suggested, the UK's accession to the European Economic Community markedly affected traditional constitutional understandings; especially, but not exclusively, regarding parliamentary sovereignty. This chapter charts the way in which this country's membership of the Community has prompted changes in the domestic constitutional order.

I. The Treaty of Rome 1: founding principles

The European Economic Community was created in 1957 by six countries which signed the Treaty of Rome (West Germany, Italy, France, Holland, Belgium, and Luxembourg). The EEC's immediate origins lie in the foundation by the same six states of the European Coal and Steel Community (ECSC) under the Treaty of Paris in 1951. The primary concern of the founders of the ECSC was to prevent another war between France, Germany, and Italy. The ECSC was intended to integrate its member countries' coal and steel industries so closely that war would become impossible. The ECSC was also motivated by a belief among many politicians that co-ordinated rebuilding of these basic industries would hasten economic recovery from the devastation inflicted by World War II. More amorphously, the ECSC offered a means for Italy and Germany to demonstrate that they could function as civilised, democratic societies.[1]

The Treaty of Rome pushed the idea of political co-operation through economic integration several steps further. The preamble asserted that the signatory States were; 'determined to lay the foundations of an ever closer union among the peoples of Europe'. It continued by identifying various economic policy objectives which would promote that purpose. The Treaty's primary concern (outlined in Arts 2 and 3) was to create a 'common market' between the EEC's

---

[1] See Craig and de Burca (op cit) ch 1; Pinder J (2nd edn, 1995) *European Community* ch 1.

members. The common market would eventually require free movement of goods, workers, services, and capital across national boundaries; a common policy on agriculture; uniform rules governing competition law; and community rules regulating imports of goods from non-Member States. It seems plausible that the Treaty's architects envisaged that increased economic interdependence would slowly lead to some kind of political union, but how widely such sentiments were shared is a matter for speculation.[2]

The organisation established by the Treaty of Rome was not a single country, and thus not 'federal' in the de jure sense. However, we have seen in previous chapters that constitutional behaviour may owe more to issues of practical politics than to legal theory. It may therefore be defensible to suggest that 'federalism' can be a de facto construct, and that specific allocations of powers between different organs of government might be of sufficient significance for us to conclude that a federal system has indeed emerged.

The types of EEC law and law-making processes

This book has suggested that most modern democracies accept the principle that their constitutions should recognise a hierarchy of laws. The more important the political value at stake, the more difficult it should be for the value to be changed. That principle is clearly expressed within the Treaty of Rome.

The Treaty itself is the original source of EEC law within the EEC's own legal order: it is a constituent document. The various governmental organisations which the Treaty created have limited competence; they can only do those things the Treaty permits. There is no doctrine equivalent to parliamentary sovereignty available to any EEC institution. The 'sovereign law-maker' within the EEC was identified by Art 236 of the Treaty. Article 236 provided for a process through which the Treaty could be amended. Amendment entails cumbersome procedures, involving an Inter-Governmental Conference between the signatory nations, and their unanimous support in accordance with their respective constitutional amendment mechanisms for any changes. So there was no possibility of a tyranny of a majority, or even of an overwhelming majority, concerning the basic scope of EEC law. Even tiny Luxembourg had a power of veto on Treaty amendment. The terms of the Treaty are therefore deeply entrenched in a procedural sense. The Treaty is often referred to as 'primary legislation' within the EEC's legal order. From a British perspective, that label can be misleading. A better characterisation might be to describe the Treaty as the Community's 'fundamental law'.

Many of the Treaty's provisions are drafted in loose terms: it is a 'traite cadre' rather than a 'traite loi'. Its text contains broadly framed objectives and basic principles about institutional structures and law-making procedures, rather than precise rules detailing what the Community could do and how it could do it. And within the Treaty, there is a clear hierarchy (or, perhaps more accurately, heterogeneity) of laws.

The Council of Ministers, Commission, and Parliament

Most EEC laws are made by a body called the Council of Ministers. Each Member State has one representative on the Council of Ministers. This is generally the Minister whose domestic responsibilities coincide with the issue the Council is addressing. The Council was empowered (per Art 148) to make laws through three types of voting system. In some areas of EEC activity, the Treaty required unanimous Member State approval. In other fields, the Council could proceed by a qualified majority, in which each Member State's voting power is (crudely) adjusted according to its population size. Thirdly, the Treaty also permits some laws to be made by a simple majority system, which gives all Member States equal weight.

---

[2] For an introduction see Pinder op cit; Urwin D (1995) *The community of Europe: a history of integration*.

In crude terms, we might conclude that the more important an issue was to the national interests of Member States, the more likely it was that the Treaty would require unanimous voting—the most inter-national law-making process. Qualified majority voting originally weighted the Member States' votes according to the following formula: Germany 4; France 4; Italy 4; Luxembourg 1; Netherlands 2; Belgium 2. Twelve votes were required to pass the law. This is a more supra-national process than unanimity, but nevertheless permitted one big state plus one other to invoke shared national interests to block integrationist legislation. Simple majority voting is clearly the most supra-national of the three processes—perhaps unsurprisingly it was rarely provided for in the EEC's initial development.

Unlike the Council, the Commission was intended to be an avowedly supra-national body. It had nine members, not more than two of whom could be nationals of the same Member State. Per Art 158, Commissioners were appointed for four-year terms by the common accord of the Member States. One Commissioner, selected by the common accord of the Member States, would serve as President of the Commission. A 'convention' emerged that Member States would approve each other's nominees. However, per Art 157, Commissioners were to be 'chosen for their general competence and of indisputable independence.' This independence was presumably to be from national pressures—whether directly, or indirectly from the Council—for Art 157(2) provided that Commissioners 'shall not seek or accept instructions from any Government or other body'. Per Art 163, the Commission would act by a simple majority. It also adopted a principle of collective responsibility—arguments among Commissioners were not made public.[3]

Article 155 charged the Commission with various powers of promoting, implementing, and monitoring measures: 'with a view to ensuring the functioning and development of the Common Market'. It was also the Commission's task to introduce much of the legislation on which the Council would vote: the Council had little power of legislative innovation. The Commission was also endowed with a limited amount of autonomous legislative power exercised without reference to the Council. Such legislation clearly had a very supra-national character.

The Parliament (originally styled the 'Assembly') was composed of delegates chosen by each Member State from their own legislatures in approximate proportion to their population size. It had few powers. Some parts of the Treaty specified that the Council had to consult the Parliament before enacting legislation, but the Treaty did not compel the Council to take any notice of the Assembly's opinions. The Parliament also had to be consulted by the Council over the Community's budgetary process, but again its views did not bind the Council's eventual decisions.

The forms of EEC 'law': Article 189

The Treaty's sensitivity to supra- and inter-national tensions is further evidenced in Art 189, which empowers the EEC to produce various types of secondary legislation to fill in the gaps left by the Treaty's nature as a traite cadre. Article 189 text identified three major types of 'secondary legislation'. 'Regulations' and 'directives' would be enacted by the Council in response to Commission proposals; 'decisions'—which applied predominantly to agricultural and competition policy issues—would be enacted by the Commission.

The Treaty's individual articles specified the type of legislation to be used for particular EEC objectives. If one links this heterogeneity with the Council's tripartite voting system and with the Commission's initiatory role and the Parliament's consultative powers, it is clear that the Treaty of Rome created a very elaborate law-making structure, with many checks and balances curbing the powers of the EEC's own institutions and of its Member States.

Since that elaborate structure could be amended only by the cumbersome Art 236 procedure, the EEC established a very complex separation of powers within its constitutional

---

[3] The 'reason' presumably being to stop the Council or Member States exploiting divisions among the Commissioners.

structure. But this separation does not comfortably correspond to orthodox British under-standings of that concept. No part of any of the EEC's institutions was directly elected by the Member States' citizens, which clearly raises some questions as to the Community's demo-cratic base. Such electoral control as citizens of Member States exercised on EEC law-making would pass through the indirect filter of their respective government's representative on the Council of Ministers, and their governments' nominees to the Commission and Assembly. But we should resist the temptation of adopting an oversimplistic definition of democracy. For in another sense, the EEC could be seen as bolstering democratic principles, by creating the pos-sibility that citizens of a Member State who did not vote for their own government would find that other governments on the Council would more accurately reflect their own preferences on matters within the EEC's competence, and thereby block or dilute a national government's majoritarian or minoritarian preferences.

In British terms, the Commission appears to serve as the executive branch of the Community's government, but one should qualify this observation. As already noted, it has some independent legislative powers. More significantly, the Commission was (and remains) a small organisation and, consequently, could not realistically be involved in the detailed implementation of Community law. For that task, the EEC was to rely primarily on Member State governments.

The EEC Parliament was obviously not comparable to Parliament in the British sense. That it was not an elected body would seem of little import, given that it had no significant powers. But this perhaps raised the longer-term question of whether the EEC should contain a powerful, directly elected legislative branch. Quite where the Parliament would stand on the supra/inter-national axis was initially unclear. Its members' status as governmental appoin-tees, rather than directly elected representatives, suggested it might simply reproduce inter-national tensions on the Council. But there was also the possibility that its members would form alliances according to political ideology rather than national origin, so that it might evolve into a pan-European forum.

The roles of the European Court of Justice (ECJ)

As stressed earlier, the Treaty is a constituent document. It was thus necessary that its framers devise some mechanism to ensure; firstly that the substance of the laws made via Art 189 and the processes by which those laws were made respected the limits imposed by the Treaty; and secondly that all the other activities of the EEC's institutions had a defensible legal base, either in the Treaty's text, or in secondary legislation passed under its authority.

Under Art 164, the ECJ was to ensure that 'in the interpretation and application of this Treaty the law is observed'. The ECJ initially had seven judges. They were (like Commissioners) to be people whose 'independence is beyond doubt', and who would be eligible for high judicial office in their own countries or were eminent legal scholars. The Treaty gave the ECJ two distinct juris-dictions. The first might be styled as 'internal': its concern being to ensure that the Community's institutions and officials acted within the boundaries of the powers given to them by the Treaty. The second jurisdiction is best characterised as having an 'external' character; its focus was on the question of whether Member States were giving proper effect to their Community obligations.

The internal jurisdiction arose primarily under Art 173. Article 173 empowered the ECJ to review the legality of acts of the Council or Commission at the instigation of the Council, Commission, or a Member State. Article 173 also seemed to enable individuals in certain cir-cumstances to initiate such proceedings. The grounds of illegality against which the acts of the EEC's institutions should be measured were also laid out in Art 173. Per Art 174, the ECJ could declare illegal acts void. This is obviously consistent with the notion that the Treaty should be regarded as 'fundamental law', and that the EEC's institutions could exercise only those powers granted by the Treaty.

The Court's 'external' jurisdiction had two elements. Articles 169–170 empowered the ECJ, if requested by the Commission or a Member State respectively, to determine if a Member

State had breached its Treaty obligations. Such a power would in itself appear rather confrontational. The potential for conflict was softened by requiring the Commission to seek a negotiated settlement before passing the matter to the ECJ, and by the absence of any measure forcing an errant state to comply with a judgment against it. Any conclusion that the ECJ reached would have only declaratory status. The judgment's efficacy as a means to ensure that the relevant Member State complied with EEC law would be wholly dependent on the Member State being willing to do so. Neither Arts 169–170 nor any other provision of the Treaty empowered the ECJ to quash domestic legislation or executive action.

The second element of the Court's external jurisdiction was less clearly spelled out. Article 177 indicated that some role would be played by national courts in litigation which raised questions as to the meaning of EEC law. Article 177 granted to the ECJ alone the power to interpret the Treaty or to decide upon the meaning or validity of any EEC secondary legislation; (and so by implication denied any such power to national courts). Article 177 also indicated that national courts and tribunals could in certain circumstances ask 'questions' of the ECJ concerning issues of EEC law, relating to the meaning of a treaty provision or the validity and meaning of secondary legislation, which arose in the course of domestic proceedings. This 'preliminary reference' procedure did not, de jure, present the ECJ as exercising an appellate jurisdiction over national courts. The procedure evidently envisaged that a domestic court would adjourn its proceedings pending the ECJ answering the question raised, whereupon the domestic legal proceedings would resume. Quite what effect and impact Art 177 was intended to have was far from clear; neither Art 177 nor any other Treaty provision revealed what should happen if the 'preliminary reference' procedure produced an answer which suggested EEC law was incompatible with domestic law.

The status of EC law within the legal systems of the Member States

The Art 169–170 jurisdiction replicated an orthodox international law dispute settlement mechanism. A treaty creates laws operating in the sphere of international law. Many treaties also create a specialised forum—again operating in the sphere of international law—for the resolution of disputes; and grant signatory States or specially created enforcement bodies the power to initiate proceedings. To state the matter simply, international law is taken to create legal relationships between countries but not within them. A treaty's terms are not presumptively enforceable in the domestic courts of a signatory State by or between individuals. Signatory States might wish a particular treaty to have such an internal legal effect, but this would be done by organising their own constitutions in a fashion which automatically gave international law an enforceable domestic status. To frame the matter more simply still, the dominant view in 1957 was that the status of international law within national legal systems was a matter for each nation state to determine.[4] Within this notion of the domestic 'status' of international law, three essential questions arise.

The first is one of 'accessibility', itself divisible into several component parts. Which domestic courts would be competent to apply international law norms to control legal relationships within the domestic territory? Who (or what) would be permitted to invoke international law rules before national courts; that is, who could be a claimant? And whom (or what) could those rules be invoked against; that is, who could be a defendant?

The second question is one of 'hierarchy'. Assuming that some or all domestic courts can apply all or parts of a particular body of international law in domestic litigation, which rule of law should a domestic court apply if it finds that international law and domestic rules demand different solutions to the case before it?

---

[4] See inter alia Brownlie I (4th edn, 1990) *Principles of public international law* ch 2; Jackson J (1992) 'Status of treaties in domestic legal systems' *American Journal of International Law* 310.

The third question—which perhaps logically precedes the first two—is one of 'interpretive competence'. Which body has the power to give authoritative answers to questions concerning the accessibility and hierarchical position of international law within a country's domestic legal system?

It is readily defensible to conclude that in 1957 most politicians and lawyers in the EEC's founding States would have concluded that the answer to the third question was: 'Whichever body is given such power by the respective constitution of each signatory State'. But while one might find widespread transnational agreement on that issue of legal competence, the ways in which individual States used that competence to answer questions relating to the domestic accessibility and hierarchal position of international law were remarkably variegated.

In 1957, the Netherlands' constitution[5] afforded an extremely high status to international law. If an international law rule protected the rights of an individual, the Dutch constitution provided both that the rule had a higher status than any rule of domestic law and was automatically and immediately enforceable by any claimant against any defendant in any national court.

The then extant Belgian constitution granted international law a much lowlier internal status. A treaty's provisions became accessible in domestic courts only to the extent to which they were expressly incorporated by an Act of the Belgian Parliament. It would be for the Belgian Parliament to determine by whom, against whom, and in which domestic courts the incorporated Treaty provisions could be invoked, and what other provisions of domestic law the incorporated terms would override. The Belgian Parliament had no power however to entrench any such incorporating statute against future repeal.[6]

The other four Member States each had different constitutional arrangements.[7] If the Treaty of Rome was simply an orthodox instrument of international law, the legal status of its provisions in the respective legal systems of Member States would vary substantially, as no explicit steps were taken by the Member States in 1957 to modify their constitutional arrangements to give EEC law an identical (and entrenched) domestic status.

The Treaty of Rome was virtually silent on each of the three 'status' questions. This silence is ostensibly surprising. It must have been appreciated by the Treaty's framers that—even if all Member State legislatures and governments consistently made bona fide attempts to ensure that national law was compatible with EEC law—numerous occasions would arise when the two sources of law were mutually inconsistent. And one would have had to have been remarkably naïve not to have assumed that in some situations Member State governments or legislatures might wilfully seek to contravene EEC law norms.

Almost 200 years earlier, such concerns about inconsistencies between rules of law emanating from different spheres of government had much exercised the minds of the framers of the US' Constitution. As noted in chapter one, substantial (and potentially overlapping) powers were given by the Constitution to the various branches of the national government and to the States. To Madison and his contemporaries, it was 'self-evident' that conflict would arise between provisions of the Constitution itself, laws enacted by Congress, and laws produced by the States. It was equally evident that the Constitution itself should give clear instructions as to according to what hierarchical criteria and in which fora such conflicts should be addressed. Article VI of the Constitution thus provided that:

> This Constitution, and the Laws of the United States which shall be made in pursuance thereof; and all treaties made or which shall be made, under the Authority of the United States, shall be the supreme Law of the Land; and the Judges in every State shall be bound thereby, any thing in the Constitution or Laws of any State to the contrary notwithstanding.

---

[5] Articles 65–66 : see Claes M and DeWitte (1998) B 'Report on the Netherlands', in Slaughter A, Stone Sweet A, and Weiler J (eds) *The European courts and national courts*.

[6] Bribosia H (1998) 'Report on Belgium', in Slaughter et al op cit.

[7] See generally the collection of essays in Slaughter et al op cit.

Article VI lays out a clear hierarchy of legal norms: the Constitution is superior to laws enacted by Congress, which in turn, if consistent with the Constitution, are superior to any laws produced by a State. Article VI also addresses questions of accessibility; all judges—and thus every court in the country—are bound by the enunciated hierarchy of laws. That principle necessarily entails that litigants in all State courts can invoke and rely upon the Constitution and Congressional legislation to override any inconsistent State law. Article VI is concerned to ensure both the *uniform impact* and the *ready enforceability* of the Constitution and Acts of Congress throughout the United States. No State may 'opt out' of any provision of the Constitution and Acts of Congress. Relatedly, by providing for the enforcement of those legal norms in all courts, Art VI provides individual citizens en masse with a vast number of local and familiar fora in which to protect their entitlements.

Invoking the US Constitution as a comparator against which to analyse the Treaty of Rome is necessarily of limited utility. The American framers were creating a country. The politicians who designed the Treaty of Rome ostensibly had no such grand ambitions. But both were much concerned with dividing law-making powers between different spheres of government, and with ensuring that the proposed divisions were effective. Why then did the Treaty of Rome not address the three status issues in clear terms? Three explanations might be advanced.

The first is that the framers of the Treaty did not expect EEC law to operate as anything other than international law, and thus pinned their hopes for its uniform and effective application throughout the six Member States on the political goodwill of the countries' respective legislatures and governments. Some support for that presumption is found in Art 5 of the Treaty:

> Member States shall take all . . . measures which are appropriate for ensuring the carrying out of the obligations arising out of this Treaty or resulting from the acts of the institutions of the Community. They shall facilitate the achievement of the Community's aims.. . . They shall abstain from any measures likely to jeopardise the attainment of the objectives of this Treaty.

Article 5 makes no express references to domestic legal systems, nor domestic courts, nor to the hierarchical relationship of EEC and domestic law. It appears no more than a declaration of political good faith.

The second—perhaps least likely—hypothesis is that the presumptions that EEC law should be hierarchically superior to all domestic law and immediately enforceable in domestic courts were so obviously essential to effective creation of a 'common market' that there was no need to express them explicitly. They were instead 'taken for granted' principles.

A third explanation is that the Treaty's framers appreciated the importance of those presumptions, but were unwilling to articulate them clearly for fear that political or public opinion in the intended Member States would find such ideas so unacceptable that support for joining the Community would evaporate. Their hope or expectation may have been that such principles could be expressly accepted by a subsequent amendment to the Treaty and the Member States' respective constitutions, or that the principles might be found already present, albeit in hidden and fragmentary form, in the original Treaty itself.

As suggested earlier, Art 177 did indicate that only the ECJ (and so by implication not national courts) was competent to determine the meaning and effect of EC law. Whether Member States would accept that proposition remained to be seen. But observers of the development of the EEC did not have to wait long to see the ECJ invoke that competence to issue judgment relating both to the accessibility and hierarchical status of EEC law within Member State constitutions.

Questions of accessibility: the 'direct effect' of treaty articles

The Court's initial response to the question of the accessibility of EEC law within domestic legal systems was to conclude that parts of the Treaty possessed a status which the ECJ termed 'direct effect'. The ECJ first articulated the principle in 1962.

Van Gend en Loos (1962)

Article 12 of the Treaty forbade Member States from increasing customs duties on goods imported from other EEC countries. Dutch legislation subsequently redesignated certain chemicals into an already existing tax band which imposed a higher duty. Van Gend challenged the legality of this redesignation before a Dutch court, asking that the court refuse to apply the Dutch law because it amounted to a new tax contravening Art 12. The Dutch court invoked Art 177 to refer two questions to the ECJ. The first concerned the substantive issue of the Netherlands' government's claim that the reclassification was not a tax increase. Unsurprisingly, the ECJ decided against the Netherlands on that point.[8]

The second, more significant issue, was the jurisdictional question of whether the Dutch court could entertain the action at all. As a matter of Dutch constitutional law, the Dutch court could do so if Art 12 created 'rights' for individuals. The ECJ concluded on that point that Art 12 did create individual rights. Although Art 12 was framed in terms of a restraint on governmental power, the corollary of that restraint was an individual entitlement. If governmental authorities cannot levy a new tax, the targeted taxpayer has a right not to pay any such tax.

From the viewpoint of the Dutch court, these answers were all that were required for it to resolve the case before it. As a result of the way in which the Dutch constitution treated international law, Art 12 immediately overrode the inconsistent provision of the domestic statute. The ECJ's primary concern was, however, with a quite different issue. Manifestly, the Dutch constitutional rule that Art 12 was accessible in Dutch courts would be of no significance in Germany or Italy or any other Member State. The ECJ's concern was therefore whether or not Art 12 of the Treaty was accessible in the domestic courts of all of the Member States simply and solely because of rules of EEC law. This question would seem in turn to raise two issues. Did EEC law require Art 12 to have that characteristic of pan-Community accessibility? And if so, did EEC law override any domestic legal rule to the contrary?

A new legal order?

The ECJ answered the first question in the affirmative. The crucial element of its reasoning for this conclusion was an assertion that the Treaty of Rome was not 'international law' in the orthodox sense:

> The Community constitutes a new legal order of international law for the benefit of which the states have limited their sovereign rights, albeit within limited fields, and the subjects of which comprise not only Member States but also their nationals. Independently of the legislation of Member States, Community law therefore not only imposes obligations on individuals but is also intended to confer upon them rights which become part of their legal heritage.[9]

Several Member State governments had intervened in the ECJ proceedings to argue that the Treaty created only one mechanism to assess the compatibility of domestic legislation with EEC law; that mechanism being an action before the ECJ via Art 169 or 170. The ECJ did not however regard this as a sufficient remedy.[10] It reasoned that to restrict legal challenges

---

[8] Case 26/62: [1963] ECR 1.   [9] Ibid, at 12.

[10] There would be several disadvantages to accepting Arts 169–170 as the only way to challenge the compatibility of domestic laws with EEC law. The first (logistical) problem is that there was only one ECJ, so it could handle only a very limited workload. Secondly, Arts 169–170 only permit actions to be brought by the Commission or another Member State; they do not allow litigation by individuals or companies. Since the Commission and Member States would constantly be co-operating with each other in the EEC's legislative process, it would be plausible to suggest that some breaches of EEC law would be 'overlooked' to maintain harmonious political relations; see Craig P (1992) 'Once upon a time in the west: direct effect and the federalisation of EEC law' *Oxford Journal of Legal Studies* 453. One might suggest that exclusive reliance on the Arts 169–170 mechanism to resolve disputes as to the compatibility of EEC and domestic law would not satisfy a 'red light', Diceyan model of the rule of law, in which citizens may challenge the legality of government action before the 'ordinary courts of the land', nor even Jones' greenishly tinged 'meaningful day in court'.

against Member States to Arts 169–170 actions 'would remove all direct legal protection of the individual rights of [EEC] nationals'.[11] If EEC law was to be effectively enforced, the national courts would have to serve as fora where the conformity of a Member State's laws with the Treaty could be gauged at the instigation of individuals; only domestic courts were sufficiently numerous and proximate and familiar to citizens. As well as acting in defence of their own EEC entitlements, citizens invoking direct effect would police Member States' compliance with EEC law.

A teleological interpretive technique

The Treaty has no obvious textual basis to support the existence of the direct effect principle. The Court made two rather unconvincing references to particular provisions in the Treaty's text to buttress its conclusion. The first noted the reference in the preamble to the 'peoples' of the Member States as well as to their respective governments. The second referred to Art 177, and suggested that the very presence of that provision in the Treaty indicated that national courts would have the capacity to apply EEC law.[12]

The ECJ found the primary justification for its conclusion in what it termed the 'spirit, scheme, and general wording' of the Treaty. The Court's search for the meaning of EEC law was premised on the assumption that the Treaty should be construed in a 'teleological' or 'purposive' manner. At the core of the ECJ's judgment lies the assumption that the effectiveness ('l'effet utile') of EEC law was substantially dependent upon there being a multiplicity of mechanisms and fora through which the law might be enforced. Legal rules which were impossible or very difficult to enforce would be of little value to the persons/organisations who/which were presumptively supposed to benefit from or be controlled by them.

The principle of direct effect initially seemed to have limited scope. *Van Gend* itself concerned a Treaty article, rather than Art 189 secondary legislation. Thus it might sensibly have been assumed that direct effect would only apply to the Treaty itself, and not to Art 189 measures.

But perhaps the most significant element of *Van Gend* is that the ECJ asserted that Art 12 acquired its status as directly effective law '*independently of the legislation* of Member States' (emphasis added).[13] In other words, the status of EC law within national legal systems was for EEC law to determine. National constitutional rules as to the domestic status of 'international law' would apparently not apply to EEC law. The law of the Community, throughout the Community, was an autonomous legal force.

Questions of hierarchy: the 'precedence' of treaty articles over domestic legislation

It would seem sensible to suggest that if the Treaty of Rome was to create a 'common market' among the six Member States, then Community law (whether it be in the form of Treaty articles or secondary legislation) on such matters as free movement of goods and persons—indeed on all areas of Community activity—would have to override any incompatible domestic laws. As noted earlier, the constitutions of the Member States adopted varying responses to that question of hierarchy. Thus if the question of 'hierarchy' remained one for Member States' own constitutions to determine, EEC law would not have uniform impact throughout the community. The practical basis of a 'common market' would therefore be substantially undermined.

---

[11] [1963] ECR 1 at 13.

[12] A more modest interpretation would be that Art 177 simply indicates that the preliminary reference procedure would be available to those Member States which wished to use it.

[13] [1963] ECR 1 at 12. The term 'legislation' here is perhaps best construed as referring to law in a generic sense (ie any law) rather than to a statute as we would understand that term in the British context.

That a Treaty article might be 'directly effective' did not address this problem. Direct effect is concerned with accessibility, not with hierarchy. If a domestic court could apply a provision of EEC law, but that provision was—according to the given Member State's own constitution—of inferior hierarchical status to an inconsistent domestic law, then the EEC law would clearly not determine the outcome of the proceedings.

The question of hierarchy was thus of enormous importance to the functioning of Community law. Yet the Treaty did not make any express statement as to the hierarchical relationship within domestic legal systems of the various provisions of EEC and national law. The nearest literal support for that proposition is found in Art 5. As suggested earlier, it is difficult to extract from this text any strong argument that provisions of EEC law—be they Treaty articles or secondary legislation—were normatively superior to incompatible national provisions. Nor had the ECJ squarely addressed this matter in *Van Gend*. The Court offered at best an oblique hint that (certain types of) EEC law might be superior to (certain types of) domestic law in its observation that: 'the Community constitutes a new legal order of international law for the benefit of which the states have limited their sovereign rights, albeit within limited fields'.[14] Two years later, the ECJ took a clearer position.

Costa v ENEL (1964)

Signor Costa was a political activist opposed to recent Italian legislation which had brought Italy's electricity supply industry under direct government control. The opponents of the legislation had invoked various political and legal challenges to the policy. Signor Costa's part in the episode involved a refusal to pay a trifling sum of his electricity bill on the basis that: firstly, the relevant legislation was incompatible with various Treaty articles; secondly, the articles concerned were directly effective; and thirdly, that the articles possessed a superior status in domestic law to the legislation. If these three propositions were correct, the outcome would be that the Italian courts would be obliged to refuse to apply the Italian legislation to the extent that it was consistent with EEC law.

That outcome was not required by Italian constitutional law at the time. As a matter of Italian law, the Treaty of Rome had the status of an ordinary statute passed by the national legislature. While it would override pre-existing statutes and lesser forms of domestic law, it was in turn inferior both to provisions of the Italian constitution and to subsequently enacted statutes. The Italian Constitutional Court had held in Signor Costa's case that the Treaty of Rome had not altered this basic principle of domestic law.[15] Both the accessibility of the Treaty articles concerned and their hierarchical status were matters for Italian law to determine. And as a matter of Italian law, the Treaty articles simply did not exist in the domestic legal system if inconsistent with subsequently enacted Italian legislation.[16]

The irrelevance of national law

Following the position laid out in *Van Gend*, the ECJ, in contrast, proceeded on the basis that the requirements of Italian constitutional law were irrelevant to the question of the status of EC law in the Member States:

> . . . By contrast with ordinary international treaties, the EEC Treaty has created its own legal system which, on the entry into force of the Treaty, became an integral part of the legal systems of the Member States and which their courts are bound to apply.[17]

---

[14] Ibid, at 12. Under Dutch law Art 12 automatically took precedence over the inconsistent national legislation.

[15] [1964] CMLR 425. For a detailed treatment see Ruggeri Laderchi P (1998) 'Report on Italy', in Slaughter et al op cit.   [16] [1964] ECR 585 at 593.

[17] Ibid. An alternative way of framing this point is that the creation of the Community automatically and invisibly amended the constitutional laws of the Member States and, more importantly, thereafter prevented the Member States from amending their respective constitutions in a way that rejected the primacy of community law.

The ECJ then turned to consider the nature of that 'independent source of law':

> The transfer by the States from their domestic legal systems to the Community legal system of rights and obligations arising under the Treaty carries with it a permanent limitation of their sovereign rights, against which a subsequent unilateral act incompatible with the concept of the community cannot prevail.[18]

The reason that such 'subsequent unilateral acts' could not prevail over Community law had an obvious, teleological, basis. If Member States could 'opt out' of Community laws which they found unpalatable, there would be no 'common market': a common market required that Community law had uniform effect throughout the Community: 'The executive force of Community law cannot vary from one State to another in deference to subsequent domestic laws, without jeopardising the attainment of the objectives of the Treaty.'[19]

The Court concluded with the observation that if its reasoning on this point was rejected, the Community simply could not exist in any meaningful sense:

> It follows from all these observations that the law stemming from the Treaty, an independent source of law, could not, because of its special and original nature, be overridden by domestic legal provisions, however framed, without being deprived of its character as Community law and without the legal basis of the Community itself being called into question.[20]

The facts of *Costa* produced an apparent conflict between Treaty articles (ie the highest form of Community law) and domestic Italian legislation (ie a form of domestic law inferior to the provisions of the Italian constitution). If narrowly construed, the ECJ's judgment might be taken to hold only that Treaty articles took precedence over national legislation. From such a perspective, it might be thought that a Treaty article did not take precedence over a national constitutional provision; nor that EEC secondary legislation would take precedence over domestic legislation or constitutional provisions. However, the ECJ's judgment did not—and one assumes by design rather than accident—draw any distinction between different types of Community law or national law. Broadly construed, *Costa* asserts the blanket principle that *all* EEC law takes precedence over *all* national law, regardless of the various laws' respective positions in their own internal normative hierarchy. Given the ECJ's evident concern with ensuring the uniform substantive impact of Community law, and given the heterogeneity of normative legal hierarchies within the domestic legal systems of the Member States, adopting a blanket approach to the precedence of Community law would make obvious sense.

The judgment did not however seem to require that domestic law incompatible with Community law be quashed or invalidated. The ECJ deployed rather less forceful terminology in identifying the practical way in which the precedence doctrine would be expressed. We are told that the domestic law 'cannot prevail', or that EEC law 'cannot be overridden' by the domestic law. This form of words might have been chosen in part for practical reasons. The ECJ presumably accepted that domestic laws which affected both EC nationals and people or organisations which did not derive any rights from the Treaty could properly be enforced by domestic courts against those non-EC nationals. It also seems likely that the ECJ was searching for a legal formula which—at least in symbolic terms—presented a less blunt challenge to the primacy of national law.

The revolutionary implications of *Van Gend* and *Costa*

This latter point might be of considerable significance when one notes that the principle of precedence would be intimately linked with the principle of direct effect. If EEC law took precedence over domestic law *and* the EEC law in issue was directly effective then—in the ECJ's view—the responsibility for not allowing domestic law to 'prevail' over EEC law would

---

[18] Ibid.   [19] Ibid.   [20] Ibid.

rest with the domestic courts. This would not cause any domestic constitutional difficulties in the Netherlands, where the constitution already mandated such a result. But in a country such as Italy, the interactive effect of the precedence and direct effect principles on the facts of a case such as *Costa* were utterly irreconcilable with orthodox constitutional understandings.

That observation highlights a point of much broader significance. In practical terms, *Van Gend* and *Costa* were simply declaratory statements of abstract legal principle. The ECJ's judgments were not backed by any coercive force. If the principles laid out in those cases were to be effective determinants of legal relationships within the Community, those principles would have to be applied by national courts, either with the approval of, or in the face of, opposition from other governmental actors within the various Member States' respective constitutional systems.[21]

This question gained increased significance in the late 1960s and early 1970s as the ECJ produced judgments holding that Art 189 secondary legislation could also be directly effective.[22] In these judgments however, the Court was inconclusive on the question of whether EEC law also required such EEC measures to possess a superior hierarchical status to some (or all) provisions of domestic law. This abstract jurisprudential question was one of profound political significance. Could it really be the case that EEC law demanded that national courts were required to grant precedence to any directly effective provision of EEC law if that provision was incompatible with a rule of domestic law? To pose the question more starkly: did EEC law require that even a piece of EEC secondary legislation—which a Member State may have opposed in Council, or which (in the case of a decision) might have been created solely by the Commission—overrode even a deeply entrenched provision of a Member State's constitution? The ECJ finally offered an answer to that question in 1970 as it encountered an acute conflict between its own effet utile jurisprudence and the provisions of the German constitution.

The German constitution had been radically remodelled after World War II. The country's system of governance was structured on a federal basis, with power divided between a bicameral national legislature and executive and a sub-national level of government (the *Lande*). The federal basis of the governmental system was substantively entrenched in the new constitution. The constitution also procedurally entrenched a series of basic human rights norms (the Basic Law) which could not be interfered with by either the national or *Lande* governments acting by simple majority. Such values could be overridden by a two-thirds majority in the national legislature. Echoing the position in the United States, the German constitution created a Federal Constitutional Court empowered to invalidate any executive or legislative measure which contravened the Basic Law.

The *Internationale Handelsgesellschaft* litigation threw up a conflict between an EEC regulation controlling flour exports, and individual rights protected in Germany's 'Basic Law'. A Frankfurt court refused to enforce the (directly effective) regulations because it considered them 'unconstitutional' under German law. In an Art 177 reference, the Frankfurt Court asked if it was obliged under EEC law to give precedence to the regulations even if they were inconsistent with the Basic Law. The ECJ's response was a forthright 'Yes':

> Recourse to the legal rules of concepts of national law in order to judge the validity of measures adopted by the institutions of the Community would have an adverse effect on the uniformity and efficacy of Community law. The validity of such measures can only be judged in the light of Community law. In fact, the law stemming from the Treaty, an independent source of law, cannot because of its very nature be overridden by rules of national law, however framed, without being deprived of its character as Community law and without the legal basis of the Community

[21] The various ways in which national courts responded to the ECJ's initial development of the effet utile doctrine are assessed at some length in the seventh edition of this book at pp 358–364.

[22] *Politi* Case 43/71: [1971] ECR 1039 (regulations); *Grad* Case 9/70: [1970] ECR 825 (decisions); *SACE Spa* Case 33/70: [1970] ECR 1213 (directives).

itself being called in question. Therefore the validity of a Community measure or its effect within a Member State cannot be affected by allegations that it runs counter to either fundamental rights as formulated by the constitution of that State or the principle of a national constitutional structure.[23]

No attempt had been made during the 1960s or early 1970s to amend the Treaty to modify the ECJ's emerging effet utile jurisprudence. And it was into this legal context that the UK's eventual accession to the EEC was to occur.

II. United Kingdom accession

British governments tried to take the country into the EEC twice during the 1960s. However new states could only be admitted with the consent of all the existing members, and on both occasions the French government vetoed British entry. In the early 1960s, the then (Conservative) Prime Minister Harold Macmillan regarded membership as a central element of his government's foreign and economic policy, and had assigned Edward Heath the task of negotiating terms of entry. Macmillan and Heath were, however, thwarted by De Gaulle's firm belief that British entry would lead to Anglo-American domination of the Community.[24] The Labour Party at that time opposed entry; its then leader, Hugh Gaitskell, suggested membership would mean 'the end of a thousand years of history' of Britain as a sovereign state. Gaitskell's historical sense was rather bizarre, but although a significant minority of Labour MPs favoured accession, most (including the next leader, Harold Wilson) then shared his sentiments.[25] Wilson subsequently changed his mind, and his government (supported by many Conservative MPs and opposed by thirty-five Labour backbenchers) applied for entry in 1967. This too was vetoed by De Gaulle.

British opponents drew on two substantial political arguments against accession. The first related to Britain's world role. Opponents of EEC entry felt that Britain should align itself with the Commonwealth countries and the US, linking those nations to the EEC, rather than risk merging into a 'European super-state'. The second argument focused on 'sovereignty'. The principles of precedence and direct effect alarmed a few British politicians. This faction feared that some of Parliament's powers would be irretrievably lost to Community institutions. Opponents of entry argued that such a transfer of political power was undesirable. But some also argued that it was constitutionally impossible for Britain to honour the obligations EEC membership entailed. We need here to recall two key elements of Diceyan theory: that Parliament cannot bind itself or its successors; and that no British court is competent to say that a statutory provision is invalid.

If we translate *Costa* and *Internationale* into orthodox British constitutional language, we seem to say that Parliament could no longer pass legislation inconsistent with EEC law; that any Parliament which incorporated the Treaty into British law would bind itself and its successors not to breach EEC law. Direct effect is equally problematic from the orthodox, Diceyan viewpoint. The principle demanded that if Parliament enacted a provision which contradicted a directly effective EEC provision, a British court would have to refuse to apply that statutory term. Thus, the courts, via the medium of EEC law, would have a higher constitutional status than Parliament on EEC matters.[26] Furthermore, the ECJ's teleological approach to Treaty and

---

[23] Case 11/70: [1970] ECR 1125 at para 3.   [24] See Horne op cit pp 444–451.

[25] Pimlott op cit pp 245–248; Jenkins R (1991) *A life at the centre* pp 144–146.

[26] It seems that few MPs grasped this point. Most viewed Parliament's 'sovereignty' as something which might be lost to the EC, not to the domestic courts; see Nicol D (1999) 'The legal constitution: United Kingdom Parliament and European Court of Justice' *Journal of Legislative Studies* 131.

legislative interpretation was incompatible with British courts' more literalist tradition; EEC membership would thus demand that the constitution abandon its traditional approach to the separation of powers.

EEC membership and parliamentary sovereignty: the legislators' views—and their votes

With the benefit of hindsight, the earliest efforts of British commentators to analyse the potential impact of EEC membership on the British constitution appear woefully inadequate.[27] By the late 1960s, such analyses were becoming more sophisticated. Professor de Smith produced a prescient article in 1971, identifying the EEC as 'an inchoate functional federation', which while not initially a federal state, was likely to evolve in a direction demanding the 'pooling' of sovereignty;[28] and (in terms echoing Wade's seminal analysis of parliamentary sovereignty) that 'full recognition of the hierarchical superiority of Community law would entail a revolution in legal thought'.[29] de Smith expected that a 'reformulation' of traditional understandings would suffice to deal with the likely eventuality of unintended conflicts between EEC and domestic law, and that such reformulation might be achieved by the simple expedient of the domestic courts presuming that Parliament never intended to breach EEC law and interpreting domestic legislation accordingly. This 'solution' might of course demand that the notion of 'interpretation' would itself have to be reinterpreted in a manner quite inconsistent with dominant British understandings of the courts' proper constitutional role.

The courts' traditional approach to international law would be inadequate for these purposes. We saw in chapter two that unincorporated treaties have no binding force in domestic law. However, that does not mean they are entirely without legal effect. British courts will assume that Parliament does not intend accidentally to legislate in breach of the country's treaty obligations. Thus in circumstances where a statute's phraseology could bear more than one meaning, the courts will choose whichever meaning best corresponds to the international obligations. Similarly, if a treaty has been incorporated into domestic law, subsequent statutes will be construed, in so far as their language is ambiguous, in a manner consistent with the obligations enacted in the incorporating statute. This interpretive technique would be of no assistance when a later statute expressly repealed or was impliedly irreconcilable with the incorporating legislation. It would also seem incompatible with the ECJ's characterisation of the Treaty as a 'new legal order', quite unlike other international law.

Professor Wade recommended more radical steps. He suggested either that a standard clause be inserted into every domestic statute enacted after accession, providing that the legislation took effect subject to the precedence of EEC law. Alternatively, Parliament might annually enact (with retrospective effect) a statute reaffirming the precedence principle.[30]

Successive governments remained unconvinced of the need for such measures. Harold Wilson's 1966–1970 Labour government had made the extraordinary suggestion that all EEC measures would take effect in the United Kingdom as delegated legislation,[31] an analysis which betokens the subordinacy rather than precedence of Community law. Edward Heath's 1970–1974 administration, which eventually secured UK accession, seemed similarly confused. The government boldly stated that while it would introduce a Bill to incorporate the Treaty into

---

[27] See Keenan P (1962) 'Some legal consequences of Britain's entry into the European Common Market' *Public Law* 327.

[28] de Smith S (1971) 'The constitution and the Common Market: a tentative appraisal' 34 *MLR* 597 at 597 and 614. Interestingly, the article made no reference at all to *Van Gend*.   [29] Ibid, at 613.

[30] (1972) 'Sovereignty and the European Communities' 88 *LQR* 1. For a survey of other contemporaneous suggestions see Trinadade F (1972) 'Parliamentary sovereignty and the primacy of community law' 35 *MLR* 375.

[31] (1967) *Legal and constitutional implications of United Kingdom membership of the European Communities* para 22 (Cmnd 3301).

domestic law, 'there is no question of any erosion of essential national sovereignty'.[32] The distinction between 'essential' and (presumably) 'non-essential' sovereignty is a novel one, but neither of the main parties seemed willing to accept that it was either desirable or possible to entrench the precedence principle.

That is, however, not a legal solution. It may be that politicians of both parties adopted such equivocal positions because they feared that candid recognition of the *Internationale* principle would further harden internal opposition to accession. Equally plausibly, it may be that they simply did not properly understand the legal significance of the step they were about to take.[33]

The European Communities Act 1972—the passage

The political question as to the desirability of EC membership exposed some unusual divisions in and between the Labour and Conservative parties. Both the Labour left and Conservative right wings opposed the idea, disliking the partial 'loss' of sovereignty they assumed accession would entail, since that would reduce their capacity (should they ever form a Commons majority) to promote legislation favouring their respective political ideologies. The support for membership of some more centrist MPs in both parties depended on the entry terms (especially Britain's budget contribution) that the government negotiated. We will return to these divisions on several occasions, but we might gain an initial appreciation of the EEC's capacity to cut across party lines by examining the Commons' vote on the 1971 Bill.

Accession would have two domestic phases: a Commons vote on whether to accept the entry terms which, if successful, would be followed by the Bill 'incorporating' the Treaty into domestic law. At the 1970 election the Conservatives had won 330 seats, Labour 287, and the small parties 13. Rebellion by twenty anti-EEC Conservatives could have deprived the Heath government of a majority. Heath himself was passionately pro-accession: most Conservative MPs supported him, but forty announced they would not approve the terms.

Labour was more deeply split. As Prime Minister in the late 1960s, Wilson had supported EEC membership, reversing his previous opposition. In 1971, he and most of his Shadow Cabinet again opposed it, and Wilson authorised a three line whip instructing Labour MPs to vote against the terms. Sixty-nine Labour MPs, led by the Shadow Chancellor Roy Jenkins, defied the whip and voted with the government; a further twenty abstained. The government majority was 112. Had the whip been respected, the terms would have been rejected. This would probably not have been regarded as a resigning issue, as Heath had allowed Conservative MPs a free vote.

But while many Labour MPs approved the terms, they would not defy the whip on votes during the Bill's passage, in part because Heath had announced he would treat the second reading as a confidence issue.[34] Only a few (Jenkins foremost among them) elevated what they saw as Britain's national interest in joining the EEC above questions of party loyalty. On the Bill's third reading, the government's majority was just seventeen. For the moment, at least, the United Kingdom had entered the EEC. What now fell to be determined was the constitutional adequacy of the legislation enacted.

The European Communities Act 1972—the terms

As we saw in chapter two,[35] a government cannot change British law by using its prerogative powers to sign a treaty. If a treaty's terms are to be effective in British law, they must be given domestic legal status by statute. Parliament sought to determine the domestic status of

---

[32] (1971) *The United Kingdom and the European Communities* para 29 (Cmnd 4715).
[33] Cf Nicol D (1999) op cit.   [34] Norton (1978) op cit pp 363–364.
[35] See 'Inconsistency with international law', ch 2, pp 29–30.

Community law in the European Communities Act 1972 (ECA 1972). Four sections of the Act merit attention here, in terms of their consistency both with orthodox British constitutional theory and the ECJ's principles of precedence and direct effect.

Section 1 listed the various treaties to which the Act would apply. It also provided that the government might add new treaties to the list by using Orders in Council. This could be seen as a form of Henry VIII clause, in so far as it effectively allowed the government (via its prerogative powers) to give domestic effect to treaties, which treaties would by virtue of the *lex posterior* principle override existing domestic legislation.

Section 2(1), while framed in ungainly language, seems to provide that all directly effective EEC law will be immediately enforceable in domestic courts:

> All such rights, powers, liabilities, obligations and restrictions from time to time arising by or under the Treaties, as in accordance with the Treaties are without further enactment to be given legal effect . . . in the United Kingdom shall be recognised and available in law, and be enforced, allowed and followed accordingly . . .

Section 2(4) then provides that '. . . any enactment passed or to be passed . . . shall be construed and have effect subject to the forgoing provisions of this section.' Section 3(1) then states that:

> For the purpose of all legal proceedings any question as to the meaning or effect of any of the Treaties, or as to the validity meaning or effect of any Community instrument shall be . . . [determined] in accordance with the principles laid down by and any relevant decision of the European Court.

There are several principles of startling constitutional significance in the ECA's few words. There is no constitutional difficulty in the ECA 1972 telling a court to give effect to EEC obligations even if there is a contradictory rule of common law. The ECA 1972 obviously overrides any inconsistent rule of common law. Nor would any problem arise if a directly effective measure of EEC law was inconsistent with a statutory provision which predated the ECA 1972. The ECA, as the later statute, would ensure that the EEC measure would prevail. But what would happen if the inconsistent British statutory provision was enacted after the ECA 1972 came into force?

The 'passed or to be passed' formula of s 2(4) seemed to instruct the courts that any such Act would not have domestic legal effect. As we saw in chapter two, Parliament had produced such forward-looking legislation before. The Treaty of Union was incorporated by an Act which said some of its provisions would endure forever.[36] But those provisions have been repealed. Similarly, the courts held that s 7(1) of the Acquisition of Land Act was impliedly repealed by an inconsistent later Act. Why should the ECA 1972 be any different? Indeed, how could it be any different? To recognise it as a 'special' statute would undermine the entire basis of the parliamentary sovereignty doctrine.

How the courts would respond to these novel instructions was a matter for speculation. Writing in an academic journal, prior to the ECA 1972 coming into force, Lord Diplock had argued:

> It is a consequence of the doctrine of [parliamentary sovereignty] that if a subsequent Act . . . were passed that was in conflict with any provision of the Treaty which is of direct application . . . the courts of the United Kingdom would be bound to give effect to the Act . . . notwithstanding any conflict.[37]

For Lord Diplock, it seemed, there could be nothing 'special' about the ECA 1972. Lord Denning was initially rather more equivocal.

---

[36] This takes a Diceyan view of the Treaty's status, rather than seeing it as a 'constituent' document establishing the British state; see 'Is parliamentary sovereignty a British or English concept?' ff, ch 2, pp 38–41.
[37] (1972) 'The Common Market and the common law' *Law Teacher* 3 at p 8.

Parliamentary sovereignty: a non-justiciable concept?

Opponents of accession had lost the political argument. In a last effort to prevent entry, they tried a legal approach. In *Blackburn v A-G*,[38] Mr Blackburn asked the Court of Appeal to declare that it would be unconstitutional for the government to sign the Treaty of Rome, because to do so would amount to an irreversible surrender of parliamentary sovereignty.

In terms of domestic constitutional principle, this was an outlandish contention in two senses. Firstly, of course, orthodox constitutional theory wholly rejected the proposition that Parliament could limit its sovereignty, still less that the government could achieve this result. Secondly, for the government to sign the Treaty would require an exercise of the prerogative. In 1971, long before *GCHQ*, hardly any prerogative powers were subject to full judicial review. Even after *GCHQ*, treaty ratification is a non-justiciable prerogative power, within Lord Roskill's 'excluded categories'. Consequently, the Court of Appeal told Mr Blackburn that it could not intervene.

Mr Blackburn's argument was however quite consistent with the ECJ's judgments in *Van Gend, Costa*, and *Internationale*. Those judgments did not simply assert the precedence and direct effect of EEC law; they also asserted that Member States lacked the legal capacity to control the domestic status of EEC law. According to the analysis offered by the ECJ, the Heath government's ratification of the Treaty of Accession would curtail the UK's (by which one means Parliament's) complete autonomy to control its constitution.

While the Court of Appeal did not appear to acknowledge this point in explicit terms, Lord Denning did make some interesting comments about the impact EEC membership would have on parliamentary sovereignty:

> We have all been brought up to believe that, in legal theory, one Parliament cannot bind another and that no Act is irreversible. But legal theory does not always march alongside political reality.[39]

Lord Denning referred approvingly to Professor Wade's 1955 article on parliamentary sovereignty in which Wade had argued that the root of the parliamentary sovereignty principle lay in 'ultimate political facts'.[40] But what is not clear from *Blackburn* is whether Denning thought that accession might entail the irrevocable surrender of sovereignty. The Court of Appeal assumed that Parliament would not legislate contrary to EEC obligations. If it did, what would the courts decide? Lord Denning was non-committal; 'We will consider that event when it happens.'[41] As one might expect, 'it' seemed to happen rather quickly. But in the interim, the UK's political argument about membership had reawakened.

The 1975 referendum

Labour's two narrow election victories in 1974 brought into power a party deeply split over the desirability of EEC membership. Labour's 1974 manifestos had promised that voters would be given the opportunity to vote on continued membership by either another general election or a referendum. A third general election was not a plausible option, so a referendum seemed inevitable. The question which then arose was how the referendum should be conducted. Having renegotiated the UK's terms of membership, Prime Minister Wilson set off down a political path along which several constitutional principles fell by the wayside.

The first casualty was the convention of Cabinet unanimity. Wilson decided to 'suspend' the convention for the referendum campaign. His justification was that the question transcended

[38] [1971] 1 WLR 1037.   [39] Ibid, at 1040.
[40] See 'Are *Trethowan, Harris*, and *Ranasinghe* relevant to the British situation?', ch 2, pp 36–38.
[41] [1971] 1 WLR 1037 at 1040.

party politics, although most commentators suggest his real motivation for both the referendum itself and the suspension was his assumption that there was no other way to keep his party together.[42] It was then announced that seven (identified) members of Wilson's Cabinet opposed continued membership, as did many backbench Labour MPs. A Commons motion approving the new terms was carried by a majority of 226; but only 137 of the 315 Labour MPs voted in favour. The success of government policy was entirely dependent on Conservative support. The second casualty was the Burkean notion of the MP as a representative law-maker rather than the delegate of her voters. Parliament had in effect chosen to divest itself of its sovereignty on membership, by allowing the people the unusual opportunity of expressing an opinion on a single matter, rather than, as in general elections, on a package of issues. Neither the government nor Parliament was legally bound to respect the outcome of the referendum, although one imagines it would have been impossible, as a matter of practical politics, to do otherwise.

The EEC thus brought to the forefront of British politics the fundamental question of the desirability of leaving all political issues to be determined by a bare parliamentary majority. Some commentators suggested the EEC referendum might have a 'ripple effect', in convincing Parliament that there were other issues on which the 'the people's' views should be directly ascertained. In the 1890s, Dicey had written approvingly of referendums as devices for 'the people' to express authoritative opinions on matters of great constitutional significance; although given his stunted perception of 'the people', it would be rash to see this approval as espousing an avowedly 'democratic' position.[43]

Such a conclusion is perhaps more justifiable in respect of the 1975 referendum. The campaign was not fought along traditional party lines, but might crudely be described as a contest in which right wing Conservatives and the left of the Labour Party united in opposing membership, while the Labour centre-right and Conservative centre-left supported it. Both sides received substantial funds from the government to publicise their arguments. The question was very simple: 'Do you think that the United Kingdom should stay in the European Community (the Common Market)?'. The result was a resounding victory for the pro-EEC lobby; 67.2% to 32.8% on a 65% turnout.

Thereafter, constitutional orthodoxies promptly reasserted themselves. The anti-EEC members of Wilson's Cabinet re-embraced the unanimity convention, and traditional inter-party rivalries rapidly reappeared.[44] Nevertheless, the mere fact that a referendum was held, the peculiar political divisions which it exposed, and the overwhelming support it revealed for EEC membership, suggested that the Treaty of Rome was undoubtedly—in political terms—a 'special' ingredient in Britain's constitutional recipe. The issue next to be decided was whether it enjoyed a similar status as a matter of law.

III. EEC law, parliamentary sovereignty, and the UK courts: phase one

The UK judiciary's earliest encounters with EEC law suggested that the radical principles of *Van Gend*, *Costa*, and *Internationale*, and Parliament's evident attempt to enact those principles in the ECA 1972, would meet a trenchant restatement of orthodox Diceyan theory. Lord Denning's non-committal attitude in *Blackburn* was followed with a firmer view in *Felixstowe Dock and Railway Co v British Docks Board*.[45] The case raised the possibility that the provisions of a Bill shortly to be enacted would contravene Art 86's rules

---

[42] Irving R (1975) 'The United Kingdom referendum, June 1975' *European Law Review* 3; Pimlott op cit pp 654–660.   [43] See Irving op cit.
[44] Lent a sharper edge by Thatcher's election as Leader of the Conservative Party.   [45] [1976] 2 CMLR 655, CA.

on competition law. However Lord Denning did not think that possibility raised a difficult constitutional issue:

> It seems to me that once the Bill is passed by Parliament and becomes a Statute, that will dispose of all this discussion about the Treaty. These courts will have to abide by the Statute without regard to the Treaty at all.[46]

It is not clear if Lord Denning felt that the ECA 1972 had not limited Parliament's sovereignty, or whether it simply could not do so. Nevertheless, in his view, the ECJ's 'new legal order' had apparently not taken root in British constitutional soil. It came therefore as a surprise when Lord Denning himself advocated a radical break with constitutional tradition some three years later.

The end of the doctrine of implied repeal? *Macarthys v Smith* (1979)

Macarthys Ltd v Smith[47] arose from an Art 119 dispute. Mrs Smith was employed at a lower wage by Macarthys than the man who previously did her job. She claimed this breached Art 119. Macarthys contended that the British courts should apply the relevant British legislation (the Equal Pay Act 1970 as amended by the Sex Discrimination Act 1975), which forbade discrimination only between men and women doing the same job for the same employer simultaneously. If Macarthys' interpretation of the domestic legislation was correct, the British courts faced a difficulty. For British purposes, Art 119 came into force in 1973. The Sex Discrimination Act was passed two years later. Should the later Act prevail, as Dicey's theory would suggest? Or should EEC law be regarded by the court as the superior form of law?

In the Court of Appeal, Lord Denning thought that a literal reading of the British legislation supported Macarthys' claim. However, he rejected a literalist approach. Rather, the Act should be construed subject to the 'overriding force' of the Treaty 'for that takes priority even over our own statute'.[48] Denning's own view of Art 119 was that its prohibition on unequal pay extended beyond 'same time' situations to successive employment.[49] Construing the Treaty and the 1975 legislation: 'as a harmonious whole . . . intended to eliminate discrimination against women',[50] Denning found in Mrs Smith's favour.

Denning suggested he was obliged to adopt this expansive interpretive strategy because of the ECA 1972 s 2. That would in itself give the ECA a somewhat 'special' status, but Denning's argument went beyond technical questions of interpretation. He also concluded that s 2 had abolished the doctrine of implied repeal for British statutes affecting EEC matters. Domestic courts should assume that if ever a British statute was impliedly inconsistent with an EEC obligation the inconsistency arose because Parliament had erred in the language chosen: legislators could not have intended to achieve such a result, so the courts would save them from the consequences of their mistake by according precedence to EEC law.

This radical contention endows the ECA with a very 'special' constitutional status.[51] In effect, Denning's judgment in *Macarthys* recognised a weak 'manner and form' entrenchment of the precedence and direct effect of EEC law (the 'manner and form' in issue being a special form of words rather than an enhanced majority). These values were not however substantively entrenched, for:

---

[46] Ibid, at 659.   [47] Case 129/79: [1979] 3 All ER 325, CA.   [48] Ibid, at 329.

[49] Ibid. Denning was in a minority on this point. The majority (Cumming-Bruce and Lawton LJJ) were uncertain as to Art 119's scope, and referred the question to the ECJ. They seemed to agree however with Denning's approach to the constitutional issue.   [50] Ibid.

[51] An excellent analysis is offered in Allan T (1983) 'Parliamentary sovereignty: Lord Denning's dexterous revolution' *OJLS* 22.

> If the time should come when Parliament deliberately passes an Act with the intention of repudiating the Treaty or any provision of it . . . and says so in express terms then I should have thought it would be the duty of our Courts to follow the statute of our Parliament. I do not envisage any such situation.. . . Unless there is such an intentional and express repudiation of the Treaty, it is our duty to give priority to the Treaty.[52]

Denning did not explain how the 1972 Parliament had managed to bind itself and its successors in this (limited) way. There is, as we have repeatedly suggested, no obvious legal principle supporting such a conclusion. One must therefore conclude that Denning was recognising a new 'ultimate political fact'—that accession to the EEC had in some (evidently rather mysterious fashion) 'revolutionised' orthodox constitutional understandings.

This argument rests on the presumption that the political, economic, and foreign policy implications of acceding to the Treaty were so profound that the courts had to assume a new, protective role. The presumption operates on two levels. The first, itself controversial, is that Parliament should be protected from the adverse political consequences of unintended breaches of the UK's EEC obligations. The second, more controversial still, is that UK citizens should be protected from unwittingly incompetent or deceptive parliamentary efforts to renege on the UK's EEC commitments.

We might think that, as an exercise in constitution building, such protective devices would be desirable. But they are constituent rather than interpretive values, and as such, beyond conventional understandings of the judicial role. Despite its obscure roots, Denning's judgment staked out new constitutional ground. But the House of Lords showed itself reluctant to disapprove it.

A matter of interpretation? *Garland v British Rail* (1983)

The issue before their Lordships in *Garland*[53] was whether the Sex Discrimination Act 1975 prohibited gender discrimination in relation to concessionary travel facilities extended to British Rail's retired employees. Such discrimination seemed as though it might contravene Art 119, so the prospect again arose of a conflict between EEC law and a subsequent domestic statute.

Somewhat peculiarly, Lord Diplock (for a unanimous House) made an extensive reference to how he would approach the question if the Treaty of Rome was ordinary international law:

> it is a principle of construction of United Kingdom statutes . . . that the words of a statute passed after the Treaty has been signed and dealing with the subject matter of the international obligation of the United Kingdom are to be construed, if . . . reasonably capable of bearing such a meaning, as intended to carry out the obligation and not to be inconsistent with it.[54]

Lord Diplock perhaps made this point to highlight the innovative nature of EEC law, for he did not decide the case on that basis. Rather he suggested that the ECA 1972 s 2 had introduced a new rule of statutory interpretation to which the courts were now subjected. A UK court should construe all domestic legislation in a manner respecting EEC obligations: 'however wide a departure from the prima facie meaning of the language of the provision might be needed in order to achieve consistency'.[55] In this case, the 1975 Act could be interpreted as compatible with EEC law 'without any undue straining of the ordinary meaning of the language used'.[56] In that respect, Diplock shared Denning's sentiment in *Macarthys*. He also agreed with Denning that UK courts must obey a statute breaching EEC law in 'express positive terms'. He was more circumspect about the doctrine of implied repeal: this was not an appropriate case to decide that question.

---

[52] [1979] 3 All ER 325 at 329, CA.   [53] [1983] 2 AC 751.   [54] Ibid, at 771.   [55] Ibid   [56] Ibid.

Barely ten years after accession, Lords Diplock and Denning had both moved considerably from their previously Diceyan position towards the EEC's constitutional impact. They had not gone far enough to satisfy *Van Gend* and *Costa*, but the dynamicism of their respective approaches to the issue of the impact of EC law on orthodox British constitutional theory is undeniable.

IV. Political development in the 1980s

The first significant amendments to the Treaty of Rome were introduced by the so-called Single European Act in 1986. The new treaty made some modest extensions to the Community's powers and to its internal organisational structure.[57] The Community had also grown larger by this time, Greece having joined in 1981 and Spain and Portugal in 1986. The driving force behind the SEA reforms had been the Commission President, Jacques Delors, a Frenchman who had served as a Minister in Francois Mitterrand's socialist government. Delors was committed to the incrementalist ideal of furthering political union between the Member States, and suggested in a speech in 1988 that the EC would evolve into a federal government akin to that of the US.

Such sentiments alarmed Prime Minister Margaret Thatcher, who promptly publicised her own view of the Community's future development in a speech delivered at the College of Europe, Bruges, on 20 September 1988. Thatcher premised her view of Europe's development on what she regarded as the essential issue of preserving British 'sovereignty':

> Willing and active co-operation between independent sovereign states is the best way to build a successful European Community . . . It would be folly to try to fit [the Member States] into some sort of identikit European personality.[58]

It would be somewhat misleading to describe this view as defending 'national' sovereignty. Rather it entailed undiluted retention of the UK Parliament's omnicompetent legal authority so that successive Thatcher governments could continue (unhindered by either domestic or EC dissent) to impose their preferred ideological agenda on the people of the United Kingdom:

> We have not successfully rolled back the frontiers of the state in Britain only to see them re-imposed at a European level with a European superstate exercising a new dominance from Brussels.. . . The lesson of the economic history of Europe in the 1970s and 1980s is that central planning and detailed control don't work, and that personal endeavour and initiative do.. . .[59]

Given the United Kingdom's poor economic performance during the 1980s, Thatcher's lauding of Hayekian theory may seem ill-founded, especially since the economically most successful state, Germany, had a highly interventionist government and advocated still closer EC integration. But the speech's main significance was that it suggested that the Thatcher government would adopt a sceptical, obstructionist approach to all integrationist EC initiatives.

The Bruges speech had not been cleared with the then Foreign Secretary, Sir Geoffrey Howe, who evidently viewed its style and content with 'weary horror'.[60] The speech lent a sharper edge to the fundamental divisions over European policy which had riven the Conservative Party ever since 1972. It was enthusiastically received in the party's Euro-sceptic wing,[61] but met

---

[57] For contemporaneous comments see inter alia Edward D (1987) 'The impact of the Single European Act on the institutions' *CMLRev* 19; Forwood and Clough (1986) 'The Single European Act and free movement' *EL Rev* 383; Corbett R (1985) 'The 1985 intergovernmental conference and the Single European Act', in Pryce R (ed) *The dynamics of European Union*. The Parliament had become an elected body in 1979, and gained modestly enhanced legislative powers under the 1986 reforms.

[58] The speech is thoroughly reported in *The Times*, 21 September 1988.

[59] Ibid.   [60] Young (1991) op cit p 550.   [61] Clark op cit pp 225–227.

with dismay by several senior Cabinet members and a substantial number of Euro-enthusiast backbenchers.[62] As we shall see later, Thatcher's perception of both the nature and location of what we might term the 'ultimate political fact' of the UK's EC membership was eventually to prove seriously flawed.

In the shorter term, it had a significant effect. In 1989, eleven Member States had adopted a *Community Charter of Fundamental Social Rights of Workers*. The so-called 'Social Charter' advocated a significant extension of the Community competence in social policy matters, to encompass workers' rights to fair remuneration and adequate protection against unfair dismissal, redundancy, and unsafe working conditions. The British government opposed such measures, seeing them as a re-expansion of the 'frontiers of the state'. The Charter was merely a 'Declaration', not a binding part of EC law. Even in this form, however, it was unacceptable to the Thatcher government, which refused to sign the Declaration.[63]

V. The end of parliamentary sovereignty? Or its reappearance?

Despite their radical practical implications, *McCarthys* and *Garland* could be portrayed in theory simply as a new innovation in judicial interpretation of statutes. They did not involve a blunt challenge to legislation which could be reconciled with EC law only by affording the concept of 'interpretation' a meaning that paid no heed at all to linguistic limitations and encompassed the presumably distinct concept of defiance. That challenge, however, was not long in coming.

The demise of the legal doctrine? *Factortame*

The *Factortame* litigation arose from a dispute over fishing rights in British waters. The Merchant Shipping Act 1894 had allowed foreign owned vessels to register as 'British', and thereby gain the right to fish in British waters. By the late 1980s, some ninety-five boats owned by Spanish companies had done so. The British government, alarmed by the impact this 'foreign' fleet was having on fishing stocks, asked Parliament to enact the Merchant Shipping Act 1988 (MSA 1988). The 1988 Act altered the registration rules to require a far higher level of 'Britishness' in a ship's owners or managers.[64] None of the ninety-five Spanish ships could meet this test. Factortame, an affected company, subsequently launched an action in the British courts claiming that the MSA 1988 was substantively incompatible with EC law.

The High Court referred the substantive question to the ECJ. It was likely that eighteen to twenty months would elapse before the ECJ issued its judgment. The High Court therefore granted Factortame an interim injunction 'disapplying' the Act and ordering the Secretary of State not to enforce it against any ship that met the previous registration criteria.[65] The Court of Appeal set aside the order for an interim injunction, on which point Factortame appealed to the House of Lords.[66]

Lord Bridge gave the sole judgment. He accepted that not issuing an interim injunction would cause irreparable damage, perhaps even bankruptcy to Factortame, since the company had no immediate prospect of using its boats elsewhere. He also accepted that the House of Lords would accord precedence to EC law if the ECJ eventually ruled that the MSA 1988

---

[62] See Young op cit ch 23.   [63] See generally Shaw op cit ch 16.

[64] Including, inter alia, requirements that individual owners had to be British citizens or residents, and that corporate owners had to be incorporated in Britain, with 75% of their shares owned by British citizens/residents.

[65] See Gravells N (1989) 'Disapplying an Act of Parliament pending a preliminary ruling: constitutional enormity or common law right' *Public Law* 568.

[66] *R v Secretary of State for Transport, ex p Factortame Ltd* [1990] 2 AC 85.

breached EC law. This apparently clear acceptance of the precedence doctrine goes consider-ably further than the formulae advanced in *Macarthys* or *Garland*. Lord Bridge suggested that the 1972 Parliament had passed legislation in the form of the ECA 1972 s 2 which in some mysterious manner was incorporated into every subsequent UK Act which affects a directly effective EC right. The inference thus appeared to be that the courts would no longer obey an Act of Parliament which breached directly effective EC law even if the Act expressly stated it was intended to achieve that result.

But that conclusion was not germane to the present appeal, the nub of which was that a British court should refuse to allow the government to apply an Act of Parliament because of the possibility the Act might subsequently prove incompatible with EC law. Lord Bridge could not find any domestic authority for such a radical proposition. Nor was he ultimately persuaded that there was an overriding principle of Community law requiring the House of Lords to issue the interim injunction. However, Lord Bridge finally concluded that any such duty on the domestic courts arose only in respect of substantive rights already clearly established under EC law. The 'rights' claimed by Factortame had yet to be pronounced upon by the ECJ. Consequently, the House of Lords referred its own question to the ECJ, asking if it should disapply domestic law in order to safeguard as yet unproven EC law rights.

The litigation before the ECJ

Shortly thereafter, the ECJ heard an Art 169 action against the United Kingdom which claimed that the MSA 1988 Act breached the UK's Treaty obligations. In *EC Commission v United Kingdom*,[67] the Commission asked the ECJ to make an interim order per Art 186 ordering the British government not to enforce the 1988 Act. The ECJ saw some merit in the UK's posi-tion, since the 1988 Act might prove a defensible means to pursue the EC's own objective of conserving long-term fish stocks. However the Act's overt discrimination against non-British EC nationals seriously undermined the UK's case. Moreover, there was no doubt that enforce-ment of the Act would inflict extremely heavy losses on the Spanish shipowners. In those circumstances, the ECJ granted an interim order requiring the United Kingdom to 'suspend' the 1988 legislation.

The ECJ subsequently gave judgment on the question referred to it by the House of Lords, in *R v Secretary of State for Transport, ex p Factortame (No 2)*.[68] The Court observed that national courts were obliged by the 'principle of co-operation laid down in Article 5' to ensure that domestic legal systems give practical legal effect to directly effective EC rights. Any provision within the national legal system which impairs this effect contravenes EC law. This principle applied as readily to questions of interim as final relief. Consequently, if the sole obstacle to interim relief is 'a rule of national law', the national court must set aside that rule.

Back in the House of Lords . . .

The House of Lords announced that it had held in Factortame's favour, and would disapply the MSA 1988, in June 1990. The announcement provoked apocalyptic denunciations from Prime Minister Thatcher about losses of national sovereignty to the Commission. The lead-ing judgment in *R v Secretary of State for Transport, ex p Factortame (No 2)*[69] was given by Lord Goff. However Lord Bridge took the opportunity to comment on claims (whose source he diplomatically chose not to name) that the decision 'was a novel and dangerous invasion by a community institution of the sovereignty of the UK Parliament'.[70] Such criticism was misconceived. Parliament had been quite aware of the precedence doctrine in 1972, so any 'limitation' of sovereignty that EC membership entailed was 'voluntary'. The ECA 1972 had

---

[67] *EC Commission v United Kingdom*: Case C–246/89R: [1989] ECR 3125, ECJ.
[68] Case C–213/89: [1990] ECR I–2433.   [69] [1991] 1 AC 603.   [70] Ibid, at 658.

ordered domestic courts to respect that 'voluntary limitation', so there was nothing novel in this judgment.[71]

The unfortunate jurisprudential and political lacuna left unfilled by the *Factortame* litigation is that the House of Lords did not grapple with the fundamental question of just how it was that in 1972 the UK Parliament managed to do something that had always been beyond its predecessors' grasp—namely 'voluntarily' to limit its sovereignty? As H R W Wade has pointed out, Lord Bridge's reasoning makes very little sense, whether as an excursion in legal theory or as a recipe for practical politics.[72] The obvious problem is that if Parliament managed in 1972 to entrench the ECA, on what basis can one sensibly maintain that it could not now or in the future entrench other legislation as well? It might be argued that the EC is 'unique' in this respect, because, perhaps, of the political significance of its powers and/or its elaborate institutional structure. But that is merely an assertion. It is no less plausible to say that other important moral or political factors could acquire a similar constitutional status, with the result that, as Wade puts it 'the new doctrine makes sovereignty a freely adjustable commodity whenever Parliament chooses to accept some limitation'.[73]

This is not as alarming a spectre as it may appear. *Factortame* entrenchment is—it seems—of an extremely weak procedural kind. It does not take the form of requiring super-majorities within Parliament, nor that there be resort to any extra-parliamentary device such as a referendum; it merely requires that a bare parliamentary majority expresses itself in unusually blunt language. A new Merchant Shipping Act which said in s 1 that it was intended to repudiate the UK's obligations under the Common Fisheries Policy would presumably have been applied by Lord Bridge and his colleagues. It is doubtful that it could have been disapplied through the judicial techniques ostensibly used in *Factortame (No 2)*.

Factortame need not therefore be read as suggesting that Parliament can grant itself a power equivalent to that given to colonial legislatures in s 5 of the Colonial Laws Validity Act 1865 to entrench any political values it chooses by altering the legislative 'manner and form' required to change them.[74] An entrenchment mechanism of this sort is a dangerous device, as it would enable a bare legislative majority enjoying only minority electoral support to set such high thresholds for the repeal of its preferred laws that they could never be altered. But if Parliament was able to create even a very weak form of entrenchment in 1972, might it not be able to create much stronger entrenchment devices in future?

Wade's conclusion that *Factortame* amounts to a 'judicial revolution' is initially enticing. It maintains in essence that it was not Parliament through the ECA 1972 but the judges themselves who have altered the constitution's rule of recognition. In other words, the old orthodoxy was correct, but it was within the power of the courts to change it at any time. This argument displaces rather than solves the problems posed by Lord Bridge's analysis. The obvious difficulty is that if the courts have managed in 1990 to entrench the European Communities Act, on what basis can one sensibly maintain that they could not now or in the future entrench other legislation as well? Wade's doctrine 'makes sovereignty a freely adjustable commodity whenever the courts choose to impose some limitation'.

Allan's analysis of *Factortame* is more satisfactory on this issue.[75] Allan has long offered a rather isolated voice in our constitutional discourse to the effect that orthodox understandings of parliamentary sovereignty are, and always have been, ill-conceived.[76] Allan's suggestion that our current constitutional settlement permits the courts to disapply legislation which is

---

[71] Lord Bridge perhaps oversimplified the issue. British judges and British governments displayed confusion in the late 1960s and early 1970s as to the nature and implications of *Costa* and *Van Gend*. Moreover, many innovative aspects of the ECJ's own constitutional jurisprudence had appeared after the UK's accession.

[72] (1996) 'Sovereignty—revolution or evolution?' *LQR* 568.   [73] (1996) op cit p 573.

[74] See '*A-G for New South Wales v Trethowan* (1931)', ch 2, pp 32–33.

[75] (1997) 'Parliamentary sovereignty: law, politics and revolution' *LQR* 443.

[76] See particularly (1983) op cit; (1985) op cit; (1993) op cit.

irreconcilable with the concepts of democracy and the rule of law offers a fascinating point of departure for discussing the *Factortame* saga.

Allan's thesis rests on the presumption that the orthodox, Diceyan view of parliamentary sovereignty misconceives the political objectives that the English Revolution of 1688 was trying to achieve. The Diceyan position, and its more modern restatements, espouse a purely formalist conception of the relationship between statute and the courts. The courts (and presumably everyone else) 'recognise' statute as the highest form of law simply because the 1688 Revolution was fought (and won) by men who wished to establish the legal superiority of measures enacted by the Commons, Lords, and Monarch acting collectively over both the actions of either house, of the Monarch acting under prerogative powers, or of the courts acting under the power of the common law. However, if, following Professor Wade, we regard parliamentary sovereignty as the ultimate political fact of the constitution, it does not seem outlandish to ask (as Dicey and Professor Wade did not) why the revolutionaries wished to achieve this objective? What political or moral purpose was the ultimate political fact intended to serve?

Questioning the 'Why' rather than the 'What' of parliamentary sovereignty

Paul Craig has latterly offered an intriguing answer to this question.[77] Craig's critique begins by noting that 'much of the current literature fails to pay attention to the reasons why Parliament should or should not be regarded as sovereign'.[78] He attempts to fill in this gap by digging deeper into and behind the legal sources underpinning the Diceyan position. Orthodox theories place much reliance, for example, on arguments voiced by Sir William Blackstone, the leading eighteenth-century jurist, in his celebrated *Commentaries* on English law. The key passage asserts that Parliament 'can in short do everything that is not naturally impossible . . . True it is, that what the Parliament doth, no authority can undo'. On its face, Blackstone's text provides unequivocal support for the orthodox position.

However, Craig's critique, unlike the analysis offered by Wade in 1955, then asks *why* Blackstone was led to this conclusion. As suggested in chapter two, the notion that sovereignty should lie in a tripartite Parliament, within which each element possessed veto powers, reflected a belief that the Commons, Lords, and Monarch acting in unison were the only legitimate arbiters of the national interest. The 1688 Revolution can thus be seen as an attempt to create an anti-majoritarian source of sovereign legal authority. It is this essentially political purpose, Craig suggests, which underlay the acceptance of Parliament as the highest source of law. To put the argument simply, Blackstone and those whose views he represented endorsed the principle of parliamentary sovereignty because they could conceive of no more broadly based mechanism for ensuring that laws enjoyed the consent of the people. Parliament was 'sovereign' for political or moral reasons—namely that it minimised the possibility that the English people[79] would be subjected to factionally motivated legislation.

The sovereign Parliament was not created for a modern society. Its proponents in 1688 had no conception that the powers of the Monarch would diminish to insignificance, nor that the House of Lords would voluntarily acquiesce in the removal of its co-equal powers in the legislative process. Still less would they have envisaged a near universal electorate for the Commons and the emergence of national political parties. Our concept of 'the people' is, of course, now much changed. We regard modern Britain as a mature democracy in which the legitimacy of a sovereign Parliament rests on the periodic consent of the electorate. Yet in our mature democracy Parliament functions as an extremely effective vehicle for the majoritarian

---

[77] (1991) 'Sovereignty of the United Kingdom Parliament after *Factortame*' *Yearbook of European Law* 221.

[78] Ibid, at 234.

[79] Narrowly defined of course as the Monarch, the Lords, and the small portion of citizens permitted to participate in electing members of the Commons.

or even minoritarian sentiments of a single political party to be given legal effect. While 1688 envisaged Parliament as a consensual forum designed to identify the national interest, it now operates as an arena of conflict intended to promote party interests.

It is at this juncture that Allan's suggestion that notions of 'democracy' and 'the rule of law' can serve as limits on Parliament's legislative competence become significant in relation to the *Factortame* conundrum. The EC Treaties stand in marked contrast to our domestic law-making process. Their terms are not the product of majoritarian or even super-majoritarian law-making. Their every provision has been arrived at through a consensual negotiatory process, demanding the unanimous approval of a growing number of nations—nations which themselves represent differing political philosophies and a multiplicity of cultural inheritances. And as the Treaties have been successively amended by the same protracted, negotiatory, consensual law-making process, so the innovate jurisprudence of the European Court and the Member States' domestic courts have implicitly been granted a unanimous, cross-national seal of legislative approval. The prospect of an EC Treaty provision being narrowly majoritarian, has been reduced almost to vanishing point. In that functional sense, Treaty provisions are a 'higher' form of law than can be produced by any of the EC's Member States within their own legal systems. The Treaties thus represent a modern manifestation of the ideal for which England's seventeenth-century 'revolutionaries' strove.[80]

In comparison with the Treaties, the Merchant Shipping Act fares very poorly when measured against this ideal. It is perhaps unfortunate that legal analysis of the *Factortame* episode has generally been confined to exploring the judgment's impact on the relationship between Parliament and the courts. Even Allan, notwithstanding his concern with substantive values of democracy and the rule of law, approaches the issue in this way. Neither Allan's nor Wade's critique addresses the individual citizen's interest in the case. What has rather been forgotten in respect of *Factortame* is that this particular constitutional episode was triggered by the deliberate decision of a xenophobic minoritarian government to use its Commons and Lords majorities (the one generated by the support of 34% of the electorate; the other derived from the principle of hereditary peerages) to enact a crudely segregationist economic policy which—in addition to clearly breaching the Treaty of Rome—was intended to bankrupt several business enterprises and throw many people into unemployment. It would be a very strange view of 'democracy' which nonetheless accorded legitimacy to such behaviour.

There is little indication that such overtly 'political' reasoning underpinned the *Factortame* decisions. It may well prove to be the case, as Craig has argued, that *Factortame* rests on no more than an adjustment to, or development of, the courts' role as interpreters of legislative intent.[81] That assertion can however only be proven 'correct' as a matter of law if political developments afforded the opportunity to put it to a legal test. This could have occurred in one of two scenarios.

Would domestic courts apply statutes which expressly contradict EC law?

The first would arise if a Euro-sceptic government, commanding a majority in the Commons and Lords, were to promote legislation (perhaps, eg, another Merchant Shipping Act unilaterally withdrawing the United Kingdom from the Common Fisheries Policy) which stated in s 1:

> This Act is intended to breach the obligations accepted by the United Kingdom in its capacity as a member state of the European Community. The courts of the United Kingdom are hereby expressly ordered to apply the terms of this Act, irrespective of any rule of law deriving from the European Communities Act 1972 or the Treaties establishing the European Community or any judgment of the European Court of Justice.

---

[80] This rationale obviously has less force in respect of EC secondary legislation, especially if that legislation can be enacted by qualified or simple majority vote.   [81] (1991) op cit.

We might then suppose that a non-UK EC national who wished to fish in UK waters in accordance with the terms of EC law launched an action in the English courts seeking an injunction to prevent the Act being applied. There would then be no scope for a domestic court to uphold the precedence of EC law through innovative techniques of interpretation. Nor could resort be made to theories distinguishing implied and express statutory commands.

If a domestic court wished to uphold the *Costa* and *Van Gend* principles in this situation, it could do so only by bluntly stating that Parliament had no power to disapply EC law while the United Kingdom remained a member of the Community. Building on *Costa* and the 'loyalty duty' contained in Art 5 of the Treaty, the argument would be that EC law cannot be 'supreme' if its supposed supremacy is divisible or suspendable at the whim of a national Parliament. If Parliament wishes unilaterally to terminate the 'effet utile' of EC law in the United Kingdom, it may do so only by passing legislation which repeals the European Communities Act 1972 and withdraws this country from the EC. This sounds, of course, like a very speculative hypothesis; but it perhaps takes a far smaller leap of the jurisprudential imagination to go to this point from *Factortame (No 2)*, than it did to reach *Factortame (No 2)* from the views which prevailed in many political and legal circles when the United Kingdom joined the EC in 1972.

Would domestic courts apply a statute withdrawing the United Kingdom from the EC?

Yet even this scenario, irreconcilable though it may seem with orthodox constitutional principles, does not betoken a permanent loss of parliamentary sovereignty. The final step in that direction could only be taken if Parliament enacted legislation purporting to withdraw the United Kingdom from the Community and the UK courts then refused to apply the Act. Thus far, little serious thought has been given to the argument that Parliament cannot expect such legislation to be applied by domestic courts.[82] But such an argument is a perfectly logical development of the foundations laid by the ECJ in *Van Gend* and *Costa* and of those set down by the House of Lords in *Factortame (No 2)*.

As noted earlier, the ECJ told us in *Van Gend* that the EC was 'more than just an agreement between Member States'. It was rather:

> ...a new legal order of international law for the benefit of which the states have limited their sovereign rights, and the subjects of which comprise not only the Member States but also their nationals.[83]

An alternative way of expressing this principle is to say that we as citizens of the United Kingdom each enjoy certain entitlements (and are subjected to certain obligations) which our domestic organs of government, acting unilaterally, are not legally competent to alter. As the Community's legal competence expanded following the Single European Act, new entitlements and obligations have been created, and the original ones bestowed by the Treaty of Rome have become more firmly rooted in our legal and political culture. This would imply that any such alteration in the UK's relationship with the EC could lawfully be accomplished only through the mechanisms of EC law. The question then becomes how can that alteration lawfully be effected?

Prior to 2009, Community law contained no express provisions for Member State withdrawal.[84] The only way that result could lawfully be achieved (as a matter of EC law, and hence, given the supremacy of EC law over contradictory domestic statutes, as a matter of domestic law) was if the EC Treaties were amended to reconstitute the Community with one fewer member. That process, as specified in Art 236, required the convening of an Inter-Governmental Conference, at which all existing Member States had to agree to alter the

---

[82] Wade hinted at the possibility; (1996) op cit at p 570: 'It may be accepted, at least at this point in time, that Parliament could indeed repeal the Act of 1972 altogether'.

[83] Case 26/62: [1963] ECR 1 at para 12.   [84] See further 'Conclusion', p 318.

Treaty's provisions. From this perspective, as a matter of EC law (and of acute political irony), any one of the other Member States would have had a veto power over UK departure from the Community.[85]

To suggest that UK courts might simply have refused to apply the provisions of legislation seeking to withdraw the United Kingdom from the Community is perhaps, a fanciful argument. The sovereignty of Parliament, as generally understood, would undoubtedly have to have been challenged in the most confrontational of ways by such judicial action. There is nonetheless some force in the contention—for the reasons outlined earlier—that for the UK courts to have denied our modern Parliament the power either expressly to breach EC law, or to leave the Community altogether, would not challenge the sovereignty of Parliament but rather restore its original purpose. Perhaps this would indeed amount to a revolution; but more in the sense of our constitutional order turning a full circle and returning to the anti-majoritarian ethos underpinning the 1688 revolution than of embarking on a wholly new and uncharted political adventure.

The reappearance of the political doctrine? Monetary union, collective ministerial responsibility, and the fall of Margaret Thatcher

Several factors contributed to Conservative MPs' decision to remove Margaret Thatcher as their leader (and thence to her decision to resign as Prime Minister) in November 1990. As chapter ten suggested, the unpopularity of the community charge led many Conservative MPs to fear defeat in the next general election. Thatcher's close personal identification with the poll tax offered an obvious reason for some Conservative MPs to want a new leader. Others remained continuingly unhappy with her evident preference for a presidential style of Cabinet government (a preference which had triggered the resignations of Heseltine in 1985 and Nigel Lawson in 1989). But the catalytic event was Thatcher's attitude towards the UK's EC membership.

The Treaty of Rome (Title II, Chapter 1) had contained various (seemingly non-justiciable) provisions heralding a co-ordinated approach to macro-economic policy. Member States undertook to maintain the stability of their respective currencies and an approximate equilibrium in their balance of payments. The Commission was empowered to monitor Member States' performances in this regard, and to offer financial assistance to Member States suffering a severe currency or balance of payments crisis.

These modest co-ordinatory policies were seen by some observers as a tentative first step towards full blown 'monetary union', which would ultimately require a single EC currency and a central EC bank controlling the Community's money supply and interest rates. This objective has an obvious economic logic in the context of creating a truly 'common' market, as it removes the transaction costs engendered by currency exchanges and ensures that businesses in particular Member States are not advantaged or disadvantaged vis-à-vis their EC competitors as a result of their own government's monetary policy.

But full monetary union also had profound political implications. A single EC currency and a central EC bank would present a distinct challenge to orthodox notions of national sovereignty. By the late 1960s, it is possible to argue that western economies were sufficiently closely interconnected for it to be practically impossible for any one European country successfully to pursue economic policies entirely independent of those adopted by neighbouring states. Nevertheless, economic and monetary union would remove such practical controls as national governments still possessed, thereby significantly extending the de facto federal nature of the Community and adding further force to arguments for a full political federalisation on the American model.

---

[85] Since the EC is (per *Van Gend*) a 'new legal order of international law', the rules in 'ordinary' international law permitting unilateral State withdrawal from treaty arrangements would not apply.

The EC's first steps towards monetary union had begun in 1969, but rapidly foundered during the recession of the early 1970s. Roy Jenkins, having resigned from the Labour government to become President of the Commission in 1977, put the issue at the top of the Commission's list of priorities, and by 1979 the European Monetary System (EMS) was in place. The EMS existed outside the legal structure of the Treaty, and so was not a Community measure in the strict sense. Its central feature was the Exchange Rate Mechanism (ERM), which placed fairly tight limits on fluctuations in currency exchange rates. Member States were not obliged to join the ERM, and successive Labour and Conservative governments chose not to do so, preferring to retain autonomy in exchange rate and interest rate policies. The SEA itself made scant reference to monetary union, beyond noting the obvious point that giving the EMS and ERM a legal basis within Community law would require further Treaty amendment. However in 1988, the European Council instructed Jacques Delors to produce a phased plan for achieving de facto and de jure economic and monetary union. The 1989 Delors *Report on Economic and Monetary Union* envisaged a three-stage process. Firstly, a gradual 'convergence' of the Member States' economies in respect of such matters as inflation rates, economic growth, and the balance of payments; secondly, the locking of all Member States' currencies into a far tighter ERM, which would tolerate only very small currency fluctuations; and thirdly, the introduction of the single currency.

While many Member State governments welcomed the plan, the UK government expressed reservations. The Conservative manifesto for the 1989 EC elections warned that monetary union would 'involve a fundamental transfer of sovereignty . . . The report, if taken as whole, implies nothing less than the creation of a federal Europe'.[86] Nevertheless, at the Madrid Summit in 1989, the European Council agreed to begin the first stage in 1990, and to initiate the process of Treaty amendment to establish a timetable for phases two and three. The British government also agreed that it would enter the ERM at some point in the near future.

It seems that the Thatcher government regarded the Madrid summit as a recipe for delay rather than prompt action. However, the other Member States took quite the opposite view, with the result that by mid-1990, the Prime Minister and some of her Cabinet colleagues were making distinctly hostile comments about the Delors plan. We noted in chapter nine that Nicholas Ridley, perhaps the Cabinet member most in sympathy with Thatcher's EC views, had resigned in July 1990 after giving an interview critical of Germany. Some parts of that interview merit further attention here. Ridley had suggested that monetary union was simply 'a German racket designed to take over the whole of Europe'; he thought that the scheme posed an intolerable threat to British sovereignty: 'You might just as well give it to Adolf Hitler, frankly'.[87]

Ridley's resignation might have been thought to suggest that Ministers holding such sentiments should at the least not express them in such terms. But the Cabinet was clearly split on the monetary union question. The United Kingdom finally joined the ERM in October 1990, yet immediately afterwards the Prime Minister herself engaged in a Ridleyesque tirade against the Delors plan. At the European Council's Rome Summit, the other eleven Member States expressed their willingness to accelerate plans for further monetary integration. Thatcher resolutely opposed any such initiative, describing the summit as 'a mess' and her fellow heads of government as living in 'Cloud Cuckoo Land'. On her return to the Commons, Thatcher accused Jaques Delors and the Commission of trying to 'extinguish democracy', and announced she would greet every 'federalist' EC measure with a resounding 'No!'.

Thatcher's outburst prompted Geoffrey Howe (the then Deputy Prime Minster) to resign from the Cabinet. His initial explanation that his resignation was over the question of government policy towards the EC was to be expanded upon in a speech to the Commons on 13

[86] Quoted in Nicoll W and Simon T (1994) *Understanding the new European Community* at p 158.
[87] *The Spectator*, 14 July 1990.

November 1990.[88] Howe was never noted as an inspiring orator. He once earned the memorable soubriquet from Dennis Healey that to be criticised by him in debate was 'like being savaged by a dead sheep'. His resignation speech did not contain any stylistic fireworks; but its content had an explosive political effect.

Howe attributed many of the country's economic difficulties to the government's refusal to join the ERM in 1985. He then revealed that the government's eventual commitment to join had been extracted from an unwilling Prime Minister only when he (then Foreign Secretary) and Nigel Lawson (the then Chancellor) had threatened to resign from the Cabinet if it did not do so. Yet Howe suggested that the question of ERM membership was merely a symptom of a more pervasive Prime Ministerial distaste for the European Community. Echoing Lord Bridge's oblique criticism in *Factortame (No 2)*, Howe asserted that it was a serious error to regard closer European integration, as the Prime Minister appeared to do, as involving the 'surrender of sovereignty'. Making an overt reference to the Bruges speech, Howe argued that such hyperbolic language served only to create:

> . . . a bogus dilemma, between one alternative, starkly labelled 'co-operation between independent sovereign states', and a second, equally crudely labelled alternative, 'centralised federal superstate', as if there were no middle way in between.[89]

Howe observed that the EC's development was more likely to proceed in a direction which coincided with British interests if the government argued its case from the centre of the EC policy-making process, rather than standing on the sidelines and eventually being dragged reluctantly into a reformed Community in which the political agenda had been set to reflect the preferences of its other members. But Howe's criticism of Thatcher did not dwell merely on tactics; it reached also to the question of her basic attitude towards the UK's EC partners. Howe saw no merit in what he termed Thatcher's 'nightmare image' of an EC 'positively teeming with ill-intentioned people, scheming in her words to 'extinguish democracy', to 'dissolve our national identities', and to lead us 'through the back-door into a federal Europe'.[90] Against such Europhobic 'background noise', it was impossible for the Chancellor of the Exchequer to be taken seriously by other Member States in any discussion of EC economic policy.

Howe's speech is a graphic example of the Commons' capacity to serve as a forum for calling the executive to account. The speech revealed not simply a disagreement between a Prime Minister and a senior colleague on a matter of major substantive importance, but also suggested that the country was being governed by a dogmatic leader who held an ill-mannered contempt for any divergent opinion (be it within Cabinet or from other EC Member States), and who utterly rejected traditional principles of Cabinet government. Such criticisms of Thatcher had frequently been made by opposition parties; but they were likely to carry more weight with Conservative MPs when delivered by the man who had served as Chancellor and Foreign Secretary for over ten years in Thatcher's Cabinets.

Thereafter, domestic political events moved with great rapidity. Michael Heseltine, five years after leaving the Cabinet, challenged Thatcher for leadership of the Conservative Party. Her failure to win an adequate majority in the subsequent election held among Conservative MPs led to her resignation as party leader and Prime Minister, and then to John Major's eventual succession.

These events reinforce the presumption that EC membership has wrought significant changes in both orthodox constitutional theory and orthodox constitutional practice. In practical terms, the constitutional history of twentieth-century Britain has been dominated (except during the two world wars) by a straightforward party political division, in which single-party governments with relatively distinct and coherent ideological beliefs have deployed a Commons majority to use Parliament's legal sovereignty to pursue their preferred policy

---

[88] *HCD* 13 November 1990 cc 461–465.   [89] Ibid, at c 463.   [90] Ibid, at c 464.

programmes. But that picture may now be changing. In part, that is attributable to the courts' recognition of supra-legislative constraints on parliamentary sovereignty on EC matters. It may be fanciful to equate *Costa* and *Factortame* with the pre-revolutionary supra-legislative notion of 'common right and reason', but the analogy is not entirely spurious. But perhaps of greater immediate significance to analysts of the British constitution is the argument that the demise of Margaret Thatcher, seen in conjunction with the extraordinary party political alignments produced in the 1972 Accession controversy and the 1975 referendum, indicates that the EC has introduced a profound ideological fault line into the very core of the traditional party political divide. In 1990, it seemed plausible to suggest that neither the Labour nor Conservative Party could any longer rely on its MPs to present a unified front on EC questions. Equally, it appeared that EC questions could never be settled in any definitive sense, for Eurosceptics seemed wedded to the belief that only a bare Commons majority would be needed to unravel whatever EC commitments Parliament had previously undertaken. In combination, these factors held out the prospect of a significant weakening of Prime Ministerial authority vis-à-vis the Cabinet, and of government authority vis-à-vis the Commons.

VI. Maastricht and Amsterdam

The substantive reforms to the Community's legal structure introduced by the Maastricht Treaty on European Union (TEU) in 1993 were perhaps less far-reaching than those in the Single European Act.[91] Yet the amendment process proved extremely problematic in several states.

The terms of the Maastricht Treaty

The least controversial amendment was one of nomenclature; the Community was formally renamed as the EC rather than the EEC. Questions of labelling retained a symbolic importance throughout the negotiatory process. The British government insisted that any reference to the creation of a 'federal' Europe be deleted from the TEU's text. An ambivalent formula was eventually adopted; that the TEU would be 'a new stage in the process of creating an ever closer union among the peoples of Europe, in which decisions are taken as closely as possible to the citizen',[92] but which would respect the 'national identities' of Member States.

The TEU introduced several minor extensions in the EC's competence.[93] The Community gained powers over consumer protection, industrial policy, and some education and cultural matters. More significantly, a specific timetable was set for phases two (1 January 1994) and three (1 January 1997 or 1999) of Delors' plan for monetary union.

Further modest efforts were made to reduce the Community's continuing democratic deficit. A new type of law-making process, requiring 'co-decision' between the Parliament and the Council in some areas, increased the Parliament's influence. Some effort was also made to strengthen the links between the Community and individual citizens by creating a (largely symbolic) status of EU 'citizenship', and by empowering EC nationals to stand for office and vote in local or European elections anywhere in the Community.[94]

But for both proponents and opponents of a United States of Europe, other aspects of the TEU may have seemed of greater long-term importance. The TEU provided that the EC itself was now to be seen as merely one 'pillar' of the 'European Union' (EU). The other two pillars

---

[91] For a longer, but accessible, guide see Hartley T (1993) 'Constitutional and institutional aspects of the Maastricht Agreement' 42 *International and Comparative Law Quarterly* 213.　　　　[92] TEU, Art A.

[93] See by Lane R (1993) 'New Community competences under the Maastricht Treaty' *CMLRev* 939.

[94] Raworth P (1994) 'A timid step forwards: Maastricht and the democratisation of the EC' *EL Rev* 16.

would be Common Foreign and Security Policy (CFSP) and Justice and Home Affairs (JHA), which in combination substantially extended the range of the former system of 'European Political Co-operation' introduced by the Single European Act. In formal, legal terms, the CFSP and JHA were not part of the EC, and should perhaps be seen as an exercise in traditional inter-governmental co-operation rather than another 'new legal order' operating in parallel to the Community. However they were serviced by the EC's institutions, and there can be little doubt that many proponents of the Maastricht reform anticipated that all three pillars would eventually merge into a single legal order. CFSP and JHA took the Member States into far less justiciable territory than that covered by the EC. Nationalist sentiment is likely to be most intense over questions of foreign and defence policy: national governments would seem unlikely to wish to cede control over so emotive an issue as involvement in foreign wars, which may dilute EU responses to the point that they are utterly ineffective. Certainly the first test of the EU's ability to operate as an effective foreign policy player, the war in former Yugoslavia, suggested that the framers of the TEU had underestimated the difficulties that would attend joint initiatives in this area.

The inference that Maastricht may have gone too far too fast may also be drawn from consideration of the fate of the plans to achieve monetary union within the EC. The ERM collapsed late in 1993, before the TEU came into effect. The Member States could not maintain exchange rate stability in the face of massive speculation on the international money markets against the weaker currencies. Consequently several countries, including Britain, left the system. The Community's failure to resist these forces undermined its credibility in the eyes of supporters of further integration, and was construed as a sign of more pervasive weakness by its opponents. It is therefore unsurprising that the ratification and incorporation of the Treaty proved so tortuous in several Member States.

The ratification and incorporation of the Maastricht Treaty

Under the terms of Art 236 of the Treaty of Rome, those parts of the TEU which amended the EC Treaty could not come into force until it had been ratified by all the Member States in accordance with their own constitutional procedures. The people of Denmark had initially rejected the terms of the Treaty in a referendum. Some rapid renegotiation between the Member States ensued, whereupon the TEU was approved by a tiny majority in a second Danish referendum. Public opinion was also sharply divided in France, in which the requisite referendum produced a very small majority in favour of the Treaty. In Germany, the political argument was clearly won by pro-Maastricht forces, although the German government subsequently faced an (unsuccessful) legal challenge which argued that the TEU was inconsistent with provisions of the Basic Law.[95] Ratification' of the TEU presented considerable political difficulties in the United Kingdom. The non-EC pillars of the Treaty were unproblematic; since there was no need to incorporate their provisions into domestic law, the government could satisfy its international law obligations simply by ratifying the measures through an exercise of the prerogative. In contrast, the TEU's reforms to the EC would have to be incorporated. Since the TEU increased the powers of the European Parliament, the government was bound by the European Parliamentary Elections Act 1978 s 6 to gain parliamentary approval of the TEU before ratifying it. Given the then small size of the government's Commons majority,[96] and the presence of a dozen anti-EC backbenchers within Conservative ranks, it was not clear that approval would be forthcoming. After a series of complex political manoeuvrings in the Commons,[97] the government was defeated by eight votes on a motion concerning the Social

---

[95] *Brunner v European Union Treaty* [1994] 1 CMLR 57.
[96] The Conservative majority at the 1992 election was twenty-one.
[97] These are described in the first edition of this book at pp 554–557.

Policy Protocol. The Prime Minister thereupon announced that the government's motion on the Protocol would be the subject of a vote of confidence the next day, and implied that a defeat would lead to a dissolution. For rebel Conservative MPs, the prospect of a general election in which they might lose their seats was sufficiently daunting to bring them back into (the party) line. The government's majority in the confidence vote was forty.

But the controversy had not run its course. In a manner reminiscent of Mr Blackburn's feeble attempt to prevent the UK's accession to the Community in 1971, right-wing Euro-sceptics launched a legal action after their cause had been defeated in the Commons.[98] The action was fronted by Lord Rees-Mogg, a cross-bench peer and former editor of *The Times*, and financed by Sir James Goldsmith, an expatriate financier. Such arguments as Rees-Mogg could muster against ratification and incorporation were peremptorily dismissed by the High Court. The litigation was a trivial event compared to the extraordinary convolutions that had gripped the Commons and divided the Conservative Party in previous months; convolutions that continued in the following months.

At the 1992 Edinburgh Summit, the Member States had agreed to a modest increase in the Community budget from 1995 onwards. When the Major government introduced legislation in November 1994 to incorporate that obligation into domestic law, it encountered a substantial rebellion from backbench Conservative MPs. For a government whose majority was then only fourteen, the prospect of a Commons defeat was very real. The Prime Minister then announced that the second reading vote would be a matter of confidence, evidently on the basis that a government which could not honour its international obligations could not continue in office. Should the government be defeated, the entire Cabinet would resign and the Prime Minister would ask the Queen to grant a dissolution.[99] Rebel Conservatives promptly accused the Prime Minister of constitutional sharp practice in elevating a minor financial matter to the status of a confidence issue, and some discussion ensued as to whether the Queen would be conventionally obliged to grant a dissolution in such circumstances. Such speculation ultimately proved of only academic interest. The threat of a general election at a time when the Labour Party enjoyed a substantial lead in the opinion polls was again sufficient to bring most potential rebels back into the government camp. Nevertheless (in a manner reminiscent of Roy Jenkins' elevation of his perception of national interest over party interest in the 1972 accession votes), eight Conservative MPs abstained at second reading. They were subsequently stripped of the party whip, and rumours abounded that their local constituency associations were being pressurised by Conservative Central Office to withdraw their support from the errant MPs at the next general election.

The Treaty of Amsterdam

The Labour Party's victory at the 1997 general election took much political heat out of the constitutional controversies attending the UK's membership of the Community. The Labour Cabinet was firmly pro-European in outlook, and while a few backbench Labour MPs fell into the Euro-sceptic camp, they were an insignificant grouping within the parliamentary party. The Conservative Party under its new leader William Hague continued its stridently Euro-sceptic tone, but given the size of the government's Commons majority Conservative Euro-scepticism had also become wholly insignificant.

The Blair government immediately demonstrated its pro-EC credentials by incorporating the Social Charter into UK law. It stood back however from participating in the launch of the

---

[98] *R v Secretary of State for Foreign and Commonwealth Affairs, ex p Rees-Mogg* [1994] QB 552, [1994] 1 All ER 457. See Rawlings R (1994a) 'Legal politics: the United Kingdom and ratification of the Treaty of European Union (part two)' *Public Law* 367.

[99] Technically, of course, Mr Major would have to have asked for the dissolution before resigning.

single European currency in 1999. The government's official position on this issue was that it supported the single currency in principle, but would not join it until economic conditions were appropriate. The government also promised that the United Kingdom would not join unless the electorate voted to do so in a referendum.[100]

The new government also found itself plunged immediately into a new round of Treaty amendment negotiations. The proposals aired in the Amsterdam Treaty were relatively modest in effect.[101] Its most significant innovation was to transfer much of the Justice and Home Affairs pillar of the EU into the EC, thereby bringing its terms within the jurisdiction of the ECJ. While the Amsterdam amendments did not incorporate the European Convention on Human Rights into the EC's legal order, the new Treaty did extend the EC's competence into a range of overtly 'political matters'. Under Art 13, the Community gained powers to address discrimination not just on the basis of nationality, but also gender, sexual orientation, disability, race and ethnicity, and religious belief. The Amsterdam Treaty also further refined the Community's institutional balance, enhancing the power of the Parliament by extending the range of legislative matters which had to be taken by the co-decision procedure. The ratification process proved less problematic than was the case with the Maastricht Treaty. It was only in Demark that there seemed any likelihood that the proposals would be rejected. In the event, they were approved by a comfortable majority in a referendum.

It might however be suggested that the proposal of any amendment proposals so soon after Maastricht damaged the EC's credibility. It becomes increasingly difficult to regard the EC treaties as containing 'constituent' principles if those principles are altered every few years. Such rapid change suggests that the treaties are more appropriately seen as part of the rather sordid world of party politics rather than as a cross-national and cross-party attempt to identify and adhere a series of fundamental political values.

Conclusion—Nice and Lisbon

The impression that the EU is now a political and legal order engaged in a process of constant constitutional amendment was reinforced when a further inter-governmental conference met at Nice in 2000. The proposals under consideration at Nice were in part issues left unresolved at Amsterdam. The primary questions to be addressed concerned the admission into the EU of as many as ten new Member States, many of them countries from the former eastern bloc, and the alterations that such enlargement would demand for voting systems within the Council and structure of the Commission and the Court.[102] A proposal was also made that the EU should add its own Charter of Rights to the Treaty framework. The United Kingdom was opposed to giving any such Charter justiciable status, and it was eventually agreed that the Charter would have the status of a 'Solemn Proclamation' appended to the new Treaty.[103] The amendments were initially rejected by Ireland, and in a manner reminiscent of Denmark's eventual ratification of Maastricht, the proposals were eventually approved by Irish voters late in 2002.

The admission of ten new members, many of them poorly developed in economic terms and lacking any deeply rooted democratic culture, presented the EU with substantial

---

[100] On shifts in Labour Party policy towards the EU in this era see Fella S (2006) 'New Labour, same old Britain? The Blair government and European treaty reform' *Parliamentary Affairs* 621.

[101] See Craig P (1998) 'The Treaty of Amsterdam: a brief guide' *Public Law* 351.

[102] A helpful guide is offered in Shaw J (2001) 'The Treaty of Nice: legal and constitutional implications' *European Public Law* 195.

[103] See Rogers I (2002) 'From the Human Rights Act to the Charter: not another human rights instrument to consider' *European Human Rights LR* 343.

challenges. The difficulties of securing consensus among so many and so very different governments and peoples for any further major change to the treaties was graphically illustrated by the ignominious collapse of attempts to introduce a 'constitution' for the Community in 2004 and 2005. The proposed 'constitution' was the result of an inquiry headed by the former French President, Giscard D'Estaing. If adopted by the Community, the constitutional Treaty would have introduced substantial changes to the scope of Community competence, to its institutional structure, and to the status of Community law within the Member States. Its terms were decisively rejected in referendums in France and Denmark, and the proposals were withdrawn without being put forward for the approval of the majority of Member States.

The capacity of 'rejected' Treaty amendments to resurface and subsequently gain acceptance from the Member States was hardly a novel feature of the Community's development by this time. It was perhaps therefore unsurprising that proposals which in the view of many commentators[104] bore a very close resemblance to those of the 'constitution' reappeared in a draft Treaty which was approved by an inter-governmental conference held at Lisbon in 2007. The Blair and Brown governments subsequently insisted that the terms of the Lisbon Treaty were so different from—and so less significant than—those of the rejected constitution that they did not regard themselves as bound (in a moral sense) by the promise made in the Labour Party's 2005 election manifesto that a referendum would be held to establish if voters wished the United Kingdom to ratify the EU constitution. The government's position on this point likely owed more to an assumption that voters might not support the new Treaty than to a sincere belief that the Treaty's contents differed meaningfully from those that had been in the constitutional Treaty. The Lisbon Treaty was then rejected by Irish voters in 2008. With admirable persistence, the Irish government re-submitted the question to a further referendum in October 2009, this time securing a positive vote. The Treaty came into force shortly thereafter.

From a lawyer's perspective, a notable feature of the Lisbon Treaty was the provision made in Art 50 for a Member State to leave the EU, either through a negotiated process or unilaterally:

> Article 50
> 1. Any Member State may decide to withdraw from the Union in accordance with its own constitutional requirements.
> 2. A Member State which decides to withdraw shall notify the European Council of its intention. In the light of the guidelines provided by the European Council, the Union shall negotiate and conclude an agreement with that State, setting out the arrangements for its withdrawal, taking account of the framework for its future relationship with the Union. That agreement shall be negotiated in accordance with Article 218(3) of the Treaty on the Functioning of the European Union. It shall be concluded on behalf of the Union by the Council, acting by a qualified majority, after obtaining the consent of the European Parliament.
> 3. The Treaties shall cease to apply to the State in question from the date of entry into force of the withdrawal agreement or, failing that, two years after the notification referred to in paragraph 2, unless the European Council, in agreement with the Member State concerned, unanimously decides to extend this period.

Should Parliament pass legislation to withdraw the United Kingdom from the EU in terms which respect Art 50, there can be no doubt that the Act would be applied by domestic courts. The more intriguing question was how the courts would react to withdrawal legislation which was not consistent with Art 50.

---

[104] Most significantly M D'Estaing himself; see his letter to *Le Monde* of 26 October 2007 : 'Traité européen: 'les outils sont exactement les mêmes, seul l'ordre a été changé dans la boîte à outils'.

For a British constitutional lawyer, however, the alterations made by the Lisbon Treaty to the powers and internal arrangements of the EU and the introduction of Art 50 were perhaps of lesser interest than the impact that accession has had on the UK's internal constitutional dynamics. It is undeniable that a substantial and continually increasing proportion of the laws applicable in the United Kingdom are found in the Treaties and secondary legislation. It is similarly clear that the gradual extension of the EU's competence beyond the nominally 'economic' sphere into a range of 'political' issues has lent the EU a far more 'federal' identity than it possessed forty years ago. In that respect, the effective 'sovereignty' of the United Kingdom as a nation has been curtailed. Article 50 of the Lisbon Treaty offers a clear route for that curtailment of 'sovereignty' to be reclaimed. But the innovative stream of jurisprudence flowing from *Macarthys* through *Garland* and *Pickstone* and *Litster* to *Factortame* and beyond has substantially restructured the *internal* balance of constitutional power between the legislature, the executive, and the courts.

In 2002, sitting in the High Court in *Thoburn v Sunderland City Council*,[105] Sir John Laws reaffirmed the proposition that the doctrine of implied repeal was no longer applicable in respect of EC matters. Intriguingly, the judgment also suggested that the ECA 1972 possessed what Sir John Laws called 'constitutional' status, which lent it a different legal character (ie being immune to implied repeal) to 'ordinary' Acts of Parliament.[106] More interestingly, the case appears to be the first instance of counsel arguing (in accordance with the ECJ's jurisprudence) that EC law takes effect in the United Kingdom simply because of its autonomous status as EC law and not through the 'incorporating' device of the ECA 1972.[107] The Court rejected that submission:

> Whatever may be the position elsewhere, the law of England disallows any such assumption. Parliament cannot bind its successors by stipulating against repeal, wholly or partly, of the 1972 Act. It cannot stipulate as to the manner and form of any subsequent legislation. It cannot stipulate against implied repeal any more than it can stipulate against express repeal. Thus there is nothing in the 1972 Act which allows the Court of Justice, or any other institutions of the EU, to touch or qualify the conditions of Parliament's legislative supremacy in the United Kingdom. Not because the legislature chose not to allow it; because by our law it could not allow it. That being so, the legislative and judicial institutions of the EU cannot intrude upon those conditions. The British Parliament has not the authority to authorise any such thing. Being sovereign, it cannot abandon its sovereignty.[108]

The Conservative/Liberal coalition was at pains to underline this reasoning in promoting a European Union Bill in 2010, which was enacted as the European Union Act 2011. The primary political purpose of the Act (in s 2) was to require that any further extension[109] of the EU's political competence could not be approved by a British government unless the proposal had been supported by a majority of voters in a referendum.[110]The autonomous effect of EU law point was addressed in s 18:

---

[105] [2003] QB 151. *Thoburn* was one of the 'metric martyr' cases, in which shopkeepers and market traders found themselves being prosecuted for failure to comply with EC sourced rules requiring weights and measures of goods offered for sale to be exclusively in metric scales. See Boyron S (2002) 'In the name of European law: the metric martyrs case' *European LR* 771.

[106] Since the judgment purports to offer principles which are not confined solely to EC law matters—and thus has broad implications for the continued vitality of the doctrine of parliamentary sovereignty—it is revisited at a later stage of this book.

[107] [2003] QB 151 at 182–184.   [108] Ibid, at 184–185.   [109] With some identified exceptions.

[110] See the speech of the then Foreign Secretary, William Hague, at the Bill's second reading; *HCD* 7 December 2010 at c191:

> Indeed, the crowning argument for the Bill was the behaviour of the last Government, who opposed a referendum on the EU constitution, then promised one, then refused to hold one on its substantially similar reincarnation as the Lisbon Treaty. The Bill will prevent Governments from being so deceptive and double-dealing when it comes to giving voters a say.

18 **Status of EU law dependent on continuing statutory basis**

Directly applicable or directly effective EU law (that is, the rights, powers, liabilities, obligations, restrictions, remedies and procedures referred to in section 2(1) of the European Communities Act 1972) falls to be recognised and available in law in the United Kingdom only by virtue of that Act or where it is required to be recognised and available in law by virtue of any other Act.

Section 18 might be thought wholly pointless from a legal (whether domestic or EU in nature) perspective. The provision will have no effect on the ECJ's view of the status of EU law. And in domestic terms, given that orthodox theories as to the sovereignty of Parliament rest on its status as an 'ultimate political fact', Parliament's reiteration of the principle in a statutory text is meaningless. Section 18 is perhaps best seen as, in part, an attempt by the coalition government to pander to the Euro-sceptic fringe of the Conservative Party, and, in part, a warning shot fired by politicians across the bows of judges who the politicians fear may be prone to succumb to the temptations of aligning their constitutional loyalties to the EU rather than Parliament.[111]

From the viewpoint of the political scientist rather than the lawyer, the UK's membership of the EU has been notable for offering us a political issue which transcends the usual rigidities of ideological loyalty within the Conservative and Labour Parties. Perhaps more significantly however, membership of the EU has lent an increasing degree of normalcy within our constitutional morality to the presumption that governmental power—be it legislative, executive, or judicial in nature—can and indeed ought to be divisible on a geographical basis. The issue of the UK's departure from the EU is discussed in the final chapter of this book. In chapter twelve, we examine the way in which our modern constitution has addressed that question of the geographical separation of governmental power in the context not of the relationship of the United Kingdom qua country with other nation states, but of the relationship within the United Kingdom of England, Scotland, and Wales.

Suggested further reading

Academic and political commentary

JACKSON J (1992) 'Status of treaties in domestic legal systems' *American Journal of International Law* 310

WEILER J (1981) 'The Community system: the dual character of supra-nationalism' *Yearbook of European Law* 267

PESCATORE P (1983) 'The doctrine of direct effect: an infant disease of Community law' *European Law Review* 155

ALLAN T (1983) 'Parliamentary sovereignty: Lord Denning's dexterous revolution' *OJLS* 22

CRAIG P (1992) 'Once upon a time in the west: direct effect and the federalisation of EEC law' *Oxford Journal of Legal Studies* 453

CRAIG P (1991) 'Sovereignty of the United Kingdom Parliament after *Factortame*' *Yearbook of European Law* 221

NICOL D (1999) 'The legal constitution: United Kingdom Parliament and European Court of Justice' *Journal of Legislative Studies* 131

WADE HRW (1996) 'Sovereignty—revolution or evolution?' *LQR* 568

ALLAN TRS (1997) 'Parliamentary sovereignty: law, politics and revolution' *LQR* 443

---

[111] The sentiments expressed in s 18 were affirmed by the Supreme Court in *R (on the application of HS2 Action Alliance Limited) v Secretary of State for Transport and another* [2014] UKSC 3; [2014] 1 WLR 324 at para 79.

Case law and legislation

Van Gend en Loos [1963] ECR 1

Costa v ENEL [1964] ECR 585

Internationale Handelsgesellschaft [1970] ECR 1125

European Communities Act 1972 ss 2–3

Macarthys Ltd v Smith [1979] 3 All ER 325

Garland v British Rail Engineering Ltd [1983] 2 AC 751

R v Secretary of State for Transport, ex p Factortame Ltd (No 2) [1991] 2 AC 603

Chapter 12

The Governance of Scotland and Wales

The *McCormick v Lord Advocate*[1] litigation in the 1950s indicated that some Scots rejected the orthodox view of the Treaty of Union that Scots MPs were simply absorbed into the English Parliament.[2] Since Scotland's population was far smaller than England's, the principle of approximate parity of constituency sizes adopted for parliamentary elections since 1948 necessarily meant that Scotland sent only a small minority of MPs to the Commons.[3] Scotland's 'separateness' was recognised by the creation of a Secretary of State for Scotland in 1926, and by the existence of a Scots 'Grand Committee' in the Commons,[4] yet neither initiative afforded Scotland any constituent political autonomy. Its Secretary was merely one member of Cabinet; the Grand Committee merely a small fraction of MPs.

But Scots discontent was not limited solely to questions of parliamentary representation. It expressed a more general perception that Scotland's historical status as a 'nation', and its contemporary status as a discrete area of the United Kingdom, had been unacceptably submerged beneath a legislative and governmental structure dominated by 'English' concerns. Such sentiments gained wider support after the 1960s, when Scots (and Welsh) nationalist parties attracted substantially increased electoral support. In response to this pressure, the Conservative and Labour Parties indicated in the late 1960s that they might introduce legislation creating distinctively Scots and Welsh 'national' governments. The second Wilson government established a Royal Commission (the Kilbrandon Commission) to address the question of the relationship between the various countries of the United Kingdom. Its report, published in 1973, recommended that Parliament enact far-reaching schemes of 'devolution'.[5]

Neither Conservative nor Labour governments in the 1970s ever suggested that Wales or Scotland should become independent sovereign states, nor that the United Kingdom should become a federal country like the USA. Any such proposal would run into the legal difficulty

---

[1] See '*McCormick v Lord Advocate* (1953)', ch 2, pp 40–41.

[2] Dicey was perhaps the prime example of this theory. As Bogdanor notes, Dicey's analysis of Anglo-Scots relations spoke always of the Act (rather than the Acts) of Union, a linguistic sleight of hand which implicitly rejects the merger theory of union: see Bogdanor V (1979) 'The English constitution and devolution' *Political Quarterly* 36.

[3] Some 11% of MPs represented Scots constituencies.   [4] See Turpin (1990) op cit pp 183–188.

[5] For a useful summary of the Commission's investigations see Mackintosh J (1974) 'The report of the Royal Commission on the Constitution 1969–1973' *Parliamentary Affairs* 115.

of the sovereignty of Parliament. In terms of strict legal theory, any grant of 'independence' that Parliament might make to Wales or Scotland (or indeed England), or any legislation that sought to reconstruct the UK's unitary state on a federal basis, would lack constituent legal status; a subsequent Parliament could at any time restore the previous arrangements. As we saw in respect of Canada, such legal niceties may be swept aside by the brute force of new 'ultimate' political facts. The political realities shaping the Kilbrandon report offered no obvious, immediate threat to the legal structure of the constitution: they did, however, point to a significant redefinition of conventional understandings.

Kilbrandon's concept of 'devolution' was distinct from either federalism or independence in the formal, legal sense. The idea suggests that Parliament is delegating or lending legal competence in certain areas of government activity. But it is not giving its sovereignty away, for it reserves the power to revoke or redefine the nature of the delegation. Scotland was to have an elected Assembly (often colloquially referred to as the Scottish Parliament), its members chosen through a process analogous to that used for the Commons. In technical terms, however, it would be problematic to describe a body implementing devolved powers within a unitary state as a legislature, or to label its 'laws' as legislation. The Scots Assembly would be an executive body, just like a local council, empowered to produce bye-laws in certain specified fields. It might prove, as a matter of practical politics, to be a tier of local government unlike any other the British constitution had ever contained; but it would nevertheless depend (at least until political realities dictated otherwise) for its continued legal existence on the whim of Parliament.

The Scotland Act 1978 and the Wales Act 1978

The schemes of devolution enacted[6] in the Scotland Act 1978 and Wales Act 1978 were presented to the Commons by the then Prime Minister James Callaghan as:

> . . . a great constitutional change . . . There will be a new settlement among the nations that constitute the United Kingdom. We shall be moving away from the highly centralised State that has characterised our system for over two and a half centuries.[7]

Whether the Acts would mark a first step in a longer march towards significant constitutional change is an open question. No answer was ever given to that question however, since the Act never came into force. The Labour government had broken with the tradition of 'parliamentary government' by including in both the Scotland and Wales Act a provision that required the proposed changes to be approved by a referendum conducted among the Scots and Welsh electorates respectively before they could be implemented.[8] The Acts required that a majority of those voting supported devolution, and also that any such majority comprised at least 40% of the eligible electorate. The government was empowered to repeal the Act if its terms were not approved by the electorates. In Wales, on a mere 59% turn-out, 80% of voters rejected the devolution proposals. In Scotland, 55% of voters approved the change. However, since the turnout was only 64%, the 40% threshold was not reached.[9]

The outcome of the referendums suggests that there was no great enthusiasm among the Scots or Welsh for the Labour government's proposals. Scots Nationalist MPs nevertheless saw the election result as sufficient reason to vote against the Labour government in a subsequent

---

[6] The Bill was opposed by the Conservative Party. Its Commons passage was secured because the Labour government, by then in a Commons minority, had the support of the Liberals and the Scots and Welsh nationalist parties.   [7] *HCD* 13 December 1976 c 993.

[8] This being perhaps another example of the 'ripple effect' of EC membership on the domestic constitution. The Wilson government deployed a referendum on the question of EEC membership in 1975; see 'The 1975 referendum', ch 11, pp 301–302.

[9] See Balsom D and McAllister I (1979) 'The Scottish and Welsh devolution referenda of 1979: constitutional change and popular choice' *Parliamentary Affairs* 394.

vote of confidence, with the result that the government resigned, Parliament was dissolved, and the first Thatcher administration was returned at the ensuing general election. The Thatcher government deployed its majorities in the Commons and Lords to repeal the Scotland and Wales Acts, and subsequent Conservative administrations saw no need to introduce devolution Bills of any sort, notwithstanding the fact that their share of the Scots vote in successive general elections was so small that barely a dozen of Scotland's seventy-two MPs were Conservatives. Throughout the 1980s, therefore, Scotland was governed by a party pursuing policies supported by only a small minority of the Scots people. In the 1995 local government elections, the Conservatives were unable to win a majority of seats on any Scots local authority.

By this time, the Scots Nationalists were committed to creating an independent Scots state, while the Labour and Liberal Parties advocated a more extensive form of devolution (including the crucial power to levy taxation) than that proposed in the Scotland Act. The status quo was preferred only by a party which had attracted little more than 40% of the popular vote in general elections since 1979; but as we have frequently seen, such minoritarian support is quite sufficient to control every level of the law-making process under the British constitution's particular form of democratic government.

I. The Scotland Act 1998

At the 1987 general election, the Conservatives won only ten of Scotland's seventy Commons seats. They nevertheless had a large Commons majority. The Conservatives' evident unpopularity in Scotland—and a growing sense of injustice that the country should be governed by an 'English' Conservative administration—led the Labour and Liberal parties in Scotland, along with various small parties and some trade union and church groups, to convene a 'Scottish Constitutional Convention' to debate radical reform to Scotland's governmental system.[10]

The Convention's discussions continued throughout the 1990s,[11] and culminated in 1995 in publication of a policy document—'*Scotland's Parliament, Scotland's Right*'—which urged establishment of a Scots legislature and executive which would exercise substantial political powers and enjoy a large degree of autonomy from the Westminster Parliament. Much of the letter and some of the spirit of the Convention's proposals found their way into the Labour Party's manifesto proposals for the 1997 election. The manifesto highlighted Scots devolution as an urgent priority for a Labour government. The extent to which the Conservative government had lost any plausible claim to legitimacy within Scotland was forcefully underlined by the election result. The Conservatives did not win a single seat in Scotland in 1997. This dire performance was partly caused by the first past the post system; the Conservatives attracted 17.5% of the Scots popular vote.

The new government acted promptly on its manifesto commitment. A white paper, *Scotland's Parliament*,[12] was published in July 1997. In its prefacer, Prime Minister Blair characterised Scotland as 'a proud historic nation' and stated that his government's reform programme was designed to enhance the Scots people's control over domestic Scottish politics. The government's plans did not extend as far as the Constitutional Convention had urged, but outlined reforms which appeared to offer the Scots substantial political autonomy.

The white paper proposed that the new structure of government within Scotland would be modelled on the existing UK system. There would be a fusion rather than separation of powers

---

[10] The Scottish Nationalist Party boycotted the Convention. It regarded complete independence for Scotland as the only acceptable reform. See McClean R (1999) 'A brief history of Scottish home rule', in Hassan G (ed) *A guide to the Scottish Parliament*.

[11] The Conservatives had won twelve Scots seats at the 1992 general election. The Major government remained implacably opposed to any reform of Scotland's governmental system.   [12] Cm 3658.

between the 'legislature' and the 'executive'. The Scots government would be headed by a First Minister, whose administration would be drawn from, and hence have to command the support of, a majority of members of the Parliament.[13]

It was proposed that the Parliament would contain 129 members. Its electoral system would be markedly different from the straightforward first past the post method used for the House of Commons, and would be loosely based on the process used to elect members of the German *Bundestag*.[14] Each elector would have two votes. Some seventy-three MSPs[15] would represent the same constituencies as the Scots members of the UK Parliament, and would be chosen by the orthodox 'first past the post' system. The electors' second vote would be for a party rather than an individual candidate. The other fifty-six MSPs would be selected from eight regional party lists, with allocation of additional members being designed to ameliorate—if not eliminate—any seats won/votes cast discrepancies arising in the constituency seat section. This system made it likely that, unless one party gained an extremely high percentage of the popular vote,[16] the Scots Parliament would always be hung. This in turn would suggest that the Scots government would be either a minority or coalition administration.

The Constitutional Convention had begun its activities with the announcement that:

> We, gathered as the Scottish Constitutional Convention, do hereby acknowledge the sovereign right of the Scottish people to determine the form of government suited to their needs.

The echoes that this statement had of the US *Declaration of Independence* were ignored in the white paper. Its text laid repeated emphasis on the legal fact that the creation of a Scots Parliament did not and could not in any way detract from the continuing sovereignty of the Westminster legislature.[17] This position implicitly repudiates any notion that the Scots people possess in the legal sense 'sovereign rights', whether over their form of government or any other matter. The government also stressed, in a less legalistic fashion, that the United Kingdom would remain as a unitary state. There was no suggestion that the reform would in legal terms attempt to restructure the constitution on a federal basis, still less that Scotland would become an independent, sovereign nation. The envisaged legislation was not a latter-day equivalent of the 1931 Statute of Westminster.[18]

In addition to believing that substantial devolution was an intrinsically correct policy to pursue, the Labour government appeared to have concluded that granting Scotland a substantial degree of self-governance would reduce rather than intensify growing pressure among some sections of the Scots electorate—particularly the Scottish Nationalist Party—for full independence. The notion that Scotland might survive and flourish as an independent nation was much less outlandish in 1997 than it was twenty years earlier. The substantial expansion of the EC's competence since 1980 made the Westminster Parliament less significant in economic terms to Scotland than hitherto, and advocates of independence could also point to the rapid emergence of small sovereign states in eastern Europe following the collapse of the Soviet Union to buttress the feasibility of their position.[19]

---

[13] The white paper did not use the formal label of 'the Cabinet' to describe the senior members of the Scots government, but it seemed likely that this would be the commonplace terminology.

[14] See 'The German system', ch 7, p 195.

[15] MSP being the accepted abbreviation for 'Member of the Scottish Parliament'.

[16] Although, given that Scotland has four major political parties, a single party could win all seventy-three constituency seats with less than 30% of the constituency vote and without receiving any party list votes at all.

[17] The white paper did not address the suggestion made in *McCormick* that the Treaty and Acts of Union may impose some limits on the Westminster Parliament's powers; see '*McCormick v Lord Advocate* (1953)', ch 2, pp 40–41.

[18] See however Bogdanor's suggestion that the relationship between the Scots and UK legislatures will in effect be quasi-federal: (1999a) 'Devolution: decentralisation or disintegration' *Political Quarterly* 185.

[19] See Bogdanor (1999a) op cit: and Brazier R (1999) 'The Constitution of the United Kingdom' *Cambridge LJ* 96.

The white paper advocated that the division of political power between the UK and Scottish Parliaments would entail certain matters being 'reserved' to the UK Parliament. But any matter not so reserved would be presumed devolved to the Scottish legislature. By a process of deduction (ie by identifying which powers were reserved), one could see that the Scots Parliament would enjoy substantial control over inter alia: all levels of education; local government; land development and environmental regulation; many aspects of transport policy; the national health service; the legal system (both civil and criminal law); agriculture and fisheries; and over sports, arts, and cultural heritage policy. Those matters reserved to the UK Parliament and government included constitutional reform, foreign policy, defence, macro-economic policy, and social security law.

As suggested in the previous discussion of local authorities, granting a government body a long list of political powers has limited meaning if the body concerned does not have the fiscal competence to exercise those powers in the way that its voters consider appropriate. Raising and spending revenue would be of crucial significance to the degree of autonomy that the Scots Parliament would enjoy.

The white paper envisaged some substantial and some minor changes to the previous financial system. From the late 1970s onwards, under what was known as the 'Barnett formula', Scotland's share of public revenues had been based increasingly on its pro rata share of the UK's overall population.[20] A 'block grant' was allocated to Scotland, which the Secretary of State could allocate to different services as he/she thought appropriate. Under the devolved system of government, the block grant system would remain unchanged, save that the Scots Parliament and government would determine how that revenue should be spent. Thus expenditure could be increased on a given service, for example schooling, but only if it was reduced by the same amount in other areas.

The devolution proposals also envisaged that the Scots Parliament should enjoy a limited tax-raising/reducing capacity to increase or cut the rate of income tax by up to three pence in the pound. The Blair government's insistence that macro-economic policy be a 'reserved' matter precluded the grant of any substantial fiscal autonomy to the Scots Parliament. The 'three pence in the pound formula' is however little more than tokenism, and makes something of a mockery of the notion that a government must possess significant tax raising powers if it is to govern in accordance with the wishes of its own electors rather than simply administer in conformity with the preferences of a hierarchically superior authority.

That the devolution proposals had as much a symbolic as a practical dimension was indicated by the white paper's insistence that a devolution Bill would only be tabled if Scots voters approved the principle of devolution in a referendum. Legislation providing for a referendum was rapidly enacted, and the vote was scheduled for 11 September 1997. The referendum posed two questions. The first was whether voters approved in principle the creation of a Scots Parliament with a substantial array of devolved, 'legislative' powers. The second was whether those powers should include a capacity to vary the rate of income tax levied by the UK Parliament by up to three pence in the pound.

The Scottish Nationalist Party—having boycotted the Constitutional Convention whose deliberations underpinned the white paper—decided to support the proposals in the referendum, albeit with the evident intention of wishing to seek full independence for Scotland at a later date. The Conservative Party maintained the stance it had adopted at the general election; that devolution was an irreversible step towards independence, and that to support it would signal the disintegration of the United Kingdom as a single country. Such sentiments evidently did not deter Scots voters. In marked contrast to the result of the 1979 referendum, the 1998

---

[20] Scotland has historically enjoyed a higher per capita share of public expenditure than England. That advantage was reduced, but not eliminated by the Barnett formula; see Mait C and McCloud B (1999) 'Financial arrangements', in Hassan op cit.

poll produced large majorities for a 'Yes' answer (on a high turnout) for both questions. The Blair government subsequently proceeded to lay a devolution Bill before the Commons and Lords.

The terms of the Act

It was a sign of the strength of the first Blair government's majority that the terms of the white paper were approved without serious quibble in the Commons. (The Lords, mindful no doubt that obstructing the Bill would be both a breach of the Salisbury Convention and a clear defiance of the referendum result, offered no resistance to the Bill.) It would nonetheless be rash to laud the promptness of the Bill's passage as a tribute to representative democracy. Given the substantial complexities of the Act's eventual provisions,[21] one cannot help but feel that few Labour and Liberal Democrat backbenchers had any detailed understanding of just exactly what they were voting for.[22] It is perhaps unrealistic to expect backbenchers to have a lawyerly grasp of all the complications of the Bill, but its rapid enactment can be seen as a further illustration of the Commons' persistent failure to act as an effective evaluator of the government's policy proposals.

The drafting of the Bill was evidently not designed to facilitate backbench scrutiny. As Brazier notes: 'Even passages of fundamental constitutional importance are not given the prominence which it may be said that they deserve, but are tucked away in the 132-section statute, leaving it to the assiduous reader to find them'.[23] That assiduity is a trait in which the Commons en bloc has been singularly lacking in recent years.

The Act is too lengthy a document to be examined in detail here, but some of its key sections might be noted. Section 1 begins with the bald announcement that; 'There shall be a Scottish Parliament'. Sections 1–10 then sketch out the electoral system through which MSPs are to be chosen, in terms which followed the proposals made in the white paper. Per the terms of ss 2–3, the Scots Parliament may sit for a maximum of four years between elections, although provision is made for more frequent elections in exceptional circumstances. Sections 22–27 and s 36 delineate the rules surrounding the legislature's internal proceedings. Section 19 creates the position of Presiding Officer (the Scots Parliament's equivalent of the Commons Speaker), and provides for her/his election by a majority of MSPs. The structure and powers of the Scots government are laid out in ss 44–58. Rules relating to the allocation of the block grant and the Parliament's tax raising powers are contained in ss 64–80.

In respect of the relationship between the Parliament and the Scots government, the Act gave a legal basis to values which in the context of the UK Parliament enjoy only conventional status. Section 45 provides, for example, that the First Minister is to be appointed by the Monarch.[24] However, that power of appointment can—per s 46—be exercised only in response to a 'nomination' by the Parliament. A similar 'legalisation' of conventional principles is imposed by s 47, which inter alia requires that Ministers of the Scots executive resign from office if the government has lost the confidence of the Parliament.

The autonomy of the Scots Parliament

Sections 28 and 29 are among the most significant of the Act's provisions. Section 28 confirms that the Parliament can pass legislation on Scots matters. Section 29 then places various substantive limits on the Parliament's legislative competence, the most significant of which is

---

[21] The Act has over 130 sections and 9 schedules.

[22] See Craig P and Walters M (1999) 'The courts, devolution and judicial review' *Public Law* 274 for a helpful outline.   [23] (1999) op cit p 103.

[24] The appointment of a First Minister is thus an exercise of a statutory power by the Monarch, and not, as is the appointment of the Prime Minister, an exercise of the prerogative.

that it may not legislate in respect of the various 'reserved matters' listed in Sch 5 of the Act.[25] Section 33 introduces a form of pre-enactment judicial scrutiny of Bills at the request of the UK or Scots government's law officers. Should a Bill be thought to exceed the Parliament's powers—in the Act's parlance 'to raise a devolution issue'—it could be referred to the Judicial Committee of the Privy Council (now to the Supreme Court) for consideration. A Bill may not be enacted unamended if the Supreme Court concludes it would breach s 29. The UK government is also empowered under s 35 to block enactment of any Scots Bill which it has reasonable grounds to believe to affect national security, international relations, or any reserved matter.[26]

The Act envisages that the Parliament may enact Bills which are not understood at the time to raise s 29 questions. Provision is therefore made for so-called 'devolution issues' to be raised by litigants in subsequent court proceedings. Schedule 6 of the Act sets out a referral procedure, (loosely modelled on the EC's Art [177] 234 device), through which lower courts may interrupt the proceedings before them to seek the opinion of the High Court or Court of Appeal (the Inner Court of Session if the proceedings are taking place in Scotland) on whether a particular legislative provision breaches s 29. A further appeal lay initially to the Privy Council (and now the Supreme Court).

The legislation itself contains a rather unusual provision in s 101. This is essentially an instruction to the courts to interpret ambiguous Scots legislation as being within, rather than beyond, the Parliament's competence if either meaning is possible. Section 101 offers a statutory echo of a much broader common law principle that has been largely obsolete in UK law for some years. Like the Scots executive, the Scots Parliament is technically a statutory executive body. When exercising justiciable powers, most statutory bodies are presumptively[27] subject to judicial review on the grounds of illegality, irrationality, and procedural impropriety. That presumption will undoubtedly apply to actions taken by the Scots government. There is however an historical exception to this general rule, rooted in Britain's former status as a colonial power,[28] which supports the argument that Scots 'legislation' could only be subject to review on the grounds of illegality.

That the Scots Parliament may not legislate incompatibly with the provisions of EU law nor (to the extent that they are 'incorporated' by the Human Rights Act 1998 into domestic law) to the provisions of the European Convention on Human Rights makes this less of a legal lacuna than would previously have been the case. Many governmental decisions previously quashed on the basis of irrationality or procedural unfairness would also fall foul of one or other provision of the 1998 Act or of EC law, to which s 29 of the Act requires the Parliament to conform.[29] (As we shall see in chapters 18 to 20, the Scots Parliament's subjection to the Human Rights

---

[25] In addition, it may not legislate with extra-territorial effect, nor in breach of any provision of European Community law. Section 30 however contains a Henry VIII clause, which empowers the Queen (de facto the UK government) to use her prerogative powers (by issuing an Order in Council) to amend the law-making authority of the Scottish Parliament. The impact of the Human Rights Act 1998 in Scotland and Wales will also be rather more dramatic than in the United Kingdom as a whole. The Scots Parliament and the Welsh Assembly (discussed later in the chapter) are both subjected to the provisions of the Human Rights Act 1998 in a way that the UK Parliament is not. All of the 'laws' that they produce, irrespective of the form that the laws take, will be liable to invalidation by the courts on the grounds of their incompatibility with the 1998 Act. See Lord Hope (1998) 'Devolution and Human Rights' *European Human Rights LR* 367. The terms and schemata of the European Convention on Human Rights and the Human Rights Act 1998 are discussed in some detail in chs 18–20.

[26] There is no ouster clause explicitly precluding judicial review of the exercise of this power, but it seems likely that its use would be regarded as non-justiciable. Conversely, the Act also contains what amounts to a Henry VIII clause in respect of s 29 in s 63. This enables the UK government to transfer additional powers on matters relating to Scotland to the Scots government by Order in Council.

[27] ie in the absence of an ouster or limitation clause in the relevant statute.

[28] See in particular the analysis offered by Craig and Walters op cit pp 288–293.

[29] One might suggest that s 29 renders the common law ground of illegality redundant. Section 29 of the Scotland Act is in essence a statutory restatement (and expansion) of the illegality principle in administrative law.

Act stands in marked contrast to the position in respect of the UK Parliament, and serves as a reminder of the non-sovereign status of the Scots legislature.) The lacuna would however be significant in respect of Scots legislation which impinged neither on requirements of the Human Rights Act nor provisions of EC law.[30] It is in respect to these powers that some rather aged case law may acquire a new significance.

Colonial case law on legislative autonomy

The issue before the Privy Council in *R v Burah*[31] concerned the validity of a statute passed by the Indian legislature which sought to alter the jurisdiction of the court system established by the British statute which created the Indian constitution. The Privy Council's judgment confirmed that Indian legislation could be overturned on the basis of illegality; that is, that the legislature was interfering with issues that the British Parliament had not empowered it to address. However the courts would not entertain challenges based on irrationality or procedural impropriety:

> If what has been done is legislation, within the general scope of the affirmative words which give the power, and if it violates no express condition or restriction by which that power is limited . . . it is not for any Court of Justice to inquire further, or to enlarge constructively those conditions and restrictions.[32]

The essentially non-democratic nature of the Indian legislature in 1878 perhaps makes *Burah* a precedent of limited utility in respect of the Scots Parliament. More assistance might be derived from Privy Council decisions on Canadian constitutional law. *Riel v R*[33] turned on the meaning to be attributed to the proviso in the British North America Act 1867 to the effect that the Canadian Parliament could pass legislation; 'for the administration, peace, order and good government' of the country. Riel contended that this provision required the courts to consider whether the policy enacted in legislation did indeed amount to 'good government'. The Privy Council saw no merit in this argument: '[T]here is not the least colour for such a contention. The words of the statute are apt to authorise the utmost discretion of enactment'.[34]

The decision in *Edwards v A-G for Canada*[35] is perhaps the most interesting judgment however; in part because of its relative historical proximity to the present day, and in part because of its subject matter, which spoke very clearly to matters of both individual human rights and the representativeness of the governmental system. As noted in chapter two, British courts had held in the nineteenth and early-twentieth century that women were incapable at common law of being regarded as 'men' or male 'persons' for the purposes of voting in elections to the Commons.[36] By the late 1920s, the UK Parliament had reversed that assumption through legislation, as had most of the provincial legislatures in Canada. Women were also by then eligible under statute to sit in the British and Canadian Houses of Commons. The question which arose in *Edwards* was whether women could sit in the Canadian Senate. Section 24

---

[30] The extent to which the courts will regulate the Parliament's non-legislative activities remains unclear. The Act affords the Parliament substantial discretion in respect of many facets of its internal proceedings. Section 29 obviously requires that those proceedings—unlike those of the Westminster legislature—respect the requirements of the European Convention; (as noted in ch 20, the Human Rights Act 1998 expressly exempts 'proceedings in Parliament' from the need to conform to the Convention). Whether the courts will also impose administrative law standards of rationality and procedural fairness on Scots parliamentary proceedings is an intriguing and thus far rather neglected question.   [31] (1878) 3 App Cas 889.

[32] Ibid, at 905; per Lord Selborne.   [33] (1885) 10 App Cas 675.

[34] Ibid, at 678; per Lord Halsbury. A similar rationale had been applied two years earlier to the activities of Canada's various provincial legislatures vis-à-vis the national Parliament in *Hodge v R* (1883) 9 App Cas 117, PC.

[35] [1930] AC 124.

[36] See the discussion of *Chorlton v Lings* and *Nairn v University of St Andrews* at '*Chorlton v Lings* (1868)' ff, ch 2, pp 41–42.

of the British North America Act 1867 provided that 'persons' could sit in the Senate. In the late 1920s, several Canadian women sought a declaration from the Canadian courts that s 24 included women. The Canadian Supreme Court held, placing much reliance on *Chorlton v Lings* and *Nairn v University of St Andrews*, that women were not 'persons' within s 24.[37]

The Privy Council reversed this judgment. At the core of its decision lay the proposition that the British North America Act 1867 was a 'constitution' rather than an ordinary statute, and so should not be subjected to orthodox techniques of statutory interpretation. As Lord Sankey put it, in a passage replete with splendidly mixed metaphors:

> The British North America Act planted in Canada a living tree capable of growth and expansion within its natural limits. Their Lordships do not conceive it to be [their] duty . . . to cut down the provisions of the Act by a narrow and technical construction, but rather to give it a large and liberal interpretation so that [Canada] to great extent . . . may be mistress in her own house.[38]

In essence, the Privy Council appeared to be holding that the intention of the British Parliament in enacting the British North America Act in 1867 was to permit the courts in future years to attach new meanings to the Act's text in response to changing political, economic, and social circumstances within Canadian society. That the Act itself made no explicit textual allusion to this principle was irrelevant; the principle was evidently to be regarded as inherent in any Westminster statute which creates a 'constitution'. On the particular facts of the case, the Privy Council concluded that gratuitous gender discrimination in relation to occupancy of legislative office had become an obsolete moral principle in Canada by 1930, an (ultimate?) political fact that was firmly evidenced by national and provincial statutes entitling women to vote in legislative elections and to occupy elected political office.

It would require something of a leap of the imagination to accept that the Scotland Act has fashioned a 'constitution' in this sense. Nonetheless, *Edwards* and the other cases mentioned earlier have led Craig and Walters to suggest that 'there is considerable scope for an interpretative approach [to the Scotland Act] that is sensitive to the fact that the courts will be reviewing the actions of democratically elected bodies'.[39] This could be considered a rather limited objective for the common law to pursue—and rather underplays the significance of the colonial case law—since just the same observation might be made in respect of the actions of local authorities.[40] Indeed, Craig and Walters' suggestion is strongly reminiscent of Lord Russell's judgment in *Kruse v Johnson*[41] that a council's power to make bye-laws be construed 'benevolently'. Adequate judicial recognition of the very different political (and thence constitutional) status of the Scots Parliament and local authorities would suggest that the courts should go considerably further than simply being 'benevolent' when assessing if the Parliament has exceeded its powers.

There is an obvious temptation to assume that the courts' approach to matters concerning the Scots Parliament will be driven by the purposive jurisprudence so firmly established in EU law. That the Scotland Act does not instruct the courts to adopt this interpretative technique is no bar to them doing so: with the exception of the provision contained in s 101,[42] the choice of interpretative principles remains a matter of common law. Any allusion to purposive interpretation obviously begs the question of just what 'purpose' the Scotland Act is intended to serve. The Act itself does not contain any preamble answering this question. A plausible line of speculation would be to suggest that the judiciary will allow its task of interpreting the Scotland Act (and subsequent related legislation, whether Scots or United Kingdom in

---

[37] [1928] SCR 276.   [38] [1930] AC 124 at 136.   [39] Op cit, at p 292.

[40] The vast difference between the Court's perception of the *vires* of a colonial parliament and a domestic local authority is forcefully conveyed if one recalls that *Edwards* was decided at much the same time as *Roberts v Hopwood*.   [41] See 'IV. The role of the judiciary', ch 10, pp 262–263.

[42] Which could perhaps be seen as a (very) mild endorsement of teleological jurisprudence.

origin) to be influenced (but obviously not determined) by the 'sovereign right of the Scots people' thesis which underpinned the final recommendations of the Scottish Constitutional Convention.[43] Re-casting this sentiment in more constitutionally orthodox terms, the courts might readily be expected to assume that the purpose underpinning the Scotland Act is to maximise the extent to which the Scots electorate, acting through its representatives in the Scots Parliament, determines the outcome of Scots political questions. To address this point, we need also to consider what impact—if any—the Act might have on the sovereignty of the UK Parliament.

The continuing sovereignty of the UK Parliament?

The question of how much autonomy the courts afford to the Scots Parliament will also be affected by the meaning that the courts attach to s 28(7) of the Scotland Act. Section 28(7) seems, from a traditionalist constitutional standpoint, to be a wholly unnecessary provision. It states simply that the power given to the Scots Parliament to enact legislation for Scotland; 'does not affect the power of the UK Parliament to make law for Scotland'. In essence, the clause is saying that Parliament cannot entrench the initial autonomy it grants to the Scots legislature. This statutory restatement of orthodox Diceyan principle has perhaps been included in the Act in response to the new constitutional climate engendered by *Factortame (No 2)*, which does indicate that Parliament can now (in a limited sense) safeguard some political values against future repeal. Section 28(7) was perhaps intended to deter the courts from allowing the *Factortame* principle to seep into non-EC related constitutional contexts. The Labour government's evident unwillingness even to attempt to entrench any part of the Scotland Act contrasted markedly with the recommendations of the Constitutional Convention. The Convention had advocated that any devolution legislation should include an entrenching device—(reminiscent of s 4 of the Statute of Westminster)[44]—namely that the Westminster Parliament should not be able to enact future legislation reducing the powers of the Scots legislature unless the Scots legislature consented to the Act in question. The white paper made no reference to this proposal, nor to the issue of entrenchment generally.[45] The presence of s 28(7) in the Act would suggest that this omission arose because the Blair government regarded entrenchment as politically undesirable, rather than legally unachievable.

However, the issue presents another example of the close coupling of law and convention in the contemporary constitution. The Act was accompanied by the Blair government's promulgation of what has come to be known as the 'Sewel Convention',[46] namely that: '[W]e would expect a convention to be established that Westminster would not normally legislate with regard to devolved matters in Scotland without the consent of the Scottish parliament'.[47] The practice subsequently emerged that the Scots Parliament would pass a 'legislative consent motion' to indicate that it did not object to a Westminster bill that affected a devolved issue.[48]

One can see two obvious 'reasons' (in Jennings' sense of the term)[49] for the Sewel Convention. The first—positive—reason is to confirm that the Westminster Parliament respects the political autonomy afforded by the Act to the Scots people. The second—negative—reason is that

---

[43] Craig and Walters op cit note that an analogous principle has been adopted by the Canadian Supreme Court in interpreting the Canadian constitution, even though that constitution initially derives from an Act of the Westminster Parliament; see *Reference Re Secession of Quebec* [1998] 2 SCR 217. Canada is of course a sovereign state, which Scotland manifestly is not.   [44] See '*Harris v Dönges (Minister of the Interior)* (1952)', ch 2, p 33.

[45] See Myles A (1999) 'Scotland's Parliament White Paper', in Hassan op cit.

[46] Lord Sewel being the Minister in the Blair government who announced the principle during the Bill's passage. See further Himsworth C and O'Neill C (3rd edn, 2015) *Scotland's constitution: law and practice* pp 166–169.

[47] *HLD* 21 July 1998 c 791.

[48] On the initial workings of the Sewel Convention and 'legislative consent motions' see Page A and Batey A (2002) 'Scotland's other Parliament: Westminster legislation about devolved matters in Scotland since devolution' *Public Law* 501.   [49] See 'The Diceyan perspective—law and conventions distinguished' ch 9, pp 224.

the convention is required because the Blair government presumed that it was not possible to entrench that autonomy as a matter of law. Notwithstanding *Pepper v Hart*, a government's wishes cannot determine a court's interpretation of a statutory provision. A court which accepted the presumption that the Scotland Act was intended to maximise the autonomy of the Scots electorate would not be sailing (and here the potential influence of the EC becomes apparent) into wholly uncharted constitutional waters if it held that s 28(7) requires the courts to apply UK legislation affecting matters devolved to the Scots Parliament by the 1998 Act only if the subsequent UK statute expressly states that the Scotland Act is being amended. To take the argument further, it might be suggested that s 28(7) could even be construed as confirming only that the Westminster Parliament can repeal the Scotland Act in its entirety. And unless and until it does so, any UK Act purportedly interfering with a devolved power will have no legal effect.

Professor Brazier offered a hypothetical but quite plausible scenario that would put a thesis of this sort to an exacting test. The Scots Nationalist Party committed itself, should it ever form a government in Scotland, to conduct a referendum to ascertain if the Scots people wish Scotland to become an independent nation. In Professor Brazier's view, an attempt by the Scots Parliament even to hold a referendum on this issue would be ultra vires s 29, as it is a 'constitutional' matter and so reserved to the UK Parliament. This is a debatable point. For the Scots Parliament to seek to discover if the electorate would welcome further constitutional reform does not necessarily amount to constitutional reform per se. Whether it does or does not do so will be dependent on the background principles that the courts invoke when interpreting ss 28–29. A court which adopted a variant of the *Edwards* rationale in determining the legal consequences of the Scotland Act would presumably conclude that it does not.

The first Scottish parliament and government

The results of the first Scottish general election, held in May 1999, were not what the Blair government had hoped for (see Table 12.1). The Labour Party failed to win a majority of seats in the new legislature, and fell far short of gathering a clear majority of votes cast. As had been widely predicted, the election produced a hung Parliament. One cannot be sure that electors would have voted the same way if the Parliament was chosen solely on the basis of the 'first past the post' system. But if one assumes they would have done so, the opposition parties (the SNP and the Conservatives) benefited hugely from the Blair government's readiness to promote legislation which provided for a proportional system.

A coalition administration was eventually formed between the Labour and Liberal Democrat Parties, within which Liberal MSPs would occupy several positions of appreciable political significance. Donald Dewar, the then Secretary of State for Scotland, became First Minister. Dewar had already indicated that he saw his political future as lying in Scotland rather than Westminster, and that he would not seek re-election to the House of Commons.

Table 12.1 Scottish Parliament election May 1999

Party	Constituency vote		Party list vote		Total seats
	%	Seats	%	seats	
Labour	38.8	53	33.8	3	56
Liberal	14.2	12	12.5	5	17
Conservative	15.6	0	15.4	18	18
SNP	28.7	7	22.0	28	35
Others	2.7	1	11.4	2	3

The Act itself is somewhat ambiguous on the issue of individuals fulfilling a dual political role in Scotland and at Westminster. A Minister in the Scots Executive is not permitted to serve as a Minister in the UK government, although Scots Ministers and MSPs are not required to resign from the House of Commons. After the 1999 election, some MSPs also had seats at Westminster. It is difficult to believe that they could adequately perform both roles, and many of the members with seats in both legislatures indicated that they would not contest seats in the Commons at the next general election.

Given that Donald Dewar was a senior member of the Blair Cabinet, it was unlikely that his administration would take policy initiatives incompatible with the Blair government's preferences. This point had indeed been made prior to the Scottish election: the Labour Party had announced in its Scots election manifesto that a Scots Labour government would not ask the Parliament to exercise its tax-raising powers in the foreseeable future. In the run-up to the 1999 election, the Liberal Democrats had stressed that the abolition of university tuition fees would be an essential component of their governmental programme. That commitment was quietly diluted in the subsequent coalition negotiations. There thus seemed no likelihood of any significant ideological friction between the Blair and Dewar governments in the first few years of the Scots Parliament's existence.

That the Scots Parliament had succeeded rapidly in establishing its political autonomy within the United Kingdom is evidenced by the successions to the office of First Minister which followed Dewar's untimely death. The second incumbent as First Secretary was Henry MacLeish, who was little known in Westminster circles. His tenure proved brief, as he resigned in 2001 following a scandal over his apparent misuse of the office expenses paid to him while he was an MP at Westminster. His successor as leader of the Labour Party in Scotland and First Minister, Jack McConnell, had no political reputation to speak of in UK circles. The choice of Scotland's First Minister, it seems, has become a matter wholly of Scots domestic politics. Such 'domestication' of the process through which major political figures emerge in Scotland is perhaps to be welcomed in one sense. It seems most unlikely that a major political party could foist a leader with no substantial and popular profile in Scotland on its Scottish members. However the corollary of this is a marginalisation of Scots politics with the United Kingdom. It was not immediately apparent that that occupying senior political office in Scotland might be a stepping stone to becoming leader of a political party at a UK level.

The 2003 and 2007 elections

Mr McConnell led the Labour Party to a victory of sorts in the 2003 parliamentary election. Labour was returned as the largest party, albeit with only a minority (50) of the Parliament's 129 seats (see Table 12.2). Negotiations between the Liberal and Labour Parties led to the formation of another coalition administration, with Mr McConnell nominated again as First Minister.

Table 12.2 Scottish Parliament election May 2003

Party	Constituency vote		Party list vote		Total seats
	%	Seats	%	seats	
Labour	34.6	46	29.3	4	50
Liberal	15.4	13	11.8	4	17
Conservative	16.6	3	15.5	15	18
SNP	23.8	9	20.9	18	27
Others	7.7	2	16.5	15	17

Table 12.3 Scottish Parliament election May 2007

Party	Constituency vote		Party list vote		Total seats
	%	seats	%	seats	
Labour	32.1	37	29.1	9	46
Liberal	16.2	11	11.3	5	16
Conservative	16.6	4	13.9	13	17
SNP	32.9	21	31.0	26	47
Others	0.2	0	8.9	3	3

The process of governance within Scotland continued without generating any significant constitutional controversy under the McConnell government. The Labour/Liberal administration continued to chart a political course that was mildly distinct from that pursued by the Blair government in several areas of social policy. By the time the third set of parliamentary elections were held in 2007, the notion that Scotland should have its own Parliament and government appeared to have become a wholly normalised presumption within contemporary constitutional morality (see Table 12.3).

Mr Salmond, leader of the SNP, took office heading a minority government. The United Kingdom was therefore faced for the first time with a UK government and a devolved government controlled by different political parties. The new government's capacity to pursue its political agenda was much compromised by its minority status within the Parliament. A governing party with barely one third of the seats in a legislature is unlikely to champion radical policies. Such proved to be the case with the first Salmond government, and the early years of SNP governance in Scotland were notable for the absence of any sharp political controversy between the Salmond and Blair/Brown administrations.

The 2011 election and the independence referendum

The potential for divergence increased following the 2011 Scots elections, in part because the SNP gained an overall majority in the Parliament and in part because of the greater gap between its own political ideology and that of the Conservative dominated British coalition government (see Table 12.4). The size of university tuition fees became a sharp point of policy difference between the two governments, as did the financing of personal care for elderly people. Conservative Ministers did appear, however, to have accepted devolution as a morally entrenched principle. No suggestions were made following the 2010 general election that the Scotland Act ought to be repealed or even amended to reduce the Scots Parliament's powers.

Table 12.4 Scottish Parliament election May 2011

Party	Constituency vote		Party list vote		Total seats
	%	Seats	%	seats	
Labour	31.7	15	26.3	22	37
Liberal	7.9	2	5.2	3	5
Conservative	13.9	3	12.4	12	15
SNP	45.4	53	44	16	69
Others	1.1	0	12.1	3	3

Indeed, the SNP's unexpected success in winning a majority at the 2011 Scottish election pushed political developments in quite the opposite direction. The Salmond government presented the election results as a justification for offering the Scots people an opportunity to express a view on whether they wished Scotland to become an independent country. The Cameron/Clegg administration eventually accepted the political inevitability of acceding to this pressure, and in December 2012 the British and Scots governments published an 'Agreement' on a referendum on independence for Scotland.[50] The Agreement identified various criteria that any referendum process should meet: it should:

- have a clear legal base;
- be legislated for by the Scottish Parliament;
- be conducted so as to command the confidence of parliaments, governments, and people; and
- deliver a fair test and a decisive expression of the views of people in Scotland and a result that everyone will respect.

Most importantly, the Agreement accepted that the details of the referendum process were to be—subject to Electoral Commission oversight—a matter for the Scots rather than UK government and Parliament. Any doubts as to the capacity of the Scots Parliament to legislate for a referendum were dispelled by the issue of an Order in Council under s 30 of the 1998 Act expressly granting such a power.[51]

The schemata for the referendum were subsequently enacted in the Scottish Independence Referendum Act 2013.[52] The question put to Scots voters in the referendum was, at least in linguistic terms, a simple one:

Should Scotland be an independent country?

The right to vote in the referendum was granted to all residents in Scotland over 16 years old on the set date for the poll, which was to be 18 September 2014. There was to be no requirement of special sized majorities for a 'Yes' vote to succeed, nor of a minimum turnout for the vote to be valid. Given that this was perhaps the most profound constitutional issue that the United Kingdom had faced for several hundred years, the notion that it could be authoritatively decided on a bare majority vote of the Scots electorate might be thought quite extraordinary.[53]

The referendum campaign was waged throughout 2014. Until the final weeks, the leading figures in the three major British political parties had not intervened substantially in the debate, albeit that all three parties clearly opposed independence. This distance was maintained in part perhaps because of a presumption that the vote was essentially a matter for the Scots to determine, but also because of a rather complacent presumption that the 'Yes' campaign had little prospects of success.

The SNP's arguments hinged substantially on the presumption that Scotland's sense of national identity was sufficiently well-developed for independence per se to be desirable. Somewhat more narrowly, the SNP made much of the point that in party political terms the

---

[50] <http://www.scotland.gov.uk/Resource/0040/00404789.pdf>.

[51] See 'The autonomy of the Scots Parliament', pp 328–330

[52] On the parliamentary passage of the Bill see <http://www.scottish.parliament.uk/parliamentarybusiness/Bills/61076.aspx>. The bulk of the Act was concerned with specifying the technical details of the organisation of the campaign and counting of the vote.

[53] Or it might be seen as a further cogent illustration of our constitution's attachment to bare majoritarianism as a legitimising force for any chosen political values. On the legitimacy issue, we might also note that voters in the rest of the United Kingdom played no part in the referendum, even though 'their' constitution would also be profoundly changed by a 'Yes' vote.

Scots electorate sat consistently to the left of UK voters overall, and were unable, even under the current devolution arrangements, to give effective expression to those values.

The 'No' campaign centred on more prosaic issues. Mr Salmond faced particular difficulties in defending a bald assertion, not obviously well-founded, that an independent Scotland would promptly be admitted to the EU.[54] The SNP also assumed—again without any obvious good reason for doing so—that an independent Scotland could continue to use the pound as its currency.

Notwithstanding these difficulties, the 'Yes' supporters continued to gain ground in the final weeks of the campaign, and in early September took the lead for the first time in several opinion polls. This prompted a distinctly panicked reaction among the Conservative, Labour, and Liberal Democrat Party leaderships. Heavyweight political figures journeyed en masse to Scotland to bolster the 'No' vote, and all three party leaders made loud but vague promises of much greater devolution of power to Scotland should independence be rejected.

In the event, on a turnout exceeding 80%, Scottish voters chose to reject independence by a clear 55% to 45% majority.[55] Political debate then moved promptly to the question of just what form further devolution would take. The Conservative/Liberal coalition government established a commission headed by Lord Smith of Kelvin (a Scots cross-bench member of the House of Lords) to which all of the political parties contributed members.[56]

The 2015 electoral landslide, the Smith Commission, and the Scotland Act 2016

The SNP's dominance of the political landscape intensified in the 2015 general election, when it won fifty-six of Scotland's fifty-nine Commons seats; (having won only six in 2010). The Conservatives obtained just one seat, and were joined in that sorry state by the Liberal Democrats. More notably, Labour's representation fell precipitously from forty-one seats to (also) just one. The distribution of seats of course bore no sensible relation to each party's share of the overall vote: the SNP's 95% share of the seats was won with 50% of the national vote (see Table 12.5). Although the SNP's new leader (and Scotland's new First Minister) Nicola Sturgeon initially made no suggestion that another independence referendum should be held, her party pressed immediately and forcefully for further extension of the powers granted to the Parliament.

That pressure contributed to the enactment of the Scotland Act 2016 in March 2016, which gave effect in broad terms to the Smith Commission recommendations. The overall thrust of the reform was a modest further extension of the powers of both the Scots Parliament and government, particularly in relation to taxation matters. But for theoretically inclined constitutional lawyers, ss 1–2 of the Act are of most interest.

Table 12.5 General election results in Scots seats 2010 and 2015

	2010		2015	
	seats	% vote	Seats	% vote
Scots Nationalist	6	19.9	56	50.0
Labour	41	42.0	1	24.3
Conservative	1	16.7	1	14.9
Liberal Democrat	11	18.9	1	7.5

[54] See the analysis of this issue in Tierney S (2013) 'Legal issues surrounding the referendum on independence for Scotland' *European Constitutional Law Review* 359.

[55] For a detailed breakdown of the results see <http://scotlandreferendum.info/>.

[56] Smith Commission (2014) *Report of the Smith Commission for Further Devolution of Powers to the Scottish Parliament*.

Section 1 is purportedly an 'entrenching' mechanism, which provides that:

1 Permanence of the Scottish Parliament and Scottish Government

In the Scotland Act 1998 after Part 2 (the Scottish Administration) insert—

'PART 2A Permanence of the Scottish Parliament and Scottish Government

63A Permanence of the Scottish Parliament and Scottish Government

(1) The Scottish Parliament and the Scottish Government are a permanent part of the United Kingdom's constitutional arrangements.

(2) The purpose of this section is, with due regard to the other provisions of this Act, to signify the commitment of the Parliament and Government of the United Kingdom to the Scottish Parliament and the Scottish Government.

(3) In view of that commitment it is declared that the Scottish Parliament and the Scottish Government are not to be abolished except on the basis of a decision of the people of Scotland voting in a referendum.'

Section 1 is a bizarre provision. On its face, it does not—like the entrenching provision in issue in *Trethowan*—add a referendum as a fourth element of the legislative process. Rather it seems to substitute a referendum for Parliament as the designated law-maker. This was presumably not what was intended either by the Smith Commission or by Parliament. Such laxity in drafting is perhaps regrettable. If we are to embrace the presumption this political value can be entrenched, a 'better' formulation of s 1(3) would surely have been:

(3) In view of that commitment it is declared that no Act of Parliament which purports to abolish the Scottish Parliament and/or the Scottish Government shall be recognised as valid by any court of the United Kingdom unless such Act has subsequent to the grant of the Royal Assent been approved by a majority of voters in Scotland in a referendum.

Consequential provisions would also have been required to (try to) 'entrench' the new s 1 itself by making its repeal subject to a referendum of Scots voters; to specify the referendum question; and to provide for the automatic repeal of the 'Act' if it was not approved at the referendum. None of those issues are addressed in the 2016 Act.

This is likely because as a matter of law those inadequacies have little significance, as we currently have no basis—other than in the context of EU law—to suppose that a court would refuse to apply any statutory provision enacted in the ordinary way, notwithstanding any previously enacted 'entrenching provision'. Section 1 may be important as a statement of political good faith and as a check on (in the sense used by Marshall)[57] the readiness of a bare Commons and Lords majority to exercise its law-making powers on that issue. It is however difficult to believe either that its express repeal or implied breach by subsequent legislation passed in the orthodox fashion would be prevented by the courts,[58] or that the legislators who voted for it believed that would be the case.

Section 2 is similarly problematic:

2 The Sewel convention

In section 28 of the Scotland Act 1998 (Acts of the Scottish Parliament) at the end add—

'(8) But it is recognised that the Parliament of the United Kingdom will not normally legislate with regard to devolved matters without the consent of the Scottish Parliament'.

Prima facie, s 2 is also an entrenching device, in which the ordinary legislative process (in respect of devolved matters) is enhanced by adding the Scots Parliament as a fourth element. Leaving aside the likely problem that 'normally' is a non-justiciable concept, we would again find ourselves in the realm of legal fantasy if we presumed that a court would refuse to apply a

---

[57] See 'Conclusion—the conventional basis of parliamentary sovereignty', ch 9, p 248.

[58] See further Himsworth C (2016) 'Legislating for permanence and a statutory footing' *Edinburgh LR* 361.

Table 12.6 Scottish Parliament election May 2016

Party	Constituency vote		Party list vote		Total seats
	%	Seats	%	seats	
Labour	22.6	3	19.1	21	24
Liberal	7.8	4	5.2	1	5
Conservative	22.0	7	22.9	24	31
SNP	46.5	59	41.7	4	63
Greens	0.6	0	6.6	6	6

(Westminster) statutory provision which affected a devolved matter on the basis that the Scots Parliament has not consented to its enactment. Such a scenario, involving a Scots court, might arise if we were to find ourselves once again in a moment of 'revolution' in Professor Wade's sense.[59] That is a question we return to in the final chapter of the book.

At the 2016 Scots Parliament election, the SNP was returned as much the largest party, but with just sixty-three of the 129 seats continued in office as a minority government. Voter turnout was notably low, reaching just 55%. The Labour Party fared a little better than in the 2015 general election, but gained fewer seats overall than the Conservatives, who formed the official opposition. Both parties owed most of their seats to the regional list category, which also provided the Greens with all of their six seats. (See Table 12.6)

Judicial evaluation of the autonomy of the Scots Parliament

The various predictions about the approach that the courts might take to interpreting the provisions of the Scots devolution legislation have now been tested in a series of Supreme Court decisions. Three cases are considered briefly here:[60] *Martin v Most*,[61] *AXA General Insurance v The Lord Advocate*,[62] and *Imperial Tobacco Ltd v Lord Advocate*.[63]

The issue before the court in *Martin v Most*[64] centred on s 45 of the Criminal Proceedings etc (Reform) (Scotland) Act 2007, which increased the sentencing powers of Scots courts in summary proceedings concerning road traffic offences. This was problematic from a devolution perspective because while the Scots Parliament is presumptively competent to modify the Scots criminal justice system, road traffic offences are expressly identified in Sch 5 E1(d) of the Scotland Act 1998 as a reserved matter. Prima facie, s 45 could credibly be viewed both as a criminal justice matter (ie within the Scots Parliament's competence) or a road traffic offence matter (ie beyond competence). That such difficulties might arise—and do so frequently—was anticipated by the Blair government. Such duality is a likely consequence of any attempt to divide law-making power among different bodies.

The primary question for the Supreme Court to resolve in *Martin* was the effect of the Scotland Act 1998 s 29(1)(b), namely that a provision would be beyond competence so far as 'it relates to reserved matters': in crude terms, what did (the Westminster) Parliament mean by the term '*relates to*'? That concept is given a more extensive definition by s 29(4):

[59] 'Are *Trethowan*, *Harris* and *Ranasinghe* relevant to the British situation?', ch 2 , pp 36–38.

[60] For a more extensive treatment see, inter alia, Elliot M (2012) 'Holyrood, Westminster and judicial review of legislation' *Cambridge LJ* 9; Dimelow S (2013) 'The interpretation of 'constitutional' statutes' *LQR* 498; Feldman D (2014) 'Statutory interpretation and constitutional legislation' *LQR* 473: Tomkins A (2013) 'The emergence of a devolution jurisprudence', UKSCblog, <http://ukscblog.com/the-emergence-of-a-devolution-jurisprudence/>; and, comprehensively, Himsworth and O'Neill op cit ch 14.   [61] [2010] UKSC 10, 2010 SC (UKSC) 40.

[62] [2011] UKSC 46, [2012] 1 AC 868.   [63] [2012] UKSC 61, 2013 SC (UKSC) 153 (SC).

[64] [2010] UKSC 10, 2010 SC (UKSC) 40.

> [T]he question whether a provision of an Act of the Scottish Parliament relates to a reserved matter is to be determined . . . by reference to the purpose of the provision, having regard (among other things) to its effect in all the circumstances.

However s 29(4) is really no more than a statement of very loose principle, which obviously affords a court considerable interpretive discretion. During the passage of the Scotland Act 1998, Lord Sewel addressed this issue, and offered an indication of how the Blair government expected the courts to resolve the question:[65]

> In interpreting what is meant by 'relates' . . . [t]he classic statement is found in the words of Lord Atkin in *Gallagher* v. *Lynn* in 1937 where he stated: 'It is well established that you ought to look at the true nature and character . . . the pith and substance of the legislation. If, on the view of the statute as a whole, you find that the substance of the legislation is within the express powers, then it is not invalidated if incidentally it affects matters which are outside the authorised field'. In other words, it is intended that any question as to whether a provision in an Act of the Scottish parliament 'relates to' a reserved matter should be determined by reference to its 'pith and substance' or its purpose and if its purpose is a devolved one then it is not outside legislative competence merely because 'incidentally it affects' a reserved matter.

The Supreme Court cited and adopted this reasoning in *Martin*. The method it followed was to explore the legislative history of s 45.[66] This could be traced to a Scots government committee established in 2001 to investigate the scope and administration of summary proceedings in Scotland, on to the approval of many of the Committee's recommendation in a 2005 government policy paper, and thereafter to the endorsement of those proposals by the sponsoring Minister during the passage of the 2007 Act. In Lord Hope's view:[67]

> [31] [T]his material shows conclusively that the purpose of s.45 of the 2007 Act was to contribute to the reform of the summary justice system by reducing pressure on the higher courts. An increase in the sentencing powers of sheriffs when they were dealing with statutory offences was seen as a necessary part of this process . . . These are pre-eminently matters of Scots criminal law . . . As it was to a rule of Scots criminal law that the provision was directed, I would hold that it does not relate to a reserved matter within the meaning of s.29(2)(b).

Legislative history can tell us much about the 'purpose' of a legislative provision in the sense of the *motives* of legislators, but has little bearing on 'purpose' in the sense (per s 29(4)) of its *effect*. The 'effect' of the provision in issue in *Martin* might be thought very modest; it increased the maximum sentence for the relevant offence on summary conviction from six months to one year. It may be more difficult for a court to conclude that Scots legislation does not 'relate' to a devolved matter if the provision's effect is much more substantial; or, to frame the matter in another way, at what point does an effect become so significant that—notwithstanding the defensibility of the legislator's motives—it loses its incidental character? This is likely a question that defies any abstract answer, demanding instead a gradual accumulation of case law before any clarity is gained.

The *Imperial Tobacco* litigation[68] turned on a slightly different dimension of the reserved powers issue. The legislation in dispute was part of the Scots Parliament's attempt to reduce smoking among the Scots population. Two provisions of the Tobacco and Primary Medical Services (Scotland) Act 2010 were challenged by Imperial Tobacco, a large multi-national corporation whose profitability was under threat from the legislation. Section 1 forbade the display

---

[65] *HLD* 21 July 1997 vol 592 cc. 818–819.

[66] [2010] UKSC 10, 2010 SC (UKSC) 40 at paras 27–31.

[67] The bench was divided on some subsidiary issues, but unanimous on this matter. For a discussion of the divisions see Himsworth C (2010) 'Nothing special about that? Martin v HM Advocate in the Supreme Court' *Edinburgh LR* 487.   [68] [2012] UKSC 61, 2013 SC (UKSC) 153 (SC).

of tobacco products in any shop other than a specialised tobacco store; that is, in a newsagent or supermarket tobacco would have to be stored out of the customer's sight. Section 9 imposed a ban on tobacco sales from vending machines. Although Imperial Tobacco accepted (in the Supreme Court) that the provisions were motivated by public health concerns—with the exception of a few very detailed issues, the promotion and preservation of public health are devolved rather than reserved matters—it argued that they were beyond competence because of their effect on two reserved matters within the Scotland Act 1998: firstly Sch 5 C7(a)—'the sale and supply of goods and services to consumers'; and secondly Sch 5 C8—'product safety'.

One might instinctively think that there is some force in that contention, especially with respect to the sale and supply of goods; bans on displays and vending machine sales seemingly affect the way in which tobacco products are sold and supplied to consumers. However, the Supreme Court (Lord Hope delivering judgment for a unanimous bench) took a more rigorous approach to the construction of those concepts. In the Court's view, 'the sale and supply of goods' caveat was limited to measures regulating the imbalance of bargaining power between consumers and commercial organisations; while 'product safety' concerned only matters in respect of the marketability of goods within the EU single market. Sections 1 and 9 therefore did not 'relate' in the s 29 sense to devolved matters. The reasoning here is not, as in *Martin*, that Scots legislation on a devolved matter impacted incidentally or consequentially on a reserved matter; instead, by lending the reserved matters a narrow meaning, the court could conclude that there was no incidental or consequential impact on them at all. The point is trite, but can perhaps be overlooked. The autonomy of the Scots Parliament can be broadened as readily by a narrow construction of 'reserved matters' as it can by a broad construction of 'devolved matters': there is in effect a see-saw like relationship between the two concepts.

Through rather different means, the techniques deployed by the Supreme Court in *Martin* and *Imperial Tobacco* arrive at the same end; namely a conclusion that enhances rather than restricts Scots legislative autonomy. But the Supreme Court emphasised firmly in *Imperial Tobacco* that it was not proceeding on the basis that there was something 'special' about the Scots devolution legislation that required the courts to adopt novel forms of statutory interpretation. The rationale offered by the Privy Council in *Edwards v A-G for Canada*[69] in respect of the British North America Act 1867 has not been endorsed by the Supreme Court in relation to the Scotland Acts. Lord Hope's sole judgment in *Imperial Tobacco* firmly disapproved of the notion that the devolution legislation had that character. The Supreme Court stated firmly that the provisions of the Scotland Act: 'must be in interpreted in the same way as any other rules that are found in a UK statute . . . [T]he legislation is [to be] construed according to the ordinary meaning of the words used'.[70] The Supreme Court accepted that the words themselves indicated that the Act: 'was intended, within carefully defined limits, to be a generous settlement of legislative authority',[71] but was not prepared to go so far as to accept that this 'generous settlement' should lead courts to interpret the Act on the basis that there was: 'a presumption in favour of competence'.[72]

There is perhaps a false dichotomy at play here. To say that the text of the Act per se points towards a 'generous settlement'—and so no unusual interpretive techniques are required—is a conclusion that can itself only be reached through a process of judicial interpretation. Section 101 is clearly a rather unusual provision insofar as it offers a systemic instruction to the courts on questions of interpretation, but it does not in terms require 'generosity'. The 'generous settlement' conclusion is a judicial deduction, not a (textual) statutory mandate. Insight into the issue of the Scots Parliament's autonomy is perhaps to be gained as much from political history as from legal doctrine: until such time as we see a stream of court decisions holding the Scots Parliament to have acted beyond competence, we might properly assume a judicial disinclination to say 'No' to the Parliament's legislative initiatives.[73] The ideal issue to test the limits of this 'generosity' would likely have been a unilateral attempt by the Scots Parliament to hold an independence referendum. However, as noted earlier, that problem was sidestepped by the use of an Order in Council per s 30 granting the Scots Parliament that power.

The Supreme Court has followed the above-referenced colonial jurisprudence in *AXA General Insurance v The Lord Advocate*[74] in concluding that even though the Scots Parliament is de jure a statutory body, its actions are not subjected to the full range of grounds of judicial review at common law, even though there is no ouster clause to that effect in the Act. *AXA* concerned the Damages (Asbestos-related Conditions) Scotland Act 2009, which reversed (in Scotland, and per s 4 with retrospective effect) a 2007 House of Lords judgment—*Rothwell v Chemical and Insulating Co. Ltd*[75]—which held that a particular variant of asbestosis-related industrial diseases could not found a personal injury claim. AXA—which stood to lose large amounts of money in compensation payments if the Act was within competence—challenged it on various grounds, including that of irrationality/unreasonableness in the *GCHQ/Wednesbury* senses.[76]

Unlike the approach he took a year later in *Imperial Tobacco*, Lord Hope held that the answer to the question before the court did not lie in the specific words of the Scotland Act 1998, but was found in: 'the general message that the words convey':[77]

> 49 The dominant characteristic of the Scottish Parliament is its firm rooting in the traditions of a universal democracy. It draws its strength from the electorate. While the judges, who are not elected, are best placed to protect the rights of the individual, including those who are ignored or despised by the majority, the elected members of a legislature of this kind are best placed to judge what is in the country's best interests as a whole. A sovereign Parliament is, according to the traditional view, immune from judicial scrutiny because it is protected by the principle of sovereignty. But it shares with the devolved legislatures, which are not sovereign, the advantages that flow from the depth and width of the experience of its elected members and the mandate that has been given to them by the electorate. This suggests that the judges should intervene, if at all, only in the most exceptional circumstances.

Those 'exceptional circumstances' did not extend to applying irrationality (and presumably by analogy procedural fairness) review to the Scots Parliament's legislative provisions. A court might properly invoke a common law review jurisdiction if a legislative measure contradicted what Lord Hope rather vaguely referred to as a 'fundamental' constitutional value, giving the example of a statute that purported to abolish judicial review. In the ordinary course of events however, the only bases on which to challenge the validity of a Scots legislative provision were those laid out in the Scotland Act itself.

II. Devolved government in Wales after 1998

The Blair government's proposals for devolution to Wales were more modest than those anticipated for Scotland. Their successful implementation also proved more problematic than those applied in Scotland. The level of popular support for Welsh devolution was pathetically low.

---

[73] Lord Hope suggested both in *Martin* (at para 4) and *Imperial Tobacco* (at para 6) that this state of affairs was due in part to the Parliament's readiness to pass legislative consent motions to approve UK legislation on devolved issues. See also the analysis in Himsworth and O'Neill op cit pp 166–168.

[74] [2011] UKSC 46, [2012] 1 AC 868.

[75] [2007] UKHL 39, [2008] 1 AC 281.

[76] See respectively 'III. Full reviewability—the *GCHQ* case (1983), ch 4, pp 94–96; 'III Judicial regulation of government behaviour: the constitutional rationale', ch 3, pp 53–55.

[77] [2011] UKSC 46, [2012] 1 AC 868 at para 46.

Some 50.3% of the voters who took part in the referendum voted in favour of devolution, while 49.7% opposed. Moreover, the turnout was a dismal 51%. This meant that the devolution proposal was positively supported by barely 25% of eligible voters. Any subsequent legislation could thus lay no convincing claim to be legitimised by popular consent, a case which could clearly be made in respect of Scots devolution. The initially ponderous momentum the proposals enjoyed was further slowed shortly after the referendum when Ron Davies, Secretary of State for Wales and the designated leader of the Labour Party in the projected Assembly, resigned from the government and his post as leader of the party in Wales, in the aftermath of a sex scandal.

The Government of Wales Act 1998

The subsequently introduced Bill was presented in the expectation within the Blair government that the resultant Act would introduce a limited scheme of devolved government that was likely to be subject to extension and expansion. The modesty of the government's initial ambitions,[78] enacted virtually unamended in the Government of Wales Act 1998, was reflected in the names attached to the new system of Welsh governance. Wales would not, like Scotland, have a Parliament, but an 'Assembly'. The Assembly would consist of sixty members. Forty members would be returned on a first past the post basis from individual constituencies. Twenty would be elected from a regional list system.

The Welsh 'government'—the term is used guardedly for reasons outlined later—would not be headed by a First Minister, but by a 'First Secretary'. And her 'Cabinet' colleagues would not be Ministers, but 'Assembly Secretaries'. The Assembly itself was not given 'legislative powers', but rather was empowered to 'enact' policy through transfers of authority from the Secretary of State for Wales.[79] The absence of any grant of 'legislative' power to the Assembly explains in large part the fact that the 1998 Act did not delineate the Assembly and the 'government' as separate legal entities, as was done in the Scotland Act 1998 in respect of the Scottish Parliament and Executive. The system of governance created by the Act did not rest in legal terms on a separation of powers between an executive and legislative branch, but designated the Assembly as a single corporate body in much the same way that Parliament had traditionally created local authorities.

The initial scope and nature of Welsh devolution were also markedly different from the model used in Scotland. Rather than grant the Assembly a general competence and then reserve specific powers to the UK Parliament, the Government of Wales Act 1998 treated the Assembly as if it were a local council that was given specific powers. The formal mechanics of this transfer of authority entailed the delegation of powers previously exercised by the Secretary of State for Wales via the device of an Order in Council.[80] The use of this technique necessarily meant that the Assembly could not acquire powers that were not already possessed by the Secretary of State. Any future broadening of the Assembly's political authority beyond those limits would be contingent upon the enactment of new enabling legislation by Parliament.

The powers initially allocated to the Assembly, designated by Sch 2 of the Act as 'fields' of authority, were reasonably extensive; including, inter alia, the provision of health services, education and training, environmental protection, town planning, housing, and social services. Significantly, however, the Act did not grant the Assembly any tax raising powers. The provision made by the Act in s 80 for financing the Assembly's pursuit of its preferred polices

---

[78] See Welsh Office (1997) *A voice for Wales* (Cm 3718).

[79] See generally Brazier op cit; Craig and Walters op cit: Rawlings R (1998) 'The new model Wales' *Journal of Law and Society* 461.   [80] Section 22.

in the designated fields was brief in the extreme, and clearly designed to afford the British government complete control over the Assembly's total expenditure:

Grants to Assembly

80 (1) The Secretary of State shall from time to time make payments to the Assembly out of money provided by Parliament of such amounts as he may determine.

(2) Any Minister of the Crown, and any government department, may make to the Assembly payments of such amounts as the Minister or department may determine.

In combination, the formal provisions of the 1998 Act would indicate that the Assembly could sensibly be seen as a powerful instrument of *local* governance, but it could in no sense be seen as a structure of *national* governance.

The Assembly nonetheless immediately proved to be of some considerable political significance. This was primarily the result of the electoral process chosen by the government to select the Labour Party's candidate as First Secretary and by the electoral process created by Parliament to select the Assembly's members. It rapidly became apparent that Labour Party members in Wales wished Rhodri Morgan, an independently minded backbench MP, to be their candidate as First Secretary. The Blair government thought Morgan too 'independent' for its taste, and so devised a rigged electoral college that ensured the candidacy was won by Alun Michael, a Cabinet Minister.

However, the first elections to the Assembly indicated that the Welsh electorate would not be as biddable to the Blair government's preferences as the Labour Party (see Table 12.7). The result of the election left Alun Michael as First Secretary of a minority Labour administration. He subsequently lost a vote of confidence in the Assembly, and resigned, to be replaced by Morgan. The devolved government thus rapidly established itself as a mechanism for delivering a salutary—if largely symbolic—rebuke to the Blair government. The episode exposed a curious inconsistency of thought within the Blair administration. Having promoted a legal structure which offered some appreciable opportunity for voters of Wales to see their preferred moral values—albeit to a limited extent and on a limited range of issues—given legal effect, the Blair government took substantial (if ultimately unsuccessful) steps to manipulate the political content of that legal structure in a fashion which minimised the likelihood of that opportunity being embraced.[81]

It also rapidly became apparent that the de jure absence of a separation of powers between the 'legislative' and 'executive' branches of the new Welsh government was not an accurate guide to the way in which the Assembly was operating in practice. In part perhaps as a

Table 12.7 Welsh Assembly election 1999

Party	Constituency vote		Party list vote		Total seats
	%	seats	%	seats	
Labour	37.6	27	35.5	1	28
Liberal	13.5	3	12.5	3	6
Conservative	15.8	1	16.5	8	9
Plaid Cymru	28.4	9	30.6	8	17
Others	4.8	0	5.0	0	0

[81] Readers may find in this an echo of Crosland's comment as to the 'ambivalence' felt by Ministers of both parties during the Butskellite era towards the principle and practicality of affording significant political autonomy to local government; see 'VI. From 'ambivalence' to 'authoritarianism', ch 10, p 267.

Table 12.8 Welsh Assembly election 2003

Party	Constituency vote		Party list vote		Total seats
	%	seats	%	seats	
Labour	39.5	30	36.6	0	30
Liberal	14.2	3	12.7	3	6
Conservative	20.5	1	19.1	10	11
Plaid Cymru	21.1	5	19.7	7	12
Others	4.7	1	11.9	0	1

consequence of the Labour Party's decision to form a minority administration rather than to engineer a broader, cross-party coalition, the Assembly promptly began to function in 'conventional' terms in a fashion which implied that its members regarded themselves as sitting in a 'Parliament' in the traditional, Westminster sense, in which they formed into 'government' and 'opposition' blocs. The suggestion was promptly made that, notwithstanding its legal form, the Assembly was functioning as a 'virtual Parliament'.[82] Political circumstances provided a further impetus for that trend in the 2003 Assembly elections, in which the Labour Party won thirty of the Assembly's sixty seats (see Table 12.8). Rhodri Morgan was again nominated and appointed as First Secretary, leading a 'virtual government' which enjoyed the statistical curiosity of being neither a majority nor minority administration.

The Assembly also took prompt steps to nudge the devolution process further along the road towards greater political autonomy for Wales by establishing a commission (the 'Richard Commission')[83] to consider how the powers and operation of the Assembly might best be developed. The report of the Commission identified various areas for reform. The Commission recommended that the legal basis of devolved governance should be altered to recognise the reality of the 'virtual Parliament' functioning of the Assembly by creating formally separate executive and legislative branches within the Assembly. Unsurprisingly, the Commission also suggested that the powers of the Assembly be extended and that new mechanisms be devised to enable the Assembly to acquire additional powers without the need for new legislation to be enacted by Parliament.

The Richard proposals were broadly welcomed by the Blair government, which responded in a white paper, *Better governance for Wales*,[84] published in 2005. The Blair government accepted that the corporate structure of the Assembly substantially blurred people's understanding of which politicians were actually responsible for particular policies and decisions and also substantially compromised the capacity of the Assembly to evaluate executive proposals and scrutinise executive action. The white paper also acknowledged the need for a more streamlined mechanism to facilitate the Assembly's acquisition of more extensive powers in the future. The government also envisaged that at some (presumably distant) point in time, it might be appropriate for the Assembly to be granted legislative powers analogous to those possessed by the Scottish Parliament, and indicated that provision would be made in a new Government of Wales Act for a referendum to be held to consider that issue.

[82] See the discussion in Rawlings R (2005) 'Hastening slowly: the next phase of Welsh devolution' *Public Law* 824.

[83] (2004) *Report of the Commission on the powers and electoral arrangements of the National Assembly for Wales*. For a helpful summary and analysis of the report see Jones T and Williams J (2005) 'The legislative future of Wales' *MLR* 642.   [84] Welsh Office (2005) *Better governance for Wales*.

The Government of Wales Act 2006

That Welsh devolution continues to be very much a constitutional work in progress is perhaps best evidenced by the fact that while the 2006 Act reformed the legal structure of the Assembly, enhanced it powers, and facilitated its acquisition of further powers in future, it did not recreate the Assembly as a 'Parliament' in a formal, titular sense. The obvious question which arises is how far the 2006 Act goes in a functional, practical sense towards investing the Assembly with a parliamentary identity.

While the Assembly was not styled as a Parliament, its members who hold executive office were renamed as 'Ministers' (rather than the previous 'Secretaries') by Part 2 of the Act. The formal identification of a 'government' drawn from the Assembly lay at the heart of the 2006 Act's legal recognition of a separation of powers within the devolved system of governance. The First Minister would be nominated by the Assembly and appointed by the Queen. The Act made provision for the government to consist of up to twelve Ministers and/or Deputy Ministers, appointed by the First Minister, all of whom must also be Assembly members.

The 2006 Act endowed the Assembly with a circumscribed area of legislative competence within specified fields of policy. These 'fields' followed the areas outlined in the 1998 Act. Within each 'field', more detailed 'matters' could be specified. Additional 'fields' and 'matters' can obviously be introduced by future Acts of Parliament. But the 2006 Act also allows for the initiative for adding 'matters' to particular fields to come from the Assembly, by way of proposals to the Secretary of State. Should the Secretary of State not approve such proposals, she must give reasons for her refusal. In the event that she does approve the proposals, she must lay them in the form of a draft Order in Council before each house of Parliament, where they are subject to the affirmative resolution procedure. The Assembly was empowered to pass laws to be known as 'Measures' in respect of any 'matter'. Subject to certain designated substantive limitations, 'measures' are given equal legal status to Acts of Parliament, which necessarily entails that within its designated fields of competence the Assembly has the power to repeal or amend existing legislative provisions.

Quite how much political autonomy the Assembly will acquire under these arrangements remains substantially in the gift of the British government. And quite how ready successive British governments will be to accept (and finance) the Welsh government's pursuit of policies which they find unpalatable remains to be seen. But certainly in formal terms, the 2006 Act could defensibly be described as a further significant step towards the creation of a constitutional order in which legal effect is given to the moral principle that citizens' varying political ideologies are afforded the opportunity to be expressed simultaneously in the practical realm of governance as well as in the abstract realm of ideas.

The 2006 Act was to come into force following the Assembly elections scheduled for May 2007. Labour remained the largest party in the Assembly, but lacked an overall majority (see Table 12.9). Somewhat unexpectedly, a Labour/Plaid Cymru coalition was subsequently

Table 12.9 Welsh Assembly election 2007

Party	Constituency vote		Party list vote		Total seats
	%	Seats	%	Seats	
Labour	32.2	24	29.6	2	26
Liberal	14.8	3	11.7	3	6
Conservative	22.4	5	21.5	7	12
Plaid Cymru	22.4	7	21.0	8	15
Others	8.3	1	16.2	0	1

Table 12.10 Welsh Assembly election 2011

Party	Constituency vote		Party list vote		Total seats
	%	Seats	%	seats	
Labour	42.3	28	36.9	2	30
Liberal	10.6	1	8.0	4	5
Conservative	25.0	6	22.5	8	14
Plaid Cymru	19.3	5	17.9	6	11
Others	2.8	0	12.7	0	0

formed, with Rhodri Morgan again nominated as First Minister, which pursued social and economic policies which diverged markedly if modestly from the policy agenda favoured by the Brown government for England.

The gradual nature of the trend towards increasing political autonomy for Wales continued in 2011, when a referendum was held to elicit the Welsh people's views on an extension of the Assembly's law-making powers to the full extent envisaged by the 2006 Act. Only 35% of the population participated in the referendum, although of those who did vote some 65% supported the proposal. In contrast to the position in Scotland, the 2011 elections in Wales did not produce any increased political pressure for consideration of independence (see Table 12.10). On a notably low turnout of barely 40% of eligible voters, the Labour Party won thirty of the sixty Assembly seats. Surprisingly perhaps, support for the Welsh nationalist Plaid Cymru party fell sharply.

The Wales Act 2014

In an echo of events in Scotland, the UK government established a Commission on Devolution in Wales (the Silk Commission) in 2011 to explore the possibilities for further legislative reform. The Commission proposals were in broad terms enacted in the Wales Act 2014. As in Scotland, the legislative trend continues to be in favour of granting greater authority to the national legislature. Although the Welsh Assembly has yet to be renamed as 'Parliament', the Wales Act 2014 took the significant step of giving the Assembly tax-raising powers (from 2018 onwards). The tax-raising powers exercisable through ordinary Welsh legislation are limited to some land-based taxes. The Assembly has also gained a power to alter rates of income tax set by the UK Parliament, but only if the alteration is approved both by a referendum and a two-thirds majority in the Assembly. Given that the 2016 election (see Table 12.11) once again left Labour as the largest party, but without even a bare majority of the seats and so governing again as minority administration, it seems rather unlikely that the income tax power will be used in the near future.

Table 12.11 Welsh Assembly election 2016

Party	Constituency vote		Party list vote		Total seats
	%	Seats	%	seats	
Labour	34.7	27	31.5	2	29
Liberal	7.7	1	6.5	0	1
Conservative	24.1	6	18.8	5	11
Plaid Cymru	20.5	6	20.8	6	12
UKIP	12.5	0	13.0	7	7

Conclusion

There seems to be something of a ratchet effect at work in the interaction of judicial construction of the Scots devolution statutes and the legislative trend since 1998. That trend has been towards gradual extension of the Scots Parliament's law-making competence. There is as yet no reason to assume that those (and future) extensions of competence will not also meet a 'generous' (per *Imperial Tobacco*)[85] response from the courts. The longer those twin processes continue, the more credible it becomes to suggest that as a matter of political practicality, if not of legal theory, Scots devolution has acquired an 'entrenched' status. In constitutional terms, as a matter both of law and of politics, the issue of devolution has thus far proved to be a much less significant event in Wales than in Scotland., but the overall significance of the devolution legislation should not be underestimated. That overall significance indicates that we have taken a substantial step towards the assertion of *simultaneous political pluralism*[86] as a fundamental (if conventional) tenet of British constitutional morality. The Blair governments knowingly and enthusiastically invited Parliament to enact legislation which created new governmental bodies within the UK constitution which—in addition to possessing significant political power—were by no means guaranteed to be controlled by the Labour Party. That a government was willing to entertain the probability that its policy initiatives would reduce its own power marks a complete break with the authoritarian ethos of the Thatcher and Major eras, and might properly be regarded as evincing a level of ideological support for the principle of simultaneous political pluralism quite unprecedented in the modern era.

In addition, the adoption of a system of proportional representation for electing the Scots Parliament and Welsh Assembly makes it unlikely that legislative policy in Scotland and Wales will regularly be determined solely by political parties enjoying only minoritarian electoral support. The adequacy of the Commons' electoral system and the minoritarian governments it almost invariably produces will thus be exposed to a constant, indigenous source of comparison. Perhaps even more importantly, the notion that a 'Parliament' can and should be a body possessing limited law-making competence will begin to become normalised within British political culture. At present, predictions as to the future development of the Scots and UK Parliaments seem to be dominated by the supposition that the former will become more like the latter.[87] We may find in the longer term that the reverse argument acquires increasing force.

Suggested further reading

Academic and political commentary

BALSOM D and McALLISTER I (1979) 'The Scottish and Welsh devolution referenda of 1979: constitutional change and popular choice' *Parliamentary Affairs* 394

BOGDANOR V (1979) 'The English constitution and devolution' *Political Quarterly* 36

---

[85] The Supreme Court had indicated it will take a similar approach to the Welsh devolution legislation; see *Attorney-General v National Assemby for Wales Commission* [2012] UKSC 53, [2013] 1 AC 792.

[86] See 'Local Government', ch 10, pp 251.

[87] One minor consequence of the initial 'success' of the devolution experiment is that the number of Scots seats in the Westminster Parliament has been reduced (by twelve) so that the 'electoral quota' for Scots and English constituencies is the same; see 'Apportionment criteria—a non-justiciable issue?', ch 7, p 178. Given that the Labour Party has enjoyed such a disproportionately high level of electoral success in Scotland in recent years, that innovation itself is a remarkable display of political generosity. Its effect is of course to make it more difficult for the Labour Party to win a Commons majority.

BOGDANOR V (1999a) 'Devolution: decentralisation or disintegration' *Political Quarterly* 185

BRAZIER R (1999) 'The Constitution of the United Kingdom' *Cambridge LJ* 96

CRAIG P and WALTERS M (1999) 'The courts, devolution and judicial review' *Public Law* 274

TIERNEY S (2000) 'Constitutionalising the role of the judge: Scotland and the new order' *European LR* 49

Case law and legislation

Martin v Most [2010] UKSC 10, 2010 SC (UKSC) 40

AXA General Insurance v The Lord Advocate [2011] UKSC 46, [2012] 1 AC 868

Imperial Tobacco Ltd v Lord Advocate [2012] UKSC 61, 2013 SC (UKSC) 153 (SC)

Part Four

Administrative Law

Chapter 13

Substantive Grounds of Judicial Review

The grounds on which the courts have traditionally been prepared to find government action unlawful have been alluded to frequently in earlier chapters. The next two chapters offer a more systematic approach to this branch of administrative law by revisiting some of those previously mentioned decisions in the context of detailed discussion of other leading cases.

Since Parliament is a sovereign law-maker, it can enact statutory rules against which the courts may assess the lawfulness of the actions of any or all governmental bodies. The provisions of the ECA 1972 are a powerful example of such *statutory grounds of judicial review*. From an administrative lawyer's perspective, one way to characterise the impact of the ECA 1972 is that it has made breach of a directly effective provision of Community law a ground of judicial review applicable to government bodies. Primarily however, as suggested in chapter three, *the grounds of judicial review are creatures of the common law*, created and developed by the courts.[1] It is with those grounds of review that the next two chapters are concerned.

The common law grounds of review fall essentially into two spheres. *Substantive* grounds of review are concerned predominantly with the content of the decision made. *Procedural* grounds of review, in contrast, address the way a decision is made. As chapter fourteen suggests, it is possible that the substance of a decision is lawful, but the decision itself is unlawful because of a procedural flaw. This chapter considers substantive grounds of review. The courts have traditionally recognised two such grounds—illegality and irrationality.[2] These are assessed in sections I and II. Section III then considers a third ground, an emergent rather than established principle in English law—that of proportionality.[3]

---

[1] See 'III. Judicial regulation of government behaviour: the constitutional rationale', ch 3, pp 53–55.

[2] 'Irrationality' is the contemporary usage for the concept once referred to as '*Wednesbury* unreasonableness': see 'III. Judicial regulation of government behaviour: the constitutional rationale', ch 3, pp 53–55. The terms are used interchangeably in this book.

[3] This chapter offers an illustrative rather than exhaustive foray into the realm of illegality. Thus for example (to the certain relief of students and the probable relief of their teachers) I have taken at face value Lord Diplock's suggestion in *GCHQ* that *Anisminic* abolished the distinction between jurisdictional and non-jurisdictional errors of law, and omitted discussion of that doctrinally impenetrable issue.

I. Illegality

Lord Greene MR's judgment in *Wednesbury*[4] noted that the various grounds of review were not discrete categories, but might often merge and overlap. The same point might be made about the various sub-categories of each ground of review. For the purposes of this book, illegality has been broken down into the following component parts: excess of power; unlawful delegation of power; unlawful fettering of power; and the estoppel doctrine.

Excess of powers

The notion that a government body's decision is unlawful because the body has attempted to exercise a power that it does not possess might be thought a straightforward concept to apply. An obvious example, mentioned in chapter three, would arise if a government body invoked a statute which empowered it to build schools as an authority for it to build houses. Such executive activity could readily be understood as involving what is sometimes termed an 'excess of power'. An alternative, and often used formulation in these circumstances is that the government body has gone 'beyond the four corners of the Act'.[5] The test becomes more complicated however when one considers that the content of legislation, (pursuing the geometrical shape metaphor), may have many curves and angles rather than resembling a neat rectangle. And even if the contours of the relevant statute might initially appear to have a readily identifiable shape, the twin processes of their application by the executive and their interpretation by the courts may produce unexpected results.

The much-cited judgment in *A-G v Fulham Corpn*[6] is a helpful way of introducing this topic. The case centred on the powers granted by a series of Baths and Washhouses Acts, passed between 1846 and 1878. Fulham Corporation had operated several such facilities to which people came to have baths and launder their clothes. It subsequently decided to offer a home delivery laundry service. The service was projected to make a substantial operating deficit each year, and would be subsidised from local taxation. The vires of this policy were then challenged by the Attorney-General.

The judgment did not rest upon a literal construction of any particular provision of the Act. Sargant J seemed instead to apply the 'golden rule' of statutory interpretation in attempting to establish the overall purpose underlying the legislation. This technique led him to conclude that 'the scheme of the Act appears to be to give washing facilities to persons who are not able to provide for themselves places where they may cleanse themselves or wash their clothes'.[7] He then observed that it was a settled facet of the illegality doctrine that a policy would be intra vires, even if it did not fall squarely within the scheme of the Act if it could be regarded as 'incidental to, or consequent upon, those things which the legislature has authorised'.[8]

The notions of incidentalism or consequentialism would seem substantially to reduce the scope for a policy to be held illegal. On these facts, however, the principle did not assist the Corporation. In Sargant J's view, the provision of a home delivery laundry service was 'a completely different enterprise'[9] from just providing facilities where people could do their own washing.

There is no compelling empirical basis for that conclusion. The case could clearly have been decided the other way just as readily, an observation which highlights the often ambiguous

---

[4] *Associated Provincial Picture Houses Ltd v Wednesbury Corpn* [1948] 1 KB 223,.
[5] That label is obviously inappropriate if the limits of a prerogative power are in question.
[6] [1921] 1 Ch 440.   [7] Ibid, at 451.
[8] Ibid, at 450; citing James LJ in *Ashbury Railway Carriage and Iron Co Ltd v Riche* (1875) LR 7 HL 653.
[9] Ibid, at 453.

reach of the illegality principle. It seems that Sargant J's decision was probably swayed by a factor which he himself described as irrelevant to the question before him—and which he then considered at some length:

> [T]he service is being performed at about half . . . of the cost to the Council. That is an instance I think, although it is immaterial for the present purpose, of the light-hearted way in which operations are conducted by persons who have not their own pockets to consider, but who have behind them what they regard as the unlimited or nearly unlimited power of the ratepayers.[10]

Sargant J's observations in *A-G v Fulham* as to the feasibility (or lack of it) of the council's scheme might be thought to have set the jurisprudential scene for the House of Lords' judgment in *Roberts v Hopwood* a few years later.[11] In *Roberts*, we may recall,[12] the House of Lords had unanimously concluded that Poplar Council's £4 per week minimum wage policy was void on the ground of illegality. The council had assumed it was acting within the limits of s 62 of the Metropolis Management Act 1855, which empowered it to pay 'such wages as it thinks fit'. The House of Lords had held that s 62 had to be construed subject to a common law 'fiduciary duty' imposed upon governmental bodies. Since the payment bore no close relation to the market value of the work performed it was not a wage at all, but a 'gift'. As such it was beyond the four corners of s 62.

In the Court of Appeal[13] however, the notion that the council was under a fiduciary duty to its ratepayers—and thus that s 62 had to be construed in that context was rejected. While the Court accepted that prevailing market rates had some bearing on establishing if a payment was indeed a 'wage', it also concluded that the concept of a 'wage' was sufficiently elastic to permit a significant departure from the sums paid in the private sector for similar work.

The origin of the fiduciary duty principle in respect of local government actions was discussed in chapter ten.[14] The doctrine can plausibly be seen as a common law mechanism designed to enhance rather than restrict an elected body's substantive autonomy. The decision of the Court of Appeal in *Roberts* is consistent with that understanding of the principle. The judgment of the House of Lords in *Roberts*, and Sargent J's observations in *Fulham*, appear to reject or ignore it.

Notwithstanding this point, one might question the accuracy of portrayals of the House of Lords' decision in *Roberts* as a simple manifestation of right-wing political bias by the judiciary.[15] Quite how well-founded that contention was in respect of the judges involved in *Roberts* is unclear. In so far as the content of the judgment reflected right wing political views, one might readily suggest that those views accurately reflected the wishes of the 1855 Parliament, whose survey of the then political landscape would not have revealed any 'socialists' controlling government bodies. The ghost of *Roberts* in the guise of the fiduciary duty doctrine re-appeared thirty years later in *Prescott v Birmingham Corpn*,[16] when the Court concluded that a council's concessionary fare scheme was illegal; and again, a further thirty years later in *Bromley v GLC*, when the House of Lords invalidated the GLC's 'Fares Fair' policy. As suggested in chapter ten, the court's reading of the relevant legislation at issue in that case was readily defensible, even if one might as readily have construed the Act to uphold the GLC's policy.

The point to draw here is perhaps that illegality, while ostensibly a straightforward concept, becomes markedly more opaque when placed—as it (generally) must be—in the context of the principles of statutory interpretation.[17] *Liversidge v Anderson* offers a compelling illustration

---

[10] Ibid, at 454.   [11] [1925] AC 578, HL.   [12] 'The role of the judiciary', ch 10, pp 262–263.

[13] *R v Roberts, ex p Scurr* [1924] 2 KB 695, CA.

[14] See 'The Municipal Corporations Act 1835' ff, ch 10, pp 255–257.

[15] See Laski op cit; Fennell op cit; 'The "fiduciary duty" doctrine revisited (and subverted?)', ch 10, pp 263–264.

[16] [1955] Ch 210, CA.

[17] That point would of course not apply when the power in issue was alleged to derive from common law rather than statute.

of this. In Lord Atkin's view, Liversidge's detention was 'illegal', as Anderson's power to detain Liversidge only arose if Anderson had 'reasonable cause' to believe him to be of hostile origins or association. However, for the majority, that power arose if the Home Secretary had a bona fide belief in Liversidge's hostile associations. As long as that belief existed, the detention would not be illegal.[18]

An equally pertinent illustration is found if one stays in the rather narrow field of a local authority's fiduciary duty when deciding on its employees' wage rates. The High Court's 1983 judgment in *Pickwell v Camden London Borough Council*[19] was triggered by the council's decision to end a strike by its employees by offering them a pay deal that was substantially (15%–20%) above the rate subsequently negotiated on a national basis by the relevant union and local authority associations. Forbes J accepted that the council was indeed under an implicit fiduciary duty to spend its money wisely. However, the council's fiduciary duty was now to be read in conjunction with another implicit but equally pervasive obligation 'to provide a wide range of services to its inhabitants'.[20] If high payments were needed to secure that objective, then those payments could defensibly be construed as a wage.[21]

That the nominally simple 'four corners' approach to illegality is more complicated than it might first appear is also well illustrated by the more recent judgment in *R v Secretary of State for Foreign Affairs, ex p World Development Movement Ltd* (popularly known as the *Pergau Dam* case).[22] The Overseas Development and Co-operation Act 1980 s 1 provided that the Foreign Secretary:

> . . . shall have power, for the purpose of promoting the development or maintaining the economy of a country . . . outside the UK, or the welfare of its people, to furnish any person or body with assistance, whether financial, technical or any other nature.

In the late-1980s, several British firms became involved in a bid to build a dam in Pergau, Malaysia. The initial project was costed at £316m. Officials from the Overseas Development Agency (ODA) subsequently visited Malaysia to examine the proposal. They concluded that the project was 'at the margin of economic viability', and the (Conservative) Foreign Secretary agreed to provide aid of £68m. In April 1989, the anticipated cost of the project was re-estimated at £397m, which led an ODA economist to conclude that the project was now 'clearly uneconomic'. In February 1990, the ODA completed a new appraisal and described the scheme as a 'very bad buy'. The World Bank considered it 'markedly uneconomic' and noted that it could have devastating consequences for the local environment. The Secretary of State nevertheless decided to grant the aid. He took the view that not to do so would 'affect the UK's credibility as a reliable friend and trading partner and have adverse consequences for our political and commercial relations with Malaysia'.[23] The Foreign Secretary maintained that s 1 did not limit provision of aid to projects viable in narrow, economic terms, but also permitted aid which served 'wider political and economic considerations, such as the promotion of regional stability, good government, human rights or British commercial interests'.[24] This argument, perhaps ironically, bears an obvious resemblance to the interpretation of the 'economic, efficient and integrated' formula in s 1 of the Transport (London) Act 1969 urged on the House of Lords by the GLC in *Bromley*.[25] Rose LJ followed the Lords' methodology in that case. The issue was a simple one: did s 1 impliedly require that development projects be economically sound?

---

[18] One might make just the same observation regarding the different view expressed by the Court of Appeal and House of Lords in *Rossminster* as to the claimed illegality of the Inland Revenue's search of the applicant's property; see '*R v IRC, ex p Rossminster Ltd* (1980)', ch 3, pp 64–65.   [19] [1983] QB 962.

[20] [1983] 2 WLR 583 at 603.

[21] A conclusion consistent with the original understanding of the fiduciary duty doctrine.

[22] [1995] 1 WLR 386.   [23] [1995] 1 WLR 386 at 399.   [24] Ibid.

[25] See 'Fares fair': *Bromley London Borough Council v Greater London Council*', ch 10, pp 271–273.

Parliament could obviously have expressly inserted the word 'sound' into s 1 had it wished to do so. The question for the court was to decide what implications should be drawn from Parliament not doing so. Does the absence of the word mean, as the government contended, that an aid project that was weak in the narrow economic sense was nonetheless legal if other, broader concerns could be invoked to support it? Or, as the World Development Movement maintained, was the requirement that development projects make good economic sense so obvious that there was no need for Parliament to say so expressly? Rose LJ favoured the latter view:

> As to the absence of the word 'sound' from s 1(1), it seems to me that if Parliament had intended to confer a power to disburse money for unsound development purposes, it could have been expected to say so expressly . . . This development, is on the evidence, so economically unsound that there is no economic argument in favour of the case.[26]

The *Pergau Dam* judgment excited considerable political controversy, but is a readily defensible exercise in literalist statutory interpretation with obvious antecedents in both *Roberts* and *Bromley*. The judgment essentially construed s 1 as containing an implied fiduciary duty on the government's aid spending. One might question whether or not the common law fiduciary duty doctrine should play any part in regulating government bodies' expenditure plans, but *Pergau Dam* would suggest that the courts do now apply the doctrine on a non-party political basis.

From a jurisprudential perspective, the courts' use of the illegality rule to invalidate government decisions is more problematic when it is premised not on the literal meaning of particular words or phrases in a statute, but—as in the *Fulham* case—when it purports to ascertain the meaning of a particular provision in the light of the overall scheme of an Act. The House of Lords' judgment in *Padfield v Minister of Agriculture, Fisheries and Food*[27] is an extreme example of this point.

An Act of 1931 had introduced the Milk Marketing Scheme, which required dairy farmers to sell all their milk to regional Milk Marketing Boards. Both consumers and producers had representation on the various Boards. The subsequent Agriculture Marketing Act 1958 made provision for two distinct bodies to hear complaints about the scheme's operation. The Act appeared to envisage that most complaints would be referred to a Consumer's Committee. However s 19(3) provided that:

> A committee of investigation shall . . . (b) be charged with the duty, if the Minister in any case so directs, of considering and reporting to the Minister on . . . any . . . complaint made to the Minister as to the operation of any scheme which, in the opinion of the Minister, could not be considered by a Consumers' Committee.

In the mid-1960s, producers in the south-east region wanted a larger price rise than the Regional Board would grant. Their preferred remedy was to rely on a 'Committee of Investigation' to consider the issue, presumably because they thought a Consumers' Committee would not be so sympathetic to their interests. The Minister refused to pass the complaint to a Committee of Investigation, on the basis that in his opinion the matter could satisfactorily be considered by a Consumers' Committee. His understanding of s 19(3) was that referral to a Committee of Investigation would only be appropriate when he felt that the relevant Regional Board was not acting in the public interest.

The text of s 19(3) seems to afford the Minister a very wide discretion. However, the House of Lords proceeded to lend s 19(3) a somewhat unexpected meaning. Rather than construing s 19(3) literally, Lord Reid's leading judgment followed an interpretative technique with

---

[26] [1995] 1 WLR 386 at 402.   [27] [1968] AC 997.

distinctly teleological overtones. He began with the ostensibly uncontroversial proposition that: 'Parliament must have conferred the discretion with the intention that it should be used to promote the policy and objects of the Act'.[28] He then deduced the 'policy and objects of the Act' by examining both its entire text and the historical circumstances surrounding its enactment. This was, he suggested, a statute with an unusual substantive effect:

> When these provisions were first enacted in 1931 it was unusual for Parliament to compel people to sell their commodities in a way to which they objected and it was easily forseeable that any such scheme would cause loss to some producers.[29]

The inference of this would seem to be that all producer complaints should be investigated, to ensure that any losses were fully justified and that producers could know their interests were being fully considered. Lord Reid therefore concluded that: '[I]t is plainly the intention of the Act that even the widest issues should be investigated if the complaint is genuine and substantial, as this complaint certainly is.'[30]

Notwithstanding Lord Reid's constant evocation of parliamentary intent as the source of his decision, cynical observers of judicial behaviour might conclude that his reasoning in *Padfield* pays as little heed to orthodox understandings of the relationship between Parliament and the courts as his contemporaneous judgment in *Anisminic*. In effect, Lord Reid ignored the plain meaning of s 19(3) and converted the power it bestowed upon the Minister into a duty whenever a complaint was 'genuine and substantial'[31]—thereby ensuring that the Minister's failure to refer the complaint to a Committee of Investigation automatically became illegal. The case perhaps suggests that the ECJ's contemporaneous embrace of the 'spirit, scheme and general wording' approach to the interpretation of the Treaty of Rome was not quite so alien to the English judicial tradition as one might have initially believed.[32]

The use of what appears de facto to be purposive judicial reasoning to bring government action within the illegality doctrine is also evident in the Court of Appeal's judgment in *Congreve v Home Office*.[33] The Wireless Telegraphy Act 1949 s 1 made it a criminal offence for any person to use a radio or television without having a licence issued by the government. Section 1 also permitted the Home Secretary to issue regulations to charge a fee for such a licence. In 1975, the fee was set at £12 per year. In an attempt to increase the revenue generated by the licence, Harold Wilson's third Labour government announced in February 1975 that the fee would be raised to £18 with effect from 1 April 1975. In the following weeks, several newspapers pointed out that licence holders whose current licences expired shortly after 31 March 1975 might save themselves some £6 by purchasing another licence before 1 April. Many citizens took this advice. The Home Office responded by revoking all such licences, and sending their purchasers letters ordering them to return the £12 licences and buy new £18 licences on the date that their original licence expired. Congreve, a solicitor in a leading city firm, refused to comply, and sought a declaration that the Home Office policy was illegal. From a purely political perspective, such an action by a government with a Commons majority of two might be thought quite asinine. But in the view of the Court of Appeal, the Home Office's behaviour was indeed illegal as well.

---

[28] Ibid, at 1030.   [29] Ibid.   [30] Ibid, at 1031.

[31] Lord Morris, the sole dissentient, rested his judgment on much more orthodox grounds; cf his comment at 705: 'If Parliament had intended to impose a duty on the Minister to refer any and every complaint, or even any and every complaint of a particular nature, it would have been so easy to impose such a duty in plain terms. I cannot read the words in s 19(3) as imposing a positive duty on the Minister to refer every complaint as to the operation of the scheme'.

[32] See the discussion of *Van Gend en Loos* at 'Van Gend en Loos (1962)', ch 11, p 292. That it is difficult to identify the interpretive technique that Lord Reid used in *Padfield* is a further indication of the broad scope of the effective power that traditional constitutional understandings accord to the judiciary.   [33] [1976] QB 629.

Lord Denning MR's leading judgment deployed the same melodramatic language later invoked in *Rossminster*. He began by expressing some suspicion about the legitimacy of s 1:

> The statute has conferred a licensing power on the Minister: but it is a very special kind of power. It invades a man in the privacy of his home, and it does so solely for financial reasons so as to enable the Minister to collect money for the Revenue.[34]

Denning regarded the purchase of a licence as creating a property right for the buyer. Nothing in the Act clearly forbade an individual from holding two or more licences which overlapped for a short period. Section 1 undoubtedly empowered the Minister to revoke a licence in some circumstances; if the purchase had been premised on fraud, for example. But in the absence of such circumstances, or some other good reason, the Act did not empower the Minister to revoke a licence. For him to attempt to do so simply because it would generate additional revenue for the Treasury was a 'misuse of power'.[35]

Congreve might broadly be construed as supporting the notion that 'misuse of power' is a distinct sub-category of the illegality doctrine. As such, it would demand that courts always be willing to inquire into the motives which underlay the impugned decision. That inquiry was unproblematic in *Congreve* itself, as the Home Secretary candidly stated that his purpose was to raise money. In other cases, where the defendant was less forthcoming, an inquiry into motives could lead the court into rather delicate political territory. The case might therefore better be construed more narrowly, as an illustration of the simple point that the courts have consistently maintained that governmental powers to levy taxation can only be created by explicit statutory language.[36]

The uncertainties inherent in the 'four corners of the Act' characterisation of illegality are further magnified when we recall the judicial presumption that many (if not most) statutory provisions can properly be regarded as 'always speaking'.[37] This point is nicely illustrated—in respect of a rather prosaic issue—by the judgment of the House of Lords in *Akumah v LB of Hackney*.[38] Mr Akumah had repeatedly parked his car on a local council housing estate in breach of the parking scheme that the local authority had established. He had received a good many penalty tickets and eventually his car was impounded. The issue before the court was whether the council derived the power to run such a scheme from s 21(1) of the Housing Act 1985. Section 21(1) was cast in very general terms:

> The general management, regulation and control of a local housing authority's houses is vested in and shall be exercised by the authority and the houses shall at all times be open to inspection by the authority.

Section 21(1) of the 1985 Act was a re-enactment of a provision first enacted in the 1930s, at a time when very few people owned cars and there was no need for councils to control parking. Seventy years later, car parking had become an important issue in many cities, but Parliament had not altered the text of the original provision to give local authorities express powers to deal with the matter.

The interpretive technique adopted by the House of Lords in *Akumah* might be seen as either teleological or always speaking in nature:

> 21. . . . [I]t is inherent in the management of houses in a housing estate that parking on the estate should be regulated. Unregulated parking could in many housing estates lead to congestion of

---

[34] Ibid, at 649.   [35] Ibid, at 651.

[36] Cf Roskill LJ, Ibid at 657–658: 'If the Secretary of State wishes to put his position in this respect beyond all argument, he should seek the necessary Parliamentary powers—if he can obtain them'; and Denning at 652: '[The Home Office letters] were an attempt to levy money for the use of the Crown without the authority of Parliament; and that is quite enough to damn them: see *A-G v Wilts United Dairies*' (1922) 38 TLR 781, HL.

[37] See 'Complicating the literal rule: (most) statutory provisions are "always speaking"', ch 3, pp 57–58.

[38] [2005] UKHL 17, [2005] 1 WLR 985.

the roads and the unavailability of places for residents to park their cars if other persons can park there at will. It is also important to ensure access for service and emergency vehicles to the houses on the estate. Those factors are clearly capable of affecting the amenity of life for the residents and their access to and enjoyment of their houses and flats on the estate. I find no difficulty in accepting that safeguarding and improving that amenity and facilitating that access and enjoyment are proper functions of a council managing a housing estate.[39]

As in *Fulham* however, it is difficult to fashion a compelling argument to support the proposition that the House of Lords could not have equally credibly come to the opposite conclusion. A conclusion that if local authorities wanted to regulate parking—and impose penalties on individuals who breached such regulations—then they should persuade Parliament to grant them such powers in express terms could be considered quite consistent with constitutional principle.

The presumption of non-interference with 'basic rights'

The narrow construction of the *Congreve* rule offered earlier is unproblematic because it speaks to a 'fundamental' constitutional principle which has an explicit basis in a statutory text—namely the Bill of Rights. But one can also find applications of the illegality doctrine which rest on the assumption that certain 'fundamental' or 'basic' rights exist at common law or are implicitly protected by statute, and that the defence of those rights provides a legitimate contextual or background principle against which a statutory text should be construed. We have encountered this point on several occasions already. The House of Lords' construction of the Defence of the Realm legislation in *De Keyser* as being intended to respect the common law rule that the government could only in the most limited circumstances take a citizen's property without paying compensation is a good example of this.[40]

Relatedly, one might offer up *Gilmore* and *Anisminic* as illustrations of a 'basic right' presumption at common law that Parliament cannot deprive citizens of access to the courts other than by the most explicit statutory formulae.[41] *R & W Paul Ltd v Wheat Commission* can also be invoked to support this contention.[42] The Arbitration Act 1889 permitted parties who had agreed to resolve commercial disputes by arbitration rather than litigation to appeal to the High Court on a point of law against the arbitrator's decision. Subsequently, the Wheat Act 1932 created a body called the Wheat Commission to regulate the wheat industry. The Wheat Act s 5 empowered the Commission to make bye-laws to give effect to the Act. Bye-law 20 made provision to refer disputes between producers and the Commission to an arbitrator, and appeared to make the arbitrator's decision on all disputes final. The company in this case wished to refer the arbitrator's decision to the courts. Bye-law 20 seemed to preclude this. The question thus raised in this action was whether the Commission had the power to pass bye-law 20. The House of Lords held that the Commission had exceeded its powers. Bye-law 20 was illegal because it interfered with the basic right of access to the courts:

> The Arbitration Act is a statute of general application, and it confers a valuable and important right of resort to the courts of law. To exclude its operation from an arbitration is to deprive the parties . . . of the rights which the Act confers . . . If that is intended, express words to that effect are in my opinion essential.[43]

---

[39] [2005] 1 WLR 985 at 993; per Lord Carswell (for a unanimous court).

[40] See 'The superiority of statute over prerogative: *A-G v De Keyser's Royal Hotel Ltd* (1920)', ch 4, pp 85–87.

[41] See 'Ouster clauses—*Gilmore* (1957) and *Anisminic* (1969)' ff, ch 3, pp 68–69.

[42] [1937] AC 139. See the discussion in Browne-Wilkinson, Lord (1992) 'The infiltration of a Bill of Rights' *Public Law* 397.   [43] [1937] AC 139 at 154, per Lord Macmillan.

A more recent example of this basic right approach to illegality—and one rooted purely in common law—is provided by *Raymond v Honey*.[44] Under the Prison Act 1952 s 47, the Home Secretary may make rules for the regulation and management of prisons. Rules 33 and 37 seemed to empower prison governors to prevent mail being sent by prisoners in certain circumstances. Raymond, the governor, prevented some of Honey's [a prisoner] mail being sent to Honey's lawyers. Honey subsequently initiated contempt of court proceedings against Raymond. Contempt of court is a broad concept in English law. The accepted definition was offered by Lord Russell in 1900 in *R v Gray*, and encompassed 'Any act done which is calculated to obstruct or interfere with the due course of justice'.[45] The governor's action clearly fell within this definition. His defence to the action was that he had been authorised to obstruct prisoners' mail by the Prison Regulations. This in turn raised the issue of whether s 47 of the Act permitted the Home Secretary to make regulations granting a governor such powers. The House of Lords concluded that s 47 did not have that effect. As Lord Wilberforce put it:

> . . . under English law, a convicted prisoner, in spite of his imprisonment, retains all civil rights which are not taken away expressly or by necessary implication . . .
>
> There is nothing in the Prison Act 1952 that confers power to make regulations which would deny, or interfere with, the right of the respondent, as a prisoner, to have unimpeded access to a court. Section 47 . . . is quite insufficient to authorise hindrance or interference with so basic a right.[46]

At this time, the English courts' use of the 'basic right' principle was patchy and erratic. One could not identify with any precision which 'basic rights' existed, nor the circumstances in which the courts would be ready to invoke them as a means to set a particular interpretative context within which particular statutory powers should be construed. As such, the principle lent the concept of illegality a still more complicated and uncertain character. As suggested in subsequent chapters, the doctrine has assumed a more coherent shape in recent years. For the moment however, we continue our analysis of the more clearly established facets of the illegality principle.

Unlawful delegation of powers

It would seem uncontroversial to assert that the illegality doctrine should limit the power of a designated decision-maker to pass on certain of her legal powers to other bodies or individuals. In respect of statutory powers, Parliament has, one assumes, given particular powers to particular people/bodies for particular reasons; such as, for example, their expertise or their representative character. Should those powers in effect be exercised by some other body or individual, Parliament's wishes would clearly be frustrated.

The basic parameters of the rule against delegation are well illustrated in *Ellis v Dubowski*.[47] The Cinematograph Act 1909 had empowered county councils to impose conditions on the grant of licences to operate cinemas in their respective areas. Middlesex County Council's licensing conditions included a provision which banned the showing of any movie which had not been approved by the British Board of Film Censors (BBFC). The High Court concluded that the provision was unlawful:

> The condition sets up an authority whose ipse dixit is to control the exhibition of films. The effect is to transfer a power which belongs to the County Council . . . [A] condition putting the matter into the hands of a third person or body not possessed of statutory or constitutional authority is ultra vires.[48]

---

[44] [1983] 1 AC 1, HL.   [45] [1900] 2 QB 36.   [46] [1983] 1 AC 1 at 10 and 12.
[47] [1921] 3 KB 621.   [48] Ibid, at 625.

The statutory scheme did permit the county council to delegate its powers to district councils, or to local magistrates. Nor would it be unlawful for the county council to have taken the BBFC's views about a particular film into account when deciding whether it could be shown in a local cinema. What it could not do, however, was grant the BBFC an effective power of veto on the issue.[49]

The rule was applied with similar clarity in *Allingham v Minister of Agriculture and Fisheries*.[50] The Defence Regulations 1939 under which Mr Liversidge had been imprisoned had a far wider scope than dealing simply with potential enemies and saboteurs. Regulation 62 gave the Minister of Agriculture a sweeping power to control the cultivation of land, be it publicly or privately owned. Regulation 66 then empowered him to delegate his power to a local executive committee. In order to make its decisions more quickly, the committee in Bedfordshire then sub-delegated its power to one of its employees. Allingham was a local farmer, who challenged the instructions he had been given in respect of his land. The basis of his challenge was that the committee had no power to sub-delegate the powers it possessed as a delegate of the Minister.

The Court accepted this contention, bringing it within the orthodox maxim of *delegatus non potest delegare*.[51] The committee had no statutory authority to allow others to carry out the tasks with which it had been entrusted. It would have been proper for the committee to allow its officers to make recommendations as to the use of land, and even for it to accord substantial weight to such recommendations in reaching its decisions. But each of those decisions had to be the product of its own collective mind.

H Lavender & Son Ltd v Minister of Housing and Local Government[52] illustrates the point that the rule against delegation works as readily between institutions as within them. Lavender had sought permission from its local council to extract gravel from a farm that it owned. When the council refused permission, Lavender exercised a right of appeal to the Minister of Housing and Local Government (MHLG). The Minister rejected the appeal, noting that as a matter of policy he would not approve such applications unless the Minister of Agriculture raised no objection to the proposal. The High Court concluded that this amounted to a de facto delegation of the MHLG's statutory powers to the Minister of Agriculture. While the MHLG was entitled to seek and consider the views of other Ministers, he was not entitled to bind himself to follow them. As Wills J characterised the situation:

> It was the decision of the Minister of Agriculture not to waive his objection that was decisive in this case, and while that might properly prove to be the decisive factor for the MHLG . . . it seems to me quite wrong for a policy to be applied which in reality eliminates all the material considerations save only the consideration, when that is the case, that the Minister of Agriculture objects.[53]

The rule that a statutory body can only delegate its powers if it has clear statutory authorisation is complicated by the proposition that such authorisation need not have an explicit textual base, but can rather arise as a matter of necessary implication. The leading example is the House of Lords' judgment in *Local Government Board v Arlidge*.[54] In that case it was considered permissible for the LGB to delegate its powers to hold inquiries concerning the closure of unfit properties to a senior official. The Court took the view that to hold otherwise would severely compromise the LGB's administrative efficiency. But the principle is not one of general application. In *Barnard v National Dock Labour Board*,[55] for example, the Court of Appeal refused to accept that the NDLB was empowered as a matter of necessary implication to delegate its powers to dismiss or suspend dock workers to a senior manager, notwithstanding the fact that

---

[49] For a more recent illustration of precisely the same point see *R v Greater London Council, ex p Blackburn* [1976] 1 WLR 550.   [50] [1948] 1 All ER 780.

[51] A delegate has no power to delegate.   [52] [1970] 1 WLR 1231.   [53] Ibid, at 1241.

[54] [1915] AC 120.   [55] [1953] 2 QB 18

such delegation would have saved the NDLB considerable time and expense.[56] The position is however rather different when one is dealing with the activities of a Minister of the Crown within her own department.

As noted in chapter nine, the convention of individual ministerial responsibility has undergone a significant change in the modern era. It is no longer presumed that a Minister is responsible—in the sense of being under a moral obligation to resign her office—for the failings of her department unless she was personally involved in the matter concerned. The scope of departmental activity has long been far too wide for such a rule to be practical.[57] This point did not escape the courts' attention when considering to what extent a Minister might lawfully 'delegate' her legal responsibilities.

The leading decision is *Carltona v Works Commissioners*.[58] The case arose from the Commissioners use of a power granted by reg 51 of the Defence Regulations 1939 to take possession of any land if it considered it necessary to do so in the interests of public safety or defence. That Parliament should grant any powers to this body was something of an oddity, since the Commissioners had no physical existence. Their powers were actually vested by statute in the Minister of Works and Planning. The notice requisitioning Carltona's property was issued by a senior civil servant in the Ministry of Works and Planning, and it was accepted that the Minister himself had not given any personal attention to the matter. Carltona thus contended that there had been an unlawful delegation of power. In the Court of Appeal, Lord Greene MR concluded that this argument was quite misplaced:

> [T]he functions which are given to ministers (and constitutionally given to ministers because they are constitutionally responsible) are functions so multifarious that no minister could ever personally attend to them . . . The duties imposed upon ministers and the powers given to ministers are normally exercised under the authority of the ministers by responsible officials of the department. Public business could not be carried on if that were not the case. Constitutionally, the decision of such an official is, of course, the decision of the Minister.[59]

If such delegation was inappropriate, Lord Greene considered that the proper remedy was for the Minister to be called to account on the floor of the Commons or Lords rather than in the courts.

Carltona tells us that, in effect, no delegation occurs in these circumstances. The official is not a delegate of the Minister, but is rather her 'alter ego'. The principle has been consistently applied by the courts.[60] It is not however without complications. Six years after *Carltona*, in *Lewisham Metropolitan Borough and Town Clerk v Roberts*, Lord Denning observed that:

> Now I take it to be quite plain that when a Minister is entrusted with administrative as distinct from legislative functions he is entitled to act by any authorised official of his department. The Minister is not bound to give his mind to the matter personally. That is implicit in the modern machinery of government . . . No question of agency or delegation . . . seems to me to arise at all.[61]

---

[56] The basis for the distinction is perhaps that while both cases concerned government interference with individual 'liberty' (ie the demolition of Arlidge's house and Barnard's dismissal from his job), the power at issue in *Arlidge* also required the LGB to take into account an obvious public interest, namely the building's structural safety and sanitary standards of the neighbourhood; see Viscount Dilhorne in *Arlidge* [1914–15] All ER Rep 1 at 6–7, HL. No such factors were relevant in *Barnard*. The inference would be that where a broad public interest in an issue clearly outweighs an individual interest, the requirement that delegation (if done to promote administrative efficiency) requires clear statutory authorisation will be relaxed. But see further the discussion of the estoppel principle later in the chapter. [57] See 'IV. Individual ministerial responsibility', ch 9, p 238.

[58] [1943] 2 All ER 560, CA.   [59] Ibid, at 563.

[60] See generally Lanham D (1984) 'Delegation and the alter ego principle' LQR 587.

[61] [1949] 2 KB 608 at 621, CA.

This comment raised the possibility that the alter ego principle applied only to 'authorised' officials, which in turn suggests that in the absence of such authorisation, an unlawful delegation would have occurred. However, it was made clear in *R v Skinner*[62] that 'authorisation' could be a very informal affair. The defendant in Skinner appealed against his conviction for drink-driving on the basis that the Minister of Transport had unlawfully delegated her statutory power to approve breath test devices of the type used on Skinner to a senior official. The argument did not attack *Carltona* as a general principle, but tried to maintain that in situations where a ministerial decision could impact upon the liberty of the individual, the Minister should act in person rather than through an alter ego. The Court saw no legal merit in that contention. The judgment also made it clear that 'authorisation' need not be explicit, but could be found simply in the official's conformity with the relevant department's established administrative routines.[63]

That the legitimate reach of the alter ego principle can be very expansive is illustrated by the House of Lords' decision in *Oladehinde v Secretary of State for the Home Department*.[64] The case involved one of the most explicit of governmental interference's with the liberty of the person; namely the power to deport foreign nationals who had overstayed their right to remain in the UK. Prior to the enactment of the Immigration Act 1988, the decision to deport had been taken in practice by a Senior Executive Officer within the Home Office. Following the passage of the Act, the Home Secretary expressly authorised a number of Immigration Inspectors to take the decision. Oladehinde's counsel suggested that since the Immigration Inspectors were technically employed under statutory powers, and so were not part of the Home Office, they could not be brought within the alter ego principle. The House of Lords rejected this proposition, observing that whatever its precise legal status, the Immigration Inspectorate had in practice 'evolved' into the Home Office's organisational structure over the years. Immigration Inspectors were comparable in seniority to the Home Office officials who had previously taken the deportation decision, and as such were appropriate figures to take those decisions after 1988. This supposition was further reinforced by the fact that the Act had explicitly required that the Home Secretary exercise certain powers in person, which raised the inference that there were no legislatively imposed limits on his/her capacity to devolve other parts of the process to his/her officials.

As Lanham has observed, the *Carltona* principle now has an expansive reach:

> [T]he courts have moved a long way from the rule against delegation so far as powers vested in Ministers are concerned. Not only can persons other than the donee of the power actually exercise the power, there is little control either of the method of authorisation or the suitability of the person by whom the power is exercised.[65]

This state of affairs undoubtedly oils the wheels of the administrative process within central government departments, increasing the speed and cutting the cost of decision-making. That is—in a narrow sense of the word—'efficient'. One might however wonder if the cost of that efficiency is that some decisions are made by officials who may not be properly fitted to take them. Any suggestion that the courts have been insufficiently rigorous in policing the *Carltona* principle might obviously be rebutted by pointing out that an inapposite use of the alter ego principle can be questioned within Parliament. But, as suggested in chapter five, it is naive to assume that the Commons and Lords exercise much effective control over the minutiae of governmental decision-making.

---

[62] [1968] 2 QB 700.

[63] See the extracts from the cross-examination of the official concerned; Ibid, at 705–706. For a similar analysis see *Re Golden Chemical Products Ltd* [1976] Ch 300.   [64] [1991] 1 AC 254.

[65] op cit p 611.

Fettering of discretion

The rule against the fettering of discretion rests on the presumption that—except in situations where a clear statutory or common law rule obliges a government body to reach one and only one particular decision—decision-makers must give a reasoned consideration on an individuated basis as to how a power should be exercised or a duty discharged.

R v LCC, ex p Corrie[66] provides a straightforward application of the rule. The London Council (General Powers) Act 1890 s 14 gave the LCC a broadly framed power to make bye-laws regulating the use of its parks. The LCC subsequently passed a bye-law which prohibited selling any goods in its parks unless the vendor had previously sought and received the council's permission. In response to a concern that the parks were being used for undesirable commercial activities, the LCC then resolved, without changing the bye-law, that no permissions would be granted in future. Corrie wished to sell pamphlets on behalf of a charity for the blind. Her application for permission to sell them met the response that, in accordance with the new resolution, no permissions would be granted in future. She then applied to the courts for a writ of mandamus to force the LCC to consider her application on its individual merits, rather than in conformity with its policy.

The court unanimously granted the writ. It concluded that the LCC had been charged with a 'judicial' function, which demanded that attention be given to the individual merits of each application. It also concluded that applicants derived a 'right' from the 1890 Act. This was not a right to receive permission, but to have their applications properly considered. The corollary of this right was that the council was under an obligation to consider each application for a permit on a case-by-case basis.

However, the rule against fettering does not preclude a government body forming strong presumptions as to the way in which discretionary powers should be exercised. In other words, while a government body may adopt a policy to structure the exercise of its powers, it may not adopt a rule which exactly controls the way they are used. This point was clearly expressed by Bankes LJ in *R v Port of London Authority, ex p Kynoch Ltd*:

> There are on the one hand cases where a tribunal in the honest exercise of its discretion has adopted a policy, and without refusing to hear an applicant, intimates to him what its policy is, and that after hearing him it will in accordance with its policy decide against him, unless there is something exceptional in his case . . . [N]o objection could be taken to such a course. On the other hand there are cases where the tribunal has passed a rule . . . not to hear any application of a particular character by whomsoever made. There is a wide distinction to be drawn between these two classes.[67]

This principle recognises that policy presumptions of this sort greatly ease the administrative process, in much the same way as the delegation of power within an organisation. The decision does of course raise the difficulty of deciding at what point a 'policy' has become so rigid that it mutates into a rule; the 'wide distinction' to which Bankes LJ alluded may on occasion be rather narrow.

The more recent House of Lords judgment in *British Oxygen Co Ltd v Minister of Technology*[68] confirms the broad thrust of the *Kynoch* doctrine, and might be seen as even more indulgent of administrative expediency. The Minister was empowered by s 1(1) of the Industrial Development Act 1966 to 'make to any person carrying on a business in Great Britain a grant towards approved capital expenditure . . . providing new machinery or plant'. In order to speed its decision-making process—by reducing the number of applications—the Ministry decided to institute a policy of not making grants for items valued at less than £25. British Oxygen, which had sought a grant for a great many gas cylinders costing £20 each, claimed that the

---

[66] [1918] 1 KB 68.   [67] [1919] 1 KB 176 at 184, CA.   [68] [1971] AC 610.

'policy' was de facto a rule, and so an unlawful fetter on the s 1 discretion. The House of Lords rejected this argument. Having approved the 'general principle' outlined in *Kynoch*, Lord Reid (in the leading judgment for a unanimous court) observed that some statutory powers might legitimately be constrained by very tight policy choices:

> I do not think that there is any great difference between a policy and a rule . . . [A] Ministry or large authority may have had to deal already with a multitude of similar applications and then they will almost certainly have evolved a policy so precise that it could well be called a rule. There can be no objection to that—provided the authority is always willing to listen to anyone with something new to say.[69]

The point—alluded to in *British Oxygen*—that the legality of any structuring of discretion turned on the precise substance of the statutory power/duty in issue was firmly reinforced in *A-G (ex rel Tilley) v Wandsworth London Borough Council*.[70] The council was potentially under a duty to provide housing to families with children through one of two statutory routes. The first duty, under the Housing (Homeless Persons) Act 1977, removed that responsibility if a family was 'intentionally homeless'.[71] The second arose—more obliquely—under s 1 of the Children and Young Persons Act 1963, which obliged local authorities 'to make available such advice, guidance and assistance as may promote the welfare of children by diminishing the need to receive children into or keep them in [local authority] care'. In 1980, Wandsworth had adopted a policy, other than in exceptional cases, to refuse to offer housing to children and their families under the 1963 Act if the child's parents were 'intentionally homeless' and so not entitled to housing under the 1977 Act. There was some dispute at trial as to whether the exceptions to the 'policy' were genuine. However the Court of Appeal (upholding the High Court) suggested that even a genuine policy (ie one that admitted of exceptions) would be an unlawful fetter in respect of this particular statutory provision. In Templeman LJ's view:

> I am not myself persuaded that even a policy resolution hedged about with exceptions would be entirely free from attack. Dealing with children, the discretion and powers of any authority must depend entirely on the different circumstances of each child before them for consideration.[72]

Tilley does not undermine the general applicability of the *British Oxygen* rationale. It does however reinforce the point that the rationale is of general and not universal application. There is a readily discernible qualitative distinction between governmental powers premised squarely on an individuated issue (ie the best interests of a child) and those relating to a generic matter (ie applications for industrial grants). One might offer as a guiding principle the suggestion that the permissible rigidity of a policy will vary in accordance with the degree of individuation inherent in the power to which the policy is applied. The formula is essentially tautological however. This is perhaps an area of law where the question of how 'rule-like' a policy may be is best answered by extrapolation from case law dealing with closely analogous powers, rather than by application of more general principle.

Estoppel

The problems posed by the doctrine of estoppel in public law also operate at several levels. The most acute difficulty is that presented by the factual scenario in *Minister of Agriculture and Fisheries v Hulkin*.[73] Let us suppose that a government body, having misunderstood its

---

[69] Ibid, at 617. For a less indulgent approach see *Eastleigh Borough Council v Betts* [1983] 2 AC 613, HL.

[70] [1981] 1 WLR 854.

[71] eg because the family had been evicted from its former home because a parent had been in rent or mortgage arrears; see generally Loveland (1995) op cit.   [72] [1981] 1 WLR 854 at 858.

[73] (1948) unreported, CA, but discussed at length in *Minister of Agriculture and Fisheries v Matthews* [1950] 1 KB 148.

statutory powers, grants a tenancy to an individual citizen in respect of land when it actually has no power to do so. To permit the tenancy to stand would require that we accept that the government body can act 'illegally', in the core sense of going beyond its legal powers. One might therefore assume that the 'tenancy' should be considered invalid. To hold otherwise would be to undermine the illegality principle, and so jeopardise both the sovereignty of Parliament and the rule of law in their orthodox senses. Yet this might work a substantial injustice on the 'tenant'. A 'tenant' who has acted in honest reliance on the government body's power to grant a tenancy may have taken such steps as giving up a former tenancy, changing her job, moving her children to new schools, or spending substantial sums on refurbishment of the property. Considerations of substantive fairness might then lead us to assume that the 'tenancy' should be upheld.[74] But the position then becomes further complicated if we suggest that a third party's interests in the land concerned may be substantially compromised if the 'tenancy' is not invalidated.

In *Hulkin*, the Court of Appeal (per Lord Greene MR) had considered the matter easily resolved. Any injustice that might be done to an individual could not be invoked to sustain a substantively unlawful decision:

> [Accepting] that the Minister had no power under the regulations to grant a tenancy, it is perfectly manifest to my mind that he could not by estoppel give himself such a power. The power given to an authority under a statute is limited to the four corners of the power given. It would entirely destroy the whole doctrine of ultra vires if it was possible for the donee to extend his power by creating an estoppel.[75]

While obviously defensible in terms of its result, the reasoning informing Lord Greene MR's judgment is conceptually problematic from a constitutional law perspective. Hulkin's objective, to remain as a tenant, cannot be achieved by any 'extension' of the Minister's power. It is a trite point that the executive branch of the UK government has no law-making powers; its legal competence derives either from statute or common law. A Minister is no more able to extend her powers through estoppel than she is by scribbling in an additional section on a statute or announcing that she has found a new common law power. Hulkin therefore cannot succeed by estopping the Minister from 'revoking' the tenancy. The Minister cannot revoke something which she had no power to create. And even if we were to accept this flawed premise, judicial enforcement of an estoppel would not entail the Minister extending her powers, but the court doing so. An alternative characterisation of the case would be to suggest that to retain his 'tenancy', Hulkin would have to establish that the court was estopped from quashing the Minister's decision. This approach is however doubly flawed. The court has no pre-existing relationship with Hulkin in respect of the tenancy, and so could not be the subject of an estoppel. But more importantly, the court has no more power than a Minister to 'extend' the powers granted to the Minister by Parliament.[76] To win his case, in a manner that is compatible with orthodox notions of parliamentary sovereignty, the rule of law and the separation of powers, Hulkin must convince the court that the relevant statute contains a provision to the effect that Parliament has instructed the courts that, in certain limited factual circumstances, they should recognise a government action as lawful even if, absent such circumstances, the action exceeds the ostensible limits of the Minister's powers.

One can offer very good reasons for assuming that a court would not embrace this approach. The imputation of such an intention to Parliament would be wholly inconsistent with orthodox principles of statutory interpretation; it would demand that the courts embrace a style of teleological construction which attached overriding importance to the avoidance of substantive injustice in certain situations. In addition to threatening orthodox notions of parliamentary

---

[74] If the grant of the tenancy was 'illegal'.   [75] Cited in *Matthews* [1950] 1 KB 148 at 154.

[76] Although it could, absent statutory limitations to the contrary, create new powers at common law.

sovereignty, such a strategy would raise acute problems of legal certainty. To which government acts would it apply? What criteria would an applicant have to meet to invoke it? There are thus very good 'constitutional law' explanations for Mr Hulkin not having his tenancy; but they have nothing to do with a Minister extending her powers.

The estoppel problem is less intractable if binding a government body to uphold a particular course of action would not result in an illegal decision. The plaintiff in *Robertson v Minister of Pensions*[77] had suffered a disability caused by a war-related injury. In seeking advice about his pension entitlements, he approached the Ministry of War. An official in that Ministry informed Mr Robertson unequivocally that the injury was attributable to his war service, and he was entitled to a pension. Acting in reliance on this statement, Mr Robertson did not seek further, expert medical confirmation of the cause of his injury. Unbeknown to Mr Robertson, and evidently to the official at the Ministry of War, responsibility for making decisions on this question had been transferred by statute to the Ministry of Pensions some years earlier. The Ministry of Pensions subsequently ordered Mr Robertson to undergo a medical examination, on the basis of which it concluded that he was not eligible for a pension. That conclusion was then upheld by a pensions appeal tribunal, against whose decision Robertson appealed on a point of law to the High Court.

The factual gist of Mr Robertson's case was that had he sought a medical examination when he first approached the War Office, that examination would have supported his claim. His point in law was that the Ministry of Pensions was estopped from resiling from the Ministry of War's letter. Denning J decided in Mr Robertson's favour. His judgment rested on two grounds. The narrower basis of his judgment was that the War Office and the Ministry of Pensions were both part of the 'Crown': a representation or decision made by one department was therefore to be regarded as being made by any other department. This is in itself a curious conclusion, in so far as it seems to extend the alter ego principle used in the delegation cases discussed earlier from being just an intra-departmental device to being an inter-departmental device. The principle is difficult to reconcile with the later judgment in *Lavender*, for example. But *Robertson* is most often cited for Denning J's rather broader statement of principle, evidently as applicable to statutory bodies as to the Crown:

> In my opinion, if a government department in its dealings with a subject takes it on itself to assume authority on a matter with which he is concerned, he is entitled to rely on it having the authority which it assumes. He does not know, and cannot be expected to know, the limits of its authority.[78]

Lord Denning took the opportunity to reiterate that broad statement of principle in the Court of Appeal in *Falmouth Boat Construction Co Ltd v Howell*.[79] Moreover, his judgment intimated that the principle would stretch to cover government officials who had made decisions that they had no legal authority to make. However, in a manner with distinct echoes of his criticism of Denning's judgment in *Magor and St Mellons*,[80] Lord Simmonds flatly rejected the proposition when the case reached the House of Lords.[81] Lord Simmonds began by restating the *Hulkin* principle: 'That which is prohibited cannot be lawfully done . . ., and if it cannot be lawfully done it cannot be the subject of a claim enforceable at law'.[82] He then poured a substantial amount of jurisprudential cold water on Denning's *Robertson* principle:

> My Lords, I know of no such principle in our law nor was any authority for it cited. The illegality of an act is the same whether or not the actor has been misled by an assumption of authority on the part of a government officer however high or low in the hierarchy.[83]

---

[77] [1949] 1 KB 227.   [78] [1949] 1 KB 227 at 232.   [79] [1950] 2 KB 16.
[80] See 'Purposive (or "teleological") interpretation', ch 3, pp 60–61.   [81] [1951] AC 837.
[82] Ibid, at 844.
[83] Ibid, at 845. See also Lord Normand at 849: ' . . . [N]either a minister nor any subordinate officer of the Crown can by any conduct or representation bar the Crown from enforcing a statutory prohibition or entitle the subject to maintain that there was no breach of it'.

This is a simple restatement of orthodox constitutional theory, and has compelling force in respect of decisions made in excess of the decision-makers' powers. But it has no obvious bearing on 'estoppel' situations where the citizen is attempting to bind an authority to a decision that would be lawful, but which for policy reasons the relevant authority decides it does not want to respect. For this reason, the High Court's judgment in *Southend-on-Sea Corpn v Hodgson (Wickford) Ltd*[84] is rather unsatisfactory. Hodgson had bought a property with a view to using it as a builder's yard. A senior official in the local authority had told them that the site had long been used for such purposes, and no planning permission was necessary for that use. It subsequently emerged that the official was mistaken. The local authority then decided not to grant planning permission, even though it was arguably entitled to do so as a matter of law. The High Court seemed to conclude that it was not possible in any circumstances for a government body to be bound by such a representation, on the basis that an estoppel would improperly fetter the exercise of its discretion. This seems an unnecessarily inflexible conclusion. A more sensible way to approach the issue might be to suggest that avoiding inflicting a substantial burden on a citizen who has relied in good faith on mistaken advice is a relevant consideration when the authority considers how to proceed. That concern should not determine the eventual outcome, since estopping the authority might work an injustice on third parties. On these facts, for example, it is likely that had Hodgson applied for planning permission, the application would have been opposed by neighbours, whose opinions may have led the council not to grant permission. If the council is bound by its official's mistake, third parties are deprived of their entitlement to participate in the decision-making process and suffer the perhaps unwelcome presence of a builder's yard near their homes.

Yet the judicial pendulum seemed to swing too far in the other direction in the Court of Appeal's judgment in *Lever Finance Ltd v Westminster (City) London Borough Council*,[85] a case resting on facts very similar to those in *Hodgson*. Denning suggested that, in practice, many planning authorities de facto delegated their powers to senior officers, even though—until the passage of s 64 of the Planning Act 1968—they had not de jure been entitled to do so.[86] A citizen acting in good faith was thus entitled to assume that decisions taken by officials within the scope of their 'ostensible authority' would be binding. That this result might prejudice the interests of equally blameless third parties did not seem to enter into Lord Denning's reasoning.[87]

This principle was rejected by a differently constituted Court of Appeal in *Western Fish Products Ltd v Penwith District Council*.[88] The Court held that an authority could only be bound to respect a representation mistakenly made by one of its officers—if the representation led to a decision within the scope of its powers—in limited circumstances. The Court laid particular stress on the need for the citizen to establish that he/she had strong grounds for believing that the representee actually had the legal power to make the relevant decision. It also intimated that an estoppel should be upheld only if the outcome would not work an injustice on third parties.

The substantive problems raised by the estoppel scenario have continued to exercise the courts in recent years. However, the classification of the problems has undergone a change—even if their substantive content has remained unaltered. As we shall see in chapter fourteen, the *Lever/Western Fish* issue now tends to be seen as a facet of the procedural irregularity doctrine; a reclassification which perhaps offers greater scope for

---

[84] [1962] 1 QB 416.   [85] [1971] 1 QB 222.

[86] The *Carltona* alter ego principle applies only to Ministers, not to non-ministerial government bodies.

[87] It is also difficult to characterise Lever Finance as an 'ignorant citizen' on these facts. It was, after all, a property development company, a body one might expect to be familiar with the legal structure of the planning process.   [88] [1981] 2 All ER 204, CA.

the innovative solution discussed earlier to the constitutional problem posed by 'illegal' estoppels.[89]

II. Irrationality

Like illegality, irrationality is primarily concerned with the substantive content of a government decision. However, it is more readily regarded as being concerned with the political or moral rather than (in the strict sense) legal character of the decision concerned.[90]

The formula used by Lord Diplock in *GCHQ* to define the irrationality doctrine might suggest that very few government decisions could be unlawful on this ground. In Lord Diplock's view, irrationality only arose if a decision was:

> . . . so outrageous in its defiance of logic or of accepted moral standards that no sensible person who had applied his mind to the question to be decided could have arrived at it.[91]

The test then is not simply that the decision defies logic or accepted moral standards; nor even that it defies these criteria to an *outrageous* extent; rather it requires the defiance to be *so* outrageous. This form of words is perhaps even more indulgent of executive autonomy on 'moral' grounds than Lord Greene MR's phraseology in *Wednesbury*: 'something so absurd that no sensible person could ever dream that it lay within the powers of the authority'.[92]

Irrationality as a 'substantive' concept: assessing 'the merits' of a governmental decision

It is often suggested that in applying the irrationality test the court has no concern with the substantive merits of the decision being challenged. That is a rather unfortunate and misleading characterisation however. The irrationality test certainly does not permit a court to impose its own preferred solution on the decision-making body. But the court is concerned to establish *if the substantive decision has any merit at all*. If the decision lacks that quality entirely, it will be unlawful. In that limited sense, the irrationality test is concerned with the political or moral merits of government decisions.

A local authority—empowered by statute to employ teachers on such terms as it thinks fit— which refused to employ a teacher because she had red hair would be making an obviously irrational decision. But one which decided to employ only teachers with Master's degrees, or more than five years previous teaching experience, would not be acting irrationally, even if many other authorities set much less exacting standards. If irrationality is construed in this expansive way, it is easy to see why the policies in issue in such cases as *Kruse v Johnson*,[93] or *Wednesbury*[94] itself, did not come within the test. The council's policies in each of those cases

---

[89] On the closely related principle of res judicata see: *Re 56 Denton Road, Twickenham* [1953] Ch 51; *Rootkin v Kent County Council* [1981] 1 WLR 1186; Bradley A (1981) 'Administrative justice and the binding effects of official acts' *Current Legal Problems* 1: Akehurst M (1982) 'Revocation of administrative decisions' *Public Law* 613.

[90] For a more sophisticated account, which breaks the ground down into several discrete sub-heads, see Walker P (1995) 'What's wrong with irrationality' *Public Law* 556.   [91] [1985] AC 374 at 410–411, HL.

[92] [1948] 1 KB 223 at 229, CA. Although one might suggest that subsequent commentators have overlooked Lord Greene MR's use of the word 'dream', rather than for example 'consider' or 'conclude'. Departures from normality are an integral element of dreams; irrationality would presumably then only arise if the content of the decision lay not just in, but at the extreme edge of the realm of fantasy.

[93] A ban on playing loud musical instruments in residential areas; see 'IV. The role of the judiciary', ch 10, pp 262–263.

[94] Excluding children from the cinema on Sunday mornings; see 'IV. The role of the judiciary', ch 10, pp 262–263.

may have struck many observers as misguided, or ineffective, or just plain stupid; but those characteristics, singly or in combination, do not amount to the extreme departure from logic or prevailing moral standards that the Diplock/Greene tests seemingly require.

Seen in this way, irrationality as a ground of review rests on a presumption that in a politically pluralist society it is entirely probable that different governmental decision-makers could quite properly produce significantly, even markedly different responses to a particular situation.[95] It is only when a given response oversteps the range of permissible responses that the decision-maker will have produced an irrational decision. This rationale has particular force when the governmental decision in issue has been made under a statutory provision couched in terms such as 'the Minister may attach such terms and conditions as she thinks fit' or 'the Minister may make such provision as she considers reasonable'. Parliament's use of such discretion-laden formulae is a statutory recognition that legislators do not expect the application of the statutory provision to lead to a particular outcome. The irrationality principle can thus be presented in an abstract, political sense as a constitutional device which requires the courts to accept that the substantive boundaries of moral consensus within which government bodies are confined are very broad.

Mis-using the irrationality test? Coming too close to the 'merits' of a governmental decision

From that perspective, the House of Lords' conclusion in *Roberts v Hopwood*[96] that Poplar's wages policy was irrational as well as illegal is difficult to defend. That a decision is illegal does not mean that it is also irrational. A decision-maker might after the most careful and sensible consideration of a particular course of action proceed on the basis of a misunderstanding of her legal powers. That may be unlawful, but it is a mistake that could be made by the most prudent of persons. But it is extremely difficult to sustain the argument that a decision is irrational if it enjoys widespread support. Poplar's wage policy undoubtedly enjoyed such support among local voters. To conclude that the substance of the policy was per se irrational thus demands that we conclude that the Labour Party's supporters at the local elections had all taken leave of their senses. Collective hysteria is, admittedly, not an unknown phenomenon. But the courts might be venturing into rather dangerous political territory if they were explicitly to maintain that a widely held belief amounted to an outrageous defiance of accepted moral standards.[97] That danger is that in adopting a narrow understanding of the boundaries of political consensus, the courts confine the limits of governmental power much more tightly than Parliament intended and so undermine the sovereignty of Parliament.

The opinions offered in the Court of Appeal in *Roberts* seem more satisfactory on this point. Scrutton LJ approached the question of irrationality in the light of the principle of 'benevolent interpretation' propounded by Lord Russell in *Kruse v Johnson*. Poplar's wages were undoubtedly in excess of market equivalents, in some instances substantially so. Such wages might have been irrational if fixed by a non-elected body. But the fact that the council was a representative assembly lent the concept of irrationality an additionally expansive character; it was therefore a test which a council was unlikely to fail.

Yet one can also point to cases in which the courts have accepted the 'benevolent interpretation' rationale but still invoked irrationality to invalidate government decisions which appear to have a plausible basis. One such case is the Court of Appeal's decision in *Hall & Co Ltd v Shoreham-by-Sea UDC*.[98] Hall had sought planning permission to develop a

---

[95] This may arise in either a sequential sense—ie to allow successive governments to adjust policy without having to persuade the Commons and Lords to pass a new Bill; and/or a simultaneous sense ie to allow different bodies (especially local authorities) to pursue different policies at the same time.

[96] See 'IV. The role of the judiciary' ff, ch 10, pp 262–263.

[97] The level of popular support for a particular policy has no bearing at all on the policy's legality; that is a technical matter which only judges are competent to determine.   [98] [1964] 1 WLR 240, CA.

plot of land close to a main road for industrial purposes. Councils were empowered by the Town and Country Planning Act 1947 s 14 to grant permission unconditionally or 'subject to such conditions as they think fit'. When approving Hall's application, the council required that the company also provide an ancillary access road, open to public traffic, which would reduce the prospect of delays being caused on the main road. Hall contended, inter alia, that the condition was irrational, as it imposed on the company the burden of building and maintaining what was in effect a public highway. The High Court rejected this argument, concluding that the condition obviously bore a sensible relation to legitimate planning concerns.[99]

This judgment was reversed in the Court of Appeal.[100] Willmer LJ's judgment accepted that; '[planning] conditions imposed by a local authority, like byelaws, should be benevolently construed, and in this connection I would venture to follow the same approach as Lord Russell of Kilowen CJ in *Kruse v Johnson*'.[101] He also accepted that the 'objective' that the planning condition was intended to achieve was 'a perfectly reasonable one'. However, while the objective was acceptable, the means chosen to achieve it were not. This was evidently because the condition imposed an unduly onerous burden on the plaintiffs. The objective would more appropriately be achieved by the council building a new public highway itself. This reasoning is difficult to support. One might accept that there were 'better' ways for the council to achieve its planning objectives. That does not per se mean that the method actually chosen was irrational.

A similar rationale was deployed by the High Court in *R v Hillingdon London Borough Council, ex p Royco Homes Ltd*[102] The council had attached several conditions to the granting of planning permission for Royco's proposed housing application. One condition required that the houses be offered to people on the council's own housing waiting list. The court held that the condition was irrational because it 'requir[ed] the applicants to take on at their own expense a significant part of the duty of the council as a housing authority'.[103]

Widgery LJ's own analysis would suggest that both *Hall* and *Royco* might better be classified as illegality cases, consistent in effect with a narrow construction of *Congreve*. In both cases the council was essentially levying a tax on the applicants, through the indirect route of demanding that they provide a substantial public service as the price of being granted planning permission.[104]

A 'better' application of the test

Two rather more satisfactory applications of the irrationality doctrine have latterly been offered by the House of Lords in *Brind v Secretary of State for the Home Department*[105] and by the Court of Appeal in *R v Ministry of Defence, ex p Smith*.[106] The *Brind* litigation was provoked by the government's efforts to address the problem of terrorism in Northern Ireland. The government formed the opinion that the terrorists' causes would be hindered if the radio and television media were not permitted to broadcast statements made by members of terrorist organisations or by members of political parties which the government designated as supportive of such groups. The ban extended however only to the speaker's actual voice; her words could be quoted verbatim by reporters, or, as frequently happened, dubbed by actors. Prime Minister Thatcher evidently believed the measure would deprive terrorists of the 'oxygen of

---

[99] (1963) 61 LGR 508.　　　[100] [1964] 1 WLR 240.　　　[101] Ibid, at 245.　　　[102] [1974] QB 720.
[103] Ibid, at 732.
[104] Cf Willmer LJ in *Hall* [1964] 1 WLR 240 at 249: '[the condition] amounts in effect to a requirement that the plaintiffs shall dedicate the ancillary road when it is built to the public'.　　　[105] [1991] AC 396.
[106] [1996] QB 517.

publicity'. The Home Secretary assumed he could impose the ban on the IBA[107] under the powers granted to him by the Broadcasting Act 1981 s 29:

> ... the Secretary of State may at any time by notice in writing require the authority to refrain from broadcasting any matter or classes of matter specified in the notice.[108]

Brind was a journalist who considered that the ban was ultra vires s 29, and thus unlawfully infringed free expression. He based his arguments on several grounds. The first is considered here. The others are addressed at a later stage. Brind firstly contended that the ban was irrational. The Court saw little merit in that argument. Lord Bridge thought it was 'impossible' to reach that conclusion: 'In any civilised country the defeat of the terrorist is a public interest of the highest importance . . . What is perhaps surprising is that the restriction is of such limited scope'.[109]

Similarly, Lord Ackner considered it entirely understandable that the government had concluded that terrorists enhanced their legitimacy by appearing on television and radio. There is little scope for disagreeing with this dismissal of the irrationality point. The test applies only to ludicrously illogical or morally outrageous decisions. The government's decision in *Brind* seems well within the range of views that reasonable people might hold. The policy may indeed have been ill-advised, and was probably counterproductive, but ineffectiveness and a lack of wisdom do not amount to irrationality.

The government policy at issue in *Smith*[110] was the long-standing practice that people of homosexual sexual orientation were not permitted to serve in the UK's armed forces. The prohibition applied simply on grounds of abstract sexual orientation; there was no requirement that the orientation manifest itself in any tangible way. Nor could the prohibition be overcome by a particular soldier's service record; even the most exemplary of recruits would be discharged from the service if it became known that he/she was not heterosexual. The justification for the policy, implemented through the government's prerogative powers, was that the presence of known homosexuals in the armed forces would compromise military efficiency, expose young recruits to sexual exploitation, and cause difficulties in the context of the communal living arrangements which the armed forces used.

Like the applicant in *Brind*, Smith contended that the policy was unlawful on several grounds. At this juncture, we consider only the irrationality argument. Smith's counsel contended that one might marshall several arguments to suggest that the policy was ill-advised and unnecessary. A soldier's sexual orientation was not a bar to military service in several other NATO and Commonwealth countries, which would suggest that military effectiveness was not compromised by employing gay men and lesbians. Similarly, within the United Kingdom, gay men and lesbians were permitted to work in the police and fire services; both of which were professions in which co-operative work was essential. It also seemed beyond dispute that—especially during World War II—a great many openly gay men had served with conspicuous distinction in the army, navy, and air force. If their presence did not, under those most acute of circumstances, compromise military efficiency, how could the presence of non-heterosexual servicemen do so in the present day?

These might all be regarded as perfectly valid arguments, and in combination would suggest there was much to be said in favour of altering the policy. It also seems evident that both the High Court and Court of Appeal in *Smith* found them to be convincing.[111] As Lord Bingham

---

[107] The Independent Broadcasting Authority, the body responsible for regulating commercial television and radio services.

[108] In respect of the BBC, the Home Secretary assumed that he could issue the ban under cl 13(4) of the BBC's licensing agreement with the government, which provided that: 'The Secretary of State may from time to time . . . require the Corporation to refrain . . . from sending any matter or matters of any class . . .'.

[109] [1991] AC 396 at 749.   [110] [1996] QB 517, CA.

[111] For further discussion see Norris M (1996) '*Ex p Smith*: irrationality and human rights' *Public Law* 590.

put it, this shift in public and professional attitudes had a significant bearing on the defensibility of the government's policy:

> I regard the progressive development and refinement of public and professional opinion at home and abroad . . . as an important feature of this case. A belief which represented unquestioned orthodoxy in Year X, may have become questionable by Year Y, and unsustainable by Year Z.[112]

But mustering a plausible, even a strong argument in favour of changing a governmental policy has no obvious bearing on whether t that policy is irrational. The pertinent test is whether there is some plausible argument in favour of the policy. In respect of the ban on gay people serving in the armed forces, that proviso seemed to be met. The Minister could point to the fact that in both 1986 and 1991 the ban had been reconsidered by the Commons Defence Select Committee; on both occasions the Committee recommended its retention. He had also conducted a survey of opinion within the armed services, which revealed widespread opposition to any removal of the ban. These reinforcements of the government's view precluded the finding that the policy was irrational: 'The threshold of irrationality is a high one. It was not crossed in this case'.[113] In Lord Bingham MR's chronological scheme, Smith was discharged in 'Year Y', and not 'Year Z'.[114]

Smith raises an important issue of what—for want of a better term—we might call common law policy. The Minister's survey of opinion in the armed forces revealed that much opposition to removing the ban was rooted in violent and bigoted beliefs. Illustrative of this point are comments such as:

> If a homosexual was on board he will have an accident waiting for him when no-one is looking . . . [Royal Naval able seaman]
>
> I would never serve in a unit where a known homosexual is serving and I like many others would quite happily smash their faces in if I found any in my unit . . . [Corporal, Royal Signals Service]
>
> I would not give first aid to a homosexual under any circumstances [RAF Senior Aircraftsman].[115]

The question of principle which then arises is whether the presumption that a government decision which enjoys appreciable levels of public support cannot be irrational should be rebutted if that support is premised on bigoted opinion. In this context, the 'red hair' scenario is an unhelpful analytical tool. One assumes that a ban on redheads serving in the army would be bigoted in a moral sense and also irrational in the legal sense. Yet that particular policy is hardly one that will attract widespread approval. The court would thus be spared the difficulty of deciding how a widely held belief could amount to an 'outrageous defiance of accepted moral standards'. If the government and members of the armed forces and the great majority of the public were to be seized with anti-red haired sentiment, however, it is difficult to conclude that a ban on redheads would be irrational.

A court would enter problematic constitutional territory if it were to assume that 'rationality' must have an objective meaning, irrespective of how widely approved a particular policy may be. Judicial excursions of that sort do perhaps take the common law too close to the moral/political merits of a decision. This is not to say that the decision must therefore be lawful; it may still fail the tests of illegality or procedural fairness. But these tests of course relate to (and here our terminology necessarily becomes rather obscure) the esoteric, legal merits of the decision; not to its exoteric, moral merits.

---

[112] [1996] QB 517, at 554.   [113] Ibid, at 558, per Lord Bingham.

[114] Intriguingly however, Lord Bingham MR indicated that we might have moved from Year Y to Year Z in the two years between Smith being discharged and the Court delivering its opinion; Ibid, at 266.

[115] The quotes are taken from a report in *The Guardian*, 5 March 1996.

There is however rather more to the irrationality than a concern with the substantive moral merits of the decision that a government body has reached. The doctrine might also be thought to have a *procedural* dimension.

Irrationality as a procedural concept: the relevant and irrelevant considerations principles

Citation of Lord Greene MR's judgment in *Wednesbury* is often just limited to the 'something so absurd . . .' comment. However the passage in which that comment appears clearly identifies the notion of 'reasonableness' in administrative law as having a rather broader reach:

> It is true the discretion must be exercised reasonably. Now what does that mean? Lawyers familiar with the phraseology commonly used in relation to exercise of statutory discretions often use the word 'unreasonable' in a rather comprehensive sense. It has frequently been used and is frequently used as a general description of the things that must not be done. For instance, a person entrusted with a discretion must, so to speak, direct himself properly in law. He must call his own attention to the matters which he is bound to consider. He must exclude from his consideration matters which are irrelevant to what he has to consider. If he does not obey those rules, he may truly be said, and often is said, to be acting 'unreasonably'. Similarly, there may be something so absurd that no sensible person could ever dream that it lay within the powers of the authority. Warrington L. J. in Short v. Poole Corporation (1) gave the example of the red-haired teacher, dismissed because she had red hair. That is unreasonable in one sense. In another sense it is taking into consideration extraneous matters. It is so unreasonable that it might almost be described as being done in bad faith; and, in fact, all these things run into one another.[116]

Lord Greene MR's comment that the decision-maker: 'must call his own attention to the matters which he is bound to consider. He must exclude from his consideration matters which are irrelevant to what he has to consider' is also significant. Lord Greene's judgment tells us that it has generally been accepted in English administrative law that a decision will be irrational if its contents were arrived at because the decision-maker either took account of irrelevant considerations or failed to take account of relevant considerations. *Roberts v Hopwood* can be advanced as the classic illustration of this principle. In *Roberts* in the House of Lords, Lord Atkinson had concluded that the £4 per week wage policy was also unlawful because the council had been influenced by 'some eccentric principles of socialist philanthropy' or by a 'feminist ambition to secure the equality of the sexes in the matter of wages in the world of labour'.[117] One might defend the House of Lords on this point by suggesting that in 1855, when s 62 of the Metropolis Management Act was passed, legislators would not have seen any 'socialists'[118] or 'feminists' in control of local authorities, and so could not have envisaged that s 62 would be used for such ends. Yet, once again, the Court of Appeal had taken a different view on this issue. The stress which both Scrutton LJ and Atkin LJ laid on the representative character of the council implicitly accepts that party political views, be they socialist, social democrat, or conservative, are a legitimate influence on the exercise of the elected body's discretionary powers. Both judges also made explicit reference to the council's concern with gender equality. For Scrutton LJ, that was 'a matter of acute controversy, which is hardly for either the auditor or the judges to determine'.[119] In Atkin LJ's view, the fact that the council may have been motivated by this factor had no bearing on the irrationality issue.[120]

---

[116] [1948] 1 KB 223 at 229.   [117] [1925] AC 578 at 594, HL.
[118] The Labour Party began to establish itself as a force in local government in the early 1900s.
[119] [1924] 2 KB 695 at 721, CA.   [120] Ibid, at 729.

The great weakness of the relevant/irrelevant consideration principle from a constitutional perspective is that it provides a nominally legitimate vehicle for the courts to steer themselves very close to the political/moral merits of a given decision.[121] Which factors are (ir)relevant to the exercise of a given governmental power is a matter on which Parliament has generally not expressed any (and certainly not an exhaustive) opinion. At an earlier point in his judgment, Lord Greene MR offered this view:

> If, in the statute conferring the discretion, there is to be found expressly or by implication matters which the authority exercising the discretion ought to have regard to, then in exercising the discretion it must have regard to those matters. Conversely, if the nature of the subject-matter and the general interpretation of the Act make it clear that certain matters would not be germane to the matter in question, the authority must disregard those irrelevant collateral matters . . .[122]

The questions of whether a matter is relevant by 'implication' or is 'germane' to the decision clearly afford the courts very substantial latitude as to whether or not they could find a decision unlawful.

Obviously, a finding that a government body has failed to take account of a relevant consideration or has considered an irrelevant matter does not necessarily preclude the decision-maker from reaching the same substantive decision again. But unlike the core substantive limb of the irrationality doctrine, this principle is much more difficult to justify in terms of clear judicial obedience to a statutory requirement. The inference thereby arises that the courts are placing tighter constraints on executive autonomy than Parliament had envisaged. That inference can be rebutted somewhat when we note that there is clear authority for the proposition that as long as the decision-maker has taken *some* account of the relevant consideration the courts will not concern themselves with whether she has attached sufficient weight to the matter concerned. This point was perhaps best put by Lord Keith in *Tesco Stores v Secretary of State for the Environment*:[123]

> It is for the courts, if the matter is brought before them, to decide what is a relevant consideration. If the decision maker wrongly takes the view that some consideration is not relevant, and therefore has no regard to it, his decision cannot stand and he must be required to think again. But it is entirely for the decision maker to attribute to the relevant considerations such weight as he thinks fit . . .

Nevertheless, the unpredictable nature of the relevancy/irrelevancy test also creates difficulties from the perspective of legal certainty; a point graphically illustrated by the differing opinions of the Court of Appeal and House of Lords in *Roberts*.

The argument that the courts might legitimately approach the substantive merits of government decisions more closely than the irrationality doctrine permits has however been a lively one since 1985, when Lord Diplock suggested in *GCHQ* that the doctrine of 'proportionality' might soon come to play a role in English administrative law.

---

[121] See the discussion in Irvine D (1996) 'The theory and practice of *Wednesbury* review' *Public Law* 59 and Beatson J, Matthews M, and Elliot M (2010) *Administrative law* pp 235–248.   [122] [1948] 1 KB 223 at 228.

[123] [1995] 1 WLR 759 at 764. And see also Lord Hoffmann at 784: 'I think that a distinction between very little weight and no weight at all is a piece of scolasticism which would do the law no credit. If the planning authority ignores a material consideration because it has forgotten about it, or because it wrongly thinks that the law or departmental policy precludes it from taking it into account, then it has failed to have regard to a material consideration. But if the decision to give that consideration no weight is based on rational planning grounds, then the planning authority is entitled to ignore it'.

III. Proportionality—a new ground of review?

By the mid-1980s, the proportionality principle was an established feature in the administrative law of several of the UK's partner countries within the EC. It was also, more pertinently, an integral part of the so-called general principles of Community law established by the ECJ.[124] This meant that whenever the UK courts were addressing the legality of government action within the area of Community competence, the doctrine would provide an additional substantive ground of review.

Bringing the courts closer to the 'merits' of a decision

There is no entirely straightforward way to define the principle. But some indication of its scope can be gleaned from consideration of the cases in which it has been applied by the ECJ. A useful example is offered in *Bela-Mühle Josef Bergmann KG v Grows-Farm GmbH & Co KG*.[125] The case concerned a regulation passed by the Council for the purpose of reducing the vast over-supply of skimmed milk powder in the Community. The regulation attempted to compel farmers to use animal feed derived from skimmed milk powder rather than soya. Soya-based feeds were however only one-third of the price of the milk products. The legality of the regulation was successfully challenged, on the basis that it imposed far too onerous a burden on farmers, and was thus a disproportionate measure.

The principle is as readily applicable to the actions of Member States as to Community institutions. *Re Watson and Belmann*,[126] concerned an attempt by the Belgian government to establish that Treaty Art 48(3) entitled it to deport workers from other Member States if they had failed to comply with administrative requirements to register their presence with the local police. The ECJ accepted that Member States had a legitimate interest in keeping accurate records of non-national workers. It also accepted that a registration requirement was a lawful means to pursue this end, and that imposing punishments on workers who failed to register was an appropriate way to enforce the requirement. However it also concluded that deportation was too serious a punishment to apply to workers who failed to register. A fine would be the proportionate response in such circumstances.

As Steiner notes in reviewing this strand of the EC's case law, proportionality: 'puts the burden on an administrative authority to justify its actions and requires some consideration of alternatives. In this respect, it is a more rigorous test than one based on reasonableness'.[127] In other words, the test requires that the court looks much more closely at the political merits of a decision than it does under the irrationality doctrine.

To re-use the terminology deployed earlier in respect of irrationality, we might also express the concept by suggesting that proportionality review can be presented in an abstract, political sense as a constitutional device which requires the courts to accept that the boundaries of moral consensus within which government bodies are confined are discernibly less broad in substantive terms than those which apply to respect of irrationality-based review.

---

[124] The leading critique is offered by Jowell J and Lester A (1988) 'Proportionality: neither novel nor dangerous', in Jowell J and Oliver D (eds) *New directions in judicial review*. See for example Hartley T (4th edn, 1998) *The foundations of European Community law* ch 5; Craig P and de Burca G (2nd edn, 1998) *EU Law* pp 349–357; de Burca G (1993) 'The principle of proportionality and its application in EC law' *YEL* 105.

[125] Case 114/76: [1977] ECR 1211, ECJ; popularly known as the 'Skimmed milk powder case'.

[126] Case 118/75: [1976] ECR 1185, ECJ.   [127] (3rd edn, 1992) *EC law* p 58.

In its Community law manifestation, the proportionality test imposes a more substantively intrusive (than irrationality) ground of judicial review on government action by requiring the court to undertake a structured, multi-stage examination of the content of the decision under challenge. In effect, the test developed by the ECJ also contains a more exacting variant of the relevant/irrelevant considerations doctrine. Firstly, the court must ask if the government body is acting in pursuit of a legitimate objective. If the answer is 'No', the action is unlawful. If the answer is 'Yes', the court will then consider if attaining that legitimate objective necessarily demands that the body interfere with a presumptively lawful entitlement possessed by an individual or company. Again, if the answer is 'No', the action is unlawful. If the answer is again 'Yes', the court will ask itself, thirdly if the government body has chosen the means to achieve its legitimate end which interferes as little as possible with the presumptive entitlements. Only if the answer to that final question is also 'Yes' will the governmental decision have survived proportionality review.

Many of the government actions we have considered against the irrationality principle would no doubt pass a substantive proportionality test. In *Wednesbury*, for example, the council's legitimate aim would be to encourage children to go to church or play sports on Sunday mornings. This interferes both with the children's entitlement to attend the cinema, and the cinema owners' entitlement to sell its seats. But the interference is a modest one. Had the prohibition extended throughout the weekend, it would most likely have failed a proportionality test, but still passed muster against the yardstick of irrationality. Similarly, in *Kruse v Johnson*, proportionality would demand that a breach of the bye-law merited only a modest fine. A large fine, while not necessarily irrational, would probably be disproportionate. Relatedly, one might sensibly conclude that the policy at issue in *Brind* would not have been disproportionate. The Home Secretary's interference with Brind's capacity to do his job as a television reporter was so trivial in scope that it is hard to imagine a less restrictive way for the government to pursue its legitimate aim of depriving terrorist supporters of publicity.

Smith raises rather different issues. In so far as the government's policy was pandering to bigotry among service personnel, it would not have been pursuing a legitimate aim. As such, it would have fallen at the first stage of the test. And if the aim was the legitimate one of safeguarding operational efficiency, that might have better been achieved by a policy forbidding inappropriate sexual behaviour than one proscribing particular sexual orientations.

A new understanding of the separation of powers?

Proportionality could thus be seen as constitutionally problematic in both a substantive and jurisdictional sense. The substantive problem arises because proportionality might be characterised as something close to an appellate jurisdiction, which requires courts to substitute their own views of the best way for a government body to achieve a particular objective for that of the designated decision-maker. The second problem arises because appellate jurisdiction is a statutory rather than common law creation. For the courts to modify the common law to produce a new ground of review which came close, in de facto terms, to giving the judiciary an appellate jurisdiction would in a functional if not formal sense amount to a usurpation of legislative power.

These objections were forcefully stated by several members of the House of Lords in *Brind*, in which the plaintiff had invoked proportionality as a second ground of challenge to the Home Secretary's action. As suggested earlier, it seems unlikely that the policy would have failed a proportionality test. But for the majority of the Court, this was not a question that ought even to be asked. Lord Roskill—having referred to Lord Diplock's suggestion in *GCHQ* that proportionality might some day emerge as a new ground of review—continued:

> I am clearly of the view that the present is not a case in which the first step can be taken for the reason that to apply that principle in the present case would be for the court to substitute its own

judgment of what was needed to achieve a particular objective for the judgment of the Secretary of State upon whom that duty has been laid by Parliament.[128]

For the same reason, Lord Ackner concluded that: 'there appears to me to be at present no basis upon which the proportionality doctrine . . . can be followed by the courts of this country'.[129] Lord Lowry was equally forceful: '[T]here can be very little room for judges to operate an independent judicial review proportionality doctrine in the space which is left between the conventional judicial review doctrine and the admittedly forbidden appellate approach'.[130]

These objections are not compelling. Notwithstanding their Lordships' sentiments to the contrary, proportionality does not by any means demand that the court adopts an essentially appellate jurisdiction. Properly construed, irrationality is such a lax test that there should be plenty of legitimate jurisprudential scope for the courts to place further limits on the political merits of government decisions without setting themselves up as appellate tribunals. The only reason for assuming that no such scope exists is if the courts are actually misapplying the irrationality doctrine, and using it improperly as a device to sail unacceptably close to the detailed political merits of government decisions: to move any closer to the merits from that position would, of course, be to assume a de facto appellate jurisdiction.

There is some indication that this has indeed happened on occasion. *Hall v Shoreham UDC* is perhaps the most obvious example of this, in so far as the Court explicitly labelled the council's policy as irrational because there were 'better' ways (ie methods that impacted much less heavily on the applicant) for the council to achieve its policies. Jowell and Lester's influential analysis of the proportionality issue also suggests that *Congreve* and *Bromley v GLC* can be explained in a similar way. This suggestion perhaps rather blurs the issue, as both cases could readily be defended as instances of the courts using a quite narrow application of the illegality doctrine.

More helpfully, Jowell and Lester identify cases in which the courts seem quite openly to have advocated use of a proportionality test. The most regularly cited illustration of this point is the Court of Appeal's judgment in *R v Barnsley Metropolitan Borough Council, ex p Hook*.[131] Hook was a stallholder in Barnsley market, whose licence was terminated by the council after he became involved in an abusive altercation with two council street cleaners who had admonished him for urinating in the street.[132] In attempting to sanction Mr Hook for this behaviour, the council was presumably pursuing a legitimate end, whether it be safeguarding its employees from threatening abuse or encouraging stallholders to respect rudimentary standards of hygiene. Lord Denning nonetheless intimated that the sanction was excessive:

> So in this case, if Mr Hook did misbehave, I should have thought the right thing would have been to take him before the magistrates under the bye-laws, when some small fine should have been inflicted. It is quite wrong that the Barnsley Council should inflict upon him the grave penalty of depriving him of his livelihood. That is a far more serious penalty than anything the magistrates could inflict.[133]

One might plausibly argue that the sanction was not disproportionately severe, given the undesirability of market traders spraying their urine over the streets and verbally abusing the council employees responsible for cleaning up the mess. Herein lies the practical difficulty of the proportionality doctrine as a substantive principle; namely that it requires courts to invalidate decisions that many observers might consider quite sensible. The difficulty would

---

[128] [1991] 1 AC 696 at 750.   [129] Ibid, at 763.   [130] Ibid, at 767.

[131] [1976] 1 WLR 1052, CA. Jowell and Lester also cite *R v Brent London Borough Council, ex p Assegai* (1987) *The Times*, 18 June.

[132] Curiously, most references to the case tend to omit the abusive altercation, which is perhaps a more serious matter than peeing in the gutter.

[133] [1976] 1 WLR 1052 at 1057–1058, CA. The case was actually decided in Mr Hook's favour on grounds of a procedural irregularity.

be compounded if a proportionality ground of review at common law was also presumed to contain a more intensive version of the relevant/irrelevant considerations doctrine which empowered the courts to consider if a decision-maker had attached the appropriate weight to a matter which she had taken into account.[134]

It is hardly surprising that many judges, unlike Lord Denning, might cavil at admitting so candidly that they are placing tight restrictions on the range of politically meritorious decisions that government bodies may lawfully make. Nonetheless, the requirement that proportionality be applied by UK courts in matters raising questions of EC law creates an obvious inconsistency in domestic administrative law, in both jurisdictional and substantive terms. Proportionality would thus have seemed another good candidate to be caught up in the 'ripple effect' of EC law. However as we shall see in subsequent chapters, the courts have latterly been spared the difficulty of taking the step that Lord Diplock canvassed in *GCHQ* by a legislative initiative promoted by the Blair government.

Conclusion

It is readily apparent that the substantive grounds of review comprise a fluid area of administrative law. This is not just because, in the broader sense, wholly new common law grounds of review may gradually emerge. It is also because the boundaries of long-established grounds are themselves somewhat unpredictable in scope. These characteristics are not however unique to the substantive grounds of review. As suggested in the following chapter, much the same argument might be made in respect of the procedural grounds of review.

Suggested further reading

Academic and political commentary

IRVINE D (1996) 'The theory and practice of *Wednesbury* review' *Public Law* 59

BROWNE-WILKINSON, LORD (1992) 'The infiltration of a Bill of Rights' *Public Law* 397

JOWELL J and LESTER A (1988) 'Proportionality: neither novel nor dangerous', in JOWELL J and OLIVER D (eds) *New directions in judicial review*

DE BURCA G (1993) 'The principle of proportionality and its application in EC law' *YEL* 105

GOODWIN J (2012) 'The last defence of *Wednesbury*' *Public Law* 445

RIVERS J (2006) 'Proportionality and variable intensity of review' *Cambridge LJ* 174.

Case law and legislation

Roberts v Hopwood [1925] AC 578

Congreve v Home Office [1976] QB 379

R v Ministry of Defence, ex p Smith [1996] QB 517

R v Secretary of State for Foreign Affairs, ex p World Development Movement Ltd [1995] 1 WLR 386

Carltona v Works Comrs [1943] 2 All ER 560

British Oxygen Co Ltd v Minister of Technology [1971] AC 610

Western Fish Products Ltd v Penwith District Council [1981] 2 All ER 204

---

[134] For a powerful defence of the original notion of the doctrine see Goodwin J (2012) 'The last defence of *Wednesbury*' *Public Law* 445. For the argument that irrationality might properly be understood as offering a more intensive standard of review see Rivers J (2006) 'Proportionality and variable intensity of review' *Cambridge LJ* 174.

Chapter 14

Procedural Grounds of Judicial Review

One might wonder what useful purpose is served by subjecting governmental action to a ground of judicial review concerned not a decision's substance, but with the way the decision was made. If the outcome of the decision-making process was neither illegal nor irrational, it would be possible for the government body whose decision was unlawful because of a procedural flaw to remake the decision, correct its procedural error, and produce precisely the same substantive result as before. It may be thought that all that is thereby achieved is to delay and increase the cost of government decision-making, while simultaneously embroiling the courts in fruitless litigation. Two forceful arguments can be asserted to rebut this proposition.[1]

The first speaks to the instrumental value of procedural standards. It maintains that there is a linkage between the substance of a decision and the way the decision is made. Insistence on rigorous procedures may enhance the likelihood that the decision is not just substantively legal/rational in the narrow sense, but that it represents—if not the best choice—then at least a good choice within the range of permissible alternatives.

The second concerns the intrinsic value of fair procedures. In a narrow vein, this argument suggests that individuals intimately affected by a particular decision will be more likely to accept its legitimacy if they consider that they have been treated with sufficient seriousness and respect by the relevant decision-maker. More broadly, it might be thought that citizens are more likely to accept the legitimacy of the governmental process if government decision-makers are known to be prevented from acting in arbitrary or capricious ways.

Within the Anglo-American political and legal tradition, the paradigmatic example of procedural fairness is the criminal trial in respect of a serious crime. In respect of this particular facet of governmental decision-making the most rigorous of procedural standards are applied. This would include such factors as the accused knowing in detail the case against her; that she be given ample time to prepare her own arguments; that she be afforded the assistance of expert legal advisers; that she or her counsel be permitted to cross-examine prosecution witnesses and to call witnesses of her own; that there be stringent rules concerning the admissibility of evidence; and that the jury (which would decide guilt or innocence) and the judge

---

[1] See Richardson G (1986) 'The duty to give reasons: potential and practice' *Public Law* 437; Craig P (2nd edn, 1989) *Administrative law* ch 7; Craig P (1994) 'The common law, reasons and administrative justice' *Cambridge LJ* 282–302.

(who would preside over the trial and if necessary impose a sentence) would approach their tasks without any pre-existing bias inclining them towards a guilty verdict. The trial process is distinctly 'red light' in nature, designed to offer substantial protection to the interests of the accused (ie in her continued liberty) against governmental interference.

Such stringent procedures maximise the possibility that the decision-making process produces the 'correct' outcome. But such trials demand extremely heavy investment in time and money. The process is expensive and slow. It would hardly seem feasible to subject all aspects of governmental decision-making processes to such a rigorous procedural regime. And as the scope of governmental intervention in economic or social affairs increases, so the need to distance the conduct of much governmental decision-making from this idealised vision becomes more acute.

That prosaic concern is reinforced by more abstract considerations deriving from the notion of the separation of powers. Determining guilt in a criminal trial is manifestly a 'judicial' function: the court's responsibility is to make a finding as to the precise merits of the issue before it. Since much governmental decision-making has been entrusted by Parliament to the executive rather than the judiciary, it can readily be presumed that there is no legislative expectation that it conform to judicial models. Nonetheless, executive decisions can impact substantially upon questions of great importance to individual citizens. Liversidge's detention by Sir John Anderson is an obvious example, as is the Inland Revenue Commissioners' seizure of Rossminster's papers. Much executive action is, in contrast, dealing with ostensibly rather trivial issues. One might intuitively suppose that this notion of there being a 'hierarchy of rights' in terms of the substantive impact of government decisions would also be reflected in common law requirements imposing varying levels of procedural rigour on the particular decision in issue.

English law on the question of procedural fairness (or as the issue was traditionally styled, 'natural justice') is essentially concerned with striking a balance between these competing considerations. This area of administrative law is generally accepted to be divisible into two distinct parts. The first is often referred to under the Latin maxim *audi alterem partem*; the literal translation is that 'the other side must be heard', and is generally taken to mean that a person affected by a governmental decision should be afforded some opportunity to present his/her case to the decision-maker and that she should be given a reasonably clear indication of the case against her. The second, often referred to under the label *nemo iudex in sua causa* (literally—'no-one shall be judge in her own cause'), addresses the question of to what extent a decision-maker may have—or to be suspected to have—a personal bias in respect of a decision she has made.

This chapter analyses a number of leading cases to identify the values which appear to be shaping the content of the procedural fairness doctrine. The bulk of the chapter analyses case law drawn from the 'modern' (ie post-1960) era. But it is helpful to begin by considering several seminal decisions from earlier periods.

I. *Audi alterem partem*—the right to a fair hearing

A recurrent (if not ever present) theme in much early *audi alterem partem* case law is the courts' attempt to draw a distinction between, on the one hand, government decisions which affected the 'rights' of individuals and, on the other, those which impacted only on matters of 'privilege'. Relatedly, much judicial energy was expended on determining if a given executive decision should be classified as '(quasi)-judicial' or 'administrative' in nature.

These distinctions may be thought to have an obvious jurisprudential root in the purpose underlying Diceyan rule of law theory. If that purpose is, inter alia, to protect private rights and liberties against the executive, it is important to establish when such rights are in issue, for the consequence of their being put in jeopardy would be that the government's decision-making process (absent a clear legislative indication to the contrary) would be expected to correspond if only in broad terms to a judicial model. Alternatively, it might be contended that Parliament has on occasion—irrespective of whether or not the statutory power in issue affects individual rights—required executive bodies to act in a quasi-judicial fashion. If this has been done explicitly, there is no difficulty in concluding that the bodies' decision-making procedures must closely resemble the judicial model. If the statute is silent on the point, that conclusion becomes more problematic, insofar as it would have to rest on judicial presumptions as to the extent to which Parliament has impliedly 'contracted in'[2] to existing common law principles.

The pervasive difficulty however, which is revealed by examining several leading cases, is in finding generalisable criteria with which to draw a distinction between 'rights' and 'privileges' and/or 'quasi-judicial' and 'administrative' functions.

The initial rise, dilution, and fall of the *audi alterem partem* principle

A forceful assertion of the *audi alterem partem* principle in the Victorian era is offered in *Cooper v Wandsworth Board of Works*.[3] Section 76 of the Metropolis Management Act 1855 introduced a limited form of land use planning control. It provided that new buildings should not be erected unless the relevant local Board of Works[4] had been given seven days' notice of the project, and also empowered the Board to demolish any buildings erected in breach of this provision. The text of the Act did not expressly require any hearing be held prior to demolition. Cooper had apparently begun to erect a building without giving the requisite notice. The Board then demolished the building overnight.

Mr Cooper commenced proceedings for trespass. The Board contended that it had lawful authority under s 76 to enter Cooper's land and raze his house. The demolition was clearly not illegal, and was probably defensible in terms of rationality. The case turned on whether the Board's decision-making process was procedurally acceptable.

The Court concluded that the Board had acted unlawfully in not granting Mr Cooper a hearing before deciding to demolish his house. The absence of an express requirement for a hearing in the Act was no obstacle to this conclusion. As Erle CJ put it: 'powers granted by that statute are subject to a qualification that has been repeatedly recognised, that no man is to be deprived of his property without his having an opportunity of being heard'.[5] Byles J made the point in similar terms: 'although there are no positive words in a statute requiring that the party shall be heard, yet the justice of the common law will supply the omission of the legislature'.[6] The more interesting point is why the 'justice of the common law' demanded that such a condition be attached to the exercise of this power.

The Court was divided on whether or not the Board's power was 'judicial' or 'administrative'. Willes J concluded that this was a 'judicial' power, while both Erle CJ and Byles J suggested that the distinction was largely irrelevant, as past case law contained many instances of the *audi alterem partem* principle being applied to what they considered administrative functions. The Court was however unanimous in concluding that because the Board's action interfered substantially with Mr Cooper's property rights, it should have afforded him a hearing before reaching its decision.

---

[2] See 'III. Judicial regulation of government behaviour: the constitutional rationale', ch 3, p 53.

[3] (1863) 14 CBNS 180.

[4] This being one of the ad hoc local government bodies created by Parliament in the nineteenth century; see 'I. Localism, tradition, and the "modernisation" of local government', ch 10, pp 254–255.

[5] (1863) 143 ER 414 at 418. The case raised a nice theoretical point, not considered by the Court; namely whether Mr Cooper could have a property right in his house if it had been built unlawfully.

[6] Ibid, at 420.

It is not clear from the judgment how closely this hearing would have to approximate to court procedures. Some indication as to what that requirement might be was subsequently offered by the House of Lords in *Board of Education v Rice*.[7] The case concerned the exercise of what was essentially an appellate jurisdiction conferred upon the Board to resolve disputes between local education authorities and their employees. The Court accepted that such a function, even if 'administrative', had to be discharged in accordance with the *audi alterem partem* principle:

> But I do not think they [the Board] are bound to treat such a question as though it were a trial. They have no power to administer an oath, and need not examine witnesses. They can obtain any information in any way they think best, always giving a fair opportunity to those who are parties in the controversy for correcting or contradicting any relevant statement prejudicial to their view.[8]

The supposition that judicial methods were an inappropriate reference point to structure the procedures of government bodies, even if the body concerned was exercising a recognisably 'judicial' function, was promptly reinforced in *Local Government Board v Arlidge*.[9] The Housing & Town Planning Act 1909 authorised a local inspector, after holding an inquiry, to issue closing orders in respect of houses he/she considered unfit for human habitation. The statute provided for an appeal against this to the Local Government Board.[10] The statute did not specify the procedures that were to be followed either at the inquiry or the appeal. Arlidge was permitted to appear in person at the inquiry, to be represented by counsel, and to cross-examine witnesses. The inspector nonetheless imposed a closure order on Arlidge's house. Arlidge was allowed to make written representations at the appeal stage, but was not granted an oral hearing, nor allowed to see the Inspector's report. He subsequently maintained that these failings constituted a breach of natural justice, in that they departed too far from a judicial model of decision-making. This argument failed at first instance, but was accepted in the Court of Appeal.

In the House of Lords, the Court of Appeal's judgment was unanimously overruled. Viscount Haldane LC rejected the Court of Appeal's presumption that in the absence of statutorily defined procedures one must assume that Parliament implicitly intended that a body follow judicial procedures. He reached this conclusion notwithstanding the fact that a 'right' was in issue:

> There is no doubt that the question is one affecting property and the liberty of a man to do what he chooses with his own. Such rights are not to be affected unless Parliament has said so. But Parliament, in what it considers higher interests than those of the individual, has so often interfered with such rights on other occasions, that it is dangerous for judges to lay much stress on what a hundred years ago would have been a presumption considerably stronger than it is today.[11]

Haldane's reasoning amounts to a recognition that the substance of government–citizen relations has undergone a profound change, and that governmental procedures must therefore change as well. The judgment offers an early but perfectly clear shift from red light to green light theory; or, if one prefers, from a rigid Hayekian concern with judicial process towards Jones' more dilute notion of a 'meaningful day in court'.[12] Somewhat confusingly, Viscount Haldane then indicated that the LGB must—since it was performing an appellate function— act 'judicially'. He followed *Rice* in determining the content of this concept in this case. The

---

[7] [1911] AC 179.   [8] Ibid, at 182 per Lord Loreburn LC.

[9] [1915] AC 120. A different facet of this case was discussed at 'Unlawful delegation of powers' ch 13, pp 361–364.

[10] The forerunner of the Department of the Environment; ie a central government department.

[11] [1915] AC 120 at 130–131. The methodology is closely comparable to that used by Lord Wilberforce in *Rossminster* sixty years later: see '*R v IRC, ex p Rossminster Ltd* (1980)', ch 3, pp 64–65.

[12] On *Hayek and Jones* see 'Hayek—the road to serfdom', ch 3, p 50.

Board need not offer an oral hearing; granting the opportunity to make written representations would suffice. Nor need it give Arlidge a copy of the Inspector's report. The requirement was simply that the Board:

> deal with the question . . . without bias and . . . give to each of the parties the opportunity of adequately presenting the case made. The decision must be come to in the spirit and with the sense of responsibility of a tribunal whose duty it is to mete out justice . . . Parliament must be taken, in the absence of any declaration to the contrary, to have intended [the Board] to follow the procedure which is its own and is necessary if it is to be capable of doing its work efficiently.[13]

These sentiments were echoed by Lord Shaw, whose judgment evinced an explicit concern that the *audi alterem partem* principle should not be invoked to impede administrative efficiency to an onerous degree:

> Judicial methods may, in many points of administration, be entirely unsuitable, and produce delays, expense, and public and private injury . . . [C]ertain ways of and methods of judicial procedure may very likely be imitated; and lawyer-like methods may find especial favour from lawyers. But that the judiciary should presume to impose its own methods on administrative or executive officers is a usurpation. And the assumption that the methods of natural justice are ex necessitate those of Courts of Justice is wholly unfounded.

A two stage question?

Cooper, *Rice*, and *Arlidge* offer a clear indication that the courts' concern with *audi alterem partem* raised two questions. The first, essentially a threshold question, was simply whether or not the principle applied to a given decision. (The cases suggest that while a formal distinction was drawn between rights/privileges and judicial/administrative decisions for this classificatory purpose, there were in practice few governmental processes impacting on individual citizens which did not pass the threshold test.) If so, the second question addressed the content of the procedural protection that the applicant should be afforded. A logical consequence of this approach would be that in situations where the first question was answered in the negative, there were no common law restraints on the decision-maker's procedural choices. This point is well illustrated by the 1920 judgment in *R v Leman Street Police Station Inspector, ex p Venicoff*.[14]

The Aliens Restriction Act 1914, enacted during World War I, empowered the Home Secretary to detain and deport aliens if he considered such action conducive to the public good. Venicoff challenged his detention and scheduled deportation on the grounds that the Home Secretary had not granted him an adequate hearing before making the decision.[15] The Court took the view that there was no requirement that the *audi alterem partem* principle be respected here:

> The legislature in its wisdom took from the Courts during the war the power of inquiry into the facts of particular cases . . . In dealing with a regulation such as that with which we are now concerned the value of the order would be considerably impaired if it could be made only after holding an inquiry, because it might very well be that the person against whom it was intended to make a deportation order would, the moment he had notice of that intention. . . . take steps to evade apprehension.[16]

The Court reached this conclusion notwithstanding the fact that the decision impacted severely upon Venicoff's 'liberty'. It might be thought that the conclusion could be limited to powers

---

[13] [1915] AC 120 at 132.   [14] [1920] 3 KB 72, DC.
[15] The action was for *habeas corpus* against the police officer detaining Venicoff in accordance with the Home Secretary's instructions.   [16] [1920] 3 KB 72 at 80, per the Earl of Reading CJ.

created in time of war, when (*Liversidge* being a primary example) 'normal' administrative law principles were relaxed to facilitate the government process. However the same rationale is evident in Goddard CJ's 1948 first instance judgment in *Russell v Duke of Norfolk*.[17] Russell was a race-horse trainer, whose licence was revoked for 'misconduct' by the Jockey Club following allegations of race fixing. As a result, Russell could no longer work in the horse-racing industry. In effect, he had lost his livelihood. He had been granted a rather perfunctory hearing prior to the decision, at which he had been permitted to make a statement but not to challenge in any meaningful way the case against him. Despite the severity of the consequences inflicted upon Russell by the withdrawal of his licence, Lord Goddard CJ saw 'no possible ground' for assuming the *audi alterem partem* principle applied.

Goddard adopted the same approach three years later in *R v Metropolitan Police Commissioner, ex p Parker*.[18] The Commissioner possessed a (properly) delegated power under the Metropolitan Public Carriage Act 1869 to revoke taxi licences. He revoked Parker's licence following Parker's conviction for various traffic offences and allegations that Parker had been using his cab as part of a prostitution operation. There is little scope to doubt that the revocation was substantively defensible. Parker had also been given the opportunity to rebut the allegations against him at a hearing before a committee chaired by an Assistant Commissioner. His complaint rested on the basis that he had not been allowed to call witnesses in his own defence. Procedures of this sort would comfortably have satisfied the *Rice/ Arlidge* test. However, Lord Goddard indicated that there was no entitlement to natural justice *at all* in respect of this decision. He offered three reasons for this conclusion.

The first was that Parker had lost only a 'privilege', not a 'right': 'The licence is nothing but a permission. As a rule, where a licence is granted, the licencor does not have to state why he withdraws his permission'.[19] The second was that the Commissioner's action was an 'administrative' rather than 'judicial' function; it is 'impossible to say that the commissioner . . . was in a judicial or quasi-judicial position. He was in fact exercising a disciplinary authority'.[20] The third explanation was rooted in more obviously policy based concerns, and betokened an extremely 'green light' approach to this facet of administrative law:

> it is most undesirable, in my opinion, that [the Commissioner] should be fettered by threats of orders of *certiorari* and so forth, because that would interfere with the free and proper disciplinary exercise of the powers that it may be expected he would otherwise use.[21]

This approach was not merely an idiosyncrasy on Lord Goddard's part. In the same year as *Parker* was decided, the Privy Council issued judgment in *Nakkuda Ali v Jayaratne*.[22] The case concerned the power of a Ceylonese government official, the Controller of Textiles, to revoke a trader's licence if he had reasonable grounds to believe that the trader was 'unfit' to hold a licence. The Court held that the *audi alterem partem* principle did not apply to this activity, on the grounds that the licence was a privilege and that its grant and withdrawal were executive and not judicial actions.

Such cases emphasise that the threshold question of whether or not a particular decision-making process was subject to the *audi alterm partem* principle had become of central importance in the immediate post-war period. That the answer to the question might be unclear is nicely illustrated by the Court of Appeal's judgment in *Russell v Duke of Norfolk*.[23] In contrast to Lord Goddard CJ's decision at first instance, the three judgments offered in the Court of Appeal (by Tucker, Asquith, and Denning LJJ) all concluded that the Jockey Club's withdrawal of a trainer's licence was subject to the *audi alterem partem* principle. However, the judges also concluded that the principle had not been breached on these facts; in respect

---

[17] [1948] 1 All ER 488.   [18] [1953] 1 WLR 1150.   [19] Ibid, at 1154.   [20] Ibid, at 1155.
[21] Ibid.   [22] [1951] AC 66, PC.   [23] [1949] 1 All ER 109, CA.

of this particular decision, the content of natural justice was quite limited. The point is best put by Tucker LJ:

> Throughout this inquiry, [the plaintiff] was . . . given an opportunity of presenting his case . . . It is true that he was not in terms asked: 'Have you got any witnesses? Do you want an adjournment?'. A layman at an inquiry of this sort is of course at a grave disadvantage compared with a trained advocate . . . Counsel for the plaintiff . . . said 'What would be said of local justices who acted in this way?'. With all due respect, the position is totally different. This matter is not to be judged by the standards applicable to local justices.[24]

Tucker LJ continued by noting that the content of a fair hearing would be highly context specific: 'The requirements of natural justice must depend on the circumstances of the case, the nature of the inquiry, the rules under which the tribunal is acting, the subject matter that is being dealt with, and so forth'.[25] In so far as there was to be a lowest common denominator, applicable to all decisions to which the *audi alterem partem* principle applied, it was the rather vague requirement that: 'the person concerned should have a reasonable opportunity of presenting his case'.[26]

That this judgment pre-dated both *Parker* and *Nakkuda Ali*, and that all three cases concerned what was in effect the loss of the plaintiff's preferred livelihood, indicates that the right/privilege and judicial/administrative dichotomies remained a powerful factor in this area of the law. But *Russell* also rather suggested that a plaintiff who successfully passed the threshold test might find herself entitled to such a low level of 'natural justice' that neither the instrumental, nor intrinsic, rationales for imposing procedural restraints on decision-making behaviour were being well-served.

This point is well illustrated by the Privy Council's decision in *University of Ceylon v Fernando*.[27] Fernando had been accused of cheating in an exam. If upheld, the charge would have ruined his reputation and career prospects. The Privy Council accepted that these proceedings were quasi-judicial, and subject to the rules of natural justice. However this did not mean that Fernando was entitled to cross-examine (either in person or through counsel) the witnesses against him.

The re-emergence of the principle? *Ridge v Baldwin*

The 1963 judgment of the House of Lords in *Ridge v Baldwin*[28] appeared decisively to reject the practical difference between judicial/administrative decisions for *audi alterem partem* purposes, although it did little to indicate that the content of the requisite hearing ought to be strengthened. Ridge was the former Chief Constable of Sussex. He had been tried for corruption, but acquitted. The Police Authority (then quaintly named 'the Watch Committee') nonetheless decided to dismiss him. The Committee was empowered to do so per the Municipal Corporations Act 1882 s 191(4) if it thought him 'negligent in the discharge of his duty, or otherwise unfit for the same'. Since Ridge's integrity and competence had been heavily criticised by the judge presiding over his trial, his dismissal would not seem to have been either illegal or irrational. However, he had been sacked immediately after the trial. He had not even been informed that the Committee was considering this course of action, and had no opportunity to make a case to its members. Following representations from Ridge's solicitor, the Committee agreed to reconvene to permit Ridge the opportunity to persuade them to revoke their decision. Ridge and his lawyer were allowed to make a statement at the hearing, but not to call witnesses or cross-examine Committee members. Ridge subsequently sought a declaration that his dismissal was void on the ground that the hearings breached the requirements of

---

[24] Ibid, at 118.   [25] Ibid.   [26] Ibid.   [27] [1960] 1 WLR 223, PC.   [28] [1964] AC 40.

natural justice.[29] Neither the High Court nor the Court of Appeal accepted that natural justice applied in this situation, on the basis that the Committee's function was administrative not quasi-judicial in nature.[30]

This conclusion was reversed in the House of Lords. Lord Reid's leading judgment suggested that the line of cases typified by *Venicoff*, *Parker*, and *Nakkuda Ali* rested on insecure jurisprudential and political foundations. This was in part because it was inappropriate to attach much significance to judgments addressing the exercise of war powers:

> It seems to me to be . . . almost an inevitable inference from the circumstances in which defence regulations were made and from their subject matter that . . . [Parliament's] intention must have been to exclude the principles of natural justice . . . But it was not to be expected that anyone would state in so many words that a temporary abandonment of the rules of natural justice was one of the sacrifices which war conditions required—that would have been almost calculated to create . . . alarm and despondency.[31]

A second, more pervasive, problem had arisen from a widespread judicial presumption that a government body's duty to act 'judicially' was not—as in *Cooper*, *Rice*, and *Arlidge*—to be inferred as a matter of course whenever its decisions impacted substantially on an individual's interests, but had rather to be 'super-added' either explicitly or as matter of necessary implication by the relevant statutory scheme.[32] Lord Reid saw no need for such a requirement.

He also suggested that the courts had rather misunderstood the changing nature of the relationship between government and the citizenry. It was undoubtedly true that since 1900 Parliament had granted the government more and more extensive powers. Many such powers addressed matters of policy which affected many people en masse. Decisions of that sort need not be subject to the rules of natural justice. However, Lord Reid implied that the courts had extended that presumption too broadly, and had overlooked the fact that many government decisions still involved a power akin to imposing a 'penalty' upon particular individuals. In respect of powers of that type, a common law presumption as to procedural rigour based on nineteenth and (very) early twentieth-century precedent was justified.[33]

The presumption was not absolute however, even in situations where what was in issue was the loss of livelihood. Lord Reid drew a careful (if somewhat formalistic) distinction between three types of 'employment' situation. In respect of contracts of employment, there seemed to be no role for common law based principles of natural justice to apply. Such procedural constraints as attached to the exercise of an employer's powers would have to be found in the relevant contract or in any statutory provisions imposed on the post. In the absence of a contract (in effect when the employment of civil servants was in issue),[34] common law restraints on procedure would apply only to office holders who were dismissible for cause (such as Ridge); those holding office at pleasure could be dismissed without any form of hearing.

Contemporary commentators have regarded *Ridge* as a landmark decision, comparable in its jurisprudential significance with contemporaneous judgments such as *Padfield* and *Anisminic*. Craig, for example argued that the judgment had two major implications for the *audi alterem partem* principle:

---

[29] Ridge's practical concern was to have the dismissal quashed. This would have the effect of reinstating him in his job. He would then immediately resign before the Committee met again. If he resigned, he retained his pension. If he was sacked for negligence or unfitness, he would not do so.

[30] [1963] 1 QB 539, CA; affg [1963] 2 All ER 523.

[31] [1964] AC 40 at 73. Lord Reid also vindicated Lord Atkin's dissent in *Liversidge* by describing the majority judgment as a 'very peculiar decision': Ibid.   [32] Ibid, at 74.

[33] Cf his criticism of the Privy Council in *Nakkuda Ali* for not considering any cases from before 1911.

[34] Courts did not accept that civil servants had 'contracts' of employment until the mid-1980s; see 'III. Full reviewability—the *GCHQ* case (1983)', ch 4, pp 94–96.

on the one hand [the majority] rediscovered the nineteenth century jurisprudence which had applied the principle to a broad spectrum of interests and a wide variety of decision-makers. On the other hand they disapproved of some of the impediments which had been erected in the twentieth century.[35]

It is however important not to overstate the significance of the case. While *Ridge* undoubtedly restored the *reach* of the *audi alterem partem* doctrine to its Victorian extent, it did little to enhance its *content*. Reid's judgment lacks any positive statement on the question of *how much* procedural protection Ridge was entitled to. In a passage towards the end of his judgment,[36] Reid implies that had the Committee actually revoked Ridge's dismissal prior to its second meeting (thereby indicating that it was addressing the issue with an open mind)[37] and given him fuller details of the case against him, it would have satisfied the requirements of natural justice.[38] Nothing in the judgment suggests that Ridge was entitled to a high level of procedural protection.[39]

The emergence of the procedural fairness doctrine and the appearance of the legitimate expectation

The indication given in *Ridge* that the common law was now to be more concerned with maximising the reach of the *audi alterem partem* principle than identifying and enhancing its content was quickly reinforced by the High Court's decision in *Re HK*.[40]

A single stage question?

Section 2(2) of the Commonwealth Immigrants Act 1962 granted a right of entry to the UK to a citizen of any Commonwealth country who: 'satisfies an immigration officer that he . . . (b) is the . . . child under sixteen years of age of a Commonwealth citizen who is resident in the United Kingdom'. HK, a citizen of Pakistan, claimed to be the 15-year-old son of a resident Commonwealth citizen. However, on his arrival at Heathrow, an immigration officer formed the initial impression that HK was over 16 years old.[41] There followed what seems to have been a rather rapid and rudimentary 'hearing' at the airport, in which HK was examined by a doctor and both HK and his father were interviewed (separately and without any form of expert representation) by immigration officers. The officers were unconvinced that HK was under 16, and arranged for him to be deported back to Pakistan the next day. This decision was challenged on the basis that the procedures adopted by the immigration officers were insufficiently rigorous.

In his leading judgment, Lord Parker CJ followed *Ridge v Baldwin* in suggesting that *Nakkuda Ali*, if not wrongly decided, was certainly poorly expressed. Lord Parker doubted that

---

[35] (1989) op cit p 204.   [36] [1964] AC 40 at 79–80.

[37] Had it done so, one assumes Ridge would not have attended the second hearing, but would have instantaneously resigned to safeguard his pension.

[38] On the more general issue of whether a governmental body can cure procedural defects in its original decision by holding a second, procedurally defensible hearing see *Calvin v Carr* [1980] AC 574,; and the analysis by Elliot M (1980) 'Appeals, principles and pragmatism in natural justice' *MLR* 66.

[39] One might contrast this position with a contemporaneous academic critique produced in the United States which was to have a profound influence on the development of constitutional and administrative law in that country. In several articles in the *Yale Law Journal*, Charles Reich argued that not only should the reach of the procedural fairness doctrine be extended to all facets of the governmental process which affected individual interests, but that its content should also be modelled on a judicial process; see Reich C (1964) 'The new property' *Yale LJ* 733–787; (1965) 'Individual rights and social welfare: the emerging legal issues' *Yale LJ* 1244.

[40] [1967] 2 QB 617, sub nom *Re K(H)(infant)*.

[41] HK's Pakistani passport recorded his date of birth as 29.2.1951; a non-existent date, as 1951 was not a leap year. This anomaly, coupled with HK's mature physical appearance, underpinned the officer's conclusion.

s 2 imposed a 'judicial' function on immigration officers. Officers were nonetheless subject to 'a duty to act fairly'. Salmon LJ echoed this reasoning:

> [D]ecisions [under s 2] are of vital importance to the immigrants since their whole future may be affected. In my judgment it is implicit in the statute that the authorities in exercising these powers and making decisions must act fairly in accordance with the procedures of natural justice.[42]

However, the Court also considered that the content of the 'duty to act fairly' was rather anodyne. As Lord Parker put it, the obligation that fell on the officer was merely to: 'give the immigrant an opportunity of satisfying him of the matters in the sub-section, and for that purpose let the immigrant know what his immediate impression is so that the immigrant can disabuse him'.[43] The brief interview which HK had been afforded at Heathrow was evidently sufficient to meet this requirement.

One might wonder if any useful purpose—intrinsic or instrumental is served by so perfunctory a standard of procedural due process. Furthermore, if so little protection was afforded to an individual interest which was (as Salmon LJ put it) 'vital' to the applicant concerned, the protection offered to 'non-vital interests' would presumably need be little more than barely discernible.

This supposition seemed to be reinforced by several cases in the late-1960s and early-1970s in which the courts accepted that a governmental decision was subject to natural justice/fair procedures, but reduced the substance of the protection almost to vanishing point. Of particular note were the decisions in *R v Aston University Senate, ex p Roffey*[44] and *Breen v Amalgamated Engineering Union*,[45] in which (respectively) the High Court and Court of Appeal indicated that procedural fairness did not always require that the individual be granted a hearing. Similarly, in *Malloch v Aberdeen Corpn*,[46] the House of Lords offered the curious suggestion that in some situations where a hearing would be required the individual need not be given any prior notice of the details of the case which she had to answer. Quite what value (other than the purely symbolic) a hearing might have in such circumstances is difficult to fathom.

It might readily be conceded that in respect of some types of governmental decision there may be strong public policy grounds both for limiting the content of any hearing and for relieving the decision-maker of any obligation to provide precise information of the case an applicant has to answer. An example is offered by *R v Gaming Board for Great Britain, ex p Benaim and Khaida*.[47] The applicants had been refused a licence to run a casino. They had been granted a hearing by the Gaming Board prior to the decision being made. They were not however permitted to know details of the evidence that the Board had considered which had led it to conclude that they were not fit persons to be granted a licence. The Board refused to provide such information, on the basis that it would jeopardise the confidentiality of its sources. This was a consideration of some importance given the suspected links between the gambling industry and organised crime. In the Court of Appeal, Lord Denning held that this was a pertinent factor for the court to consider. He also observed that the plaintiffs were not being deprived of any existing entitlement, but were rather seeking a permission to begin a new venture. In these circumstances, the Board's duty to act fairly demanded that Benaim and Khaida be given:

> an opportunity of satisfying them of the matters specified . . . They must let him know what their impressions are so that he can disabuse them. But I do not think that they need quote chapter and verse against him as if they were dismissing him from an office as in *Ridge*: or depriving him of his property, as in *Cooper*.[48]

---

[42] [1967] 2 QB 617 at 633.   [43] Ibid, at 630.   [44] [1969] 2 QB 538.   [45] [1971] 2 QB 175 CA.
[46] [1971] 1 WLR 1578.   [47] [1970] 2 QB 417.   [48] Ibid, at 430.

Such a conclusion obviously runs the risk that the Board is acting on the basis of flawed evidence, or indeed of no evidence at all. Lord Denning's judgment implies that this is a lesser evil than running the risk that potentially useful sources of information be deterred from offering evidence to the Board.

Lord Denning's own readiness to trust unhesitatingly in the competence and integrity of government decision-makers is perhaps best revealed by his absurd comments a few years later in *R v Secretary of State for Home Affairs, ex p Hosenball*.[49] Hosenball was an American journalist, whose activities were embarrassing the (then Labour) government. The Home Secretary subsequently sought to deport Hosenball. He claimed that 'national security' was in issue, although he declined to give any explanation as to how Hosenball's activities had this effect. In Lord Denning's view, notwithstanding the severe consequences for Mr Hosenball of the Home Secretary's decision, the government was under no obligation to give Hosenball details of the case against him so that he might convince the Home Secretary that the government's suspicions were ill-founded:

> There is a conflict here between the interests of national security on the one hand and the freedom of the individual on the other. The balance between these two is not for a court of law. It is for the Home Secretary. He is the person entrusted by Parliament with the task. In some parts of the world national security has on occasions been used as an excuse for all sorts of infringements of individual liberty. But not in England . . . Ministers . . . have never interfered with the liberty or freedom of movement of any individual except where it is absolutely necessary for the safety of the state.[50]

These sentiments do Denning little credit. The proposition that no government Minister has ever taken inappropriate advantage of the courts' general unwillingness to accept the justiciability of national security issues is risible. To empty the procedural fairness doctrine of all meaningful content in such circumstances may be justifiable, but it is done at the certain cost that the autonomy thereby afforded to the government *may* be abused and the probable cost that it *will* be.[51]

Benaim and Khaida obviously did not raise a 'national security' issue—nor did it concern a ministerial decision—but nonetheless addressed a public policy issue of sufficient sensitivity to persuade the Court of Appeal that only a dilute level of procedural rigour need be attached to the Gaming Board's licensing decisions. The matters in issue in cases such as *Roffey*, *Breen*, and *Malloch* had no such 'delicate' ramifications however.[52] The dilution of the content of procedural fairness in such cases appeared to rest largely on the grounds that it would ease the administrative process.

This line of decisions attracted forceful academic criticism from DH Clark, in an article published in *Public Law*.[53] While welcoming the evident extension in the reach of the natural justice principle since *Ridge*,[54] Clark took a less sanguine view of the way in which some decisions had treated the question of its content. His concern essentially was that there was little point in saying that in principle the safeguard of procedural fairness applies to all

---

[49] [1977] 1 WLR 766.   [50] Ibid, at 461.

[51] See the discussion of *GCHQ* at 'III. Full reviewability—the *GCHQ* case' (1983)', ch 4, pp 94–96. See also Geoffrey Robertson's analysis of the way in which Denning's hyperbolic rhetoric in *Hosenball* has been deployed in some Commonwealth countries whose democratic credentials are less firmly established than those of the United Kingdom: (1999) *The justice game* ch 10.

[52] *Roffey* concerned the expulsion of students from university on the grounds of poor academic performance; *Breen* the (non)-appointment of a trade union official; and *Malloch* the dismissal of a teacher.

[53] (1975) 'Natural justice: substance or shadow' *Public Law* 27. The paper merits careful attention.

[54] '*Ridge v Baldwin* restored light to an area benighted by the narrow conceptualism of the previous decade . . . It would not be immoderate to describe as dramatic the pace of consequent advancement beyond the old frontiers': Ibid, at 27.

governmental decisions (unless removed by statute) if the concept is so flexible that the benefit thereby bestowed on the individual may be worthless: 'even as the doctrine finds new fields to conquer it is being emasculated from within, honoured in name, but dangerously devalued in substance'.[55] Clark argued in contrast that *audi alterem partem* ought to be viewed as: 'a basic procedural minimum standard irreducible without negating its *raison d'etre*';[56] that *raison d'etre* being to enhance the likelihood that 'good' substantive decisions were produced, and that the legitimacy of the decision-making process be maximised. To achieve those objectives, the 'basic minimum' had to include an entitlement to a hearing and a clear indication of the case that had to be met.

Other commentators took a more positive view of these developments. Mullan, drawing a comparison between recent English, Canadian, and New Zealand decisions saw merit in what he termed a 'spectrum theory' approach to natural justice.[57] Mullan suggested that the two extreme ends of his 'spectrum' should be set not by archaic or formalistic distinctions between 'rights and privileges' and/or 'judicial and administrative' decisions, but by the criterion of justiciability. The extent to which governmental decisions would be required by the common law to approximate to an idealised, court-based standard of procedural rigour would depend upon the nature of the decision and the immediacy and intensity of its impact upon a particular individual. As a given decision appeared less and less justiciable, so the process of making it would become subject to less and less legalistic procedural constraints, until eventually a concern with due process would almost disappear.

While 'spectrum theory' may have a certain conceptual neatness, and might seem a useful analytical tool with which (given the benefit of hindsight) to critique some of the post-*Ridge* case law, its value as a practical, prescriptive tool with which to assess just 'how much fairness' should be applied to particular governmental decisions would appear limited. This was in part due to the intrinsic limitations of the idea itself. But such force as the idea had was also overshadowed by the appearance and rapid consolidation of a new principle in English administrative law—that of the 'legitimate expectation'.

Legitimate expectation—an entitlement to a procedural benefit or a substantive benefit?

The notion of the 'legitimate expectation' emerged in the Court of Appeal's 1969 decision in *Schmidt v Secretary of State for Home Affairs*.[58] The British government had, by the mid-1970s, taken a dim view of the 'religion' of Scientology, to the extent that EC nationals (see *Van Duyn v Home Office*)[59] found themselves barred from working for the Church of Scientology in the UK. This governmental disapproval had become clear in 1968, when the then Labour government announced that it would take steps to curb the growth of the sect. Among the measures to be taken were a ban on non-British citizens studying at the Church's British headquarters. No new students would be admitted to the country, and those already in the UK would not have their permission to stay in the UK renewed. This new policy posed an acute problem to Mr Schmidt and fifty other non-British citizens studying with the Church, as their permissions to stay would expire before they completed their studies. Their application for an extension of their permission to stay was refused by the Home Secretary. Among various grounds of

---

[55] Ibid, at 28. Cf also his suggestion at p 63 that the doctrine was 'undergoing a metamorphosis that would convert it into a mere slogan or ill-defined aspiration'.   [56] Ibid, at 37.

[57] Mullan D (1975) 'Fairness: the new natural justice' *University of Toronto LJ* 280–316. For (respectively) a more jurisprudential analysis and a helpful critique of this area of administrative law see Loughlin M (1978) 'Procedural fairness: a study of the crisis in administrative law theory' *University of Toronto LJ* 215; and Harlow and Rawlings (1984) op cit pp 78–94.   [58] [1969] 2 Ch 149, CA.

[59] Case 41/74: [1974] ECR 1337.

challenge to this decision was the contention that Schmidt should have been granted a hearing before the Home Secretary reached his decision.

The Court rejected this argument, on the narrow ground that aliens had no right of entry into the United Kingdom in the first place, and so had no concomitant right to have any permission to stay that they may have been granted extended. Lord Denning indicated that he thought *Venicoff* correctly decided in terms of its result, although the reasoning underpinning the judgment was now outmoded insofar as it was based on:

> the fact that the Home Secretary was exercising an administrative power and not doing a judicial act. But that distinction is no longer valid. The speeches in *Ridge v Baldwin* show that an administrative body, may in a proper case, be bound to give a person who is affected by their decision an opportunity of making representations. It all depends on whether the person has some right or interest, or, I would add, some legitimate expectation of which it would not be fair to deprive him without hearing what he has to say.[60]

Lord Denning was prepared to accept that Mr Schmidt had a legitimate expectation that he could remain in the United Kingdom until the expiry of his permission to stay. In the event that the Home Secretary revoked that permission prematurely, Mr Schmidt would be entitled to a hearing in order to attempt to persuade the Home Secretary not to frustrate his expectation. Non-renewal of permission did not however create such an entitlement. Widgery LJ's judgment also recognised the existence of a legitimate expectation as a trigger for procedural fairness. While no such expectation arose on these facts, he indicated—more broadly—that in cases involving the economic interests of citizens a non-renewal of a licence or permission by a government body might be subject to a requirement of procedural fairness. This would suggest that a case such as *Parker* would now be decided differently.

Schmidt suggested that while the courts saw no little merit in the judicial/administrative decision dichotomy, they would prefer to embellish rather than abolish the former distinction drawn in natural justice cases between rights and privileges by adding the legitimate expectation as a third, intermediate category of individual interest. Which individual interests would fall within this new category was however far from certain, as was the level of procedural protection such interests would attract.

Procedural not substantive protection?

That the first question might attract a very broad answer was indicated three years later by the Court of Appeal's judgment in *R v Liverpool Corpn, ex p Liverpool Taxi Fleet Operators' Association*.[61] The decision in issue concerned the council's power to licence taxi-cab drivers in its area. In the late-1960s, the council issued some 300 licenses each year for one-year periods. It subsequently considered whether to increase the number of licences. As part of its decision-making process, it invited the trade association representing existing licence holders to make representations to its relevant committee during which the association was represented by counsel. The council decided to increase the number of licences quite substantially, but promised (in writing on several occasions through senior councillors and officers) that no increase would be given effect until the council had succeeded in persuading Parliament to pass a private Act[62] empowering the council to ban the operation of unlicenced mini-cabs in the area. The council subsequently sought to break that promise. The association then asked the Court to hold that the council was bound to respect the substance of its promise.

In a narrow sense, one might doubt if *Liverpool Taxi* can properly be regarded as a 'legitimate expectation case', since that phrase does not appear anywhere in any of the three judgments delivered in the Court of Appeal.[63] In Denning's analysis, this was an estoppel case,

---

[60] [1969] 2 Ch 149 at 170, CA.   [61] [1972] 2 QB 299.   [62] On which see 'Private Bills', ch 5, p 120.
[63] By Lord Denning MR, Roskill LJ, and Sir Gordon Willmer.

to be decided in accordance with his own judgments in *Robertson* and *Lever Finance*.[64] He proceeded on the assumptions that: firstly, this particular licensing function was subject to the requirements of procedural fairness; and secondly, the council's promise to delay an increase in the number of licences granted until the relevant Act had been passed was substantively intra vires—that is, that it did not unlawfully fetter the council's discretion.[65] Lord Denning then invoked the amorphous notion of 'the public interest' to support the proposition that the council was not at liberty to resile from the substance of its promise: 'except after the most serious consideration and hearing what the other party has to say: and then only if they [sic] are satisfied that the overriding public interest requires it'.[66]

The implications of this reasoning are significant. Firstly the entitlement to a hearing (which entails a reasonably high level of procedural protection) seems to be triggered not by the association's economic interest in the decision, but by the council's own promise. This is an innovative, but not radical proposition, resting on the premise that it is per se procedurally unfair for a government body to break clear, substantively intra vires promises, and then to continue to make a new decision (whatever its content) without affording a new hearing to those individuals intimately affected by the new decision. This was the basis upon which both Roskill LJ and Sir Gordon Willmer decided the case and so should be taken as the opinion of the Court.[67] Much more radical—and much more constitutionally problematic—is the second limb of Denning's formula; (which is strictly merely obiter). In effect, Denning is saying that the council's promise had taken it into a position where the Court could subject the range of substantive decisions the council might then make in exercising its powers *in so far as they applied to individuals who legitimately expect the promise to be honoured* to much narrower limits than would be applied if the promise had not been made.[68] This is essentially to subject the council to a proportionality test in these particular circumstances, although Denning did not acknowledge (or perhaps perceive) that his judgment had that effect.[69] Roskill LJ and Sir Gordon Willmer made no such allusion; their judgments indicated that as long as a new hearing was held, the council could lawfully make just the same range of decisions as it could if its initial promise had not been made.[70]

The possibility that the legitimate expectation—as Denning construed it—might provide a backdoor route through which courts might in some circumstances come much closer to the political merits of a decision than was permitted by the *Wednesbury* unreasonableness test did not seem to be immediately appreciated after *Liverpool Taxi*. The presumption seemed rather to be—following Roskill and Willmer—that a legitimate expectation, whether it derived from a government body's action or was inherent in an applicant's interest, could give rise only to

---

[64] See 'Estoppel', ch 13, pp 366–369. See also Ganz G (1986) 'Legitimate expectation: a confusion of concepts', in Harlow C (ed) *Public law and politics*.   [65] See 'Fettering of discretion', ch 13, pp 365–366.

[66] [1972] 2 QB 299 at 308.

[67] An important point to note here is that a hearing would have been required before the council could resile from its promise to delay any increase in licences until the Bill had been passed even if it had not additionally promised to hold such a hearing; ie it was not the promise of a hearing that triggered the requirement of a hearing.

[68] It seems tolerably clear that, like Roskill and Willmer, Denning considered that the substantive benefit which the association could legitimately expect was that no new licences would be issued until the Act regulating minicabs had been passed.

[69] This is a distinct position from raising an estoppel in respect of the council's decision. If the court were to estop the council from breaking its promise, the court would essentially be exercising an appellate function by determining the precise outcome of the decision-making process. The 'overriding public interest' formula, in contrast, gives the council some room for substantive manoeuvre, albeit markedly less than it previously enjoyed. Lord Denning was also shortly to stress in *Cinnamond v British Airports Authority* ([1980] 1 WLR 582, CA) that any expectation on which an applicant sought to rely had to be 'legitimate', a quality that would not attach to (as in *Cinnamond*) an expectation generated by repeated criminal behaviour.

[70] Nor did Roskill LJ refer to estoppel as a source for his conclusion. Rather he regarded it as a new administrative law principle which he styled as 'fairness': [1972] 2 QB 299.

a procedural benefit. Thus in *R v Hull Prison Board of Visitors, ex p St Germain* the Court of Appeal invoked the concept to conclude (for the first time) that the disciplinary functions of prison Boards of Visitors could be quashed if they failed to conform to the requisite standard of fairness: a prisoner's interest in not being subject to disciplinary punishment was not a right in the orthodox sense, but was an interest of sufficient importance to be interfered with only through fair procedures.[71] Mr St Germain had been punished for his part in a riot at Hull prison by the revocation of some two years of expected remission of his sentence, a 'punishment' which was clearly of major significance.

The majority in *St Germain* had arguably limited its extension of the procedural fairness doctrine to the disciplinary functions of Boards of Visitors.[72] These were presumed to be 'judicial'. Disciplinary powers exercised by prison Governors were however classified as 'administrative'; (the old dichotomy clearly had not passed into obsolescence). These powers should not be subjected to the natural justice doctrine because (echoing Lord Goddard in *Parker*) that would place too great a burden on the Governor's decision-making behaviour. In *Leech v Deputy Governor of Parkhurst Prison*,[73] the House of Lords rejected this formalistic distinction. It held that a Governor's functions could be divided into disciplinary and management issues, and that the disciplinary element would be subject to the requirements of natural justice. More broadly, Lord Bridge suggested that this principle would extend to any governmental power which affected 'the rights or legitimate expectations' of individuals. In a clear break with the *Parker* rationale, Lord Bridge also attached unusually explicit significance to the intrinsic value of procedural fairness, observing that any burdens this extension of natural justice might impose upon prison Governors would be outweighed by the benefits resulting from prisoners knowing that their grievances about disciplinary decisions would have a full airing at a fair hearing.

A tripartite approach to the requisite level of procedural protection

The legitimate expectation idea was also used in *McInnes v Onslow Fane*[74] to offer rather more precise guidance on the issue of the content rather than just applicability of the procedural fairness doctrine. Mr McInnes, after an extremely chequered career in and around the fringes of the boxing industry, had by 1976 made five successive but unsuccessful applications to the British Boxing Board of Control for a licence to operate as a manager. All his applications were rejected without him being granted a hearing, and without him being apprised in any detail of the factors which led to the Board's refusals.

Megarry VC's judgment suggested that licensing decisions of this sort could be divided into three categories for procedural fairness purposes. The first category was 'forfeiture' cases, in which the decision under challenge had revoked or abridged a still extant licence. The third category was 'application' cases, in which a licence was being sought for the first time. Between these two extremes lay the second category, in which 'the applicant has some legitimate expectation from what has already happened that his application will be granted'.[75]

---

[71] [1979] QB 425. This case was argued only on a preliminary, jurisdictional question. On the (once again rather low) level of protection subsequently held appropriate, see *R v Hull Prison Board of Visitors, ex p St Germain (No 2)* [1979] 1 WLR 1401. Four years earlier, in *Fraser v Mudge* [1975] 1 WLR 1132, the High Court had hinted that Boards of Visitors might be subject to the rules of natural justice, but did not decide the issue; see the discussion in *St Germain*. *Fraser v Mudge* is revisited in a slightly different context later in this chapter.

[72] The point is not wholly clear. See the discussion by Webster J in *R v Secretary of State for the Home Department, ex p Tarrant* [1985] QB 251 at 271–272.   [73] [1988] AC 533.

[74] [1978] 1 WLR 1520.

[75] [1978] 1 WLR 1520 at 1529. Megarry VC intimated that already possessing a licence triggered a legitimate expectation of renewal, as would presumably—although he was not explicit on this—representations that a licence would be granted by the Board's officials.

The first category would attract a high level of procedural protection: 'the right to an unbi-ased tribunal, the right to notice of the charges, and the right to be heard in answer to the charges'.[76] The mere application cases, in contrast, would apparently merit no worthwhile pro-tection at all. No hearing would be necessary, and the applicant need not be given even the gist of the case against her. Megarry VC did not offer any details of the protection to be provided in the intermediate category; such 'intermediate' decisions would presumably attract an 'inter-mediate' level of procedural rigour.[77]

That a legitimate expectation might trigger a particular level of procedural protection may have raised practical difficulties in deciding how much was enough, but it was not a concep-tually problematic idea. The possibility that a legitimate expectation might have the effect of narrowing a government body's substantive discretion was more contentious. That idea had been given some currency by the Court of Appeal in *Chief Constable of North Wales Police v Evans*, but was then firmly rejected by the House of Lords.[78] Evans was a probationer consta-ble. Under the relevant statutory scheme, the Chief Constable could dismiss a probationer if she considered that he would not be a 'reliable and competent officer'. Evans was dismissed on the basis of unfounded rumours about his personal life, and was not given any opportunity to rebut the allegations. In the House of Lords, Lord Hailsham had described Evans' treatment as 'little short of outrageous'. Evans' status was clearly comparable to that of Ridge, and as such he was entitled to procedural protection. As in *Ridge*, the Court set the content of fairness at a low level. Evans need not be granted an oral hearing, but had to be given at least an opportunity to refute the charge.

However perhaps the most important aspect of the judgment is noted by Craig:

> The House of Lords explicitly disapproved of statements made in the Court of Appeal that a court should exercise a general power to consider whether the decision reached was fair and reason-able. It was firmly stated that where review was based upon breach of natural justice the court should only be concerned with the manner in which the decision was reached and not with the correctness of the decision itself.[79]

Construed in this way, the judgment implicitly rejects Lord Denning's reasoning in *Liverpool Taxi*. But the judgment may also be seen as indicative of a pervasive judicial failure or unwill-ingness to distinguish between a proportionality-based level of substantive review and an appellate jurisdiction.[80] To decide if the substantive content of a decision is correct is de facto to exercise appellate powers; to decide whether or not it is defensible within a narrower range of options than permitted by the *Wednesbury* unreasonableness test need not have this effect at all. The judgment, whether ill-conceived or not, is nonetheless clear authority for the proposi-tion that a government body's procedural failings should not be used as a stepping stone for a court to narrow its substantive discretion.

Blurring the edges of the procedural/substantive dichotomy

This evident clarity was then rather obscured by several decisions in the mid-1980s.[81] The applicant in *A-G of Hong Kong v Ng Yuen Shiu*[82] was an illegal immigrant to Hong Kong from Macau. As part of a general tightening of its policy towards illegal immigration, the Hong Kong

---

[76] Ibid.

[77] This tripartite analysis of licensing decisions has a superficial conceptual neatness. However, it may be diffi-cult to generalise significantly from *McInnes*. Megarry VC paid no obvious attention, eg, to the scale of or public interest in the licence concerned. Should, eg, the revocation of a market stallholder's licence merit greater proce-dural protection than an application to renew a licence to run an airline?   [78] [1982] 1 WLR 1155.

[79] (1989) op cit at p 213.

[80] See the discussion at 'III. Proportionality—a new ground of review?', ch 13, pp 377–380.

[81] A very helpful and incisive analysis is provided in Forsyth C (1988) 'The provenance and protection of legiti-mate expectations' *Cambridge LJ* 238.   [82] [1983] 2 AC 629 PC.

government announced that illegal entrants from Macau would not be deported until they had been granted an individuated hearing so that their claim to stay could be carefully considered. Such a hearing was not specifically required by the relevant statutory scheme, but it is clear that the government was acting substantively intra vires in making the promise. Mr Ng was not afforded such a hearing. The Privy Council subsequently held that Mr Ng had a legitimate (or as Lord Fraser styled it 'reasonable') expectation that this promise be honoured. Lord Fraser, who delivered the sole judgment, also held that a legitimate expectation could arise in several ways:

> The expectations may be based on some statement or undertaking by, or on behalf of, the public authority which has the duty of making the decision, if the authority has, through its officers, acted in a way that would make it unfair or inconsistent with good administration for him to be denied such an inquiry.[83]

In other respects, however, the judgment seemed to restrict the scope of the principle. Lord Fraser stressed that 'this is a very narrow case on its facts'.[84] He also emphasised that whatever the source of the legitimate expectation, it could trigger only procedural entitlements which would have no impact on the range of substantive decisions that might eventually be reached.

This seems clear. The seeds of potential confusion sown by *Ng Yuen Shiu* derive from two sources. The first was that the substantive benefit Mr Ng was seeking was itself a procedural right. All he was asking for was a hearing, not that he be permitted to stay in Hong Kong. He thus left the Court having succeeded in binding the Hong Kong government to the precise substance of its promise. The second derives from Lord Fraser's reliance on *Liverpool Taxi*, and his failure to note the significantly different implications of Lord Denning's opinion and the judgments of Roskill LJ and Sir Gordon Willmer in that case. In Lord Fraser's view, those three judgments all held that the council's substantive autonomy was not changed by its generation of a legitimate expectation on the part of the association. That is however incorrect, and by failing to draw the distinction, and by quoting at length from Lord Denning's opinion, Lord Fraser perhaps lent an unintended credibility to its substantive implications.

Those implications were certainly afforded great credibility in *R v Secretary of State for the Home Department, ex p Khan*.[85] Mr Khan was seeking to adopt his nephew, who then lived in Pakistan. A Home Office policy letter detailed the criteria which a person in his situation would have to meet to bring a child to the United Kingdom for adoption. Having complied with these criteria Mr Khan was informed that the letter incorrectly represented Home Office policy, that more restrictive criteria actually applied, and that he could not meet them. Parker LJ's leading judgment in the Court of Appeal invoked *Ng Yuen Shiu* as approving Lord Denning's opinion in *Liverpool Taxi*. Parker LJ held that Mr Khan had a legitimate expectation that the policy outlined in the statement would be followed. This legitimate expectation had no *general* impact on the Home Secretary's power to apply a different policy, located at any point within the boundaries of irrationality. But, the substantive autonomy the Home Secretary retained *in respect of Mr Khan*, and anyone in his position, had apparently shrunk:

> The Home Secretary, if he undertakes to allow in persons if certain conditions are satisfied, should not in my view be entitled to resile from that undertaking without affording interested parties a hearing and then only if the *overriding public interest* demands it.[86]

With respect to Mr Khan, the Home Secretary had it seemed engaged in a course of conduct which essentially subjected his substantive discretion to something akin to proportionality rather than irrationality review.

---

[83] Ibid, at 350.   [84] Ibid, at 352.   [85] [1984] 1 WLR 1337.

[86] Ibid, at 1344; emphasis added. Cf also at 1347: 'vis à vis the recipient of such a letter, a new policy can only be implemented after such recipient has been given a full and serious consideration whether there is some overriding public interest which justifies a departure from the procedures stated in the letter'.

In *R v Secretary of State for the Home Department, ex p Ruddock*[87] the intimation that a legitimate expectation placed tight limits on a public body's capacity to depart from published policy promises was made more strongly than in *Khan*. The applicant was a prominent member of CND, who suspected her phone was being tapped by the security services. If her suspicion was correct, the security services were acting in breach of guidelines issued by the Home Secretary which identified the criteria she/he would invoke to authorise such tapping.[88] The Court of Appeal concluded that the policy statement created a legitimate expectation (presumably to all citizens) that phones would not—absent overriding public policy considerations—be tapped unless the guideline criteria were satisfied. This would have to be more than a procedural benefit; given the nature of the power in issue, the idea that a potential surveillance target be invited to a hearing to discuss whether the policy should be changed is absurd.[89] The substantive benefit claimed is however modest; the Home Secretary may change his policy, but must announce he is doing so and may not depart, except in limited circumstances, from whatever policy is currently in force.

Despite the modesty of this jurisprudential ambition, it appeared to be dismissed as constitutionally inappropriate by the House of Lords in *Re Findlay; Re Hogben; Re Honeyman; Re Matthews*.[90] The policy in question here was when prisoners became eligible for parole. In late-1983, the Home Secretary altered government policy on this matter. The previous policy was that prisoners became eligible for parole after serving one-third of their sentence; under the new policy, half of the sentence would have to be served. The applicants argued, inter alia, that the change of policy was unlawful in so far as it frustrated their legitimate expectations to be eligible for parole after one third of their sentence. This was perhaps too ambitious an argument. It goes much beyond *Khan*, in that it leaves no scope for 'overriding public policy considerations' to enable the Home Secretary to amend the initial policy. As such, it essentially invited the court to adopt an appellate jurisdiction. That invitation was unsurprisingly refused. Lord Scarman's sole judgment held that while the prisoners may have had a legitimate expectation, it could only be an expectation to be treated in a procedurally fair fashion in accordance with whatever policy the government had in force at the time: 'Any other view would entail the conclusion that the unfettered discretion conferred by the statute upon the minister can in some cases be restricted so as to hamper, or even to prevent, changes of policy'.[91] It is unfortunate that Lord Scarman should suggest that the Home Secretary's discretion in this matter was 'unfettered', as it was obviously subject to *Wednesbury* constraints. The thrust of his conclusion is however clear; that no procedural failing can initiate a change in the scope of a government body's substantive discretion.[92]

The opposing lead counsel in *Findlay* (Stephen Sedley QC for the applicant and John Laws for the government) were both sitting as High Court judges in the mid-1990s, when they produced very different opinions on the substantive legitimate expectation issue. In *R v Secretary of State for Transport, ex p Richmond-upon-Thames London Borough Council*,[93] Laws J faced

---

[87] [1987] 1 WLR 1482.

[88] Ten years later, the supposedly subversive Ms Ruddock was a Minister in the first Blair government.

[89] Cf Forsyth C (1997) '*Wednesbury* protection of substantive legitimate expectations' *Public Law* 375. The point being that a hearing would obviously alert a suspect to the benefit of no longer using her phone.

[90] [1985] AC 318.   [91] Ibid 338.

[92] Astute commentators might have suggested that Lord Scarman's endorsement of orthodox principle was confined to this particular power, as, following the earlier quotation, he continued: 'Bearing in mind the complexity of the issues which the Secretary of State has to consider and the importance of the public interest in the administration of parole I cannot think that Parliament intended the discretion to be restricted in this way': Ibid. This supposition is rather contradicted, however, by Lord Diplock's approval of Lord Scarman's reasoning in *Hughes v Department of Health and Social Security* ([1985] AC 776 at 788, HL), a case concerning the ostensibly far more justiciable issue of civil servants' retirement ages. It was at this time, we might recall, that Lord Diplock floated in *GCHQ* the possibility that proportionality could become a ground of review. He too evidently saw no link between proportionality and the recognition of substantive legitimate expectations.

[93] [1994] 1 WLR 74.

an attempt by several London councils to bind the Secretary of State—unless overriding public policy reasons justified a contrary decision—to respect the substance of a promise made to limit the number of flights permitted to land at and depart from Heathrow airport. Richmond's counsel, Richard Gordon QC, invoked Lord Denning in *Liverpool Taxi* and Parker LJ in *Khan* to support the existence of this limited notion of a substantive legitimate expectation. Laws J dismissed Mr Gordon's argument as 'barren'. One might however suggest that Laws J's approach perpetuated the judiciary's familiar unwillingness to accept that there is a clear distinction to be drawn between ordering a Minister to reach one particular decision (ie an appellate jurisdiction) and limiting his/her room for substantive manoeuvre to decisions underpinned by overriding public policy considerations. The scope inherent in the latter concept may be substantial; it will just not be so wide as permitted by the irrationality test.[94]

Sedley J's judgment in *R v Ministry of Agriculture, Fisheries and Food, ex p Hamble (Offshore) Fisheries Ltd*[95] accepted that the creation of a legitimate expectation by a government body did entitle the court to assess if a decision which would disappoint that expectation was 'fair' in substantive terms. He recognised that this did not equate to the court assuming an appellate jurisdiction (although he did not explicitly characterise his principle as a proportionality test):

> To postulate this is not to place the judge in the seat of the minister . . . [I]t is the court's task to recognise the constitutional importance of ministerial freedom to formulate and to reformulate policy; but it is equally the court's duty to protect the interests of those individuals whose expectation of different treatment has a legitimacy which in fairness outtops the policy choice which threatens to frustrate it.[96]

The principle may better have been framed with a qualifying adverb ('clearly' or 'markedly' perhaps) attached to 'outtops'; unqualified, the verb does rather hint at an (almost) appellate power. Unqualified or not, however, Sedley J's reasoning was promptly refuted as 'heretical' and explicitly overruled by the Court of Appeal in *R v Secretary of State for the Home Department, ex p Hargreaves*.[97] Hargreaves' position was closely analogous to that of Findlay, although the benefit in issue in his case was a prisoner's entitlement to 'home leave' rather than parole. At the time of Hargreaves' commitment to prison, the government's policy was that prisoners would be eligible for home leave, subject to good behaviour, after serving a third of their sentence. This policy was outlined in a letter given to prisoners on arrival in gaol. Prisoners also signed something called a 'compact', in which they were informed that certain benefits (including home leave) would be available to them if their behaviour was satisfactory. After Hargreaves was gaoled, the Home Secretary altered government policy on home leave, extending the qualifying period from one-third to one-half of the sentence.[98]

Rather curiously, the Court of Appeal held that no legitimate expectation arose on the facts of this case, on the basis that no clear indication had ever been given to the prisoners that home leave became available at a particular point in their sentences.[99] Even if such an expectation had arisen, however, it could do no more than had been identified in *Findlay*; that is entitle Hargreaves to have his case considered in accordance with whatever (rational) policy was in force at the time. The Court approved the reasoning as well as the result of Lord Scarman's judgment in *Findlay*.

The scope of the legitimate expectation principle was then further elaborated by the Court of Appeal in *R v Secretary of State for Education, ex p Begbie*.[100] The case concerned the 'Assisted Places' scheme, promoted by the first Thatcher administration and enacted in the Education Act 1980, under which some children had their fees to attend private sector schools paid by the

---

[94] See especially the passage at ibid 92–96.   [95] [1995] 2 All ER 714.   [96] Ibid, at 731.
[97] [1997] 1 WLR 906.   [98] There was no suggestion that this was an irrational decision.
[99] See the forceful criticism of the Court's conclusion on this point in Forsyth (1997) op cit.
[100] [2000] 1 WLR 1115.

government. Prior to the 1997 general election, the Labour Party had indicated that it would abolish the scheme should it be elected to form a government. The issue raised in *Begbie* was whether various statements made by Labour politicians before and after the 1997 election about continued funding of places for children who had entered the scheme prior to its projected abolition had generated a substantive legitimate expectation on the part of the applicant (who had a child in that position).

The Court of Appeal saw no basis for assuming that any statements made by politicians while in opposition could generate a substantive legitimate expectation when such politicians subsequently gain government office. That conclusion seems unavoidable, given that in legal terms the politician had no governmental authority when the representation was made. The judgment also indicated that where a government body's initial position rested on a mistake or incompetence on its part, it should be permitted to resile from that position. A further welcome development from a government body's perspective was that the Court firmly indicated that some degree of detrimental reliance on the applicant's part was required in cases where the representation relied upon was made to a specific person rather than the public at large. Perhaps rather confusingly however, the Court also suggested that a substantive legitimate expectation could arise from a policy statement to the public at large; in which case no detrimental reliance would be required.[101]

It thus seemed likely that widespread judicial acceptance of even a partial substantive legitimate expectation would have to await judicial recognition of proportionality as a legitimate ground of substantive review.

A substantive legitimate expectation by another name?

The judgment of the Court of Appeal in *R v North and East Devon Health Authority, ex p Coughlan*[102] appeared to circumvent this potentially thorny question by labelling the ground of substantive review that the courts should apply in such circumstances as 'unfairness' or 'abuse of power'. Ms Coughlan was a severely disabled person, who had been placed by the health authority in a particular residential facility and promised that the facility would be 'a home for life'. For financial reasons, the authority subsequently wished to close the facility and relocate Ms Coughlan. The Court of Appeal expressly approved the reasoning deployed in *Khan* and *Hamble Fisheries*; the health authority should be permitted to resile from the substance of its promise to Ms Coughlan only to satisfy 'an overriding public interest'. More significantly, the Court confirmed that the evaluation of whether there was such an interest was a matter for the court itself. On the basis of the information before it, the Court of Appeal concluded that no such overriding public interest existed.

The 'fairness' label has a pedigree in legitimate expectation case law. As noted, it formed the basis of Roskill LJ's decision in *Liverpool Taxi*. In that case however, its reach was limited to procedural rather than substantive matters. Its invocation in *Coughlan* as a ground of substantive review lends an unnecessary opacity to this point of law. At one point in the Court's

---

[101] Ibid, at 133 per Sedley LJ:

But, Mr Beloff [counsel for Ms Begbie] submits, reliance is not a necessary precondition of enforcement of a legitimate expectation. He cites the passage at paragraph 13–030 of *de Smith, Woolf & Jowell, Judicial Review of Administrative Action*, 5th ed., p. 574, from which Peter Gibson L.J. has quoted the key passage. I have no difficulty with the proposition that in cases where government has made known how it intends to exercise powers which affect the public at large it may be held to its word irrespective of whether the applicant had been relying specifically upon it. The legitimate expectation in such a case is that government will behave towards its citizens as it says it will. But where the basis of the claim is, as it is here, that a pupil-specific discretion should be exercised in certain pupil's favour, I find it difficult to see how a person who has not clearly understood and accepted a representation of the decision-maker to that effect can be said to have such an expectation at all. A hope no doubt, but not an expectation.

[102] [2001] QB 213.

judgment, Lord Woolf MR observed that; 'labels are not important'.[103] This might be thought rather disingenuous. While no doubt of little significance to Ms Coughlan and the health authority, the label applied by the court to the ground of review on which it premised its judgment is important in constitutional terms. De facto, the Court of Appeal's judgment was subjecting the health authority to proportionality review. It is perhaps unfortunate that the Court did not say so explicitly, as it thereby exposes itself to the accusation that it was seeking to expand the reach of judicial review by covert rather than transparent means.[104]

The Court of Appeal confirmed its preference for the notion of 'abuse of power' as a covering label for the analysis of legitimate expectation cases in *R v London Borough of Newham, ex p Bibi*.[105] The Court also suggested that no distinction need be drawn between substantive and procedural expectations; the same approach should be adopted in either situation. The Court's reasoning, which drew heavily on Craig's analysis[106] of the problem, suggested that:

> In all legitimate expectation cases, whether substantive or procedural, three practical questions arise. The first question is to what has the public authority, whether by practice or promise, committed itself; the second is whether the authority has acted or proposes to act unlawfully in relation to its commitment; the third is what the court should do.

In *Bibi*, the local authority had mistakenly believed itself to be under an obligation to grant a secure tenancy[107] in one of its own properties to the applicant. Having promised to do so in a letter to the applicant, the authority then realised that it was not under any such obligation, and resiled from its representation. The Court was not prepared to apply the *Coughlan* test on these facts; that is, to insist that a secure tenancy be granted unless the local authority could demonstrate overriding public policy reasons to justify why that should not be done. The judgment that the local authority had acted unlawfully was ultimately premised on the local authority's failure to consider what weight it should attach to the fact that it had actually made the promise before deciding not to provide the substantive benefit in issue.

In addition to subsuming the legitimate expectation concept within a wider notion of 'abuse of power', *Bibi* also weakened the relevance of the principle of estoppel in the administrative law context. In a conclusion that is difficult to reconcile with its earlier judgment in *Begbie*, the Court considered that it was not necessary to found a legitimate expectation—as it would be to found a claim in estoppel—that the claimant had relied to her detriment on the representation made.[108]

The severance between the legitimate expectation and estoppel principles was subsequently underlined by the House of Lords in *R v East Sussex County Council, ex p Reprotech Ltd*[109] The case rested on facts similar to those in the *Lever Finance* and *Western Fish* litigation, but the House of Lords indicated that such facts should in future be approached in a quite different way:

> It is true that in early cases such as . . . *Lever (Finance) Ltd v Westminster Corp* . . ., Lord Denning MR used the language of estoppel in relation to planning law. At that time the public law concepts of abuse of power and legitimate expectation were very undeveloped and no doubt the analogy of estoppel seemed useful. In the *Western Fish* case the Court of Appeal tried its best to reconcile these invocations of estoppel with the general principle that a public authority cannot

---

[103] Ibid, at para 76.

[104] In contrast to the view expressed in *Begbie*, the Court indicated that the principle of a substantive legitimate expectation should be limited to; 'cases where the expectation is confined to one person or a few people, giving the representation the character of a contract'; (Ibid, at para 59). One might also note that the judgment did not necessarily mean that Ms Coughlan will indeed have a 'home for life' in that particular facility. The authority might well succeed at some future date in convincing a court that changing circumstances have lent an 'overriding' character to its wish to close the facility down.   [105] [2001] EWCA Civ 607; [2002] 1 WLR 237.

[106] Craig P (5th edn, 2003) *Administrative* law pp 418–431.

[107] This being the type of tenancy introduced by the Housing Act 1980: see 'Housing—individuated and collective privatisation', ch 10, pp 275–277.   [108] [2002] 1 WLR 237 at paras 27–31.

[109] [2002] UKHL 8, [2003] 1 WLR 348.

be estopped from exercising a statutory discretion or performing a public duty . . . It seems to me that in this area, public law has already absorbed whatever is useful from the moral values which underlie the private law concept of estoppel and the time has come for it to stand upon its own two feet.[110]

It has been suggested that the *Reprotech* decision marks the 'end of estoppel' as a ground of judicial review.[111] That contention seems soundly based in respect of land use planning law, and indeed in respect of other areas of government activity which raise broad questions of public interest. Whether it will have a pervasive effect remains to be seen.[112]

But, notwithstanding the innovations which appear to have been introduced by the substantive legitimate expectation case law, it must be emphasised that all of the cases discussed in this section have involved attempts to bind government bodies to substantively intra vires decisions. The argument that the common law could recognise the concept of a substantive legitimate expectation as a device to overcome the classic *Hulkin* estoppel dilemma (ie whether one should, to avoid substantive injustice to an innocent citizen, bind a government body to a decision it had no power to reach) has yet to be successfully made.[113] It would at present seem no more feasible to reach that destination through the legitimate expectation route than through the mechanism of estoppel.[114]

The content of procedural fairness—legal representation and an obligation to give reasons for decisions

An entitlement to representation by counsel is regarded as an essential element of the procedural protection afforded to litigants in a criminal trial. The entitlement is however far less widely available in respect of hearings held by governmental bodies other than courts.

The applicant in *Pett v Greyhound Racing Association Ltd*[115] had been accused of doping his greyhounds. The Association, which policed the ethics of greyhound racing, announced that he would be subject to disciplinary proceedings and refused to allow him to be represented by counsel. Pett subsequently sought an interlocutory injunction to prevent the hearing being held until he had established whether he had a right to counsel at the hearing. Lord Denning indicated that he thought Pett's claim was well-founded:

> It is not every man who has the ability to defend himself on his own. He cannot bring out the points in his own favour, or the weaknesses in the other side. He may be tongue-tied or nervous, confused or wanting in intelligence . . . If justice is to be done he ought to have the help of someone to speak for him. And who better than a lawyer . . . [116]

Lord Denning (supported by Davies and Russell LJJ) appeared to limit this principle to cases where a person's reputation and livelihood was at stake. The above passage was however strictly

---

[110] [2003] 1 WLR 348 at para 35.

[111] Purdue M (2002) 'The end of estoppel in public law' *Journal of Planning and Environmental Law* 509.

[112] Interestingly in the light of *Reprotech*, the broad thrust of recent legitimate expectation decisions might be characterised as lending the idea a character which is increasingly akin to estoppel, in the sense both of requiring that the representation be targeted at a specific audience and that, in general, the applicant can demonstrate reliance on the representation; see eg *Nadarajah v Secretary of State for the Home Department* [2005] EWCA Civ 1363; *R (Wheeler) v Office of the Prime Minister and Secretary of State for Foreign and Commonwealth Affairs* [2008] EWHC 1409 (Admin); and *R (Bancoult) v Secretary of State for Foreign Affairs (No 2)* [2008] UKHL 61, [2009] 1 AC 453. See further Knight, C (2009) 'Expectations in transition' *Public Law* 15. For a more reflective conceptual analysis see Watson J (2010) 'Clarity and ambiguity: a new approach to the legitimacy in the law of legitimate expectations' (2010) *Legal Studies* 633.   [113] See 'Estoppel', ch 13, pp 366–370.

[114] It does now seem that such an outcome could arise through the provisions of the Human Rights Act 1998; see *Stretch v United Kingdom* [2003] EHRR 320.   [115] [1969] 1 QB 125, CA.

[116] Ibid, at 132.

obiter. At the full trial, *Pett v Greyhound Racing Association Ltd (No 2)*,[117] Lyell J reached the conclusion that even applicants in Mr Pett's position had no automatic right to representation. That their reputations and livelihoods might be at stake was not sufficient to trigger this level of protection.

Nor was the Court of Appeal prepared to accept that this entitlement should be extended to prisoners facing disciplinary proceedings by a Governor or Board of Visitors. In *Fraser v Mudge*, Roskill LJ offered what—from a policy perspective—might be regarded as the other side of the coin to the reasoning advanced by Lord Denning in *Pett*:

> One looks to see what are the broad principles underlying these rules. They are to maintain dis-
> cipline in person by proper, swift and speedy decisions, whether by the governor or the visitors;
> and it seems to me that the requirements of natural justice do not make it necessary that a person
> against whom disciplinary proceedings are pending should as of right be entitled to be repre-
> sented by a solicitor or counsel or both.[118]

A parallel line of case law addressed the separate question of whether, even if an applicant had no automatic right of representation, the decision-maker might nonetheless be obliged to consider if in the circumstances of the particular case, such representation should be permitted. The Court of Appeal had lent this principle a potentially expansive reach in *Enderby Town Football Club Ltd v Football Association Ltd*,[119] emphasising that no body should adopt a rigid rule never to permit representation.

In *R v Secretary of State for the Home Department, ex p Tarrant*,[120] the High Court held that it would be irrational for a Board of Visitors to refuse to allow representation where there was scope for doubt as to whether a prisoner's behaviour fell within the legal definition of a particular offence (in this case 'mutiny'). Representation need not however be permitted if all that was in issue was a question of fact, even if the offence charged (in this case assault) could attract substantial penalties. Some indication that *Tarrant* applied this principle too gener-ously was subsequently given by the House of Lords in *R v Board of Visitors of HM Prison, The Maze, ex p Hone*, in which the Court stressed that allowing legal representation on a routine basis would have the unwelcome results of causing: 'wholly unnecessary delays in many cases, to the detriment of all concerned including the prisoner charged, and to wholly unnecessary waste of time and money, contrary to the public interest'.[121]

The common law had until very recently been as reluctant to recognise a general duty that government bodies give reasons for their decisions as it has been to grant applicants an entitle-ment to legal representation. In the aftermath of the Crichel Down controversy,[122] Parliament imposed such a duty on a wide range of statutory bodies in the Tribunals and Inquiries Act 1958. That bodies were not brought within the remit of this Act might imply that Parliament did not intend that the common law should subject them to a similar obligation. The argument against the recognition of this doctrine as a general facet of procedural fairness is largely one of the time and expense that it would impose upon decision-makers. A lesser argument is that giving reasons may compromise the anonymity of informants, as for example in *Benaim and Khaida*. It is however clear that both the instrumental and intrinsic justifications for a concern with procedural fairness have especial resonance in respect of this particular content issue.[123] In addition, the giving of reasons would make subsequent review of or appeal against the deci-sion in question more straightforward. These factors may explain the courts' evidently greater willingness to apply the doctrine in a more extensive, if piecemeal fashion in recent years.

---

[117] [1970] 1 QB 46   [118] [1975] 1 WLR 1132 at 1134, CA.   [119] [1971] Ch 591.
[120] [1985] QB 251.   [121] [1988] 2 WLR 177 at 186, HL.
[122] See 'Issues of competence', ch 9, pp 238–240.
[123] Richardson G (1986) op cit; Craig (1993) op cit pp 310–316.

The Court of Appeal's judgment in *R v Civil Service Appeal Board, ex p Cunningham*[124] is a good illustration of this trend. The Civil Service Appeal Board (CSAB) performed the role of an industrial tribunal in relation to civil servants. Under the terms of the Civil Service Code, the CSAB was to treat civil servants no less favourably than they would be treated by an industrial tribunal applying the terms of the Employment Protection (Consolidation) Act 1978. Cunningham, a prison officer, maintained that the compensation awarded to him by the CSAB was far lower than he would have been given by an industrial tribunal. The CSAB had not offered any reasons for its decisions. The Court of Appeal rejected the proposition that the common law imposed a general duty to give reasons on government bodies. It nonetheless concluded that reasons should be given in this situation. This was in part because the CSAB's function 'mirrored' that of industrial tribunals, which were required to give reasons; in part because the Code had generated a legitimate expectation that reasons should be given; and in part because the imposition of that requirement would not have any obviously adverse implications for the administrative process. The obligation was however to be limited to 'outline reasons'; the CSAB did not have to provide full details of its reasoning. In Lord Donaldson MR's opinion 'fairness requires a tribunal such as the board to give sufficient reasons for its decision to enable the parties to know the issues to which it addressed its mind and that it acted lawfully'.[125]

Subsequently in *R v Parole Board, ex p Wilson*,[126] the Court of Appeal imposed a similar duty on the Parole Board's decision as to whether a prisoner serving a life sentence should be refused parole on the basis that his release would pose a danger to the public. The principle was extended in *R v Secretary of State for the Home Department, ex p Doody*[127] to encompass the Home Secretary's powers to fix the minimum period that prisoners sentenced to life had to serve before they became eligible for parole.[128] This conclusion was presented by Lord Mustill as part of; 'a perceptible trend towards an insistence on greater openness, or if one prefers the contemporary jargon, "transparency", in the making of administrative decisions'.[129]

This approach appeared to spill over into other areas of the government process. In *R v London Borough of Lambeth, ex p Walters*, the High Court held that such a duty to give reasons attached to all aspects of the homelessness provisions of the Housing Act 1985, notwithstanding the fact that a local authority was placed under specific statutory duty to give reasons in respect of particular decisions under the Act.[130] *Walters* was however promptly disapproved by the Court of Appeal in *R v Kensington and Chelsea Royal London Borough Council, ex p Grillo*.[131] The Court ruled that this was not an area where the common law 'should supply the omission of the legislature'. While the giving of reasons might be desirable as an element of 'good and courteous administration', the terms of the Act negated the inference of any general duty to do so.

Sedley J's judgment in *R v Higher Education Funding Council, ex p Institute of Dental Surgery* reinforced the view that there would be limits to the scope of the duty to give reasons. The decision in issue was an evaluation of the research activity of an academic institution. Sedley J regarded this as an essentially non-justiciable question, and thus one which the common law would not require to be supported with reasons.[132] The judgment was also however notable

---

[124] [1991] 4 All ER 310, CA.   [125] Ibid, at 320.   [126] [1992] QB 740.   [127] [1994] 1 AC 531.
[128] See Craig P (1994) 'The common law, reasons and administrative justice' *Cambridge LJ* 282.
[129] [1994] 1 AC 531 at 561.
[130] [1994] 2 FCR 336. The rationale of the authority's argument was that the explicit requirement that an authority give reasons in respect of particular parts of the Act implied that it need not do so in respect of the remaining parts of the Act.   [131] [1996] 2 FCR 56, 28 HLR 94.
[132] 'It may be a misfortune for the applicant that the court, which in *Cunningham's* case could readily evaluate the contrast between what the board awarded and what an industrial tribunal would have awarded, cannot begin to evaluate the comparative worth of research in clinical dentistry; but it is a fact of life': [1994] 1 All ER 651 at 670.

for Sedley J's suggestion that certain classes of decisions should be subject to a duty to give reasons; these being those which affected personal liberty or which appeared aberrant in substantive terms.

These categories were extended by the Court of Appeal in *R v Secretary of State for the Home Department, ex p Fayed*.[133] Fayed had made an unsuccessful application for British nationality under the terms of the British Nationality Act 1981, which had been rejected by the Home Office in the most cursory of terms; ('after careful consideration your application has been refused'). Section 44(2) of the Act expressly provided that the Home Secretary need not give any reasons for any decision granting or refusing citizenship. The Court concluded that but for that provision, the common law would have imposed a duty to provide clear reasons for a refusal of citizenship, given the importance of the decision to the applicant concerned.

Conclusion

The *Fayed* decision exemplifies the argument that in recent years the courts have been applying a more stringent set of procedural criteria to the making of governmental decisions. In addition to extending the reach of the procedural fairness principle, the courts have been taking (modest) steps also to enhance its content. This area of law still retains however a considerable degree of imprecision, especially on the question of exactly what procedural fairness entails. The point is perhaps best put by Lord Bridge's now oft-quoted comment in *Lloyd v McMahon*:

> My Lords, the so-called rules of natural justice are not engraved on tablets of stone . . . [W]hat the requirements of fairness demand when any body . . . has to make a decision which will affect the rights of individuals depends on the character of the decision-making body, the kind of decision it has to make and the statutory or other framework in which it operates . . . [T]he courts will not only require the procedure in the statute to be followed, but will readily imply so much and no more to be introduced by way of additional procedural safeguards as will ensure the attainment of fairness.[134]

II. The rule against bias

The second limb of the natural justice doctrine has proven rather less complicated than the *audi alterem partem* principle.[135] The rule against bias (*nemo iudex in sua causa*—'no-one may be a judge in his own cause') is concerned to ensure that government decision-makers do not have a personal interest in decisions that they take. This has long been held to be a fundamental tenet of English public law. The strength and longevity of the rule is neatly illustrated by recalling *Dr Bonham's Case*.[136] The legislation which Coke CJ had suggested was 'against common right or reason' in that case had in effect allowed a governmental body to settle disputes in which it was a party. In the post-revolutionary era, Parliament may if it wishes (subject now to the constraints of EU law) permit such bias, but the undesirability of such situations is now so deeply embedded in the common law that only the most explicit of statutory authorisations could achieve that effect.

The types of bias considered problematic at common law might crudely be labelled as either 'financial' or 'ideological' interests. Such interests may give rise (depending on the intensity of the interest) to the automatic disqualification of a particular decision-maker, or to

---

[133] [1998] 1 WLR 763.   [134] [1987] AC 625 at 702–703.

[135] A thorough and incisive view of the complexities of this issue is offered in Beatson, Matthews, and Elliot op cit ch 7.   [136] See 'Pre-1688—natural or divine law', ch 2, pp 19–20.

disqualification if it is established that a suspicion of bias could be thought to be well-founded. The courts' concern has generally been focused not on *actual* bias, but on the possibility that bias may arise. Much case law in this area has been concerned with 'judicial' decision-making, a term broadly defined to include judges per se, magistrates, jurors, and executive bodies performing judicial or quasi-judicial functions. The relevance of the principle to purely 'administrative' decisions is less pronounced.

Direct financial interests

The objections to a decision-maker having a direct financial interest in a given decision are obvious. She may favour her own financial concerns above the public interest and so produce a substantively undesirable decision; and even if she does not do so anyone else affected by the decision might reasonably suspect that she has. The rule against bias had been forcefully applied in this situation.

The leading case is *Dimes v Grand Junction Canal*.[137] The case involved a claim that Lord Cottenham LC had sat in proceedings involving a company in which he had shares. There was no suggestion that he had acted in a biased way; the applicant's objection was to the obvious risk that Lord Cottenham's financial involvement would undermine public confidence in the court's impartiality. The judgment thus had to be set aside. Lord Campbell put the point very clearly:

> it is of the last importance that the maxim that no man is to be a judge in his own cause should be held sacred . . . This will be a lesson to all inferior tribunals to take care not only that in their decrees they are not influenced by their personal interest, but to avoid the appearance of labouring under such an influence.[138]

The incompatibility of a judge's financial interest with the unbiased administration of justice was reiterated in 1866 by Blackburn J in *R v Rand*: 'There is no doubt that any direct pecuniary interest, however small, in the subject of inquiry, does disqualify a person from acting as a judge in the matter'.[139] A judge who has such an interest is subject to what was later termed 'automatic disqualification' from the case concerned. The strength of the suspicion that has to arise before bias is established is largely unproblematic when direct financial interests are at stake, but it becomes a much more difficult question when the financial interest is rather more oblique.

Indirect financial interests—a mere suspicion or a real likelihood

The difficulties that may be caused by claims of indirect financial bias are well illustrated by the judgments in *R v Sussex Justices, ex p McCarthy*[140] and *R v Barnsley Licensing Justices, ex p Barnsley and District Licensed Victuallers' Association*.[141] *McCarthy* arose because a solicitor who worked on a part-time basis as clerk to the Justices had sat in a criminal case concerning a car accident which involved a defendant who a client of his firm was suing in a civil action arising from the same accident. There was no suggestion that the clerk/solicitor had actually acted in a biased fashion in the criminal case. But this was not a relevant issue. Lord Hewart CJ again stressed that it was appearances that mattered:

> A long line of cases shows that it is . . . of fundamental importance that justice should not only be done, but should manifestly and undoubtedly be seen to be done . . . Nothing is to be done which creates even a suspicion that there has been an improper interference with the course of justice.[142]

---

[137] (1852) 3 HL Cas 759, 10 ER 301, HL.   [138] 10 ER 301 at 315.

[139] (1866) LR 1 QB 230 at 232. The Court nonetheless concluded that the financial interest in issue in this case—local justices' status as trustees of a hospital and friendly society which had a financial stake in the outcome of the decision—did not amount to a direct interest.   [140] [1924] 1 KB 256.

[141] [1960] 2 QB 167, CA.   [142] [1924] 1 KB 256 at 259.

The notion of a mere 'suspicion' is however a very wide test; it seems to suggest there need only be a possibility of bias, not a strong probability. This was narrowed somewhat by the presumption that the 'suspicion' is supposed to arise in the mind of a dispassionate observer, not a party to the proceedings (who would be likely, because of her own bias, to magnify any suspicions as to the impartiality of the decision-maker).

In *R v Barnsley Licensing Justices, ex p Barnsley and District Licensed Victuallers' Association*, the decision at issue was the justices' grant of a licence to sell alcohol to the local co-operative society—an organisation of which all the justices were members. As such, they were entitled to a share of any profits that the society might make. The Court of Appeal concluded that this interest was sufficient to raise a real likelihood of bias. The case is however most notable for Devlin LJ's judgment, in which he intimated that Lord Hewart CJ's 'even a suspicion' test in *McCarthy* was too broadly stated:

> [I]n my judgment, it is not the test. We have not to inquire what impression might be left on the minds of the present applicants or on the minds of the public generally. We have to satisfy ourselves that there was a real likelihood of bias, and not merely satisfy ourselves that that was the sort of suspicion which might reasonably get abroad.[143]

Both Ormerod LJ and Lord Evershed MR also used the 'real likelihood' formulation in their judgments, which led to the suggestion that the bias test would now be less easily satisfied than hitherto.

The law was then thrown into a state of some confusion by the subsequent Court of Appeal judgment in *R v London Rent Assessment Panel Committee, ex p Metropolitan Properties Co (IFGC) Ltd*[144] Lannon was a solicitor who also chaired a rent assessment committee. His father was in dispute with his (the father's) landlord. Lannon was advising his father. Lannon subsequently sat on a rent assessment committee which set the rents (at an extremely low level) at another property owned by the landlord. Lord Denning MR accepted that Mr Lannon's financial interest in the rent level set was 'remote . . . indirect and uncertain'. He nevertheless quashed the committee's decision. He did so by invoking the 'real likelihood' formula, but lent that formula a meaning that seemed to come close to the 'even a suspicion' test by observing that in *Barnsley* Devlin LJ 'appears to have limited [the *McCarthy*] principle considerably, but I would stand by it'.[145] He then offered a test which seemed to include elements of both Lord Hewart CJ's and Devlin LJ's ostensibly disparate approaches to this issue:

> [I]n considering whether there was a real likelihood of bias . . . the court looks at the impression which would be given to other people . . . [I]f right-minded persons would think that, in the circumstances, there was a real likelihood of bias on his part, then he should not sit . . . Nevertheless, there must appear to be a real likelihood of bias. Surmise or conjecture is not enough . . . The reason is plain enough. Justice must be rooted in confidence: and confidence is destroyed when right-minded people go away thinking; 'The judge was biased'.[146]

The result of this rather opaque reasoning was that administrative law now seemed to harbour two formulae in respect of indirect pecuniary interests; 'suspicion of bias' (on the part of dispassionate observers) or 'real likelihood of bias' (in the view of the Court). Presumably these two formulae did not mean the same thing; the latter test seems to be harder to satisfy. As Beatson and Matthews suggest,[147] this uncertainty generated a good deal of contradictory case law, including judgments which advanced the unlikely proposition that the two formulae did indeed produce just the same test.[148] The point was not subject to exhaustive analysis by the House of Lords until 1993, in *R v Gough*.[149]

---

[143] [1960] 2 QB 167 at 187.   [144] [1969] 1 QB 577.   [145] Ibid, at 599.   [146] Ibid.
[147] Op cit pp 287–290.   [148] *R v Liverpool City Justices, ex p Topping* [1983] 1 WLR 119.
[149] [1993] AC 646.

Clarifying the law? The *Gough* formulae

Gough had been convicted of robbery. After the trial, he recognised one of the jurors as his brother's next door neighbour, and made the rather speculative assertion that this created a suspicion of bias sufficient for the verdict to be quashed. The claim received short shrift from the Court. The primary concern in the judgment was to clarify what Lord Goff referred to as the 'bewildering' state of the law on this point.

Lord Goff (with whom the rest of the Court concurred) rooted this uncertainty primarily in the co-existence of the 'suspicion' and 'real likelihood' formulae. He attempted to clarify matters by confirming that a direct pecuniary interest should lead to automatic disqualification. In respect of indirect financial interests—and it seems non-financial interests—the Court offered the following test:

> I think it unnecessary . . . that the court should look at the matter through the eyes of the reasonable man, because the court in cases such as these personifies the reasonable man . . . [H]aving ascertained the relevant circumstances, the court should ask itself whether, having regard to those circumstances, there was a real danger of bias on the part of the relevant member of the tribunal in question, in the sense that he might unfairly regard . . . with favour or disfavour, the case of a party to the issue.[150]

Lord Goff stressed that he was thinking in terms of a possibility rather than probability of bias, but also managed to convey the impression that his 'real danger' formula was not a simple assertion of the 'mere suspicion' test. The test formulated by Lord Woolf in his concurring judgment seemed, in contrast, to owe rather more to Devlin LJ's views, being framed in terms of: 'a real danger of injustice having occurred as a result of the alleged bias'.[151] One might doubt that *Gough* allayed the doctrinal confusion over this issue, but its significance has latterly come to be overshadowed by an evident extension of the automatic disqualification principle to ideological as well as financial interests.

Ideological bias in 'judicial' decisions

The question before the House of Lords in *R v Bow Street Metropolitan Stipendiary Magistrate, ex p Pinochet Ugarte (No 2)*[152] was triggered by the attempts of the Spanish government to have Pinochet, the Chilean dictator, extradited from Britain to face trial in Spain for various human rights abuses committed against Spanish citizens in Chile. In *Pinochet*,[153] the House of Lords had approved the extradition by a majority of three to two. Somewhat unusually, the Court had allowed various interested parties, including Amnesty International, to participate in the proceedings by offering their respective views of the relevant law.

It then emerged that one of the majority, Lord Hoffmann, in addition to being a member of Amnesty, served as a director of an associated charity. Pinochet then argued that this interest amounted to bias which should automatically have excluded Lord Hoffmann from sitting.

The House of Lords subsequently reconvened and concluded that Lord Hoffmann was disqualified from sitting, and that the judgment had to be 'set aside'. The principle outlined in Lord Browne-Wilkinson's leading judgment was clearly expressed:

> if the absolute impartiality of the judiciary is to be maintained, there must be a rule which automatically disqualifies a judge who is involved, whether personally or as a Director of a company, in promoting the same causes in the same organisation as is a party to the suit.[154]

It might readily be thought that Lord Hoffmann's interest was sufficiently remote on these facts to preclude any finding of automatic disqualification. The *Gough* test would then have come

---

[150] Ibid, at 670.   [151] Ibid, at 671.   [152] [2000] 1 AC 119.   [153] [2000] 1 AC 61.
[154] [2000] 1 AC 119 at 135.

into play, and it would have been for Pinochet to establish that there was 'a real danger of injustice having occurred'. That would seem a stiff test to surmount on the facts, even if one accepts the questionable contention that a judge's support for an organisation whose *raison d'etre* is to promote respect for international law could amount to 'bias' in the first place.

The judgment does imply that no automatic disqualification would have arisen if Amnesty had not actually intervened in the case, or if Hoffmann had—in previous judgments or academic writings—expressed support for Amnesty's view of the law but was not a member of the group. Whether the *Gough* test would be met in such circumstances is a matter for speculation.[155]

The supposition that *Pinochet* might prompt a flood of spurious bias claims from disgruntled litigants appeared to be borne out by the various cases joined in *Locabail (UK) Ltd v Bayfield Properties Ltd*[156] The alleged bias in *Locabail* itself was that the judge (who was a QC sitting in a part-time capacity) was a partner in a firm of city solicitors which was acting for a client which was suing the husband of the (de facto) defendant in the action. The contention was that this 'conflict of interest' might be thought to dispose the judge to find in the plaintiff's favour. The Court of Appeal concluded that any financial interest the judge might have was far too tenuous to fall within the *Dimes* principle of 'automatic disqualification'.[157]

Nor did it think the *Gough* test was met. The judge had no knowledge that his firm (which was very large) was acting against the defendant's husband; thus, as the Court put it: 'How can there be any real danger of bias, or any real apprehension or likelihood of bias, if the judge does not know of the facts that, in argument, are relied upon as giving rise to the conflict of interest'.[158]

The same rationale was invoked to dismiss the bias claim raised in *O'Callaghan*. Here the judge's family firm owned property leased to a company against which the applicant was conducting extensive litigation. The judge had no knowledge of the leases, and played no active part in the firm's business decision. His interest was 'nominal and indirect', and thus could not substantiate a bias claim.

The allegation in *Williams* was wholly absurd. The applicant was engaged in litigation for sexual harassment and racial discrimination against the Inland Revenue. Having lost her claim before an industrial tribunal, Williams then claimed that the *Gough* test was met because the tribunal chair, some forty years earlier, had spent three years working for the Inland Revenue. The Court saw no merit in this claim: '[N]o right-thinking person knowing of the connection of [the chair] with the Inland Revenue would feel that there was any danger of bias in this case. The suggestion that there might be was fanciful'.[159]

However, in *Timmins*, the Court did accept that the *Gough* test was met. The litigation was a personal injury action, in which the plaintiff had been awarded an ostensibly surprisingly large sum. The defendant's insurance company claimed that the judge fell within *Gough* because he had in recent years written several scathing critiques in professional journals about the way in which insurance companies attempted to refute or minimise their liability in personal injury cases. The Court of Appeal saw no basis for assuming that a judge's extra-judicial

---

[155] See Malleson K (2000) 'Judicial bias and disqualification after *Pinochet (No 2)*' *MLR* 119: Jones J (1999) 'Judicial bias and disqualification in the *Pinochet* case' *Public Law* 391.

[156] [2000] QB 451. The case was joined with *Timmins v Gormley; Williams v Inspector of Taxes; R v Bristol Betting and Gaming Licensing Committee, ex p O'Callaghan*.

[157] The Court of Appeal did seem somewhat to limit the extensive meaning that could be lent to *Dimes* and *Rand*, noting that: 'In the context of automatic disqualification the question is not whether the judge has some link with a party involved in a cause before the judge but whether the outcome of that cause could, realistically, affect the judge's interest' ([2000] QB 451 at para 8). It also intimated that it approved recent Australian decisions on this issue which accepted that a *de minimis* exception should apply to the automatic disqualification principle.

[158] [2000] QB 451 at para 55. This does not imply that *McCarthy* was wrongly decided. The Court stressed in this case that the solicitors' firm in question was very large, employing 500 lawyers; there could be no sensible expectation that any partner could be familiar with its entire caseload. [159] Ibid, at para 96.

writings could per se amount to apparent bias. But a judge who engaged in such activities had to be 'circumspect in the language he uses and the tone in which he expresses himself. It is always inappropriate for a judge to use intemperate language about subjects on which he has adjudicated or will have to adjudicate'.[160] Because the judge in question had used particularly trenchant language in his articles, a real danger of bias could be thought to arise.

Locabail will no doubt deter bias allegations based on a judge's indirect and tenuous financial interest or institutional affiliations.[161] *Timmins* may however prompt dissatisfied litigants to trawl academic and professional journals for any hint that a judge holds them or their ilk in disfavour. The Court noted it reached its conclusion with 'misgiving'; which may indicate that the judgment was an unfortunate one which ought soon to be reversed. As in *Pinochet* itself, the conclusion raises the unwelcome inference that we must assume that judges are incapable of recognising and discounting their 'political' views when presiding over litigation.

Further clarifying the law? The *Porter v Magill* formula

The flurry of litigation on the bias point following *Pinochet* and *Gough* promptly led the Court of Appeal, and thereafter the House of Lords, to offer a further refinement of the correct test to apply in respect of this aspect of the procedural fairness doctrine. The Court of Appeal in *Re Medicaments and Related Classes of Goods (No 2)*[162] concluded that:

> The court must first ascertain all the circumstances which have a bearing on the suggestion that the judge was biased. It must then ask whether those circumstances would lead a fair-minded observer to conclude that there was a real possibility, or a real danger, the two being the same, that the tribunal was biased.[163]

The House of Lords subsequently endorsed this test in *Porter v Magill*,[164] save for the further minor modification that the reference to 'real danger' be removed from the formula.

It might be suggested that this drift in the case law evinces a concern to attach greater significance to the second of the two 'intrinsic reasons' identified at the start of this chapter for applying procedural fairness rules to the activities of governmental bodies. But it might also be argued that this strand of administrative law doctrine was becoming bedevilled with an evermore elaborate linguistic superstructure which positively invites disgruntled litigants to engage in ingenious semantic arguments in attempting to overturn unfavourable decisions.

The Court of Appeal's robust conclusion in *Taylor v Lawrence*[165] might therefore be welcomed as sending such litigants a clear signal that claims of tenuous bias would not succeed. The claimed bias in *Taylor* arose from the fact that the judge in the case had previously instructed the firm of solicitors representing the successful party to draw up his will. The Court of Appeal held that this was not a matter that could be thought to have any bearing on the judge's conduct. The Court also indicated that it could see little scope for assuming that any credible suspicion of bias could arise simply because a judge and a party's lawyers had a pre-existing professional relationship.

Bias in non-judicial proceedings

A further way of holding that Poplar Council's wage policy that was in issue in *Roberts v Hopwood* was unlawful would be to suggest that the council had succumbed to bias in making its decision. This bias would be found in the councillor's evident embrace of 'eccentric principles of socialist philanthropy' and 'feminist ambition', motives which the House of Lords considered wholly improper. The obvious problem with such a rationale is that it wholly excludes

---

¹⁶⁰ Ibid, at para 85.   ¹⁶¹ See now also *Taylor v Lawrence* [2003] QB 528.   ¹⁶² [2001] 1 WLR 700.
¹⁶³ Ibid, at para 85.   ¹⁶⁴ [2002] 2 AC 357.   ¹⁶⁵ [2003] QB 528.

any legitimate role for political ideology in the making of governmental decisions, a proposition which is obviously nonsensical in the modern era.

It was subsequently made clear in *Franklin v Minister of Town and Country Planning*[166] that a decision-maker was not 'biased' simply because she formulated policy in accordance with her pre-existing political beliefs. Lord Thankerton indicated that the nemo iudex rule has no application to this type of 'political decision':

> My Lords, I could wish that the use of the word 'bias' should be confined to its proper sphere. Its proper significance, in my opinion, is to denote a departure from the standard of even handed justice which the law requires from those who occupy judicial . . . or quasi-judicial office . . . [167]

Personal financial interests will however be just as unacceptable in this context as in respect of judicial decisions. This is clearly illustrated by *R v Hendon RDC, ex p Chorley*,[168] in which it was held that a suspicion of bias arose if a member of a council planning committee was an estate agent with a financial interest in a piece of land being considered for a grant of planning permission.

Conclusion

The concept of procedural fairness has generated a vast body of case law in the modern era, and will no doubt continue to do so in future. But the law on this point, even when seen in conjunction with the law relating to the traditional substantive grounds on which government action can be held unlawful, offers only a partial picture of the way in which administrative law fits into the broader constitutional principles of the rule of law and the sovereignty of Parliament. Chapters fifteen and sixteen add to that picture by exploring two vital, related issues: which legal procedures must an applicant follow when challenging a government decision; and who is entitled to initiate legal proceedings?

Suggested further reading

Academic and political commentary

REICH C (1964) 'The new property' *Yale LJ* 733

CLARK D (1975) 'Natural justice: substance or shadow' *Public Law* 27

FORSYTH C (1988) 'The provenance and protection of legitimate expectations' *Cambridge LJ* 238

CRAIG P (1994) 'The common law, reasons and administrative justice' *Cambridge LJ* 282

MALLESON K (2000) 'Judicial bias and disqualification after *Pinochet (No 2)*' *MLR* 119

Case law and legislation

Ridge v Baldwin [1964] AC 40

R v North and East Devon Health Authority, ex p Coughlan [2001] QB 13

Re HK [1967] 2 QB 617

Schmidt v Secretary of State for Home Affairs [1969] 2 Ch 149

R v Gough [1993] AC 646

Porter v Magill [2002] 2 AC 357

R v Liverpool Corpn, ex p Liverpool Taxi Fleet Operators' Association [1972] 2 QB 299

R v East Sussex County Council, ex p Reprotech Ltd [2002] UKHL 8; [2003] 1 WLR 348

---

[166] [1948] AC 87, HL.   [167] Ibid, at 92, HL.   [168] [1933] 2 KB 696.

Chapter 15

Challenging Governmental Decisions: The Process

Questions as to the legal process which should be followed by claimants challenging the lawfulness of governmental decisions have assumed heightened importance within English administrative law since 1977. This trend was triggered by a 1997 modification to the Rules of the Supreme Court, which was given statutory form in the Supreme Court Act 1981.[1] The reform introduced a procedural device called the 'application for judicial review' (hereafter referred to as AJR). The terminology can cause confusion, as a substantial part of constitutional and administrative law litigation—which in its entirety is often referred to loosely as 'judicial review'—was not initiated through the AJR process or its immediate predecessors.

The starting point for analysing this subject is the historical duality within English administrative law of the mechanisms through which citizens might question the lawfulness of government action. This duality might be categorised as one between 'private law' and 'public law' remedies. Legal actions against government bodies might often take exactly the same procedural form as actions against private individuals. *Entick v Carrington*, for example, was technically an action for trespass—that is a private law tort—even though its real concern was to establish the lawfulness of the government's claimed power to suppress sedition through the use of general warrants. Similarly, *Liversidge v Anderson*, an action for unlawful imprisonment, was nominally a private law action (as was *habeas corpus*), even though the real concern was to ascertain the meaning of the government's powers under reg 18B. Equally, the question of whether a government body's actions were illegal, irrational, or procedurally unfair might arise in an action for breach of contract or restitution. In addition, the private law stream contained the remedies of declaration or injunction; (the former designed to 'declare' the law on a particular point, the latter being a coercive order requiring a defendant to cease a particular course of behaviour). These remedies might be sought through procedural devices known as a 'writ' or 'originating summons'.

---

[1] Now re-named as the Senior Courts Act 1981.

The 'public law' stream contained the three so-called 'prerogative remedies' of certiorari, prohibition, and mandamus. Certiorari was a device to quash (or invalidate) unlawful decisions; prohibition had the same effect as the injunction; and mandamus was intended to force a government body to exercise its legal powers when it was refusing to do so.

The private and public law streams had developed for different reasons, and had different characteristics. The declaration and injunction were initially designed solely to regulate disputes between private individuals. (This is evidenced quite clearly in the way such cases are styled; eg *Anisminic v Foreign Compensation Commission*.) The actions took for granted firstly that litigants would have a direct interest in the dispute, and secondly that trivial or vexatious litigation would rarely occur. The development of the private law remedies was informed by two central assumptions. Firstly, that the court's role would often be as finder of both fact and law; that is, to determine the precise merits of a particular issue. Secondly, because the action was designed to resolve disputes between 'individuals', the efficient administration of government would rarely be compromised by such litigation.[2]

The prerogative remedies, in contrast, developed to ensure that all government bodies remained within the limits of their lawful powers; individual litigants here were theoretically acting on the Monarch's behalf to establish if the law had been breached.[3] Had *Anisminic* been an action for certiorari, it would have been styled *R v Foreign Compensation Commission, ex p Anisminic*. One obvious consequence of this is that the prerogative remedies were traditionally assumed not to be available against the Crown, on the basis that the Crown could not bring legal proceedings against itself.[4] The development of the remedies also rested on the presumptions firstly that the court's role would generally be simply to establish if an obviously unlawful decision had occurred (ie it would not be looking closely at questions of fact nor reaching any conclusion as to the detailed merits of the governmental decision in issue); and secondly that all prerogative remedy applications would necessarily have implications for the efficient administration of government.

To put the matter crudely, remedies in the private law stream—whether the remedy sought be an action in breach of contract or in tort or an attempt to seek a declaration or injunction through the writ or originating summons route—offered applicants several substantial procedural advantages compared to the prerogative remedies.

Firstly, the private law stream had much longer time limits than the prerogative remedies. Time limits for the declaration or injunction could be as long as six years, while for the prerogative remedies they were generally limited to six months. This difference could obviously be vital if evidence of unlawful government action did not come to light until a year or more after the decision in issue was made. If a six-month limit was enforced, the lawfulness of such decisions could not be assessed, a consequence which would obviously compromise purist understandings of the rule of law. On the other hand, the short time limits for the prerogative remedies served an obvious purpose. Once the limit had expired, a government body could be sure that its decisions could not be quashed by the courts, a factor which might be of great significance to activities such as land or property development.

Secondly, the prerogative remedies required that the applicant be granted 'leave' to proceed by the court before a full hearing was initiated. Leave was a filter mechanism intended to

---

[2] The one—major—caveat to this point being that the Crown was regarded as an 'individual' for the purposes of a declaration. It was not possible until the enactment of the Crown Proceedings Act 1947 to sue the Crown de jure in contract or tort. Instead, litigants proceeded through the arcane device of a 'petition of right', in which a nominated official would stand as a defendant, and the Crown would underwrite the official's liability; see the first edition of this book at pp 98–99.

[3] See the reference to *Baggs' Case* at 'III. Judicial regulation of government behaviour: the constitutional rationale', ch 3, p 53.

[4] They would however be available against Ministers if the Minister was exercising a statutory power given to the Minister in her personal capacity, rather than to the Crown per se.

protect government bodies (and indeed the courts themselves) from having to spend large amounts of time dealing with hopeless or mischievous cases. If the court took the view—on a brief perusal of the applicant's case—that the claim was wholly unmeritorious, leave would be refused, and no time need be spent on assessing the details of the claim. The application for leave, which placed the burden of proof on the plaintiff, was not required for a private law action. Unmeritorious claims could only be struck out at the instigation of the defendant.

Thirdly, the private law remedies came with a strong presumption that extensive discovery of documents and cross-examination of witnesses would be permitted. This was an obvious consequence of the assumption that private law remedies dealt with matters of fact as well as of law, and would often be concerned with imposing a detailed solution on the merits. Discovery and cross-examination were, in contrast, not widely available within the public law stream, as the prerogative remedies had not been designed as fact-finding mechanisms. Clearly, if a government body's allegedly unlawful activity was 'hidden' in its papers or the minds of its officers, the private law stream would have been far more useful to an applicant. Additionally, it was possible to combine declaratory or injunctive relief with damages, which were not available with the prerogative remedies.

Simply put, if the allegedly unlawful nature of the government body's decision was not immediately apparent, a plaintiff was much more likely to win if she could proceed by the declaration or injunction rather than a prerogative remedy. In more theoretical terms, this public/private dichotomy can readily be presented as raising a rule of law issue. The more widely that private law procedures were available to applicants, the more rigorously the decisions of government bodies would be examined by courts.

It is important to stress the significance of the linkage between what might ostensibly seem to be 'mere' matters of procedure within administrative law and the grounds of review themselves. There would be little point in having, for example, rules against unlawful delegation of power, or the fettering of discretion, or rules requiring fair procedures, if strict time limits prevented many decisions from being challenged, or if restrictive provisions as to discovery and cross examination meant that vital information needed to prove that such actions had occurred could not be obtained.[5]

There were nonetheless disadvantages to the declaration and injunction. They were accepted as remedies available only at the court's discretion, not as of right. A court might conclude that an application was made too late, or that discovery and cross-examination were not appropriate. Or it might even hold that a claim was well-founded but then refuse to grant relief. Furthermore, it was traditionally held (a tradition lasting until *Factortame (No 2)*) that injunctions were not available against the Crown. This placed a substantial portion of central government beyond the reach of the injunction, although it was never wholly clear exactly which parts of central government should be regarded as 'the Crown' for these purposes.[6] Both the declaration and injunction were also subject to restrictive tests of 'locus standi' or 'standing'. We consider this issue in chapter sixteen: here we might simply note that it was appreciably more difficult for many applicants to convince the courts that they had locus standi for a declaration or injunction than for the public law remedies. And if an applicant lacked standing (ie was not permitted to 'stand' before the court and argue her case), she could not pursue her action at all.

---

[5] To frame the matter in crude theoretical terms, the private law route offers a 'red light' approach to controlling government action, while the public law route is notably more 'green light'; see "Red light" and "green light" theories', ch 3, pp 52–53.

[6] In *Nireaha Tamaki v Baker* [1901] AC 561, the Privy Council had held that an injunction could lie against a Minister acting in a personal capacity, but not against a Minister acting in an official capacity, when she was in theory the Crown itself. As noted earlier, this was also an issue in respect of the scope of the prerogative remedies, since the Crown could not act against itself. The Crown could however in theory act against central government bodies which were not part of the Crown.

The detailed history of the inter-relationship between the public and private law streams of administrative law is too complex a matter to be addressed here. For our limited purposes, it suffices to say that in the first half of the twentieth century the courts appeared reluctant to permit the declaration and injunction to be widely used as a means to challenge the exercise of governmental powers. Insofar as challenges were permitted, they were steered primarily through the public law route.[7] In effect, this amounted to the courts favouring a diluted version of the rule of law.

The turning point? *Barnard v National Dock Labour Board*

The applicant in *Barnard v National Dock Labour Board*[8] was a dock worker suspended from his job. The power to suspend workers had been given by Parliament to the NDLB. The applicant suspected that, as a matter of routine, this power had been unlawfully delegated to the port manager.[9] There was however no way of establishing this from the notice of suspension. Proof could only be gathered through having discovery of the NDLB's documents and/or by cross-examining its members. Barnard therefore sought a declaration; certiorari would have been a useless remedy. Rather oddly, the defendant made such documents available on receipt of the writ, instead of arguing immediately that the declaration was an inappropriate remedy. The unlawful delegation was thereby revealed. It was not until the case came to court that the NDLB sought to have the action struck out on procedural grounds.

Given that the Court knew that the NDLB's action had been substantively unlawful in this case, the striking out motion was unlikely to succeed. The rationale informing the judgment was well put by Denning LJ:

> If the tribunal does not observe the law, what is to be done? The remedy by certiorari is hedged round by limitations and may not be available. Why, then, should not the court intervene by declaration and injunction? If it cannot so intervene, it would mean that the tribunal could disregard the law . . . In certiorari there is no discovery, whereas in an action for a declaration there is. The plaintiffs only discovered the true position shortly before the trial, about two and a half years after the suspension. That shows that, but for these proceedings, the truth would never have been known.[10]

Whether the Court would have been so ready to lift any procedural barriers to Mr Barnard gaining a substantively just result if he had come to court only with a strong suspicion that unlawful delegation had occurred is open to question. The case is nonetheless of crucial significance in illustrating the intimacy of the linkage between matters of 'mere' procedure and the substantive reach of administrative law. Had the Court held that certiorari was the appropriate remedy, the result would have been that both the rule of law and the sovereignty of Parliament (in their orthodox senses) would have been compromised. In broad terms, *Barnard* can be seen as heralding a shift in the courts' attitudes both towards government bodies (ie being more willing to subject executive action to scrutiny) and towards the citizen (ie being more willing to protect individual interests against government encroachment). In broader terms, it endorsed a more purist understanding of the rule of law.

The *Barnard* rationale was reinforced by the 1959 decision in *Pyx Granite Co Ltd v Ministry of Housing and Local Government*.[11] The applicant was challenging the lawfulness of conditions attached to planning permission. It was out of time to proceed by certiorari, and so sought a declaration. The MHLG argued that certiorari was an exclusive remedy in these

---

[7] As noted in ch 14, this was also the period in which the courts frequently took the view that the rules of natural justice did not apply to 'administrative' decisions, or those affecting 'privileges' rather than 'rights'.

[8] [1953] 2 QB 18, CA.   [9] See 'Unlawful delegation of powers', ch 13, pp 361–364.

[10] [1953] 2 QB 18 at 41, CA.   [11] [1960] AC 260, HL.

circumstances. The Court rejected the contention that the public law route should be the only means through which a plaintiff might challenge the lawfulness of decisions of this sort:

> I know of no authority for saying that if an order or decision can be attacked by certiorari the court is debarred from granting a declaration in the appropriate case. The remedies are not mutually exclusive, though no doubt there are some orders, notably convictions before justices, where the only appropriate remedy is certiorari.[12]

This judicial initiative was reinforced in a political sense by the report of the Franks Committee in the mid-1950s following the Crichel Down episode.[13] Franks had urged that a more judicialised approach be taken to the administrative decision-making processes. This created a climate of opinion which regarded government with suspicion, thereby legitimising more extensive court intervention through relaxing procedural barriers to effective redress. Many of the seminal administrative law decisions of the 1960s and 1970s would not have happened without the procedural innovation accepted in *Barnard*. *Anisminic* is perhaps the best example, but we might also recall that both *Ridge v Baldwin* and *Padfield* were initiated through private law rather than public law procedures. In the early 1960s, there was, Craig suggests, a presumption that: 'The declaration was meant . . . to be the shining white charger cutting through outmoded limitations encrusted upon the pick and shovel prerogative orders'.[14] That this did not in fact happen seems to be due largely to the restrictive standing tests applied to the declaration.[15] The result was that by the early-1970s English administrative law, notwithstanding the large strides being made respecting the grounds of judicial review that might be invoked to challenge government action, was riven with a profound ambiguity on matters of legal process; an ambiguity which might sometimes mean that entirely meritorious cases were never properly argued in court.

The Order 53 reforms

The Law Commission addressed this conceptual confusion in 1971. Its first proposal was that English administrative law should recognise an entirely separate procedural system for public law matters, akin in some senses to the rigid divide between public and private law in France. This proposal attracted substantial criticism, on the grounds that the Law Commission had not satisfactorily defined what was meant by 'public law', that the proposal was not compatible with the English legal tradition, and that an exclusive public law system—if modelled on the existing prerogative remedies—might substantially weaken the courts' capacity to subject government decision-making to effective scrutiny.

The reforms the Commission proposed in 1976 were nominally simpler.[16] They envisaged a dual procedure in which the declaration and injunction would be available either through private law procedures (technically the 'writ' or 'originating summons') or, along with the prerogative remedies, through a new mechanism known as the 'application for judicial review' (AJR). Actions in contract or tort against governmental bodies would not be affected by the new procedure.

The Commission's proposals represented a balanced approach towards the supposedly competing concerns of protecting citizens against unlawful executive decision-making, and protecting lawful government decision-making from vexatious or frivolous applicants. It is certainly clear that the Law Commission did not intend the AJR to be an exclusive remedy; that is to say there would be some situations (although precisely which was unclear) where an

---

[12] Ibid, at 290; per Lord Goddard CJ.   [13] See 'Issues of competence', ch 9, pp 238–240.
[14] (1994) op cit p 549.   [15] Ibid; the issue is discussed in detail in ch 16.
[16] Law Commission (1976) *Report on remedies in administrative law*.

applicant would seem to have a choice of using either the AJR or the declaration or injunction through a writ or originating summons.

The reforms were initially implemented by an amendment to the Rules of the Supreme Court, which introduced a modified Order 53. The changes were subsequently given a statutory basis in s 31 of the Supreme Court Act 1981 (now the Senior Courts Act 1981).[17] The new Order 53 encompassed all the prerogative remedies and the declaration and injunction in a single procedural form.[18] The declaration and injunction could be granted in situations where any of the prerogative remedies are available, if having considered all the circumstances of the case in issue, the court considered it just and convenient to do so. The AJR retained the requirement of leave, and also introduced a strict time limit of three months. However, even within that period, an application could be ruled out of time if there had been undue delay. These two factors obviously indicated that the reform was intended to protect public bodies against tardy and vexatious claims. In contrast, r 8 seemed to relax the previously tight limits on the availability of discovery and cross-examination; these could now be granted at the court's discretion in respect of all five remedies. There was nothing explicit in the text of the new Order 53 to confirm that the declaration or injunction would no longer be available through the writ or originating summons procedure, although it was unclear what the relationship between the public and private law streams would be. Some hint was given by r 9(5), which empowered the court to transfer applications begun through the AJR to private law procedures, but did not permit movement in the other direction. This raised the possibility that some applicants could find that the substantive merits of their cases would not be heard simply because they chose the wrong procedure. Initially, however, it seemed that the courts might interpret Order 53 in a way that did not permit procedural technicalities to have such an important substantive effect.[19]

The initial Order 53 case law

The crucial issue to be resolved was whether the applicant had a choice between the private law and public law procedures. The policy implications of this issue are obvious. Giving applicants a choice would suggest that the courts are more concerned with protecting citizens' interests, and ensuring that the executive acts within legal limits, than with protecting government from scrutiny and thereby expediting administrative processes.

In *De Falco v Crawley Borough Council*,[20] Lord Denning's Court of Appeal evidently favoured that approach. The case concerned a council's decision under the homeless persons legislation (then the Housing (Homeless Persons) Act 1977). The challenge had been initiated as a breach of statutory duty action, in effect a private law action in tort. Lord Denning (while

---

[17] For the rest of this chapter, the term 'Order 53' is used to include the relevant provisions of s 31.

[18] Order 53 r 1 provided:

(1) An application for (*a*) an order of mandamus, prohibition or certiorari, or (*b*) an injunction under section 9 of the Administration of Justice (Miscellaneous Provisions) Act 1938 restraining a person from acting in any office in which he is not entitled to act, shall be made by way of an application for judicial review in accordance with the provisions of this Order.

(2) An application for a declaration or an injunction (not being an injunction mentioned in paragraph (1)(*b*)) may be made by way of an application for judicial review, and on such an application the Court may grant the declaration or injunction claimed if it considers that, having regard to (*a*) the nature of the matters in respect of which relief may be granted by way of an order of mandamus, prohibition or certiorari, (*b*) the nature of the persons and bodies against whom relief may be granted by way of such order, and (*c*) all the circumstances of the case, it would be just and convenient for the declaration or injunction to be granted on an application for judicial review.

[19] Some more prosaic reforms were introduced in an attempt to speed up the judicial process in administrative law cases. From 1981 onwards, a single judge (rather than the previous three) would hear both leave applications and inter partes hearings, and a more concerted attempt was made to ensure that the High Court contained a de facto 'administrative division'; see Blom-Cooper L (1982) 'The new face of judicial review: administrative changes in Order 53' *Public Law* 250.   [20] [1980] QB 460, CA.

finding for the council on the merits) rejected the council's suggestion that Order 53 was now the sole route for applicants to question decisions under the 1977 Act:

> [T]he Housing (Homeless Persons) Act 1977, contained nothing about remedies . . . It has been held by this court that, if the council fails to provide accommodation as required by s 3(4), the applicant can claim damages in the county court: see *Thornton v Kirklees Metropolitan Borough Council* [1979] 2 All ER 349, [1979] QB 626. I am very ready to follow that decision and indeed to carry it further, because this is a statute which is passed for the protection of private persons, in their capacity as private persons. It is not passed for the benefit of the public at large . . . No doubt such a person could, at his option, bring proceedings for judicial review under the new RSC Ord 53 . . . So the applicant has an option.[21]

Lord Denning's advocacy of a procedural choice for applicants challenging homelessness decisions might be contrasted with Goulding J's judgment in *Heywood v Board of Visitors of Hull Prison*.[22] Heywood, like Mr St Germain,[23] had been involved in the Hull prison riots, and had subsequently been punished by the Board of Visitors by loss of remission. He had sought a declaration through a writ. The Board argued that he must use Order 53. If so, he would be time barred, and the litigation would never reach the merits of his claim. Goulding J supported this argument:

> [I]t is obviously undesirable that the plaintiff should seek relief by action rather than by application for judicial review . . .
> There are very good reasons (among them an economy of public time and the avoidance of injustice to persons whom it is desired to make respondents) for that requirement of preliminary leave. If an action commenced by writ or originating summons is used instead of the machinery of Ord 53, that requirement of leave is circumvented.[24]

Goulding J was particularly concerned that what he considered (evidently notwithstanding Order 53, r 8) the much more generous rules relating to discovery and cross-examination available through the private law route would have an undesirable impact on the board's decision-making:

> [T]he machinery of an action as to discovery and giving of evidence may result in placing members of the tribunal concerned in a position not really compatible with the free and proper discharge of their public functions, or at least result in attempts to put them in that position . . . [25]

Goulding J distinguished *De Falco*, on the basis that the homelessness legislation was designed to create individual rights (ie it raised a *private law issue*), while the prison system is run for the public interest (ie it raised a *public law issue*). There is no express indication in the text of Order 53 that such a distinction should be drawn. Nor, one might add, that it should not. *De Falco* and *Heywood* thus seemed to present quite divergent, policy-driven interpretations of the reforms.

The twin issues of homelessness and prison discipline continued to lend an aura of uncertainty to the impact of Order 53. In *Parr v Wyre Borough Council*,[26] another homelessness case, Lord Denning's Court of Appeal again implied that applicants should have a choice of procedure, although here the suggestion was that an Order 53 action could sometimes prove more effective, and considerably quicker, than a county court claim. However, Lord Denning then (without proper explanation) appeared to conclude that his approach in *De Falco* and *Parr* had been misconceived. In *Lambert v Ealing London Borough Council*,[27] he indicated that the AJR should be an exclusive remedy in homelessness cases. This ambiguity then appeared equally starkly in respect of prison disciplinary proceedings.

---

[21] Ibid, at 468.   [22] [1980] 1 WLR 1386.   [23] See 'Procedural not substantive protection?', ch 14, p 393.
[24] [1980] 1 WLR 1386 at 1390.   [25] Ibid, at 1390–1391.   [26] (1982) 2 HLR 71, CA.
[27] [1982] 1 WLR 550, CA.

I. *O'Reilly v Mackman* (1982)

O'Reilly v Mackman[28] was another case emerging from the aftermath of the Hull Prison riots. The action was not begun until some three years after the impugned decision (here the imposition of a loss of remission by the Board of Visitors) was made. The applicants were time-barred from proceeding via Order 53. Additionally, they claimed that their action would require extensive discovery and cross-examination, which rendered it more suitable to proceed in the private law rather than public law stream.

In the High Court, the Board invoked *Heywood* as authority for a rule that only the AJR could be used in such circumstances. To accept that argument would necessarily mean that Mr O'Reilly would have no effective remedy. Peter Pain J rejected the argument, and indicated that *Heywood* had been wrongly decided:

> The law offers the plaintiff a choice . . . It seems to me to be an abuse of language to say that the plaintiff is abusing the process of the court because he exercises the choice in the way he thinks best in his own interest.[29]

The 'rule of law' argument underpinning Peter Pain J's conclusion is well brought out by his observation that only express words in a statute could convince him that Order 53 was intended to operate as an 'exclusive' remedial route. This echoes Lord Denning's approach to the ouster clause in issue in *Gilmore*,[30] and emphasises the point that a judicial decision to consign a case to a worthless procedure amounts de facto to the court ousting its own jurisdiction.

It is perhaps therefore ironic that Lord Denning sat in the Court of Appeal in *O'Reilly* that overturned Pain J's judgment. Building upon his rejection of *De Falco* in *Lambert*, Lord Denning (supported by Ackner and O'Connor LJJ) concluded that the availability of the AJR should preclude applicants resorting to the declaration through the private law stream, not only for challenges to homelessness decisions and those of prison Boards of Visitors, but for all governmental decisions. To allow private law actions:

> would open the door to great abuse. Nearly all these [applicants] are legally aided. If they were allowed to proceed by ordinary action, without leave, I can well see that the public authorities of this country would be harassed by all sorts of claims, long out of time, on the most flimsy grounds.[31]

Lord Denning MR observed that the Law Commission's insistence that its proposed reforms should not be an exclusive remedy 'does not appeal to me, at any rate so far as the remedy by action for a declaration is concerned'.[32] To allow such an action would be 'an abuse of process of the court'. Lord Denning seemed to assume that the purpose of the Order 53 reforms was to provide additional protection to government bodies by the requirement of leave, the limited availability of discovery, and the equally limited availability of cross-examination—which should be 'rarely allowed'.[33]

The Court of Appeal's judgment was upheld in the House of Lords, where Lord Diplock issued the sole judgment.[34] The crucial point on which the House rested its decision was that,

---

[28] [1983] 2 AC 237, CA and HL. For an extremely cogent analysis see McBride J (1983) 'The doctrine of exclusivity and judicial review' *Civil Justice Quarterly* 268.

[29] [1982] 3 All ER 680 at 688. He considered that a loss of remission was no less a 'private right' from the individual applicant's perspective than an entitlement to be rehoused.

[30] See 'Ouster clauses—*Gilmore* (1957) and *Anisminic* (1969)', ch 3, pp 68–70.

[31] [1983] 2 AC 237 at 257–258.

[32] Ibid, at 254. It is not clear if Lord Denning intended to limit his argument solely to declarations. This passage supports that assumption, but he also expressly disapproved *Thornton*, a breach of statutory duty action.

[33] Ibid, at 256.   [34] Ibid.

for procedural purposes, a sharp distinction had to be drawn between matters of 'private law' and 'public law'. While Mr O'Reilly stood to spend more time than he had expected in prison if the Board's conclusion was not overturned, this did not amount to a private right. As Lord Diplock put it:

> It is not, and it could not be, contended that the decision of the board awarding him forfeiture of remission had infringed or threatened to infringe any right of the appellant derived from private law, whether a common law right or one created by a statute. Under the Prison Rules remission of sentence is not a matter of right but of indulgence . . . [35]

Lord Diplock acknowledged that before 1977, the prerogative remedies did not adequately protect applicants' interests, and it was therefore acceptable, and often indeed necessary, to allow an applicant to proceed by way of declaration or injunction. But, he continued:

> The position of applicants for judicial review has been drastically ameliorated by the new Ord 53. It has removed all those disadvantages, particularly in relation to discovery, that were manifestly unfair to them and had, in many cases, made applications for prerogative orders an inadequate remedy if justice was to be done . . . [36]

Since Order 53 had now removed these obstacles. Lord Diplock concluded that:

> Therefore it would in my view as a general rule be contrary to public policy, and as such an abuse of the process of the court, to permit a person seeking to establish that a decision of a public authority infringed rights to which he was entitled to protection under public law to proceed by way of an ordinary action and by this means to evade the provisions of Order 53 for the protection of such authorities.[37]

Lord Diplock's presumption that discovery and cross-examination would be much more readily available under the Order 53 procedure than they had been previously in respect of the prerogative writs could be little more than speculation, given the limited body of Order 53 litigation by then undertaken.[38] The integrity of *O'Reilly* would thus depend in large part on the way in which the High Court would respond to applicants' requests for discovery and cross-examination.

If Lord Diplock's presumption on this point was to prove correct, then the 'protection' that was being extended to public authorities via Order 53 was limited essentially to the matters of leave and of short time limits. As a policy choice, this conclusion is readily understandable. The rationale in respect of short time limits necessarily accepts that the arguably (or even obviously) unlawful actions of government bodies will go unremedied; but this (it can be argued) is a price worth paying if it means that government decisions acquire a veneer of legal certainty within a short time, and thereby enable policies to be pursued and decisions to be acted upon.

Whether that price was worth paying in Mr O'Reilly's case might give us pause for thought. The outcome of the case is that we simply do not know if the Board acted lawfully in revoking his remission; his argument on the merits was never made because he failed to surmount a procedural obstacle. He had undoubtedly come very late to court—some three years after the Board of Visitors' decision. The delay was however readily explicable. The legal rule that Boards of Visitors were subject to the rules of natural justice had only been established in 1979—by Mr St Germain, one of Mr O'Reilly's fellow rioters.[39] O'Reilly himself (and Mr Heywood) could

---

[35] Ibid, at 275. As noted earlier, Peter Pain J had concluded that O'Reilly was raising an issue of private rights.

[36] Ibid, at 285.   [37] Ibid.

[38] The case law then decided offered little support for Lord Diplock's view; see *George v Secretary of State for the Environment* (1979) 38 P & CR 609, CA, and *Air Canada v Secretary of State for Trade (No 2)* [1983] 2 AC 394, HL. Both cases indicate that discovery should only be granted sparingly under Order 53, and *Air Canada* intimates that it should only be granted in exceptional cases.

[39] See 'Procedural not substantive protection?', ch 14, p 393.

not have known that he had any legal remedy available until *St Germain* had run its course. To deprive a plaintiff in this situation of a remedy seems, in terms of substantive justice, a harsh decision for the court to reach; a point which perhaps explains Peter Pain J's judgment at first instance. Order 53 did leave the courts a residual discretion to extend the three-month time limit; but it would seem that a generous approach to that issue would undermine the 'protection' that Lord Diplock assumed the legal reforms were intended to introduce.[40]

Lord Diplock took some considerable care to root his 'exclusivity principle' in parliamentary intent, rather than—as Lord Denning had done—to present it as a judicial choice. This is perhaps because the House of Lords did not wish to take full responsibility for a procedural initiative which might increase the likelihood that unlawful government action would go unchecked.

Exceptions to the general principle?

Lord Diplock's 'exclusivity principle' was not however to be a principle of universal application. It would, it seemed, apply only to 'public law' issues. There was an unfortunate lacuna in the judgment, in so far as Lord Diplock did not explain how—over the broad range of government activities—we might distinguish 'public law' and 'private law' matters for these purposes. Craig has argued that it is doubtful if we could find a convincing theoretical rationale for distinguishing between the two types of interest:

> statements that a public body must have a sufficiently 'public' element or must be exercising a public duty cannot function as anything other than conclusory labels for whatever we choose to pour into them: they cannot guide our reasoning in advance.[41]

Craig has suggested that there are three possible ways to construct a predictable distinction, but notes that all of them have flaws.[42] The first would focus on the *source* of the decision. If the defendant organisation was a government body we might safely assume that a public law issue arose. However, there are obvious problems in defining 'government'. This is a familiar problem in the context of the vertical direct effect of EC directives,[43] and would be no less difficult to resolve in the purely domestic sphere. Equally, it is perfectly clear that government bodies often engage in purely 'private' activities, such as making contracts or acting negligently. Should we assume that the defendant's identity would override the basis of its relationship with the applicant for procedural purposes?

A second approach might focus on the *nature* of the power. A decision would be a public law matter, irrespective of the identity of the defendant, if its content impacted significantly on the public interest. But it would not seem any easier to define the 'public interest' than to define 'government'.

A third, rather formalistic approach might equate 'public law' with the traditional scope of the prerogative remedies. But as Craig notes, the scope of these remedies has always been dynamic, and would therefore offer a rather unstable test.

The elusive nature of 'public law' can be seen as a major definitional fault line running through Lord Diplock's opinion in *O'Reilly*. Assuming we could identify the concept however, Lord Diplock also anticipated that even when a public law issue was raised, there would be two—and perhaps more—exceptions to the requirement that the AJR be invoked:

---

[40] Case law suggests that three months is a maximum; cases brought within that limit may be refused on grounds of delay; see eg *R v Stratford-on-Avon, ex p Jackson* [1985] 1 WLR 1319, CA; *Caswell v Dairy Produce Quota Tribunal for England and Wales* [1990] 2 AC 738, HL.   [41] (1989) op cit p 420.

[42] See Craig P (1997) 'Public law and control over private power', in Taggart M (ed) *The province of administrative law*.   [43] See 'V. Direct effect—the saga continues', at ch 11, pp 379–382 of the seventh edition.

My Lords, I have described this as a general rule; for, though it may normally be appropriate to apply it by the summary process of striking out the action, there may be exceptions, particularly where the invalidity of the decision arises as a collateral issue in a claim for infringement of a right of the plaintiff arising under private law, or where none of the parties objects to the adoption of the procedure by writ or originating summons. Whether there should be other exceptions should, in my view, at this stage in the development of procedural public law, be left to be decided on a case to case basis . . . [44]

II. The Post-*O'Reilly* case law

O'Reilly appeared to have created the clear split between public law and private law which the Law Commission had toyed with in the early-1970s, but then rejected in its 1976 report. The policy implications of *O'Reilly* were potentially profound; the case moved away from the Law Commission's advocacy of procedural choice towards a procedural regime apparently balanced in favour of protecting public bodies.

That *O'Reilly* should not be read in quite so draconian a fashion was hinted at by a subsequent House of Lords' judgment issued on the same day. In *Cocks v Thanet District Council*,[45] the Court arrived at the convoluted and essentially nonsensical proposition[46] that the homelessness legislation could be divided into 'private law' and 'public law' issues for procedural purposes. It also emphasised that most such decisions would fall within the AJR procedure.

The suggestion that *O'Reilly* and *Cocks* may have been underpinned by a judicial concern that government bodies were being subjected to too many challenges—especially in the fields of housing and immigration—was reinforced by the House of Lords' extraordinary 1985 decision in *Puhlhofer v Hillingdon London Borough Council*.[47] In *Puhlhofer*, the Court (per Lord Brightman) explicitly disapproved of the use of judicial review to challenge local authority decision-making towards homeless persons. Since *Cocks* had already restricted the availability of private law procedures in this area, *Puhlhofer* effectively placed homeless persons in a position of having virtually no effective protection against ultra vires decision-making. In effect, it seemed, the courts had read an ouster clause into the legislation.

Contemporary empirical evidence suggested that such judicial concerns were misplaced. Sunkin's innovative 1987 study found no evidence that government bodies were being, or ever had been, deluged by legal challenges.[48] In respect of the homelessness legislation, for example, Sunkin noted that local authorities had received some 219,000 applications in 1986. Some thirty-two of these decisions had led to an Order 53 application.

It was also evident, following the *GCHQ* decision, that there was an arguable inconsistency between the House of Lords' evident readiness to pull more types of governmental decision-making within the field of judicial supervision, and its unwillingness to allow challenges to be raised through the most effective procedural route. This possible tension perhaps underlay the House of Lords' clear statement in *Davy v Spelthorne Borough Council*[49] that an action for damages in negligence against a government body was not precluded by the availability of the Order 53 procedure. Describing the case as 'a sequel' to *O'Reilly*, Lord Fraser

---

[44] [1983] 2 AC 237 at 285.   [45] [1983] 2 AC 286, HL.

[46] See Loveland I (1993) 'An unappealing analysis of the public-private law divide: the case of the homelessness legislation' *Liverpool LR* 39.

[47] [1986] AC 484 HL. For a discussion see Loveland (1995) op cit pp 98–101.

[48] Sunkin M (1987) 'What is happening to applications for judicial review?' *MLR* 432; (1987) 'Myths of judicial review' *LAG Bulletin* (September) 8; (1991) 'The judicial review caseload' *Public Law* 490.

[49] [1984] AC 262, HL.

saw no grounds for thinking that the litigation was a 'public law' matter at all: 'The present proceedings, so far as they consist of a claim for damages, appear to me to be simply an ordinary action for tort. They do not raise any issue of public law as a live issue'.[50] More broadly, Lord Wilberforce appeared to caution counsel and judges against regarding the 'public-private divide' as an organising principle for procedural purposes:

> the expressions 'private law' and 'public law' have recently been imported into the law of England from countries which, unlike our own, have separate systems concerning public and private law. In this country they must be used with caution, for, typically, English law fastens, not upon principles, but upon remedies.[51]

In *Wandsworth London Borough Council v Winder*[52] the House of Lords offered a further exception to the *O'Reilly* principle. Wandsworth used the evidently broad discretion left to it by the Housing Act 1980 over the matter of council house rents[53] to raise rents by 50%. Mr Winder, a tenant refused to pay the entire increase, but paid his old rent plus an amount to cover inflation. A year later, the council began possession proceedings against Mr Winder in the county court—in effect an action for breach of contract.

Mr Winder then sought to raise the defence that the rent rise was irrational and thus void, with the result that he had not breached the terms of his lease. The council claimed that this was a public law issue, which could only be addressed via Order 53. The administrative consequences if Mr Winder was permitted to raise the defence and then win on the merits would have been profound; every rent that Wandsworth had collected for the past year might have been unlawful, money might have had to be returned to thousands of tenants, a new rent (with retrospective effect) would have to be set[54] and then collected. This would seem to be just the type of scenario against which Lord Diplock might have wished public bodies to be protected. Mr Winder could obviously have initiated Order 53 proceedings as soon as the rent increase was passed. However, the House of Lords held that *O'Reilly* did not prevent a public law matter being raised in private law proceedings in these circumstances. There appeared to be two reasons for this conclusion. The first was that Mr Winder was addressing a public law matter that impacted on his existing private legal right, that is, his tenancy. Secondly, perhaps more importantly, Mr Winder himself had not chosen the form of action. He was merely responding to the council's challenge to his legal right. In Lord Fraser's view:

> It would in my opinion be a very strange use of language to describe the respondent's behaviour in relation to this litigation as an abuse or misuse by him of the process of the court. He did not select the procedure to be adopted. He is merely seeking to defend proceedings brought against him by the appellants. In so doing he is seeking only to exercise the ordinary right of any individual to defend an action against him on the ground that he is not liable for the whole sum claimed by the plaintiff.[55]

---

[50] Ibid, at 273. Cf Lord Fraser's approval of Fox LJ's comment in the Court of Appeal (1983) 81 LGR 580 at 596: 'The claim, in my opinion, is concerned with the alleged infringement of the plaintiff's rights at common law. Those rights are not even peripheral to a public law claim. They are the essence of the entire claim so far as negligence is concerned'.   [51] [1984] AC 262 at 276, HL.

[52] [1985] AC 461.   [53] See 'V. Council housing', ch 10, pp 264–267.

[54] Which obviously would have required new legislation.

[55] [1985] AC 461 at 509. For a review of these cases, and a powerful analysis of the flaws in *O'Reilly*, see Forsyth C (1985) 'Beyond *O'Reilly v Mackman*: the foundations and nature of procedural exclusivity' *Cambridge LJ* 415. See also Beatson J (1987) '"Public" and "private" in English administrative law' *LQR* 34. For a critical analysis of Winder see Woolf H (1986) 'Public law—private law: why the divide?' *Public Law* 220. Mr Winder's argument as to the lawfulness of the rent increase was unsuccessful; see *Wandsworth LBC v Winder* (No.2) (1988) 20 HLR 400.

The flip side of the *O'Reilly* coin

As indicated in the *Pett* decisions discussed in chapter fourteen,[56] prior to the Order 53 reforms it appeared to be broadly accepted that the activities of bodies regulating sports industries could be challenged by private law proceedings. However in *Law v National Greyhound Racing Club Ltd*,[57] the NGRC argued that a trainer who alleged that there were procedural flaws in his suspension following a dog-doping accusation should have to proceed through the AJR. The NGRC argued in effect that it performed a 'governmental function' in regulating the greyhound racing industry; that is, that the activity was so important that 'but for' the existence of the NGRC itself, the government would have to step in to perform this role. As such, the NGRC should benefit from the protections alluded to by Lord Diplock in *O'Reilly*.

While the Court of Appeal could readily see why the NGRC was making this argument,[58] it considered that the contention had little merit. Even if one could identify a 'public law' element in the NGRC's activities, the nature of the relationship between the Club and Mr Law was the quintessentially private law matter of a contract. In consequence, a private law procedure was the only suitable route for the applicant to take.[59]

In *Law* and the other cases discussed so far, the applicant has been seeking to gain access to the private rather than public law stream, on the basis that that stream is the most likely to lead her to her desired outcome. However, there are some situations in which an applicant might prefer to proceed through a public law mechanism while the government defendant wished to have her steered into a private law remedy.

Employment disputes are a primary example of this. The United Kingdom now has a substantial body of law (much of it EC generated) protecting employees against their employers. But it is only in very rare circumstances that these statutory provisions offer employees the remedy of 'specific performance'—namely that they are reinstated in their jobs. Certiorari would however have this effect; if the employee's dismissal was quashed and thus held to be void, she would never have been dismissed at all.

This concern underpinned the applicant's procedural choice in *R v BBC, ex p Lavelle*.[60] Ms Lavelle had been sacked from the BBC following allegations of theft. She argued that because the BBC was a publicly financed body, created by royal charter, its activities should all be regarded as raising a public law issue. Woolf J rejected this contention. Following *Law*, he concluded that Ms Lavell's dispute with the BBC was a pure master/servant question, which should be resolved through private law remedies.

A different approach was taken by Hodgson J in *R v East Berkshire Health Authority, ex p Walsh*, in which he had concluded that the political significance of the National Health Service in modern Britain was sufficiently pronounced to make the dismissal of NHS employees a 'public law' matter as well as a case of breach of contract.[61] This conclusion was promptly

---

[56] See 'The content of procedural fairness—legal representation and an obligation to give reasons for decisions', ch 14, pp 402–405.   [57] [1983] 1 WLR 1302, CA.

[58] Ibid, at 1311; per Slade LJ: '[I]t is easy to understand why the NGRC would prefer that any person who seeks to challenge the exercise of its disciplinary functions should be compelled to do so, if at all, by way of an application for judicial review. In this manner the NGRC would enjoy the benefit of what Lord Diplock in *O'Reilly v Mackman* described as "the safeguards imposed in the public interest . . . on the validity of decisions made by public authorities in the field of public law". Notwithstanding recent procedural changes, these safeguards are still real and substantial. Leave is required to bring proceedings . . . There is a time-bar of three months . . . The court retains firm control over discovery and cross-examination . . .'.

[59] Cf Lawton LJ, Ibid at 1307: 'In my judgment, such powers as the stewards had to suspend the plaintiff's licence were derived from a contract between him and the defendants . . . There was no public element in the jurisdiction itself . . . [T]he courts have always refused to use the orders of certiorari to review the decisions of domestic tribunals'.   [60] [1983] ICR 99.

[61] The judgment is reported, only at (1983) *The Times*, 15 November, and is discussed in the Court of Appeal's decision: [1984] ICR 743.

overturned in the Court of Appeal, on the basis that the existence of a contractual relationship precluded an action via Order 53.

Notwithstanding the fact that he had been overruled in *Walsh*, Hodgson J concluded in *R v Home Secretary, ex p Benwell*[62] that employment as a prison officer fell within the scope of Order 53. This conclusion seems readily defensible, since at that time (pre-*GCHQ*) it was assumed that prison officers did not have contracts. Unless the AJR was available to such applicants, there would be no means at all of assessing whether their employer had acted lawfully.[63]

A 'nature' not 'source' of power test—the *Datafin* (1987), *Aga Khan* (1993), *Servite Houses* (1999), and *Wachmann* (1993) decisions

The 'but for' argument that failed to sway the Court of Appeal in *Law* was made successfully in *R v Panel on Take-overs and Mergers, ex p Datafin*.[64] The Take-over Panel, created in 1968, was the body responsible for policing the ethics of merger and take-over activities in the United Kingdom. It was neither a statutory nor common law body, nor were any of its members government appointees. The Panel's members were representatives of major financial institutions, and applied a non-binding code of ethical practice to firms engaged in take-over or merger activities. Breach of the code did not entail legal sanctions, but would in effect lead to the blackballing of the firms concerned. The Panel effectively exercised monopolistic control over this area of economic activity. Datafin had complained to the Panel that it had been the victim of unethical practices by another firm. Its complaint was investigated but rejected. Datafin then sought judicial review of the Panel's decision.

The Panel argued that since it was de jure a non-governmental body, its decisions could not be challenged via Order 53. Since it did not have a contractual relationship with any of the firms it policed, there was no possibility of a breach of contract action being initiated. Nor did there seem to be any realistic prospect of Datafin being able to found an action in negligence against the Panel. If the Panel was not subject to challenge via Order 53, its activities would seemingly be wholly beyond judicial control.

Hodgson J had accepted this consequence at first instance. His judgment was then reversed in the Court of Appeal. Sir John Donaldson MR's leading judgment offered several reasons which, in combination, led him to the conclusion that the Panel was subject to judicial review.[65]

The first was that the quantitative significance of the Panel's activities—in contrast to that of the NGRC for example—was immense. The Panel dealt with issues involving hundreds of millions of pounds, and in so doing affected the financial interests of hundreds of thousands of shareholders. Secondly, it was clear that 'but for' the Panel, the government would have to take a central role in this field. The issue was simply too important to be left unregulated. Thirdly, it was already apparent that the Department of Trade played a significant background role underpinning the Panel's activities. Fourthly, since the Panel exercised monopolistic powers in this area, it would be inappropriate to suggest that Datafin had 'consented' to its supervision. Fifthly, as applicants would not have any plausible remedy in either contract or

---

[62] [1985] QB 554. The judgment contains a fierce criticism of the Court of Appeal's decision in *Walsh*.

[63] An excellent analysis is offered in Walsh B (1989) 'Judicial review of dismissal from employment: coherence or confusion?' *Public Law* 131. Subsequently, in *McClaren v Home Office* [1990] ICR 824, the Court of Appeal held that prison officers should be regarded as having an employment relationship with the government which, if not contractual in the narrow sense, was nonetheless sufficiently contractual to permit challenges to the Home Office's decisions through private law proceedings.　　[64] [1987] QB 815, CA.

[65] Datafin failed on the merits, on the basis that it was essentially asking the Court to exercise an appellate rather than supervisory jurisdiction over the Panel's decisions.

negligence, or through the somewhat esoteric action in unlawful restraint of trade, against the Panel, Order 53 provided the only means of legal control. Citing the celebrated judgment of Scrutton LJ in *Czarnikow v Roth Schmidt & Co*,[66] Sir John Donaldson reasoned that: ' . . . to exclude this safeguard for the administration of the law is contrary to public policy. There must be no Alsatia in England where the King's writ does not run'.[67] He then concluded that: '[I]t is really unthinkable that, in the absence of legislation such as affects trade unions, the panel should go on its way cocooned from the attention of the courts'.[68]

This conclusion seems wholly defensible. To have upheld Hodgson J's judgment would, in effect, have been to issue the government with an invitation to manouevre governmental behaviour beyond judicial supervision by transferring public functions to private sector bodies.[69] That outcome would have been difficult to reconcile with any meaningful notion of the rule of law.[70] The caveat that might however be attached to the *Datafin* judgment is that the facts of the case presented a substantial number (the five listed earlier) of factors which pointed firmly towards the conclusion that the Panel's activities should be subject to judicial review. In circumstances where some of those factors were not present, or were less significant in quantitative terms, it might transpire that the courts would feel compelled to accept that little outposts of 'Alsatia' could be found on our administrative law landscape.

The Jockey Club: a public or private body?

In terms of its financial significance, the Jockey Club lies somewhere between the NGRC and the Take-over Panel. Since 1970, when it was granted a Royal Charter, the Jockey Club's legal origins have lain in the prerogative. As such it had—unlike the NGRC and the Take-over Panel, a de jure 'governmental' source. Despite these distinctions, in *R v Jockey Club, ex p Massingberd-Mundy*,[71] the High Court considered that it was bound by the Court of Appeal's judgment in *Law* to the effect that anyone who had a contractual relationship with the Jockey Club (as in fact did everyone involved in the horse racing industry) should challenge its decisions through private law rather than public law procedures.

This analysis was upheld in *R v Disciplinary Committee of the Jockey Club, ex p Aga Khan*.[72] One of the Aga Khan's horses had 'won' the Oaks at Epsom in 1992. The horse was subsequently disqualified after traces of a prohibited substance were detected in its urine. A challenge to this decision through contract, even if successful, could not have given the Aga Khan the outcome that he desired—namely to have his horse reinstated as the winner of the race. Consequently, he attempted to proceed via Order 53 in order to have the disqualification quashed. His counsel marshalled several arguments to convince the Court that the AJR procedure was appropriate. Firstly, the Jockey Club's source in the prerogative lent it a governmental character. Secondly, it performed functions of such public importance that 'but for' its existence, an explicitly governmental body would have to take over its role. Thirdly, its role gave it monopolistic control over a major industry; anyone wishing to participate in the horse racing industry had to submit to its terms and conditions.

The Court of Appeal found these arguments unconvincing. At least in respect of applicants who had a contractual relationship with the Club, private law procedures were the appropriate mechanism to bring challenges. The Court did imply that the AJR procedure might be

---

[66] [1922] All ER Rep 45 at 50, CA.

[67] [1987] QB 815 at 827. 'Alsatias' being a colloquial name for the medieval areas known as 'sanctuaries', where criminals could shelter from the attentions of the criminal law.

[68] Ibid, at 839.

[69] See Forsyth C (1987) 'The scope of judicial review: "public duty" not source of power' *Public Law* 356.

[70] See the analysis by Murray Hunt; Hunt M (1997) 'Constitutionalism and the contractualisation of government', in Taggart M (ed) *The province of administrative law*. Hunt engages with the case law at a distinctly more abstract 'constitutional' level than much of the analytical literature.   [71] [1993] 2 All ER 207.

[72] [1993] 1 WLR 909.

available to applicants who did not have a contractual relationship with the Club, but declined to decide the point.[73]

'Private' actors and 'public' functions: the *Servite Houses* case (1997)

To observers on many points of the political spectrum, it might seem that there are few more quintessentially 'public' functions than the provision of residential nursing care to people who are unable to look after themselves. Responsibility for providing such care to certain types of people was placed on local authorities by s 21 of the National Assistance Act 1948, which was an important element of the Atlee government's programme of extending the reach of the welfare state. The enthusiasm of the Thatcher and Major administrations for privatisating of public welfare provisions led Parliament to amend the 1948 Act in 1993 (by inserting a new s 26) to permit local authorities to discharge their s 21 duties by making contractual arrangements with private sector care providers. The London Borough of Wandsworth embraced this reform with substantial vigour, and made contracts with—inter alia—a charity called Servite Houses to provide s 21 facilities.

The applicants in *R v Servite Houses and Wandsworth LBC, ex p Goldsmith and Chatting*[74] were elderly disabled women placed by Wandsworth in accommodation owned and managed by Servite. Servite had decided that the relevant care home (called Mary Court) was too expensive to continue to run, and in accordance with its contract with Wandsworth gave notice to terminate the arrangement. At the end of the notice period, all of the residents of Mary Court placed there by Wandsworth would have to leave. The applicants contended that Servite had promised them 'a home for life' in Mary Court. Neither applicant had a contractual relationship with Servite in which to root such a commitment, and so they sought to argue that Servite had generated a substantive legitimate expectation in the *Coughlan* sense[75] towards them. In order to succeed with that argument, however, the applicants first had to convince the Court that Servite was subject to the grounds of judicial review.

In a carefully reasoned judgment which showed particular awareness of the 'constitutional' implications of the 'privatisation' of governmental activities, Moses J concluded with evident reluctance on the basis of authorities such as *Datafin* and *Aga Khan* that Servite's decision could not be challenged by way of judicial review. The mere fact that Servite was contracting with a government body did not in itself lend Servite a governmental character for judicial review purposes. Nor could Moses J discern any provisions in the amended Act which gave a sufficient degree of 'statutory underpinning' to Servite's activities:

> In those circumstances, it seems to me wrong for a court of first instance to identify Servite's function as a public function absent any of the features upon which courts have in the past relied. That is not to say that a fresh approach ought not to be adopted so that the court can meet the needs of the public faced with the increasing privatisation of what were hitherto public law functions. But any advance can, in my judgment, only be made by those courts which have the power to reject the previous approach enshrined in past authority. I conclude that Servite was not exercising a public function.[76]

---

[73] For comment see Bamforth N (1993) 'The scope of judicial review: still uncertain' *Public Law* 239. See eg the factual situation raised in *R v Jockey Club, ex p RAM Racecourses Ltd* [1993] 2 All ER 225. See also *R v Football Association, ex p Football League* [1993] 2 All ER 833, in which the High Court rejected the argument that the FA's activities could be subject to judicial review. This may be largely attributable to the existence of a contractual relationship between the League and the FA. Perhaps surprisingly however, given the economic significance of soccer in this country, the Court also held that the 'but for' argument did not assist the League. Rose J suggested that if the FA did not exist, the regulation of football would more likely be undertaken by companies in the entertainment industry rather than by government.

[74] (2001) 33 HLR 35. For further comment see Handy C (2001) 'Housing associations: public or private law revisited' *Journal of Housing Law* 11.

[75] See 'A substantive legitimate expectation by another name?', ch 14, pp 400–401.

[76] (2001) 33 HLR 35 at para 93.

Servite offers a powerful illustration of the intimate linkage between the grounds of review and the mechanisms through which those grounds can be invoked; or in more grandiose terms, between the substance-based and process-based dimensions of the rule of law. *Coughlan* marked a notable advance in terms of the entitlement that individuals could successfully assert against government bodies. But in the context of s 21 residential provision, the significance of the *Coughlan* principle of a substantive legitimate expectation would be much reduced if s 21 accommodation were to be contracted out by a local authority. Any representation as to 'a home for life' (or indeed any lesser period) in a given facility made by the private sector provider would not create a substantive legitimate expectation because the provider would not be subject to judicial review, and any such representation made by the relevant local authority would likely be worthless as it is not credible to assume that any private sector provider would contract with a council to honour any representations that the authority might make to individual residents.

While the ratio of *Servite* would be limited to s 21 provision, the reasoning that underlies the judgment might be thought to offer an unhappy incentive to governmental bodies to privatise any and all of their service provision whenever Parliament has permitted them to do so. For that reason, it is perhaps unfortunate that *Servite* was not appealed so that the 'fresh approach' alluded to by Moses J might have been adopted by the Court of Appeal.

The relevance of justiciability

The High Court was presented with a rather different problem in *R v Chief Rabbi of the United Hebrew Congregations of Great Britain and the Commonwealth, ex p Wachmann*.[77] Wachmann was a rabbi who had been suspended by the Chief Rabbi following complaints about Wachmann's alleged professional misconduct. The Chief Rabbi's conclusion in effect made Wachmann unemployable as a rabbi. Wachmann did not have a contractual relationship with the Chief Rabbi, so the only possible means of legal challenge (Wachmann claimed bias and procedural irregularities in the Chief Rabbi's decision) would be the AJR. The Court held that Mr Wachmann was not raising a public law issue, although Simon Brown J's judgment rather suggests that he felt Mr Wachmann was not even raising a justiciable issue:

> [T]he court is hardly in a position to regulate what is essentially a religious function—the determination whether someone is morally and religiously fit to carry out the spiritual and pastoral duties of his office. The court must inevitably be wary of entering so self-evidently sensitive an area . . . [T]o entertain this challenge would involve a clear departure from and extension of the principles established by the *Datafin* case.[78]

III. Retreating from *O'Reilly*? The *Roy* case

The applicant in *Roy v Kensington and Chelsea and Westminster Family Practitioner Committee*[79] was a general medical practitioner working in the National Health Service. NHS general practitioners have a statutory entitlement to a scale of fees based on a statutory formula. However, Family Practitioner Committees could withhold a portion of those fees if they considered a practitioner had failed to carry out his/her duties adequately. The dispute in *Roy's* case arose when the FPC withheld part of his fee. Roy challenged the decision by seeking a declaration

---

[77] [1992] 1 WLR 1036.   [78] Ibid, at 1042–1043.
[79] [1992] 1 AC 624. For contemporaneous comment see Cane P (1992) 'Private rights and public procedure' *Public Law* 193.

via a writ. The FPC's initial response was that since its relationship with Dr Roy was not contractual, he was raising a purely public law issue and could thus proceed only via Order 53.

Lord Lowry's judgment for a unanimous House of Lords indicated that *O'Reilly*, if not misconceived per se, had certainly been lent an inappropriate interpretation in subsequent years.
Lord Lowry accepted counsel's suggestion that *O'Reilly* could be construed in two ways.[80] The
'broad view' of the case—which would reduce the scope of the exclusivity principle—was that
the AJR would be the sole remedy to be used only where there was no private law element at
all to the decision in issue. The 'narrow view'—which would extend the reach of the exclusivity
principle—was that the AJR would be the sole remedy whenever a public law issue is raised,
unless the case comes within the specified exceptions.

Lord Lowry observed that he instinctively preferred the 'broad view', an observation which
one assumes the House of Lords intended lower courts to follow in future. However, he managed to decide the case in Dr Roy's favour by adopting the 'narrow view'. He suggested that
there were three reasons for regarding Dr Roy's claim as an exception to the exclusivity principle. The first was that while Dr Roy's relationship with the FPC was not contractual in the
orthodox sense, it nonetheless had 'contractual echoes', in that Dr Roy was laying claim to
what Lord Lowry characterised as a 'private statutory' right. The second was that the private
right 'dominated' the public law issue in the case. The third reason was that the claim required
examination of a disputed issue of fact.

The second point is little more than a re-affirmation of the *Winder* principle. The first point
illustrates neatly the instability of the public or private right dichotomy offered in *O'Reilly*. The
scope of that case could be fundamentally altered without modifying the exclusivity principle
at all by the alternative mechanism of lending a 'private' character to previously 'public' rights.
That technique would of course simply displace rather than solve the dilemma that *O'Reilly*
throws up, and has the added disadvantage of exposing the courts to accusations that they are
engaging in a jurisprudential sleight of hand in order to evade, rather than overrule, an inconvenient principle.[81] The third point—the reference to disputes as to fact—is significant, for it
implies that the House of Lords did not envisage that discovery and cross-examination (which
would be vital if factual disputes were in issue) would be routine elements of AJR proceedings.

That supposition was echoed by Rose LJ in *R v Secretary of State for Foreign Affairs, ex
p World Development Movement Ltd*, in rejecting the WDM's request for access to detailed
minutes of the Foreign Secretary's deliberations on the Pergau dam aid grant:

> [It is] common ground that in judicial review proceedings general discovery is not available as it is
> in a writ action under Ord 24, rr 1 and 2, that an application can be made under Ord 24, r 3, which
> by virtue of Ord 24, r 8 will be refused if discovery is not necessary for disposing of the case fairly.[82]

Despite Lord Diplock's predictions to the contrary in *O'Reilly*, it appeared that this issue
remained of considerable importance over twenty years later.

It may however be that the most significant element of the *Roy* judgment is Lord Lowry's
clear intimation that the House of Lords was no longer as exercised by the prospect of applicants 'abusing the process of the court' as Lord Diplock and his colleagues had been:

> unless the procedure adopted is ill-suited to dispose of the question . . ., there is much to be said in
> favour of the proposition that a court having jurisdiction ought to let a case be heard rather than
> entertain a debate concerning the form of proceedings.[83]

This apparent reassertion of the courts' primary responsibility as being to establish if an applicant's claim is well-founded, rather than to be bogged down in arguments as to procedure, has

---

[80] Neither of which—unfortunately—was very clearly formulated.
[81] See also the discussion by Cane P (1992) op cit.   [82] [1995] 1 WLR 386 at 396.
[83] [1992] 1 AC 624 at 655.

obvious (if much less melodramatic) echoes of Lord Denning's judgment in *Barnard*.[84] But any hopes that *Roy* would lead the courts to clarify rather than complicate this area of the law were at least initially disappointed by the judgment in *Bugg v DPP*.[85]

IV. Public law principle as a defence in criminal proceedings

From the mid-1980s onwards, Mr Bugg made a considerable nuisance of himself to the Ministry of Defence. He was one of several anti-nuclear protesters who (updating Mr Chandler's preferred form of activism in the 1960s)[86] engaged in persistent incursion into MoD airbases. Such incursions nominally amounted to a breach of certain criminal bye-laws, produced by the MoD under statutory powers. Mr Bugg had taken great delight in frequently demonstrating that he and his colleagues had not breached the bye-laws or—the issue at stake in this case—that the bye-laws concerned were themselves ultra vires.

In *Bugg v DPP*,[87] Mr Bugg convinced the High Court that several MoD bye-laws under which he and his colleagues had been prosecuted were indeed invalid. However the case is most notable for its procedural implications. The prosecutions had taken place in a magistrates' court. When Mr Bugg had attempted to raise the alleged invalidity of the bye-laws as a defence, the prosecuting authorities—building on *O'Reilly*—had contended that this issue could only be addressed via an AJR. Mr Bugg would obviously have been long out of time to pursue this course. Unless he could raise the defence, the risk arose that he would be prosecuted, convicted, and sentenced in respect of a 'crime' which might lack any lawful basis.

In a most peculiar judgment, the High Court concluded that a defendant in such circumstances could plead the unlawful nature of the bye-law as a defence if that claim was rooted in either illegality or irrationality. However she could not do so if the claim lay in procedural impropriety. The Court did not contend that such a defence would amount to 'an abuse of process', so the case should not strictly be seen as an extension of *O'Reilly*. Rather Woolf LJ concluded that the criminal courts had no jurisdiction to enter such an inquiry and were not 'properly equipped to do so'.[88] The distinction was evidently drawn because illegality and irrationality would be obvious flaws, which would not require any examination of 'evidence', whereas procedural impropriety might well be identifiable only after extensive perusal of such evidence.

Quite what rationale underpinned this analysis is a mystery, as the distinction is nonsensical. A criminal court, concerned as it must be with detailed evaluation of evidence, is perfectly competent in the technical sense to consider factual allegations about procedural impropriety. If Woolf LJ's point was really intended to suggest that criminal courts lacked the expertise to apply principles of administrative law, two further problems arise. The first is that High Court judges who deal with administrative law litigation often sit as trial judges in criminal cases; their administrative law expertise presumably does not disappear when they do so. Secondly, while it is plausible to argue that a lay magistrate may lack the legal skills properly to apply the legal esoterica of the procedural impropriety jurisprudence, she would presumably be equally at sea when faced with a problem rooted for example in the rule against unlawful delegation, or the fettering of discretion, or whether irrelevant considerations had been taken into account. More obviously, it is readily apparent that procedural impropriety (in the form for example of bias or a complete failure to hold a hearing) could be discerned without any detailed evidential

---

[84] See also the judgment of the Court of Appeal in *Clark v University of Lincoln and Humberside* [2000] 1 WLR 1988.   [85] [1993] QB 473.

[86] See 'V. "Justiciability" revisited—are all statutory powers subject to full review?', ch 4, pp 99–100.

[87] [1993] QB 473.

[88] The form of words was perhaps inspired by Lord Lowry's closing comments in *Roy*.

questions being addressed, and that conversely (*Barnard* and *Anisminic* being prime examples) substantive illegality may be well hidden within the decision-making body.[89]

The judgment also represented a departure from recent[90] and more long-established authority. In the latter category, *DPP v Head*[91] is perhaps the most helpful case. Head was prosecuted under the Mental Deficiency Act 1915 s 56(1) for having sex with a person classified as 'mentally defective' under s 9 of that Act. At trial, it emerged that the victim of the 'crime' may not have been lawfully classified under s 9. If so, she was not 'a mental defective', and Head would not have committed the s 56 offence. Head obviously had not challenged the victim's classification (nor had anyone else) when it was made. Even under the more generous pre-1977 time limits, a certiorari action would have been time barred. In the view of the majority of the House of Lords, there was no room to doubt that Head should be able to rely on this defence:

> It is conceded that the court had material before it which would have led to the [classification] being quashed on certiorari or other appropriate proceedings. The next question, as it appears to me, can be stated in this way. Is a man to be sent to prison on the basis that an order is a good order when the court knows it would be set aside if proper proceedings were taken? I doubt it.[92]

The Court rejected the suggestion that any distinction could be drawn between different types of unlawful order for these purposes. As such the judgment is a forceful assertion of an expansive notion of the rule in respect of criminal liability. *Bugg* clearly compromised that principle.

Woolf LJ's reasoning in *Bugg* was questioned by the House of Lords in *R v Wicks*,[93] although the decision was not overruled. Mr Wicks had rebuilt his house in a manner which required planning permission without having troubled to seek it. He then refused to stop the rebuilding, and was eventually served by his council with an enforcement notice under s 172 of the Town and Country Planning Act 1990. He nonetheless continued building, even though non-compliance with an enforcement notice is a criminal offence. At the subsequent criminal trial—having unsuccessfully exercised a statutory right of appeal under the 1990 Act to the Secretary of State for the Environment—he attempted to argue that the enforcement notice was unlawful. The House of Lords accepted that the common law recognised a 'guiding principle' that a defendant should always be able to raise the alleged invalidity of a government measure which formed the root of a criminal prosecution. The substantial judgments delivered by Lords Hoffmann and Nicholls overtly cast doubt on the *Bugg* distinction. The Court was nonetheless prepared to conclude that Mr Wicks should not be able to raise this administrative law point in the criminal proceedings. The 'guiding principle' could be rebutted by considerations specific to the decision in issue. In this case, the provision of a statutory appeal against the enforcement notice in addition to a potential AJR proceeding afforded the defendant an adequate remedy, and the intensity of the public interest in having planning laws promptly enforced militated against permitting a challenge other than by way of Order 53.

The unworkable distinction introduced by *Bugg* was subsequently removed entirely by the House of Lords in *Boddington v British Transport Police*.[94] Boddington was an inveterate smoker, who took exception to the fact that the operator of his daily train into London had exercised powers under a bye-law wholly to forbid smoking on trains. Boddington decided to ignore the ban and, when subsequently prosecuted for so doing, sought to raise the alleged irrationality of the bye-law as his defence. Predictably, the BTP contended that a challenge

---

[89] See Feldman D (1993) 'Collateral challenge and judicial review: the boundary dispute continues' *Public Law* 37.

[90] *DPP v Hutchinson* [1990] 2 AC 783, HL; *Plymouth City Council v Quietlynn* [1988] QB 144.

[91] [1959] AC 83, HL.   [92] Ibid, at 687; per Lord Somervell.

[93] [1998] AC 92. See Bradley A (1997) 'Collateral challenge to enforcement decisions—a duty to apply for judicial review?' *Public Law* 365.

[94] [1999] 2 AC 143, HL. See Forsyth C (1999) 'Collateral challenge and the foundations of judicial review: orthodoxy vindicated and procedural exclusivity rejected' *Public Law* 364; Craig P (1998) 'Collateral attack, procedural exclusivity and judicial review' *LQR* 535.

of this sort could only be initiated under Order 53. The magistrate accepted this argument. Boddington was convicted and fined £10. He then appealed against his conviction to the High Court, claiming that he should have been permitted to raise the public law defence.

This view was rejected at first instance by Auld J, who appeared to extend the reach of *Bugg* by holding that a magistrate's court would not be competent to entertain any challenge to the validity of a bye-law or of delegated legislation in the course of criminal proceedings. To allow this to happen would, he suggested, cause chaos in the criminal courts.

The House of Lords reversed Auld J's judgment, and unanimously concluded that Boddington was entitled to raise the defence. Lord Steyn offered a carefully argued judgment which convincingly married detailed points of administrative law with broader questions of constitutional principle and condemned *Bugg* as 'contrary to authority and principle'.[95]

Lord Steyn (apparently adopting Lord Lowry's broad view of *O'Reilly*) observed that *O'Reilly's* exclusivity principle should be limited to 'situations in which an individual's sole aim was to challenge a public law act or decision'.[96] The principle did not apply when private rights were at stake, or when an individual was defending an action initiated by a government body. Lord Steyn also rejected the idea that Woolf LJ's distinction between procedurally and substantively unlawful decisions had a defensible base, either in pragmatic[97] or conceptual terms.[98]

In a more overtly constitutional vein, Lord Steyn observed that: 'the rule of law requires a clear distinction to be made between what is lawful and what is unlawful. The distinction put forward in *Bugg* undermines that axiom of constitutional principle'.[99] The constitutional consequences of *Bugg*, namely that a person might be convicted of a 'crime' which might be found not to exist if subject to legal challenge were 'too austere and indeed too authoritarian to be compatible with the traditions of the common law'.[100] This was not however to be an absolute rule. Rather it should be construed as an extremely strong presumption which could only be rebutted if the statutory scheme surrounding the decision in issue made it wholly clear that a departure from orthodoxy was warranted.

Lord Irvine's judgment is perhaps more effective in identifying the constitutional implications of the Order 53 litigation. In forceful terms, he concluded that Boddington had to be allowed to raise his defence: 'It would be a fundamental departure from the rule of law if an individual were liable to conviction for contravention of some rule which is itself liable to be set aside by a court as unlawful . . .'.[101]

Conclusion

To accept *Boddington* as (for the moment) the last word on Order 53 issues would be rather ill-advised. Notwithstanding the grand constitutional terms in which Lords Steyn and Irvine

[95] [1992] 2 AC 143 at 172.   [96] Ibid.

[97] 'An issue of substantive illegality may involve daunting issues of fact . . . In such a case, the issues of law may also be complex. In contrast, an issue of procedural invalidity of a bye-law may involve minimal evidence . . . And the question of law may be straight-forward': Ibid, at 169–170.

[98] 'There is also a formidable difficulty of categorisation created by *Bugg's* case. A distinction between substantive and procedural invalidity will often be difficult to draw . . . In *Wednesbury*, Lord Greene MR pointed out that different grounds of review 'run into one another': Ibid, at 170.   [99] Ibid, at 171.

[100] Ibid, at 173.

[101] Ibid, at 153. It would nonetheless seem that *Wicks* is still good law. Lord Irvine's judgment in *Boddington* drew a clear distinction in respect of governmental actions which precipitated criminal liability between bye-laws issued to the world at large (as in *Boddington*) and administrative decisions targeted at a specific individual (as in *Wicks*). In the latter scenario, the individual would have ample opportunity to impugn the lawfulness of the decision, whether by—as in Mr Wick's case—a statutory appeal and then an AJR application, or through an AJR alone. We might note, for the sake of completeness, that the House of Lords saw no merit in Boddington's irrationality defence, and upheld the conviction.

dressed their judgments in that case, *Boddington* deals only with a narrow area of the public law–private law divide. The case tells us little about the way in which procedural questions should be resolved when the action in issue is being instigated rather than defended by the individual citizen. It may be that we might apply the same constitutional logic found in *Boddington* to the broader *O'Reilly* issue, and find that it points us very strongly in the direction of (at least) adopting the 'broad view' of *O'Reilly* propounded by Lord Lowry in *Roy*.[102] But it would seem unlikely that this technique could plausibly take us as far as re-embracing the unhindered procedural duality apparently offered in *Barnard* and *Pyx Granite* and supported by the Law Commission in 1976.

In October 2000, various technical and linguistic changes were introduced to the application for judicial review procedure. Order 53 was replaced by what is now Part 54 of the Civil Procedure Rules. A 'claimant' (rather than a 'plaintiff') now makes a 'claim' (rather than an 'application') for judicial review. The names of the prerogative remedies were also altered: certiorari became a 'quashing order'; mandamus became a 'mandatory order'; and prohibition became a 'prohibitory order'. De jure recognition was also given to a state of affairs long existing de facto, namely that the High Court contained a specialist Administrative division. The style of citation of judicial review cases was also amended; from *R v Government Body, ex p Claimant* to *R (Claimant) v Government Body*. A 'pre-action protocol' for judicial review claims under Part 54 was also introduced within the Civil Procedure Rules. The protocol specifies a number of steps which parties ought to follow before commencing proceedings; the objectives being either to lead parties to resolve their dispute without the need for litigation or, if that is not possible, to clarify the issues that will have to be pursued before the court.

The object underlying the alterations was to simplify and expedite the conduct of litigation raising administrative law issues.[103] Whether the changes have that effect remains to be seen. What they are unlikely to do is finally resolve the conceptual difficulties generated by *O'Reilly v Mackman* and its progeny.[104]

Notwithstanding its intrinsic complexity, the Order 53/part 54 case law is of great importance in constitutional terms, since it lays out so clearly the extent to which our legal system's understanding of the rule of law and the sovereignty of Parliament are conditioned not so much by the content of judicially generated constraints on governmental behaviour, as by the issue of access to them within a procedural regime which enhances rather than restricts the likelihood that a claimant can prove her case. But the Order 53 debate forms only one element of this 'access to justice' question within our modern constitutional law. Of equal significance is the topic considered in chapter sixteen—the matter of locus standi.

Suggested further reading

Academic and political commentary

HUNT M (1997) 'Constitutionalism and the contractualisation of government', in TAGGART M (ed) *The province of administrative law*

MCBRIDE J (1983) 'The doctrine of exclusivity and judicial review' *Civil Justice Quarterly* 268

---

[102] See eg *Mercury Communications Ltd v Director General of Telecommunications* [1996] 1 WLR 48, HL. A caveat against this point is raised by a short line of cases addressing the inter-relationship between the AJR and *habeas corpus*. See in particular *R v Secretary of State for the Home Department, ex p Muboyayi* [1992] QB 244, CA, and the critique by Sir William Wade (1996) 'Habeas corpus and judicial review' *LQR* 55.

[103] See Fordham M (2001) 'Judicial review: the new rules' *Public Law* 4; Cornford T and Sumkin M (2001) 'The Bowman Report: access and the recent reforms of the judicial review procedure' *Public Law* 11.

[104] See Ingman T (2002) *The English legal process* pp 607–610.

HUNT M (1997) 'Constitutionalism and the contractualisation of government', in TAGGART M (ed) *The province of administrative law*

FORSYTH C (1985) 'Beyond *O'Reilly v Mackman*: the foundations and nature of procedural exclusivity' *Cambridge LJ* 415

CRAIG P (1997) 'Public law and control over private power' in TAGGART M (ed) *The province of administrative law*

BEATSON J (1987) '"Public" and "private" in English administrative law' *LQR* 34

WOOLF H (1986) 'Public law—private law: why the divide?' *Public Law* 220

BLOM-COOPER L (1982) 'The new face of judicial review: administrative changes in Order 53' *Public Law* 250

Case law and legislation

Barnard v National Dock Labour Board [1953] 2 QB 18

O'Reilly v Mackman [1983] 2 AC 237, HL

R v Panel on Take-overs and Mergers, ex p Datafin [1987] 1 All ER 564

DPP v Head [1959] AC 83

Boddington v British Transport Police [1999] 2 AC 143

Roy v Kensington and Chelsea and Westminster Family Practitioner Committee [1992] 1 AC 624

Wandsworth London Borough Council v Winder [1985] AC 461

R v Chief Rabbi of the United Hebrew Congregations of Great Britain and the Commonwealth, ex p Wachmann [1993] 2 All ER 249

Chapter 16

Locus Standi

One obvious question arising from discussion of the public/private divide that informed the procedural element of administrative law before 1977 is: 'Why would any applicant ever challenge government action through a prerogative remedy rather than seek a declaration or injunction via a writ or originating summons?' Pursuing a public law remedy would not seem a rational choice, since the applicant would be handicapped by short time limits, restrictive rules as to discovery of documents and cross-examination of witnesses, and the non-availability of damages.

The answer is in part offered by the historical intricacies of the ways in which the various remedies developed. Among the more significant of these esoterica was the principle—which survived until *Factortame*—that injunctions could not (generally) be issued against the Crown.[1] Declarations were available against the Crown, but as indicated by *Dyson v A-G* in 1911[2]—there remained uncertainty as to their exact scope. As noted in chapter fifteen, the reach of the various administrative law remedies has never been fixed,[3] and the possibility always existed that an applicant might persuade a court to step in hitherto untrodden directions. But notwithstanding such intricacies, an important influence on the form of remedy an applicant sought was provided by the law of locus standi (standing).

The division between public law and private remedies raises rule of law questions at a fairly sophisticated level. We saw in chapter three that one of the most obvious challenges to orthodox understandings of the rule of law is posed by Parliament's use of ouster clauses, which—unless imaginatively construed by the courts as in *Gilmore* and *Anisminic*—preclude applicants from arguing their cases at all. The rule of law issue raised in cases such as *O'Reilly* is more subtle. Mr O'Reilly was not de jure denied access to the courts to challenge the government body's decision. Rather he was directed down a procedural route which made it much less likely that he could win his case.[4] In rule of law terms, locus standi raises, like

---

[1] See Beatson and Matthews op cit ch 9. On the exceptions, see Wade H.R.W (6th edn, 1988) *Administrative law* pp 588–590.   [2] [1911] 1 KB 410, CA.

[3] See 'Exceptions to the general principle?', ch 15, pp 421–422.

[4] It might be suggested he was de facto so excluded, both because under the public law route he was out of time and—even if he had been within time—he could not have won his case without discovery of the Board's documents and cross-examination of its members.

ouster clauses, the question of whether the applicant can gain access to the courts at all. We might characterise the law on locus standi as asking: 'Who is allowed to stand before the court to challenge a government action?' If an applicant was not granted standing, she simply could not reach the question of whether the government action she was challenging was unlawful. This might mean that 'unlawful' government actions were not quashed, a consequence with obvious (and presumably adverse) implications for orthodox perceptions both of the rule of law and the sovereignty of Parliament.

This topic is intimately connected to the application for judicial review, both because of the present law's roots in Order 53 and the Senior Courts Act 1981, and because of the competing policy issues that it throws up. Those policy concerns are essentially threefold. How does administrative law balance the protection of individual citizens' interests with the desire to ensure that government decision-making remains within legal limits and with the concern to protect government bodies (including the courts) from vexatious litigants? The concept of locus standi is perhaps the most important way in which administrative law deals with this complex question.

The subject is best studied by a three-part chronological division. The first period addresses the law prior to the introduction of Order 53 in 1977. The second covers the short period between 1977 and the House of Lords' decision in *IRC v National Federation of Self-Employed and Small Businesses* ('*IRC*').[5] The third runs from the mid-1980s to the present day.

I. The 'old' case law

The law on locus standi developed in distinct ways in respect of the public law (certiorari, mandamus, and prohibition) and the private law remedies (declaration or injunction).[6] At the risk of oversimplification, one might at this initial stage suggest that the courts applied significantly more stringent standing tests for the declaration and injunction than for the public law remedies. This is the primary explanation for what might on occasion seem the surprising fact that an applicant chose to proceed (assuming the choice were available) by prerogative writ rather than a declaration or injunction. While an action for certiorari or prohibition might offer lesser prospects of succeeding at trial than an action for a declaration, it offered a better chance of surmounting the standing test and so being able to begin the action at all.

This point is reinforced when one considers that standing was widely perceived as a 'threshold issue'—that is, an obstacle an applicant had to overcome before she argued the merits of her case. If this view was correct, then the ostensible strength of an applicant's legal argument and the political significance of the decision contested would be irrelevant to the standing question, which would presumably have to focus solely on the applicant's identity and the intimacy of her connection to the decision challenged. Although this notion of locus standi being a preliminary issue enjoyed widespread judicial and academic approval,[7] it was something of a legal fiction. As suggested later, many leading standing judgments were clearly influenced by the respective court's views of the merits of the claim, and in many cases where one might have thought there was considerable doubt as to the applicant's standing, the question was never broached at all.

The following pages sketch out the main currents in the orthodox view of standing prior to 1977, and also identify some decisions which might suggest we should regard the orthodoxy sceptically.

---

[5] [1982] AC 617.

[6] Standing is not an issue in private law actions such as tort or breach of contract.

[7] Cf Cane P (1980) 'The function of standing rules in administrative law' *Public Law* 303 at 303–304; Harlow and Rawlings (1984) op cit pp 284–285.

Declaration and injunction—a restrictive test?

A cursory glance at several leading judgments might lead the reader to assume that the courts have consistently—over a long period—set very high tests for the grant of standing for these two remedies. In the 1858 case of *Ware v Regent's Canal Co*,[8] the applicant landowner sought a declaration that the defendant had undertaken works on his land not authorised by the relevant Act of Parliament permitting construction of a canal. Lord Chelmsford LC's judgment offered what Professor Wade describes as a 'classic statement' of this restrictive perception of standing:

> Where there has been an excess of the powers given by an Act of Parliament, but no injury has been occasioned to any individual, or is imminent and of irreparable consequences, I apprehend that no-one but the Attorney-General on behalf of the public has a right to apply to this court to check the exorbitance of the party in the exercise of the powers confided to him.[9]

Much attention has also been given to Buckley J's judgment in *Boyce v Paddington Borough Council*.[10] Boyce owned a block of flats adjacent to a churchyard owned by the council. Statutory provisions limited the types of development that could be carried out in the churchyard. To prevent Boyce claiming the arcane right of 'ancient lights', the council erected a billboard in the churchyard pending more permanent development. Boyce subsequently sought a declaration that the billboard was a 'building' of a type prohibited by the statute.

The council argued that individuals could never have standing to seek a declaration against it. Buckley J rejected this argument, and suggested that standing for a declaration could be satisfied on two grounds. The first, more restrictive ground, was that the applicant had a '*private legal right*' which was affected by the decision being challenged. The second, less restrictive ground (often referred to as 'special damage') was that the applicant was *atypically and intensely affected* by the decision's adverse impact on a *public right*.

One can discern obvious reasons for a restrictive standing test for these two remedies. In formal terms, their origin in the private law field would point to their availability being dependent upon infringement of private law rights. From a functionalist perspective, a difficult standing test offered important protections to the defendants against the lengthy time limits and presumptive entitlement to discovery of documents and cross-examination of witnesses that an action for a declaration/injunction brought with it.

The rule in *Ware v Regent's Canal* clearly compromises both the sovereignty of Parliament and the rule of law in their purist, orthodox senses, insofar as it hindered a citizen's attempt to prove that a government body has acted unlawfully. But it did not ignore either concept entirely. In particular, as Lord Chelmsford stressed, the Court's view was shaped by the fact that the applicant had known about the works for some eighteen months before he began his action. Had he come promptly, the Court's conclusion may have been different. Furthermore, Lord Chelmsford accepted that the applicant had other legal paths open to him, provided for by the Act itself. And it should also be noted that while the Court denied the applicant standing, it nonetheless examined the merits of his claim—and found it unproven.

A skilled lawyer would have little difficulty in constructing a plausible argument to the effect that *Ware* offered a rule of narrow rather than general application. And even if *Ware* was construed broadly, the judgment in *Boyce* would suggest that its scope had been attenuated by the 'public right' limb of Buckley J's two-part formula.

It must also be remembered that Parliament could at any time have introduced a more relaxed standing test had it wished to do so. That Parliament did not take such an initiative

---

[8] (1858) 3 De G & J 212.

[9] Ibid, at 228; quoted in Wade (1988) op cit p 690, fn 7. On the role of the Attorney-General see '*Gouriet* (1978)—a division of judicial opinion', ch 4, p 92. [10] [1903] 1 Ch 109.

indicates that legislators were content with the common law position, even if this might mean that some unlawful government actions would never be corrected.

More recent case law was markedly ambiguous in its approach. Some seminal cases discussed in earlier chapters which were initiated as actions for a declaration clearly fell within even the *Ware* test of locus standi. The applicant's interest in *Anisminic*[11] was money; in *Barnard* and *Ridge v Baldwin*[12] it was continuance in employment. Standing was not an issue in those cases. Yet the applicant in *Prescott v Birmingham Corpn*[13] also sought—and was granted—a declaration. Prescott successfully challenged the legality of the council's policy to offer concessionary bus fares to old age pensioners. His interest (as a ratepayer) did not fall within either *Ware* or *Boyce*, but the standing issue was not even argued in that case, still less addressed by the Court.

The suspicion that the grant or refusal of standing for a declaration or injunction was determined largely by the courts' views of the merits of applicants' claims rather than the nature of the applicants' interests is reinforced by several leading cases from the 1960s and 1970s. The issue in *Gregory v Camden London Borough Council*[14] was the grant of planning permission to open a school on the site of a former convent. There was allegedly a procedural flaw in the grant of permission. But before reaching that question, the Court had to decide if Gregory, who lived next door to the convent and was concerned by the additional noise and traffic that the school would generate, had standing. The Court concluded that he did not:

> One has to consider the legal rights of someone . . . I may be very much affected by the noise of the children coming out to play, by the shouts, by the laughter and everything else. But unless I can establish it is a nuisance then I have lost no legal right . . . The next point is this. In this case no question of public rights is involved, as where there is interference with the highway . . .'[15]

The Court was obviously influenced in reaching this decision however by its view that to grant a declaration would be a useless remedy in the circumstances. Paull J indicated that had the applicant sought an injunction, which might have had some practical effect, the Court might have taken a different view on the standing point.

The paradigmatic 'hopeless case' is perhaps *Thorne v BBC*.[16] Thorne sought an injunction to prevent the BBC broadcasting what he regarded as anti-German propaganda. He claimed that the programmes breached s 6 of the Race Relations Act 1965, which created a criminal offence of incitement to racial hatred. The applicant's bizarre statement of claim[17] would suggest he was mentally disturbed, but the Court of Appeal saw no need to address this matter. In this case, standing was treated as a threshold issue. As Lord Denning put it:

> It is a fundamental rule that the court will only grant an injunction at the suit of a private individual to support a legal right . . . [The applicant] does not allege, and indeed he does not have, any legal right in himself personally in this matter.[18]

The Court[19] observed that the very high standing test set for a declaration served an important political purpose in situations such as this; namely to prevent individual citizens invoking civil law remedies to pre-empt or second guess governmental decisions as to whether to initiate criminal law proceedings.

---

[11] See '*Anisminic Ltd v Foreign Compensation Commission* (1969)', ch 3, pp 68–70.

[12] See 'The re-emergence of the principle? *Ridge v Baldwin*', ch 14, pp 387–389 and 'The turning point? *Barnard v National Dock Labour Board*', ch 15, pp 412–414 respectively.

[13] [1955] Ch 210, CA; 'Excess of Powers', ch 13, pp 354–361.   [14] [1966] 1 WLR 899.

[15] Ibid, at 907, per Paull J. On this second test see eg *Brownsea Haven Properties Ltd v Poole Corpn* [1958] Ch 574. The plaintiff owned a hotel in a road which he claimed had been unlawfully designated as a one-way street. The standing issue was not even broached.   [16] [1967] 1 WLR 1104, CA.

[17] Reproduced at ibid, 1106–1107.   [18] Ibid, at 1109.

[19] Danckwerts and Winn LJJ concurred with Lord Denning.

Some exceptions to the general rule?

Gregory and *Thorne* appear difficult to reconcile with the Court of Appeal's decision in *Blackburn v A-G*.[20] The merits of Blackburn's challenge to the UK's ratification of the Treaty of Rome were discussed in chapter eleven.[21] What is pertinent here is that the application was for a declaration and that the applicant's substantive claim was quite outlandish. Blackburn manifestly had no 'private legal right' in issue; nor could he plausibly maintain that he would be atypically affected by the public law consequences of the United Kingdom's accession to the Community. Yet Lord Denning MR's leading judgment certainly did not treat the locus standi question as a preliminary issue. He did not reach it until the end of his judgment, and dealt with it in the following way:

> [Standing] is not a matter which we need rule on today. [Mr Blackburn] says that he feels very strongly and that it is a matter in which many persons in this country are concerned. I myself would not rule him out on the ground that he has no standing.[22]

Whether the Court would have 'ruled Mr Blackburn out' on that ground if the merits of his case indicated that he might have won his action is a matter for speculation.

There is some further indication that Lord Denning's Court of Appeal would allow the declaration and injunction to be invoked by citizens with no particular link to the government decision being challenged if they had (in the Court's view) a strong case on the merits. *A-G (ex rel McWhirter) v Independent Broadcasting Authority*[23] is a good example. McWhirter sought an injunction against the Independent Broadcasting Authority. His specific concern was to prevent the television broadcast of a documentary about Andy Warhol, which he considered obscene.[24] The point of law on which he relied arose under s 3(1) of the Television Act 1964, which required members of the IBA Board to 'satisfy themselves' that broadcast programmes did not offend against good taste. On the facts, it appeared that the Board's members had unlawfully delegated that responsibility to their officials. While McWhirter seemed to have a strong case on the merits, the suggestion that he fell within either of the categories identified in *Boyce* is risible. But the Court did not rule out the possibility that an applicant in such circumstances could have standing. Lord Denning expressed this point in grandiloquent language:

> I regard it as a matter of high constitutional principle that if there is good ground for supposing that a government department or a public authority is transgressing the law . . . in a way which offends or injures thousands of Her Majesty's subjects, then in the last resort any one of those injured or offended can draw it to the attention of the courts and seek to have the law enforced.[25]

This conclusion is readily defensible if we assume that the primary purpose of an injunction is to prevent what seems prima facie to be unlawful government[26] activity. If its purpose is however to protect private rights, the majority's conclusion is absurd. Lord Denning was aware of the shaky doctrinal foundations of his conclusion, observing that: 'in these days we have to mould procedural requirements so as to see that the duty which the statute ordains is fulfilled'.[27] 'Moulding' is perhaps a polite way of describing what the Court did to traditional

---

[20] [1971] 1 WLR 1037.   [21] At 'Parliamentary sovereignty: a non-justiciable concept?, ch 11', p 301.

[22] [1971] 1 WLR 1037 at 1041.   [23] [1973] QB 629, CA.

[24] The case is a mark of how far notions of obscenity have relaxed since 1973. Much press indignation (papers had been given a pre-broadcast screening of the film) was engendered by scenes which might appear only comical today. Thus, per the *Sunday Mirror*, the film was: 'the most permissive shocker to be shown on British screens . . . It includes: A FAT GIRL, stripping to the waist, daubing her breasts with paint and then painting a canvas with them'. ibid, at 633.   [25] Ibid, at 649.

[26] 'Government' in the context of an injunction at this time did not include the Crown.

[27] [1973] QB 629 at 635, CA.

doctrine. A more satisfactory approach would have been for the Court explicitly to break with past practice and to suggest that in cases involving manifestly unlawful government behaviour, any citizen could bring an action for an injunction or a declaration.[28]

We have seen in earlier chapters that Lord Denning's time in the Court of Appeal was marked by occasional disagreement on matters of constitutional principle with the House of Lords; *Magor and St Mellons RDC* and *Rossminster* being primary examples.[29] A similar tension was evident in *Gouriet v Union of Post Office Workers*.[30] The background to this case was outlined in chapter four, which addressed the question of whether the Attorney-General's power to initiate relator proceedings was susceptible to full review. Gouriet had also sought to proceed in his own right, seeking a declaration that the proposed mail boycott was illegal and an injunction to prevent it taking place. The Court of Appeal unanimously concluded that Gouriet had standing to seek a declaration. Since he had unsuccessfully sought a relator, the declaration was presumably (per *McWhirter*) his remedy of 'last resort'.

The House of Lords rejected this conclusion. Lord Wilberforce forcefully restated the rule in *Boyce*: 'where there is no interference with a private right and no personal damage, declaratory relief cannot be sought without joining the Attorney-General as a party (sc as relator)'.[31] (As noted in chapter four, the House of Lords also concluded that the High Court had no jurisdiction to examine the merits of the Attorney-General's refusal to begin relator proceedings.) One might argue that Mr Gouriet would have fared better on the standing question had he presented himself to the court as the owner of a business that communicated frequently with South African customers, or if he had friends in South Africa with whom he regularly corresponded.[32] It is conceivable that he might then, particularly on the first ground, have fallen within Lord Wilberforce's rule. This would however demand that we ignored the political context in which the judgment was issued, which would perhaps be unwise. Lord Wilberforce had indicated that a grant of standing would be futile, since Gouriet was challenging a decision so intensely political in nature that it was effectively non-justiciable.

In discussing the House of Lords' judgment, Craig suggested that: 'The decision illustrates a conception of standing which in itself reflects a view of administrative law: the vindication of private rights'.[33] Craig's comment is readily defensible. But their Lordships' decision in *Gouriet* offered just *one* conception of locus standi. As this relatively cursory discussion of the early case law has suggested, other conceptions could readily be found, some of which intimated that in certain circumstances the declaration and injunction could be available to litigants with only the most remote personal connections to the substantive question in issue. As Craig noted a few pages after the comment quoted earlier: 'To describe the common law as unnecessarily confused would be to pay it a compliment'.[34] That view applied as readily to the prerogative orders as to the declaration and injunction.

---

[28] McWhirter was not given standing. His own action was not 'the last resort', as he could have attempted to persuade the Attorney-General to initiate relator proceedings.

[29] See 'Purposive (or "teleological") interpretation', ch 3, pp 60–61 and 'R v IRC, ex p Rossminster Ltd (1980)', ch 3, pp 64–65 respectively.   [30] [1978] AC 435, HL.

[31] Ibid, at 484. Cf also Viscount Dilhorne at 494: 'In my opinion the cases establish that the courts have no jurisdiction to entertain such claims by a private individual who has not suffered and will not suffer damage'. These comments presumably mean that *Prescott*, *Blackburn*, and *McWhirter* should not be regarded as 'authorities' on the locus standi issue.

[32] Cf Cane P (3rd edn, 1996) *An introduction to administrative law* pp 43–44.

[33] (1989) op cit p 354. Cf Beatson and Matthews: 'A survey for locus standi prior to *Gouriet* would have revealed that consistency was also lacking in respect of that remedy'; op cit p 482.

[34] Craig (1989) op cit p 358.

Certiorari and prohibition—an expansive test?

Since the prerogative remedies initially developed as mechanisms to control the activities of government bodies, one might expect that they would incorporate a broader test of standing than the declaration and injunction. Their original purpose was, after all, not to protect private rights but to ensure that government bodies did not exceed their jurisdiction.[35] The dominant view appeared to be that standing for certiorari could be satisfied on either of two grounds. These are perhaps best illustrated by the Court of Appeal's judgment in *R v Thames Magistrates' Court, ex p Greenbaum*.[36]

The case concerned the allocation of licences for market pitches. Greenbaum, a licencee, complained that the magistrate's court had exceeded its jurisdiction in ordering that a rival trader be given a specific pitch which had previously been allocated to him. Greenbaum clearly had a pecuniary interest in this decision, and it seems plausible that he would have had standing for a declaration had he sought one. He undoubtedly met the first of the two standing tests for certiorari; namely was he 'a person aggrieved'? This test bears some resemblance to the second limb of the *Boyce* test for a declaration. As Lord Ellenborough put it in *R v Taunton St Mary Inhabitants*:

> Certainly a person does not answer to the character of a person aggrieved who is only in common with the rest of the subjects inconvenienced by the nuisance; but here it appears that persons have by reason of their local situation, a grievance of their own.[37]

Greenbaum confirmed the proposition that a person aggrieved would be given standing *ex debito justiciae*, that is as a 'matter of right'. Lord Denning also confirmed that standing for certiorari could be granted to a 'stranger' to the challenged decision. In these circumstances, standing would be granted if the court considered it in the public interest for the action to proceed. Lord Denning was not explicit as to which factors would be weighed to determine this issue. He referred to the 1870 decision of *R v Surrey Justices*[38] to illustrate this point, but all that this case tells us is that standing is unlikely to be granted to a stranger if 'no good would be done to the public' by the applicant succeeding in the action.[39] One would assume that 'the public good/interest' embraced matters relating to the merits of the case, and in particular the apparent strength of the applicant's legal argument and the political significance of the decision challenged. If those factors were indeed taken into account, one cannot plausibly maintain that locus standi was a threshold question.

A 'citizen's action' test for standing for certiorari?

That 'strangers' could seek certiorari is a strong indication that the court was willing to accept what is sometimes referred to as a 'citizen's action' or 'actio popularis' basis for standing for this remedy. Private rights are irrelevant under this conception of standing, which regards the purpose of the remedy as a means to control unlawful government decision-making.

The Court of Appeal seemed to step further in this direction in *R v Paddington Valuation Officer, ex p Peachey Property Corpn Ltd*,[40] in which Lord Denning suggested that one could be a 'person aggrieved' (and so entitled to standing as of right) even if one had no financial

---

[35] Cf Wade (1988) op cit p 625: 'Nominally [prohibition and certiorari] are granted to the Crown and the Crown always has sufficient interest to call upon public bodies to act lawfully'.   [36] (1957) 55 LGR 129.

[37] (1815) 3 M & S 465 at 472.   [38] (1870) LR 5 QB 466.

[39] Ibid, at 473, per Blackburn J. The case is in fact not about standing at all, but rather about the analytically distinct issue of whether the court should withhold a remedy from an applicant who has standing and succeeds on the merits.   [40] [1966] 1 QB 380.

interest affected by the challenged decision. Peachey Property was a landlord whose purpose-built flats had been given a higher rateable value than similar converted flats. It sought to have the rating list quashed on the grounds that the valuation was unlawful. The company clearly had a financial interest in the rateable value of its property, but Lord Denning indicated that this was not necessary for it to be a 'person aggrieved':

> I do not think grievances are to be measured in £.s.d. If a ratepayer or other person finds his name included in a valuation list which is invalid, he is entitled to come to the court and apply to have it quashed. He is not to be put off by the plea that he has suffered no damage.[41]

The judgment thus seemed to widen the category of individuals who could expect to be granted standing *ex debito justiciae* to seek certiorari. Lord Denning also held that the courts should construe the notion of a 'stranger' broadly, suggesting that the only type of litigant who would not satisfy this test was 'a mere busybody who was interfering in things which did not concern him'.[42]

The 'busybody' seemed a narrow residual category. Mr Blackburn appeared again as the applicant in *R v Greater London Council, ex p Blackburn*.[43] His complaint was that the GLC had unlawfully delegated its film censorship functions to the British Board of Film Censors by automatically accepting the Board's classification of particular porno-graphic films rather than evaluating the films itself. He sought an order of prohibition forbidding the GLC from doing this. Lord Denning's judgment is of interest because (rather like his treatment of locus standi for an injunction in *McWhirter*) it manifestly views standing for prohibition as being concerned almost exclusively with ensuring that public bodies do not act unlawfully, regardless of whether the impugned decision affects individual rights:

> I regard it a matter of high constitutional principle [that] if the government transgresses the law . . . in a way which offends thousands . . . anyone offended can draw it to the attention of the courts.[44]

The standing test to be adopted was therefore a (very) loose one:

> Mr Blackburn is a citizen of London. His wife is a ratepayer. He has children who may be harmed by the exhibition of pornographic films. If he has no sufficient interest, no other citizen has.[45]

Lord Denning's test is apparently even more expansive than the one deployed in *McWhirter*, since he has here dropped any reference to an individual's action being admissible only as a matter of last resort.

But, unlike in *McWhirter*, there is an obvious flaw in Lord Denning's reasoning on the matter of 'high constitutional principle' here. One could not know if a government body had 'transgressed the law' until the court issued judgment. Mr Blackburn could at most 'draw the attention of the courts' to a strong prima facie argument that an unlawful act had occurred.[46] Denning's text rather suggests that he did not address the standing question until after he had reached a conclusion on the merits; which in turn raises the inference that he allowed his answer on locus standi to be determined by his view on the substantive law. One might be forgiven for concluding that all that was required to gain standing for certiorari and prohibition was that an applicant present a prima facie convincing legal argument in respect of a decision which the court regarded as touching upon a matter of political or moral importance.

---

[41] Ibid, at 401.　　[42] Ibid.　　[43] [1976] 1 WLR 550.　　[44] Ibid, at 559.　　[45] Ibid.
[46] This is the point Lord Denning made in *McWhirter*.

Mandamus—a broad or narrow test?

Case law on the standing requirements for mandamus offers support for the conflicting views that the remedy demanded an applicant have something approximating the *Boyce* 'special damage' interest and that he/she need only be a concerned citizen.[47] The first line of case law is best illustrated by *R v Hereford Corpn, ex p Harrower*;[48] the second by *R v Metropolitan Police Comr, ex p Blackburn*.[49]

Harrower was a building contractor who tendered unsuccessfully for a contract with the council. The applicants alleged that the council had failed to comply with its own standing orders in allocating the contract, and that its decision was therefore procedurally unfair. Harrower applied for an order of mandamus to make the council go through the tendering process again.

The Court considered the merits—finding in the applicant's favour—before broaching the standing issue. Lord Parker CJ felt that the test set was a high one:

> It has always been recognised that there is a quite different criterion of interest which would justify an application for certiorari and one which would justify an application for mandamus. It is said that a far more stringent test applies in the case of mandamus, and that the applicant must have, as it is put, a specific legal right.[50]

This 'right' was not satisfied by the mere fact that the applicants had an economic interest qua potential contractor in the outcome of the tendering process; nor by the fact that the company was a ratepayer in the council's area. However Lord Parker CJ held that the combined effect of these two dilute economic interests was sufficient to give the applicant standing on these facts. The judgment implies that the applicant would have to show a specific pecuniary interest in the decision made by the council. The case is not authority for the proposition that being a ratepayer was per se sufficient to give standing for mandamus.

However, the Court of Appeal took a different view in *R v Metropolitan Police Comr, ex p Blackburn*.[51] Blackburn alleged that the Commissioner had taken a policy decision not to enforce the anti-gambling laws since he considered such enforcement an inefficient use of manpower. Blackburn sought mandamus to compel the Commissioner to reverse this policy. As in *R v GLC, ex p Blackburn*, Lord Denning approached the case from an explicitly constitutional perspective. He seemed to doubt that Mr Blackburn had standing:

> it is I think an open question whether Mr Blackburn has a sufficient interest to be protected. No doubt any person who was adversely affected by the action of the commissioner in making a mistaken policy would have such an interest. The difficulty is to see how Mr Blackburn himself has been affected.[52]

Lord Denning saw no need to decide this issue however. Instead he moved straight away to considering whether the policy was unlawful. Observing that 'The rule of law must prevail', Lord Denning characterised the non-enforcement of the gambling laws as 'a deplorable state of affairs'.[53] The Commissioner's policy was undoubtedly unlawful.

The judgment suggests that the Court's concern was primarily with the legality of police policy, irrespective of the policy's impact on Blackburn himself. The case indicates that the merits of the case and the applicant's standing were intertwined issues. In the event, the commissioner had reversed his policy before judgment was issued, so no remedy was granted.

---

[47] Compare for example *R v Lewisham Union Guardians* [1897] 1 QB 498, requiring a 'specific legal right', with *R v Cotham* [1898] 1 QB 802, demanding only a 'substantial interest'.

[48] [1970] 1 WLR 1424.   [49] [1968] 2 QB 118.   [50] [1970] 1 WLR 1424 at 1428.

[51] [1968] 2 QB 118, CA.   [52] Ibid, at 137.   [53] Ibid, at 138.

II. Section 31(3) of the Supreme Court (now Senior Courts) Act 1981 and the *Inland Revenue Commissioners* case

Prior to 1977 the law on standing varied markedly not just between remedies but also within them.[54] This is not necessarily undesirable. If one sees the purposes of standing 'rules' as ensuring that the courts have a wide discretion to ration access to judicial review, the diversity in the case law would be quite satisfactory. For applicants however, the uncertainty could be problematic. There would for example be little reason to seek prohibition or certiorari rather than a declaration or injunction if the court adopted the very relaxed test of standing for the declaration favoured in *Blackburn v A-G*, or ignored the standing question altogether as in *Prescott v Birmingham*. But it would have been foolhardy for counsel to affirm with any certainty whether a court would take that line in an individual case. From that perspective, the law was ripe for reform.

The same policy issues that underlay the amended application for judicial review informed the changes that Order 53, and subsequently the Supreme Court Act 1981 s 31(3), promised to bring with respect to standing. Section 31(3) provided that—at the leave stage—standing would be granted to an applicant who had a 'sufficient interest in the matter to which the application relates'. The text of s 31 did not differentiate between the five remedies in this respect. But while the standing test was now nominally a statutory rather than common law issue, s 31(3) was cast in very loose terms. The notion of 'sufficient interest' is itself a flexible concept.[55] When one adds to this the 'in the matter to which the application relates' limb of the formula, the legitimate scope for judicial discretion in deciding whether a given applicant meets the test seems virtually boundless.[56] It was also unclear if s 31(3)'s explicit reference to the leave stage meant that locus standi was not to be considered at the full hearing stage; or, if it was to be considered, whether the 'sufficient interest . . .' formula was the test to be applied. Two further issues in particular remained to be resolved by subsequent case law. The first was whether s 31(3) introduced a uniform locus standi test for all five remedies. The second was whether, irrespective of the answer to the first question, s 31(3) should be taken as indicating a parliamentary preference for the relaxation or the restriction of standing requirements.

The House of Lords offered answers to these questions shortly afterwards, in *IRC v National Federation of Self Employed and Small Businesses*.[57] The IRC had given a tax 'amnesty' to casual workers in the newspaper industry who had previously evaded taxes in return for accurate returns in future. The National Federation subsequently sought a declaration to have the amnesty declared illegal and mandamus to force the IRC to assess and collect the tax.

All five judges issued judgments. Although there were many points of agreement between the opinions, there were also some significant differences, which makes it very difficult to identify the clear ratio of the case. It would perhaps be more accurate to suggest that the various judgments laid out a series of principles which might be expected to exert a strong influence on the development of the law on locus standi in future.

---

[54] But see Cane P (1981) 'Standing, legality and the limits of public law' *Public Law* 322 at p 335: 'The "old" law of standing was, it is true, couched in terms of greater or lesser vagueness—legal rights, special damage, genuine grievance. But the content of these vague concepts was in principle and in practice capable of being rendered relatively concrete and certain . . . Rules of standing could be stated in terms of classes of plaintiffs—ratepayers, commercial competitors, neighbours, taxpayers'.

[55] Cf Cane (1980) op cit pp 325–326.

[56] On the background to the new test see Harlow and Rawlings (1984) op cit pp 299–301; Craig (1989) op cit pp 358–359.

[57] [1982] AC 617. Despite the styling of the case (ie *NFSESB v IRC*), it was argued before the House of Lords as an AJR, not as a private law stream case. The significance of this point is returned to later in the chapter.

The judges differed on the question of whether s 31 had created a uniform standing test. Lord Diplock clearly felt that a uniform test now applied. Lords Scarman and Roskill appeared to support this view. Lord Wilberforce, in contrast, firmly rejected the idea of a uniform test. Lord Fraser was more equivocal, suggesting that not all of the old law had been swept away.

Should standing be a threshold issue?

With the exception of Lord Fraser,[58] the Court took the view that standing should no longer be a threshold issue. There might on occasion be situations where an applicant's interest in the matter was so tenuous that she could be denied standing at the leave stage. In most cases however, the questions of standing and the merits of a claim would be explicitly fused. This fusion implied that if an applicant approached the court with an ostensibly convincing legal argument in respect of a gross illegality committed by a government body, she could expect to be granted leave even if she herself had only a remote, personal interest in the matter.[59] This reasoning indicated that the court was rejecting a preoccupation with formal rules of standing, and embracing instead a functionalist approach; that function being not so much the protection of private rights, but ensuring that potentially unlawful government action did not escape judicial scrutiny. In Lord Diplock's opinion:

> It would in my view be a grave lacuna in our system of public law if a pressure group, like the federation, or even a single public spirited taxpayer, were prevented by outdated technical rules of locus standi from bringing the matter to the attention of the court to vindicate the rule of law and get the unlawful action stopped.[60]

On the facts, all five law lords concluded that the Federation did not have standing. This was in (small) part because the relationship between the IRC and taxpayers was regarded as confidential, and should not be open to breach by third parties. The primary reason for denying standing however lay in the fusion of locus with the merits. Simply put, the Court considered that the IRCs' actions had been well within the limits of their statutory discretion:

> [T]he Inland Revenue were acting in this matter genuinely in the care and management of the taxes, under the powers entrusted to them. This has no resemblance to any kind of case where the court, at the instance of a taxpayer, ought to intervene.[61]

The judges nonetheless did not rule out the possibility that there might be some types of allegedly unlawful IRC behaviour in respect of which any taxpayer would be granted standing; a conclusion which certainly countenances the possibility of an *actio populares* basis to the locus standi issue.[62]

Lord Wilberforce rooted the explicit fusion of *standing* and merits in the wording of s 31(3); that is, that the applicant show 'sufficient interest *in the matter to which the application relates*'. Lord Diplock, in contrast, indicated that this step was a natural progression in the evolution of common law understandings of the courts' role in regulating the relationship between citizens and government bodies. Whether we see the source of the *IRC* principle in statute or common law, its policy implications are clear. Craig characterised the judgment as confirming that:

---

[58] '[W]hether the respondents have a sufficient interest to make the application at all is a separate, and logically prior, question which has to be answered affirmatively before any question on the merits arises': Ibid, at 645.

[59] Cf Lord Diplock: 'If on a quick perusal of the material then available, the court thinks that it discloses what might on further consideration turn out to be an arguable case in favour of granting to the applicant the relief claimed, it ought, in the exercise of a judicial discretion, to give him leave to apply for that relief': Ibid, at 644.

[60] Ibid, at 618–619.   [61] Ibid, at 635; per Lord Wilberforce.

[62] There is obviously another side to the 'fusion' coin. An applicant who had a close connection to the matter in dispute, but who came to court with an apparently weak legal argument, could be denied standing.

'archaic limitations on standing should be discarded in order that public law can meet the new challenges of a developing society'.[63]

Yet it would be a mistake to assume that the *IRC* case is the *starting point* for the current law of standing. It is perhaps more instructive to view it as a *turning point*. Its constitutional significance can only properly be understood if the judgments are set in the contexts of both the previous case law and the competing policy objectives that case law was attempting to address. Professor Wade suggested in the sixth edition of his influential *Administrative law* textbook that in the *IRC* case:

> The House of Lords gave a new and liberal but somewhat uncertain character to the law of standing. . . . In general [the decision] may be said to crystallise the elements of a generous and public-oriented doctrine of standing which had previously been sporadic and uncoordinated.[64]

Standing in the private law stream

The extent to which the 'new' law of standing has lent that liberality a more coherent form is the subject we address in the remainder of this chapter.[65] Before doing so, however, it is important to note that whatever liberalisation of locus standi the *IRC* decision produced, it was a liberalisation that operated only in the public law stream of remedies. The judgment was concerned only with locus standi for the AJR: it had no obvious bearing on the standing test for a declaration or injunction sought via a writ or originating summons. *O'Reilly v Mackman* was to be decided shortly after *IRC*. After that judgment was issued, it was apparent that a relaxation of the standing test for a declaration or injunction through Order 53 might not in fact make it any easier at all for an applicant to gain access to the long time limits and entitlement to cross-examination and discovery associated with the private law stream. A grant of standing might therefore prove of limited utility to some (or perhaps many) applicants.

In *Steeples v Derbyshire County Council*,[66] decided in 1981, Webster J had concluded that the standing test for both the public law and private law routes to a declaration should be the same. To hold otherwise 'would seem to me to make an ass of the law'.[67] However, this view was not widely shared.

Thus in *Barrs v Bethell*,[68] decided shortly after *IRC*, the High Court refused to grant standing for a private law route declaration to a ratepayer who alleged that Camden council had unlawfully mismanaged its finances. Warner J indicated that he felt standing should not have been granted in *Prescott*, and doubted that some of Lord Denning's more extravagant locus standi claims were supported by authority. In Warner J's view, the fact that an applicant might satisfy the s 31(3) test did not mean she had standing for a declaration in the private law stream. The *Boyce* test would still apply in these circumstances. And it would apply in order to ensure that the protections (by way of leave and short time limits) offered to public bodies by Order 53 could not be circumvented by applicants who lacked an intimate interest in the matter in issue.[69]

Similarly, in *Ashby v Ebdon*,[70] Warner J held that s 31(3) and *IRC* made no difference to the *Gouriet* rationale.[71] An applicant could not seek a declaration through a writ if the effect of so doing would be to sidestep the need to gain the Attorney-General's consent to a relator action

---

[63] (1983) op cit p 362. [64] (1988) op cit p 701.

[65] Cf Cane's suggestion that *IRC* would create 'a large degree of uncertainty and unpredictability' (1981) op cit p 339. [66] [1985] 1 WLR 256.

[67] Ibid, at 500. [68] [1982] Ch 294.

[69] Warner J placed considerable reliance on *Heywood* (see 'The initial Order 53 case law', ch 15, pp 417–419) in support of this point. [70] [1985] Ch 394.

[71] See 'Some exceptions to the general rule?', p 439.

in circumstances where the civil law was to be used as an indirect means of pursuing criminal proceedings, unless the applicant could demonstrate that she fell within the *Boyce* test. This view was upheld by the House of Lords in *Stoke-on-Trent City Council v B & Q (Retail) Ltd*[72] The Court held that the council had no standing to seek an injunction through a writ against B&Q (a home improvement retailer) in an attempt to stop the store breaching the provisions of the Sunday Trading Act 1950, that breach being a criminal offence.

III. Post-*IRC* developments

Several cases decided shortly after *IRC* indicated that Lord Diplock's preference for more liberal standing rules within the AJR was well supported in the lower courts. The applicant in *R v HM Treasury, ex p Smedley*[73] approached the court 'in his capacity of British taxpayer and elector'. Mr Smedley's complaint was that the government was about to make (unlawfully) a payment of some £120m to the EC. The Court of Appeal concluded that his claim was ill-founded on the merits. Lord Donaldson MR did not expressly decide the standing issue, but indicated he would be 'extremely surprised'[74] if he found himself upholding the government's submission that Mr Smedley did not have sufficient interest in this matter. Slade LJ was more explicit: 'I do not feel much doubt that Mr Smedley, if only in his capacity as a taxpayer, has sufficient locus standi to raise this question . . .'[75]

A 'citizen's action' test for standing under s 31(3)?

Smedley is perhaps a good indication that the 'matter' identified in s 31(3) could include the scale of the practical consequences of the decision under challenge as well as the prima facie flagrancy of its breach of legal norms. Mr Smedley's argument appeared to be weak on its merits, but since £120m was in issue the 'matter' he raised was a serious one. Slade LJ's grant of locus to Mr Smedley qua taxpayer does not contradict *IRC*, since the applicant was not seeking confidential information about another individual.

The *Smedley* decision is not without pre-*IRC* precedent. It may be recalled that the Court of Appeal in *Blackburn v A-G* had permitted a 'concerned citizen' to seek a declaration, on quite hopeless grounds, concerning the legality of the government's ratification of the Treaty of Accession. *Smedley* may help us to explain that decision as prompted by the Court's concern about the consequences (enormous) of accession. Given that the UK's accession to the EC has prompted radical alteration to the doctrine of parliamentary sovereignty,[76] it would be unsurprising if it has also prompted the courts effectively to abandon any concern with the status of the applicant in cases raising important, EC-related constitutional questions. Lord Rees-Mogg's challenge to the government's ratification of the Maastricht Treaty reinforces that hypothesis.[77] He was granted standing—in respect of an argument as legally feeble as that deployed by Mr Blackburn thirty-five years earlier—because of his 'sincere concern for constitutional issues'.

There is however reason for believing that a locus standi test of this breadth is not confined to EC matters, but may extend to other 'constitutional issues'. The applicant in *R v Felixstowe Justices, ex p Leigh*[78] was a journalist who sought—inter alia—a declaration that a policy adopted by the Felixstowe magistrates' courts of concealing the identity of magistrates in certain types of case was unlawful. Having concluded that Mr Leigh's argument succeeded on

---

[72] [1984] AC 754.   [73] [1985] QB 657.   [74] Ibid, at 667.   [75] Ibid, at 670.

[76] See 'V. The end of parliamentary sovereignty? Or its reappearance?', ch 11, pp 306–312.

[77] *R v Secretary of State for Foreign and Commonwealth Affairs, ex p Rees-Mogg* [1994] QB 552; see 'The ratification and incorporation of the Maastricht Treaty', ch 11, pp 316–317.   [78] [1987] QB 582.

the merits, the Court then accepted that he met the s 31(3) test, characterising him as 'the guardian of the public interest in the maintenance and preservation of open justice in the magistrates' courts, a matter of vital concern in the administration of justice'.[79]

Watkins LJ then went rather further, and held that any 'public spirited citizen' would have standing in this matter. This raises the inference that, as in *Smedley*, it was the political significance of the impugned government action, rather than the ostensible strength of the applicant's legal argument, that drove the decision on locus.

The argument that *IRC* was de facto if not de jure pushing the courts towards accepting a citizen's action test is buttressed by *R v Independent Broadcasting Authority, ex p Whitehouse*.[80] The case concerned the IBA's decision to broadcast a controversial movie, *Scum*, about life in a gaol for young offenders. Whitehouse sought a declaration that the IBA's members had acted unlawfully by delegating the decision about whether to screen the film to its Director General. The Court held that she had sufficient interest in the matter. Watkins LJ indicated that every television licence-holder would have standing in litigation relating to the broadcast of television programmes likely to give offence to children or adults. That the applicant identified herself as a licence-holder, rather than simply a citizen or viewer, or—as Whitehouse was—the leader of a long-established pressure group concerned with broadcasting standards—suggests that the courts were still looking for a pecuniary interest as a justification for granting standing. But that interest is so remote in *Whitehouse* that the licence-holder point seems little more than a fig leaf to conceal a locus decision driven wholly by the merits of the case.

The Court of Appeal's judgment in *R v Monopolies and Mergers Commission, ex p Argyll Group plc*[81] lent a more complicated gloss to the position by suggesting (building on the intimations given in *IRC*) that standing was to be regarded both as a threshold issue at the leave stage and as an issue fused with the merits of the claim at the full hearing. As Lord Donaldson MR put it:

> The first stage test, which is applied on the application for leave, will lead to a refusal if the applicant has no interest whatsoever and is, in truth, no more than a meddlesome busybody. If, however, the application appears to be otherwise arguable and there is no other discretionary bar, such as dilatoriness on the part of the applicant, the applicant may expect to get leave to apply, leaving the test of interest or standing to be re-applied as a matter of discretion on the hearing of the substantive application. At this second stage, the strength of the applicant's interest is one of the factors to be weighed in the balance.[82]

It would make little practical sense for the court to make precisely the same inquiry at both the leave and full hearing stages: a distinction between a 'quick glance' and a 'close scrutiny' test for locus standi at the leave and full hearing stages has much to commend it. Lord Donaldson's test is however difficult to square with the wording of s 31(3); it requires something of a feat of the interpretive imagination to construe 'sufficient interest in the matter to which the application relates' as 'so long as she is not a busybody'. The case perhaps confirms the point that in this particular field, the text of the relevant statutory provisions has had little substantive impact on how the courts are developing the law.

'Representative standing'

The cases discussed in the previous section would suggest that *IRC* had triggered a pervasive shift towards a more expansive notion of standing. All of them had involved actions brought by an individual citizen. However, each applicant was 'representing' a broader constituency. This is most evident in respect of Mrs Whitehouse, who provided a legal mouthpiece for her pressure group. Smedley and Rees-Mogg were in effect acting as representatives of that swathe

---

[79] Ibid, at 598.   [80] (1984) *The Times*, 14 April.   [81] [1986] 2 All ER 257, CA.   [82] Ibid, at 265.

of political opinion hostile to the UK's membership of the EC. Mr Leigh, more broadly, represented the public at large, albeit not in any formal, organisational capacity.

The courts face rather different standing issues when the prospective applicant is a formal, organised group, created for the purpose of pursuing a particular political agenda.[83] The applicant itself may not have an interest in any sense comparable with the private right/special damage test of standing.[84] It would however seem evident that granting standing to representative bodies increases the prospect that an unlawful government action will be challenged. An interest group may have greater financial resources than an individual and is less likely to be intimidated by the potentially adverse personal consequences of beginning an action. It is also probable that an expert pressure group will present a case to the court in the most effective way. These considerations would of course also offer government defendants an incentive to argue that standing should not be granted; that is if we adopt the essentially cynical position of assuming that government bodies are invariably predisposed to exceed the limits of their powers and to resist being called to legal account for doing so. Furthermore, the ready grant of standing to such applicants raises the potential problem that the courts would find themselves being used as a surrogate or alternative political process by interest groups which had failed to convince the government of the merits of adopting its particular view on a given political issue.[85]

The High Court had shown a willingness to permit such representative actions shortly after *IRC* in *Covent Garden Community Association Ltd v Greater London Council*.[86] The applicant company had been formed by residents and traders living in the Covent Garden neighbourhood of central London, with the specific purpose of promoting their particular view of how the area should be developed. The litigation concerned a GLC decision to grant planning permission for an office development on a site previously allocated for residential use. The Association alleged that there had been a breach of natural justice in the decision-making process. It was unable to convince the Court on this point. Woolf J was nonetheless prepared to accept that the Association had standing. His reasoning seemed to rest primarily on the fact that the Association was an aggregation of the interests of many individuals each of whom, because they had been consulted about and participated in the planning process, had an individual entitlement to locus standi.

It is perhaps neither conceptually nor empirically problematic to grant standing to a representative group when many or all of the members of the group would have been entitled to standing qua individuals. Indeed, it may not even be appropriate to regard such bodies as 'representative' at all, but rather to see them as 'associational' bodies.[87] A slightly different issue is thrown up when the court is dealing with an interest group whose members would not obviously be granted standing in an individual capacity. This question arose in *R v Secretary of State for Social Services, ex p Child Poverty Action Group*.[88] The case concerned a challenge by the CPAG to a government decision which had occasioned substantial delays in the payment of welfare benefits. The Court of Appeal did not explicitly decide the locus standi issue, but indicated that it would have granted standing to the CPAG on the grounds that:

> the issues raised are agreed to be important in the field of social welfare and not ones which individual claimants for supplementary benefit could be expected to raise. Furthermore, the CPAG . . . play a prominent role in giving guidance, advice and assistance to such claimants.[89]

---

[83] 'Political' is used in a broad sense, to encompass cross-party or non-party political concerns such as health or environmental or social policy matters.

[84] Although it could have such an interest, for example in respect of planning permission decisions affecting its own land and premises.

[85] For an illuminating discussion see Cane P (1995) 'Standing, representation and the environment', in Loveland (1995a) op cit; and Cane P (1995) 'Standing up for the public' *Public Law* 276. The 'surrogate political process' label comes from Stewart R (1975) 'The reformation of American administrative law' *Harvard LR* 1667 at 1670; see the discussion in Harlow and Rawlings (1984) op cit pp 307–309.   [86] [1981] JPL 183.

[87] Cane (1995) op cit.   [88] [1990] 2 QB 540, CA.   [89] Ibid, at 546

The presumption that the courts would invariably welcome representative actions from responsible and expert bodies was however rebutted by Schieman J's judgment in *R v Secretary of State for the Environment, ex p Rose Theatre Trust*.[90] The case concerned the site of the sixteenth-century Rose Theatre in London, which was newly rediscovered in the 1980s. Property developers wished to build on the site. The Rose Theatre Trust was formed specifically to lobby to save the site from development. The Trust comprised archaeologists, actors and writers, and other members interested in preserving the country's cultural heritage. The Trust wished to have the theatre site 'listed' under the Ancient Monuments and Archaeological Areas Act 1979. The Secretary of State refused to list the building, reasoning that the developers had agreed to delay their works to facilitate archaeological digs and that economic development was more important than preserving the site.

Schieman J denied standing to the Trust.[91] His judgment was driven by explicit policy considerations. He did not accept that standing rules should invariably be interpreted to facilitate challenges to government decisions, even if those challenges were brought by informed and non-partisan applicants. But neither did he assume that standing would invariably be granted even to an applicant who possessed a legal right in the matter in dispute. As Schieman J put it, the fact that a government body may have acted unlawfully did not in itself mean *anyone at all* had the right to challenge the decision:

> the law does not see it as a function of the courts to be there for every individual who is interested in having the legality of an administrative action litigated . . . We are not all given by Parliament the right to apply for judicial review.[92]

According to Schieman J, the reason for standing rules was 'to avoid chaos'. By this he seemed to mean in part that locus standi was a mechanism to protect the courts from being overloaded with litigation, and, more importantly, to lend a degree of certainty to government decisions by safeguarding them from legal challenge.[93] As Cane has suggested this perspective has little to commend it.[94] If avoiding 'chaos' in respect of a particular area of government activity is of paramount importance, Parliament could make that clear by using an ouster clause. Similarly, the imposition of a three-month maximum time limit for initiating litigation under Order 53/Part 54 protects government bodies against the possibility of having to undo major works should they turn out to be premised on unlawful actions. Furthermore, it is always open to the court to find in an applicant's favour and yet avoid 'chaos' by either denying a remedy or tailoring that remedy in a fashion sensitive to the facts of a particular case.[95]

There would seem to be good reasons for thinking that the Trust should have been granted standing for its challenge. The site was arguably of great importance to the country's cultural heritage. The Trust represented a collectivity rather than just an individual, and thus increased the likelihood that the application was motivated by 'serious' and 'non-partisan' considerations. Schieman J was unconvinced by any of these points. Even though the Trust was not a 'busybody', it had no locus standi. He laid considerable stress on the point that mere 'weight of numbers' could not produce standing: if the members of the Trust qua individuals lacked standing, they could not gain it by banding together into an association.[96] *Rose Theatre* was not

---

[90] [1990] 1 QB 504.

[91] Schieman J devoted most of his judgment to the merits, and concluded the SOSE's action was lawful. He only turned to the issue of standing at the end of his opinion.   [92] [1990] 1 QB 504.

[93] For a fuller exposition of the judge's views see Schiemann K (1990) 'Locus standi' *Public Law* 342.

[94] (1990) 'Statutes, standing and representation' *Public Law* 307.

[95] Schieman J's judgment on this point might be contrasted with Lord Denning's 1968 decision in *Bradbury v Enfield London Borough Council* ([1967] 1 WLR 1311 at 1319).

[96] Cf Lord Wilberforce in *IRC* [1982] AC 617 at 633: 'an aggregate of individuals each of whom has no interest cannot of itself have an interest'. It would however seem plausible that Lord Wilberforce was here alluding to the specific issue of the relationship between taxpayers and the Inland Revenue, rather than advancing a rule of general application.

taken to appeal. Had that happened, it seems probable that Schieman J's decision would have been reversed. That the judgment was something of a restrictive aberration within a generally facilitative trend is suggested by several subsequent cases.

In 1993, British Nuclear Fuels wished to begin to test a new method of treating radioactive waste, involving the discharge of waste into the sea at the Sellafield nuclear reactor. In order to do so, BNF needed a licence from the Inspectorate of Pollution under the Radioactive Substances Act 1960. The inspectorate issued the licence. In *R v HM Inspectorate of Pollution, ex p Greenpeace Ltd (No 2)*,[97] Greenpeace contended that the method was not safe, and sought certiorari to quash the Inspectorate's decision plus an injunction to prevent BNFL discharging any more waste.

As in *Rose Theatre*, the Court examined the merits first. Again as in *Rose Theatre*, the Court concluded that the impugned action was lawful. But it took a different view on standing. In holding that Greenpeace did satisfy s 31(3), the Court emphasised the following factors. Greenpeace had 5,000,000 members worldwide, 400,000 in the UK and (of especial importance) 2,500 living close to Sellafield. This might be seen as rejecting the *Rose Theatre* presumption that individuals who all lacked standing qua individuals could gain it by acting as a group. It should however be noted that each of the 2,500 local members might have been granted standing in an individual capacity. It may be that what most strongly influenced the Court were the considerations that: firstly, Greenpeace was a long-established and widely respected body (the Court noted that the United Nations has given Greenpeace consultant status on pollution issues); and secondly, Greenpeace had far more expertise on this question than an individual living near Sellafield would have and could thus assist the Court in evaluating the issues. Otton J indicated that this conclusion was not compatible with *Rose Theatre*, but stressed that his judgment should not be seen as de facto abolishing standing tests in representative actions; 'it must not be assumed that Greenpeace (or any other interest group) will automatically be afforded standing for judicial review in whatever field it and its members may have an interest'.[98]

That there is now a strong, if not 'automatic' presumption that 'respectable' pressure groups will be granted standing in representative actions was underlined in *R v Secretary of State for Foreign Affairs, ex p World Development Movement Ltd*.[99] The merits of the applicant's case were considered in chapter thirteen.[100] At this point, we might ask on what basis did the WDM have standing? It had no personal financial interest in the outcome. Nor did its members have a direct financial interest. It might perhaps have been argued that all citizens had a remote financial interest in the project, in so far as the tax we pay goes in part towards this activity. However the Court did not follow this line: rather, it dwelt on two different issues.

The first concerned the 'expertise' and 'respectability' of the WDM. Rose LJ stressed the WDM attracted members from all political parties and none; that is, it was not a partisan troublemaker. It had 13,000 members in the UK, with 200 local branches, so could not be dismissed as part of a lunatic fringe. It also enjoyed official consultative status with UNESCO and the OECD; that is, it was recognised by powerful bodies as a source of useful advice and so would not be wasting the court's time with spurious argument. All these factors pointed toward the grant of standing. The second issue was a more familiar one. Rose LJ observed that if the WDM did not have standing, no-one else would have it either. This would mean that the legality of the decision would be left unquestioned, a state of affairs compatible neither with (at a theoretical level) a rigorous understanding of the rule of law nor with (in more prosaic terms) the satisfactory stewardship of large amounts of taxpayers' money. In combination, these considerations brought the WDM comfortably within what Rose LJ referred to as 'an increasingly liberal approach to standing'.[101]

---

[97] [1994] 4 All ER 329.   [98] Ibid, at 351.   [99] [1995] 1 WLR 386.

[100] See 'Excess of powers', ch 13, pp 354–361.

[101] [1995] 1 WLR 386 at 395. As noted in ch 15, success on the standing point did not mean that the WDM received discovery of the government documentation that it considered necessary to support its case; see 'III. Retreating from *O'Reilly*? The *Roy* case', ch 15, pp 428–430.

Conclusion

It would be a rash commentator who suggested that trends in this area of the law had now been set with cast iron certainty. *Greenpeace* and *Pergau Dam* suggest that there is now a strong body of case law indicating that the courts' key concern when interpreting s 31(3) is with establishing the legality of government action. That the issue remains riven by ambiguity was however forcefully illustrated by two contrasting 1997 High Court decisions, in respect of similar facts, in *R v North Somerset District Council and Pioneer Aggregates (UK) Ltd, ex p Garnett*[102] and *R v Somerset County Council and ARC Southern Ltd, ex p Dixon*.[103] In each case, the objectors were local residents who contended that the challenged decisions, which granted quarrying rights on publicly owned land, would have substantial adverse effects on their use of the land. Neither applicant could plausibly be regarded as a 'busybody'. In each case, the Court (Popplewell J in *Garnett* and Sedley J in *Dixon*) concluded that the applications failed on the merits. In *Garnett*, the applicant was denied standing. Popplewell J did not explain his reasoning on this point, although his suggestion that the applicant had not acted promptly might suggest he was endorsing Schieman's locus standi version of 'chaos theory'. In *Dixon*, in contrast, Sedley J did grant standing, and did so on the basis of a carefully reasoned and explicitly constitutional law rationale:

> Public law is not at base about rights, even though abuses of power may and often do invade private rights; it is about wrongs—that is to say misuses of public power; and the courts have always been alive to the fact that a person or organisation with no particular stake in the issue or the outcome may, without in any sense being a meddler, wish and be well placed to call the attention of the court to an apparent misuse of public power.[104]

In this particular case, the applicant was:

> neither a busybody nor a mere troublemaker . . . He is, on the evidence before me perfectly entitled as a citizen to draw the attention of the court to, what he contends is an illegality in the grant of a planning consent which is bound to have an impact on our natural environment.[105]

The decision thus appears to recognise a citizen's action basis to standing when major planning applications are in issue. Indeed, by alluding only to the applicant's 'contention' of illegality, Sedley J seems almost to be 'de-fusing' the question of standing and the merits, and recasting locus as a preliminary question to be answered on the basis not of the identity of the plaintiff and her relationship to the issue in question, but of the substantive content of the issue itself. That Sedley J's judgment is flatly irreconcilable with *Garnett* is perhaps of little significance, given the patent inadequacy of Popplewell J's reasoning in that case. That *Dixon* goes rather further towards the *actio popularis* may be attributable to its particular facts, or it may herald a further extension of the principles articulated by the House of Lords in *IRC*.[106]

The relaxation of locus standi rules, together with the House of Lords' subsequent retreat from the strict public/private dichotomy propounded in *O'Reilly v Mackman*, gives a clear indication that the procedural obstacles to the enforcement of a rigorous notion of the rule of law in respect of government action have become less substantial in recent years. More citizens can now question the legality of government action in court, and more can do so under

---

[102] [1997] JPL 1015.   [103] [1997] JPL 1030.   [104] Ibid, at 1037.   [105] Ibid.

[106] For an illustration of the limits to this trend see *R (Bulger) v Secretary of State for the Home Department* [2001] EWHC Admin 119, [2001] 3 All ER 449.

a procedural regime which enhances their prospects of ultimate success.[107] It is appropriate at this juncture to recall the *GCHQ* case. In chapter four, the House of Lords' judgment in *GCHQ* was presented as a radical break with past orthodoxies on an important matter of the courts' jurisdiction.[108] But it occurred at much the same time—the mid-1980s—as the courts were also reforming the key procedural elements of administrative law. As such, it should be seen as part of a wider, judicially-led rebalancing of the separation of powers between Parliament, the executive, the courts, and the citizenry.

It might sensibly be suggested that any attempt to assess the extent to which administrative law principles subject governmental behaviour to a rigorous[109] understanding of the rule of law must address five inter-related questions: what do we mean by the notion of a 'government' body; what types of government action are amenable to review; on what grounds can review be sought; who is entitled to seek such a review; and through what legal process must that review be conducted? As we have now begun to see in some detail, the answers to those questions might simultaneously point in rather different directions.

In the next chapter we continue to explore this rebalancing by focusing not on matters of process, nor on questions of jurisdiction, but on the grounds for review of administrative action. Chapters thirteen and fourteen dealt primarily with traditional grounds of review. Some cases discussed there had what we might now regard as 'human rights' or 'civil liberties' implications, insofar as the government actions in issue touched upon the political values which the Americans had so long ago identified in their Bill of Rights. The lack of entrenched values in the UK's constitution presented an obvious obstacle to the construction of a systematic body of 'human rights' jurisprudence within our constitutional and administrative law.[110] But the concern has, in a somewhat erratic and eclectic form, frequently been visible either on or just below the surface of judicial decisions. As noted in chapter thirteen, the courts have long recognised the (admittedly patchy and elusive) principle that certain 'basic rights' are recognised at common law and may be invoked as yardsticks to measure the lawfulness of government action.[111] Chapters seventeen to twenty-two trace the way in which that episodic presence has latterly—as a result of judicial, governmental and finally parliamentary intervention—been lent a more expansive and coherent form.

Suggested further reading

Academic and political commentary

CANE P (1995) 'Standing up for the public' *Public Law* 276

STONE C (1972) 'Should trees have standing? Towards legal rights for natural objects' *Southern California LR* 450

CANE P (1980) 'The function of standing rules in administrative law' *Public Law* 303

---

[107] Cf Harlow and Rawlings (1984) op cit at p 299 who presciently offered the following comment from an even more prescient (but unpublished) paper by David Feldman, written in 1981: 'Arguments which concentrate on the position of the individual applicant, to the extent of excluding the social interest in maintaining the rule of law, are not properly admissible in a public law context. Others may benefit more than the applicant. In particular, society may benefit as a whole when the courts impress on government agencies the need to act strictly within their legal powers'.

[108] 'III. Full reviewability—the *GCHQ* case (1983)', ch 4, pp 94–96.   [109] Or 'Diceyan' or 'red light'.

[110] Any such 'rights' would of course be enforceable only against government bodies, and not (as in the US) against the legislature.

[111] See 'The presumption of non-interference with "basic rights"', ch 13, pp 360–361.

CANE P (1981) 'Standing, legality and the limits of public law' *Public Law* 322

SCHIEMANN K (1990) 'Locus standi' *Public Law* 342

Case law and legislation

IRC v National Federation of Self-Employed and Small Businesses [1982] AC 617

Boyce v Paddington Borough Council [1903] 1 Ch 109

A-G (ex rel McWhirter) v Independent Broadcasting Authority [1973] QB 629

R v Thames Magistrates' Court, ex p Greenbaum (1957) 55 LGR 129

R v Greater London Council, ex p Blackburn [1976] 1 WLR 550

R v HM Inspectorate of Pollution, ex p Greenpeace Ltd (No 2) [1994] 4 All ER 329

R v Somerset County Council and ARC Southern Ltd, ex p Dixon [1997] JPL 1030

R v Secretary of State for the Environment, ex p Rose Theatre Trust [1990] 1 QB 504

Part Five

Human Rights

Chapter 17

Human Rights I: Traditional Perspectives

As chapter one suggested, the Framers of the US Constitution reached a broad consensus concerning the moral values which should not be left at the mercy of the federal legislature or executive. Madison's assumption that 'the people' could not always rely on the integrity and competence of government institutions was expressed in part by imposing a rigid separation of powers on the national government, and by constituting America as a federal country where States retained extensive law-making authority.

America's third anti-majoritarian/minoritarian safeguard was that the Constitution should provide deeply entrenched legal protection for the various civil liberties identified in the Bill of Rights. The Bill of Rights amendments outlined broad principles, based on ideas which several States had already accepted as fundamental tenets of their own constitutional orders. The Bill of Rights was in no sense a detailed code, but its constitutional purpose was, and remains, clear. One hundred and fifty years after it was framed, the moral values underpinning Madison's creation were powerfully restated by the US Supreme Court:

> The very purpose of a Bill of Rights was to withdraw certain subjects from the vicissitudes of political controversy, to place them beyond the reach of majorities and officials and to establish them as legal principles to be applied by the courts. One's right to life, liberty, and property, to free speech, a free press, freedom of worship and assembly, and other fundamental rights may not be submitted to vote; they depend on the outcome of no elections.[1]

The consequence of this is that courts have the power to hold that the Congress, or the President, or a State does not have power to give legal effect to certain moral or political values. As a matter of formal constitutional principle, the United States adheres to an understanding of democracy which places substantive limits on the content of 'ordinary' law-making processes.

The British understanding of democracy is of course quite different, and is best expressed by a judicial comment we initially met at the end of chapter two, namely Lord Reid's observation in *Madzimbamuto v Lardner-Burke*:

> it is often said that it would be unconstitutional for…Parliament to do certain things, meaning that the moral, political and other reasons against doing them are so strong that most people

---

[1] *West Virginia State Board of Education v Barnette* 319 US 624 (1943) per Jackson J.

would regard it as highly improper if Parliament did these things. But that does not mean it is beyond the power of Parliament to do such things. If Parliament chose to do any of them, the courts could not hold the Act of Parliament invalid.[2]

Within the British constitution, it has traditionally been presumed that every social value is constantly prey to 'the vicissitudes of political controversy'; that no moral principles were 'beyond the reach of majorities'; and that no constituent concepts enjoyed protection from the 'outcome of parliamentary elections'. The UK's EU membership has perhaps imbued EU law with constituent, 'fundamental' status. That proposition has yet however to be put to a determinative test. (Nor, at least on its face, does the EU Treaty reach, in respect of all the Member States,[3] the 'political' or 'moral' principles safeguarded in the US Bill of Rights.[4]) Leaving this question aside for the moment, the organising principle in respect of civil liberties in Britain is that individuals (including government officials) may engage in any activity not prohibited by statute or common law. Relatedly, neither other individuals nor government officials may interfere with an individual's legal entitlements unless they can identify a statutory or common law justification for so doing.

The principle is very clear. Civil liberties or human rights in UK law are 'residual' concepts. People may do anything which is not legally forbidden. The principle is also, as a practical long-term guide to the substance of citizen–state relations, quite meaningless. This relates in part to the discretion exercised by the courts when interpreting statutes or developing the common law. As we saw in cases such as *Liversidge v Anderson* and *Aninismic*, judges sometimes produce unexpected decisions. More significantly, the principle accommodates the blunt political reality that Parliament can at any time forbid activities hitherto permitted, or conversely, permit activities previously forbidden. Civil liberties in Britain are extremely precarious *legal* concepts.[5] They may enjoy a more assured *conventional* status, in so far as the courts, the executive, and the legislature may fear the political or moral consequences of undermining them; but, as we saw in chapters nine and ten conventional understandings about constitutional morality may themselves be nebulous creatures.

This chapter does not offer a substantial survey of either the history or current status of civil liberties in Britain; so large a task is quite beyond its scope.[6] Instead, more modestly, it focuses on several discrete issues raising principles of general applicability. Sections I and II address the traditional approach taken by Parliament and the courts to the protection of personal privacy and to certain aspects of freedom of expression.

I. Privacy

The actions of the government officials in *Entick v Carrington* clearly amounted to a tortious intrusion against both Mr Entick's home and his possessions. His home was physically invaded, and his belongings physically removed. The tort in issue was however trespass. As

---

[2] [1969] 1 AC 645 at 723, PC.

[3] The reluctance of successive British governments to accept the EU Charter of Rights as a universally applicable element of EU law being the obvious example of this.

[4] It now seems to be doing so indirectly however, albeit only in respect of a limited range of issues. See Phelan D (1992) 'Right to life of the unborn v promotion of trade in services' *MLR* 670; Coppell J and O'Neill A (1994) 'The European Court of Justice: taking rights seriously' *Legal Studies* 227.

[5] One might respond to this by saying that any values contained in the US Constitution are also 'precarious'—the Constitution's text may be changed via the Art 5 amendment process. But this mechanism is very cumbersome, very time-consuming, and also extremely visible. Amendment is difficult to achieve. In contrast, any aspect of the UK constitution could be changed in a day by a government enjoying majority support in the Commons and Lords.

[6] It has however been admirably undertaken recently by several authors. See particularly Feldman (1993) op cit; and successive editions of Bailey S, Harris D, and Jones B *Civil liberties*.

we saw in our discussion of *Rossminster*,[7] Parliament has in recent times explicitly authorised government bodies to undertake law enforcement activities which would otherwise
amount to trespass in the most obvious of senses: the 'invasion' of Rossminster's premises
had a 'clear' statutory base.[8] But it would be a mistake to assume that such authorisation is
needed to lend a lawful character to governmental attempts to investigate even the most
intimate elements of a citizen's life. The 'invasion' suffered by Mr Malone in the 1970s took
a less tangible form.

Speech and communication

The Metropolitan Police Commissioner, suspecting Mr Malone was involved in criminal
activities, arranged with the Post Office for a tap to be made on Mr Malone's phone calls. This
was done by Post Office engineers in Post Office premises recording Mr Malone's phone calls
and passing tapes to the police. The tap therefore did not involve physical interference with
Malone's home or property, and so was not a trespass in any traditional sense. The tap was thus
not obviously unlawful. However, the Commissioner could not point to any statutory or common law power expressly permitting taps to be made.

Malone v Metropolitan Police Commissioner (1979)

Mr Malone subsequently challenged the legality of the Commissioner's action by seeking a
declaration (through a writ rather than the AJR) that the tapping was unlawful. His argument rested in part on provisions of the European Convention on Human Rights, which
we consider in chapter eighteen. But he also made contentions based purely on domestic
law. In effect, Mr Malone was asking the court to recognise that the common law had (by
1979) developed sufficiently to treat telephone tapping by government bodies with the same
opprobrium that Lord Camden had regarded a physical trespass in *Entick* 200 years earlier:
to restrict the concept of trespass to tangible interference with a person's body or possessions would be to adopt an unduly formalist interpretation of the law. In the modern era,
he argued, listening-in to a person's phone conversations should be seen as just as much of
a trespass as confiscating her books or letters. To frame the matter somewhat differently,
Malone was contending that the common law should now recognise an individual right to
privacy which could be protected through legal action in the courts against interferences not
authorised by common law or statute.[9]

In considering, and rejecting, Malone's argument, Megarry VC offered a cogent analysis of
the common law's innovatory power:

> I am not unduly troubled by the absence of English authority: there has to be a first time for eve-
> rything, and if the principles of English law . . . together with the requirements of justice and com-
> mon sense, pointed firmly to such a right existing, then I think the court should not be deterred
> from recognising the right.[10]

However, Megarry VC's perception of 'justice and common sense' did not lead him to accept
that the common law now recognised a right to 'privacy' which could be compromised by
phone taps only if the listener had explicit legal authority for her intrusion. Since neither

---

[7] See 'R v IRC, ex p Rossminster Ltd (1980)', ch 3, pp 64–65.

[8] To the House of Lords, if not in the view of the Court of Appeal; see 'R v IRC, ex p Rossminster Ltd (1980)', ch
3, pp 64–65.

[9] Mr Malone placed great reliance on an academic article, published in the *Harvard Law Review* in the 1890s,
which suggested that such a right was already discernible in English law. The article had subsequently exercised
much influence on the development of American law—and virtually none on English law; Warren S and Brandeis
L (1890) 'The right to privacy' *Harvard LR* 193.   [10] [1979] Ch 344 at 372.

Parliament nor the common law had prohibited phone tapping, the practice was not unlawful, irrespective of who conducted it. And since it was not unlawful, it could not infringe Mr Malone's legal rights.

Megarry VC's opinion was it seems heavily influenced by questions of justiciability. He suggested that the whole question of privacy in telecommunications was so complex that it could only be settled by legislation. No such package of rights could properly 'spring from the head of a judge'.

Megarry's judgment is open to several criticisms.[11] His reasoning on the privacy argument is wholly circular. The Commissioner's action was not unlawful because it did not affect Mr Malone's legal entitlements: and Mr Malone's legal entitlements were not affected because the Commissioner's action was not unlawful. Admittedly, a decision in Mr Malone's favour would have been similarly tautological in conceptual terms. The question which then arises however is, in the event of uncertainty, should the courts construe the common law in a manner that facilitates or impedes governmental interference with a citizen's privacy? That Megarry VC chose the former course is perfectly defensible as a matter of narrow legalism; whether his choice shares that characteristic in respect of its political legitimacy is a rather different question.

The justiciability point is also quite specious. Mr Malone was not asking the court to create an elaborate scheme to regulate all interceptions of telecommunications. He sought merely to establish that the tap made in his case was unlawful. It seems plausible that had he succeeded on this point, the government would have found space in its legislative timetable to introduce the comprehensive statutory scheme which Megarry VC evidently thought desirable. If we (cynically) accept that governments are happiest when their actions escape legal control, it makes little sense merely to invite them to promote legislation subjecting unregulated powers to judicial supervision. If the court's purpose was to seek legislative clarification of ambiguous common law principles, it would be more likely to achieve that purpose if it resolved ambiguities in a manner which inconvenienced central government. It is not surprising that the first Thatcher government declined Megarry VC's invitation.

The existence of statutory authority does not settle the question of the legitimacy of intrusive governmental action, even if it does—following judicial interpretation—settle the question of its legality. Whether or not the substance of the MPC's activities at issue in *Malone* was defensible in political or moral terms is an obviously debatable issue. A more recent case, however, throws up a 'privacy' issue in which even the question of the legality of government behaviour—when measured against traditional, domestic yardsticks—seems to prompt quite different answers.

Sado-masochistic sexual behaviour

The UK's domestic law had maintained several sharp distinctions prior to the late-1960s in the way it treated private, consensual sexual activity between adults, depending upon whether the participants were engaging in heterosexual or homosexual behaviour. Until the passage of s 1 of the Sexual Offences Act 1967, consensual sexual relations between adult men were a crime. Section 1(1) decriminalised the activity when it involved only two participants, although retained a much higher age of consent (twenty-one years old) for homosexual activities than for heterosexual ones (sixteen years old). The discrimination between heterosexual and homosexual private consensual acts was not wholly eliminated, however, as homosexual activities involving more than two persons remained a crime, whereas group sex among heterosexuals was not illegal.

---

[11] See Bevan V (1981) 'Is anybody there?' *Public Law* 431; Ewing and Gearty op cit pp 56–61.

The law did not evidently draw any further distinction between homosexual and heterosexual behaviour when the acts concerned involved physical violence. English law on assault had been (somewhat imprecisely) codified in the 1861 Offences Against the Person Act. The Act recognised, inter alia, an offence of assault occasioning actual bodily harm (s 47) and the more serious offence of assault resulting in wounding or grievous bodily harm (s 20). The common law offence of assault did not require that any bodily harm be inflicted. It had long been accepted that a common law assault did not arise if the 'victim' had consented to the physical contact concerned. It also appeared to be accepted—conversely—that it was not possible for a victim of 'wounding or grievous bodily harm' per s 20 to consent to such injury, in the sense that his/her consent was irrelevant to the question of the assailant's guilt. It was rather less clear if consent was a relevant issue in respect of the infliction of actual bodily harm.[12] The courts had accepted that the infliction of actual or grievous bodily harm, or wounding, would not be an offence if the injury was the incidental result of the victim's consensual participation in certain types of lawful activity—surgery, cosmetic procedures such as tattooing or body piercing, and contact sports such as boxing or rugby, being obvious examples. The previously unresolved question presented to the Court of Appeal in *R v Donovan*[13] was whether the victim's consent was a relevant issue in respect of a s 20 injury inflicted upon her by a man for the purpose of sexual gratification.[14] The Court concluded that:

> As a general rule, although it is a rule to which there are well-established exceptions, it is an unlawful act to beat another person with such a degree of violence that the infliction of bodily harm is a probable consequence, and where such an act is proved, consent is immaterial.[15]

The Court also held that it would be 'absurd' and 'repellent to the ordinary intelligence' to classify this kind of nominally deviant sexual activity as one of the exceptions to the rule.

R v Brown (1994)

Some sixty years later, the defendants in *R v Brown*[16] found themselves facing prosecution under s 20 and s 47. The defendants were all homosexual men, who engaged in consensual sado-masochistic activities, involving burning, beating, and wounding each other's bodies, sometimes carried out under the influence of drugs and alcohol. They were convicted at trial. On appeal before the House of Lords, the gist of their defence was to argue that *Donovan* should no longer be regarded as good law, and that infliction of injury in the course of private, consensual sexual activities should not be an offence unless the injury was sufficiently severe to impose costs upon the public at large, either because the 'victim' required hospital treatment or became eligible as a result of the injury for some kind of social security benefit. The House of Lords rejected this argument. The texts of the majority judgments[17] indicate that their authors' conclusions were driven in part by policy considerations, and in part by the way in which the judges organised their analyses.

The majority judges appeared to take as their analytical starting point the presumption that, prima facie, a crime of violence had been committed by the accused. The secondary question was then whether the circumstances of the particular activities in question fell within an exception to the presumption. The secondary question raised matters of public policy. While the majority could see a policy argument in favour of permitting an exception for such activities as boxing, they could see little to invoke in favour of granting an exemption for sado-masochistic sex. They could in contrast see many good policy reasons for not exempting such activities from the general rule: for example that being in a state of sexual arousal would

---

[12] See the variously phrased judgments in *R v Coney* (1882) 8 QBD 534. [13] [1934] 2 KB 498, CCA.
[14] The conduct being whipping the victim's backside with a cane.
[15] [1934] 2 KB 498 at 502, per Swift J. [16] [1994] 1 AC 212, HL.
[17] Lords Jauncey, Lowry, and Templeman.

compromise the 'sadist's' capacity to notice a 'masochist's' withdrawal of consent; that the use of alcohol and drugs undermined the certainty that consent was properly informed; that wounding might lead to infections; and that the drawing of blood raised the possibility of the transmission of disease, particularly HIV. If consent was to be a relevant factor in such circumstances, the legal initiative should come from Parliament through new legislation rather than from the courts through a re-interpretation of the 1861 Act. Lord Jauncey appeared neatly to sum up the majority's rationale in the following passage:

> If it is to be decided that such activities as the nailing by A of B's foreskin or scrotum to a board or the insertion of hot wax into C's urethra followed by the burning of his penis with a candle or the incising of D's scrotum with a scalpel to the effusion of blood are injurious neither to B, C and D nor to the public interest then it is for Parliament with its accumulated wisdom and sources of information to declare them to be lawful.[18]

The convictions were upheld by a three-to-two majority. The two dissenting judgments (by Lords Slyn and Mustill) approached the analytical task before the Court in a quite different way, and—presumably as a result of this divergence in approach—viewed the policy considerations informing their reasoning in a very different light. The point is best put by the opening words of Lord Mustill's judgment: 'My Lords, this is a case about the criminal law of violence. In my opinion it should be a case about the criminal law of private sexual relations, *if about anything at all*'.[19] Lord Mustill's analytical starting point appeared to be a presumption that an interference with the accused's entitlement to engage in consensual sexual activities had been committed by the government. The secondary question was then whether the circumstances of the particular interference in question fell within the limits on individual autonomy contained in ss 20 and 47:

> The point from which I ask your Lordships to depart is simply this, that the state should interfere with the right of the individual to live his or her life as he or she may choose no more than is necessary to ensure a proper balance between the interests of the individual and the general interests of the individuals who together comprise the populace at large.[20]

Lord Mustill could discern no overriding force in the public policy arguments advanced by the majority to justify conviction. In consequence, he could not accept that any crime had been committed.

II. Freedom of speech

One can identify many celebrated judicial pronouncements by American judges concerning the centrality of the First Amendment's protection of freedom of speech and freedom of the press to the American constitutional tradition. In the landmark case of *Palko v Connecticut*, Cardozo J characterised freedom of speech as 'the matrix, the indispensable condition of nearly every other form of freedom'.[21] Brandeis J's judgment in *Whitney v California* enjoys a similarly oft-quoted status. In his view the First Amendment existed to protect the principle that:

> freedom to think as you will and to speak as you think are indispensable to the discovery and spread of political truth; that without free speech and assembly discussion would be futile; . . . that public discussion is a political duty; and that this should be a fundamental principle of the American government.[22]

---

[18] [1994] 1 AC 212 at 247.   [19] Ibid, at 257 (emphasis added).   [20] Ibid, at 273.
[21] 302 US 319 at 327 (1937).   [22] 274 US 357 (1927).

Judge Learned Hand advanced a similarly expansive view in *United States v Associated Press* in 1943:

> The First Amendment presupposes that right conclusions are more likely to be gathered out of a multitude of tongues, than through any kind of authoritative selection. To many, this is, and always will be, folly; but we have staked upon it our all.[23]

William Brennan's celebrated judgment in *New York Times v Sullivan*[24] formulated a legal rule which rested on the broadest of political foundations: '[W]e consider this case against the background of a profound national commitment that debate on public issues should be uninhibited, robust, and wide-open'.[25]

The functional core of this presumption is that whenever freedom of speech questions arise before a court, the starting point for analysis of the issues involved is the principle that the citizenry has an entitlement to disseminate and receive all kinds of information, and that any attempt by a governmental agency—be it legislative, executive, or judicial—to erode that entitlement should be regarded with the most intense suspicion. Brennan characterised this ethos as 'a fundamental departure from the English and other forms of government . . . [it] was this country's great contribution to the science of government'.[26] Quite how wide a departure the Americans made from the English tradition is addressed—in a limited fashion—in the following pages.[27]

Official secrecy

The Official Secrets Act 1911 was enacted at the instigation of Asquith's Liberal government. The legislation was prompted by a public panic about the supposed presence of German spies and saboteurs, at a time when war with Germany no longer seemed a distant prospect.[28] The Act passed all of its Commons' stages in one hour. This might suggest that it was not subject to searching scrutiny and consideration, an omission which is perhaps all the more surprising when one notes the very wide terms in which it was framed.

As we saw in our earlier discussion of *Chandler v DPP*,[29] s 1 of the 1911 Act forbade entry to any 'prohibited place' for 'any purpose prejudicial to the safety or interests of the State'. Section 1 also criminalised the making of any 'note, sketch or plan' for such purposes, or the communication to any other person of any information 'which is calculated to be or might be or is intended to be directly or indirectly useful to an enemy'. Section 2 was drafted in even broader terms; it penalised the passing of *any* official information (irrespective of whether the information compromised national security) to anybody 'other than a person to whom he is authorised to communicate it, or a person to whom it is in the interest of the State his duty to communicate it'. The potential reach of s 2 was subject to frequent criticism; the most oft-quoted being that of Sir Lionel Heald that the Act: 'makes it a crime . . . to report the number of cups of tea consumed per week in a government department'.[30]

Legal rules which punish or otherwise restrict the publication of information which arguably compromises the security of the state invariably raise difficult questions.[31] The evident flaw of s 2 however was that it was not restricted to national security questions. Nor did it appear to offer the discloser any opportunity to defend his/her actions on the basis that disclosure was in the public interest.[32] It is not difficult to envisage circumstances in which such disclosure

---

[23] 52 F Supp 362 at 372 (1943).   [24] 376 US 254 (1964).   [25] Ibid, at 270.   [26] Op cit at 11.

[27] For a more detailed treatment see the essays in Loveland I (ed) (1998) *Importing the First Amendment?*

[28] French D (1978) 'Spy fever in Britain 1900–1915' *Historical Journal* 355.

[29] See 'V. "Justiciability" revisited—are all statutory powers subject to full review?', ch 4, pp 99–100.

[30] See Bailey, Harris, and Jones (1992) op cit pp 421–422.

[31] For a helpful discussion see Marshall G (1986) 'Ministers, civil servants and open government', in Harlow C (ed) *Public law and politics*.

[32] See *R v Fell* [1963] Crim LR 207, CCA; *R v Berry* [1979] Crim LR 284.

might be desirable; when for example it exposed corruption in the award of arms contracts, or revealed that government officials were misleading Ministers, or that Ministers were misleading the Commons. On its face, s 2 could, as the following cases suggest, be invoked simply to punish the disclosure of information which the government for reasons of either administrative expediency or party political convenience preferred to keep secret.

The *Tisdall* (1984 and 1985) and *Ponting* (1985) cases

In the early-1980s considerable controversy arose over the Thatcher government's decision to allow the United States to keep cruise missiles at its air force bases in Britain. The government had apparently decided to announce the missiles' arrival at the very end of Commons questions to the Defence Secretary, Michael Heseltine. Heseltine would then leave the chamber without giving MPs the chance to question him immediately. A civil servant, Sarah Tisdall, subsequently leaked a memo disclosing this plan to *The Guardian* newspaper. Tisdall evidently believed that Heseltine's planned behaviour was 'immoral', in so far as it denied the Commons the opportunity to question the government on a policy question of major significance.[33]

The government demanded the return of the memo, seemingly because markings on the text would enable the leak's source to be identified. *The Guardian* claimed it was not obliged to return the documents. The Contempt of Court Act 1981 s 10 empowered the courts to order disclosure of the media's sources only if 'necessary in the interests of justice or national security'.[34] The government contended that national security questions did make such disclosure necessary in this case. The information itself posed no such threat, but the government contended that the mere presence of a leaker within the Defence Ministry would so undermine our allies' confidence in the government's defence capabilities that it was vital that she/he be identified.

The High Court and the Court of Appeal accepted the government's argument, and ordered *The Guardian* to return the documents.[35] Tisdall was subsequently identified as the leaker, convicted under s 2 and imprisoned for six months. The House of Lords (by a three-to-two majority) later upheld the Court of Appeal's interpretation of s 10 and its application of s 10 to these facts.[36] On the next occasion that the government resorted to a prosecution under s 2 of the Official Secrets Act 1911, however, the outcome was perhaps not what it had expected.

Clive Ponting was, in the early 1980s, an apparently high-flying civil servant in the Ministry of Defence, who had been singled out for praise by the Prime Minister. However, after the Falklands War, Ponting formed the conclusion that his Secretary of State, Michael Heseltine, was systematically misleading the Commons over the circumstances surrounding the sinking of the Argentine battleship, the *Belgrano*. Ponting subsequently leaked information which he regarded as accurate to Tam Dalyell, a backbench Labour MP who had been harrying the government on this question. Dalyell passed the information to the Chair of the Commons Foreign Affairs Select Committee, who (in an act exemplifying the Committee's deference to the executive) returned it to Heseltine.[37]

Ponting was subsequently prosecuted under s 2.[38] The government accepted that the information released did not compromise national security. The issue was simply one of enforcing

---

[33] See Ewing and Gearty op cit pp 137–142; Barker R (1986) 'Obedience, legitimacy and the state', in Harlow (ed) op cit.   [34] On the origins of this legislation see ch 19.

[35] *Secretary of State for Defence v Guardian Newspapers Ltd* [1984] Ch 156, CA.

[36] [1985] AC 339, HL. Lord Scarman and Lord Fraser dissented. Neither felt a threat to national security had been established. Lord Scarman seemingly thought that the government's main motive was to spare itself party political embarrassment; ibid, at 364.

[37] See Drewry G (1985b) 'Leaking in the public interest' *Public Law* 203; Thomas R (1987) 'The British Official Secrets Act 1911–1939 and the Ponting case', in Chapman R and Hunt M (eds) *Open government*.

[38] *R v Ponting* [1985] Crim LR 318.

the civil servant's supposed duty of confidentiality to the Crown. Ponting did not deny leaking the information. He claimed however that Mr Dalyell was a person 'to whom it was in the interest of the State' that the information be passed. The nub of Ponting's argument was that Heseltine was deliberately misleading the House of Commons, and thereby subverting the doctrine of ministerial responsibility.[39] It could not be in 'the interests of the state' that the Commons (and thence the public) formed conclusions about government behaviour based on information which the government knew was false. Since Mr Dalyell would raise the matter in the house, giving him the information would in fact advance the public interest.

However at Ponting's trial, McCowan J instructed the jury that this argument had no legal basis. Section 2, he maintained, adopted a highly factionalised interpretation of 'the interests of the state'. This was not a matter that concerned 'the people', nor even the House of Commons. Rather:

> The policies of the State mean the policies laid down by the those recognised organs of government and authority . . . The government and its policies are for the time being the policies of the State.[40]

In formal terms, therefore, Ponting was guilty. The jury nevertheless declined to convict him. British juries are not permitted to disclose their reasoning, but it seems plausible to assume that the jurors hearing Ponting's case concluded that the government was invoking narrowly legal means to justify broadly immoral ends, and decided it should not be permitted to do so. The jury nevertheless remains a somewhat unreliable defender of 'just' solutions when faced with clear legal arguments: Tisdall's jurors seemingly took a less robust view of constitutional morality than their counterparts in *Ponting*.

The *Spycatcher* saga (1987–1991)

The Thatcher government was obviously not unique in invoking legal proceedings to restrain publication of information which would enable the Commons and the electorate to make more informed choices about the adequacy of government behaviour. The *Crossman Diaries* case,[41] instigated by a Labour government, served in effect the same purpose as the *Tisdall* and *Ponting* trials—namely to deter people with access to sensitive information about government behaviour from making their knowledge available to the general public. But the Thatcher government was perhaps atypical in respect of the patently absurd lengths to which it would go in order to deter civil servants and the media from revealing 'secret' information.

Peter Wright had been employed in the 1960s and 1970s by MI5.[42] Exactly what Wright did in that capacity remains unclear. He was however disgruntled with the financial benefits the work provided, and some years after retiring published a book, *Spycatcher*, which alleged that MI5 agents had plotted to destabilise Harold Wilson's Labour governments.[43] Rather than ensure that such extraordinary accusations (which amounted, if proven, to treason) were thoroughly and publicly investigated, the Thatcher government devoted its energies to trying to prevent Wright's story being made available to the British public.

The case raised several rather different issues. One might readily suggest that Mr Wright should not have been permitted to profit financially from any disclosures he made, irrespective of their content. However that presumption is quite separate from the question of whether or not his allegations should have been discussed in the press. If the allegations posed a present

---

[39] For a less benevolent view of Ponting's motives and behaviour see Marshall (1986) op cit.

[40] [1985] Crim LR 318.

[41] See 'Can conventions become laws? 1: The *Crossman Diaries* case', ch 9, pp 230–231.

[42] The exact nature of the security services, their effective powers, and the extent to which they are meaningfully controlled by elected politicians is, as one might expect, a mystery. For an overview see Lustgarten L and Leigh I (1994) *In from the cold: national security and parliamentary democracy*.

[43] Wilson had long thought that such plots had been hatched against him; Pimlott op cit pp 697–715.

threat to national security, one could see strong arguments for prohibiting disclosure. Yet if they exposed illegal or treasonable behaviour, one would presumably favour disclosure in the expectation that public discussion and criticism might lead both to the prosecution and conviction of those engaged in such treasonable plots and prevent a recurrence of such activities in future. The practical difficulty attending either viewpoint is of course that citizens could not form a view on whether the allegations threatened national security or revealed subversive behaviour until they had been made public. Essentially therefore, the issue is reduced to a question of whether one can (or should) trust government to identify and remedy any wrongdoing among the security services. Diceyan or Madisonian orthodoxies might suggest that would be a dangerous assumption to make; especially when the allegations apparently have a party political dimension, and the government is composed solely of members of one political party.

As noted in earlier chapters, the British courts have tended to adopt a very deferential stance towards government claims that litigation raised 'national security' questions. One can trace an unbroken thread of judicial acquiescence from *Ship Money*, through to *The Zamora*, to *Liversidge v Anderson*, to *Chandler v DPP*, and on to *GCHQ*. The *Spycatcher* litigation suggested that this tradition still enjoyed appreciable judicial support in the late-1980s.[44]

Mr Wright had taken the precaution of going to live in Tasmania before publishing his book. He could thus not be prosecuted under s 2. The government therefore resorted to the civil law to stop publication and discussion of the book. As we saw in the *Crossman Diaries* case, the common law principle of confidentiality was an elastic concept. In the *Spycatcher* litigation, the government suggested that Wright owed his employer (the Crown) a lifelong duty of confidentiality in respect of any official information he acquired during his employment. The government argued that this duty prevented Wright from publishing any such material, and that if he did so, any profits made would belong to the Crown. But the government further contended that its interest in maintaining confidentiality also prevented *the media* from reporting Wright's allegations.

In 1986, both *The Observer* and *The Guardian* ran stories commenting on Wright's claims. The government immediately sought a temporary injunction prohibiting such stories, pending a full trial to determine if such publication could be prevented permanently. This was granted by Millet J. It remained in place for a year, until the newspapers persuaded the High Court to lift it. The judge, Sir Nicolas Browne-Wilkinson, saw no point in retaining the injunction, given that the book had by then been published in the United States and its contents were widely known to British citizens who had access to foreign newspapers or had imported copies from foreign sellers.[45] However both the Court of Appeal and the House of Lords reinstated the constraint on publication.[46]

The Lords' decision in *Spycatcher (No 1)* upheld the injunctions, albeit only by a three-to-two majority. The majority were strongly influenced by the government's claim that publication would damage the public interest in maintaining efficient security services, because it would undermine officers' morale. Lord Bridge's dissent took a different view of the 'public interest', employing grandiloquent language reminiscent of Lord Atkin's speech in *Liversidge*:

> Freedom of speech is always the first casualty under a totalitarian regime . . . . The present attempt to insulate the public from information which is freely available elsewhere is a significant step down that very dangerous road . . . . [The government's] wafer thin victory in this litigation has been gained at a price which no government committed to upholding the values of a free society can afford to pay.[47]

---

[44] See Barendt E (1989) 'Spycatcher and freedom of speech' *Public Law* 204–212; Ewing K and Gearty C (1990) *Civil liberties under Thatcher* pp 152–174.   [45] *A-G v Guardian Newspapers Ltd* [1987] 1 WLR 1248.
[46] Ibid.   [47] Ibid, at 1286.

The Thatcher administration seemed however quite ready to pay this price. In *Spycatcher (No 2)*, the government sought permanent injunctions against *The Guardian* and *The Observer*, and against *The Sunday Times* which intended to publish Wright's book in serial form. At first instance, Scott J discharged the temporary injunction and refused to grant permanent restraints.[48] His decision was upheld by a two-to-one majority in the Court of Appeal, and by a four-to-one majority in the House of Lords.[49] However Lord Keith's leading judgment in the Lords seemingly did not wish to be drawn into consideration of the large constitutional issues which the government's conduct appeared to raise:

> I do not base this upon any balancing of public interests nor upon any considerations of freedom of the press, nor upon any possible defences of . . . just cause or excuse, but simply upon the view that all possible damage to the interest of the Crown has already been done by the publication of *Spycatcher* abroad and the ready availability of copies in this country.[50]

It would thus be misleading to characterise the decision as a forceful judicial assertion of the constitutional right of the British people to be informed of their government's alleged inadequacies. The protection afforded by *Spycatcher (No 2)* to free expression seems at best oblique, premised on the fact that the laws of other countries had permitted both the publication and export of Wright's allegations.

In the interim, the government had also trailed around the courts of the world in an effort to prevent publication of *Spycatcher* in foreign jurisdictions. The government suffered defeats in Australia and New Zealand, before obtaining the dubious benefit of a victory in Hong Kong—a British colony which then had no elected legislative assembly. There was no point in pursuing such an action in the United States, where publication would clearly have been protected by the First Amendment. It is instructive to compare the House of Lords' judgments in *Spycatcher (No 1)* and *(No 2)* with the decision of the US Supreme Court in *New York Times v United States*, the famous 'Pentagon Papers' case.[51] The Pentagon Papers were a comprehensive (and secret) analysis of the US involvement in Vietnam. The papers were leaked to *The New York Times*, which planned to publish them. The Court rejected the government's efforts to prevent publication. Its rationale for so doing was best expressed by Black J:

> In the First Amendment the Founding Fathers gave the free press the protection it must have to fulfil its essential role in our democracy. The press was to serve the governed, not the governors. The government's power to censor the press was abolished so that the press would remain forever free to censure the government. The press was protected so that it could bare the secrets of government and inform the people. Only a free and unrestrained press can effectively expose deception in government.[52]

The Official Secrets Act 1989

These were not sentiments for which the Thatcher government showed any greater enthusiasm than had the majority of the House of Lords in the *Spycatcher* litigation. The combined impact of the *Ponting* and *Spycatcher* embarrassments prompted the third Thatcher government to reform the 1911 Official Secrets Act.[53] The 1989 Act did remove the catch-all provisions of s 2 of its 1911 predecessor, but it is difficult to portray the new legislation as an exercise

---

[48] *A-G v Guardian Newspapers (No 2)* [1990] 1 AC 109.   [49] Ibid.   [50] Ibid, at 260.

[51] 403 US 713 (1971).   [52] Ibid, at 739.

[53] For a helpful summary and critique see Palmer S (1988) 'In the interests of the state' *Public Law* 523; (1990) 'Tightening secrecy law: the Official Secrets Act 1989' *Public Law* 243.

in enhancing the transparency and accountability of the government to its citizens. One com-mentator has suggested that the Act's:

> stated purpose . . . is to reduce the amount of information protected by criminal sanctions to areas where disclosure would be harmful to the public interest. Yet it is tempting to conclude that the primary rationale behind this reform is to tighten the criminal law of secrecy, with the aim of making convictions more likely.[54]

Section 1 imposes an absolute and permanent duty of confidentiality on all members and ex-members of the security services. Any disclosure of any official information by any such person under any circumstances is now a crime. Thus, to take an extreme example, it would apparently be illegal for an MI5 or MI6 agent to reveal that her superior officers were planning to assassinate the Prime Minister. At the other extreme, even the most trivial of information may not be disclosed by security service officers. There is no requirement that the prosecution prove the disclosure to have damaged the national interest. Nor may officers argue that their action was designed to defend the public interest. Furthermore, under s 1(1)(b) the govern-ment may extend this absolute obligation to any person it wishes.

Other civil servants and government contractors are caught by widely-framed provisions which criminalise the disclosure of 'damaging' information in the specific areas of defence (s 2), international relations (s 3), or the investigation of crime (s 4). This is clearly a less expansive prohibition than the one contained in the former s 2. Additionally, accused per-sons have a defence if they can establish that disclosure would not be 'damaging'. However, the Act does not permit a 'public interest defence'—it is a crime to reveal 'damaging' infor-mation even if one believes one thereby exposes government behaviour that would be even more 'damaging'.

Palmer rather overstates the case in suggesting that Lord Keith's judgment in *Spycatcher (No 2)* approved the principle that:

> It is unacceptable in our democratic society that there should be a restraint on the publication of information relating to government when the only vice of that information is that it enables the public to discuss, review and criticise government action'.[55]

It would be more accurate to suggest that Lord Keith's judgment piggybacked on the judg-ment of the US Supreme Court in the *Pentagon Papers* case—a judgment expressing moral values subsequently adopted by the constitutions of other western democracies—which ensured that Peter Wright's book was published and subjected to extensive press analysis in many other parts of the world. Palmer is however surely correct in observing that the Thatcher government seemed wholly unpersuaded by this principle. The thrust of the 1989 Act appears to be a rejection of the idea that government employees' duty of loyalty lies anywhere other than to the government of the day. That a government should make such an assumption is an entirely logical consequence of the supposed 'ultimate political fact' of the contemporary constitution—namely that having a Commons majority generally enables a government to do whatever it wishes. This is, as suggested in earlier chapters, a theme which pervades every aspect (except perhaps issues involving EU law) of our current constitutional arrangements. We turn to the broad question of whether and how this ultimate political fact might be reformed in the final chapter of this book. Yet while litigation involving freedom of expression often arises as a result of governmental attempts to curb public access to infor-mation that allegedly has a 'national security' dimension, official secrecy is by no means its only trigger.

---

[54] Palmer (1990) op cit p 243. For similarly critical comment see Ewing and Gearty op cit pp 189–208.

[55] (1990) op cit p 247, citing Lord Keith's approval of the quote by Mason J of the Australian High Court in *Commonwealth of Australia v John Fairfax & Sons Ltd* (1980) 147 CLR 39 at 51–52.

Blasphemy

In addition to providing safeguards for freedom of speech and the press, the First Amendment provides in specific terms that 'Congress shall make no law respecting an establishment of religion, nor prohibiting the free exercise thereof'. The Supreme Court concluded in *Watson v Jones* in 1872 that 'the law knows no heresy, and is committed to the support of no dogma, the establishment of no sect'.[56] It was thus impossible for blasphemy to be made an offence either by Congressional statute or federal common law. Despite its trenchant rhetoric, *Watson* provided little practical protection for speech attacking religious beliefs, since at that time it was assumed that the First Amendment did not control the activities of state governments.[57] By the early-1950s however, the Court had concluded that a criminal offence of blasphemous libel—whether fashioned by an organ of federal or state government—was wholly incompatible with First Amendment principles. This conclusion was powerfully laid out in *Joseph Burstyn Inc v Wilson*:

> [F]rom the standpoint of freedom of speech and the press, it is enough to point out that the state has no legitimate interest in protecting any or all religions from views distasteful to them . . . It is not the business of government in our nation to suppress real or imagined attacks upon a particular religious doctrine, whether they appear in publications, speeches or motion pictures.[58]

The *Wilson* decision stands in stark contrast to the British constitutional tradition, within which the common law offence of blasphemous libel imposed an acute restraint on freedom of speech.

Blasphemy at English common law in the 'modern' era: *R v Lemon* (1979)

Prior to the litigation in *R v Lemon*[59] in the mid-1970s, a prosecution for blasphemy had not been brought in England for over fifty years. The offence emerged within the common law in the seventeenth century. It was closely linked to the crime of sedition. Sedition dealt with attacks on the integrity and adequacy of the government; blasphemy addressed attacks on the integrity and adequacy of the established church and the Christian religion. In its initial form, the offence did not concern itself with the style of the attack.[60] A calm and measured assault upon Christian doctrine was as much blasphemy as the most abusive or offensively presented criticism. This principle was relaxed in the mid-nineteenth century, so that religious criticism expressed in temperate terms unlikely to insult or ridicule believers in Christianity would not be blasphemous.[61]

Lemon published *Gay News*, a magazine intended primarily for a non-heterosexual readership. The June 1976 edition contained an illustrated poem, entitled 'The love that dares to speak its name'. The poem drew on the imagery of Jesus Christ being executed, and alluded to a homosexual relationship between him and John the Baptist. This poem apparently outraged the delicate religious sensibilities of Mrs Mary Whitehouse, who having failed to persuade the Attorney-General to initiate a prosecution, did so herself.[62]

It is perhaps indicative of the very primitive understanding of freedom of expression principles that then informed English law that the *Lemon* case was not argued on the grounds of

---

[56] 20 L Ed 66 at 676 (1872)—quoted in Feldman op cit, p 690.

[57] The Court began to apply aspects of the First Amendment to the States in *Gitlow v New York* 45 S Ct 625 (1925).

[58] 343 US 495 at 505 (1952). This did not preclude the possibility that blasphemous material could be the subject of criminal or civil regulation if it was also obscene.   [59] [1979] QB 10, CA; affd [1979] AC 617, HL.

[60] See generally Kenny C (1922) 'The evolution of the law of blasphemy' *Cambridge LJ* 127; Feldman (1993) op cit pp 684–695.   [61] *R v Hetherington* (1841) 4 State Tr NS 563.

[62] On *Whitehouse* see 'A "citizen's action" test for standing under s 31(3)?', ch 16, p 447–448. On the background to and conduct of the prosecution see Robertson G (1999) *The justice game* ch 6.

the basic, substantive point that the common law in a modern, multi-faith and largely secular democratic society should find no place for an offence such as blasphemy to restrict debate about religious matters. Judgment turned instead on a narrow question of law, relating to the mens rea element of the offence. The first possibility was that the prosecution need only prove that the defendant intended to publish a blasphemous article. The second possibility was that the prosecution also has to prove that the defendant intended to offend, shock, and arouse resentment among adherents to the Christian faith. It is evident that had the House of Lords accepted that the more expansive version of mens rea was the correct one, the reach of the offence would have been reduced, if not necessarily substantially.

However, by a three-to-two majority, the House of Lords held that the prosecution need only prove an intention to publish. It appeared to be common ground among the Court that, as Lord Russell put it: 'The authorities embrace an abundance of apparently contradictory or ambivalent comments. There is no authority of your Lordships' House on the point. The question is open for decision'.[63] The question was answered without any systematic consideration being given to the way in which blasphemy laws, however construed in terms of mens rea, interfered with the freedom of expression of publishers and readers on religious matters. Neither Lord Diplock (dissenting) nor Lord Russell and Viscount Dilhorne made any mention at all of freedom of expression in their judgments. Lord Scarman, the third member of the majority, briefly addressed the free expression issue only to note that the common law did not permit people to publish offensive criticisms of Christianity. Indeed, in Lord Scarman's view, the real vice of the blasphemy law was that it covered only Christianity, and did not also restrict freedom of expression in respect of other religions as well. The only judge to accept that promoting freedom of expression on religious matters was a factor that should push the court towards accepting the more expansive mens rea test was Lord Edmund-Davies,[64] the second dissentient. It might also be noted that the arguments offered by Lemon's counsel were equally silent on the significance of free expression principles to the decision before the court.

That the principle of freedom of expression was either (for three judges) wholly irrelevant or (for two) of marginal significance to the content of the law of blasphemy is indicative of a broader ambivalence within the judiciary in this era. *Lemon* is a startling illustration of the potential illiberality of the common law. Even if we accept—and this is a dubious premise— that a majority of the population in the 1970s adhered sincerely to the Christian faith, the existence of blasphemy as a discrete offence was a blatant example of the common law pandering to majoritarian intolerance. Neither Mrs Whitehouse, nor any other Christian of delicate sensibilities was in any sense compelled to read the poem. Nor were they likely to encounter it by chance. In essence the crime permitted self-righteous proponents of the Christian faith to rest secure in the knowledge that anyone who had the temerity to cause them offence on a matter of religious doctrine or practice faced the prospect of a substantial fine or a prison sentence.[65] Lord Scarman's professed wish to extend the reach of the offence is even more unpalatable, in so far as it would grant the same repressive entitlement to a still larger proportion of the population.

But as the following case suggests, it would be quite misleading to conclude that the public's interest in being able to read and evaluate certain types of information—as opposed to the publisher's interest in being able to disseminate it—was never accorded importance by the courts. Yet the principle was undoubtedly invoked inconsistently, and certainly did not enjoy the status of being deployed as the starting point for judicial analysis.

---

[63] [1979] AC 617 at 657, HL.

[64] Ibid, at 652–653; quoting a sentiment expressed in a textbook as to 'the splendid advantages which result to religion and truth from the exertion of free and unfettered minds'.

[65] Of perhaps greater significance was the likelihood that fear of prosecution would deter people from even expressing such criticism—the so-called 'chilling effect'.

Contempt of court

A-G v Times Newspapers Ltd[66] concerned two newspaper articles scheduled for publication in *The Sunday Times*. Both articles dealt with the on-going controversy caused by the drug thalidomide. The drug had been marketed by a multi-national drug company, Distillers, in the 1960s as a remedy for morning sickness suffered by pregnant woman. The drug caused severe birth defects in thousands of children throughout the world. Litigation against Distillers was initiated in the United Kingdom by several hundred parents of the affected children. The key issue to be decided was whether Distillers had been negligent in testing the drug before its release. The litigation had not been concluded by the early-1970s, as Distillers and some of the plaintiffs were conducting protracted negotiations about a possible settlement.

In September 1972, *The Sunday Times* published a long article which urged Distillers not to stand on whatever legal defences it might muster, but rather to make a generous settlement to ensure that justice—in a broad, moral sense—was done. Distillers claimed that the article amounted to a contempt of court, but the Attorney-General did not accept that view and declined to begin proceedings. *The Sunday Times* then prepared a second article, which examined the evidence that might be put before a trial court on the negligence issue. The paper sent the article to the Attorney-General prior to publication. The Attorney-General concluded that this article would amount to contempt. His assumption was that the article would prejudice the fairness of any subsequent trial, by creating a climate of opinion in which Distillers would already stand condemned. This would compromise the overwhelming public interest in ensuring that litigation was conducted free from inappropriate external pressure. The Attorney-General thus sought an injunction preventing publication of the article. The injunction was granted in the High Court.

The injunction was promptly discharged by the Court of Appeal. All three members of the Court were clearly influenced by what they regarded as a legitimate public interest in citizens knowing what progress was being made in settling the thalidomide controversy. This was never, it seems, to be regarded as a dominant interest, but in some circumstances could be a powerful one. Lord Denning MR expressed the point in the following way:

> It must always be remembered that besides the interests of the parties in a fair trial or a fair settlement of the case there is another important interest to be considered. It is the interest of the public in matters of national concern, and the freedom of press to make fair comment on such matters. The one interest must be balanced against the other.[67]

When set in the context of his opinion as a whole, however, Lord Denning's above-quoted characterisation of the problem before the Court is somewhat misleading. The key factor in his decision seems to have been that the litigation against Distillers was dormant, and that there was no likelihood of any hearings actually beginning in the foreseeable future. Since there was no trial in prospect, there was no possibility that its fair conduct could be jeopardised.

Readers of Lord Denning's judgment could be forgiven for concluding that the purpose of contempt of court in such circumstances was to protect one or other of the parties to the litigation. As was made abundantly clear in the House of Lords, its actual purpose is to protect the public's interest in the proper administration of justice.[68] Nonetheless, the House of Lords framed the question raised in much the same way as the Court of Appeal. In Lord Reid's

---

[66] [1974] AC 273. For more detailed treatment of the litigation see Miller C (1976) *Contempt of court* pp 126–134; Duffy P (1980) 'The Sunday Times case: freedom of expression, contempt of court and the ECHR' *Human Rights Review* 17.   [67] [1973] QB 710 at 739.

[68] This point is conveyed with great clarity in the opening paragraphs of Lord Diplock's opinion. See also Lord Reid, [1974] AC 273 at 294: 'The law on this subject is and must be founded entirely on public policy. It is not there to protect the private rights of the parties. It is there to prevent interference with the administration of justice'.

view, the Court was faced with responsibility of balancing 'the public interest in freedom of speech and the public interest in protecting the administration of justice from interference'.[69] Lord Reid and his colleagues reached however a different conclusion from that adopted in the Court of Appeal.

The Court saw no scope for accepting that the first *Sunday Times* article could amount to contempt. For a newspaper or broadcaster to urge a powerful litigant such as Distillers to accept a moral obligation not to stand on its legal rights was quite legitimate as long as the persuasion was delivered in 'a fair and temperate way and without any oblique motive'.[70] The second article, however, was seen as much more problematic. Lord Reid considered that *The Sunday Times*' analysis of the negligence issue raised a real risk of pre-judging the issue that would be of vital importance at any trial. He observed that: 'There has long been and there still is in this country a strong and generally held belief that trial by newspaper is wrong and should be prevented'.[71] In Lord Reid's view, *The Sunday Times*' second article would have that effect; it was thus quite proper for the Court to suppress its publication.[72]

Judicial law-making by the invocation of slogans—in this case 'trial by newspaper'—might immediately raise suspicions that the decision produced may lack a rigorous logical basis. Lord Reid's judgment explicitly acknowledged this point by suggesting it was much driven by intuitive feelings which defied written elucidation.[73]

Those feelings led Lord Reid to offer the following principle as a guide to the way in which such issues should be resolved:

> Responsible 'mass media' will do their best to be fair, but there will also be ill-informed, slapdash or prejudiced attempts to influence the public. If people are led to think that it is easy to find the truth disrespect for the processes of the law could follow and, if mass media are allowed to judge, unpopular people and unpopular causes will fare very badly . . . . I do not think that the freedom of the press would suffer, and I think that the law would be clearer and easier to apply in practice if it is made a general rule that it is not permissible to prejudge issues in pending cases . . . [74]

This principle was to apply only to litigation at first instance. In Lord Reid's opinion, it was evidently 'scarcely imaginable' that law lords or Lord Justices of Appeal could ever be swayed in discharging their judicial functions by any stories in the press. This comment makes explicit an assumption on Lord Reid's part that seems to permeate the court's reasoning. The result produced takes a very condescending view of the citizenry's capacity to draw a meaningful distinction between a newspaper's view of a legal issue and the way that issue should be dealt with in a court. The crux of the conclusion is that citizens cannot be trusted with such material.

As one might expect, the informed consent philosophy underpinning the First Amendment had led the US Supreme Court to adopt a far more robust approach to the analytical capacity of American citizens than that favoured in respect of their British counterparts even by the Court of Appeal in *The Sunday Times* case. In *Nebraska Press Association v Stuart*,[75] decided in 1976, the Supreme Court affirmed a line of case law that indicated there

---

[69] Ibid, at 301.   [70] Ibid, at 299.   [71] Ibid, at 300.

[72] The House of Lords also took the view that the litigation was not dormant, but was simply in something of a negotiatory lull.

[73] For example the following passage at [1974] AC 273 at 300: 'If we were to ask the ordinary man or even a lawyer in his leisure moments why he has that feeling, I suspect that the first reply would be—well look at what happens in some other countries where that is permitted. As in so many other matters, strong feelings are based on one's general experience rather than on specific reasons, and it often requires an effort to marshall one's reasons. But public policy is generally the result of strong feelings, commonly held, rather than of cold argument. If the law is to be developed in accord with public policy we must not be too legalistic in our general approach. No doubt public policy is an unruly horse to ride but in a chapter of the law so intimately associated with public policy as contempt of court we must not be too pedestrian . . .'.   [74] Ibid.

[75] 427 US 539 (1976).

were virtually no conceivable circumstances in which an injunction could be granted to restrain publication of press stories analysing either the moral or legal merits even of ongoing, still less pending litigation.[76] A similarly profound distinction between 'traditional' American and English law is also evident in respect of the final topic we consider in this chapter—the issue of political libels.

Political libels

The tort of libel is something of a curiosity within the field of tort law. In general, a plaintiff in a tort action has to prove that the defendant's actions have caused her a quantifiable loss. She usually also has to demonstrate that the loss was caused by some level of fault (usually negligence) on the defendant's part. The damage at issue in a libel action is to the plaintiff's reputation, which has allegedly been undermined by a book or article published by the defendant. In a libel action, damage is presumed to flow automatically from the publication of libellous material; that is, material that damages the reputation of the victim in the eyes of fair-minded observers. That the material is true is a defence, but it is for the defendant to prove truth. In general, under English law, the publisher had no defence if she did not know the material was false even if she had taken reasonable care to establish its accuracy.

The US—a constitutional law perspective

In the United States, the English law of libel has come to be seen as imposing an unacceptable restriction on freedom of speech in relation to political issues. This is because it is feared that politicians and government bodies would be able to suppress media criticism of their activities by threatening a libel action. If the publisher was not wholly confident she/he could prove truth—which might be difficult in respect of many political stories— she might be deterred by the prospect of a large damages award against her from running stories which might well prove to be true. Consequently, by the early-twentieth century, many American states had accepted the principle that a *government body* should not be able to initiate any form of legal action at all to suppress criticism of its activities—unless the speech concerned threatened an imminent breach of the peace. The leading case is *City of Chicago v Tribune Co.*[77]

The press stories which provoked the litigation had accused the Mayor and the city council of Chicago of being so corrupt and incompetent that the city itself was bankrupt. Such stories could obviously undermine the city's reputation, both as an institution of government and as a commercial actor. Yet the Illinois Supreme Court, its unanimous opinion delivered by Thompson CJ, held that the city could do nothing at all to suppress the dissemination of such stories.

The judgment was formally rooted in Art 2, s 4 of the Illinois Constitution: 'Every person may freely speak, write and publish on all subjects, being responsible for the abuse of that liberty', but the reasoning the Court deployed had an overtly functionalist base. Thompson CJ observed that State and federal government in the United States were 'founded upon the fundamental principle that the citizen is the fountain of all authority'.[78] Such powers as government bodies possessed were granted on trust by the relevant electorate. Informed electoral choices demanded that citizens be afforded *absolute* protection against prosecution for criticising government bodies, except in the narrow instance of criticism likely to promote violent disorder.

---

[76] For a concise analysis of the leading cases see Lockhart W, Kamisat Y, Choper J, and Shiffrin S (6th edn, 1986) *Constitutional law* pp 830–836.

[77] 139 NE 86 (1923). For a detailed discussion and analysis see Loveland I (1998) '*City of Chicago v Tribune Co—in contexts*', in Loveland I (ed) *Importing the First Amendment*. [78] 139 NE 86 at 90 (1923).

Having thus limited the legitimate scope of criminal libel, Thompson CJ drew an analogy between criminal and civil actions. He suggested that civil actions could be substantially more effective prohibitors of speech than criminal prosecutions: civil libel actions, unlike criminal prosecutions, did not grant the defendant the presumption of innocence; they imposed a lesser standard of proof on the plaintiff; and there was no ceiling to the damages that might be awarded.

Thompson CJ stressed that the protection against civil liability for criticising a government body was *absolute*; no action of any sort would be permissible. There was no question of the Court trying to strike a 'balance' between freedom of political speech and the government's reputation; the government body had no corporate or public interest in its reputation to weigh in the scales.

Thompson CJ accepted that the rule the Court had propounded would sometimes lead to unfounded and malevolent criticism being aired. This however was a price worth paying:

> [I]t is better that an occasional individual or newspaper that is so perverted in its judgment and so misguided in his or its civic duty should go free than that all of the citizens should be put in jeopardy of imprisonment or economic subjugation if they venture to criticise an inefficient or corrupt government.[79]

American States which adopted this principle recognised that there would be little point in preventing government bodies launching libel actions if such bodies could indirectly achieve the same deterrent effect on freedom of political speech through actions initiated by individual politicians under the ordinary libel laws. Thus, importantly, these States also accepted that individual politicians or government officials could only succeed in a libel action in relation to their political beliefs and behaviour if they could prove that the defendant had knowingly or recklessly published false information.[80] The device used to achieve this objective was the long recognised English law defence of 'qualified privilege', which in English law had only ever been applied to a narrow range of types of information, such as commercial or familial matters, in which it was assumed that both the disseminee and the recipient of the libellous information were under a duty to exchange it.[81] The American rationale, not embraced in England, was that in a representative democracy all citizens (and all media organisations) were under a reciprocal duty to disseminate, analyse, and discuss political information in so far as it related to the fitness for office of elected politicians, candidates for such office, and senior appointed government officials. By the 1960s, these principles had been embraced by the US Supreme Court in the landmark case of *New York Times v Sullivan*,[82] and applied through the First Amendment to all of the American States.

Britain—a tort law perspective

English law had, in contrast, adopted a very limited understanding of the extent to which individuals and the press should be protected from the ordinary law of libel when publishing political information. In the 1868 case of *Wason v Walter*,[83] the Court accepted that newspapers which offered verbatim accounts of parliamentary proceedings should enjoy a common

---

[79] Ibid, at 91. The passage echoes Madison's celebrated observation, which Thompson CJ had earlier quoted (at 89), that: 'Some degree of abuse is inseparable from the proper use of everything, and in no instance is this more true than in that of the press. It has accordingly been decided by the practice of the states that it is better to leave a few of the noxious branches to their luxuriant growth than by pruning them away to injure the vigour of those yielding the proper fruits'.

[80] See especially *Coleman v McClennan* 98 PAC 201 (1908) (Kansas); *Ambrosious v O'Farrell* 199 Ill App 265 (1905) (Illinois); *Briggs v Garrett* 11 Pa 406 (1886) (Pennsylvania);. For a detailed discussion see Loveland (1998) op cit.   [81] See Loveland I (2000) *Political libels* ch 1.

[82] 376 US 254 (1964). The case is discussed in some detail in Loveland (2000) op cit ch 5; and in great detail in Lewis A (1991) *Make no law*.   [83] (1868) LR 4 QB 73.

law protection analogous to that bestowed upon proceedings in Parliament by Art 9 of the Bill of Rights. The Court's reasoning in *Wason*—unusually in the English context—framed the issue as one essentially of constitutional law and political morality. Common law libel rules should not be allowed to prevent voters reaching informed conclusions about what was happening in the Houses of Parliament. The task of the common law was to give expression to the public interest; and, as Cockburn CJ saw the matter: 'There is perhaps no subject matter in which the public have a deeper interest than in all that relates to the conduct of public servants of the state'.[84]

Perhaps ironically, it was the reasoning in this case which provided the inspiration which led American courts in the next fifty years to extend protection for political libels to a much wider range of political information, on the grounds that coverage of legislative proceedings was by no means sufficient to enable citizens to acquire the knowledge they would need in order to offer their informed consent to the government process.[85] Such developments were as often rooted in common law as in interpretation of the texts of state constitutions. These courts took Cockburn's CJ's reference in *Wason* to 'all' political information quite literally.

Notwithstanding English law's evident fondness for literalism as a jurisprudential technique, this American development was not systematically mirrored either by Parliament or the courts in the United Kingdom,[86] with the result that even by the 1980s English law drew no obvious distinction between libels dealing with political issues and those affecting purely private matters. Two cases illustrate this point with great clarity.

The defendant in *Bognor Regis UDC v Campion*[87] had waged a campaign against what he claimed was corruption in his local authority. The suit was triggered by a pamphlet authored by Campion which contained an hysterical polemic accusing the ruling group on the council of ineptitude and dishonesty. Rather than ignore the pamphlet, the council's ruling group resolved that the council itself should sue Mr Campion in libel.

The issue before Browne J in the High Court was whether the authority could maintain such an action. He saw no difficulty in concluding that it could. A council was simply an individual for these purposes:

> Just as a trading company has a trading reputation which it is entitled to protect by bringing an action for defamation, so in my view the plaintiffs as a local government corporation have a 'governing reputation' which they are equally entitled to protect in the same way . . . [88]

Judgment was eventually delivered against Mr Campion. The award of damages was only £2,000, but this was accompanied by an order to pay the council's costs, which amounted to some £30,000.[89] A bill of £32,000 (at 1972 prices) might be thought to have a decidedly deterrent effect on citizens or newspapers wishing to criticise a local authority's behaviour. But there is nothing in Browne J's judgment to indicate that he perceived the case to have any 'political' or constitutional dimension at all. The action was characterised simply as a matter of tort law.

Ten years later, in *Blackshaw v Lord*,[90] the Court of Appeal acknowledged the argument that political libels might raise a 'constitutional law' issue; but having acknowledged the argument, the judges accorded it no weight. The litigation concerned a *Daily Telegraph* story written by Lord which alleged that the Department of Energy had apparently breached Treasury guidelines and overpaid some £52m in grants to various oil companies. Several civil servants were reprimanded following internal disciplinary proceedings. The Commons

---

[84] Ibid, at 89.   [85] Loveland (2000) op cit ch 3.

[86] For an account of some exceptions to this general trend see ibid, chs 4 and 6.   [87] [1972] 2 QB 169.

[88] Ibid, at 175.

[89] Weir A (1972) 'Local authority v critical ratepayer—a suit in defamation' *Cambridge LJ* 238.

[90] [1984] QB 1, CA.

Public Accounts Committee investigated the affair, and issued a report. The article linked the report to the resignation of a senior civil servant, Blackshaw, who held the rank of Under-Secretary. The Permanent Secretary at the Department of Energy had told the PAC that an Under-Secretary had been reprimanded. Just after Lord's story ran, the Permanent Secretary informed the PAC that this was false; no Under-Secretary had been reprimanded. Blackshaw claimed that the story libelled him, in that it implied that his professional incompetence had cost the taxpayer £52m.

At trial, Lord claimed that a story dealing with so obviously political a matter should attract qualified privilege. This argument was accepted by the trial judge. His conclusion was however overturned in the Court of Appeal, which held that the press had no duty to publish stories of this type to the public at large. Fox LJ doubted that the general public had any 'audience interest' in this sort of story. He concluded simply that 'an allegation of improper or negligent conduct against a public servant may be privileged if made to persons having a proper interest to receive it—such as the police or senior officials'.[91] The electorate had no legitimate interest in such information.

Conclusion

Fox LJ's suggestion that the electorate had 'no proper interest' in being provided with press analysis (which was neither deliberately dishonest nor reckless as to truth) of important political issues offers a most compelling illustration of the antediluvian state of the common law's human rights jurisprudence in the mid-1980s. It is no answer to this criticism to explain it away as a necessary consequence of the doctrine of parliamentary sovereignty; that, in the absence of a codified statement of entrenched, fundamental civil liberties such as those in the US's Bill of Rights, the courts simply had no legitimate scope to fashion a systematic approach to the issue of human rights protection. Even within the constitutional constraints imposed on the judiciary by the existence of a sovereign legislature, there was scope for such principles to have emerged and hardened as moral yardsticks against which to measure responses to purely common law problems or to structure the task of statutory interpretation. As we have seen in this, and previous chapters, there were undoubtedly exceptions to this general proposition. But English law could not lay any plausible claim at this time even to have addressed, still less embraced, any systematic methodology for the identification and protection of human rights issues. The lacuna is perhaps all the more surprising because by the mid-1980s the United Kingdom had been for almost forty years a signatory to an extensive body of international law dealing with civil liberties questions—the European Convention on Human Rights.

Suggested further reading

Academic and political commentary

COPPELL J and O'Neill A (1994) 'The European Court of Justice: taking rights seriously' *Legal Studies* 227

WARREN S and BRANDEIS L (1890) 'The right to privacy' *Harvard LR* 193

BARENDT E (1987) *Freedom of speech* ch 3

ROBERTSON G (1999) *The justice game* ch 6

---

[91] Ibid, per Fox LJ at 41.

Drewry G (1985b) 'Leaking in the public interest' *Public Law* 203

Palmer S (1990) 'Tightening secrecy law: the Official Secrets Act 1989' *Public Law* 243

Case law and legislation

Malone v Metropolitan Police Commissioner [1979] Ch 344

City of Chicago v Tribune Co. (1923) 139 NE 86

Bognor Regis UDC v Campion [1972] 2 QB 169

Attorney-General v Guardian Newspapers Ltd (No. 2) [1990] 1 AC 109

Secretary of State for Defence v Guardian Newspapers Ltd [1985] AC 339

Chapter 18

Human Rights II: Emergent Principles

This chapter offers a limited introduction to the European Convention on Human Rights. Section I discusses the main procedural and substantive features of the Convention itself. Section II assesses the status of the Convention in English law up until (approximately) the early-1990s. And sections III and IV examine the leading judgments of the European Court on Human Rights in the areas of privacy and freedom of expression addressed in chapter seventeen.

I. The European Convention on Human Rights— introductory principles

The European Convention on Human Rights[1] is an international treaty, originating like the EC, in the reconstruction of Europe's political order following World War II. In 1949, twenty-five European states formed a body known as the Council of Europe.[2] The Council's broad concern was to foster the growth and entrenchment of democratic government within western Europe. One means of doing so was to persuade its members to become signatories to the Convention.

The Convention's terms cover a wide sweep of political issues, broadly comparable to those in the US's Bill of Rights. Article 2 safeguards the right to life. Article 3 prohibits the use of torture, and the infliction of degrading or inhuman treatment and/or punishment. Articles 5 and 6 are aimed primarily at the conduct of criminal proceedings. Article 7 places strict limits on retrospective criminal laws. Article 8 addresses the right to privacy and family life, while Art 12 concerns the right of adults to marry and found a family. Articles 9 and 10 focus on freedom

---

[1] <http://www.echr.coe.int/Documents/Convention_ENG.pdf>.

[2] Which should not be confused either with the EC's Council of Ministers or the EU's European Council. On the Council of Europe's formation, and the subsequent production of the Convention, see Robertson A and Merrill J (3rd edn, 1994) *Human rights in Europe* ch 1.

of thought, conscience, religious belief, and expression,[3] and Art 11 concerns the right to freedom of assembly and association, including the right to join a trade union.

Institutional and jurisdictional issues

The Council of Europe also established several institutions to enforce and monitor the Convention's provisions. The European Commission of Human Rights (EComHR) was established to perform both an investigatory and conciliatory role. Its members were distinguished lawyers, their number being equal to the number of states which have ratified the Convention; no state could have more than one of its nationals sitting on the Commission.[4] The Commission was the body to which complaints of a breach of the Convention were initially notified. The Commission was also empowered to determine if the complaint was admissible. The Commission would not admit complaints which it considered 'manifestly ill-founded'. Furthermore, per Art 26, the applicant must have exhausted all effective domestic remedies before the Commission would intervene. Nor could the Commission act if the applicant raised a question which was 'substantially the same' as one with which the Commission or Court had already dealt. Admissibility proved a formidable hurdle for applicants to surmount. By 1990, the Commission had entertained over 17,000 applications; fewer than 700 were admitted.[5] It would thus be inaccurate to portray the Commission as a body which was constantly interfering with the internal affairs of the Convention's Signatory States.

Should the Commission have concluded that the complaint was justified, it attempted to negotiate a 'friendly settlement' between the parties. If no settlement could be reached, the Commission drafted an 'opinion' detailing its view of the breach, which was sent to the Committee of Ministers (comprising the foreign ministers of each Signatory State). The Committee could either (by a two-thirds majority) produce its own 'judgment', or could refer the case to the European Court of Human Rights (ECtHR). The term 'judgment' is used guardedly. The Convention does not require the Committee to adopt court-style procedures. Its decision-making process is conducted in secret, and the impugned Member State can vote on the outcome. This process is obviously unsatisfactory from a narrowly legalistic perspective, but it does alert observers to the important fact that the Convention was designed to retain a substantial 'inter-national' element.

Approximately 25% of the Commission's opinions were dealt with in this way. The majority were in contrast referred to the European Court on Human Rights (ECtHR). The Court's members were selected by the Committee of Ministers, generally for a nine-year term; the Court's total membership could not exceed the number of Signatory States, and no state could have more than one of its nationals sitting on the bench. The applicant was not formally a party to the ECtHR proceedings, although she could appear and be legally represented. Her case was presented on her behalf by the Commission, although the Commission's role in such proceedings was technically the 'defender of the public interest', rather than the applicant's advocate.

Article 46 of the Convention provides: '1. The High Contracting Parties undertake to abide by the final judgment of the Court in any case to which they are parties.' Responsibility for ensuring compliance is entrusted to the Committee of Ministers. Compliance generally requires the offending state to alter its domestic law in a manner which satisfies the ECtHR's judgment. Thus far, such amendments have almost always been forthcoming. The Convention has therefore to some extent 'federalised' the constitutional orders of some of its signatory nations. Its provisions are the supreme source of legal authority in some states. For those countries whose constitutions provide that treaty obligations automatically become part of domestic

---

[3] The scope of the initial Convention has been expanded by various protocols, although not all the original Signatory States have acceded to all of these.   [4] See Robertson and Merrill op cit ch 7.

[5] Bailey, Harris, and Jones (1992) op cit p 757.

law, or have made specific arrangements to accord the Convention that status, it is also (to borrow familiar terminology) 'directly effective'; their own courts must apply the ECtHR's case law, a situation which greatly speeds their citizens' access to their Convention entitlements. Yet there is no requirement in the Convention itself that Signatory States make its provisions directly effective at all in domestic law. The Convention does not demand that its terms can be enforced by national courts. In many states, citizens were instead required to exhaust all their domestic remedies before invoking a right of direct complaint to the Commission itself. However, the Convention does not even insist that Signatory States grant individuals this right of petition to the EComHR. In those countries, the Convention operates more as a source of diplomatic rather than legal obligation; it exists in the realm of international law rather than constitutional law. The conformity of such states' laws with the Convention can be challenged only at by another Signatory State.[6]

The absence of a direct effect requirement within the Convention has meant that citizens of states which granted the right of petition might find that pursuing a complaint to the Court proved a very time-consuming process. Suits are rarely concluded in under two years, and time spans of five years between the first action in a domestic court and the eventual ECtHR judgment were not uncommon.

In 1999, in a significant procedural reform, the Commission and the Court merged into a single body, styled as the ECtHR.[7] It was hoped that the reform would make the ECtHR more accessible to citizens, speed up litigation, and also reduce costs. The merged Court is substantially larger than its predecessor, and will do much of its work in 'Chambers' of a few members, rather than in a plenary session in which all judges will sit.[8] Article 43 of the Convention now provides for an appeal from the court in session to lie in some circumstances to the full court, which is now referred to as the 'Grand Chamber'.

The jurisprudential methodology of the Convention

In one important sense, albeit not necessarily a supra-legislative legal sense, the Convention articulates a series of 'higher law' moral principles ostensibly embedded within the political cultures of its Signatory States. It might readily be thought that in some of those states, where democratic traditions enjoy only a precarious foothold in political culture, accession to the Convention was intended more as a sop to international opinion rather than a sincere attempt to restrain the potential abuse of governmental power.[9] Yet one should not equate the Convention's embrace of supposedly fundamental moral principles with the imposition of a rigid constitutional orthodoxy on those Signatory States which have committed themselves bona fide to respect its terms.

Contingent rather than absolute entitlements

The Convention does not impose a uniform coda of detailed legal rules. Its text is itself liberally sprinkled with provisions allowing states to derogate from its formal provisions. Article

---

[6] ie the equivalent of an Art 170 action under the Treaty of Rome: see 'The roles of the European Court of Justice (ECJ)', ch 11, pp 288–289. There have been very few such actions: see Bailey, Harris, and Jones (1992) op cit pp 756–757.

[7] For the background to the reform, and an indication of its details, see Schermers H (1993) 'The European Court of Human Rights after the merger' *European Law Review* 493.

[8] On the final shape of the reforms see Mowbray A (1999) 'The composition and operation of the new European Court of Human Rights' *Public Law* 219.

[9] In 2000, for example, the countries adhering to the Convention included Romania, Bulgaria, and the Ukraine, in respect of which it was then absurd to suggest that the governmental system was in any meaningful sense democratic. It might of course be argued that such countries should ratify the ECHR, in the hope that so doing might make a contribution to the consolidation of democratic governance within their constitutional orders.

15, for example, is a derogation clause of wide application in respect of many Convention entitlements, through which a state can seek permission de jure to 'opt out' of Convention obligations for limited periods. Similarly, the 'rights' protected in specific articles of the Convention are often immediately qualified by provisions permitting state interference. For example, the 'right to life' protected in Art 2 contains an exception for 'the execution of a sentence of a court following . . . conviction for a crime for which this penalty is provided by law'.

Similarly, while Art 10(1) provides that:

Freedom of expression

1. Everyone has the right to freedom of expression. This right shall include freedom to hold opinions and to receive and impart information and ideas without interference by public authority and regardless of frontiers. This Article shall not prevent States from requiring the licensing of broadcasting, television or cinema enterprises.

Art 10(2) substantially qualifies that 'right' in these terms:

> The exercise of these freedoms, since it carries with it duties and responsibilities, may be subject to such formalities, conditions, restrictions or penalties as are prescribed by law and are necessary in a democratic society, in the interests of national security, territorial integrity or public safety, for the prevention of disorder or crime, for the protection of health or morals, for the protection of the reputations or rights of others, for preventing the disclosure of information received in confidence, or for maintaining the authority and impartiality of the judiciary.

This constitutional methodology pervades the Convention. In the main, the Convention's articles identify and afford protection to a broadly defined civil right (what we might call 'the presumptive entitlement'); the text then permits Signatory States to interfere with the presumptive entitlement in defence of certain specified objectives (what we might call 'legitimate interference'); but it then in turn requires that intrusion to comply with certain safeguards; that is, that it be 'prescribed by law' and 'necessary in a democratic society'.

The same scheme of reasoning can be seen in the text of Art 8, which protects 'privacy and family life':

1. Everyone has the right to respect for his private and family life, his home and his correspondence.
2. There shall be no interference by a public authority with the exercise of this right except such as is in accordance with the law and is necessary in a democratic society in the interests of national security, public safety or the economic well-being of the country, for the prevention of disorder or crime, for the protection of health or morals, or for the protection of the rights and freedoms of others.

A four stage inquiry

The way in which this textual methodology has been applied by the ECtHR is perhaps best illustrated by examining the Court's decision-making process in Art 10 cases. Its technique can be broken down into four stages.

Firstly, the Court will ask if a governmental body has in some way interfered with the applicant's presumptive entitlement to free expression? If the answer is 'No' then the claim will obviously fail.

Secondly, if the first answer is 'Yes', the ECtHR will ask if the government body has interfered with the entitlement in pursuit of a legitimate objective arising from one or more of the factors identified in Art 10(2); that is, national security, territorial integrity etc. This test is generally unproblematic from a state's perspective. If however the ECtHR considers that the objective being pursued is not a legitimate one a breach of the Convention will be established without any need to consider stages three and four.

If the answer is again 'Yes' (ie the state's objective is legitimate), the Court moves to stage three, in which it considers if the restriction is 'prescribed by law'; that is, is its content accurately identified in the domestic legal system? The primary point of reference for the meaning of this concept is now provided by the ECtHR in its 1979 judgment in *Sunday Times v United Kingdom*:

> a norm cannot be regarded as a 'law' unless it is formulated with sufficient precision to enable the citizen to regulate his conduct; he must be able, if need be with appropriate advice—to foresee to a degree that is reasonable in all the circumstances, the consequences which a given action may entail.[10]

The ECtHR has not accepted that a measure can only be 'prescribed by/according to law' if it has a legislative base. The Court has recognised that a body of judge-made rules such as the common law may pass that test, even if—as is the case with common law—the state's indigenous legal principles permit the substance of that law to change in response to altered social and economic circumstances or moral perceptions. Thus, in *The Sunday Times* case, the ECtHR continued after the above quotation in the following way:

> Those consequences need not be attainable with absolute certainty: experience shows this to be unattainable. Again, whilst certainty is highly desirable, it may bring in its train excessive rigidity and the law must be able to keep pace with changing circumstances. Accordingly many laws are inevitably couched in terms which, to a greater or lesser extent, are vague and whose interpretation and application are questions of practice.[11]

Should the government's interference fail that test, a breach of Art 10 is established. The 'prescribed by law' test speaks to what was earlier described as the 'How?' element of the rule of law.[12] Its concern is—to put the matter somewhat simplistically—with the procedural rather than the substantive dimension of the relationship between government and citizens.[13]

If the interference in issue is 'prescribed by law', the ECtHR then moves to the fourth and final stage of its analysis: is the measure taken 'necessary in a democratic society'? This is the most complex and controversial area of the ECtHR's jurisprudence. Its concern is explicitly with the 'What?' element of the rule of law; namely what substantive restraints may a Signatory State legitimately impose upon its citizens?

In interpreting this aspect of the Convention, the ECtHR has developed a principle known as 'the margin of appreciation'. In formulating its approach to the 'necessary in a democratic society' provision, the ECtHR has repeatedly stressed that it does not see the Convention's role as imposing a series of common, detailed legal rules on all of the Signatory States. The Court's jurisdiction is not de jure appellate, nor—in most situations—could its jurisdiction be so classified in a de facto sense. In much of its activity, the Court's task could be seen—if one were searching for an indigenous British comparator—as supervisory in a rather loose, almost *Wednesbury* irrationality sense. Neither does the Court quash or invalidate national laws. Its remedial role is

---

[10] (1979) 2 EHRR 245 at para 49. The case, which dealt with the *A-G v Times Newspapers* litigation (see 'Contempt of court', ch 17, pp 471–473) is discussed in detail later in the chapter.

[11] Ibid. The ECtHR is quite accommodating to this common law tradition. The best illustration of the point is perhaps provided by the Court's eventual decision in the *R v R (marital rape exemption)* case: [1992] 1 AC 599, HL: see 'Retrospectivity at common law? Rape within marriage', ch 3, pp 71–74. The ECtHR's judgment is given in *SW v United Kingdom; CR v United Kingdom* (1995) 21 EHRR 363. R challenged his conviction on the basis that the House of Lords' judgment had breached the Art 7 prohibition on retrospective criminal laws. The ECtHR saw no merit in this argument. The Court held that the orderly evolution of the common law did not per se amount to retrospectivity. On this particular issue, the Court considered that it was perfectly clear by the time R 'raped' his wife that the scope of the marital consent defence was diminishing and that it was plausible to assume that it might at any point be narrowed further or be removed altogether.

[12] See 'The rule of law and the separation of powers', ch 3, p 44.

[13] The term 'citizen' is used here loosely, simply to denote any individual who falls within the state's jurisdiction.

essentially declaratory in nature, although it also has the power under Art 41 to order a state to pay 'damages' (the term used in the text is 'just satisfaction') to successful applicants. Subsequent compliance with the Court's judgments is a matter for the Signatory State concerned.

This point is well conveyed by the ECtHR's judgment in *Handyside v United Kingdom*.[14] The applicant, a book publisher, had been convicted under English obscenity laws for distributing a publication called *The Little Red Schoolbook*.[15] Before the ECtHR, the UK government argued that this interference with freedom of expression was justified 'for the protection of morals'. Having accepted this argument, and having agreed that the UK's obscenity laws met the 'prescribed by law' test, the Court then turned to consider whether the laws were 'necessary in a democratic society'. The Court stressed that when questions of 'the protection of morals' were in issue, it would be reluctant to conclude that state measures were not necessary:

> By reason of their direct and continuous contact with the vital forces of their countries, state authorities are in principle in a better position than the international judge to give an opinion ... on the necessity of a 'restriction' or 'penalty'.[16]

This did not mean that the ECtHR had no role to play in such circumstances; but rather that its jurisdiction would be secondary, almost residual, in nature:

> Nevertheless, Art 10(2) does not give the contracting states an unlimited power of appreciation. The Court is empowered to give the final ruling on whether a 'restriction' or 'penalty' is reconcilable with freedom of expression as protected by Art 10.[17]

This principle speaks to a limited notion of justiciability in both a substantive and transnational sense. The Court accepts that the classification and regulation of 'obscene' material is an intensely 'moral' question. This does not per se render the matter non-justiciable, since prosecutions for obscenity are necessarily judged on their detailed merits by national courts. However, moral questions evidently acquire a much less justiciable status when they are exported beyond their indigenous national boundaries. In describing itself as an 'international' rather than 'constitutional' court, the ECtHR seems to suggest that it lacks the cultural competence to conduct a close examination of the merits of a state's laws. Thus, while the Court would insist that a measure was only 'necessary' if it met what the Court termed 'a pressing social need' and was 'proportionate' in the sense of not interfering unduly with the presumptive entitlement, it would not subject the state's own conclusions on these points to rigorous scrutiny.

The consequences of this relaxed standard of review could be spun in either a positive or negative light. It could be seen as having the desirable outcome of respecting the autonomy of Signatory States on moral matters. Alternatively, it might be viewed as abandoning the liberties of individuals or small minorities to the intolerance of national majorities.[18]

It is however clear that as a matter of general principle—we explore the point in a more detailed context later—the breadth of the margin of appreciation afforded to Signatory States (and thence the practical nature of the EComHR's and the Court's jurisdiction) is not uniform

---

[14] [1976] 1 EHRR 737.

[15] Hansen S and Jensen J (1969). The original version of the book (published in 1969) was in Danish, authored by two politically radical Danish teachers. The book—aimed at teenagers—urged them to question the authority of their parents and teachers, especially in relation to matters of sexuality and drug use. For further background see Fiengold C (1978) 'The Little Red Schoolbook and the ECHR' *Human Rights Review* 21. For an interesting retrospective on the book (and the mores of the era) listen to Jenkins J (2008) 'The little red schoolbook' (BBC Radio 4 series '*In living memory*' available at: <http://www.bbc.co.uk/radio4/inlivingmemory/pip/62r6s/>.

[16] (1976) 1 EHRR 737 at para 48.   [17] Ibid, at para 49.

[18] For a powerful critique from this perspective see Jones T (1996) 'The devaluation of human rights under the European Convention' *Public Law* 430. See also Warbrick C (1998) 'Federalism and free speech', in Loveland I (ed) *Importing the First Amendment?*

in respect of all the Convention's provisions; rather it varies according to the particular presumptive entitlements and/or legitimate interferences in issue. In many situations, the ECtHR will seem to function more as a 'constitutional' than 'international' court; it will look closely at the merits of the legitimate interference, and will accept that it is 'necessary' only if the Court itself is convinced that, given the detailed circumstances of the case, the measure has indeed been undertaken to satisfy a 'pressing social need' and if the means chosen to achieve the desired end are 'proportionate' in the sense of interfering as little as possible with the presumptive entitlement. An examination of the intricacies of the way in which the Court has pursued this approach across the whole spectrum of Convention entitlements is beyond the scope of this book.[19] We return to the issue later in the chapter, but at this point we might just note that the Court subjects state laws to quite varying standards of scrutiny depending on the issue at stake.

II. The initial status of the ECHR in domestic law

It is perhaps worth repeating the point that, in contrast to the status of EC law, the Convention does not require that its terms be given 'direct effect' in the Signatory States. Nor did the Convention even require that states grant their citizens direct access to the Commission and the ECtHR. In countries where the Convention is neither directly effective, nor actionable by individuals before the ECtHR itself, compliance with its terms would be a matter to be resolved through the political rather than the legal process.

    Although Attlee's 1945–1950 Labour government was closely involved in drafting and promoting the Convention, his Cabinet was bitterly divided on the question of whether this country should even be a signatory.[20] Atlee's government did eventually accede to the Convention. However, it was not until the mid-1960s that a UK government (Harold Wilson's first Labour administration) allowed UK citizens the right of direct access to the ECtHR. And, prior to 1997, no post-war government ever introduced a Bill to give any domestic legal effect to the Convention before UK courts.[21] UK citizens were thus apparently unable to enforce its terms before their courts.

Political responses—why did Parliament not 'incorporate' the ECHR?

Parliament's failure to give any provisions of the ECHR any degree of enforceability before the domestic courts cannot be explained on simple party political grounds. Both Labour and Conservative governments consistently refused to promote the necessary legislation. It is also misleading to suggest that this reluctance stemmed from an objectively defensible concern to ensure that the wishes of a democratically elected legislature are not frustrated by the unelected judiciary. That argument fails on several counts. The shortcomings in 'Parliament's' democratic credentials have already been alluded to; the Commons' electoral system was (and remains) crudely minoritarian, and the Lords' composition was until 1999

---

[19] Both Janis, Bradley, and Kay op cit and Harris, O'Boyle, and Warbrick op cit undertake the task admirably.

[20] On the Atlee government's views see Lester A (1984) 'Fundamental rights: the United Kingdom isolated' *Public Law* 46. Much the most informative guide to and analysis is provided by Simpson A (2001) *Human rights and the end of empire*.

[21] It is perhaps best to avoid simplistic use of the term 'incorporate' to refer to Parliament's use of statute to give domestic legal force to provisions of internal law. As suggested in ch 2 and ch 11, the question of the domestic status which Parliament accords to international law has several discrete dimensions; relating to matters of accessibility, hierarchy, and interpretive competence respectively. See 'Inconsistency with international law', ch 2, pp 29–30 and 'The status of EC law within the legal systems of the Member States', ch 11, pp 289–291.

entirely indefensible.[22] Moreover, if the ECHR were to be incorporated (on terms analogous to those used in the ECA 1972), the government and Parliament's subordination would not be to the domestic courts, but to the ECtHR, on whose behalf the British courts would act as an agent. Rather, the Convention's formal constitutional status as merely international law seems to derive from the traditional unwillingness of either the Labour or Conservative Parties to accept the moral premise that they are not each entitled to make whatever use they wish of Parliament's sovereignty whenever their electoral fortunes afford them a Commons majority.

The legal education of many law students in Britain in the past thirty years has included exposure to successive editions of Professor John Griffith's celebrated work on *The Politics of the judiciary*. Griffith promoted considerable controversy in suggesting that the judiciary's social and educational background predisposed most judges to adopt a highly conservative attitude when faced with contentious political questions. Griffith was not accusing judges of acting in a crudely party political sense:

> But it is demonstrable that on every major social issue which has come before the courts during the last 30 years—concerning industrial relations, political protest, race relations, governmental secrecy, police powers, moral behaviour—the judges have supported the conventional, established and settled interests. And they have reacted strongly against challenges to those interests.[23]

Griffith suggested that such judicial bias may explain the Labour Party's historic reluctance to embrace the idea of a supra-legislative constitution. The Griffith thesis—which enjoyed considerable influence on the political left despite its rather simplistic arguments—draws much of its force from its attachment to such a crude notion of 'democracy'. The unelected judiciary's 'conservatism' was undesirable because it obstructed the policies preferred by the 'democratically elected' government of the day. Such assumptions are themselves vulnerable to criticism on the ground that they leave a rather more important question unasked—namely whether it is 'democratic' for a constitution to permit barely majoritarian or even minoritarian ideologies to exercise ultimate control of the law-making process. In a democracy which had placed its basic moral principles beyond the reach of bare majorities, one would of course expect the judiciary to adopt a conservative stance in defence of constituent moral values. By doing so, they evince loyalty to a rather broader conception of 'the people' than one is likely to find in a transient electoral majority. This might suggest that in so far as judicial conservatism reveals a 'problem' within the constitution, it is a problem that stems from the doctrine of parliamentary sovereignty rather than from the courts.

Nonetheless, the notion that it was 'undemocratic' to place supra-legislative authority in the hands of the judges—both domestic and European—exercised a sufficiently strong grip on both the Labour and Conservative Party leaderships to make legislative incorporation of the Convention a non-issue in British political circles until the late-1990s. The notion that the Convention should restrain the power of Parliament itself was regarded as absurd, and even the more modest proposition that the Convention should operate as a de jure check on government power in the field of administrative law attracted minimal political support.

The suggestion that this opposition to incorporation rested on an implacable hostility to the possibility of the imposition of 'foreign' legal solutions to domestic political problems is not easy to sustain. The UK's record in complying with adverse ECtHR judgments through the eventual enactment of legislation was almost flawless. As noted in section I of this chapter, it is also generally misleading to suggest that the Convention imposes rules on Signatory States. Defeat before the Court usually means no more than that the Signatory State must accept that its discretion in respect of certain matters is not quite as broad as it would like. And, as is indicated by the cases discussed in the final sections of this chapter, the EComHR and the

---

[22] Quite how defensible it is now is obviously a matter of some controversy: see 'The "reformed" House of Lords', ch 6, pp 160–161.   [23] Op cit pp 239–240. The thirty years in question being the mid-1940s to the mid-1970s.

Court have often found governmental decisions which generated acute political controversy in the United Kingdom to be perfectly compatible with the Convention. Before reaching that question however, it is helpful to spend some time exploring the way in which the Convention was deployed in domestic law by the courts.

Legal responses—the ECHR as a source of principle at common law

Murray Hunt's influential analysis of the Convention's role in domestic law records that for the first twenty years of its existence—between 1953 and 1973—the Convention was cited only once in domestic law reports, and that was in a case involving the institutional status of the EComHR.[24] The first allusions made to it (Hunt describes them as 'fleeting' and 'passing' references)[25] as a potential influence on individual rights under English law appeared in *Cassell & Co Ltd v Broome*,[26] a House of Lords' judgment on damages in libel cases, and *Waddington v Miah*,[27] an immigration case which addressed whether a particular statutory provision imposed retrospective criminal liability.

The Convention's virtual invisibility in domestic law in this period is something of a puzzle. As suggested in discussing in chapters two and eleven the relationship between statute and international law, English courts had long accepted that while the terms of an unincorporated treaty could not override the clear meaning of an Act of Parliament, they could be invoked as an aid to the interpretation of ambiguous statutory provisions. Thus the fact that the Convention had not been incorporated into domestic law by Parliament did not mean that it was invariably irrelevant in domestic proceedings. This principle as to the general status of international law had been clearly recognised in *Mortensen v Peters*.[28] As Lord Kyllachy put it—in somewhat equivocal terms:

> [I]t may probably be conceded that there is always a certain presumption against the legislature of any country asserting or assuming the existence of a territorial jurisdiction going beyond limits established by the common consent on nations—that is to say by International law.[29]

The principle was reiterated in a much more forceful and expansive form sixty years later by Diplock LJ in *Salomon v Customs and Excise Comrs*:

> If the terms of the legislation are clear and unambiguous they must be given effect to whether or not they carry out Her Majesty's treaty obligations . . . If the terms of the legislation are not clear, however, but are reasonably capable of more than one meaning, the treaty itself becomes relevant, for there is a prima facie presumption that Parliament does not intend to act in breach of international law . . . ; and if one of the meanings that can reasonably be ascribed to the legislation is consonant with the treaty obligations and another or others are not, the meaning which is consonant is to be preferred.[30]

That neither counsel nor the judges made any resort to the Convention as an interpretive aid when faced with ambiguous legislation or common law rules impacting upon civil liberties may perhaps be explained by a complacent assumption that UK law—being the product of a 'democratic' legislature and an independent judiciary—was invariably as protective of human rights as the Convention itself. *Jordan v Burgoyne*,[31] for example, in 1963 and *Brutus v Cozens*[32] ten years later, were both cases affecting freedom of expression and assembly (protected by Arts 10 and 11 ECHR) which turned on issues of statutory interpretation. Neither case made any reference to the Convention.

---

[24] (1997) *Using human rights law in English courts* p 131.   [25] Ibid.
[26] [1972] AC 1027. See Loveland I (2000) *Political libels* pp 90–91.   [27] [1974] 1 WLR 683.
[28] (1906) 14 SLT 227; see 'Inconsistency with international law', ch 2, pp 29–30.
[29] (1906) 14 SLT 227 at 232.   [30] [1967] 2 QB 116 at 143, per Diplock LJ, CA.   [31] [1963] 2 QB 744.
[32] [1973] AC 854, HL.

A sudden—short-lived—legal shift?

Yet in 1975—if only initially for a brief period—the Convention seemed suddenly to have acquired prominent (even perhaps dominant status) in domestic law. As Hunt notes, this may be attributable to the fact that the first few cases against the United Kingdom had by then reached the ECtHR.[33] It may also stem from the fact that as a result of applying (directly effective) EC law, domestic judges were more aware of other 'European' treaty provisions.

Whatever the explanation, Lord Denning was among the first to recognise that—at the very least—the normal status of international law attached to the ECtHR. In *Birdi v Secretary of State for Home Affairs*, he indicated that the imaginative rules of statutory interpretation he later applied in respect of EC law in *Macarthys v Smith* should also apply to the Convention: '[judges]—could and should take the Convention into account in interpreting a statute. An Act of Parliament should be construed so as to conform with the Convention.'[34]

Lord Denning does not require ambiguity in statutory provisions as a trigger for considering the ECtHR: his assumption seems to be that the Convention would always be a relevant factor. In the same case, Lord Denning also claimed (which Hunt, with admirable understatement describes as 'surprising')[35] that the ECtHR might be viewed as a higher form of law than statute: '[I]f an Act of Parliament did not conform to the Convention, I might be inclined to hold it invalid.'[36]

If acted upon, this would have been a 'revolutionary' proposition. It would entail the denial of parliamentary sovereignty, not by virtue as subsequently seems to have been the case in respect of EC law of an entrenching statute passed by Parliament itself,[37] but as result of a judicial assertion (triggered by successive government's continuing affirmation of the Convention treaties) of the supreme legal status of the moral values laid out in the ECHR's text.

A prompt return to orthodoxy

It thus came as no surprise that Lord Denning promptly stepped back from his position in *Birdi*. In *R v Secretary of State for the Home Department, ex p Bhajan Singh*,[38] Lord Denning dropped any suggestion that the Convention could be used to 'invalidate' legislation. He retained, however, his presumption that it could be used as an aid to statutory interpretation even if there was no apparent ambiguity in the relevant statutory text.[39]

For no obviously discernible reason however, the courts (led by Lord Denning) then discarded this more radical interpretive principle and reasserted the orthodox understanding of the use that might be made of international law. Thus, in *R v Chief Immigration Officer, Heathrow Airport, ex p Salamat Bibi*,[40] a case turning on the meaning of provisions of the Immigration Act 1971, Lord Denning made the following statement:

> The position, as I understand it, is that if there is any ambiguity in our statutes or uncertainty in our law, then these courts can look to the convention as an aid to clear up the ambiguity and uncertainty. But I would dispute altogether that the convention is part of our law. Treaties and declarations do not become part of our law until they are made law by Parliament.[41]

The courts were still holding firmly to this proposition in the early-1990s. There was nothing 'special' about the ECHR which required that its status in domestic law could be any different

---

[33] Op cit pp 135–136.   [34] (1975) 119 Sol Jo 322, CA.   [35] Op cit at p 134.

[36] (1975) 119 Sol Jo 322, CA.

[37] See the discussion of *Factortame* at 'The demise of the legal doctrine? *Factortame*', ch 11, pp 306–311.

[38] [1976] QB 198, CA.

[39] A similar presumption seemed to have been embraced at this time in respect of purely common law rules; see Hunt op cit pp 139–140.   [40] [1976] 1 WLR 979, CA.

[41] Ibid, at 984. Cf also Geoffrey Lane LJ at 988: 'It is perfectly true that the convention was ratified by this country. Nevertheless the convention, not having been enacted by Parliament as an Act, does not have the effect of law in this country. Whatever persuasive force it may have in resolving ambiguities it certainly cannot have the effect of overriding the plain provisions of the 1971 Act . . .'.

from any other unincorporated treaty. Thus, for example, in *R v Secretary of State for the Home Department, ex p Brind*, Lord Ackner observed that: 'It is well settled that the convention may be deployed for the purpose of the resolution of an ambiguity in English primary or subordinate legislation'.[42] In the absence of such an ambiguity however—and Lord Ackner felt that s 29 of the Broadcasting Act 1981 was unambiguous in bestowing an extremely wide discretion on the Home Secretary—the Convention was not a relevant factor for the Court to consider. Nor did Lord Ackner discern any merit in Mr Brind's suggestion that, as matter of domestic law, the Court should at least insist that the Home Secretary considered whether or not the ban was consistent with Art 10. Lord Ackner suggested that accepting this argument: 'inevitably would result in incorporating the convention into English law by the back door'.[43] That contention is poorly founded. Requiring Ministers to pay attention to the Convention as part of the government's decision-making process would not bind them to follow the ECtHR's judgments.

We revisit the question of the Convention's changing status at common law at the beginning of chapter nineteen. Before doing so however, we consider the judgments that the ECtHR eventually reached in respect of the controversial English 'human rights' cases discussed in the previous chapter in an attempt to form a preliminary conclusion on the question of how much difference the ECtHR might actually have made to the substance of civil liberties and human rights protection in the UK's constitutional order.

III. The impact of the ECHR on domestic law 1: privacy

The UK's record before the Court has not been an entirely happy one, although it is overly simplistic to suggest that British law has been found wanting significantly more often than that of the Convention's other signatories.[44] Successive governments have generally responded to defeats before the ECtHR by introducing Bills to amend domestic law,[45] although if one adds the time needed to pass legislation to the lengthy time period required to bring a claim before the ECtHR, it is clear that British citizens did not enjoy speedy access to the Convention's protection. Mr Malone, for example, found himself having to wait some five years before his challenge to Megarry VC's High Court judgment was heard.

Speech and communication

In his judgment in *Malone v Metropolitan Police Comr*, Megarry VC had closely examined the ECtHR's decision in *Klass v Germany*.[46] *Klass* addressed the compatibility with Art 8 ECtHR of Germany's legislation authorising the interception of mail and the tapping of phone conversations. German law constrained such powers very tightly, and established an elaborate series of legal and political controls which had to be complied with before the powers could be used. Given these extensive controls, the ECtHR concluded that the German rules were both 'in accordance with the law' and 'necessary in a democratic society'.

Malone had been argued shortly after *Salamat Bibi* had been decided, and Megarry VC intimated that he was not certain to what extent this judgment had modified the principle expressed in *Birdi*. He thus concluded that: 'I take note of the Convention, as construed in the *Klass* case, and I shall give it due consideration in discussing English law on the point'.[47] That

---

[42] [1991] 1 AC 696 HL. On the background to the case, see 'A "better" application of the test', ch 13, pp 372–373.

[43] [1991] 1 AC 696 at 76–762.

[44] For a helpful analysis see Bradley A (1991) 'The UK before the Strasbourg court', in Finnie W, Himsworth C, and Walker N (eds) *Edinburgh essays in public law*. For a listing of the cases involving the UK up until 1993 see *HCD*, 17 December 1993 c 964. See also Farran S (1996) *The UK before the European Court of Human Rights*.

[45] See Bradley (1991) op cit.   [46] (1978) 2 EHRR 214.   [47] [1979] Ch 344 at 366.

consideration led Megarry VC to suggest that the wholly unregulated nature of domestic law on telephone tapping certainly breached Art 8:

> [I]t is impossible to read the judgment in the *Klass* case without its becoming abundantly clear that a system which has no legal safeguards whatever has small chance of satisfying the requirements of [the ECtHR].[48]

This proved of no help to Mr Malone in the High Court however. Megarry VC observed that had he been faced with an ambiguity in domestic law, he would have resolved that ambiguity in accordance with the *Klass* formula. But here there was no ambiguity in the law; there simply was no law at all. The Court was faced with a legal void. In such circumstances, Megarry VC suggested, the Court would be compromising traditional understandings of the separation of powers if it granted Mr Malone a remedy:

> It seems to me that where Parliament has abstained from legislating on a point that is plainly suitable for legislation, it is indeed difficult for the court to lay down new rules of common law . . . that will carry out the Crown's treaty obligations, or to discover for the first time that such rules have always existed.[49]

When Mr Malone's case finally reached the ECtHR,[50] the Court saw no difficulty in concluding that telephone conversations were within Art 8's concepts of 'private life' and 'correspondence'. Accepting also that the MPC's interference had been in pursuit of a legitimate Art 8(2) objective—namely the prevention of crime—the question which then arose was whether the Commissioner's interference with this right had been exercised 'according to law'. The meaning afforded to the concept in *Malone* was broadly in line with the test laid out in *The Sunday Times* case:

> law must be sufficiently clear in this terms to give citizens an adequate indication as to the circumstances in which and the conditions on which public authorities are empowered to resort to this secret and potentially dangerous interference with the right to respect for private life . . . [51]

No such clarity could be found in British law. The Post Office Act 1969 s 80 required the Post Office to pass information to the police when requested to do so. However the Act itself did not specify the circumstances under which such a requirement arose. Furthermore, William Whitelaw (when Home Secretary) had explained to the Commons in 1980 that he considered such guidance as existed regarding use of s 80 unsuited to enactment. These factors led the Court to conclude that the tapping power had not been exercised 'according to law'. The Court answered the question before it in terms evocative of Diceyan principle: 'it would be contrary to the rule of law for the legal discretion granted to the executive to be expressed in terms of an unfettered power'.[52]

On this occasion, the government appeared willing to amend domestic law accordingly. The Interception of Communications Act 1985 (ICA 1985) introduced a statutory framework to regulate phone tapping. Unauthorised tapping was made a criminal offence, although the Act permitted government bodies to authorise taps in a wide range of circumstances.[53]

Sado-masochistic sexual behaviour

The three-to-two basis of the House of Lords' decision in *R v Brown* indicated that the criminal nature of sado-masochistic sexual behaviour was a precarious concept in domestic law. Brown subsequently came before the ECtHR as *Laskey, Jaggard and Brown v United Kingdom*.[54] Unlike

---

[48] Ibid, at 379.   [49] Ibid.   [50] *Malone v United Kingdom* (1984) 7 EHRR 14.   [51] Ibid, at para 67.

[52] (1984) 7 EHRR 14 at para 68.

[53] See Ewing and Gearty op cit pp 66–81: Leigh I (1986) 'A tapper's charter' *Public Law* 8.

[54] (1997) 24 EHRR 39.

the House of Lords, the Court was unanimous in its judgment: Brown's prosecution and conviction did not breach Art 8. The ECtHR observed (obiter) that it doubted there had been any interference with private life at all in this case, on the rather curious basis that the group nature of Brown's activities implied that they could not be regarded as private.[55] Nonetheless, accepting that there had been such interference, it was also accepted by all parties that the interference was undertaken in pursuit of a legitimate objective (the protection of health or morals) and was imposed according to law. The Court confined its observations to the protection of health, and offered no clear indication of the breadth of the margin of appreciation that the United Kingdom would have been granted if its objective had been limited solely to protecting morals.[56] The breadth accorded on health grounds, however, was sufficient for the Court to conclude that Brown's conviction had been 'necessary in a democratic society'. Rejecting any assertion that the prosecution or conviction had been prompted by the fact that the defendants had been engaging in homosexual rather than heterosexual practices, the Court noted both that the 'extreme' activities undertaken had caused serious injuries and could cause even more serious damage. It thus concluded that: 'The state authorities therefore acted within their margin of appreciation in order to protect its citizens from real risk of serious physical harm or injury'.[57]

IV. The impact of the ECHR on domestic law 2: freedom of expression

The contrasting outcomes (from the government's perspective) of *Malone* and *Brown/Laskey* indicate the varying impact that the Convention would be likely to have on domestic treatment of civil liberties issues. The following section continues to explore that question by focusing on several judgments in the area of freedom of expression.

Official secrecy

That the ICA 1985 afforded the government wide discretion is itself a powerful reminder that compliance with the Convention does not impose detailed or uniform standards on its Signatory States. That point is reinforced when one considers the reasoning and conclusions of the ECtHR when *Spycatcher* eventually came before it.

The litigation concerned both the temporary and continuing injunctions granted against *The Guardian* and *The Observer* in *Spycatcher (No 1)* by Millet J and the House of Lords respectively. The ECtHR's judgment in *Observer and Guardian v United Kingdom*[58] began by articulating two general principles which might initially seem redolent of the ethos which has informed the US Supreme Court's interpretation of the First Amendment:

> (a) Freedom of expression constitutes one of the essential foundations of a democratic society; subject to para (2) of Art 10, it is applicable not only to 'information' or 'ideas' that are favourably received or regarded as inoffensive or as a matter of indifference, but also to those that offend, shock or disturb. Freedom of expression, as enshrined in Art 10, is subject to a number of exceptions which must be narrowly interpreted and the necessity for any restrictions must be convincingly established.

---

[55] Ibid, at para 36.

[56] Cf para 42: 'The scope of this margin of appreciation is not identical in each case but will vary according to the context. Relevant factors include the nature of the Convention right in issue, its importance for the individual and the nature of the activities concerned'.   [57] Ibid, at para 41.

[58] (1991) 14 EHRR 153.

(b) These principles are of particular importance as far as the press is concerned. While it must not overstep the bounds set, inter alia, 'in the interests of national security' . . . it is nevertheless incumbent upon it to impart information and ideas on matters of public interest. Not only does the press have the task of imparting such information: the public also has a right to receive them. Were it otherwise, the press would be unable to play its vital role of public watchdog.[59]

On closer reading, this statement seems to attach great significance to the Art 10(2) exceptions, a significance only partly reduced by the subsequent assertion that the scope for legitimate interference with freedom of expression should be narrowly constrained. The Court's application of these principles in *Spycatcher* did not amount to an expansive protection of freedom of expression. Despite the intensely political content of the information contained in Wright's book, the Court concluded that the initial injunction did not contravene Art 10: it was entirely reasonable for Millet J to have assumed that the book may have contained information that jeopardised national security; in such circumstances, pending a full trial, a temporary restraint could be regarded as 'necessary in a democratic society'. However, the Court also held that the House of Lords' continuation of the injunction did breach Art 10. Since the book had by then been published in the United States, its contents were common knowledge; the ban on media discussion therefore served no useful purpose.

For advocates of an expansive notion of 'informed consent', the ECtHR's judgment is rather unsatisfactory, in that it seemed to hinge (as did the House of Lords' decision in *Spycatcher (No 2)*), on the fact that the book had been published in the United States. As Leigh has suggested,[60] one might therefore wonder if the Convention per se would have permitted the newspapers to discuss *Spycatcher* if not for the more extensive protection of free expression afforded to the book in America under the First Amendment.

Political libels

There would however appear to have been a divergence between domestic law and the requirements of the Convention in respect of libel actions initiated by politicians. By the early-1990s, the ECtHR had yet to be faced with a civil law libel action initiated either by a politician or a government body. It had however delivered several judgments declaring convictions for criminal libel against journalists disseminating political information to be in breach of Art 10.

The *Lingens* (1986) judgment of the ECtHR

The Court's decision in *Lingens v Austria*[61] seemed to rest on an organising principle concerned with the *effect* rather than the *form* of restraints on freedom of expression. The *Lingens* litigation arose following Lingens' publication of two articles in a political magazine which suggested that Austria's then Chancellor, Kreisky, had shielded the leader of a minor political party from investigations into that person's alleged role in Nazi atrocities to secure the smaller party's participation in a coalition government. Kreisky issued private criminal proceedings against Lingens under Art 111 of the Austrian Criminal Code. This provided that the publisher of material which accuses any person of 'possessing a contemptible character or attitude or of behaviour contrary to honour or morality and of such a nature . . . to lower him in public esteem' could be fined or imprisoned for up to a year. The disseminator had a defence if he proved truth, or that he had a reasonable belief that the material was true. Lingens was convicted by the Austrian courts.

The ECtHR began its judgment with a broad evaluation of the functions to be performed by Art 10. In the Court's view, the Convention recognised freedom of speech as 'one of the

---

[59] Ibid, at para 59.   [60] Leigh I (1992) 'Spycatcher in Strasbourg' *Public Law* 200.
[61] (1986) 8 EHRR 407.

essential foundations of a democratic society and one of the basic conditions for its progress and for each individual's self-fulfilment'.[62] Freedom of speech on political questions enjoyed an elevated status: 'freedom of political debate is at the very core of the concept of a democratic society which prevails throughout the Convention'.[63]

That the Austrian law in issue did not restrain political debate by preventing publication of the article at all was regarded as irrelevant by the ECtHR. Fines or gaol sentences imposed after publication could still deter journalists from voicing useful political information and opinions in future, thereby depriving the public of access to political discussion and undermining the press' role as a watchdog on governmental behaviour.

The ECtHR held that the 'core' status of political speech had significant implications for the extent to which states could restrict its dissemination in order to protect the reputation of individuals. Politicians did not forfeit all entitlement to have their reputations protected by defamation laws, but nor could they expect to be treated as 'private citizens'. In respect of attacks on a politician's political beliefs and behaviour: 'the requirements of such protection have to be weighed in relation to the interests of the open discussion of political issues'.[64] In the Court's view, that weighing demanded that: 'The limits of acceptable criticism are accordingly wider as regards a politician as such than as regards a private individual'.[65] The unavoidable inference to be drawn from this conclusion was that the ECHR required that the obstacles presented by domestic libel law to a politician plaintiff in respect of stories concerning her political beliefs or behaviour had to be appreciably more onerous than those facing a private plaintiff suing over a non-political story.

Derbyshire County Council v Times Newspapers (1992) in the Court of Appeal

This point seemed however to elude the Court of Appeal, which invoked *Lingens* as a persuasive authority in *Derbyshire County Council v Times Newspapers Ltd*, a case triggered by a *Sunday Times'* story alleging that Derbyshire had been improperly using its pension funds. When sued for libel by the council, *The Sunday Times* argued that local authorities lacked the legal capacity to bring a libel action over criticism of their 'governing reputations'. This contention was initially rejected by Morland J, who followed the lead given some twenty years earlier by Browne J in *Bognor Regis UDC v Campion*.[66] A unanimous Court of Appeal reversed Morland J's decision.[67] All three judges (Balcombe, Ralph Gibson, and Butler Sloss LJJ) thought that the common law position on this question was ambiguous. Consequently, the Court felt that it was appropriate to examine the provisions of the Convention to assist it in finding the 'correct' solution to the problem before it. Indeed, both Balcombe LJ and Butler Sloss LJ, while observing that the Convention was not formally part of domestic law, went so far as to say they considered it appropriate to 'apply' the case law of the ECtHR in this instance. On examining the ECtHR's case law, the Court of Appeal concluded that allowing a local council to launch a libel action was an 'unnecessary' restriction on free expression.

This conclusion was reached largely because the Court considered that the council could deploy other legal remedies to defend its reputation. It would be possible, for example, for the council to initiate a criminal prosecution for libel. It might also begin an action in malicious falsehood. This tort is less helpful to plaintiffs than libel, as they must prove the falsity of the material published and that the publisher was motivated by 'malice' in disseminating it. Thirdly, the council's reputation could be indirectly protected through a libel action begun by a councillor or officer libelled in the relevant story, who could evidently proceed on the same basis as a private individual.

The Court of Appeal had apparently misunderstood the implications of Art 10 by failing to draw a distinction between elected politicians and private individuals for libel law purposes.

---

[62] Ibid, at para 41.   [63] Ibid, at para 42.   [64] Ibid, at para 42.   [65] Ibid.
[66] See 'Britain—a tort law perspective', ch 17, pp 474–476.   [67] [1992] QB 770.

Its failure to do so was technically obiter rather than part of the ratio of the judgment, but the substance of the point was perfectly clear. The presumption that the Court had misconstrued Art 10 was strengthened by the ECtHR's decision in *Castells v Spain*, delivered shortly after the Court of Appeal's judgment in *Derbyshire*.

Developing the *Lingens* doctrine in the ECtHR: *Castells v Spain* (1992)

The applicant in *Castells v Spain*[68] was a member of the Spanish Senate. He had published articles in a Basque newspaper which accused 'the government' of complicity in violence against the Basque people. He was convicted under Art 162 of Spain's criminal code, which made it a crime to 'insult, falsely accuse or threaten the government'. Article 162 did not permit a defence of truth.

The Court accepted that the government had brought this action not to protect any person's reputation, but to preserve public order—the Basque area was in considerable turmoil when the articles were published in 1979. The restraints 'necessary' to achieve this objective were more severe than those justified by the protection of reputation: criminal law sanctions could be imposed against untruths or accusations 'formulated in bad faith'. However, if such sanctions were to comply with Art 10, the defendant had to have the chance (denied to Castells) to prove the truth of his claims and his good faith.

Like *Lingens*, *Castells* has no direct bearing on civil defamation law. But the conceptual framework surrounding the Court's narrow holding was broadly framed. Thus the Court observed that:

> [T]he pre-eminent role of the press in a State governed by the rule of law must not be forgotten ... [F]reedom of the press affords the public one of the best means of discovering and forming an opinion on the ideas and attitudes of their political leaders.[69]

Building from this political presumption, the Court suggested that domestic legal systems had to recognise a tripartite division within their defamation laws. The Court observed that 'the limits of political criticism are wider with regard to government than in relation to a private citizen, or even a politician'.[70] This clearly implies that the 'government' qua corporate body must endure more criticism than a 'politician', who in turn must endure more than a private citizen. The Court of Appeal in *Derbyshire* correctly predicted the first part of the *Castells* formula, but seemed to neglect the second.

As will be suggested in chapter nineteen, the common law has subsequently been amended in a manner which would seem to satisfy Art 10. For the present, however, we return to litigation in which the ECtHR held that English law on freedom of expression fell far short of the Convention's requirements.

Contempt of court

The ECtHR's judgment in *Sunday Times v United Kingdom*[71] case was eventually delivered in April 1979, almost six years after the House of Lords had upheld the injunction forbidding publication of the paper's article on the thalidomide controversy.[72] The EComHR had concluded—albeit not unanimously—that the injunction had breached Art 10. The Court subsequently reached the same conclusion. There could be no doubt that the injunction had amounted to an interference with freedom of expression. The ECtHR also accepted without difficulty that the purposes served by the contempt jurisdiction were intended to promote one of the legitimate objectives identified in Art 10(2) to justify such interference—namely to protect 'the authority

---

[68] (1992) 14 EHRR 445.   [69] Ibid, para 43.   [70] Ibid, para 46.   [71] (1979) 2 EHRR 245.
[72] See 'Contempt of court', ch 17, pp 471–473. The House of Lords had issued judgment on 25 July 1973.

and impartiality of the judiciary'.[73] The Court further accepted that the interference with free expression imposed by contempt of court met the 'prescribed by law' criterion of Art 10(2). As noted earlier, the Court's formulation of that principle in this case now serves as the standard point of reference for its meaning. The outcome of the case turned on whether the grant of the injunction had been 'necessary in a democratic society'.

In addressing this issue, the Court stressed that the nature of its Art 10 jurisdiction would vary according to which of the legitimate objectives identified in Art 10(2) was in issue. The approach to the margin of appreciation doctrine laid out in *Handyside* (ie that 'State authorities are in principle in a better position than the international judge to give an opinion on the exact content of these requirements')—was not appropriate here. The governmental interference with free expression under consideration in *Handyside*—a case involving obscenity—was pursued 'for the protection of morals'. 'Moral' principles might legitimately vary substantially among the Signatory States. The ECtHR's jurisdiction in such matters would be of a loosely supervisory kind. However, the Court reasoned that:

> [T]he same cannot be said of the far more objective notion of the 'authority' of the judiciary. The domestic law and practice of the Contracting States reveal a fairly substantial measure of common ground in this area . . . Accordingly, here a more extensive European supervision corresponds to a less discretionary power of appreciation.[74]

To frame the matter rather differently, one might suggest that evaluating interferences with judicial authority was a far more 'justiciable' task than gauging moral standards.[75] In consequence, the Court could legitimately exercise a jurisdiction which came very close to being appellate rather than just supervisory in character. The ECtHR thus went on to make its own evaluation of the facts at issue in the litigation. The Court laid particular stress on what it regarded as the even-handed substance of the censored article, and doubted that so balanced a piece could in any meaningful sense prejudge the result of any trial.[76] Perhaps more broadly, the Court observed that stories addressing important matters of public controversy 'did not cease to be a matter of public interest merely because they formed the background to pending litigation'.[77] Indeed, it was suggested that publication of *The Sunday Times* article could actually enhance rather than prejudice the conduct of any subsequent trial: 'By bringing to light certain facts, the article might have served as a brake on speculative and unenlightened discussion'.[78]

It is tempting to assume that the ECtHR reached a different conclusion from the House of Lords largely because the two courts adopted different analytical starting points. In the House of Lords, preserving the impartial administration of justice was the initial consideration. In the ECtHR, that value was assigned only secondary status, as a potential justification for an interference with the dominant value of freedom of expression.[79] It should however be noted that the Court's judgment was an eleven to nine majority verdict. This rather precludes the conclusion that the English law of contempt was 'clearly' incompatible with Art 10, and also emphasises

---

[73] On this point, the ECtHR concluded that it was not relevant to ask if the litigation was dormant: 'preventing interference with negotiations towards the settlement of a pending suit is no less legitimate an aim under Art 10(2) than preventing interference with a procedural situation in the strictly forensic sense' (1979) 2 EHRR 245 at para 64.   [74] Ibid, at para 59.

[75] It might be suggested that this raises a 'political' question—not in the *GCHQ* sense of being non-justiciable— but in the sense which the ECtHR later emphasised in *Lingens* and *Castells* that freedom of expression on political/governmental issues (which would include judicial law-making) lies at the 'core' of Art 10, and thus any interference with it must surmount exacting standards of review.

[76] 'The proposed *Sunday Times* article was couched in moderate terms and did not present just one side of the evidence or claim that there was only one result at which a court could arrive': (1979) 2 EHRR 245 at para 63.

[77] Ibid, at para 66.   [78] Ibid.

[79] For a detailed critique see Duffy P (1980) 'The Sunday Times case: freedom of expression, contempt of court and the ECHR *Human Rights Review* 17.

the point that there is a certain contingency about the substance of the ECtHR's jurisprudence. It would seem quite plausible to expect that the same issue could be decided quite differently within a few years simply as result of a change of personnel on the Strasbourg bench.

The judgment was accorded a mixed reception from British commentators. In a ludicrously melodramatic critique, Mann condemned the majority's reasoning as 'diffuse and imprecise',[80] and castigated the decision as: '[T]he gravest blow to the fabric of English law that has ever occurred'.[81] In Mann's view, the judgment evidently posed an immediate threat to the integrity of the British legal system. One might note that Mann's critique afforded no explicit significance to the public's interest in reaching informed conclusions about the thalidomide saga, and offered the extraordinary suggestion that the House of Lords decision was perfectly consistent with the First Amendment.[82] Other commentators offered a more measured response.[83]

The Contempt of Court Act 1981

Notwithstanding the potential ephemerality of the ECtHR's judgment—and the criticism it had attracted—the first Thatcher government moved promptly to bring domestic law into line with the ruling by promoting a Contempt of Court Bill, which was enacted in 1981. The Bill was not wholly a response to the ECtHR's judgment; it was also intended to implement some of the recommendations of a *Report on contempt of court*, chaired by Phillimore LJ, which had conducted a general review of the contempt jurisdiction.[84]

Section 2(2) of the Act addressed *The Sunday Times* judgment. It provided that contempt in respect of pressurising litigants or prejudging issues would only arise if a particular story created 'a substantial risk that the course of justice in the proceedings in question will be seriously impeded or prejudiced'. The Act also made it clear (in Sch 1) that in a civil action 'proceedings' were only occurring if a date had been set down for trial; if no date was set, proceedings would be 'dormant' and so no possibility of contempt could arise. A contemporary commentator suggested that s 2 did enhance press freedom in respect of issues such as the thalidomide controversy: '[T]he fact that the matter under discussion is one of legitimate public interest and concern and that the issues are addressed in a fair and balanced way will now weigh more strongly in favour of allowing publication, where previously these factors would have been discounted'.[85] Others were more sceptical. Lowe commented that, notwithstanding s 2(2): 'The Act nevertheless maintains the basic stance of the ultimate supremacy of the administration of justice over free speech, although it does attempt to shift the balance a little further in favour of the latter'.[86] Lowe doubted that s 2(2) actually met the ECtHR's requirements. Given that the margin of appreciation doctrine—even when narrowly construed—grants states some appreciable discretion, that claim was perhaps overstated. But as we shall see later in the chapter, the Act—or at least its interpretation by the House of Lords—was subsequently to prove an inadequate response to the ECtHR's interpretation of the Convention.

---

[80] Mann F (1979) 'Contempt of Court in the House of Lords and the European Court of Human Rights' *LQR* 348.

[81] Ibid, at 349.

[82] For a more sensible view see Nathanson N (1979/1980) 'The Sunday Times case: freedom of the press and contempt of court under English law and the European Convention on Human Rights' *Kentucky Law Journal* 972; noting at 972: 'the gulf between constitutional law of freedom of the press and the British common law on the same subject'.

[83] Cf Gray C (1979) 'European Convention on Human Rights—freedom of expression and the thalidomide case' *Cambridge LJ* 242 at 245: 'Perhaps this case will remind English courts of the potentially embarrassing consequences of ignoring the existence of the ECHR and encourage in them a more constructive approach to its application'.

[84] (1974, Cmnd 5794). Phillimore LJ had sat in the Court of Appeal in *A-G v Times Newspapers*. For contemporaneous critiques of the Act see Lowe N (1981) 'Contempt of Court Act' *Public Law* 20; Boyle A (1981) 'The Contempt of Court Act 1981' *Human Rights Review* 148; Bailey S (1982) 'The Contempt of Court Act 1981' *MLR* 301.

[85] Boyle (1981) op cit p 148.   [86] Lowe op cit p 28.

Blasphemy

Observers who assumed that Art 10 might protect freedom of expression to an extent closely comparable to that provided by the First Amendment in the United States would also have been dismayed by the outcome of the *Lemon v United Kingdom* litigation. Lemon's challenge to the House of Lords' judgment did not even reach the ECtHR: the Commission dismissed it as manifestly 'ill-founded'.[87]

Lemon v United Kingdom (1982)

The Commission recognised that Lemon's conviction[88] interfered with the entitlement to freedom of expression, but it found little merit in the rest of his contentions. The EComHR considered that blasphemy laws did pursue a legitimate Art 10(2) objective, namely the 'protection of the rights of others':

> The Commission considers that the offence of blasphemous libel as it is construed under the applicable common law in fact has the main purpose to protect the right of citizens not to be offended in their religious feelings by publications.[89]

This is an extremely expansive proposition, which simply endorses without question the common law presumption that Christians in the United Kingdom—unlike adherents to other religious faiths or atheists—need not endure scathing criticism of their beliefs, even if that criticism was published in a forum which it was unlikely that any of them would ever encounter in their daily lives. This constitutes a markedly illiberal approach to freedom of expression.

Lemon's argument under Art 10 rested in part on the contention that the crime of blasphemy was too imprecisely defined to be 'prescribed by law'. The Commission rejected this argument. While the fact that the House of Lords' judgment had been divided three-to-two indicated that the law was somewhat uncertain, the Commission concluded that the majority judgment: 'did not go beyond the limits of a reasonable interpretation of the existing law'—the decision was: 'reasonably foreseeable with the assistance of appropriate legal advice'.[90] That would seem a largely uncontentious conclusion. Much more problematic, in contrast, was the Commission's conclusion on the final stage of its inquiry—was the law of blasphemy 'necessary in a democratic society'?

The EComHR's views on this point were evidently determined by its earlier conclusion that the law pursued a legitimate objective:

> If it is accepted that the religious feelings of the citizen may deserve protection against indecent attacks on the matters held sacred by him, then it can also be considered as necessary in a democratic society to stipulate that such attacks, if they attain a certain level of severity, shall constitute a criminal offence at the request of the offended person.[91]

There is little independent logical force to the Commission's argument on this point. It seemed to rest wholly on the twin propositions that because Mary Whitehouse was so offended by the poem, and because the judges considered the poem blasphemous, the law was necessary. That Whitehouse may have been unduly sensitive, or ideologically intolerant, or a religious zealot, were not matters that the Commission addressed. Nor did it entertain the point that the absence of blasphemy prosecutions in the fifty years prior to *Lemon* indicated that the law was obsolescent. In effect, the Commission was extending an extremely wide margin of appreciation to the United Kingdom on this point, with the result that its own jurisdiction was clearly perceived as supervisory in the most relaxed (perhaps comatose) of forms, and could in no sense be seen as involving quasi-appellate functions.

---

[87] (1982) 5 EHRR 123.   [88] See 'Blasphemy' ff, ch 17, pp 469–471.   [89] (1982) 5 EHRR 123 at para 11.
[90] Ibid, at para 10.   [91] Ibid, at para 12.

It might readily be thought that the legitimate objective which the Commission upheld in *Lemon*—namely that Christian sensibilities should not be offended—is very difficult to reconcile with the principle subsequently outlined by the ECtHR in *Spycatcher*; namely that freedom of expression extends 'not only to 'information' or 'ideas' that are favourably received or regarded as inoffensive or as a matter of indifference, but also to those that offend, shock or disturb'.[92] The reasoning deployed in *Lemon* would suggest that the Art 10(1) entitlement to publish and receive information and ideas which 'offend' others is trumped by those others' Art 10(2) entitlement not to be offended. One cannot of course—unless one adheres to a ludicrously formalistic notion of law—publish 'offensive' material if nobody is offended by it.

A further point not addressed by the Commission in *Lemon* was whether blasphemy should be seen as 'political/public interest' speech in the sense to which the ECtHR subsequently alluded in *Lingens*. The irresistible inference to be drawn from this omission is that the Commission did not consider that blasphemy raised political questions at all, but simply moral ones. Quite how one draws the line between 'political' and 'moral' is unclear, but one might have thought the divide was particularly obscure in the British context, given the privileged legal status enjoyed by the Church of England.[93]

Otto-Preminger Institute v Austria (1994) and *Wingrove v United Kingdom* (1996)

Twelve years later, in *Otto-Preminger Institute v Austria*,[94] the ECtHR confirmed both that religious speech was not 'political' speech in the *Lingens* sense, and that the entitlements of citizens who wished to publish or consume religiously offensive material could indeed be subordinated to the interests of adherents to the particular religion in not being offended.

The applicant was an arts organisation located in Innsbruck, Austria. The Institute had arranged to exhibit a movie, *Das Liebeskonzil*, which presented a forceful attack on the Catholic church. A very substantial majority of citizens in the Institute's area were practising Catholics, and the state authorities took the view that showing the movie would both cause grave offence to such people and raise the possibility of public order offences. The film was therefore banned under Austria's blasphemy laws, and the Institute's copy of it seized and destroyed.

The ECtHR found no breach of Art 10 on these facts. At the core of its judgment lay the proposition that Art 10's protection would not extend to expression that did 'not contribute to any form of public debate capable of furthering progress in human affairs'.[95] *Das Liebeskonzil* evidently fell into this pariah category of expression, and could thus be banned entirely. The Court drew a distinction between offensive attacks on political issues (presumptively of some value) and those addressing religious questions (presumptively worthless):

> Whereas there is little scope for restrictions on political speech or on debate of questions of public interest . . . a wider margin of appreciation is generally available to the Contracting States when regulating freedom of expression in relation to matters liable to offend intimate personal convictions within the field of morals or, especially, religion.[96]

The Court's insistence on 'depoliticising' religious belief seems myopic in this situation, given that such beliefs are likely to exercise a considerable influence on political issues. It is a formalistic rather than functionally based differentiation. The judgment has been subjected to a

---

[92] *Observer and Guardian v United Kingdom* (1991) 14 EHRR 153 at para 59.

[93] For a happily unsuccessful attempt to extend the intolerance of the blasphemy laws to non-Christian religions after the publication of Salman Rushdie's satirical novel, *The Satanic Verses*, see Modood T (1990) 'British Asian Muslims and the Rushdie affair' *Political Quarterly* 143; *R v Chief Metropolitan Stipendiary Magistrate, ex p Choudhury* [1991] 1 QB 429; *Choudhury v United Kingdom* (1991) 12 *Human Rights LJ* 74.

[94] (1994) 19 EHRR 34.   [95] Ibid, para 49.   [96] Ibid, at para 58.

compelling critique by Warbrick, who suggests that it 'makes an unfortunate collapse of the nature of the expression in issue and the justification for interfering with it'.[97] In particular, Warbrick observes that the Court has been less than astute in appreciating the 'political' or 'public interest' dimension of ideological attacks on the supposed sanctity of (some) religious sentiment.

The Court's decision was by a six-to-three majority. The three dissentients took particular issue with the majority's suggestion that some ideas were per se incapable 'of furthering progress in human affairs'. To allow a state to impose that opinion: 'could be detrimental to that tolerance on which pluralist democracy depends'.[98] The ratio of the dissent was however rather timid, resting primarily on the fact that the Institute had taken steps to ensure that the film was not seen by young people or those with strongly held Catholic beliefs.

The poverty of the ECtHR's ambition in this respect, and the consequent feebleness of its jurisprudence, provide perhaps the most compelling of rebuttals to any of those opponents of incorporating the Convention into UK law whose case rested on the argument that the ECtHR would impose alien cultural values on our domestic law. Indeed, in respect of blasphemy the domestic courts and Parliament showed themselves to be a better protector of freedom of expression than the ECtHR. The rationale adopted by the House of Lords in *Lemon* had been substantially undermined by the High Court's judgment in *R (on the application of Green) v City of Westminster Magistrates' Court*.[99] The applicant ran a pressure group called Christian Voice. He took exception to the BBC's decision to transmit a broadcast of a scurrilous musical, *Jerry Springer; the Opera,* which had been running in a London theatre for a several years. The show was notably more offensive in its tone and content than the poem at issue in *Lemon*. The High Court however concluded it was not blasphemous by focusing on an element of the offence which had been rather overlooked in *Lemon* in the House of Lords:

> 5 This development of the law of criminal blasphemous libel was carefully traced by Roskill L.J. when R. v Lemon was in the Court of Appeal, [1979] Q.B. 10, in an analysis which received clear endorsement when the case reached the House of Lords. Roskill L.J. observed (at 18G): 'The state only became interested in the offence if the actions of the alleged offender affected the safety of the state . . .
>
> 16 There is therefore ample basis for the common ground before us that the gist of the crime of blasphemous libel is material relating to the Christian religion, or its figures or formularies, so scurrilous and offensive in manner that it undermines society generally, by endangering the peace, depraving public morality, shaking the fabric of society or tending to be a cause of civil strife . . .'. What is necessary to make such material a crime is that the community (or society) generally should be threatened. This element will not be shown merely because some people of particular sensibility are, because deeply offended, moved to protest.

The Court considered that the fabric of British society was sufficiently robust not to be 'shaken' by a rude play and so no offence had been committed, notwithstanding the damage to Mr Green's sensibilities. Gordon Brown's Labour government subsequently considered that the judgment effectively made the offence entirely obsolete, and the offence was abolished by s 79 of the Criminal Justice and Immigration Act 2008[100] shortly thereafter.[101]

---

[97] (1998) op cit p 189.   [98] (1994) 19 EHRR 34 at 61.

[99] [2007] EWHC 2785 (Admin), [2008] EMLR 15.

[100] The provision is admirably succinct:

79 Abolition of common law offences of blasphemy and blasphemous libel

(1) The offences of blasphemy and blasphemous libel under the common law of England and Wales are abolished.

[101] See Sandberg R and Doe N (2008) 'The strange death of blasphemy' *MLR* 971–986.

Conclusion

Despite the UK's evidently mixed record before the ECtHR on freedom of expression issues, it was not uncommon in the early-1990s to encounter judicial pronouncements that the common law and the Convention bestowed identical levels of civil liberties protection on British citizens. A typical example is Lord Goff's comment in *A-G v Guardian Newspapers Ltd (Spycatcher) (No 2)*:

> I can see no inconsistency between English law on this subject and art 10 . . . This is scarcely surprising, since we pride ourselves on the fact that freedom of speech has existed in this country perhaps as long as, if not longer than, it has existed in any other country in the world.[102]

Such protestations would seem poorly based. *Spycatcher* was decided in the same way both domestically and in the ECtHR, as was *Lemon*, but there is little doubt that the Court of Appeal's judgment in *Derbyshire* was irreconcilable with *Lingens*. This spasmodic rather than pervasive consistency between domestic law and Art 10 is reinforced if one contrasts *Brind* with the *Morgan Grampian/Goodwin* litigation.

Mr Brind's efforts to raise his case before the ECtHR did not even win the approval of the Commission. In July 1994, the Commission concluded that Brind's application was ill-founded. Even if—and the Commission seemed to have doubts on this point—the government's policy amounted to an interference with freedom of expression, that interference was undoubtedly in pursuit of a legitimate objective, it was prescribed by law, and it was necessary in a democratic society. That the policy was just plain silly did not seem to found an Art 10 claim.[103] The Commission's conclusion was perhaps surprising, but it did perform the useful function of suggesting that advocates of incorporating the Convention overestimated its capacity to forbid government behaviour which impinged upon freedom of expression, while opponents of incorporation had a similarly exaggerated view of the extent to which it would impinge upon the sovereignty of Parliament and the autonomy of the government.

The *Goodwin* case, in contrast, revealed a substantial (if not obviously predictable) divergence between UK law and Art 10.[104] Mr Goodwin was a journalist, working for *The Engineer*, a specialist trade magazine. Goodwin was provided with some sensitive financial information about a firm Tetra (the 'X' in the case name) by a source who must have been either a disloyal Tetra employee or a thief who had stolen the information. Goodwin then wrote an article about the firm, drawing on the leaked information. Before *The Engineer* published any story, Tetra successfully applied to the High Court for an injunction preventing publication. Tetra also sought a court order requiring the publishers and Mr Goodwin to identify their source.

Prior to 1981, the question of whether a court could order a journalist to reveal her sources had been a matter of common law. The courts accepted that competing interests might be at stake in such circumstances. An order to disclose could have a 'chilling effect'—much like the threat of a libel action—on press freedom, in so far as sources might not come forward in future and so potentially valuable stories might not be written. That interest would of course be particularly strong in respect of leaked information revealing criminal behaviour, or unethical or incompetent activities by government bodies. On the other hand, allowing the press to keep their sources secret could mean that a firm like Tetra (X) would have to continue to operate knowing that it may be employing a disloyal employee, and that none of its operations (which may be wholly legal and ethical) could be kept secret from commercial rivals.

---

[102] [1990] 1 AC 109 at 283, HL.

[103] For a critical comment see Pannick D 'No logic behind gagging terrorists' empty rhetoric' *The Times*, 2 August 1994.   [104] *X Ltd v Morgan-Grampian (Publishers) Ltd* [1991] 1 AC 1, HL.

In *British Steel Corpn v Granada Television Ltd*, decided in 1980,[105] the House of Lords ordered Granada to identify the source who had provided it with 250 confidential BSC documents. BSC, then a state-owned industry, was in the throes of major industrial action by its workers. It had for many years been making vast operating losses. The leaked documents charted major incompetence within the firm, and revealed that the Thatcher government—contrary to its public protestations—was taking covert steps to assist BSC to break the strike. Granada argued that the documents concerned a matter of acute public interest, and that an order to disclose its source would have the effect of deterring comparable leaks in future, with the result that the public would be denied access to important political information.

The High Court, Court of Appeal, and four members of the House of Lords rejected this argument.[106] In a manner that foreshadowed the Court of Appeal's decision in *Blackshaw v Lord* a few years later,[107] the majority in the House of Lords failed to see any 'political' or 'constitutional' issue at stake in the case. As Lord Wilberforce put it: 'this case does not touch on freedom of the press even at its periphery'.[108] His sentiment was echoed by Lord Russell: 'this case has not even marginal connection with any concept of "the freedom of the press"'.[109]

The principle on which the majority decided the case was framed in the following way. Newspapers, television stations, and journalists 'have no immunity based on public interest which protects them from the obligation to disclose in a court of law their sources of information, when such disclosure is necessary in the interest of justice'.[110] While such a public interest might arise in respect of information exposing criminality or wrongdoing, no such activities were in issue here. All that was at stake was the continued confidentiality of commercially sensitive information. The 'interest of justice'—namely that BSC not be subjected to breaches of confidentiality or thefts—therefore demanded that the source be revealed.

Lord Salmon issued a powerful and wholly convincing dissent. He started from the premise that this case was primarily about the freedom of the press, and especially about the public's interest in knowing about huge mismanagement of public funds by a state-owned industry. BSC was as much a governmental body as a commercial enterprise. He thus had no difficulty in concluding that Granada need not disclose its source:

> The freedom of the press depends on this immunity. Were it to disappear, so would the sources from which [press] information is obtained; and the public would be deprived of much of the information to which the public of a free nation is entitled.[111]

Section 10 of the Contempt of Court Act 1981 ostensibly attempted to strengthen press protection in such circumstances by replacing the common law rule with a new statutory formula. The presumption would be against disclosure unless disclosure was 'necessary in the interests of justice or national security or for the prevention of disorder or crime'. Whether s 10 actually modified the *BSC* decision is debatable;[112] much would obviously depend on the way the new provision was interpreted. As noted in the previous discussion of the *Tisdall* case, s 10 was not being lent an expansive definition in the mid-1980s.[113]

The *X v Morgan-Grampian* case seemed to lack the 'political' or 'constitutional' overtones of either *BSC* or the *Tisdall* episode. In contrast to its decision in *BSC*, the House of Lords clearly recognised that the case did raise freedom of expression questions, even if no 'political'

---

[105] [1981] AC 1096.   [106] The cases are reported together at [1981] AC 1096.

[107] See 'Britain—a tort law perspective', ch 17, pp 474–476.   [108] [1981] AC 1096 at 1168.

[109] Ibid, at 1203.   [110] Ibid, at 1169; per Lord Wilberforce.   [111] Ibid, at 1195.

[112] Cf Boyle (1981) op cit p 149: 'the section appears to do no more than adopt the very test employed by the majority judgments in [*BSC*]'.

[113] See 'The *Tisdall* (1984 and 1985) and *Ponting* (1985) cases', ch 17, pp 464–465.

information was in issue. It also indicated—the point is put most clearly by Lord Bridge—that it accepted that s 10 had tipped the balance in favour of maintaining the confidentiality of press sources:

> In this balancing exercise it is only if the judge is satisfied that disclosure in the interests of justice is of such preponderating importance as to override the statutory privilege against disclosure that the necessity will be reached.[114]

On these facts, there was no obvious public interest in disclosure of the relevant information, while the continued presence of a potential leaker within Tetra posed an acute and serious problem for the company. It thus seems unobjectionable from a human rights perspective that Morgan-Grampian and Mr Goodwin were ordered to disclose their source. Mr Goodwin—who had not revealed the source to his employers—chose not to comply with the court order. He was thus fined £5,000 for contempt. While this was an unfortunate consequence for Mr Goodwin—and while one might admire his (in the Court's view misguided) determination to respect his source's confidentiality[115]—the judgment need not have any 'chilling effect' on sources providing political or public interest information; it can be seen as limited solely to cases involving purely 'private' information.[116]

Lord Bridge's methodology in *X v Morgan-Grampian* has obvious similarities to the ECtHR's approach to Art 10 claims. It was perhaps therefore something of a surprise that Mr Goodwin's subsequent Art 10 action before the ECtHR was successful.[117] The Court adopted an essentially appellate role in remaking the balancing equation that the House of Lords had conducted. On the Court's view of the facts, Tetra's interest in uncovering the identity of the leaker/thief did not outweigh 'the vital public interest in the protection of the applicant's journalist's source'.[118] The House of Lords' order—and Mr Goodwin's subsequent committal for contempt—therefore breached Art 10.

Goodwin is a rather unsatisfactory decision, marred by the ECtHR's peculiar failure—given the position it had staked out in *Lingens* and *Castells*—to distinguish between different types of information. Had it respected the 'core status' of political speech identified in those two cases, its judgment would presumably have approved the House of Lords' decision since there was no 'political' element to Tetra's internal financial secrets. One could hardly cast any blame on the English courts for failing to conform with Art 10 on this point, since the ECtHR seemed to go markedly further than its previous case law would suggest was possible.

Even if one accepted that proposition that domestic law on freedom of expression issues was generally in conformity with the Convention in the early-1990s, it was certainly arguable that the protection thereby obtained often fell far short of that provided in the United States by the First Amendment. On this issue at least, the Convention did not set particularly exacting civil liberties standards. Nonetheless by this time the Convention had become a quite 'normal' ingredient of domestic administrative law—albeit in a context in which 'normalcy' meant it enjoyed only a limited effect. In chapter nineteen, our attention turns to the way in which the constitution's approach to the issue of civil liberties and human rights has altered in the past thirty years; an alteration which while falling some way short of a 'revolution', has nonetheless involved evolution at an unusually rapid pace and lent that 'normalcy' a rather different—and initially constitutionally problematic—character.

---

[114] [1991] 1 AC 1 at 44, HL.

[115] Cf Lord Bridge, ibid, at 49: 'To contend that the individual litigant, be he a journalist or anyone else, has a right of "conscientious objection" which entitles him to set himself above the law if he does not agree with the court's decision, is a doctrine which undermines the rule of law and is wholly unacceptable in a democratic society'.

[116] For an insightful discussion see Palmer S (1992) 'Protecting journalists' sources: section 10, Contempt of Court Act 1981' *Public Law* 61.   [117] (1996) 22 EHRR 123.   [118] Ibid, at para 45.

Suggested further reading

Academic and political commentary

HUNT M (1997) *Using human rights law in English courts* chs 1 and 4

DUFFY P (1980) 'The Sunday Times case: freedom of expression, contempt of court and the ECHR' *Human Rights Review* 17

JONES T (1996) 'The devaluation of human rights under the European Convention' *Public Law* 430

SANDBERG R and DOE N (2008) 'The strange death of blasphemy' *MLR* 971

WARBRICK C (1998) 'Federalism and free speech', in LOVELAND I (ed) *Importing the First Amendment*

LEIGH I (1992) 'Spycatcher in Strasbourg' *Public Law* 200

Case law and legislation

Birdi v Secretary of State for Home Affairs (1975) 119 Sol Jo 322

Malone v United Kingdom (1984) 7 EHRR 14

Laskey, Jaggard and Brown v United Kingdom (1997) 24 EHRR 39

Observer and Guardian v United Kingdom (1991) 14 EHRR 153

Handyside v United Kingdom (1976) 1 EHRR 737

Derbyshire County Council v Times Newspapers [1992] QB 700

Lingens v Austria (1986) 8 EHRR 407

Lemon v United Kingdom (1982) 5 EHRR 123

Chapter 19

Human Rights III: New Substantive Grounds of Review

That UK law was so frequently found to have breached the Convention by the ECtHR is explained largely by the fact that the Convention could not be applied directly by domestic courts; it became a relevant factor only when statutory provisions or common law rules were ambiguous. If Parliament had enacted a statute which gave Convention articles a superior status to common law rules, and/or to delegated legislation, and/or to previously enacted statutes, many cases which eventually reached the ECtHR would have been resolved domestically. It is likely that some national law would have been held to have contravened the Convention; but those outcomes would have been produced by judgments of UK courts, not the ECtHR.

Such judgments would not have been enforcing the Convention directly, but would have been applying the statute through which the Convention had been given domestic legal effect. An 'incorporation' statute of that sort would not of course have challenged the doctrine of parliamentary sovereignty. The courts would still have been required to apply the terms of any subsequently enacted legislation inconsistent with the 'incorporated' provisions of the Convention.

Members of the House of Lords frequently promoted private members' Bills from 1970 onwards intended to give (varying types of) domestic legal effect to the ECHR. Some Bills proposed unambiguously supra-legislative, entrenched status for the Convention. That would obviously be, from an orthodox perspective, a futile exercise. An alternative scenario was that an incorporating statute should seek to protect Convention Rights from implied, but not express repeal. This too would not seem to have been possible in a legal sense at that time. The most modest proposals envisaged only that some of the provisions of the Convention should be used as additional grounds of review in administrative law, which would have been an achievable objective in an abstract doctrinal sense, with no binding effect on Parliament. These initiatives invariably triggered brief media interest in the question of fundamental rights, and as such exemplify the House of Lords' (qua legislative chamber) useful role as a forum for debate on issues of public concern. No such Bill, however, even came close to being enacted.[1] Several senior judges in their academic writings also suggested that Parliament should enact legislation which would give some elements of the Convention the status of statutory grounds of review.[2] The Liberal Party had long been committed to incorporation in this sense, and by

---

[1] See Bailey, Harris, and Jones (1992) op cit pp 19–20.
[2] Scarman L (1987) 'Human rights in an unwritten constitution' *Denning LJ* 129: Bingham T (1993) 'The European Convention on Human Rights: time to incorporate' *LQR* 393.

the mid-1990s the Labour Party (under the leadership of John Smith and then Tony Blair) also accepted this position. In the meantime however, there were indications that some senior judges were embracing the view that the common law might properly be more receptive to the substantive values articulated in the Convention.

I. The (re-)emergence and consolidation of fundamental human rights as an indigenous principle of common law

The following section focuses on several leading decisions in which the courts appeared to recognise that the common law contained a significant and as yet under-explored capacity to mirror the moral principles contained in the Convention.

Derbyshire County Council v Times Newspapers Ltd in the House of Lords

Lord Keith delivered the leading judgment in the Lords. Unlike the judges in the Court of Appeal,[3] he did not either 'apply' the Convention, nor resort to judgments of the ECtHR to resolve a common law 'ambiguity'. Lord Keith considered the common law quite clear. There was no ambiguity: *Bognor Regis UDC v Campion* had simply been wrongly decided:

> [N]ot only is there no public interest favouring the right of organs of government, whether central or local, to sue for libel, but it is contrary to the public interest that they should have it . . . because to admit such actions would place an undesirable fetter on freedom of speech.[4]

In reaching this conclusion, Lord Keith had focused on the function served by criticism of government in a modern democratic society. He thought this purpose was best described by Lord Bridge in *Hector v A-G of Antigua and Barbuda*:

> [T]hose . . . responsible for public administration must always be open to criticism. Any attempt to stifle or fetter such criticism amounts to political censorship of the most insidious and objectionable kind . . . . [T]he very purpose of criticism . . . is to undermine public confidence in their stewardship and to persuade the electorate that the opponents would make a better job of it than those presently holding office.[5]

Lord Keith found further support for his perception of the requisite 'public policy' concerns in several US decisions, primarily *City of Chicago v Tribune Co*[6] and *New York Times v Sullivan*.[7]

Lord Keith's concern was obviously to remove an undesirable fetter on free speech. As such, his judgment can readily be seen as enhancing the protection afforded to freedom of expression. However, on closer reading, both the substance of the judgment and the methodology that underpinned it are flawed. The substantive problems are twofold. Firstly, like the Court of Appeal, Lord Keith placed no additional barriers in the path of libel actions brought by elected politicians. This omission provided an obvious route to sidestep the ratio of the judgment. Secondly, the ratio itself is problematic, as indeed is that of the *Chicago* judgment on which Lord Keith relied. A complete ban on libel actions initiated by government bodies provides the press and political parties with a perverse incentive to tell deliberate lies on political matters; that is knowingly and wilfully to mislead voters. If one's primary concern when addressing

---

[3] See '*Derbyshire County Council v Times Newspapers* (1992) in the Court of Appeal', ch 18, pp 492–493.

[4] [1993] AC 534 at 549.

[5] [1990] 2 AC 312 at 318, PC. The case is incisively analysed in Bradley A (1990) 'Press freedom, governmental constraints and the Privy Council' *Public Law* 453.

[6] 139 NE 86 (1923); 'The US—a constitutional law perspective', ch 17, pp 473–474.

[7] 376 US 254 (1964); 'Political libels', ch 17, pp 473–476.

freedom of expression issues concerning political matters is to promote informed consent, such an incentive may well prove counter-productive.

The methodological flaw lies in the House of Lords' evident failure to appreciate the subtle question of balance between encouraging the circulation of information and restricting the circulation of misinformation that the US Supreme Court struck in *Sullivan*. The judgment seems to have been read rather simplistically, and used to underpin propositions which it did not really support. This raises a danger of general application when civil liberties questions are in issue in domestic law; namely that courts may invoke authorities from other jurisdictions to buttress innovative common law developments without properly appreciating the reasons for and implications of the judgments concerned.[8]

R v Secretary of State for the Home Department, ex p Leech (No 2)

The expansion of the notion of fundamental rights at common law in respect of freedom of expression issues continued—this time rooted in wholly indigenous principles—in *R v Secretary of State for the Home Department, ex p Leech (No 2)*.[9] As noted in the previous discussion of *Raymond v Honey*,[10] the common law has long accepted that 'access to the courts' should be regarded as a 'basic right', in the sense that it could only be abridged by legislation either explicitly or by necessary implication. *Raymond* concerned a prison governor's attempts to prevent a prisoner initiating legal action, a power which the Court held had not been given to him by the loosely framed powers in s 47 of the Prison Act 1952. The applicant in *Leech* was seeking to extend that principle.

Mr Leech, a prisoner, was an inveterate litigator on matters of prison discipline. His action was aimed at preventing the prison authorities from intercepting or stopping his letters to his solicitor. The relevant prison rules which the prison governor invoked to justify this activity were said to be authorised by s 47. The case was concerned simply with deciding whether those rules were ultra vires s 47.

Two rules were in issue. Rule 33(3) provided that:

> Except as provided by these Rules, every letter or communication to or from a prisoner may be read or examined by the governor . . . and the governor may at his discretion, stop any letter or communication on the grounds that its contents are objectionable or that it is of inordinate length.

Rule 37A removed this limit in respect of correspondence between an inmate and his/her solicitor in respect of ongoing litigation.[11] It did not however apply to letters preparatory to actual or potential litigation. It was correspondence of this sort with which Mr Leech was concerned. His action failed in the High Court, but that judgment was then reversed by a unanimous Court of Appeal, for which Steyn LJ delivered the sole judgment.[12]

The opinion was framed in terms which bore an obvious resemblance to the jurisprudence of the ECtHR. Steyn LJ accepted that a 'presumptive entitlement' was in issue; 'It is a principle of our law that every citizen has a right of unimpeded access to a court . . . Even in our unwritten constitution it must rank as a constitutional right'.[13] The significance of the 'constitutional

---

[8] See Loveland I (1995) 'Introduction: should we take lessons from America?' in Loveland I (ed) *A special relationship?*. *Derbyshire* itself attracted considerable academic attention. For various perspectives see Tomkins A and Bix B (1993) 'Local authorities and libel again' *MLR* 738; Barendt E (1993) 'Libel and freedom of speech in English law' *Public Law* 449; Loveland I (1994) 'Defamation of 'government': taking lessons from America' *Legal Studies* 206.

[9] [1994] QB 198, CA.

[10] [1983] 1 AC 1, HL: 'The presumption of non-interference with 'basic rights', ch 13, pp 360–361.

[11] This amendment had been introduced in response to an ECtHR judgment which found r 33(3) to breach Art 6 of the Convention: see *Golder v United Kingdom* (1975) 1 EHRR 524.   [12] [1994] QB 198.

[13] Ibid, at 210.

right' designation was that the entitlement could be removed or abridged only by explicit legislation or as a matter of necessary implication from the relevant statutory text. Steyn LJ made it clear that courts should be reluctant to accept implied statutory interferences with such rights:

> . . . in relation to rule-making powers alleged to arise by necessary implication, it can fairly be said that the more fundamental the right interfered with, and the more drastic the interference, the more difficult becomes the implication.[14]

While one might welcome this conclusion, the methodology is open to criticism on two obvious grounds. The first is the absence of any supra-judicial catalogue of 'constitutional rights'. They are purely common law creations, susceptible to change at any time. The second is Lord Steyn's suggestion that the common law recognises a hierarchy of constitutional rights, some 'more fundamental' than others. If the rights themselves are elusive, their respective positions on the constitutional ladder are even more so. What Steyn LJ did de facto here was to construe the Prison Act 1952 and the rules made under it in a way that rendered them compatible with the requirements of Arts 6 and 10 ECHR but, presumably for the reasons discussed earlier, he was unable to acknowledge this explicitly.

Having established its methodology, the Court defined the notion of 'access to a court' quite broadly. Steyn LJ argued that the common law clearly recognised that:

> a prisoner's unimpeded right of access to a solicitor for the purpose of receiving advice and assistance in connection with the possible institution of civil proceedings in the courts forms an inseparable part of the right of access to the courts themselves.[15]

Steyn LJ's reasoning on the latter point is somewhat disingenuous. That the reach of that proposition extended to a prisoner in Leech's situation was made entirely clear only by Steyn LJ's own judgment. His purpose perhaps was to suggest that the Court of Appeal was merely declaring existing law rather than creating new law. That is an unconvincing distinction. The conclusion is obviously teleological in its source, resting on the premise that a prisoner will be deterred from initiating legal actions at all if he/she knows that she cannot discuss the pros and cons of such action with her/his legal advisers on a confidential basis.

While the Court accepted that s 47—as a matter of necessary implication—authorised *some* interference with prisoner's mail, the question to be answered was whether r 33(3) was drawn too widely. In addressing this issue, Steyn LJ effectively adopted a proportionality test:

> The question is whether there is a self-evident and pressing need for an unrestricted power to read letters between a prisoner and a solicitor and a power to stop such letters on the ground of prolixity and objectionality.[16]

In applying the test, the Court looked unusually closely—given that this was an AJR action—at the merits of the policy issues involved. It considered the Home Office's arguments on this point to be unconvincing. Drawing on a recent Canadian authority,[17] Steyn LJ offered a series of 'illustrative' safeguards which might be attached to such a governmental power to make it compatible with the prisoner's right of access to the courts. Since the Prison Rules contained no such safeguards, rule 33(3) was ultra vires s 47.[18]

---

[14] Ibid, at 209.   [15] Ibid, at 210.

[16] Ibid, at 209. He framed the test in somewhat different terms, even more redolent of the proportionality principle, at 555; 'The authorised intrusion must, however, be the minimum necessary to ensure that the correspondence is in truth bona fide legal correspondence'.   [17] *Solosky v R* (1979) 105 DLR (3d) 745.

[18] This technique invites comparison with Megarry VC's much less assertive strategy in *Malone*: see '*Malone v Metropolitan Police Commissioner* (1979)', ch 17, pp 458–459.

R v Secretary of State for Social Security, ex p Joint Council for the Welfare of Immigrants

In February 1996, Peter Lilley (then Secretary of State for Social Security) introduced delegated legislation[19] denying welfare benefits to any asylum seekers who did not declare themselves as such immediately upon entering the United Kingdom and to those who chose to appeal (as they were entitled by statute to do) against an initial refusal of their application. Such people would have to rely on charitable support. The measure attracted much criticism, on the basis that many asylum seekers were likely to be too afraid or disorientated to approach the Home Office straight away and that, de facto, the change would abrogate rights of appeal. In June 1996, the Court of Appeal held the policy unlawful.[20] The Court reached this conclusion by in effect applying the 'fundamental human rights' rationale: indeed, the argument deployed had undertones of a 'natural law' philosophy. Simon Brown LJ expressed his conclusion in very forceful terms:

> [T]he 1996 regulations necessarily contemplate for some a life so destitute that, to my mind, no civilised nation can tolerate it. So basic are the human rights here at issue, that it cannot be necessary to resort to the [ECHR] . . . Nearly 200 years ago Lord Ellenborough CJ in *R v Eastbourne (inhabitants)* ((1803) 102 ER 769 at 779) said: 'As to there being no obligation for maintaining poor foreigners . . . the law of humanity, which is anterior to all positive laws, obliges us to afford them relief, to save them from starving'.[21]

The Court considered that when Parliament had passed the relevant 'parent Act', it had not given the government any power to negate this common law principle.

Simon Brown LJ concluded by observing that:

> Parliament cannot have intended a significant number of genuine asylum seekers to be impaled upon the horns of so intolerable a dilemma—the need either to abandon their claims to refugee status or alternatively to maintain themselves as best they can but in an utter state of destitution. Primary legislation alone could in my judgement achieve that sorry state of affairs.[22]

II. The 'judicial supremacism' controversy

The increasing assertiveness of the domestic courts, coupled with a series of forceful judgments by the ECJ and the ECtHR in the mid-1990s, triggered something of a political controversy in the early- to mid-1990s. The controversy was kindled and stoked by a mix of government Ministers (the second Major government then being in power), backbench MPs, and right-wing newspapers. It was cast in terms of a need to defend 'sovereignty' and 'democracy', which were apparently both being undermined by a judicial conspiracy embracing domestic judges and the 'foreigners' sitting on the two European courts, all of whom were supposedly intent on giving themselves a more powerful, essentially illegitimate constitutional role within the United Kingdom.

Judgments of the ECJ and the ECtHR

In November 1995, the ECJ delivered its judgment in *R v Secretary of State for the Home Department, ex p Gallagher.*[23] Gallagher was an Irish citizen, who had been convicted in

---

[19] The Social Security (Persons From Abroad) Miscellaneous Amendments Regulations 1996, SI 1996/30.

[20] *R v Secretary of State for Social Security, ex p Joint Council for the Welfare of Immigrants* [1997] 1 WLR 275, CA.

[21] Ibid, at 292.   [22] Ibid, at 293.

[23] Case C–175/94: [1995] ECR I–4253; [1996] 1 CMLR 557. See the comment by O'Leary S (1996) '*R v Secretary of State for the Home Department, ex p Gallagher*' CMLR 777.

Ireland some years previously of firearms offences. The then Home Secretary, Michael Howard, invoked powers under the Prevention of Terrorism (Temporary Provisions) Act 1989 to exclude Gallagher from the United Kingdom. Gallagher challenged his exclusion before the English courts on the basis that it breached his EC-derived right of free movement as a worker. Gallagher relied specifically on Directive 64/221, Art 9 of which required that an individual be able to challenge any exclusion decision before a 'competent authority'. Following a reference from the Court of Appeal, the ECJ indicated that the UK's procedures on this point were incompatible with EC law. The judgment was hardly surprising, being well-rooted in existing ECJ judgments.[24] Nor was it as far reaching as it might have been. The ECJ did not require, for example, that prospective deportees be provided with reasons for the government's actions. The effect and legitimacy of the ECJ's conclusion were nonetheless derided by Conservative Ministers and backbench MPs,[25] who were it seems distinctly disturbed to see how the nominally 'economic' basis of Community law could cut across into 'human rights issues'.[26]

Their indignation was rather more forceful in response to the ECJ's judgment in *Factortame (No 3)/Brasserie du Pêcheur*,[27] handed down on 5 March 1996. The judgment indicated that a Member State could be liable in damages to individuals or organisations which had suffered economic loss caused by the Member State's breach of EU law, and so raised the possibility that an English court might soon award Factortame substantial damages for losses caused by the Merchant Shipping Act 1988. The notion that—in effect—Parliament could be liable in damages was not welcomed by the Major government and Conservative MPs. The then Fisheries Minister, Tony Baldry, described the judgment as: 'a crazy law'.[28] A backbench MP, Iain Duncan Smith, proposed drastic action to prevent any damages being awarded:

> The government should therefore act now to stop these cases going ahead until it had resolved the matter. It should pass a simple act of Parliament amending the European Communities Act 1972 to stop the ruling applying in English courts.[29]

Duncan Smith's presumption that the government could pass an Act is itself a telling indictment of the extent to which Conservative MPs had discarded orthodox understandings of the separation of powers. It is perhaps unfortunate that Parliament did not enact such a Bill. Factortame would no doubt have sought to have the resultant statute disapplied. The ensuing litigation would have provided a marvellous opportunity for the courts to confirm just how significantly the UK's accession to the Community had compromised traditional understandings of the sovereignty of Parliament.

Factortame (No 3) was immediately followed by the judgment in the '*Working Time Directive*' case.[30] The Council had enacted Directive 93/104 to place maximum limits on the hours that employees could be required to work. The Council claimed it had the power to do so under Art 118a of the Treaty of Rome; which provided, inter alia, that: 'Member States shall pay particular attention to encouraging improvements, especially in the working environment, as regards the health and safety of workers. . . .' Limiting working hours (to a maximum of forty-eight per week) would seem obviously to be a 'health and safety' matter. The Major government, which opposed the substance of the measure, was unable to veto it in Council, because Art 118(a) allowed secondary legislation to be adopted by a qualified

---

[24] See the discussion in O'Leary op cit.   [25] See *The Times* and *The Guardian* 1 December 1995.

[26] Cf O'Leary op cit at 787: 'indeed it is surprising that the PTA was adopted and successively renewed in the form it was, given the clear rulings of the Court of Justice . . . Perhaps it was thought that national anti-terrorist legislation did not come within the scope of Community law'.

[27] Cases C–46/93 and C–48/93: [1996] 1 CMLR 889.   [28] *The Guardian* 6 March 1996.

[29] 'This writ should not run over us' *The Times* 12 March 1996. Duncan Smith was elected as leader of the Conservative Party in 2001. He proved remarkably inept in that role.

[30] *United Kingdom v EU Council*: C–84/94 [1996] ECR I–5755.

majority. It thus argued that the measures of this sort were properly regarded as parts of the 'internal market' strategy,[31] and should thus be enacted under Art 100a. Since Art 100a required unanimity in the Council, success on this point would enable the government to veto the measure altogether. The Advocate-General's preliminary opinion found against the United Kingdom, and was met with the comment from the Prime Minister that: 'It is precisely because of legislation like this and stupidities like this that the EU is becoming uncompetitive and losing jobs to other parts of the world'.[32] When the ECJ subsequently upheld the Advocate-General's opinion, the most splenetic reaction came from John Redwood, one of the Prime Minister's Cabinet colleagues: 'The court is off the leash and on the loose, overturning Acts of Parliament, destroying our fishing industry, and changing our employment laws. Parliament should immediately assert its rights'.[33]

Shortly afterwards, in *P v S and Cornwall County Council*,[34] the ECJ held that the notion of 'gender' within the Equal Treatment Directive[35] included transsexualism. Thus a person who was dismissed from his/her job because he/she had undergone surgical and hormonal treatments to change his/her sex from male to female had been unlawfully discriminated against under EC law. No such protection then existed under domestic law. The gist of the political reaction within the Conservative Party on this issue was nicely characterised by a hysterical leading article in the right-wing newspaper *The Daily Mail*, on 2 May 1996:

> Until and unless we have a government prepared to mount a fundamental and unyielding challenge to the supremacy of this alien jurisdiction, then Britain will continue to face nothing less than the death of its nationhood by a thousand cuts of the Euro-scalpel.

The government received several similarly unwelcome setbacks before the ECtHR in this period. In June 1996, the Court's judgment in *Benham v United Kingdom*[36] found the United Kingdom in breach of Art 6 ECHR.[37] Benham had refused to pay his poll tax, and was eventually gaoled for thirty days for continuing to withhold payment. He had not been able to afford to employ counsel at his trial, and no legal aid was available for such hearings. Given the severity of the punishment he faced (ie a gaol sentence), and the complexity of the legal issues that the trial raised, the ECtHR considered that the government's failure to provide legal representation had denied Mr Benham a fair hearing.[38]

Benham followed the judgment in *Hussain v United Kingdom*.[39] Hussain was convicted of murder while a juvenile, and sentenced to be detained 'at her Majesty's pleasure'. Under domestic law, his release was a matter for the Home Secretary not for a judge. The applicant argued that this amounted to a breach of Art 5(4) ECHR.[40] The Court accepted this submission, thereby in effect requiring a transfer of particular sentencing powers from the government to the courts.

---

[31] See 'I. The Single European Act—the terms', discussed in the seventh edition of this book, ch 11, pp 386–388, which is available in the online resources supporting this edition of the book.   [32] *The Guardian* 13 March 1996.

[33] *The Times* 13 March 1996.

[34] Case C–13/94: [1996] ECR I–2143. Judgment was given on 1 May 1996.

[35] Secondary legislation which gave detailed effect to Art 119; see 'The justiciability test and the horizontal direct effect principle reaffirmed and expanded...' discussed in the seventh edition of this book, ch 11, pp 373–374 (available in the online resources for this edition).   [36] (1995) 21 EHRR 97.

[37] Art 6 (1): 'In the determination of his civil rights and obligations or of any criminal charge against him, everyone is entitled to a fair and public hearing within a reasonable time by an independent and impartial tribunal established by law...'

[38] The judgment goes substantially further than domestic administrative law rules concerning the 'right' to legal representation: see 'The content of procedural fairness—legal representation and an obligation to give reasons for decisions', ch 14, pp 402–405.   [39] (1996) 22 EHRR 1.

[40] Article 5 (4): 'Everyone who is deprived of his liberty by arrest or detention shall be entitled to take proceedings by which the lawfulness of his detention shall be decided speedily by a court....'

To Conservative MPs, however, the ECtHR's most controversial judgment was *McCann v United Kingdom*.[41] McCann was an Art 2 case.[42] The applicants were relatives of several IRA terrorists, who, while plotting to explode a bomb in Gibraltar, had been shot dead by British soldiers. In a judgment which involved an extremely detailed examination of the facts of the episode,[43] the Court concluded by a ten to nine majority that the killings could not be justified under Art 2(2).

In response to these decisions, the Major government evidently gave serious consideration to withdrawing UK citizens' right of individual petition to the Commission. It decided instead to try to pressurise the Council of Europe to curb the ECtHR's jurisdiction and to set much wider limits to the 'margin of appreciation' doctrine. A Foreign Office memorandum to the Council (leaked to the British press) contained the extraordinary proposal that the Court be required to respect 'long-standing laws and practices' within Member States even if they were 'manifestly contrary to the Convention'.[44] The Council of Europe was apparently unimpressed by these suggestions. This is hardly surprising, for by then it was wholly clear that the Major government's penchant for making unlawful decisions arose as often in respect of matters of domestic law as it did in respect of the law of the EC and the ECHR.

Judgments in domestic courts on immigration policies

Two of the more important judgments which figured in the judicial supremacism controversy have already been discussed in previous chapters. The *Pergau Dam* case proved a substantial embarrassment to the Major government, as did the House of Lords' decision in the *Fire Brigades Union* litigation. Neither judgment could be regarded as particularly radical in nature. *Pergau Dam* turned on a long-rooted principle of statutory interpretation,[45] while *Fire Brigades Union* was concerned with safeguarding the sovereignty of Parliament from governmental misuse of the royal prerogative.[46] The government's most acute and consistent cause for concern however lay in judgments dealing with its immigration policies, especially concerning the treatment of people who had come to the United Kingdom to escape from what they claimed was political persecution in their home countries.

Michael Howard's legal difficulties as Home Secretary prompted much of the Conservative MPs' anti-judicial ire in this period. However his predecessor, Kenneth Baker, had set the scene for this supposed conflict between the Home Office and the courts through a course of action which ultimately led to the House of Lords' judgment in *Re M*.[47]

Re M

M was a teacher from Zaire who sought political asylum in Britain, claiming that he would be subject to political persecution if he returned to his homeland. The Home Secretary[48] decided

---

[41] (1995) 21 EHRR 97.

[42] '1 Everybody's right to life shall be protected by law. No-one shall be deprived of his life intentionally save in the execution of a sentence of a court following his conviction of a crime for which this penalty is provided by law.

2 Deprivation of life shall not be regarded as inflicted in contravention of this Article when it results from use of force which is no more than is absolutely necessary:

(a) in defence of any person from unlawful violence;

(b) in order to effect a lawful arrest or to prevent the escape of a person lawfully detained;

(c) in action lawfully taken for the purpose of quelling a riot or insurrection.'

[43] ie the ECtHR was in effect exercising an appellate jurisdiction.   [44] See *The Guardian*, 2 April 1996.

[45] See 'Excess of powers', ch 13, pp 354–361.

[46] See 'Extending *Laker: R v Secretary of State for the Home Department, ex p Fire Brigades Union* (1995)', ch 3, pp 89–90.   [47] [1994] 1 AC 377, sub nom *M v Home Office*.

[48] It appears that the decision was actually made by a junior Minister, and that the Home Secretary himself, Kenneth Baker, was not familiar with the case.

that M did not qualify for asylum under the relevant legislation, and ordered his deportation. M's counsel then presented new evidence to the Court. By this time, M was on his way to Heathrow airport. The judge, Garland J, considered that the Home Office's counsel had given the Court an undertaking that M would not be deported until the new evidence was heard, and made an order (which was in effect an interim injunction) in those terms. However, M was then flown to Paris and placed on a flight to Zaire. M's solicitor then woke up Garland J in the middle of the night, and the judge immediately (by phone) ordered the Home Secretary to return M to Britain. The Home Secretary was then informed by his legal advisers that Garland J had no power to make such order, and the Home Secretary decided to ignore it. The case raised several important issues. Much of the argument centred on complex questions of administrative law, which need not concern us here.[49] There are however, two points of constitutional significance which we need to address. Firstly, did the High Court have the power to issue an injunction against the Crown, represented here by the Home Office? And if so, was Kenneth Baker, the Home Secretary, in either his personal or ministerial capacity, in contempt of court for ignoring it?

If we recall *Entick* and *Liversidge*, we see that the citizen's legal actions were not against the 'government' (or the Crown), but against individual government officials. In both instances, the government official was being sued for allegedly committing a tortious action; trespass in *Entick* and false imprisonment in *Liversidge*. In neither 1765 nor 1942 was it possible for those actions to be commenced against the Crown per se. As previously noted, while the 1688 revolution had established the supremacy of statute over common law, it did not in itself alter common law principles in any systematic way. One such principle, encapsulated in the aphorism that 'the King could do no wrong', was that the courts had no jurisdiction to entertain suits in tort or contract against the Crown. Citizens could pursue such actions only via 'the petition of right' device. Relatedly, it had always been thought that an injunction could not lie against the Crown per se.[50] Similarly, while an individual government official who deliberately defied an injunction against her would be in contempt of court, the non-availability of such a remedy against the Crown would logically imply that there could be nothing in respect of which the Crown per se could be in contempt.

It was not until the Crown Proceedings Act 1947 that Parliament exercised its sovereign legal power to abolish the petition of right device. The Act made it clear that the Crown itself could now be sued in contract or tort. However the Act did not explicitly confirm that injunctions and the contempt jurisdiction could also issue against the Crown per se, rather than just against individual officials. Prior to the *M* case, the weight of judicial authority in matters purely of domestic law suggested such remedies were not available. In effect, this case law seemingly suggested that remedies which citizens might enforce against other citizens were only available against the Crown when Parliament had explicitly legislated to that effect.

This left something of a gap in the legal regulation of government activity. On the facts of *M*, for example, an interim injunction against Mr Baker in person would not have prevented other Home Office Ministers or employees from placing M on the plane to Zaire. Had Mr Baker wilfully defied the courts and breached such an order, he personally would have been in contempt, but that consequence would neither be of assistance to M nor underline the principle that the government as a corporate body must respect court orders. Thus, if the 'rule of law' was not to be undermined in practice, we would have to rely on the integrity of government in never doing anything that might be the subject of an injunction or a contempt order, a reliance that fits uneasily with the Diceyan principle that the rule of law demands that we should always be suspicious of government's bona fides. In the context of EC law, that position had been changed by the *Factortame* judgments,[51] but it did not necessarily follow that this principle would spill over into domestic law.

---

[49] See Gould M (1993) '*M v Home Office*: government and the judges' *Public Law* 568.
[50] See further 'Challenging Governmental Decisions: the Process', ch 15, pp 412–414.
[51] See 'The demise of the legal doctrine? *Factortame*', ch 11, pp 306–312.

The leading judgment in *M* was given by Lord Woolf. The Court concluded that the High Court had the power to issue an interim injunction against the Crown, that the Crown was in theory amenable to the contempt jurisdiction, and that, on the facts of this case, such a contempt had been committed. Lord Woolf's judgment is much concerned with technical questions of administrative law. For our purposes, perhaps the key passage in the decision comes from Lord Templeman's speech:

> [T]he argument that there is no power to enforce the law by injunction . . . against a Minister in his official capacity would, if upheld, establish the proposition that the executive obey the law as a matter of grace and not as a matter of necessity, a proposition which would reverse the result of the civil war.[52]

The logic of his contention seems unassailable; namely that the revolution had created a situation in which the Crown's legal status was equivalent to that of an ordinary legal person; thus all legal remedies which are available against individuals should be available against the Crown, unless Parliament has clearly provided to the contrary.

Lord Woolf drew on similarly expansive principles in confirming the availability of the contempt jurisdiction. The Home Secretary, in either his personal or official capacity, could be in contempt for disregarding the terms of such an injunction. The only bodies capable of overturning the order of a High Court judge would be the Court of Appeal and House of Lords; if Ministers could ignore the courts on the basis of the advice of their lawyers, the rule of law would clearly be being subverted. As Lord Woolf explained:

> [T]he ability of the court to make a finding of contempt is of great importance. It would demonstrate that a government department has interfered with the administration of justice. It will then be for Parliament to determine what should be the consequences of that finding.[53]

M should thus be seen as a long overdue embrace of traditional principle. The judgment plugged an unfortunate gap in the coverage of the rule of law principle in modern society, while making it perfectly clear that if Parliament took the view that it was appropriate for government Ministers to enjoy this immunity (in non-EC matters) it could create it for them in statute.

R v Secretary of State for the Home Department, ex p Moon

Kenneth Baker's successor as Home Secretary, Michael Howard, threw further fuel onto the political fire by making a series of patently unlawful decisions which were subsequently invalidated in the courts. In *R v Secretary of State for the Home Department, ex p Moon*,[54] Sedley J quashed Howard's attempt to exclude the Revd Sun Il Moon—the leader of the 'Moonie' religious cult—from the United Kingdom under powers granted by the Immigration Acts. The decision promoted an outcry among Conservative MPs and the tabloid and broadsheet press, who felt Moon was so unpleasant a character that he should never be allowed into the country. This response was wholly ill-informed about both the nature of the decision and the basic features of the judicial review jurisdiction. Sedley J had not held that Howard could not exclude Moon. His decision was based on a procedural irregularity in the Home Secretary's decision-making process. The judgment held simply that Howard could exclude Moon only after giving him an opportunity to argue that he should be admitted: that is, it was a straightforward application of the procedural fairness doctrine. Having heard such arguments, the Home Secretary could admit or exclude Moon as he thought fit, subject only to *Wednesbury* irrationality constraints.

One might expect tabloid papers to misrepresent or misunderstand such principles. It was more surprising to find *The Times* displaying similar ignorance. In a leader engagingly entitled 'Judicial Moonshine', *The Times* castigated Sedley's judgment on the grounds that Moon was a thoroughly undesirable alien who should never be allowed into Britain. That substantive conclusion may have

---

[52] [1994] 1 AC 377 at 395.   [53] Ibid, at 425.   [54] (1995) 8 Admin LR 477.

much to commend it; but it has nothing to do with Sedley J's judgment, which concerned only the procedures through which the Home Secretary acted. *The Times* was either misinformed or mendacious in suggesting the judgment overturned established legal understandings.

The *al-Mas'ari* case

Professor al-Mas'ari's legal action against the Home Secretary had rather graver implications. Saudi Arabia, while an important economic and political ally for the United Kingdom, could hardly be described as having a constitutional system which operated as a model of enlightened and humane government. The regime is intolerant of internal political opposition, and dissidents who escape imprisonment tend to conduct their political campaigns from abroad. Professor al-Mas'ari was one such dissident who had sought political asylum in the United Kingdom. The Home Secretary, again exercising statutory powers, declined to grant asylum. His reason for so doing was a fear that Saudi Arabia's government would be less inclined to buy British arms and other goods if the United Kingdom sheltered one of its critics.

Al-Mas'ari's legal challenge to this refusal was unsurprisingly successful. The case turned on a simple and long-established administrative law point: were calculations as to arms' sales a 'relevant consideration' in the exercise of statutory powers concerning asylum decisions? In this case, Judge Pearl had little difficulty in concluding that considerations of commercial advantage were not relevant factors. On relevant grounds—such as the asylum seeker's personal characteristics, the regime from which she or he fled, the likelihood that she or he would suffer harm if returned there—al-Mas'ari presented a strong case. For the Home Secretary to allow such factors to be trumped by the prospect of losing arms sales was an abuse of the powers Parliament had granted him. The government did not appeal against this judgment, which indicates it realised that its legal position was untenable.

However, the government did not let the matter rest. Rather than challenge the judgment in court, the government attacked it in the media. On Radio 4's *Today* programme on 14 March 1996, John Major elided the *al-Mas'ari* judgment with recent terrorist outrages in Israel and suggested that Parliament might reconsider whether Britain should shelter critics of 'friendly' regimes. His government could have asked Parliament to enact legislation achieving such an outcome; or providing specifically for al-Mas'ari's deportation; or expressly permitting the Home Secretary to take into account the beneficial impact on arms sales that deporting political dissidents might have. Should Parliament have enacted such laws, a future Home Secretary could follow Howard's lead without fear of court intervention. That the Major government did not choose to pursue any of these options might suggest it knew the ends it sought might be regarded as immoral by both the Commons and the Lords.

The Court's decision can therefore be seen as protecting not just Professor al-Mas'ari, but also the principle of parliamentary sovereignty, against government whims. Both the *Moon* and the *al-Mas'ari* cases, as well as the *Fire Brigades Union* and *Pergau Dam* judgments, underline this basic constitutional truth. Ministers may do only what Parliament permits. The limits of parliamentary intent are, and always have been, policed by the High Court. If Ministers find these limits uncongenial, they must ask Parliament to change them.

R v Secretary of State for Social Security, ex p Joint Council for the Welfare of Immigrants

Perhaps the most graphic example of Conservative MPs either denying or not understanding this principle was provided in the aftermath of the *R v Secretary of State for Social Security, ex p Joint Council for the Welfare of Immigrants* judgment.[55] As noted earlier, the Court of Appeal

---

[55] [1997] 1 WLR 275.

had concluded in that case that only primary legislation could achieve 'the sorry state of affairs' of removing all benefit entitlements from certain categories of asylum seekers. Spectators in the Commons' public gallery the week after judgment was issued saw Peter Lilley announce that the government would seek to persuade Parliament to enact new legislation to achieve that objective.[56] The Minister did not enter debates about judicial supremacism. His backbench colleagues showed no such restraint, and coupled their copious indignation with magnificent ignorance.

Tony Marlow MP simply failed to grasp the essential distinction between primary and delegated legislation. His contribution to the debate was to ask: 'Have I missed something? Do the judiciary now have a democratic mandate to decide which laws are acceptable?'[57] His colleague Toby Jessell apparently found the distinction between politics and law too confusing to grasp: 'My constituents [do not] expect the Court of Appeal to do other than uphold public policy. [They] do not expect the Court of Appeal to make up the law as it goes along.'[58]

The answer to both of Marlow's questions is manifestly: 'Yes'. Mr Marlow had apparently 'missed' the Glorious Revolution, the structure of constitutional law built upon its foundations, and the long-established principle that the courts do indeed have a 'democratic mandate': namely, to ensure that the executive in making delegated legislation does not exceed the limits of powers delegated by the parent Act. What Marlow and his ilk on the Tory backbenches did not understand was that what the Court invalidated in the *JCWI* case was not 'a law' at all, but government abuse of the law.

There is a certain comedy in listening to MPs' politically closed minds rattling around in their legally empty heads, but the comedy is underpinned by a serious constitutional point. The MPs' substantively illiterate criticism of the Court was echoed in much of the press, which accused Simon Brown LJ in particular of overstepping the limits of his powers. It might be argued that the style of Simon Brown LJ's judgment was atypically trenchant. It might even be suggested that his recognition of what was in essence a 'fundamental human right' to subsistence, abrogable only by explicit statutory language, somewhat extended the reach of the courts' resurgent fundamental rights jurisprudence.[59] But the judgment can hardly be seen as an example of judicial supremacism. It would be much more accurate to categorise it as removing an element of 'executive supremacism'.

'Executive supremacism' is of course not a concept which sits happily in a constitution where, in theory, sovereign authority lies with Parliament rather than the government. However, as has been suggested repeatedly in earlier chapters of this book, 'executive supremacism' would seem an accurate description of the way the constitution works in practice, in so far as a government is generally able to 'persuade' both Houses of Parliament to enact whatever legislation it wishes. The defining feature of the judicial supremacism episode was that Ministers, Conservative MPs, and much of the press seemed either to ignore or forget that point. Their argument was, in effect, that as long as a Commons majority approves of what a Minister does, nothing more need be said about the legality of her or his behaviour. A governing party which had for over fifteen years possessed a substantial and generally loyal majority in both houses may well have forgotten that the constitution requires the house's majority views to be placed on a statutory basis before the courts accord them legal significance. It is no more the task of backbench MPs, individually or en masse, to determine if a Minister's action is lawful than it is for a Minister to do so.

A judicial response

Michael Howard's criminal justice policies also brought him into public confrontation within the political arena with several senior judges and ex-judges. In December 1995,

---

[56] *HCD* 24 June 1996 cc 37–38.   [57] Ibid, at c 42.   [58] Ibid, at c 44.
[59] Cf his own acknowledgement of the relevance of *Leech* to his judgment: [1997] 1 WLR 275 at 282.

Lord Donaldson, the former Master of the Rolls, suggested in a *Guardian* article that the government and its media supporters were mounting 'a campaign of abuse and criticism of the judiciary as a whole'.[60] In so doing, the government was attacking orthodox understandings of the rule of law and thereby opening a path towards despotic government. As Lord Donaldson acknowledged, Parliament could enact any policy which the government wanted to pursue. But he argued that it was wholly unacceptable that Ministers should, by constantly vilifying judicial decisions, seek to intimidate the courts into toeing the government line.

The former Lord Chief Justice, Lord Taylor, also joined the fray, arguing in a speech at King's College London in March 1996 that Howard's plans to impose mandatory sentences for particular kinds of criminal offence were dictated by 'the vagaries of fashion'. The Home Secretary responded to the Lord Chief Justice's speech on the *Today* programme the following morning, suggesting that Lord Taylor was 'soft on crime'. One particular line of Howard's diatribe was reprinted as the front-page headline of the same day's London *Evening Standard* in the form of a question to Lord Taylor: 'DO YOU WANT RAPISTS TO GO FREE?' The question is absurd—a gratuitous insult, which could not be taken seriously by any rational observer. But that does not mean it was ineffective. Rather, it suggested that if judges offered reasoned criticism of any aspect of the Major government's policy agenda, they would face a ministerial reply designed only to foster prejudice and intolerance among the public.

Any thought that Lord Donaldson's claim that the judiciary was being subjected to an orchestrated government campaign was the result of paranoia was dispelled in December 1995 by the curious episode of Lord Mackay's non-existent speech. *The Daily Telegraph* ran a story on 7 December headed 'Judges Warned to Keep in Line', explaining that the Lord Chancellor, the formal head of the judiciary, would deliver a speech that evening warning the judges not to exceed their powers. That day's *Times* predicted that Lord Mackay would tell judges to 'refrain from using their judicial powers to challenge ministerial decisions'. Lord Mackay evidently intended no such thing. He had circulated a paper on recent judicial decisions for internal Cabinet discussion; in it he defended traditional understandings of the courts' powers. He had no wish to make his views public. However, the then Conservative Party Chairman, Brian Mawhinney, evidently thinking that such comment from the head of the judiciary would undermine the position of 'liberal' judges, arranged (without Lord Mackay's approval) to leak the paper to *The Telegraph*. Mawhinney's initiative reinforced what *The Times* had already identified on 3 November 1995 as an acute judicial concern: that the government was fanning, in one judge's words, 'a hate campaign coming through sections of the media, to pour poison on the views of the judiciary'. Another judge who was quoted felt, more charitably, that the government's behaviour resulted not from mendacity, but from ignorance: Ministers and backbench MPs simply did not understand the basic constitutional principles underpinning the role of judicial review, had no grasp of the legitimacy of the common law as a dynamic source of legal authority, and did not appreciate the distinction between parliamentary majorities and Parliament itself.[61]

These points are axiomatic as to the way the constitution has been structured since 1688. That structure also makes it clear that the *only* way Ministers can ultimately be rendered answerable to *Parliament* is through judges in the courts ensuring that Ministers do not deploy powers that Parliament has not given them. Of course, members of the judiciary may misconstrue Parliament's intentions in their interpretation of statutes. If Parliament considers a court has misconstrued its intention, it may pass legislation amending the court's decision. A Commons majority plays a vital part in that process—but only a part.

---

[60] *The Guardian* 11 December 1995. Lord Donaldson was not regarded as a particularly liberal judge.

[61] For a more detailed treatment of this issue see Loveland I (1997) 'The war against the judges' *Political Quarterly* 162.

Lord Mustill's analysis

Perhaps the most coherent and revealing exposition of the relationship between the courts and the Thatcher and Major governments is offered by a lengthy passage in Lord Mustill's (dissenting) judgment in the *Fire Brigades Union* case.[62] The passage merits substantial reproduction here, as it raises important and controversial questions as to the inter-relationship of the sovereignty of Parliament, the rule of law, and the separation of powers in late-twentieth-century British society:

> The courts interpret the laws, and see that they are obeyed. This requires the courts on occasion to step into the territory which belongs to the executive, to verify . . . that the powers asserted accord with the substantive law created by Parliament . . .
>
> Concurrently with this judicial function Parliament has its own special means of ensuring that the executive, in the exercise of delegated functions, performs in a way which Parliament finds appropriate. Ideally, it is these latter methods which should be used to check executive errors and excesses; for it is the task of Parliament and the executive in tandem, not of the courts, to govern the country. In recent years, however, the employment in practice of these specifically Parliamentary remedies has on occasion been perceived as falling short, and sometimes well short, of what was needed to bring the performance of the executive into line with the law . . . To avoid a vacuum in which the citizen would be left without protection against a misuse of executive powers the courts have had no option but to occupy the dead ground in a manner, and in areas of public life, which could not have been foreseen 30 years ago. For myself, I am quite satisfied that this unprecedented judicial role has been greatly to the public benefit. Nevertheless, it has its risks, of which the courts are well aware. As the judges themselves constantly remark, it is not they who are appointed to administer the country. Absent a written constitution much sensitivity is required of the parliamentarian, administrator and judge if the delicate balance of the unwritten rules evolved (I believe successfully) in recent years is not to be disturbed . . .[63]

In a fascinating critique of judicial politics during the Thatcher and Major eras, Simon Lee argued that the courts effectively donned the mantle of 'the opposition' to the minoritarian preferences of the elected central government.[64] But this was not 'opposition' in a party political sense; the judiciary was not simply plugging the constitutional holes left by the feebleness of the Labour Party during the 1980s, or more systemically, by the Commons' pervasive inadequacy as a monitor of and restraint on governmental extremism. Lee is not suggesting that the courts' allegedly more interventionist ideas were intended to compete on equal terms with those of politicians, but rather that they existed above party political dispute, in a kind of constitutional moral stratosphere.

 Lee's thesis receives some support from essays and articles written by members of the judiciary in addition to Lord Mustill's critique in *Fire Brigades Union*. In a series of academic articles, Sir John Laws characterised the judiciary's more interventionist stance in administrative law as an attempt to give legal expression to a series of moral principles; 'about whose desirability there can be no serious argument'.[65] Sir John Laws suggests that much of the impetus for this development has come from the judiciary's increasing exposure to the constitutional orders of the EC, the European Convention, and the domestic legal systems of the EC's and the Convention's Member States.

 A perhaps more significant analysis, given its author's then status as a law lord, was offered by Lord Browne-Wilkinson.[66] Lord Browne-Wilkinson also acknowledged that the ECHR and the ECJ had had a significant influence on the judicial consciousness. However he also

---

[62] *R v Secretary of State for the Home Department, ex p Fire Brigades Union* [1995] 2 AC 513, HL.

[63] Ibid, at 567.   [64] Lee S (1994) 'Law and the constitution', in Kavanagh D and Seldon A (eds) *The Major effect*.

[65] Sir John Laws (1993) 'Is the High Court the guardian of fundamental constitutional rights?' *Public Law* 59. See also (1995) 'Law and democracy' *Public Law* 72; (1998) 'The limitations of human rights' *Public Law* 254.

[66] Browne-Wilkinson op cit.

suggested that British courts have increasingly been returning to a more rigorous (and often overlooked) schemata of statutory interpretation, in which judges should assume that; 'a presumption in favour of individual freedom almost certainly reflects the true intention of Parliament'.[67]

Conclusion

It would however be rash to assume that such sentiments pointed towards an inviolable truth in recent judicial decisions. The common law has always been, and remains, a pluralistic source of legal authority. Its balance may shift, but it is implausible to expect either that the new balance will be set in stone, or that even firmly established trends could not be reversed. More significantly, notwithstanding the force of Lord Mustill's speech in *Fire Brigades Union*, there will always be doubts raised as to the legitimacy of judges determining the meaning of 'human rights' or 'individual liberties' without the benefit of guidance from a supra-parliamentary constitution. With such an instrument to hand, courts may plausibly claim not to be imposing their own values on governmental bodies, but to be demonstrating instead a loyalty to 'the people' who decided upon the values to be placed beyond governmental reach. In the 1990s, the domestic courts were—with the limited exception of EC law—denied such luxuries. Every innovative principle—even any traditional principle—invoked to defend individual rights could be expected to serve as a trigger for political controversy should it inconvenience a government not prepared to accept orthodox constitutional principles.

The Labour Party evidently harboured few such fears in the mid-1990s. Its attraction to the idea of incorporating the Convention in some fashion into domestic law was evidently growing stronger, for it committed itself to do so in the party's 1997 election manifesto. Barely a year after coming to power in May 1997, the Blair government had successfully piloted the Human Rights Act 1998 through Parliament. In chapters twenty and twenty-one, we consider both the terms of the Act and its initial impact on the status of human rights principles in the UK's constitutional law.

Suggested further reading

Academic commentary

BROWNE-WILKINSON, LORD (1992) 'The infiltration of a Bill of Rights' *Public Law* 397

LAWS J (1993) 'Is the High Court the guardian of fundamental constitutional rights?' *Public Law* 59

SCARMAN L (1987) 'Human rights in an unwritten constitution' *Denning LJ* 129

BINGHAM T (1993) 'The European Convention on Human Rights: time to incorporate' *LQR* 393

GOULD M (1993) '*M v Home Office*: government and the judges' *Public Law* 568

Case law and legislation

Re M [1994] 1 AC 377

R v Secretary of State for Social Security, ex p Joint Council for the Welfare of Immigrants [1996] 4 All ER 385 (CA)

R v Secretary of State for the Home Department, ex p Leech (No 2) [1994] QB (CA)

---

[67] Ibid, at p 408. Lord Browne-Wilkinson suggests *R & W Paul Ltd v Wheat Commission* [1937] AC 139, HL; *National Assistance Board v Wilkinson* [1952] 2 QB 648; and *Raymond v Honey* [1983] 1 AC 1, HL, as examples.

Chapter 20

Human Rights IV:
The Human Rights Act 1998

The Labour Party's 1997 election manifesto commitment to redefine the status of the ECHR in domestic law[1] was overseen by Lord Irvine, the Lord Chancellor, following the formation of the first Blair administration. Speaking shortly after the election, Lord Irvine outlined the government's intentions:

> The government's position is that we should be leading in the development of human rights in Europe, not grudgingly driven to swallow the medicine prescribed for us by the Court in Strasbourg when we are found in breach of the Convention. Our citizens should be able to secure their human rights not only from a court in Strasbourg but from our own judges.[2]

The detailed contents of the proposed Act were signalled in a white paper—*Rights Brought Home: the Human Rights Bill*[3]—which proposed that the moral values articulated in the Convention should be given substantially enhanced status in domestic law. The white paper identified several cogent reasons for dissatisfaction with the current position:

> 1.14 . . . It takes on average five years to get an action into the ECtHR . . . ; and it costs an average of £30,000. Bringing these rights home will mean that the British people will be able to argue for their rights in the British courts—without this inordinate delay and cost. It will also mean that the rights will be brought much more fully into the jurisprudence of the courts throughout the United Kingdom and their interpretation will thus be far more subtly and powerfully woven into our law . . .
>
> 1.15. Moreover, in the government's view, the approach which the United Kingdom has so far adopted towards the Convention does not sufficiently reflect its importance . . . [4]

The white paper's main proposals were reflected in a Bill published in October 1997, the contents of which were in broad terms subsequently enacted in the 1998 legislation.

---

[1] **Real rights for citizens**
Citizens should have statutory rights to enforce their human rights in the UK courts. We will by statute incorporate the European Convention on Human Rights into UK law to bring these rights home and allow our people access to them in their national courts. The incorporation of the European Convention will establish a floor, not a ceiling, for human rights. Parliament will remain free to enhance these rights, for example by a Freedom of Information Act.

[2] Lord Irvine (1997) 'Constitutional reform and a Bill of Rights' *European Human Rights LR* 483 at 485.

[3] (1997) (Cm 3782).

[4] Ibid. Publication of the white paper coincided with the ECtHR concluding that—for the fiftieth time, UK law breached the Convention; see *Johnson v United Kingdom* [1997] 27 EHRR 296. Mr Johnson's case had taken four years to reach the ECtHR.

The Act was widely portrayed in the popular press as tantamount to a 'Bill of Rights'—an analogy presumably intended to suggest that Parliament had succeeded by embracing European jurisprudence in Americanising the UK's constitutional order. Campaigners for constitutional reform afforded the Bill a warm welcome. The then chairperson of the pressure group Charter 88 hailed the Bill as a measure which would; 'tip the balance of power from politicians to the people'.[5] The director of the human rights group Liberty announced that; 'We're absolutely delighted'.[6]

I. The terms of the Act

The analysis of the Act offered here makes no attempt to be comprehensive.[7] Such a task is more appropriately undertaken in a text dealing specifically with human rights issues. This chapter simply discusses the Act's main provisions, and identifies some of the Act's implications for the understandings we attach to the core constitutional principles of parliamentary sovereignty, the rule of law, and the separation of powers.

An 'incorporation' of 'fundamental' rights?

The device of 'entrenching' basic human rights by requiring super-majoritarian legislative procedures to alter their content is a widely established feature within the constitutions of western democratic nations. There is substantial variation on the types of entrenching techniques deployed in different countries, as well as in the depth of the entrenchment thereby achieved. The various methods however all share a common rationale—namely that those moral principles considered fundamental to societal ordering must not be left at the mercy of transient political majorities which might temporarily control a national legislature.

The European Convention articulates just such a set of fundamental moral and political principles. And in many of the Convention's Signatory States, its terms have been afforded supra-legislative constitutional status. That status enables those countries' courts to invoke the Convention terms as a moral yardstick against which to measure national legislation, and thereafter to strike down or disapply such legislation if it falls short of the necessary standards.

Rejecting entrenchment

The Human Rights Act makes no attempt to achieve similar results in the United Kingdom; it does not seek to endow the moral values in the Convention with an 'entrenched', supra-legislative legal status which would override any *future* legislation that breached its terms. Nor does the Human Rights Act 'incorporate' the Convention in the limited sense of permitting the courts to invoke the Convention to invalidate *pre-existing* legislation.[8] The preamble identifies a more modest purpose; 'An Act *to give further effect to* rights and freedoms guaranteed under the European Convention on Human Rights'.[9]

---

[5] *The Guardian* 25 October 1997.   [6] Ibid.

[7] For various perspectives see Lord Irvine (1997) 'Constitutional reform and a Bill of Rights' *European Human Rights LR* 483; Boateng P and Straw J (1996) *Bringing Rights Home*; (1997) 'Bringing rights home: Labour plans to incorporate the ECHR into UK Law' *European Human Rights LR* 71; Tierney S (1998) 'The Human Rights Bill' *European Public Law* 299; Ewing K (1999) 'The Human Rights Act and parliamentary democracy' *MLR* 79; Bamforth N (1998) 'Parliamentary sovereignty and the Human Rights Act 1998' *Public Law* 572; Loveland I (1999) 'Constitutional law or administrative law? The Human Rights Act 1998' *Contemporary Issues in Law* 124.

[8] ie a statutory provision which simply stated that 'The terms of the European Convention on Human Rights shall henceforth be enforceable by all domestic courts and tribunals in all legal proceedings' would by virtue of the doctrine of implied repeal render any previously enacted statutory provisions ineffective if they were inconsistent with a Convention article.   [9] Emphasis added.

The white paper reiterated the orthodox proposition that Parliament lacks the legal capacity to entrench an Act against repeal by a future Parliament through the simple majority plus royal assent formula; even if the (then) present Parliament and the government—wished to do so. Almost a decade after *Factortame (No 2)* had been decided, that seemed an odd view to adopt.[10] By quite what constitutional mechanism directly effective EC law achieved a minimal degree of entrenchment in UK law remains conceptually unclear,[11] but the principle does seem to have become embedded ('entrenched' being perhaps too loaded a word) in contemporary understandings of constitutional propriety. Unless we accept the contention that EC law is a unique jurisprudential creature, the political fact that it has achieved embedded status in UK law would indicate that other moral values might also—in similarly mysterious fashion—acquire that characteristic.

That the Blair administration did not think it appropriate to invite Parliament to try to entrench the Human Rights Act indicates that for the New Labour government the old constitutional orthodoxies retained a potent force. The government's unwillingness to try to tackle the entrenchment issue would suggest that the Human Rights Act is, in formal legal terms, a statute just like any other. Its provisions may be amended or repealed by any future legislation.

Advocates of incorporation who accept that the Convention cannot be entrenched in the legal sense have suggested that a measure such as the Human Rights Act might gain a degree of 'moral entrenchment', in that its hold on the political consciousness of politicians of all mainstream parties might quickly become so firmly established that no government would promote a Bill seeking to dilute its effect. But one might readily doubt if a future right-wing Conservative government which re-embraced the rigours of Thatcherite authoritarianism would feel morally constrained not to introduce a Bill substantially amending or wholly repealing the Human Rights Act.

The Blair government's evident reluctance to seek to achieve such unconventional constitutional objectives as entrenching a panoply of fundamental moral principles can perhaps be explained by its members' intrinsic attachment to Diceyan orthodoxies. More cynically, one might suggest, the government had no wish to limit the law-making autonomy it derived from its de facto control of Parliament's unlimited legislative powers. What is more difficult to understand is why the Blair government set its face against the principle that the Human Rights Act should empower courts to invalidate *previously enacted* statutory provisions incompatible with the ECHR. The white paper portrayed this scenario as politically undesirable:

> To make provision in the Bill for the courts to set aside Acts of Parliament would confer on the judiciary a general power over the decisions of Parliament which under our present constitutional arrangements they [sic] do not possess, and would be likely on occasions to draw the judiciary into serious conflict with Parliament.[12]

The Blair government was vigorously opposed to the proposal floated at the Nice Summit that the EC treaties should be amended to include a fundamental human rights element. Such an amendment to EC law would—post-*Factortame*—have empowered domestic courts and tribunals to disapply both existing and future legislation which was inconsistent with the requirements of EC human rights jurisprudence.[13] Having set its face so firmly against such

---

[10] In so far as the *Factortame* principle is limited to matters within the EU's competence, it is admittedly not a 'general' power in the sense that the white paper may be using that term. But given the very wide competence that the EU by then enjoyed (ie after the Amsterdam treaty), it was hardly credible to suggest that the *Factortame* rationale was not applicable to broad swathes of legislative activity.

[11] See 'The demise of the legal doctrine? *Factortame*', ch 11, pp 306–312.

[12] *Rights Brought Home, the Human Rights Bill*, at para 2.13. One should also note that the Act contains a broad definition of 'legislation', to include not just statutes but also certain elements of the prerogative: s 21.

[13] Craig P and de Burca G (2002, 3rd edn) *EU law* pp 358–369. See also Rogers I (2002) 'From the Human Rights Act to the Charter . . . ' *European Human Rights LR* 343.

innovations as an element of EC law, there was little likelihood that the Blair administration would attempt to produce a similar effect through engineering a 'revolutionary' change to domestic law. It is this lack of will or ambition in the Act's reach which perhaps most clearly points to its status as an innovation in administrative rather than constitutional law. The point was put with perfect clarity in political terms by the then Home Secretary, Jack Straw, at the Bill's second reading in the Commons:

> What the [HRA] makes clear is that Parliament is supreme, and that if Parliament wishes to maintain the position enshrined in an Act that it has passed, but which is incompatible with the Convention in the eyes of a British court, it is that Act which will remain in force.[14]

Sections 1 and 2: 'Convention Rights' under the HRA and Convention articles under the ECHR

The point has already been made that when Parliament 'incorporates' an international law into the domestic legal system, domestic courts are not being ordered to give effect to the international law per se but to the relevant statutory provisions.[15] Parliament might require in the incorporating statute that the substantive content of those statutory provisions should be identical to the international law norms concerned, which might in turn entail domestic courts being bound to adjust the meaning of the statutory provisions in accordance with the meaning lent to the international law instrument by the international court competent under the particular treaty regime to perform that role.[16] To put the matter crudely, according to an orthodox understanding of our existing constitutional arrangements, international law cannot be 'directly effective' within the domestic legal system.[17]

In respect of the treatment accorded to the Convention by the HRA, this principle was starkly stated by Lord Irvine at the report stage of the Bill in the House of Lords: 'I have to make this point absolutely plain. The ECHR under [the HRA] is not made part of our law . . . it does not make the Convention directly justiciable'.[18]

The scheme of the HRA is to create a set of statutory human rights principles (in s 1) which are labelled 'Convention Rights'. The Convention Rights are identified in Sch 1 of the HRA. In textual terms, the Convention Rights are identical to the analogous articles of the Convention; the schedule simply recites the words of the relevant articles.[19]

However, *a Convention Right need not have the same substantive meaning as the textually identical Convention article.* The Act does not grant the ECtHR any kind of appellate status within the domestic legal system. That Court's determinations as to the meaning of a Convention article do not have binding effect on domestic courts' construction of the meaning of a textually identical Convention Right.

Rather, s 2 imposes a duty on any court or tribunal hearing litigation involving a Convention Right to 'take into account' any judgment of the ECtHR, opinion of the EComHR, or decision of the Committee of Ministers when considering the case before it. Section 2(1) makes it clear that it is for the domestic court or tribunal to decide if any such judgment, opinion, or decision is indeed relevant. But even if such a judgment is considered relevant and is 'taken into account' by the domestic court, the domestic court is not obliged to follow it. Parliament has it

---

[14] *HCD* 16 February 1998 c 773.   [15] See 'Inconsistency with international law', ch 2, pp 29–30.

[16] For so long of course as the 'incorporating statute' was not expressly or impliedly overridden by later legislation.

[17] As noted in ch 11, Parliament also asserted in the European Union Act 2011 that even EU law is dependent for its status in domestic law on its incorporation via the ECA 1972.   [18] *HLD* January 29 1998 c 421.

[19] Not all parts of the Convention appear in Sch 1 of the Act. Those parts of the Convention which are not identified as 'Convention Rights' have effect in domestic law only to the extent that orthodox common law principles permit.

seems envisaged the possibility that Convention Rights and their Convention article counterparts will bear different meanings. The meaning of Convention Rights is a matter for domestic courts within the sphere of domestic law; the meaning of Convention articles is a matter for the ECtHR within the sphere of international law. Presumably, a Convention Right could afford more, less, or the same degree of legal protection as its Convention article counterpart.

The Act itself gives no indication of the degree of divergence permissible between the meaning of a Convention Right and that of the textually equivalent Convention article. Nor did the Act offer any guidance as to the circumstances in which such divergence would be appropriate.

Section 3—new rules of statutory interpretation?

At an abstract, theoretical level, s 3 of the Act marks a clear departure from orthodox understandings of the separation of powers.[20] Parliament has traditionally regarded the question of the principles which courts should apply when interpreting legislation as a matter of common law as an issue determined by the courts. Legislation rarely instructs the courts as to the principles of statutory interpretation which they should deploy. An exception is provided by ss 2–3 of the European Communities Act 1972;[21] but as we have seen, the issue of EC membership occupies an apparently distinct position within the UK's constitutional law.

Section 3 contains the following instruction to courts and tribunals:

> (1) So far as it is possible to do so, primary legislation and subordinate legislation must be read and given effect to in a way which is compatible with Convention rights.
> (2) This section—
>   (a) applies to primary legislation and subordinate legislation whenever enacted;
>   (b) does not affect the validity, continuing operation or enforcement of any incompatible primary legislation.[22]

The constitutional significance of s 3 depends largely on the meaning which courts attach to the notion of 'possible'. This is a term which might plausibly be thought to bear several meanings. Narrowly construed, s 3 requires courts to reject literalist approaches to statutory interpretation if such approaches would produce results incompatible with Convention Rights, and to adopt instead other indigenous, established techniques (viz the golden rule or the mischief rule) if those techniques would produce a Convention Right compatible outcome. More broadly construed, s 3 might require courts to embrace a teleological or purposive approach to interpretation in the sense advocated by Lord Denning in *Magor and St Mellens RDC*[23] if established techniques would not render a statutory term consistent with the requirements of Convention Rights; (the purpose being of course to respect Convention Rights). If lent a very broad meaning, s 3 might authorise domestic courts to adopt interpretive techniques which encompasses such innovations as ignoring particular words or phrases in a statutory text, or reading in words and phrases that do not appear in the text itself.[24] Such an initiative would obviously be very hard to reconcile with traditional understandings of the courts' interpretive role.

Varying views were expressed in political, judicial, and academic fora as to how s 3 itself should be interpreted. The white paper suggested that the instruction to be given to the courts

---

[20] See 'IV. Principles of statutory interpretation', ch 3, p 55.

[21] See 'The European Communities Act 1972—the terms', ch 11, pp 299–301.

[22] Section 21(1) extends the notion of 'primary legislation' to Orders in Council made under the prerogative.

[23] See 'Purposive (or "teleological") interpretation', ch 3, pp 60–61.

[24] The phrase 'as far as possible' has been lent such a meaning in EC law; see *Marleasing SA v La Comercial Internacional di Alimentation SA*, Case C-106/89: [1990] ECR I-4135 at para 8; discussed in the seventh edition of this book at pp 391–397.

by s 3 would go 'far beyond the present rule which enables the courts to take the Convention into account in resolving any ambiguity in legislative provisions'.[25] At the Bill's committee stage in the Commons, the Home Secretary appeared to favour giving s 3 a narrow meaning: '[I]t is not our intention that the courts, in applying [s 3] should contort the meaning of words to produce implausible or incredible results'.[26] He then went on to offer a magnificently tautological construction of the term 'possible' in s 3: 'It means, 'What is the possible interpretation?' Let us [ie the courts] look at this set of words and the possible interpretations'.[27] Lord Irvine, in a public lecture, indicated that he anticipated that s 3 would empower the courts to adopt a *Marleasing*-type approach to the construction of legislation: it would be acceptable for the courts to 'strain the meaning of words or read in words which are not there'.[28]

Quite what the government and Parliament intended s 3 to do—and quite what the courts would make of it—prompted considerable debate among academic commentators. Geoffrey Marshall suggested that s 3 was 'a deeply mysterious provision'.[29] Bennion's view that; 'There was much vagueness and confusion in the minds of the Act's promoters about the intended meaning of the rule'[30] seems eminently defensible.[31] Some hint as to the judiciary's view of the effect of s 3 was offered by Lord Cooke (a former President of the New Zealand Court of Appeal, and then sitting as a law lord), during the Bill's Committee Stage in the Lords. Lord Cooke suggested that s 3 'enjoins a search for possible meanings as distinct from the true meaning which has been the traditional approach'; it would require courts and tribunals to adopt not 'a strained interpretation, but one that is fairly possible'.[32]

Notwithstanding such divergences of opinion, it would seem safe to conclude that the real question raised by s 3 would not be *whether* it required the courts to make a radical break with orthodox interpretive principles—but rather *to what extent* it required them to do so. One can readily identify individual judgments decided before 1998 in which British courts pursued unorthodox interpretive strategies in order to safeguard human rights values.[33] But s 3 could sensibly be construed as requiring all domestic courts in all cases to match the most imaginative and expansive use of the Convention occasionally made by some courts prior to 1998.[34]

Section 3 of the HRA 1998 was modelled on the approach taken by the New Zealand Parliament when it enacted a Bill of Rights.[35] The thinking behind both countries' adoption of this technique is rooted in a concern to preclude the courts from straying into the legislative arena; by explicitly identifying the judiciary's competence as one of 'interpretation', it might be thought possible to present the Act as an initiative which does not impinge upon traditional understandings of the separation of powers and therefore does not compromise the sovereignty of Parliament.

---

[25] At para 2.7.   [26] *HCD* 3 June 1998 c 421.   [27] Ibid, at c 423.

[28] Cited in Klug F (1999) 'The Human Rights Act 1998, *Pepper v Hart* and all that' *Public Law* 246 at p 254.

[29] Marshall G (1998) 'Interpreting interpretation in the Human Rights Bill' *Public Law* 167 at 167.

[30] Bennion F (2000) 'What interpretation is "possible" under s 3(1) of the Human Rights Act?' *Public Law* 77 at 88.

[31] See also Pannick D (1998) 'Principles of interpretation of Convention Rights.' *Public Law* 545; Klug F (1998) op cit; Lester A (1998) 'The Act of the possible.' *European Human Rights LR* 665.

[32] Lord Cooke's views might be thought particularly persuasive here, given his status as a senior law lord and his previous role as President of the Court of Appeal of New Zealand, where he heard many cases involving the New Zealand Bill of Rights, a measure which strongly influenced the design of the HRA 1998 itself.

[33] The Court of Appeal's judgment in *Ex p Leech* [1994] QB 198 being a clear example of this: see '*R v Secretary of State for the Home Department, ex p Leech (No 2)*', ch 19, p 505. See also the Court of Appeal's judgment in *Rantzen v Mirror Group Newspapers (1986) Ltd* [1994] QB 670; discussed in Loveland (2000) op cit pp 129–132.

[34] It might also be thought that the term 'possible' encompasses domestic presumptions as to matters of precedent and judicial hierarchy; ie it would not be 'possible' for a court to lend a statutory provision a meaning inconsistent with a meaning already arrived at by a higher court, even if the lower court considered that the original meaning was not compatible with a Convention Right. By analogy we might also assume that the Act does not empower or require a lower court to depart from the view of a higher court as to the content of a Convention Right.

[35] Lord Cooke (1997) 'Mechanisms for entrenchment and protection of a Bill of Rights: the New Zealand experience' *European Human Rights LR* 490.

This is perhaps a naive assumption, and one which rests on a rather limited understanding of the relationship between Parliament and the courts. If we are to accept that orthodox perceptions of parliamentary sovereignty hinge upon the presumption that courts adopt a literalist approach to statutory interpretation, s 3 does impact upon—at least de facto—Parliament's sovereignty. It was after all judgments, both of domestic courts and the ECJ and ECtHR, couched in the language of interpretation which so enraged many backbench Conservative MPs during the judicial supremacism controversy.[36] Labour Ministers in the Blair governments might be thought less likely than their Conservative predecessors to indulge media and backbench hysteria concerning alleged 'judicial usurpations of legislative functions' in respect of innovative 'interpretations' of legislative provisions that might emerge from the courts, but whether they would wholly resist the temptation to engage in cheap political populism at the judiciary's expense remained to be seen.[37]

Section 4–the 'declaration of incompatibility'

While the Act does not empower any court to question the *legality* of primary legislation, it does offer the superior courts[38] the opportunity to challenge a statute's *legitimacy*. Section 4 introduces a device called the 'Declaration of Incompatibility'. Section 4 is directed at those statutory provisions which a court cannot interpret in a fashion that is compatible with a Convention Right, even if those provisions are subjected to the unorthodox canons of constructions evidently introduced by s 3.[39]

The declaration of incompatibility empowers—but does not oblige—a court to identify the way in which a statutory provision breaches a Convention Right. Section 4(6) provides that the declaration does not invalidate the provision concerned: the court is obliged to apply the incompatible parts of the statute. Nor does the Act contain any requirement the government or Parliament take remedial action to repeal or modify the statute. Section 4 is not therefore an entrenching device in the traditional sense.

The purpose of the Declaration of Incompatibility mechanism seems twofold. Firstly, assuming the government's pro-Convention *bona fides*, a Declaration will alert the government to unintended breaches of a Convention Right which it might then seek to remedy. Or secondly, should the government wish to condone a breach of the Convention Right, the Declaration will expose Ministers to the pressure of public and/or opposition opinion to take remedial action.

In either case, the Declaration mechanism relieves the courts of the responsibility of having to deploy controversial interpretative strategies which might lead to them being accused of 'usurping the legislative function'. Section 4 empowers judges openly to express their loyalty to the notion that the HRA identifies moral principles which Parliament cannot legitimately override while simultaneously avoiding any covert undermining of Parliament's intentions through use of s 3 in an inappropriately expansive way.

The mechanism has strong echoes of the tactic adopted by the Canadian Supreme Court in the early 1980s when it found itself faced with a national government attempt to amend the constitution in a way which was constitutional in the narrow legal sense, but which breached established constitutional conventions. The Supreme Court's judgment in *A-G of Manitoba v A-G of Canada*[40] confirmed that there were no legal obstacles in the government's path, but did so in language so condemnatory of the political mores of the government's plans that it became impossible for the government to proceed.[41]

---

[36] See 'II. The 'judicial supremacism' controversy', ch 19, pp 507–514.

[37] On which point see further 'Judicial supremacism revisited?', ch 21, pp 583–586.

[38] In England and Wales these are the High Court, the Court of Appeal, and the House of Lords: s 4(5).

[39] Again, we might note that the notion of 'primary legislation' includes Orders in Council made under the prerogative.   [40] [1981] 1 SCR 753.

[41] See 'The judgment of the Canadian Supreme Court', ch 9, p 246.

The Canadian episode was an isolated instance of a court undermining the moral foundation of governmental and parliamentary intentions, and one fashioned by the Supreme Court rather than the national legislature. That the UK Parliament created a similar device, without knowing with any certainty how often a declaration of incompatibility might be made, may be thought a rather radical innovation. Section 4 does not bind the legislature in a legal sense, but it could be read as inferring that the judiciary need no longer adhere to the traditional administrative law notion that courts should adopt a deferential attitude towards Parliament's clearly expressed intentions. A judge may not be empowered by the Act to overturn legislation, but she has it seems been invited, even perhaps instructed, by Parliament to make clear her reasons for assuming it lacks a defensible moral base.

The inter-relationship between s 3 and s 4

The frequency with which the Declaration device would be used would turn in large part on the way in which the courts construed s 3. The more expansively the courts construed their interpretive jurisdiction, the less likely it would be that a particular statutory provision could not be reconciled with the pertinent Convention Right. One might sensibly suggest that if the courts were to construe s 3 as requiring the insertion of qualificatory clauses into legislation, then the Declaration of Incompatibility would become a relevant factor only in respect of statutory provisions which were stated in express terms as being intended to breach Convention Rights.[42] The interplay between s 3 and s 4 of the Act thus promised to pose the courts a complicated question to answer. The Blair government—implicitly endorsing an expansive interpretation of s 3—evidently expected that Declarations would rarely be necessary. As the Home Secretary put it during the Bill's committee stage; 'We want the courts to strive to find an interpretation . . . that is consistent . . . and only in the last resort to conclude that legislation is simply inconsistent'.[43]

Sections 3 and 4 create consequential or secondary jurisdictions

It is important to note that the scheme of the Act only brings ss 3 and 4 into play if a court has already reached the anterior conclusion that the particular statutory provision under consideration is—literally construed—incompatible with a Convention Right. This in turn requires the court to have already determined the content of the particular Convention Right in issue. If domestic courts were to hold that the meaning of a Convention Right could diverge significantly from the meaning of the analogous Convention article as interpreted by the ECtHR in the sense of providing less human rights protection, there might be little need for ss 3 and/or 4 to be invoked at all.

Convention Rights and the common law

While s 3 obviously contained some uncertainties as to its precise meaning and effect, it does clearly require that the moral underpinnings of all statutory provisions fall to be re-evaluated by the courts in the light of their compatibility with the moral values which the courts consider

---

[42] And so would be completely irrelevant to any provision enacted before the HRA came into force. The government indicated during the Bill's passage that its view of s 3 was shaped by a principle of EU law offed by the ECJ in *Marleasing* (Case C-106/89: [1990] ECR I-1435) which used the formula 'as far as possible' (at para 8) to encompass the reading into domestic legislation of words which were not there in order to achieve consistency with EU law. The House of Lords had accepted the validity of this approach in *Pickstone v Freemans* [1989] AC 66. See pp 391–394 of the seventh edition of this book.   [43] *HCD* 3 June 1998 cc 421–422.

inherent in Convention Rights. It might seem odd that the Act does not in express terms impose the same obligation on the courts in respect of the common law; that is, that the Act does not contain a provision (modelled on s 3) to the effect that: 'So far as it is possible to do so, the common law must be developed and given effect in a way which is compatible with the Convention rights'.

The omission is odd in two senses. The first oddity derives from a question of policy. While we might accept that most of our contemporary law has a statutory rather than common law base, there are still many common law rules and principles, many of which might be thought to have an impact on Convention Rights. Why should that body of law not be subject to re-evaluation? The second oddity is a normative one. Given that statutory provisions are a hierarchically superior form of law to the common law, why would Parliament require re-evaluation of the superior form of law but not of the inferior one?

Those questions might be answered at an abstract theoretical level by suggesting that the common law's amenability to re-evaluation from a Convention Rights perspective is a necessary implication arising from the subjection of statutory provisions to that new regime. To conclude otherwise would have the perverse effect of affording (in a generic sense) common law rules a superior status to statutory provisions. Had Parliament wished to achieve that odd result, it would have said so expressly. At a more prosaic level, an answer can perhaps be drawn from the interactive effect of ss 2, 3, and 6.

Section 6—the reach of the act: vertical (and horizontal?) effect

Section 6 is a rather opaque provision. Section 6(1) expressly provides that it is unlawful for a 'public authority' to act incompatibly with a Convention Right. In essence, this provision makes incompatibility with a Convention Right a new statutory ground of judicial review, best categorised perhaps as a new sub-category of illegality.

Many of the Convention's provisions require that government action be measured against a rigorous standard: the requirements that interferences with Art 8 or Art 10 rights be 'necessary in a democratic society' are obvious examples.[44] This level of judicial scrutiny of the lawfulness of government action would in many circumstances seem to be akin to what English administrative lawyers would regard as proportionality review. As noted in chapter thirteen,[45] English courts have traditionally rejected suggestions that the common law should recognise proportionality as a new ground of review. Section 6 might be thought to render such judicial innovation unnecessary when Convention Rights are in issue. If the domestic courts accepted that Convention Rights contained an identical (or similar) proportionality requirement to that recognised by the ECtHR in respect of Convention articles, then administrative law would become a more intensive mechanism through which the courts could police the lawfulness of 'government' action.[46]

What is a public authority within s 6?

A major difficulty thrown up by s 6(1) is identifying which decision-makers are caught by this expanded notion of review; that is, what is the meaning of 'public authority'. The issue of how to draw a line between 'public' and 'private' organisations/individuals has been a vexed

---

[44] See 'Contingent rather than absolute entitlements', ch 18, pp 480–481.

[45] See 'III. Proportionality—a new ground of review?', ch 13, pp 377–380.

[46] For a contemporary assessment of what this might entail see the essays in Ellis E (ed) (1999) *The principle of proportionality in the laws of Europe*; and in particular the contrasting views expressed by Lord Hoffmann—'The influence of the European principle of proportionality upon UK law' and David Feldman—'Proportionality and the Human Rights Act 1998'.

question both in domestic administrative law over the past forty years.[47] The white paper had offered a reasonably lengthy list of 'public authorities'. This included:

> . . . central government (including executive agencies); local government; the police; immigration officers; prisons; courts; and, to the extent that they are exercising public functions, companies responsible for areas of activity which were previously within the public sector, such as privatised utilities.[48]

The Act, in contrast, makes no attempt to identify all the various bodies which Parliament envisages should be 'public authorities'. The definition offered in s 6 of the Act includes 'courts and tribunals' and—in a disquieting display of imprecision in s 6(3)(b)—'any person certain of whose functions are of a public nature'.[49] Section 6(3)(b) offers a limited, negative definition of the public authority concept. The sub-section states that neither house of Parliament is a public authority for these purposes, nor is a person 'exercising functions in connection with proceedings in parliament'.

Much interpretative work would thus have to be done by the courts to decide whether a particular person or body was a 'public authority', or whether she or it was performing functions having 'a public nature'. This prospect evidently alarmed several Conservative MPs who criticised the vagueness of the 'public authority' formula during the Bill's passage. It remained to be seen whether the courts' definition of public authorities would borrow wholesale from common law doctrine on this question, or follow the ECJ's reasoning, or blend common law and EC law, or create a whole new line of 'Convention Right' specific 'public authorities'. It would be most unfortunate if we were to end up with three quite distinct streams of law on this question for domestic, EC, and Convention Right purposes.

Lawful breaches of Convention Rights by public authorities

The Act does not designate a specific procedure through which Convention Rights issues may be raised. Section 7 states that such issues can be addressed; 'in any legal proceedings'. Section 8 then provides that if a public authority has acted unlawfully per s 6(1), the court may; 'grant such relief or remedy, or make such order, within its powers as it considers just and appropriate'.[50]

However, s 6(2) provides that a public authority which breaches a Convention Right does not act unlawfully if it is required to adopt the course it has taken by 'primary legislation'. The bite of s 6(2)—which effectively provides public authorities with a justification for breaching Convention Rights—would be contingent both on the way in which the courts construed s 3 of the Act and the anterior question of deciding what the content of the invoked Convention Right actually is.[51]

Should a court conclude that the statutory provision under which the public authority was proceeding could be construed in a manner compatible with Convention Rights, s 6(2) would not come into play. In these circumstances, a court exercising a judicial review jurisdiction (which does not permit it to substitute its own judgment for that of the initial decision-maker)[52] would invalidate the initial decision and remit it to be determined afresh in

---

[47] 'II. The Post-*O'Reilly* case law', ch 15, pp 422–428.   [48] At para 2.2.

[49] Section 6(5) then tells us that: 'In relation to a particular act, a person is not a public authority by virtue of subsection (3)(b) above if the nature of the act is private'.

[50] Subsequent provisions of s 8 indicate that courts should be slow to award damages against public authorities for breaches of Convention Rights; and if they do so, awards should be set at a low level.

[51] Assume a public authority wishes to do X. It acts unlawfully per HRA s 6(1) only if the court holds that: (i) X is incompatible with a Convention Right; and (ii) the public authority is not required by 'primary legislation' to do X. A court could conclude that the public authority is not acting unlawfully per HRA s 6(1) either by holding (i) X is not incompatible with a Convention Right or (ii) X is incompatible but is nonetheless the result required by 'primary legislation'.

[52] See 'III. Judicial regulation of government behaviour: the constitutional rationale', ch 3, pp 53–55.

accordance with a Convention Right compliant construction of the relevant statutory provision.[53] If the Convention Right issue was raised in private law litigation, such as an action in tort or contract, the court's jurisdiction would of course be as the primary decision-maker. If, in contrast—in either a judicial review or private law action context—the court concluded that the public authority's breach of a Convention Right was unavoidable, s 6(2) precludes a finding of unlawfulness. A court empowered to issue a Declaration of Incompatibility would then consider whether its s 4 power should be invoked.[54]

Section 6(2) is obviously another manifestation of the principle that the Human Rights Act does not (at least directly and overtly) limit the sovereignty of Parliament. The provision's impact was characterised earlier as providing public authorities with a justification for breaching Convention Rights. An alternative characterisation would be to regard s 6(2) as affirming Parliament's capacity to order executive bodies to act in defiance of accepted human rights norms. That conclusion might be regarded as undesirable in moral or political terms. Its legal impact is nonetheless quite clear. On another important question, however, s 6 seemed woefully lacking in clarity.

Convention Rights and the common law ... again ...

The identification of courts as 'public authorities' in s 6(3) provides a further basis for assuming that the Act requires the judiciary to re-evaluate rules of common law to ensure that those rules are compatible with Convention Rights. A court which resolved litigation on the basis of a rule of common law which was incompatible with a Convention Right would presumably itself be acting unlawfully in a s 6(1) sense, but could not be said to be required to do so by primary legislation. Since—subject to principles of precedent and judicial hierarchy—the courts may alter the common law as they think fit, it would seem that a court should take that course to avoid an incompatibility. The assertion is really no more than a restatement of the analysis offered by Lord Keith in *R v R (marital rape exemption)*.[55] In this instance it would be the HRA itself which provided the 'changing social, economic developments' which would prompt a modification of the common law.[56]

Do Convention Rights have 'horizontal effect'?

It is an important characteristic of the 'fundamental' nature of many provisions of EU law that the rights and obligations they create are both 'vertically' and 'horizontally' directly effective; that is, enforceable against both government bodies (vertically) and private companies or individuals (horizontally).[57] Similarly, many common law rules are as enforceable against

---

[53] If the courts accept that the Human Rights Act requires application of proportionality review to some or all interferences with Convention Rights, a judicial review jurisdiction will more closely approach a substitution of judgment power; see the discussion at 'III. Proportionality—a new ground of review?', ch 13, pp 377–380.

[54] Section 6(2) clearly has no bearing on government action taken through a direct exercise of prerogative powers, although per s 21 it would impact upon prerogative powers exercised through Orders in Council.

[55] See '*R v R (rape: marital exemption)* (1981)', ch 3, pp 71–72.

[56] To similar effect see *Kleinwort Benson v Lincoln CC* [1999] 2 AC 349 per Lord Browne-Wilkinson at p 358: 'The whole of the common law is judge-made and only by judicial change in the law is the common law kept relevant in a changing world'; and per Lord Goff at p 377: 'It is universally recognised that judicial development of the common law is inevitable. If it had never taken place, the common law would be the same now as it was in the reign of King Henry II; it is because of it that the common law is a living system of law, reacting to new events and new ideas, and so capable of providing the citizens of this country with a system of practical justice relevant to the times in which they live'.

[57] See 'The horizontal direct effect of treaty articles—*Walrave and Koch* (1974)', in the seventh edition of this book, ch 11, pp 372–373 (available in the online resources).

companies or individuals as against government bodies.[58] Whether the Human Rights Act bestows this universalistic character on the Convention Rights was not however made clear by the Act's text. Might an individual, for example, invoke Art 8's right to privacy against a newspaper which publishes stories about her sex life?[59] Could a court apply Art 9 to prevent a plc from refusing to hire Buddhist or Muslim employees? Could a newspaper, qua defendant in a libel action brought by a politician, invoke Art 10 and rely on *Lingens* and *Castells*?[60]

There is no explicit, textual provision in the Act to the effect that individual or private sector organisations are legally required to respect Convention Rights. Had Parliament wished the Act to have horizontal effect, such a term could certainly have been placed in the legislation.[61] The absence of any such provision can be taken as strong evidence that Parliament intended that Convention Rights operate only in the vertical plane.

That inference can be reinforced in a contextual sense by considering the reach of the Convention itself as an international law instrument. In proceedings before the ECtHR, the 'defendant' is invariably one of the Convention's Signatory States. As already noted, the Convention contains provisions which enable (but do not require) a state to empower its citizens to initiate actions against it before the ECtHR. The ECHR does not make any provision however for individual citizens to litigate against other individuals or private sector organisations before the Strasbourg court. Actions before the ECtHR instigated by individuals are always 'vertical' in nature; at least in formal terms.[62]

The courts qua public authority as the route to horizontal effect?

Section 6 can however be read as implicitly lending Convention Rights horizontal effect. The starting point for this argument is the fact that Convention Rights are creatures of domestic law, not—as are Convention articles—of international law. A litigant in a 'horizontal' action would not be relying on the ECHR but on the HRA. Secondly, we might note that s 6(3) designates courts as 'public authorities'. Per s 6(1), therefore, it is 'unlawful' for a court to act incompatibly with a Convention Right; (unless of course it is required so to act by legislation which cannot be interpreted in a Convention Right compliant manner). So far, so simple. But the jurisprudential map drawn by s 6 becomes much more difficult to read from this point on.

A problem arises because one might take rather different points of view as to who—or what—is really 'the defendant' in HRA litigation. This in turn has profound consequences for the effective horizontality of the Act's effect. The uncertainties can be illustrated by considering several mundane hypothetical scenarios.

Scenario 1: A judicial review action brought by citizen A against the Home Secretary's use of a prerogative power. Since no statutory power is in issue, neither s 3 nor s 6(2) are relevant. In this scenario, the action is vertical. The Home Secretary is obviously a 'public authority'. If the High Court concludes that the Home Secretary's action does not breach a Convention Right, we might assume that in any subsequent appeal the Home Secretary would still be the defendant. However, it could also be suggested that the breach of the Convention Right is triggered

---

[58] Obviously a 'private sector body' is not amenable to judicial review in a direct sense. But, and this is a point sometimes overlooked in the modern era, much of what we now regard as administrative law principle was generated by cases involving bodies which we would not class as 'governmental' in nature. There is a fair amount of common law principle regulating the way in which clubs and societies must conduct their relationships with their members. In effect, these cases apply what we now regard as administrative law ideas as implied terms of the contractual relationship between an individual and a club or society of which she is a member. *Dawkins v Antrobus* (1881) LR 17 Ch D 615; *Lee v Showman's Guild of Great Britain* [1952] 2 QB 329; and *McInnes v Onslow-Fane* [1978] 1 WLR 1520 provide good examples.

[59] See for example Markesinis B (1986) 'The right to be let alone versus freedom of speech' *Public Law* 671; (1990) 'Our patchy law of privacy' *MLR* 802.   [60] See 'Political libels', ch 18, pp 491–493.

[61] ie s 6(1) might read; 'It is unlawful for a public authority or any natural or legal person . . .'.

[62] The reason for this caveat is outlined below.

here by the High Court's first instance judgment; that the High Court qua public authority is breaching s 6(1); and that the 'real' defendant on appeal is the High Court. The identity of the defendant is of no obvious significance in this scenario—all of the candidates are 'vertical' entities.

Scenario 2: We might reach a similar conclusion in scenario 2. Here, a judicial review action is brought by citizen A against the Home Secretary's use of a statutory power. The Home Secretary is a public authority. The High Court is also a public authority, and is additionally obliged by s 3 to interpret the relevant statutory provision in a manner consistent with the Convention Right. Again, it could be suggested that if the first instance judgment is in the Home Secretary's favour, either she or the High Court could be seen as the 'real' defendant on appeal. The defendant's identity is not significant in this scenario as all candidates are 'vertical' entities.

Scenario 3: An action brought by citizen A against company B, the solution to which turns on the conclusion reached by the court as to the meaning of a particular statutory provision. An action of this sort is nominally horizontal. Company B is not a public authority; (and we may assume that s 6(3)(b) is not relevant here). Three questions then arise. Firstly; notwithstanding the lack of a public authority defendant at first instance, is the court nonetheless obliged by s 3 to give the relevant statutory term a Convention Right compliant interpretation? Secondly; alternatively or additionally, does s 6 require the court to construe the term in a manner compatible with the relevant Convention Right; the rationale being that if the court adopted an orthodox, Convention non-compliant meaning of the provision the court itself would be acting unlawfully? Thirdly, assuming that neither of the first two questions are answered affirmatively, would the first instance court nonetheless become de facto the defendant in a subsequent appeal?

Scenario 4: An action brought by citizen A against company B, the solution to which turns on the conclusion reached by the court as to the content of the common law. Section 3 would not bite here, as no statutory term is in issue. But the second and third questions outlined in scenario 3 above would still be pertinent.

The argument made in scenarios 3 and 4 would afford the Human Rights Act at least de facto horizontal effect through the indirect mechanism of placing the courts through either s 3 or s 6 under a duty to ensure that domestic law conforms to Convention Right requirements. This is an imaginative but by no means implausible reading of the Act's text.

This textual justification for according Convention Rights de facto horizontal impact can be buttressed by contextual considerations. It is clear that the ECtHR has interpreted some elements of the Convention as founding what would seem to be a 'horizontal' remedy. This situation can arise in one of two ways.

Firstly, it arises when the action before the Strasbourg court has emerged from what was ostensibly horizontal litigation in the domestic sphere. *Goodwin v United Kingdom*[63] is a good example. The litigation began as a suit between private parties, but turned on the interpretation of the Contempt of Court Act 1981 s 10. Before the ECtHR, the 'real' defendant was s 10 itself as interpreted by the House of Lords in *X Ltd v Morgan-Grampian (Publishers)*.[64] The ECtHR's judgment illustrates the proposition that a Signatory State may breach the Convention if its laws allow individuals to invoke legal protections which unacceptably hamper other individuals' access to rights identified by the Convention.

The second situation is illustrated by cases such as *X and Y v The Netherlands*.[65] X was the father of a mentally handicapped teenager (Y) allegedly raped in the residential facility where she lived. The crux of the Court's judgment was that both the father and child's Art 8 rights to private and family life were breached because Dutch criminal law made no effective provision

---

[63] At 'Conclusion', ch 18, pp 499–502.   [64] Ibid.   [65] (1985) 8 EHRR 235.

for the prosecution of such alleged crimes. The ECtHR concluded that Art 8 imposed a positive obligation on the Netherlands to introduce such a law because; 'This is a case where fundamental values and essential aspects of private life are at stake. *Effective deterrence* is indispensible in this area . . .'.[66] Similarly, in *Marckx v Belgium*,[67] the ECtHR held that Belgium was in breach of Art 8 because Belgian law did not allow parents and their illegitimate children to enjoy any legally recognised family relationship at all. The Court's decision in *Malone v United Kingdom* can be analysed in a similar way. The United Kingdom was in breach of Art 8 because domestic law contained no provisions at all to safeguard Mr Malone's Art 8 rights against intrusion by government tapping of his phone. In all three cases, the state's first step in remedying the breach would be to introduce *some* law dealing with the relevant issues.[68]

There is an unhappy lack of clarity in the ECtHR's jurisprudence as to which articles of the Convention—and in what circumstances—can create such a 'positive obligation'. And of course it is not necessarily the case that domestic courts would accept that such a positive obligation would arise in respect of any Convention Right. But the principle per se lends weight to the argument that the Human Rights Act might impose a comparable responsibility on domestic courts in some instances of ostensibly horizontal litigation.

A division of academic opinion on the horizontal effect issue?

Prior to the Human Rights Act coming into force, academic and judicial opinion on the horizontal effect issue was sharply divided. The argument against horizontal effect was strongly put by Buxton LJ in the *Law Quarterly Review*.[69] Buxton LJ's argument rested primarily on the fact that, under the Convention itself, actions are brought only against Signatory States; that is, that they are only vertically effective. The argument is supposedly buttressed, as a matter of implication, by the very mention of 'public authorities' in s 6; the inference being that had Parliament intended the Act to be horizontally and vertically effective, it would have inserted the clause 'or any natural or legal person' into s 6.

The counter argument was raised by Professor Wade and Murray Hunt.[70] Their central contention is that since a major element of the courts' role as 'public authorities' is to settle disputes between individuals, the Act's horizontal impact arises as a matter of necessary implication. Wade further makes the point that accepting the horizontality of the Act would much reduce the problem of deciding whether or not a body is a 'public authority' for this purpose.[71] Hunt also suggests that the Fourteenth Amendment jurisprudence of the US Supreme Court on the construction of common law ruled as 'State action' may prove particularly instructive to UK judges on this issue. The Fourteenth Amendment is notionally directed only at 'State action' which infringes certain human rights principles, notably a freedom from racial discrimination. However the US Supreme Court's 1948 judgment in *Shelley v Kramer*[72] clearly gave the Fourteenth Amendment an effective horizontal impact. In *Shelley*, the Supreme Court held that a racist restrictive covenant negotiated between individuals could not be enforced by State courts in an action between private individuals as any judgment issued by a court would be 'state action' within the Fourteenth Amendment.

---

[66] Ibid, at para 27 (original emphasis).   [67] (1979) 2 EHRR 330.

[68] That law would in turn be subject to evaluation against the yardsticks (cf the 'necessary in a democratic society' test) applied by the Convention.   [69] (2000) 'The Human Rights Act and private law' *LQR* 48.

[70] Wade HRW (2000) 'Horizons of horizontality' *LQR* 217; Hunt M (1998) 'The "horizontal effect" of the *Human* Rights Act' *Public Law* 423. See also Bamforth N (1999) 'The application of the Human Rights Act to public authorities and private bodies' *Cambridge LJ* 159; Phillipson G (1999) 'The Human Rights Act, "horizontal effect" and the common law: a bang or a whimper' *MLR* 824.

[71] (2000) op cit at p 223. The obvious point against this assertion is that the Act expressly recognises in s 6(5) that persons who are 'public authorities' when discharging functions of a 'public nature' are not public authorities when discharging functions of a private nature. This seems implicitly to accept a public/private or vertical/horizontal divide within the Act.   [72] 334 US 1 (1948).

One might also note that if Buxton LJ's view is correct, an applicant whose 'Convention rights' have been infringed by a 'private body' can still make an application direct to the ECtHR to begin an action against the United Kingdom.[73] If the point of the Act is indeed to 'bring rights home', that consequence would seem rather silly.

Anthony Lester and David Pannick urged the courts to adopt a more subtle technique to give Convention Rights horizontal effect. Their proposition essentially suggested that the court should regard the Human Rights Act as a parliamentary invitation to accelerate innovation at common law to prevent individuals interfering unjustifiably with other people's Convention Rights:

> The correct way involves approaching the Convention rights through domestic law rather than round domestic law . . . The central legislative purpose [of the 1998 Act] is that of bringing the Convention rights home, that is of domesticating them so that they are not regarded as alien rights protected exclusively by a 'foreign' European Court . . . [I]t is especially important to weave the Convention rights into the principles of the common law and of equity . . . [74]

The Blair government's intention as to horizontal effect?

Which of these various views would prove the more compelling to the courts remained to be seen. It is however an unhappy indictment of Parliament's approach to this legislation that so important a matter was not clearly settled by the text of the Act itself. Reference to *Hansard* along the lines permitted by *Pepper v Hart*[75] will apparently not provide the courts with obvious assistance on this point. Lord Irvine observed at the Bill's second reading in the Lords:

> [I]t is right as a matter of principle for the courts to have the duty of acting compatibly with the Convention not only in cases involving other public authorities but also in developing the common law in deciding cases between individuals. Why should they not? In preparing this Bill, we have taken the view that it is the other course, that of excluding Convention considerations altogether from cases between individuals, which would have to be justified.[76]

While that passage points firmly towards the conclusion that the Act was intended to have horizontal effect, at a later point in his speech Lord Irvine said that; '[The Act] should apply only to public authorities, however defined, and not to individuals'.[77] Lord Irvine's evidently inconsistent views have unsurprisingly been invoked as persuasive authority by both Buxton LJ and Professor Wade to support their respective arguments. One can also find passages in Lord Irvine's speeches on the Bill in the Lords which seem strongly to approve the Lester/Pannick strategy.[78] The only conclusion we might safely draw from this is that resort to *Hansard* is by no means a panacea to cure all the interpretative ills caused by textual ambiguities in legislation.

At the point when the Bill was enacted, commentators could do little more than surmise that once the Act came into force, a significant portion of domestic 'administrative law' might have to concern itself with regulating relationships between individuals, rather than between individuals and various state bodies. In effect, the Act could introduce a public law dimension to what have previously been regarded as issues purely of private law.

A special status for churches and the press?

Few substantial amendments were made to the Bill during its passage. The Church of England expressed grave concern—voiced by the bishops in the House of Lords—that its religious

---

[73] Wade cites *Young, James and Webster v United Kingdom* (1981) 4 EHRR 38 and *A v United Kingdom* (1998) 27 EHRR 611 to support this point; (2000) op cit at p 219.

[74] (2000) 'The impact of the Human Rights Act on private law: the knight's move' *LQR* 380 at 383.

[75] See 'Opening Pandora's box?', ch 8, pp 212–213.   [76] *HLD* 24 November 1997 c 783.

[77] Ibid, at cc 1231–1232.   [78] See eg *HLD* 24 November 1997 cc 784–785.

freedom would be unacceptably curbed if it were to be subject to the Act. The government was evidently moved by these plaintive representations, although whether from a belief in their intrinsic desirability or a concern to avoid possible obstruction of the Bill in the Lords is not entirely clear. Section 13 of the Act requires that courts pay 'particular regard' to the Convention's protection of religious freedom. The inference would seem to be that should, for example, the Church of England or any other religious body wish to discriminate against its employees on grounds of race, gender, or sexual orientation, it might be able to invoke the principle of freedom of religious belief to trump these competing entitlements. The amendment is a substantive obscenity, as are the sentiments of the Church of England which lies behind it—namely that there is no obvious linkage between Christian values and respect for human rights. It is unfortunate that the concession was made, and one might hope that it proves of little substantive value to its progenitors when it comes to be interpreted by the courts.

Some media organisations were evidently also much concerned that the Act would curb media freedom, primarily by stimulating the growth of an indigenous privacy law. The concern seemed hugely overstated, as the European Court on Human Rights has shown little willingness to allow privacy considerations to trump press freedom in respect of news coverage with a political or public interest dimension.[79] Lobbying of Ministers, particularly by Lord Wakeham, the Chairman of the Press Complaints Commission, nonetheless led to the insertion of what would seem a wholly superfluous amendment. Mirroring the favoured status afforded to religious groups in s 13, s 12 requires courts to have 'particular regard' to freedom of expression principles when, inter alia, the litigation before it concerns information which it would be in the 'public interest' to be published.

Questions of procedure

While the Act undoubtedly expands the substantive scope of administrative law, its procedural implications seem more ambiguous. The Act's locus standi requirements raise a potentially awkward problem for the courts to resolve.[80] As noted earlier, s 7 permits Convention Rights issues to be raised in; 'any legal proceedings'. However, s 7 also provides that only a 'victim' of an alleged infringement of the Convention may bring an action under the Act. The concept of 'victim' is borrowed from Art 25 of the Convention itself.[81] The concept is a narrow one, which requires claimants to be personally affected by the action being impugned. The ECHR test is undoubtedly more expansive than the restrictive notion of a 'private legal right' which used to govern the grant of standing for the declaration and injunction in English law prior to the introduction of the Order 53 reforms in 1977.[82] Thus, for example, in *Dudgeon v United Kingdom*[83] and *Norris v Ireland*,[84] the gay male applicants would have been regarded as 'victims' of their countries' criminalisation of homosexual practices even though they themselves had not been subject to a prosecution. Conversely, in *Leigh, Guardian Newspapers Ltd and Observer Ltd v United Kingdom*,[85] the Commission did not accept that all journalists were 'victims' of a House of Lords' decision upholding a lower court's refusal to disclose documents to journalists even though the documents concerned had been read out in court.

There is an obvious tension in the ECtHR's case law on this point. On the one hand, as the Court made clear in *Klass v Germany*, that it would not allow procedural questions to frustrate

---

[79] See Tierney S (1998) 'Press freedom and public interest' *European Human Rights LR* 419.

[80] See Marriot J and Nicol D (1999) 'The Human Rights Act, representative standing and the victim culture' *European Human Rights LR* 730.

[81] For a helpful summary of the European Court's case law on Art 25 see Harris, O'Boyle, and Warbrick op cit pp 630–638.   [82] See 'Declaration and injunction—a restrictive test?', ch 16, pp 437–439.

[83] (1981) 4 EHRR 149.   [84] (1988) 13 EHRR 186.   [85] (No 10039/82) (1984) 38 DR 74.

achievement of the Convention's substantive objectives.[86] This concern points towards a liberal interpretation of Art 25. On the other hand, a more restrictive test would be helpful in ensuring that cranks and busybodies are excluded from the Court, in reducing the likelihood that litigation is used by pressure groups as in effect a surrogate political process, and in preventing the Court being overwhelmed with work.

Domestic courts will now also face this tension. But the Act's importation of Art 25 into domestic law creates a further problem for UK judges. The Act does not abolish—but rather expressly preserves in s 11—an individual citizen's right to maintain an action for an infringement of an existing common law right as an addition or alternative to an action alleging breach of a Convention Right entitlement.[87]

This raises a difficulty from a locus standi perspective, since, as noted in chapter sixteen, the UK courts have latterly made it easier for individuals and pressure groups to challenge the legality of government decisions against a common law yardstick. Recent judgments on standing have taken significant steps towards the point where a reputable claimant with a plausible legal argument can use a judicial review action and the publicity such hearings provide as an alternative or supplement to the political process. But the claimants who feature in these cases are not obviously 'victims' in the sense envisaged by the Human Rights Act. They are more accurately seen as 'representatives' of victims.[88] They arguably perform a useful public service in bringing potentially unlawful government action into a forum where that action's lawfulness can be assessed.

That they should not be permitted to do so in respect of alleged breaches of human rights seems most curious. Many individuals who are personally affected by an alleged breach of the Convention may lack the financial resources and the expertise to marshall an effective legal argument, particularly as the Act has been introduced at a time when the legal aid budget is being reduced. It also seems improbable that many lawyers will accept conditional fee arrangements to pursue Convention cases, given that the European Court has traditionally set 'damages' for breaches of the Convention at a very low level. Section 8 of the Act explicitly links any awards of damages for a breach of Convention Rights to the ECtHR's 'just satisfaction' principles. While it is conceivable that a court might under s 8 depart from these principles or that the courts will recognise breach of human rights as a head of damage at common law—it seems at present most unlikely that the quantum available will be substantial. Some lawyers may expand their provision of *pro bono* work to pick up Convention litigation, particularly in high profile cases, but this offers no guarantee of effective representation on any systemic scale.

The Act's attempts to use standing rules to close the Convention door to well-resourced, expert pressure groups might thus be thought appreciably to reduce the efficacy of its substantive provisions. During the Bill's passage, the government acknowledged in the House of Commons that it was quite likely that groups such as Amnesty and Greenpeace could achieve locus standi de facto by sponsoring and funding any action launched by a 'real' victim. If that is indeed the case, the Act's restrictive position de jure seems unnecessary. Even at its most benevolent, the English law of standing has never opened the doors of the courts to cranks, busybodies, and vexatious litigants.

We were thus faced with the unwelcome prospect that our public law procedures could contain two streams of administrative law controls on government running side-by-side. The one a common law stream which offers claimants easy access to the courts but limited

---

[86] (1978) 2 EHRR 214.

[87] **Section 11. Safeguard for existing human rights.**
A person's reliance on a Convention right does not restrict–
(a) any other right or freedom conferred on him by or under any law having effect in any part of the United Kingdom; or
(b) his right to make any claim or bring any proceedings which he could make or bring apart from sections 7 to 9.

[88] See the discussion by Cane (1995) op cit.

grounds against which to measure the acceptability of the impugned government action; the other a Convention Right stream which, while offering significantly more extensive grounds of review, will be more difficult for a claimant to enter.

The government made some attempt to address this problem in what is now s 7(3). This provides that a claimant who raises a Convention Right claim via proceedings for judicial review will only have 'sufficient interest in the matter to which the application relates'[89] if she is a 'victim' of the action impugned. This seems an unnecessarily illiberal provision. But it would also seem to be ineffective. This becomes apparent when one considers that our courts have been suggesting with increasing frequency that many Convention Right principles already have precise counterparts in the common law. The non-victim applicant could therefore seek locus standi for an application for judicial review on the basis that a common law right, not a Convention Right, has been infringed. Having been granted standing in accordance with our increasingly liberal domestic law, she might then argue that the common law right she is invoking should now be construed in a way that mirrors the protections offered by the Convention Right. By adopting this strategy, the claimant will by-pass the Human Rights Act's less accommodating locus standi rules without depriving herself de facto of the substantive protection the Act is intended to provide.

The courts would seem to have two choices in attempting to resolve this contradiction. The first would be to adopt a more expansive interpretation of 'victim' than is favoured by the ECtHR. That would seem undesirable, both because it runs counter to Parliament's evident intentions and because it would involve an outright rejection by domestic courts of the legal principles developed by the ECtHR itself. The second would be for our domestic law of standing to become more restrictive. There is no legal impediment to the courts reversing the recent trend towards more liberal standing laws, but it would seem unlikely that they would be willing to do so given that the consequences of such a reversal would be to reduce the extent to which government action is subject to judicial scrutiny. Neither option seems particularly attractive, which would suggest that in respect of this part of the Act the unhappy result the courts will have to pursue is to decide which choice amounts to the lesser evil.

This concern is reinforced when one considers the issue of time limits. The rather brief presumptive three-month limit for initiating actions via judicial review has been one of the main reasons for claimants seeking to challenge government action through private law proceedings, in which time limits are considerably more generous. Section 7(5)(a) of the Act imposes a maximum time limit of one year on the commencement of action relying on Convention Rights, while s 7(5)(b) provides that this 'is subject to any rule imposing a stricter time limit in relation to the procedure in question'. This presumably means that any Convention based challenge brought by judicial review will have to be begun at most within three months.[90]

It would seem that if a claimant wishes to raise a Convention argument in an action in tort, contract, or restitution, she must begin that action within a year, or run the risk of the Convention points being struck out.[91] Section 7(5)(b) grants the court a power to disregard the time limit if it considers that would be equitable in the circumstances, but this is a provision which—to put it kindly—is rather vague.

On the separation of powers

There appear to be firm grounds for accepting the argument that the Act gives too much power to the government at the expense of 'Parliament'. In its original form, cl 10 of the Human Rights Bill proposed to empower the government to respond to a declaration of

---

[89] The formula is taken from s 31(3) of the Supreme Court (now re-named Senior Courts) Act 1981.

[90] See Nicol D (1999) 'Limitation periods under the Human Rights Act 1998 and judicial review' *LQR* 216.

[91] The stricter limit clearly does not apply to Convention points raised as a defence in proceedings initiated by another person or institution, but does apply to counter-claims initiated in response to another action.

incompatibility by issuing an Order in Council amending or repealing the relevant statutory provision concerned. Except in 'urgent' cases, the Order would not have legal effect unless issued in draft form and subsequently approved by a resolution of both houses within sixty days. In urgent cases however, a draft Order would have immediate effect, and while it would lapse if it were not approved by a resolution of both houses within forty days, the government could have re-issued it (seemingly *ad infinitum*).

From a separation of powers/parliamentary sovereignty perspective, the objections to these proposals were obvious. In an 'urgent' case, cl 10 would empower the government to repeal legislation even if it could not command majority support for its views in both houses. Assessing 'urgency', it seemed, was a matter for the subjective discretion of the relevant Secretary of State. In non-urgent cases, cl 10 would have required the government to command majority support for its proposed remedy in each house. What it did not require was that the measure receive the same degree of scrutiny—and hence the same level of publicity—as would attach to a proposed reform effected by new primary legislation.

The clause clearly proposed a substantial extension of de facto legislative power to the government, a step manifestly incompatible with the constitutional presumption that Parliament is the only legislative body within the United Kingdom. The government's response to such criticisms of cl 10 was rather modest. As enacted, s 10(2) provides that:

> If a Minister of the Crown considers that there are compelling reasons for proceeding under this section, he may by order make such amendments to the legislation as he considers necessary to remove the incompatibility.

Professor Ewing has suggested that s 10(2) represented a substantial concession by the government: 'The result is to restore the principle that primary legislation should be amended or repealed only by primary legislation'.[92] The 'compelling reasons' caveat is seen as a residual power, and one that will in any event be subject to judicial review. This seems a curious conclusion. The initial responsibility for deciding if an issue is 'compelling' will rest with the Minister. While framed in subjective terms, her power under s 10(2) is obviously subject to the limitations imposed by administrative law. But it is arguable that these will be extremely loose constraints. If one takes human rights seriously, it might be thought any breach of a Convention Right provides 'compelling' grounds for immediate remedial action. What is being infringed is, after all, a fundamental human right. At most, judicial control of this particular power is likely to be premised on grounds of *Wednesbury* unreasonableness. It seems improbable that a court would be pre-disposed to obstruct a ministerial action which is intended to remedy a legal wrong which a superior court had itself identified a short time previously.

It could be suggested that this entire debate on the way the 1998 Act affects the balance of power between 'Parliament' and the executive is a silly indulgence in abstract theorisation, which has minimal relevance to the realities of political power. Governments with reliable Commons majorities have for most practical (ie legislative) purposes been Parliament in the post-war era. This might suggest that the only sensible way to give some worthwhile empirical effect to an idealised understanding of the separation of powers is to break the link between bare Commons majorities and legislative authority when fundamental human rights are in issue. But this is one thing the Human Rights Act makes no attempt to do.

Political entrenchment? A new 'rights' culture within government and parliament

Whether the Act produces a degree of 'moral entrenchment' for Convention Rights would be dependent as much on Ministers' and Parliament's ability to avoid taking decisions or enacting

---

[92] (1999) op cit at p 93.

statutes which breached Convention Rights as on their readiness to respond to judicial con-demnation of measures which already exist. The Act contains several provisions designed to prevent, rather than just cure, contravention of Convention principles.

Section 19 requires a Minister piloting a Bill through either house to certify prior to the second reading either that she is satisfied that the measure is compatible with the Convention, or that she believes it to be incompatible but nevertheless wishes it to proceed. The white paper argued that this obligation; 'will ensure that all ministers, their depart-ments and officials are fully seized of the gravity of the Convention's obligations in respect of human rights'.[93] The white paper also anticipated that the requirement would lead to the creation of inter-departmental working groups of lawyers and administrators within central government; 'meeting on a regular basis to ensure that a consistent approach is taken and to ensure that developments in case law are well understood'.[94]

What actually happens within Parliament in respect of s 19 may also raise contentious legal questions. MPs who fancied themselves—with or without good cause—as legal experts would surely not resist the temptation to challenge the accuracy of the Minister's certification. This would obviously make the Bill's conformity with the Convention a subject of sustained debate during second reading, at the committee and report stages, and again at third reading. The white paper did not seem to anticipate this. The Commons in particular is much pressed for time in discharging its legislative business. Section 19 might well encourage every opponent of a government Bill[95] to eat up significant amounts of time by questioning the measure's vires vis-à-vis the Convention. While this might have what many observers would consider the welcome consequence that less legislation would be passed, what might alternatively ensue is that the substantive merits of Bills (above and beyond their conformity with the Convention) would receive an even more cursory examination in the Commons than is offered at present.

Nor was it clear what the legal position would be if a Minister fails to make a s 19 certifica-tion, or is alleged to have done so in bad faith, or to have come to a wholly unsustainable con-clusion as to the Bill's compatibility with the Convention. There would presumably not be any scope for a court subsequently to hold that an Act which has not been certified in accordance with s 19 is invalid, since that would entail a rejection of parliamentary sovereignty.

Conclusion

The Blair government's rapid and determined efforts to convince Parliament to pass the Human Rights Act offers clear confirmation that members of the first New Labour administration did not share the simplistic view of 'democracy' embraced by the Conservative Party during the judicial supremacism episode. The 1998 Act may obviously be criticised on the basis that it transfers a dangerous amount of political power from the government to the judges. But the sentiments evinced by many Conservative MPs on this issue had little to commend them from a constitutional perspective. Properly construed, Convention Rights have no role at all to play within the field occupied by mainstream party politics. Rather, their whole purpose is to try to lift certain basic moral values *above* the sphere of party politics. The Convention offers an understanding of democracy which has a substantive rather than just a procedural dimension. It is concerned not just with how governmental power is won, but also with how it is subse-quently used. It rejects the simple homily that everything a democratically elected government does must be democratic just because the government was elected.

The Convention represents an attempt to fashion a wide-ranging substantive notion of democracy based on broad consensus. It rests on moral principles which are assumed to cut

---

[93] At para 3.4.   [94] At para 3.5.
[95] Section 19 seems not to reach to private members Bills or private Bills.

across not just party political boundaries, but also historical and geographical frontiers. It is unarguable that a judgment of a UK court which concludes that the action of a public authority has breached a Convention Right, or a declaration that a statute is incompatible with a Convention Right, does indeed disclose 'undemocratic' behaviour. However it is not necessarily the court's behaviour which has that characteristic; rather it may be the behaviour of the government or Parliament. What the Blair government seemed clearly to have understood—and the point that eludes critics of so-called 'judicial supremacism'—is that the Human Rights Act does not subordinate government to the courts, but to the moral principles articulated in the Convention. The courts figure in this new constitutional equation only because Parliament has taken the view that judges are better equipped than politicians to draw the *preliminary* conclusion as to whether those moral principles have been compromised.

This is however an innovation—albeit a radical one—which operates only in the sphere of administrative law. For it leaves the power to draw the *final* conclusion in the same hands—namely those of a bare majority of members of the Commons[96] who between them may have garnered the electoral support of barely one third of the voting population. The Human Rights Act thus readily lends itself to characterisation as a repository of legally contingent political values. It provides further mechanisms for preventing the exercise of political power in extremist directions, be they to the left or the right, only for so long as centrist political sentiment commands the support of a majority of members of the House of Commons. What it does not do is provide any long-term legal underpinnings for centrist values if majoritarian sentiment should at some future date lurch violently to the left or right. For this reason, it is regrettable the Blair government seemed to write off any attempt to engineer a new legal settlement premised on legally entrenched fundamental rights. It is not until a government grasps that particular nettle that talk of a constitutional revolution will be well-founded.

While the Act received the Royal Assent in 1998, most of its provisions did not come immediately into effect. Section 22(3) granted the Home Secretary the power to decide at what date(s) the other parts of the legislation would be effective. The government had made it clear that full implementation of the Act could not occur until the many tribunal members, magistrates, and judges who would be required to apply its terms had received extensive training with respect both to the Act itself and the relevant provisions of the Convention. This process evidently took longer than the government had initially expected, with the result that the target date for bringing the Act fully into force was set for October 2000. Further delay was apparently caused by the government's dawning realisation that the impact of the Act would touch upon many more areas of domestic law than had hitherto been anticipated.[97] In the interim period, however, the status of fundamental rights at common law had not been standing still.

Rather than construe the Act as a legislative 'takeover' of the common law's emergent fundamental human rights jurisprudence, some judges seem to have seen it as a spur to continuing innovation. In *R v Secretary of State for the Home Department, ex p Simms*,[98] the House of Lords substantially extended the principle set out by the Court of Appeal in *Leech*.[99] In *Simms*, the Court broadened still further the concept of 'access to the courts' to include a prisoner's entitlement to conduct face-to-face interviews with journalists who the prisoner was trying to persuade to investigate his claims that he was the victim of a miscarriage of justice. Lord Steyn's leading judgment appeared to proceed on the basis that the common law had by this point absorbed both the substantive values and the methodological requirements of Art 10 ECHR. In a concurring opinion Lord Hoffmann underlined the constitutional principle that it was entirely proper for the courts to approach the construction of legislation issues in a

---

[96] I assume that the Commons majority could if necessary invoke the Parliament Act 1949 to override a Lords veto.
[97] *The Times* 5 May 1999.   [98] [2000] 2 AC 115, [1999] 3 All ER 400, HL.
[99] See '*R v Secretary of State for the Home Department, ex p Leech (No 2)*', ch 19, pp 505–506.

way that required Parliament to use absolutely explicit language if it wished to impinge upon human rights entitlements:

> Parliamentary sovereignty means that Parliament can, if it chooses, legislate contrary to funda-mental principles of human rights. The Human Rights Act 1998 will not detract from this power. The constraints upon its exercise by Parliament are ultimately political, not legal. But the principle of legality means that Parliament must squarely confront what it is doing and accept the political cost. Fundamental rights cannot be overridden by general or ambiguous words. *This is because there is too great a risk that the full implications of their unqualified meaning may have passed unno-ticed in the democratic process.*[100]

In a similar, if more significant, extension of the common law's protection of freedom of expression, the House of Lords accepted in *Reynolds v Times Newspapers Ltd*[101] that a vari-ant of the qualified privilege defence would frequently be available to defendants who had published libellous stories about elected politicians.[102] This innovation in the content of the common law may have occurred without the prospect of the Human Rights Act coming into force, but it is apparent that the Court considered that the Act legitimised such a development and—filling a gap left by the text of the Act—suggested that the legislation would *as a matter of general principle* require courts to alter the common law in order to ensure its compatibility with Convention Rights.[103]

In *Fitzpatrick v Sterling Housing Association Ltd*,[104] the House of Lords offered an illustra-tion of the way in which developments of common law principles—here the approach taken to statutory interpretation—could render the vertical/horizontal debate in respect of the Human Rights Act quite redundant. The judgment rested on an innovative use of the 'always speak-ing' principle[105] to read legislation initially passed in the 1920s to hold that non-heterosexual couples could be regarded as members of the same (ie each other's) family for the purposes of inheriting a tenancy in a flat owned by a private individual.

Such developments indicated that the courts would approach the implementation of the Human Rights Act with considerable enthusiasm for the project of 'giving better effect' in the domestic legal system to Convention jurisprudence. In the following chapter, we assess whether that prediction was well-founded.

---

[100] [2000] 2 AC 115 at 131; emphasis added. This reference to the 'democratic' basis for a rigorous standard of judicial review is more fully developed by Lord Steyn in a subsequently published lecture; (2002) 'Democracy through law' *European Human Rights LR* 723. The lecture is a powerful corrective to the viewpoint that judicial law-making is an 'undemocratic' phenomenon.   [101] [2001] 2 AC 127.

[102] See Loveland I (2000) '*Reynolds v Times Newspapers* in the House of Lords' *Public Law* 351: Williams K (2000) 'Defaming politicians: the not so common law' *MLR* 748.

[103] See especially Lord Nicholls [2001] 2 AC 127 at 200 (emphasis added):

> My starting point is freedom of expression. The high importance of freedom to impart and receive informa-tion and ideas has been stated so often and so eloquently that this point calls for no elaboration in this case. At a pragmatic level, freedom to disseminate and receive information on political matters is essential to the proper functioning of the system of parliamentary democracy cherished in this country. This freedom ena-bles those who elect representatives to Parliament to make an informed choice, regarding individuals as well as policies, and those elected to make informed decisions. Freedom of expression will shortly be buttressed by statutory requirements. Under section 12 of the Human Rights Act 1998, expected to come into force in October 2000, the court is required, in relevant cases, to have particular regard to the importance of the right to freedom of expression. *The common law is to be developed and applied in a manner consistent with article 10 of the European Convention . . .* , and the court must take into account relevant decisions of the European Court of Human Rights (sections 6 and 2). To be justified, any curtailment of freedom of expression must be convincingly established by a compelling countervailing consideration, and the means employed must be proportionate to the end sought to be achieved.

[104] [2001] 1 AC 27.

[105] See 'Complicating the literal rule: (most) statutory provisions are "always speaking"', ch 3, pp 57–58.

Suggested further reading

Academic commentary

STEYN, LORD (2002) 'Democracy through law' *European Human Rights LR* 723

BAMFORTH N (1998) 'Parliamentary sovereignty and the Human Rights Act 1998' *Public Law* 572

BOATENG P and STRAW J (1996) *Bringing Rights Home*

BOATENG P and STRAW J (1997) 'Bringing rights home: Labour plans to incorporate the ECHR into UK Law' *European Human Rights LR* 71

EWING K (1999) 'The Human Rights Act and parliamentary democracy' *MLR* 79

HUNT M (1998) 'The "horizontal effect" of the Human Rights Act' *Public Law* 423

LESTER A and PANNICK D (2000) 'The impact of the Human Rights Act on private law: the knight's move' *LQR* 380

WADE HRW (2000) 'Horizons of horizontality' *LQR* 217

FELDMAN D (1999) 'Proportionality and the Human Rights Act 1998', in ELLIS E (ed) *The principle of proportionality in the laws of Europe* (Oxford: Hart Publishing)

Case law and legislation

R v DPP, ex p Kebilene [2000] 2 AC 326

R v Secretary of State for the Home Department, ex p Simms [2000] 2 AC 115, HL

Lord Chancellors's Department (1997) *Rights Brought Home: the Human Rights Bill*

Chapter 21

Human Rights V: The Impact of the Human Rights Act 1998

The Act has now been in force for eighteen years.[1] This chapter analyses its constitutional implications in several areas: firstly, the interlinked issues of the extent to which the courts differentiate between Convention articles and Convention Rights, the approach taken to statutory interpretation mandated by s 3, and the use of s 4 Declarations of Incompatibility; secondly, the doctrine of judicial 'deference' to legislative policy decisions; thirdly, the Act's 'horizontality' and its impact on the common law; and fourthly, the status of proportionality as a ground of review. The conclusion considers whether the Act has triggered a shift in understandings as to the scope of the doctrines of the sovereignty of Parliament and the rule of law within the modern constitutional order.

I. Convention Rights and Convention articles under s 2, statutory interpretation under s 3, and the use of declarations of incompatibility under s 4

The interactive effect of ss 2–4 is perhaps the most important issue raised by the Act. To what extent have the courts accepted (through s 2) that the substantive meaning of Convention Rights is the same as that of the textually identical Convention article and (through s 3) that they should now abandon traditional attachments to literalist approaches to statutory interpretation and adopt instead a teleological technique in which the telos (purpose) is to uphold

---

[1] On the Act's immediate impact see Selgado E and O'Brien C (2001) 'Table of cases under the Human Rights Act' *European Human Rights LR* 376; Arkinstall J and O'Brien C (2002) 'Table of cases under the Human Rights Act' *European Human Rights LR* 364; and Klug F and Starmer K (2001) 'Incorporation through the "front door": the first year of the Human Rights Act' *Public Law* 654.

Convention Rights in a manner consistent with ECHR jurisprudence? An acceptance that Convention Rights and Convention articles are substantively as well as textually identical coupled with a radical divergence from orthodox techniques of statutory interpretation in defence of those Convention Rights would have significant implications for the meaning of the separation of powers. Any such judicial innovation would transfer effective governmental power away from executive bodies and towards the (European and domestic) judiciary.

Furthermore, insofar as our perceptions as to the correct nature of the relationship between Parliament and the courts rests on the presumption that judges take a literalist approach to statutory interpretation, s 3 also raises questions about the meaning of the sovereignty of Parliament. It is undoubtedly possible to identify judgments in which the courts have embraced expansive understandings of s 3. It would however be an exaggeration to suggest that such an approach had become a new dominant paradigm within domestic law.

The initial judicial reaction

One of the most radical departures from orthodox approaches to statutory interpretation is the *Marleasing/Litster* methodology mandated by the ECJ, which requires courts to add 'missing' clauses to domestic legislation to secure compatibility with EU law.[2] In *R v A (No 2)*,[3] the House of Lords indicated that HRA s 3 could have a similar effect in relation to Convention Rights.

R v A (2001): the divergent views of Lord Steyn and Lord Hope

The issue in *R v A (No 2)* was the admissibility of evidence in a rape trial relating to a complainant's previous sexual behaviour. Section 41 of the Youth Justice and Criminal Evidence Act 1999 seemed to bar any evidence being adduced during a rape trial which might support the assertion that the defendant had had a consensual sexual relationship with the alleged victim, unless the evidence related to consensual sexual relations which occurred (per s 41(3) (b)); 'at or about the same time' as the alleged rape. Section 41 was enacted to prevent defence counsel seeking to discredit alleged rape victims by subjecting them to irrelevant questioning about past sexual behaviour. The difficulty from a Convention Right perspective was that s 41 could rule out the admission of evidence relevant to the trial, and thereby breach the 'fair trial' requirements of Art 6 of Sch 1 of the HRA.

Lord Steyn's leading judgment held that such a rule was inconsistent with Art 6 ECHR and therefore—without discussion—with Art 6 of Sch 1 as well. His primary focus was on s 3. Lord Steyn suggested that domestic courts should not immediately resort to s 3 in construing other legislation. If it appeared prima facie that a literal construction of a statutory provision would breach a Convention Right, courts should first consider whether; 'ordinary methods of purposive and contextual interpretation'[4] could yield Convention compliant results. Only if 'ordinary methods' were inadequate should s 3 be invoked.

In this case, Lord Steyn doubted that 'ordinary methods' would suffice. He thus turned to s 3:

> The interpretive principle under s 3 of the 1998 Act is a strong one . . . [It] goes far beyond the rule which enabled the courts to take the Convention into account in resolving any ambiguity in a legislative provision . . . In accordance with the will of Parliament as reflected in s 3 it will sometimes be necessary to adopt an interpretation which linguistically may appear strained. The techniques to be used will not only involve the reading down of express language in a statute, but also the implication of provisions . . .[5]

---

[2] See 'Making sense of *Marshall*. The emergence of indirect effect' in the seventh edition of this book, ch 11, pp 380–382; and 'The "indirect effect" of directives—continued' in the seventh edition of this book, ch 12, pp 391–392. Both chapters are available in the online resources.   [3] [2001] UKHL 25, [2002] 1 AC 45.

[4] [2002] 1 AC 45 at para 43.   [5] Ibid, at para 44.

Adopting this approach, Lord Steyn construed the relevant statutory provision in a way compatible with the Convention Right by reading into s 41 an addendum that permitted use of such evidence where it was obviously relevant to the particular case.

Lord Hope also accepted that there was no divergence between the substantive meanings of Art 6 ECHR and Art 6 of Sch 1, although in his view s 41 was compatible with Art 6. However, Lord Hope's judgment indicated that he felt Lord Steyn's approach to s 3 overstepped appropriate constitutional boundaries:

> The rule of construction which s 3 lays down is quite unlike any previous rule of statutory interpretation. There is no need to identify an ambiguity or an absurdity. Compatibility with convention rights is the sole guiding principle. That is the paramount objective which the rule seeks to achieve. But the rule is only a rule of interpretation. It does not entitle the judges to act as legislators.[6]

It is not problematic to support the abstract assertion that our constitutional traditions allocate the task of making legislation to Parliament and of interpreting legislation to the courts. It is lending practical meaning to such abstractions that causes difficulty.

In the context of Human Rights Act adjudication, that task is further complicated by the higher courts' s 4 power to issue declarations of incompatibility in respect of statutory provisions which cannot be construed in a Convention Right compliant way. Lord Steyn's judgment in *R v A (No 2)* echoed the Home Secretary's assumption during the Act's passage that s 4 would rarely be invoked: 'A declaration of incompatibility is a measure of last resort . . . It must be avoided unless it is plainly impossible to do so.'

The frequency with which s 4 is used depends largely on how the courts construe their interpretive powers under s 3. Lord Steyn's 'last resort' approach to s 4 obviously has greater credibility when viewed alongside his readiness to 'strain' or 'add to' the text of ostensibly Convention non-compliant statutory terms. In contrast, Lord Hope's more conservative interpretive technique might be thought to lead to more frequent use of declarations of incompatibility.

Wilson v First County Trust (2001) in the Court of Appeal

That Lord Steyn and Lord Hope's respective analyses in *A* indicated a diversity of views within the judiciary as to the nature of s 3 (and thence the role of s 4) is illustrated by the Court of Appeal's almost contemporaneous treatment of an apparently Convention Right non-compliant statutory provision in *Wilson v First County Trust (No 2)*.[7] The case concerned s 127 of the Consumer Credit Act 1974—a statute which might not initially be thought to raise Convention Right issues at all. Section 127 of the Act placed an absolute bar on recovery of assets by a creditor from a debtor if certain formalities had not been complied with when the credit agreement between the parties had been concluded. In *Wilson*, the creditor succeeded in convincing the trial court and the Court of Appeal that this provision, if literally construed, would breach Art 1 of the First Protocol to the ECHR[8] (which is concerned with the protection of people's property) and also the fair trial provisions of ECHR Art 6.

The references above to the ECHR rather than to Convention Rights are deliberate, and reflect the Court of Appeal's apparent assumption that Convention Rights were merely a

---

[6] Ibid, at para 108. As noted in ch 12, Lord Hope was shortly to take a similarly conservative approach to statutory interpretation in the context of the devolution legislation; see 'Judicial evaluation of the autonomy of the Scots Parliament' ch 12, pp 339–342. [7] [2001] EWCA Civ 633, [2002] QB 74.

[8] The Convention Right textual equivalent of which is HRA 1998 Sch 1 Part II para 1.

device to give domestic effect to the identical Convention articles; that is, that there was simply no scope for substantive divergence between the two:

> The Convention rights to which the Act gives 'further effect' are not, themselves, new rights introduced by the Act; they are existing rights set out in the Convention and its Protocols, to which the United Kingdom is party: see section 1(1) of the Act. The object of the Act is to incorporate those rights into domestic law and to give an effective domestic remedy.[9]

This analysis seems to ignore s 2 of the Act and the clear statement given by Lord Irvine during the Act's passage that the government was not asking Parliament to make the ECHR directly effective. Its consequence however is that s 3 would be used to reconcile domestic legislation with the judgments of the ECtHR without the Court going through the anterior stage of asking if the Convention article and Convention Right bore the same meaning.

In addressing that issue, the Court of Appeal construed s 3 in rather opaque terms:

> The court is required to go as far as, but not beyond, what is legally possible. The court is not required, or entitled, to give words a meaning which they cannot bear . . .[10]

The Court concluded that it could not use s 3 to read words into s 127 which would limit the provision's effect to situations where recovery would work an injustice on the debtor, and thereby render s 127 compatible with the Convention. The immediate consequence of this conclusion was that the Court of Appeal issued a declaration of incompatibility with respect to s 127.[11]

A similar rationale was employed in *R (on application of H) v London North and East Mental Health Review Tribunal*.[12] Section 73 of the Mental Health Act 1983 seemed to provide—literally construed—that persons detained in a mental hospital because they had committed serious crimes could not be released unless they proved that they are no longer dangerous. The Court of Appeal regarded this as a deprivation of personal liberty and reversal of the burden of proof in a criminal matter, and so incompatible with Art 5 and Art 6 ECHR.[13] As in *Wilson*, the Court did not consider that s 3 would permit the reading in of a qualification to the 1983 Act. This breach of the Convention could be cured only by new legislation.

Quite what qualitative methodological difference can be drawn between reading in a clause to s 41 of the Youth Justice and Criminal Evidence Act 1999 which made evidence of consensual sexual relationships admissible when it was obviously relevant, and reading in a saving proviso to s 127 of the Consumer Credit Act which lifted the bar to recovery of assets in situations where non-compliance with legal formalities had not worked any substantive injustice on the debtor, is less than obvious.[14]

---

[9] Ibid, at 87–88 per Sir Andrew Morritt VC. See also at pp 92–93, where Sir Andrew suggests the test of compatibility is not against a Convention Right but against: 'the right guaranteed by art 6(1) of the convention and Art 1 of the First Protocol of the Convention'.   [10] Ibid, at para 42.

[11] The judgment was reversed in the House of Lords ([2003] UKHL 40; [2004] 1 AC 816) on the basis that the relevant agreement pre-dated the coming into force of the HRA and that Parliament had not intended the HRA to have 'retrospective' effect, and that there was in any event no incompatibility between s 127 and Art 1 of the First Protocol. We return to *Wilson* on another point later. For present purposes however, perhaps the most interesting part of the House of Lords' judgment is in the speech of Lord Nicholls: '10 As everyone knows, the purpose of the Human Rights Act 1998 was to make the human rights and fundamental freedoms set out in the European Convention on Human Rights directly enforceable in this country as part of its domestic law'. Again the judicial assumption appears to be that there can be no gap between the meanings of ECHR articles and Convention Rights.   [12] [2002] QB 1.

[13] Again, the Court assumed that it was applying the Convention per se; as indeed did the government in its submissions. See especially [2002] QB 1 at 10–11.

[14] One might suggest that the impact on the individual of the alleged breach of Convention Rights would be far more severe in *R v A (No 2)* than in *Wilson*, and that a court's readiness to 'stretch' the notion of interpretation should be greater in cases involving serious criminal charges than issues of civil law. Section 3's text does not expressly support any such distinction.

A more structured approach to the meaning of 'possible' in s 3? A distinction between 'systemic' and 'individuated' consequences

Subsequently, the Court of Appeal identified a more principled means to determine when innovative judicial construction of a statutory term stops being 'interpretation' and becomes 'legislation'. In *Poplar Housing and Regeneration Community Association Ltd v Donoghue*, Lord Woolf offered the following suggestion:

> If it is necessary in order to obtain compliance [with the Convention] to radically alter the effect of the legislation this will be an indication that more than interpretation is involved.[15]

We might instinctively agree that the notion that 'radical' change to a statute's meaning is beyond s 3 is attractive in formal or rhetorical terms. We would presumably also ask what does 'radical' mean here? A helpful indication was offered in *R (International Transport GmbH) v Secretary of State for the Home Department*.[16] The case was triggered by the government's use of provisions in the Immigration and Asylum Act 1999 which empowered the Home Secretary to impose automatic fines on transport companies on whose lorries or trains asylum seekers had hidden to enter the United Kingdom illegally. Nearly 1,000 fines had been imposed by 2001. This seemed incompatible with the fair trial provisions of Art 6 ECHR.[17] The Court of Appeal (per Simon Brown LJ) considered s 3 did not assist here:

> It appears to me quite impossible to recreate this scheme by any interpretive process as one compatible with Convention rights . . . To achieve fairness would require a radically different approach . . . As the authorities clearly dictate, the Court's task is to distinguish between legislation and interpretation and confine itself to the latter. We cannot create a wholly different scheme . . . so as to provide an acceptable alternative means of immigration control. That must be for Parliament itself.[18]

As in *Wilson*, the Court of Appeal's reasoning on the scope of s 3 led it to issue a declaration of incompatibility in respect of the relevant statutory provisions.

This tentative distinction between 'schematic' and 'isolated' legislative incompatibility with Convention Rights may provide a helpful way of demarcating boundary lines between s 3 and s 4 of the Act. Where a non-literal reading of a specific statutory provision would unravel a wide-ranging regulatory system, it may be that courts will and should be unwilling to construe their s 3 powers broadly. In those circumstances, s 4 offers the courts a mechanism to pass responsibility for securing compliance with Convention Rights to the government and to Parliament.

There is obvious scope to argue that greater judicial resort to s 4—which would be the result of adopting a less expensive understanding of the power arising under s 3—would better fit traditional understandings of the separation of powers. Lord Steyn's judgment in *A* was for example criticised as being 'outlandish' and 'far-fetched' by Professor Nicol, on the basis that Lord Steyn's method could not convincingly be categorised as 'interpretation' in any meaningful sense.[19] Professor Nicol also suggests that in several subsequent judgments, the House of Lords has taken a less expansive view of s 3.

---

[15] [2001] EWCA Civ 595, [2002] QB 48 at 73.   [16] [2002] EWCA Civ 158, [2003] QB 728.

[17] Once more the case was argued on the basis of incompatibility with the Convention per se, not the relevant Convention Right. Indeed the judge at first instance (Sullivan J) made a s 4 order that the legislation was incompatible with Art 6 of the Convention; see [2003] QB 728 at para 2. There is no statutory basis for such a remedy.

[18] [2002] EWCA Civ 158, [2003] QB 728.

[19] Nicol D (2004a) 'Statutory interpretation and human rights after *Anderson*' *Public Law* 273.

Re S (Care Order . . .) (2001): preserving the 'fundamental' features of an Act

In *Re S (Care Order: Implementation of Care Plan)*,[20] the Court of Appeal invoked s 3 to create an entirely new procedure within the Children Act 1989 to make the provisions of that Act in relation to care proceedings compatible with Arts 6 and 8.[21] The 1989 Act had largely removed the High Courts' previous jurisdiction to supervise closely the way in which a local authority implemented orders made by the court which placed children in local authority care. The Court of Appeal in *S* considered that this scheme was inconsistent with Arts 6 and 8, and so read into the 1989 Act a judicial power for the court to specify particular targets in the care order which, if breached by the local authority, would entitle the court to intervene.

Lord Nicholls, delivering the only substantial judgment in the House of Lords,[22] offered a principle of general application to the scope of s 3:

> [39] . . . Interpretation of statutes is a matter for the courts; the enactment of statutes, and the amendment of statutes, are matters for Parliament.
>
> [40] Up to this point there is no difficulty. The area of real difficulty lies in identifying the limits of interpretation in a particular case. This is not a novel problem . . . . For present purposes it is sufficient to say that a meaning which departs substantially from a fundamental feature of an Act of Parliament is likely to have crossed the boundary between interpretation and amendment. This is especially so where the departure has important practical repercussions which the court is not equipped to evaluate. In such a case the overall contextual setting may leave no scope for rendering the statutory provision Convention compliant by legitimate use of the process of interpretation . . .

In this 'particular case', Lord Nicholls considered that the Court of Appeal had undermined a 'fundamental feature' of the Children Act 1989; namely that Parliament had sought to prevent the courts exercising the kind of supervisory role within the child care system which would be created by the Court of Appeal's conclusion.[23] This reasoning underlines the presumption that s 3 cannot be used to alter the schematic nature of particular statutory regimes, but is instead limited in scope to statutory provisions which have an essentially isolated, free-standing character.

Lord Nicholls also advanced a further principle which would likely restrict the range of substantive results which s 3 could be invoked to achieve:

> [41] . . . When a court, called upon to construe legislation, ascribes a meaning and effect to the legislation pursuant to its obligation under s 3, it is important the court should identify clearly the particular statutory provision or provisions whose interpretation leads to that result. Apart from all else, this should assist in ensuring the court does not inadvertently stray outside its interpretation jurisdiction.

This observation seems to re-inject a dose of literalism into the s 3 interpretive process, and might be thought to make it more difficult to justify a *Marleasing* approach to s 3 which empowers a court to read particular words or even entire phrases into a statutory text. That is of course what was done in *R v A*, albeit in respect of an 'isolated' rather than 'schematic' legislative provision. Lord Nicholls did not in terms disapprove the method used in *R v A*,

---

[20] [2001] EWCA Civ 757, [2001] 2 FCR 450.

[21] The judicial assumptions variously being that either the Court was giving effect to Art 8 ECHR per se or (without discussion) that Art 8 ECHR and Art 8 Sch 1 HRA had the same meaning.

[22] [2002] UKHL 10; [2002] 2 AC 291. The House of Lords saw no distinction between the ECHR articles and the Convention Rights: cf Lord Nicholls at para 36: 'Even if the Children Act is inconsistent with articles 6 or 8 of the Convention . . .'; and para 50: '. . . even if there is incompatibility between the Children Act 1989 and articles 6 or 8 of the Convention, . . .'.   [23] See especially paras [42]–[44] of the judgment.

but it is difficult to conclude otherwise than that his judgment in *S* could sensibly be read by judges in lower courts as intended to limit the circumstances in which such an approach could be applied.[24]

Bellinger v Bellinger (2003): rejecting a systemic change of meaning

This conclusion is reinforced by *Bellinger v Bellinger*,[25] in which Lord Nicholls again gave the leading judgment. The claimant in *Bellinger* had been classified (correctly as a matter of then extant law)[26] as male at birth. The claimant subsequently had gender reassignment treatment, and had conducted herself as a woman since 1975. In 1981, the claimant underwent a marriage ceremony with a male partner. Under the terms of the Matrimonial Causes Act 1973 s 11(c), any 'marriage' would be void if the partners were not respectively a 'man' and a 'woman'. Domestic law equated gender for this purposes with the gender assigned to a person at birth. Thus the claimant and her husband were both 'men', and consequently no marriage had occurred. The Bellingers contended that domestic law was incompatible with Arts 8 and 12 of Sch 1 of the HRA.[27]

In several decisions in the 1980 and 1990s,[28] the ECtHR had held that the United Kingdom's refusal to allow post-operative transsexual persons to alter their legal gender classification was not incompatible with the Convention. It would therefore seem that the conclusion reached by the High Court in *Corbett* would not have been inconsistent with Art 12 ECHR and presumably Art 12 Sch 1 HRA. However, by the time the Bellingers' case reached the House of Lords, the ECtHR had changed its view, and had concluded in *Goodwin v the United Kingdom*[29] that UK law breached Art 12 ECHR insofar as it prevented a transsexual person marrying another person of the 'same' gender.[30]

No suggestion was made in *Bellinger* that *Goodwin* did not also settle the meaning of Art 12 of Sch 1 HRA 1998. The point might appear pedantic, but it is not without significance. Under the scheme of the HRA, it would have been possible for the House of Lords to conclude that the moral basis of modern British society was such that the principle recognised as part of Art 12 of the Convention by the ECtHR was not an element of the Convention Right articulated in Art 12 Sch 1 HRA. This conclusion would have placed the United Kingdom under an obligation in the international law sphere to alter s 11 accordingly, but it would have had no impact on domestic law. Equally of course, had the ECtHR in *Goodwin* held that s 11 was consistent with Art 12 ECHR, it would still be open to Mrs Bellinger to argue that s 11 was incompatible with her statutory Convention Right under Art 12 of Sch 1 HRA 1998.[31] It is curious that this issue, so clearly envisaged by the scheme of the Act and so bluntly stated by

---

[24] Professor Nicol also invokes the House of Lords' judgment in *R (on the application of Anderson) v Secretary of State for the Home Department* [2002] UKHL 46, [2003] 1 AC 837 in support of this argument. For an alternative perspective see Kavanagh A (2004) 'Statutory interpretation and human rights after *Anderson*: a more contextual approach' *Public Law* 537.   [25] [2003] UKHL 21, [2003] 2 AC 467.

[26] See *Corbett v Corbett (otherwise Ashley) (No 1)* [1970] 2 WLR 1306. The judgment offers a fascinating snapshot of social history and the role of the law in making it.

[27] Which concern the right to private and family life and to marry. Interestingly, even though the Bellingers expressly framed their case with reference to their Convention Rights, the House of Lords conducted its analysis on the basis of whether s 11 was compatible with the ECHR: see especially Lord Hope at para 70 and Lord Nicholls at para 50.

[28] *Rees v United Kingdom* (1986) 9 EHRR 56; *Cossey v United Kingdom* [1993] 13 EHRR 622.

[29] [2002] 2 FCR 577.

[30] Under domestic law, the claimant in *Bellinger* could have married a person classified at birth as a 'woman', even if that person had undergone gender reassignment treatment to live as a 'man'.

[31] Cf the assertion in the white paper that the Act would set a floor, not a ceiling for the scope of human rights protection; see 'Human Rights IV: The Human Rights Act 1998', n 1, ch 20, p 518. The argument has particular resonance if the ECtHR is divided in its judgment. HRA s 2 is as applicable to dissenting judgments of the ECtHR as to unanimous or majority opinions.

Lord Irvine during the Bill's passage, passed most lawyers by in the early years of the HRA's implementation.

In the event, the primary question before the House of Lords in *Bellinger* was whether HRA s 3 empowered the Court to read s 11 of the Matrimonial Causes Act 1973—and specifically the terms 'man' and 'woman'—in a fashion consistent with the ECtHR's judgment in *Goodwin*. All members of the Court held that the answer to this question was 'No', but the unanimous conclusion rested on rather different reasons.

Lord Hope concluded that since it was then (and presumably remains) beyond the capacity of medical science to provide a person with what he termed 'the equipment'[32] needed to make that person fertile in his/her chosen gender identity, it is simply not 'possible' as a matter of objective fact for 'man' and 'woman' within s 11(c) to mean anything other than the gender assigned at birth.

The other substantive judgments (by Lords Hobhouse and Nicholls respectively) approached the issue in a fashion better attuned to the sensitivities of the claimant and people in her position. Both opinions accepted that whether a person was a 'man' or a 'woman' was a question of law, not of biological fact. The question to be answered was not whether the claimant was a 'man' or a 'woman', but which law-makers could legitimately decide that point. Lords Hobhouse and Nicholls considered that Mrs Bellinger's claim raised a profoundly systemic question. Whether she was a 'woman' had implications going far beyond the validity of her marriage. Lord Nicholls identified; 'education, child care, occupational qualifications, criminal law (gender specific offences), prison regulations, sport, the needs of decency and birth certificates'[33] as areas of social policy on which gender reassignment would have an obvious impact. Equally problematic, in Lord Nicholls' view, was what degree of transgender medical treatment would a person have to undergo before he/she should be regarded as having altered his/her initial gender for a particular purpose?[34]

When are the implications of change 'systemic' rather than 'individuated' ?

The initial cogency of this 'systemic implications' justification for concluding it was not 'possible' to use s 3 in this case should perhaps be questioned. It was manifestly open to the House of Lords to limit the ratio of *Bellinger* to the question of the validity of a marriage. Mrs Bellinger could be a 'woman' for that purpose. Whether she, or persons in like circumstances, would be a 'woman' for other legal purposes would then be left to be litigated on a case-by-case basis as and when particular questions arose. That conclusion would have no disabling effect upon Parliament's legal capacity to revisit the 'marriage' question in any subsequent legislative initiative dealing with the legal gender classification of persons who had undergone gender reassignment treatment. Such a judgment would perhaps have injected an additional sense of urgency and importance into the respective minds of government ministers and MPs as they considered how best to respond to this issue.[35]

The point to be made here is a simple, if somewhat cynical, one. Whether a particular statutory provision has a systemic or isolated character is itself a matter for judicial determination. The use of such dichotomous classification criteria as tools with which to structure the use of s 3 displaces rather than resolves the difficult question which s 3 creates.

Bellinger also offered further guidance on the use of s 4. There is no requirement in the HRA that a court which cannot 'save' a Convention non-compliant term through s 3 must then issue

---

[32] [2003] UKHL 21, [2003] 2 AC 467 at para 57.   [33] [2003] 2 AC 467, at para 45.

[34] Ibid, paras 39–44. For more extensive comment see Kavanagh (2004) op cit; Nicol D (2004) 'Gender reassignment and the transformation of the Human Rights Act' *LQR* 194.

[35] The position adopted by the House of Lords—and the criticism that can be levelled at it—are precisely the same as those arising from Megarry VC's conclusion in *Malone* that he should not recognise even a narrowly drawn right to privacy at common law; see '*Malone v Metropolitan Police Commissioner* (1979)', ch 17, pp 459–460.

a declaration of incompatibility. Section 4 creates a power, not a duty. The government intervened in the proceedings to argue that, inter alia, no declaration should be issued as it accepted that domestic law breached the Convention and was formulating proposals for new legislation. That the Blair government took this position, notwithstanding the rather contentious political nature of eliminating discrimination against transgender people, is perhaps in itself a good illustration of the power of the ECHR and the HRA to safeguard some human rights norms against domestic bigotry even within the political—rather than judicial—arena.[36] The new legislation was subsequently enacted as the Gender Recognition Act 2004.

In *Bellinger,* however, the House of Lords saw little weight in the government's contention that a Declaration of Incompatibility should not be issued. It is perhaps not an exaggeration to suggest that *Bellinger* supports the proposition that s 4 creates a very strong, if not quite irrebuttable, presumption that a declaration of incompatibility should be made whenever a statutory term's breach of a Convention Right cannot be avoided by use of s 3.

Ghaidan v Mendoza (2004): an individuated not systemic change of meaning

That this aspect of HRA jurisprudence remains mired in uncertainty is confirmed by the House of Lords' judgment in *Ghaidan v Godin-Mendoza*.[37] Mr Godin-Mendoza was the same-sex partner of a man who had occupied a house leased from Mr Ghaidan with the status of a 'protected tenant' under the Rent Act 1977. Under the 1977 Act (as amended in 1988) the husband or wife or spouse (a term taken to include non-married cohabitees of different genders) of a deceased protected tenant could succeed to a statutory continuation of the tenancy. A 'family member' (if he/she had resided in the property for the year prior to the tenant's death) was entitled to succeed to a less beneficial 'assured' tenancy.[38] A resident who was neither a spouse nor family member had no extra-contractual occupancy rights at all on the death of the tenant. Shortly before the HRA came into effect, the House of Lords held in *Fitzpatrick v Sterling Housing Association*[39] that a person in Mr Ghaidan-Mendoza's position could be a 'family member' of the deceased tenant, but not his/her spouse. The outcome clearly discriminated against same-sex couples on the basis of their sexual orientation.

Shortly after *Fitzpatrick*, the ECtHR held for the first time that sexual orientation discrimination was presumptively prohibited by Art 14 and Art 8 ECHR. The issue in *Salgueiro v Portugal*[40] was a custody dispute in which an appellate Portuguese court overruled a first instance judgment awarding custody of a child to S, the child's father. The Court's reason for overruling the lower court was based solely on S's homosexuality. The ECtHR concluded that such discrimination breached the Convention. In 2003, in *Karner v Austria*,[41] the ECtHR applied the *Salgueiro* principle squarely to succession rights in tenancies.

Mr Ghaidan-Mendoza argued that domestic law breached Arts 8 and 14 ECHR, and his case was analysed in that way by the court.[42] The precise wording of the phrase in issue within the relevant statutory provision[43] was: 'a person who was living with the original tenant as his husband or wife shall be treated as the spouse of the original tenant . . . ' Mr Mendoza's argument was that para 2(2) should be read to expand the literal formulation 'as his husband and

---

[36] Or, more prosaically, of the Blair government's determination to pursue policies that it thought morally correct even in the face of 'bigoted' opposition.

[37] [2004] UKHL 30, [2004] 2 AC 557. See Young A (2005) *Ghaidan v Godin-Mendoza*: avoiding the deference trap' *Public Law* 23; Loveland I (2003) 'Making it up as they go along: the Court of Appeal on succession rights in tenancies to same sex partners' *Public Law* 222.

[38] A protected statutory tenancy is subject to rigorous rent control, while an assured tenancy is not.

[39] [2001] AC 127; see 'Conclusion', ch 20, p 537.   [40] (2001) 31 EHRR 47.

[41] [2003] 2 FLR 623, [2004] 2 FCR 563, (2004) 38 EHRR 24.

[42] See especially Lord Steyn at [2004] UKHL 30, [2004] 2 AC 557 at para 38; Lord Nicholls at para 6.

[43] Rent Act 1977, Sch 1, para 2(2).

wife' beyond mere categories of physical gender—which if *Bellinger* is to be taken as correct are concepts beyond judicial redefinition—to include the particular types of emotional and physical relationship which characterised a marriage or heterosexual cohabitation partnership and which could just as readily be met in a same-sex partnership.

Accepting this argument, Lord Nicholls reviewed and attempted to clarify the body of principle which had built up around the use of s 3. He began his analysis with a question:

> [27] . . . What is the standard, or the criterion, by which 'possibility' [in s 3] is to be judged? A comprehensive answer to this question is proving elusive. The courts, including your Lordships' House, are still cautiously feeling their way forward as experience in the application of s 3 gradually accumulates.

The point at which Lord Nicholls seemed to have arrived was that courts should eschew use of s 3 to lend Convention compliant meanings to statutory terms if this would produce a meaning 'inconsistent with a fundamental feature of [the] legislation'.[44] What this notion of 'fundamental' appears to mean is that the Court should satisfy itself that the meaning it might give to a statutory provision is consistent with the policy objectives that Parliament was seeking to achieve when the term was enacted. In addition to introducing this 'fundamental feature' barrier to an expansive use of s 3, Lord Nicholls also reiterated the views expressed in *Re S* and *Anderson* that it was not constitutionally appropriate for courts to deploy s 3 to produce results that would have far-reaching systemic implications.

If neither a fundamental nor systemic matter was in issue however, Lord Nicholls indicated that it was appropriate for s 3 to be used to achieve what would from a traditional understanding of the sovereignty of Parliament and the separation of powers be regarded as very unorthodox results:

> [32] . . . Section 3 enables language to be interpreted restrictively or expansively. But s 3 goes further than this. It is also apt to require a court to read in words which change the meaning of the enacted legislation, so as to make it convention-compliant. In other words, the intention of Parliament in enacting s 3 was that, to an extent bounded only by what is 'possible', a court can modify the meaning, and hence the effect, of primary and secondary legislation.

Lord Nicholls saw no systemic implications for a modification of the previously accepted meaning and effect of the Rent Act provision in issue.[45] Nor did he consider that construing that provision to include same-sex partners ran counter to the social policy purpose underlying the legislation, which policy he took to be extending the benefit of succession to; 'couples living together in a close and stable relationship'.[46]

It would therefore be appropriate for the Court to change the original meaning of para 2.2 by reading in additional words. Perhaps surprisingly, Lord Nicholls did not think any particular linguistic exactitude was needed in this regard: 'The precise form of words read in for this purpose is of no significance. It is their substantive effect which matters.'[47]

Lord Steyn's view: a wrong turning

While Lord Steyn agreed with both the result reached by Lord Nicholls and the reasons underlying it, his judgment advocated a rather more forceful approach to s 3 and—consequentially— less frequent use of s 4. Lord Steyn had not sat in *Bellinger*. In *Mendoza*, he expressed concerns

---

[44] [2004] UKHL 30, [2004] 2 AC 557 at para 33.

[45] That he reached this conclusion without offering any considered discussion of the point nicely illustrates the way displacement tools can be invoked to gloss over difficult analytical questions.

[46] [2004] UKHL 30, [2004] 2 AC 557 at para 35.

[47] [2004] 2 AC 557 at para 35. One might wonder if para 2(2) could have been construed to produce the effect for which Mr Mendoza argued through a quite conservative form of literalism. If one's attention focuses on the word 'as' in the phrase 'as his husband or wife' one might quite credibly assert that the 'as' denotes the nature of the couple's emotional and physical relationship rather than their physiological identities.

that courts when faced with a non-Convention compliant statutory term were making insufficient use of s 3. Lord Steyn identified twenty-five such cases. In ten, the incompatibility had been removed by use of s 3. In fifteen, a s 4 declaration had been issued. These statistics, Lord Steyn suggested, 'reinforce the need to pose the question whether the law has taken a wrong turning'.[48]

That 'wrong turning' arose from the relative priority afforded to s 3 and s 4 as remedial devices in the event of a Convention article/Right being breached. Lord Steyn asserted that s 3 was intended by Parliament to be the dominant remedy in such circumstances. As such, the notion of 'possible' within s 3 should be accorded a very expansive meaning. Unlike Lord Nicholls, Lord Steyn held that *Marleasing* and the consequential judgment of the House of Lords in *Pickstone*[49] provided the proper guide to the potential of s 3 as an interpretive device. Lord Steyn appeared to accept that s 3 should not be used to undermine the scheme of a particular statute, but in terms of principle his approach towards s 3 is rather difficult to reconcile with the arguments offered by Lord Nicholls in the same case.

Assessing the effect of declarations of incompatibility

By the time *Mendoza* was decided, the ECtHR had indicated on several occasions that it did not regard a declaration of incompatibility per se as an effective remedy for Convention purposes. In *Walker v United Kingdom*[50] it held:

> Nor is the Court minded to change the view expressed in previous cases that a declaration of incompatibility issued by the domestic courts to the effect that the legislation infringed provisions of the Convention cannot be regarded as an effective remedy within the meaning of Art.35 (1). As stated in Hobbs (cited above [App No 63684/00, *Hobbs v United Kingdom*, Dec.06.06.2002]):
>
> > 'In particular, a declaration is not binding on the parties to the proceedings in which it is made. Furthermore, by virtue of section 10(2) of the 1998 Act, a declaration of incompatibility provides the appropriate minister with a power, not a duty, to amend the offending legislation by order so as to make it compatible with the Convention. The minister concerned can only exercise that power if he considers that there are "compelling reasons" for doing so.'
>
> The government's arguments have not given any basis for departing from this analysis in the present case.

The ECtHR's view had softened four years later. In *Burden v United Kingdom*[51] it observed:

> 43 . . . [I]t cannot be excluded that at some time in the future the practice of giving effect to the national courts' declarations of incompatibility by amendment of the legislation is so certain as to indicate that s.4 of the Human Rights Act is to be interpreted as imposing a binding obligation. In those circumstances, except where an effective remedy necessitated the award of damages in respect of past loss or damage caused by the alleged violation of the Convention, applicants would be required first to exhaust this remedy before making an application to the Court.

The ECtHR was likely prompted to modify its view by the empirical reality of how the Blair governments and Parliament responded to s 4 declarations.[52] That reality was usually a prompt amendment to the relevant law (either through primary legislation or the delegated legislative route provided for by HRA s 10). The incompatibility identified in *R (on application of H) v London North and East Mental Health Review Tribunal*[53] (the reverse burden of proof proviso

---

[48] Ibid, at para 39.

[49] See 'III. EC law. Parliamentary sovereignty and the courts: phase two' in the seventh edition of this book, ch 12, pp 393–397 (available in the online resources).   [50] (App No 37212/02); (2004) 39 EHRR SE4 at 27.

[51] (App No 13378/05); (2008) 47 EHRR 38.

[52] See the helpful analysis offered in Chandrachud C (2014) 'Reconfiguring the discourse on political responses to declarations of incompatibility' *Public Law* 624.   [53] [2002] QB 1.

in s 73 of the Mental Health Act 1983) was amended by a s 10 order; the problem raised in *R (International Transport GmbH) v Secretary of State for the Home Department*[54] was remedied by the Nationality, Immigration and Asylum Act 2002; and as noted earlier the incompatitbilty in *Bellinger* was removed by the Gender Recognition Act 2004.

Chandrachud's (2014) study[55] suggests that this presumption of compliance has continued. Of the eighteen s 4 orders made by that point, all had led to legislative amendment with the exception—as we shall see later[56]—of those concerning the voting rights of prisoners. Chandrachud suggests that we may be witnessing the emergence of a constitutional convention prompting both governments and Parliament towards responding positively to s 4 orders. This trend presumably provided the initial basis for the ECtHR's comments in *Burden*. It is a little early to form a strong view on this point. The more significant short-term implication of presumptive compliance may be that courts become more willing to use s 4 and so eschew very radical approaches to s 3.

Notwithstanding the statistics noted by Lord Steyn in *Mendoza*, there is as yet little indication of any deluge of declarations of incompatibility flooding across the UK's legal landscape. This consequence can be seen as—in part—an indication of the judiciary's initial willingness to read ss 3–4 of the Human Rights Act as an invitation to redefine the courts' interpretive role in an expansive way. We might also attribute it however to the emergence of a new common law principle informing the courts' approach to human rights issues.

The notion of 'deference' to legislative judgment

In an early review of the court's use of the Human Rights Act,[57] Craig argued that the Court of Appeal and House of Lords have developed a doctrine of 'deference' in respect of questions arising under the Act; that deference being owed by the courts to the decisions made by elected executive and legislative bodies. The doctrine appeared to be an indigenous version (and variation) of the 'margin of appreciation' principle within the jurisprudence of the EComHR and the ECtHR.[58]

The margin of appreciation principle is generally taken as recognising that the Convention requires that the ECtHR affords Signatory States some autonomy in determining if a prima facie derogation from a Convention entitlement can be permitted; that is, it is a doctrine existing in international law, the purpose of which is to 'save' or 'justify' a nation's intrusion into the sphere of a given ECHR provision. However, in Craig's view, the emergent concept of deference in domestic law goes rather further than this:

> [I]t is equally clear that deference may be of relevance in determining the initial scope and applicability of Convention rights, as well as the application of limitations placed on those rights . . . . The early jurisprudence has however applied deference at an earlier stage. It has done so as part of the initial determination as to the scope of the right in question. . .[59]

To use the terminology deployed in chapter eighteen, Craig's argument is that domestic courts appear to be accepting that the scope of the 'presumptive entitlement' element[60] of certain Convention Rights is a matter for political as well as judicial definition. He draws on several authorities raising Art 6 issues to support this proposition.

The issue before the Court of Appeal in *R v Lambert, Ali and Jordan*[61] was the compatibility of various provisions of the Homicide Act 1957 and the Misuse of Drugs Act 1971 with Art 6

---

[54] [2002] EWCA Civ 158, [2003] QB 728.   [55] Chandrachud (2014) op cit.

[56] See 'Conclusion', p 586.

[57] Craig P (2001) 'The courts, the Human Rights Act and judicial review' *LQR* 592; (original emphasis).

[58] See 'A four stage inquiry', ch 18, pp 481–484.   [59] Craig (2001) op cit p 592; original emphasis.

[60] See 'A four stage inquiry', ch 18, pp 481–484.   [61] [2002] QB 1112, [2001] 2 WLR 211.

ECHR. In finding that neither provision was incompatible with the Convention, Lord Woolf CJ (giving the sole judgment) offered a general statement of principle as to the appropriate method for the courts to follow in HRA cases:

> It is also important to have in mind that legislation is passed by a democratically elected [sic] Parliament and therefore the Courts under the Convention should, as a matter of constitutional principle, pay a degree of deference to the view of Parliament as to what is in the interest of the public generally when upholding rights of the individual under the Convention.[62]

The concept does not seem to entail the domestic court saying that: 'The meaning of the Convention article is X, but—in deference to the views of Parliament—we hold that the meaning of the relevant Convention Right is Y'. Rather the proposition appears to be: 'In the absence of an ECtHR judgment dealing squarely with this precise issue, we do not think that the legislative provision in issue can breach the Convention because Parliament is a democratically elected law-maker'. To put it slightly differently, the concept seems to rest on a second-guessing by UK courts of how the ECtHR would decide a particular case; that is, because the domestic court assumes that the ECtHR would conclude that the impugned law/action falls with the margin of appreciation that the ECtHR would extend to the United Kingdom as a country, then it is appropriate for a domestic court to defer to Parliament's view of what Convention Rights require.

This principle was reiterated by Lord Hoffmann in the House of Lords in *Alconbury*, a case concerning the compatibility of aspects of the land use planning system with Art 6 ECHR:

> In a democratic country, decisions as to what the general interest requires are made by democratically elected bodies or persons accountable to them. . .
>
> There is no conflict between human rights and the democratic principle. Respect for human rights requires that certain basic rights of individuals should not be capable in any circumstances of being overridden by the majority, even if they think that the public interest so requires. Other rights should be capable of being overridden only in very limited circumstances. These are rights which belong to individuals simply by virtue of their humanity . . . But outside these basic rights there are many decisions which have to be made every day (for example about the allocation of resources) in which the only fair method of decision is by some person or body accountable to the electorate.[63]

Lord Hoffman's dichotomy between 'basic rights' (in respect of which courts should be unwilling to defer to legislative conclusions) and 'allocation of resources' questions (when deference to legislative opinion is more appropriate) echoes Lord Hope's analysis in *R v DPP, ex p Kebilene*:

> The Convention should be seen as an expression of fundamental principles rather than as a set of mere rules. . . . In some circumstances, it will be appropriate for the courts to recognise that there is an area of judgment within which the judiciary will defer, on democratic grounds, to the considered opinion of the elected body or person whose act or decision is said to be incompatible with the Convention. . . . It will be easier for it [ie deference] to be recognised where the questions involve issues of social or economic policy, much less so where the rights are of high constitutional importance or are of a kind where the courts are especially well placed to assess the need for protection.[64]

This judicial recognition of a 'hierarchy' of Convention Rights jurisprudence lends a further layer of elaboration to the way in which the HRA can be applied by the courts. The need to apply s 3 expansively—or to invoke 4—diminishes if one accepts that it is legitimate within a

---

[62] [2002] QB 1112 at para 17.
[63] *R (Alconbury Developments Ltd and others) v Secretary of State for the Environment, Transport and the Regions* [2001] UKHL 23, [2003] 2 AC 325 at paras 69–70.   [64] [1999] UKHL 43, [2000] 2 AC 326, at 380–381.

scheme of human rights protection for politicians to determine through majoritarian legislation what the content of those fundamental human rights should be.[65]

This is illustrated by the outcome of *Wilson v First County Trust* in the House of Lords.[66] The view taken by the Court was that, even if the HRA had been applicable to the contract in question, s 127 of the Consumer Credit Act 1974 was not incompatible with Art 1 of the First Protocol ECHR. While it was accepted that s 127(3) worked 'drastic' or 'harsh' consequences even on a lender who had acted throughout in good faith,[67] the Court approached its assessment of s 127 vis-à-vis Art 1 with a clear preconception as to the correct allocation of decision-making responsibility on such a question:

> [70] In approaching this issue . . . courts should have in mind that theirs is a reviewing role. Parliament is charged with the primary responsibility for deciding whether the means chosen to deal with a social problem are both necessary and appropriate. Assessment of the advantages and disadvantages of the various legislative alternatives is primarily a matter for Parliament. The possible existence of alternative solutions does not in itself render the contested legislation unjustified. . . . The court will reach a different conclusion from the legislature only when it is apparent that the legislature has attached insufficient importance to a person's convention right. The readiness of a court to depart from the views of the legislature depends upon the circumstances, one of which is the subject matter of the legislation. The more the legislation concerns matters of broad social policy, the less ready will be a court to intervene.[68]

If lent a broad meaning, as in *Wilson* in the House of Lords, the 'deference' principle might often spare courts the difficulty of grappling with the meaning of s 3 and thence the inter-relationship between s 3 and s 4. This might seem an attractive proposition. It becomes much less so when one considers that 'deference' has the potential to be a mechanism for the abdication of judicial responsibility, in that it transfers interpretive authority from the courts to the legislature.

The deference principle is rooted in a perception of the separation of powers which speaks to the courts' acceptance of their constitutionally subordinate position to Parliament. But this notion of subordination needs to be deployed carefully, for it is one in which quite discrete aspects of the judiciary/legislature relationship can easily—and misleadingly—be conflated.

The courts' 'subordination' to Parliament is a matter concerned primarily with those institutions' respective capacities to give legal effect to substantive moral values. It is a question of *hierarchy*. A court which regards a legislative value as morally abhorrent when measured against orthodox common law principles cannot refuse to apply the legislative provision in issue; although it can of course lend meanings to legislative texts which defy any rational linguistic explanation and appear de facto at least to reject the court's formally subordinate position.[69]

This is a wholly distinct proposition from the suggestion that the courts are 'subordinate' to Parliament in the sense that Parliament has any legitimate claim to expect its understanding—or that of an executive body—of the legal meaning of the measures it enacts to prevail over the meaning arrived at by the courts. This is a question of *function*. Notwithstanding occasional invocation of the romantic shibboleth of Parliament as 'the High Court of Parliament', neither Parliament qua legislature—nor the House of Commons within it—is a judicial body.[70] That

---

[65] The proposition ignores the arguable inadequacies of the parliamentary process as a source of law. At this juncture one might usefully place the notion of 'deference' alongside the analysis of the judiciary's constitutional role offered by Lord Mustill in *Fire Brigades Union*; see 'Lord Mustill's analysis', ch 19, pp 516–517.

[66] [2003] UKHL 40, [2004] 1 AC 816.   [67] [2004] 1 AC 816, per Lord Nicholls at para 72.

[68] Per Lord Nicholls at para 70.

[69] Obvious examples being *Liversidge* ('*Liversidge v Anderson* (1942)', ch 3, pp 61–64) and *Anisminic* ('*Anisminic Ltd v Foreign Compensation Commission* (1969)', ch 3, pp 68–70.).

[70] See eg Stephen J in *Bradlaugh v Gossett* (1884) 12 QB and Lord Browne-Wilkinson in *Pepper v Hart* [1993] AC 593.

Parliament might have the power to accord itself through statute a nominally 'judicial' jurisdiction is beyond dispute. But while that might make Parliament a 'court' in a formalistic legal sense, it would not do so legitimately if we measure legitimacy against accepted tenets of the Anglo-American constitutional tradition.[71]

Unhappily, our courts seemed to have blurred this distinction between hierarchy and function, and used the notion of deference in effect to relinquish their traditional constitutional responsibilities to determine what Parliament has actually done in enacting legislation. 'Deference' has been presented as a concept of general application, although the extent to which courts should 'defer' is already established as dependent on the context of the case under consideration. If lent too broad a meaning, the deference principle could substantially compromise the 'fundamental' (in the sense of supra-party political) nature of Convention Rights.[72] A second concern is more prosaic. The notion of a hierarchy of rights may seem a coherent concept in principle, but will surely prove complex and prone to inconsistency when put into practice.

The difficulty that the idea of deference creates for an expansive understanding of human rights protection is best put by Professor Allan:

> . . . [T]here is no role for any distinct doctrine of deference to fulfil. Its invocation above and beyond the ordinary constraints inherent in judicial review amounts to an abdication of the judicial role and a failure to protect legal rights.[73]

And deference to the ECtHR?

It was not until 2009 that the higher courts appeared to recognise the possibility of a co-existence between Convention articles and Convention Rights whose identical texts bore different legal meanings. The point was clearly made in *R v Horncastle*,[74] in which the Supreme Court approved the Court of Appeal's conclusion (which was in effect if not in express terms) that the meaning of Art 6 of Sch 1 of the HRA should not be the same as that of Art 6 ECHR. The substantive issue at stake in *Horncastle* was the admissibility in criminal trials of hearsay evidence from witnesses who were either dead or too frightened to give oral evidence. The Supreme Court declined to follow the ECtHR's Grand Chamber's ruling in *Al-Khawaja and Tahery v United Kingdom*[75] that admitting such evidence would breach Art 6 if it was the 'sole or decisive' reason for conviction.

The Court underlined the impact of HRA s 2 as lending only persuasive and not binding status to ECtHR authority:

> 10 Mr Tim Owen QC, for Mr Horncastle and Mr Blackmore, submitted that we should treat the judgment of the Chamber in Al-Khawaja as determinative of the success of these appeals. He submitted that this was the appropriate response to the requirement of section 2(1) of the Human Rights Act 1998 that requires a court to 'take into account' any judgment of the European Court of Human Rights in determining any question to which such judgment is relevant . . .
> 11 I do not accept that submission. The requirement to 'take into account' the Strasbourg jurisprudence will normally result in the domestic court applying principles that are clearly established

---

[71] See the discussion of South Africa's 'High Court of Parliament' at '*Harris v Minister of the Interior*—the aftermath', ch 3, pp 49–50.

[72] See Leigh I (2002) 'Taking rights proportionately' *Public Law* 265: Edwards R (2002) 'Judicial deference under the Human Rights Act' *MLR* 859; Jowell J (2003) 'Judicial deference: servility, civility or institutional capacity' (2003) *Public Law* 592.

[73] Allan T (2006) 'Human rights and judicial review: a critique of "due deference" *Cambridge LJ* 671.

[74] [2009] EWCA Crim 964, [2010] 2 AC 373.

[75] (2009) 49 EHRR 1. See Metcalfe E (2010) 'Free to lead as well as to be led: Section 2 of the Human Rights Act and the relationship between the UK Courts and Strasbourg' *Justice Journal* 7.

by the Strasbourg court. There will, however, be rare occasions where the domestic court has concerns as to whether a decision of the Strasbourg court sufficiently appreciates or accommodates particular aspects of our domestic process. In such circumstances it is open to the domestic court to decline to follow the Strasbourg decision, giving reasons for adopting this course . . .

In rejecting *Al-Khawaja* and related ECtHR authorities as authoritative determinants of the meaning of Art 6 of Sch 1 of the HRA, Lord Phillips observed:

107 [T]hat case law appears to have developed without full consideration of the safeguards against an unfair trial that exist under the common law procedure. Nor, I suspect, can the Strasbourg court have given detailed consideration to the English law of admissibility of evidence, and the changes made to that law, after consideration by the Law Commission, intended to ensure that English law complies with the requirements of article 6(1)(3)(d).

The Court did not bluntly reject the legitimacy of ECtHR authority. Rather Lord Phillips suggested that it was appropriate for domestic courts to enter into a 'dialogue' with the ECtHR in such cases, his assumption apparently being that in a subsequent judgment the ECtHR might be persuaded by the reasoning of the domestic court to modify its previous judgment. This would in turn enable the domestic courts to accept that Art 6 of Sch 1of the HRA bore the same meaning as Art 6 ECHR. Lord Phillips did not specify what the Court would do if the ECtHR confirmed its previous conclusions.

Some indication on this point and on the potentially fractious nature of this process of 'dialogue' more generally was given between 2004 and 2012 by a series of ECtHR and House of Lords/Supreme Court judgments dealing with the effect of Art 8 on English law regulating residential possession proceedings.[76] The House of Lords had initially concluded in *LB Harrow v Qazi*[77] that Art 8 provided no protection to people at risk of being evicted from their homes. The ECtHR promptly indicated in *Connors v United Kingdom*[78] that Art 8 required that the proportionality of eviction be assessed by a court. The House of Lords thereafter responded (in *LB Lambeth v Kay*)[79] by saying that any such requirement was met by ordinary principles of judicial review. Shortly afterwards in *McCann v United Kingdom*[80] the ECtHR held that ordinary principles of judicial review did not suffice for proportionality purposes. The House of Lords in *Birmingham City Council v Doherty*[81] subsequently declined to accept this position, with both Lord Hope and Lord Scott noting intemperately that the ECtHR did not understand English law. In *Kay v United Kingdom*[82] (the Strasbourg sequel to *LB Lambeth v Kay*) the ECtHR reiterated its position, whereupon the Supreme Court (including Lords Hope and Scott) accepted in *Manchester City Council v Pinnock*[83] that Art 8 of Sch 1 of the HRA did require there to be proportionality review in such circumstances and that proportionality review had to involve the court in more intensive evaluation of the merits of the landlord's decision than provided for by *Wednesbury* irrationality.

The episode is of especial interest to housing lawyers, but *Pinnock* is also significant in broad constitutional terms for indicating the extent to which the Supreme Court will allow the content of domestic law to be de facto determined by the ECtHR:

48 . . . This Court is not bound to follow every decision of the EurCtHR. Not only would it be impractical to do so: it would sometimes be inappropriate, as it would destroy the ability of the Court to engage in the constructive dialogue with the EurCtHR which is of value to the

---

[76] See Loveland I (2009a) 'A tale of two trespassers: reconsidering the impact of the Human Rights Act on rights of residence in rented housing' *European Human Rights Law Review* 148 (part 1) and 495 (part 2); (2010) 'The shifting sands of Art 8 jurisprudence in English housing law' *European Human Rights Law Review* 151.

[77] [2003] UKHL 43, [2004] 1 AC 983.   [78] (2004) 40 EHRR 189.

[79] [2006] UKHL 10, [2006] 2 AC 465.   [80] (2008) 47 EHRR 40.

[81] [2008] UKHL 57, [2009] 1 AC 367.   [82] [2011] HLR 2.   [83] [2011] UKSC 6, [2001] 2 WLR 220.

development of Convention law (see e g *R v Horncastle*). . . . Where. . .there is a clear and constant line of [ECtHR] decisions whose effect is not inconsistent with some fundamental substantive or procedural aspect of our law, and whose reasoning does not appear to overlook or misunderstand some argument or point of principle, we consider that it would be wrong for this Court not to follow that line.

The Supreme Court's phraseology in *Pinnock* obviously leaves scope for domestic courts to reject ECtHR authority as determining the meaning of Convention Rights. As such, the principle forcefully underlines the autonomous character of Convention articles and Convention Rights and is perfectly consistent with the meaning of HRA s 2. It remains to be seen however if this realisation becomes normalised within HRA litigation.

The question of precedent

The issue of precedent and internal judicial hierarchies is one question which perhaps entirely escaped the MPs who supported enactment of the HRA. Several hypothetical scenarios might be explored to illustrate this point.[84] The question we might ask in respect of each scenario is whether the High Court and/or Court of Appeal should regard themselves as bound to follow precedent set by the House of Lords/Supreme Court if that precedent appears to articulate a legal rule incompatible with a Convention Right.

In scenario A, a post-2000 case, the House of Lords/Supreme Court concludes, having considered relevant ECtHR jurisprudence as required by HRA s 2, that law X (be it a statutory provision or a common law rule) is consistent with a particular Convention Right. Shortly afterwards, the ECtHR rules that the precise domestic law in issue is incompatible with the relevant Convention article.

In scenario B, a post-2000 case, the House of Lords/Supreme Court concludes, having considered relevant ECtHR jurisprudence as required by HRA s 2, that law X is compatible with a particular Convention Right. Shortly afterwards, the ECtHR rules that a similar law existing in another Signatory State is incompatible with the relevant Convention article.

In scenario C, in a case decided before (perhaps many years before) the HRA came into force, the House of Lords decided that the meaning of a statutory provision or common law rule was X. Many years later, before the issue of whether such a law is compatible with a Convention Right is considered by the House of Lords/Supreme Court, the ECtHR rules that the precise domestic law in issue (if its meaning is X) is incompatible with the relevant Convention article.[85]

In scenario D, in a case decided before (perhaps many years before) the HRA came into force, the House of Lords decided the meaning of a statutory provision or common law rule is X. Many years later, before the issue of whether such a law is compatible with a Convention Right is considered by the House of Lords/Supreme Court, the ECtHR rules that a similar law existing in another Signatory State is incompatible with the relevant Convention article.

Ordinarily we expect the High Court and Court of Appeal simply to follow and apply judgments of the House of Lords/Supreme Court. There is no express provision in the HRA to rebut that presumption. But each of the scenarios outlined earlier raises a difficulty from an HRA perspective if we assume both that the lower courts must follow the precedents set by the House of Lords/Supreme Court and that the meaning of Convention Rights is determined by the ECtHR judgments as to the meaning of the relevant Convention article.

[84] I assume for these purposes that domestic courts have appreciated the distinction drawn by the HRA between Convention Rights and Convention articles.

[85] A case may reach the ECtHR without it having been considered by the Supreme Court or Court of Appeal. One has exhausted domestic remedies if one is refused permission to appeal at a lower level of the court hierarchy.

The difficulty is most acute in scenario C. Here, there is no House of Lords/Supreme Court ruling that law X is compatible with the Convention Right in issue. The question has never been considered by a domestic court. The meaning of law X is clear, but that meaning is evidently also incompatible with the meaning of the ECHR.

One might suggest that if the lower court nonetheless followed the House of Lords' ruling it would be acting unlawfully per HRA s 6, given that s 6 does not in terms indicate that a lower court may lawfully breach Convention Rights if it does so because it is applying a precedent set by a higher court. The inference then arising is that the lower court might be 'saved' from acting unlawfully if we assume that s 6 impliedly incorporates the rules of precedent and judicial hierarchy.[86] That assumption might however be thought constitutionally problematic because it could be seen as allowing a common law principle to override the statutory protection of Convention Rights.

The issue came before the House of Lords in *D v East Berkshire Community NHS Trust*.[87] The rule of domestic law in issue was the House of Lords' judgment in *X (Minors) v Bedfordshire County Council*,[88] which had held that children who had suffered mistreatment while in the care of a local authority social services department could not sue the local authority in negligence for any physical or psychiatric injuries they had received. The conclusion rested on the assumption that it would be contrary to public policy to allow any such claims to go forward because the prospect of being sued would deter local authorities from carrying out their statutory duties with sufficient rigour.

Six years later the claimants in *X* established before the ECtHR—in *Z v United Kingdom*[89]—that they had been subject to inhuman and degrading treatment contrary to Art 3 ECHR and that the rule in *X* denied them any effective remedy contrary to Art 13 ECHR. Several subsequent ECtHR judgments involving other states also indicated that such a 'blanket immunity' provision in relationship to government bodies' child care powers breached various provisions of the Convention.

In *D*, the Court of Appeal held that it was not bound by the House of Lords' judgment in *X*. The Court appeared to hold[90] that the effect of the Human Rights Act was that in circumstances where the ECtHR had held that a specific rule of domestic law promulgated by a higher court breached the Convention then any binding effect that rule once had in domestic law was removed. The Court of Appeal also suggested that any such precedential effect would be lost if the ECtHR subsequently held that similar domestic laws breached the Convention. The House of Lords approved this reasoning. Both courts—and these we must recall were judgments which pre-dated *Horncastle* and *Pinnock*—evidently considered that the meanings of Convention Rights and Convention articles were invariably the same.

The House of Lords/Supreme Court may alter the rules of precedent and judicial hierarchy, with respect both to its own powers (as it did in 1966)[91] and the powers of lower courts. The rules exist at common law, and the House of Lords/Supreme Court can amend the common law as it thinks fit. For *the Court of Appeal* to have taken that step is conceptually more problematic, for if the Court of Appeal has such a power presumably so does the High Court. It is unfortunate that the House of Lords' judgment in *D* did not make this point more forcefully. That it did not do so makes it hard to avoid the conclusion that both the Court of Appeal and the House of Lords were according the ECtHR what was in effect an appellate (ie final court of appeal) status within the schemata of the HRA.

In *Kay*,[92] the House of Lords resiled substantially from the suggestion that its reasoning in *D* created a rule of general application. The general rule should in fact be that lower courts

---

[86] This assumption would rest on an empirical fiction. The point does not appear to have been considered by MPs during the passage of the Bill.   [87] [2005] UKHL 23, [2005] 2 AC 373.

[88] [1995] 2 AC 663.   [89] (2001) 34 EHRR 97.

[90] [2003] EWCA Civ 1151, [2004] QB 558 at paras 79–84.   [91] See 'The 1966 Practice Statement', ch 3, p 67.

[92] [2006] UKHL 10, [2006] 2 AC 465 at paras 40–45.

would continue to be bound by ordinary rules of precedent, even if it seemed clear that a particular domestic law breached a Convention article/Right. The primary reason for that conclusion had little to do with the de facto hierarchical relationship between domestic courts and the ECtHR implied by *D*, but lay in concerns about legal certainty. Because there would often be substantial scope for domestic courts to disagree about the precise meaning of ECtHR judgments, a rule which allowed lower courts to invoke those judgments to justify departing from otherwise binding domestic authority would be a recipe for confusion. The proper course for a lower court to follow would be to apply the domestic law but to hear argument on the Convention (Right) point and if it regarded those arguments as well-founded to say so and grant permission for an appeal. A lower court could depart from binding authority only if several preconditions were met. Firstly the judgment in issue had been decided before the HRA came into force. Secondly, no consideration has been given to ECHR issues by the domestic court. And thirdly the specific domestic judgment has subsequently been found by the ECtHR to breach the Convention in an action brought by the individuals who lost the domestic proceedings.[93]

In essence, *Kay* tells us that there is no HRA equivalent to the EU law precedence doctrine articulated in *Factortame*.[94] Whether that substantive conclusion is morally desirable from an abstract rule of law perspective is obviously disputable. But from the viewpoint of a rather more pragmatic concern with legal certainty, the position taken in *Kay* appears eminently sensible.

II. The horizontality of the Act

The courts have charted a rather erratic course through the murky waters of HRA s 6. As commentators had predicted, two major questions have arisen. The first relates to the breadth of the concept of a 'public authority' for s 6(1) purposes. The second concerns the Act's effect on legal relationships between private parties.

As suggested earlier, the definition of 'public authority' within s 6 was a question likely to generate considerable litigation. The answer given by the courts on this point might have a substantial bearing on the Act's impact, insofar as that answer would determine which legal actors were bound by Convention Rights. The point also bears closely on the distinction between de facto and de jure understandings of the 'horizontal effect' argument.

The identification of a particular individual or body as a 'public authority' means that any action against her or it based on the HRA 1998 would be (nominally) 'vertical' in nature. But one must beware of allowing labels to obscure realities. By interpreting the notion of a public authority broadly, the courts could pull many ostensibly 'private' individuals or corporations within s 6 without formally recognising horizontal effect at all. Conversely, a narrow construction of 'public authority' would be irrelevant if the courts assumed that s 3 and their own status as public authorities per s 6 compelled them to issue Convention-compliant judgments irrespective of the identities of the parties to litigation.

The meaning of 'public authorities'

An ostensibly straightforward question as to the reach of the public authority principle was raised in *Aston Cantlow and Wilmcote with Billesley Parochial Church Council v Wallbank*.[95] The Chancel Repairs Act 1932 empowers parochial church councils (PCCs) to impose costs of

---

[93] [2006] UKHL 10, [2006] 2 AC 465 at para 45 per Lord Bingham; 'But such a course is not permissible save where the facts are of that extreme character'   [94] 'The demise of the legal doctrine: Factortame' pp 306–312.
[95] [2001] EWCA Civ 713, [2002] Ch 51, [2001] 3 WLR 1323.

maintaining church buildings on owners of land previously owned by the church. The defendants had received a substantial bill from their local PCC, and claimed that this infringed Art 1 of the First Protocol. The Court of Appeal accepted that the PCC was a public authority within s 6. In part this was because the PCC derived its powers from statute. This should not per se be regarded as a conclusive point however. It may be that a more important factor underpinning the Court's conclusion was the nature of the PCC's power. The power in issue was regarded by the Court of Appeal as essentially one of taxation, which is generally seen as a government function.[96]

An early analytical principle: the 'close assimilation' test

A different factual situation arose in *Poplar Housing and Regeneration Community Association v Donoghue*.[97] The appellant was a notionally private sector housing association. However, de facto the housing association was a management takeover of the housing operation previously controlled by the London Borough of Tower Hamlets.[98] The litigation was triggered by the association's attempt to evict a tenant whose tenancy had been granted when the housing was owned by the local authority. The central issue before the Court of Appeal was whether the association fell within s 6(3)(b); that is, was it—a 'person certain of whose functions are of a public nature'. Lord Woolf CJ's leading judgment accepted that the notion of public authority in s 6: 'should be given a generous interpretation'.[99] Lord Woolf suggested that guidance as to the meaning of public authority could be found in administrative law cases concerned with whether particular bodies should be subject to judicial review.[100] But, in terms of broad principle, the Court of Appeal rejected the suggestion that private individuals or organisations which contracted with public authorities to provide the means for those authorities to discharge legal obligations themselves became public authorities for s 6 purposes:

> The fact that a body performs an activity which otherwise a public body would be under a duty to perform cannot mean that such a performance is necessarily a public function. A public body in order to perform its public duties can use the services of a private body. S 6 should not be applied so that if a private body provides such services, the nature of the functions are inevitably public.[101]

On the facts, the Court of Appeal considered that the Association was performing a public function because it was 'so closely assimilated' with the local authority.

[T]he 'close assimilation' test led to a different conclusion in *R (Heather) v Leonard Cheshire Foundation*.[102] The National Assistance Act 1948 s 21(1) requires local authorities to provide accommodation for certain vulnerable people. Section 26 allows local authorities to discharge the s 21 duty by placing people in facilities owned and run by charities.[103] Several local authorities placed residents in a home run by a charity, the Leonard Cheshire Foundation. The Foundation subsequently decided to close the particular home where Mrs Heather lived. The Court of Appeal concluded that the Foundation was not a public authority. The Court accepted that *Poplar* required that s 6 be given a broad interpretation. However it distinguished the

---

[96] The Court further concluded that the tax imposed on the defendants breached Art 1 of the First Protocol, in that it was arbitrary and disproportionate as it bore no relation to the value of the land itself. See Dawson I and Dunn A (2002) 'Seeking the principle: chancel, choices and human rights' *Legal Studies* 238; Oliver D (2001) 'Chancel repairs and the Human Rights Act' *Public Law* 651.

[97] [2001] EWCA Civ 595, [2002] QB 48, [2001] 3 WLR 183.

[98] See the discussion of the privatisation of council housing at 'X. Privatising local government', ch 10, p 274.

[99] [2001] EWCA Civ 595, [2002] QB 48 at 67.

[100] See the discussion in ch 15.   [101] [2001] EWCA Civ 595, [2002] QB 48 at 67.

[102] [2002] EWCA Civ 366, [2002] 2 All ER 936.

[103] See the discussion of *Servite Houses* at '"Private" actors and "public" functions: the *Servite Houses* case (1997)', ch 15, p 427.

factual position of the Foundation and the Housing Association in *Poplar*. The Court saw no reason for assuming that there was a 'close assimilation' between the local authorities and the Foundation. This conclusion was clearly driven by policy concerns. As in *Poplar*, the Court evidently saw no merit in the argument that every privately owned hotel or nursing home should be regarded as a public authority just because a government body bought its services to house people to whom the government body owed a duty.

A more refined analytical principle? 'Core' and 'hybrid' or 'functional' public authorities

The *Poplar* 'close assimilation' test has obvious attractions as a means to determine if a body is a public authority. Its main shortcoming however is that it focuses primarily on the *identity* of the body (and/or the intimacy of its relationship with an organisation that is obviously a public authority) rather than on the *function* that the body performs. HRA s 6(3)(b) is cast in terms of function rather than identity, and in later cases the higher courts cast doubt on the appropriateness of an assimilation test.

Aston Cantlow in the House of Lords

The House of Lords in *Aston Cantlow* took a different approach to the Court of Appeal.[104] The Court indicated that s 6 required a distinction to be drawn between 'core' and 'hybrid' public authorities. This dichotomy was substantially shaped by a consideration not pursued before the Court of Appeal. Article 34 of the Convention empowers the ECtHR to receive petitions from 'persons, groups of individuals and non-governmental organisations'. Section 7 of the HRA identifies such petitioners as potential 'victims' of infringements of Convention Rights for the purposes of domestic law. The House of Lords was concerned to avoid the potential difficulty of defining 'public authorities' under s 6 in a fashion which effectively negated the capacity of a 'non-governmental organisation' to present itself as a 'victim' in respect of Convention Rights. That incapacity should apply only to a 'core' public authority.

There is some circularity in this reasoning.[105] But members of the Court did offer some freestanding criteria to be used in assessing whether a body was a 'core' body for this purpose. Lord Nicholls' formulation was perhaps the most expansive:

> [T]he phrase 'a public authority' in s 6(1) is essentially a reference to a body whose nature is governmental in a broad sense of that expression. It is in respect of organisations of this nature that the government is answerable under the convention. Hence, under the Human Rights Act a body of this nature is required to act must compatibly with convention rights in everything it does. The most obvious examples are government departments, local authorities, the police and the armed forces. Behind the instinctive classification of these organisations as bodies whose nature is governmental lie factors such as the possession of special powers, democratic accountability, public funding in whole or in part, an obligation to act only in the public interest, and a statutory constitution . . .[106]

No member of the Court felt that the PCC could be classified in this way:

> Its functions. . . . clearly include matters which are concerned only with the pastoral and organisational concerns of the diocese and the congregation of believers in the parish. It acts in the sectional not the public interest. . . . [I]t is essentially a domestic religious body. The fact that

---

[104] [2003] UKHL 37, [2004] 1 AC 546, [2003] 3 WLR 283.

[105] Complications may arise on the domestic impact of the ECtHR's jurisprudence on this point: cf Davis H (2005) 'Public authorities as victims under the HRA' *Cambridge LJ* 315; Quane H (2006) 'The Strasbourg jurisprudence and the meaning of a "public authority" under the HRA' *Public Law* 106.

[106] [2004] 1 AC 546 at para 7.

the Church of England is the established Church of England may mean that various bodies within that Church may as a result perform public functions. But it does not follow that PCCs themselves perform any such functions.[107]

The Court's conclusion on this point was reinforced by the ECtHR's own decision in *Holy Monasteries v Greece*[108] in which the ECtHR held that the 'established' Greek Church could bring an action against the Greek state in respect of the confiscation of its property.

Nor did the House of Lords accept that the PCC was performing a 'function of a public nature' within s 6(3)(b). The Court indicated that it would not be possible to offer any definitive answer to what might amount to a public function for these purposes. Any such answer would have to be substantially dependent upon the factual character of the particular body and function in issue. On the facts of *Aston Cantlow*, the Court concluded that the 'function' under consideration lacked a 'public' character. Rather than characterise what the PCC was doing as analogous to levying a tax, the House of Lords regarded the PCC as simply enforcing a private law obligation comparable to a restrictive covenant or a civil debt.[109]

R (Beer) v Hampshire Farmers Market Ltd (2004)

The impact of *Aston Cantlow* was promptly considered in the Court of Appeal in *R (on the application of Beer) v Hampshire Farmers Market Ltd*.[110] Hampshire Farmers Market Ltd was de jure a private company. However it had initially been created by Hampshire County Council as a device to stimulate the agricultural sector of the local economy by promoting weekend markets at which local farmers sold their produce to the public. The Council subsequently handed control of the operation to the local farmers involved. It assisted them in establishing a limited company, provided office space and logistical support, and a former council employee took on a senior position in the new company. The company was given control, inter alia, of granting licences to farmers who wished to participate in the market. Mr Beer was refused a licence, in a fashion which—by the time the case reached the Court of Appeal—was accepted to have been procedurally unfair. The issues before the Court were whether the company was subject to judicial review at common law, and whether it was a public authority within s 6.

Dyson LJ's judgment observes that the answer to these two questions would often—but not always—be the same on any given set of facts. Two factors in this case led him to conclude that the company was both a 'hybrid' public authority and amenable to judicial review. The first was the very close assimilation between the company and the county council; the council had created the company; the company 'stepped into the council's shoes' in terms of its functions; and the council continued to provide substantial support to the company. This element of the judgment is essentially an endorsement of the Court of Appeal's reasoning in *Poplar*. The second, and perhaps more idiosyncratic, factor was that the venues where the markets were held had traditionally been regarded as places to which the general public had a right of access. As such, the company was in a sense acting as a steward of a public rather than private interest.

---

[107] Ibid, per Lord Hobhouse at para 86.

[108] (1994) 20 EHRR 1. In emphasising the importance of the ECtHR's case law on this point, the House of Lords indicated that no reliance should be placed for s 6 purposes on the ostensibly similar issue of whether a body was amenable to judicial review.

[109] See generally Meisel F (2004) 'The *Aston Cantlow* case: blots on English jurisprudence and the public/private law divide' *Public Law* 2; Donnelly C (2005) '*Leonard Cheshire* again and beyond: private contractors, contract and s 6(3)(b) of the Human Rights Act' *Public Law* 785; Sunkin M (2004) 'Pushing forward the frontiers of human rights protection; the meaning of public authority under the Human Rights Act' *Public Law* 643.

[110] [2003] EWCA Civ 1056, [2004] 1 WLR 233. For an interesting discussion see Hough B (2005) 'Public regulation of markets and fairs' *Public Law* 586.

YL v Birmingham and Others (2007)

The Court of Appeal's decision in *Leonard Cheshire* was not appealed to the House of Lords, but the matter was revisited in 2007 in *YL v Birmingham and Others*.[111] Birmingham council had contracted with a private company, Southern Cross, for Southern Cross to provide the residential care which Birmingham was obliged to offer under s 21 of the National Assistance Act 1948. Southern Cross had such agreements with many local authorities. In 2007, it provided 29,000 residential care places, of which 80% were s 21 placements.

YL was an elderly lady, suffering from Alzheimer's disease. Southern Cross wished to evict her from her care home because of her erratic behaviour. YL had no contract with Southern Cross; nor, as matters then stood following *Servite Houses*,[112] could she challenge her eviction by judicial review. Unless Southern Cross was a public authority, YL would have no means of bringing the matter before the courts. It seems likely that the care home was YL's home for the purposes of Art 8, and that her eviction would have interfered with her Art 8 entitlements. However the case was argued on the basis of the preliminary issue of whether Southern Cross was a public authority.

Both Lord Bingham and Baroness Hale considered that Southern Cross was performing a public function in accommodating YL and was thus a public authority within HRA s 6. Lord Bingham evidently saw little difficulty in reaching that conclusion:

> 20. When the 1998 Act was passed, it was very well known that a number of functions formerly carried out by public authorities were now carried out by private bodies. Section 6(3)(b) of the 1998 Act was clearly drafted with this well-known fact in mind. The performance by private body A by arrangement with public body B, and perhaps at the expense of B, of what would undoubtedly be a public function if carried out by B is, in my opinion, precisely the case which section 6(3)(b) was intended to embrace. It is, in my opinion, this case.

Lord Bingham and Baroness Hale identified four factors leading to this conclusion. The first was that Parliament in enacting the 1948 legislation had assumed a positive obligation towards people accommodated under s 21. The second was that such people were atypically vulnerable to abuse and exploitation and so, correspondingly, needed greater protection. The third was that the service performed by the private contractor was, in effect, the service that would otherwise have to be performed by Birmingham Council. And the fourth was that the service was being substantially financed by public funds.[113]

Baroness Hale and Lord Bingham were however in a minority. The majority view, put perhaps most forcefully by Lord Scott (supported by Lords Mance and Neuberger), did not accept that Southern Cross was caught by HRA s 6. Lord Scott rejected the suggestion that just because Southern Cross was providing services which the council could have provided meant that Southern Cross itself was performing a public function. Lord Scott was concerned that if this argument were accepted, there would be no limit to the functions and bodies falling within HRA s 6:

> [30] . . . If every contracting out by a local authority of a function that the local authority could, in exercise of a statutory power or the discharge of a statutory duty, have carried out itself, turns the contractor into a hybrid public authority for section 6(3)(b) purposes, where does this end? Is a contractor engaged by a local authority to provide lifeguard personnel at the municipal swimming pool a section 6(3)(b) public authority? If so, would a local authority employee engaged by the local authority as a lifeguard at the pool become a public authority? Could it be argued that his or her function was a function of a public nature? If Southern Cross is a section 6(3)(b) public

---

[111] [2007] UK HL 27, [2008] 1 AC 95, [2007] 3 WLR 112.

[112] See '"Private" actors and "public" functions: the *Servite Houses* case (1997), ch 15, pp 427–428.

[113] Cf Baroness Hale at para 65: '. . . While there cannot be a single litmus test of what is a function of a public nature, the underlying rationale must be that it is a task for which the public, in the shape of the state, have assumed responsibility, at public expense if need be, and in the public interest'.

authority, why does it not follow that each manager of each Southern Cross care home, and even each nurse or care worker at each care home would, by reason of his or her function at the care home, be a section 6(3)(b) public authority?

This is an extravagant reading of the minority position. There is little difficulty in drawing a qualitative distinction between a contractor providing lifeguards at a swimming pool and a contractor providing intensively supportive residential care to elderly people suffering from debilitating medical conditions. Local authorities are, for example, required to provide s 21 care: they are not obliged to provide swimming pools. Nor are swimming pool attendants qua swimming pool attendants in a position to impact significantly on any person's human rights. Conceivably a swimming pool might refuse entry to a person on a basis which breaches Art 9 or Art 10, and one might concede (having swum in our imaginations to the deep end of barely credible empirical example) that a 'public authority' lifeguard who declined to rescue a drowning child because of the child's race or gender or religious belief would breach—inter alia—Art 2 and/or Art 9 and/or Art 14. A care home, in contrast, is always intimately involved with a resident's Art 8 entitlements. Additionally, very few patrons of a local authority swimming pool will be 'vulnerable' in the sense identified by Lord Bingham and Baroness Hale. In contrast, all of Southern Cross's s 21 residents would be vulnerable persons.

Nor did the majority seem to attach any significance to the fact that Southern Cross derived so much of its income—and profit—from residents placed by local authorities and paid for by public funds. As Lord Scott put it:

> 26. Southern Cross is a company carrying on a socially useful business for profit. It is neither a charity nor a philanthropist. It enters into private law contracts with the residents in its care homes and with the local authorities with whom it does business. It receives no public funding, enjoys no special statutory powers, and is at liberty to accept or reject residents as it chooses (subject, of course, to anti-discrimination legislation which affects everyone who offers a service to the public) and to charge whatever fees in its commercial judgment it thinks suitable. It is operating in a commercial market with commercial competitors.
>
> 27 . . . There is no element whatever of subsidy from public funds. It is a misuse of language and misleading to describe Southern Cross as publicly funded.

Lord Scott's reasoning here resembles the 'close assimilation' test: since Southern Cross was not in any sense 'assimilated' to Birmingham Council it was not a public authority. The majority view provides an obvious and—it might be thought—unhappy incentive for local authorities and other government bodies to 'contract-out' provision of public services to organisations whose primary concern is simply to make profits rather than provide appropriate services.[114]

One might also question the assertion that Southern Cross received 'no public funding'. The frailty of this reasoning is readily demonstrable. Had Birmingham offered Southern Cross a rent free building to accommodate residents and so paid the company a much lower weekly fee for its s 21 placements, the public funding paid would be both obvious and substantial. If Southern Cross pays for its own buildings by using a portion of the much higher fee it therefore charged to Birmingham, the element of public funding is less obvious but no less substantial.[115]

---

[114] The majority did accept that private service providers which exercised coercive powers over their 'customers' might be public authorities in respect of some of their functions. The obvious examples would be privatised prisons or hospitals accommodating people detained under mental health legislation.

[115] See also Lord Mance at para 105: 'Public funding takes various forms. The injection of capital or subsidy into an organisation in return for undertaking a non-commercial role may be one thing: payment for services under a contractual arrangement with a company aiming to profit commercially thereby is potentially quite another': and Lord Neuberger at para 165: 'It seems to me much easier to invoke public funding to support the notion that a service is a function of a 'public nature' where the funding effectively subsidises, in whole or in part, the cost of the service as a whole, rather than consisting of payment for the provision of that service to a specific person'.

Some indication that the minority position in *YL* was closer to the Blair government's perception of what types of activities the public authority concept was supposed to cover was given immediately after the judgment, when the government announced that legislation would be promoted to designate care providers such as Southern Cross as public authorities for HRA s 6 purposes.[116]

Weaver v London and Quadrant Housing (2008)

Shortly after *YL* was decided, the High Court surprisingly produced a much more expansive application of the public authority concept in *R (on the application of Weaver) v London and Quadrant Housing Trust*.[117] Ms Weaver was an 'assured tenant' of London and Quadrant. The assured tenancy regime is laid out in the Housing Act 1988, and includes a provision (known as 'ground 8') which gave landlords an absolute right to regain possession of a leased property if the tenant is more than eight weeks in arrears with her rent when proceedings are begun and at the date of the trial. London and Quadrant began ground 8 proceedings against Ms Weaver, whose sole defence to the claim was that she had a substantive legitimate expectation that such proceedings would only be initiated as a last resort.

To argue that point, Ms Weaver had to establish either that London and Quadrant was amenable to judicial review or/and that it was a public authority. Given the High Court's judgment in *Servite Housing* and that of the House of Lords in *YL*, it might have been thought that both arguments would be difficult to make out.

London and Quadrant is a charity, its purpose being to provide housing. It also had the status of a 'registered social landlord' ('RSL'). It is not a body created by statute, nor (unlike Poplar HARCA) did it come into being following privatisation of council housing stock. Nevertheless, the High Court[118] held that London and Quadrant was both a public authority within HRA s 6 and amenable to judicial review in respect of its housing management functions. Several factors led to this conclusion.

Firstly, London and Quadrant received substantial financial support from the Housing Corporation (a government body) to buy or develop new properties. Secondly, most of its lettings were to persons nominated by local authorities; and as an RSL it was statutorily required to co-operate with local authorities for this purpose. Thirdly, as a charity, London and Quadrant could not be categorised as a commercial, profit-making (and thus presumptively private for HRA purposes) organisation. Fourthly, perhaps most importantly, the thrust of recent government housing policy had been to have RSLs increasingly take over the role of providing low cost accommodation previously performed by local councils.[119]

The judgment is significant in practical terms. Its immediate effect would provide tenant defendants in possession proceedings with grounds of defence—namely the various grounds of judicial review—which would not previously have been available to them. In many circumstances, these grounds would add little to the explicit statutory protection which Parliament has granted to housing association tenants. But since that protection does not extend to all such tenants in all situations, nor to residents who were not tenants at all, *Weaver* introduced a significant change to domestic residential possession law.

The conclusion reached by the High Court in *Weaver* was subsequently upheld by the Court of Appeal.[120] The Court of Appeal suggested however that the proper way to analyse such a

---

[116] The Health and Social Care Act 2008 s 148. On the broader issue of the impact of privatisation of public services on HRA protections see Donnelly C (2010) 'Positive obligations and privatisation' *Northern Ireland Legal Quarterly* 209.   [117] [2008] EWHC 1377 (Admin), [2009] 1 All ER 17.

[118] Sitting as a two judge court; Richards LJ and Swift J.

[119] As noted in ch 10, this policy shift was initiated by the Thatcher governments in the 1980s. The trend was continued by the Blair and Brown administrations; see '"Opting out" and Housing Action Trusts', ch 10, pp 276–277.   [120] [2009] EWCA Civ 587, [2010] 1 WLR 363.

case was to consider whether the claimant's attempt to evict the defendant from her home was a 'public function' for s 6 purposes rather than whether the claimant was per se a 'public authority'. That reasoning is of course wholly consistent with the *Aston Cantlow* judgment.

In more general terms, the cases discussed in this section could be taken to suggest that the courts have got into something of a muddle in respect of the meaning which should be accorded to the public authority concept. But even an entirely coherent body of authority on this issue would not settle the question as to the reach of the Human Rights Act. Of equal significance on that point is how the courts have dealt with what were referred to earlier as 'scenario 3' and 'scenario 4' situations.

Imposing Convention Rights on private individuals and organisations

The Court of Appeal's judgment in *Wilson v First County Trust (No 2)*[121] took a conservative approach to the impact of s 3. The House of Lords saw no need to tackle that issue as it concluded that the HRA did not impact upon the contract in question and in any event the relevant statutory provision was compatible with the Convention. But the decision also has implications for the Act's reach into the ostensibly 'private' sphere.

Wilson concerned the construction of the Consumer Credit Act 1974 s 127. Insofar as s 127 regulates the relationship between private lenders and borrowers it creates a 'horizontal' relationship. The Court of Appeal however (without evidently giving any thought to the horizontality question) 'verticalised' the dispute by in effect treating the first instance judgment as the defendant on appeal.[122] The Court (whether by design or happy accident is not clear) cut through much of the conceptual difficulty attending the horizontal/vertical effect debate by essentially making Parliament—in the sense of s 127 as construed by the trial court—the 'defendant'. The action in the case was 'horizontal' only inasmuch as Ms Wilson provided the procedural peg on which the substantive argument as to the compatibility of the Consumer Credit Act 1974 s 127 with the Convention (Right) could be hung. The question of horizontality was not pursued before the House of Lords. To put the point differently; one issue of principle which could be extracted from *Wilson* is that Human Rights Act litigation in which the substance of the relationship between the parties turns on the interpretation of statutory provisions is always 'vertical' in nature irrespective of the identity of the parties.[123]

The same conclusion can be drawn from *Mendoza*. No issue was taken by either counsel or the various courts which heard *Mendoza* as to the 'horizontality' of the action. Mr Mendoza's landlord was not a public authority in either a core or functional sense. Mr Ghaidan had conceded the point that the HRA was applicable to the case because of the interactive effect of the court's twin obligations under s 3 to read the relevant provisions of the Rent Act in a Convention compliant fashion and under s 6 (qua public authority) not to act in an unlawful manner unless required to do so by primary legislation. The point was best put by Keene LJ in the Court of Appeal:[124]

> [37] . . . First, the concession made on behalf of the respondent that the appellant's rights under the European Convention on Human Rights are relevant to the construction of para 2 of Sch 1 to the Rent Act 1977, even though this is litigation between two private individuals, was a proper one. Section 6(1) of the Human Rights Act 1998 ('the 1998 Act') makes it unlawful for a public authority to act in a way which is incompatible with a Convention right, and by virtue of s 6(3)(a) this court is

---

[121] [2001] EWCA Civ 633, [2002] QB 74, [2001] 3 WLR 42.

[122] [2002] QB 74 at paras 18–19; per Sir Andrew Morrit VC.

[123] This would not require the conclusion that *Leonard Cheshire* was wrongly decided. In that case, there was no direct statutory relationship between the Foundation and the applicant; the parties were indirectly linked together through their respective statutory relationships with a local authority.

[124] [2002] EWCA Civ 1533, [2003] Ch 380.

a public authority. It follows that this court cannot act incompatibly with a Convention right, unless (see s 6(2)) the court is acting to give effect to or enforce provisions of or made under primary legislation which cannot be read or given effect in a way which is compatible with such a right. [38] That patently takes one to s 3 of the 1998 Act, with its obligation on the court to read and give effect to primary and secondary legislation in a way compatible with Convention rights 'so far as it is possible to do so'. . . .

On this analysis of the HRA—which was not questioned in the House of Lords—the 'real' defendant in *Ghaidan v Mendoza*, as in *Wilson*, was the statutory term which mandated a particular outcome in any dispute between private parties in the respective positions of the litigants.

If the HRA is read this way, the designation of courts as 'public authorities' within HRA s 6 simply reiterates their s 3 obligation when questions of statutory interpretation arise. The consequences of the courts' designation as 'public authorities' within s 6 for the purposes of 'horizontalising' Convention Rights in actions between private parties then becomes pertinent only in litigation which raises the question of whether existing common law rules should be modified or—if the court faces a legal void—whether new common law rules should be recognised/created to limit the autonomy of private parties in their dealings with each other. The initial case law suggested that the courts might be inclined de facto—but not de jure—to give certain Convention Rights horizontal effect.

As noted in ch 20, the House of Lords had suggested in *Reynolds* that the HRA might trigger important developments in the common law.[125] Immediately prior to the HRA coming into force, Sedley LJ in *Redmond-Bate v Director of Public Prosecutions*[126] (a judgment dealing with the inter-relationship between freedom of expression and the common law concept of breach of the peace)—echoed the suggestion that the HRA would have a significant impact on the content of the common law:

(10) . . . Parliament has now enacted the Human Rights Act 1998, requiring every public authority, including the police and the courts, to give effect to the scheduled Convention rights unless statutory provision makes it impossible to do so. The bulk of the Act is not yet in force: Ministers have announced their intention to bring it into force on October 2, 2000. But in this interregnum it is far from immaterial. *Not only is it now accepted that the common law should seek compatibility with the values of the Convention insofar as it does not already share them; executive action which breaches the Convention already runs the risk, if uncorrected by law, of putting the United Kingdom in breach of the Convention and rendering it liable to proceedings before the European Court of Human Rights.* There is, therefore, and has been for a long time, good reason for policing and law in this field to respect the Convention . . . (emphasis added).

(13) To speak of rights at all in this context is to recognise *the constitutional shift which is now in progress* . . . (emphasis added).

Sedley LJ subsequently sat in one of the first HRA cases before the Court of Appeal. The applicants in *Douglas and Zeta-Jones v Hello! Ltd*[127] were unlikely candidates for the roles of flag-bearers of a right to privacy in English law. As noted earlier, prior to 2000 neither the courts nor Parliament had thought it desirable to introduce such a law.[128] Douglas and Zeta-Jones, both film stars, had signed a lucrative deal with a popular magazine—*OK*—for exclusive coverage of their wedding. Elaborate security precautions were established to prevent any unauthorised photos or sound recordings being made. Another magazine, *Hello!*, nonetheless acquired photos of the event and planned to publish them. Douglas and Zeta-Jones then successfully sought an injunction to prevent publication.

---

125 'Conclusion', ch 20, p 537.   126 ((QBD) [2000] HRLR 249.   127 [2001] QB 967, CA.
128 See the discussion of *Malone* at '*Malone v Metropolitan Police Commissioner* (1979)', ch 17, pp 459–460.

The Court of Appeal subsequently lifted the injunction, but did so in a judgment which seemed to have significant implications for both the emergence of a right to privacy at common law and the likely horizontal impact of the HRA. All three judges (Sedley, Brooke, and Keene LJJ) appeared to approve the approach to horizontality advocated by Pannick and Lester;[129] namely that the courts should see the HRA as providing a legislative spur for more rapid development of common law principles.[130] For Sedley LJ, the spur was sufficient for him to accept that; 'We have reached a point at which it can be said with confidence that the law recognises and will appropriately protect a right of personal privacy.'[131] Keene LJ appeared to endorse this view. Brooke LJ adopted a more conservative approach, preferring to conclude that the claimants would find a remedy in an extended version of the tort of breach of confidence.

The subtleties of the various judgments prompted divergent analyses of the degree of horizontalisation which the Act might subsequently attain.[132] Even cautiously construed however, *Douglas and Zeta-Jones* supports the proposition that the HRA has provided a stimulus to the courts to stretch existing common law principles to cover interferences with Convention Rights by bodies other than 'public authorities'. The Court considered that the existing law of breach of confidence could extend in these circumstances to protect the claimant's Art 2 and Art 8 rights.

Further powerful support for that viewpoint was provided by a High Court judgment— *Venables v Newsgroup Newspapers Ltd.*[133] Venables had been convicted of murder when a child. He was shortly to be released from imprisonment, and feared he would be the subject of vigilante vengeance attacks if his identity and whereabouts became matters of public knowledge. He therefore sought an injunction against all media sources to prevent publication of any information that could reveal his new identity and home, on the basis that such publicity would unacceptably jeopardise his right to privacy under Art 8 and his right to life under Art 2.

Dame Butler Sloss P followed the reasoning in *Douglas* in drawing the following conclusion:

> That obligation [ie of s 6(1)] on the court does not seem to me to encompass the creation of a free standing cause of action based directly on the articles of the convention. . . . The duty on the court, in my view, is to act compatibly with convention rights in adjudicating on existing common law causes of action, and that includes a positive as well as a negative obligation.[134]

The House of Lords subsequently addressed this issue in *Wainright v Home Office*.[135] *Wainright* was not a case in which horizontality was strictly in issue, as the defendant was a public authority. However the judgment offered guidance as to the intensely important question in respect of both 'horizontal' and 'vertical' actions of whether or not the HRA directly or indirectly created a right to privacy at common law. The claimants had been strip searched—in a fashion which breached Home Office guidelines—while visiting a family member in prison. One had

---

[129] See 'A division of academic opinion on the horizontal effect issue ?', ch 20, pp 531–532.

[130] Cf Sedley LJ [2001] QB 967 at 1002; '[I]f the step from confidentiality to privacy is not simply a modern restatement of the scope of a known protection but a legal innovation—then I would accept . . . that this is precisely the kind of incremental change for which the Human Rights Act is designed . . .' : Keene LJ at 1011: '[T]he courts as a public authority cannot act in a way which is incompatible with a convention right: s 6(1). That arguably includes their activity in interpreting and developing the common law, even where no public authority is a party to the litigation'.   [131] [2001] QB 967 at 997.

[132] See Moreham N (2001) '*Douglas v Hello! Ltd*—the protection of privacy in English private law' *MLR* 767: Young A (2002) 'Remedial and substantive horizontality: the common law and *Douglas v Hello! Ltd*' *Public Law* 232. On subsequent developments see Beyleveld D and Pattinson S (2002) 'Horizontal applicability' *LQR* 623; Morgan J (2002) 'Questioning the "true effect" of the Human Rights Act' *Legal Studies* 259.

[133] [2001] Fam 430.   [134] Ibid, at 446.   [135] [2003] UKHL 53, [2004] 2 AC 406.

been subject to a battery which caused him psychiatric damage. The other claimant had not been the victim of a battery, but was left feeling humiliated by the search. That one claimant had an existing remedy in damages in respect of the battery was uncontentious. The difficult point before the House of Lords was whether the claimants also had an action for breach of privacy.

The House of Lords rejected the assertion that English law should recognise a general remedy for breach of privacy in English law. The Court approvingly referred to Megarry VC's analysis in *Malone*[136] to explain why it was inappropriate for such an initiative to be taken at common law. Nor did the Court consider that such a wide-ranging right was required by the Convention. Its reading of the ECtHR's jurisprudence led it to conclude that what was required was that remedies be available to deal with specific instances of breaches of Art 8. Nor, on the facts, did the Court accept that a breach of Art 8 had even occurred. That the claimants were distressed or humiliated by the search did not in itself amount to an invasion of the claimants' privacy entitlement under the ECHR.

The contention that the HRA could not found 'new' causes of action at common law might however be qualified (as a matter of substance if not of form) by the House of Lords' judgment in *Campbell v MGN*.[137] In *Campbell*, the Court held (unanimously in principle but by a three to two majority on the facts) that the model Naomi Campbell had a remedy in breach of confidence in respect of the publication by a newspaper of photographs of her attending a drug rehabilitation programme. This conclusion had a radical effect on the substance of the common law. The tort of breach of confidence had previously been assumed to require a pre-existing relationship between the parties which per se generated an expectation of confidence, as between a husband and wife or an employer and employee for example. In *Campbell*, the House of Lords accepted that a pre-existing relationship was unnecessary. What was important was the nature of the information disclosed. There is certainly force to the argument that the judgment effectively created a new tort rather than simply extended an existing one.

In respect of the broader issue of the HRA's impact on the propriety of courts altering the common law, two passages of the judgment are especially significant. Lord Nicholls observed at para 19:

> In applying this approach, and giving effect to the values protected by article 8, courts will often be aided by adopting the structure of article 8 in the same way as they now habitually apply the Strasbourg court's approach to article 10 when resolving questions concerning freedom of expression. *Articles 8 and 10 call for a more explicit analysis of competing considerations* than the three traditional requirements of the cause of action for breach of confidence identified in *Coco v A N Clark (Engineers) Ltd* [1969] RPC 41; (emphasis added).

Lord Hope made the same substantive point at para 86:

> The language has changed following the coming into operation of the Human Rights Act 1998 and the incorporation into domestic law of article 8 and article 10 of the Convention. We now talk about the right to respect for private life and the countervailing right to freedom of expression. The jurisprudence of the European Court offers important guidance as to how these competing rights ought to be approached and analysed. I doubt whether the result is that the centre of gravity, as my noble and learned friend, Lord Hoffmann, says, has shifted. *It seems to me that the balancing exercise to which that guidance is directed is essentially the same exercise, although it is plainly now more carefully focused and more penetrating.* (emphasis added).

---

[136] '*Malone v Metropolitan Police Commissioner* (1979)', ch 17, pp 459–460.

[137] [2004] UKHL 22, [2004] AC 457. For (a very) critical comment see Morgan J (2004) 'Privacy in the House of Lords, again' *LQR* 563.

Nor did the House of Lords (per Lord Nicholls) see any difficulty in applying this concept in an action between private parties:

> 17 . . . The values embodied in articles 8 and 10 are as much applicable in disputes between individuals or between an individual and a non-governmental body such as a newspaper as they are in disputes between individuals and a public authority.
>
> 18 . . . It is sufficient to recognise that the values underlying articles 8 and 10 are not confined to disputes between individuals and public authorities. This approach has been adopted by the courts in several recent decisions, reported and unreported, where individuals have complained of press intrusion.

Although these cases deal primarily with privacy entitlements, there is no obvious barrier to the concepts of a 'more explicit analysis of competing considerations'(per Lord Nicholls) or a 'more carefully focused and more penetrating' balancing exercise (per Lord Hope) being of general application. The very nature of common law reasoning is to find the proper balance for the law to strike between competing considerations. The effect of HRA s 2 is to make the ECtHR's views on the meaning of Convention articles a matter which must be taken into account by domestic courts in determining the meaning of Convention Rights. The s 2 duty is no less applicable when common law rules rather than statutory provisions are in issue. Common law rules formulated without adequate judicial attention being given to such considerations will necessarily be subject to re-evaluation when they come before the courts.[138]

The principle articulated by Lord Nicholls and Lord Hope in *Campbell* is the methodological equivalent—when common law rules are before the court—of the HRA s 3 requirement imposed on the courts in respect of statutory provisions. That this duty in respect of the common law may sensibly be seen as a corollary of the court's obligations under HRA s 3 in respect of statutory provisions is underlined in the Court of Appeal's judgment in *HRH Prince of Wales v Associated Newspapers Ltd*:[139]

> 25 . . . Section 3 of the Human Rights Act 1998 requires the court, so far as it is possible, to read and give effect to legislation in a manner which is compatible with the Convention rights. *The English court has recognised that it should also, in so far as possible, develop the common law in such a way as to give effect to Convention rights. In this way horizontal effect is given to the Convention.* This would seem to accord with the view of the European Court of Human Rights as to the duty of the court as a public authority . . . ; (emphasis added).

An alternative framework for analysis

The extent to which the HRA has a horizontal impact has presented the courts with a difficult question to which we have thus far been given a complex answer. Several propositions might however be advanced.

Firstly, where the substantive outcome of litigation is dependent upon the meaning attached to a statutory provision, the identity of the parties is irrelevant. All such situations are lent a vertical character by s 3.

Secondly, the courts have adopted a sufficiently expansive approach to the meaning of 'public authority' per s 6 to ensure that some notionally horizontal actions acquire a vertical character because of the identity of the claimant/defendant.

---

[138] Cf. Clayton R and Tomlinson H (2nd edn, 2008) *The law of human rights* at 5.136–5.137:

(5) The impact on the common law and rules of precedent

5.136 The inclusion of the court as a public authority under section 6(3) of the HRA places the court under a duty to ensure that the common law is not developed incompatibly with Convention rights . . . 5.137 One of the most striking effects of the HRA has been its impact on the law of precedent. The Act comprehensively affects most areas of English law: and requires that common law principles be re-examined in the light of the new approach . . . .

[139] [2007] EWHC 522 (Ch), [2008] Ch 57 per Lord Phillips CJ.

Thirdly, if no statutory provision is in issue and neither party is a public authority, the court qua public authority per HRA s 6:

(a) is obliged where the substantive outcome of the case is dependent on an existing rule of common law to alter that rule of common law to ensure that the common law is Convention Right-compliant;

(b) is obliged where the existing common law does not produce a Convention Right-compliant outcome but could do so if it were extended in a modest and orderly fashion to make that extension;

(c) is not obliged, where no extendable rule of common law exists, to create an entirely new rule to render the relationship between the parties Convention Right-compliant.

This perspective takes us towards the universalistic understanding of HRA horizontality favoured by Professor Wade and Murray Hunt. The strength of these analyses is that they invite us to see the identification of 'courts' in s 6 as being concerned primarily with a jurisdictional rather than institutional phenomenon. From this viewpoint, the target of s 6 is not the (common) law-maker but what the (common) law-maker makes. The target is the (common) law. And the court acts unlawfully if it creates (or for the more traditionally minded 'discovers') or applies a rule of common laws incompatible with a Convention Right.

One might however analyse this understanding of the notion of 'horizontal' effect rather differently. A better way of framing the issue may be to identify four types of 'verticality'—only one of which is concerned with the identity of the parties. Type 1 arises when the party allegedly contravening a Convention Right is a public authority. Type 2 occurs when the outcome of litigation depends upon the meaning given by the court to a legislative provision. Type 3 is in issue when the outcome of litigation depends upon the meaning given by the court to an existing rule of common law. And type 4 comes into play when the outcome of litigation depends on the courts' capacity to extend an existing rule of common law.

The House of Lords/Supreme Court has been reluctant to offer any definitive view on this question. The matter will no doubt fall to be decided within the next few years. But the only certain conclusion which might yet be drawn is that the precise nature of the horizontal impact of the Act will at least in the short term continue to be a subject on which much judicial and academic attention will be focused.

III. Proportionality as a ground of review of executive action

Domestic courts have traditionally been unwillingly (at least overtly) to apply proportionality as a ground of review of executive action. It is quite clear however that the 'necessary in a democratic society' test used in many provisions of the Convention may require that courts subject the merits of government action to more rigorous scrutiny than required by orthodox principles of English administrative law. This proposition has been endorsed cautiously by domestic courts, with the result that government actions interfering with Convention Rights will in some circumstances be subjected to 'proportionality' review. Much the larger—and more difficult question—is just what the notion of 'proportionality' might mean.

The initial judicial response: the *Daly* and *Alconbury* cases

This development is well-illustrated by the House of Lords' judgment in *R (Daly) v Secretary of State for the Home Department*.[140] The case concerned the legality of a policy adopted by the Home Secretary to exclude prisoners from their cells while the cells were being searched.

---

[140] [2001] UKHL 26, [2001] 2 AC 532.

Mr Daly contended that the policy breached Art 8, inasmuch as such searches could be conducted even if the prisoner had legally privileged correspondence in his cell at the time. The policy had been adopted to minimise the possibility that searches for contraband material could be compromised by prisoners being able to intimidate or obstruct prison officers during the search. These are obviously rational objectives, and there would be little scope for thinking such a policy *Wednesbury/GCHQ* irrational. Daly's challenge was tightly focused: he argued that it was not 'necessary' per Art 8(2) to achieve those objectives to leave privileged correspondence in the cell during the search.

Lord Steyn framed the issue in the following way:

> There is an overlap between the traditional grounds of review [irrationality] and the approach of proportionality. Most cases would be decided in the same way whichever approach is adopted. But the intensity of review is somewhat greater under the proportionality approach . . .[141]

The primary distinction between the two approaches was, in Lord Steyn's view, that: 'the doctrine of proportionality may require the reviewing court to assess the balance which the decision-maker has struck, not merely whether it is within the range of rational or reasonable decisions'.[142] On the facts, the House of Lords suggested that the policy was disproportionate. To comply with Art 8, the policy should be modified to permit legally privileged correspondence to be safely sealed prior to any search.

Both Lord Steyn and Lord Bingham indicated that proportionality review would arise in respect of Convention Rights as a result of the requirements imposed on the courts by the HRA. They did not advocate that it should be accepted as a principle of domestic common law. Lord Cooke's concurring judgment took that larger step. He concluded that Lord Greene MR's very loose test of irrationality in *Wednesbury*: 'was an unfortunately retrogressive decision in English administrative law, in so far as it suggested that there are degrees of unreasonableness and that only a very extreme degree can bring an administrative decision within the legitimate scope of judicial invalidation'.[143]

Lord Slynn adopted a similar viewpoint—not expressly shared by his colleagues—in *R (Alconbury Developments) v Secretary of State for the Environment*.[144] The case concerned the compatibility of the land use planning system with Art 6 HRA, and in particular the degree of judicial scrutiny applied to planning decisions taken by the Secretary of State for the Environment in which central government had a financial interest. The House of Lords concluded in *Alconbury* that if a Convention Right was engaged by a government decision that could be characterised as being a 'policy' matter, a loose regime of judicial supervision akin to *Wednesbury* irrationality might suffice to make the overall process Convention Right compliant; that is, for such decisions proportionality review in a more searching or rigorous sense would not be required to satisfy the 'necessary in a democratic society' element of the HRA's various articles.

The House of Lords initially also applied that latter rationale to more individuated decisions in the context of housing law. In *Harrow LBC v Qazi*,[145] a majority held that Art 8 made no difference at all to the rigour with which a court should review a local council's decision to seek possession of a house from an occupant who lacked statutory security of tenure. Proportionality review was not required: the traditional understanding of *Wednesbury* would suffice. That proposition was repeated two years later in *LB Lambeth v Kay*.[146]

---

[141] [2001] 2 AC 532 at 547.   [142] [2001] 2 AC 532.   [143] Ibid, at 549.

[144] [2001] UKHL 23, [2003] 2 AC 295.   [145] [2003] UKHL 43, [2004] 1 AC 983.

[146] [2006] UKHL 10, [2006] 2 AC 465. *Qazi* and *Kay* were discussed from a different perspective at 'And deference to the ECtHR?', pp 555–557.

A more elaborate approach: the *Denbigh High School* and *Miss Behavin* cases

'Proportionality' is an umbrella term. It could bear a purely substantive meaning, entailing only a narrowing of the range of permissible substantive outcomes that a government body might produce compared to the range possible under the more expansive notion of irrationality. Proportionality in that sense necessarily entails an effective shift of decision-making power as to matters of substance from the executive to the courts. But the shift could be significant or trivial, depending upon the extent to which the range of outcomes is narrowed. A second form of proportionality review might entail a procedural enhancement of judicial control over executive behaviour by insisting that an executive body's decision-making process goes through certain specified steps and/or that a particular set of factors are taken into account before the substance of the decision is determined. Proportionality in that sense increases the likelihood that government decisions will fall within a narrower range than is permissible under irrationality review, but does not guarantee that they will do so. This approach to proportionality necessarily entails an effective shift of decision-making power as to matters of procedure from the executive to the courts, but does not necessarily rebalance powers in substantive terms.

The approach taken by the Convention and the ECtHR to proportionality review combines both procedural (that a government decision pursues one of more of various specified objectives) and substantive (that it interferes no more than is 'necessary' with Convention entitlements) elements.[147] In *Alconbury* and *Daly*, the House of Lords approach to proportionality view within the context of HRA litigation appeared to be concerned primarily, perhaps wholly, with matters of substance; that is, that proportionality was simply what we might call an 'outcome value'. Shortly thereafter, however, the Court of Appeal suggested that a procedural approach to proportionality review was also required; that is, that proportionality might also be a 'process value'.

The applicant in *R (SB) v Governors of Denbigh High School*[148] was a schoolgirl whose adherence to a particular understanding of Islam led her to feel that she could only attend a school which allowed her to wear a form of clothing known as a jilbab. The students at the (state) school were predominantly Muslim in religious orientation, as was the headteacher and several of the school governors. The relevant statutory regime left the power to decide whether state schools would have a uniform to the governing bodies of individual schools. The governing body at Denbigh High had consulted widely on its uniform policy, and had adopted various options, including a shalwar kamazee for girls considered consistent with mainstream Islamic beliefs as to appropriate dress for girls. The uniform policy had been in force before the applicant entered the school, and she had complied with it for some years. There were several other state schools nearby where the jilbab was permitted.

The applicant contended that the school's refusal to allow her to wear the jilbab breached her entitlements under Art 9 to manifest her religious beliefs.[149] That contention seemed extravagant given existing ECtHR authority, which indicated—primarily in the context of employment cases—that Art 9 was not engaged, still less breached, by restrictions on

---

[147] See 'The jurisprudential methodology of the convention' ff, ch 18, pp 480–483.

[148] [2006] UKHL 15, [2007] 1 AC 100.

[149] **Article 9. Freedom of thought, conscience and religion**

1   Everyone has the right to freedom of thought, conscience and religion; this right includes freedom to change his religion or belief and freedom, either alone or in community with others and in public or private, to manifest his religion or belief, in worship, teaching, practice and observance.

2   Freedom to manifest one's religion or beliefs shall be subject only to such limitations as are prescribed by law and are necessary in a democratic society in the interests of public safety, for the protection of public order, health or morals, or for the protection of the rights and freedoms of others.

an individual's capacity to express her/his religious beliefs in circumstances where the individual was at liberty to seek other employment.[150] That view was taken by the High Court in *Denbigh*.[151]

However, the Court of Appeal[152] subsequently held that Art 9 was engaged on these facts, and that the school's policy was presumptively not 'necessary in a democratic society'—that is, that it failed the proportionality test—because in making the policy the school had not structured its decision-making procedure in the correct way:

> 75 The decision-making structure should therefore go along the following lines. (1) Has the claimant established that she has a relevant Convention right which qualifies for protection under article 9(1)? (2) Subject to any justification that is established under article 9(2), has that Convention right been violated? (3) Was the interference with her Convention right prescribed by law in the Convention sense of that expression? (4) Did the interference have a legitimate aim? (5) What are the considerations that need to be balanced against each other when determining whether the interference was necessary in a democratic society for the purpose of achieving that aim? (6) Was the interference justified under article 9(2)?[153]

This 'process value' understanding of proportionality did not exclude the possibility that the substance of the uniform policy could be reconciled with Art 9. It did however mean that a substantive choice to that effect could not be arrived at if it was not made through the *rigidly structured process* which the Court of Appeal laid down.

The Court of Appeal's reasoning was sharply criticised by several academic commentators.[154] The concern expressed was that it was wholly impracticable to expect all decision-makers in public authorities to adopt what was an essentially judicial approach to the decision-making process. This is a point strongly reminiscent of the judicial debate as to the content of the procedural fairness doctrine in the early part of the twentieth century.[155]

The approach was nonetheless followed in an Art 10 context in *Belfast City Council v Miss Behavin Ltd*[156] The case concerned a local authority power to licence sex shops in its area. Belfast City Council had refused to grant a licence to a shop owned by the Miss Behavin company in a particular neighbourhood. It had done so for a variety of reasons, any one or combination of which would certainly have meant that the decision was not irrational in a *Wednesbury* sense. The council's decision had not however been structured in a way that obviously considered and applied Art 10 criteria in a manner analogous to the test laid out in *Denbigh*. As in *Denbigh*, the Court of Appeal held that this failure to follow a tightly structured decision-making process rendered the decision itself disproportionate.

The Court of Appeal's judgments in both *Denbigh* and *Miss Behavin* were reversed in the House of Lords. The Lordships (unanimously in both cases) considered that the Court of Appeal had misunderstood the scope of the proportionality principle in HRA litigation. There was no basis for assuming that proportionality should be given a procedural meaning. Proportionality review should be concerned solely with *the result* of the decision-making process. It was an 'outcome value' not a 'process value':

> The Court of Appeal's decision-making prescription would be admirable guidance to a lower court or legal tribunal, but cannot be required of a head teacher and governors, even with a solicitor to help them. If, in such a case, it appears that such a body has conscientiously paid attention to all

---

[150] Cf *X v Denmark* (1976) 5 DR 157; *Kjeldsen v Denmark* (1976) 1 EHRR 711; *Ahmad v United Kingdom* (1981) 4 EHRR 126.   [151] [2004] EWHC 1389 (Admin), [2004] ELR 374.

[152] [2005] EWCA Civ 199, [2005] 1 WLR 3372.   [153] [2005] 1 WLR 3372 per Brooke LJ.

[154] See eg Poole T (2005) 'Of headscarfs and heresies: The *Denbigh High School* case and public authority decision-making under the Human Rights Act' *Public Law* 685.

[155] See 'The initial rise, dilution and fall of the *audi alterem partem* principle', ch 14, pp 383–387.

[156] In the High Court of Northern Ireland [2004] NIQB 61; in the Court of Appeal [2005] NICA 35, [2006] NI 181; in the House of Lords [2007] UKHL 19, [2007] 1 WLR 1420.

human rights considerations, no doubt a challenger's task will be the harder. But what matters in any case is the practical outcome, not the quality of the decision-making process that led to it.[157]

The judgments also confirmed that the intensity of review arising under the proportionality test might often be greater than required under the irrationality test.

The point is perhaps best put by Lord Bingham in *Denbigh*:

> 30 Secondly, it is clear that the court's approach to an issue of proportionality under the Convention must go beyond that traditionally adopted to judicial review in a domestic setting. The inadequacy of that approach was exposed in *Smith and Grady v United Kingdom* (1999) 29 EHRR 493 para 138, and the new approach required under the 1998 Act was described by Lord Steyn in *R (Daly) v Secretary of State for the Home Department* [2001] 2 AC 532, paras 25–28, in terms which have never to my knowledge been questioned. There is no shift to a merits review, but the intensity of review is greater than was previously appropriate, and greater even than the heightened scrutiny test adopted by the Court of Appeal in *R v Ministry of Defence, ex p Smith* [1996] QB 517, 554. The domestic court must now make a value judgment, an evaluation, by reference to the circumstances prevailing at the relevant time. . . .

In both cases, the House of Lords indicated that the relevant Convention Rights were not interfered with at all by the decisions in issue. But even if Arts 9 and 10 respectively were engaged, the House of Lords was satisfied that there were entirely credible reasons for both the school and the local authority to have reached the substantive conclusions that they did. In such circumstances, there could be no basis for concluding that the decisions were disproportionate.

Denbigh should be considered alongside the House of Lords' almost contemporaneous judgment in *Huang v Secretary of State for the Home Department*,[158] an immigration case. The claimant was an elderly Chinese lady who had been refused permission for indefinite leave to remain in the United Kingdom where her daughter, son-in-law, and grandchildren (all British citizens) resided, because she fell outside the scope of the Immigration Rules. At that time, the leading authority as to the intensity of review which should be applied to such a decision was the Court of Appeal's (2003) judgment in *Edore v Secretary of State for the Home Department*.[159] *Edore*, in a vein reminiscent of the House of Lords' view in *Qazi* and *Kay* of the impact of the HRA on council housing decision-making, had held that the Home Secretary's decision[160] need only be subject to review on orthodox grounds to satisfy the requirements of Art 8.

In *Huang*, a unanimous court rejected the Home Secretary's advocacy of that position. But the Court also seemed to go further than simply adopting the rather vague 'slightly more intensive' basis of review it had endorsed in *Denbigh*. Although the House of Lords did not suggest that the very tightly structured procedural notion of proportionality applied in *Denbigh* to the school should be imposed upon *the Home Secretary*, it did accept that a similarly structured approach should be taken *by any court or tribunal* which was assessing the lawfulness of the Home Secretary's decision. The Court drew on authority from several Commonwealth jurisdictions in holding that the reviewing court should ask itself: 'whether: (i) the legislative objective is sufficiently important to justify limiting a fundamental right; (ii) the measures designed to meet the legislative objective are rationally connected to it; and (iii) the means used to impair the right or freedom are no more than is necessary to accomplish the objective'.[161] The

---

[157] [2006] UKHL 15, [2007] 1 AC 100 at para 31, per Lord Bingham. That reasoning might not apply however if the Convention Right in issue was an entitlement to a particular type of procedure.

[158] [2007] UKHL 11, [2007] 2 AC 167.   [159] [2003] EWCA Civ 716, [2003] 1 WLR 2979.

[160] Formally the decision was the Home Secretary's. In practice the decision was made by an immigration officer. See the discussion of *Oladehinde* in 'Unlawful delegation of powers', ch 9 pp 361–365.

[161] [2007] UKHL 11, [2007] 2 AC 167 at para 19.

Court also considered that this formulation should be supplemented by a final question which asked if a fair balance was being struck; 'between the rights of the individual and the interests of the community which is inherent in the whole of the Convention'.

The Court expressly rejected the Home Secretary's suggestion that the *Qazi/Kay* approach to HRA proportionality should apply in this context. One might have thought that one basis for distinguishing those two scenarios would be a 'hierarchy of rights' argument; that is, that what was at stake for Mrs Huang was far more important than what was at stake for Mr Qazi or Mr Kay. While that might have been an unspoken assumption on the court's part, its explicit reason for doing so was rooted in a facet of the deference question:

> [17] . . . The analogy is unpersuasive. Domestic housing policy has been a continuing subject of discussion and debate in Parliament over very many years, with the competing interests of land-lords and tenants fully represented, as also the public interest in securing accommodation for the indigent, averting homelessness and making the best use of finite public resources. The outcome, changed from time to time, may truly be said to represent a considered democratic compromise. This cannot be said in the same way of the Immigration Rules and supplementary instructions, which are not the product of active debate in Parliament, where non-nationals seeking leave to enter or remain are not in any event represented.

To put the matter rather simplistically, this early tranche of cases offered three different under-standings of 'proportionality' for HRA purposes. These were respectively what we might call: 'Changing orthodox administrative law principles is not required at all' (*Qazi/Kay*); 'The intensity of review is somewhat greater' (*Daly/Denbigh*); and 'Structured review' (*Huang*). These three categories manifestly have (at least presumptively) differing implications from a separation of powers perspective: *Kay* leaves the balance of power between the executive and the courts unchanged; *Denbigh* tilts the balance slightly in the courts' favour; and *Huang* tilts the balance in the courts' direction to a possibly significant extent. In formal doctrinal terms neither *Denbigh* proportionality nor *Huang* proportionality are problematic from a par-liamentary sovereignty viewpoint, since the judicial innovations are expressly rooted in the demands posed by the HRA itself.

For observers concerned with issues of legal certainty, a trichotomous response of this sort makes the question of allocating a challenged government decision to a particular category of review very important. The challenger's prospect of success likely increases as one moves up the scale of intensity of review from *Kay* to *Denbigh* to *Huang*. We return to the way in which the Supreme Court has more recently classified different types of governmental decisions for this purpose. Before doing so we might consider a trio of judgments which generated con-siderable confusion concerning the inter-relationship bewteen *Wednesbury* irrationality and HRA proportionality.

Blurring the issue? *Doherty* (2008), *Pinnock* (2009), and *Powell* (2010)

The question before the House of Lords in *Doherty v Birmingham City Council*,[162] as in *Qazi* and *Kay*, was what level of scrutiny should apply to a public authority landlord's decision to commence proceedings seeking possession of a person's home in circumstances where the relevant legal regime did not grant the trial court full jurisdiction over all matters of fact and law. Given that many thousands of such proceedings are issued every year, the answer to that question would be significant in a quantitative systemic sense. Unhappily, the various opinions offered by members of the Court in *Doherty* were—to put it kindly—rather lacking in clarity.

---

[162] [2008] UKHL 57, [2009] 1 AC 367.

At para 52 of his judgment, Lord Hope observed that the: 'grounds on which the decision to claim possession could be judicially reviewed were whether it was arbitrary, unreasonable or disproportionate'. This might be taken as suggesting that proportionality is being offered here as an *additional* ground of review. Then in para 53, Lord Hope refers only to *Wednesbury* unreasonableness as the basis of review. In para 55, Lord Hope seemed to approve a more intensive (than irrationality) version of proportionality: 'It would be unduly formalistic to confine the review strictly to traditional *Wednesbury* grounds'; and also to an endorsement of irrationality review: 'The test of reasonableness should be . . . whether the decision to recover possession was one which no reasonable person would consider justifiable'.

In para 70 Lord Scott used irrationality and proportionality interchangeably: 'The question for the court would be whether the local authority's decision to [seek to] recover possession of the property in question was so unreasonable and disproportionate as to be unlawful'. Such inter-changeability is hard to understand. A decision which is irrational will always be disproportion-ate, but it by no means follows that a decision which is disproportionate will be irrational. Matters become more uncertain in para 76, when Lord Scott stated that a public law challenge could not succeed unless the trial court considered that a decision to seek possession was: 'one to which the council could not reasonably have come'. That formula is redolent of the much-quoted Lord Greene MR definition of irrationality,[163] but para 76 continues by saying that if the decision passes the Lord Greene test then it would also be 'proportionate'. The analysis is repeated at para 85:

> . . . An article 8 defence requires the judge to review the lawfulness of the local authority's deci-sion to recover possession of the property in question and, in doing so, to review the factors that a responsible local authority ought to have taken into account in reaching its decision. The propor-tionality of the decision in all the circumstances of the case would be central to the review and if the local authority's decision could be shown to be outside the range of reasonable decisions that a responsible local authority could take, having regard both to the circumstances of the defendant as well as to all the other relevant circumstances, the decision would be held to be unlawful as a matter of public law.

Lord Mance (at para 135) referred with evident approval to the short line of 'anxious scrutiny' cases which predate the coming into force of the HRA,[164] and quoted Laws LJ's comment in *Begbie* that: 'The *Wednesbury* principle itself constitutes a sliding scale of review, more or less intrusive according to the nature and gravity of what is at stake'.[165] After suggesting that public authority landlords are also bound to regard respect for a person's home as a relevant consid-eration when exercising their discretion to initiate possession proceedings, Lord Mance then concluded (at para 136) that in possession proceedings the court should 'relax' *Wednesbury* perceptions of review so that trial courts engage in a 'more straightforward' examination of reasonableness than the orthodox understanding of irrationality would permit.

As noted earlier, *Doherty* was one of a long line of cases in which the House of Lords engaged in what we might (perhaps euphemistically) call a 'dialogue' with the ECtHR as to the require-ments of the proportionality principle in the context of residential possession proceedings. Shortly after *Doherty*, in *Manchester City Council v Pinnock*[166] the Supreme Court formally accepted that proportionality review was an element of Art 8 Sch 1 HRA in such litigation. Yet the Supreme Court also suggested that this 'new' level of review would affect the outcome only of 'very exceptional' cases. This might be thought a surprising assertion, which must rest on the presumption that there really is very little difference between proportionality and irrationality review. Guidance of this sort may prove rather difficult for trial courts to apply.

---

[163] See 'II. Irrationality', ch 13, pp 370–377.

[164] Especially *R v Secretary of State for the Home Department, Ex p Bugdaycay* [1987] AC 514.

[165] *R v Secretary of State for Education and Employment, Ex p Begbie* [2000] 1 WLR 1115 at 1130; cited in para 135 of *Doherty*.   [166] [2001] UKSC 6, [2010] 3 WLR 1441.

Shortly after *Pinnock*, in *Hounslow LBC v Powell*,[167] the Supreme Court firmly rejected the suggestion that *Huang's* 'structured' approach to proportionality should apply to possession proceedings:

> 41 A structured approach of the kind that Mr Luba [counsel for the defendant occupants] was suggesting may be appropriate, and indeed desirable, in some contexts such as that of immigration . . . But in the context of a statutory regime that has been deliberately designed by Parliament, for sound reasons of social policy, so as not to provide the occupier with a secure tenancy it would be wholly inappropriate. I agree with Mr Stilitz for the Secretary of State that to require the local authority to plead its case in this way would largely collapse the distinction between secured and non-secure tenancies. It would give rise to the risk of prolonged and expensive litigation, which would divert funds from the uses to which they should be put to promote social housing in the area.

There is an obvious temptation to see *Pinnock/Powell's* analysis of Art 8 proportionality in the possession proceedings context as no more than dressing up orthodox understandings of *Wednesbury* substantive unreasonableness in differently labelled juridic clothes, and thus as being a mere symbolic initiative intendedly devoid of any practical effect: there is very little reported case law in which such a defence has succeeded; and there are many cases in which it has not.[168] But even if that view is correct in respect of this particular (and quantitatively very important) area of government activity, subsequent recent cases have indicated that the more general impact in doctrinal and practical terms of the 'irrationality vs proportionality' debate has been and will continue to be significant.

'Un-blurring' the issue? *Quila* (2012), *Pham* (2015), and *Keyu* (2016)

The claimants in *R (Aguilar Quila) v Home Secretary*[169] were a young married couple, who had married when Mr Quila was 18 and Mrs Quila 17. Mrs Quila was a British citizen, and her husband was Chilean. They wished to live together in Britain, but were prevented from doing so by an immigration policy recently adopted by the Brown/Blair governments which imposed a simple rule that spouses or civil partners of British citizens would not be permitted to enter the United Kingdom if either spouse/partner was under 21 years old. (The policy was adopted in 2008. Before then, a similar policy had applied but with an age limit of 18 years.)[170] The policy was—according to the government—introduced not to control immigration per se, but to discourage the practice of forced marriage.[171] There was no suggestion that the Quila marriage was forced in any way, but since the policy permitted no exceptions the claimants would have to wait until Mr Quila was 21 before he could apply for admission to the United Kingdom.

The Supreme Court had no difficulty in accepting that the policy interfered with the Quilas' Art 8 right to respect for their family life, and did so in a very serious manner: they had been subjected to: 'a colossal interference with [their] rights to respect for their family life'.[172]. It was equally clear that the lawfulness of the policy required that the policy be proportionate. The taxing question was whether 'proportionate' should have a '*Denbigh*' or '*Huang*' meaning in this context.

---

[167] [2011] UKSC 8, [2011] 2 AC 186.

[168] See the discussion in Loveland I (2017) 'Twenty years later—assessing the significance of the Human Rights Act 1988 to residential possession proceedings' *The Conveyancer and Property Lawyer* 174.

[169] [2011] UKSC 45, [2012] 1 AC 621.

[170] When the case reached the Supreme Court, the Cameron/Clegg coalition government was in power. That administration had adopted the former policy.

[171] The rationale supposedly being that young British women—primarily of south Asian ethnicity—were being subject to forced marriages as a means for foreign men to sidestep immigration controls. That would clearly be a legitimate objective in the Art 8 sense, and the clarity of the policy meant that it was also prescribed by law for Art 8 purposes.   [172] [2011] UKSC 45 at para 32 per Lord Wilson for the majority.

Writing for the majority, Lord Wilson referred to both the *Denbigh* and *Huang* judgments and clearly adopted the latter approach.[173] In part that conclusion was surely driven by a 'hierarchy of rights' concern—the Quilas had suffered a 'colossal' interference with their Art 8 rights. However the majority devoted a great deal of attention to assessing if the new policy had what Lord Wilson referred to—harking back to *Huang*—as: 'the imprimatur of democratic approval'.[174]

In Lord Wilson's view, the question for the Home Secretary to address was to balance the benefits that the policy would produce in terms of deterring forced marriages against the burdens it would create in terms of delaying or preventing genuine marriages. The key failing which Lord Wilson identified in the Home Secretary's position was that she had no sound evidential basis to conclude that any benefits accruing from the new policy would not be outweighed—perhaps substantially—by the burdens it would impose. The majority attached particular importance to a Commons Home Affairs Select Committee report published in response to the Home Office's proposed change to the policy which suggested there was no good evidence as to how many forced marriages would be prevented by altering the age limit. The report called for further research to provide conclusive evidence that the policy presumptions were soundly based. Lord Wilson concluded that the Home Secretary's response to this report was: 'wholly inadequate'.[175]

The significant rebalancing of decision-making power from the executive to the judiciary triggered by the intensive variant of proportionality adopted by the majority in *Quila* is forcefully illustrated by the passage[176] in which Lord Wilson set ten questions which would have had to be addressed and properly answered by the government in order for a view to be formed on whether the merits of the new policy would outweigh its drawbacks. The ten questions were of the court's own devising. In effect, they amounted to a rigorous judicial cross-examination of the evidential adequacy of the Home Secretary's decision-making process. Lord Wilson was far from satisfied on that point, and concluded by adapting an oft-used proportionality metaphor: 'On any view [the new policy] is a sledgehammer, but she has not attempted to identify the size of the nut'.[177]

It is (just about) conceivable that a court could have found the Home Secretary's new policy unlawful on the orthodox basis that since she did not have evidence as to the number of forced marriages that would be deterred she had failed to take account of a relevant consideration. But there could be no justification for the court's 'ten question' methodology within traditional understandings of the judicial review function. Nor is it credible to argue that the new policy would be *Wednesbury* irrational in the normal sense of the principle, even if the policy had been premised on the assumption that many more genuine marriages would be delayed than forced marriages prevented. Such a policy might in such circumstances be silly, or mean-spirited, or counter-productive; but that would not make it irrational.[178] *Quila* therefore stands as a powerful example of the way in which the HRA has altered the balance of power between the different branches of government.

The claimant in *Pham v Secretary of State for the Home Department*[179] was born in Vietnam in 1983, and as such became a Vietnamese citizen. His family subsequently emigrated to Britain when he was a child, and Mr Pham acquired British Nationality in 1995. In 2011, the

---

[173] See especially his comment at para 46: 'Lord Brown's [dissenting] call at para 91 below, for the courts in this contest to afford a government a very substantial area of discretionary judgment is at odds with my understanding of the nature of their duty'.   [174] [2012] 1 AC 621.

[175] Ibid, at para 27.   [176] At paras 49–55.

[177] At para 59. See also what we might call the 'We have no idea . . .' passage in Baroness Hale's judgment at paras 75–76.

[178] Cf 'Irrationality as a "substantive" concept: assessing "the merits" of a governmental decision', ch 13 pp 370–375.

[179] [2015] UKSC 19, [2015] 1 WLR 1591. Readers seeking a more detailed picture of developments in this period might also refer to *Bank Mellat v HM Treasury (No 2)* [2013] UKSC 39, [2014] AC 700 and *Kennedy v Information Commissioner* [2014] UKSC 20, [2014] 2 WLR 808.

Home Secretary made an order against him under the British Nationality Act 1981 s 40(2) which deprived him of his British nationality and provided for his deportation on the basis that it was conducive to the public good.[180] Per s 40(4), such an order could not be made if it would render the person concerned stateless. The primary issue before the Court was whether or not Mr Pham was actually a Vietnamese citizen when the Home Secretary made her order. If he was a Vietnamese citizen, the s 40(2) order would not have made him stateless. The Court found in the government's favour on that question. For present purposes, the judgment is of interest for what was said by several members of the Court—especially Lords Mance and Sumption—both about the nature of proportionality review and about the desirability of taking a uniform approach to the question of substantive review irrespective of whether the point in issue concerned EU law, the HRA, or a purely domestic administrative law question.

Lord Mance reiterated the analysis he had offered the previous year in *Kennedy v Information Commissioner*: [181]

> [94] . . . The common law no longer insists on the uniform application of the rigid test of irrationality once thought applicable under the so-called Wednesbury principle: see Associated Provincial Picture Houses Ltd v Wednesbury Corpn [1948] 1 KB 223. The nature of judicial review in every case depends on the context.

This suggestion that drawing a sharp distinction between irrationality and proportionality was (becoming) a false dichotomy was underlined by Lord Mance's observation that 'fundamental' rights (such as, here, not being stripped of citizenship) could arise at common law as well as under the HRA or EU law, and could therefore attract similar levels of judicial protection. Lord Mance concluded that what he termed a 'correspondingly strict standard of review' should apply in this case, although rather confusingly given his comment at para 94 he held that this 'strict standard' should be seen as deriving from the concept of proportionality rather than irrationality.

The notion that 'the nature of judicial review in every case depends on the context' points us towards the ostensibly rather unhappy conclusion—from a legal certainty perspective—that irrationality and proportionality might mean the same thing and that they both might mean a level of review equating to the supine indifference of the classic *Wednesbury* formulation (we might style this as 'supine review') or the rigorously intrusive 'ten questions' methodology in *Quila* (styled perhaps as 'searching review') or any point in between those two extremes.

Lord Sumption ruminated on the issue at some length in his opinion. He suggested that ever since Lord Diplock's judgment in *GCHQ*, the English courts had been 'stumbling towards' an indigenous version of proportionality: '[105] . . . The solution adopted, albeit sometimes without acknowledgment, was to expand the scope of rationality review so as to incorporate at common law significant elements of the principle of proportionality'.[182]

Lord Sumption doubted that a hard and fast line could be drawn between 'fundamental' and 'non-fundamental rights', with differing levels of review applying according to which side of the line a particular issue fell. Rather, he advocated adoption of a 'sliding scale' of intensity of review:

> [107] . . . It is for the court to assess how broad the range of rational decisions is in the circumstances of any given case. That must necessarily depend on the significance of the right interfered with, the degree of interference involved, and notably the extent to which, even on a statutory

---

[180] The 'reason' for the s 40(2) order was that Mr Pham was believed by the Home Secretary to be linked to the Al-Qaeda terrorist group.   [181] [2014] UKSC 20, [2014] 2 WLR 808.

[182] [2014] 2 WLR 808 at para 105. The stumbling metaphor is also at para 105. On the 'without acknowledgment' point, Lord Reed at para 114 identified *Shoreham* and *Hook* as proportionality cases; see 'Mis-using the irrationality test? Coming too close to the "merits" of the decision', ch 13, p 377 and 'A new understanding of the separation of powers?', ch 13 p 378.

appeal, the court is competent to reassess the balance which the decision-maker was called on to make given the subject matter.

There are obvious echoes here of the 'how much procedural protection does the audi alterem partem principle require' debate which informed administrative law doctrine in the post-*Ridge v Baldwin* era, and Lord Sumption's 'sliding scale' has clear parallels with Mullan's 'spectrum theory' in relation to the procedural fairness issue. The pressing question which such analysis raises is 'How do we establish where on the scale a particular issue lies?'.

We can confidently predict that a defendant in a residential possession claim brought by a local council would be wasting her time invoking a *Quila* version of substantive review; her case sits—per *Pinnock* and *Powell*—at the 'supine review' bottom of the sliding scale. It would presumably be similarly fruitless for the Home Secretary to rely on 'supine review' in cases analogous to *Quila* or *Huang* which evidently sit at the 'searching review' top of the scale. Lord Sumption's obvious allusion to justiciability issues in para 107 of *Pham* perhaps also enables us to suppose that 'national security' issues will prove as much a trump card in relation to the intensity of substantive review as they did in relation to the procedural fairness principle in *GCHQ*,[183] at least to the extent of pushing the intensity of review firmly towards the bottom of the scale. And we might also realistically expect that the 'democratic imprimatur' criterion would play a significant role in any 'sliding scale' approach to substantive review.

Considerable interest was therefore raised by *R (Keyu) v Secretary of State for Foreign and Commonwealth Affairs*,[184] in which the claimant invited the Supreme Court formally to hold that *Wednesbury* irrationality should no longer be applied as the ground of substantive review in English administrative law, and that it should be replaced by proportionality even in cases where there was no EU or HRA dimension. That step would manifestly be problematic for the court to take in constitutional terms. In the EU and HRA contexts, proportionality review (whatever it might mean) is rooted in a statutory imperative; that is, Parliament has ordered the courts to apply this new (and statutory) ground of review. Expressly replacing irrationality with proportionality as a principle of common law would be a wholly judicial innovation, and one which in *Keyu* the Supreme Court was unwilling to take.

The Keyu claimants were challenging the Foreign Secretary's refusal to establish a public inquiry under the Inquiries Act 2005 s 1 to investigate the killing of twenty-four civilians in Malaya in 1948 (Malaya then being a British protectorate) by British soldiers. Initial investigations by British authorities had suggested that nothing untoward had occurred, but a steady trickle of new evidence—including testimony from soldiers deployed in Malaya at the time—raised serious concerns that the army had carried out an unjustifiable massacre.[185] Despite this new evidence, the government declined to establish an inquiry, on the various bases that the lapse of time since the events in issue made it unlikely that reliable evidence could be gathered.

The Supreme Court held that the historical nature of the massacre meant that the claimants could not assert an HRA right as the basis for review; any proportionality assessment would have to be rooted in the common law. The claimants had advanced that argument in the expectation that an orthodox irrationality argument would—as it did on the facts—fail. Lord Neuberger's leading judgment observed that the claimant's argument:

> has implications which are profound in constitutional terms and very wide in applicable
> scope . . . [I]t would involve the court considering the merits of the decision at issue: in partic-
> ular, it would require the courts to consider the balance which the decision-maker has struck

---

[183] See 'The "nature" not the "source" of power as the determinant of reviewability', ch 4, pp 95–96.

[184] [2015] UKSC 69, [2016] AC 1355.

[185] Lord Kerr referred (at para 204) to: '[T]he shocking circumstances in which, according to the overwhelming preponderance of currently available evidence, wholly innocent men were mercilessly murdered and the failure of the authorities of this state to conduct an effective inquiry into their deaths . . .'.

between competing interests (often a public interest against a private interest) and the weight to be accorded to each such interest.[186]

Lord Neuberger acknowledged—referring inter alia to *Pham*—that the common law might be moving away 'to some extent' from irrationality review,[187] but felt that this was too significant an issue to be dealt with by a five member court, and would require a nine judge bench. He considered that step unnecessary however, as he also concluded that the claimant would fail even if proportionality review were available; (although curiously he did not specify what variant of that principle he had applied to reach that decision).

The case perhaps serves more to raise questions than provide answers, a point nicely illustrated by Lord Kerr:

> [278] . . . Final conclusions on a number of interesting issues that arise in this area must await a case where they can be more fully explored. These include whether irrationality and proportionality are forms of review which are bluntly opposed to each other and mutually exclusive; whether intensity of review operates on a sliding scale, dependent on the nature of the decision under challenge and that, in consequence, the debate about a 'choice' between proportionality and rationality is no longer relevant; whether there is any place in modern administrative law for a 'pure' irrationality ground of review ie one which poses the question, 'could any reasonable decision-maker, acting reasonably, have reached this conclusion'; and whether proportionality provides a more structured and transparent means of review.

As yet, we still await that fuller exploration. While it is tempting to suggest that the Supreme Court's vacillation on this question is lending this aspect of the law an unnecessarily uncertain character, such criticism rather assumes that there is an easy answer waiting to be found. But, rather paradoxically, the many vagaries inherent in the Supreme Court's case law both on proportionality as an HRA value and more latterly its status at common law provide a legitimising context for a subsequent judgment to redefine this area of constitutional and administrative law in possibly far-reaching ways. Knight and Cross offered a rather weary characterisation of the way ahead: '[T]he seemingly endless proportionality debate trudges on in the light of *Keyu* . . . '[188]. Perhaps, to put matters in a more positive light, we must acclimatise ourselves to the fact that continuing complexity of the governmental process, infused as it is with ever-changing and always contested moral perceptions about the very existence of legal rights and—if they do exist—their relative importance, inevitably means that judicial attempts to identify the proper limits of executive and, to a much lesser extent, legislative autonomy will present us with a similarly complex legal landscape.

Conclusion

The focus of these last five chapters has been in explicit terms on the changing moral and legal status of 'human rights' norms within the UK's constitutional order. But, at a higher level of abstraction, the concern of the chapters has been very much—if thus far only implicitly—with our understanding of the concept of the rule of law. In charting the way in which the politics and law of the constitution have dealt with the issue of human rights protection, we have constantly been analysing a familiar issue: namely 'what government can do and how government can do it'.[189]

---

[186] At paras 132–133.
[187] Lord Sumption did not sit in *Keyu*, and so had no opportunity further to develop his 'sliding scale' analysis.
[188] Knight C and Cross T (2017) 'Public law in the Supreme Court 2015–2016' *Judicial Review* 215 at para 8.
[189] See 'The Rule of Law and the Separation of Powers', ch 3, p 44.

The Human Rights Act has appreciably changed the way in which those questions might now be answered. The Act has already had a significant impact on domestic administrative law and has triggered extensive changes in the balance of power between executive bodies and the courts. Furthermore, in so far as our understanding of the sovereignty of Parliament rests on an assumption that judges should adopt a literalist approach to construing legislation, the way in which the judiciary has thus far used s 3 also has important implications for the balance of power between Parliament and the courts.

It is trite—but nonetheless important—to reiterate the point that none of the moral values identified in the text of the HRA and in its initial application by the courts are entrenched in a legal sense. The Act itself, and the body of case law built upon it, could be swept away in part or in their entirety should Parliament choose to do so. It is also too soon to make any definitive assertions about the extent to which—if any—the HRA has acquired a status of 'moral entrenchment' or to which it has lent greater legitimacy and practical force to pre-existing moral suppositions about the proper scope of constitutional governance in a democratic society. Nonetheless, some plausible suggestions might be offered. And in pursuit of that objective, we might consider two controversies which arose in 2003 and 2004 in the always politically sensitive field of immigration policy.[190]

IV. Judicial supremacism revisited?

In his speech to the Labour Party conference in October 2001, delivered following the terrorist attacks in the US on September 11, Prime Minister Blair linked the issue of people seeking asylum in this country with terrorism, and promised that the way in which asylum seekers were treated by the law would be changed:

> New extradition laws will be introduced; new rules to ensure asylum is not a front for terrorist entry. This country is proud of its tradition in giving asylum to those fleeing tyranny. We will always do so. But we have a duty to protect the system from abuse. It must be overhauled radically so that from now on, those who abide by the rules get help and those that don't, can no longer play the system to gain unfair advantage over others.[191]

The Blair government lost little time in persuading Parliament to give those sentiments legal effect.

The Nationality, Immigration and Asylum Act 2002 s 55

One step promptly taken by the Blair government to discourage 'bogus' asylum seekers was to insert a provision into an immigration and asylum Bill (at a very late stage of the Bill's parliamentary passage)[192] which forbade the provision of any welfare support to asylum seekers who had not declared themselves as such as soon as it was reasonably practical for them to have done so after entering the country. The policy was a watered-down version of the initiative taken through delegated legislation by the Major government some years earlier, which initiative had been held ultra vires by the Court of Appeal in the *Joint Council for the Welfare of Immigrants* case.[193] The new policy was enacted in s 55 of the 2002 Act. However, s 55 provided that support should not be withheld if to do so would breach an applicant's Convention Rights.

---

[190] See Le Sueur A (2004) 'Three strikes and it's out . . . ' *Public Law* 225: and McGarry J (2005) 'Parliamentary sovereignty, judges and the Asylum and Immigration (Treatment of Claimants etc) bill' *Liverpool LR* 1.

[191] <http://www.guardian.co.uk/politics/2001/oct/02/labourconference.labour6>.

[192] See Bradley A (2003) 'Judicial independence under attack' *Public Law* 397.

[193] See '*R v Secretary of State for Social Security, ex p Joint Council for the Welfare of Immigrants*', ch 19, pp 513–514.

A refusal of support under s 55 was challenged in *R (on the application of Q) v Secretary of State for the Home Department*.[194] Collins J held the refusal unlawful on various grounds, including a lack of procedural fairness and a failure by decision-makers to consider if leaving the applicants in a state of effective destitution was compatible with Arts 3 and 8 ECHR. There then followed a very public denunciation of Collins J by the then Home Secretary, David Blunkett. Echoing the way in which Conservative MPs had attacked the democratic creden-tials of the courts a few years earlier,[195] Mr Blunkett and some Labour MPs attacked the consti-tutional propriety of Collins J's decision.[196] Mr Blunkett greeted the judgment in the following terms in an interview with the BBC:[197]

> Frankly, I'm personally fed up with having to deal with a situation where Parliament debates issues and the judges then overturn them. I don't want any mixed messages going out so I am making it absolutely clear today that we don't accept what Justice Collins has said. We will seek to overturn it. We will continue operating a policy which we think is perfectly reasonable and fair.

Mr Blunkett then held a series of interviews with newspapers, and wrote an article for the Sunday tabloid newspaper the *News of the World*, in which he made similarly derogatory com-ments about judges in general and Collins J in particular. Mr Blunkett had evidently failed to appreciate the constitutional distinction between his view of what the law allowed him to do and what the law actually did allow him to do. From a senior member of the government which had promoted the HRA just five years earlier, such disdain for or ignorance of orthodox constitutional principles is quite remarkable.[198]

Collins J's judgment was largely upheld by the Court of Appeal.[199] Mr Blunkett appeared to accept the correctness of this conclusion, and the Home Office modified its decision-making procedures to ensure that the new policy could be lawfully applied. Shortly thereafter, the government returned to address in even clearer terms its concern to limit the role played by the judiciary in immigration matters.

The ouster clause provisions in the Immigration and Asylum Bill 2003

One of the government's subsequent proposals to prevent asylum seekers 'playing the system' appeared in the Asylum and Immigration (Treatment of Claimants) Bill in 2003. Until 2002, appeals against a Home Office decision to refuse an asylum application were initially heard by Immigration Adjudicators, who were in effect equivalent in status and expertise to district judges, the lowest tier of the professional judicial hierarchy. Thereafter, an appeal on a point of law lay to a more specialised Immigration Appeal Tribunal (IAT), generally consisting of two lay members and a legal qualified 'vice president', equivalent in status to a circuit judge. If the IAT refused to hear an appeal, its decision was open to challenge by judicial review.

The judicial review challenge was replaced by a statutory right of review by the High Court in the National Immigration and Asylum Act 2002 s 101. This was a fast track form of judicial super-vision. The application was to be entirely on paper, and had to be made within ten days of the IAT decision being made. The 'hearing' itself would then be conducted within a further ten days.

---

[194] [2003] EWHC 195 (Admin), (2003) 100(15) LSG 26, *The Times*, 20 February 2003.

[195] See 'The judicial supremacism controversy', ch 19, pp 507–510.

[196] For details see Bradley (2003) op cit. See also Hickman T (2008) 'The courts and politics after the Human Rights Act: a comment' *Public Law* 84 at 95: 'The reaction of government ministers to adverse judicial decisions is rarely charitable and, moreover, frequently so misrepresents the judgment that one hopes they have not had the time to read it and have relied instead on a brief from a political adviser.'

[197] <http://news.bbc.co.uk/1/hi/uk/2779343.stm>.

[198] See the analysis of Mr Blunkett's reaction in *The Daily Telegraph*, 21 February 2003 and *The Independent*, 20 February 2003. For a broader selection of Mr Blunkett's views see Blunkett D (2006) *The Blunkett tapes: my life in the bear pit* pp 282, 288, 327, 332, 344, 365, 637.   [199] [2003] EWCA Civ 364, [2004] QB 36.

This streamlined procedure was evidently not sufficiently expeditious for the Blair government. The 2003 Bill proposed that the Adjudicators and IAT be merged into a single body, the Asylum and Immigration Tribunal (AIT), which would offer a single hearing to replace the two-stage process. The Bill also included the following provision (cl 11) (formulated no doubt with *Gilmore* and *Anisminic* in mind)[200] to amend the 2002 Act:

108A Exclusivity and finality of Tribunal's jurisdiction
> (1) No court shall have any supervisory or other jurisdiction (whether statutory or inherent) in relation to the Tribunal.
> (2) No court may entertain proceedings for questioning (whether by way of appeal or otherwise)—
>   (a) any determination, decision or other action of the Tribunal . . .
> (3) Subsections (1) and (2)—
>   (a) prevent a court, in particular, from entertaining proceedings to determine whether a purported determination, decision or action of the Tribunal was a nullity . . .

The proposal attracted substantial criticism within Parliament and among the legal profession including—perhaps most notably—senior members (both retired and serving) of the judiciary. The former (Conservative) Lord Chancellor, Lord Mackay of Clashfern, described the Bill as: 'Very obnoxious . . . I just hope that Parliament is not prepared to see the ordinary courts of law prevented from intervening to protect claimants from breaches of natural justice'.[201] Lord Steyn, in a lecture delivered at the Inner Temple, made similar comments.[202] The theme common to all such criticism was the accusation that the government was seeking to use its effective control of Parliament's sovereignty to enact a provision which was manifestly inconsistent with orthodox understandings of the rule of law. The most significant criticism came from Lord Woolf CJ. Ten years earlier, Lord Woolf had written an academic article in which he had mused about circumstances in which judges might be inclined overtly to deny the sovereignty of Parliament and to invalidate certain statutory provisions:

> There are however situations where already, in upholding the rule of law, the courts have had to take a stand. The example that springs to mind is the *Anisminic* case . . . Since that case Parliament has not again mounted such a challenge to the reviewing power of the High Court. There has been, and I am confident there will continue to be, mutual respect for each other's roles.
>
> However, if Parliament did the unthinkable, then I would say that the courts would also be required to act in a manner which would be without precedent. Some judges might choose to do so by saying that it was an unrebuttable presumption that Parliament could never intend such a result. I myself would consider there were advantages in making it clear that ultimately there are even limits on the supremacy of Parliament which it is the courts' inalienable responsibility to identify and uphold. They are limits of the most modest dimensions which I believe any democrat would accept. They are no more than are necessary to enable the rule of law to be preserved.[203]

In March 2004, shortly after the new asylum Bill was published, and speaking as the senior member of the judiciary, Lord Woolf returned to that theme in a public lecture and placed cl 11 squarely in the context of axiomatic presumptions as to constitutional morality:

> In discussions which have taken place between the judiciary and the Government, there have been attempts to justify the clause, but these are specious and unsatisfactory. It is particularly regrettable that the Lord Chancellor and Secretary of State should find it acceptable to have responsibility for promoting this clause.

---

[200] See 'Ouster clauses—*Gilmore* (1957) and *Anisminic* (1969)', ch 3, pp 67–70.
[201] *The Times*, 27 February 2004.   [202] *The Times*, 4 March 2004.
[203] (1995) 'Droit public: English style' *Public Law* 57.

> I understand that the Lord Chancellor has recently said that the clause is not intended to exclude habeas corpus. In view of the language of the clause this surprises me. It also surprises me because, if the clause does not exclude habeas corpus, then I would have thought it inevitable that it will, in practice, lead to an increase in delay. This is because the right to apply for habeas corpus does not involve the safeguard of a requirement as to leave. It also surprises me that the Government does not see it as inconsistent to promote a clause designed to exclude the courts from performing their basic role of protecting the rule of law at the same time that it is introducing the present constitutional reforms. Their actions are totally inconsistent and I urge the Government to think again. . . . The implementation of the clause would be a blot on the reputation of the Government and undermine its attempts to be a champion of the rule of law overseas. I trust the clause will have short-shrift in the Lords, but, even then, the attempt to include it in legislation could result in a loss of confidence in the commitment of the Government to the rule of law.[204]

Effective judicial resistance to ouster clauses is not without precedent. The *Anisminic* episode in the late 1960s provides an obvious example of this happening, and that in an era when the notion of human rights protection played little meaningful part in our constitutional discourse. Lord Woolf's intervention in 2004 was not however in the form of a judgment. It was essentially a political initiative, albeit one in which the notion of 'politics' bore a constitutional rather than party-based meaning. The speech excited a flurry of comment to the effect that members of the judiciary were preparing themselves to invoke Diceyan notions of the rule of law to overturn Diceyan notions of the sovereignty of Parliament by accepting jurisdiction to review the AIT actions (or indeed its 'purported' actions) notwithstanding the ouster clause.[205]

Whether such 'revolutionary' intent would have been acted upon was—perhaps unfortunately—never put to the test. Thirty-five Labour backbenchers voted against the proposal at second reading, and the Blair government was sufficiently persuaded (or alarmed) by the force (and the sources) of opposition to cl 11 that the proposal was withdrawn ten days after Lord Woolf's speech.

Conclusion

These two episodes nicely illustrate both the potential and limitations of human rights norms as a mechanism to prompt reconsideration of constitutional orthodoxies above and beyond the narrower question of assessing the legal impact of the HRA itself. Both the narrow and broader questions are further explored in chapter twenty-two, which focuses on the issue of governmental powers to deprive individuals of their physical liberty because of their suspected involvement in 'criminal' activities. In concluding this chapter however, we might return to the issue of the 'moral entrenchment' of the HRA.

While Leader of the Opposition, David Cameron had called for the repeal of the Human Rights Act.[206] In the run-up to the 2010 general election, the Conservative Party announced in its election manifesto that: 'To protect our freedoms from state encroachment and encourage greater social responsibility, we will replace the Human Rights Act with a UK Bill of Rights'.

---

[204] 'The rule of law and a change in the constitution'; available at <http://www.dca.gov.uk/judicial/speeches/lcj030304.htm>.

[205] See eg the article by Jeffrey Jowell (2004) 'Immigration wars' *The Guardian* March 2; available online at: <http://www.guardian.co.uk/world/2004/mar/02/law.immigration>; and a longer treatment of the issue by the same author (2004) 'Heading for constitutional crisis' *New Law Journal* (19 March) 401. Dyer C (2004) 'Profile of Lord Woolf' *The Guardian* March 5; available at: <http://www.guardian.co.uk/politics/2004/mar/05/ukcrime.immigrationandpublicservices>.

[206] See eg <http://www.telegraph.co.uk/news/uknews/1560975/David-Cameron-Scrap-the-Human-Rights-Act.html>.

The Liberal Democrat Party, in contrast, firmly supported the HRA.[207] The Liberal Democrat leader (and Deputy Prime Minister) Nick Clegg put his party's position bluntly at the 2011 Liberal Democrat Annual conference: '[L]et me say something really clear about the Human Rights Act. In fact I'll do it in words of one syllable: It is here to stay'.[208]

These differing views were an obvious potential source of tension within the coalition administration. Those differences were initially at least subsumed within a wide-ranging expression of intent in the coalition's programme for government:

> We will establish a Commission to investigate the creation of a British Bill of Rights that incorporates and builds on all our obligations under the European Convention on Human Rights, ensures that these rights continue to be enshrined in British law, and extends and protects British liberties. We will seek to promote a better understanding of the true scope of these obligations and liberties.[209]

The depth of this ostensibly bi-partisan commitment was put to the test early in 2011 when the ECtHR held that UK law which denied voting rights to all prisoners serving custodial sentences was incompatible with the Convention.

The immediate roots of the controversy lay in the ECtHR's 2005 judgment in *Hirst v United Kingdom*.[210] *Hirst* considered the compatibility of the Representation of the People Act 1983,[211] s 3 with Art 3 of the First Protocol ECHR.[212] Section 3 automatically removes voting rights from any person serving a custodial sentence (of any length and for any crime). The automatic exclusion is of relatively modern vintage, introduced in the RPA 1969 on the recommendation of a Speaker's Conference which reported in 1968.[213] The policy rationale underpinning the provisions appeared to be that by committing a crime prisoners had forfeited their presumptive entitlement to participate in the electoral process. In more grandiose theoretical terms, we might say that Parliament had decided that prisoners were no longer to be seen as part of the people whose consent underpinned the legitimacy of the governmental system.

The ECtHR in *Hirst* accepted that on a matter such as this States would enjoy a wide margin of appreciation. It indicated however that the breadth of that margin might be affected by the extent to which the domestic law in issue had been the subject of recent and reasoned debate by the country's law-makers. Since neither the Commons nor Lords had addressed the issue, the margin would be rather narrower than it could be. The Court also noted that it had been accepted in previous ECHR litigation that a voting disqualification imposed on persons

---

[207] Liberal Democrats (2010) *Our manifesto* at p 94; (<http://www.politicsresources.net/area/uk/ge10/man/parties/libdem_manifesto_2010.pdf>).

[208] 21 September 2011; <http://www.telegraph.co.uk/news/politics/nick-clegg/8779738/Nick-Clegg-The-Human-Rights-Act-is-here-to-stay.html>.

[209] At p 11: (<https://www.gov.uk/government/uploads/system/uploads/attachment_data/file/78977/coalition_programme_for_government.pdf>).

[210] (2006) 42 EHRR 41.

[211] **3.—Disfranchisement of offenders in prison etc.**
(1) A convicted person during the time that he is detained in a penal institution in pursuance of his sentence . . . is legally incapable of voting at any parliamentary or local government election.
(2) For this purpose—
(a) 'convicted person' means any person found guilty of an offence . . . but not including a person dealt with by committal or other summary process for contempt of court . . .
(c) a person detained for default in complying with his sentence shall not be treated as detained in pursuance of the sentence . . . [eg for non-payment of a fine] . . .

(3) It is immaterial for the purposes of this section whether a conviction or sentence was before or after the passing of this Act.

[212] 'The High Contracting Parties undertake to hold free elections at reasonable intervals by secret ballot, under conditions which will ensure the free expression of the opinion of the people in the choice of the legislature'.

[213] See generally White I (2011) *Prisoner's voting rights* pp 9–11.

serving a seven-year sentence for possession of explosives and a three-year sentence for tax fraud did not breach Art 3 of the First Protocol.[214] The difficulty which the ECtHR identified in *Hirst* was the automatic and universal nature of the RPA 1983 s 3 provision. The most trivial sentence attracted the same disqualificatory consequence as the most serious sentence and there was no scope in any circumstances for a domestic court to consider the proportionality of the loss of voting rights. It was for these reasons that the Court held that the United Kingdom was in breach of its treaty obligations.[215] There is nothing novel about the application of this principle in Convention jurisprudence. The ECtHR has been consistently sceptical about the acceptability of laws which have a 'blanket' character of this sort.[216]

Hirst therefore did not hold that restrictions on voting rights for prisoners was per se incompatible with the Convention. The judgment very clearly accepts that domestic law-makers can legitimately conclude disenfranchisement is an acceptable element of conviction for a serious crime and also suggests that removal of voting rights could be attached to less substantial crimes so long as some mechanism existed in domestic law for a judicial consideration of the proportionality of disqualification in a given case. It was certainly quite credible to assume that any change to the law need not encompass Mr Hirst per se, given that he was serving a life sentence for manslaughter.

The (then) Labour government appreciated this point, and began a consultation process to explore how domestic law might be altered. It seemed however that the Blair and Brown governments were in no hurry to resolve this issue, presumably because relaxing the ban would have been unpopular with many voters. No proposals had been put before Parliament before the 2010 general election. By that point, the domestic courts had accepted that RPA 1983 s 3 was incompatible with the Convention, rejected the suggestion that it was 'possible' per HRA 1998 s 3 to construe RPA 1983 s 3 in a Convention-compliant manner, and issued a Declaration of Incompatibility.[217] The Committee of Ministers of the Council of Europe had criticised the United Kingdom for its tardy response to the issue. And then in November 2010 the ECtHR ruled in *Greens and MT v United Kingdom*[218] that the United Kingdom should modify its law within six months.

Greens prompted a vast outpouring of bucolic criticism in much of the populist press, the criticism rooted in part in moral distaste for the enfranchisement of any prisoners and in part in the familiar assertion that British 'sovereignty' was under attack from 'foreign judges'. *The Daily Mail* newspaper led the charge, greeting the judgment in *Greens* with the headline 'Toasting victory with cannabis and bubbly, the axe killer who won convicts the vote'.[219] A follow up article in April 2011 announced: 'Euro judges trample UK sovereignty and insist: You WILL give prisoners the vote'.[220] Both articles were notable for their substantial misrepresentation (whether willful or ignorant) of the reasoning behind and implications of *Hirst* and *Greens*.

---

[214] In *Holland v Ireland* (App no 24827/94), Comm. Dec. 14.04.1998 and *Mathieu-Mohin v Belgium* (A/113): (1988) 10 EHRR 1 respectively.

[215] For a thoughtful analysis supportive of the ECtHR's conclusion see Easton S (2006) 'Electing the electorate: the problem of prisoner disenfranchisement' *MLR* 443.

[216] See eg the discussions at 'Blurring the issue? *Doherty* (2008), Pinnock (2009), Powell (2010)', pp 576–577.

[217] *Smith v Scott* (2007) SLT 137; *Chester v Secretary of State for Justice* [2010] EWCA Civ 1439, [2011] 1 WLR 1436. The judgment of Laws LJ in *Chester* merits attention for its broader treatment of the implications of the HRA for the relationship between Parliament, the government, and the courts. This is one of the few s 4 orders that has not been met with amending legislation.

[218] (2011) 53 EHRR 21. The time for compliance was subsequently extended to mid-2012.

[219] 3 November 2010; <http://www.dailymail.co.uk/news/article-1325930/Axe-killer-toasts-prison-vote-victory-cannabis-Champagne-Youtube.html#ixzz1YOn6X5QS>.

[220] <http://www.dailymail.co.uk/news/article-1376350/Prisoner-vote-ban-Euro-judges-trample-UK-sovereignty-dismiss-appeal.html#ixzz1YOoTvXYh>. An analysis of the legal accuracy of the assertions made in the text of the article might provide the basis of an enlightening term paper for students.

One should perhaps not have high expectations of the intellectual rigour and political integrity of tabloid journalists, but it is rather more concerning (if not surprising) to see such sentiments voiced by members of the Commons. In a manner reminiscent of the assertions made by Conservative MPs during the 'judicial supremacism' episode,[221] some members of the house fulminated with indignant fury at the temerity of the ECtHR during debates held in January and February 2011. In February, the Commons debated a motion moved by the Conservative MP David Davis and the Labour MP (and former Foreign and Home Secretary) Jack Straw that:

> [T]his House notes the ruling of the European Court of Human Rights in Hirst v the United Kingdom in which it held that there had been no substantive debate by members of the legislature on the continued justification for maintaining a general restriction on the right of prisoners to vote; acknowledges the treaty obligations of the UK; is of the opinion that legislative decisions of this nature should be a matter for democratically-elected lawmakers; and supports the current situation in which no prisoner is able to vote except those imprisoned for contempt, default or on remand.[222]

Mr Davis and Mr Straw proceeded on the basis that the debate would in itself meet the concern expressed by the ECtHR in *Hirst* that the issue of prisoner disenfranchisement had not properly been considered in Parliament. It would rather perhaps overstate the case to say that Mr Straw and Mr Davis were entering into a dialogue with the ECtHR. Both MPs suggested that *Hirst* extended the reach of the Convention beyond its proper moral boundaries and saw no likelihood of alteration in domestic law in response to the judgment.

The debate highlighted the seemingly widely held view among contemporary MPs that it could never be legitimate for any moral values to be beyond the reach of ordinary parliamentary majorities, and an apparently similarly widespread view that the United Kingdom should withdraw from the Convention altogether. [223]

The Prime Minister David Cameron had perhaps invited disdain for the ECtHR's judgments (and the Court itself) from Conservative MPs by expressing a personal disinclination to see any alteration in domestic law. The government's formal position was presented to the Commons in a much more thoughtful fashion by the Attorney-General, Dominic Greive, who recognized that *Hirst* by no means held that the Convention required all prisoners to be allowed to vote and saw the central task facing the government as promoting an amendment to domestic law which satisfied the respective demands of the ECtHR and Parliament.[224] MPs seemed to be initially unpersuaded by this approach. The Davis/Straw motion was carried by 234 votes to 22, which rather suggested that the government would face great difficulty in eventually persuading Parliament to make any alteration at all to domestic law.

The difficult position in which this imbroglio placed the Supreme Court was subsequently demonstrated in *R (Chester) v Secretary of State for Justice*.[225] Since Chester was serving a life

---

[221] See 'III. The judicial supremacism controversy', ch 19, pp 507–510.

[222] *HCD* 10 February 2011 c 493.

[223] Ibid c 495: David Evennett (Bexleyheath and Crayford) (Con): '...Giving votes to any prisoners is quite incomprehensible to our constituents, who sent us here to make the rules and the laws, not to have the European Court make them for us?'; ibid at c 496: Robert Halfon (Harlow) (Con): '[I]t is rather strange that we are being forced to do this by the European Court of Human Rights, many of whose own judges come from authoritarian regimes? Is it not time to withdraw from its jurisdiction?'; ibid at 505: Gary Streeter (South West Devon) (Con) '[T]here comes a time when it is necessary to take a stand. I argue that right now, on this issue, it is right for this House, today, to assert its authority. The judgment of the ECHR in the *Hirst* case flies in the face of the original wording and purpose of the European convention on human rights, in which it was clearly intended that each signatory should have latitude in making decisions on the electoral franchise in that country'; ibid at 505.'

[224] Ibid at c 509 et seq. See also the contribution of Dennis McShane ibid at c 507 et seq. The debate is informatively analysed by Professor Nicol (2011) 'Legitimacy of the Commons debate on prisoner voting' *Public Law* 681–691.   [225] [2013] UKSC 63; [2014] AC 271.

sentence for murder, it would seem clear that he was a person who, per *Hirst*, could properly have been disenfranchised. His challenge, however, was obviously to the blanket nature of the ban. The Supreme Court held unanimously that the relevant provisions of the RPA 1983 were incompatible with Art 3 of the First Protocol to the Convention, and the incompatibility could not be cured through use of s 3. The Court however declined to make a declaration of incompatibility per s 4. This was in part because the matter was 'under active consideration'[226] by Parliament, and it would be inappropriate for the Court to pre-empt legislative reconsideration of the question. The Court also seemed to be influenced on this point by the fact that denying the vote to a person convicted of murder could not be thought to breach the Convention.[227]

The 'active consideration' to which the Court referred culminated in the publication of a joint House of Lords and House of Commons report in December 2013.[228] In marked contrast to the tone of the earlier debate in the Commons, the report offered a carefully considered view both of the ECtHR's case law and the relevant policy issues. The Committee recommended two alterations to the RPA 1983.[229] The first was that voting rights should not be removed from persons sentenced to twelve months or shorter terms of imprisonment. The second was that all prisoners should be entitled to reclaim their voting rights when they had only six months or less of their sentence to serve. There is little doubt that reform of that sort would remove any incompatibility with the Convention. As of late 2017, nether the Cameron or May governments had shown any inclination to support either proposal.[230]

Chester is perhaps significant in general HRA terms because it links the notion of judicial 'deference' to Parliament with legislators actually taking steps to place the relevant matter 'under active consideration'. The Supreme Court indicated quite clearly that it was not inclined to engage in a minute assessment of the quality (or indeed quantity of that consideration).[231] Given the obvious limitations of the parliamentary law-making process, that reluctance might strike some observers as unduly benevolent. Nonetheless, the inference does arise therefore that in respect of statutory provisions (or indeed common law rules) which have not, in terms of their compliance with Convention Rights, been subject to any legislative consideration at all, there is nothing to which a court needs to defer.[232]

More broadly still, *Chester* suggests that—for the judiciary at least—the Human Rights Act has prompted a new understanding of the meaning of 'democracy' in our modern constitution. The point was forcefully put by Baroness Hale:

> 88 Of course, in any modern democracy, the views of the public and Parliamentarians cannot be the end of the story. Democracy is about more than respecting the views of the majority. It is also about safeguarding the rights of minorities, including unpopular minorities. 'Democracy values everyone equally even if the majority does not': *Ghaidan v Godin-Mendoza* [2004] 2 AC 557, para 132. It follows that one of the essential roles of the courts in a democracy is to protect those rights.

---

[226] [2014] AC 271 per Lord Mance at para 39.   [227] Ibid, at para 83, para 101.

[228] House of Lords and House of Commons Joint Committee (2013) *Draft Voting Eligibility (Prisoners) Bill* (HL paper 103; HC 924); <http://www.publications.parliament.uk/pa/jt201314/jtselect/jtdraftvoting/103/103.pdf>.

[229] Ibid, at 64–65.

[230] The ECtHR appeared to wish to limit the political hostility of the Cameron government to the *Hirst* principle by holding in August 2014 in *Firth v United Kingdom* (App no 47784/09) that, notwithstanding that the United Kingdom remained in breach of the Convention there was no basis to award either damages or costs to the complaint prisoners, concluding at para 18 that '[T]he finding of a violation constitutes sufficient just satisfaction for any non-pecuniary damage sustained by the applicants'.   [231] [2014] AC 271 at paras 80, 136.

[232] The ECtHR has continued to emphasise that that quality of the domestic law-making process will be a very pertinent factor in its assessment of whether a state has strayed beyond the boundaries of the margin of appreciation. See in particular *Animal Defenders International v United Kingdom* (2013) 57 EHRR 607: '108. It emerges from that case-law that, in order to determine the proportionality of a general measure, the Court must primarily assess the legislative choices underlying it (James and Others, § 36). The quality of the parliamentary and judicial review of the necessity of the measure is of particular importance in this respect, including to the operation of the relevant margin of appreciation'.

and also by Lord Sumption:

[112] . . . Of course, as Baroness Hale DPSC has pointed out, it does not follow that a democracy can properly do whatever it likes, simply by virtue of the democratic mandate for its acts. The protection of minorities is a necessary concern of any democratic constitution.

How widely this judicial decoupling of democracy and majoritarianism will spread into our wider political culture remains to be seen. It might readily be thought however that the denial of the right to vote to a convicted murderer does not present a particularly taxing question in democratic terms. In the next chapter, we turn our attention to several rather more 'difficult' issues.

Suggested further reading

Academic commentary

ALLAN T (2006) 'Human rights and judicial review: a critique of "due deference"' *Cambridge LJ* 671

BRADLEY A (2003) 'Judicial independence under attack' *Public Law* 397

NICOL D (2011) 'Legitimacy of the Commons debate on prisoner voting' *Public Law* 681

KAVANAGH A (2004) 'Statutory interpretation and human rights after *Anderson*: a more contextual approach' *Public Law* 537

NICOL D (2004) 'Statutory interpretation and human rights after *Anderson*' *Public Law* 273

CRAIG P (2001) 'The courts, the Human Rights Act and judicial review' *LQR* 592

HICKMAN T (2008) 'The courts and politics after the Human Rights Act: a comment' *Public Law* 84

JOWELL J (2003) 'Judicial deference: servility, civility or institutional capacity' (2003) *Public Law* 592

WOOLF H (2004) 'The rule of law and a change in the constitution'; available online at <http://www.dca.gov.uk/judicial/speeches/lcj030304.htm>

Case law and legislation

Aston Cantlow . . . [2003] UKHL 37, [2003] 3 WLR 283

Bellinger v Bellinger [2003] UKHL 21, [2003] 2 AC 467

Campbell v MGN [2004] UKHL 22, [2004] AC 457

Ghaidan v Godin-Mendoza [2004] UKHL 30, [2004] 2 AC 557

R v A [2001] UKHL 25, [2001] 3 All ER 1

R (SB) v Governors of Denbigh High School [2006] UKHL 15, [2007] 1 AC 100

R (Daly) v Secretary of State for the Home Department [2001] UKHL 26, [2001] 2 AC 532

Re S (Care Order: Implementation of Care Plan) [2001] EWCA Civ 757, [2001] 2 FCR 450

YL v Birmingham and Others [2007] UK HL 27, [2008] 1 AC 95, [2007] 3 WLR 112

R (Chester) v Secretary of State for Justice [2013] UKSC 63, [2014] AC 271

Animal Defenders International v United Kingdom (2013) 57 EHRR 607

Chapter 22

Human Rights VI: Governmental Powers of Arrest and Detention

We could hold a wide range of wholly credible views on the question of the relative hierarchical positions particular moral values should occupy within a society's constitutional order, and relatedly, on the question of whether or not (and if yes, to what extent) that hierarchy should be enforceable in the courts rather than left to the realm of self-restraint by legislators or government officials. Several scenarios raising sharp moral conflicts were broached in chapter one, and as our journey through the political and legal topography of the British constitution has progressed we have encountered many examples of the ways these often difficult questions of weighting competing values have been resolved. This chapter focuses on an axiomatic illustration of the moral issues constitutional law must address in a democratic society: the powers of government officials in respect of persons suspected of involvement in 'criminal' activities.[1]

That our constitution's adherence to the 'rule of law' may have a formalistically legal rather than substantively moral basis because of Parliament's unconfined law-making power is illustrated by the fate of Mr Liversidge, detained for five years at the instigation of Sir John Anderson, the Home Secretary in Churchill's war-time coalition government.[2] Mr Liversidge was locked up in a prison camp. He had not been convicted of a crime; nor tried for or even charged with any criminal offence. But as the House of Lords told us, Parliament had enacted a law which meant that Mr Liversidge had been quite lawfully detained.

There is little difficulty in concluding that—for five years—Mr Liversidge had been deprived of his liberty in an acute sense. We might also safely conclude that the nature of Mr Liversidge's imprisonment was seen then (and all the more so now) as an extraordinary consequence of extraordinary times. That we draw that conclusion is a powerful indicator that traditional constitutional morality attaches great importance to preserving people's physical liberty, a supposition leading in turn to the assumption that governmental attempts to restrict that

---

[1] Important constitutional questions—often as a matter of law and always as a question of morality—may arise over whether particular conduct should be criminal at all; see for example the discussion of, inter alia, *R v Brown* at '*R v Brown* (1994)', ch 17, pp 461–462; *R v R (martial rape exemption)* at 'Retrospectivity at common law? Rape within marriage' ff, ch 3, pp 72–73; and *R v Lemon* at 'Blasphemy at English common law in the "modern" era: *R v Lemon* (1979)', ch 17, pp 469–471. For the limited purposes of this chapter the constitutionality (in both the legal and moral sense) of crimes is taken as given.

[2] See '*Liversidge v Anderson* (1942)', ch 3, pp 61–64.

liberty should be narrowly constrained as a matter of substance and rigorously proven as a matter of process.[3]

'Liberty' under Art 5 ECHR

Less than a decade after *Liversidge* was decided, the framers of the ECHR identified preservation of individual liberty as a vital element of human rights protection:

Article 5. Right to liberty and security

1 Everyone has the right to liberty and security of person. No one shall be deprived of his liberty save in the following cases and in accordance with a procedure prescribed by law:

   a the lawful detention of a person after conviction by a competent court;

   b the lawful arrest or detention of a person for non-compliance with the lawful order of a court or in order to secure the fulfillment of any obligation prescribed by law;

   c the lawful arrest or detention of a person effected for the purpose of bringing him before the competent legal authority on reasonable suspicion of having committed an offence or when it is reasonably considered necessary to prevent his committing an offence or fleeing after having done so; . . .[4]

The ECtHR's perception of what is meant by 'liberty' is perhaps best illustrated by its 1980 judgment in *Guzzardi v Italy*.[5] Mr Guzzardi had been detained under a law which authorised the detention of—inter alia—'idlers and vagrants' even though the persons concerned had not been convicted of any criminal offence. Mr Guzzardi's detention took the form of an order which required him to live in a designated area of a small, sparsely populated island. He was under house arrest at night, had limited access to the telephone, was required to report to the police daily, and could only leave the island with police permission. The order lasted for over a year. The ECtHR considered that the cumulative effect of these restrictions was tantamount to Mr Guzzardi being in an open prison. The Court also offered general guidance for assessing whether there had been a deprivation of liberty:

[92] In order to determine whether someone has been deprived of his liberty with the meaning of Article 5, the starting point must be his concrete situation and account must be taken of a whole range of criteria such as the type, duration, effects and manner of implementation of the measure in question.

While a condition analogous to detention in gaol would seem clearly to amount to a deprivation of liberty, the 'whole range of criteria' principle adumbrated in *Guzzardi* has also led the Court to conclude that situations falling short of imprisonment in the orthodox sense might engage Art 5. In several judgments, the Court has indicated that twenty-four hour 'house arrest' can amount to a deprivation of liberty.[6] In contrast, the ECtHR has also held that night time or weekend curfews which required a person to be in her home for designated periods did not engage Art 5.[7] The

---

[3] Lest it be thought that such governmental action would be prevented by such constitutional devices as giving liberty an entrenched legal status as in the Fifth Amendment to the US Constitution, we might recall that the US government imprisoned without trial for several years over 100,000 Americans of Japanese descent during World War II on the sole grounds that—because of their ancestry—they might threaten the American war effort; see *Korematsu v United States* (1944) 323 US 214. For a fierce critique see Rostow E (1945) 'The Japanese-American cases—a disaster' *Yale LJ* 489.

[4] Article 5's text differs from provisions such as Art 8 or 10, in that it states specified exceptions to the presumptive entitlement of liberty rather than using the 'necessary in a democratic society' formula.

[5] (1980) 3 EHRR 333. See also the wide-ranging discussion in *Engel v The Netherlands* (1976) 1 EHRR 647.

[6] Cf *Vachev v Bulgaria* (App no 42987/98) [2004] ECHR 325; *Mancini v Italy* (App no 44955/98) [2001] ECHR 502.

[7] *Raimondo v Italy* (1994) 18 EHRR 237.

issue appears to be another aspect of the Convention in respect of which Signatory States enjoy a broad margin of appreciation.

Nonetheless, the Commission and Court have held that involuntary detention which lasts only for very short periods of time can engage Art 5. In *X and Y v Sweden*,[8] for example, the EComHR concluded that detention of only one hour (prior to deportation) could amount to a deprivation. A similar conclusion was reached in *X v Austria*,[9] in which the applicant had been detained for barely an hour so that a blood sample could be taken from him.

This chapter considers the extent to which the government can restrict the physical liberty of persons who have not been put on trial for, nor convicted of a criminal offence. Much English law, even in the relatively modern era, was formulated and applied without explicit reference being made to Art 5, an historical circumstance which provides a useful opportunity to evaluate the consistency of domestic law with Art 5's requirements. That objective is pursued in a series of discrete sections. Sections 1 and 2 consider police powers lawfully to restrict an individual's physical autonomy by subjecting her to involuntary detention. Section 1 assesses those powers in the context of what are termed 'ordinary' offences: section 2 is concerned with 'terrorist offences'.[10]

The Police and Criminal Evidence Act 1984

Much domestic law delineating governmental powers of detention and investigation addressed in this chapter now derives from a single piece of legislation, the Police and Criminal Evidence Act 1984 (a measure generally referred to by the acronym 'PACE'). The Act is perhaps better seen as an attempt to codify and clarify a hitherto disparate and sometimes obscure collection of statutory and common law powers than as marking a fundamental break with the previous law. PACE was enacted to implement the proposals of a Royal Commission on Criminal Procedure established by a Labour government in 1977. The Commission reported in 1980. Its proposals received a broad welcome. An initial Bill published in 1982 was eventually enacted in 1984. The second Thatcher government had proposed many amendments to the Bill, but most were—somewhat unusually—withdrawn or modified in the face of significant opposition both within and outside Parliament. The leading commentator on the Act, Professor Zander, suggests the history of the Act is a good example of the law-making process operating as constitutional idealists would wish:[11]

> The Committee stage in the House of Commons broke the record for the highest number of sittings . . . . There was extensive debate about the proposals before the Conservative government introduced first one and then a second Bill. Both Bills were massively amended by the government . . . [T]he vast majority of amendments were moved by the Government because Ministers and officials were persuaded that they represented genuine improvements in the proposed legislation . . . [12]

The then Home Secretary Leon Brittan described PACE as:

> . . . A long overdue reform and modernisation of the law governing the investigation of crime. The Government's aim has throughout been to ensure that the police have the powers they need to bring offenders to justice, but at the same time to balance those powers with new safeguards to ensure that these powers are used properly, and only where and to the extent that they are necessary.[13]

---

[8] (1976) 7 DR 123.   [9] (1979) 18 DR 154.

[10] The treatment of these issues in this chapter is brief and selective. Readers seeking a more extensive introduction to the subject might refer to the excellent studies in Fenwick H (2007, 4th edn) *Civil liberties and human rights* chs 11–14; and Feldman D (2002, 2nd edn) *Civil liberties and human rights in England and Wales* part II.

[11] Cf the Burkean ideal alluded to in ch 5; see 'Crown and commons—the original intent and the subsequent rise of "party" politics' ff, ch 5, pp 107–108.

[12] See Zander M (1995, 3rd edn) *The Police and Criminal Evidence Act 1984* pp x–xi.   [13] Ibid, p v.

PACE dealt with many police powers. The Act sought to structure and refine the content and use of such powers both by explicit and closely targeted provisions in the legislation itself, and also by empowering the Home Secretary to issue 'Codes of Practice' specifying how particular powers ought to be used. Codes were initially required in respect of powers of search without arrest, the treatment (including questioning) of detained persons, search of premises and seizure of property, and the tape-recording of interviews with detained persons. No provision was initially made for a Code in respect of powers of arrest, an omission not remedied until 2005. The legal status of Codes was somewhat uncertain. PACE did not provide that a police breach of a relevant Code rendered police action unlawful, nor that breach was per se a criminal or tortious act. Section 67(11) did state that a breach of a Code could be taken into account by a court in any related proceedings, but what that might mean was far from clear.

I. Deprivation of liberty for 'ordinary' offences

This section divides its analysis of police powers to restrict an individual's physical liberty into three parts. The first considers powers of 'arrest'. The second addresses powers of detention which arise consequent upon arrest but before the detained person is charged with any offence. The final part considers situations in which a person can lawfully be detained without actually being arrested.

Powers of arrest

An arrest occurs when an individual has been deprived of her liberty: the concept is more a matter of fact than of legal nicety.[14] Presumptively, an arrest could be both a tort and a crime upon the part of the person carrying it out. And just as Mr Carrington had to try (unsuccessfully as it turned out) to find a lawful justification for his intrusion into Mr Entick's printshop in order to rebut Mr Entick's claim for trespass,[15] so a person making an arrest must find lawful justification for his actions either in statute or common law.[16]

Most lawful arrests are now made under statutory authority. The few situations in which a power of arrest still arises at common law are considered briefly below. There are also situations, arising both under common law and statute, where arrest can lawfully be made by any person.[17] The focus of this section remains limited however to arrests made by police officers.

At common law

The most significant common law power of arrest now available to the police relates to situations in which a breach of the peace is occurring or about to occur.[18] The leading modern authority on the meaning of a 'breach of the peace' (which is not per se a criminal offence)[19] is the Court of Appeal's 1984 judgment in *R v Howell*:[20]

> We entertain no doubt that a constable has a power of arrest where there is reasonable apprehension of imminent danger of a breach of the peace; so for that matter has the ordinary citizen . . .

---

[14] For relatively recent House of Lords discussions of the point see *Spicer v Holt* [1977] AC 987; and *Holgate-Mohammed v Duke* [1984] AC 437.

[15] See 'Entick v Carrington (1765)', ch 3, pp 46–47.

[16] Cf Diplock LJ in *Dallison v Caffery* [1965] 1 QB 348 at 370: 'Since arrest involves trespass to the person and any trespass to the person is prima facie tortious, the onus lies on the arrestor to justify the trespass by establishing reasonable and probable cause for the arrest.'

[17] See Bradley A and Ewing K (2002, 13th edn) *Constitutional and administrative law* pp 481–7; Parpworth N (2006, 4th edn) *Constitutional and administrative law* pp 436–46.

[18] See Williams G (1954) 'Arrest for breach of the peace' *Criminal LR* 578.

[19] Cf *Williamson v West Midlands Chief Constable* [2003] EWCA Civ 337, [2004] 1 WLR 14.

[20] [1982] QB 416, (1981) 73 Cr App R 31.

> We are emboldened to say that there is a breach of the peace whenever harm is actually done or is likely to be done to a person or in his presence to his property or a person is in fear of being so harmed through an assault, an affray, a riot, an unlawful assembly or other disturbance. It is for this breach of the peace when done in his presence or the reasonable apprehension of it taking place that a constable, or anyone else, may arrest an offender without warrant.

Howell can be taken as restricting police powers, insofar as there was previously a widespread perception that breach of the peace did not require a fear of immediate physical violence. However, the case also confirmed that the power of arrest arose when the breach of the peace could reasonably be apprehended; it was not necessary that the breach actually occurred.

The Court of Appeal subsequently stressed (in 1998) that the power should not be regarded as a routine element of police conduct. In *Foulkes v Chief Constable of Merseyside*, Beldam J observed that:

> . . . the common law power of a police constable to arrest where no actual breach of the peace has taken place but where he apprehends that such a breach may be caused by apparently lawful conduct is exceptional . . . [A]lthough I am prepared to accept that a constable may exceptionally have power to arrest a person whose behaviour is lawful but provocative, it is a power which ought to be exercised by him only in the clearest of circumstances and when he is satisfied on reasonable grounds that a breach of the peace is imminent . . . there must . . . be a sufficiently real and present threat to the peace to justify the extreme step of depriving of his liberty a citizen who is not at that time acting unlawfully.[21]

Howell (a 1981 case) was decided without any reference to Art 5 ECHR. Prima facie, the power appears compatible with Art 5 ECHR, since any arrest would notionally be made pursuant to the Art 5(1)(c) proviso. That supposition seems to be confirmed by *Foulkes*, which was also decided without considering Art 5.

Shortly after *Foulkes* the ECtHR in *Steel v United Kingdom*[22] held that while breach of the peace was not per se a crime in English law, it could be an 'offence' within the meaning of Art 5(1)(c). The Court also considered that in the aftermath of *Howell*, the notion of a breach of the peace was sufficiently precisely (and narrowly) defined to provide a lawful basis for arrest:

> 55. In this connection, the Court observes that the concept of breach of the peace has been clarified by the English courts over the last two decades, to the extent that it is now sufficiently established that a breach of the peace is committed only when an individual causes harm, or appears likely to cause harm, to persons or property or acts in a manner the natural consequence of which would be to provoke others to violence. It is also clear that a person may be arrested for causing a breach of the peace or where it is reasonably apprehended that he or she is likely to cause a breach of the peace.
>
> Accordingly, the Court considers that the relevant legal rules provided sufficient guidance and were formulated with the degree of precision required by the Convention.

Breach of the peace and 'wilful obstruction' of a police officer

The power of arrest at common law for breach of the peace is also significant in respect of the criminal offence of obstructing a police officer in the execution of her duty; (now found in the Police Act 1996 s 89(2)).[23] That duty extends to preventing breaches of the peace. In circumstances where a prosecution is brought against a person for failing to comply with a police officer's instructions issued because the officer considered a breach of the peace was occurring or likely to occur, the person can obviously raise in her defence the argument that

---

[21] [1998] 3 All ER 705 at 711.   [22] [1999] 28 EHRR 603.
[23] The offence is one of considerable longevity; previously it was contained in the Police Act 1964 s 51.

the officer had no proper basis for reaching that conclusion. The effect of the judgments in *Howell* and *Foulkes* was to enhance the utility of the defence by narrowing the circumstances in which a breach of the peace could reasonably be apprehended. Shortly after the HRA came into force, the judgment of the High Court (per Sedley LJ) in *DPP v Redmond-Bate*[24] provided an important analysis of the inter-relationship between this common law principle and various articles of the ECHR.

Ms Redmond-Bate, a fundamentalist Christian, had been espousing her religious beliefs from the steps of Wakefield Cathedral. Her speech eventually attracted a crowd, which crowd a police officer considered was sufficiently antagonised by what she was saying that a breach of the peace was likely. When Ms Redmond-Bate refused the officer's request that she stop speaking, the police officer arrested her under s 89 and she was convicted in the Crown Court. The High Court quashed the conviction. Sedley LJ was led to this conclusion in part by his understanding of longstanding common law principles. On a proper understanding of the facts, any threat of a breach of the peace came from the crowd, not from Ms Redmond-Bate, whose actions were not per se unlawful. In that sense, the judgment forcefully restated an old common law principle laid out over a century ago in *Beatty v Gillbanks*,[25] that police action in the face of threatened disruption to peaceful protest should be targeted at the putative disrupters rather than at the protestor. In Sedley LJ's view, an individual who persisted in lawful conduct when told to stop by a police officer could not be guilty of wilful obstruction.

Although the HRA was not then in force, Sedley LJ assessed the compatibility of this common law rule with various provisions of the Convention.[26] As noted in chapter twenty-one,[27] Sedley LJ suggested that the coming into force of the HRA was part of a 'constitutional shift' in which notions of 'rights' were gaining increased prominence and significance. In relation to this specific area of human rights protection, he took the view that the common law as he understood it was quite consistent in substantive terms with the requirements of the Convention.

What one might term the express suffusion of ECHR principles into domestic understandings of the breach of the peace concept was demonstrated by the Court of Appeal's subsequent judgment in *Bibby v Chief Constable of Essex*,[28] in which the Court drew upon *Redmond-Bate* to provide a more systematic exposition of what was meant by 'exceptional' per *Foulkes*. Schiemann LJ indicated that six tests would have to be satisfied before the power of arrest could be deployed:

1. There must be the clearest of circumstances and a sufficiently real and present threat to the peace to justify the extreme step of depriving of his liberty a citizen who is not at the time acting unlawfully.

2. The threat must be coming from the person who is to be arrested.

3. The conduct must clearly interfere with the rights of others.

4. The natural consequence of the conduct must be violence from a third party.

5. The violence in 4 must not be wholly unreasonable.

6. The conduct of the person to be arrested must be unreasonable.

Many leading cases on breach of the peace and obstruction of police officers have involved mundane social situations in which disputes over trivial matters have escalated out of hand. *Howell*, for example, arose from a fracas when police attended at a rowdy, middle of the night

---

[24] (1999) 163 JP 789, [2000] HRLR 249.

[25] (1882) 9 QBD 308. *Beatty* is discussed in the seventh edition of this book at pp 561–562.

[26] Since Ms Redmond-Bate was making a religious/political speech at the time of her detention, Arts 9, 10, and 11 ECHR as well as Art 5 were relevant to this inquiry.

[27] See 'Imposing Convention Rights on private individuals and organisations', ch 21, pp 566–571.

[28] (2000) 164 JP 297.

party which was disturbing local residents. Mr Bibby was a bailiff, who had been arrested by a police officer during an altercation with a debtor.[29] The 'human rights' dimension of cases such as *Redmond-Bate* are perhaps more readily apparent. The significance of a case such as *Bibby* perhaps lies in its evident normalisation of ECHR ideas within the Court's analysis of the proper scope of common law powers of arrest.

Statutory powers of arrest

Common law powers of arrest are now quantitatively insignificant compared with those arising under statutory provisions. There is a long and complex history of particular police forces being empowered by private Acts of Parliament to exercise a power of arrest in particular circumstances,[30] but the enactment of powers of arrest through public Acts on a nationwide basis is a more recent development. Many such arrests are carried out in pursuance of a warrant of arrest granted by a magistrate under the terms of s 1 of the Magistrates' Courts Act 1980 in respect of a person who has committed or is suspected of having committed an offence.[31] Should the warrant prove on later examination invalid, the arrest effected under it would be unlawful. However, as long ago as 1750 Parliament had enacted a provision (s 6 of the Constables Protection Act)[32] to prevent any action for unlawful arrest being brought against a police officer in such circumstances.[33]

Until the mid-1960s, police officers had extensive but ill-defined powers at common law to arrest without a warrant any person who they had reasonable grounds to suspect had committed, was committing, or was about to commit, a felony.[34] This and various other common law powers were first put on a statutory basis in the Criminal Law Act 1967, as part of wide-ranging initiative by the then Labour Home Secretary, Roy Jenkins, to modernise all aspects of the criminal justice system. Those reforms were subsequently taken further by PACE.

The Police and Criminal Evidence Act 1984—and its 2005 amendments

Section 26 of PACE expressly repealed most existing statutory powers of arrest, and introduced a stark distinction between two sets of circumstances in which a police officer would be entitled to arrest a person without having a warrant to do so.

Arrestable and non-arrestable offences

PACE drew a sharp (but now redundant) distinction between 'arrestable offences' under s 24 and 'non-arrestable offences' under s 25. As the label implies, 'arrestable offences' were the

---

[29] The Court of Appeal overturned the trial judge's conclusion that the arrest was lawful, on the basis that insofar as a breach of the peace could have been regarded as imminent, the threat came from the debtor not the bailiff.

[30] Which would mean that invoking the power when the requisite circumstances did not exist would be unlawful; see *Christie v Leachinsky* [1947] AC 573.

[31] **1 Issue of summons to accused or warrant for his arrest**.

(1) On an information being laid before a justice of the peace that a person has, or is suspected of having, committed an offence, the justice may issue—

(a) a summons directed to that person requiring him to appear before a magistrates' court to answer the information, or

(b) a warrant to arrest that person and bring him before a magistrates' court.

[32] '[N]o action shall be brought against any constable . . . or against any person or persons acting by his order and in his aid, for anything done in obedience to any warrant under the hand or seal of any justice of the peace.'

[33] Cf the judgment of McNaghten J in *Horsfield v Brown* [1932] 1 KB 355: If the constable acts in obedience to the warrant, then, though the warrant be an unlawful warrant, he is protected by the statute of 1750, but if the warrant be a lawful warrant, and he executes it in an unlawful way, then no action is maintainable against the magistrate, but an action is maintainable against the constable.

[34] See the discussion by Lord Diplock in *Dallison v Caffery* [1965] 1 QB 348. For a rather antiquated overview see Turner J (1962, 18th edn) *Kenny's Outlines of criminal law* pp 561–567. See also Williams G (1954) 'Arrest for felony at common law' *Criminal LR* 408.

more serious crimes, such as—inter alia—murder, kidnapping, theft, and causing grievous bodily harm.

Section 24(4)–(7) empowered a police officer to arrest any person whom she had 'reasonable grounds' for suspecting had committed, is committing, or was about to commit an arrestable offence. The Act did not itself further define the notion of 'reasonable suspicion'. The meaning lent to that concept by the courts would therefore be of great significance in determining the reach of the power. The higher the court set the bar of 'reasonableness'—and the more rigorously judges investigated if the bar was passed in a given case—the less scope there would be for the power to be used. An approach to reasonableness in s 24 which simply equated the term with the administrative law concept of irrationality would afford the power a very broad scope.

Prior to PACE coming into effect, authoritative guidance as to the meaning of the notion of 'suspicion' in relation to powers of arrest had been provided by Lord Devlin's judgment in *Hussein v Chong Fook Kam*, which drew a clear distinction between 'suspicion' and 'proof':

> Suspicion in its ordinary meaning is a state of conjecture or surmise where proof is lacking; 'I suspect but I cannot prove'. Suspicion arises at or near the starting point of an investigation of which the obtaining of prima facie proof is the end. When such proof has been obtained, the police case is complete; it is ready for trial and passes on to its next stage. It is indeed desirable as a general rule that an arrest should not be made until a case is complete. But if an arrest before that were forbidden, it would seriously hamper the police . . . [35]

There was no reason to assume that this guidance would not remain authoritative in respect of powers created by PACE.

The Act was introduced in the same year as the House of Lords offered authoritative guidance as to the meaning of 'reasonable' in s 24's statutory predecessor, the Criminal Law Act 1967 s 2(4), which was worded in the same way as s 24.[36] The appellant in *Holgate-Mohammed Appellant v Duke*[37] had been arrested on suspicion of having carried out a burglary. The basis of the arresting officer's reasonable suspicion was identification evidence from the victim. Lord Diplock's leading judgment held that an arrest made under s 2(4) would be unlawful only if the officer had no bona fide belief that the arrested person was guilty of the offence or that the belief was *Wednesbury* unreasonable. Such a test would mean that the power could be exercised on the basis of little evidence or evidence which was not prima facie especially credible.

The Court of Appeal subsequently developed a three stage test to be applied to assess if an officer's suspicion met the requirements of s 24. The appellant in *Castorina v Chief Constable of Surrey*[38] had been arrested on suspicion of burgling a company from which she had recently been sacked. The Court of Appeal underlined the point that s 24 did not require the officer to believe that the person arrested was indeed guilty of the offence, but merely that such a suspicion was honestly held. More prescriptively, the Court of Appeal held that a trial court in assessing the lawfulness of an arrest under s 24(6) should ask itself three questions:

(a) Did the arresting officer suspect that the person arrested was guilty of the offence;

(b) were there reasonable grounds for that suspicion;

(c) did the officer exercise his discretion to make the arrest in accordance with *Wednesbury* principles.[39]

---

[35] [1970] AC 492 at 498. See also the judgment of Scott LJ in *Dunbell v Roberts* [1944] 1 All ER 326. *Hussein* is a Privy Council rather than House of Lords judgment, and therefore strictly only of persuasive authority. It has however consistently been followed by domestic courts.

[36] '2 (4) Where a constable, with reasonable cause, suspects that an arrestable offence has been committed, he may arrest without warrant anyone whom he, with reasonable cause, suspects to be guilty of the offence'.

[37] [1984] AC 437.   [38] (1996) 160 LG Rev 241.   [39] [1996] LG Rev Rep 241 at p 249.

Castorina indicates that there is both a subjective and objective dimension to the reasonable suspicion test. If the arresting officer herself had no belief in the person's guilt when the arrest was made, the existence of even a substantial body of relevant information known to other officers cannot stop the arrest from being unlawful.

Professor Zander characterised the *Castorina* test as: '[N]ot a very exacting standard'.[40] The courts' evident unwillingness to subject the PACE 'reasonable suspicion' regime to rigorous scrutiny is nicely illustrated by the Court of Appeal's judgment in *Hough v The Chief Constable of the Staffordshire Constabulary*.[41] Mr Hough was arrested, at gunpoint, by a police officer who had been told over the radio that there was an entry on the police national computer that Mr Hough was suspected of illegal possession of a gun and was considered armed and dangerous. The information proved erroneous. The issue before the Court was whether the s 24 reasonable suspicion test applied only to the belief of the arresting officer or whether it should also be applied to the officer who entered the relevant information on the computer. The trial judge had applied the latter test, and since the Chief Constable led no evidence as to the reasonableness of the computer entry, found the arrest to be unlawful. The Court of Appeal reversed that conclusion, holding that it was the belief only of the arresting officer that was relevant and that in most circumstances it was perfectly reasonable for an officer to rely on such information without attempting to evaluate its credibility.

In 2003, in *Cumming v Chief Constable of Northumbria*,[42] the Court of Appeal considered if—in the post-HRA era—the notion of irrationality should be lent a tighter meaning. Cumming was one of a group of local authority employees who monitored CCTV cameras. During an investigation into car theft, the police formed the view that an employee must have altered a CCTV tape that might contain evidence relating to a theft. All the employees were arrested on the assumption that one of them must have altered the tape (which would have amounted to the offence of attempting to pervert the course of justice), and that the formal process of arrest would be more likely to induce the employees to provide useful information than merely inviting them to be interviewed.

The Court of Appeal saw no basis for concluding that an enhanced level of scrutiny should apply to the third branch of the *Castorina* test:

> It has to be remembered that the protection provided by Article 5 is against arbitrary arrest . . . I do not therefore consider that Article 5 required the court to evaluate the exercise of discretion in any different way from the exercise of any other executive discretion, although it must do so, as I have said, in the light of the important right to liberty which was at stake.[43]

The s 25 power of arrest in respect of 'non-arrestable offences'[44] was more tightly drawn. The power was exercisable when a lesser offence had been, was being or was about to be committed and a police officer believed that one or more of specified (in s 25(3)) 'general arrest conditions' were satisfied. These conditions include circumstances where the officer did not know and could not easily find out the name or address of the person arrested (which would make issue of an arrest warrant problematic); and those where the officer has reasonable grounds for thinking—inter alia—that the person is injured, and/or may injure himself or others or damage property.

The High Court confirmed in *Edwards v DPP*[45] that s 25 created a dual test comparable to the one outlined in respect of s 24 in *Castorina*. It would not suffice that there was a credible,

---

[40] (1995) op cit at p 69. He cites more forceful criticism of *Castorina* from Clayton R and Tomlinson J (1988) 'Arrest and reasonable grounds for suspicion' *Law Society Gazette* (September 7) 22 at p 26; 'If the police are justified in arresting a woman of good character on such flimsy grounds, without even questioning her as to her alibi or possible motives, the law provides very scant protection for those suspected of crime'.

[41] [2001] EWCA Civ 39, [2001] Po LR 6.   [42] [2003] EWCA Civ 1844, [2004] Po LR 61.

[43] [2004] Po LR 61 at para 44.   [44] The terminology is unhappily oxymoronic.

[45] [1993] 97 Cr App R 301. The case is significant for other reasons and is discussed more fully later.

even strong reason to think that an arrest condition was satisfied. It was also necessary that the arresting officer had the conditions in his/her mind when she made the arrest.[46]

The 2005 amendments

PACE has now been amended by the Serious Organised Crime and Police Act 2005. The 2005 reforms were an element of what Tony Blair described in a 2004 speech as his governments' 'war on crime',[47] a policy which he portrayed as rejecting what he termed the 'liberal consensus' on crime issues of recent years which placed too much emphasis on the interests of those accused or suspected of crimes and too little emphasis on the interests of victims of crime and ordinary 'law-abiding citizens'.[48] The Home Office had previously indicated in a consultation paper—*Policing: modernising police powers to meet community needs*[49]—that the PACE regime should be amended by: '[M]oving towards a straightforward, universal framework which focuses on the nature of an offence in relation to the circumstances of the victim, the offender and the needs of the investigation'.[50]

The Home Office proposed that this end could best be achieved by abolishing the distinction between arrestable and non-arrestable offences. This policy was enacted in what is now PACE s 24A. The amended legislation creates a police power of arrest for any offence in the following terms:

24A Arrest without warrant: constables

(1) A constable may arrest without a warrant—
    (a) anyone who is about to commit an offence;
    (b) anyone who is in the act of committing an offence;
    (c) anyone whom he has reasonable grounds for suspecting to be about to commit an offence;
    (d) anyone whom he has reasonable grounds for suspecting to be committing an offence.
(2) If a constable has reasonable grounds for suspecting that an offence has been committed, he may arrest without a warrant anyone whom he has reasonable grounds to suspect of being guilty of it.
(3) If an offence has been committed, a constable may arrest without a warrant—
    (a) anyone who is guilty of the offence;
    (b) anyone whom he has reasonable grounds for suspecting to be guilty of it.

Taken alone, these elements of s 24A extend powers of arrest. The section continues however by providing that the power may only be used if the police officer has reasonable grounds to believe that it is necessary to arrest the person concerned for one or more of a list of specified reasons in s 24(5). Many of these echo 'grounds of arrest' in the former s 25, (which has now been repealed), but several other factors have been added, including protecting a child or vulnerable person from the person to be arrested, and—in s 24(5) (e): 'to allow the prompt and effective investigation of the offence or of the conduct of the person in question'.

The insertion of the word 'necessary' is certainly a linguistic nod towards the sentiments of the ECHR[51] If the courts take a rigorous approach to the issue of necessity the presumptive extension of police powers displayed in s 24A might turn out to have little effect in practice.

---

[46] 'The first requirement is that the relevant condition shall have appeared to the officer at the time and then secondly the question whether that condition was in fact fulfilled or not': ibid, at 307 per Evans LJ.

[47] Available at <http://www.guardian.co.uk/politics/2004/jul/19/immigrationpolicy.ukcrime>.

[48] The accuracy of Mr Blair's historical premise is calmly and comprehensively undermined by David Feldman in (2006) 'Human rights, terrorism and risk; the roles of politician and judges' *Public Law* 364.

[49] (2004); <http://www.statewatch.org/news/2004/aug/police-powers-consult.pdf>.   [50] At para 2.5.

[51] Although as noted earlier Leon Brittan used the word in describing the objectives of PACE itself.

Giving reasons for arrest

Art 5(2) ECHR requires that:

> Everyone who is arrested shall be informed promptly, in a language which he understands, of the reasons for his arrest and of any charge against him.

In *Christie v Leachinsky*,[52] decided three years before the ECHR came into being, the House of Lords held that a similar principle existed at common law. Mr Leachinsky was a dealer in waste fabrics, arrested by Christie, a police officer who suspected him of handling stolen cloth. Christie had however purported to arrest Leachinsky under powers conferred on him by a private Act of Parliament promoted by Liverpool Council. Christie knew he had no such power, since it could only be used in respect of persons whose name or address were unknown to the arresting officer, but evidently invoked it because doing so was 'more convenient' than seeking a warrant.

The House of Lords held that arrest without a warrant in such circumstances was unlawful. Viscount Simon's judgment drew upon what he considered to be several long established[53] propositions on this point:

1. If a policeman arrests without warrant on reasonable suspicion of felony, or of other crime of a sort which does not require a warrant, he must in ordinary circumstances inform the person arrested of the true ground of arrest. He is not entitled to keep the reason to himself or to give a reason which is not the true reason . . . [A] citizen is entitled to know on what charge or on suspicion of what crime he is seized.

2. If the citizen is not so informed, but is nevertheless seized, the policeman, apart from certain exceptions, is liable for false imprisonment.

3. The requirement that the person arrested should be informed of the reason why he is seized naturally does not exist if the circumstances are such that he must know the general nature of the alleged offence for which he is detained.

4. The requirement that he should be so informed does not mean that technical or precise language need be used. The matter is a matter of substance, and turns on the elementary proposition that in this country a person is, prima facie, entitled to his freedom and is only required to submit to restraint on his freedom if he knows in substance the reason why it is claimed that this restraint should be imposed.

Viscount Simon's judgment laid great stress—in both substantive and rhetorical terms—on a common law tradition of maximising individual liberty.[54] The sentiments echo those offered

---

[52] [1947] AC 573.

[53] Viscount Simon began his review of the authorities by turning to a textbook first published in 1755: 'Burn's Justice Of The Peace is a work of acknowledged authority which has gone through more than thirty editions. It originally appeared in 1755, and the author, the Rev Richard Burn, DCL (who also brought out three successive editions of Blackstone's Commentaries), deals in detail with the law of arrest without warrant. He says (vol. I, p 302) that "where a constable acts without warrant by virtue of his office of constable, he should, unless the party be previously acquainted with it, notify that he is a constable, or that he arrests in the Queen's name, and for what, . . . "'; ibid, at 586.

[54] 'If a policeman who entertained a reasonable suspicion that X had committed a felony were at liberty to arrest him and march him off to a police station without giving any explanation of why he was doing this, the prima facie right of personal liberty would be gravely infringed. No one, I think, would approve a situation in which, when the person arrested asked for the reason, the policeman replied: "That has nothing to do with you. Come along with me." Such a situation may be tolerated under other systems of law, as, for instance, in the time of lettres de cachet in the eighteenth century in France, or in more recent days when the Gestapo swept people off to confinement under an overriding authority which the executive in this country happily does not in ordinary times possess. This would be quite contrary to our conceptions of individual liberty. If I may introduce a reference to the well known book, Dalton's Country Justice, that author, dealing with arrest and imprisonment, says: "The liberty of a man is a thing specially favoured by the common law".; ibid, at 588.

by Lord Atkin five years earlier in *Liversidge v Anderson*, sentiments which the majority of the Court considered had been rejected by Parliament in approving the text of reg 18b. Like any rule or principle of common law, the propositions advanced so firmly by Viscount Simon could be abrogated in 'ordinary' as well as in 'extraordinary times'.

The *Christie* principle does now have a statutory basis in PACE s 28, which provides that:

28 Information to be given on arrest

(1) Subject to subsection (5) below, where a person is arrested, otherwise than by being informed that he is under arrest, the arrest is not lawful unless the person arrested is informed that he is under arrest as soon as is practicable after his arrest . . .

(3) Subject to subsection (5) below, no arrest is lawful unless the person arrested is informed of the ground for the arrest at the time of, or as soon as is practicable after, the arrest.

(4) Where a person is arrested by a constable, subsection (3) above applies regardless of whether the ground for the arrest is obvious

The common law principles outlined in *Christie* are echoed in the requirements of s 28. The appellant in *Edwards v Director of Public Prosecutions*[55] was one of several suspected cannabis users arrested by police officers late one evening in a busy street after a violent altercation. It was entirely likely on the facts that the officer could lawfully have arrested Ms Edwards on the basis that Ms Edwards was committing a non-arrestable offence (possession of cannabis) and that one or more of the grounds of arrest in PACE s 25 was satisfied. The officer had, however, in nicely prosaic terms, told Ms Edwards that she was 'nicked for obstruction'. Unhappily for the officer, the previously extant statutory power of arrest for obstruction had been repealed by PACE s 26. The arrest was therefore unlawful.[56]

Edwards shows clearly the two purposes inherent in the requirement to give reasons for arrest. The first is that it removes the possibility that a person can be—or feels she can be—arrested arbitrarily. The second is that it provided a yardstick against which the lawfulness of the arrest can subsequently be measured. The importance of these considerations led Evans LJ in *Edwards* to observe—notwithstanding his evident sympathy for the difficult position in which the officer found himself—that: '[I]t has to be borne in mind that giving correct information as to the reason for an arrest is a matter of the utmost constitutional significance in a case where a reason can be and is given at the time'.[57]

Edwards was decided in 1993, without any reference to Art 5. The compatibility of s 28 with Art 5(2) came before the ECtHR in *Fox, Campbell and Hartley v United Kingdom*.[58] The Court concluded in *Fox* that the Art 5(2) requirement that reasons be given for a deprivation of liberty did not necessarily require that those reasons be especially detailed:

40 . . . Whilst this information must be conveyed 'promptly' (in French: 'dans le plus court délai'), it need not be related in its entirety by the arresting officer at the very moment of the arrest. Whether the content and promptness of the information conveyed were sufficient is to be assessed in each case according to its special features.

There is no obvious basis to assume that the test in *Edwards* would not suffice for these purposes. The Court of Appeal's 2004 judgment in *Taylor v Chief Constable of Thames Valley Police*[59] confirmed the presumption that s 28 met Art 5's requirements. The appellant in Taylor was a 10-year-old boy arrested on 31 May 1998 in respect of his activities at an anti-vivisection rally on 18 April 1998, when it appeared he had engaged in violent

---

[55] (1993) 97 Cr App R 301.

[56] Zander equally prosaically observes that the officer should simply have said: 'You're nicked for suspected possession of cannabis': (1995) op cit at p 71.   [57] [1993] Cr App Rep 301 at 308.

[58] (1990) 13 EHRR 157. The case is discussed more extensively in section II later in the chapter.

[59] [2004] EWCA Civ 898, [2004] 1 WLR 3155.

disorder by—inter alia—throwing stones. The reason given for his arrest was that he had been engaged in violent disorder at Hillgrove Farm on 18 April. In an action for unlawful arrest, the trial judge held that the arresting officer should have been more specific in the information he gave (ie by saying the appellant had been throwing stones), bearing in mind the 'special features of the case'; namely the appellant's age and the lapse of time since the events occurred.

The Court of Appeal held that such specificity was not required either by s 28 or Art 5:

> Neither the claimant nor his mother could be expected to be in any doubt why he was being arrested. It was for his part in the previous violent disorder. There was no need to specify the precise way in which he was said to be taking part. Whatever are the various ways in which violent disorder can be committed, 'violent disorder' was a good description of what had happened on the previous occasion without more. Associated with its time and place, it permitted the claimant and his mother to respond, if either had wished, that the claimant was not there or that he was doing nothing wrong.[60]

The powers of arrest which Parliament (through statute) and the courts (through the common law) have bestowed upon government officials clearly amount to a deprivation of liberty, albeit in a chronologically limited sense. Perhaps of more significance—certainly for arrested persons who are not subsequently prosecuted for having committed any offence—are the powers which government officials possess in respect of an arrested person after she has been arrested. In what circumstances, and for what period of time, can the person continue to be deprived of her physical freedom?

Powers of detention after arrest

PACE was significant in amending the police's statutory powers to detain arrested persons for questioning prior to them being charged or released. PACE's immediate predecessor was the Magistrates Court Act 1980. Section 43 of that Act required that a person detained for an offence which was not 'serious' had to be brought before a court or released within twenty-four hours. If the offence was 'serious', however, s 43(4) did not place express limits on the duration of detention, but provided that the arrested person be brought before the court 'as soon as practicable'. The distinction between a 'serious' and 'non-serious' offence was not drawn by the Act, which given the significance of the difference was a thoroughly unsatisfactory abdication of responsibility by Parliament. Munro's review of the law at the time[61] described the law on the point as 'notoriously inadequate'.[62] Munro noted that as long ago as 1825 the courts had identified a common law principle to the effect that a period of three days' detention without charge was unacceptably long, and would amount to false imprisonment,[63] but that there was little in the way of contemporary authority on the question. The High Court's 1981 judgment in *Re Sherman and Apps*[64] indicated that 'as soon as practicable' in s 43[65] should read as authorising a maximum of forty-eight hours' detention. Moreover, Donaldson LJ also held that it was a 'fundamental' common law principle: 'That when a police officer who is making inquiries of

---

[60] [2004] 1 WLR at 3167; per Clarke LJ. Contrast the Court's approval of a finding of unlawful arrest on rather different facts; '[I]n Murphy v Oxford 15 February 1985 a person arrested for burglary was told that he was being arrested on suspicion of burglary in Newquay. As Sir John Donaldson MR put it, no mention was made either of the fact that the premises in Newquay were a hotel or of the date on which the offence was committed. The arrest was held to be unlawful'; ibid, at 3166.

[61] Munro C (1981) 'Detention after arrest' *Crim LR* 802.   [62] Ibid, at 802.

[63] *Wright v Court* (1825) 4 B & C 596.   [64] (1981) Cr App Rep 266.

[65] At the time of Apps' arrest, the provision in force was the identically worded s 38 of the Magistrates Courts Act 1952.

any person about an offence has enough evidence to prefer a charge against that person for the offence, he should without delay cause that person to be charged or informed that he may be prosecuted for the offence'.[66]

PACE treats the issue more systematically. The Act divides powers of detention into distinct time periods.[67] Section 30 requires any arrested person to be brought as soon as practicable to a police station. On arrival at the police station, or twenty-four hours after her arrest (whichever time is earlier), the detention clock in relation to the arrested person begins to run. Section 41 authorises an initial detention period of twenty-four hours. If the arrest has been for an indictable offence,[68] that period may then be extended (per s 42) to thirty-six hours by a senior officer if certain conditions are met.[69] Under s 43, a further period of detention up to ninety-six hours in all may be authorised by two magistrates at a hearing which the arrested person is entitled to attend.

The rationale underpinning ss 41–43 is that an arrested person should have her liberty restored to her if the police cannot gather sufficient evidence to sustain her being charged with an offence. In more grandiloquent constitutional terms, PACE manifests Parliament's conclusion that a person's physical liberty is (ordinarily) a sufficiently important moral value that it may not be abrogated for more than ninety-six hours on the basis merely of police suspicion that the person has committed a serious criminal offence.

The ninety-six hour maximum detention provided for in PACE is also presumptively consistent with Art 5(3) ECHR, which provides that:

> Everyone arrested or detained in accordance with the provisions of paragraph 1.c of this article shall be brought promptly before a judge or other officer authorised by law to exercise judicial power and shall be entitled to trial within a reasonable time or to release pending trial. Release may be conditioned by guarantees to appear for trial.

The ECtHR has been unwilling to specify an acceptable maximum period of detention in these circumstances.[70] The reluctance is no doubt attributable both to the wide variety of circumstances in which arrests are made, and to the presumption that states should enjoy a fairly wide margin of appreciation on such matters. In a decision issued in 1966, the EComHR indicated that a four-day period would not be inconsistent with Art 5.[71] More recently, in *Brogan v United Kingdom*[72] (discussed later in the context of 'terrorism' cases), the Court suggested that a narrower view ought to be taken of acceptable time limits in relation to persons arrested for 'ordinary' criminal offences.

Powers of detention without arrest

It is one of the more widely held myths of English law that the police have—and have always had—a general power to detain people for short periods in order that the person concerned

---

[66] (1981) Cr App Rep 266 at 269.

[67] This summary is both concise and selective. No discussion is offered of the potentially significant role of the 'custody officer' (see PACE ss 35–36) nor of the distinction drawn by the Act between 'designated' and 'non-designated' police stations for detention purposes.

[68] ie an offence of sufficient seriousness to be triable in the Crown Court.

[69] **42. Authorisation of continued detention.**
   (1) Where a police officer of the rank of superintendent or above who is responsible for the police station at which a person is detained has reasonable grounds for believing that—
      (a) the detention of that person without charge is necessary to secure or preserve evidence relating to an offence for which he is under arrest or to obtain such evidence by questioning him;
      (b) an offence for which he is under arrest is a serious arrestable offence; and
      (c) the investigation is being conducted diligently and expeditiously, he may authorise the keeping of that person in police detention for a period expiring at or before 36 hours after the relevant time.

[70] See the discussion in Starmer K (1999) *European human rights law* pp 227–231.

[71] *X v Netherland* (1966) 9 Yearbook 564.   [72] (1989) 11 EHRR 117.

can 'help the police with their inquiries'. The reality is nicely illustrated by the oft-cited case of *Kenlin and another v Gardner*.[73] Kenlin and his friend (a Mr Sowoolu) were teenage boys, who were calling round at friends' houses to inform their friends about a forthcoming rugby match. Their activities aroused the suspicions of two plain clothes policeman, who sought to question the boys about what they were doing, but did not purport to arrest them. The boys did not believe that the officers were indeed police officers, and struggled when the officers sought to detain them. The boys were subsequently convicted of assaulting a police officer in the execution of his duty.[74]

The conviction was overturned in the High Court. The Court's brief judgment is comprised mostly of a recitation of the facts of the case. Winn LJ's leading opinion does not cite nor discuss a single authority, and is not couched at any point in a style which deals overtly with matters of constitutional principle. The Court's characterisation of the officers' actions portrays them as prosaic, even mundane:

> What was done was not done as an integral step in the process of arresting, but was done in order to secure an opportunity, by detaining the boys from escape, to put to them or to either of them the question which was regarded as the test question to satisfy the officers whether or not it would be right in the circumstances, and having regard to the answer obtained from that question, if any, to arrest them.[75]

One might almost be forgiven for missing the constitutional significance of the conclusion Winn LJ reached in the next paragraph of his judgment; namely that the officer had committed an assault on the boys because he had no power either at common law or rooted in statute to detain the boys for questioning without having first arrested them. The officer was therefore not acting in the 'execution of his duty' at the time of the altercation, and therefore the boys could not have committed an offence under s 51.

Some ten years later, in *R v Lemsatef*, the Court of Appeal restated the *Kenlin* principle in more forceful terms:

> First, it must be clearly understood that neither customs officers nor police officers have any right to detain somebody for the purposes of getting them to help with their inquiries. Police officers either arrest for an offence or they do not arrest at all. Customs either detain for an offence or they do not detain at all. The law is clear. Neither arrest nor detention can properly be carried out without the accused person being told the offence for which he is being arrested. There is no such offence as 'helping police with their inquiries.' This is a phrase which has crept into use, largely because of the need for the press to be careful about how they report what has happened when somebody has been arrested but not charged. If the idea is getting around amongst either Customs and Excise officers or police officers that they can arrest or detain people, as the case may be, for this particular purpose, the sooner they disabuse themselves of that idea, the better.[76]

It should also be noted that Art 5 does not expressly identify 'helping police with their inquiries' as a legitimate basis for depriving a person of her liberty, an omission which underlines the sentiment that government officials should have a reasonable basis for assuming a person to have engaged in criminal activities before detaining her.

At common law

Notwithstanding the mythical nature of the supposed requirement that the police may detain persons to help with their inquiries, there has long been and remains a power at common law for officers (and indeed private individuals) to exercise a power of detention without arrest

---

[73] [1967] 2 QB 510.   [74] Under what was then Police Act 1964 s 51.   [75] [1967] 2 QB 510 at 519.
[76] [1977] 1 WLR 812 at 816 per Lawton LJ.

when a breach of the peace is occurring or seems likely to occur. The existence of the power was confirmed by the House of Lords in *Albert v Lavin*,[77] in which Lord Diplock observed:

> [E]very citizen in whose presence a breach of the peace is being, or reasonably appears to be about to be, committed has the right to take reasonable steps to make the person who is breaking or threatening to break the peace refrain from doing so; and those reasonable steps in appropriate cases will include detaining him against his will. At common law this is not only the right of every citizen, it is also his duty, although, except in the case of a citizen who is a constable, it is a duty of imperfect obligation.[78]

Albert v Lavin arose out of trivial facts. Mr Albert had tried to jump a bus queue, and was prevented from doing so by an off-duty police constable. A more recent judgment of the House of Lords—*R (Laporte) v Chief Constable of Gloucestershire*[79]—illustrates clearly the constitutional significance of the power to detain people because of an anticipated breach of the peace. The claimant in *Laporte* was among three coachloads of protestors who in March 2003 were travelling by coach from London to join a protest against the Iraq war at an RAF base in Gloucestershire. The coaches were heading towards a protest planned at Fairford, where several demonstrations—of varying degrees of legality—had been held in the previous few months.

Gloucestershire police had been monitoring the convoy and were under the impression that the party included a substantial number of militant protestors known as Wombles,[80] whose reputation evidently indicated to the police that violent protest might occur when the protestors got to Fairford. The Gloucestershire constabulary therefore decided to 'stop and search' the convoy when it came to Lechlade, within a few miles of the protest site. Quite how many 'Wombles' were among the protestors was never ascertained, but the police did find and confiscate a number of items, some of which—such as 'a can of red spray paint . . . a safety flare . . . and 5 polycarbonate home-made shields'[81]—might obviously have been used for non-peaceful purposes.

This evidence, along with their pre-existing intelligence, led the police to believe it was justifiable to stop the coaches, to detain all of the passengers on board (albeit not to arrest them), to require the drivers to turn the coaches around and then—accompanied by a police escort—to drive the coaches and their passengers back to London; thereby not only preventing the protestors from expressing their views in the planned demonstration but also—since the coaches had no toilets and the police did not allow them to stop en route during the two and a half hour trip—subjecting them to some appreciable discomfort and inconvenience.

All of this was done on the presumed basis that the police had reasonable grounds to believe that a breach of the peace would occur if the coaches were allowed to proceed to Fairford, and that such reasonable belief justified the detention of the passengers in the sense both of stopping them joining the protest and sending them all the way back to London.

Ms Laporte challenged the lawfulness of the police action on the basis of its alleged breach of Arts 5, 10, and 11 ECHR. The challenge was made both to the police's decision to prevent her going to Fairford and to the decision to force her to return to London. At first instance, the High Court upheld the decision to prevent the passengers joining the protest, but held that their subsequent forced return to London was unlawful.[82] Those conclusions were subsequently upheld by the Court of Appeal.[83] The House of Lords took a less indulgent view of the police's powers to interfere with Ms Laporte's physical liberty and freedom of expression, holding unanimously that both elements of the police's actions were unlawful.

---

[77] [1982] AC 546. [78] Ibid, at 565. [79] [2006] UKHL 55, [2007] 2 AC 105.
[80] An acronym for the clumsily named 'White Overalls Movement Building Libertarian Effective Struggles'.
[81] [2006] UKHL 55, [2007] 2 AC 105 at para 11. [82] [2004] EWHC 253 (admin), [2004] 2 All ER 874.
[83] [2004] EWCA Civ 1639, [2005] QB 678.

The argument in all three courts had proceeded on the common assumption that the police's power to *arrest* a person on the basis of an officer's belief that a breach of the peace was about to occur required that there be a reasonable basis for the police to believe that violent disorder would occur and would do so imminently.[84] The police did not contend that these conditions were satisfied when the protestors' coaches were stopped at Lechlade. Any arrest in those circumstances would have been unlawful at common law and thus also a breach of Arts 5, 10, and 11 ECHR. Ms Laporte and her fellow protestors were however not arrested. Rather they were prevented from going to their planned destination, forcibly detained on a bus, and then driven against their wills some eighty miles back to London.

The Chief Constable's argument in *Laporte* was in essence that interferences with individual liberty falling short of arrest would be lawful if the interference was 'reasonable' in the circumstances and that police assessment of reasonableness was something which courts should be slow to second guess. The submission rested largely on the High Court's judgments in *Piddington v Bates*,[85] and *Moss v McLachlan*,[86] in both of which the Court had upheld the detention of protestors even though there was no evidential basis to believe that a breach of the peace was *immediately* likely to occur.

Ms Laporte's rebuttal was that the common law, properly construed, drew no meaningful distinction between arrest and other forms of detention, and required imminence in either circumstance. Alternatively, she contended that the Chief Constable's action on the particular facts of her case could not withstand scrutiny under the 'necessary in a democratic society' limb of Arts 10 and 11.

The House of Lords accepted both of Ms Laporte's arguments. Lord Bingham felt that the weight of domestic legal authority pointed towards a requirement of 'imminence' of a breach of the peace to justify both arrest and detention or interference falling short of arrest.[87] *Piddington v Bates* was dismissed as an 'aberrant' decision, while *Moss* was read as a case which properly accepted an unusually lengthy notion of immediacy because of the particular facts of the case and the context in which they arose.[88]

From the perspective of preserving freedom of expression on political issues, *Laporte* is an obviously welcome development. The legal principle being argued for by the police in *Laporte* was one which would have lent considerable uncertainty to the substantive scope of lawful police interference with per se peaceful speech and protest and which would likely have had a significant deterrent effect on many citizens' readiness to engage in such activities. But the judgment also has a more general narrowing effect on the polices' common law powers of detention. *Laporte* also provides us with another example of the courts concluding that the common law has independently developed to a point of substantive compatibility with the Convention. It is perhaps plausible to conclude however that the presence of the HRA on the constitutional landscape has nudged common law development on this point further and faster than would otherwise have occurred.

Under statute

In addition to their limited common law powers, police officers traditionally had various narrowly tailored statutory powers which permitted them to detain people without arrest in

---

[84] Lord Bingham offered (at para 30) Glanville Williams' analysis as a correct statement of the law: see (1954) 'Arrest for breach of the peace' *Crim LR* 578. The case law most relied upon by the police to sustain the proposition was *Albert v Lavin* [1982] AC 546 and *Foulkes v Chief Constable of Merseyside* [1998] 3 All ER 705.

[85] [1961] 1 WLR 162.   [86] [1985] IRLR 76.   [87] At para 50.

[88] At para 51. *Moss* arose during the miner's strike of the 1980s. The Court upheld the arrest of miners who refused police instructions to abandon their plans to join a demonstration at a colliery several miles from where the arrest took place. Police action in that era had often been attended by extraordinary violence and brutality towards protesters, sometimes in response to similar behaviour by striking miners towards the police. See the collection of essays in Fine B and Millar R (1985) *Policing the miners' strike*.

certain circumstances. A good example of such a power is s 23(2) of the Misuse of Drugs Act 1971, which provides that:

> (2) If a constable has reasonable grounds to suspect that any person is in possession of a controlled drug in contravention of this Act or of any regulations made thereunder, the constable may—
>   (a) search that person, and detain him for the purpose of searching him;
>   (b) search any vehicle or vessel in which the constable suspects that the drug may be found, and for that purpose require the person in control of the vehicle or vessel to stop.[89]

As with powers of arrest, various Acts of Parliament also gave geographically limited and subject specific powers of detention—usually for the purposes of conducting a search—to some police forces. For example, the Metropolitan Police Act 1839 s 66 gave officers in London a power to stop and search people whom it was thought might be carrying stolen goods.

The patchwork nature of these powers was regarded as both inadequate and unhappily uncertain by the Phillips Commission and by Parliament in the early 1980s,[90] which led Parliament to enact a much more wide-ranging power in PACE s 1. This proved a controversial initiative, in part as a matter of principle but also because of the somewhat arbitrary way in which it seemed that existing statutory powers of 'stop and search' were being used. Zander notes that the 'success rate' (in terms of the numbers of arrests of people stopped) of searches under s 23 in the late 1970s was little more than 20%, while in the same era barely 10% of people stopped under s 66 were subsequently arrested.[91]

The core of the power lies in s 1(2):

> (2) [A] constable—
>   (a) may search
>   (i) any person or vehicle:
>   (ii) anything which is in or on a vehicle,
>   for stolen or prohibited articles . . .
> (3) This section does not give a constable power to search a person or vehicle or anything in or on a vehicle unless he has reasonable grounds for suspecting that he will find stolen or prohibited articles . . .

Like powers of arrest under PACE, the stop and search power requires both that the officer has a suspicion that she will find stolen or prohibited goods, and that the suspicion has a reasonable basis. The category of 'stolen articles' is self-explanatory. 'Prohibited articles' encompasses weapons or items (such as tools) which might be used in carrying out other criminal activities; (burglary and car theft being the obvious examples). In a nod to the 'Englishman's home is his castle' principle, the power did not extend to people or vehicles on land used as a dwelling unless the officer had reasonable grounds to believe that the person did not live in the dwelling or have permission from the occupier to be there, or that the vehicle was not controlled by the occupier or there with her permission.

The s 1(2) power was also subject to provisions in s 2 which—inter alia—required the officer to identify herself to the persons searched, and state what she was searching for and on what grounds she considered the search to be justified. Section 3 then made provision for a record of searches to be made by the officer. A particular concern was that 'stop and search' powers—especially under s 23—were used by the police on the basis of empirically unfounded presumptions about the propensity of particular ethnic or cultural groups to be in possession of illegal drugs, and that a similarly unfounded discriminatory ethos would inform the use of the much broader powers granted under PACE.

---

[89] The Firearms Act 1968 gave a similar power to search persons and vehicle for—obviously—guns.
[90] See Zander (1995) op cit pp 3–4.   [91] Ibid, at 4.

The second Thatcher government sought to meet or diffuse the controversy on this point by producing a Code of Practice (Code A) on the way the powers should be used. The most oft-quoted part of the original Code stressed that an officer's reasonable suspicion must have both an objective and an individuated basis:

> 1.6 . . . Reasonable suspicion may exist for example where information has been received such as a description of an article being carried or of a suspected offender; a person is seen acting covertly or warily or attempting to hide something; or a person or a person is carrying a certain article at an unusual time or in a place where a number of burglaries or thefts are known to have taken place recently . . .
>
> 1.7 Reasonable suspicion can never be supported on the basis of personal factors alone. For example a person's colour, age, hairstyle, or manner of dress, or the fact that he is known to have a previous conviction for possession of an unlawful article, cannot be used alone or in combination with each other as the sole basis on which to search that person. Nor may it be founded on the basis of stereotyped images of certain persons or groups as more likely to be committing offences . . .

Similar provisions are found at paras 2.1–2.3 of the 2009 version of the Code. Notwithstanding these provisions, empirical evidence indicates that stop and search powers under PACE are used disproportionately frequently against non-white persons.[92]

Both the Act and the Code address the manner of any search in some detail. Para 3.1 of the Code says that: 'Every reasonable effort must be made to reduce to the minimum the embarrassment that a person being searched may experience'. That rather vague objective is buttressed by more explicit prohibitions in the Act itself, such as s 2(9) which provides that the s 1 power does not extend to requiring a person to remove items of clothing other than a coat, jacket, or gloves in public.[93] The Code also suggests (in para 3.3) that officers should make efforts to secure the person's consent to a search rather than have her submit to an involuntary search; that the period of detention should not exceed the time needed for the search, and that the search itself should be conducted expeditiously.

The Act also makes extensive provision (in s 3) for a record to be kept of all searches. The supposed importance of that requirement—which if met would provide both a basis for assessing the propriety of police behaviour in a given case and a body of empirical evidence relating to overall use of the power—is reiterated in para 4 of Code A.

Pre-arrest powers of detention are, in the main, powers of extremely limited chronological duration, often measured in minutes rather than hours. If exercised in a bona fide manner, they will often be no more than an irritation to the persons detained. As yet, the ECtHR has not given any clear indication that detention of this sort will necessarily amount to a deprivation of liberty within Art 5. It may of course do so if a particular individual is subjected to such searches on a frequent or regular basis and no evidence of criminal activity is ever uncovered.

II. Deprivation of liberty for 'terrorist' offences

While the ECtHR has consistently held that a 'deprivation' within Art 5 is not limited to detention in a jail in the orthodox sense, it should also be stressed that the scheme of the Convention permits states to derogate from Art 5—and most other provisions of the ECHR—in certain circumstances. The scenario in which Art 15[94] has most often been invoked in relation to governmental powers of arrest and detention has been when states have felt that their internal security is threatened by the actual or expected activities of 'terrorist' groups.

---

[92] See Fenwick (2007) op cit pp 1124–1126 and the sources cited therein.

[93] The Code (para 3.5) but not the Act specifies that a search involving the removal of any other clothing shall not be done by officers of the opposite sex to the person detained unless the person so requests.

[94] See 'Contingent rather than absolute entitlements', ch 18, pp 480–481.

One of the first Art 5 cases with which the ECtHR had to deal was *Lawless v Ireland*.[95] Mr Lawless was a member of the IRA, and had been detained without trial for five months by the Irish government. Such a detention would presumptively breach Art 5 since the Irish government had not detained Mr Lawless for any of the purposes identified in Art 5(1), but Ireland argued before the Court that it was entitled under the derogation provisions of Art 15 to permit such actions. Art 15 provides:

1. In time of war or other public emergency threatening the life of the nation any [State] may take measures derogating from its obligations under the Convention to the extent strictly required by the exigencies of the situation . . .

The Court held in *Lawless* that the notion of 'public emergency . . . ' meant: 'an exceptional situation of crisis or emergency which affects the whole population and constitutes a threat to the organised life of the community'.[96] It then accepted that the activities of the IRA in Ireland were sufficiently grave to meet that test.[97] The ECtHR also concluded that prolonged detention of persons without trial was not a measure that went beyond what was; 'strictly required by the exigencies of the situation'. Equally significantly, the Court held that when Art 15 was in issue states would enjoy a wide margin of appreciation in respect both of whether an emergency existed and what steps should be taken to address it.

For successive British governments in the post-war era, the political instability of Northern Ireland has until very recently been the major reason for promoting legislation which interferes in an 'extraordinary' fashion with individual liberty. Until 1922, Ireland had been part of the United Kingdom, and had been so since the Act of Union of 1800. Following what was in effect revolution and civil war in the early decades of the twentieth century, the Republic of Ireland came into being as a separate nation state in 1922, while the northern parts of Ireland ('Northern Ireland') remained part of the United Kingdom. Unlike Scotland and Wales at that time however, Northern Ireland had a form of devolved government, the composition and powers of which were set by the Government of Ireland Act 1922. Parliament also granted the Northern Ireland government (in the Civil Authorities (Special Powers) Act 1922 s 1) a very broad 'legislative' authority:

1(1) The [government] shall have power, in respect of persons, matters and things within the jurisdiction of the Government of Northern Ireland, to take all such steps and issue all such orders as may be necessary for preserving the peace and maintaining order, . . .

Provided that the ordinary course of law and avocations of life and the enjoyment of property shall be interfered with as little as may be permitted by the exigencies of the steps required to be taken under this Act.

Section 1 provided an obviously broad base for the government of Northern Ireland to pursue its preferred policies in respect of suspected 'terrorists'. From the 1950s onwards, the extent to which the use of those powers diverged from ordinary constitutional presumptions became increasingly apparent.

Powers of arrest and detention in the 1945–1977 era

In much the same way as the Irish government had reacted to IRA terrorism in the mid-1950s, the Northern Irish government in the mid-1950s made several orders under the Special

---

[95] (1961) 1 EHRR 15.   [96] At para 28.

[97] 28 . . . [T]he existence at the time of a 'public emergency threatening the life of the nation' was reasonably deduced by the Irish Government from a combination of several factors, namely: in the first place, the existence in the territory of the Republic of Ireland of a secret army engaged in unconstitutional activities and using violence to attain its purposes; secondly, the fact that this army was also operating outside the territory of the State, thus seriously jeopardising the relations of the Republic of Ireland with its neighbour [ie Northern Ireland]; thirdly the steady and alarming increase in terrorist activities from the autumn of 1956 and throughout the first half of 1957'.

Powers Act which were prima facie inconsistent with ECHR Art 5. Regulation 10 empowered a police officer to arrest without a warrant any person for the purposes of interrogation.[98] The only other precondition for the arrest was that the officer considered that arresting the person would assist the 'preservation of peace and maintenance of order'. Regulation 10 allowed for up to forty-eight hours detention of the arrested person.

Like reg 10, reg 11(1) did not refer explicitly to 'terrorism'. Regulation 11 permitted arrest without warrant by a police officer, a member of the armed forces, or any other person authorised by the government. There was, in contrast to reg 10, no specified purpose for the arrest. However the arresting officer did have to suspect that the person arrested had acted, was acting, or was about to act 'in a manner prejudicial to the preservation of peace or the maintenance of order'. There was no express requirement that the suspicion be reasonable. Regulation 11(1) also permitted detention of an arrested person before charge for up to seventy-two hours. This period could be consequential on the forty-eight hour detention permitted by reg 10, so allowing for a 120 hour (five day detention) in all.

Regulation 11(2) authorised the continuing detention of a person arrested under reg 11(1). No express limit was placed on the duration of the time for which the arrested person could be held before being charged with any offence, although as a matter of practice it seemed that a twenty-eight day maximum was observed.

Regulation 12 made provision for a further period of detention (referred to as 'internment'). Regulation 12 empowered a government Minster to order the detention of any person who he/she suspected of acting in a manner prejudicial to public order if the Minister considered it expedient to do so. No limit was placed on the length of internment, which would continue for as long as the Minister wished. The scheme of reg 12 was much like that used in reg 18b of the Defence Regulations during World War II. An interned person was entitled to have her detention examined by a Committee of a judge and two non-legal members. However the detainee was not granted any express entitlement to appear before the committee, nor call witnesses nor cross-examine any witnesses appearing for the Minister, nor be legally represented at a hearing. The Committee could recommend, but not order, a person's release.

The compatibility of these measures with Art 5 was not tested until the 1970s. The regulations provoked huge controversy in 1971, when after an escalation of IRA activities the Northern Ireland government invoked regs 10, 11, and 12 to arrest, detain, and intern hundreds of people it suspected of being IRA activists or supporters. Nearly 3,000 people were arrested under reg 10, some 1,200 of whom were also subsequently detained under reg 11(1). 1,250 detention orders were made under reg 11(2), and almost 800 people were interned under reg 12. This policy appeared to exacerbate rather than calm the political situation. The continuation of both terrorist activities and widespread political unrest prompted Edward Heath's (Conservative) government to promote a Bill, enacted as the Northern Ireland (Temporary Provisions) Act 1972 to—in effect—suspend the existence of Northern Ireland's devolved government and institute a system of 'direct rule' through prerogative powers (taking the form of Orders in Council) exercised by a newly created Secretary of State for Northern Ireland. The regs 10, 11, and 12 powers were retained (with 'internment' being renamed 'interim custody' and 'detention'), but given a new statutory source; the Detention of Terrorists (Northern Ireland) Order. The powers were then enacted as primary legislation within the Northern Ireland (Emergency Provisions) Act 1973. The Heath government considered that these powers of arrest would breach Art 5, and had sought a derogation under Art 15 ECHR. That position was maintained by the subsequent Labour government.

That derogation was sought is perhaps in itself a good indication of the level of political legitimacy—if not legal enforceability—that the ECHR then enjoyed within governmental

---

[98] This was essentially a statutory creation of a police power to require persons 'to help police with their inquiries'; ie the power held in *Kenlin* not to exist at common law.

circles in Britain.[99] The then Irish government (overlooking perhaps the policies pursued by its 1950s predecessor) promptly initiated proceedings against the United Kingdom before the ECtHR, seeking to establish that the powers were incompatible with Art 5 and not justifiable through a derogation under Art 15.

When the matter reached the Court in 1978, everyone detained under the order had either been released or charged with an 'ordinary' crime. Nonetheless, some of the persons detained or interned had spent a period of several years in jail without having been convicted of nor even charged with any offence. The United Kingdom government did not contest that the measures breached Art 5, relying instead on the validity of its derogation.

The ECtHR accepted that reasoning. It considered (echoing its view in *Lawless*) that the level of terrorist violence in Northern Ireland in the 1970s amounted to 'an emergency threatening the life of the nation'. It was also persuaded that the policies pursued in the order went no further than was 'strictly required'. The Court noted in particular the scale of the violence,[100] the military nature of the IRA, and the difficulties of gathering evidence securing convictions through the ordinary criminal process because of widespread IRA intimidation of potential witnesses.

Powers of arrest after *Ireland v United Kingdom*

By the mid-1980s, the level of political violence in Northern Ireland had declined significantly. Parliament had also taken steps to clarify the nature of the extraordinary powers available to the government, not least by expressly framing the problem in issue as 'terrorism' rather than using the euphemistic notion of 'peace and order'. Parliament offered a definition of 'terrorism' in s 31(1) of the Northern Ireland (Emergency Provisions) Act 1978 Act:

> '[T]errorism' means the use of violence for political ends and includes any use of violence for the purpose of putting the public or any section of the public in fear; 'terrorist' means a person who is or has been concerned in the commission or attempted commission of any act of terrorism or in directing, organising or training persons for the purpose of terrorism; . . . [101]

The statutory definition of terrorism may have had certain symbolic ends, but in a narrower legal sense it served the instrumental purpose of lending lawful status to police powers that would be regarded as legally excessive (because morally indefensible) in respect of ordinary crimes. Both Conservative and Labour governments were sufficiently alarmed by the terrorist activities of extremist political groups (including, but not only the IRA) in Northern Ireland during the 1970s and 1980s to promote Bills which created powers of arrest which gave greater authority to police officers than they possessed in respect of 'ordinary' crimes. Provision was made for example in the Northern Ireland (Emergency Provisions) Act 1978 s 11 that: 'Any constable may arrest without warrant any person whom he suspects of being a terrorist'. Thus there was no requirement in the text of s 11 that the officer's suspicion should have a 'reasonable' basis.

The House of Lords subsequently confirmed in *McKee v Chief Constable for Northern Ireland*[102] that no such presumption should be read into the provision. The arresting officer's basis for suspicion in McKee was simply that he had been told by his sergeant that Mr McKee

---

[99] The United Kingdom (and Ireland) joined the EC in 1972. While the Convention was not part of the EC's legal structure, for the United Kingdom to have breached the Convention on such a high profile issue within months of joining the EC would not have played very well with other Member State governments.

[100] Cf at (1978) 2 EHRR 25 at para 44: '[F]rom August to December 1971 . . . there were a total of 146 persons killed, including 47 members of the security services and 99 civilians, 729 explosions and 1437 shooting incidents'.

[101] That definition was retained throughout the latter part of the twentieth century; cf Prevention of Terrorism (Temporary Provisions) Act 1989; '[T]errorism means the use of violence for political ends and includes any use of violence for the purpose of putting the public or any section of the public in fear.'   [102] [1984] 1 WLR 1358.

was suspected of being a terrorist. The House of Lords unanimously held that this was sufficient to make the arrest lawful:

> On the true construction of section 11(1) of the statute, what matters is the state of mind of the arresting officer and of no one else. That state of mind can legitimately be derived from the instruction given to the arresting officer by his superior officer. The arresting officer is not bound and indeed may well not be entitled to question those instructions or to ask upon what information they are founded . . .
>
>   [O]n the true construction of the statute the powers of arrest under section 11 are not qualified by any words of 'reasonableness.' The suspicion has to be honestly held but it need not be a reasonable suspicion as well.[103]

The compatibility of that reasoning with Art 5 ECHR came before the ECtHR in *Fox, Campbell and Hartley v United Kingdom*.[104] The Court concluded that the absence of any requirement at all in s 11 that the belief be reasonable as well as bona fide could not be reconciled with Art 5:

> [35] The 'reasonableness' of the suspicion on which an arrest must be based forms an essential part of the safeguard against arbitrary arrest and detention which is laid down in article 5(1)c . . . [A] 'reasonable suspicion' presupposes the existence of facts or information which would satisfy an objective observer that the person concerned may have committed the offence. What may be regarded as 'reasonable' will however depend upon all the circumstances.

The ECtHR accepted that when terrorism was in issue, the basis of any 'reasonable' suspicion could not fully be disclosed in any court proceedings as this might jeopardise the effectiveness of the police investigation and/or the safety of informants:

> [34] . . . Nevertheless the Court must be enabled to ascertain whether the essence of the safeguard afforded by Article 5(1)(c) has been secured. Consequently the respondent Government has to furnish at least some facts or information capable of satisfying the Court that the arrested person was reasonably suspected of having committed the alleged offence. This is all the more necessary where, as in the present case, the domestic law does not require reasonable suspicion, but sets a lower threshold by merely requiring honest suspicion . . .

The only basis of suspicion for the detention of the appellants which the government advanced in *Fox* was that the appellants had previous convictions for terrorist related activities. The ECtHR held that this could not suffice to justify the arrest.

By the time *Fox* was decided, the mere suspicion test in s 11 had been repealed and replaced with a requirement that the suspicion was 'reasonable' under (what was initially) s 12(1) of the Prevention of Terrorism (Temporary Provisions) Act 1984:

> Subject to subsection (2) below, a constable may arrest without warrant a person whom he has reasonable grounds for suspecting to be— . . .
>
>   (b) a person who is or has been concerned in the commission, preparation or instigation of acts of terrorism . . .[105]

Some indication as to quite how much (or how little) difference this new form of words made to the nature of police powers of arrest in relation to suspected terrorists was given by the House of Lords in *O'Hara v Chief Constable of the RUC*.[106] Mr O'Hara had been arrested by a police officer acting on the orders of a senior officer, following a murder that was presumed to be a terrorist act. The sole basis for the officer's belief that Mr O'Hara was a terrorist was a

---

[103] Ibid, at 1361–1362; per Lord Roskill.   [104] (1990) 13 EHRR 157.

[105] Re-enacted verbatim in the Prevention of Terrorism (Temporary Provisions) Act 1989.

[106] [1997] AC 286.

briefing given by the senior officer concerned. The trial judge had characterised the evidential basis of the officer's belief as 'scanty'.[107] A unanimous House of Lords held that even 'scanty' evidence could suffice for these purposes. The s 12 test would not be satisfied if an officer simply followed an order to arrest a person without forming the view that the person might indeed be guilty of a terrorist offence.[108] However, the notion of 'reasonable' was to be given a broad, *Wednesbury*-type meaning:

> The information acted on by the arresting officer need not be based on his own observations, as he is entitled to form a suspicion based on what he has been told. His reasonable suspicion may be based on information which has been given to him anonymously or it may be based on information, perhaps in the course of an emergency, which turns out later to be wrong. As it is the information which is in his mind alone which is relevant however, it is not necessary to go on to prove what was known to his informant or that any facts on which he based his suspicion were in fact true. The question whether it provided reasonable grounds for the suspicion depends on the source of his information and its context, seen in the light of the whole surrounding circumstances.[109]

A briefing given by a senior officer would presumptively satisfy this test. The House of Lords also considered that this understanding of the law was consistent with the view of Art 5 ECHR advanced by the ECtHR in *Fox*. That assumption was subsequently approved by the ECtHR in *O'Hara v United Kingdom*.[110] Echoing the position adopted by Lord Devlin in *Chong Fook Kam*, the ECtHR stressed that the evidential threshold necessary to justify an arrest could fall substantially short of that required to justify a charge against the arrested person.[111] The Court was also satisfied by the bona fides of the UK government's submissions that the information which underlay the briefing that led to the arrest had come from four separate informers, all of whom were regarded as reliable. Furthermore, the Court reiterated its observation in *Fox* that Art 5 did not require states to disclose the identities of informants in terrorist cases.

The ECtHR's seal of approval for the principle inherent in s 12 and its application on the facts of *O'Hara* goes some substantial way to legitimising the moral preferences expressed by Parliament in the PT(TP)A s 12. But the legislation itself and its construction by the domestic courts are not beyond criticism.

The House of Lords' judgment in *O'Hara* was drawn upon in both and *Cumming* and *Hough* as a guide to the meaning of reasonable suspicion in PACE s 24. That might be thought to be an unfortunate use of precedent. While the words used in s 24 and s 12 of the PT(TP) A were the same, they were found in statutes which had very different purposes. The matters before the courts in *Hough* and *Cumming* were morally mundane instances of everyday criminality—elements of the ordinary business of law enforcement. *O'Hara*—in contrast—occurred in the realm of the morally extraordinary.

Conceding—for the sake of argument—that a potent terrorist threat or state of war does indeed exist, the supposition that Parliament should afford government officials greater

---

[107] Surprisingly, Mr O'Hara's lawyers had chosen not to cross-examine the officer as to the contents of the briefing.　　　　　[108] What Lord Steyn referred to as the 'subjective' element of the test.

[109] Per Lord Hope; [1997] AC 286 at 298. This being the 'objective' element of the test. Lord Steyn agreed that Parliament had not required much judicial scrutiny of the objective element: '[A] constable must be given some basis for a request to arrest somebody under a provision such as section 12(1), e.g. a report from an informer'. [1977] AC 286 at 294.　　　　　[110] (2002) 34 EHRR 32.

[111] At para 36; '[T]he standard imposed by Article 5(1)(c) does not presuppose that the police have sufficient evidence to bring charges at the time of arrest. The object of questioning during detention under sub-paragraph (c) of Article 5(1) is to further the criminal investigation by way of confirming or dispelling the concrete suspicion grounding the arrest. Thus facts which raise a suspicion need not be of the same level as those necessary to justify a conviction, or even the bringing of a charge . . .'.

authority in countering those threats than it grants to those officials in respect of 'ordinary' crime is unproblematic. Legislators might therefore be properly criticised for using identical or very similar textual formulae to express their preferences as to the extent of governmental powers to address those two very different scenarios. And courts which construed such powers on the basis of the legislative text without regard to the text's context might be thought to be engaging in an overly formalistic approach to the task of statutory construction.[112]

Powers of detention after *Ireland v United Kingdom*

Although no government used the power of internment in Northern Ireland after 1975, Parliament underlined the distinction between 'ordinary' crimes and 'terrorist' activity by enacting s 12(4)–(5) of the Prevention of Terrorism (Temporary Provisions) Act 1984. This provided that:

(4) A person arrested under this section shall not be detained for more than forty eight hours after his arrest; but the Secretary of State may, in any particular case, extend the period of forty eight hours by a period or periods specified by him.

(5) Any such further period or periods shall not exceed five days in all.

Section 12(4)–(5) therefore extended, by two days, the period of post-arrest detention previously available under the Detention of Terrorists (Northern Ireland) Order. Given that the scale of the terrorism problem in Northern Ireland had diminished since the early 1970s, the extension of the time period might seem surprising.

It might also be recalled that PACE, enacted in the same year as s 12(4)–(5), imposed a ninety-six hour maximum period of pre-charge detention on arrested persons. PACE also required that detention beyond thirty-six hours had to be approved by a court. The requirement of judicial supervision is a clear manifestation in a practical sense of the theoretical principle of the separation of powers: Parliament has recognised that detention for more than thirty-six hours is such a grave interference with individual liberty that it is not appropriate to place such a power solely in the hands of the executive branch of government. A similar provision was applicable in Northern Ireland in respect of non-terrorist offences.[113]

However the seven day period authorised by s 12(4)–(5) of the PT(TP)A 1984 did grant that power exclusively to the Home Secretary, and expressly excluded any role for the courts. It appeared that the Secretary of State for Northern Ireland routinely granted extensions when asked to do so. Between 1984 and 1987 an extension was refused in barely 2% of cases.[114]

The use of the s 12 powers of post-arrest, pre-charge detention came before the ECtHR in *Brogan v United Kingdom*.[115] The main submission made by the applicants, who had been detained for periods of between four and six days, was that s 12 was inconsistent with the requirement of Art 5(3) ECHR which provides that every person arrested: 'shall be brought promptly before a judge or other officer authorized by law to exercise judicial power . . .'. There was no Art 15 derogation in force at this time. The United Kingdom therefore argued before the Court that the substantially longer period of detention applicable to 'terrorist' arrestees than to persons arrested for ordinary crimes was a necessary response to the difficulties of

---

[112] Although if one's concern was to maximize individual autonomy and constrain governmental power, one might welcome judicial use of interpretive presumptions formulated in the context of 'ordinary' police powers to define the meaning of anti-terrorist provisions.

[113] Magistrates Courts (Northern Ireland) Order 1981 Art 131.

[114] *Brogan v United Kingdom* (1989) 11 EHRR 117 para 17.   [115] (1989) 11 EHRR 117.

evidence gathering in respect of terrorist offences, and to the impracticality of revealing in court details of the suspicions which underlay the arrest. The ECtHR was not persuaded by this argument. It concluded that the concept of 'promptly' demanded that arrested persons be brought before a court very quickly,[116] and that the difficulties cited by the UK government were not sufficient to justify so prolonged a period of detention.[117]

The presumption that anti-terrorism legislation enacted in the 1970s and 1980s imposed 'extraordinary' limitations on individual liberty is underlined by the fact that the Acts invariably included a requirement that their continued applicability was dependent upon annual approval by the two Houses of Parliament, although in practical terms one should perhaps not expect that governments would face exacting scrutiny when seeking such approval. More significantly perhaps, the PT(TP)A 1979 and the PT(TP)A 1984 were each enacted only for a five-year period, a proviso which compelled any government which wished to retain such powers to take on the political challenge of pushing a new Bill through the Commons and Lords.

Powers of arrest and detention in the post-1977 era

David Feldman has latterly referred to a problem of 'legislative creep' within criminal justice policy generally and anti-terrorist measures particularly:

> The law of criminal procedure in England and Wales is full of powers originally granted to deal with very serious offences . . . which come to be normalised, or regarded as equally applicable to other offences, over the course of five, ten or twenty years.[118]

It might also be suggested that a second and third dimension of this phenomenon are, respectively, a government predilection to promote (and a parliamentary predilection to approve) Bills which both expand the definition of 'very serious offences' and also grant evermore substantial powers to government to address them.

In 2000, Parliament enacted a Blair government Bill (as the Terrorism Act 2000) which contained a notably more far-reaching definition of 'terrorism' than had previously been used:

1.–Terrorism: interpretation
(1) In this Act 'terrorism' means the use or threat of action where—
    (a) the action falls within subsection (2),
    (b) the use or threat is designed to influence the government or to intimidate the public or a section of the public, and
    (c) the use or threat is made for the purpose of advancing a political, religious or ideological cause.
(2) Action falls within this subsection if it—
    (a) involves serious violence against a person,
    (b) involves serious damage to property,
    (c) endangers a person's life, other than that of the person committing the action,
    (d) creates a serious risk to the health or safety of the public or a section of the public, or
    (e) is designed seriously to interfere with or seriously to disrupt an electronic system.
(3) The use or threat of action falling within subsection (2) which involves the use of firearms or explosives is terrorism whether or not subsection (1)(b) is satisfied.

[116] The French language version of the ECHR uses 'aussitot' in Art 5(3), the English translation of which would be 'immediately'.

[117] The Court expressly declined (at para 60) to indicate what maximum period of detention was permissible for 'ordinary' offences.   [118] (2006) op cit at p 370.

Since Parliament has also chosen to give s 1 extra-territorial effect,[119] it is difficult to disagree with Professor Walker's observation that: 's.1 is significantly broader than its predecessor'.[120] The broadening of the definition is per se of limited intrinsic significance. The importance of the breadth of the definition lies in its consequential application as a justification for the exercise of governmental powers against 'terrorists' (actual or suspected) which could not be used in respect of 'non-terrorist' activities. To put the matter perhaps rather simplistically, the grant of quite extraordinary powers of arrest and detention to police officers in respect of 'terrorist' activities would be of minimal importance if 'terrorism' itself were defined in extremely narrow terms, since very few people would fall within the 'terrorist' test.[121] In contrast, even a minor extension of police powers of arrest and detention would represent a substantial threat to orthodox notions of individual liberty if the definition of 'terrorism' which permitted the use of those powers was very broad.

The 'temporary' nature of the anti-terrorism legislation of the 1970s–1990s was also brought to an end by the Terrorism Act 2000, which overhauled, extended, and gave 'permanent' status to governmental powers to interfere with the liberty of persons suspected of involvement with terrorist activity. The Act may be seen in part as a legislative response to one of the worst terrorist actions in Northern Ireland, the Omagh bombing in 1998. However, the issue of the extent of the proper extent of governmental powers in relation to terrorism had been the subject of a bipartisan inquiry chaired by the law lord, Lord Lloyd in the mid-1990s, and much of the Act gave legal force to the inquiry's recommendations.[122]

In respect of powers of arrest without a warrant, s 41 retained the formula that a police officer may arrest a person whom she 'reasonably suspects to be a terrorist'. Section 41 and Schedule 8 of the Act permit pre-charge detention of arrested persons for up to fourteen days, but—consistent with the ECtHR's interpretation of Art 5 in *Brogan*—detention beyond forty-eight hours must be authorised by a court. The Blair government sought to justify the substantially increased maximum period of detention by suggesting that modern day terrorists were far more sophisticated in concealing their activities than their predecessors had been.[123]

The primary source of terrorist activity in the United Kingdom at that time continued to be various extremist political groups in Northern Ireland. That position was shortly however to change. In his speech to the Labour Party conference in October 2001, delivered a month after the terrorist attacks in New York and Washington DC, then Prime Minister Blair painted an apocalyptic picture of a western world under imminent threat of further terrorist outrages, a danger that would have to lead to profound changes in our views of human rights in general and personal liberty in particular:

> It was the events of September 11 that marked a turning point in history, where we confront the dangers of the future and assess the choices facing humankind . . .
>
> Here in this country and in other nations round the world, laws will be changed, not to deny basic liberties but to prevent their abuse and protect the most basic liberty of all: freedom from terror.[124]

---

[119] Per s 1(4): (a) 'action' includes action outside the United Kingdom, (b) a reference to any person or to property is a reference to any person, or to property, wherever situated, (c) a reference to the public includes a reference to the public of a country other than the United Kingdom, and (d) 'the government' means the government of the United Kingdom, of a part of the United Kingdom or of a country other than the United Kingdom.

[120] See the thoughtful discussion of the way in which terrorism is defined in Walker C (2007) 'The legal definition of terrorism in United Kingdom law and beyond' *Public Law* 331. It is perhaps a trite point to note that many 'terrorists' have subsequently come to be regarded as freedom fighters and great statesman. Madison would have been a terrorist within the terms of the 2000 Act, as presumably would Nelson Mandela. Closer to home—in the chronological and jurisdictional senses—the former Deputy First Minister of Northern Ireland, Martin McGuiness, was for many years regarded as a 'terrorist' by successive British governments.

[121] It would of course be very significant to persons caught by the test.

[122] Lord Lloyd (1996) *Inquiry into legislation against terrorism.*

[123] For a forceful critique of the Act and its rationale see Fenwick (2007) op cit pp 1146–1148.

[124] <http://www.guardian.co.uk/politics/2001/oct/02/labourconference.labour6>.

From 2001, the Blair and Brown governments sought substantially to increase the government's powers to detain suspected terrorists prior to the persons concerned being charged with any offence. In 2005, the government promoted a Bill which allowed for ninety (90) days pre-charge detention of terrorist suspects. Such a long period of detention was considered inappropriate both by opposition parties and a sufficiently large number of backbench Labour MPs that—as noted in chapter five[125]—the Blair governments suffered their first defeat in the Commons. Both houses did however approve a twenty-eight day limit, doubling the previous maximum period. The policy was enacted as s 23 of the Terrorism Act 2006.

That the bombings of 7 July 2005 were the only significant 'Al-Qaeda' related terrorist attack carried out in the United Kingdom since 2001 would suggest either that the Blair governments were indeed much exaggerating the threat and/or that the twenty-eight day period of detention was sufficient for the police and security services to establish if detained suspects were involved in terrorist activities. Gordon Brown's Labour government nonetheless thought it necessary to become embroiled in an intense political battle early in 2008 in both houses and in the media over its proposal to increase the period of post-arrest detention of suspected 'terrorists' from a maximum of twenty-eight days to forty-two days. The purported rationale underlying the proposal was that modern day terrorists were so sophisticated in their operation that twenty-eight days could not suffice for evidence gathering purposes. The moral premise in issue here—which Mr Brown seemed unwilling to acknowledge—was that it was preferable to take the chance that 'innocent' people be detained for a much longer period than risk 'guilty' people not being charged. The passage of the measure in the Commons again produced the unlikely spectacle of the Conservative Party opposing the measure on the basis that it interfered excessively with civil liberties. Few backbench Labour MPs were prepared to vote against the government on the issue, a state of affairs which rather weakens Cowley's recent arguments that Labour MPs have latterly been much more independently minded than they were in the past.[126] The proposal was subsequently rejected in the House of Lords, at which point the government accepted defeat.[127] It seems unlikely that the forty-two day detention period would be regarded by the ECtHR as compatible with Art 5 ECHR, or indeed by the domestic courts, which have taken a reasonably rigorous approach to other 'extraordinary' legislative initiatives promoted by the Blair government.

Indefinite detention without charge, trial, or conviction under the Anti-Terrorism, Crime and Security Act 2001

Mr Liversidge was lawfully detained—but not arrested, charged, or convicted—because the Home Secretary presumably took the view that to leave Mr Liversidge at liberty might present a threat to the successful prosecution of the war. We will likely never know whether there was any credible basis for Sir John Anderson's evident suspicions about Mr Liversidge. But we can safely assume that 'the life of the nation' has never been in graver jeopardy than it was in 1940. We might accept—but should perhaps do so with some scepticism—that the threat to life, limb, and property in Britain posed by 'Al-Qaeda' terrorist activity in the early years of the twentieth century was sincerely perceived by Ministers in the Blair government to be substantial. We might also accept—with more scepticism—that the perception was well-founded. But however severe the threat, it was clearly *de minimis* compared with the dangers posed by German military forces during World War II, and might strike many observers as distinctly less substantial than that posed by IRA activities in the 1970s and 1980s.[128]

---

[125] See 'A more assertive and independent house?', ch 5, pp 134–135.   [126] Ibid.

[127] See *The Guardian* 13 October 2008.

[128] Cf at (1978) 2 EHRR 25 at para 44: '[F]rom August to December 1971 . . . there were a total of 146 persons killed, including 47 members of the security services and 99 civilians, 729 explosions and 1437 shooting incidents'.

The Anti-Terrorism Crime and Security Act 2001 was nonetheless rushed through Parliament in the aftermath of the September 11 bombings in New York and Washington DC, a context in which members of the government, vociferously assisted by much of the mass media, painted a picture of the United Kingdom as being at immediate risk of large scale terrorist attacks. Faced with what were apparently extraordinary times, Parliament accepted the government's invitation to enact extraordinary measures. That the Blair government exaggerated the dangers and deliberately fanned media hysteria on the issue seems entirely likely. What is beyond dispute, however, is that any suggestion that careful consideration was given by MPs to the measures (the Act had 129 sections) contained in the Bill is utterly implausible.[129]

The Act included new powers of detention of persons who had not been charged with nor convicted of any crime. But in contrast to the situation which pertained in World War II (in respect of suspected German sympathisers) and in the 1970s (in respect of suspected Irish terrorists), these powers would fall to be measured by the domestic courts against the requirements of the ECHR and the HRA 1998.

The provision before the House of Lords in *A v Secretary of State for the Home Department*[130] (widely known as the *Belmarsh* case, after the name of the prison where the defendants were detained) was s 23 of the Act. Section 23 empowered the Home Secretary to detain without criminal charge for an indefinite period any foreign national whom the Home Secretary certified to be a terrorist if the person did not consent to being deported to his home country. The policy—which rested in part on a presumption that the government would not be able to prove that suspects had committed any criminal offence—was prima facie incompatible with Art 5(1) ECHR. The government therefore sought to avoid the possibility of a declaration of incompatibility in respect of s 23 by claiming that the threat posed by terrorists was such as to justify a derogation under Art 15 ECHR from Art 5 ECHR, on the basis that the United Kingdom was faced with a 'public emergency threatening the life of the nation'.[131]

The House of Lords—sitting as a nine judge court to emphasise the importance of the case—accepted (over a notable dissent by Lord Hoffmann) that the requisite 'public emergency' existed. However, it also held that s 23 did not meet the requirement in Art 15 that any derogation be limited to 'the extent strictly required by the exigencies of the situation.' The Court considered that s 23 clearly failed to satisfy a key element of the proportionality test. The supposed purpose of s 23 was to protect the public against terrorist attacks. But since a putative detainee could in effect free herself from detention by agreeing to be deported, the Court understandably reasoned that s 23 was not a rational means to achieve that purpose. The notion that a 'terrorist' would be unable to plot terrorist attacks against targets in Britain from her/his homeland and then to re-enter the country and carry out the attacks and/or use other individuals to do so was clearly risible. The Court also concluded that s 23 breached Art 14's prohibition on nationality based discrimination. Assuming there was indeed a real emergency in existence, there was no convincing basis for assuming that terrorist attacks would not be planned or carried out by British nationals.[132] Given that s 23 lent itself to only one Convention non-compliant meaning, no issue arose as to the use of s 3 of the HRA. The Court therefore issued a declaration of incompatibility.[133]

---

[129] A point which might be recalled when considering the propriety of domestic courts' development of the 'deference' principle in HRA cases; see 'I. The notion of "deference" to legislative judgment, ch 21, pp 552–555.

[130] [2004] UKHL 56, [2005] 2 AC 68.

[131] The mechanism by which the HRA gives domestic effect to a derogation is per s 14 by empowering the government to issue a 'derogation order'—which is strictly speaking a statutory instrument. A prima facie breach of a Convention Right loses its unlawful domestic nature if the derogation is in force.

[132] Indeed, the only Al-Qaeda related terrorist attack in Britain—the bombings of July 2005—were carried out by four British citizens.

[133] See further Dwyer D (2005) 'Rights brought home' *LQR* 359; Feldman D (2005) 'Proportionality and discrimination in anti-terrorism legislation' *Cambridge LJ* 270; Shah S (2005) 'The UK's anti-terror legislation and the House of Lords: the first skirmish' *Human Rights LR* 403.

The judgment was (predictably) denounced in some media and political quarters as an affront to democracy. As has been suggested repeatedly in this book, the presumption that any political value favoured by elected law-makers is 'democratic' simply because its makers are elected is at best grossly over-simplistic and at worst dangerously misleading. Any sophisticated notion of democratic governance would identify two major objections to s 23. The first would relate to the rushed and truncated nature of the deliberative process within the Commons and Lords as to the merits of the proposed Act. The second would focus on the ludicrously ineffective and grossly discriminatory substantive provisions. If one's understanding of democratic governance embraces the proposition that politicians should be prevented from giving legal effect to policies which impose grotesque restrictions on basic liberties, or even the more modest proposition that it should very difficult for politicians to achieve such results, s 23 was an obscenity and in saying so the House of Lords was upholding rather than undermining notions of democratic governance.

While the judgment of the House of Lords is per se significant as an indicator of the way in which the HRA has led the courts to feel they may now appropriately venture into areas of political controversy which might previously have been regarded as having a demonstrably 'non-justiciable character', it may be that we should attach even more importance to the way in which the government responded to the judgment. The government did not choose, as it was legally entitled to do, to proceed on the basis that s 23 should remain in effect notwithstanding its incompatibility with the Convention. Instead, the government promoted—and Parliament enacted—a new provision which would replace s 23 with a less draconian 'control order' applicable to nationals and non-nationals which restricted the movements of suspected terrorists.

'Control orders' under the Prevention of Terrorism Act 2005

The episode continued when the compatibility of the 'control order' regime with Art 5 came before the courts in 2006 and 2007. The powers were enacted in the Prevention of Terrorism Act 2005. A 'control order' was defined in s 1 as a measure which placed restrictions on individual autonomy in respect of such matters as—inter alia—her place of residence, the hours during which she may leave her residence, where she may travel, whom she might meet and talk to, and her access to communication and information media. The Act distinguished between 'derogating' and 'non-derogating' control orders. The former could only be imposed by a court which was satisfied that there is some evidentiary basis for believing the individual concerned to be involved in terrorist activity, that the order was necessary to protect the public, and that an Art 15 state of emergency existed. A non-derogating order, in contrast, could be imposed by the Home Secretary if she had reasonable cause to believe the individual was involved in terrorist activity and the order was necessary to protect the public. In neither case was it necessary that the person subject to the order had been charged with or even arrested for any offence, although breach of an order was itself a crime, punishable with up to five years' imprisonment.

The control order at issue in *Secretary of State for the Home Department v JJ and others*[134] was a non-derogating order that required JJ to live in a designated one bedroom flat, and to remain there other than between 10 am and 4 pm, during which time he could go out within a prescribed area. He was not permitted access to a mobile phone or the internet, and could only receive visitors approved by the Home Office.

At trial, the primary matter before the Court was whether the restrictions imposed upon JJ amounted to a deprivation of liberty. Sullivan J had considered that the combined effect of

---

[134] [2007] UKHL 45, [2008] 1 AC 385. *JJ* is one of several linked cases dealing with control order issues. See also *Secretary of State for the Home Department v MB* [2007] UKHL 46, [2008] 1 AC 440: *Secretary of State for the Home Department v E* [2007] UK HL, [2008] 1 AC 499.

these restrictions was sufficiently close to detention in an open prison to amount to a deprivation of liberty within Art 5.[135] That conclusion was subsequently upheld both in the Court of Appeal[136] and (albeit only by a three to two majority) in the House of Lords. The majority view—most fully expressed by Lord Bingham—was wholly supportive of Sullivan J's reasoning and conclusion. In a related appeal, however, the House of Lords was unanimous in holding that a similar order which imposed only twelve rather than eighteen hours per day of house arrest, would not engage Art 5.

Rather than resort to the type of vehement attack on the judiciary sometimes favoured by some of her predecessors, the then Home Secretary Jacqui Smith responded quietly to the judgment in *JJ* by modifying the period of house arrest in the order, thereby bringing the policy within what the House of Lords had indicated were acceptable Art 5 parameters.

Conclusion

It is possible that—if the HRA had not been enacted—domestic courts would have identified some flaw in the way that the powers of indefinite detention created by the Anti-Terrorism Crime and Security Act 2001 were used by the Home Secretary, and that particular detention orders would have been found unlawful. It is also possible that senior judges would have taken the opportunity in judgments concerning s 23 to have made comments as to the difficulty of reconciling the provision with traditional ideas of constitutional propriety. Either or both eventualities would have to some extent undermined the legitimacy of the power. Neither would have done so however to the extent of the declaration of incompatibility that the HRA enabled the House of Lords to issue. Whether the government's response to *A*—and thereafter to *JJ*—represented a sincere desire by Ministers to remain within the confines of a more tightly drawn notion of governance according to the rule of law or was rather attributable to a fear of the political consequences of ignoring the House of Lords' rulings is perhaps of little importance. The most significant point to be taken from the episode is that a government with majority support in Parliament for policies which the domestic courts held to be inconsistent with the ECHR chose to respect those judicially identified limits on the *legitimate* (but not, of course, the *legal*) boundaries of legislative power. The episode provides important evidential support for the suggestion made by Chandrachud that a convention may be emerging that governments will make a good faith response to have the relevant law amended when a s 4 order is issued.[137]

The constitutional landscape thus far marked out by the HRA is complicated, and likely to become more so the longer that the Act remains in force. But it would be premature to regard the Human Rights Act as having had in any systemic sense a *revolutionary* effect in the sphere of constitutional law. The crucial point to labour (perhaps painfully) here is that the HRA does not—and makes no attempt to—endow the Convention with the status of a constituent framework of political values, existing beyond the reach of reform or repeal by a simple legislative majority. The protection offered to civil liberties by the Human Rights Act is in legal terms ephemeral and (at this point in time) in political terms precarious. Its substance may be promptly modified by whichever political faction can command even a bare Commons and Lords majority. As suggested in chapter twenty-one, some Labour Ministers and MPs were not averse to castigating judges who produced judgments which upheld ECHR principles, and both Prime Minister Blair and senior members of his Cabinet occasionally intimated that the Act should be amended. Prominent members of the Conservative Party were more forthright

---

[135] [2006] EWHC 1623 Admin.   [136] [2006] EWCA Civ 1141, [2007] QB 446.
[137] Chandrachud (2014) op cit. See 'Assessing the effect of declarations of incompatibility' ch 21, pp 551–552.

in expressing their dislike of the Act,[138] and had the party secured an outright majority in the Commons at the 2010 general election a Bill to abolish or restrict the scope of the Act may very well have been promoted by the government. The commitment was retained in the Conservative's 2015 election manifesto, but was not acted upon before the 2017 election.

Rights recognised as 'fundamental' at common law prior to the HRA coming into force are obviously no less ephemeral than those contained in legislation. The Human Rights Act does not even attempt to embrace the basic moral principles that, over two hundred years ago, Jefferson, Madison, and their colleagues articulated in the US Constitution: namely that, as Madison put it, in the United States: 'the censorial power is in the people over the government, and not in the government over the people'.[139] (The people being of course not a minority or bare majority of an electorate, but the sovereign law-maker identified by the process of constitutional amendment).[140]

Once made, this observation raises a larger question. It takes little reflection to lead one to ask whether the greatest threat to the pervasive, long-term respect for human rights in modern British society stems from the constitution's continuing failure to offer a means legally to entrench fundamental moral and political values. The vehicle in which we explore these questions is the proposed departure of the United Kingdom from membership of the European Union.

Suggested further reading

Academic commentary

FELDMAN (2006) 'Human rights, terrorism and risk; the roles of politician and judges' *Public Law* 364

WALKER C (2007) 'The legal definition of terrorism in United Kingdom law and beyond' *Public Law* 33

MUNRO (1981) 'Detention after arrest' *Crim LR* 802

Case law and legislation

A v Secretary of State for the Home Department [2004] UKHL 56, [2005] 2 AC 68.

R (Laporte) v Chief Constable of Gloucestershire [2006] UKHL 55, [2007] 2 AC 105

Ireland v United Kingdom (1978) 2 EHRR 25

Guzzardi v Italy (1980) 3 EHRR 333

R v Howell [1982] QB 416

Steel and others v United Kingdom [1999] 28 EHRR 603

Home Office (2004) Policing: modernising police powers to meet community needs

Albert v Lavin [1982] AC 546

Christie v Leachinsky [1947] AC 573

---

[138] See eg *The Guardian*, 23 August 2004 ('Tories may repeal Human Rights Act'; *The Guardian*, 12 May 2006 ('Cameron calls for repeal of Human Rights Act'); *The Independent*, 13 May 2006 ('Cameron threatens to scrap Human Rights Act').

[139] Cf. Madison's views in his speech in the House of Representatives in June 1789, when he moved adoption of the First Amendment; see Fisher L (3rd edn, 1996) *Constitutional law* vol 2, pp 551–555).

[140] See 'Constitutional values as fundamental law', ch 1 pp 14–15.

Part Six

Conclusions

Chapter 23

A Revolution by Due Process of Law? Leaving the European Union

This book began by considering the constitutional settlement eventually arrived at by the American revolutionaries after the successful conclusion of their war of independence against British rule.[1] That settlement rested on the basic premise that a country's constitution should require that issues of fundamental political significance be legally entrenched in a fashion and to an extent that made it very difficult for them to be changed. In the United States, that power of change lies with 'the People'. In the context of amendment to the US Constitution, 'the People' as a law-maker are defined in a very specific way—namely a two-thirds majority in Congress coupled with a three-quarters majority among the (now fifty) States.

The very large majority required for constitutional amendment is per se a direct safeguard against the content of the US' fundamental law being controlled by ephemeral or ill-considered political ideologies. A second, indirect but no less important safeguard, arises from the inescapable fact that securing such a large majority for legal change in so many different polities takes a very long time, which in turn increases the likelihood that the evidential underpinnings of proposals for amendment are clearly identified and rigorously evaluated by politicians, the mass media, and (at least some) members of the voting public. It is not enough that super-majoritarian support for constitutional amendment be created at a given moment; it must also be sustained over an extensive period. The (mini-) peoples of States which might initially favour amendment may very well change their collective minds before the requisite three-quarters majority is consolidated, either because new political majorities emerge within them or because new information about the proposed amendment leads voters who previously supported it to change their view. Consensus for change must be demographically wide-ranging and chronologically stable.

The UK's attribution of sovereign power to the bare majoritarian process of enacting legislation in Parliament means that we lack such safeguards.[2] Profound political change may be given legal effect on the basis of quite modest levels of public support which reflect transient ideologies resting on a basis of poorly explored and evaluated evidence. The saga of the UK's

---

[1] See 'The first 'modern' constitution', ch 1, pp 9–17.
[2] See 'The Diceyan (or orthodox) theory', ch 2, pp 20–21.

effort to depart from the European Union has—to this point[3]—exposed many inadequacies in our country's constitutional arrangements and culture. The episode offers a fascinating case study of the interaction between law, politics and populist ideologies within the contemporary constitutional order: this chapter tries to disentangle some of the most important threads.[4]

I. The 2016 referendum

As noted in chapter eleven,[5] both the Conservative and Labour parties had been consistently riven by factional disagreement about the desirability of the United Kingdom being a member of the EC/EU, and if it was to be a member what the terms of that membership would be. That factionalism was especially acute within the Conservative Party during the Major government's (eventually successful) attempts during the early 1990s to ratify the Maastricht Treaty.[6] Intra-party strife over EU policy was less of an issue for the Blair/Brown governments between 1997 and 2010, but the period in opposition did little to quell so-called Euro-sceptic sentiment with the parliamentary Conservative Party.

While Prime Minister during the 2010–2015 Conservative/Liberal coalition government, David Cameron had been broadly if unenthusiastically supportive of EU membership. In what was apparently an attempt to out-manoeuvre Euro-sceptic sentiment within his own party and to reduce the electoral threat to the Conservative Party from the United Kingdom Independence Party (UKIP), Cameron announced in January 2013 that if the Conservatives formed a single party government after the 2015 general election it would promote legislation offering voters a referendum on the question of whether the United Kingdom should remain in the EU.[7]

The Conservative Party's 2015 election manifesto subsequently devoted several pages to the EU, all of which were excoriatingly critical of the EU's institutions and functions.[8] The tone of the manifesto was presumably intended to appease Euro-sceptic Conservative voters and attract wavering UKIP voters, but its unrelentingly hostile nature towards the EU likely did little to suggest to Conservative voters that continued EU membership was something they should support. The Conservatives won a very small overall majority at the 2015 general election, and promptly took steps to promote the necessary referendum legislation.[9]

The 2015 election had significant consequences for the opposition parties. Ed Miliband resigned as leader of the Labour Party in the light of the party's poor performance at the polls, to be replaced (to the surprise of most commentators) by the avowedly left-wing backbencher Jeremy Corbyn. Similarly, Nick Clegg quit as leader of the Liberal Party, from among whose eight MPs Tim Farron emerged as the new leader. In Scotland, the success of the Scots Nationalist Party (winning fifty-six of fifty-nine seats) propelled the SNP's new leader Nicola Sturgeon into a position of considerable political prominence. Farron and Sturgeon led parties

---

[3] The final draft of this chapter was completed in September 2017, and some of what is said here may, since then, have been overtaken by events.

[4] Lest it is not self-evident from what follows in the rest of this chapter, I should say here that I regard the (currently prospective) exit of the United Kingdom from the EU as an action of utter political folly and aspects of the processes through which it is being/has been effected as sorely lacking in moral integrity.

[5] 'United Kingdom accession', ch 11, pp 297–302.

[6] 'The ratification and incorporation of the Maastricht Treaty', ch 11, pp 316–317.

[7] For coverage of the speech and initial reaction to it from various sources see <http://www.bbc.co.uk/news/uk-politics-21148282>.

[8] Conservative Party (2015) *The Conservative party manifesto* 2015 pp 72–73; available at <https://www.bond.org.uk/data/files/Blog/ConservativeManifesto2015.pdf>.

[9] 'Counting the vote' and Table 7.5, ch. 7 pp 190–193. In another graphic illustration of the votes/seats discrepancy inherent in the Commons electoral system, UKIP won 11% of the votes (3.8 million in total) in the 2015 election but did not win a single seat in the house. The SNP gained fifty-six seats on the basis of 4.7% of the vote.

that were firmly supportive of continued EU membership. However Corbyn had never displayed any particular liking for the EU, and since many of the Labour Party's more senior and pro-EU members decided 'on principle' to refuse to serve in Corbyn's shadow Cabinet in protest against his overly left-wing political preferences, it seemed unlikely that the Labour Party would adopt an enthusiastically pro-EU stance in any referendum.

The government issued a white paper[10] in February 2016 entitled *The process for withdrawing from the European Union*. In distinct contrast to the Conservative election manifesto, both the substance and the tone of the white paper appeared distinctly hostile to the political implications of withdrawal. Repeated emphasis was laid on the uncertain nature of the withdrawal process,[11] on the immense complexity of renegotiating trade relationships with the EU and other nations after withdrawal,[12] on the great difficulties the EU had experienced in concluding much more modest trade arrangements with non-member countries,[13] and on the improbability that other EU States would adopt a benevolently indulgent attitude towards UK interests during the withdrawal negotiations:

> 3.11 It is therefore probable that it would take up to decade or more to negotiate firstly our exit from the EU, secondly our future arrangements with the EU, and thirdly our trade deals with countries outside of the EU, on any terms that would be acceptable to the UK. This would be a long period of uncertainty, which would have consequences for UK businesses, trade and inward investment . . .
>
> 3.13. . . [W]e should expect the remaining 27 Member States to be driven by their own national political and economic interests, and would fight for them as hard as we would for the UK's position.

The white paper suggested that withdrawal from the EU would prove to be an extremely difficult and complex enterprise, with profound implications for many areas of economic and social policy. However, the referendum statute which prompted it seems to be a rather simplistic document.

The referendum legislation

The legal basis of the referendum was set out in the European Union Referendum Act 2015,[14] several parts of which merit attention here.

The question

Section 1 of the Act contained the 'question' which was to be put to the vote:

1 The referendum

(1) A referendum is to be held on whether the United Kingdom should remain a member of the European Union.

(2) The Secretary of State must, by regulations, appoint the day on which the referendum is to be held . . .

(4) The question that is to appear on the ballot papers is—
'Should the United Kingdom remain a member of the European Union or leave the European Union?'

The question itself might be thought rather inept in textual terms by any observer with a more than rudimentary familiarity with the history of the EEC/EC/EU. That history has entailed a

---

[10] Foreign and Commonwealth Office (2016) *The process for withdrawing from the European Union* (Cm 9216).
[11] See especially paras 2.3 and 3.4.   [12] Paras 2.7–2.10 and 3.6.   [13] Para 3.8.
[14] The most illuminating element of its passage is the second reading debate in the Commons on 9 June 2015, which can be found at: <https://www.parliament.uk/business/news/2015/june/commons-second-reading-european-union-referendum-bill/>.

continuous broadening and deepening of areas of integration between the various Member States. On the narrowest of readings, a withdrawal of UK representation in the Parliament, on the Commission and in the Council would amount to 'leaving' the EU. But a country could quite feasibly be a member of the single market, and/or of the customs union, and/or of Euratom without being a member of the European Union. It may well be that many voters would take the question to mean that 'leaving' the EU would entail an immediate severing of all legal ties with the EU. Others might assume it meant retaining all or many or some aspects of the single market.[15] Yet others might assume that 'leaving the EU' would be done in a fashion which preserved the substance of EU free movement rights for UK nationals living or working in other EU States, and for nationals of those states living or working in the UK. But none of these possibilities were canvassed by 'the question'. Anyone who voted to leave on the basis of the s 1 question was therefore voting for a wholly unknown and unknowable future relationship between the United Kingdom and the EU.

That rather fundamental issue seemed to pass most legislators by during the Bill's passage. A more overt point of controversy within Parliament was the text of the question itself. The Bill had originally provided that the question would be: 'Should the United Kingdom remain a member of the European Union?'; to which voters would tick either a 'Yes' or 'No' box. Euro-sceptic Conservative MPs had been concerned that the very style of such a question would bias the likely outcome of the vote, on the rather dispiriting but apparently empirically well-founded grounds that a small section of the population would simply tick the 'Yes' box irrespective of the substantive issue being raised.[16] Under the terms of the Political Parties, Elections and Referendum Act 2000 (PPERA) s 104, the Electoral Commission is tasked with assessing the merits of any proposed referendum question. On the basis of the research it conducted, the Commission concluded there was indeed a prospect of a 'Yes' bias, and so proposed the question be re-worded to offer distinct 'Remain' and 'Leave' answers.[17] The Bill was amended accordingly before its enactment.

The 2015 Act—and its governmental promoters—might be further criticised because it did not make any provision[18] for the proposed terms of the UK's departure from the EU to be subjected to legislative approval or a resolution of either house (or both houses), and/or a further referendum in which the obvious question (with 'Leave' and 'Remain' tick box answers) would be:

> Should the United Kingdom leave the European Union on the basis of the terms agreed between the United Kingdom and the European Union or should the United Kingdom remain a member of the European Union?

It may be that the Cameron/Osborne faction of the Cameron government did not pursue this issue in the Bill because it had not countenanced the possibility that the referendum would be lost, and so the need to negotiate terms of departure would never arise. However, the difficulty is in part a consequence of the design of Art 50 itself. Article 50 provides a mechanism for withdrawal of a Member State from the EU but offers no indication at all as to what that country's future relationship with the EU might be. Prima facie Art 50 does not enable a Member State to leave the EU having already negotiated what that future relationship would be. Nor, prima facie, does Art 50 permit a country to revoke its notice of departure. It would therefore seem

---

[15] See eg the discussion in Bogdanor V (2016) 'Brexit, the constitution and the alternatives' *Kings LJ* 314.

[16] Shipman T (2016) *All out war: the full story of Brexit* pp 83–84. Shipman's book provides an engaging and hugely detailed account of the political machinations which were generated in the campaign.

[17] Electoral Commission (2015) *Referendum on membership of the European Union: assessment of the Electoral Commission on the proposed referendum question*; available at <https://www.electoralcommission.org.uk/__data/assets/pdf_file/0006/192075/EU-referendum-question-assessment-report.pdf>.

[18] Although Parliament could enact such legislation at any future date.

that it is not possible for a Member State's particular 'constitutional requirements' to allow it to change its constitutional mind on the departure question. As a matter of EU law, a more nuanced or conditional question might not be permissible. It is perhaps unfortunate that the Court of Justice (CJEU)[19] was not given the opportunity to identify the limits of Art 50 before the United Kingdom took any steps to trigger it.

The voters

Mr Cameron's belief that public opinion favoured (and by a comfortable margin) remaining in the EU may also explain various aspects of the Act concerning the 'who' and the 'how' of the referendum process. The Bill's passage was apparently conducted on the assumption in much political and media discourse that a 'referendum' would obviously and unproblematically express the views of the 'people', and—consequently—that there could be no more legitimate and thus 'democratic' way for the political controversy over EU membership to be resolved.[20]

The larger question of the legitimacy of the referendum is addressed in Section II of this chapter.[21] But in the narrow sense of the composition of the referendum electorate as a vehicle for securing 'the consent of the governed'[22] the conclusions expressed in the Act were open to some criticism. Eligibility to vote was controlled by s 2. This broadly mirrored the franchise for parliamentary elections, with the addition of residents of Gibraltar and members of the House of Lords.

There was some controversy of whether the default voting age limit of 18 years should be lowered to 16[23] (as had been the case in the Scots independence referendum), but the Cameron government showed no enthusiasm for that modification to the original Bill. Two further categories of people who would likely be very significantly affected by any eventual withdrawal of the United Kingdom from the EU were not included within the referendum electorate. The larger group, some three million people, was non-UK EU nationals residing in the United Kingdom in accordance with treaty rights. The second group, comprising just over a million people, was UK nationals exercising such rights in other EU countries; (many of whom had been living in Spain for a considerable period). Several claimants who fell into one or other of these unrepresented categories initiated legal proceedings to try to establish that their exclusion was inconsistent with EU law, but the action failed in the domestic courts (essentially on the basis that the composition of the referendum electorate did not raise an EU law issue at all) and did not come before the CJEU.[24] If the Cameron/Osborne faction within the Cabinet was indeed hoping to secure a Remain majority in the referendum, then the exclusion of these groups from the referendum electorate was an unfortunate error as they might all be expected to lean quite heavily in favour of a Remain vote.[25]

The Act did not give any recognition to the increasingly devolved structure of governance within the nations of the United Kingdom. The result of the referendum would be determined by a single, UK-wide referendum electorate. If it transpired for example that the requisite UK majority in favour of Leave or Remain arose because a sufficient majority of voters in England

---

[19] Referred to henceforth as the CJEU (Court of Justice of the European Union) rather than the ECJ to reflect its current formal nomenclature.

[20] Readers might at this point refer briefly to some of the abstract discussions of 'democratic' law-making processes (and outcomes) at 'What is democratic governance? Some hypothetical examples', ch 1, pp 5–7.

[21] See also Eleftheriadis P (2017) 'Constitutional illegitimacy over Brexit' *Political Quarterly* 182.

[22] This being the issue explored in ch 1 in both hypothetical terms and in respect of the founding of the US Constitution.

[23] See the second reading debate in the Commons at: <https://www.parliament.uk/business/news/2015/june/commons-second-reading-european-union-referendum-bill/>.

[24] *Shindler v Chancellor of the Duchy of Lancaster* [2016] EWCA Civ 469, [2017] QB 226; discussed in Davies B (2016) 'Who were the British people?' *Kings LJ* 323.

[25] See the discussion in Shipman op cit at 88–89.

(England containing some 55.2 million of the UK's 65.8 million population in 2016)[26] supported that outcome, but majorities in Scotland, Wales, and Northern Ireland chose the other result, the Leave voters would have 'won' the referendum. A result of that sort might have created substantial political difficulties, but those difficulties would not have any legal significance. The SNP had moved an amendment to the Bill at committee stage, proposing that a so-called 'quadruple lock' or 'double majority lock' be placed in the legislation; that is, that a 'Leave' victory would require both a majority in the United Kingdom overall and in each of its four component countries.[27] The government was not receptive to that amendment and the SNP could not attract the necessary support for it in the Commons.

Having thus defined 'the people', the 2015 Act also provided that 'the people' it created would 'speak' through a bare rather than enhanced majority of those who voted. The legal significance of the result (whether for Remain or Leave) would not be contingent on the size of the voting majority. Nor was there any requirement that turnout should pass any particular threshold in order for the result to have any legal validity. In the event that turnout in the referendum matched the level at recent general elections (ie 70% would be a high figure),[28] the 'people' whose preferences decided the issue might amount to as little as 36% of the eligible voting population. That might be thought a rather flimsy basis on which to rest the legitimacy of such a profound constitutional change.

But while the Act provided the legal basis of who 'the People' would be for this purpose, and of how they would speak, it was notably lacking in telling us what the legal consequences of their answer—should it favour withdrawal—would actually be.

The legal consequences of a Leave majority vote on the mechanism for triggering Art 50

A glaring omission from the Act—perhaps a consequence of the Prime Minister's assumption that 'the People' would not wish to have the United Kingdom leave the EU—was an express grant of statutory authority to the Crown to trigger the Art 50 process in the event of a Leave vote. As we have noted on many previous occasions, UK entry into treaty arrangements is achieved by exercise of the prerogative, a common law power.[29] Presumptively, the prerogative can also be used to enable the United Kingdom to depart from or modify treaty arrangements. However—and this might be thought a simple point—if a precursor or consequence of entering a particular treaty arrangement has been the prior and/or subsequent enactment by Parliament of statutory provisions, legislative authority would surely be needed for that departure to be effected. If that were not the constitutional position, then the prerogative would in normative terms be superior to statute: a proposition wholly inconsistent with basic constitutional principles.

Such authority might be found in one of the existing EU-related statutes. The ECA 1972 and any/or subsequent legislation might have provided for example that all its provisions would automatically be repealed if the government were ever to exercise its prerogative power to withdraw the UK from (what was then) the EEC. One might argue—and lawyers undoubtedly would—over whether such a statutory provision had de jure replaced the prerogative power with a statutory equivalent for the purpose of departing the EEC or was expressly preserving the prerogative and lending it an unusual remit.[30] We are spared such difficulties however by

---

[26] <https://www.ons.gov.uk/peoplepopulationandcommunity/populationandmigration/populationestimates>.

[27] See McCorkindale C (2016) 'Scotland and Brexit: the state of the Union and the Union State' *Kings LJ* 354 at 356–358. The political complexion of Scotland in the past forty to fifty years has been notably to the left of England. EU membership—which has required States to accept a great deal of economic and social policy laws which have a distinctly social democratic character—has to a significant extent protected Scotland from legislation which might otherwise have been imposed upon the entire United Kingdom by Parliaments dominated by a more right-leaning English majority.   [28] See ch 7, Table 7.5, pp. 190–193.

[29] eg 'Inconsistency with international law' ch 2, pp 29–30; 'United Kingdom accession' ch 11, pp 297–302.

[30] This would be in essence a form of Henry VIII clause.

the fact that the ECA 1972 did not contain such a clause, and nor did any other domestic legislation, including the European Union Act 2011.

As we saw in chapter four, the domestic courts have repeatedly asserted in the modern era that prerogative powers dealing with particular political issues are displaced or suspended by the enactment of statutory schemes dealing with the same or closely inter-related matters. The line of authority—beginning with *DeKayser* and running on through *Laker Airways* to the *Fire Brigades Union*[31] case is both clear and consistent. Relatedly, since the United Kingdom's accession to the EEC in 1972, our courts have held with similar consistency and clarity that one effect of the European Communities Act 1972 is to endow directly effective EC/EU law rights and obligations with a status which is statutory in nature (or is equivalent to statute) and so superior to the prerogative in normative terms.[32] Indeed, the post-*Factortame* orthodoxy appears to be that directly effective EU law provisions have an enhanced statutory status in a normative sense, insofar as they are safeguarded from implied repeal by subsequent legislation.[33] Parliament apparently endorsed that judicial analysis in the European Union Act 2011 s 18, which stated that that the legal source in the United Kingdom of rights created by EU law was the ECA 1972.[34]

Consequently it is very surprising that the Referendum Act 2015 did not specify what legal consequences would flow from a 'Leave' vote for the purposes of triggering Art 50. The 2015 Conservative manifesto had included a pledge that a Conservative government would: 'honour the result of the referendum, whatever the outcome,'[35] but that could not have any legal significance. *The process for withdrawing from the European Union* white paper had also been unequivocal:

> 2.1 The result of the referendum on the UK's membership of the European Union will be final. The Government would have a democratic duty to give effect to the electorate's decision. The Prime Minister made clear to the House of Commons that 'if the British people vote to leave, there is only one way to bring that about, namely to trigger Article 50 of the Treaties and begin the process of exit, and the British people would rightly expect that to start straight away' [*HCD* 22 February 2016 c 24].

An assertion in a white paper has no more legal effect than a manifesto 'commitment'[36]. But the presumption that exit could 'start straight away' implies that the government expected to be able to invoke Art 50 by use of prerogative powers, since it had taken no steps to seek statutory authorisation to do so. Given the obvious difficulty of reconciling that presumption with basic tenets of orthodox constitutional theory and practice, one would have expected the 2015 Act to contain a simple clause to the following (or similar) effect:

> If a majority of votes cast in the referendum are in favour of the UK leaving the European Union, the Prime Minister may at a time of her/his choosing initiate the process provided for by Art 50 of the Treaty of Lisbon.

---

[31] *A-G v DeKayser's Royal Hotel* [1920] AC 508; *Laker Airways v Department of Trade* [1977] QB 643; *R v Secretary of State for the Home Department* [1995] 2 AC 513 respectively; discussed at 'The relationship between statute, prerogative and the rule of law', ch 4, pp 83–90.

[32] *Macarthys v Smith* [1979] 3 All ER 325; *Garland v British Rail* [1983] 2 AC 751: discussed at 'EEC law, parliamentary sovereignty and the UK courts: phase one', ch 11, pp 302–305.

[33] See 'The end of parliamentary sovereignty? Or its reappearance?' ch 11, pp 306–312.

[34] That provision was likely intended to negate any possibility that a domestic judge might accept the suggestion—central to the ECJ's jurisprudence (see 'The revolutionary implications of *Van Gend* and *Costa*', ch 11, pp 295–296)—that EC/EU law took effect in domestic legal systems because of its sui generis and autonomous character and not because of any domestic constitutional provision. But s 18 serves just as effectively to underline the orthodox presumption that the domestic UK status of EU law, precisely because it is rooted in statute, is not amenable to change through the exercise of the prerogative.

[35] *Conservative Party* (2015) op cit p 73.

[36] Albeit that the white paper is a product of the government rather than just—as is a manifesto—of a political party.

That formulation assumes that a 'Leave' vote would not bind the government to invoke Art 50. A formulation in accordance with the apparent spirit of the Conservative's 2015 manifesto pledge (and the subsequent assumption in the white paper) would have been:

> If a majority of votes cast in the referendum are in favour of the United Kingdom leaving the European Union, the Prime Minister shall promptly, and in any event no later than two months after the date of the referendum, initiate the process provided for by Art 50 of the Treaty of Lisbon.

Either clause would have spared the country a rather obvious difficulty if the vote was in favour of leaving the EU; namely that Art 50 could not be invoked unless and until Parliament enacted legislation permitting that to happen. The failure to anticipate and deal with this issue in the 2015 Act is quite remarkable.

Such a clause would obviously have had only a contingent legal basis. There is presumably no form of words which could—in the legal sense—bind Parliament to follow the result of the referendum. Parliament could have responded to a majority Leave vote by enacting legislation forbidding the government to invoke Art 50; or it could have responded to a majority Remain vote by enacting legislation requiring the government to do so. Such legislation might be widely regard as 'highly improper' in the *Madzimbamuto* sense of unconstitutionality,[37] even if was produced as the result of a painstaking application by supportive MPs of a Burkean presumption of independence of inquiry, evaluation, and action.[38] But—at risk of repetition—there could be no legal impediment to Parliament following either a course.

The campaign

Both the Liberal Democrats and the Scots Nationalists identified themselves as firm supporters of the United Kingdom remaining within the EU. UKIP was equally clearly attached to withdrawal. The positions adopted by the Conservative and Labour Parties were distinctly more complicated.

Like the parliamentary Conservative Party, the Cabinet was from the outset clearly divided on the EU membership issue. Prime Minister Cameron followed the precedent set by Harold Wilson in the 1975 referendum of suspending collective Cabinet responsibility so that Ministers could campaign for either position.[39] As with Wilson in 1975, Cameron had little choice to do so; any attempt to impose collective responsibility in pursuit of a Remain majority would likely have prompted multiple resignations from the Cabinet. Cameron and his Chancellor of the Exchequer, George Osborne, placed themselves firmly in the Remain camp. Several Ministers, the most prominent among them Michael Gove, joined the Leave campaign, which was also boosted from within Conservative ranks by the support of Boris Johnson, the former Mayor of London and then a backbench MP.

The Labour Party's official strategy seemed to be at best a lukewarm approval of the Remain cause. The new leader of the party, Jeremy Corbyn, and his shadow Chancellor of the Exchequer, John McDonnell, made no positive interventions of note during the course of the campaign,[40] raising the obvious suspicion that they would be quite content for Leave supporters to win.

'Designation' of the Leave and Remain campaigns—'Vote Leave' and 'Stronger In'

Schedule 1 of the Act laid out an extensive and elaborate system of controls for the conduct of the referendum campaign. The most important issue was perhaps the process through

---

[37] See 'Conclusion', ch 1, p 17.   [38] 'The MP—representative or delegate', ch 5, p 108.

[39] 'The 1975 referendum', ch 11, p 301.

[40] Shipman's analysis (see especially op cit ch 19) strongly and credibly suggests that Corbyn's closest advisers were deliberately obstructive to the Remain campaign.

which one—and only one—organisation was to be 'designated' by the Electoral Commission as the official voice or representative of the respective Leave and Remain campaigns; (per the Commission's statutory responsibility under the PPERA 2000 ss 108–110).[41] The significance of designation related primarily to the two-month period immediately prior to the vote, when each designated campaigner would be permitted a spending limit of £7 million, would qualify for radio and television broadcasts, free mail shots to voters, and a grant of as much as £600,000.[42]

The Electoral Commission has a broad discretion in identifying the evaluative criteria it uses for designation applications.[43] For the EU referendum, it produced five (all rather vague) principles relating to inter alia the applicant's level of cross-party support and its organisational competence. Only one group put itself forward for the Remain designation—*Britain Stronger in Europe* (hereafter referred to as '*Stronger in*'). Stronger in was formally headed by Will Straw, a young Labour politician. George Osborne led the Conservatives' input into the campaign, with the Labour Party's activities headed by the former Home Secretary Alan Johnson. The 'Leave' designation was contested by three groups. The winner, '*Vote Leave*', was primarily the tool of mainstream Conservative Euro-sceptics, with the support of a few Labour MPs and some UKIP members.

Lies, damned lies, and statistics

Although the Electoral Commission played an important legal role in setting and policing the ground rules for the conduct of campaign, it had no power to ensure that the campaign was conducted in a fashion that was 'honest, decent and truthful'.[44] Both '*Vote Leave*' and '*Stronger in*' engaged in fairly substantial amounts of what any informed observer would have regarded as unsubstantiated speculation as to the consequences of withdrawal. Among the sillier of the assertions made by Remain campaigners was George Osborne's suggestion that a Leave vote would cost every household in the country the (remarkably precise) sum of £4,300. The claim was patently nonsense and its main effect was likely to suggest to voters that other claims made by *Stronger in* were equally silly. In a like vein, evidently panicked by the prospect of defeat, Osborne announced shortly before the vote that a Leave majority would require him to introduce an emergency budget that would raise taxes and slash public spending.[45] Such scaremongering enabled *Vote Leave* convincingly to describe the Remain campaign as 'Project Fear'. But for anyone who had hoped that the campaigns would present voters with a thorough and carefully reasoned description and analysis of relevant issues, Osborne's statements appeared largely unobjectionable when set alongside key elements of the '*Vote Leave*' campaign.

Vote Leave founded its campaign substantially on the slogan 'Take back control'. In a general sense, the slogan built on the argument that had been being made for many years by Eurosceptic Conservatives and more latterly by UKIP that it was per se undesirable that significant amounts of UK law should be made by EU institutions and overseen by the CJEU. In broad terms, that argument is wholly unobjectionable. But there were several particularly contentious aspects to the 'Take back control' strategy.[46]

---

[41] Electoral Commission (2016) *Designation of lead campaigners for the EU referendum*.

[42] The PPERA 2000 s 125 imposes a so-called 'purdah' period on government bodies (national and local) in referendum campaigns in the last twenty-eight days preceding the vote which prevents publication of materials relating to the referendum issue, whether designed to influence voters one way or another or even in general terms. The restraint was a significant one in the context of the EU referendum, given that the Cameron government supported the Remain position.

[43] For an account of the process see:<https://www.electoralcommission.org.uk/__data/assets/pdf_file/0015/200904/2016-04-13-EC-27-16-EU-Referendum-Designation-of-Lead-Campaigners.pdf>.

[44] See "Decent, honest and truthful"? The content of political advertising', ch 7 pp 189–190.

[45] Shipman op cit pp 376–380.

[46] A detailed account is provided in Shipman op cit chs 14 and 16 respectively.

The first was the use of a large red 'battle bus' in which *Vote Leave* campaigners toured the country, on the sides of which were plastered the slogan:

We send the EU **£350 million** a week

Let's fund our **NHS** instead - Vote Leave

Let's take back control

The £350 million a week figure was a crude (and deliberately so) misrepresentation of the sums that the United Kingdom contributed to the EU budget. Although £350 million could defensibly be seen as a headline figure, it took no account of the substantial amount of that sum which was rebated to the United Kingdom, nor of any EU funds spent on activities within the United Kingdom. Nor did the slogan give any recognition to the point that in large part the UK's financial contribution was a price paid for access to the single market.

The second was a consistent and conscious attempt to use the issue of immigration control to exploit concerns about large-scale immigration among sections of the British public. In particular *Vote Leave* raised the spectre that Turkey was about to join the EU, and that consequently millions of Turks would invade their towns and villages, stealing their jobs, and overburdening the local housing market, schools, and other public service provision.[47] There was—and remains—no credible prospect of Turkey becoming an EU Member State even in the medium term. *Vote Leave* did not however allow such inconvenient truths to qualify the message it promoted to potential supporters.

Both *Vote Leave* and *Stronger in* had spent a substantial part of their permitted £7 million campaign expenditure on digital media activities. The balance of forces in the traditional newsprint media firmly favoured the Leave cause: the *Daily Mail*, *Daily Express*, *Sun*, and *Daily Telegraph* all adopted a fervently Leave editorial line: *The Guardian*, *Daily Mirror*, *The Times*, and *Financial Times* supported the Remain position.

The result

Until the final days of the campaign, opinion polls consistently suggested that the outcome of the referendum was likely to be a small majority for the Remain campaign.[48] The political ground seemed to shift in the Leave direction in those last few days, and the eventual balance of the vote was 51.9% in favour of Leave and only 48.1% favouring Remain. 'The people'—or rather a very slender majority of the 72% of them who had participated in the vote—had spoken.

An analysis of the voting patterns identifies several significant cleavages within the electorate (see Table 23.1).[49] Perhaps the most striking division was between the various 'nations' of the United Kingdom. In England, 53.2% of voters favoured Leave and 46.8% Remain. Wales

---

[47] See Shipman op cit pp 207–302. *Vote Leave* published a poster on the point on May 22, with an accompanying facebook thread available at: <https://www.facebook.com/voteleave/posts/598515206992074:0>. Former Conservative Minister Penny Mordant gave a television interview on May 22 in which she raised the spectre of an influx of Turkish criminals, and made the patently untrue assertion that the United Kingdom could not veto Turkish accession. The interview is available at: <http://www.dailymail.co.uk/news/article-3603212/Staying-EU-expose-Britain-terrorists-gangsters-12–7m-guns-Turkey-join-claims-defence-minister-Penny-Mordaunt-campaign-accuses-stoking-prejudice.html>.

[48] Uberoi E (2016) 'The EU referendum' *House of Commons Library Briefing Paper* No CBP 7639; available at: <http://researchbriefings.parliament.uk/ResearchBriefing/Summary/CBP-7639#fullreport>.

[49] For analysis of voting patterns see Clarke H, Goodwin M, and Whitely P (2017) 'Why Britain voted for Brexit: an individual level analysis of the 2016 referendum vote' *Parliamentary Affairs* 439: Goodwin M and Heath O (2017) 'The 2016 referendum, Brexit and the left behind: an aggregate level analysis of the result' *Political Quarterly* 323: Shipman op cit pp 583–612.

Table 23.1 European Union referendum 2016

Area	Leave %	[total]	Remain %	[total]	Turnout
United Kingdom	51.9%	[17.4m]	48.1%	[16.1m]	72.2%
Country					
England	53.4%	[15.1]	46.6%	[13.5]	73.0
Scotland	38.4%	[1.0m]	61.6%	[1.6m]	67.2%
Wales	52.6%	[0.8m]	47.4%	[0.7m]	71.7%
Northern Ireland	44.3%	[0.4m]	55.7%	[0.3m]	62.7%
English regions					
London	40.5%	[1.5m]	59.5%	[2.2m]	69.7%
South East	51.9%	[2.6m]	48.1%	[2.4m]	76.8%
South West	52.7%	[1.7m]	47.3%	[1.5m]	76.7%
North East	58.1%	[0.8m]	41.9%	[0.6m]	69.3%
North West	53.7%	[2.0m]	46.3%	[1.7m]	70.0%
East Midlands	58.9%	[1.5m]	41.1%	[1.0m]	74.2%
East	56.4%	[1.8m]	43.6%	[1.4m]	75.7%
Yorkshire/Humber	57.8%	[1.6m]	42.2%	[1.2m]	70.7%
West Midlands	59.3%	[1.8m]	40.7%	[1.2m]	72.0%

Source: <https://www.electoralcommission.org.uk/find-information-by-subject/elections-and-referendums/past-elections-and-referendums/eu-referendum/electorate-and-count-information>.

also supported the Leave cause, by a majority of 52% to 47%. In Northern Ireland, in contrast, the votes cast were 56% for Remain and 44% for Leave. The Remain majority was substantially larger in Scotland at 62%, where only 38% of voters supported the Leave position.[50] There was also a striking variation in voting patterns within the various regions of England. In London, the vote was 59%–41% in favour of Remain. In every other English region, the vote favoured Leave, with over 57% of voters choosing that option in the East Midlands, the West Midlands, the North East, and Yorkshire.

The Leave campaign appeared to have been very successful in motivating what psephologists have termed 'left behind' voters,[51] and especially voters in economically deprived areas in the north of England. Turnout in those areas was notably higher than in recent general elections. Whether this was because *Vote Leave's* focus on immigration prompted usually non-voting people to support the Leave cause, or was indicative of a more diffuse perception among such voters that voting Leave would somehow improve their economic circumstances, or was just an unreasoned protest vote against the status quo are questions which will intrigue political scientists and party politicians for many years.[52]

Equally significantly, turnout was generally higher in Leave rather than Remain voting areas. In contrast to the position in general elections, there could be no 'wasted votes' in the referendum; every vote would have the same value. A voter who favoured candidate X in a

[50] McCorkindale C (2016) 'Scotland and Brexit: the state of the Union and the Union State' *Kings LJ* 354.

[51] Goodwin and Heath op cit. See also Clarke et al op cit; Dodds A (2016) 'Why people voted to leave and what to do now: a view from the doorstep' *Political Quarterly* 360.

[52] One of the apparent curiosities of the vote was that Leave support was highest in areas with no significant immigrant populations, whether from EU or non-EU countries. The area with by far the highest immigrant population, London, voted very strongly to Remain.

parliamentary election but who did not bother to vote would not affect the outcome of the election if candidate X was nevertheless the most-supported candidate in her constituency: but in a referendum which is essentially a single constituency two candidate election, that voter's non-participation can affect the result.

David Cameron announced on the day after the referendum[53] that he would stand down as Prime Minister and leader of the Conservative Party, apparently only on the basis that it would not be appropriate for a Prime Minister to pursue a policy of which he did not approve:

> I fought this campaign in the only way I know how, which is to say directly and passionately what I think and feel - head, heart and soul. I held nothing back, I was absolutely clear about my belief that Britain is stronger, safer and better off inside the European Union . . . But the British people have made a very clear decision to take a different path and as such I think the country requires fresh leadership to take it in this direction. I will do everything I can as Prime Minister to steady the ship over the coming weeks and months but I do not think it would be right for me to try to be the captain that steers our country to its next destination.

The ensuing leadership process within the Conservative Party presented the extraordinary spectacle of the senior Leave politician Michael Gove running the leadership campaign of his fellow Leaver Boris Johnson, and then at the last minute announcing that he considered Johnson unfit to be Prime Minister and would stand himself. Many Conservative MPs evidently took a very dim view of such duplicity, and Gove's candidacy rapidly disintegrated.[54] Theresa May was subsequently selected as the next leader of the Party—and thus also as Prime Minister. While May had nominally supported the Remain position, she had done so in a notably lukewarm fashion,[55] prompting subsequent suggestions that her primary concern in the campaign had been to position herself for a successful leadership bid irrespective of the referendum result.[56]

Within the Labour Party, Remain supporting MPs placed substantial blame for the defeat on Jeremy Corbyn and his close advisers. Corbyn's support within the parliamentary party had fallen to extremely low levels, and his opponents launched a leadership election in the hope of removing him. Election of the leader lay in the hands of Party members rather than MPs however, and in the ensuing election Corbyn defeated his rather lacklustre and little-known opponent, Owen Smith, by a large margin.[57]

The referendum, the campaign, the result, and its immediate aftermath provide fascinating political contexts within which to place questions of constitutional law. However, a more overtly 'legal' issue soon assumed centre stage.

II. The *Miller* litigation

Unsurprisingly it took little time for a legal challenge to appear. The lead claimant in the legal challenge[58] to the May government's assertion that it could trigger Art 50 through the prerogative was a woman named Gina Miller.[59] The argument she brought before the High Court was

---

[53] The full text and video of his statement can be found at <http://www.telegraph.co.uk/news/2016/06/24/david-cameron-announces-his-resignation---full-statement/>.   [54] Shipman op cit chs 28–30.

[55] Cf Shipman op cit pp 132 and 268.

[56] See generally Allen N (2017) 'Brexit, butchery and Boris: Theresa May and her first Cabinet' *Parliamentary Affairs* 633.   [57] Shipman op cit ch. 27.

[58] Reported as *R (Miller and another) v Secretary of State for Exiting the European Union* [2016] EWHC 2768 (Admin) in the High Court and [2017] UKSC 5 in the Supreme Court. Both judgments are at [2017] 2 WLR 583.

[59] Ms Miller was no more affected by the prospect of withdrawal than any other UK citizen, but that status per se would clearly be sufficient to give her locus standi to bring her claim; see 'III. Post-*IRC* developments', ch 16, 447–452; and especially the discussion of *Smedley* and *Rees-Mogg* at p 447.

an obvious one, apparently resting on quite basic propositions of constitutional law: if membership of the EU created rights and obligations for individuals which were or were equivalent to statutory rights, and if the triggering of Art 50 would end or undermine such rights and obligations, then surely statutory authorisation—rather than an exercise of the prerogative—would be required in order for Art 50 to be invoked?

Rather than promote a simple one clause bill to have Parliament grant the Prime Minister such statutory authority—and it is very difficult to envisage that such a bill would not have been promptly enacted with cross-party support—the government chose to contest the claim. In essence, the government's case was that the court should assume firstly that Parliament did not create a statutory power for this purpose in the EU Referendum Act 2015 because legislators had thought—correctly—that it was so obvious that the prerogative could be used to trigger Art 50 that there was no need to enact a statutory power; and secondly that this assumption arose because the ECA 1972 did not expressly remove the government's presumptive prerogative power to withdraw from any treaty arrangements it had entered.

In the High Court

It cannot have surprised any informed and honest observer that the High Court held[60] that Ms Miller's argument was well-founded: the triggering of Art 50 required statutory authority; and since no such authority had been included in the Referendum Act—and could not be found anywhere else—new legislation would be required. What was perhaps surprising was the significant number of media organisations and Conservative politicians who must have known the High Court's decision was correct but who nevertheless attacked it as being morally illegitimate. The episode had strong echoes of the 'judicial supremacism' controversy that flared in the mid-1990s,[61] and was—as then—pervaded by indications that Conservative MPs and many media commentators were unable to understand and/or unwilling to accept orthodox propositions concerning the sovereignty of Parliament, the rule of law, and the separation of powers.

A unanimous court

The High Court's judgment proceeded through a series of straightforward steps. It began by invoking Dicey to reiterate the principle of parliamentary sovereignty, and also referred to Dicey to make the point that the wishes of electors were per se a matter of no legal significance:

> 22 . . .[I]t cannot be said that a law is invalid as being opposed to the opinion of the electorate, since as a matter of law:
>
> 'The judges know nothing about any will of the people except in so far as that will is expressed by an Act of Parliament, and would never suffer the validity of a statute to be questioned on the ground of its having been passed or being kept alive in opposition to the wishes of the electors.' (*[Introduction to the study of the law of the constitution* (1915, 8th edn) p 72].)

The Court then referred inter alia to the *Case of Proclamations*, the Bill of Rights, *The Zamora* and *De Keyser*[62] to illustrate the normative inferiority of the prerogative to statute:

> 29 The legal position was summarised by the Privy Council in The Zamora [1916] 2 AC 77, 90:

---

[60] The case was argued in mid-October 2016, and judgment handed down on 3 November.

[61] See 'II. The "judicial supremacism" controversy', ch 19, 507–514.

[62] Respectively (1611) 12 Co rep 74, [1916] 2 AC 77; *A-G v DeKayser's Royal Hotel* [1920] AC 508; and discussed respectively at 'Prerogative cases before the 1688 revolution', ch 4, pp 78–81; 'The political source of parliamentary sovereignty—the 'glorious revolution', ch 2, pp 21–25; 'The relationship between statute, prerogative and the rule of law', ch 4, pp 83–84.

'The idea that the King in Council, or indeed any branch of the Executive, has power to prescribe or alter the law to be administered by Courts of law in this country is out of harmony with the principles of our Constitution. It is true that, under a number of modern statutes, various branches of the Executive have power to make rules having the force of statutes, but all such rules derive their validity from the statute which creates the power, and not from the executive body by which they are made. No one would contend that the prerogative involves any power to prescribe or alter the law administered in Courts of Common Law or Equity.'

These principles are not only well settled but are also common ground. It is therefore not necessary to explain them further.

The Court accepted that the ECA 1972 had 'created'[63] various types of domestically enforceable legal rights, some or all of which would inevitably be compromised by the triggering of Art 50; (the government having conceded that such triggering was not revocable). The notion that the ECA 1972 'created' those rights suggests that the Court regarded them as per se statutory constructs. Moreover, following the House of Lords judgment in *Factortame*, it was necessary to regard the ECA 1972 as at least in a limited sense an entrenched measure, inasmuch as the rights that the Act created were: 'not subject to the usual wide principle of implied repeal by subsequent legislation'.[64]

As such, to allow them to be interfered with by an exercise of the prerogative would run counter to orthodox constitutional principles. The only way for the government to succeed would therefore be to persuade the Court that it was Parliament's 'intention' (in the ECA 1972 and subsequent EU related statutes) that in respect of the UK's membership of the EU the Crown's prerogative power to withdraw from the relevant treaties should be preserved. Since that 'intention' had no express textual basis in any statute, it could exist only if it was proper for the Court to infer it to do so from relevant constitutional principles and political circumstances. The Court could not see any basis for drawing such an inference. Triggering of Art 50 would require explicit statutory authorisation.

Reaction(s) to the judgment

The lead-in to the High Court hearing had been pock-marked by a substantial campaign of racist and often violent abuse targeted at Ms Miller (who is of mixed-race heritage) on various social media fora. Ms Miller was also vilified in somewhat more refined terms in mainstream media outlets for having the evident temerity to ask a court to rule on this important legal question.[65] That our constitution's understanding of such principles as the rule of law and sovereignty of Parliament is largely built on court judgments prompted by individuals (sometimes people, sometimes companies) challenging government policy (and more latterly statutory provisions) is an axiomatic element of our constitutional tradition was a principle and indeed a fact that these commentators were either ignorant of or unwilling to accept.[66]

The tirades fired at Ms Miller continued when the judgment was announced. They were accompanied by fusillades of vitriolic abuse levelled at the members of the court. The peak of

---

[63] [2017] 2 WLR 583 at para 66.   [64] Ibid, at paras 43–44.

[65] <https://www.theguardian.com/politics/2017/may/13/gina-miller-interview-article-50-brexit-tactical-voting>.

[66] To offer a few familiar examples: Mr Entick (see '*Entick v Carrington* (1765)', ch 3, pp 46–47); John Wilkes (see 'John Wilkes', ch 8, pp 203–204); Freddie Laker (see 'Extending *De Keyser: Laker Airways v Department of Trade* (1977)' ch 4, pp 88–89); Anisminic (see '*Anisminic v Foreign Compensation Commission* (1969)' ch 3, pp 68–70); Chief Constable Ridge (see 'The re-emergence of the principle? *Ridge v Baldwin*' ch 14, pp 387–389); Ms Smith (see 'The end of the doctrine of implied repeal? *Macarthys v Smith*' ch 11, pp 303–304); and Factortame (see 'The demise of the legal doctrine? *Factortame*' ch 11, pp 306–312).

this trend ('bottom of this pit' might be a better metaphor) was the headline in *The Daily Mail* on 4 November 2016:[67]

Enemies of the people:

Fury over 'out of touch' judges who have 'declared war on democracy' by

defying 17.4m Brexit voters and who could trigger constitutional crisis

The Daily Mail also thought it appropriate to highlight that one member of the Court (Sir Terence Etherton MR) was Jewish, gay, and married to a man; that another (Thomas LCJ) was a 'committed Europhile'; and the third (Sales LJ) was regarded in some circles as a crony of former Prime Minister (and presumably similarly Europhile) Tony Blair. The clumsy smear was presumably intended to suggest to readers that the Court was biased against withdrawal in political terms and had allowed that bias to shape its judgment.

The headline offered by *The Daily Telegraph* was:

The judges versus the people.

The Sun adopted a more xenophobic tone, running a front page with a picture of Ms Miller smiling beneath headlines which read:

WHO DO YOU THINK EU ARE?

Loaded foreign elite defy will of Brit voters

It is perhaps difficult to believe that the journalists who produced such headlines were really ignorant of the constitutional principles in issue, and were not consciously seeking to mislead their (more ill-informed and impressionable) readers rather than just being ill-informed themselves.[68] It is also perhaps surprising that some politicians echoed such sentiments.

The Conservative MP Dominic Raab, a leading light of the Leave campaign and previously (and subsequently) a Minister in the Department of Justice, offered the following comment on the judgment:

> On 23 June the British people gave a clear mandate for the UK Government to leave the EU. This case is a plain attempt to block Brexit by people who are out of touch with the country and refuse to accept the result . . . An unholy alliance of diehard Remain campaigners, a fund manager, an unelected judiciary and the House of Lords must not be allowed to thwart the wishes of the British public. It would trigger a constitutional crisis if the Supreme Court upheld this vague and undemocratic verdict.[69]

Iain Duncan-Smith MP, a prominent player in the Maastricht episode[70] and the Leave campaign, weighed in through *The Sun*.[71] The column perhaps merits reading in full as an illustration of the quite staggering constitutional illiteracy or mendacity that can be a characteristic

[67] <http://www.dailymail.co.uk/news/article-3903436/Enemies-people-Fury-touch-judges-defied-17-4m-Brexit-voters-trigger-constitutional-crisis.html#ixzz4rEVlYSb2>. An overview of similar press coverage is offered at <http://www.politico.eu/article/how-the-british-press-reacted-to-high-court-brexit-ruling/>. For analysis see Constitution Unit and McNeil A (2017) 'Miller and the media: Supreme Court judgment generates more measured response'; available at: <https://constitution-unit.com/2017/02/09/miller-and-the-media-supreme-court-judgement-generates-more-measured-response/>.

[68] It should be stressed that not all right-leaning media organisations subscribed to this view; see eg Massie A (2106) 'The unhinged backlash to the High Court's Brexit ruling' *The Spectator*, available at: <https://blogs.spectator.co.uk/2016/11/unhinged-backlash-high-courts-brexit-ruling/>.

[69] Quoted in <http://www.dailymail.co.uk/news/article-3903436/Enemies-people-Fury-touch-judges-defied-17-4m-Brexit-voters-trigger-constitutional-crisis.html#ixzz4rEp85X2U>.

[70] 'The ratification and incorporation of the Maastricht Treaty', ch 12, pp 316–317.

[71] <https://www.thesun.co.uk/news/2125187/out-of-touch-judges-have-set-up-a-clash-between-parliament-and-the-british-people-over-brexit/>.

even of people who have held high political office, but the following passage conveys the gist of the 'analysis':

> The latest betrayal and perhaps the worst is that three unelected judges have decided that the vote the British people cast wasn't binding on the Government and that Parliament should instead decide if we should leave the EU. Twisting and turning in their out of touch world, the Judges have dismissed the vote the British people cast.
>
> I don't know where they were during the referendum debate or whether they even bothered to listen, (maybe judges don't read newspapers or watch television) but they should have noticed that the government said again and again that there was no going back from the public vote—it would be final—leave meant leave. In deliberately ignoring the instruction given by the British people that the UK must leave the EU, the judges have instead set up a clash between Parliament and the British people. We, who voted to leave, have every reason to be angry and feel we were duped by the ruling elite, who now deny the vote.

Prime Minister May was notably reticent in even criticising let alone condemning comments of this sort from the press or her own party's backbench MPs. The then Lord Chancellor, Liz Truss, initially appeared to not consider that her statutory duty under the Constitutional Reform Act 2005 s 17[72] extended to voicing any support for the competence and integrity of the court. Her later intervention was seen as too little, too late.

In contrast to the silence displayed by Ministers, several Conservative MPs offered a robust defence of the Court's position.[73] The former Attorney-General Dominic Grieve described such criticisms of the Court as:

> [E]ntirely unjustified and are either made in ignorance or out of malice, it's impossible to know which. The judges are the safeguarders of our unwritten constitution. Nothing they have done ought to take anybody by surprise. To accede to the principle that you can change primary legislation by royal prerogative is a constitutional monstrosity and would totally undermine everything that our forebears struggled to give us. It would trash the constitution.[74]

The government was happily not swayed by the wilder claims of the tabloid press and some of its own MPs, and took prompt steps to have the case appealed directly to the Supreme Court. Argument before the Court began in early December. At the same time, the House of Commons debated and approved[75] on a cross-party basis a resolution to the effect that the house wished to see that Art 50 was triggered by the end of March 2017. Most of the MPs who participated in the debate appeared to understand and accept that if the government did not succeed in its appeal then legislation for that purpose would be required.

In the Supreme Court

Miller was argued before the Supreme Court sitting as a full bench of eleven judges. By a majority of eight to three the Court upheld the result reached in the High Court, albeit through a slightly different route.

---

[72] Which requires that on taking office the Lord Chancellor swears an oath that she will inter alia 'respect the "rule of law" and "defend the independence of the judiciary"'.

[73] See the coverage at <https://www.theguardian.com/media/2016/nov/04/labour-condemns-newspaper-attacks-on-judges-after-brexit-ruling>.

[74] Ibid. In more pungent terms Lord Macdonald of River Glaven QC characterised the criticism of the Court as: '[C]onstitutionally illiterate attacks from politicians who should know better. The high court has reaffirmed the sovereignty of parliament within the rule of law. In other words, it has fulfilled precisely its most critical function in a democratic society. The idea that judges would be better employed kowtowing to the executive is shameful heresy from political pygmies'.

[75] <http://hansard.parliament.uk/commons/2016-12-07/debates/CA09D9B2-9634-41C8-8979-8B9CD82DBB8F/TheGovernmentSPlanForBrexit>.

The case continued to be argued (and decided) on the basis that giving notice under Art 50 was not a revocable action.[76] The May government's concession on that point is in one sense surprising. If Art 50 notice could indeed be withdrawn at any point within the presumptive two year withdrawal period, then it would be perfectly credible to argue that no legal rights of any sort would be affected by giving notice; that issue would arise only when the terms of withdrawal were agreed and given effect.

The main plank of the May government's argument before the Supreme Court again rested on a reversal of constitutional orthodoxies; that is, that (contra *DeKeyser*, *Laker*, and *Fire Brigades Union*) prerogative powers dealing with matters that had acquired a statutory character should be presumed to be continuingly effective unless the relevant statute had expressly provided that they would not be:

> 37 [Counsel for] the Secretary of State . . . argued that the fact that significant legal changes will follow from withdrawing from the EU Treaties does not prevent the giving of Notice, because the prerogative power to withdraw from treaties was not excluded by the terms of the 1972 Act, and that, in any event, 'acts of the Government in the exercise of the prerogative can alter domestic law'. More particularly, he contended that the 1972 Act gave effect to EU law only in so far as the EU Treaties required it, and that that effect was therefore contingent upon the United Kingdom remaining a party to those treaties. Accordingly, he said, in the 1972 Act Parliament had effectively stipulated that, or had sanctioned the result whereby, EU law should cease to have domestic effect in the event that minsters decided to withdraw from the EU Treaties.

The crux of Ms Miller's case was put through the use of a gun metaphor:[77] that giving the Art 50 notice would pull 'the trigger which causes the bullet to be fired, with the consequence that the bullet will hit the target and the Treaties will cease to apply' with the necessary consequence that (at least) some of the legal rights deriving from the Treaties would be lost. If, as Ms Miller maintained, such rights had a statutory basis, then statutory authorisation would be required for the trigger to be pulled.

Prerogative powers could not be used to override or compromise statutory provisions

The majority's response to these divergent propositions amounted to little more than a recitation of introductory constitutional history. Like the High Court, the Supreme Court referred[78] to Coke's assertion in the pre-revolutionary *Case of Proclamations*, to Art 1 of the Bill of Rights 1689, and the House of Lords' 1916 judgment in *The Zamora* to illustrate the basic proposition that prerogative powers could not be used to alter the content of laws enacted by Parliament or the common law:

> 50 . . . [I]t is a fundamental principle of the UK constitution that, unless primary legislation permits it, the Royal prerogative does not enable ministers to change statute or common law . . .

The judgment then invoked *DeKeyser*, *Burmah Oil*, and *Laker Airways*[79] to underline the related proposition that:

> 51 Further, ministers cannot frustrate the purpose of a statute or a statutory provision, for example by emptying it of content or preventing its effectual operation . . .

---

[76] [2017] 2 WLR 583, at para 26.   [77] Ibid, at para 36.   [78] Ibid, at paras 44 and 45 respectively.
[79] Respectively [1920] AC 508; [1977] QB 643; [1995] 2 AC 513: and respectively discussed at 'The superiority of statute over prerogative: *A-G v De Keyser's Royal Hotel*', ch 4, pp 85–88; 'Extending *De Keyser: Laker Airways v Department of Trade*', ch 4, pp 88–89; 'Extending *Laker: R v Secretary of State for the Home Department ex parte Fire Brigaded Union*', ch 4, pp 89–90.

Having underlined these very basic points, the Court then turned to the question of whether or not the various rights and obligations created by EU law should properly be regarded as statutory provisions.

What is the domestic status of EU law?

At the outset of this section of its judgment, the majority reiterated (what has become since *Factortame* in 1991) the dominant understanding of the legal effect of the ECA 1972:

> 60 Many statutes give effect to treaties by prescribing the content of domestic law in the areas covered by them. The 1972 Act does this, but it does considerably more as well. It authorises a dynamic process by which, without further primary legislation (and, in some cases, even without any domestic legislation), EU law not only becomes a source of UK law, but actually takes precedence over all domestic sources of UK law, including statutes. This may sound rather dry or technical to many people, but in constitutional terms the effect of the 1972 Act was unprecedented. Indeed, it is fair to say that the legal consequences of the United Kingdom's accession to the EEC were not fully appreciated by many lawyers until the Factortame litigation in the 1990s . . . Of course, consistently with the principle of Parliamentary sovereignty, this unprecedented state of affairs will only last so long as Parliament wishes: the 1972 Act can be repealed like any other statute. For that reason, we would not accept that the so-called fundamental rule of recognition (ie the fundamental rule by reference to which all other rules are validated) underlying UK laws has been varied by the 1972 Act or would be varied by its repeal.

However, the majority's view was that rights deriving from EU law were not (domestic) statutory rights in the ordinary sense; it did not adopt the High Court's view that the ECA 1972 'created' EU law rights. Nor did the majority suggest that the effect of the ECA 1972 was somehow to convert EU law rights into UK statutory rights. It is certainly correct that s 2 of the ECA 1972 does not expressly provide for that consequence, and to arrive at that conclusion would demand some departure from traditional canons of statutory interpretation.[80] Rather than pursuing that course, the majority held that the ECA 1972 should be seen a 'conduit pipe'[81] through which EU law flowed into the domestic legal system. The metaphor was taken from an article by Professor Finnis[82] written in response to the first instance judgment in *Miller*. The Court did not acknowledge that Finnis used the metaphor in opposition to Ms Miller's case, to attack what he referred to as: 'the glaringly fallacious syllogism on which he [David Pannick QC for Ms Miller] has rested the claim': that is, that if EU rights were not statutory rights the use of the prerogative to remove them was legally unobjectionable. That argument rests of course on the assumption that the normative domestic status of EU rights if they were not statutory in the ordinary sense was not equivalent to or superior to statute. Unhappily for the government, the majority of the Supreme Court did not accept that proposition flowed from applying the conduit pipe metaphor.

The metaphor may seem an apposite analytical tool insofar as although the majority appeared to accept that the ECA 1972 was 'the source' of EU law rights in the United Kingdom in a formal sense, it suggested that: '[I]n a more fundamental sense, and we consider, more realistic sense, it is the EU institutions which are the relevant sources of that law.'[83] One might wonder if it was sensible for the Supreme Court to offer a distinction between the 'formal' legal position and the 'realistic' legal position when both analyses seem to lead to the same

---

[80] 'Traditional' in the non-EU-related sense. Strict literalism is at best only a marginal player in the 'traditions' of EU law, whether before the ECJ or before UK courts; see 'IV. EEC law, parliamentary sovereignty and the UK courts: phase one', ch 11 pp 302–304; and the seventh edition of this book at pp 393–97.   [81] At para 65.
[82] Finnis J. (2016) 'Terminating Treaty-based UK rights'; available at:<https://ukconstitutionallaw.org/2016/10/26/john-finnis-terminating-treaty-based-uk-rights/>.   [83] [2017] 2 WLR 583 at para 61.

normative conclusion: namely that—per *Factortame*—these EU rights were not just equivalent to statutory rights; they were actually superior to domestic statutory rights insofar as they were not subject to implied repeal. The High Court's conclusion that the ECA 1972 'creates' a statutory basis for EU law is a rather more straightforward (and post-*Factortame* 'orthodox') means through which to accord such rights a normative status superior to the prerogative than the Supreme Court's identification of a new 'third (and external) source' of domestic legal authority.

It is also difficult to reconcile the majority's conduit pipe/third source of EU law analysis with its conclusion that the ECA 1972 did not change the constitution's basic rule of recognition. If we accept that the orthodox understanding of the rule of recognition encompasses implied as well as express repeal,[84] then a court's refusal to apply the implied repeal doctrine in the EU context produces a form of entrenchment. Admittedly that entrenchment is only linguistic in nature, and thus can quite easily be overcome; but if we take the Diceyan position on Parliament's sovereignty as our 'rule of recognition' it is untenable to suggest that the passage of the ECA 1972 did not alter that rule; just as Professor Wade argued had occurred in his analysis of *Factortame* in 1997.[85]

This wrinkle in the majority's reasoning has little practical significance. The Court's conclusion was that the domestic normative superiority of EU law went no further than being safeguarded against implied repeal/amendment, as Parliament has always been competent to remove the 'conduit pipe' by repealing the ECA 1972 in express terms. But if the pipe was laid and opened by statute, then prima facie it could only be closed and dismantled by the same legal mechanism. Might it be the case however, that the insertion of the referendum per se into the governmental process should be taken to have altered the orthodox presumption that prerogative powers could not be used to affect 'statutory' rights and obligations?

The significance of the referendum

In essence, the government's primary argument on the prerogative point was tantamount to advocacy of revolution in a legal sense. That it received such short shrift from the majority of the Supreme Court is unsurprising. But the government's resort to what we might benevolently call 'novel' legal principles had a second string:

> 116 . . . The Attorney General submitted that the traditional view as to the limits of prerogative power should not apply to a ministerial decision authorised by a majority of the members of the electorate who vote in a referendum provided for by Parliament. In effect, he said that, even though it was Parliament which required the referendum, the response to the referendum result should be a matter for ministers, and that it should not be constrained by the legal limitations which would have applied in the absence of the referendum.

The contention is so preposterous that one instinctively feels both an embarrassed sympathy on behalf of the Attorney-General who advanced it and an admiration for the Court's patience in rejecting it in such polite terms.[86] As noted earlier, the legal consequences of the referendum result were a matter for Parliament to determine pre-emptively in the 2015 Act. Parliament chose—whether through ignorance or design is of no significance—not to enact any provisions addressing that question. That government Ministers might suggest that the referendum was binding would most likely have *political consequences* in terms of what might happen

---

[84] Cf. 'The doctrine of implied repeal', ch 2, pp 28–29.   [85] See 'Back in the House of Lords', ch 12, pp 307–308.

[86] The bulk of the government's case was argued by James Eadie QC, a very eminent member of the public law bar. That the referendum point was argued by the Attorney-General, Jeremy Wright MP, a lawyer of no evident distinction as either an advocate or theorist, might suggest that Mr Eadie's concern for his own professional reputation disinclined him to offer the Court such a ludicrous submission.

within Parliament or at subsequent elections if Ministers followed a different path, but such suggestions carried *no legal weight* at all.

The government did not however suggest that the December 2016 Commons resolution could have any bearing on the Crown's capacity to trigger Art 50 through the prerogative. As we saw in chapter eight, a Commons resolution per se has no legal effect on either the common law or statute.[87]

The voice of the devolved legislatures

The devolution issue had not been pursued in the hearing before the High Court. It was however raised by all of the devolved governments before the Supreme Court. In simple terms, their argument was that triggering Art 50 would not just affect the rights of their respective populations but would also have a profound effect on their respective legislatures and executives powers to control various devolved issues. The first branch of this argument was that since those matters were statutory in nature, they could not be interfered with by the exercise of prerogative powers. Given the majority's conclusion on Ms Miller central proposition, there was no need for that point to be pursued at any length. The second branch of the argument (again stated in simple terms) was the more speculative assertion that Parliament could not enact a statute permitting invocation of Art 50 unless the devolved legislatures had agreed to that Act.

It was suggested in chapter twelve that one could credibly argue that a constitutional convention (the 'Sewel convention')[88] was emerging to the effect that the UK Parliament would not legislate on matters within the competence of the devolved legislatures without the consent of the respective legislature. The 'moral' force of that proposition was apparently given legislative reinforcement in 2016 by the addition to s 28 of the Scotland Act 1998 of the new s 28(8) of which reads:

> (8) But it is recognised that the Parliament of the United Kingdom will not normally legislate with regard to devolved matters without the consent of the Scottish Parliament.

The Scots government relied upon both the Sewel convention and s 28(8) to support its argument.

The majority's[89] treatment of the question was rather odd in several respects. As to the argument based on convention, the Supreme Court again referred to long established constitutional orthodoxies, referring inter alia to the familiar passage from Lord Reid's judgment in *Madzimbamuto*[90] to the effect that breach of a convention might be 'unconstitutional' in a moral sense, but not in a legal sense, and to the judgment in the *Crossman Diaries* case (*Attorney-General v Jonathan Cape Ltd*).[91] The Court might sensibly have looked no further in reaching the conclusion that the Sewel convention was not relevant to the legal issue it had to resolve. Unfortunately however the majority also drew—and at some length—on the Canadian Supreme Court's *Patriation Reference* judgment[92] to bolster its conclusion. Reliance on that authority sits rather unhappily with the Court's decision to adopt a 'realist' rather than 'formalist' approach to the domestic status of EU law.

---

[87] It is of course possible that Parliament can lend such a resolution legal effect, but in those circumstances the House would be exercising a statutory power.

[88] See 'The continuing sovereignty of the UK Parliament?', ch 12, pp 332–333.

[89] The three judges who dissented on the prerogative point joined the majority on this issue.

[90] [1969] 1 AC 645 at 723; see 'Conclusion', ch 2, p 42.

[91] [1976] QB 752; see 'Can conventions become law? 1: The *Crossman Diaries* case' ch 9, pp 230–231.

[92] [1981] SCR 753; see 'V. Can conventions become laws? 2: Patriating the Canadian constitution', ch 9, pp 243–246.

In formal terms, of course, the Canadian Supreme Court concluded that the convention that the national government should not seek an amendment by the UK Parliament to the British North America Act 1867 which affected Provincial powers unless it did so with the approval of a substantial number of the provinces did not trump the government's legal power to do so. The 'reality' of that judgment however was that the Canadian Supreme Court ascribed the convention such a high degree of political and moral importance and portrayed the Trudeau government's intended breach of it in such a pejorative fashion that it became politically impossible for the government to proceed.[93] The Supreme Court in *Miller* did not follow either of those leads. It may therefore have been better for the Supreme Court to have steered well clear of that particular episode in resolving this question.[94]

As to s 28(8)—which is a law and not a convention—the Supreme Court considered that its purpose was: 'to entrench [the Sewel convention] as a convention'.[95] Consequently, it should not be regarded as having created a justiciable obligation giving rise to a legal remedy. Quite how one 'entrenches' a moral principle without giving it legal effect is something of a puzzle. More troubling perhaps is the Court's readiness to accept that Parliament can enact provisions which are *never* intended to have any legal effect. A more conservative—and thence orthodox—analysis might have been simply to conclude that s 28(8) was a legal rule which would in all likelihood *very rarely* have any justiciable effect, and that this was not such an occasion, whether because of the nature of the (at that point hypothetical) legislation in issue and/or because sufficient time had not yet passed for any sensible view to be formed on what 'normally' might mean.

The dissenting judgments

Three members of the Supreme Court accepted the government's arguments. Lords Reed, Carnwarth, and Hughes were the dissentients, each delivering a separate judgment, although the gist of their analysis is conveyed by Lord Reed's opinion.

Lord Reed started from the premise that the conduct of foreign policy through prerogative powers was a 'basic principle' feature of the constitutional order. As such, the prerogative power could only be removed or controlled by legislation which did so either in *express terms* or by *necessary* implication. While Lord Reed obviously accepted that there was no express term, he rejected from the majority's conclusion that such an implication *necessarily* arose.

This was in part a question of chronology. The passage of the ECA 1972 preceded ratification of the Treaty of Accession, and Lord Reed considered it was: 'not difficult to imagine circumstances in which ratification might not have occurred':[96] a change of government for example (Labour then being in the main opposed to entry), or a serious breakdown in diplomatic relationships with an existing Member State.

More significantly, Lord Reed held that the ECA 1972 gave rise to legal rights which were contingent in nature. In some respects, that contingency lay in matters over which the United Kingdom had no control. If another Member State left the EU, for example, then any EU rights its nationals exercised in the United Kingdom would disappear without the need for any intervention by the UK government or Parliament. In respect of the issue before the Court, that

---

[93] Ibid.

[94] Alternatively, maintaining a 'realist' approach, the Supreme Court might have noted that 'Canada' was created (by the British North America Act 1867) de jure as a federal polity and that the convention of provincial assent had been recognised and acted upon for many decades prior to 1980, so that the 'reason' for it (in Jennings' sense) was much stronger than the reason underpinning the Sewel convention. For a forceful criticism of this aspect of the Supreme Court's judgment see Elliot (2017) op cit.

[95] [2017] 2 WLR 583 at para 149.

[96] Ibid, at paras 195–196.

contingency was rooted in successive governments' continuing decisions not to exercise the prerogative to withdraw from the Treaties. In short terms:

> [204] . . . If Parliament chooses to give domestic effect to a Treaty containing a power of termination, it does not follow that Parliament must have stripped the Crown of its authority to exercise that power. In the present context, the impact of the exercise of the power on EU rights given effect in domestic law is accommodated by the 1972 Act: the rights simply cease to be rights to which section 2(1) applies. Withdrawal under article 50EU alters the application of the 1972 Act, but is not inconsistent with it. The application of the 1972 Act after a withdrawal agreement has entered into force (or the applicable time limit has expired) is the same as it was before the Treaty of Accession entered into force. As in the 1972 Act as originally enacted, Parliament has created a scheme under which domestic law tracks the obligations of the UK at the international level, whatever they may be.

Lord Reed also suggested that the majority had attached insufficient importance to the dual nature of controls over the exercise of governmental powers.[97] Ministers individually and the government collectively could be called to account by either or both houses of parliament in relation to the exercise of the foreign policy prerogative:

> [240] . . . For a court to proceed on the basis that if a prerogative power is capable of being exercised arbitrarily or perversely, it must necessarily be subject to judicial control, is to base legal doctrine on an assumption which is foreign to our constitutional traditions. It is important for courts to understand that the legalisation of political issues is not always constitutionally appropriate, and may be fraught with risk, not least for the judiciary.

Reaction(s) to the judgment

The highly biased coverage by some media organisations and politicians which had greeted the High Court's *Miller* judgment was echoed in reaction to the Supreme Court's opinion. The most extraordinary comment perhaps came from the veteran Conservative MP Iain Duncan-Smith:[98]

> You've got to understand that, of course, there's the European issue but there's also the issue about who is supreme—Parliament or a self-appointed court . . . This is the issue here right now, so I was intrigued that it was a split judgment, I'm disappointed they've decided to tell Parliament how to run its business. After all, there was a vote before in December overwhelmingly to trigger Article 50, so they've stepped into new territory where they've actually told Parliament not just that they should do something but actually what they should do and I think that leads further down the road to real constitutional issues about who is supreme in this role.

Leaving aside the bizarre assertion that the Supreme Court is 'self-appointed', Duncan-Smith's 'critique' rests on (yet again) a failure to recognise a distinction between the government and Parliament or—more prosaically—between what a government is politically inclined to do and what it is legally allowed to do.

In contrast to Mr Duncan-Smith's continuing embrace of a fantasy-land constitutional order, the newspapers which had been so scathing in their denunciation of the High Court's opinion afforded the Supreme Court's judgment a much more muted response. *The Daily Mail's* leading article forswore any criticism of the court as an institution or the judges as

---

[97] For a very different judicial perspective on that issue see the speech of Lord Mustill in the *Fire Brigades Union* case, discussed at 'Lord Mustill's analysis', ch 19, 516–517.

[98] For text and video coverage see <http://www.express.co.uk/news/uk/758244/Iain-Duncan-Smith-Supreme-Court-judges-Brexit-attack>.

individuals, reserving its criticism instead for any MPs who might seek to block the passage of the required legislation.[99] *The Daily Telegraph* offered similar coverage.[100] *The Sun* was unable to be quite so restrained: although it did not criticise the Supreme Court its leading headline in response to the judgment again included a personalised attack on Ms Miller:[101]

> Chief Brexit wrecker Gina Miller claims her
> Supreme Court win is 'about the legal process, not politics'

In legal terms, the most significant consequence of the judgment was the May government's promotion of a Bill to acquire the statutory power to invoke Art 50. The European Union (Notification of Withdrawal) Act 2017 received the Royal Assent in March 2017, having passed though both houses without attracting any significant opposition.[102] Section 1 provides simply that:

1. Power to notify withdrawal from the EU

    (1) The Prime Minister may notify, under Article 50(2) of the Treaty on European Union, the United Kingdom's intention to withdraw from the EU.

    (2) This section has effect despite any provision made by or under the European Communities Act 1972 or any other enactment.[103]

That legal issue having been resolved, the constitutional implications of withdrawal moved from the legal sphere to the political, as the May government set about clarifying its policy objectives for the UK's future relationship with the EU. Article 50 was triggered on March 29 2017, which meant that the (presumptive) date for withdrawal would be 29 March 2019.

III. Negotiating the terms of departure

There has likely never been a more asinine mantra within British political discourse than the slogan repeatedly offered up by May and her Cabinet in the aftermath of the referendum that 'Brexit means brexit'. If one asked a meaningful question—'I am a British retiree living in Spain. Will I still be able to live there and have access to Spanish medical services at no cost after brexit?'; or 'I am a British law student. Will I be able to study for an LLM at the University of Amsterdam and only pay EU level fees after brexit?'; or 'I work at the BMW Mini plant in Oxford. Will BMW be able to export Minis to the EU without paying an import duty after brexit?' then the government could offer no worthwhile answer.

In (very) crude terms, the political debate as to what brexit might actually mean polarised around two extreme positions. The so-called 'soft brexit' option envisaged that the United Kingdom would seek to remain within the EU's customs union and the single market. This would safeguard freedom of movement of UK goods and workers into other EU countries. But the United Kingdom would not regain any substantial control over immigration by EU nationals and remain subject to judicial oversight by CJEU on all single market and customs union issues. Proponents of the alternative extreme, styled as 'hard brexit', attached such importance

---

[99] <http://www.dailymail.co.uk/news/article-4150822/Judges-ruling-PM-executive-powers-trigger-Brexit.html>.

[100] <http://www.telegraph.co.uk/news/0/article-50-ruling-does-mean-brexit-happens-next/>.

[101] <https://www.thesun.co.uk/news/2691568/chief-brexit-wrecker-gina-miller-claims-her-supreme-court-win-is-about-the-legal-process-not-politics/>.

[102] A smattering of MPs voted against the Bill (even though the Leave vote had been in a majority in their particular constituencies) on the basis that they considered withdrawing from the EU to be a politically ludicrous policy which could only harm the national interest. The Conservative Ken Clarke was the most notable of these MPs. See <https://www.theguardian.com/politics/2017/feb/01/full-list-mps-voted-against-brexit-bill>.

[103] Section 1(2) was presumably included to deal with the *Factortame* implied repeal entrenchment point, in that it is an express repeal of whatever effect the ECA might have on deploying Art 50.

to the United Kingdom having complete control over immigration and escaping the jurisdiction of the CJEU that wished to leave both the single market and the customs union as quickly as possible, even if that were to occur without any agreement being reached between the EU and United Kingdom as to their future economic and political relationship.

May's initial actions as Prime Minister sent conflicting signals as to her own preferences. Michael Gove, a primary player in the Leave campaign was sacked from the Cabinet, as was the Chancellor of the Exchequer, George Osborne, who had been a prominent Remainer. May appointed three of the more extreme Leave campaigners to the three Cabinet offices which would be primarily responsible for negotiating the terms of departure and subsequent trade relationships with the EU and other countries; Boris Johnson as Foreign Secretary, Liam Fox as Secretary of State for International Trade, and David Davis as head of the newly created Department for Exiting the European Union. Suggestions were aired that May had appointed these 'Three Brexiteers' in the expectation that they would make such a mess of protecting the UK's interests that the entire brexit project would have to be abandoned. A more plausible explanation is that the Prime Minister was trying to appease Euro-sceptic members of her parliamentary party, while her appointment of the reputedly soft brexit favouring Phillip Hammond as Chancellor of the Exchequer was designed to placate—if not reassure—Conservative MPs who had favoured Remain.[104] Before any greater clarity emerged however, a purely domestic event unexpectedly intervened.

The 2017 general election

Prime Minister May had said on several occasions early in 2017 that she saw no need to call a general election to secure a mandate for her pursuit of the 'hard brexit' she seemed to prefer. However her sense of party political opportunism, in the face of the evident disarray of the Labour Party under Jeremy Corbyn's leadership trumped the country's need to make a prompt and well-prepared start to the departure negotiations and led her to seek to call an election for the Spring of 2017 in the apparent hope of securing a large Commons majority.

As noted in chapter seven, the Conservative/Liberal coalition government had promoted legislation (enacted as the Fixed Term Parliaments Act 2011) which removed the prerogative power to call elections at any time and introduced a presumptive five-year period between general elections.[105] That presumption could be rebutted (per s 2(1)) by a two-thirds (of all members)[106] Commons majority vote. Prime Minister May announced in April 2017 that she wished to hold an election in early June. Despite its then dreadful ratings in recent opinion polls, the Labour Party supported the proposal, which was passed with some 522 votes in favour.

The election campaign did not unfold as Prime Minister May evidently expected (see Table 23.2). The substantial poll lead that the Conservatives initially held began to evaporate in the face of u-turns in party policy, an unexpectedly able performance by Jeremy Corbyn as Labour leader, and suggestions of readiness among many voters to vote tactically for whichever local candidate had the best prospect of defeating the Conservative nominee. The eventual result revealed May's decision to seek an early election to be a spectacular self-inflicted wound. Although the Conservatives 'won' the election in the sense of being returned as much the largest party in the Commons, it lacked an overall majority and clung to power by negotiating an informal alliance—a so-called 'confidence and supply agreement'—with Northern Ireland's Democratic Unionist Party.

The election was also notable for the entirely unexpected resurgence of the Conservative Party in Scotland. Of the fifty-nine Scots seats in the Commons, the SNP won thirty-five [59.3%]

---

[104] For further analysis see Allen (2017) op cit.   [105] 'The prospects of reform', ch 7, pp 196–197.

[106] ie at least 434 members would have to support the motion.

Table 23.2 Votes won and seats gained at the general election 2017

Party	Vote %	Seats	[%]
Conservative	42.5	318	[48.9]
Labour	40.0	262	[40.3]
Liberal	7.4	12	[1.8]
Scots Nationalist	3.0	35	[5.3]
Democratic Unionist	0.9	12	[1.8]

(with a 36.9% share of the vote); the Conservatives won thirteen [22 %] (28.6% share of the vote); Labour won seven [11.8%] (27.1% of the vote); and the Liberals won four [6.7] (6.1% of the vote). The voting pattern suggested that one consequence of devolution had been effectively to decouple the Conservative Party in Scotland from the Party in England (and Wales), where its resurgence was due at least in part to its (compared to May) charismatic and popular party leader, Ruth Davison. The Labour Party performed much better in the election than many commentators had expected. It had done so without adopting any clear position on its brexit policy, although subsequent analysis of voting patterns suggested that it had attracted significant numbers of pro-Remain voters who had formerly supported other parties.

The May government's policy objectives

As leader of a minority government, Prime Minister May's capacity to command a Commons majority for any politically contentious policy was quite weak. That weakness was compounded by the fact that the unnecessary loss of the government's previous (albeit slender) Commons majority had undermined her personal credibility in the eyes of many Conservative MPs. Within the Conservative Party, proponents of both hard and soft brexit jostled for position after the 2017 election. It rapidly became apparent that the conventions of unanimity and confidentiality[107] within the Cabinet had broken down as ministers on both sides of the argument regularly leaked accounts of developments and disputes within Cabinet over brexit policy.

The government published a series of position papers during the summer and early autumn of 2017 outlining its hopes for various aspects of the UK's future relationship with the EU. Although negotiations between the United Kingdom and the EU had begun in the spring of 2017, little progress had been made by the autumn. The EU had indicated that it would not begin to discuss the question of the future relationship until agreement was reached on several issues that it regarded as crucial to the terms of withdrawal; namely the continued rights of EU citizens reside in the United Kingdom, the regulation of the UK's land border with Ireland, and the level of the UK's still to be discharged contributions to the EU budget.

At this point (September 2017), Art 50's apparent presumption that exit terms could be successfully negotiated within the two-year period ending in March 2019 might seem wildly optimistic. The two-year period may be extended with the unanimous consent of all the Member States. It may well be that that power will have to be used if we are to avoid what has been referred to as a 'cliff edge' departure; that is, that the withdrawal occurs without any agreement having been reached between the EU and the United Kingdom on any significant aspects of their future commercial and political relationships.

The May government resisted any suggestions that the negotiation of withdrawal was a matter that might properly be conducted on a cross-party basis. No invitation was offered to any

---

[107] See respectively 'Unanimity' and 'Confidentiality', ch 9 pp 227–230 and 230–231.

other political party to be part of the UK's negotiating team. Nor did the government offer any role to the devolved legislatures or governments to participate directly in the process. Such input as the other parties might have into the withdrawal process would arise largely through their contribution within Parliament to the passage of the May government flagship brexit legislation—the so-called 'Great Repeal Bill'.

The 'Great Repeal Bill'

The European Union (Withdrawal) Bill—colloquially referred to as the 'Great Repeal Bill'—received its first reading in the Commons in July 2017, and its second reading in September 2017.[108] In crude terms, the objective underlying the Bill was to provide that all EU law applicable to the United Kingdom on the date of leaving the EU would be converted into domestic legislation, and thereafter the domestic law-making process would be used to determine which such laws to keep, which to amend, and which to repeal entirely.

The phrase 'domestic law-making process' is used advisedly here. That process could entail either primary legislation on all issues or the use—to varying degrees—of delegated legislative power to Ministers. The balance struck between those two alternatives has significant implications for the effective meaning of the separation of powers.

In hypothetical terms, a 'Great Repeal Act' might simply provide that:

> Section 1 Upon the day that the United Kingdom withdraws from the European Union, all European Union treaty articles and secondary legislation which immediately prior to withdrawal were applicable to and enforceable in the United Kingdom shall take effect in the United Kingdom as if they were statutory provisions enacted by Parliament.

However, a quite different consequence would ensue if one were to add a second section to the Act in the terms below:

> Section 2 Any Minister of the Crown may at any time she considers appropriate make such regulations as she considers desirable to repeal or amend in any fashion any measure identified in s 1.

Taken in isolation, section 1 of a Bill cast in those terms is a straightforward reassertion of Parliament's control over the content of domestic law as a matter both of theory and fact. The hypothetical section 2 would not of course affect Parliament's sovereignty in any theoretical sense, but its immediate practical effect (until such time as Parliament might repeal or amend it) would be to afford the government very extensive legislative powers. It would be a Henry VIII clause of extraordinarily sweeping extent.

The objections to Henry VIII clauses were rehearsed in chapter five.[109] Those objections are intensified when the power is exercised by a government which could not reliably command majority support in the Commons for a legislative programme pursued through primary legislation. The dominant characteristic of the May government's 'Great Repeal Bill' was to grant Ministers very expansive Henry VIII clause powers.

Clause 1 simply announced the repeal of the ECA 1972 on 'exit day'.[110] Clause 3 then provided that (most) EU law applicable to the United Kingdom immediately before exit day would be 'part of' domestic law. Such measures would be known collectively as 'retained law'. Clause 3 did not specify what normative status this notion of 'part of' entailed. The implication of cl 5(2), which expressly endorsed the principle of the supremacy of EU law to any existing (ie pre exit day) domestic law, suggest that 'part of' must mean (at least) equivalent to statute. Clause 5(1) expressly removed the supremacy principle with respect to any post-exit day domestic law.

---

[108] The text of the original version of the Bill is available at: <https://publications.parliament.uk/pa/bills/cbill/2017-2019/0005/18005.pdf>.   [109] 'Henry VIII clauses' ch 5, pp 123–124.
[110] Ibid.

Those provisions were not contentious in constitutional terms. Clause 7 in contrast contained a very contentious provision:

7 Dealing with deficiencies arising from withdrawal

(1) A minister of the Crown may by regulations make such provision as the Minister considers appropriate to prevent, remedy or mitigate—
   (a) any failure of retained EU law to operate effectively, or
   (b) any other deficiency in retained EU law, arising from the withdrawal of the United Kingdom from the EU . . .
(4) Regulations under this section may make any provision that could be made by an Act of Parliament.

Clause 7(2) then defined the notion of 'deficiencies' in an expansive fashion which would accord Ministers virtually untrammelled discretion; although cl 7(6) proposed that the cl 7(1) could not be used—inter alia—to raise taxes, introduce retrospective law, or create criminal offences. We noted in chapter five Professor Turpin's characterisation of Henry VIII clauses as granting a: 'circumscribed portion of legislative competence to a subordinate Minister'.[111] In abstract terms that description remains apposite for cl 7. What is striking about cl 7 however is that the 'portion of legislative competence' it sought to assign to the government was essentially unlimited in scale.

Clause 7 would create sweeping Henry VIII powers *subsequent to withdrawal*. An equally problematic provision was advanced for the *pre-withdrawal period* by cl 9:

9 Implementing the withdrawal agreement

(1) A Minister of the Crown may by regulations make such provision as the Minister considers appropriate for the purposes of implementing the withdrawal agreement if the Minister considers that such provision should be in force on or before exit day.
(2) Regulations under this section may make any provision that could be made by an Act of Parliament (including modifying this Act).

An even broader ministerial power seemed to be envisaged in cl 17:

17 Consequential and transitional provision

(1) A Minister of the Crown may by regulations make such provision as the Minister considers appropriate in consequence of this Act.
(2) The power to make regulations under subsection (1) may (among other things) be exercised by modifying any provision made by or under an enactment.
(3) In subsection (2) 'enactment' does not include primary legislation passed or made after the end of the Session in which this Act is passed

In essence, the May government was inviting Parliament to enact a statue dealing with the most politically important issue the country had faced in many years which would contain a term allowing the government to alter the provisions of the Act itself whenever the government thought it appropriate to do so.

Schedule 7 of the Bill made various provisions about the scrutiny of such regulations. Some would be subject to the affirmative resolution procedure: most however would be subject only to the negative resolution procedure.[112] There is little basis for thinking that the negative resolution procedure will permit extensive parliamentary evaluation of the likely very large numbers of regulations that will spew forth from various government departments both before and after the exit date. If enacted in its original form, the primary consequence of the Act—given

---

[111] Which, per cl 14 would be 'such day as a Minister of the Crown may by regulations appoint'.
[112] See 'The Statutory Instruments Acts 1946', ch 5, pp 121–122.

the huge range of laws to which it applies—would be a de facto transfer of Parliament's sovereignty to the government.

The second reading debate was prefigured by requests from Prime Minister May and her Chancellor Phillip Hammond to Conservative backbenchers not to obstruct the passage of the Bill or weaken its contents by proposing amendments.[113] While such entreaties may have persuaded some backbench MPs, others were not deterred from expressing disapproval of the Bill and intimating that they would oppose or seek to amend it. As one might expect, the second reading debate was peppered with contributions from hard brexit Conservatives suggesting that any MP who questioned any provision of the Bill was in effect defying the will of the people, but several Conservatives—Kenneth Clarke and Dominic Grieve again foremost among them—voiced strong criticism of the Bill itself, primarily on the basis that it accorded far too much legislative power to the government.[114]

The Labour Party had performed a remarkable volte face shortly before the Bill's second reading and announced that its preferred brexit policy would be for the United Kingdom to remain within both the single market and the customs union in the medium term, and perhaps in the long term as well if that could be achieved alongside some modification to the requirement that it accept existing EU rules concerning the free movement of persons. Neither Jeremy Corbyn nor the shadow Chancellor John McDonnell were especially conspicuous in announcing this new policy.

However, the Party's decision to oppose the Bill at second reading was rooted in the constitutional concerns expressed by Conservative MPS such as Kenneth Clarke and Dominic Grieve. The shadow brexit secretary, Keir Starmer, critiqued the Bill in forceful terms as an unprecedented grant of law-making power to the executive. The following passage, dealing with the scope of cl 9 and Sch 7, conveys both the flavour and force of Keir Starmer's analysis:[115]

> Part 2 of schedule 7 deals with clause 9. It makes it clear that unless the delegated legislation creates a public authority, or the function of a public authority, affects a criminal offence or affects a power to make legislation, it is to be dealt with by—what? The negative procedure for statutory instruments, which means the least possible scrutiny: it means that the widest possible power, with no safeguards, will be channelled into the level of least scrutiny.
>
> That is absolutely extraordinary. Let us be clear about what it means, because I am sure that the Secretary of State and others will say that notwithstanding the number of statutory instruments for which the schedule provides, they can be called up and annulled, and Parliament will have its say. I looked up the last time a negative-procedure statutory instrument had been annulled in the House, and it was 38 years ago. I do not know how many Members have been in the House for 38 years, but many of us will not have had that opportunity. So much for 'taking back control'.
>
> There is no point in the Secretary of State or the Prime Minister saying, 'We would not use these powers: take our assurance.' If they would not use them, they are unnecessary, and if they are unnecessary they should not be put before the House for approval today.

Conclusion

The 'Great Repeal Bill' offered an extraordinary opportunity for the Commons (and to a lesser extent the Lords) as a part of Parliament to function in de facto as well as de jure terms independently of the government. The Bill before the house dealt with a matter of enormous political

---

[113] The government had also proposed allocating only two days for the second reading debate and just eight days for the standing committee stage. These might be thought rather modest periods for considering so significant a Bill.

[114] *HCD* 7 September 2017 c 342 et seq; available at: <http://hansard.parliament.uk/Commons/2017-09-07/debates/3861F3BE-F7F1-4C3C-893E-194E14185F5C/EuropeanUnion(Withdrawal)Bill>.

[115] Ibid, at c 359.

significance: it was a Bill promoted by a government which lacked a reliable Commons majority; that government was drawn from a party riven with factional division over the withdrawal issue; and members of the house from both the governing and opposition parties delivered powerful speeches at the start of the second debate critiquing the constitutional implications of the Bill in its original form.

Whether that opportunity would be taken as the passage of the Bill played out in the autumn of 2017 presented constitutional lawyers with a case study of almost unparalleled importance. The Bill passed its second reading quite comfortably, although several Conservative MPs indicated that they would expect significant amendments to be made in committee. But up to that point, if one is seeking a powerful example of how the constitution of a modern democratic nation should make arrangements for resolving issues of huge political significance, the ongoing saga of the UK's attempts to withdraw from the EU provides a perfect illustration at the levels both of broad principle and narrow technicality of how *not* to proceed. In a more positive vein, the episode throws into sharp relief the issue with which this book began and to which we return in the final chapter; namely the desirability of maintaining a constitutional order in which sovereign legal power rests with a law-maker which represents in only a quite limited sense 'the people' who consent to live according to its laws.

Suggested further reading

Academic commentary

ALLEN N (2017) 'Brexit, butchery and Boris: Theresa May and her first Cabinet' *Parliamentary Affairs* 633

BOGDANOR V (2016) 'Brexit, the constitution and the alternatives' *Kings LJ* 314

ELEFTHERIADIS P (2017) 'Constitutional illegitimacy over Brexit' *Political Quarterly* 182

SHIPMAN T (2016) *All out war: the full story of Brexit*

Case law and legislation

R *(Miller and another) v Secretary of State for Exiting the European Union* [2016] EWHC 2768 (Admin) and [2017] UKSC 5, [2017] 2 WLR 583

Chapter 24

Conclusion

I.   Entrenchment of fundamental law revisited   657

In analysing the EU withdrawal referendum result and its aftermath, Professor Bogdanor was one among several commentators who apparently welcomed the consolidation of the convention of deploying referenda in respect of major constitutional issues as heralding the replacement of the sovereignty of Parliament with 'the Sovereignty of the People':[1]

> The referendum gives us a form of constitutional protection –perhaps the only from of constitutional protection for a country without a written constitution in which Parliament is sovereign and can do what it likes. The referendum is a safeguard against major constitutional changes which the people do not want. It is the people's veto.[2]

This seems an unfortunately positive way to characterise the referendum process. It has been consistently argued in this book that Parliament's possession of sovereign law-making power is a profoundly undesirable characteristic of the UK's constitution. Although one could credibly suggest (in an obviously pre-democratic sense) that the recognition in 1688 as a sovereign law-maker was an effectively anti-majoritarian initiative, it has bequeathed us an institutional structure which is not well-suited to exercising such power in a society in which relatively sophisticated notions of democracy are widely regarded as underpinning the legitimacy of the governmental process. It has owed more perhaps to good fortune than good design that we have thus far been spared the consequences of that power being used in pursuit of grossly oppressive ends in the modern era.

There may be something—perhaps much—to be said in favour of using a referendum (even so poorly designed a version of it as the EU withdrawal referendum) as *an addition* to the existing parliamentary law-making process when fundamentally important matters are in issue. In respect of EU withdrawal however we have seen it used as an *alternative* to the usual parliamentary methods, and as such it has done nothing to remedy the defects that the usual methods entail. The EU referendum did not in any sense cure or even mitigate these difficulties. It did not spare us from the consequences of narrow majoritarianism producing

---

[1] Bogdanor V (2016) 'Europe and the sovereignty of the people' *Political Quarterly* 348. Professor' Bogdanor's analysis gained wider coverage and currency through publication of condensed versions in the mainstream press; see <http://www.telegraph.co.uk/news/2016/06/26/the-eu-referendum-shows-how-the-sovereignty-of-britains-people-c/> and <https://www.ft.com/content/9b00bca0-bd61-11e6-8b45-b8b81dd5d080>.

[2] Ibid, at 348.

significant constitutional reform. Nor did it relieve us of the shortcoming of votes being cast on the basis of incomplete or downright misleading (from both sides of the debate) propaganda. Replacing an inadequate method for constitutional reform with a still more inadequate method is a cause for regret rather than rejoicing.

The question of constitutional reform is in itself worthy of book length examination. This final chapter does not offer a detailed prescription of the ways in which the UK's constitution should be structured. Its concern rather is briefly to address the issue which is perhaps of most interest to constitutional lawyers, and which logically precedes any discussion of the substance of truly radical constitutional realignment. That issue is whether it is legally possible to entrench legislation in a manner which safeguards it from repeal by the traditional 'simple majority in the Commons and Lords plus Royal Assent' formula; and, if such a legal device can be found, under what political circumstances might it legitimately be employed?

I. Entrenchment of fundamental law revisited

As suggested in chapter two, it now seems rather less difficult to construct a legal argument supporting the idea of entrenched legislation than it was in the 1950s, when the *Harris* and *McCormick* cases triggered a rash of interest in the possibility of finding domestic limitations to Parliament's evidently sovereign legal status. The orthodox Diceyan view, so persuasively restated by Professor Wade in 1955, need not be repeated here. The argument that such orthodoxy need no longer be construed as binding rests on several premises, both formalist and functionalist in nature. Some of these were evident but underdeveloped when Wade and indeed Dicey himself outlined the traditionalist viewpoint; others have emerged far more recently, as a result both of modern political history and contemporary judicial practice.

Issues of legality and legitimacy

The first issue we might address is a problem raised by linguistic imprecision, an imprecision that has in turn produced considerable conceptual confusion. The conceptual confusion may arise if one fails to distinguish between two quite different routes to achieve the same moral/political ends. If one should somehow succeed in legally 'binding' future Parliaments to respect particular values, then one has necessarily succeeded in entrenching those values. But one need not necessarily have to achieve the former result to bring about the latter consequences; it may be that one can now entrench legislation without having to destroy 'Parliament's' legal sovereignty. This argument assumes that entrenchment need not place any limits at all on 'Parliament's' legislative capacities; rather it need only convince the High Court that it has—if invited to do so by Parliament in a particular political context—an appropriate role to play in controlling the internal proceedings of the Commons and the Lords and the prerogative powers of the Monarch.

A different way of analysing the problem

To illustrate this argument, we might begin with a hypothetical entrenching provision, contained in a 'Constitution Act' passed in the ordinary manner. The Constitution Act specifies that a statutory provision (whether enacted prior or subsequent to the Constitution Act) affecting an entrenched value detailed in the Constitution Act (which would include the entrenching provision itself) would have legal force only if the court was satisfied that the following criteria had been met:

1. the Act concerned had begun its parliamentary passage in the Commons;
2. the Commons had voted for it by a two-thirds majority at third reading before sending it to the Lords;

3.   the Lords had voted for it by a two-thirds majority at third reading before sending it for the Royal Assent;

4.   the Monarch had granted the Royal Assent only after establishing that the requisite majorities had been achieved in both houses.

We may then assume that a subsequent 'Parliament' purports to pass an 'Act' by the traditional simple majority plus Royal Assent formula that contains terms breaching the provisions of the Constitution Act.

It is tempting to conclude simply that a citizen who asked the court to obey the Constitution Act and disapply or invalidate a later statute would be asking the judiciary to override the wishes of Parliament, which had seemingly enacted the subsequent provision. However, steps 1–3 of the entrenchment process can be analysed in a rather different way. They could be seen as merely asking the courts to 'question' the proceedings adopted in each house in respect of a Bill. Step 4, in contrast, could be seen as simply requiring the courts to undertake the now uncontentious task of reviewing an exercise of the prerogative.[3]

The argument assumes that 'Parliament' has the legal capacity to regulate the powers of its component parts—that the Commons, the Lords, and the Monarch as parts of Parliament are legally inferior to Parliament itself. If this view is accepted, it seemingly follows that Parliament may enact legislation placing specific limits on the legal competence of either house or of the Monarch. The hypothetical Constitution Act essentially provides that the Commons would be acting ultra vires its powers in sending a Bill which infringed the Constitution Act to the Lords if the Bill had not attracted a two-thirds majority; similarly, the House of Lords would be acting ultra vires in sending that Bill for the Royal Assent if it was not supported by that enhanced majority of peers; while the Monarch would be acting ultra vires if she assented to such a measure without having established that the requisite majorities in each house had been achieved.

There is similarly a need here for precision in describing what the High Court would be doing if it declined to disapply a subsequent statute which infringed the Constitution Act, on the basis of the orthodox theory that no Parliament can bind its successors. In refusing to disapply such a statute, the courts would in effect be concluding that the privileges of each house (steps 1–3)[4] and/or privilege plus the royal prerogative (steps 1–4) and/or the royal prerogative alone (step 4) outrank legislation in the constitution's legal hierarchy.

This rationale would draw us into a rather bizarre series of conclusions. It was suggested in chapter two that the orthodox view does indeed recognise one limit on Parliament's sovereign authority—namely that it cannot bind itself and its successors. But the orthodox view seemingly also requires us to accept three further constraints to Parliament's omnipotent legal power—namely that it cannot remove the Commons and Lords' powers to approve a Bill by simple majority vote, nor attach conditions to the Monarch's legal capacity to give the Royal Assent. To accept one limit to a nominally unlimited power might perhaps be accommodated as an inconvenient necessity: to accept four suggests that the integrity of the central argument is seriously flawed.

It is most unfortunate that the common elision in constitutional parlance of Parliament itself and the two houses of Parliament (but particularly the Commons) has so thoroughly pervaded analysis of the question of sovereignty as well as the question of privilege.[5] A perfect

---

[3] It is perhaps feasible to argue that the granting of the Royal Assent is itself a 'proceeding in Parliament'. This would however seem implausible, given that privilege and Art 9 emerged as devices to protect the two houses against the Monarch. But for the purposes of this argument, the legal source of the Royal Assent is irrelevant.

[4] *Wauchope* and *Pickin* might thus be reclassified as cases which did not concern the sovereignty of Parliament at all, but the non-justiciability of the privileges of the two houses. That analysis gains additional force when we recall that the 'rules' in issue in those cases were the internal rules of the Commons, not rules imposed on the house by statute.   [5] See 'Conclusion', ch 8 pp 221–222.

example of this is provided by Lord Simon's previously quoted observation in *Pickin*,[6] that the exclusive right of each house to control its own proceedings is a 'concomitant' of the sovereignty of Parliament. That view is however fundamentally misconceived, as a matter both of simple logic and of constitutional history. To allow each house an unfettered and apparently unfetterable power to control its own proceedings is not a concomitant of parliamentary sovereignty, but a blatant denial of it. By suggesting that each house has such an 'exclusive power', Lord Simon is setting privilege above both common law and statute. One thus finds oneself facing the oxymoronic proposition that Parliament possesses its legal sovereignty not because it cannot bind itself and its successors, but because it cannot bind its component (and hence inferior) parts.

The suggestion that one might entrench legislation in Britain by placing limits on the powers of the respective houses of Parliament rather than on those of Parliament itself is not, it should be stressed, a novel idea. Heuston had advanced a very similar thesis in 1964.[7] Heuston chose to support his argument with reference to the litigation in Commonwealth countries which we discussed in chapter two. This might be thought to weaken both the legal and political force of his thesis. As Wade observed in 1955, there is little point in invoking this case law in the British context.[8] The entrenchment formulae in issue in *Trethowan* and *Harris* each enjoyed a certain, unambiguous legal and political status because they were 'created' by a British statute which the 'peoples' of New South Wales and South Africa had accepted as expressing their preferred constituent moral values.[9] Since the British Parliament has no 'creator' in this sense,[10] we might assume (as traditionalists always have) that the 'manner and form' principle cannot be applied here.

But this involves perhaps too ready a dismissal of the *Trethowan* rationale. Heuston's argument has also been offered more recent support by Paul Craig, in a thesis premised on a discussion of basic, indigenous constitutional principles rather than a speculative importation of inapposite foreign case law.[11] This was discussed at some length in chapter eleven in the context of the *Factortame* judgments.[12] Both authors operated under something of a disadvantage when advancing their ideas. Heuston, writing in 1964, laboured under the handicap of courts' adherence to the principle that exercise of the prerogative was not reviewable under any circumstances, a common law rule which would presumably incline the judiciary to consider the Royal Assent beyond legal scrutiny. In post-*GCHQ* era, that principle no longer presents an obstacle to entrenchment. Similarly, both Heuston and Craig's critiques were formulated when the courts were seemingly not prepared to examine events that occurred in either house during the passage of a Bill in order to ascertain the meaning of a statute. In the aftermath of *Pepper v Hart*, it seems clear that Art 9 of the Bill of Rights (whatever its legal status)[13] is no longer regarded by the courts as an insuperable barrier to questioning either house's proceedings.

There is a clear danger here that one simply ends up suggesting that entrenchment is now possible because the courts have embraced an increasingly expansive notion of justiciability, in which the legitimacy of judicial intervention is determined not by the legal identity of the institution whose actions are being impugned, but by the nature of the question the courts

---

[6] At 'Substance or procedure? the enrolled Bill rule', ch 2, pp 27–28.

[7] Heuston R (2nd edn, 1964) *Essays in constitutional law* ch 1.

[8] See 'Are *Trethowan, Harris,* and *Ranasinghe* relevant to the British situation?', ch 2, pp 36–38.

[9] In the case of South Africa, 'the people' was obviously an extremely narrow concept, which would not be regarded as legitimate in the modern context.

[10] I leave aside for present purposes any arguments rooted in the Treaty/Acts of Union; see 'Is parliamentary sovereignty a British or English concept?', ch 2, pp 38–41.

[11] (1991) op cit.

[12] See 'V. The end of parliamentary sovereignty? Or its reappearance?', ch 11, pp 306–312.

[13] See 'Redefining parliament'—*Pepper v Hart* (1993)', ch 8, pp 210–215.

assume they are being asked. (In the hypothetical Constitution Act, the terms of the entrenchment procedure itself simply require the courts to perform a simple arithmetic calculation, and are thus obviously justiciable. Care would also have to be taken that the Act's substantive terms were similarly amenable to judicial analysis: we might accept here for the sake of argument that those terms simply embraced the provisions of the Convention, which are also clearly matters courts can address.)[14] To do so would in effect return us to Jennings' view that the 'rule of recognition' is a common law concept.[15] This would however be no solution at all to the entrenchment conundrum, rather it makes the legal problem even more vexed.

As Jennings suggested, accepting that the rule of recognition was a common law concept implies that it could be redefined by Parliament. But equally (and this is a point on which we did not dwell in chapter two) it could be redefined by the courts without any parliamentary initiative having been undertaken at all. In formal terms, if the rule of recognition is a purely common law phenomenon, there is no legal barrier to the House of Lords suddenly deciding that it would not 'recognise' any statute that impinged upon particular moral or political values, or that it would 'recognise' such statutes only if they had been enacted with an enhanced Commons and/or Lords majority. Jennings' thesis, taken to its logical conclusion, suggests that the common law is legally superior to Acts of Parliament, that the courts and not the legislature are the ultimate source of legal authority, and that we might, as a matter of law, find that at any moment the courts had exercised a power explicitly to refuse to apply statutes of which they disapproved. The extravagant interpretation of the principle espoused in *Dr Bonham's Case* would thereby be reasserted, and the 1688 revolution would have been waged in vain.

Some commentators—one thinks primarily of Professor Griffith—might find that alarming prospect made rather too real by Laws LJ's judgment in *Thoburn v Sunderland City Council*.[16] *Thoburn* was an EC-related case, focused on the ostensibly prosaic issue of whether fruit and vegetables had to be sold in metric rather than imperial measurements. In the course of his judgment, Laws LJ endorsed the presumption that the European Communities Act 1972 possessed 'special' constitutional status, and was as such immune to the doctrine of implied repeal. Laws LJ also made two assertions of perhaps broader interest. The first was that the doctrine of implied repeal was itself a creature of the common law—rather than, as Wade's analysis of orthodox theory would suggest—an element of the constitution's 'ultimate political fact'. As a creature of the common law, of course, the doctrine of implied repeal would always be subject to extension, contraction, or abolition at the behest of the higher courts. The second was that other statutes—which Laws LJ termed 'constitutional' statutes—enjoyed the same status as the European Communities Act:

> We should recognise a hierarchy of Acts of Parliament: as it were 'ordinary' statutes and 'constitutional' statutes. The two categories must be distinguished on a principled basis. In my opinion a constitutional statute is one which (a) conditions the legal relationship between citizen and State in some general, overarching manner, or (b) enlarges or diminishes the scope of what we would now regard as fundamental constitutional rights . . . Examples are the Magna Carta, the Bill of Rights 1688, the Act of Union, the Reform Acts which distributed and enlarged the franchise, the HRA, the Scotland Act 1998 and the Government of Wales Act 1998. The ECA clearly belongs in this family.[17]

---

[14] Although one lesson that we should learn from the *Harris* saga in South Africa is that the requirement of super-majorities to protect entrenched rights can be sidestepped by cynical governments unless both the mechanism for selecting members of the legislature and the process of appointing judges are themselves entrenched values; see further '*Harris v Minister of the Interior*—the aftermath', ch 3, 49–50 and Loveland (1999) op cit ch 11.

[15] See 'Jennings' critique and the "rule of recognition"', ch 2, pp 31–37.   [16] [2002] 1 CMLR 1461.

[17] Ibid, at para 62.

Thoburn was not appealed to the Court of Appeal. It initially stood therefore as little more than a point of departure for further speculation about the nature of Parliament's legislative authority. As a mechanism within the sphere of administrative law to force Parliament in the text of legislation—and by extension the government in the text of the Bills it promotes—to be utterly candid about the objectives an Act it is intended to achieve, Laws LJ's conclusion perhaps had much to commend it. Characterised in this way, the judgment may be seen as little more than an extension of developing principles of statutory interpretation. Very generously construed, however, the judgment might be seen as advocating a 'revolutionary' limitation of Parliament's law-making powers.

Further judicial fuel was added to this particular jurisprudential fire by the obiter comments of several members of the House of Lords in *R (on the application of Jackson and others) v Attorney-General*.[18] Lord Steyn put the point in this way:

> 81. . . . But, apart from the traditional method of law making, Parliament acting as ordinarily constituted may functionally redistribute legislative power in different ways. For example, Parliament could for specific purposes provide for a two-thirds majority in the House of Commons and the House of Lords. This would involve a redefinition of Parliament for a specific purpose. Such redefinition could not be disregarded.

Lord Hope made similar observations:

> 104. . . . Our constitution is dominated by the sovereignty of Parliament. But Parliamentary sovereignty is no longer, if it ever was, absolute. It is not uncontrolled in the sense referred to by Lord Birkenhead LC in *McCawley v The King* [1920] AC 691, 720. It is no longer right to say that its freedom to legislate admits of no qualification whatever. Step by step, gradually but surely, the English principle of the absolute legislative sovereignty of Parliament which Dicey derived from Coke and Blackstone is being qualified.
>
> 105. For the most part these qualifications are themselves the product of measures enacted by Parliament. Part I of the European Communities Act 1972 is perhaps the prime example.

Baroness Hale took the argument one step further:

> 163. If the sovereign Parliament can redefine itself downwards, to remove or modify the requirement for the consent of the Upper House, it may very well be that it can also re-define itself upwards, to require a particular Parliamentary majority or a popular referendum for particular types of measure. In each case, the courts would be respecting the will of the sovereign Parliament as constituted when that will had been expressed. But that is for another day.

The Supreme Court subsequently gave something of a seal of approval to Laws LJ's *Thoburn* analysis in *R (HS2 Action Alliance Ltd) v Secretary of State for Transport*.[19] Describing Laws LJ's judgment as a 'penetrating discussion',[20] Lords Neuberger and Mance (with whom all the other judges concurred) indicated that the courts now recognised—in effect as a new orthodoxy—both 'constitutional statutes' and 'ordinary statutes'; and, going beyond *Thoburn*, that there might also be principles existing at common law that should be accorded 'constitutional' status:

> 207 The United Kingdom has no written constitution, but we have a number of constitutional instruments. They include Magna Carta, the Petition of Right 1628, the Bill of Rights and (in Scotland) the Claim of Rights Act 1689, the Act of Settlement 1701 and the Act of Union 1707. The European Communities Act 1972, the Human Rights Act 1998 and the Constitutional Reform Act 2005 may now be added to this list. The common law itself also recognises certain principles as

---

[18] [2005] UKHL 56, [2006] 1 AC 262. See 'One parliament or three? *Jackson v Attorney-General*', ch 6, pp 165–168.
[19] [2014] UKSC 3, [2014] 1 WLR 324.   [20] [2014] 1 WLR 324 at para 206.

fundamental to the rule of law. It is, putting the point at its lowest, certainly arguable (and it is for United Kingdom law and courts to determine) that there may be fundamental principles, whether contained in other constitutional instruments or recognised at common law, of which Parliament when it enacted the European Communities Act 1972 did not either contemplate or authorise the abrogation.[21]

The Court's reasoning is couched in tentative language. It does not take us to the 'another day' to which Baroness Hale referred, but it does reinforce the proposition that the orthodox Diceyan understanding of Parliament's wholly unconstrained sovereign authority is becoming an increasingly contingent rather than settled feature of the constitutional landscape. Or, to invoke a familiar but non-legal authority, it gives us further cause to recognise that the most pertinent question to ask in this context may not be whether 'parliamentary sovereignty', like all other words and phrases, 'can mean different things', but who—in deciding what it means— 'is to be master'?[22]

It is readily apparent that any search for a purely legal solution to the entrenchment question in that more expansive sense—namely that Parliament cannot through even the most express of statutory formulae achieve certain objectives—is likely to be severely hampered by the conceptually tangled constitutional undergrowth which has now grown so luxuriantly from the soil of the 1688 settlement. But Craig's critique is also helpful to advocates of entrenchment in that it asks us to consider not what the traditional rule is, but what the traditional rule is *for*. This approach then forces us to consider that entrenchment should not be analysed as a legal issue, but as a moral one. The central question that is raised is 'Are there sound reasons for regarding particular political values as so important that they should not be subject to amendment or repeal by simple parliamentary majorities?'

Questions of legitimacy

The parliamentary sovereignty doctrine appears to have emerged as a crude device to prevent enactment of factional legislation in a pre-democratic society. Yet it is quite clear that by the early-twentieth century, shifts in the political context in which the doctrine operated meant that it had evolved into a constitutional device which would in most circumstances facilitate achievement of entirely the opposite result. The combined impact of the Commons' dominance within Parliament, and of minoritarian governments within the Commons, generally places uninhibited legislative power within the grasp of political factions which represent the preferred political views of only a minority of the population. It is perhaps in this political reality, rather than in tortuous arguments about legal practicality, that the real difficulties posed by entrenchment actually lie. For in such a context, we might plausibly wonder whether even if the entrenchment of particular political values was possible as a matter of law, would it be defensible as a matter of morality if it was triggered simply by a legislative initiative enacted by Parliament?

The entrenching device upheld by the Privy Council in *Trethowan* offers a very poor model for the creation of fundamental, supra-parliamentary values in the British context. The effect of such a provision would be to place the power to entrench laws in the hands of a barely majoritarian or even minoritarian faction. There would seemingly have been no legal impediment to a legislature introducing 'manner and form' legislation which rooted the preferences of the then governing party so deeply that they could not in practice be changed—by insisting

---

[21] For further discussion of this analysis, and of the theoretical and practical issues which it raises, see inter alia, Ahmed F and Perry A (2017) 'Constitutional statutes' *Oxford Journal of Legal Studies* 461; Craig P (2014) 'Constitutionalising constitutional law' *Public Law* 373.

[22] See '*Liversidge v Anderson* (1942)', ch 3 pp 61–64.

for example on 75% or 80% majorities in both houses, or requiring similar levels of support in a referendum.

Transposed to the modern British context, this would have permitted the Thatcher or Major governments to impose their own preferred brand of minoritarian ideology on the substantial majority of the electorate which consistently chose not to support them. Similarly, a future Labour government which took the view that it should attempt to entrench certain social democratic moral values against an extremist right wing administration would be doing so with (on the most optimistic of electoral predictions) 50% of the vote on an 85% turnout.

One would have to embrace a rather peculiar view of democracy to discern any moral legitimacy in a process which allowed minority factions within modern British society to impose entrenched 'fundamental' political values on the entire population. Such 'reform' would be the very antithesis of the supra-majoritarianism required to shape the outlines of the US Constitution and the unanimity needed to fashion and subsequently amend the provisions of the EC Treaties. Its terms would be not consensual but coercive: its rationale would be not pluralist but authoritarian: its effect would be not to empower 'the people' but to oppress them.

Thus even if we assume entrenchment is legally possible, we do not thereby prove that it is constitutionally desirable. As has been stressed throughout this book, constitutional law forms but one ingredient (albeit an important one) of a complex constitutional recipe. Issues of politics and morality as well as mere legality pervade the much larger and more complex issue of constitutionality.

There would seem to be only two ways that entrenchment could plausibly claim to have a legitimate constitutional basis. The legitimacy of constituent moral values appears to depend primarily on the breadth of consensus that they attract. The rationale underpinning this principle was perhaps best articulated, as we saw in chapter one, in Madison's celebrated critique of factionalism: the higher the level of support required to enact a law, the less likely it is that the law concerned will be arbitrary, oppressive, or intolerant, because its terms will express a compromise between groups of citizens holding different moral and political views. The Americans chose the 'two thirds of Congress plus three quarters of the States' rule to protect the terms of this initial compromise. We have seen that other constitutions have adopted devices which differ in their detailed form—the 'substantial provincial support' formula discovered by the Canadian Supreme Court in 1982, or the two-thirds of both chambers sitting in joint session criterion originally upheld by the South African Supreme Court in *Harris (No 1)* and *Harris (No 2)*, or the legislative majority plus referendum approach favoured in New South Wales—but which serve a broadly similar function.[23]

Two-thirds or three-quarters legislative majorities clearly do not eliminate the possibility that a country will produce oppressive laws. Such countries are however less likely to do so than those whose constitutions permit unfettered minoritarian or bare majoritarian lawmaking. But in the British context, this 'enhanced legislative majority' route to entrenchment could be followed only by a government which enjoyed hitherto unachieved levels of electoral support, in terms both of Commons seats *and* share of the popular vote. There would seem no prospect of a single political party coming remotely close to achieving such levels of popular approval. The position could presumably only be reached if the Labour Party won a comfortable Commons majority, attracting perhaps 45% of the vote, but rather than govern as a single party chose to initiate major constitutional reform with the support of a Liberal Party which had maintained its recent average electoral support of around 20%. Ideally, such a coalition would also detach at least a handful of MPs from the left-wing of the Conservative Party, and attract the support of Scots, Welsh, and Irish nationalist members of the Commons. The

[23] See respectively 'A-G for New South Wales v Trethowan (1931)' ff, ch 2, pp 32–34 and 'V. Can conventions become laws? 2: Patriating the Canadian constitution', ch 9, pp 244–245.

legitimacy of such reform would be further enhanced if the various governing parties had announced their intentions prior to the general election; the government could then more convincingly argue that the consent of their supporters to a constitutional revolution was informed.

In the absence of such a broad coalition, a minoritarian or barely majoritarian government seeking to entrench certain basic values could only stake a plausible claim to legitimacy by promoting substantive reforms which would both reduce its own share of political power and enhance the political influence wielded by opposition parties. The claim would however be a weak one, since many observers might genuinely doubt that any political party could ever be motivated by such selfless objectives. In these circumstances, a reformist government would necessarily be embarking on an elitist and ostensibly unrepresentative course of action.

It would nevertheless be rash to assume a reform of this nature could not be 'democratic'. The moral quandary such a government would face forces us rather to focus again on the intimate linkage between matters of substance and process in the context of constitution building which were adverted to in chapter one. One should perhaps add that this observation applies, albeit perhaps with less force, to a context in which reform attracted overwhelming popular support. Even a super-majoritarian coalition government could not defensibly claim much legitimacy for its plans unless it sought to entrench principles which both restricted its own authority and increased the political power exercised by citizens who did not support its 'revolution'.

Legitimacy in process? A Liberal Democrat proposal

The Liberal Democrat Party offered a relatively detailed vision of a reformed British constitution in a 1990 policy paper, entitled '*We the people . . .*'. As might be surmised from its title, the paper drew heavily on the American constitutional model, in matters both of abstract theory and practical detail. *We the people* devoted considerable attention to planning a reform process which would enhance the legitimacy of the 'fundamental' values it hoped to introduce.

As suggested earlier, any attempt by a single party government returned under the existing electoral system to entrench constitutional values with any significant degree of fixity would be most unlikely to have a legitimate moral base: the breadth of popular consent such a government attracted would simply be too narrow to justify the imposition of constituent principles. *We the people* clearly recognised this difficulty, and offered an ingenious mechanism to overcome it.

Had the Liberals won a Commons majority at the 1992 general election, its government would have promoted Bills to reform the Commons' electoral system on the basis of the single transferable vote (STV) mechanism, and to establish a body to be called the 'Constituent Assembly'. Parliament would then be dissolved, and a general election fought on the basis of the new STV electoral system. The Constituent Assembly would be composed of the members of the Commons returned under the basis of the new STV electoral system. The Assembly would have been empowered by the previous Parliament to adopt (by a two-thirds majority) a new constitutional settlement, within which certain political values (inter alia the ECHR, the STV electoral system, and (extensive) devolved powers to the Scots, Welsh and Northern Irish and regional governments) would all assume supra-parliamentary status. These values would be entrenched in the procedural sense; they could be amended only with the approval of two-thirds of both houses sitting separately.

In legal terms, using the Constituent Assembly to implement a constitutional revolution might be thought something of a nonsense: Parliament presumably cannot create something more powerful than itself. It would however seem that *We the people* proceeded on the assumption that its proposals were at root designed to achieve a political rather than legal objective. By requiring a two-thirds majority of a body chosen by the STV system to create the new constitution, the Liberal programme ensured that its terms could not be given legal effect unless they enjoyed a very high level of popular support. The proviso that the Commons should in effect wear a different political hat when assessing the merits of fundamental reform would also have served a useful legitimising purpose, in so far as it would focus both MPs and the public's attention on the gravity of the task being undertaken.

For adherents to a pluralist perception of democracy, the Liberal Party's inability to mobilise greater electoral support is something of a disappointment. There is no doubt that *We the people* offered a radical and far-reaching programme to modernise Britain's constitutional arrangements. One might of course suggest that the Liberals' limited electoral support is in itself indicative of 'the people's' disinclination to have the constitution reformed in any meaningful way. The only immediate prospect of the Liberal programme being implemented would be for the party to hold the balance of power in a hung Commons, and to convince one of the main parties that pursuing its reforms was an acceptable price to pay for the benefit of forming a coalition government for one parliamentary term. It would however seem unlikely that either the Labour or Conservative Parties would accept such reasoning. Certainly the balance of power in the aftermath of the 2010 general election did not enable the Liberal Democrats to make such radical constitutional reforms the price of its participation in the coalition government. Nor, indeed, would the reforms enjoy much legitimacy if their opponents could plausibly argue that the major partner in the coalition had been 'blackmailed' into accepting them.

Conclusion

Prime Minister Blair stressed in the preface to the *Scotland's Parliament* white paper that Scots devolution was best seen as just one part of a much broader programme of constitutional reform. There is no doubt that—in terms of its commitment to establishing a pluralist political culture—the Blair governments stand head and shoulders above any of their twentieth-century predecessors. This is obviously evidenced in its devolution legislation. But it is also apparent in the government's embrace of the ECHR and the provisions of the Amsterdam Treaty: the protection of individual rights is an essential element of a diverse democratic polity. The same observation may be made about the Blair government's promotion of the Constitutional Reform Act 2005. The Act's objectives were more modest than its grandiose title would suggest but we might still accept that the Act's transfer of the judicial functions of the House of Lords to a new Supreme Court and the creation of a Judicial Appointments Commission to select judges are valuable reforms which further underline the Blair government's atypical (among its post-war predecessors of either party) readiness to use its Commons majority to promote laws which limited its own powers.

Yet these initiatives, desirable though they may be, can hardly be seen as engineering a constituent reformation of our political system. Their longevity is by no means assured. It is perhaps something of a misnomer to speak at all of the *law* of the British constitution, whether we are considering legislation of great or recent vintage, or rules of common law. This misdescription does not simply arise from the obvious fact that so much of the organisation and behaviour of contemporary government rests on the non-justiciable basis of convention. More seriously, it derives from the constant vulnerability of those principles which are expressed in justiciable form to whichever political faction has temporary control of the House of Commons. To search for constitutional law in a society which has thus far rejected the concept of subjecting its system of governance to constituent legal principles is to embark upon a generally fascinating, often frustrating, but ultimately always fallacious journey.

Having begun that journey in this book with a quotation from Thomas Jefferson's *Declaration of Independence*, we might, in the interests both of substantive and stylistic symmetry, end it with the words of Jefferson's great friend and colleague, James Madison:

> No doctrine can be sound that releases a legislature from the control of a constitution. The latter is as much a law to the former, as the acts of the former are to individuals; and although alterable by the people who formed it, it is not alterable by any other authority; certainly not by those chosen by the people to carry it in to effect. This is so vital a principle . . . that a denial of it cannot possibly last long or spread far.[24]

Britain has of course denied the principle for over 300 years. To many observers that may suggest the principle is an unnecessary ingredient of a democratic society. To others, it may in contrast indicate that an attempt to grapple with this elemental ingredient of constitutional morality is long overdue.

Suggested further reading

Academic commentary

CORWIN (1928) 'The higher law background of American constitutional law Parts I and II' *Harvard LR* 149 and 365

HEUSTON (2nd edn, 1964) *Essays in constitutional law* ch 1

ALLAN (1985) 'Legislative supremacy and the rule of law' *Cambridge LJ* 111

BAILYN (1967) *The ideological origins of the American revolution*

Case law and legislation

R (on the application of Jackson and others) v Attorney-General [2005] UKHL 56, [2006] 1 AC 262

---

[24] Padover S (ed) (1953) *The complete Madison* p 344.

Bibliography

ADONIS A (1988) 'The House of Lords in the 1980s' *Parliamentary Affairs* 380–401.

ADONIS A (1990) *Parliament today* (Manchester: Manchester University Press).

ADONIS A (2nd edn, 1993) *Parliament today* (Manchester: Manchester University Press).

AHIER J AND FLUDE M (eds) (1983) *Contemporary education policy* (London: Croom Helm).

AHMED F AND PERRY A (2017) 'Constitutional statutes' *Oxford Journal of Legal Studies* 461–481.

AKEHURST M (1982) 'Revocation of administrative decisions' *Public Law* 613–627.

ALDER J (1994) *Constitutional and administrative law* (London: Macmillan).

ALDERMAN R AND SMITH M (1990) 'Can British Prime Ministers be given the push by their parties?' *Parliamentary Affairs* 260–276.

ALDERMAN R AND CARTER N (1991) 'A very Tory coup: the ousting of Mrs Thatcher' *Parliamentary Affairs* 125–139.

ALLAN T (1983) 'Parliamentary sovereignty: Lord Denning's dexterous revolution' *Oxford Journal of Legal Studies* 22–33.

ALLAN T (1985) 'Legislative supremacy and the rule of law' *Cambridge LJ* 111–143.

ALLAN T (1986) 'Law convention and prerogative' *Cambridge LJ* 305–320.

ALLAN T (1993) *Law, liberty and justice* (Oxford: Clarendon Press).

ALLAN T (1995) 'Equality and moral independence: public law and private morality', in Loveland I. (1995a) *infra*.

ALLAN T (1997) 'Parliamentary sovereignty: law, politics and revolution' *LQR* 443–452.

ALLAN T (2006) 'Human rights and judicial review: a critique of "due deference"' *Cambridge LJ* 671–692.

ALLEN C (1942) 'Regulation 18B and reasonable cause . . .' *LQR* 232–242.

ALLEN N (2017) 'Brexit, butchery and Boris: Theresa May and her first Cabinet' *Parliamentary Affairs* 633–644.

ALLEN N AND BIRCH S (2011) 'Political conduct and misconduct: probing public opinion' *Parliamentary Affairs* 61–81.

ALTER K (2001) *Establishing the supremacy of European law* (Oxford: OUP).

ANDERSON O (1967) 'The Wensleydale peerage and the position of the House of Lords in the mid-nineteenth century' *English Historical Review* 486–502.

ANSON W (5th edn, 1922) *The law and custom of the constitution* (Oxford: Clarendon Press).

ARKINSTALL J AND O'BRIEN C (2002) 'Table of cases under the Human Rights Act' *European Human Rights LR* 364–388.

ARNSTEIN W (1983) *The Bradlaugh case* (Columbia, Missouri: University of Missouri Press).

ARNULL A (1987) 'The incoming tide: responding to *Marshall*' *Public Law* 383–399.

ASCHER K (1983) 'The politics of administrative opposition—council house sales and the right to buy' *Local Government Studies* 12–20.

ATRILL S (2005) 'Nulla poena sine lege in comparative perspective . . .' *Public Law* 107.

AUDIT COMMISSION (1990) *The administration of the community charge* (London: HMSO).

BAGEHOT W (1963 ed by Crossman R) *The English constitution* (London: Fontana).

BAILEY S (1982) 'The Contempt of Court Act 1981' *MLR* 301–316.

BAILEY S AND PADDISON R (eds) *The reform of local government finance in Britain* (London: Routledge).

BAILEY S, HARRIS D, AND JONES B (1977; 2nd edn, 1992; 3rd edn, 1998; 4th edn) *Civil liberties* (London: Butterworths).

BAILYN B (1967) *The ideological origins of the American revolution* (Cambridge, Mass: Harvard University Press).

BAINES P (1985) 'The history and rationale of the 1979 reforms', in Drewry G (ed) *The new Select Committees* (Oxford: Clarendon Press).

BAKER D, GAMBLE A, AND LUDLUM S (1993) 'Whips or scorpions? The Maastricht vote and Conservative MPs' *Parliamentary Affairs* 147–166.

BAKER K (1993) *The turbulent years* (London: Faber).

BALDWIN N (1999) 'The membership and work of the House of Lords', in Dickson and Carmichael (eds) *The House of Lords: its parliamentary and judicial roles* (Oxford: Hart Publishing).

BALL W, GULAM W, AND TROYNA B (1990) 'Pragmatism or retreat? funding policy, local government, and the marginalisation of anti-racist education', in Ball and Solomos *infra*.

BALL W AND SOLOMOS J (eds) *Race and local politics* (London: Macmillan).

BALSOM D AND MCALLISTER I (1979) 'The Scottish and Welsh devolution referenda of 1979' *Parliamentary Affairs* 394–409.

BAMFORTH N (1993) 'The scope of judicial review—still uncertain' *Public Law* 239–248.

BAMFORTH N (1998) 'Parliamentary sovereignty and the Human Rights Act 1998' *Public Law* 572–582.

BAMFORTH N (1999) 'The application of the Human Rights Act to public authorities and private bodies' *Cambridge LJ* 159–170.

BANNER C AND BOUTLE T (2004) 'Challenging the Commons' *New law Journal* 1466.

BARENDT E (1987) *Freedom of speech* (Oxford: Clarendon Press).

BARENDT E (1989) 'Spycatcher and freedom of speech' *Public Law* 204–212.

BARENDT E (1993) 'Libel and freedom of speech in English law' *Public Law* 449–464.

BARENDT E (1995) 'Constitutional law and the Criminal Injuries Compensation Scheme' *Public Law* 357–366.

BARENDT E (1998) *An Introduction to Constitutional Law* pp 86–93 (Oxford: Clarendon Press).

BARKER R (1986) 'Obedience, legitimacy and the state', in Harlow C (ed) *Public law and politics* (London: Sweet and Maxwell).

BASH L AND COULBY D (eds) *The Education Reform Act: competition and control* (London: Cassell).

BATES ST J (1988) 'Scrutiny of administration', in Ryle M and Richards P (eds) *The Commons under scrutiny* (London: Routledge).

BATES S., ET AL. (2012) 'Questions to the Prime Minister: a comparative study of PMQs from Thatcher to Cameron' *Parliamentary Affairs* 1.

BEALEY F (1988) *Democracy in the contemporary state* (Oxford: Clarendon Press).

BEARD C (1990) 'An economic interpretation of the Constitution', in Birmbaum J and Ollman *infra*.

BEATSON J (1987) '"Public" and "private" in English administrative law' *LQR* 34–65.

BEATSON J, MATTHEWS M, AND ELLIOT M (4th edn, 2010) *Administrative law* pp 235–248 (Oxford: OUP).

BEIBR R (1984) 'The settlement of institutional conflicts on the basis of Article 4 of the Treaty' *CMLRev* 505–523.

BENNET P AND PULLINGER S (1991) *Making the Commons work* (London: Institute for Public Policy Research).

BENNION F (1997) *Statutory interpretation* (Oxford: OUP).

BENNION F (2000) 'What interpretation is "possible" under s.3(1) of the Human Rights Act?' *Public Law* 77–91.

BEVAN V (1981) 'Is anybody there?' *Public Law* 431–453.

BEYLEVELD D AND PATTINSON S (2002) 'Horizontal applicability' *LQR* 623–647.

BINGHAM T (1993) 'The European Convention on Human Rights: time to incorporate' *LQR* 390–400.

BIRMBAUM J AND OLMANN B (eds) (1990) *The United States Constitution* (New York: New York University Press).

BLAKE R AND LOUIS W (eds) (1993) *Churchill* (Oxford: Clarendon Press).

BLOM-COOPER L (1982) 'The new face of judicial review: administrative changes in Order 53' *Public Law* 250–261.

BLUNKETT D (2006) *The Blunkett tapes: my life in the bear pit* (London: Bloomsbury).

BOATENG P AND STRAW J (1996) *Bringing rights home* (London: Labour Party).

BOATENG P AND STRAW J (1997) 'Bringing rights home: Labour plans to incorporate the ECHR into UK law' *European Human Rights LR* 71–80.

BOGDANOR V (1976) 'Freedom in education' *Political Quarterly* 149–159.

BOGDANOR V (1979) 'The English constitution and devolution' *Political Quarterly* 36–49.

BOGDANOR V (1983) *What is proportional representation?* (Oxford: Martin Robertson).

BOGDANOR V (1988) 'Introduction', Bogdanor V (ed) *Constitutions in democratic politics* (Dartmouth Publishing: Aldershot).

BOGDANOR V (1999) 'Reform of the House of Lords: a sceptical view' *Political Quarterly* 375–381.

BOGDANOR V (1999a) 'Devolution: decentralisation or disintegration' *Political Quarterly* 185–194.

BOGDANOR V (2009) *The new British constitution* (Oxford: Hart Publishing).

BOGDANOR V (2016) 'Brexit, the constitution and the alternatives' *Kings LJ* 314–322.

BOGDANOR V (2016a) 'Europe and the sovereignty of the people' *Political Quarterly* 348–354.

BORTHWICK R (1973) 'Public Bill Committees in the House of Lords' *Parliamentary Affairs* 440–453.

BORTHWICK R (1979) 'Questions and debates', in Walkland S (ed) *The House of Commons in the twentieth century* (Oxford: Clarendon Press).

BORTHWICK R (1988) 'The floor of the house', in Ryle M and Richards P (eds) *The Commons under scrutiny* (London: Routledge).

BOULTON C (ed) (21st edn, 1989) *Erskine May's treatise on the law, privileges, proceedings and usage of Parliament* (London: Butterworths).

BOWLEY M (1985) *Housing and the state 1919-1945* (London: Allen & Unwin).

BOYCE B (1993) 'The democratic deficit of the European Community' *Parliamentary Affairs* 458–477.

BOYLE A (1981) 'The Contempt of Court Act 1981' *Human Rights Review* 148–150.

BOYLE A (1986) 'Political broadcasting, fairness and administrative law' *Public Law* 562–596.

BOYRON S (2002) 'In the name of European law: the metric martyrs case' *European LR* 771–779.

BRADLEY A (1981) 'Administrative justice and the binding effects of official acts' *Current Legal Problems* 1–20.

BRADLEY A (1988) 'Police powers and the prerogative' *Public Law* 298–303.

BRADLEY A (1991) 'The UK before the Strasbourg Court', in Finnie W, Himsworth C, and Walker N (eds) *Edinburgh essays in public law* (Edinburgh: Edinburgh University Press).

BRADLEY A (1997) 'Collateral challenge to enforcement decisions—a duty to apply for judicial review' *Public Law* 365–370.

BRADLEY A (1990) 'Press freedom, governmental constraints and the Privy Council' *Public Law* 453–461.

BRADLEY A (2003) 'Judicial independence under attack' *Public Law* 397–407.

BRADBURY J AND MITCHELL J (2005) 'Devolution; between governance and territorial politics' *Parliamentary Affairs* 287–302.

BRADLEY K (1987) 'Maintaining the balance' *Common Market LR* 41–64.

BRANSON N (1979) *Popularism* (London: Lawrence and Wishart).

BRAZIER M (9th edn, 1993) *Street on torts* (London: Butterworths).

BRAZIER R (1990) *Constitutional texts* (Oxford: OUP).

BRAZIER R (1992) *Constitutional reform* (Oxford: OUP).

BRAZIER R (1994) 'It is a constitutional issue: fitness for Ministerial office in the 1990's' *Public Law* 431–451.

BRAZIER R (1999) 'The constitution of the United Kingdom' *Cambridge LJ* 96–128.

BRIDGES LC ET AL. (1987) *Legality and local politics* (Aldershot: Avebury).

BRIGGS A (ed) (1959) *Chartist studies* (London: Macmillan).

BROCK M (1973) *The Great Reform Act* (London: Hutchinson).

BROGAN H (1986) *History of the USA* (Harmondsworth: Pelican).

BROWN K (ed) (1985) *The first labour party* (London: Croom Helm).

BROWN L AND KENNEDY T (1994) *The Court of Justice of the European Communities* (London: Sweet and Maxwell).

BROWN R (1987) 'The Beard thesis attacked: a political approach', in Birmbaum and Olson *supra*.

BROWN W (1899) 'The Hare system in Tasmania' *LQR* 51–70.

BROWNE-WILKINSON, LORD (1992) 'The infiltration of a Bill of Rights' *Public Law* 397–410.

BULL D (1980) 'School admissions: a new appeals procedure' *Journal of Social Welfare Law* 209–233.

BURROWS H. (1964) 'House of Lords: change or decay?' *Parliamentary Affairs* 403–417.

BURTON I AND DREWRY G (1972) 'Public legislation a survey of the session of 1971–1972' *Parliamentary Affairs* 145–185.

BURTON I AND DREWRY G (1978) 'Public legislation: a survey of the sessions of 1975/77' *Parliamentary Affairs* 140–162.

BUSH M (1983) 'The Act of Proclamations: a reinterpretation' *American Journal of Legal History* 33–53.

BUTLER D (1953) *The electoral system in Britain 1918–1951* (Oxford: Clarendon Press).

BUTLER D (1976) 'The Australian crisis of 1975' *Parliamentary Affairs* 201–210.

BUTLER D, ADONIS A, AND TRAVERS T (1994) *Failure in British Government: the politics of the poll tax* (Oxford: OUP).

BUTLER D AND BOGDANOR V (eds) (1983) *Democracy and elections* (Cambridge: CUP).

BUTLER D AND KAVANAGH D (1984; 1988; 1993; 1998) *The British general election of 1982; 1987; 1992; 1997* respectively (London: Macmillan).

BUTLER D AND KAVANAGH D (2002) *The British general election of 2002* (London: Macmillan).

BUTLER D AND KAVANAGH D (2005) *The British general election of 2005* (Basingstoke: Palgrave Macmillan).

BUTLER D, PENNIMAN H, AND RANNEY A (1981) *Democracy at the polls* (Washington DC: American Enterprise Institute).

BUTLER D AND SLOMAN A (1975) *British political facts* (London: Macmillan).

BUXTON, LORD JUSTICE (2000) 'The Human Rights Act and private law' *LQR* 48–67.

BUXTON R (2nd edn, 1973) *Local Government* (Harmondsworth: Penguin).

CANE P (1980) 'The function of standing rules in administrative law' *Public Law* 303–328.

CANE P (1981) 'Standing, legality and the limits of public law' *Public Law* 322–339.

CANE P (1992) 'Private rights and public procedure' *Public Law* 193–200.

CANE P (1995) 'Standing, representation and the environment', in Loveland I (ed) *A special relationship?* (Oxford: Clarendon Press).

CANE P (1995) 'Standing up for the public' *Public Law* 276–285.

CANE P (3rd edn, 1996) *An introduction to administrative law* (Oxford: Clarendon Press).

CANNON J (1973) *Parliamentary reform 1640–1832* (Cambridge: CUP).

CENTRE FOR CONTEMPORARY CULTURAL STUDIES (1981) *Unpopular education* (London: Hutchinson).

CHADWICK A (2011) 'Britain's first live televised leaders' debate: from the news cycle to the political information cycle' *Parliamentary Affairs* 24–44.

CHANDRACHUD C (2014) 'Reconfiguring the discourse on political responses to declarations of incompatibility' *Public Law* 624–641.

CHAPMAN R AND HUNT M (eds) (1987) *Open government* (London: Routledge).

CHESTER N (1977) 'Questions in the House', in WALKLAND S and Ryle M (eds) *The Commons in the seventies* (London: Martin Robertson).

CHESTER N AND BOWRING M (1962) *Questions in parliament* (London: OUP).

CLAES M AND DEWITTE (1998) 'Report on the Netherlands', in Slaughter A, Stone Sweet A and Weiler J (eds) *The European courts and national courts* (Oxford: Hart Publishing).

CLARK A (1993) *Diaries* (London: Weidenfeld and Nicolson).

CLARK D (1975) 'Natural justice: substance or shadow' *Public Law* 27–63.

CLARKE H, GOODWIN M, AND WHITELY P (2017) 'Why Britain voted for Brexit: an individual level analysis of the 2016 referendum vote' *Parliamentary Affairs* 439–464.

COHN, M (2009) 'Judicial review of non-statutory executive powers after Bancoult: a unified anxious model' *Public Law* 260–282.

COLEMAN D AND SALT J (1992) *The British population* (Oxford: OUP).

COLLEY L (1996) *Britons* (London: Vintage).

CONSTITUTION UNIT (2001 —December) *Monitor* p 2.

CONSTITUTION UNIT AND MCNEIL A (2017) 'Miller and the media: Supreme Court judgment generates more measured response'.

COOKE, LORD (1997) 'Mechanisms for entrenchment and protection of a Bill of Rights: the New Zealand experience' *European Human Rights LR* 490–495.

COOPERS AND LYBRAND (1988) *Local management of schools* (London: Coopers and Lybrand).

COPPEL J AND O'NEILL A (1994) 'The European Court of Justice: taking rights seriously' *Legal Studies* 227–245.

CORBETT R (1985) 'The 1985 intergovernmental conference and the Single European Act', in Pryce R (ed) *The dynamics of European integration* (London: Croom Helm).

CORBETT R (1989) 'Testing the new procedures; the European Parliament's first experiences with its new "Single Act" powers' *Journal of Common Market Studies* 362–372.

CORNFORD T AND SUNKIN M (2001) 'The Bowman Report: access and the recent reforms of the judicial review procedure' *Public Law* 11–20.

CORWIN E (1928) 'The higher law background of American constitutional law (parts I and II)' *Harvard LR* 149–175 and 365–409.

COULBY D (1989) 'From educational partnership to central control', in Bash L and Coulby D (eds) *The Education Reform Act* (London: Cassell

COWEN D (1952) 'Legislature and judiciary: part I' *MLR* 282–296.

COWEN D (1953) 'Legislature and judiciary: part II' *MLR* 273–298.

COWLEY P AND STUART M (2001) 'Parliament: a few headaches and a dose of modernisation' *Parliamentary Affairs* 238 at 253–255.

COWLEY P AND STUART M (2002) 'Parliament: mostly continuity, but more change than you'd think' *Parliamentary Affairs* 270.

COWLING M (1967) *1867: Disraeli, Gladstone and revolution* (Cambridge: CUP).

CRAIG J (1959) 'Parliament and Boundary Commissions' *Public Law* 23–45.

CRAIG P (1991) 'Sovereignty of the UK Parliament after *Factortame*' *Yearbook of European Law* 221–255.

CRAIG P (1992) 'Once upon a time in the west: direct effect and the federalization of EEC law' *Oxford Journal of Legal Studies*.

CRAIG P (1993) '*Francovich*, remedies and the scope of damages liability' 109 *LQR* 595–621.

CRAIG P (1994) 'The common law, reasons and administrative justice' *Cambridge LJ* 282–302.

CRAIG P (3rd edn, 1994) *Administrative law* (London: Sweet & Maxwell).

CRAIG P (1996) 'Substantive legitimate expectations in domestic and Community law' *Cambridge LJ* 289–312.

CRAIG P (1997) 'Formal and substantive conceptions of the rule of law' *Public Law* 467–487.

CRAIG P (1997a) 'Public law and control over private power', in Taggart M (ed) *The province of administrative law* (Oxford: Hart Publishing).

CRAIG P (1998) 'The Treaty of Amsterdam: a brief guide' *Public Law* 351–355.

CRAIG P (1998a) 'Collateral attack, procedural exclusivity and judicial review' *LQR* 535–538.

CRAIG P (4th edn, 1998b) *Administrative law* (London: Sweet and Maxwell).

CRAIG P (2001) 'The courts, the Human Rights Act and judicial review' *LQR* 592–612.

CRAIG P (2014) 'Constitutionalising constitutional law' *Public Law* 373–392.

CRAIG P AND DE BURCA G (2nd edn, 1998) *EU law* (Oxford: Clarendon Press).

CRAIG P AND DE BURCA G (3rd edn, 2002) *EU law* (Oxford: OUP) pp 358–369.

CRAIG P AND WALTERS M (1999) 'The courts, devolution and judicial review' *Public Law* 274–308.

CRAWFORD C (1915) 'The suspension of the Habeas Corpus Act and the Revolution of 1689' *The English Historical Review* 613–630.

CROSBY S (1991) 'The Single market and the rule of law' *EL Rev* 451–465.

CROSLAND C (1952) 'The transition from capitalism', in Crossman R (ed) *New Fabian Essays* (London: Turnstile

CROSS C (1961) *The fascists in Britain* (London: Barrie Books).

CROSS J (1967) 'Withdrawal of the Conservative party whip' *Parliamentary Affairs* 169–175.

CULLINGWORTH J (1979) *Essays in housing policy* (London: Allen & Unwin).

CURTICE J (2005) 'Turnout: electors stay home again' *Parliamentary Affairs* 776–785.

CURTIN D (1990) 'The province of government: delimiting the direct effect of directives in the common law context' *EL Rev* 195–223.

DALE R (1983) 'Thatcherism and education', in Ahier J and Flude M (eds) *Contemporary education policy* (London: Croom Helm

DAUSES M (1985) 'The protection of fundamental rights in the Community legal order' *EL Rev* 398–417.

DAVIES B (2016) 'Who were the British people?' *Kings LJ* 323–332.

DAVIES H AND STEWART J (1994) *The growth of government by appointment: implications for democracy* (Birmingham: Local Government Management Board).

DAVIES H AND STEWART J (1994) 'A new agenda for local governance' *Public Money and Management* (October) 29–36.

DAVIS H (2005) 'Public authorities as victims under the HRA' *Cambridge LJ* 315–328.

DAWSON I AND DUNN A (2002) 'Seeking the principle: chancel, choices and human rights' *Legal Studies* 238–258.

DE BURCA G (1993) 'The principle of proportionality and its application in EC law' *YEL* 105–130.

DE COSTA C (2009) 'The King versus Aleck Bourne' *Medical Journal of Australia* 230–231.

DENNING, LORD (1985) 'Re Parliamentary Privilege Act 1770' *Public Law* 80–92.

DENNIS I (2010) 'The right to confront witnesses: meanings, myths and human rights' *Criminal Law Review* 255–267.

DE SMITH S (1951) 'The prerogative writs' *Cambridge LJ* 40.

DE SMITH S (1955) 'Boundaries between Parliament and the courts' *MLR* 281–286.

DE SMITH S (1971) 'The constitution and the Common Market: a tentative appraisal' 34 *MLR* 597–614.

DE SMITH S (5th edn, 1985) *Constitutional and administrative law* (by Brazier R and Street H) (Harmondsworth: Penguin).

DICKSON B AND CARMICHAEL P (eds) (1998) *The House of Lords* (Oxford: Hart Publishing).

DIKE C (1976) 'The case against parliamentary sovereignty' *Public Law* 283–297.

DIMELOW S (2013) 'The interpretation of "constitutional" statutes' *LQR* 498–503.

DIPLOCK, LORD (1972) 'The common market and the common law' *The Law Teacher* 3–12.

DoE (1971) *Local government in England* p 6 (London: HMSO; Cmnd 4584).

DoE (1976) *Report of the Committee of Inquiry into local government finance* (London: HMSO; Cmnd 6453).

DoE (1977) *Housing policy: a consultative document* (London: HMSO).

DoE (1983) *Rates* (London: HMSO; Cmnd 9008).

DoE (1983) *Streamlining the cities* (London: HMSO; Cmnd 9063).

DoE (1986) *Paying for local government* (London: HMSO; Cmnd 9414).

DoE (1988) *The conduct of local authority business* (London: HMSO; Cmnd 433).

DEPARTMENT OF THE ENVIRONMENT, TRANSPORT AND THE REGIONS (1998) *A Mayor and Assembly for London* (London: HMSO; Cm 3897).

DODDS A (2016) 'Why people voted to leave and what to do now: a view from the doorstep' *Political Quarterly* 360–364.

DOHERTY M (1988) 'Prime Ministerial power and ministerial responsibility in the Thatcher era' *Parliamentary Affairs* 49–67.

DOIG A (2002) 'Sleaze fatigue in "The house of ill-repute"' *Parliamentary Affairs* 389–401.

DONNELLY C (2005) '*Leonard Cheshire* again and beyond: private contractors, contract and s 6(3)(b) of the Human Rights Act' *Public Law* 785–805.

DONNELLY C (2010) 'Positive obligations and privatisation' *Northern Ireland Legal Quarterly* 209–223.

DONOUGHMORE, LORD (1932) *Report of the Committee on Minister's powers* (London: HMSO; Cmnd 4060).

DREWRY G (1983) 'The National Audit Act— half a loaf' *Public Law* 531–537.

DREWRY G (ed) (1985) *The new select committees* (Oxford: Clarendon Press).

DREWRY G (1985a) 'Select committees and backbench power' in Jowell J and Oliver, D (eds 2nd edn) *The changing constitution* (London: OUP).

DREWRY G (1985b) 'Leaking in the public interest' *Public Law* 203–212.

DREWRY G (1988) 'Legislation', in Ryle M and Richards P (eds) *The Commons under scrutiny* (London: Routledge).

DREWRY G (1993) 'Mr Major's Charter' *Public Law* 248–256.

DREWRY G AND BUTCHER T (1988) *The civil service today* (Oxford: Basil Blackwell).

DU BOIS W (1990) 'Slavery and the Founding Fathers', in Birmbaum and Olson *supra*.

DUFFY P (1980) 'The Sunday Times case: freedom of expression, contempt of court and the ECHR' *Human Rights Review* 17–53.

DUNLEAVY P, JONES G, AND O'LEARY B (1990) 'Prime Ministers and the Commons: patterns of behaviour 1868–1987' *Public Administration* 123–140.

DWYER D (2005) 'Rights brought home' *LQR* 359–364.

EDELMAN M (1964) *The symbolic uses of politics* (Urbana: University of Illinois Press).

EDWARD D (1987) 'The impact of the Single European Act on the institutions' *CMLRev* 19–30.

EDWARDS R (2002) 'Judicial deference under the Human Rights Act' *MLR* 859–875.

EHLERMANN C (1975) 'Applying the new budgetary procedure for the first time' *CMLRev* 325–343.

EHLERMANN C (1987) 'The internal market following the Single European Act' *CMLRev* 361–409.

EKINS R (2007) 'Acts of Parliament and the Parliament Acts' 123 *LQR* 91–115.

ELCOCK H (2nd ed, 1986) *Local government* (London: Methuen).

ELECTORAL COMMISSION (2002) *Modernising elections*.

ELECTORAL COMMISSION (2004) *The funding of political parties*.

ELECTORAL COMMISSION (2005) *Spending by political parties and campaign groups at the 5 May UK parliamentary election.*

ELECTORAL COMMISSION (2005a) *Securing the vote.*

ELECTORAL COMMISSION (2011) *UK general election 2010 campaign spending report.*

ELECTORAL COMMISSION (2015) *Referendum on membership of the European Union: assessment of the Electoral Commission on the proposed referendum question.*

ELECTORAL COMMISSION (2016) *Designation of lead campaigners for the EU referendum.*

ELEFTHERIADIS P (2017) 'Constitutional illegitimacy over Brexit' *Political Quarterly* 182–188.

ELLIOT M (1980) 'Appeals, principle and pragmatism in natural justice' *MLR* 66–69.

ELLIOT M (2012) 'Holyrood, Westminster and judicial review of legislation' *Cambridge LJ* 9–11.

ELLIOT M (2017) 'The Supreme Court's judgment in Miller: in search of constitutional principle' *Cambridge LJ* 257–288.

ELLIOT M AND PEARRAU-SAUSSINE A (2009) 'Pyrrhic public law: Bancoult and the sources, status and content of common law limitations on prerogative power' *Public Law* 697.

ELLIS D (1980) 'Collective ministerial responsibility and collective solidarity' *Public Law* 367–396.

ELLIS E (ed) (1999) *The principle of proportionality in the laws of Europe* (Oxford: Hart Publishing).

ELTON G (1953) *The Tudor Revolution in government* (Cambridge: CUP).

ELTON G (1960) 'Henry VIII's Act of Proclamations' *English Historical Review* 208–222.

EMILIOU N (1994) 'Subsidiarity: panacea or figleaf', in O'Keefe D and Twomey P (eds) *Legal issues of the Maastricht Treaty* (London: Wiley).

EWING K (1987) *The funding of political parties in Britain* (Oxford: Clarendon Press).

EWING K (1999) 'The Human Rights Act and parliamentary democracy' *MLR* 79–99.

EWING K (2001) 'Transparency, accountability and equality: the Political Parties, Elections and Referendums Act 2000' *Public Law* 542–565.

EWING K AND GEARTY C (1990) *Civil liberties under Thatcher* (Oxford: OUP).

FARRAN S (1996) *The UK before the European Court of Human Rights* (London: Blackstone Press).

FELDMAN D (1993) *Civil liberties and human rights in England and Wales* (Oxford: Clarendon Press).

FELDMAN D (1993a) 'Collateral challenge and judicial review: the boundary dispute continues' *Public Law* 37–48.

FELDMAN D (1999) 'Proportionality and the Human Rights Act 1998', in Ellis E (ed) *The principle of proportionality in the laws of Europe* (Oxford: Hart Publishing).

FELDMAN D (2005) 'Proportionality and discrimination in anti-terrorism legislation' *Cambridge LJ* 270–272.

FELDMAN D (2006) 'Human rights, terrorism and risk; the roles of politician and judges' *Public Law* 364–384.

FELDMAN D (2014) 'Statutory interpretation and constitutional legislation' *LQR* 473–497.

FELDMAN D (2017) 'Pulling a trigger or starting a journey? Brexit in the Supreme Court' *Cambridge LJ* 217–223.

FELLA S (2006) 'New Labour, same old Britain? The Blair government and European treaty reform' *Parliamentary Affairs* 621–637.

FENNEL P (1986) '*Roberts v Hopwood*: the rule against socialism' *Journal of Law and Society* 401–422.

FENWICK H (4th edn, 2007) *Civil liberties and human rights* (London: Routledge-Cavendish).

FIENGOLD C (1978) 'The little red schoolbook and the ECHR' *Human Rights Review* 21–47.

FINER S (1956) 'The individual responsibility of Ministers' *Public Administration* 377–396.

FINNIE W, HIMSWORTH C, AND WALKER N (eds) (1991) *Edinburgh essays in public law* (Edinburgh: Edinburgh University Press).

FINNIS J (2016) 'Terminating Treaty-based UK rights' <https://ukconstitutionallaw. org/2016/10/26/john-finnis-terminating-treaty-based-uk-rights/>.

FITZPATRICK B (1989) 'The significance of EEC Directives in UK sex discrimination law' *Oxford Journal of Legal Studies* 336–355.

FORDHAM M (2001) 'Judicial review: the new rules' *Public Law* 4–10.

FOREIGN AND COMMONWEALTH OFFICE (2016) *The process for withdrawing from the European Union* (Cm 9216).

FORREST R AND MURIE A (1988) *Selling the welfare state* (London: Routledge).

FORSYTH C (1985) 'Beyond *O'Reilly v Mackman*: the foundations and nature of procedural exclusivity' *Cambridge LJ* 415–434.

FORSYTH C (1987) 'The scope of judicial review: "public duty" not "source of power"' *Public Law* 356–367.

FORSYTH C (1988) 'The provenance and protection of legitimate expectations' *Cambridge LJ* 238–260.

FORSYTH C (1997) '*Wednesbury* protection of substantive legitimate expectations' *Public Law* 375–384.

FORSYTH C (1999) 'Collateral challenge and the foundations of judicial review: orthodoxy vindicated and procedural exclusivity rejected' *Public Law* 364–370.

FORWOOD N AND CLOUGH M (1986) 'The Single European Act and free movement' *EL Rev* 383–408.

FOWLER N (1988) *Ministers decide* (London: Chapman).

FOXTON D (2003) '*R v Halliday, ex parte Zadig* in retrospect' *LQR* 455–494.

FREEDLAND M (1995) 'Privatising *Carltona*: Part II of the Deregulation and Contracting Out Act 1994' *Public Law* 21–27.

FRENCH D (1978) 'Spy fever in Britain 1900–1915' *Historical Journal* 355–370.

FRIEDMANN W (1950) 'Trethowan's case, parliamentary sovereignty and the limits of legal change' 24 *Australian Law Journal* 103–108.

FRY G (1970) 'The Sachsenhausen concentration camp case and the convention of ministerial responsibility' *Public Law* 336–357.

GAMBLE A (1981) *Britain in decline* (London: Papermac).

GANZ G (1986) 'Legitimate expectations: a confusion of concepts', in Harlow C (ed) *Law and politics* (London: Sweet and Maxwell).

GANZ G (1990) 'The depoliticisation of local authorities: the Local authorities: the Local Government and Housing Act 1989' *Public Law* 224–242.

GASH N (1953) *Politics in the age of Peel* (London: Longmans).

GENN H AND RICHARDSON G (eds) (1994) *Administrative law and government action* (Oxford: Clarendon Press).

GEORGE V AND WILDING P (1976) *Ideology and state welfare* (London: RKP).

GHANDI S AND JAMES J (1998) 'The English law of blasphemy and the European Convention on Human Rights' *European Human Rights LR* 430–451.

GOODHART A (1942) 'Note' [on *Liversidge*] *LQR* 3–8.

GOODWIN J (2012) 'The last defence of *Wednesbury*' *Public Law* 445.

GOODWIN M AND HEATH O (2017) 'The 2016 referendum, Brexit and the left behind: an aggregate level analysis of the result' *Political Quarterly* 323–332.

GOLBY M (1993) 'Parents as school governors', in Munn P (ed) *Parents and schools* (London: Routledge).

GOLDSWORTHY J (1999) *The sovereignty of Parliament* (Oxford: Clarendon Press).

GORDON M (2009) 'The conceptual foundations of parliamentary sovereignty: reconsidering Jennings and Wade' *Public Law* 519–543.

GORDON P (1990) 'A dirty war', in Ball and Solomos *supra*.

GOUGH I (1983) 'Thatcherism and the welfare state': in Hall and Jacques *infra*.

GOULD M (1993) '*M v Home Office*: government and the judges' *Public Law* 568–578.

GRANT J (2017) 'Prerogative, Parliament and creative constitutional adjudication: reflections on Miller' *Kings LJ* 35–61.

GRAVELLS N (1989) 'Disapplying an Act of Parliament pending a preliminary ruling: constitutional enormity or common law right' *Public Law* 568–586.

GRAY C (1979) 'European Convention on Human Rights—freedom of expression and the thalidomide case' *Cambridge LJ* 242–245.

GRIEF N (1991) 'The domestic impact of the ECHR as mediated through Community law' *Public Law* 555–567.

GRIFFITH J (1966) *Central departments and local authorities* (London: Allen & Unwin).

GRIFFITH J (1974) *Parliamentary scrutiny of government bills* (London: Allen & Unwin).

GRIFFITH J (1985) 'Judicial decision making in public law' *Public Law* 564–582.

GRIFFITH J (1993) *Judicial politics since 1920* (Oxford: Basil Blackwell).

GRIFFITH J AND RYLE M (1989) *Parliament* (London: Sweet and Maxwell).

GRISWOLD E (1952) 'The coloured vote case in South Africa' *Harvard LR* 1361–1374.

GYFORD J (1985) *The politics of local socialism* (London: Allen & Unwin).

HALL S (1983) 'The great moving right show' in Hall and Jacques *infra*.

HALL S AND JAQUES M (eds) (1983) *The politics of Thatcherism* (London: Lawrence and Wishart).

HALL W (1986) 'Contracts compliance at the GLC' *Local Government Studies* 17–24.

HAMPSON W (2nd edn, 1991) *Local government and urban politics* (London: Longman).

HAMSON C (1954) 'The real lesson of Crichel Down' *Public Administration* 383–400.

HANDY C (2001) 'Housing associations: public or private law revisited' *Journal of Housing Law* 11.

HANSARD SOCIETY (2000) *The challenge for Parliament: making government accountable* (London: Vacher Dod).

HARLOW C (ed) (1986) *Public law and politics* (London: Sweet and Maxwell).

HARLOW C (1995) 'A special relationship? American influences on judicial review in England', in Loveland (1995a) *infra*.

HARLOW C AND RAWLINGS R (1984) *Law and administration* (London: Weidenfeld and Nicolson).

HARRIS N (1993) *Law and education: regulation, consumerism and the education system* (London: Sweet and Maxwell).

HART H (2nd edn, 1994) *The concept of law* (Oxford: Clarendon Press).

HART J (1992) *Proportional representation: critics of the British electoral system 1820–1945* (Oxford: Clarendon Press).

HARTLEY T (2nd edn, 1988) *The foundations of European Community law* (Oxford: Clarendon Press).

HARTLEY T (1993) 'Constitutional and institutional aspects of the Maastricht Agreement' *International and Comparative Law Quarterly* 213–237.

HARTLEY T (3rd edn, 1994) *The foundations of European Community law* (Oxford: Clarendon Press).

HARTLEY T (4th edn, 1998) *The foundations of European Community law* (Oxford: Clarendon Press).

HASSAN G (ed) (1999) *A guide to the Scottish Parliament* (Edinburgh: Centre for Scottish Public Policy).

HATTERSLEY R (1992) 'The beggaring of PM's question time' *The Guardian* January 28.

HAWES D (1992) 'Parliamentary select committees: some case studies in contingent influence' *Policy and Politics* 227–235.

HAY J (1975) *The origins of the Liberal welfare reforms 1906–1914* (London: Macmillan).

HAYEK F (1944) *The road to serfdom* (London: RKP).

HENNESSY P (1986) 'Helicopter crashes into Cabinet: Prime Minister and constitution hurt' *Journal of Law and Society* 423–432.

HENNESSY P (1986a) *Cabinet* (Oxford: Basil Blackwell).

HEUSTON R (1964) *Essays in constitutional law* (London: Stevens).

HEUSTON R (1970) 'Liversidge v Anderson in retrospect' *LQR* 33–68.

HICKMAN T (2008) 'The courts and politics after the Human Rights Act: a comment' *Public Law* 84–100.

HIMSWORTH C (1991) 'Poll tax capping and judicial review' *Public Law* 76–92.

HIMSWORTH C (1995) 'The delegated powers scrutiny committee' *Public Law* 34–44.

HIMSWORTH C (2010) 'Nothing special about that? Martin v HM Advocate in the Supreme Court' *Edinburgh LR* 487–492.

HIMSWORTH C (2016) 'Legislating for permanence and a statutory footing' *Edinburgh LR* 361–367.

HIMSWORTH C AND O'NEILL C (3rd edn, 2015) *Scotland's Constitution: law and practice* (Haywards Heath: Bloomsbury).

HOAR F (2001) 'Public or personal character in election campaigns: a review of the implications of the judgment in Watkins v Woolas' *MLR* 607.

HOFFMAN N, LORD (1999) 'The influence of the European principle of proportionality upon UK law' Ellis E (ed) *The principle of proportionality in the laws of Europe* (Oxford: Hart Publishing).

HOGG Q (1947) *The case for Conservatism* (West Drayton: Penguin).

HOLDEN B (1988) *Understanding liberal democracy* (Oxford: Phillip Allan).

HOLDSWORTH W (1919) 'The power of the Crown to requisition British ships in a national emergency' *LQR* 12–42.

HOLDSWORTH W (1942) 'Note' [on *Liversidge*] *LQR* 1–3.

HOME OFFICE (1993) *Compensation for victims of violent crime* (London: HMSO; Cm 2434).

HOME OFFICE (1997) *Rights brought home* (London: HMSO; Cm 3782).

HOOD-PHILLIPS O (1982) 'A Garland for the Lords: Parliament and Community law again' *LQR* 524–526.

HOPE, LORD (1998) 'Devolution and Human Rights' *European Human Rights LR* 367–375.

HORNE A (1987) *Macmillan 1957–1986* (London: Macmillan).

HORWITZ H (1974) 'Parliament and the glorious revolution' *Bulletin of the Institute of Historical Research* 36–52.

HOUGH B (2005) 'Public regulation of markets and fairs' *Public Law* 586–607.

HOUGHTON, LORD (1976) *Report of the committee on financial aid to political parties* (London: HMSO; Cmnd 6601).

HOUSE OF COMMONS FOREIGN AFFAIRS COMMITTEE (1981) *British North America Acts* (London: HMSO).

HOUSE OF COMMONS INFORMATION SERVICE (2009) *Members' pay, pensions and allowances*; available at: <http://www.parliament.uk/documents/commons-information-office/fymp/m05.pdf>.

HOUSE OF COMMONS PUBLIC ADMINISTRATION SELECT COMMITTEE (2002) *Continuing the reform* (HC 4941 2001–2002) (London: HMSO).

HOUSE OF LORDS AND HOUSE OF COMMONS JOINT COMMITTEE (2013) *Draft Voting Eligibility (Prisoners) Bill* (HL paper 103; HC 924).

HUGHES D AND POLLARD D (1990) *Cases and materials on constitutional and administrative law* (London: Butterworths).

HUME D (1978) 'Of the original contract', in Locke J (ed) *Social contract: essays by Locke, Hume and Rousseau* (London: OUP).

HUNT M (1997) *Using human rights law in English courts* (Oxford: Hart Publishing).

HUNT M (1997a) 'Constitutionalism and the contractualisation of government', in Taggart M (ed) *The province of administrative law* (Oxford: Hart Publishing).

HUNT M (1998) 'The 'horizontal effect' of the Human Rights Act' *Public Law* 422–423.

HUTTON R (1985) *The Restoration* (Oxford: Clarendon Press).

INGMAN T (9th edn, 2002) *The English legal process* (London: OUP).

INGMAN T (13th edn, 2011) *English legal process* (London: OUP).

INSTITUTE OF FISCAL STUDIES (1990) *Local government finance* (London: IFS).

IRVINE D (1996) 'The theory and practice of *Wednesbury* review' *Public Law* 59.

IRVINE, LORD (1997) 'Constitutional reform and a Bill of Rights' *European Human Rights LR* 483–493.

IRVING R (1975) 'The United Kingdom referendum, June 1975' *EL Rev* 3–12.

IRWIN H (1988) 'Opportunities for backbenchers', in Ryle and Richards infra.

JACKMANN R (1984) 'The Rates Bill: a measure of desperation' *Political Quarterly* 161–170.

JACKSON P (1964) 'The royal prerogative' *MLR* 709–717.

JACKSON P (1965) 'War Damage Act 1965' *MLR* 574–576.

JAFFE L AND HENDERSON G (1956) 'Judicial review and the rule of law: historical origins' *LQR* 345.

JENKINS D (2007) 'The European legal tradition against torture and implementation of Article 3 of the European Convention on Human Rights' *Public Law* 15–22.

JENKINS J (1987) 'The green sheep in Colonel Gadaffi Drive' *New Society*, 9 January 1987.

JENKINS R (1952) 'Equality', in Crossman R. (ed) *New Fabian Essays* (London: Turnstile).

JENKINS R (1968) *Mr Balfour's Poodle* (London: Heinemann).

JENKINS R (1991) *A life at the centre* (London: Pan).

JENKINS R (1994) 'Churchill: the government of 1951–1955', in Blake and Louis *supra*.

JENKINS R (1999) *Report of the independent commission on the voting system* (London: HMSO).

JENNINGS I (5th edn, 1959) *The law and the constitution* (London: Hodder and Stoughton).

JENNINGS I (3rd edn, 1959) *Cabinet government* (Cambridge: CUP).

JENNINGS I (4th edn, 1960) *Principles of local government law* (London: University of London Press).

JENNINGS I AND TAMBIAH H (1952) *The dominion of Ceylon* (London: Stevens and Sons).

JENSEN M (1990) 'The Articles of Confederation', in Birmbaum and Ollman *supra*.

JOHNSON N (1988) 'Departmental select committees', in Ryle and Richards *infra*.

JOINT COMMITTEE ON HOUSE OF LORDS REFORM (2002) *First Report* (HL 171/HC 17) (London: HMSO).

JONES A (1972) *The politics of reform 1884* (Cambridge: CUP).

JONES B AND KAVANAGH D (6th edn, 1998) *British politics today* (Manchester: Manchester University Press).

JONES G (1973) 'Herbert Morrison and Popularism' *Public Law* 11–31.

JONES G (1973) 'The Prime Minister and parliamentary questions' *Parliamentary Affairs* 260–272.

JONES H (1958) 'The rule of law and the welfare state' *Columbia LR* 143–156.

JONES T (1996) 'The devaluation of human rights under the European Convention' *Public Law* 430–449.

JONES T (1999) 'Judicial bias and disqualification in the *Pinochet* case' *Public Law* 391–398.

JONES T AND WILLIAMS J (2005) 'The legislative future of Wales' *MLR* 642–653.

JOWELL J (2003) 'Judicial deference: servility, civility or institutional capacity' (2003) *Public Law* 592–614.

JOWELL J (2004) 'Heading for constitutional crisis' *New Law Journal* (19 March) 401–403.

JOWELL J (2006) 'Parliamentary sovereignty under the new constitutional hypothesis' *Public Law* 562–580.

JOWELL J AND LESTER A (1988) 'Proportionality: neither novel nor dangerous', in Jowell J and Oliver D (eds) *New directions in judicial review* (London: Stevens and Sons).

JOWELL J AND OLIVER D (1985; 2nd edn, 1989; 3rd edn, 1994; 4th edn) *The changing constitution* (London: OUP).

JUDSON M (1936) 'Henry Parker and the theory of parliamentary sovereignty', in Wittke C (ed) *Essays in honour of McIlwain* (Cambridge, Mass: Harvard University Press).

KAVANAGH A (2004) 'Statutory interpretation and human rights after *Anderson*: a more contextual approach' *Public Law* 537–545.

KAVANAGH A (2005) '*Pepper v Hart* and matters of constitutional principle' 121 *LQR* 98–122.

KAVANAGH D AND SELDON A (eds) (1994) *The Major effect* (London: Macmillan).

KAVANAGH D AND COWLEY P (2010) *The British General election of 2010* (Basingstoke: Palgrave Macmillan).

KAY A, LEGG C, AND FOOT J (1985) *The 1980 Tenant's Rights in Practice* (London: City University).

KEENAN P (1962) 'Some legal consequences of Britain's entry into the European Common Market' *Public Law* 327–343.

KEIR D (1936) 'The case of shipmoney' *LQR* 546–574.

KEIR D (8th edn, 1966) *The constitutional history of modern Britain* (London: Adam and Charles Black).

KEIR D (6th edn, 1978) *Cases in constitutional law* (Oxford: Clarendon Press).

KEITH-LUCAS B (1962) 'Popularism' *Public Law* 52–80.

KELLY A, HARBISON W, AND BEIZ H (1983) *The American Constitution* (New York: W. W. Norton).

KELSO A (2006) 'Reforming the House of Lords: navigating representation, democracy and legitimacy at Westminster' *Parliamentary Affairs* 563.

KENNY C (1922) 'The evolution of the law of blasphemy' *Cambridge LJ* 127–142.

KENNY M (2009) 'Taking the temperature of the British political elite 3: when grubby is the order of the day' *Parliamentary Affairs* 503–513.

KENT S (1989) *Sex and suffrage in Britain 1860–1914* (New Jersey: Princeton University Press).

KLOTT J (1998) 'Report on Germany' in Slaughter A, Stone Sweet A, and Weiler J (eds) *The European courts and national courts* (Oxford: Hart Publishing).

KLUG F. (1999) 'The Human Rights Act 1998, *Pepper v Hart* and all that' *Public Law* 246–273.

KLUG F AND STARMER K (2001) 'Incorporation through the "front door": the first year of the Human Rights Act' *Public Law* 654–665.

KNIGHT C (2009) 'Expectations in transition' *Public Law* 15–25.

KNIGHT C AND CROSS T (2017) 'Public law in the Supreme Court 2015–2016' *Judicial Review* 215.

KOOPMANS T (1992) 'Federalism: the wrong debate' *CMLRev* 1047–1052.

LAFFIN M (1986) *Professionalism and policy* (Aldershot: Gower).

LAIRD V (1992) 'Reflections on R. v R' *MLR* 386–392.

LANE R (1993) 'New Community competencies under the Maastricht Treaty' *CMLRev* 929–980.

LANHAM D (1984) 'Delegation and the alter ego principle' *LQR* 587–611.

LARDY H (2001) 'Democracy by default: the Representation of the People Act 2000' *MLR* 263–281.

LARGE D (1963) 'The decline of the party of the Crown' *English Historical Review* 669–695.

LASKI H (1926) 'Judicial review of social policy in England' *Harvard LR* 832–848.

LASLETT P (1998) 'The social and political theory of Two Treatises of Government', in Laslett *infra*.

LASLETT P (1988) 'Two Treatises of Government and the revolution of 1688', in Laslett *infra*.

LASLETT P (ed) (1988) *Locke—Two Treatises of Government* (Cambridge: CUP).

LASOK D AND BRIDGE J (1991) *Law and institutions of the European Community* (London: Butterworths).

LAUNDY P (1979) 'The Speaker and his office in the twentieth century' in Walkland S (ed) *The House of Commons in the twentieth century* (Oxford: Clarendon Press).

LAW COMMISSION (1976) *Report on remedies in administrative law* (London: HMSO; Cmnd 6407).

LAWRENCE I (2006) 'Punishment without law: how ends justify the means in marital rape' *Denning LJ* 37–50.

LAWS, SIR JOHN (1993) 'Is the High Court the guardian of fundamental constitutional rights?' *Public Law* 59–79.

LAWS, SIR JOHN (1995) 'Law and democracy' *Public Law* 72–93.

LAWS, SIR JOHN (1998) 'The limitations of human rights' *Public Law* 254–265.

LAWSON N (1992) *The view from No. 11* (London: Lawrence and Wishart).

LEACH S (1989) 'Strengthening local democracy? The government's response to Widdicombe', in Stewart J and Stoker G (eds) *The future of local government* (London: Macmillan).

LEE S (1985) 'Prerogative and public principles' *Public Law* 186–193.

LEE S (1994) 'Law and the constitution' in Kavanagh D and Seldon A (eds) *The Major effect* (London: Macmillan).

LEIGH I (1986) 'A tapper's charter' *Public Law* 8–18.

LEIGH I (1992) 'Spycatcher in Strasbourg' *Public Law* 200–208.

LEIGH I (2002) 'Taking rights proportionately' *Public Law* 265–280.

LE MAY G (1957) 'Parliament, the constitution and the doctrine of the mandate' *South African Law Journal* 33–42.

LENEMAN L (1991) 'When women were not "persons": the Scottish women graduates case, 1906-1908' *Juridical Review* 109–118.

LEOPOLD P (1981) 'References in court to Hansard' *Public Law* 316–321.

LEOPOLD P (1984) 'Parliamentary privilege and an MP's threats' *Public Law* 547–550.

LEOPOLD P (1986) 'Leaks and squeaks in the Palace of Westminster' *Public Law* 368–374.

LEOPOLD P (1989) 'The freedom of peers from arrest' *Public Law* 398–406.

LEOPOLD P (1998) 'The application of the civil and criminal law to members of Parliament and parliamentary proceedings', in Oliver and Drewry *infra*.

LEOPOLD P (1999) 'The report of the Joint Committee on parliamentary privilege' *Public Law* 604–615.

LESTER A (1984) 'Fundamental rights: the United Kingdom isolated' *Public Law* 46–72.

LESTER A (1998) 'The Act of the possible' *European Human Rights LR* 665–680.

LESTER A AND PANNICK D (2000) 'The impact of the Human Rights Act on private law: the knight's move' *LQR* 380–392.

LE SUEUR A (2004) 'Three strikes and it's out . . .' *Public Law* 225–235.

LE SUEUR A (2008) 'Gordon Brown's new constitutional settlement' *Public Law* 21–27.

LEVY L (1987) 'Introduction', in Levy L (ed) *The Making of the Constitution* (New York: OUP).

LEWIN J (1956) 'The struggle for law in South Africa' *Political Quarterly* 176–181.

LEWIS A (1991) *Make no law* (New York: Vintage Books).

LEWIS T AND CUMPER P (2009) 'Balancing freedom of political expression against equality of opportunity: the courts and the UK broadcasting ban on political advertising' *Public Law* 89–111.

LIDDINGTON J AND NORRIS J (1979) *One hand tied behind us* (London: Virago).

LLOYD, LORD (1996) *Inquiry into legislation against terrorism* (London: HMSO; Cm 3420).

LOACH J (1990) *Parliament under the Tudors* (Oxford: Clarendon Press).

LOCK G (1988) 'Information for Parliament', in Ryle and Richards *infra*.

LOCK G (1989) 'The 1689 Bill of Rights' *Political Studies* 541–556.

LOCK G (1999) 'The report of the Joint Committee on parliamentary privilege' *Study of Parliament Group Newsletter* (summer) 13–19.

LOCKHART W, KAMISAT Y, CHOPER J, AND SHIFFRIN S (6th edn, 1986) *Constitutional law* (West Publishing: St Paul, Minnesota).

LOCKE J (1988) *Two treatises of government* (Cambridge: CUP).

LOUGHLIN M (1978) 'Procedural fairness: a study of the crisis in administrative law theory' *University of Toronto LJ* 280–316.

LOUGHLIN M (1985) 'Municipal socialism in a unitary state', in MacAuslan P and McEldowney J (eds) *Law, legitimacy and the constitution* (London: Sweet and Maxwell).

LOUGHLIN M (1985a) 'The restructuring of central-local government legal relations' *Local Government Studies* 59–73.

LOUGHLIN M (1986) *Local government in the modern state* (London: Sweet and Maxwell).

LOUGHLIN M (1992) *Public law and political theory* (Oxford: Clarendon Press).

LOUGHLIN M (1994) 'The restructuring of central-local government relations', in Jowell and Oliver *supra*.

LOUGHLIN M (1988) *Legality and locality* (Oxford: Clarendon Press).

LOVELAND I (1992) 'Labour and the Constitution: the "right" approach to reform' *Parliamentary Affairs* 173–187.

LOVELAND I (1993) 'Racial segregation in state schools: the parent's right to choose?' *Journal of Law and Society* 341–355.

LOVELAND I (1993a) 'An unappealing analysis of the public-private divide: the case of the homelessness legislation' *Liverpool LR* 39–59.

LOVELAND I (1994) 'Defamation of government: taking lessons from America?' *Legal Studies* 206–225.

LOVELAND I (1995) *Housing homeless persons* (Oxford: Clarendon Press).

LOVELAND I (ed) (1995a) *Frontiers of criminality* (London: Sweet and Maxwell).

LOVELAND I (ed) (1995b) *A special relationship?* (Oxford: Clarendon Press).

LOVELAND I (1995c) 'The criminalisation of racist violence', in Loveland (1995b) *supra*.

LOVELAND I (1995d) 'Introduction: should we take lessons from America?', in Loveland (ed) *A special relationship?* (Oxford: Clarendon Press).

LOVELAND I (1996) *Constitutional law* (London: Butterworths).

LOVELAND I (1997) 'The war against the judges' *Political Quarterly* 162–171.

LOVELAND I (1998) *Importing the First Amendment* (Oxford: Hart Publishing).

LOVELAND I (1998a) '*City of Chicago v Tribune Co*—in contexts', in Loveland I (ed) *Importing the First Amendment* (Oxford: Hart Publishing).

LOVELAND I (1999) *By due process of law: racial discrimination and the right to vote in South Africa 1850-1960* (Oxford: Hart Publishing).

LOVELAND I (1999a) 'Constitutional law or administrative law? The Human Rights Act 1998' *Contemporary Issues in Law* 124–140.

LOVELAND I (1999b) 'Local authorities' in Blackburn R and Plant R (eds) *Constitutional reform* (London: Longman).

LOVELAND I (2000) '*Reynolds v Times Newspapers* in the House of Lords' *Public Law* 351–357.

LOVELAND I (2000a) *Political libels* (Oxford: Hart Publishing).

LOVELAND I (2003) 'Making it up as they go along: the Court of Appeal on succession rights in tenancies to same sex partners' *Public Law* 222–235.

LOVELAND I (2009) 'A tale of two trespassers: reconsidering the Impact of the Human Rights Act on rights of residence in rented housing' *European Human Rights LR* Part 1 at 148–169; Part 2 at 495–511.

LOVELAND I (2010) 'The shifting sands of Art 8 jurisprudence in English housing law' *European Human Rights Law Review* 151–163.

LOVELAND I (2017) 'Twenty years later—assessing the significance of the Human Rights Act 1988 to residential possession proceedings' *The Conveyancer and Property Lawyer* 174.

LOWE N (1979) 'Contempt of Court Act' *Public Law* 20–28.

LUSTGARTEN L (1989) *The governance of police* (London: Sweet and Maxwell).

LUSTGARTEN L AND LEIGH I (1994) *In from the cold: national security and parliamentary democracy* (Oxford: Clarendon Press).

MacCormick N (1978) 'Does the United Kingdom have a constitution?' *NILQ* 1–20.

Mackintosh J (1962) *The British Cabinet* (London: Stevens and Sons).

Mackintosh J (1974) 'The report of the Royal Commission on the Constitution 1969-1973' *Parliamentary Affairs* 115–123.

Madgwick P (1966) 'Resignations' *Parliamentary Affairs* 59–76.

Magnus P (1963) *Gladstone* (London: John Murray).

Maidment R (1992) *The Supreme Court and the New Deal* (Buckingham: Open University Press).

Maier P (1963) 'John Wilkes and American disillusionment with Britain' *William and Mary Quarterly* 373–395.

Mait C and McCloud B (1999) 'Financial arrangements', in Hassan *infra*.

Maitland F (1908) *The Constitutional history of England* (Cambridge: CUP).

Malleson K (2000) 'Judicial bias and disqualification after *Pinochet (No.2)*' *MLR* 119–127.

Malpass P and Murie A (1987) *Housing policy and practice* (1987) (London: Macmillan).

Mandler P (1990) *Aristocratic government in the age of reform* (Oxford: Clarendon Press).

Mann F (1979) 'Contempt of court in the House of Lords and the European Court of Human Rights' *LQR* 348–354.

Markesenis B (1973) 'The royal prerogative revisited' *Cambridge LJ* 287–309.

Markesenis B (1986) 'The right to be let alone versus freedom of speech' *Public Law* 67–81.

Markesenis B (1990) 'Our patchy law of privacy' *MLR* 802–809.

Marriot J (2005) 'Alarmist or relaxed? Election expenditure limits and free speech' *Public Law* 764–784.

Marriot J and Nicol D (1999) 'The Human Rights Act, representative standing and the victim culture' *European Human Rights LR* 730–741.

Marshall G (1954) 'What is Parliament? The changing concept of Parliamentary Sovereignty' *Political Studies* 193–209.

Marshall G (1979) 'The House of Commons and its privileges', in Walkland *infra*.

Marshall G (1984) *Constitutional conventions* (Oxford: Clarendon Press).

Marshall G (1986) 'Ministers, civil servants and open government' in Harlow *supra*.

Marshall G (1992) 'Ministerial responsibility, the Home Office and Mr Baker' *Public Law* 7–12.

Marshall G (1998) 'Hansard and the interpretation of statutes', in Oliver and Drewry *infra*.

Marshall G and Loveday B (1994) 'The police: independence and accountability', in Jowell and Oliver *supra*.

Mason D (1985) *Revising the rating system* (London: Adam Smith Institute).

Mather F (1962) 'The government and the Chartists', in Briggs A (ed) *Chartist studies* (London: Macmillan).

Matthew C (1986) *Gladstone 1809-1874* (Oxford: Clarendon Press).

Maude A and Szemerey J (1981) *Why electoral reform? The case for electoral reform examined* (London: Conservative Political Centre).

McAuslan P (1983) 'Administrative law, collective consumption and judicial policy' *MLR* 1–21.

McAuslan P (1987) 'The Widdicombe Report: local government business or politics' *Public Law* 154–162.

McAuslan P and McEldowney J (eds) (1985) *Law, Legitimacy and the constitution* (London: Sweet and Maxwell).

McBride J (1983) 'The doctrine of exclusivity and judicial review: *O'Reilly v Mackman*' *Civil Justice Quarterly* 268–281.

McClean I (1999) 'The Jenkins Commission and the implications of electoral reform for the UK' *Government and Opposition* 145–160.

McClean R (1999) 'A brief history of Scottish home rule', in Hassan *supra*.

McCorkindale C (2016) 'Scotland and Brexit: the state of the Union and the Union State' *Kings LJ* 354–365.

McEldowney J (1985) 'Dicey in historical perspective', in McAuslan and McEldowney *supra*.

McEldowney J (1988) 'The contingencies fund and the Parliamentary scrutiny of public finance' *Public Law* 232–245.

McGarry J (2005) 'Parliamentary sovereignty, judges and the Asylum and Immigration (Treatment of Claimants etc) bill' *Liverpool LR* 1–12.

McHarg A (2006) 'What is delegated legislation?' *Public Law* 539–561.

McKay D (1989) *American politics and society* (Oxford: Basil Blackwell).

Meisel F (2004) 'The *Aston Cantlow* case: blots on English jurisprudence and the public/private law divide' *Public Law* 2–10.

Merret S (1979) *State housing in Britain* (London: RKP).

Metcalfe E (2010) 'Free to lead as well as to be led: Section 2 of the Human Rights Act and the relationship between the UK courts and Strasbourg' *Justice Journal* 7–41.

Miers D (1983) 'Citing Hansard as an aid to interpretation' *Statute LR* 98–102.

Miliband R and Smith J (eds) (1975) *Socialist Register* (London: Merlin).

Miller C (1976) *Contempt of court* (London: Paul Elek).

Miller J (1982) 'The Glorious Revolution: "contract" and "abdication" reconsidered' 25 *The Historical Journal* 541–555.

Ministry of Justice (2007) *The governance of Britain* (London: HMSO; Cm 7170).

Ministry of Justice (2008) *An elected second chamber* (London: HMSO; Cm 7438).

Ministry of Justice (2009) *Bribery: draft legislation* (London: HMSO; Cm 7570).

Mirfield P (1979) 'Can the House of Lords be lawfully abolished?' *LQR* 36–58.

Mitchell A (1974) 'Clay Cross' *Political Quarterly* 165–175.

Moddod T (1990) 'British Asian Muslims and the Rushdie affair' *Political Quarterly* 143–160.

Montesquieu C (1989) *The spirit of the laws* (Cambridge: CUP).

Moreham N (2001) '*Douglas and others v Hello! Ltd*—the protection of privacy in English private law' *MLR* 767–775.

Morgan J (2002) 'Questioning the "true effect" of the Human Rights Act' *Legal Studies* 259–275.

Morgan J (2004) 'Privacy in the House of Lords, again' *LQR* 563–566.

Morris G and Fredman S (1991) 'Judicial review and civil servants' *Public Law* 485–490.

Mount F (1992) *The British constitution now* (London: Heinemann).

Mowbray A (1999) 'The composition and operation of the new European Court of Human Rights' *Public Law* 219–231.

Mullan D (1975) 'Fairness: the new natural justice' *University of Toronto LJ* 280–316.

Mullan K (1999) 'The impact of *Pepper v Hart*' in Carmichael and Dickson (eds) *The House of Lords: its parliamentary and judicial roles* (Oxford: Hart Publishing).

Munro C (1976) 'Elections and expenditure' *Public Law* 300–304.

Munro C (1987) *Studies in constitutional law* (London: Butterworths).

Munro C (1989) (2nd edn, 1989) *Studies in constitutional law* (London: Butterworths).

Munro C (2011) 'Parliamentarians, privilege and prosecutions' *Scots Law Times* 1–4.

Murdie A (1990) 'Bailiffs, Henry III, the community charge and all that' *Municipal Journal* August 17–23.

Myles A (1999) 'Scotland's Parliament White Paper', in Hassan *supra*.

Nally S and Dear J (1990) 'No surrender' *Municipal Journal*, October 12–18.

Nathanson N (1979 /1980) 'The Sunday Times case: freedom of the press and contempt of court under English law and the European Convention on Human Rights' *Kentucky LJ* 971–1025.

Neville-Brown L and Kennedy T (1994) *The Court of Justice of the European Communities* (London: Sweet and Maxwell).

NICOL D (1996) 'Disapplying with relish? The Industrial Tribunals and Acts of Parliament' *Public Law* 579–589.

NICOL D (1999) 'The legal constitution: United Kingdom Parliament and European Court of Justice' *Journal of Legislative Studies* 131–151.

NICOL D (1999a) 'Limitation periods under the Human Rights Act 1998 and judicial review' *LQR* 216–220.

NICOL D (2004) 'Gender re-assignment and the transformation of the Human Rights Act' *LQR* 194–198.

NICOL D (2004a) 'Statutory interpretation and human rights after Anderson' *Public Law* 273–281.

NICOL D (2011) 'Legitimacy of the Commons debate on prisoner voting' *Public Law* 681–691.

NICOL W (1984) 'The Luxembourg compromise' *Journal of Common Market Studies* 35–43.

NICOL W AND SIMON T (1994) *Understanding the new European Community* (London: Harvester Wheatsheaf).

NIXON J AND NIXON N (1983) 'The social services committee' *Journal of Social Policy* 331–355.

NORRIS M (1996) '*Ex p Smith*: irrationality and human rights' *Public Law* 590–600.

NORTON P (1978) 'Government defeats in the House of Commons' *Public Law* 360–378.

NORTON P (1979) 'The organisation of parliamentary parties', in Walkland *infra*.

NORTON P (1980) *Dissension in the House of Commons 1974-1979* (London: Macmillan).

NORTON P (1982) '"Dear Minister" . . . The importance of MP to minister correspondence' *Parliamentary Affairs* 59–72.

NORTON P (1985) *The Commons in perspective* (London: Martin Robertson).

NORTON P (1988) 'Opposition to government', in Ryle and Richards *infra*.

NORTON P (2nd edn, 1991) *The British polity* (London: Longman).

NORTON P (2005) *Parliament in British politics* (Basingstoke: Palgrave Macmillan).

O'KEEFE D AND TWOMEY P (eds) *Legal issues of the Maastricht Treaty* (London: Wiley).

O'LEARY B (1987) 'Why was the GLC abolished' *International Journal of Urban and Regional Research* 192–217.

O'LEARY B (1987) 'British farce, French drama amid tales of two cities' *Public Administration* 369–389.

O'LEARY C (1962) *The elimination of corrupt practices in British general elections 1868-1911* (Oxford: Clarendon Press).

O'LEARY S (1996) '*R v Secretary of State for the Home Department, ex parte Gallagher*' *Common Market LR* 777–793.

OLIVER D (1982) 'Why electoral reform? The case for electoral reform examined' *Public Law* 236–239.

OLIVER D (1990) *Government in the United Kingdom* (Buckingham: Open University Press).

OLIVER D (1992) 'Written constitutions: principles and problems' *Parliamentary Affairs* 135–152.

OLIVER D (1999) 'An Electoral Commission: an ingenious idea' *Public Law* 585–588.

OLIVER D (2001) 'Chancel repairs and the Human Rights Act' *Public Law* 651–653.

OLIVER D (2004) 'Constitutionalism and the abolition of the role of the Lord Chancellor' *Parliamentary Affairs* 754–766.

OLIVER D AND DREWRY G (eds) (1998) *The law and parliament* (London: Weidenfeld and Nicolson).

OUSLEY H (1984) 'Local authority race initiatives', in Boddy M and Fudge C (eds) *Local socialism* (London: Macmillan).

PADOVER S (ed) (1953) *The complete Madison* (Norwalk, Conn: Eastern Press).

PAGE A AND BATEY A (2002) 'Scotland's other Parliament: Westminster legislation about devolved matters in Scotland since devolution' *Public Law* 501–523.

PALMER S (1988) 'In the interests of the state' *Public Law* 523–535.

PALMER S (1990) 'Tightening secrecy law: the Official Secrets Act 1989' *Public Law* 243–256.

PALMER S (1992) 'Protecting journalists' sources: section 10, Contempt of Court Act 1981' *Public Law* 61.

PANNICK D (1984) 'The Law Lords and the needs of contemporary society' *Political Quarterly* 318–328.

PANNICK D (1988) 'What is a public authority?', in Jowell J and Oliver D (eds) *New directions in judicial review* (London: Sweet and Maxwell).

PANNICK D (1994) 'No logic behind gagging terrorists' empty rhetoric' *The Times* August 2.

PARPWORTH N (2010) 'The Parliamentary Standards Act 2009: a constitutional dangerous dogs measure' *MLR* 262–281.

PEDLEY R (1958) 'Lord Hailsham's legacy' *Journal of Education* 4–5.

PEDLEY R (1966) *The comprehensive school* (Harmondsworth: Penguin).

PESCATORE P (1972) 'The protection of human rights in the European Communities' *CMLRev* 73–79.

PESCATORE P (1983) 'The doctrine of direct effect: an infant disease of Community Law' *EL Rev* 155–177.

PETERSON J (1994) 'Subsidiarity: a definition to suit any vision' *Parliamentary Affairs* 116–132.

PHELAN D (1992) 'Right to life of the unborn v promotion of trade in services' *MLR* 670–689.

PHILLIMORE, LORD JUSTICE (1974) *Report on contempt of court* (London: HMSO; Cmnd 5794).

PHILLIPSON G (1999) 'The Human Rights Act, "horizontal effect" and the common law: a bang or a whimper?' *MLR* 824–849.

PIMLOTT B (1992) *Harold Wilson* (London: Harper Collins).

PLOTNER J (1998) 'Report on France' in Slaughter A, Stone Sweet A, and Weiler J (eds) *The European courts and national courts* (Oxford: Hart Publishing).

PLUCKNETT T (1928) 'Dr Bonham's Case and judicial review' *Harvard LR* 30–70.

PLUCKNETT T (11th edn, 1960) Taswell-Langmead's *English constitutional history* (London: Sweet and Maxwell).

PLUMB J (1937) 'Elections to the Convention Parliament of 1689' *Cambridge Historical Journal* 235–254.

POOLE T (2005) 'Of headscarfs and heresies: *The Denbigh High School* case and public authority decision-making under the Human Rights Act' *Public Law* 685–695.

PRYCE R (ed) (1985) *The dynamics of European Union* (London: Croom Helm).

PUGH M (1980) *Women's suffrage in Britain 1867-1928* (London: The Historical Association).

PUGH M (1985) 'Labour and women's suffrage', in Brown K (ed) *The first Labour Party* (London: Croom Helm).

PULZER P (1983) 'Germany', in Butler and Bogdanor *supra*.

PUNNET R (1968) *British government and politics* (London: Heinemann).

PURDUE M (2002) 'The end of estoppel in public law' *Journal of Planning and Environmental Law* 509–510.

QUANE H (2006) 'The Strasbourg jurisprudence and the meaning of a "public authority" under the HRA' *Public Law* 106–123.

RAAB C (1993) 'Parents and schools: what role for education authorities?', in Munn *supra*.

RADCLIFFE, VISCOUNT (1976) *Report on Ministerial Memoirs, Cmnd* 6386 (London: HMSO).

RANSON S (1988) 'From 1944-1988: education, citizenship and democracy' *Local Government Studies* 1–19.

RANSON S AND THOMAS H 'Educational reform: consumer democracy or social democracy', in STEWART J and STOKER G (eds) *The future of local government* (London: Macmillan).

RAWLINGS H (1988) *Law and the electoral process* (London: Sweet and Maxwell).

RAWLINGS R (1994) 'Legal politics: the UK and ratification of the Treaty on European Union (parts one and two)' *Public Law* 254–278 and 367–391.

RAWLINGS R (1998) 'The new model Wales' *Journal of Law and Society* 461–512.

RAWLINGS R (2005) 'Hastening slowly: the next phase of Welsh devolution' *Public Law* 824–852.

RAWORTH P (1994) 'A timid step forwards: Maastricht and the democratisation of the EC' *EL Rev* 16–33.

RAYNER G AND WINNETT R (2009) *No expenses spared* (London: Bantam Press).

RAZ J (1977) 'The rule of law and its virtue' *LQR* 195–211.

REICH C (1964) 'The new property' *Yale LJ* 733–787.

REICH C (1965) 'Individual rights and social welfare: the emerging legal issues' *Yale LJ* 1244–1257.

REID (Lord) (1972–1973) 'The judge as lawmaker' *Journal of the Society of Public Teachers of Law* 22–28.

RHODES R (1986) *The national world of local government* (London: Allen & Unwin).

RICHARD (2004) *Report of the Commission on the powers and electoral arrangements of the National Assembly for Wales* (Cardiff: National Assembly for Wales).

RICHARDS P (1970) *Parliament and conscience* (London: Allen & Unwin).

RICHARDSON G (1986) 'The duty to give reasons: potential and practice' *Public Law* 437–469.

RICHARDSON T (1995) 'The War Crimes Act 1991', in Loveland (1995a) *supra*.

RIVERS J (2006) 'Proportionality and variable intensity of review' *Cambridge LJ* 174.

ROBERTSON A AND MERRILL J (3rd edn, 1995) *Human rights in Europe* (Manchester: Manchester University Press).

ROBERTSON G (1999) *The justice game* (Harmondsworth: Penguin).

ROBERTSON G AND NICOL A (3rd edn, 1992) *Media law* (Harmondsworth: Penguin).

ROBINSON R (1988) 'The House of Commons and public money', in Ryle and Richards *infra*.

RODGER (Lord) (2005) 'A time for everything under the law: some reflections on retrospectivity' *LQR* 57–71.

ROGERS R AND WALTERS R (eds) *How Parliament works* (6th edn, 2006).

ROGERS I (2002) 'From the Human Rights Act to the Charter: not another human rights instrument to consider' *European Human Rights LR* 343–356.

ROMANOV R, WHYTE J, AND LEESON H (1984) *Canada notwithstanding* (Toronto: Carswell/ Metheun).

ROSE H (1973) 'The Immigration Act 1971: a case study in the work of Parliament' *Parliamentary Affairs* 69–91.

ROSTOW E (1945) 'The Japanese-American cases—a disaster' *Yale LJ* 489–533.

ROUSSEAU J (1987) *The social contract* (edited and translated by C Betts) (Oxford: OUP).

ROVER C (1967) *Women's suffrage and party politics in Britain* (London: RKP).

ROWBOTTOM J (2005) 'The electoral Commission's proposals on the funding of political parties' *Public Law* 468–476.

RUDE G (1962) *Wilkes and liberty* (Oxford: Clarendon Press).

RUSH M (1998) 'The law relating to members' conduct', in Oliver and Drewry *supra*.

RUSSELL C (1971) *The Crisis of Parliaments* (Oxford: Clarendon Press).

RUSSELL M (2000) *Reforming the House of Lords. Lessons from overseas* (London: OUP).

RYLE M AND RICHARDS (1988) *The Commons under scrutiny* (London: Routledge).

SANDBERG R AND DOE N (2008) 'The strange death of blasphemy' *MLR* 971–986.

SCARMAN, LORD (1987) 'Human Rights in an unwritten constitution' *Denning LJ* 129–139.

SCHERMERS H (1993) 'The European Court of Human Rights after the merger' *European LR* 493–505.

SCHIEMANN K (1990) 'Locus standi' *Public Law* 342–353.

SEDLEY S (1994) 'Governments, constitutions and judges', in Genn and Richardson *supra*.

SELGADO E AND O'BRIEN C (2001) 'Table of cases under the Human Rights Act' *European Human Rights LR* 376.

SEYMOUR C (1970) *Electoral reform in England and Wales* (Newton Abbot: David and Charles).

SEYMORE-URE C (1964) 'The misuse of the question of privilege in the 1964-65 session of Parliament' *Parliamentary Affairs* 380–388.

SEYMORE-URE C (1970) 'Proposed reforms of parliamentary privilege' *Parliamentary Affairs* 221–231.

SHAH S (2005) 'The UK's anti-terror legislation and the House of Lords: the first skirmish' *Human Rights LR* 403–421.

SHANNON R (1982) *Gladstone Vol. 1* (London: Hamish Hamilton).

SHARLAND A AND LOVELAND I (1997) 'The Defamation Act 1996 and political libels' *Public Law* 113–124.

SHARP A (1983) *Political ideas of the English civil war* (London: Longman).

SHARPE J (1970) 'Theories and value of local government' *Political Studies* 153–174.

SHAW J (1993) *EC law* (London: Macmillan).

SHAW J (2001) 'The Treaty of Nice: legal and constitutional implications' *European Public Law* 195–207.

SHELL D (1985) 'The House of Lords and the Thatcher government' *Parliamentary Affairs* 16–32.

SHELL D (1992) *The House of Lords* (London: Harvester Wheatsheaf).

SHELL D (1999) 'The future of the second chamber' *Political Quarterly* 390–395.

SHELL D (2000) 'Reforming the House of Lords' *Public Law* 193.

SHIPMAN T. (2016) *All out war: the full story of Brexit* (London: William Collins).

SILK P (1992) *How Parliament works* (London: Longman).

SILLS P (1968) 'Report of the Select Committee on parliamentary privilege' *MLR* 435–439.

SIMON B (1988) *Bending the rules* (London: Lawrence and Wishart).

SIMPSON A (1991) *In the highest degree odious* (Oxford: Clarendon Press).

SIMPSON A (2001) *Human rights and the end of empire* (Oxford: OUP).

SKIDELSKY R (1968) 'Great Britain', in Woolf S (ed) *European fascism* (London: Weidenfeld and Nicolson).

SKLAIR L (1975) 'The struggle against the Housing Finance Act', in Miliband R and Smith J (eds) *The socialist register* (London: Macmillan).

SLAUGHTER A, STONE SWEET A, AND WEILER J (eds) *The European courts and national courts* (Oxford: Hart Publishing).

SLAUGHTER T (1981) '"Abdicate" and "contract" in the Glorious Revolution' *The Historical Journal* 323–337.

SMITH E (1992) *The House of Lords in British politics and society 1815-1911* (London: Longman).

SMITH H (1926) 'The residue of power in Canada' *Canadian Bar Review* 432.

SMITH T (1957) 'The Union of 1707 as fundamental law' *Public Law* 99–121.

SPECK W (1986) *Reluctant revolutionaries* (Oxford: Clarendon Press).

STARMER K (1999) *European human rights law* (London: Legal Action Group).

STEINER J (1990) 'Coming to terms with EC directives' *LQR* 144–159.

STEINER J (3rd edn, 1992) *EC law* (London: Blackstone).

STEINER J (1993) 'From direct to *Francovich*: shifting means of enforcement of community law' *EL Rev* 3–22.

STELLMAN H (1985) 'Israel: the 1984 election and after' *Parliamentary Affairs* 73–85.

STEWART J (1983) *Defending public accountability* (London: Demos).

STEWART J (2006) 'A banana republic? The investigation into electoral fraud by the Birmingham election court' *Parliamentary Affairs* 654–667.

STEWART J AND STOKER G (eds) *The future of local government* (London: Macmillan).

STEWART R (1975) 'The reformation of American administrative law' *Harvard LR* 1667–1812.

STEYN, LORD (2002) 'Democracy through law' *European Human Rights LR* 723–726.

STONE C (1972) 'Should trees have standing? Towards legal rights for natural objects' *Southern California LR* 450–501.

SUNKIN M (1987) 'What is happening to applications for judicial review' *MLR* 432–467.

SUNKIN M (1987a) 'Myths of judicial review' *LAG Bulletin* (September) 8.

SUNKIN M (1991) 'The judicial review caseload, 1987-1989' *Public Law* 490–499.

SUNKIN M (2004) 'Pushing forward the frontiers of human rights protection; the meaning of public authority under the Human Rights Act' *Public Law* 643–658.

SZYSZCZAK E (1990) 'Sovereignty: crisis, compliance, confusion, complacency' *EL Rev* 480–488.

SZYSZCZAK E (1993) 'Interpretation of Community Law in the courts' *EL Rev* 214–225.

TAYLOR/DES (1977) *A new partnership for schools* (London: HMSO).

TEW Y (2011) 'No longer a privileged few: expense claims, prosecution and parliamentary privilege' *Cambridge LJ* 282.

THOMAS R (1987) 'The British Official Secrets Act 1911-1939 and the Ponting case', in Chapman R and Hunt M (eds) *Open government* (London: Routledge).

THOMPSON E (1975) *Whigs and hunters* (London: Penguin).

THOMPSON L (2013) 'More of the same or a period of change? The impact of Bill Committees in the twenty first century House of Commons' *Parliamentary Affairs* 459.

THOMPSON R AND GAME C (1985) 'Section 137: propaganda on the rates?' *Local Government Studies* 11–18.

THORNE S (1938) 'Dr Bonham's case' *LQR* 543–552.

TIERNEY S (1998) 'The Human Rights Bill: incorporating the European Convention on Human Rights into UK law' *European Public Law* 299–311.

TIERNEY S (1998a) 'Press freedom and public interest' *European Human Rights LR* 419–431.

TIERNEY S (2000) 'Constitutionalising the role of the judge: Scotland and the new order' *European LR* 49–72.

TIERNEY S (2000a) 'Devolution issues and s 21(1) of the Human Rights Act' *European Human Rights LR* 380–392.

TIERNEY S (2013) 'Legal issues surrounding the referendum on independence for Scotland' *European Constitutional Law Review* 359–390.

TITMUSS R (1971) 'Welfare rights, law and discretion' *Political Quarterly* 133–151.

TOMKINS A (2005) *Our republican constitution* (Hart: Oxford).

TOMKINS A (2013) 'The emergence of a devolution jurisprudence', UKSC blog, <http://ukscblog.com/the-emergence-of-a-devolution-jurisprudence>.

TOMKINS A AND BIX B (1993) 'Local authorities and libel again' *MLR* 738–744.

TOTH A (1986) 'The legal status of declarations attached to the SEA' *CMLRev* 803–812.

TOTH A (1994) 'Is subsidiarity justiciable?' *EL Rev* 268–285.

TRINADADE F (1972) 'Parliamentary sovereignty and the primacy of community law' *MLR* 375–402.

TURBEVILLE A (1927) *The House of Lords in the eighteenth century* (Oxford: Clarendon Press).

TURBEVILLE A (1958) *The House of Lords in the Age of Reform* (London: Faber and Faber).

TURNER J (18th edn, 1962) *Kenny's Outlines of criminal law* (Cambridge: CUP).

TURPIN C (1985; 2nd edn, 1990) *British government and the constitution* (London: Weidenfeld and Nicolson); (3rd edn, 1995) (London: Butterworths).

UBEROI E (2016) 'The EU referendum' *House of Commons Library Briefing Paper* No CBP 7639.

UNDERDOWN D (1985) *Revel, riot, and rebellion* (Oxford: Clarendon Press).

UPTON M (1989) 'Marriage vows of the elephant: the constitution of 1707' *LQR* 79.

VILE M (1967) *Constitutionalism and the separation of powers* (Oxford: Clarendon Press).

VINCENT-JONES P (1986) 'The hippy convoy and criminal trespass' *Journal of Law and Society* 343–370.

WADE HRW (1955) 'The basis of legal sovereignty' *Cambridge LJ* 172–197.

WADE HRW (1969) 'Constitutional and administrative aspects of the Anisminic case' *LQR* 198–212.

WADE HRW (1972) 'Sovereignty and the European Communities' *LQR* 1–5.

WADE HRW (1977) 'Judicial control of the prerogative' *LQR* 325–327.

WADE HRW (1980) *Constitutional fundamentals* (London: Steven & Sons).

WADE HRW (1985) 'The civil service and the prerogative' *LQR* 190–199.

WADE HRW (1996) 'Sovereignty—revolution or evolution' *LQR* 568–575.

WADE HRW (1996a) 'Habeas corpus and judicial review' *LQR* 55–70.

WADE HRW (2000) 'Horizons of horizontality' *LQR* 217–224.

WADE HRW AND FORSYTH C (1994) *Administrative law* (Oxford: Clarendon Press).

WAKEHAM COMMISSION (2000) *A House for the future* (London: HMSO; Cm 4534).

WALKER C (1987) 'Review of the prerogative: the remaining issues' *Public Law* 63–84.

WALKER C (2007) 'The legal definition of terrorism in United Kingdom law and beyond' *Public Law* 331–352.

WALKER P (1995) 'What's wrong with irrationality?' *Public Law* 556–576.

WALKLAND S (ed) (1979) *The House of Commons in the twentieth century* (Oxford: Clarendon Press).

WALKLAND S AND RYLE M (eds) (1977) *The Commons in the seventies* (London: Martin Robertson).

WALLINGTON P AND MCBRIDE J (1976) *Civil Liberties and a Bill of Rights* pp 28–29 (London: Cobden Trust).

WALSH B (1989) 'Judicial review of dismissal from employment: coherence or confusion' *Public Law* 131–155.

WARBRICK C (1998) 'Federalism and free speech', in Loveland I (ed) *Importing the First Amendment*? (Oxford: Hart Publishing).

WARREN S AND BRANDIES L (1890) 'The right to privacy' *Harvard LR* 193–220.

WATSON J (2010) 'Clarity and ambiguity: a new approach to the legitimacy in the law of legitimate expectations' *Legal Studies* 633–655.

WEARE V (1964) 'The House of Lords—prophecy and fulfilment' *Parliamentary Affairs* 422–433.

WEILER J (1981) 'The Community system: the dual character of supra-nationalism' *Yearbook of European Law* 267–306.

WEILER J (1986) 'Eurocracy and distrust . . .' *Washington Law Review* 1103–1152.

WEILER J AND LOCKHART N (1995) 'Taking rights seriously: the European Court and its fundamental rights jurisprudence (parts one and two)' *CMLRev* 51–94 and 579–627.

WEIR A (1972) 'Local authority v critical ratepayer—a suit in defamation' *Cambridge LJ* 238–249.

WELFARE D (1992) 'The Lords in defence of local government' *Parliamentary Affairs* 205–219.

WELSH OFFICE (2005) *Better governance for Wales* (London: HMSO; Cm 6582).

WESTON C (1965) *English constitutional theory and the House of Lords* (London: RKP).

WHITAKER R (2006) 'Backbench influence on government legislation? A flexing of parliamentary muscles at Westminster' *Parliamentary Affairs* 350–359.

WHITE I AND GAY O (2010) *Reducing the size of the House of Commons* (London: House of Commons).

WICKS E (2001) 'A new constitution for a new state? The 1707 union of England and Scotland' *LQR* 109.

WICKS E (2006) *The evolution of a constitution* (Oxford: Hart Publishing).

WILLIAMS G (1978) *Textbook of criminal law* (London: Stevens).

WILLIAMS K (2000) 'Defaming politicians: the not so common law' *MLR* 748–756.

WILKS-HEEG S (2005) *Purity of elections in the UK: causes for concern* (Joseph Rowntree Reform Trust: York).

WILSON D (2001) 'Local government: balancing diversity and uniformity' *Parliamentary Affairs* 289–307.

WILSON H (1979) *Final term* (London: Weidenfeld and Nicolson).

WINTER J (1972) 'Direct applicability and direct effect: two distinct and different concepts in Community law' *CMLRev* 425–438.

WINTERTON G (1976) 'The British grundnorm: parliamentary sovereignty re-examined' *LQR* 591–617.

WINTERTON G (1979) 'Is the House of Lords immortal?' *LQR* 386–392.

WINTERTON G (1981) 'Parliamentary supremacy and the judiciary' *LQR* 265–275.

WITTKE C (ed) (1936) *Essays in history and political theory in honour of Charles Howard McIlwain* (Cambridge, Mass: HUP).

WITTKE C (1970) *The history of English parliamentary privilege* (New York: Da Capo Press).

WOLFFE W (1987) 'Values in conflict: incitement to racial hatred and the Public Order Act 1986' *Public Law* 85–95.

WOODHOUSE D (1994) *Ministers and Parliament* (Oxford: Clarendon Press).

WOODWARD R (1991) 'Mobilising opposition: the campaign against housing action trusts in Tower Hamlets' *Housing Studies* 44–56.

WOOLF H (1986) 'Public law—private law: why the divide?' *Public Law* 220–238.

WOOLF H (1995) 'Droit public: English style' *Public Law* 57–71.

WOOLF H (2004) 'The rule of law and a change in the constitution'; available at <http://www.dca.gov.uk/judicial/speeches/lcj030304.htm>.

WOOLF S (ed) (1968) *European fascism* (London: Weidenfeld and Nicolson).

YOUNG A (2002) 'Remedial and substantive horizontality: the common law and *Douglas v Hello! Ltd*' *Public Law* 232–241.

YOUNG A (2005) *Ghaidan v Godin-Mendoza*: avoiding the deference trap' *Public Law* 23–34.

YOUNG H (1991) *One of us* (London: Pan).

ZANDER M (1994) *The law-making process* (London: Butterworths).

ZANDER M (3rd edn, 1995) *The Police and Criminal Evidence Act 1984* (London: Sweet and Maxwell).

Index